Renaissance Drama

BLACKWELL ANTHOLOGIES

Renaissance Drama An Anthology of Plays and Entertainments
Edited by Arthur F. Kinney

Editorial Advisers

Blackwell Anthologies are a series of extensive and comprehensive volumes designed to address the numerous issues raised by recent debates regarding the literary canon, value, text, context, gender, genre, and period. While providing the reader with key canonical writings in their entirety, the series is also ambitious in its coverage of hitherto marginalized texts, and flexible in the overall variety of its approaches to periods and movements. Each volume has been thoroughly researched to meet the current needs of teachers and students.

BRITISH LITERATURE
Victorian Women Poets: An Anthology
edited by Angela Leighton and Margaret Reynolds

Romanticism: An Anthology. Second Edition
edited by Duncan Wu

Romantic Women Poets: An Anthology
edited by Duncan Wu

British Literature 1640–1789: An Anthology
edited by Robert DeMaria, Jr

Chaucer to Spenser: An Anthology of Writings in English 1375–1575
edited by Derek Pearsall

Renaissance Drama: An Anthology of Plays and Entertainments
edited by Arthur F. Kinney

Restoration Drama: An Anthology
edited by David Womersley

The Victorians: An Anthology of Poetry and Poetics
edited by Valentine Cunningham

Old and Middle English: An Anthology
edited by Elaine Treharne

Forthcoming
Medieval Drama: An Anthology
edited by Greg Walker

Renaissance Literature: An Anthology
edited by Michael Payne and John Hunter

Gothic Novels: An Anthology
edited by Nicola Trott

Modernism: An Anthology
edited by Lawrence Rainey

AMERICAN LITERATURE
Nineteenth-Century American Women Writers: An Anthology
edited by Karen L. Kilcup

Nineteenth-Century American Women Poets: An Anthology
edited by Paula Bernat Bennett

American Gothic: An Anthology 1787–1916
edited by Charles L. Crow

Forthcoming
Early African-American Literature: An Anthology
edited by Phillip M. Richards

Native American Women Writers *c.* 1800–1925: An Anthology
edited by Karen L. Kilcup

RENAISSANCE DRAMA

AN ANTHOLOGY OF PLAYS AND ENTERTAINMENTS

EDITED BY **ARTHUR F. KINNEY**

First published 1999
2 4 6 8 10 9 7 5 3 1

Blackwell Publishers Inc.
350 Main Street
Malden, Massachusetts 02148
USA

Blackwell Publishers Ltd
108 Cowley Road
Oxford OX4 1JF
UK

Library of Congress Cataloging-in-Publication Data
Renaissance drama: an anthology of plays and entertainments/edited by Arthur F. Kinney.
p. cm. – (Blackwell anthologies)
Includes bibliographical references.
ISBN 0-631-20802-X (acid-free paper). – ISBN 0-631-20803-8 (pbk.: acid-free paper)
1. English drama – Early modern and Elizabethan, 1500–1600.
2. English drama – 17th century. 3. Renaissance – England.
I. Kinney, Arthur F., 1933– . II. Series.
PR1263.R45 1999
822'. 308 – dc21
99-25286
CIP

British Library Cataloguing in Publication Data
A CIP catalogue record for this book is available from the British Library.

Commissioning Editor: Andrew McNeillie
Desk Editor: Brigitte Lee
Production Controller: Lisa Eaton
Picture Researcher: Leanda Shrimpton

Typeset in 9 on 10.5 pt Garamond
by Kolam Information Services Pvt Ltd, Pondicherry, India
Printed in Great Britain by T.J. International, Padstow, Cornwall
This book is printed on acid-free paper

For past, present, and future
scholars, teachers, and
readers at the
Massachusetts Center
for Renaissance Studies,
Amherst

Contents

Acknowledgments

From the start of this project, Andrew McNeillie, my editor at Blackwell, has been a warm and wise supporter, and Eric Salehi, a graduate student at New York University, has been a wonderfully able assistant. Many illustrations were chosen in consultation with Janet Moulding, Curator of the collection at the Massachusetts Center for Renaissance Studies. As ever, I am grateful to my colleague and co-teacher, R. Malcolm Smuts, of the Department of History at the University of Massachusetts, Boston, for spotting historical inaccuracies. The faults that remain are my own.

The publishers wish to thank Stan Sherer for the new photography.

The editor and publishers gratefully acknowledge the following for permission to reproduce copyright material: Manchester University Press for songs from *A Chaste Maid in Cheapside*, Revels edition, Methuen, 1969 (edited by R. B. Parter, Music prepared by John P. Cutts) and 'O let us howl, some heavy note', from *The Duchess of Malfi*, Revels edition, Methuen, 1964 (edited by John Russell Brown, music transcription by David Greer).

A Note on the Texts

The texts of all the plays and entertainments in this anthology have been newly edited and modernized from the earliest extant quartos and any substantive changes are listed with the Textual Variants for each work. The single exception is Sir Philip Sidney's *Lady of May*, where the copytext is the first extant publication of the work in the 1598 edition of Sidney's *Arcadia*. Ben Jonson's *Masque of Blackness* has also been collated with the extant manuscript.

No text is innocent

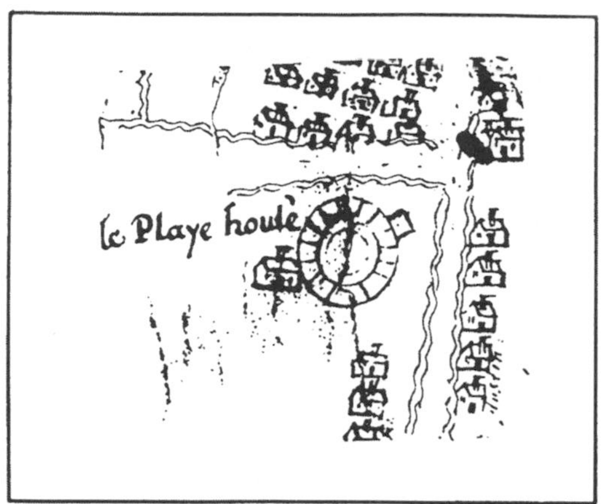

The Swan:
detail from the Paris Garden Manor *map, 1627*

The Swan:
detail from the Visscher view of London, *1616*

The Swan:
detail from the Merian view of London, *1638*

The Swan:
detail from the Civitas Londini view, *1600*

Introduction

On February 25, 1601 – not coincidentally on Ash Wednesday, the beginning of Christian Lent, a period of forbearance and reconsecration – Robert Devereux, the Earl of Essex, was the fifth person under the Tudors to be beheaded publicly on the green in the Tower of London for treason. Once the favorite courtier of Elizabeth I and her loyal servant, he was accused of leading his men in a bold, brash attempt to depose her. For several days before his public execution he was said to be hysterical with remorse and terror. If so, his steady composure on that fatal day came as a dramatic change. Eyewitnesses testified that he mounted the scaffold calmly and steadily, and once on the platform he swept off his black hat – the color of melancholy and the sign of repentance – and bowed to the peers of the realm who had gathered to see his end. He confessed his past sins, lamented his wasted youth, and prayed for forgiveness from God. With a speech that would long be remembered, he talked of his special regret for the rebellion and prayed for the Queen's welfare. Then, pausing dramatically while a clergyman prompted him, he went on to forgive his enemies, to pray against the fear of death, and to ask God to uphold the realm. He said the Lord's Prayer. He absolved his executioner, recited the Creed, and then began disrobing. He removed his outer garments, including the black cloak that signified mourning; he passed from the public dress of the condemned to the private dress of a man alone before God. He was now seen in a long-sleeved scarlet waistcoat, the rich red color symbolizing the bloody death that faced him but also the martyrdom he wished his death to become. Then he lay down, put his head on the executioner's block, and commending his spirit to the Lord gave the axeman the cue to strike. The Christian knight who had served his lady the Queen with such magnanimity, devotion, and obedience was transformed into a Christian servant of the Lord now reconciled to his Maker.

Just how much of this scripted spectacle performed before a limited audience dramatized a man's conflict with guilt and how much was simply convention – in 1587 the rebellious Mary, Queen of Scots, had been executed in much the same way at Fotheringhay Castle on February 18 – is difficult to discern. Both were moments of extravagant theater before an audience for which life and theater, history and art, were often interchangeable. Shakespeare's plays make repeated use of this fact: the mechanicals' show before the Athenian Duke Theseus and his court in *A Midsummer Night's Dream*; the pageant of the Nine Worthies staged in *Love's Labors Lost*; the wedding masque in *The Tempest*; the revival of Hermione in *The Winter's Tale*; and even the whole play of Kate and Petruchio put on for Christopher Sly in *The Taming of the Shrew* demonstrate how art might grow out of life, life might turn into art, or art might mock or transform human existence. "All the world's a stage, And all the men and women merely players" Jaques says in *As You Like It* – the word *merely* then meaning *entirely* – and he goes on to describe all the stages of man's life as stock theatrical characters with stock dramatic behavior. Everything is contained here – from the praise of Henry V by Shakespeare's Chorus to the poor players left to strut an hour on the stage of Macbeth's imagination. All of life, seen as representational, was also seen as enactment.

But if all the world was a stage in the English Renaissance, it follows that the stage may be the world. Surely this was so at the Globe playhouse, where a round building representing the world contained a stage in which the trapdoor represented hell while the actors spoke their lines in earthly settings beneath a roof painted to look like the heavens. Plays of the period, moreover, grew out of earlier village plays sponsored by the church and the guilds in which local folk enacted their own world history with biblical texts from Genesis to Revelation, from the dawn of creation to the Last Judgment; here ordinary men might become Adam or Moses or Christ or Judas for a day and ordinary women could play Eve or Noah's wife, the Virgin Mary or Mary Magdalene. Alongside plays of all sorts in the Renaissance in England, there were other public spectacles and entertainments, such as jousts, tournaments, pageants, processionals, and masques. These too followed scripts, usually implicit, often condensed, but essentially narrative when they unfolded, presenting life's moments of celebration and conflict. So theatrical beheadings – usually reserved for nobility – and hangings for offenders of other stations or rank or of no rank at all were essentially performative, as were the lesser punishments of scolds and witches carried in carts to the jeers of spectators, or cuckolds asked to ride backwards through the streets, or, in an equally theatrical if more static way, those condemned to the stocks or to whipping posts. The rule of state might be dramatized through the orations of town heralds reading royal proclamations; the word of God might be made dramatic by the delivery and gestures of preachers in their indoor and their outdoor pulpits. At London's Inns of Court law students turned mock trials into serious theater or comic mockery. Indeed, Renaissance England was a world which measured time, welcomed ambassadors, and installed royal and local officials with plays, disguisings, and mummings as well as even more spectacular juggling, fencing, and the setting off of fireworks. The theatrical culture that inspired Renaissance plays and entertainments gave them its substance and drama responded by not only representing but interrogating that culture. No performance was simply make-believe; and no performance was innocent of truth. They were, indeed, inherently analogous to the life they portrayed and inherently a comment on it.

The recorded coronation procession of Queen Elizabeth through the streets of London in 1559 is a case in point. The shows along the procession were designed to celebrate the new monarch and to entertain the broadest possible populace as they lined the streets; but these shows also had their political purposes. At the Conduit in Fleet Street, for example, the obligatory welcome of Elizabeth reinstated the sovereign as Deborah and her role as *rex iustus*, a queen of law and even-handed justice. The pageant, moreover, points out that she was not only the heir to the throne but, more importantly, God's judge and agent. At the Great Conduit a second pageant cast her in a different role. There eight children invoking the beatitudes from Protestant scripture recast her as a holy virgin full of grace, their bearer of grace. She is blessed because she is sanctioned by the Word, but it is the Word of Tyndale and Coverdale, Calvin and Luther; it is not the Word of her Catholic sister and predecessor Mary. Such shows, intended to guide and propagandize, were designed and financed by Londoners, especially merchant members of the guilds, but this procession was followed in later years by similar shows in royal visits to Cambridge in 1564 and to Oxford in 1566; to cities like Bristol in 1574; and to the homes of nobility such as the visit to the Earl of Leicester's new residence at Kenilworth in 1575. While such journeys and entertainments were costly and occasional, there were annual celebrations on the Queen's Accession Day, November 17, from 1570 onwards, a mixture of tournament and masque with the Queen's own Office of Revels providing costumes and scenery.

Such plays and entertainments might be not only instructive but also deliberately distracting. Armigal Waad, clerk to the Privy Council under Edward VI, described "The Distresses of the Commonwealth" at the time of Elizabeth's coronation procession: "The Queen poor. The realm exhausted. The nobility poor and decayed. Want of good captains and soldiers. The people out of order. Justice not executed. All things dear [costly]. The French King bestriding the realm." Slowly, Spain, too, was becoming a threat to Elizabeth's sovereignty, aligning itself with the Catholic nobility of Scotland, Ireland, and northern England in allegiance to the imprisoned Mary Stuart. "Seldom shall you see any of my country men above eighteen or twenty years old to go without a dagger at the least at his back or by his side," William Harrison records; "Our nobility wear commonly swords or rapiers with their daggers as doth every common servingman." In part, then, Elizabeth I was defending her claim to absolute power and to the divinity of her rule through a drama of state self-consciously displayed in her pageantry, processions, and progresses among the towns and villages as well as in the great houses of the counties surrounding London and her palace at Whitehall. When her people wished to stabilize the realm by urging the Queen to marry and create a new line of succession to the throne she temporized while performing – perhaps seriously at first – an abortive courtship with the French Duke of Anjou. When the Privy Council urged her to execute Mary, Queen of Scots, who seemed an indestructible magnet for dissidents and rebels of all kinds, Elizabeth undertook the role of a beleaguered ruler, unable to dictate the death of a fellow sovereign. When the Invincible Armada of Spain threatened the invasion of England in 1588, she put on the armor of a soldier and visited the military camp at Tilbury. Wearing a white gown and a silver breastplate, she inspired her army by proclaiming that "I know I have the body of a weak and feeble woman, but I have the heart and stomach of a king, and of England too." While events conspired to permit such performances – she was never *wholly* in control – she had a genius for public appearance reinforced by those who witnessed the events. Even as she contracted a network of spies abroad and a system of surveillance within her own borders, she herself publicly appeared stoutly in control. "We princes," she proposed, "are set on stages in the sight and view of all the world." The French ambassador agreed. "She is a Princess," he remarked, "who can act any part she pleases."

Acts of political theater might not only reestablish the role of supreme ruler, relax tension, moderate opposition, and stem attack from rebellion; in a peculiarly inverse way, theater also played to the unstable, the transparent, and the ever-changing sense of life where, as in a play, nothing is ever fully predictable and roles are often subject to change. Drama came to resemble as well as portray the condition of English life in the Renaissance; it seems symbolic now that Queen's College, Cambridge, putting up its first scaffolding for plays when Elizabeth took office, began to use it annually for the next ninety years and that other Cambridge colleges followed suit. The sense of instability in national life was further emphasized by the Protestant religion that Elizabeth championed in 1559. With the increasing use of the Geneva Bible that preached Calvin's doctrine of the elect and the reprobate, Puritans were quick to uphold the sanctity of each individual conscience even when a person's moral sense might conflict with that of the government. Parliamentarians like the Puritan Peter Wentworth in the House of Commons were, by the 1580s, openly criticizing royal practices. Some radical Puritans separated from the Church of England – joined by the monarch to the state by its use of state sermons or homilies – and formed independent congregations. Others began satiric attacks on the Elizabethan bishops under the pseudonym of Martin Marprelate. In 1590 nine ministers headed by the Presbyterian Thomas Cartwright were summoned before the royal Court of High Commission; when they refused to take an oath of allegiance all of them save Cartwright were deprived of their benefices. In May 1591 they were brought before Star Chamber, charged with refusing the oath and thereby seditiously denying the royal supremacy; but the final trial was consistently postponed. By 1597 Commons had turned from religious to economic matters, protesting royal monopolies which were seen as unequal and unfair taxation of the poorer ranks of society; and in this instance, in 1601, the Queen herself apologized for any harm she had done even to the least of her subjects. "I do assure you there is no prince that loveth his subjects better." When in September of 1599 Essex, returning precipitously and unannounced from Ireland, entered her privy chamber, he found her wrinkled, scared, toothless, and nearly bald without her wig. Aging, she took to more elaborate uses of costumes and cosmetics – the very stuff of theater.

The troubled years of Elizabeth's reign were not immediately settled by her successor, who inherited her military debts amounting to £350,000. James VI of Scotland and James I of England's claim to the throne was objected to since he was an alien and the son of the proclaimed traitor Mary, Queen of Scots. His candidacy was contested by his first cousin Arbella Stuart, great-great-granddaughter to Henry VIII and English by birth; by Lord Beauchamp, the son of Catherine Grey by a doubtful marriage; and by the Earl of Derby. James's politics were also unsettling. He set as an early goal a claim to absolute authority and, by the fact of his twin titles of king, his practice of imperialism; he urged that England be united with Scotland as "Great Britain." All these practices raised concerns about possible infringement of English laws and liberties. He remarked to Parliament in 1604, the second year of his reign, "What God hath conjoined then, let no man separate. I am the husband, and all of the whole isle is my lawful wife; I am the head and it is my body; I am the shepherd and it is my flock." His personal and political aspirations were aided by a liberal bestowal of titles – he established new nobility and hundreds of new knights – in order to forge his own political base, but this attempt at stabilization led to intrigue, jealousy, and bitter or cynical competition for places at the new court. His style of life was luxurious, self-indulgent, and costly, a striking contrast to Elizabeth's parsimony. "It is a horror to me," he remarked to his Principal Secretary, Robert Cecil, "to think of the height of my place, the greatness of my debts, and the smallness of my means." His generosity was especially apparent with his male favorites – the Duke of Somerset, Robert Carr, and the Duke of Buckingham, George Villiers – with whom he had romantic interests. "God so love me," he once wrote Buckingham, "as I desire only to live in the world for your sake, and that I had rather live banished in any part of the earth with you than live a sorrowful widow's life without you." Such personal gratification also sought outlet in court spectacles. James had advocated and even sponsored drama in Edinburgh when he was King of Scotland in the 1590s; he took Shakespeare's company under his patronage as the King's Men shortly after he arrived in England. His wife, Queen Anne, shared a love of court entertainments with him, especially the masques which elaborated on simple scripts with music and dance. Indeed, the notorious personal indulgences of James now – and perhaps even then – overshadowed his shrewdness at governance and his ability to handle both peace with foreign countries (he managed a lasting treaty with Spain) and toleration at home (factionalism arising in connection with Essex's death in the last years of Elizabeth continued to smolder with his friends' opposition to Cecil).

The same order and discipline that government required, especially in light of continuing resistance, was true of social practices as well. The all-pervasive system of social inequality reinforced by a hierarchy of status and a distinction of social functions is recorded in 1577 in William Harrison's description of England at the close of Raphael Holinshed's chronicle history. According to Harrison, there were four "degrees" of people. Highest were "gentlemen," including titular nobility, knights, and squires who are characterized as "those whom their race and blood or at least their virtues do make noble and known." Next down the social scale were citizens and burgesses who because of their occupation possessed freedom of the city in which they practiced their trades. Third were country yeomen, either freeholders of land to the value of forty shillings or farmers to gentlemen. At the bottom of the ladder were commoners: day laborers, poor husbandmen, artificers, and servants, or those who had "neither voice nor authority in the commonwealth, but are to be ruled and not to rule other." Each class was marked by income, residence, diet, and dress as shown graphically in the sumptuary legislation of 1597 this way:

Men's Apparel

	Material		Article		Persons excepted
None shall wear	Cloth of gold, Silver tissued, Silk of purple color			Except	Earls and above that rank and Knights of the Garter in their purple mantles
	Cloth of gold or silver, tinselled satin, silk or cloth mixed or embroidered with gold or silver. Foreign Woolen Cloth			Except	Barons and above that rank. Knights of Garter, and Privy Councillors
	Any lace of gold or silver mixed with gold and silver, or with gold or silver and silk. spurs, swords, rapiers, daggers, buckles or studs of girdles, etc.		Gilt or damasked with gold or silver silvered	Except	Baron's sons and all above that rank. Gentlemen attending upon the Queen in house or chamber. Those who have been employed in embassies. Those with net income of 500 marks per year for life. Knights (as regards daggers, spurs, etc.); Captains
	Velvet Embroidery with silk. Netherstocks of silk	in	Gowns Cloaks Coats and upper garments	Except	Knights, and all above that rank; their heirs apparent; those with net income of £200, and all excepted in preceding article
	Velvet	in	Jerkins Hose Doublets	Except	Knights' eldest sons, and all above that rank. Those with net income of £100. Those excepted above
	Satin Damask Taffeta Grograin	in	Gowns Cloaks Coats, etc.		
	Velvet Gilding Silvering, etc. Studs Buckles, or other garniture, gilt, silvered, etc.	in	Saddles Bridles Stirrups, and all furniture of horse	Except	Baron's sons and all above that rank; Knights; Men with incomes of 500 marks etc. as above

Women's Apparel

None shall wear any:

Cloth of gold or silver tissued, purple silk		Except	Countesses and all above that rank
(Viscountesses may wear cloth of gold or silver tissued only in their kirtles)			
Silk or cloth, mixed or embroidered with pearl, gold or silver		Except	Baronesses and all above that rank
Cloth of gold and silver only in linings of garments, etc.		Except	Wives of Barons' eldest sons and all above that rank. Barons' daughters
Cloth of silver in kirtles only		Except	Knights' wives and all above that rank
Embroideries of gold or silver. Lace of gold or silver or mixed with gold, silver or silk. Headdresses trimmed with pearl		Except	Wives of Barons' eldest sons and all above that rank. Barons' daughters Wives of Knights of Garter or of Privy Councillors. Maids of honor, Ladies, etc. of Privy Chamber. Those with income of 500 marks a year
Velvet in upper garments Embroidery with silk. Netherstocks of silk		Except	Knights' wives and all above that rank and those excepted above Those with incomes of £200
Velvet in	Kirtles Petticoats Gowns	Except	Wives of Knights' eldest sons, and all above that rank. Gentlewomen attendant upon countesses, viscountesses, etc. Those with incomes of £100
Satin in	Cloaks and other outer garments		
Satin in Kirtles		Except	Gentlemen's wives, bearing arms, and all above that rank, etc.
Damask Tufte taffeta Plain taffeta Grograin	in Gowns		

Social order was further reinforced by the custom of endogamy, marrying within social ranks. Status and prestige could change within social rank by the accumulation of power or wealth. A successful merchant might be elected to office and become in time an alderman or mayor of a city; a clergyman might rise from small to larger parishes and even, on occasion, to the bishopric; successful lawyers could progress from local benches to offices of state. Status, that is, could change, but not rank: bloodlines caused and secured stations in life, not wealth. Like the royal bloodlines that established a lineage of rule in England, society dictated its own perpetuation of order although with some family lines dying out, new ones infrequently emerged. As with national events, social events could also hold out possibilities of change and opportunities for the ambitious. Such a system, even as it proclaimed and fostered order, could also breed discontent and even at times outright denial. The very regimentation of such life could encourage evasion or plot exceptions so that fathers might make marriage arrangements for their children based more on property and status than on devotion.

The culture attempted to police such exceptions by advocating that each household was "a small commonwealth" or "a little church"; according to William Vaughan, "Every man's a king in his own house." To insure the family structure English common law practiced primogeniture; when a marriage failed to produce a son, as it did in about 40 percent of marriages, property went to the daughter rather than to brothers, nephews, or male cousins. In those instances where the father died before the eldest son came of age, the property was often left temporarily in the hands of his wife as a protection, giving to the family the same sort of absolute rule and continuation that marked government in the country at large. Families were as patriarchal as descent was patrilineal. A good wife was one who was essentially submissive to her husband, a person patient, sweet, loving, modest, obedient, largely silent. A bad wife was one who was unruly, quarrelsome, inconstant, foolish, or extravagant. Perpetuating the paradox whereby royalty rules what was termed a commonwealth, husbands strove to establish partnerships with their wives. William Whately writes in 1623 that husband and wife were complementary, the wife being a "subordinate," a "deputy" or "associate"; William Perkins saw husband and wife as "yokefellows." Lady Margaret Hoby writes in her diary of an exemplary marriage. She and her husband regularly set aside time to talk and walk together. They discussed business together, attended religious services together, and attended each other whenever one of them was ill. He read aloud to her at night and they exchanged letters frequently when they were apart. Those lower in rank were encouraged to spend as much time together as their larger workloads might allow.

As a public institution, marriage did not mean privacy. Every room was shared; servants lived in. Small private rooms or closets and occasionally large galleries might allow an occasional moment of privacy or refuge, but generally isolation and seclusion within the house as well as outside it were unknown. The internal affairs of families were also of knowledge and interest to the neighborhood, to the parish, to the village, even to the state. A priest in Kent is recorded to have received a woman when naked in his bed and when he put out his candle "very suspiciously," half the parish was assembling to witness the event. In another instance, a man in Faversham saw his neighbor spying on a man and woman meeting in the churchyard but when he approached them he cried, "Shall I suffer the arrant whore to undo the husband?" Government surveillance thus resonated on local and personal levels. Nor were these isolated cases. Petitions of villagers of Yardley to the Worcestershire justices in 1617 complained of a neighboring householder who beat his wife; at the Ely assizes in 1652, one John Barnes, who kicked and beat his wife when drunk "Out of a hasty choleric humor" so badly that she died of her injuries, was condemned by his neighbors. Such unruly or unwarranted behavior was also punished by a kind of street theater in which cuckolds or unruly marriage partners were given "rough ridings" – "skimmingtons" and "charivaris" – through village and city streets, exposing their private failings to public mockery. Such attempts to regulate and regularize marriage practices, however, may well have resulted from a society that refused to tolerate divorce. While ecclesiastical courts had the power to nullify marriage that was unconsummated or legally invalid, separation on grounds of adultery, apostasy, or cruelty was generally denied, and an actual divorce took an Act of Parliament. The other side of regulation and tradition was repression.

Life could not only be difficult; it could also be fragile. Life expectancy, for example, was then much lower than today; the average life expectancy was thirty or forty years. At the same time, infant mortality rates were high: in the parish records of London, only half the children born survived until the age of fifteen among poorer members of a parish, and those of higher status often did not fare much better. Births and deaths were household affairs; there were no hospitals except a handful in London for charity, for the incurable, or for the insane. There were no antiseptics or anesthetics, and there was little understanding of disease, of the thousand natural shocks that Hamlet says man is heir to. Epidemics were little understood if at all; and repeated outbreaks of bubonic plague, sudden and sweeping, could eliminate large segments of a town's population. "The dreadfulness," writes Thomas Dekker, "is unutterable." As a stay against such mortality, married couples conceived children early and often. Statistics from villages in Cambridgeshire, Surrey, Sussex, and Lancashire show that over one-third of all brides bore their first child within the first year of marriage, while between two-thirds and four-fifths did so within two years. Other demographic studies show that across England one-third of all deaths (34.4 percent) were of children under ten. Grief was assuaged by large families or by time. The Elizabethan Marquis of Winchester notes that "the love of the mother is so strong, though the child be dead and laid in the grave, yet always she hath him quick in her heart." Fathers suffered too. Nehemiah Wallington, a London furniture maker, also recorded the death of his three-year-old daughter: "Says she to me, father I go abroad tomorrow and buy you a plum pie." Childbirth was also frequent because, given the need to provide second households at marriage, many people needed to save money and married relatively late, between the ages of twenty-five and thirty in the cases of both men and women. Conversely, bastardy was a growing social problem, increasing by 50 percent in the reign of Elizabeth to a total of 4.5 percent of the birthrate by 1603 and causing a related rise in infanticide. Abortions were more frequently resorted to. In 1560 a defamation case in Yorkshire revealed a woman drinking white lavender and reeve to terminate pregnancy; in 1600 Alice Bradley told the Colchester authorities that the father offered her some powders for a posset to prevent the birth of their child. By 1600, too, networks of brothels were rapidly spreading through the suburbs of London. Despair (as well as madness and idiocy) also gave way to suicide. The King's Bench ruled on sixty-one suicides between 1500 and 1509, but this number escalated to 801 in 1590–9, 894 in 1600–9, and 976 in 1610–19. Just as loveless marriages which trapped the partners gave rise to *Arden of Faversham* and *A Woman Killed with Kindness*, shrewishness was not lost on Thomas Dekker, bastardy on Thomas Middleton, prostitution on Ben Jonson, nor the terror of child mortality and suicide on John Webster.

The fears and dangers of mortality were also addressed by religious thought and practice. Sensing clearly the power and centrality of religion, Elizabeth and James attempted to regulate church life by regulating the church. They encouraged the Protestant faith established first in the reign of Edward VI and took every opportunity to curtail any practices of a Catholic church which challenged the Established Church of Edward and Elizabeth. Catholic rituals and images were seen as pagan or sacrilegious and always subversive. While the Queen was thought to keep a Catholic crucifix in her own private chambers, she ordered that the royal arms replace the crucifixes and rood crosses in all her parish churches. London visitors in 1599 purged St. Paul's Cathedral of all its images and altars, and ordered the clergy to get rid of all priestly vestments except surplices; rood crosses and the rood-loft were taken from the cathedral and two great bonfires in Cheapside burned "all the roods and Maries and Johns and many other of the church goods." "The Queen did fish for men's souls," remarked Christopher Hatton, "and had so sweet a bait, that no one could escape her network." But enforced conformity was difficult and sometimes impossible to establish or sustain. Some hardened Catholics still served Rome, but a great many more were "Church papists," those of all ranks who attended Protestant services yet could still think and act like unreformed Catholics and could quickly revert if a national situation allowed or advocated it. And there were other unsettling conditions. Trained ministers for the Established Church, replacing Catholic priests, were hard to come by. In 1576 some 14 percent of church livings in Lincolnshire were still vacant; even as late as 1610 thirty out of eighty-five chapelries in Lancashire were unfilled. Nor were clergy always sufficiently educated in the new religion. Of 396 clergy tested by the archdeaconries of Lincoln and Stow in 1576, only 123 were found adequate while in the archdeaconry of Leicester in that year only twelve of ninety-three clergy were found "sufficient" in their knowledge of scripture. At the same time, individual Puritans, persuaded by Calvinism that they were among the elect, were in their own ways subversive. One of them in Bury St. Edmunds, critical of the Queen, inscribed below the royal arms words from Revelation: "Because thou art lukewarm, and neither cold nor hot, I will spew thee out of my mouth"; he was hanged for treason. Still Puritan resistance flourished. In 1603, on his way to Westminster to be crowned King of England, James was presented with a petition signed by one thousand ministers requesting him to eliminate traces of Catholics still evident. They had cause. In Lancashire in 1590 evidence was uncovered of the use of rosary beads, of Catholic sacraments, of wakes, and of genuflection, all banned by the state-supported church. Their use was encouraged by some sixty-six Catholic priests, part of the 452 who immigrated to England in the reign of Elizabeth despite the fact that her government executed 131 priests and sixty lay Catholics between 1581 and 1603. Others suffered financial loss. The Catholic Sir Thomas Tresham was fined a total of £8,000 between 1581 and 1605, and many Catholic families were ruined financially. Others were brutally invaded and searched. The priest John Gerard records one such search at Braddocks, Essex, where pursuivants broke down the doors, locked up the mistress and her daughters, lifted tiles, knocked down the walls of "suspicious-looking places," stripped off plaster, and forced confessions which amounted to treason against the state. Henry, the brother of the poet John Donne, was arrested for harboring a priest in London, imprisoned, and died in Newgate jail of the plague. Religion, like so much else, became grounds for regulation and repression. Matters of belief were matters both of personal salvation and state governance – just as Essex demonstrated as he prepared to die in 1601.

In the course of the troubled and troubling sixteenth and seventeenth centuries in England, the population of the country doubled: London itself grew from a population of 50,000 to 60,000 in the 1520s, to 200,000 by 1600, and again to 400,000 by 1650. Part of this growth was due to the increased land market caused by the massive amounts of property passing into private and state holdings with the dissolution of the monasteries in the 1540s, much as Thomas Arden finds new wealth by accruing lands once held by Faversham Abbey. At the beginning of the Tudor age, the church had owned nearly a quarter of the country; by the end of Elizabeth's reign nearly all of that property was owned by successful merchants, manufacturers, and investors. The rate of sales and turnovers was sizeable; by 1640 nearly half of the gentility owning land had acquired it since the beginning of the sixteenth century. The yeomanry was, in fact, especially well placed. Farming or overseeing increasingly substantial acreage, they were either freeholders immune from rent increases or tenant farmers whose holdings were sufficient to insure large crops that, combined with low labor costs, meant insulation even from poor harvests. In some places, such as the Midlands, arable land was enclosed for pasturage, reducing labor costs even farther. Wealth became more and more conspicuous, in fact, with the advent of new country houses – Hardwick Hall at £70,000 and Audley End at £80,000 were the most spectacular – as the new expression of power and taste at the turn of the century; but the smaller manor houses of gentry and the houses of yeomen were a part of this "great rebuilding."

Industry expanded swiftly. Coal shipped from Newcastle to London grew from 32,951 tons in 1563–4 to 162,550 tons in 1597–8. Exports in lead, tin, grain, and skins also grew rapidly, but cloth and cloth goods remained primary. The Merchant Adventurers Company took cloth as far as Russia and Morocco, and English tin, lead, and fabric were sold abroad in Tuscany and in Turkey. By 1600 London was a major port, shipping more than 100,000 woollen cloths a year valued at least £75,000. England further fostered such growth of business and the economy by encouraging foreign workers to settle in London and granted some industries and individuals exclusive rights or patents to produce and sell certain goods, returning some of the profit as payment for such patents to the government. Hard white soap was given a patent in 1561, ovens and furnaces in 1563, window glass in 1567, sailcloths and drinking glasses in 1574, sulfur, brimstone, and oil in 1577, armor and horses' harnesses in 1587, starch in 1588, white rag paper in 1589, aqua vitae and vinegar in 1594, playing cards in 1598, and mathematical instruments in 1598. Middleton is attracted to the bustle of the new life based in capital investment and active markets and Jonson sees it invading what was once a fair that dealt only in livestock and staples. Many rural cottagers, no longer able to farm land, turned their homes into domestic factories, working as spinners, carders, weavers, nailmakers, and cutlers; Dekker captures the domesticity of small industry and craft at the same time he attacks the alien workforce, producers of the New Draperies that, freed from guild regulations, were able to establish practices that undermined native craftsmen. The ability to get rich quick was in the air; and economic regulations like those of church, society, and state were not so much directives as challenges to overcome.

But the haves, the upwardly mobile and the entrepreneurial, turned profits at the expense of those who had little or nothing, constituting a world of privilege and exclusion. Many farmers and tenant farmers were turned off the land when acreage was combined for large sheep pastures. The unemployed drifted to cities for employment and choked London streets and alleys, suffering from poverty and want. Those feeling the pinch were further victimized by the weather: droughts for three successive years in the mid-1590s caused dearth and starvation. Royal proclamations against enclosure or exploitation of scarcities were inadequate, and in 1596 a crowd rioted in Canterbury, rising to prevent grain from leaving the city for sale elsewhere. The same year in Somerset a crowd seized a load of cheese, motivated by hatred of those of higher station and by the belief that "rich men had gotten all into their hands and will starve the poor." Riots were more often than not relatively controlled, defying authority only to make clear the needs and inequality of distribution of foodstuffs and other goods. At Sydenham, Kent, where over half the freeholders held less than five acres and two-fifths had only a cottage and garden to their name, 500 householders protested against the possible loss of common land for pasturage, claiming they were greatly relieved by the said common and would be utterly undone if it should be unjustly taken from them. England was still overwhelmingly rural (85 percent); even by 1640 London housed perhaps 8 percent of the nation's people. But here too there was unrest. There were at least thirteen insurrections, riots, and unlawful assemblies in a dozen parts of London and Southwark in 1595, twelve of them between June 6 and 29; even the life of the Lord Mayor, Sir John Spencer, a clothmaker, was for a time seriously threatened. But food riots did not cease with improved harvests. In 1620 some Wiltshire weavers noted that "to starve is woeful, to steal ungodly and to beg unlawful, whereunto we may well add that to endure our present estate anywhile is almost impossible." Need was expressed in other forms too, among the vagrants and vagabonds and petty criminals who had once been farmers or soldiers or sailors or laborers but were now among the unemployed, sometimes unemployable. They too knew what it meant to change roles, to play different parts through the ages of man on the world's stage. In 1600 roughly half were men, another 25 percent women, while 12 percent were married couples and 10 percent children. Some eventually found permanent work and settled into a local neighborhood; others, temporarily out of work, were hustled along the road, whipped out of parishes where they were not native, and seen taking refuge in barns, haystacks, and even ditches at night. Many of them died as the winter months came on, memorialized only in parish records where they are entered anonymously: "a poor woman which died in a barn at the parsonage whose name we could not learn." The charity of monasteries had been replaced in London by five hospitals – St. Bartholomew's and St. Thomas's for the sick poor; Christ's for orphaned children; Bethlem for the mad poor; and Bridewell for correction – but they were woefully inadequate. "Hospitals abound," said Francis Bacon in 1618, "and beggars abound never a whit less."

The Golden Age of the Renaissance in England was thus largely legendary, yet in the trials and turbulence of life, in its constant inconstancy and change, drama found its natural place. Some early records of performances have survived, such as payments to actors and others, court cases against players, descriptions of dramatic performances in the chronicles, and infrequent drawings. The first public playhouse in London was the Red Lion, built in the courtyard of a farmhouse in 1567 by John Brayne. The stage, 40 by 30 feet, was raised 5 feet off the ground and had a trapdoor; on or abutting the stage was a 30-foot-high turret with a floor 7 feet from the top. Around the yard were scaffolds or galleries for the playgoers. This seems to have been the crude forerunner of other public playhouses first in Shoreditch to the north of London, and later in Southwark to the south – the Theatre, the Curtain, the Rose, the Fortune, the Hope, the Swan, and the Globe. They too had a thrust stage with a trap beneath and a roof overhead supported by pillars. Those who paid a penny stood on the open ground before the stage; those who paid more sat in galleries, often covered, with seats costing more the higher one went, with the Lord's Rooms, over and behind the stage, the most expensive of all. It might seem as if this stage-play world replicated the real one by separating the audience by ranks, but it in fact was even more authentic by separating them in terms of wealth. Better seats went to those who paid more money. The largest and most crowded theater district was in the parish of St. Savior south of the Thames, where the public playhouses took their place among the Beargarden, the Clink prison, and numerous brothels. Inside the city walls the Children of the Chapel and on occasion St. Paul's Boys played at a smaller indoor theater located in the old Blackfriars priory where much higher prices guaranteed a more homogenous audience.

Smaller touring companies – with six to twelve actors instead of sixteen – played the provinces, especially in times of plague. Most frequently they followed circuits along the Roman road east of London to Canterbury and the Cinque Ports, northeast into East Anglia, Ipswich, and Norwich, north on the Great North Road to Cambridge and on to York, and then west to Bristol. They played in all sorts of venues, including the great halls of noble households, churches and churchyards, inns and innyards, streets, private houses, and at least one purpose-built theater – the Wine Street Playhouse in Bristol, which opened around 1605. The most common space, however, was the town hall. Someone named R. Willis has left a description of what seems customary practice by the end of the sixteenth century:

> In the City of Gloucester the manner is (as I think it is in other like corporations) that when the players of interludes come to town, they first attend the Mayor to inform him what nobleman's servant they are, and so get license for their public playing, and if the Mayor like the actors, or would show respect to their Lord and Master, he appoints them to play their first play before himself and the Aldermen and Common Council of the city and that is called the Mayor's play, where everyone that will come in without money, the Mayor giving the players a reward as he thinks fit to show respect unto them.

They were thus guaranteed some income, but subsequent local performances at local inns or yards or halls also allowed them to pass the hat for additional payment. Two innyards that are known to have housed theaters are the Boar's Head at Whitechapel and the Red Bull at Clerkenwell. Audiences varied too in background, sophistication, and size: the public playhouses in Southwark could perform to 2,000 spectators or more, while the smaller private theaters at Blackfriars and Whitefriars could at best seat about 600.

Actors formed their own playing companies under the patronage of a nobleman or an officer of the Queen's household with Elizabeth, and under the patronage of the royal family with James. They needed to act about forty weeks of any year to turn a profit; the manager Philip Henslowe's takings at the Rose Playhouse show little seasonal variation in attendance and profits. Plays were tried out and if they attracted an audience were added to the company's repertory and repeated until they had run their course. Henslowe's diary records thirty-five performances of Marlowe's *Jew of Malta* between February 26, 1592 and June 21, 1596; but the play was still in the repertoire of the Admiral's Men as late as May 1601. Henslowe's entries between March 1591 and January 1593 show the popularity of Kyd's *Spanish Tragedy* (referred to as *Hieronimo*).

Rd at Jeronymo the 14 march 1591	iij li xj s
Rd at Joronymo the 20 marche 1591	xxxviij s
Rd at doneoracio the 30 of marche 1591	xxxix s
Rd at Jeronymo the 7 of ap^{r}ell 1591	xxvj s
Rd at the comodey of Jeronymo the 10 of ap^{r}ell 1591	xxviij s
Rd at Jeronymo the 14 ap^{r}elle 1591	xxxiij s
Rd at the comodey Jeronymo the 22 of ap^{r}ell 1591	xvij s
Rd at Jeronymo the 24 of ap^{r}ell 1592	xxviij s
Rd at Jeronymo the 2 of maye 1592	xxxiiij s
Rd at Jeronymo the 9 of maye 1592	xxvj s
Rd at Jeronymo the 13 of maye 1592	iij^{li}4^{s}
Rd at the comodey of Jeronymo the 21 of maye 1592	xxviij s
Rd at Jeronymo the 22 of maye 1592	xxvij s
Rd at Jeronymo the 27 of maye 1592	xxiij s
Rd at Jeronymo the 9 of June 1592	xxviij s
Rd at Joronymo the 18 of June 1592	xxiiij s
Rd at the comodey of Jeronymo the 20 of June 1592	xv s
Rd at Joronymo the 30 of desember 1592	iij^{li} x^{s}
Rd at Jeronymo the 8 of Jeneway 1593	xxij s
Rd at Jeronymo the 22 of Jeneway 1593	xx^{s}

Alternatively, the record for a single month – September 1594 – shows the range of a company's active repertory.

2 of septmb*er* 1594	Rd at the Jew of malta	xxiijs vjd
3 of septmb*er* 1594	Rd at Tasso	xxxxvjs
4 of septmb*er* 1594	Rd at phillipo & hewpolito	xxijs
5 of septmb*er* 1594	Rd at the venesyon comodey	xxxvjs vjd
6 of septmb*er* 1594	Rd at cvtlacke	xjs
7 of septmb*er* 1594	Rd at masacar	xvijs vjd
8 of septmb*er* 1594	Rd at godfrey	xxxxs
9 of septmb*er* 1594	Rd at mahemett	xxxvs
10 of septmb*er* 1594	Rd at galiaso	xxvs
11 of septmb*er* 1594	Rd at bellendon	xxiiijs vjd
12 of septmb*er* 1594	Rd at tamberlen	xxxxvs
13 of septmb*er* 1594	Rd at phillipo & hewpolito	xxs
15 of septmb*er* 1594	Rd at the venesyon comedy	xxxvjs vjd
16 of septmb*er* 1594	Rd at the Rangers comodey	xvs
17 of septmb*er* 1594	ne*–Rd at palamon & arsett	ljs
18 of septmb*er* 1594	Rd at tasso	xxvijs vjd
19 of septmb*er* 1594	Rd at phillipo & hewpolyto	xiiijs vjd
20 of septmb*er* 1594	Rd at godfrey	xxxs
21 of septmb*er* 1594	Rd at mahemett	xxviijs
22 of septmb*er* 1594	Rd at the venesyon comodey	xxvs
23 of septmb*er* 1594	Rd at bellendon	xvjs vjd
24 of septmb*er* 1594	ne–Rd at venesyon & the love of & Ingleshelady	xxxxvis
25 of septmb*er* 1594	Rd at masacar	xiiijs
26 of septmb*er* 1594	Rd at cvttlacke	xiijs
28 of septmb*er* 1594	Rd at tamberlen	xxxjs
29 of septmb*er* 1594	Rd at galiaso	xvijs
30 of septmb*er* 1594	Rd at docter ffostose	iijli xijs

* (=new)

Some plays, such as Kyd's *Spanish Tragedy* and Marlowe's *Dr. Faustus*, were rewritten and updated to extend their life, but any play performed ten or twelve times was considered a success. To learn their lines, actors rehearsed each morning, played in the afternoon, and often learned new lines in the evenings. The fact that they played similar parts from play to play and often spoke in conventional or formulaic language, with stock gestures and stock positions on the stage, allowed them to keep many plays in their minds at the same time. They were given only their "parts" to memorize – the "fair copy," or readable copy of all the parts – was used as a promptbook. Such practices, however, encouraged improvisation as well, and players played to their audiences as well as to each other and to events of the day: drama was also analogous to life in its malleability, its fluidity, and its ability to improvise. Like life too, it was a collaborative art, as well as one which could be personal with its audiences, addressing almost intimately those closest to the stage.

In and about London this commercial drama was totally unlike shows and pageants; here drama thus established in a playhouse an entire world that was both an analogy and an alternative to the world just outside the theater's walls. Men and women might dress up to attend, to see a play and be seen at a play, but theaters also beckoned children playing truant from school and apprentices truant from work as well as prostitutes, pickpockets, and those ready for a fight. Cobblers, merchants, gallants, and gentry were all in attendance: if a world apart, it was also a part of much of the real world. Courtiers could play roles daily as they do in Marlowe's *Edward II*. The witchcraft and diabolism of *Dr. Faustus* paralleled unruly citizens and the religious practices of exorcism. Thus playgoers' fascination with the world of illusion – Francis Beaumont's major concern – threatened those who, like many Puritans, some preachers, and fearful city magistrates, felt that these representations of life might attract some to authentic acts of villainy or foolishness. Despite the approval of the Queen's and the King's

Privy Councils and the nobility and royalty who served the acting companies as patrons, the London city aldermen distrusted the large and riotous crowds as a real and potential danger of crime, disease, plague, and general misbehavior. Meantime, the crown, aware of the stage as a place open to commentary on and criticism of the life and culture from which and to which it played, set forth its own regulations. In 1581 the Queen's Master of the Revels, an official on the staff of the Lord Chamberlain, was obliged

> to warn, command, and appoint in all places within this our realm of England, as well within franchises and liberties as without, all and every player or players with their playmakers, either belonging to any nobleman or otherwise ... to appear before him with all such plays, tragedies, comedies, or shows as they shall in readiness or mean to set forth, and them to recite before our said Servant or his sufficient deputy, whom we ordain, appoint, and authorize by these presents of all such shows, plays, players, and playmakers, together with their playing places, to order and reform, authorize and put down, as shall be thought meet or unmeet unto himself or his said deputy in that behalf.

The regulation, meant to enforce order and discipline, was also repressive, providing a means of censorship. We may find Renaissance English drama entertaining and pleasurable, but it was also seen, always, as potentially instructive and possibly dangerous. If we fail to see how the drama represented the triumphs and the failures of the culture, as well as its problems, we risk both underestimating its power and misunderstanding its full meaning. The struggle to convey and the struggle to comment were then as now part of drama's needful and privileged struggle to mean. The English drama of the Renaissance that survives gives us our most accurate portrayal – and so our deepest understanding – of that moment in history that gave it birth.

Brief Lives

FRANCIS BEAUMONT was born at his family's country seat at Grace-Dieu in Leicestershire in 1584. Both his grandfather and father were distinguished judges and he may have planned to follow in their footsteps. He entered Broadgates Hall (now Pembroke College), Oxford, as a gentleman commoner but left without a degree in 1600 to enter the Inner Temple, one of London's law schools. His first known publication is an erotic poem, "Salmacis and Hermaphroditus" (1602). In 1607 he must have known John Fletcher, with whom he would collaborate on about twelve plays between 1609 and 1611, because they both wrote commendatory poems then for Ben Jonson's *Volpone*. Beaumont also wrote plays alone and with others, often contributing satiric scenes. But he seems to have retired from writing on his marriage to Ursula Isley, the coheiress to a decayed Kentish house, in 1613. He died on March 25, 1616, about one month before Shakespeare.

THOMAS DEKKER was probably born in London, descended from Dutch craftsmen, but nothing is known from his life except what we might infer from his works. In the earlier 1590s he worked with Shakespeare and others on the unpublished play of *Sir Thomas More*. But he was an extremely popular and prolific playwright who worked on salary for Philip Henslowe and his acting company, the Admiral's Men, who played largely at the Rose Theater in Southwark. He wrote at high speed, in all dramatic genres, and usually with others: in 1599, for instance, he wrote *The Shoemakers' Holiday* and *Old Fortunatus* as well as *Patient Grissil*, a comedy, and history plays and tragedies with others. His work consistently shows particular sensitivity to the lives of citizens and working men, often plagued by insecurity or poverty; he himself was imprisoned for debt in 1598 and again in 1599, and released only when Henslowe advanced him money. After 1600 he began writing with major playwrights, such as Middleton, Webster, and Ford, and turned to journalistic pamphlets about daily life in London. The best known of these is *The Wonderful Year* (1603), describing public reaction to the death of Elizabeth I and the devastation of a plague that killed 30,000 persons in London; *News from Hell* and *The Seven Deadly Sins of London* (both 1606) and *Lanthorn and Candlelight* (1608) focus on social and moral issues of city life. In 1603 the city of London commissioned Dekker and Ben Jonson to write the civic pageant welcoming King James, and Dekker went on to write similar civic pageants for the installation of Lord Mayors. Despite this festivity he often focused on the crime, poverty, and disease of city life, doubtless from first-hand knowledge: from 1612 to 1619 he was again in jail for debt. Apparently he also died in debt in 1632, since his wife renounced her right to administer his estate, presumably to avoid his further indebtedness.

JOHN FORD was baptized on April 17, 1586, at Islington, Devonshire. Nothing is known of his early life; on November 16, 1602, he was admitted to the Middle Temple in London. Many of his family were already members, and others were to follow. In Hilary Term, 1606, he was expelled for failing to pay his buttery bill, a common offense, but he was readmitted in June 1608. He was resident there until at least 1617. In 1606 he began publishing prose and poetry, much of it heavily moralistic, but between 1621 and 1625 he published at least five works with Dekker (probably his mentor in the genre), including *The Witch of Edmonton* and a masque, *The Sun's Darling*. His three major works, *'Tis Pity She's a Whore*, *The Broken Heart*, and *Perkin Warbeck*, were written between 1625 and 1634 and are distinguished by his interest in the psychology of his characters. Nothing more is known of him subsequent to the publication of his last play, *The Lady's Trial*, in 1639.

THOMAS HEYWOOD was the most prolific playwright of Renaissance English drama: his career stretches from the mid-1590s to 1641, and well before its end, in 1633, he remarked he had written all or part of 222 plays. Still, his life is reasonably obscure. He attended Cambridge University and apparently was interested in the classics, since one of his early works is a translation of Sallust. He was writing plays for Henslowe by October 1596 – his most famous was *A Woman Killed with Kindness* – and he became a professional actor in 1598, his acting career continuing with the Earl of Worcester's Men (later the Queen's Men) until 1620. But this did not stop his productivity; in 1598 Francis Meres noted he was "among our best for comedy." Beginning with his *History of Women* in 1624, he wrote a number of works which praised women; from 1630 to 1639 he wrote a number of Lord Mayors' pageants. He was proud of the theater and defended it in his well-known *Apology for Actors*. He died in 1641 and was buried on August 16 in the Church of St. James in Clerkenwell.

Ben Jonson's life is more fully recorded than that of any other playwright of the time. He was born in 1572, in or near London, the posthumous son of "a grave minister of the gospel." Soon after, his mother married a master bricklayer from Westminster. Although Jonson later claimed a childhood of poverty, a friend paid for his early education at Westminster School, where he studied under the famous historian William Camden. He was later removed and taught bricklaying, remaining for much of his life a guild member. He served as a volunteer in the war in Flanders, killing a man in single combat. Sometime between 1592 and 1595 he married "a shrew yet honest," by whom he had two children – a daughter who died at six months and a son who died at the age of seven. His theater life began as a strolling player in the country where he acted in *The Spanish Tragedy*, but by 1597 he was back in London, arrested and jailed for two months for his part in a satiric and "seditious" play called *The Isle of Dogs* (now lost). His first successful work was *Every Man in His Humor* (1598) with Shakespeare in the cast, but the same year he was arrested for killing the actor Gabriel Spencer in another duel. He pleaded guilty but escaped hanging by benefit of clergy; his goods were confiscated and his thumb branded. His early comedies often lampooned his contemporaries, who satirized him in turn. In 1603 he turned to serious drama with *Sejanus* and later *Catiline*, but they were far less successful and in 1604 he was again jailed for his comments on Scots in the play *Eastward Ho!* Then followed the decade of highest achievement in playwriting, with the highly popular comedies *Volpone* (1605), *Epicoene* (1609–11), *The Alchemist* (1610), and *Bartholomew Fair* (1614). Another comedy on London life, *The Devil Is an Ass*, followed in 1616, when Jonson oversaw publication of the great folio of his *Works*. During this period he also wrote poetry and, beginning with the *Magnificent Entertainment* for James I's entry into London in 1604, he began writing pageants and especially masques for the Jacobean court, often in collaboration with the scenic designer Inigo Jones. He wrote very little drama between 1616 and 1624, although in 1619 Oxford University awarded this self-educated man an M.A. He returned to the stage with *The Staple of News* (1626), but Charles I did not share his father's enthusiasm for Jonson's work. He was stricken with paralysis in 1628 but lived another nine years. He died on August 6, 1637, and was buried in the Poets' Corner of Westminster Abbey, where his tombstone reads "O rare Ben Jonson," traditionally a phrase used after the "popular applause" for *Bartholomew Fair*.

Thomas Kyd was baptized on November 6, 1558, in the Church of St. Mary Woolnoth, London, the son of prosperous parents. His father was Warden of the Company of Scriveners in 1580. In 1565, at the age of seven, he entered Merchant Taylors' School studying, along with Edmund Spenser, Lancelot Andrewes, and Thomas Lodge, under the acclaimed Richard Mulcaster. There he learned Latin, French, Italian, and some Greek and acted with his schoolmates before Elizabeth I at court. By 1585 he was writing plays for the Queen's Company, the leading London players, although none of these survives. The only works certainly his that are extant are *The Spanish Tragedy* and a translation of Tasso entitled *The Householder's Philosophy* (1588), although he may also have written *Soliman and Perseda* and an early version of *Hamlet*. He was arrested in 1593 when libelous papers were found in his chambers; taken before the Privy Council on May 11, he claimed they were the work of Marlowe, with whom he had shared rooms. His imprisonment may have hastened his death; he was buried at St. Mary Colchurch, London, on August 15, 1594.

Christopher Marlowe, the first son of John Marlowe, a Canterbury shoemaker, and his wife Katherine, was baptized on February 26, 1564, the year John Marlowe became a freeman of the city. Marlowe's father was notoriously improvident and quarrelsome, as were two of his sisters, and the playwright may have shared their nature in his later outspokenness. He was educated at King's School, Canterbury, and then, on a scholarship offered by Matthew Parker, at Corpus Christi, Cambridge, destined for the clergy. He was awarded the B.A. by examinations in February 1584, but his M.A. was delayed by university authorities who noted his frequent absences from Cambridge until the government intervened, noting he had "done Her Majesty good service." That service is thought to be spying on the Continent, but there is no hard evidence extant for this. He never presented himself for ordination, however. His first play, in collaboration with his fellow Cambridge student Thomas Nashe, was *Dido, Queen of Carthage* (ca. 1586) for the Children of the Chapel, but it was his epic play on Tamburlaine in magnificent blank verse (1587) that made him sensationally successful. Four public tragedies followed: *Dr. Faustus* (ca. 1588), *The Jew of Malta* (ca. 1589), *The Massacre at Paris* and *Edward II* (ca. 1591–2). In this brief span he also wrote two well-known poems, a sexually explicit translation of Ovid's *Amores* (probably at Cambridge) and an erotic epyllion, *Hero and Leander* (1593). In later years he was frequently in trouble: he was arrested in a street fight in September 1589 and spent two weeks in jail; he was arrested for counterfeiting coins in Flushing in 1592, and in September of that year for an assault on a Canterbury tailor; on May 30, 1593, he was killed in a tavern fight in Deptford. The tavern brawl may have been caused by his perpetual indebtedness, his quick temper, or his involvement in spying and counterspying for the Queen's Lord Treasurer, Sir Francis Walsingham, but there is no conclusive evidence. Equally ambiguous may be his sexual orientation, for his sympathy with homosexuality in *Hero and Leander* and *Edward II* is offset by the pronounced heterosexuality of *Tamburlaine* and *Dr. Faustus.*

THOMAS MIDDLETON was born in 1580 and christened at St. Lawrence Jewry, London, on April 18. His father, William, a bricklayer and gentleman with his own coat of arms owning property near the Curtain Theater in Shoreditch and at Limehouse, died when Thomas was seven. His mother then married Thomas Harvey, an adventurer who clearly was after her property, and financial squabbles for the family fortune by Thomas's stepfather and later his sister occupied the family until 1603. He matriculated at Queen's College, Oxford, in 1598, but left in 1601 to help his mother with lawsuits, having already surrendered his own property rights to his brother-in-law a year earlier in order to continue his studies. By the time he was twenty, Middleton had published poetry (*The Wisdom of Solomon Paraphrased*), a Marstonian satire (*Micro-Cynicon*), and a complaint (*The Ghost of Lucrece*). In 1602 he was collaborating on plays with Munday, Drayton, and Webster and in 1602 he wrote his own play (now lost), *Caesar's Fall*, as well as, in 1604, two prose works attacking the vices of urban life. His first play, *The Family of Love* (1602), is a lively satire on sex and wealth and on the Brownists, based in part, perhaps, on the brother-in-law to whom he had given his property who had been imprisoned in Newgate for his Brownist beliefs. His early work in drama was for the children's companies of Paul's and Blackfriars; when they disbanded in 1606 he wrote for Prince Henry's Men, Lady Elizabeth's company and (largely) for the King's Men, Shakespeare's company, but in all of these he remained influenced by his early family quarrels and the city life around his father's house in Ironmonger's Lane off Cheapside. His major works demarcate three periods: those of city comedies culminating in *A Chaste Maid in Cheapside* (1611–13); romances such as *The Widow* (1616); and the late great tragedies including *The Changeling* (with William Rowley, 1622); *Women Beware Women* (1621–7); and *A Game at Chess* (1624), a brilliant satire which resulted in the players being summoned before the Privy Council although no action was finally taken. His comic attacks on property could, at times, turn to bitterness and dismay. He died in 1627 and was buried on July 4 at St. Mary's, Newington Butts, about a mile south of Southwark.

RICHARD MULCASTER was born, probably in Carlisle, in 1530 or 1531, the son of an old border family that traced its ancestry back to the time of William Rufus. He was first educated under the playwright Nicholas Udall, master of Eton College; in 1548 he was elected scholar at King's College, Cambridge; in 1555 he was elected a scholar at Christ Church, Oxford, where he received the M.A. in 1556. He went down to London as a schoolmaster and in 1561 he was appointed headmaster at the new Merchant Taylors' School, where his most famous pupil was Edmund Spenser. He was educationally liberal, but strict by temper and, after much trouble with the governing body, he resigned his position in 1586. He was named vicar of Cranbrook, Kent, in 1590, and prebendary of Gatesbury, Sarum, in 1594. At the age of sixty-six, on August 5, 1596, he was elected High Master of St. Paul's School, London, where he served until his resignation in the spring of 1608. He was noteworthy in his progressive ideas for education, teaching music and singing, the performance of plays and masques, urging physical education and vocational education alongside the classics, and arguing that girls should receive education equal to that of boys, mounting a strong case in two books, *Positions* (1581) and *The Elementarie* (1582). He died on April 15, 1611, and was buried alongside his wife at Stanford Rivers Church.

ANTHONY MUNDAY was born in 1560 and baptized on October 13, the son of Christopher Munday, a freeman of the Draper's Company who made his living as a stationer. Both Munday's parents died when he was young, and he was taken as an apprentice by the stationer John Allde, where he remained until 1578. He then went with Thomas Nowell on a trip to the Continent, first to Boulogne, then to Amiens, and ultimately to Rome, where he stayed at the English College founded to train Jesuits. On his return he turned against papists, attacking them in his account of the English College and of the execution of Edmund Campion. For a while he served the government under Walsingham and Richard Topcliffe. But he also began acting and writing in various genres – in prose fiction, ballads, news pamphlets and even attacks on the theater. He wrote a comedy, *Mother Redcap*, with Michael Drayton, and several other plays with Chettle, Wilson, and Dekker; among his best-known works are *John a Kent and John a Cumber*; *The Downfall of Robert, Earl of Huntingdon*; and *Histriomastix*. Known primarily for his versatility, Munday was commissioned to write the city pageants for 1605, 1609, 1611, 1614–16, 1618, and 1623, and he seems to have been authorized to keep the properties for such shows, since Middleton applied to him in 1613 for the use of some of them. Since he signs some of these shows as a citizen and draper, he may have inherited his father's trade. But in later years he devoted much time to writing and translating romances, including *Amadis de Gaul.* He died in 1633 and was buried on August 10 in the Church of St. Stephen, Coleman Street, London.

William Rowley was born around 1585. Little is known of his life; his first recorded acting is in 1607, the same year his first two plays – *Fortune by Land and Sea* with Thomas Heywood and *The Travels of the Three English Brothers* with John Day and George Wilkins – were produced. From 1609 to 1621 he was a member of the Duke of York's Men (later Prince Charles's Men), usually taking the part of the clown. He was apparently congenial, for he was in demand as a collaborator by a great many playwrights, although he was better at his understanding of human nature than in writing good poetry. He began collaborating with Thomas Middleton on several important plays in 1617, writing the subplot for *A Fair Quarrel*; two years later he played the clown's role in Middleton's *The Inner Temple Masque.* That same year, 1619, he wrote his only extant play without others, *All's Lost by Lust.* He wrote the subplot for *The Changeling* in 1622 and in 1623 joined the King's Men, offending the Spanish ambassador while playing the part of the fat bishop in Middleton's *A Game at Chess* (1624). He may have worked with Middleton on *The Spanish Gipsy*, he wrote the comedy *A Cure for a Cuckold* with John Webster, and, finally, with the well-known clown Compass, a city comedy entitled *A Woman Never Vexed.* He died in February 1626.

Sir Philip Sidney, a descendant of the powerful Dudley family, was born on November 30, 1554, at the family home at Penshurst, Kent, and (ironically) was christened Philip for his godfather Philip II, King of Spain. He was educated at Shrewsbury School, not far from the official residence of his father, Lord President of the Marches of Wales, in Ludlow, and then went on to Christ Church, Oxford, where he translated a part of Aristotle's *Rhetoric.* His father thought him too serious a student and sent him on a Grand Tour of Europe, where he met and was influenced by many humanists and heads of state. He returned in the winter of 1575, presumably to help his uncle, the Earl of Leicester, prepare to entertain Elizabeth I at Kenilworth. In 1576 he was made Cupbearer to the Queen, and the following year led an embassy touring Europe to determine the possibility of a Protestant League against Spain; in the course of his travels he became especially friendly with William of Orange, the Protestant leader of the Low Countries. He followed his uncle in opposing the Queen's marriage to the French Catholic Duke of Anjou. The Queen took offense, and Sidney retired to Wilton, the country house of his sister, the Countess of Pembroke, where he wrote a long politically inspired romance, the *Arcadia*, which has claim to being the first major English novel (and the most popular until 1740). He was elected to Parliament in 1581 and wrote a sonnet sequence, perhaps on his failed romance with Penelope Devereux, *Astrophil and Stella*, in 1582. In 1583 he was knighted to be proxy for Prince Casimir's Garter installation in March; in September he married Frances, the daughter of Sir Francis Walsingham, then Elizabeth I's Principal Secretary. In 1586 he met his uncle in the Netherlands, where they joined battle against the invasion of Spain. He was wounded in a skirmish at Zutphen on September 22 which attempted to break the main Spanish supply lines; infection spread from his leg wound and he died at Arnheim on October 17. On February 16, 1587, he was buried in a great state ceremony at St. Paul's Cathedral, financed by Walsingham.

John Webster was born around 1578, the eldest son of the owner of a business of making, hiring, and selling coaches, wagons, and carts in Cow Lane, London, who, because there was no guild for coachmakers, was a freeman of the Merchant Taylors' Company. He was educated at Merchant Taylors' School before passing to the New Inn and being admitted to Middle Temple on August 1, 1598. He seems to have been especially studious, for his plays are full of quotations and allusions to law. He first collaborated on a play for Henslowe in 1602 and contributed to John Marston's *The Malcontent* (1604), as well as two city comedies with Thomas Dekker for Paul's Boys, *Westward Ho!* (1604) and *Northward Ho!* (1605). His first major tragedy, *The White Devil* (1612), was not an initial success, but it was followed closely by *The Duchess of Malfi* (1612–13), which was better received. He continued to supply material for the work of others, including the sixth edition of Sir Thomas Overbury's *Characters* (1615) and a popular play for which no text survives, *The Late Murder of the Son Upon the Mother* (1624), which led to proceedings in the Court of Star Chamber. In 1615 he seems to have exercised his inherited right to become a freeman of the Merchant Taylors' guild, and in 1624 he wrote the civic pageant when one of their members was elected Lord Mayor. Later collaborations include *Anything for a Quiet Life* (1620–1) with Middleton, *The Fair Maid of the Inn* (with Fletcher), *A Cure for a Cuckold* (1624–5) with William Rowley and possibly Thomas Heywood, and *Appius and Virginia.* He is presumed to have died in the 1630s.

The Queen's Majesty's Passage

Richard Mulcaster

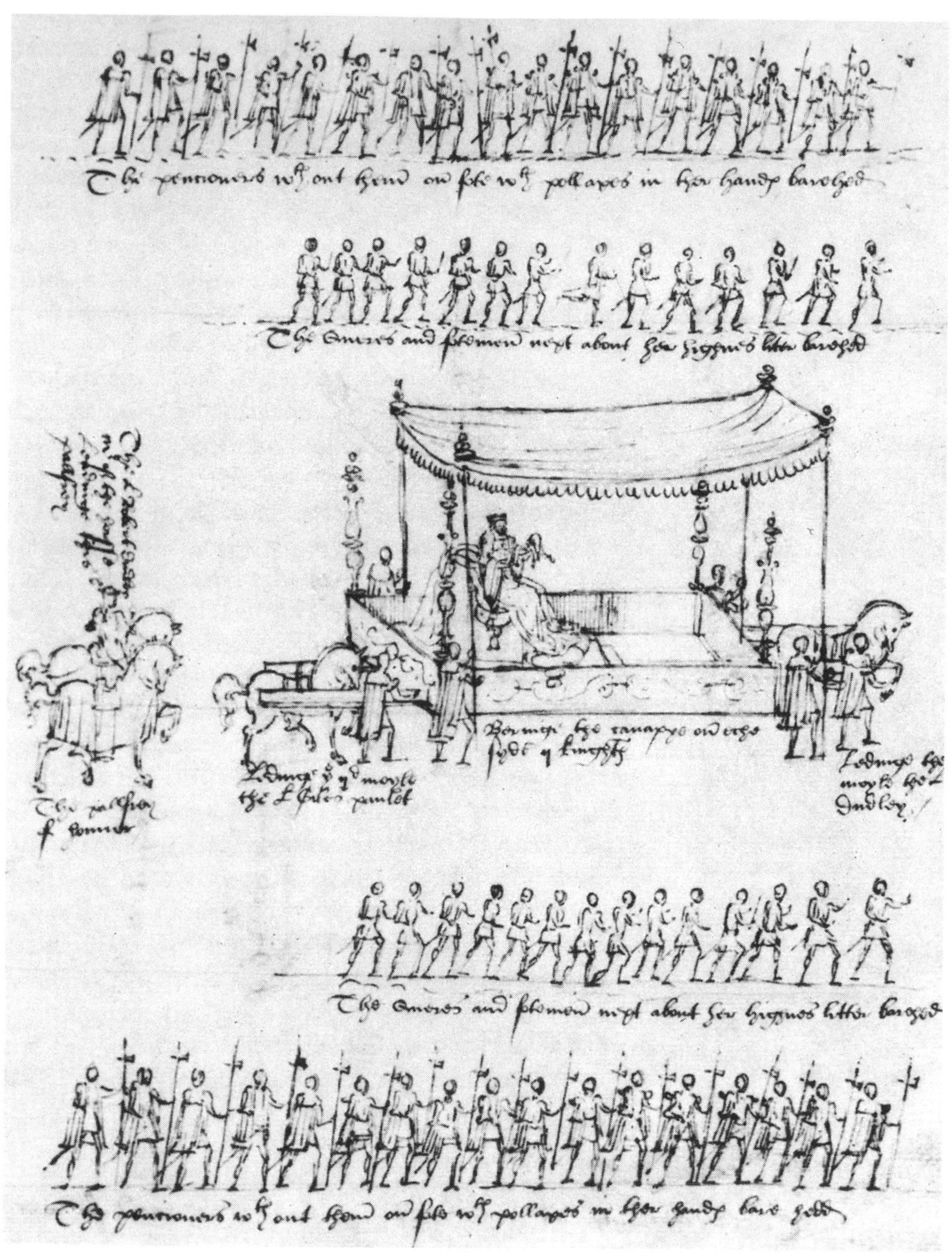

The Queen in her litter on her way from Whitehall to her coronation at Westminster. This was on Sunday, January 15, the day following her passage through the city of London; and undoubtedly the same litter was used on both occasions. Reproduced from Egerton MS 3320, by courtesy of the Trustees of the British Library.

Thousands upon thousands attended the first Elizabethan performance – rich and poor; men, women, and children; nobility, courtiers, citizens, merchants, and masterless men – in a joyful, noisy crowd that would fill a Fortune, Rose, or Globe Theater several times over: Richard Mulcaster's account calls it "a stage wherein was shown the wonderful spectacle of a noble hearted princess toward her most loving people." The occasion was the passage of Princess Elizabeth through the streets of London the day before her coronation. The entertainment may seem to us more pageant than drama; indeed, Elizabeth resembled the sacred wafer once beneath a canopy in the Corpus Christi processions of an earlier age. But there is forceful dramatic action between the virtues and vices at Cornhill Street, and, even more importantly, sustained dramatic tension between the show and the intention, the actors and the audience (where the princess played with both). The account and script that have come down to us as they frame and interpret the actual presentations force us to unlock the drama on the streets of London on Saturday, January 14, 1559. Clearly these presentations are the root for the Renaissance English drama that flourished later, and the emblems, metaphors, and issues staged for the Queen's passage, if more or less implicit, remain at the center of all the plays, pageants, and entertainments that followed throughout the reigns of Elizabeth I and James I and VI.

The records for the Corporation of London dated December 7, 1558, reveal the splendor and the cost:

> Item this day the Worshipful Commoners hereunder named were nominated, appointed, and charged by the whole Court to take the charge, travail, and pains to cause at the City's costs and charges all the places hereafter mentioned to be very well and seemly trimmed and decked for the honor of the City against the coming of our Sovereign Lady the Queen's majesty that now is to her Coronation through the City with pageants, fine paintings, and rich cloths of arras, silver, and gold in such and like manner and sort as they were trimmed against the coming of our late Sovereign lady Queen Mary to her Coronation and much better if it conveniently may be done.

The city gates, walls, churches, and the streets themselves were covered with cloths and tapestry bright with color. The city of at least 150,000 must have been congested, noisy, and electrifyingly alive in preparation and anticipation. The Venetian ambassador, Il Schifanoya, writes to Mantua nine days later that "The houses on the way were all decorated; there being on both sides of the street, from Blackfriars to St. Paul's, wooden barricades, on which the merchants and artisans of every trade leant in long black gowns lined with hoods of red and black cloth ... with all their ensigns, banners, and standards, which were innumerable, and made a very fine show." Still others pushed and shoved to get the best view along the proposed route of the princess or to see as well as possible one of the many stations where the shows would be staged.

Snow fell lightly the morning of January 14 and by afternoon the streets were muddy with residue; gravel and sand were shoveled before shops and houses. Il Schifanoya notes that shortly after two in the afternoon, Elizabeth appeared "dressed in a royal robe of very rich cloth of gold, with a double-raised stiff pile, and on her head over a coif of cloth of gold, beneath which was her hair, a plain gold crown without lace, as a princess, but covered with jewels, and nothing in her hands but gloves." She was carried on a litter, accompanied by one thousand people on horseback. Before her went her household staff: lesser officers of state; the bench of bishops and temporal peers; foreign ambassadors; the king of arms; Arundel, as Lord Steward, bearing the sword of state; Norfolk, as Earl Marshal; and Oxford, as High Constable. Elizabeth's litter was open, trimmed to the ground with gold brocade, and borne by two mules which were also covered with brocade. She was followed by Robert Dudley, as master of the horse, leading a spare mount; thirty-nine ladies of honor, twenty-four on palfreys and the rest in three chariots; wives and daughters of the chief peers; henchmen; and royal guards. All about there were footmen in crimson velvet jerkins with gilt silver and, on back and front, a white and red rose with the letters E. R. for Elizabeta Regina. She quickly and securely made her first point: there could not have been greater splendor – nor a greater demonstration of power and authority. During her passage from the Tower of London to Temple Bar and so on to Westminster Abbey for the actual crowning ceremony, she made eleven stops and saw five pageants, together reinforcing the day's thematics: her legitimate descent to rule England with a rule as forceful as that of her father Henry VIII and as Protestant as that of her brother Edward VI. Both her love of her own nation and her love of the newly established church displayed her again and again as the deliberate antitype of her late sister Mary, whose brief reign had been characterized by the horrors of bloody Catholic persecution: the fires at Smithfield, the unholy marital alliance with Philip of Spain, and the humiliation of losing the vital French port of Calais – the last English part of the Continent – in what was then called "King Philip's War." As such an antitype, she too became a character in the pageantry, but so did the audience when they elected to side with her personally and politically.

Richard Hilles, a member of Parliament and a merchant taylor; Lionell Ducket, a mercer and (in 1572) Lord Mayor of London; Francis Robinson, a grocer; and Richard Grafton, a printer, were commissioned by the Corporation to write the five pageants. The first of these, "The uniting of the two houses of Lancaster and York," might at first seem to provide an historical prologue. But it did more than that: by demonstrating Elizabeth's hereditary right to the crown of England, it answered the Catholic charge of bastardy (introducing the anti-Marian strain) and, deliberately, was placed at Gracechurch Street where, decades before, Elizabeth's mother Anne Boleyn, later executed for treason, had herself seen a coronation pageant for her own installation as Queen of England. Such pointedness continues. The first staging, centered on unity, leads to the second, centered on peace, "The seat of worthy governance," in which Elizabeth uses her claim to the throne to insure the end of strife and so give testament to the nation's need for her. Here vices battle virtues and the victory of the virtues is related directly to Elizabeth's accession to the throne; that this inset morality play underscored the new reign's Protestantism was not lost on the Italian ambassador: he understands this pageant to mean "that hitherto religion had been misunderstood and misdirected, and that now it will proceed on a better footing." Elizabeth's abiding right to rule is guaranteed by the principles set forth in the third pageant, stressing the beatitudes from the gospel of Matthew: she will especially bless (and so in turn be blessed by) the poor in spirit, those that mourn, the meek, the hungry, the merciful, those who have been persecuted for righteousness, the pure in heart, and the peacemakers. The opposition, now clearly linked to Mary Tudor and Philip of Spain, are those who are superstitious, ignorant, rebellious, insolent, foolish, vainglorious, full of bribery and false adulation – the eight beatitudes are trampling the eight sins of Elizabeth's predecessor and the characteristics of her rule. The second and third pageants thus join forces to lay the groundwork for the final two: the ruined commonwealth of the fourth pageant (as the fourth act in what is now clearly a drama of mind and belief) where the country is rescued by Time – Henry VIII's will and legacy made good – through his daughter of Truth, Elizabeth, known as such because she holds the Book of Truth, the Protestant Bible. Handed to her in the course of this public proclamation she will hold it up, kiss it, and hold it tightly to her breast. The final pageant, having dismissed Mary Tudor as a model for Elizabeth (and with her the Catholic Virgin for whom she was named), supplies the new model for the new realm in the Old Testament hero of Deborah. Such a judge reasserts biblical authority, but in a new Protestant mode.

The various stages that produce the five-act drama for the Queen's passage through London, then, reenact the states of the mystery cycle of plays that were still widely performed, in city and village, during Corpus Christi Day each year; indeed, if originating in the medieval Catholic church, they would continue to flourish in Coventry, York, and Chester until midway through Elizabeth's reign. But civic pageantry began simultaneously with the Corpus Christi celebrations – in a mimetic pageant in 1377 and with elaborate Latin speeches added, as here, by 1392; the coronation pageantry for Richard II (and for all those who succeeded him) display him as a Christian king and London as his continually renewing New Jerusalem. The Venetian ambassador adds details to the report of Richard Mulcaster when he describes the Standard and the Cross at Cheap: on the Standard "there were painted to the life all the kings and queens chronologically in their royal robes down to her present Majesty" while the Cross was "like a pyramid, completely gilt and somewhat renovated, with all the saints in relief, they being neither altered nor diminished." The Queen's passage would convert them all to *her* New Jerusalem.

If the show called *The Queen's Majesty's Passage* is emblematic rather than realistic in its mode of presentation, it is not meant only to impress the spectators and indoctrinate the readers of Mulcaster's pamphlet below; it is also meant to direct the incoming Queen. The Queen may have been complicit in formulating this script; she is surely complicit by the end of it when, accepting nosegays from the poor, rosemary from one who would have her remember those who have been repressed, and laughing at a joke about her father, she turns the previous emblems and the present acts into metaphors and signs for her realm. The author of *The Queen's Majesty's Passage* is clear about this, too. He introduces a certain amount of general and classical learning – the legendary founding of Britain as well as biblical texts – in part, perhaps, because it was his instinct to do so, as the famed headmaster of Merchant Taylors' School in London. Yet we do well to remember that Mulcaster was also a Member of Parliament himself, sitting for Carlisle. He had interests in education and in government both, and he understood ways in which a playscript could conscript Elizabeth. Sacred monarchy was itself of two perspectives: it could awaken fear and obedience through awe ("dread" in the pamphlet) or it could provide peace and healing through beneficence (advanced in reciting the beatitudes). To contain such variety, the pageants invite Elizabeth to declare Protestantism openly; to conclude with a student of Christ's Hospital forces her to recognize, sympathize with, and advocate the causes of the poor (in time her reign would enact the nation's first poor laws). Nor does the show itself end its intentional purposes there: Mulcaster's account is filled with adjectives describing the princess as loving, caring, pacific, Protestant, and responsible – that is, it turns her into a real-life character far more complicated (and so more contained and confined) than any of the boy speakers or adult actors in the shows. The pamphlet also, just as consciously, is meant to teach its readers, promulgating among them not simply support of the new Queen but support of a particular kind of rule and a particular political and social perspective. In the end, pageant, play, and pamphlet are all propagandistic. This too is obvious: the account we have appeared only nine days after the events it records, which suggests either that Mulcaster knew of events in advance, or the printers cleared their printshops to publish this before anything else, or both; it went through three editions (and perhaps more) limited to 1,500 copies each by the Stationers' Company with only a partial (and minimal) resetting of type. This work is not only the first show of Elizabeth's reign but the first published drama of her period.

Further Reading

Anglo, Sydney, *Spectacle, Pageantry, and Early Tudor Policy*. Oxford: Clarendon Press, 1969.

Bergeron, David M., *English Civic Pageantry 1558–1642*. Columbia: University of South Carolina Press, 1971.

DeMolen, Richard L., "Richard Mulcaster and Elizabethan Pageantry," *Studies in English Literature 1500–1900* 14:2 (Spring 1974): 209–21.

Frye, Susan, *Elizabeth I: The Competition for Representation*. New York: Oxford University Press, 1993.

Kipling, Gordon, "Richard II's 'Sumptuous Pageants' and the Idea of the Civic Triumph," in *Pageantry in the Shakespearean Theater*, ed. David M. Bergeron (Athens: University of Georgia Press, 1985), pp. 85–103.

——, "'He That Saw It Would Not Believe It': Anne Boleyn's Royal Entry into London," in *Civic Ritual and Drama*, ed. Alexandra F. Johnston and Win Hüsken (Amsterdam: Rodopi V. C., 1997), pp. 39–79.

Smuts, R. Malcolm, "Public Ceremony and Royal Charisma: The English Royal Entry in London, 1485–1642," in *The First Modern Society*, ed. A. L. Beier, David Cannadine, and James M. Rosenheim (Cambridge: Cambridge University Press, 1989), pp. 65–94.

Wirthington, Robert, *English Pageantry in Historical Outline*, 2 vols. Cambridge, Mass.: Harvard University Press, 1918–20.

The Queen's Majesty's Passage through the City of London to Westminster the Day before Her Coronation

The receiving of the Queen's Majesty.

Upon Saturday, which was the thirteenth day of January in the year of our Lord God 1558 about two of the clock at afternoon, the most noble and Christian princess, our most dread sovereign Lady Elizabeth by the grace of God Queen of England, France, and Ireland, Defender of the Faith, etc. marched from the Tower to pass through the city of London toward Westminster, richly furnished and most honorably accompanied, as well with gentlemen, barons, and other the nobility of this

Textual Variants

72 on] Q in **167** estate] Q state **227** before] Q tofore **404** Cheapside] Q Cheap **420** before] Q tofore **517** before] Q tofore **760** platform] Q plat **766** damaging] Q endamaging **944** shouting] Q shooting

7 Tower it was customary for kings of England to spend one or more nights in the Tower of London before their coronation processional to Westminster Abbey

realm, as also with a notable train of goodly and beautiful ladies richly appointed. And entering the city was of the people received marvelous entirely, as appeared by the assembly, prayers, wishes, welcomings, cries, tender words, and all other signs which argue a wonderful earnest love of most obedient subjects toward their sovereign. And on the other side, Her Grace, by holding up her hands and merry countenance to such as stood far off, and most tender and gentle language to those that stood nigh to Her Grace, did declare herself no less thankfully to receive her people's good will than they lovingly offered it unto her. To all that wished Her Grace well she gave hearty thanks, and to such as bade God save Her Grace, she said again "God save them all," and thanked them with all her heart. So that on either side there was nothing but gladness, nothing but prayer, nothing but comfort. The Queen's Majesty rejoiced marvelously to see that so exceedingly showed toward Her Grace which all good princes have ever desired, I mean so earnest love of subjects, so evidently declared even to Her Grace's own person being carried in the midst of them. The people again were wonderfully ravished with the loving answers and gestures of their princess, like to the which they had before tried at her first coming to the Tower from Hatfield. This Her Grace's loving behavior preconceived in the people's heads upon these considerations was then thoroughly confirmed, and indeed implanted a wonderful hope in them touching her worthy government in the rest of her reign. For in all her passage she did not only show her most gracious love toward the people in general, but also privately, if the baser personages had either offered Her Grace any flowers or such like as a signification of their good will, or moved to her any suit, she most gently, to the common rejoicing of all the lookers-on and private comfort of the party, stayed her chariot and heard their requests. So that if a man should say well, he could not better term the city of London that time than a stage wherein was shown the wonderful spectacle of a noble-hearted princess toward her most loving people, and the people's exceeding comfort in beholding so worthy a sovereign. And hearing so princelike a voice which could not but have set the enemy on fire, since the virtue is in the enemy always commended, much more could not but inflame her natural, obedient, and most loving people, whose weal leaneth only upon Her Grace and her government. Thus therefore the Queen's Majesty passed from the Tower until she came to Fanchurch, the people on each side joyously beholding the view of so gracious a Lady their Queen, and Her Grace no less gladly noting and observing the same. Near unto Fanchurch was erected a scaffold richly furnished, whereon stood a noise of instruments, and a child in costly apparel, which was appointed to welcome the Queen's Majesty on the whole city's behalf. Against which place when Her Grace came, of her own will she commanded the chariot to be stayed, and that the noise might be appeased until the child had uttered his welcoming oration which he spoke in English meter as here followeth:

O peerless sovereign Queen, behold what this thy town
Hath thee presented with at thy first entrance here:
Behold with how rich hope she leads Thee to Thy crown
Behold with what two gifts she comforteth Thy cheer.

The first is blessing tongues, which many a welcome say
Which pray thou mayest do well, which praise Thee to the sky,
Which wish to thee long life which bless this happy day,
Which to Thy kingdom heaps, all that in tongues can lie.

The second is true hearts, which love Thee from their root
Whose suit is triumph now, and ruleth all the game,
Which faithfulness have won, and all untruth driven out,
Which skip for joy, when as they hear thy happy name.

Welcome, therefore, Oh, Queen, as much as heart can think,
Welcome again, Oh, Queen, as much as tongue can tell:
Welcome to joyous tongues, and hearts that will not shrink.
God Thee preserve we pray, and wish Thee ever well.

At which words of the last line the whole people gave a great shout, wishing with one assent

34 carried the Queen was transported in a litter of yellow cloth of gold in a quilt of white damask with satin lining and eight matching cushions. Four knights carried a canopy over her and on either side marched an escort of pensioners with axes

38 Hatfield the royal palace in Hertfordshire, 19 miles NNW of London, where Mary had kept Princess Elizabeth detained in state

51 chariot i.e., litter

65 Fanchurch Fenchurch Street, a major street in Aldsgate Ward leading from the Tower

70 noise melody; consort

as the child had said. And the Queen's Majesty thanked most heartily both the city for this her gentle receiving at the first, and also the people for confirming the same. Here was noted in the Queen's Majesty's countenance during the time that the child spoke, besides a perpetual attentiveness in her face, a marvelous change in look, as the child's words touched either her person or the people's tongues and hearts. So that she with rejoicing visage did evidently declare that the words took no less place in her mind than they were most heartily pronounced by the child as from all the hearts of her most hearty citizens. The same verses were fastened up in a table upon the scaffold, and the Latin thereof likewise in Latin verses in another table as hereafter ensueth:

Vrbs tua quae ingressu dederit tibi munera primo,
O Regina paren non habitura, vide.
Ad diadema tuum, te spe quam diuite mittat,
Quae duo laetitae det tibi dona, vide.
Munus habes primum, linguas bona multa precantes,
Quae te quum laudant, tum pia vota sonant,
Foelicemque diem hunc dicunt, tibi secula longa
Optant, et quic quid denique lingua potest.
Altera dona fertes, vera, et tui amantia corda,
Quorum gens ludum iam regit vna tuum:
In quibus est infracta fides, falsumque perosa,
Quaequm tuo audito nomine laeta salit
Grata venis igitur, quantum cor concipit vllum,
Quantum lingua potest dicere, grata venis.
Cordibus infractis, linguisque per omnia laetis
Grata venis: saluam te velit esse deus.

Now when the child had pronounced his oration and the Queen's Highness so thankfully had received it, she marched forward toward Gracious Street where, at the upper end before the sign of the Eagle, the city had erected a gorgeous and sumptuous ark as here followeth:

A stage was made which extended from the one side of the street to the other, richly vaulted with battlements containing three ports, and over the middlemost was advanced three several stages in degrees. Upon the lowest stage was made one seat royal wherein were placed two personages representing King Henry the VII and Elizabeth his wife, daughter of King Edward the IV, either of these two princes sitting under one cloth of estate in their seats, not otherwise divided, but that the one of them which was King Henry the VII proceeding out of the house of Lancaster was enclosed in a red rose, and the other which was Queen Elizabeth being heir to the house of York enclosed with a white rose, each of them royally crowned, and decently appareled as appertaineth to princes, with scepters in their hands, and one vault surmounting their heads, wherein aptly were placed two tables, each containing the title of those two princes. And these personages were so set that the one of them joined hands with the other with the ring matrimony perceived on the finger. Out of the which two roses sprang two branches gathered into one, which were directed upward to the second stage or degree, wherein was placed one, representing the valiant and noble Prince King Henry the VIII which sprang out of the former stock, crowned with a crown imperial, and by him sat one representing the right worthy Lady Queen Anne, wife to the said King Henry VIII, and mother to our most sovereign Lady Queen Elizabeth that now is, both appareled with scepters and diadems and other furniture due to the estate of a king and queen, and two tables surmounting their heads, wherein were written their names and titles. From their seat also proceeded upwards one branch directed to the third and uppermost stage or degree, wherein likewise was planted a seat royal, in the which was set one representing the Queen's most excellent Majesty Elizabeth now our most dread sovereign Ladie, crowned and appareled as the other princes were. Out of the forepart of this pageant was made a standing for a child which, at the Queen's Majesty's coming, declared unto her the whole meaning of the said pageant. The two sides of the same were filled with loud noises of music. And all empty places thereof were furnished with sentences concerning unity, and the whole pageant garnished with red roses and white and in the forefront of the same pageant in a fair wreath was written the name and title of the same, which was *The uniting of the two houses of Lancaster and York*. This pageant was grounded upon the Queen's Majesty's name. For like as

98 **gentle** courteous
109 **table** printed board
131 **Gracious Street** Gracechurch Street, a major street going N from the Thames which served as a boundary of [London] Bridge Ward Within
132 **sign of the Eagle** a public house by that name
133 **ark** arch
136 **ports** gates; openings
138 **degrees** tiers
142 **cloth** canopy
166 **furniture** furnishings
174 **dread** awesome
177 **standing** platform

the long war between the two houses of York and Lancaster then ended, when Elizabeth, daughter to Edward the IV, matched in marriage with Henry the VII heir to the house of Lancaster so since that the Queen's Majesty's name was Elizabeth, and forsomuch as she is the only heir of Henry the VIII, which came of both the houses as the knitting up of concord, like as Elizabeth was the first occasion of concord, so she another Elizabeth might maintain the same among her subjects, so that unity was the end whereat the whole devise shott, as the Queen's Majesty's names moved the first ground. This pageant now against the Queen's Majesty's coming was addressed with children representing the forenamed personages, with all furniture due unto the setting forth of such a matter well meant, as the argument declared, costly and sumptuously set forth, as the beholders can bear witness. Now the Queen's Majesty drew near unto the said pageant, and forsomuch as the noise was great by reason of the press of people, so that she could scarce hear the child which did interpret the said pageant and her chariot was passed so far forward that she could not well view the personages representing the kings and queens above named she required to have the matter opened unto her, which so was, and every personage appointed, and what they signified, with the end of unity and ground of her name, according as is before expressed. For the sight whereof, Her Grace caused her chariot to be removed back and yet hardly could she see, because the children were set somewhat with the farthest in. But after that Her Grace had understood the meaning thereof, she thanked the city, praised the fairness of the work, and promised that she would do her whole endeavor for the continual preservation of concord, as the pageant did import. The child appointed in the standing above named to open the meaning of the said pageant spoke these words unto Her Grace.

The two princes that sit under one cloth of state,
The man in the red rose, the woman in the white,
Henry the VII and Queen Elizabeth his mate,
By ring of marriage as man and wife unite.

Both heirs to both their bloods, to Lancaster the King
The Queen to York, in one the two houses did knit,
Of whom, an heir to both, Henry the VIII did spring,
In whose seat his true heir thou Queen Elizabeth doth sit.

Therefore as civil war and shed of blood did cease
When these two houses were united into one
So now that jar shall stint, and quietness increase,
We trust, Oh, noble Queen, thou wilt be cause alone.

The which also were written in Latin verses, and both drawn in two tables upon the forefront of the said pageant as hereafter followeth.

Hii quos iungit idem solum quos annulus idem:
Haec albente nitens, ille rubente Rosa:
Septimus Henricus Rex, Regina Elizabetha,
Scilicet Haeredes gentis vterque suae:
Haec Eboracenis, Lancastrius ille dedrunt
Connubio, e geminis quo foret vna domus
Excipit hos haeres Henricus copula regum
Octauus, magni Regis imago potens
Regibus hinc succedis auis, Regique parenti
Patris iusta haeres Elizabetha tui.

Sentences placed therein concerning unity.

Nullae concordes animos vires domant.
Qui iuncti terrent, deiuncti timent.
Discordes animi soluunt, concordes ligant.
Augentur parua pace, magna bello cadunt.
Coniunctae manus fortius tollunt onus.
Regno pro menibus aeneis ciuium concordia.
Qui diu pugnant diutius lugent.
Discidentes principes sulditorum lues.
Princeps ad pacem natus non ad arma datur
Filia concordiae copia, neptis quies.
Dissentiens respublica hostibus placet.
Qui idem tenent, diutius tenent.
Regnum diuisum facile dissoluitur.
Ciuitas concors armis frustra tentatur.
Omnium gentium consensus firmat fidem etc.

These verses and other pretty sentences were drawn in void places of this pageant, all tending

---

214 required inquired

236 two houses did knit Henry Tudor, Duke of Richmond, a Lancastrian sympathizer, married Elizabeth, eldest daughter of Edward IV, a Yorkist, in January 1486

239 civil war War of the Roses, 1455–85

241 jar disagreement; **stint** stop

246–255 *Hii . . . tui* (translated at lines 231–42)

257–71 *Nullae . . . etc.* "No force can subdue united souls. Those who inspire fear when united must fear when they are divided. Souls in conflict divide, united souls bind together. Small things are made greater by peace, great things fall in war. Joined hands can bear a heavier burden. Unity among the citizens will act as a firm defense of a kingdom. Those who fight long, mourn longer. Warring rulers are the plague of their subjects. A prince born to peace is not given to arms. Plenty is the daughter of concord, peace its granddaughter. A divided state lays itself open to its enemies. Those who hold the same thing will hold for longer. A kingdom divided against itself is easily destroyed. A united city is attacked in vain by force of arms. Concord between nations strengthens the faith"

272 pretty artful; astute

273 void unutilized

to one end that quietness might be maintained and all dissention displaced, and that by the Queen's Majesty, heir to agreement and agreeing in name with her, which before had joined those houses which had been the occasion of much debate and civil war within this realm as may appear to such as will search chronicles, but be not to be touched in this treatise only declaring Her Grace's passage through the city, and what provision the city made therefore. And ere the Queen's Majesty came within hearing of this pageant, she sent certain as also at all the other pageants to require the people to be silent for Her Majesty was disposed to hear all that should be said unto her.

When the Queen's Majesty had heard the child's oration, and understood the meaning of the pageant at large, she marched forward toward Cornhill, always received with like rejoicing of the people, and there as Her Grace passed by the conduit which was curiously trimmed against that time with rich banners adorned, and a noise of loud instruments upon the top thereof, she espied the second pageant, and because she feared for the people's noise that she should not hear the child which did expound the same, she inquired what that pageant was ere that she came to it. And there understood that there was a child representing Her Majesty's person, placed in a seat of government, supported by certain virtues which suppressed other vices under their seat and so forth, as in the description of the said pageant shall hereafter appear.

This pageant standing in the nether end of Cornhill was extended from the one side of the street to the other, and in the same pageant was devised three gates all open, and over the middle part thereof was erected one chair, a seat royal with cloth of estate to the same appertaining, wherein was placed a child representing the Queen's Highness with consideration had for place convenient for a table which contained her name and title and in a comely wreath artificially and well devised with perfect sight and understanding to the people. In the front of the same pageant was written the name and title thereof, which is *The seat of worthy governance*, which seat was made in such artificial manner as to the appearance of the lookers-on, the forepart seemed to have no stay, and therefore of force was stayed by lively personages, which personages were in number four, standing and staying the forefront of the same seat royal, each having his face to the Queen and people, whereof every one had a table to express their effects, which are virtues, namely, *Pure religion*, *Love of subjects*, *Wisdom and Justice*, which did tread their contrary vices under their feet, that is to wit, *Pure religion* did tread upon *Superstition* and *Ignorance*, *Love of subjects* did tread upon *Rebellion* and *Insolency*, *Wisdom* did tread upon *Folly* and *Vainglory*, *Justice* did tread upon *Adulation* and *Bribery*. Each of these personages, according to their proper names and properties, had not only their names in plain and perfect writing set upon their breasts easily to be read of all, but also every of them was aptly and properly appareled so that his apparel and name did agree to express the same person that in title he represented. This part of the pageant was thus appointed and furnished. The two sides over the two side ports had in them placed a noise of instruments, which immediately, after the child's speech, gave an heavenly melody. Upon the top or uppermost part of the said pageant stood the arms of England royally portrayed with the proper beasts to uphold the same. One representing the Queen's Highness sat in this seat crowned with an Imperial crown, and before her seat was a convenient place appointed for one child which did interpret and apply the said pageant as hereafter shall be declared. Every void place was furnished with proper sentences commending the seat supported by virtues and defacing the vices, to the utter extirpation of rebellion, and to everlasting continuance of quietness and peace. The Queen's Majesty approaching nigh unto this pageant thus beautified and furnished in all points, caused her chariot to be drawn nigh thereunto that Her Grace might hear the child's oration which was this.

While that religion true shall ignorance
    suppress,
And with her weighty foot break superstition's
    head,
While love of subjects shall rebellion distress
And with zeal to the prince, insolence down tread.

While justice can flattering tongues and bribery
    deface,

---

292 Cornhill the next ward s, at the w end of Leadenhall, named for a flourishing corn market there

294 conduit fountain; Cornhill Conduit which drew sweet water in lead pipes was formerly part of a prison cistern; it was restored as a town well in 1546; **curiously** skillfully; **against** in preparation for

307 nether lower

321 artificial artful

348 proper beasts a lion rampant and dragon (adopted from arms borne by Henry VIII)

While folly and vainglory to wisdom yield their
hands
So long shall government not swerve from her
right race
But wrong decayeth still and rightwiseness
upstands.

Now all thy subjects' hearts, Oh, prince of
peerless fame,
Do trust these virtues shall maintain up thy throne,
And vice be kept down still, the wicked put to
shame
That good with good may joy, and naught with
naught may moan.

Which verses were painted upon the right side of the same pageant and the Latin thereof on the left side in another table, which were these:

Quae subnixa alte solio regina superbo est,
Effigiam sanctae principis alma refert,
Quam ciuilis amor fulcit, sapientia firmat,
Iustica illustrat, Relligioque beat.
Vana superstitio et crassae ignorantia frontis
Pressae sub pura relligine iacent.
Regis amor domat effroenes, animosque rebelles
Iustus adulantes, Domiuorosque terit.
Cum regit imperium sapiens, sine luce sedebunt
Stultitia, atque hurus numen inanis honor.

Beside these verses there were placed in every void room of the pageant both in English and Latin such sentences as advanced the seat of governance upheld by virtue. The ground of this pageant was that like as by virtues (which do abundantly appear in Her Grace) the Queen's Majesty was established in the seat of government so she should sit fast in the same so long as she embraced virtue and held vice under foot. For if vice once got up the head, it would put the seat of government in peril of falling. The Queen's Majesty when she had heard the child and understood the pageant at full, gave the city also thanks there, and most graciously promised her good endeavor for the maintenance of the said virtues, and suppression of vices, and so marched on until she came against the Great Conduit in Cheapside which was beautified with pictures and sentences accordingly against Her Grace's coming thither.

Against Soper Lane's end was extended from the one side of the street to the other a pageant which had three gates all open. Over the middlemost whereof were erected three several stages, whereon sat eight children as hereafter followeth. On the uppermost one child; on the middle three; on the lowest four, each having the proper name of the blessing that they did represent written in a table and placed above their heads. In the forefront of this pageant before the children which did represent the blessings was a convenient standing cast out for a child to stand, which did expound the said pageant unto the Queen's Majesty as was done in the other before. Every [one] of these children were appointed and appareled according unto the blessing which he did represent. And on the forepart of the said pageant was written in fair letters the name of the said pageant in this manner following.

The eight beatitudes expressed in the fifth chapter of the gospel of St. Matthew, applied to our Sovereign Lady Queen Elizabeth.

Over the two side ports was placed a noise of instruments. And all void places in the pageant were furnished with pretty sayings commending and touching the meaning of the said pageant, which was the promises and blessings of Almighty God made to His people. Before that the Queen's Highness came unto this pageant, she required the matter somewhat to be opened unto her that Her Grace might the better understand what should afterward by the child be said unto her. Which so was that the city had there erected the pageant with eight children representing the eight blessings touched in the fifth chapter of St. Matthew. Whereof every one upon just considerations was applied unto Her Highness, and that the people thereby put Her Grace in mind that as her good doings before had given just occasion why that these blessings might fall upon her, that so if Her Grace did continue in her goodness as she had entered, she should hope for the fruit of these promises due unto them that do exercise themselves in the blessings which Her Grace heard marvelous graciously, and required that the chariot might be removed towards the pageant that she might perceive the child's words, which were these, the Queen's Majesty giving most attentive

389 **room** space
403 **marched** proceeded
404 **against** to; **Great Conduit in Cheapside** a large fountain in the E part of the market square of West Cheaping Street which transported water from Paddington. The fountain was built in 1285 and rebuilt and enlarged in 1479
407 **Against** At; **Soper Lane** a lane beginning at the market square of West Cheaping, headquarters for cordwainers (shoemakers) and curriers (those who dressed and colored leather)
424 **fair** neat (i.e., for a presentation copy)
427 ***St. Matthew*** Matt. 5:3–10
436 **opened** revealed; explained

ear, and requiring that the people's noise might be stayed.

Thou hast been eight times blest, Oh, Queen of worthy fame,
By meekness of thy spirit, when care did thee beset,
By mourning in thy grief, by mildness in thy blame,
By hunger and by thirst, and justice could none get.

By mercy showed, not felt, by cleanness of thine heart
By seeking peace always, by persecution wrong.
Therefore trust thou in God, since He hath helped thy smart
That as His promise is, so He will make thee strong.

When these words were spoken, all the people wished that as the child had spoken, so God would strengthen Her Grace against all her adversaries, whom the Queen's Majesty did most gently thank for their so loving wish. These verses were painted on the left side of the said pageant, and other in Latin on the other side which were these.

Qui lugent hilares fient, qui mitia gestant
Pectora, multa soli iugera culta metent
Iustitiam esuriens sitensue replebitur, ipsum.
Fas homini puro corde videre deum
Quem alterius miseret dominus miserebitur huius,
Pacificus quisquis, filius ille Dei est.
Propter iustitiam quisquis patietur habetque
Demissam mentem, caelica regna capit.
Huic hominum generi terram, mare, sidera vouit
Omnipotens, horum quisque beatus erit.

Besides these, every void place in the pageant was furnished with sentences touching the matter and ground of the said pageant. When all that was to be said in this pageant was ended, the Queen's Majesty passed on forward in Cheapside.

At the Standard in Cheap which was dressed fair against the time was placed a noise of trumpets with banners and other furniture. The Cross likewise was also made fair and well trimmed. And near unto the same, upon the porch of St. Peter's Church door stood the waits of city, which did give a pleasant noise with their instruments as the Queen's Majesty did pass by, which on every side cast her countenance and wished well to all her most loving people. Soon after that Her Grace passed the Cross, she had espied the pageant erected at the Little Conduit in Cheap and incontinent required to know what it might signify. And it was told Her Grace that there was placed Time. "Time?" saith she, "and Time hath brought me hither." And so forth the whole matter was opened to Her Grace as hereafter shall be declared in the description of the pageant. But in the opening, when Her Grace understood the Bible in English should be delivered unto her by Truth, which was therein represented by a child, she thanked the city for that gift and said that she would oftentimes read over that book, commanding Sir John Perrot, one of the knights which held up her canopy, to go before and to receive the book. But learning that it should be delivered unto Her Grace down by a silken lace, she caused him to stay, and so passed forward until she came against the aldermen in the high end of Cheap before the Little Conduit, where the companies of the city ended, which began at Fanchurch, and stood along the streets one by another enclosed with rails, hanged with cloths, and themselves well

463 **smart** sorrow

473–82 ***Qui . . . erit*** "Those who mourn shall be made joyful; those who are of meek heart alone shall reap many fertile acres; those who hunger and thirst after righteousness shall be filled. It is right that the pure in heart shall see God. God will be merciful to him who shows mercy on others. Anyone who is a peacemaker is the son of God. Whosoever suffers for the sake of righteousness and has a humble mind, shall receive the kingdom of heaven. The Almighty promised the earth, the sea and the stars to men of this kind, each one of whom shall be blessed"

488 **Standard** a column next to the fountain used as a market cross and a landmark midway between the w end of the Poultry and Paul's Gate; a popular place for reading proclamations, holding executions, and burning condemned documents

490 **Cross** Cheapside Cross was not part of the city's fabric, but was one of the series of memorial crosses, from Hardeby, Lincolnshire, to Westminster, which Edward I erected to mark the stages in the funeral procession of his wife, Queen Eleanor of Castile. The cross was renovated with new leadwork in the fifteenth century and gilded, burnished, and regilded in 1554

491 **fair** beautifully

492–3 **St. Peter's Church** in Wood Street, Cheap, near Cripplesgate; **waits** wind instrumentalists maintained by the city of London at public charge

499 **Little Conduit** in West Cheapside by Paul's Gate

499–500 **incontinent** anxious

501–8 **Time . . . Truth** the allegorical presentation takes its special force from the presentation of the Bible

511 **Sir John Perrot** (?1527–92), reputedly the son of Henry VIII, he was one of four gentlemen chosen to carry the Queen's canopy of state; shortly afterwards, the Queen appointed him vice-admiral of the seas about south Wales and keeper of the jail at Haverfordwest

517 **companies** London corporations of tradesmen who produced the pageants and whose activities stopped by custom and law at the city gates

appareled with many rich furs and their livery hoods upon their shoulders in comely and seemly manner, having before them sundry persons well appareled in silks and chains of gold, as wiflers and garders of the said companies, beside a number of rich hangings as well of tapestry, arras, cloths of gold, silver, velvet, damask, satin, and other silks plentifully hanged all the way as the Queen's Highness passed from the Tower through the city. Out at the windows and penthouses of every house did hang a number of rich and costly banners and streamers until Her Grace came to the upper end of Cheap. And there, by appointment, the right worshipful Master Randolph Cholmley, Recorder of the city, presented to the Queen's Majesty a purse of crimson satin richly wrought with gold, wherein the city gave unto the Queen's Majesty a thousand marks in gold, as Master Recorder did declare briefly unto the Queen's Majesty, whose words tended to this end, that the Lord Mayor, his brethren, and commonalty of the city to declare their gladness and good will towards the Queen's Majesty, did present Her Grace with that gold, desiring Her Grace to continue their good and gracious Queen, and not to esteeme the value of the gift but the mind of the givers. The Queen's Majesty with both her hands took the purse, and answered to him again marvelous pithily, and so pithily that the standersby, as they embraced entirely her gracious answer, so they marveled at the couching thereof, which was in words truly reported these: "I thank my Lord Mayor, his brethren, and you all. And whereas your request is that I should continue your good Lady and Queen, be you insured that I will be as good unto you as ever queen was to her people. No will in me can lack, neither do I trust shall there lack any power. And persuade yourselves that for the safety and quietness of you all, I will not spare, if need be, to spend my blood, God thank you all." Which answer of so noble and hearted princess, if it moved a marvelous shout and rejoicing it is nothing to be marveled at, since both the heartiness thereof was so wonderful and the words so jointly knit. When Her Grace had thus answered the Recorder, she marched toward the Little Conduit, where was erected a pageant with square proportion, standing directly before the same conduit with battlements accordingly. And in the same pageant was advanced two hills or mountains of convenient height. The one of them being on the north side of the same pageant was made cragged, barren, and stony, in the which was erected one tree, artificially made, all withered and dead, with branches accordingly. And under the same tree at the foot thereof, sat one in homely and rude apparel crookedly, and in mourning manner, having over his head in a table, written in Latin and English, his name, which was *Ruinosa Respublica*, A decayed commonweal. And upon the same withered tree were fixed certain tables, wherein were written proper sentences, expressing the causes of the decay of a commonweal. The other hill on the south side was made fair, fresh, green, and beautiful, the ground thereof full of flowers and beauty, and on the same was erected also one tree very fresh and fair, under the which stood upright one fresh personage well appareled and appointed, whose name also was written both in English and in Latin, which was *Respublica bene instituta*, A flourishing commonweal. And upon the same tree also, were fixed certain tables containing sentences which expressed the causes of a flourishing commonweal. In the middle between the said hills was made artificially one hollow place or cave with door and lock enclosed, out of which a little before the Queen's Highness coming thither, issued one personage whose name was *Time*, appareled as an old man with a scythe in his hand, having wings artificially made, leading a personage of lesser stature than himself which was finely and well appareled, all clad in white silk, and directly over her head was set her name and title in Latin and English, *Temporis filia*, the daughter of Time. Which two so appointed went forward toward the south side of the pageant. And on her breast was written her proper name, which was *Veritas*, Truth, who held a book in her hand upon the which was written, *Verbum veritatis*, the word of truth. And out of the south side of the pageant was cast a standing for a child which should interpret the same pageant. Against whom, when the Queen's Majesty came, he spoke unto Her Grace these words.

This old man with the scythe, old Father Time
they call,
And her his daughter Truth, which holdeth
yonder book

524–5 wiflers and garders ornamental borders and trimmings
530–1 penthouses shop canopies
538 marks coins of varying weights, but usually around 8 ounces
541 brethren aldermen and city council
541–2 commonalty citizens below the rank of peer
565 jointly smoothly
577 rude poor; coarse

Whom he out of this rock hath brought forth to us all
From whence this many years she dare not once out look.

The ruthful wight that sitteth under the barren tree,
Resembleth to us the form when commonweals decay,
But when they be in state triumphant, you may see
By him in fresh attire that sitteth under the bay.

Now since that Time again his daughter Truth hath brought,
We trust O worthy Queen, thou wilt this truth embrace.
And since thou understands the good estate and nought,
We trust wealth thou will plant, and barrenness displace.

But for to heal the sore, and cure that is not seen,
Which thing the book of truth doth teach in writing plain:
She doth present to thee the same, Oh, worthy Queen,
For that, that words do fly, but writing doth remain.

When the child had thus ended his speech, he reached his book towards the Queen's Majesty, which a little before Truth had let down unto him from the hill, which by Master Perrot was received, and delivered unto the Queen. But she as soon as she had received the book, kissed it, and with both her hands held up the same and so laid it upon her breast with great thanks to the city therefore and so went forward towards Paul's Churchyard. The former matter which was rehearsed unto the Queen's Majesty was written in two tables, on either side the pageant eight verses, and in the midst these in Latin:

Ille, vides falcem laeua qui sustinet vncam,
Tempus is est, cui stat filia vera comes
Hanc pater exesa deductam rupe reponit
In lucem, quam non viderat ante diu
Qui sedet a laeua cultu male tristis inepto
Quem duris crescens cautibus orbis obit
Nos monet effigie, qua sit respublica quando
Corruit, at contra quando beata viget.
Ille docet iuuenis forma spectandus amictu
Scitus, et aeterna laurea fronde virens.

The sentences written in Latin and English upon both the trees, declaring the causes of both estates, were these.

Causes of a ruinous commonweal are these.

Want of the fear of God.	*Blindness of guides*
Disobedience to rulers.	*Bribery in magistrates*
Rebellion in subjects.	*Unmercifulness in rulers.*
Civil disagreement.	*Unthankfulness in subjects.*
Flattering of princes.	

Causes of a flourishing commonweale.

Fear of God.	*Obedient subjects.*
A wise prince.	*Lovers of the commonweal.*
Learned rulers.	*Virtue rewarded.*
Obedience to officers.	*Vice chastened.*

The matter of this pageant dependeth of them that went before. For as the first declared Her Grace to come out of the house of unity, the second that she is placed in the seat of government stayed with virtues to the suppression of vice, and therefore in the third the eight blessings of Almighty God might well be applied unto her, so this fourth now is, to put Her Grace in remembrance of the state of the commonweal, which Time with Truth his daughter doth reveal, which Truth also Her Grace hath received, and therefore cannot but be merciful and careful for the good government thereof. From thence the Queen's Majesty passed toward Paul's Churchyard. And when she came over against Paul's School, a child appointed by the schoolmaster thereof pronounced a certain oration in Latin, and certain verses, which also were there written as followeth:

Philosophus ille diuinus Plato inter multa preclare ac sapienter dicta, hoc posteris proditum reliquit, Rempublique illam, faelicissimam fore, cui princeps sophiae studiosa, virtutibusque ornata contigerit. Quem si vere dixisse censeamus (vt quidem verissime) cur non terra Britannica plauderet? cur non populus gaudium atque

620 **ruthful wight** lamentable man

640–1 **Paul's Churchyard** the N churchyard of St. Paul's, the city cathedral, which is connected to West Cheaping by Friday Street

645–54 ***Ille . . . virens*** (translated approximately in lines 616–27)

687–716 ***Philosophus . . . Amen*** "The divine philosopher Plato left this observation for posterity, among many wise and valuable sayings: that a state would be most fortunate if its princes should be interested in matters favorable to wisdom and conspicuous for their virtues. And if it seems to us that he was right (and he was indeed entirely right), why should Britain not rejoice? Why should the people not leap with joy and pleasure? Why should this day not be marked (as they say) with a white stone? A day when we have with us a prince whose like was never seen by our ancestors, and whose like our descendants are unlikely ever to see, most excellently endowed with all bodily and spiritual gifts. The bodily

laetitiam agitaret? immo, cur non hunc diem albo (quod aiunt) lapillo notaret? quo princeps talis nobis adest, qualem priores non viderunt, qualemque posteritas haud facile cernere poterit, dotibus quum animi, tum corporis undique faecilissima. Casti quidem corporis dotes ita apertae sunt, vt oratione non egeant. Animi vero tot tantaeque, vt ne verbis quidem exprimi possint. Haec nempe Regibus summis orta, morum atque animi nobilitate genus exuperat. Huius pectus Cristi religionis amore flagrat. Haec gentem Britannicam virtutibus illustrabit, clipeoque iustitiae teget. Hac literis graecis et latinis eximia, ingenioque prepollems est. Hac imperante pietas vigebit, Anglia florebit, aurea secula redibunt. Vos igitur Angli tot commoda accepturi Elizabetham Reginam nostram celeberrimam ab ipso Christo huibus regni imperio destinatam, honore debito prosequimini. Huius imperiis animo libentissimo subditiestote, vosque tali principe dignos prebete. Et quoniam pueri non viribus sed precibus officium prestare possunt, non Alumni huius scholae ab ipso Coleto olim Templi Paulini Decano, extructae, teneras palmas ad caelum tendentes Christum Opt: Maxi: precaturi sumus vt tuam celsitudinem annos Nestoreos summo cum honore Anglis imperitare faciat, matremque pignoribus charis beatam reddat. Amen.

Anglia nunc tandem plaudas, laetare, re sulta,
Presto iam vita est, praesidiumque tibi
En tua spes venit tua gloria, lux, decus omne
Venit iam solidam quae tibi prestat opem.
Succurretque tuis rebus quae pessum abiere.
Perdita quae fuerant haec reparare volet
Omnia florebunt, redeunt nunc aurea secla.
In melius surgent quae cecidere bona.
Debes ergo illi totam te reddere fidam
Cuius in accessu commoda tot capies.
Salue igitur dicas, imo de pectore summo.
Elizabeth Regni non dubitanda salus,
Virgo venit, veniatque optes comitata deinceps.
Pignoribus charis, laeta parens veniat
Hoc deus omnipotens ex alto donet olympo
Qui caelum et terram condidit atque regit.

Which the Queen's Majesty most attentively harkened unto. And when the child had pronounced, he did kiss the oration which he had there fair written in paper and delivered it unto the Queen's Majesty, which most gently received the same. And when the Queen's Majesty had heard all that was there offered to be spoken, then Her Grace marched towards Ludgate where she was received with a noise of instruments, the forefront of the gate being finely trimmed up against Her Majesty's coming. From thence by the way as she went down toward Fleet Bridge, one about Her Grace noted the city's charge, that there was no cost spared. Her Grace answered that she did well consider the same, and that it should be remembered. An honorable answer, worthy a noble prince, which may comfort all her subjects, considering there can be no point of gentleness or obedient love showed toward Her Grace which she doth not most tenderly accept and graciously weigh. In this manner, the people on either side rejoicing, Her Grace went forward toward the Conduit in Fleet Street, where was the fifth and last pageant erected in form following. From the Conduit which was beautified with painting, unto the north side of the street, was erected a stage embattled with four towers and in the same a square platform rising with degrees, and upon the uppermost degree was

---

gifts are so apparent that they do not lack for description. But the spiritual gifts are so manifold and so great that they cannot possibly be expressed in words. Although she is descended from the noblest kings, in nobility of manners and mind she far surpasses her race. Her breast burns with love of Christ's religion. She will bring fame to the British people by her virtues, and still protect them with the shield of justice. She is most learned in Greek and Latin literature, and outstanding in intellectual gifts. Under her rule religion will flourish, England will prosper, the Golden Age will return. Oh, Englishmen, who are about to receive so many benefits, attend with due honor on our most celebrated Queen Elizabeth, destined by Christ Himself to rule this empire. Be her most willing subjects, and show yourselves worthy of such a prince. And since boys can show their loyalty not by their strength but by their prayers, we the pupils of this school, founded by [John] Colet, sometime Dean of St. Paul's, raising our tender hands towards heaven will pray Christ, the Best and Mightiest, that He will cause your Highness to rule England with great honor until you reach the age of Nestor, and that he will grant you to become a joyful mother of children. Amen"

717–32 ***Anglia . . . regit*** "Oh, England, now rejoice, clap your hands, leap and dance; your life is at hand, and your help. Behold, your hope comes, your glory, your light, and your salvation. Now she comes who will surely bring you succor. She will help your affairs which have gone astray; she will bring back those things which were lost. All will flourish, the Golden Age returns. Good things which fell will rise again as better things. You must therefore give yourself up to her in complete trust, for by her accession you will receive so many benefits. You should therefore hail her from the depths of your heart. The merit of Elizabeth's reign is not to be doubted; she comes a virgin; may she return later accompanied by dear children, may she come as a joyful parent. May the omnipotent God, creator and ruler of both heaven and earth, grant this from highest Olympus"

740 **Ludgate** the most western of the city's six gates, leading to Westminster

744 **Fleet Bridge** a stone bridge over Turnemill Brook (alternatively Fleet Dike) which emptied into the Thames. The bridge was decorated in 1431 with the same coping of angels as Cheap Standard; the stream, however, was considerably diminished by 1559

745 **charge** expense

755 **Conduit in Fleet Street** a cistern built by the citizens of Fleet Street at Fleet Bridge in 1478

759 **embattled** fortified

placed a chair, or seat royall, and behind the same seat in curious, artificial manner was erected a tree of reasonable height and so far advanced above the seat as it did well and seemly shadow the same, without damaging the sight of any part of the pageant, and the same tree was beautified with leaves as green as art could devise, being of a convenient greatness and containing thereupon the fruit of the date, and on the top of the same tree in a table was set the name thereof which was *A Palm tree*, and in the aforesaid seat or chair was placed a seemly and mete personage richly appareled in Parliament robes, with a scepter in her hand, as a queen, crowned with an open crown, whose name and title was in a table fixed over her head in this sort: *Deborah the judge and restorer of the House of Israel. Jdic. 4.* and the other degrees on either side were furnished with six personages, two representing the nobility, two the clergy, and two the commonalty. And before these personages was written in a table *Deborah with her estates, consulting for the good government of Israel.* At the feet of these and the lowest part of the pageant was ordained a convenient room for a child to open the meaning of the pageant. When the Queen's Majesty drew near unto this pageant, and perceived, as in the other, the child ready to speak, Her Grace required silence, and commanded her chariot to be removed nearer, that she might plainly hear the child speak, which said as hereafter followeth:

> Jaben of Canaan King had long by force of arms
> Oppressed the Israelites, which for God's people went
> But God minding at last for to redress their harms,
> The worthy Deborah as judge among them sent.
>
> In war she, through God's aid, did put her foes to flight,
> And with the dint of sword the band of bondage braced.
> In peace she, through God's aid, did always maintain right
> And judged Israel until forty years were past.
>
> A worthy precedent, Oh, worthy Queen, thou hast,
> A worthy woman judge, a woman sent for stay.
> And that the like to us endure always thou mayest
> Thy loving subjects will with true hearts and tongues pray:

Which verses were written upon the pageant and the same in Latin also.

> *Quando dei populum Canaan, res pressit Iaben,*
> *Mittitur a magno Debora magna deo:*
> *Quae populum eriperet, sanctum seruatet Iudan,*
> *Milite quae patrio frangeret hostis opes.*
> *Haec domino mandante deo lectissima fecit*
> *Faemina, et aduersos contudit ense viros*
> *Haec quater denos populum correxerat annos*
> *Iudico, bello strenua, pace grauis.*
> *Sic, O sic populum belloque et pace guberna,*
> *Debora sis Anglis Elizabetha tuis.*

The void places of the pageant were filled with pretty sentences concerning the same matter. The ground of this last pageant was that forsomuch as the next pageant before had set before Her Grace's eyes the flourishing and desolate states of a commonweal, she might by this be put in remembrance to consult for the worthy government of her people, considering God oftentimes sent women nobly to rule among men, as Deborah which governed Israel in peace the space of forty years; and that it behooveth both men and women so ruling to use advice of good counsel. When the Queen's Majesty had passed this pageant, she marched toward Temple Bar. But at St. Dunstan's Church where the children of the Hospital were appointed to stand with their governors, Her Grace perceiving a child offered to make an oration unto her, stayed her chariot, and did cast up her eyes to Heaven, as who should say, "I here see this merciful work toward the poor whom I must in the midst of my royalty needs remember," and so turned her face toward the child, which in Latin pronounced an oration to this effect, that after the Queen's Highness had passed through the city and had seen so sumptuous, rich, and notable spectacles of the citizens which declared their most hearty receiving and

---

766 damaging impaired

773 seemly appropriate; **mete** suitable

774 Parliament robes i.e., royal robes as ordained by Parliament

777 *Deborah* (see Judg. 4: 4–5)

785 open reveal

793 Jaben the king of Canaan who oppressed the Israelites for twenty years (see Judg. 4: 2, 3)

798 braced strengthened

807–16 *Quando . . . tuis* (approximate translation of lines 793–804)

830 Temple Bar the entrance to Westminster from the Duchy of Lancaster, the area between Westminster and the old city of London

831 St. Dunstan's Church St. Dunstan's in the West, a parish church extending along Fleet Street from the conduit to Fetter (Fetwars) Lane

832 the Hospital Christ Hospital, a school founded for poor boys by Henry VIII in a former Greyfriars monastery and supported by the people of London

joyous welcoming of Her Grace into the same, this one spectacle yet rested and remained, which was the everlasting spectacle of mercy unto the poor members of Almighty God, furthered by that famous and most noble prince King Henry the VIII, Her Grace's father, erected by the city of London, and advanced by the most godly virtuous and gracious prince King Edward the VI, Her Grace's dear and loving brother, doubting nothing of the mercy of the Queen's most gracious clemency by the which they may not only be relieved and helped, but also stayed and defended, and therefore incessantly they would pray and cry unto Almighty God for the long life and reign of Her Highness with most prosperous victory against her enemies.

The child, after he had ended his oration, kissed the paper wherein the same was written and reached it to the Queen's Majesty which received it graciously both with words and countenance, declaring her gracious mind toward their relief. From thence Her Grace came to Temple Bar, which was dressed finely with the two images of Gotmagot the Albion and Corineus the Briton, two giants big in stature furnished accordingly, which held in their hands even above the gate a table, wherein was written in Latin verses the effect of all the pageants which the city before had erected, which verses were these:

Ecce sub aspectu iam contemplaberis vno
O princeps populi sola columna tui.
Quicquid in immensa passim perspexeris vrbe
Quae cepere omnes vnus hic arcus habet.
Primus te solio regni donauit auiti,
Haeres quippe tui vera parentiis eras.
Suppressis vitiis, domina virtute, Secundus
Firmauit sedem regia virgo tuam.
Tertius ex omni posuit te parte beatam
Si, qua caepisti pergere velle, velis.
Quarto quid verum, respublica lapsa quid esset
Quae florens staret te docuere tui
Quinto magna loco monuit te Debora, missam
Caelitus in regni gaudia longa tui.
Perge ergo regina, tuae spes vnica gentis,
Haec postrema vrbis suscipe vota tuae.
Viue diu, regnaque diu, virtutibus orna
Rem patriam, et populi spem tucare tui.
Sic o sic petitur caelum Sic itur in astra
Hoc virtutis opus, caetera mortis erunt.

Which verses were also written in English meter in a less table as hereafter followeth:

Behold here in one view, thou mayst see all that plain,
Oh, Princess, to this thy people the only stay:
What eachwhere thou hast seen in this wide town, again
This one arch whatsoever the rest contained, doth say.

The first arch as true heir unto thy father dear,
Did set thee in the throne where thy grandfather sat,
The second did confirm thy seat as princess here,
Virtues now bearing sway, and vices beaten down flat.

The third, if that thou wouldest go on as thou began,
Declared thee to be blessed on every side,
The fourth did open Truth and also taught thee when
The commonweal stood well, and when it did thence slide.

The fifth as Deborah declared thee to be sent
From heaven, a long comfort to us thy subjects all,
Therefore go on, Oh, Queen, on whom our hope is bent,
And take with thee this wish of thy town as final,

Live long, and as long reign, adorning thy country,
With virtues, and maintain thy peoples' hope of thee,
For thus, thus heaven is won, thus must they pierce the sky,
This is by virtue wrought, all other must needs die.

On the south side was appointed by the city a noise of singing children, and one child richly attired as a poet, which gave the Queen's Majesty her farewell in the name of the whole city, by these words:

As at thine entrance first, Oh, Prince of high renown,
Thou wast presented with tongues and hearts for thy fair,

866 two images according to the (legendary) history of Britain by Geoffrey of Monmouth (d. 1155), two Trojans, Corineus and Brutus, the great grandson of Aeneas, settled Britain by exterminating the giants living there. Corineus, the eponymous founder of Cornwall, destroyed the giant Goēmagot (Gogmagog), bringing order and peace to the founding of Britain (New Troy)

873–92 ***Ecce . . . erunt*** (translated in lines 895–914)

So now since thou must needs depart out of this town
This city sendeth thee firm hope and earnest prayer,

For all men hope in thee that all virtues shall reign,
For all men hope that thou none error will support,
For all men hope that thou will truth restore again,
And mend that is amiss, to all good men's comfort.

And for this hope they pray thou mayst continue long,
Our Queen among us here, all vice for to supplant,
And for this hope they pray that God may make thee strong
As by His Grace puissant, so in His truth constant.

Farewell, Oh, worthy Queen, and as our hope is sure,
That into errors place thou will now truth restore,
So trust we that thou will our sovereign Queen endure,
And loving Lady stand, from henceforth evermore.

While these words were in saying, and certain wishes therein repeated for maintenance of truth and rooting out of error she now and then held up her hands to heavenward and willed the people to say "Amen."

When the child had ended, she said, "Be ye well assured, I will stand your good Queen." At which saying, Her Grace departed forth through Temple Bar toward Westminster with no less shouting and crying of the people than she entered the city with a noise of ordinance which the Tower shot off at Her Grace's entrance first into Tower Street.

The child's saying was also in Latin verses written in a table which was hanged up there.

O Regina potens, quum primam vrben ingredereris
Dona tibi, linguas fidaque corda dedit
Discedenti etiam tibi nunc duo munera mittit.
Omina plena spei, votaque plena precum.
Quippe tuis spes est, in te quod prouida virtus
Rexerit, errori nec locus vllus erit.
Quippe tuis spes est, quod tu verum omne reduces
Solatura bonas, dum mala tollis, opes.
Hac spe freti orant, longum vt Regina gubernes,
Et regni excindas crimina cuncta tui.
Hac spe freti orant, diuina vt gratia fortem,
Et verae fidei te velit esse basin.
Iam Regina vale, et sicut nos spes tenet vna,
Quod vero inducto, perditus error erit.
Sic quoque speramus quod eris Regina benigna
Nobis per regni tempora longa tui.

Thus the Queen's Highness passed through the city which without any foreign person of itself beautified itself, and received Her Grace at all places as has been before mentioned, with most tender obedience and love, due to so gracious a Queen and Sovereign Lady. And Her Grace likewise of her side in all Her Grace's passage showed herself generally an image of a worthy Lady and Governor, but privately these special points were noted in Her Grace as signs of a most princelike courage, whereby her loving subjects may ground a sure hope for the rest of her gracious doings hereafter.

Certain notes of the Queen's Majesty's great mercy, clemency, and wisdom used in this passage.

About the nether end of Cornhill toward Cheap, one of the knights about Her Grace had spied an ancient citizen which wept and turned his head back and therewith said this gentleman, "Yonder is an Alderman (for so he termed him) which weeps and turns his face backward. How may it be interpreted that he so doth, for sorrow or for gladness?" The Queen's Majesty heard him and said, "I warrant you it is for gladness." A gracious interpretation of a noble courage which would turn the doubtful to the best. And yet it was well known that as Her Grace did confirm the same, the party's cheer was moved for very pure gladness for the sight of Her Majesty's person, at the beholding whereof he took such comfort that with tears he expressed the same.

In Cheapside Her Grace smiled and being thereof demanded the cause, answered for that she had heard one say, "Remember old King Henry the VIII." A natural child which at the very remembrance of her father's name took so great a joy that all men may well think that as she rejoiced at his name whom this realm doth hold of so worthy memory, so in her doings she will resemble the same.

947–8 Tower Street the main street of Tower Street Ward, at the E side of the city, running from the Tower of London along the Thames almost to Billingsgate

951–66 *O . . . tui* (translation at lines 920–35)

When the city's charge without partiality and only the city was mentioned unto Her Grace, she said it should not be forgotten. Which saying might move all natural Englishmen heartily to show due obedience and entireness to their so good a queen which will in no point forget any parcel of duty lovingly showed unto her.

The answer which Her Grace made unto Master Recorder of London, as the hearers know it to be true, and with melting hearts heard the same, so may the reader thereof conceive what kind of stomach and courage pronounced the same.

What more famous thing do we read in ancient histories of old time than that mighty princes have gently received presents offered them by base and low personages. If that be to be wondered at (as it is passingly) let me see any writer that in any one prince's life is able to recount so many precedents of this virtue, as Her Grace showed in that one passage through the city. How many nosegays did Her Grace receive at poor women's hands? How often stayed she her chariot when she saw any simple body offer to speak to Her Grace? A branch of rosemary given to Her Grace with a supplication by a poor woman about Fleet Bridge was seen in her chariot until Her Grace came to Westminster, not without the marvelous wondering of such as knew the presenter and noted the Queen's most gracious receiving and keeping the same.

What hope the poor and needy may look for at Her Grace's hand, she as in all her journey continually, so her hearkening to the poor children of Christ's Hospital with eyes cast up into heaven did fully declare as that neither the wealthier estate stand without consideration had to the poverty, neither the poverty be duly considered unless they were remembered as commended to us by God's own mouth.

As at her first entrance she as it were declared, herself prepared to pass through a city that most entirely loved her, so she at her last departing, as it were bound herself by promise to continue good Lady and Governor unto that city which by outward declaration did open their love to their so loving and noble prince in such wise as she herself wondered thereat.

But because princes be set in their seat by God's appointing and therefore they must first and chiefly tender the glory of Him from whom their glory issues, it is to be noted in Her Grace that forasmuch as God hath so wonderfully placed her in the seat of government over this realm, she in all doings doth show herself most mindful of His goodness and mercy showed unto her, and among all other. Two principal signs thereof were noted in this passage. First, in the Tower, where Her Grace before she entered her chariot lifted up her eyes to Heaven and said, "Oh Lord, almighty and everlasting God, I give thee most hearty thanks that thou hast been so merciful unto me as to spare me to behold this joyful day. And I acknowledge that thou hast dealt as wonderfully and as mercifully with me as thou did with thy true and faithful servant Daniel, thy prophet, whom thou delivered out of the den from the cruelty of the greedy and raging lions; even so was I overwhelmed and only by thee delivered. To thee therefore only be thanks, honor, and praise, forever. Amen."

The second was the receiving of the Bible at the Little Conduit in Cheap [Street]. For when Her Grace had learned that the Bible in English should there be offered, she thanked the city therefore, promised the reading thereof most diligently, and incontinent commanded that it should be brought. At the receipt whereof, how reverently did she with both her hands take it, kiss it, and lay it upon her breast to the great comfort of the lookers-on. God will undoubtedly preserve so worthy a prince, which at his honor so reverently taketh her beginning. For this saying is true, and written in the Book of Truth: he that first seeks the kingdom of God shall have all other things cast unto him.

Now, therefore, all English hearts, and her natural people, must needs praise God's mercy which hath sent them so worthy a prince, and pray for Her Grace's long continuance among us.

1018 stomach spirit
1026 nosegays bouquets of flowers or herbs
1030 rosemary herb signifying remembrance
1071 Daniel (see Dan. 6: 16–24)
1089–91 he... him (Matt. 6: 33; Luke 12: 31)

The Lady of May

Sir Philip Sidney

Elizabeth I in progress. Sherborne Castle Estate.

The first literary work of one of the greatest of Elizabethan poets, Sir Philip Sidney, *The Lady of May* (an untitled text when it first appeared in the 1598 Folio of Sidney's *Arcadia*) also lays claim to being the first English pastoral drama. On the surface, this country-house revel follows the classical pastoral debate in which the shepherd Espilus and the forester Therion engage in a singing match to win the May Lady; they are introduced to Queen Elizabeth by the old shepherd Lalus and the highly ridiculed village schoolmaster, Master Rombus. On the evidence of their arguments Elizabeth I is asked to determine the winner. Their causes are championed by two associates, the old shepherd Dorcas, who defends the pastoral way of life, and the young forester Rixus, who defends Therion. But as the May Lady then reminds the Queen, "in judging me, you judge more than me in it." What that something more to be judged is remains a crucial question, but it is the crux of the work and may help to explain the Queen's unexpected verdict and her unspecified reasons for it.

The single substantive text from which all other texts and manuscripts derive is not authorial, for it does not follow Sidney's peculiar spelling habits. But it is most likely either the playscript used or a record of the performance staged on May 1, 1579, apparently to the Queen's surprise. The drama was enacted during her visit to Wanstead Garden near her royal palace at Greenwich, since 1577 the home of her favorite courtier, Robert Dudley, Earl of Leicester, Sidney's uncle. (The title was first assigned to the play in an edition of Sidney's *Works* published in 1725.)

At first glance, the debate that forms the heart of the play looks commonplace, too. The shepherd defends the life of contemplation while the forester defends a life of activity; the shepherd seems dreamy while the forester urges the value of experience. But this easy convention soon breaks down. Espilus preaches worldly wealth while Therion points out the naive dangers of a life of contemplation. Espilus uses sentimental similitudes; Therion uses moral metaphors. Espilus allows figurative language to displace even the truths of his own existence, while Therion counters by pointing out that such tropes are at best only partially true. Thus *The Lady of May* seems to set up conventions only to undermine them.

Such reversals, however, were indicative of May Day ceremonies. These celebrations were a common feature of Tudor village life, where young people went into the woods for games, decked themselves in flowers and their homes with hawthorn, and danced around the village maypole, a symbol of fertility and marriage. At country houses like Wanstead, aristocratic festivities were more sophisticated; there might be plays and pageants, tournaments and contests in archery, and the leader was often not a May Queen but the Lord of May, who frequently dressed up as Robin Hood. The 1574 account books for the Sidney family show that (although Philip was then on his Grand Tour of the Continent) Sir Henry Sidney, Elizabeth's Lord Deputy in Ireland, paid out for May Day celebrations one shilling for "singers" and three shillings for those who "played Robin Hood," while the family children were given bows and arrows. Like the Lord of Misrule, the May Lord presided over a short-lived regime in which those of high status were rendered low and those of low status high, just as the May Lady is at first harshly treated while Rombus assumes an authority he cannot successfully maintain. Thus too the simple shepherd Espilus promotes wealth and sensuous pleasures while Therion delights in liberty, binding himself only to the service of his own choosing. Indeed, Therion's vitality and license qualify him much more readily as the May Lord, or Robin Hood, translating misrule into potential service to the monarch, and Sidney's play seems written in a way that will require the Queen to choose Therion at the conclusion.

This may well be the intention, for *The Lady of May* is as much propaganda as pageant. The implicit link is Leicester's pet name – the Queen called Robert Dudley "Robin." Read this way, Sidney is using the license of the occasion of the play's performance to defend his uncle as a suitor, too, in this case for the Queen herself. After all, her special affection for him was widely known. But his attraction to her had also been fading. As the leader of the Puritan faction of her Privy Council, he had been arguing aggressively since 1572 for military intervention in the Low Countries where the Protestant Dutch were threatened by Catholic Spain. Both Leicester and Sidney were ready to wage war on behalf of the Dutch, although such decisive events always made Elizabeth nervous – indeed, she never approved of subjects rising against their rulers no matter what the cause. Because of her intransigence, Leicester's effectiveness had been eroding and Sidney may have devised this play and the debate at its center to promote Leicester's case and structured the play so that she would choose his representative in Therion. While the Queen was free to make any choice, she is required at the end to make some choice and this would, in any event, force her to reveal her own attitudes. The text of the play also requires the Queen to explain her reasons for her selection and here Sidney's silence calls attention to her position and invites speculations about it.

But Sidney might also be using *The Lady of May* to explain, defend, and promote himself. For years Sidney had been frustrated in his attempts to win a place at court or on the battlefield; his own religious and political beliefs may well have been ways of expressing his felt aristocratic need to prove himself in war. In June 1574 his mentor, Hubert Languet, had been advocating just such a life and had tried to enlist him under General von Schwendi, a plan that never materialized. By 1579, Philip was writing to his brother Robert, then on the Continent, to join an army; as Robert wrote their father, Philip had advised him "that if there were any good wars, I should go to them." Philip's own vitality, then, is represented in Therion's attitude and Rixus' promulgation of it. As Philip wrote Languet, "For to what purpose should our thoughts be directed to various kinds of knowledge, unless room be afforded for putting it into practice, so that public advantage may be the result, which in a corrupt age we cannot hope for? Who would learn music except for the sake of pleasure? or architecture except with a view to building?" At the same time, Sidney creates characters who display those qualities he opposes: Espilus with his passivity and simplicity; Rombus with his outmoded Ciceronianism, his humanist learning employed for its own sake rather than for the sake of others.

Yet the more we study *The Lady of May* the more complex and problematic it becomes. The supplication of the May Lady's mother which opens the play pleads for justice, but seeks justice (and order) on May Day, a day of misrule and injustice. The Lady of May herself, as she enters, seems equally torn between the shepherds and the foresters, an object of contention more than an object of pursuit. And in the abrupt and deconstructive end of the play, when the Queen chooses the passive shepherd, upsetting the design of the work, both shepherds and foresters join in consort, their harmony allowing both groups to escort the Lady of May off the stage as if the unresolved debate had led to some kind of resolution. It has not. By turning pageantry and drama into political and social interrogation, Sidney's script confronts the Queen herself. And in the Queen's sudden and resolute silence, such urgent issues pass on to spectators and to us as readers to adjudicate.

Further Reading

Berry, Edward, "Sidney's May Game for the Queen," *Modern Philology* 86 (1989): 252–64.

Hager, Alan, "Rhomboid Logic: Anti-Idealism and a Cure for Recusancy in Sidney's *Lady of May*," *ELH* 57 (1990): 485–502.

Montrose, Louis, "Celebration and Insinuation: Sir Philip Sidney and the Motives of Elizabethan Courtship," *Renaissance Drama* n.s. 7 (1977): 3–35.

Orgel, S. K., "Sidney's Experiment in Pastoral: *The Lady of May*," *Journal of the Warburg and Courtauld Institutes* 26 (1963): 198–203.

Stillman, Robert E., "Justice and the 'Good Word' in Sidney's *The Lady of May*," *Studies in English Literature 1500–1600* 24 (1984): 23–38.

[The Lady of May]

Her most excellent Majesty walking in Wanstead Garden, as she passed down into the grove, there came suddenly among the train one appareled like an honest man's wife of the country; where, crying out for justice, and desiring all the lords and gentlemen to speak a good word for her, she was brought to the presence of her Majesty, to whom upon her knees she offered a supplication, and used this speech:

The Suitor

Most fair lady; for as for other your titles of state statelier persons shall give you, and thus much mine own eyes are witnesses of: take here the

Textual Variants

59 foresters] F fosters **87** eloquence] F loquence **89** Rombus] F schoolmaster **197** bore] F bare **264** sheepish] F sleepish **333** bore]: F bear **396** brains]: F trains

1 Her most excellent Majesty Elizabeth I; **Wanstead** home of Robert Dudley, Earl of Leicester, in Waltham Forest near the royal palace of Greenwich, purchased in 1577

3 train royal procession

4 honest chaste

10 Suitor mother of the May Lady

complaint of me, poor wretch, as deeply plunged in misery, as I wish to you the highest point of happiness.

One only daughter I have, in whom I had placed all the hopes of my good hap, so well had she with her good parts recompensed my pain of bearing of her, and care of bringing her up. But now, alas, that she is come to the time that I should reap my full comfort of her, so is she troubled with that notable matter, which we in the country call matrimony, as I cannot choose but fear the loss of her wits, at least of her honesty. Other women think they may be unhappily cumbered with one master husband; my poor daughter is oppressed with two, both loving her, both equally liked of her, both striving to deserve her. But now lastly (as this jealousy, forsooth, is a vile matter) each have brought their partakers with them, and are at this present, without your presence redress it, in some bloody controversy; my poor child is among them. Now, sweet lady, help; your own way guides you to the place where they encumber her. I dare stay here no longer, for our men say here in the country the sight of you is infectious.

And with that she went away a good pace, leaving the supplication with her Majesty, which very formally contained this:

Supplication

Most gracious Sovereign:

To one whose state is raised over all,
Whose face doth oft the bravest sort enchant,
Whose mind is such, as wisest minds appal,
Who in one self these diverse gifts can plant:
How dare I (wretch) seek there my woes to rest,
Where ears be burned, eyes dazzled, hearts oppressed?
Your state is great, your greatness is our shield,
Your face hurts oft, but still it doth delight,
Your mind is wise, your wisdom makes you mild;
Such planted gifts enrich even beggars' sight:
So dare I, wretch, my bashful fear subdue,
And feed mine ears, mine eyes, mine heart in you.

Herewith, the woman suitor being gone, there was heard in the woods a confused noise and forthwith there came out six shepherds, with as many foresters, haling and pulling to whether side they should draw the Lady of May, who seemed to incline neither to the one nor other side. Among them was Master Rombus, a schoolmaster of a village thereby, who, being fully persuaded of his own learned wisdom, came thither with his authority to part their fray; where for an answer he received many unlearned blows. But the Queen coming to the place, where she was seen of them, though they knew not her estate, yet something there was which made them startle aside and gaze upon her: till old father Lalus stepped forth (one of the substantiallest shepherds) and making a leg or two, said these few words:

May it please your benignity to give a little superfluous intelligence to that which, with the opening of my mouth, my tongue and teeth shall deliver unto you. So it is, right worshipful audience, that a certain she-creature, which we shepherds call a woman, of a minsical countenance, but by my white lamb, not three quarters so beauteous as yourself, hath disanulled the brainpan of two of our featioust young men. And will you wot how? By my mother Kit's soul, with a certain fransical malady they called "love"; when I was a young man they called it flat folly. But here is a substantial schoolmaster can better disnounce the whole foundation of the matter, although in sooth, for all his eloquence our young men were nothing duteous to his clerkship. Come on, come on, Master Rombus, be not so bashless; we say that the fairest are ever the gentlest. Tell the whole case, for you can much better vent the points of it than I.

Then came forward Master Rombus, and with many special graces made this learned oration:

Now the thunderthumping Jove transfund his dotes into your excellent formosity, which have

18 hap fortune
25 honesty virginity
31 partakers supporters; allies (as seconds in a duel)
38 infectious dazzling
40 supplication (probably read aloud)
43 Most gracious Sovereign this address makes Elizabeth I a necessary participant
45 bravest stoutest, strongest
57 confused noise the following action after the supplication to the Queen is similar to an antimasque
62 Master Rombus (rhombus is an equilateral parallelogram, a figure with no right angles)
68 estate position
70 Lalus (name means "babbler")
71 substantiallest oldest
71–2 leg or two (courteous gesture to the Queen)
78 minsical mincing
81 featioust elegant
82 wot know; By my mother Kit's soul (invented oath)
83 fransical frenzied
85 disnounce affected form of *announce*
87 sooth truth
89 bashless shameless (perhaps said in confusion)
91 vent air; explain
95 transfund transfer
96 dotes foolish students; **formosity** beauty

with your resplendent beams thus segregated the enmity of these rural animals. I am, *Potentissima Domina*, a schoolmaster; that is to say, a pedagogue, one not a little versed in the disciplinating of the juvental fry, wherein (to my laud I say it) I use such geometrical proportion, as neither wanteth mansuetude nor correction, for so it is described:

Parcare subjectos et debellire superbos.

Yet hath not the pulchritude of my virtues protected me from the contaminating hands of these plebeians; for coming, *solummodo*, to have parted their sanguinolent fray, they yielded me no more reverence than if I had been some *Pecorius Asinus*. I, even I, that am, who I am. *Dixi. Verbus sapiento satum est.* But what said that Trojan Aeneas, when he sojourned in the surging sulks of the sandiferous seas: *Haec olim memonasse iuvebit.* Well well, *ad propositos revertebo*; the purity of the verity is, that a certain *pulchra puella profectò*, elected and constituted by the integrated determination of all this topographical region, as the sovereign lady of this, Dame Maia's month, hath been *quodammodo* hunted, as you would say, pursued by two, a brace, a couple, a cast of young men, to whom the crafty coward Cupid had *inquam* delivered his dire dolorous dart.

But here the May Lady interrupted his speech, saying to him:

Away, away you tedious fool, your eyes are not worthy to look to yonder princely sight, much less your foolish tongue to trouble her wise ears.

At which Master Rombus in a great chafe cried out:

O Tempori, O Moribus! In profession a child, in dignity a woman, in years a lady, *in ceteris* a maid, should thus turpify the reputation of my doctrine with the superscription of a fool! *O Tempori, O Moribus!*

But here again the May Lady, saying to him:

Leave off, good Latin fool, and let me satisfy the long desire I have had to feed mine eyes with the only sight this age hath granted to the world.

The poor schoolmaster went his way back, and the Lady kneeling down said in this manner:

Do not think, sweet and gallant Lady, that I do abase myself thus much unto you because of your gay apparel; for what is so brave as the natural beauty of the flowers? nor because a certain gentleman hereby seeks to do you all the honor he can in this house; that is not the matter; he is but our neighbor, and these be our own groves; nor yet because of your great estate, since no estate can be compared to be the Lady of the whole month of May, as I am. So that since both this place and this time are my servants, you may be sure I would look for reverence at your hands, if I did not see something in your face which makes me yield to you. The truth is, you excel me in that wherein I desire most to excel, and that makes me give this homage unto you, as the beautifullest Lady these woods have ever received. But now, as old father Lalus directed me, I will tell you my fortune, that you may be judge of my mishaps, and others' worthiness. Indeed so it is that I am a fair wench, or else I am deceived, and therefore by the consent of all our neighbors have been chosen for the absolute Lady of this merry month. With me have been (alas I am ashamed to tell it) two young men, the one a forester named Therion, the other Espilus a shepherd, very long even in love forsooth. I like them both, and love neither. Espilus is the richer, but Therion the livelier. Therion doth me many pleasures, as stealing me venison out of these forests, and many other such like

98–9 ***Potentissima Domina*** Most Powerful Lady
100 **disciplinating** disciplining
101 **juvental** youthful; **laud** praise
103 **mansuetude** gentleness
104 ***Parcare . . . superbos*** "spare the humble and war on the proud" (*Aeneid* VI.853)
107 **plebeians** commoners; ***solummodo*** alone (*solus*)
108 **sanguinolent** bloody
109–10 ***Pecorius Asinus*** asinine brute (*pecus asininus*)
110–11 ***Dixi . . . est*** "A word to the wise man is enough"
112 **sulks** troughs between waves
113 **sandiferous** sandy; ***Haec . . . iuvebit*** "One day it will be a joy to remember these things" (*Aeneid* I.203)
114 ***ad . . . revertebo*** revert to the proposition
115 ***pulchra . . . profecto*** a pretty girl indeed
118 **Maia's** May's
118–19 ***quodammodo*** to a certain measure
120 **cast** two (term in hunting)
121 ***inquam*** it is said
130 ***O . . . Moribus!*** Oh, Time, Oh, Death! (misquoting Cicero, *Against Cataline* I.1)
131 ***in ceteris*** in certainty
132 **turpify** befoul
133 **superscription** overwriting
143 **brave** splendid
146 **that** i.e., beauty
161 **wench** maid
165 **Therion** (name means "wild beast")
166 **Espilus** (name means "felt presser," hatter)
167 **forsooth** truly

pretty and prettier services; but withal he grows to such rages, that sometimes he strikes me, sometimes he rails at me. This shepherd, Espilus, of a mild disposition, as his fortune hath not been to do me great service, so hath he never done me any wrong; but feeding his sheep, sitting under some sweet bush, sometimes, they say, he records my name in doleful verses. Now the question I am to ask you, fair Lady, is whether the many deserts and many faults of Therion, or the very small deserts and no faults of Espilus be to be preferred. But before you give your judgment (most excellent Lady) you shall hear what each of them can say for themselves in their rural songs.

Thereupon Therion challenged Espilus to sing with him, speaking these six verses:

Therion

Come, Espilus, come now declare thy skill,
Show how thou canst deserve so brave desire,
Warm well thy wits, if thou wilt win her will,
For water cold did never promise fire:
Great sure is she, on whom our hopes do live,
Greater is she who must the judgment give.

But Espilus, as if he had been inspired with the Muses, began forthwith to sing, whereto his fellow shepherds set in with their recorders, which they bore in their bags like pipes; and so of Therion's side did the foresters, with the cornets they wore about their necks like hunting horns in baldricks.

Espilus

Tune up, my voice, a higher note I yield:
To high conceits the song must needs be high;
More high than stars, more firm than flinty field
Are all my thoughts, in which I live or die:
Sweet soul, to whom I vowed am a slave,
Let not wild woods so great a treasure have.

Therion

The highest note comes oft from basest mind,
As shallow brooks do yield the greatest sound;
Seek other thoughts thy life or death to find;
Thy stars be fall'n, ploughed is thy flinty ground:
Sweet soul, let not a wretch that serveth sheep
Among his flock so sweet a treasure keep.

Espilus

Two thousand sheep I have as white as milk,
Though not so white as is thy lovely face;
The pasture rich, the wool as soft as silk,
All this I give, let me possess thy grace,
But still take heed lest thou thyself submit
To one that hath no wealth, and wants his wit.

Therion

Two thousand deer in wildest woods I have,
Them can I take, but you I cannot hold:
He is not poor who can his freedom save,
Bound but to you, no wealth but you I would:
But take this beast, if beasts you fear to miss,
For of his beasts the greatest beast he is.

Espilus kneeling to the Queen

Judge you to whom all beauty's force is lent.

Therion

Judge you of love, to whom all love is bent.

But as they waited for the judgment her Majesty should give of their deserts, the shepherds and foresters grew to a great contention whether of their fellows had sung better, and so whether the estate of shepherds or foresters were the more worshipful. The speakers were Dorcas, an old shepherd, and Rixus, a young forester, between whom the schoolmaster Rombus came in as moderator.

Dorcas the shepherd

Now all the blessings of mine old grandam (silly Espilus) light upon thy shoulders for this honeycomb singing of thine. Now, by mine honesty, all the bells in the town could not have sung better. If the proud heart of the harlotry lie not down to thee now, the sheep's rot catch her, to teach her that a fair woman hath not her fairness to let it grow rustish.

Rixus the forester

Oh, Midas, why art thou not alive now to lend thine ears to this drivel? By the precious bones of a huntsman, he knows not the blaying of a calf from the song of a nightingale. But if yonder great gentlewoman be as wise as she is fair, Therion, thou shalt have the prize; and thou, old Dorcas,

---

177 **records** sings
185 **challenged** derived from classical singing matches in Greek and Latin (e.g., Theocritus V and Virgil, *Eclogues* III)
200 **baldricks** richly ornamented leather belts or girdles
206 **Sweet soul** i.e., the Queen
221 **wants** is lacking
227 **beast . . . beasts** (a play on shepherd and sheep)
235 **whether** which
243 **grandam** grandmother
244 **silly** foolish
245 **honeycomb** intricate; excessively sweet
247 **harlotry** harlot
248 **sheep's rot** disease of the liver
250 **rustish** rusty
253 **ears** Midas had ass's ears awarded for his foolishness
253–4 **By the precious bones of a huntsman** (another invented oath)
254 **blaying** bleating
255–6 **great gentlewoman** the Queen

with young master Espilus, shall remain tame fools, as you be.

Dorcas

And with cap and knee be it spoken, is it your pleasure, neighbour Rixus, to be a wild fool?

Rixus

Rather than a sheepish dolt.

Dorcas

It is much refreshing to my bowels, you have made your choice; for my share, I will bestow your leavings upon one of your fellows.

Rixus

And art not thou ashamed, old fool, to liken Espilus, a shepherd, to Therion, of the noble vocation of huntsmen, in the presence of such a one as even with her eye only can give the cruel punishment?

Dorcas

Hold thy peace, I will neither meddle with her nor her eyes. They say in our town they are dangerous both; neither will I liken Therion to my boy Espilus, since one is a thievish prowler, and the other is as quiet as a lamb that new came from sucking.

Rombus the schoolmaster

Heu, Ehem, Hei, Insipidum, Inscitium vulgorum et populorum. Why, you brute nebulons, have you had my *corpusculum* so long among you, and cannot yet tell how to edify an argument? Attend and throw your ears to me, for I am gravidated with child, till I have indoctrinated your plumbeous cerebrosities. First you must divisionate your point, *quasi* you should cut a cheese into two particles – for thus I must uniform my speech to your obtuse conceptions; for *prius dividendum oratio antequam definiendum, exemplum gratia*: either Therion must conquer this, Dame Maia's nymph, or Espilus must overthrow her; and that *secundum* their dignity, which must also be subdivisionated into three equal *species*, either according to the penetrancy of their singing, or the meliority of their functions, or lastly the superancy of their merits. *De* singing *satis. Nunc* are you to argumentate of the qualifying of their estate first, and then whether hath more infernally, I mean deeply, deserved.

Dorcas

Oh poor Dorcas, poor Dorcas, that I was not set in my young days to school, that I might have purchased the understanding of Master Rombus' mysterious speeches. But yet thus much I conceive of them, that I must even give up from the bottom of my stomach what my conscience doth find in the behalf of shepherds. Oh sweet honey milken lambs, and is there any so flinty a heart, that can find about him to speak against them, that have the charge of so good souls as you be, among whom there is no envy and all obedience; where it is lawful for a man to be good if he list, and hath no outward cause to withdraw him from it; where the eye may be busied in considering the works of nature, and the heart quietly rejoiced in the honest using them? If contemplation, as clerks say, be the most excellent, which is so fit a life for templars as this is, neither subject to violent oppression, nor servile flattery? How many courtiers, think you, I have heard under our field in bushes make their woeful complaints, some of the greatness of their mistress' estate, which dazzled their eyes and yet burned their hearts; some of the extremity of her beauty mixed with extreme cruelty; some of her too much wit which made all their loving labors folly? Oh, how often have I heard one name sound in many mouths, making our vales witnesses of their doleful agonies! So that with long lost labor, finding their thoughts bore no other wool but despair, of young courtiers they grew old shepherds. Well, sweet lambs, I will end with you as I began. He that can open his mouth against such innocent souls, let him be hated as much as a filthy fox; let the taste of him be worse than musty cheese, the sound of him more dreadful than the howling of a wolf, his sight more odible than a toad in one's porridge.

Rixus

Your life indeed hath some goodness.

Rombus the schoolmaster

261 cap and knee respect (to doff cap and bend knee)
283 *Heu . . . Hei* (nonsensical Latin)
283–4 *Insipidum . . . populorum* of the ignorant multitudes and peoples
284 nebulons worthless fellows
285 *corpusculum* small body
287 gravidated made pregnant
288 plumbeous leaden; **cerebrosities** mad or stubborn ideas
289 divisionate divide; ***quasi*** as it were
291 uniform render, make compatible
292–3 *prius . . . gratia* first a speech must be divided before it is defined; for instance,
295 *secundum* secondly
297 penetrancy penetrating quality
298 meliority superiority
299 superancy surpassing quality
299 *De . . . satis* enough of singing; ***Nunc*** Now
300 argumentate argue
301 estate condition; **whether** which
315 list please
321 templars (1) those who contemplate; (2) barristers (at the Inner and Middle Temple law courts in London)
340 odible hateful

Oh, *tace*, *tace*, or all the fat will be ignified. First let me dilucidate the very intrinsical marrowbone of the matter. He doth use a certain rhetorical invasion into the point, as if indeed he had conference with his lambs; but the truth is, he doth equitate you in the mean time, master Rixus, for thus he saith that sheep are good, *ergo* the shepherd is good: an *enthymeme a loco contingentibus*, as my finger and my thumb are *contingentes*. Again, he saith, who liveth well is likewise good: but shepherds live well, *ergo* they are good; a syllogism in Darius King of Persia *a conjugatis*: as you would say, a man coupled to his wife, two bodies but one soul. But do you but acquiescate to my exhortation, and you shall extinguish him. Tell him his *major* is a knave, his *minor* is a fool, and his conclusion both: *et ecce homo blancatus quasi lilium.*

Rixus

I was saying the shepherd's life had some goodness in it because it borrowed of the country quietness something like ours. But that is not all, for ours, besides that quiet part, doth both strengthen the body and raise up the mind with this gallant sort of activity. Oh, sweet contentation, to see the long life of the hurtless trees; to see how in straight growing up, though never so high, they hinder not their fellows; they only enviously trouble which are crookedly bent. What life is to be compared to ours, where the very growing things are samples of goodness? We have no hopes, but we may quickly go about them, and going about them, we soon obtain them; not like those that have long followed one (in truth) most excellent chase, do now at length perceive she could never be taken; but that if she stayed at any time near pursuers, it was never meant to tarry with them, but only to take breath to fly further from them. He therefore that doubts that our life doth not far excel all others; let him also doubt that the well deserving and painful Therion is not to be preferred before the idle Espilus, which is even as much to say, as that the roes are not swifter than sheep, nor stags more goodly than goats.

Rombus

Bene, bene, nunc de questione propositus: that is as much to say, as well, well, now of the proposed question, that was, whether the many great services and many great faults of Therion, or the few small services and no faults of Espilus, be to be preferred, incepted or accepted the former.

The May Lady

No, no, your ordinary brains shall not deal in that matter. I have already submitted it to one whose sweet spirit hath passed through greater difficulties; neither will I that your blockheads lie in her way.

Therefore, oh, Lady, worthy to see the accomplishment of your desires, since all your desires be most worthy of you, vouchsafe our ears such happiness, and me that particular favor, as that you will judge whether of these two be more worthy of me, or whether I be worthy of them; and this I will say, that in judging me, you judge more than me in it.

This being said, it pleased her Majesty to judge that Espilus did the better deserve her; but what words, what reasons she used for it, this paper, which carrieth so base names, is not worthy to contain. Sufficeth it that upon the judgment given, the shepherds and foresters made a full consort of their cornets and recorders, and then did Espilus sing this song, tending to the greatness of his own joy, and yet to the comfort of the other side, since they were overthrown by a most worthy adversary. The song contained two short tales, and thus it was:

Espilus

Sylvanus long in love, and long in vain,
At length obtained the point of his desire,
When being asked, now that he did obtain
His wished weal, what more he could require:

---

344 *tace* quiet; **ignified** ignited
345 **dilucidate** make clear; **intrinsical marrowbone** inner qualities
348 **equitate** ride (as on horseback, perhaps confused with the word for equation)
350 *ergo* therefore
351 ***enthymeme*** **...** ***contingentibus*** implicit syllogism at the place joined
352 ***contingentes*** joined
355 **Darius King of Persia** reference is to *Darii*, in formal logic a syllogism where the major premise is a universal affirmation and the minor premise and conclusion are particular affirmations; ***conjugatis*** coupling
357 **acquiescate** acquiesce
359 ***major*** **...** ***minor*** major and minor premises in a syllogism
360 ***et*** **...** ***lilium*** he will turn white in dismay (apparently invented proverb)
389 ***Bene*** **...** ***propositus*** Good, good; now to the subject under question
394 **incepted** begun
401 **Lady** i.e., the Queen
414 **consort** concert; harmonious music
422 **Sylvanus** god of foresters
425 **weal** happiness

"Nothing," said he, "for most I joy in this,
That Goddess mine, my blessed being sees."

Therion

When wanton Pan, deceived with lion's skin,
Came to the bed, where wound for kiss he got,
To woe and shame the wretch did enter in,
Till this he took, for comfort of his lot:
"Poor Pan," he said, "although thou beaten be,
It is no shame, since Hercules was he."

Espilus

Thus joyfully I in chosen tunes rejoice,
That such a one is witness of my heart,
Whose clearest eyes I bliss, and sweetest voice,
That see my good, and judgeth my desert.

Therion

Thus woefully I in woe this salve do find,
My foul mishap came yet from fairest mind.

The music fully ended, the May Lady took her leave in this sort:

Lady your self, for other titles do rather diminish than add unto you: I and my little company must now leave you. I should do you wrong to beseech you to take our follies well, since your bounty is such as to pardon greater faults. Therefore I will wish you good night, praying to God according to the title I possess, that as hitherto it hath excellently done, so henceforward the flourishing of May may long remain in you and with you.

429 Pan god of shepherds; **deceived . . . skin** alludes to the story in which Pan mistakes the bed of Hercules for that of his mistress Omphale

The Spanish Tragedy

Thomas Kyd

The Spanish Tragedie:

OR,

Hieronimo is mad againe.

Containing the lamentable end of *Don Horatio*, and *Belimperia*; with the pittifull death of *Hieronimo*.

Newly corrected, amended, and enlarged with new Additions of the *Painters* part, and others, as it hath of late been diuers times acted.

LONDON,
Printed by W. White, for I. White and T. Langley, and are to be sold at their Shop ouer against the Sarazens head without New-gate. 1615.

Title page of the 1615 edition

Frontispiece, 1614.

From the 1570s to the 1590s – as Europe approached the end of the sixteenth century – a number of geological and astrological occurrences, along with increasing epidemics of plague, led to an apocalyptic dread and numerous eschatological works. A nova suddenly appeared to alter the heavens in 1572; a comet appeared in 1577; there was an earthquake in 1580 and ominous conjunctions of planets in 1583, 1588, and 1593. Scientists like moralists were increasingly concerned with the corruption of the air and the apparent decline in the fertility of the soil and growth of vegetation. A growing belief in an irreversible process of decay was applied to human affairs: increasing battles between nations and religions also seemed to mark humanity's decline in physical and moral stature and even life span. Aggressive acts of major European powers such as France and Spain and the ominous presence of the magnetic Mary Stuart – imprisoned in the northern English castle of Fotheringhay – suggested imminent danger of invasion and rebellion, while the English Reformation had put each man's and woman's conduct alone before the heavenly court of justice without the aid or consolation of sacraments and beliefs of a discredited Catholicism. In short, there could be no more fitting (or likely) time for a play called *The Spanish Tragedy* than the period between 1585 and 1589 when it was written. Catching the age's deep malaise and even deeper anxiety, it was the first major play of the English Renaissance as well as its first great tragedy, the first work to confront the fact of vengeance and the need for justice, and the first play to study the emergent cunning politician like the Spanish King and the Machiavellian villain such as Lorenzo. Even as Kyd attempted to lighten such matters with the grim comedy concerning the death of Pedringano, these characters became, in Kyd's hands, the subject of a tragedy of intrigue.

Nor was Kyd unaware of the conditions of his time. By naming the character who inspires much of the action in the play Bel-imperia, the beauty of empire or conquest, and by setting his play in Spain – the imperialist nation that was settling much of the New World in a contest with England for markets and plunder and threatening to send warships up the English Channel to restore the Catholic faith – Kyd addressed the deeper anxieties of his day. He may not have been the first. George Peele's *The Battle of Alcazar* (written around 1588–9) is about the struggle for the Portuguese crown, Spain's conquest of Portugal in 1580, and the installation of a subordinate viceroy to rule that annexed country in 1582; one character remarks of the treachery of the Spanish King Philip II, and of Spain,

> The heavens will right the wrongs that they sustain.
> Philip, if these forgeries be in thee,
> Assure thee, King, 'twill light on thee at last,
> And when proud Spain hopes soundly to prevail,
> The time may come that thou and thine shall fail.

The Catholic Philip II had, in fact, been a significant threat to England and to the future of English Protestantism since his marriage to Mary Tudor four years before her sister Elizabeth succeeded her to the throne. But there were other historic matters in the recent past, too, such as the horrifying massacre of French Huguenots in Paris on St. Bartholomew's Day following the failed attempt to reconcile faiths through the marriage of the Catholic Margaret, daughter of the Queen-mother, Catherine de Medici, to the Protestant Henry of Navarre. Such a bloodbath anticipates the deaths at the end of Kyd's play following the fears of a marriage between Bel-imperia and Horatio. What Kyd does, however, that Peele and others do not, is announce – through the use of the framing device of Revenge and the Ghost of Andrea and the judgments of Hades – that for him the action of the play, like the art of playwriting itself, is a matter of analogy. That Kyd chose Spain rather than France for his setting, however, followed recent history. While both countries were Catholic, and therefore naturally antagonistic towards England, the danger of Spain had grown exponentially since Elizabeth's forces under Leicester had been sent to the Protestant Netherlands to prevent the incursion of Spain and to keep those Low Countries as a buffer zone for her own further protection. "The state of the world is marvelously changed," Elizabeth's Principal Secretary Burghley remarked, when the threat of war came from Spain and no longer from France. Kyd mirrors his country's suspicious hatred of Spain by portraying a government that is self-indulgent, unfeeling, and corrupt and plays to the fervent English chauvinism by inserting – odd as it seems in the plot – Hieronimo's own actions as a playwright in the masques of Act I that show both Spain and Portugal defeated by an earlier, medieval England. Indeed, Spanish deception seems to be everywhere in the world of the play – in the uneven battle that kills Andrea in the first place; in Villuppo's false story that nearly kills Alexandro; in Lorenzo's endless scheming; and even in Horatio's presumptuous affair with Bel-imperia – all of which feed the perversity of the will and manipulate others for personal ends. It may be no coincidence that the one character who appeals consistently to a Christian god in this play about blood vengeance is Isabella, but that she does so only when she is mad and on the verge of suicide. The chief visual spectacle at the play's center is the dead Horatio, hanged and stabbed in the side by enemies he once thought his friends: a kind of crucifix, the idolatrous center of the Catholic faith that the Reformers had obliterated from all the Protestant English parish churches. The age of Reformation was said to be appointed by God before the end of the world as the time of the downfall of the Antichrist. In portraying Spain as the home of corruption and Antichrist, Kyd is appealing to the prejudices of his own audiences; but in the midst of all this he is also appealing to the playgoers' desire for redemption with such characters as Hieronimo, Horatio, Bel-imperia – and, we should not forget, Andrea.

From the first staging, *The Spanish Tragedy* was an overwhelming success; extant records find it the third most popular play between 1592 and 1599, with more productions than even *Dr. Faustus*. At least four companies performed it – Strange's Men (in what may have been the London premiere in 1594), the Admiral's Men, Pembroke's Men, and the Chamberlain's Men. And it played at many venues – in the Rose and Fortune theaters in London and, most likely, in the Theatre, the Cross Keys Inn, Newington Butts, the Curtain, and the first Globe. Additions were requested of Ben Jonson and others in 1602 and it took on renewed life; the citations, quotations, and parodies of it in subsequent years suggest it was a fundamental work of Tudor and early Stuart culture. So long a life – well past the defeat of the Spanish Armada and the eventual peace with Spain under James I – suggests that the play meant more than the kind of apocalyptic Babel/Babylon that Hieronimo suggests when he presents his final play to the Spanish court in Act IV. Clearly it addressed playgoers on a much more personal level as well. For one thing – in an age heavy with litigation – it examined the efficacy of law, the desirability (or undesirability) of vengeance (that is, taking the law into one's own hands), and the possibility of equity – that is, of special cases and special consideration. The play is set in motion by desires of revenge: Andrea wants revenge for his battledeath; Bel-imperia seeks revenge for the death of her beloved; Balthazar and Lorenzo seek revenge on Horatio for winning Bel-imperia for himself; and Hieronimo seeks revenge for the death of his son. All of them seek redress for deep personal grievances which martial law and the country's courts seem to refuse to address. Thus at a deeper level the acts of vengeance really raise questions about the possibilities for justice. This is what the Ghost of Andrea demands of Revenge; what Hieronimo seeks as he goes crying through the court; and what Isabella at her death seeks anxiously from religion. But justice for Kyd is a complicated matter, as many of the scenes demonstrate in an astonishing variety of ways. Pedringano's comeuppance, for instance, suggests that crimes do get punished but that perhaps the criminals who engineer them do not. The supplication of Bazulto suggests injustice stems from ineffectual laws and hearings – that the legal process rather than the identification of the villain is at fault. The incident of Villuppo's initially successful charge against Alexandro suggests that law working too hastily may make errors. Isabella's trust in the eventual justice of providence – that truth is the daughter of time – goes unfulfilled until, at last, she takes her own life.

Of all the characters, the one most central and most sympathetic is Hieronimo, and his sorrowful appeal – "I will go plain me to my Lord the King, And cry aloud for justice through the court," linking the King's court and the law courts – becomes choric for others, the earthbound cries of the Hades-imprisoned Andrea. It is proper for the Knight Marshal, as the King's chief law officer, to investigate the possibilities of justice and, given his position, his failures are far more unsettling. He refuses to admit the limitation or the absence of law at first; rather, he suspends judgment while seeking evidence and, when Bel-imperia's letter miraculously appears, he waits still longer for confirmation of its charges. Yet he has also – at the private moment of discovering his son's death when awakened in his nightshirt – made that very secret crime public with his outcry to the very heavens. But the heavens prove as silent, perhaps as disinterested, as the court will prove to be:

> Oh, sacred heavens! if this unhallowed deed,
> If this inhuman and barbarous attempt,
> If this incomparable murder thus
> Of mine, but now no more my son,
> Shall unrevealed and unrevengèd pass,
> How should we term your dealings to be just,
> If you unjustly deal with those that in your justice
> trust?

Justice itself no longer comprehends justice. Law and fortune seem oblivious to individual circumstance. Principles fail before so ruthless and selfish an individualism as Lorenzo's, as he uses the ceremonies of politics and the fabrications of words to achieve his own closely guarded ends. He is the ultimate cynic. He knows how to motivate others without revealing himself; to the foolish and gullible Pedringano, he remarks, "Where words prevail not, violence prevails," then adds, "But gold doth more than either of them both." His reticence obscures his motives, but the play will not let us off so easily. Does he act out of injured pride? wounded family pride? a hatred of the lower ranks invading his social realm? the arrogance of those who will not do his bidding? his own delight in the manipulation of others, the intricacies of his own plotting, the love of sheer cruelty? Does he live only for power and victory?

Such matters can be urgent at any time; the threat to justice always is. But at this unsettled time in England when the law courts of chancery were advancing the possibility of equity into a legal system but could not accommodate the cases, the issues can become crucial. In this sense, Hieronimo is a critical point man. The injustice he faces not only provides him no relief in his tragic quest for just punishment but questions the very validity of the position of Knight Marshal, the validity of law itself. Before the implacable ambition and ruthless solipsistic powers of a person like Lorenzo, how does an aggrieved party (or an aggrieved society) react? Hieronimo moves towards solitude and despair; his path veers towards the self-destructive route his wife takes. He avoids her fate only by protesting in a larger, if still a mute and unresponding, world, the cost to his own mind tragically measured by the way he treats petitioners who come to him seeking their own justice. In an important soliloquy that reveals his own self-assessments of the possibilities of justice left in a world of private interests, he turns to Romans 12: 19, "Vengeance is mine, saith the Lord," but in looking to heavenly justice as a guide to earthly justice the slippage is telling:

> *Vindicta mihi!*
> Aye, heaven will be revenged of every ill,
> Nor will they suffer murder unrepaid,
> Then stay, Hieronimo, attend their will,
> For mortal men may not appoint their time.

Attending to the will of God as life's final arbiter and judge, he moves on to represent God, to become His agent in a transformation that, in the end, looks very much like Lorenzo's agency. He becomes a schemer, too, enlisting the aid of Bel-imperia, designing his own plots secretively, and feigning obedience which he neither believes nor feels: "therefore will I rest me in unrest, Dissembling quiet in unquietness." When he takes up the rope and dagger – the halter and the poniard, the traditional stage signs of the suicide – he deliberately takes up the instruments that Lorenzo used to kill Horatio and that he in turn will use to accomplish his own ritualized revenge later when once again he ceremoniously turns playwright. There is something both neat and desperate about this; but Kyd makes it grimmer, more provocative, and more debatable by suggesting at the play's end that all of this has been, after all, merely a dream – a show desired by Andrea's Ghost at the hands of Revenge after they have exited Hades not by the gates of horn (their entrance, providing true visions) but the gates of ivory, which provide false ones. What now, this play asks, are we to make of justice?

But *The Spanish Tragedy*, introducing a subgenre of revenge tragedies, charts other dislocations in the unsettled Elizabethan society as well. Like the rest of Europe, English society was highly stratified; government and society alike functioned and even flourished because they depended on a hierarchy of power and a traditional network of obligations. All people were bound to the will of the monarch and, in addition, retainers to aristocrats, servants to masters, government officials to government itself, playwrights to patrons and audiences. Political and social custom marked dominance and submission, as Hieronimo's initial obsequiousness in Act I and his feigning in Act IV illustrate. But especially after the Reformation, newly emerging persons, such as William Cecil, Lord Burghley, applied to the College of Heralds for a coat of arms and sought a new genealogical pedigree. In such instances, there were no real precedents and no longer any permanent regulations of behavioral codes, admitting a kind of self-reliance which could easily turn into self-interest. In Kyd's play, this situation characterizes both Lorenzo and Hieronimo and, by making two such dissimilar members of society analogous in reaction to their changing times, Kyd's play explores and questions the causes and consequences of such changes. In *The Spanish Tragedy*, for instance, birth, lineage, rank, and station become increasingly important as the means for a stable society, something which Kyd himself seems to upset by making the legal functionary Hieronimo rather than the aristocratic Cyprian or his son Lorenzo the moral center of his play.

What at first unifies this stratified society of *The Spanish Tragedy* is its throwback to a kind of medieval chivalry where fealty – such as Portugal's obligations to Spain, the Duke of Castile to the King of Spain and Balthazar to the Viceroy of Portugal, and Andrea and Horatio to their country, defending it against the Portuguese insurgence – is linked to personal codes of honor such as those that join fathers to sons and knights to their ladies. This is clearly a premise to the play which begins by disrupting it: Andrea is killed on the battlefield because he is overpowered by a host of the enemy; he is not killed in a fair and honorable battle. When his death is avenged honorably by Horatio, the Spanish King cannot at first decide whether the captive murderer Balthazar should go to Horatio or to Lorenzo, whose claim rests on his assertion that he first seized the enemy's weapon. When Bel-imperia seems to find some solace (and a replacement) in the love of Horatio after the death of Andrea, Lorenzo counters with the proposed courtship of Balthazar. In each one of these instances, honor is said to determine the issue while in fact social rank determines it. Balthazar out*ranks* Andrea on the battlefield and has superior forces to support him. Lorenzo out*ranks* Horatio in the defeat of Balthazar and so, while Horatio gets the ransom money, station dictates that Balthazar is more acceptably at home with the family of Castile. For the same reason, as Lorenzo tells his sister, Balthazar will make a proper marriage for her; Horatio will not. Aristocracy as a way of keeping bloodlines pure and secure is thus a private way in which Kyd examines the more public issues of justice and warfare. Honor in the play, then, becomes the means and value of the relatively disempowered; Andrea, we are told, whose death begins the play's whole chain of events, " 'both lived and died in love,' " according to Minos, " 'And for his love tried fortune of the wars, And by war's fortune lost both love and life.' " He is therefore unable to judge the disposition of Andrea's spirit, for he is neither, finally, a lover nor a martialist because he has scrambled the two. Yet Minos only confirms Andrea's own innocent admission: "By duteous service and deserving love," he tells Revenge, "In secret I possessed a worthy dame." How "dutiful" and "deserving" is it to "possess" one of higher social rank by clandestine meetings? This standard trope of chivalric literature here taints Andrea's courtship and his military service long before Balthazar overpowers him on the battlefield. That illicit relationship is one that neither Castile nor Lorenzo was willing to entertain although it flourished, if only briefly, because of Lorenzo's support: "Since I did shield thee from my father's wrath For thy conveyance in Andrea's love, For which thou wert adjudged to punishment." What is at stake is the dynastic purity and the dynastic ambition of the House of Castile against which it would appear, with Horatio, Bel-imperia continues to rebel. Horatio, like his predecessor, chooses to court Bel-imperia only at night and in secret, and Kyd requires that we determine whether he does so in the innocence of love or the desire to rise socially. It is a bone of contention. Hieronimo would see it as innocent (as he himself seems, strangely, to be) but surely Lorenzo does not. Nor does Bel-imperia: "I'll love Horatio, my Andrea's friend, The more to spite the Prince that wrought his end." Exercise of power and self-interest – here motivated by vengeance – inspired Bel-imperia and in turn seduces Horatio and goes unrecognized by Hieronimo, until, in the end, they join forces to seek both vengeance and self-interest in a kind of diabolically shared purpose. It may be no accident, then, that Balthazar fought unevenly with Andrea on the battlefield in order to keep status and rank protected; and it may, further, be no accident that Lorenzo finds a way to claim Balthazar for his own captive (and the King provides it) to rank social like with like. In both cases neither Andrea nor Horatio is willing to see the possible motives for such actions; and their very blindness may make them as culpable of the tragedies of the play as anyone is.

If this is a significant part of Kyd's play, then rank becomes the sole determinant not only of romance and war but of government and justice as well. At best, the Knight Marshal can only be the Knight Marshal and his son's case is no different from that of the old man in whom, in a moment of the illumination of madness, Hieronimo sees himself reflected. But where does Thomas Kyd, the son of a scrivener, stand in such matters? Through his trade, Kyd's father had access to the court, but he was never of the court. To compound matters, he sent his son to the well-endowed Merchant Taylors' School in London which had a curriculum – in classics, modern languages, and mathematics – designed to teach aristocratic ideas and values to the gentry and merchant class. The school's headmaster, the talented and informed Richard Mulcaster, was openly aware of such a clear and present danger: "Before that time we pardon many things and use points of ambition and courage, to enflame the little ones onward, which we cut off afterward, for making them too malapert [impudent; presumptuous], as in their apparel freize is successor to silk." There is an eerie resonance of this precise remark in the silk handkerchief or scarf which Bel-imperia gives to Andrea as a token of their love to take into battle, that Horatio retrieves and returns to her and gets in turn as Andrea's successor, and that Hieronimo takes, drenched in blood, as the love token of his son that will prescribe his duty of justice and ultimately of vengeance. But Kyd himself was trained up to be another Andrea, another Horatio. What, then, might be his intention in writing a revenge tragedy such as this play: to expose and challenge the unspoken social codes that control government and society and so, like Andrea, Bel-imperia, Horatio, and Hieronimo, challenge the rigidity of a culture that will not honor talent as much as bloodline? Or, in asking that those who seek vengeance themselves pay with their lives, as Bel-imperia and Hieronimo do, as well as Lorenzo and Balthazar, Andrea and Horatio, does the play work to reinstate the old order as a way of stabilizing a restless and threatened world?

The execution of justice in Elizabethan England as a flashpoint for such questions is not surprising: 6,160 persons received theatrically spectacular public deaths by hanging at Tyburn during Elizabeth's reign – it was a common enough sight, mirroring Pedringano's onstage death as well as the onstage preparations to burn Alexandro at the stake. In fact, on August 28, 1588, John Stow records, there was a virtual joining of the two as one W. Gunter, a foreign priest, was hanged "at the Theater" while on October 1 another priest, William Hartley, was executed "nigh the Theater." The Knight Marshal's masques of his own prescriptions for justice near the start and conclusion of *The Spanish Tragedy* also make the connection, but to see them as simply justified or unjustified is to simplify Kyd's play. For nothing in this play, which is filled with masques, dumb shows, pageantry and multiple staging (as when Revenge and the Ghost watch Balthazar and Lorenzo watching Horatio and Bel-imperia, all seen by the playhouse audience), is simply either/or. Rather *The Spanish Tragedy* is a play of multiple perspectives as well as delayed consequences. In the first scene, none of the three judges of Hades is able to determine the fate of Andrea and when Minos refers his case to Pluto and Proserpine, even they do not decide, referring the case instead to Revenge to work out. Similarly, when the King of Spain asks about the battle that caused the death of Andrea in the land above the underworld, his General's report emerges at sharp disagreement with that of Villuppo to the Portuguese Viceroy and Horatio to Bel-imperia. Whom are we to believe, if anyone at all, in this play of various schemers and playmakers within the play about Spain within the classical frame of Revenge's perspective? Since Revenge announces that he and Andrea will "see the mystery" and then decisively "serve for Chorus in this tragedy," does his own singular interest make his own seeing unreliably myopic? He does combine both – the mystery and the revenge – that has so bothered critics in what they generally see as Hieronimo's final gratuitous murder of the "innocent" Cyprian, Duke of Castile, but Revenge's play (and Kyd's) have made it clear enough in III.xiv that in this play no one is innocent, and everyone, in some way, complicit. Like Lorenzo, Cyprian would not condone a second "illicit" match for Bel-imperia, like that clandestine affair with Andrea, but this time one that is licit because socially correct. In the same scene he can plead for patience and understanding for the frustrated Hieronimo and yet renew that frustration:

> Welcome brave Prince, the pledge of Castile's peace.
> And welcome Bel-imperia. How now, girl?
> Why com'st thou sadly to salute us thus?
> Content thyself, for I am satisfied,
> It is not now as when Andrea lived,
> We have forgotten and forgiven that,
> And thou art graced with a happier love.

In forgiving Bel-imperia of her clandestine affair with Andrea, Cyprian establishes his own court and makes his own judgment, in line with family honor and family preservation. Hieronimo understands that it is Castile himself who has engineered the murder of his son by the values he holds; and it is Castile who thus must become the last of Hieronimo's victims if he is to restore some last possibility for his sense of honor. Thus the once-sympathetic Hieronimo sets out to annihilate the Spanish succession. He stops short, however, at the King himself, content, it might seem, only to instruct him about the consequences of family honor and the anguish of injustice and thus risk keeping the old order firmly in place after all. Through the play until its very last words – Revenge's pronouncement of a lack of closure, an "endless tragedy" – Kyd seems on the one hand to portray all events within the long shadow of Andrea's infernal desires expressed in the underworld, and, on the other, to suggest that in contemporary society free will is only another illusion, another dream.

Justice, then, like rank and honor, remains deeply problematic in *The Spanish Tragedy*. It insists we interrogate what constitutes justice and what must be guaranteed a citizenry if government is to function. Kyd knew these issues at first hand. In 1593 the Privy Council launched an investigation for subversive writings of all kinds and in due course they arrested Kyd, finding among his papers some atheistical writings which he said were not his, but Marlowe's, mistakenly shuffled among his own work when they once shared a room. Kyd was imprisoned in Bridewell where he underwent the dreadful torture of the strappado, in which his hands were tied behind his back and he was hoisted by a pulley and then his body suddenly dropped and jerked. At the very time *The Spanish Tragedy* was probably playing the provinces of England by a touring company of strolling players – where, Dekker claims, Ben Jonson played the part of Hieronimo – Kyd was sending a confession to Sir Thomas Puckering, Lord Keeper of the Great Seal and a member of the Court of Chancery, that protested his continuing loyalty: "If I knew any whom I could justly accuse of that damnable offense to the awful Majesty of God or of that other mutinous sedition toward the state I would as willingly reveal them as I would request your Lordship's better thoughts of me that never have offended you." It could well be Hieronimo speaking – or Castile. *The Spanish Tragedy*, like the procession of Elizabeth through London or the entertainment at Wanstead Garden, demonstrates how perilously thin the line was between public performance and the culture that produced and saw it – and suggests that sometimes there may have been no dividing line at all.

FURTHER READING

Adams, Barry B., "The Audiences of *The Spanish Tragedy*," *Journal of English and Germanic Philology* 48:2 (April 1969): 221–36.

Ardolino, Frank, *Apocalypse and Armada in Kyd's "Spanish Tragedy."* Kirskville, Mo: Sixteenth Century Essays and Studies, 1995.

Barish, Jonas A., "*The Spanish Tragedy*, or The Pleasures and Perils of Rhetoric," in *Elizabethan Theatre*, ed. John Russell Brown and Bernard Harris (London: Edward Arnold, 1966), pp. 59–85.

Hamilton, Donna B., "*The Spanish Tragedy*: A Speaking Picture," *English Literary Renaissance* 4:2 (Spring 1974): 203–17.

Hill, Eugene D., "Senecan and Vergilian Perspectives in *The Spanish Tragedy*," *English Literary Renaissance* 15:2 (Spring 1985): 143–65.

Jensen, Ejner J., "Kyd's *Spanish Tragedy*: The Play Explains Itself," *Journal of English and Germanic Philology* 44:1 (January 1965): 7–16.

McMillin, Scott, "The Figure of Silence in *The Spanish Tragedy*," *ELH* 39 (1972): 27–48.

Murray, Peter B., *Thomas Kyd*. New York: Twayne Publishers, 1969.

Siemon, James R., "Dialogical Formalism: Word, Object, and Action in *The Spanish Tragedy*," *Medieval and Renaissance Drama in England* 7 (1991): 87–115.

——, "Sporting Kyd," *English Literary Renaissance* 24:3 (Autumn 1994): 553–82.

Shapiro, James, "'Tragedies naturally performed': Kyd's Representation of Violence," *Staging the Renaissance: Reinterpretations of Elizabethan and Jacobean Drama*, ed. David Scott Kastan and Peter Stallybrass (London: Routledge, 1991), pp. 99–113.

The Spanish Tragedy

CONTAINING THE LAMENTABLE END OF DON HORATIO AND BEL-IMPERIA: WITH THE PITIFUL DEATH OF OLD HIERONIMO.

[*DRAMATIS PERSONAE*]

Ghost of Andrea.
Revenge.

King of Spain ("Spanish King").
Cyprian, Duke of Castile ("Castile", "Duke"), *his brother.*
Lorenzo, *the Duke's son.*
Bel-imperia, *Lorenzo's sister.*
General *of the Spanish Army.*

Viceroy of Portugal ("King").
Pedro, *his brother.*
Balthazar ("Prince"), *his son.*
Alexandro, } *noblemen at the Portuguese court.*
Villuppo, }
Ambassador *of Portugal to the Spanish court.*

Hieronimo, *Knight Marshal of Spain.*
Isabella, *his wife.*
Horatio, *his son.*
Pedringano, *servant to Bel-imperia.*
Serberine, *servant to Balthazar.*
Christophil, *servant to Lorenzo.*
Page ("Boy") *to Lorenzo.*
Three Watchmen.
Messenger.
Deputy.
Hangman.
Maid *to Isabella.*
Two Portuguese.
Servant.
Three Citizens.
An Old Man, Bazulto ("Senex").

Portuguese Nobles, Soldiers, Officers, Attendants, Halberdiers.

Three Knights, Three Kings, a Drummer *in the first Dumb show.*
Hymen, Two Torch-bearers *in the second Dumb show.*

In Hieronimo's play:

Soliman, Sultan of Turkey (Balthazar).
Erasto ("Erastus"), Knight of Rhodes (Lorenzo).
Bashaw (Hieronimo).
Perseda (Bel-imperia).

Act I

[I.i]

Enter the Ghost *of* Andrea, *and with him* Revenge.

Ghost. When this eternal substance of my soul
Did live imprisoned in my wanton flesh,
Each in their function serving other's need,
I was a courtier in the Spanish court.
My name was Don Andrea, my descent,
Though not ignoble, yet inferior far
To gracious fortunes of my tender youth.
For there in prime and pride of all my years,
By duteous service and deserving love,
In secret I possessed a worthy dame,
Which hight sweet Bel-imperia by name.
But in the harvest of my summer joys
Death's winter nipped the blossoms of my bliss,
Forcing divorce betwixt my love and me.
For in the late conflict with Portingale
My valor drew me into danger's mouth,
Till life to death made passage through my wounds.
When I was slain, my soul descended straight
To pass the flowing stream of Acheron.
But churlish Charon, only boatman there,
Said that my rites of burial not performed,
I might not sit among his passengers.
Ere Sol had slept three nights in Thetis' lap
And slaked his smoking chariot in her flood,
By Don Horatio, our Knight Marshal's son,
My funerals and obsequies were done.
Then was the ferryman of hell content
To pass me over to the slimy strond
That leads to fell Avernus' ugly waves.
There pleasing Cerberus with honeyed speech,
I passed the perils of the foremost porch.
Not far from hence, amid ten thousand souls,
Sat Minos, Aeacus, and Rhadamanth,
To whom no sooner gan I make approach,
To crave a passport for my wandering ghost,
But Minos, in graven leaves of lottery,
Drew forth the manner of my life and death.
"This knight," quoth he, "both lived and died in love,
And for his love tried fortune of the wars,

TEXTUAL VARIANTS

I.i.65 shake] Q shakes **I.ii.162** spoke] Q spake **164** won] Q wan **I.iii.9 s.d.**] Q has s.d. at line 12 **I.iv.31** carcass] Q carkasse **II.i.41** *qui*] Q *que* **II.ii.16** choir] Q quire **II.iii.49** thought] Q thoughts **II.iv.24** leafy] Q leavy **44** withal] Q with **II.v.27** vile] Q vild **29** lose] Q leese **48** stayed] Q stained **69** *animis*] Q annum **73** *herbarum*] Q irraniue *nenia*] Q menia **II.vi.5** On] Q Or **III.i.l s.d.**] Q adds Alexandro **70 s.d.** Viceroy] Q King **77** Lord] Q lord, unbind him (too long a line may mean compositor added stage direction at this point) **III.ii.26**] Q has speech prefix for Bel-imperia for lines 26–31 "For] Q For **32**] Q adds speech prefix for Hieronimo **117** live, for me] Q live for me, **III.iii.32** ha't] Q ha'te **III.iv.5** inexpected] Q in expected **45** help] Q holp **87** E] Q Et **88** *io, nessun lo*] Q It nessum le **III.v.l s.d.**] Q has no speech prefix **III.vi.40** And] Q Had **103** Heaven] Q heavens **III.vii.l s.d.**] Q has no speech prefix **42** helped] Q holp **43** Helped] Q holp **III.x.102** *Et*] Q *Est* **III.xii.46** inexplicable] Q inexecrable **III.xiii.l s.d.**] Q has no speech prefix **45 s.d.**] Q has s.d. at line 44 **127** pounds] Q pound **151** fate] Q Father **III.xiv.1–2**] Q sets as prose **128**] Q has no speech prefix **144** Lord] Q love **163** thus] Q that **168** suole] Q sule **III.xv.3** Erebus] Q Ericus **5**] syntax of lines 4 and 6 suggests compositor omitted something **7** sees!] Q see? **14** prevalence] Q prevailance **17** begone] Q degone **IV.i.9**] Q reads "With what excuses canst thou shew thy self?"; the printer's eyeskip has set the same line twice **114** was] Q way **185–6**] Q reverses these lines, but syntax suggests the order given here **IV.iv.l s.d.**] Q has no speech prefix **IV.iv.201**] Q has no speech prefix **214** gulf] Q grief **217 s.d.** Viceroy] Q King **IV.v.27** haul] Q hale

Playsource

The Spanish Tragedy has no known source, although Kyd may well have known the parallel story of Adilon and Clorinda in *A Courtlie Controversie of Cupid's Cautels* (1578), Henry Wotton's translation of the tales of Jacque Yver. Another of Yver's tales may have suggested Hieronimo's play-within-a-play and still another the story of Solimon and Perseda. Pedringano's death may have been drawn from the anonymous *Copie of a Letter* (1584) where the Earl of Leicester rids himself of the accomplice Gates while pretending to protect him. But the form – with its emphases on revenge, ghosts, dumb shows, and blood – is taken from Senecan tragedy, common to Elizabethan grammar schools, and some of the ideas may derive from Book VI of Virgil's *Aeneid* with its account of a trip to Hades.

I.i s.d. *Enter* (probably from under the stage through the trap to suggest the underworld)
1–14 When . . . me (later this was frequently parodied; cf. Beaumont, V.i)
8 prime early manhood; **pride** most flourishing condition
10 possessed made love to
11 hight was called
14 divorce separation
15 Portingale Portugal
18–85 When . . . eye (derived from Virgil, *Aeneid* VI)
19 Acheron river in Hades, more customarily it was the Styx
20 boatman Charon ferried dead souls into Hades
23 Sol . . . lap i.e., the sun had not passed three times over the ocean (Thetis, here the sea, was the daughter of the sea god Nereus)
24 slaked extinguished the flame of
25 Knight Marshal Marshal of the King's House whose authority in England extended to hearing and determining all pleas of the crown; he also handled lawsuits and judged and awarded punishments for any illegalities within 12 miles of the court
28 strond shore
29 Avernus lake near Puteoli thought to be the entrance to the underworld
30 Cerberus the monstrous three-headed dog who was sentry
31 porch entry
33 Minos . . . Rhadamanth judges in the underworld
35 passport letters for safe conduct
36 graven engraved, written; **leaves . . . lottery** (Virgil claims the place the dead souls finally occupied was determined by lot)
37 manner biography

And by war's fortune lost both love and life."
"Why then," said Aeacus, "convey him hence,
To walk with lovers in our fields of love,
And spend the course of everlasting time
Under green myrtle trees and cypress shades."
"No, no," said Rhadamanth, "it were not well
With loving souls to place a martialist,
He died in war, and must to martial fields,
Where wounded Hector lives in lasting pain,
And Achilles' Myrmidons do scour the plain."
Then Minos, mildest censor of the three,
Made this device to end the difference.
"Send him," quoth he, "to our infernal king,
To doom him as best seems his majesty."
To this effect my passport straight was drawn.
In keeping on my way to Pluto's court,
Through dreadful shades of ever-glooming night,
I saw more sights than thousand tongues can tell,
Or pens can write, or mortal hearts can think.
Three ways there were: that on the right-hand side
Was ready way unto the foresaid fields,
Where lovers live, and bloody martialists,
But either sort contained within his bounds.
The left-hand path, declining fearfully,
Was ready downfall to the deepest hell,
Where bloody Furies shake their whips of steel,
And poor Ixion turns an endless wheel.
Where usurers are choked with melting gold,
And wantons are embraced with ugly snakes,
And murderers groan with never-killing wounds,
And perjured wights scalded in boiling lead,
And all foul sins with torments overwhelmed.
'Twixt these two ways, I trod the middle path,
Which brought me to the fair Elysian green,
In midst whereof there stands a stately tower,
The walls of brass, the gates of adamant.
Here finding Pluto with his Proserpine,
I showed my passport humbled on my knee.
Whereat fair Proserpine began to smile,
And begged that only she might give my doom.
Pluto was pleased and sealed it with a kiss.
Forthwith, Revenge, she rounded thee in th' ear,
And bade thee lead me through the gates of horn,
Where dreams have passage in the silent night.
No sooner had she spoke but we were here,
I wot not how, in twinkling of an eye.

Revenge. Then know, Andrea, that thou art arrived
Where thou shalt see the author of thy death,
Don Balthazar the prince of Portingale,
Deprived of life by Bel-imperia.
Here sit we down to see the mystery,
And serve for Chorus in this tragedy.

[I.ii]

Enter Spanish King, General, Castile, Hieronimo.

King. Now say, Lord General, how fares our camp?

Gen. All well, my Sovereign Liege, except some few
That are deceased by fortune of the war.

King. But what portends thy cheerful countenance,
And posting to our presence thus in haste?
Speak, man, hath fortune given us victory?

Gen. Victory, my Liege, and that with little loss.

King. Our Portingals will pay us tribute then?

Gen. Tribute and wonted homage therewithal.

---

46 **martialist** warrior
48–9 **Hector . . . plain** Hector, a Trojan hero, was killed by the Myrmidons outside the city walls of Troy
49 **Myrmidons** followers of Achilles; **scour** range over
50 **censor** judge
51 **device** compromise
52 **infernal king** Pluto
53 **doom** pronounce final judgment on
56 **glooming** (1) dark; (2) threatening
60 **fields** Elysian Fields
62 **either** each; **his** i.e., his own
64 **downfall** gulf; **deepest hell** Tartarus
65 **Furies** mythical avengers of crime
66 **Ixion . . . wheel** Ixion was sentenced to an eternal treadmill for seeking the love of Hera
67 **usurers** moneylenders
68 **wantons** knaves, loose or lascivious persons
70 **wights** people
72 **middle path** (Virgil has only two paths; perhaps this is meant to suggest Andrea's homelessness and restlessness)
73 **fair . . . green** home of the blessed
75 **adamant** (1) hard stone; (2) diamond
76 **Proserpine** i.e., Persephone, Queen of the Underworld; at first abducted there, her union with Pluto represented the reconciliation of life and death
77 **humbled . . . knee** i.e., kneeling in respect
79 **doom** sentence
81 **rounded** whispered
82 **gates of horn** entrance for true dreams or visions as opposed to the gates of ivory
85 **wot** know
90 **mystery** i.e., the forthcoming events of the play
I.ii.1 **camp** army in the field
2 **Liege** Lord
8 **tribute** money paid to the victors as part of the settlement following war

King. Then blest be Heaven, and guider of the heavens,
From whose fair influence such justice flows.

Cast. O multum dilecte Deo, tibi militat aether, Et conjuratae curvato poplite gentes
Succumbunt: recti soror est victoria juris.

King. Thanks to my loving brother of Castile.
But, General, unfold in brief discourse
Your form of battle and your war's success,
That adding all the pleasure of thy news
Unto the height of former happiness,
With deeper wage and greater dignity
We may reward thy blissful chivalry.

Gen. Where Spain and Portingale do jointly knit
Their frontiers, leaning on each other's bound,
There met our armies in their proud array,
Both furnished well, both full of hope and fear,
Both menacing alike with daring shows,
Both vaunting sundry colors of device,
Both cheerly sounding trumpets, drums and fifes,
Both raising dreadful clamors to the sky,
That valleys, hills, and rivers made rebound,
And heaven itself was frighted with the sound.
Our battles both were pitched in squadron form,
Each corner strongly fenced with wings of shot.
But ere we joined and came to push of pike,
I brought a squadron of our readiest shot
From out our rearward to begin the fight.
They brought another wing to encounter us.
Meanwhile our ordnance played on either side,
And captains strove to have their valors tried.
Don Pedro, their chief horsemen's colonel,
Did with his cornet bravely make attempt
To break the order of our battle ranks.
But Don Rogero, worthy man of war,
Marched forth against him with our musketeers,
And stopped the malice of his fell approach.
While they maintain hot skirmish to and fro,
Both battles join and fall to handy blows,
Their violent shot resembling th' ocean's rage,
When, roaring loud and with a swelling tide,
It beats upon the rampiers of huge rocks,
And gapes to swallow neighbor-bounding lands.
Now while Bellona rageth here and there,
Thick storms of bullets rain like winter's hail,
And shivered lances dark the troubled air.
Pede pes et cuspide cuspis,
Arma sonant armis, vir petiturque viro.
On every side drop captains to the ground,
And soldiers, some ill-maimed, some slain outright.
Here falls a body scindered from his head,
There legs and arms lie bleeding on the grass,
Mingled with weapons and unbowelled steeds,
That scattering overspread the purple plain.
In all this turmoil, three long hours and more,
The victory to neither part inclined,
Till Don Andrea, with his brave lanciers,
In their main battle made so great a breach,
That, half dismayed, the multitude retired.
But Balthazar, the Portingales' young prince,
Brought rescue and encouraged them to stay.
Here-hence the fight was eagerly renewed,
And in that conflict was Andrea slain –
Brave man at arms, but weak to Balthazar.
Yet while the Prince, insulting over him,
Breathed out proud vaunts, sounding to our reproach,
Friendship and hardy valor, joined in one,

12–14 *O ... juris* "Oh, one much loved of God, for thee the Heavens contend, and the united peoples fall down on bended knee: victor is sister to just right" (Claudian, *De Tertio Consulatu Honorii*, lines 96–8)
16 unfold divulge
20 deeper wage greater reward
21 blissful chivalry extraordinary skill at arms
22–84 Where ... retreat (this reliable account expands the Ghost in I.i and will correct Villuppo's biased report in I.iii)
23 bound i.e., boundary
25 furnished equipped
27 vaunting boasting; **colors of device** heraldic banners
28 cheerly cheerfully
32 battles squadrons; **squadron form** square formation
33 fenced (1) defended; (2) reinforced; **wings of shot** soldiers carrying firearms on the outer edges of the formation
34 push of pike hand-to-hand fighting
38 ordnance heavy artillery; **played** directed fire
41 cornet squadron of cavalry
45 malice danger; **fell** savage
47 handy hand-to-hand
48 shot exchange of fire
50 rampiers ramparts
52 Bellona Roman goddess of war
54 shivered broken; splintered
55–6 *Pede ... viro* "Foot against foot and spear against spear, arms ring on arms and man is assailed by man" (partly Statius, *Thebais* VIII.399)
58 ill-maimed seriously injured
59 scindered sundered
61 unbowelled disembowelled
62 purple i.e., bloody
65 lanciers lancers
70 Here-hence as a result of this
72 man at arms (i.e., he was a cavalryman)
73 insulting exulting
74 sounding tending

Pricked forth Horatio, our Knight Marshal's son,
To challenge forth that Prince in single fight.
Not long between these twain the fight endured,
But straight the Prince was beaten from his horse
And forced to yield him prisoner to his foe.
When he was taken, all the rest they fled,
And our carbines pursued them to the death,
Till Phoebus waning to the western deep,
Our trumpeters were charged to sound retreat.

King. Thanks good Lord General, for these good news,
And for some argument of more to come,
Take this and wear it for thy sovereign's sake.
Give him his chain.
But tell me now, hast thou confirmed a peace?

Gen. No peace my Liege, but peace conditional,
That if with homage tribute be well paid,
The fury of your forces will be stayed.
And to this peace their Viceroy hath subscribed,
Give the King a paper.
And made a solemn vow that during life
His tribute shall be truly paid to Spain.

King. These words, these deeds, become thy person well.
But now Knight Marshal, frolic with thy King,
For 'tis thy son that wins this battle's prize.

Hier. Long may he live to serve my Sovereign Liege,
And soon decay unless he serve my Liege.
A tucket afar off.

King. Nor thou nor he shall die without reward.
What means the warning of this trumpet's sound?

Gen. This tells me that Your Grace's men of war,
Such as war's fortune hath reserved from death,
Come marching on towards your royal seat
To show themselves before your Majesty,
For so I gave in charge at my depart.
Whereby by demonstration shall appear
That all (except three hundred or few more)
Are safe returned and by their foes enriched.

The Army enters, Balthazar *between* Lorenzo *and* Horatio, *captive.*

King. A gladsome sight, I long to see them here.
They enter and pass by.
Was that the warlike Prince of Portingale,
That by our nephew was in triumph led?

Gen. It was, my Liege, the Prince of Portingale.

King. But what was he that on the other side
Held him by th' arm as partner of the prize?

Hier. That was my son, my gracious Sovereign,
Of whom though from his tender infancy
My loving thoughts did never hope but well,
He never pleased his father's eyes till now,
Nor filled my heart with overcloying joys.

King. Go let them march once more about these walls,
That staying them we may confer and talk
With our brave prisoner and his double guard.
Hieronimo, it greatly pleaseth us,
That in our victory thou have a share,
By virtue of thy worthy son's exploit.

Enter [the Army] again.

Bring hither the young Prince of Portingale,
The rest march on, but ere they be dismissed,
We will bestow on every soldier
Two ducats, and on every leader ten,
That they may know our largess welcomes them.
Exeunt all [the Army] but Balthazar, Lorenzo, Horatio.
Welcome, Don Balthazar; welcome, nephew,
And thou, Horatio, thou art welcome too.
Young Prince, although thy father's hard misdeeds,
In keeping back the tribute that he owes,
Deserve but evil measure at our hands,
Yet shalt thou know that Spain is honorable.

Bal. The trespass that my father made in peace
Is now controlled by fortune of the wars,
And cards once dealt, it boots not ask why so.

76 **Pricked forth** spurred on
80 **him** i.e., himself
82 **carbines** armed men
83 **Phoebus** the sun; **deep** the sea
86 **argument** indication
89 **but** save for
91 **stayed** (1) halted; (2) restrained
92 **subscribed** signed his name
96 **frolic** (1) rejoice; (2) celebrate
99 **decay** decline in health and fortune
99 **s.d.** ***tucket*** trumpet flourish (for cavalry)
100 **Nor** neither
106 **depart** departure
110 **s.d.** ***pass by*** cross over the stage
112 **our nephew** i.e., Balthazar; **triumph** captivity
116 **son** Horatio
120 **overcloying** satiating
122 **staying** stopping
131 **largess** money and gifts bestowed by a king
134 **hard** unyielding
139 **controlled** brought to an end
140 **boots** avail

His men are slain, a weakening to his realm,
His colors seized, a blot unto his name,
His son distressed, a corsive to his heart.
These punishments may clear his late offense.
King. Aye, Balthazar, if he observe this truce
Our peace will grow the stronger for these wars.
Meanwhile live thou, though not in liberty,
Yet free from bearing any servile yoke,
For in our hearing thy deserts were great,
And in our sight thyself art gracious.
Bal. And I shall study to deserve this grace.
King. But tell me, for their holding makes me doubt,
To which of these twain art thou prisoner?
Lor. To me, my Liege.
Hor. To me, my Sovereign.
Lor. This hand first took his courser by the reins.
Hor. But first my lance did put him from his horse.
Lor. I seized his weapon and enjoyed it first.
Hor. But first I forced him lay his weapons down.
King. Let go his arm, upon our privilege.
Let him go.
Say, worthy Prince, to whether didst thou yield?
Bal. To him in courtesy, to this perforce.
He spoke me fair, this other gave me strokes.
He promised life, this other threatened death.
He won my love; this other conquered me.
And, truth to say, I yield myself to both.
Hier. But that I know your Grace for just and wise,
And might seem partial in this difference,
Enforced by nature and by law of arms
My tongue should plead for young Horatio's right.
He hunted well that was a lion's death,
Not he that in a garment wore his skin.
So hares may pull dead lions by the beard.
King. Content thee, Marshal, thou shalt have no wrong,
And for thy sake thy son shall want no right.
Will both abide the censure of my doom?
Lor. I crave no better than your Grace awards.
Hor. Nor I, although I sit beside my right.
King. Then by my judgment thus your strife shall end.
You both deserve and both shall have reward.
Nephew, thou took'st his weapon and his horse,
His weapons and his horse are thy reward.
Horatio, thou didst force him first to yield,
His ransom therefore is thy valor's fee.
Appoint the sum as you shall both agree.
But nephew, thou shalt have the Prince in guard,
For thine estate best fitteth such a guest.
Horatio's house were small for all his train.
Yet in regard thy substance passeth his,
And that just guerdon may befall desert,
To him we yield the armor of the Prince.
How likes Don Balthazar of this device?
Bal. Right well, my Liege, if this proviso were
That Don Horatio bear us company,
Whom I admire and love for chivalry.
King. Horatio, leave him not that loves thee so.
Now let us hence to see our soldiers paid,
And feast our prisoner as our friendly guest.
Exeunt.

[I. iii]

Enter Viceroy, Alexandro, Villuppo [, Attendants].

Vice. Is our ambassador despatched for Spain?
Alex. Two days, my Liege, are passed since his depart.
Vice. And tribute payment gone along with him?
Alex. Aye, my good Lord.
Vice. Then rest we here awhile in our unrest,
And feed our sorrows with some inward sighs,
For deepest cares break never into tears.
But wherefore sit I in a regal throne?
This better fits a wretch's endless moan.
Falls to the ground.
Yet this is higher than my fortunes reach,
And therefore better than my state deserves.
Aye, aye, this earth, image of melancholy,

---

142 colors standards
143 distressed taken prisoner; **corsive** corrosive
144 clear be full compensation for; **late** recent
155 courser horse
159 our privilege royal prerogative
160 whether which of these two men
167 partial (because one captor is his own nephew while the other is Hieronimo's son)
170–2 He . . . beard (even timid hares may beard a dead lion; proverbial)
175 censure . . . doom outcome of my judgment
177 sit beside (1) demonstrate; (2) (perhaps forgo)
185–90 nephew . . . Prince (differences in social status require the victors receive different treatment by the King)
187 train attendants
188 in regard since
189 guerdon reward; **desert** deserving
190 him Horatio
191 device strategy; decision
I.iii.10 this . . . reach my circumstances are now worse than even this
11 state present condition
12 earth . . . melancholy (in the theory of the four elements making up all temperaments these two were traditionally associated)

Seeks him whom fates adjudge to misery.
Here let me lie, now am I at the lowest.
Qui jacet in terra non habet unde cadat.
In me consumpsit vires fortuna nocendo,
Nil superest ut jam possit obesse magis.
Yes, Fortune may bereave me of my crown.
Here take it now. Let Fortune do her worst.
She will not rob me of this sable weed.
Oh, no, she envies none but pleasant things:
Such is the folly of despiteful chance!
Fortune is blind and sees not my deserts,
So is she deaf and hears not my laments.
And could she hear, yet is she willful mad,
And therefore will not pity my distress.
Suppose that she could pity me, what then?
What help can be expected at her hands,
Whose foot is standing on a rolling stone
And mind more mutable than fickle winds?
Why wail I then, where's hope of no redress?
Oh, yes, complaining makes my grief seem less.
My late ambition hath distained my faith,
My breach of faith occasioned bloody wars,
Those bloody wars have spent my treasure,
And with my treasure my people's blood,
And with their blood, my joy and best beloved,
My best beloved, my sweet and only son.
Oh, wherefore went I not to war myself?
The cause was mine. I might have died for both.
My years were mellow, his but young and green,
My death were natural, but his was forced.
Alex. No doubt, my Liege, but still the Prince survives.
Vice. Survives! aye, where?
Alex. In Spain, a prisoner by mischance of war.
Vice. Then they have slain him for his father's fault.
Alex. That were a breach to common law of arms.
Vice. They reck no laws that meditate revenge.
Alex. His ransom's worth will stay from foul revenge.
Vice. No, if he lived the news would soon be here.
Alex. Nay, evil news fly faster still than good.
Vice. Tell me no more of news, for he is dead.
Vill. My Sovereign, pardon the author of ill news,
And I'll bewray the fortune of thy son.
Vice. Speak on, I'll guerdon thee whate'er it be.
Mine ear is ready to receive ill news,
My heart grown hard 'gainst mischief's battery.
Stand up, I say, and tell thy tale at large.
Vill. Then hear that truth which these mine eyes have seen.
When both the armies were in battle joined,
Don Balthazar, amid the thickest troops,
To win renown did wondrous feats of arms.
Among the rest I saw him hand to hand
In single fight with their Lord-General.
Till Alexandro, that here counterfeits
Under the color of a duteous friend,
Discharged his pistol at the Prince's back
As though he would have slain their general.
But therewithal Don Balthazar fell down,
And when he fell, then we began to fly.
But had he lived, the day had sure been ours.
Alex. Oh, wicked forgery! Oh, traitorous miscreant!
Vice. Hold thou thy peace! But now Villuppo, say,
Where then became the carcase of my son?
Vill. I saw them drag it to the Spanish tents.
Vice. Aye, aye, my nightly dreams have told me this.
Thou false, unkind, unthankful, traitorous beast,
Wherein had Balthazar offended thee,
That thou shouldst thus betray him to our foes?
Was't Spanish gold that bleared so thine eyes
That thou couldst see no part of our deserts?

15–17 ***Qui . . . magis*** "If one lies on the ground, one has no further to fall. Towards me Fortune has exhausted her power to injure; there is nothing further that can happen to me"
18 **bereave** deprive
20 **sable weed** black clothing (denoting royalty)
22 **despiteful** malicious
23 **Fortune is blind** (the common iconographic representation of Fortune shows her blindfolded)
25 **willful mad** deliberately closed to reason
29 **rolling stone** (the changeable nature of Fortune associates her with moving things such as a rolling stone or wheel)
33 **distained** tarnished, sullied
37 **joy . . . beloved** i.e., Balthazar, now captured
40 **cause** i.e., withholding tribute to Spain
42 **My . . . forced** my age is closer to the point of death than his
45 **mischance** fortunes
46 **fault** wrongdoing
48 **They . . . revenge** they heed no laws that contemplate revenge
49 **stay** restrain
53 **author** messenger
54 **bewray** disclose
57 **mischief's** evil's; **battery** arsenal (of bad news)
58 **at large** without reservation or omission of detail
66 **color** pretense
72 **forgery** (1) fabrication; (2) deliberate lie; **miscreant** villain
74 **carcase** body
80 **bleared** dazzled

Perchance because thou art Terceira's lord
Thou hadst some hope to wear this diadem,
If first my son and then myself were slain.
But thy ambitious thought shall break thy neck.
Aye, this was it that made thee spill his blood,

Take the crown and put it on again.

But I'll now wear it till thy blood be spilled.

Alex. Vouchsafe, dread Sovereign, to hear me speak.

Vice. Away with him, his sight is second hell,
Keep him till we determine of his death.

[*Exeunt Attendants with* Alexandro.]

If Balthazar be dead, he shall not live.
Villuppo, follow us for thy reward.

Exit Viceroy.

Vill. Thus have I with an envious forged tale
Deceived the King, betrayed mine enemy,
And hope for guerdon of my villainy.

Exit

[I.iv]

Enter Horatio *and* Bel-imperia.

Bel. Signior Horatio, this is the place and hour
Wherein I must entreat thee to relate
The circumstance of Don Andrea's death,
Who, living, was my garland's sweetest flower,
And in his death hath buried my delights.

Hor. For love of him and service to yourself,
I nill refuse this heavy doleful charge,
Yet tears and sighs, I fear will hinder me.
When both our armies were enjoined in fight,
Your worthy chevalier amid the thick'st,
For glorious cause still aiming at the fairest,
Was at the last by young Don Balthazar
Encountered hand to hand. Their fight was long,
Their hearts were great, their clamors menacing,
Their strength alike, their strokes both dangerous.
But wrathful Nemesis, that wicked power,
Envying at Andrea's praise and worth,
Cut short his life to end his praise and worth.
She, she herself, disguised in armor's mask
(As Pallas was before proud Pergamus),
Brought in a fresh supply of halberdiers,
Which paunched his horse and dinged him to the ground.
Then young Don Balthazar with ruthless rage,
Taking advantage of his foe's distress,
Did finish what his halberdiers begun,
And left not till Andrea's life was done.
Then, though too late, incensed with just remorse,
I with my band set forth against the Prince,
And brought him prisoner from his halberdiers.

Bel. Would thou hadst slain him that so slew my love.
But then was Don Andrea's carcass lost?

Hor. No, that was it for which I chiefly strove,
Nor stepped I back till I recovered him.
I took him up and wound him in mine arms,
And welding him unto my private tent,
There laid him down and dewed him with my tears,
And sighed and sorrowed as became a friend.
But neither friendly sorrow, sighs nor tears,
Could win pale death from his usurpèd right.
Yet this I did, and less I could not do:
I saw him honored with due funeral.
This scarf I plucked from off his liveless arm,
And wear it in remembrance of my friend.

Bel. I know the scarf, would he had kept it still,
For had he lived he would have kept it still,
And worn it for his Bel-imperia's sake.
For 'twas my favor at his last depart.
But now wear thou it both for him and me,
For after him thou hast deserved it best.
But for thy kindness in his life and death,
Be sure while Bel-imperia's life endures,
She will be Don Horatio's thankful friend.

Hor. And, Madam, Don Horatio will not slack
Humbly to serve fair Bel-imperia.
But now if your good liking stand thereto,
I'll crave your pardon to go seek the Prince,
For so the Duke your father gave me charge.

Exit.

---

82 **Terceira's lord** captain (as discoverer and colonizer) of Terceira, an island in the Azores where the ruler was perhaps despotic
83 **diadem** crown
93 **envious** malicious
I.iv.4 **garland's . . . flower** (as her beloved)
7 **nill** will not
10 **chevalier** a lady's gallant
11 **glorious . . . fairest** was a brave soldier because inspired by you
14 **great** brave
16 **Nemesis** goddess of retribution
19–20 **She . . . Pergamus** (as in *Aeneid* II.615–16)
20 **Pallas** Athena, patron goddess of Athens; **Pergamus** Troy
21–6 **Brought . . . done** (Andrea is outnumbered; he is therefore not killed in a fair or even battle)
21 **halberdiers** soldiers with halberds, poles with spears
22 **paunched** stabbed in the belly; **dinged** struck
27 **just remorse** righteous indignation and pity
29 **brought** took
31 **lost** left behind
34 **wound** embraced
35 **welding** carrying
42 **scarf** (Bel-imperia's favor; by taking it, Horatio volunteers to be her new champion)

Bel. Aye, go Horatio, leave me here alone,
For solitude best fits my cheerless mood.
Yet what avails to wail Andrea's death,
From whence Horatio proves my second love?
Had he not loved Andrea as he did,
He could not sit in Bel-imperia's thoughts.
But how can love find harbor in my breast,
Till I revenge the death of my belovèd?
Yes, second love shall further my revenge.
I'll love Horatio, my Andrea's friend,
The more to spite the Prince that wrought his end.
And where Don Balthazar, that slew my love,
Himself now pleads for favor at my hands,
He shall in rigor of my just disdain
Reap long repentance for his murd'rous deed.
For what was't else but murd'rous cowardice,
So many to oppress one valiant knight,
Without respect of honor in the fight?
And here he comes that murdered my delight.

Enter Lorenzo *and* Balthazar.

Lor. Sister, what means this melancholy walk?
Bel. That for a while I wish no company.
Lor. But here the Prince is come to visit you.
Bel. That argues that he lives in liberty.
Bal. No, Madam, but in pleasing servitude.
Bel. Your prison then belike is your conceit.
Bal. Aye, by conceit my freedom is enthralled.
Bel. Then with conceit enlarge yourself again.
Bal. What if conceit have laid my heart to gage?
Bel. Pay that you borrowed and recover it.
Bal. I die if it return from whence it lies.
Bel. A heartless man and live? A miracle!
Bal. Aye, lady, love can work such miracles.
Lor. Tush, tush my lord, let go these ambages,
And in plain terms acquaint her with your love.
Bel. What boots complaint, when there's no remedy?
Bal. Yes, to your gracious self must I complain,
In whose fair answer lies my remedy,
On whose perfection all my thoughts attend,
On whose aspect mine eyes find beauty's bower,
In whose translucent breast my heart is lodged.
Bel. Alas, my Lord, these are but words of course,
And but device to drive me from this place.

She, in going in, lets fall her glove, which Horatio, *coming out, takes up.*

Hor. Madam, your glove.
Bel. Thanks, good Horatio, take it for thy pains.
Bal. Signior Horatio stooped in happy time.
Hor. I reaped more grace than I deserved or hoped.
Lor. My Lord, be not dismayed for what is past,
You know that women oft are humorous;
These clouds will overblow with little wind.
Let me alone, I'll scatter them myself.
Meanwhile let us devise to spend the time
In some delightful sports and reveling.
Hor. The King, my Lords, is coming hither straight,
To feast the Portingal ambassador.
Things were in readiness before I came.
Bal. Then here it fits us to attend the King,
To welcome hither our ambassador
And learn my father and my country's health.

Enter the Banquet, Trumpets, the King, *and* Ambassador.

King. See, Lord Ambassador, how Spain entreats
Their prisoner Balthazar, thy Viceroy's son?
We pleasure more in kindness than in wars.
Amb. Sad is our King, and Portingale laments,
Supposing that Don Balthazar is slain.
Bal. So am I slain, by beauty's tyranny.
You see, my Lord, how Balthazar is slain:
I frolic with the Duke of Castile's son,
Wrapped every hour in pleasures of the court,
And graced with favors of his Majesty.
King. Put off your greetings till our feast be done,
Now come and sit with us and taste our cheer.
Sit to the banquet.
Sit down, young Prince, you are our second guest.
Brother, sit down, and nephew take your place.
Signior Horatio, wait thou upon our cup,

71 **disdain** indignation
74 **oppress** (1) oppose; (2) overwhelm
77–89 **Sister . . . miracles** (stichomythia, or one-line exchanges, was a convention of high classical tragedy deriving from Seneca)
77 **melancholy** (1) sorrowful; (2) brooding (for the Elizabethans, melancholy could be an illness)
82 **belike** perhaps; **conceit** metaphor, reference (sarcastically)
83 **enthralled** enslaved
84 **enlarge** set free
85 **laid . . . gage** given as a pledge; **gage** pawn
90 **ambages** circuitous, evasive speeches; circumlocutions
92 **complaint** compliments, requests
98 **words of course** conventional expressions
99 **device . . . place** (a technique used to change my mind)
99 s.d. ***lets fall*** (1) accidentally drops; (2) drops as a sign of favor
102 **happy** successful
105 **humorous** moody, temperamental
113 **fits** befits
116 **entreats** shows hospitality to
118 **pleasure** take pleasure
127 **cheer** banquet; refreshments
128 **second guest** (Balthazar, although he is a captive, is here elevated to second position after Horatio)
130 **our cup** (for a toast)

For well thou hast deserved to be honored.
Now, Lordings, fall to; Spain is Portugal,
And Portugal is Spain. We both are friends,
Tribute is paid, and we enjoy our right.
But where is old Hieronimo, our Marshal?
He promised us, in honor of our guest,
To grace our banquet with some pompous jest.

Enter Hieronimo *with a* Drum, *three* Knights, *each his scutcheon: then he fetches three* Kings, *they take their crowns and them captive.*

Hieronimo, this masque contents mine eye,
Although I sound not well the mystery.
Hier. The first armed knight that hung his scutcheon up,
He takes the scutcheon and gives it to the King.
Was English Robert, Earl of Gloucester,
Who when King Stephen bore sway in Albion,
Arrived with five and twenty thousand men
In Portingale, and by success of war
Enforced the King, then but a Saracen,
To bear the yoke of the English monarchy.
King. My lord of Portingale, by this you see
That which may comfort both your King and you,
And make your late discomfort seem the less.
But say, Hieronimo, what was the next?
Hier. The second knight that hung his scutcheon up,
He doth as he did before.
Was Edmund, Earl of Kent in Albion,
When English Richard wore the diadem.
He came likewise and razed Lisbon walls,
And took the King of Portingale in fight.
For which, and other suchlike service done,
He after was created Duke of York.
King. This is another special argument
That Portingale may deign to bear our yoke
When it by little England hath been yoked.
But now, Hieronimo, what were the last?
Hier. The third and last, not least in our account,
Doing as before.
Was as the rest a valiant Englishman,
Brave John of Gaunt, the Duke of Lancaster,
As by his scutcheon plainly may appear.
He with a puissant army came to Spain,
And took our King of Castile prisoner.
Amb. This is an argument for our Viceroy,
That Spain may not insult for her success,
Since English warriors likewise conquered Spain,
And made them bow their knees to Albion.
King. Hieronimo, I drink to thee for this device,
Which hath pleased both the Ambassador and me.
Pledge me, Hieronimo, if thou love the King.
Takes the cup of Horatio.
My Lord, I fear we sit but over-long,
Unless our dainties were more delicate:
But welcome are you to the best we have.
Now let us in, that you may be despatched,
I think our council is already set.
Exeunt omnes.

[I.v]

Ghost. Come we for this from depth of underground,
To see him feast that gave me my death's wound?
These pleasant sights are sorrow to my soul,
Nothing but league, and love, and banqueting!
Revenge. Be still, Andrea, ere we go from hence.
I'll turn their friendship into fell despite,
Their love to mortal hate, their day to night,
Their hope into despair, their peace to war,
Their joys to pain, their bliss to misery.

Act II

[II.i]

Enter Lorenzo *and* Balthazar.

Lor. My Lord, though Bel-imperia seem thus coy,
Let reason hold you in your wonted joy.
In time the savage bull sustains the yoke,
In time all haggard hawks will stoop to lure,
In time small wedges cleave the hardest oak,

137 **pompous jest** i.e., stately entertainment
137 **s.d. Drum** drummer; ***scutcheon*** shield with crest
139 **sound** understand, perceive; **mystery** (1) hidden meaning; (2) significance
142 **Albion** England
146 **the yoke** captivity, defeat
154 **razed** destroyed
158 **special** suitable
159 **deign** vouchsafe, grant
166 **puissant** powerful
169 **insult** boast
172 **device** masque, show
174 **Pledge** toast
174 **s.d. of** from
I.v.4 **league** companionship
6 **fell despite** cruel hatred (this is Revenge's job)
II.i.1 **coy** unresponsive
2 **wonted** accustomed
3–10 **In ... wall** (these lines paraphrase a popular contemporary poem by Thomas Watson)
4 **haggard** untamed; wild; **lure** decoy
5 **wedges** pieces of metal used to fell trees

In time the flint is pierced with softest shower,
And she in time will fall from her disdain,
And rue the sufferance of your friendly pain.
Bal. No, she is wilder, and more hard withal,
Than beast, or bird, or tree, or stony wall.
But wherefore blot I Bel-imperia's name?
It is my fault, not she, that merits blame.
My feature is not to content her sight,
My words are rude and work her no delight.
The lines I send her are but harsh and ill,
Such as do drop from Pan and Marsyas' quill.
My presents are not of sufficient cost,
And being worthless, all my labor's lost.
Yet might she love me for my valiancy,
Aye, but that's slandered by captivity.
Yet might she love me to content her sire,
Aye, but her reason masters his desire.
Yet might she love me as her brother's friend,
Aye, but her hopes aim at some other end.
Yet might she love me to uprear her state,
Aye, but perhaps she hopes some nobler mate.
Yet might she love me as her beauty's thrall,
Aye, but I fear she cannot love at all.
Lor. My Lord, for my sake leave these ecstasies,
And doubt not but we'll find some remedy:
Some cause there is that lets you not be loved:
First that must needs be known and then removed.
What if my sister love some other knight?
Bal. My summer's day will turn to winter's night.
Lor. I have already found a stratagem
To sound the bottom of this doubtful theme.
My Lord, for once you shall be ruled by me,
Hinder me not whate'er you hear or see.
By force or fair means will I cast about
To find the truth of all this question out.
Ho, Pedringano!
Ped. Signior!
Lor. *Vien qui presto.*

Enter Pedringano.

Ped. Hath your Lordship any service to command me?
Lor. Aye, Pedringano, service of import;
And not to spend the time in trifling words,
Thus stands the case: it is not long, thou know'st,
Since I did shield thee from my father's wrath
For thy conveyance in Andrea's love,
For which thou wert adjudged to punishment.
I stood betwixt thee and thy punishment.
And since thou know'st how I have favored thee.
Now to these favors will I add reward,
Not with fair words, but store of golden coin,
And lands and living joined with dignities,
If thou but satisfy my just demand.
Tell truth and have me for thy lasting friend.
Ped. Whate'er it be your Lordship shall demand,
My bounden duty bids me tell the truth,
If case it lie in me to tell the truth.
Lor. Then, Pedringano, this is my demand:
Whom loves my sister Bel-imperia?
For she reposeth all her trust in thee.
Speak, man, and gain both friendship and reward –
I mean, whom loves she in Andrea's place?
Ped. Alas, my Lord, since Don Andrea's death,
I have no credit with her as before,
And therefore know not if she love or no.
Lor. Nay, if thou dally then I am thy foe,
[*Draw his sword.*]
And fear shall force what friendship cannot win.
Thy death shall bury what thy life conceals,
Thou diest for more esteeming her than me.
Ped. Oh, stay, my lord!
Lor. Yet speak the truth and I will guerdon thee,
And shield thee from whatever can ensue,
And will conceal whate'er proceeds from thee,
But if thou dally once again, thou diest.
Ped. If Madam Bel-imperia be in love –
Lor. What, villain, ifs and ands?
[*Offer to kill him.*]
Ped. Oh, stay my Lord, she loves Horatio.
Balthazar starts back.
Lor. What, Don Horatio, our Knight Marshal's son?
Ped. Even him, my Lord.
Lor. Now say but how know'st thou he is her love,

8 rue pity; **sufferance** patient endurance
11 blot blacken
13 feature bearing, person
16 Pan and Marsyas (gods who challenged Apollo in flute-playing and lost); **quill** (1) musical pipe; (2) pen
19 valiancy valor
20 slandered brought into disrepute
25 uprear...state improve her social and political position (estate)
29 ecstasies irrational passions (suggesting Balthazar exaggerates)
36 sound measure (i.e., get to the bottom of the matter)
41 *Vien...presto* "Come here quickly"
43 import significance
47 conveyance (1) secret undertaking; (2) service as a go-between
52 store abundance
58 If...me in case I am able
65 credit special closeness
71 stay stop

And thou shalt find me kind and liberal.
Stand up, I say, and fearless tell the truth.
Ped. She sent him letters which myself perused,
Full fraught with lines and arguments of love,
Preferring him before Prince Balthazar.
Lor. Swear on this cross, that what thou say'st is true,
And that thou wilt conceal what thou hast told.
Ped. I swear to both by him that made us all.
Lor. In hope thine oath is true, here's thy reward,
But if I prove thee perjured and unjust,
This very sword whereon thou took'st thine oath,
Shall be the worker of thy tragedy.
Ped. What I have said is true, and shall for me
Be still concealed from Bel-imperia.
Besides, your Honor's liberality
Deserves my duteous service, even till death.
Lor. Let this be all that thou shalt do for me:
Be watchful when, and where, these lovers meet,
And give me notice in some secret sort.
Ped. I will, my Lord.
Lor. Then shalt thou find that I am liberal.
Thou know'st that I can more advance thy state
Than she; be therefore wise and fail me not.
Go, and attend her as thy custom is,
Lest absence make her think thou dost amiss.
Exit Pedringano.
Why so: *tam armis quam ingenio:*
Where words prevail not, violence prevails.
But gold doth more than either of them both.
How likes Prince Balthazar this stratagem?
Bal. Both well, and ill. It makes me glad and sad.
Glad, that I know the hinderer of my love,
Sad, that I fear she hates me whom I love.
Glad, that I know on whom to be revenged,
Sad, that she'll fly me if I take revenge.
Yet must I take revenge or die myself,
For love resisted grows impatient.
I think Horatio be my destined plague:
First in his hand he brandished a sword,
And with that sword he fiercely waged war,
And in that war he gave me dangerous wounds,
And by those wounds he forced me to yield,
And by my yielding I became his slave.
Now in his mouth he carries pleasing words,
Which pleasing words do harbor sweet conceits,
Which sweet conceits are limed with sly deceits,
Which sly deceits smooth Bel-imperia's ears,
And through her ears dive down into her heart,
And in her heart set him where I should stand.
Thus hath he ta'en my body by his force,
And now by sleight would captivate my soul.
But in his fall I'll tempt the Destinies,
And either lose my life, or win my love.
Lor. Let's go my Lord, your staying stays revenge.
Do you but follow me and gain your love.
Her favor must be won by his remove.
Exeunt.

[II.ii]

Enter Horatio *and* Bel-imperia.

Hor. Now, Madam, since by favor of your love
Our hidden smoke is turned to open flame,
And that with looks and words we feed our thoughts
(Two chief contents, where more cannot be had),
Thus in the midst of love's fair blandishments,
Why show you sign of inward languishments?

Pedringano showeth all to the Prince and Lorenzo, placing them in secret [*above*].

Bel. My heart, sweet friend, is like a ship at sea:
She wisheth port, where riding all at ease,
She may repair what stormy times have worn,
And, leaning on the shore, may sing with joy
That pleasure follows pain, and bliss annoy.
Possession of thy love is th' only port
Wherein my heart, with fears and hopes long tossed,
Each hour doth wish and long to make resort,

85 fraught laden
87 this cross (i.e., the hilt of his sword near the cross-piece)
91 unjust dishonest
100 in . . . sort by some secret means
103 state (1) status; (2) financial condition
107 *tam . . . ingenio* "by equal parts of force and skill"
123 slave (1) captive; (2) servant
125 conceits figures of thought and speech
126 limed made traps (lime was a gluey substance used for trapping birds)
127 smooth seduce
131 sleight trick, stratagem
132 fall downfall; **Destinies** gods of fate
136 remove removal; i.e., death
II.ii.2 smoke emotions; **flame** passion
4 contents sources of contentment
5 blandishments alluring speeches
6 languishments (1) weariness; (2) suffering
9 repair restore
10 sing celebrate

There to repair the joys that it hath lost,
And sitting safe, to sing in Cupid's choir
That sweetest bliss is crown of love's desire.

Bal. [*Above.*] Oh, sleep mine eyes, see not my love profaned,
Be deaf, my ears, hear not my discontent;
Die, heart, another joys what thou deservest.

Lor. [*Above.*] Watch still mine eyes, to see this love disjoined,
Hear still mine ears, to hear them both lament,
Live heart, to joy at fond Horatio's fall.

Bel. Why stands Horatio speechless all this while?

Hor. The less I speak, the more I meditate.

Bel. But whereon dost thou chiefly meditate?

Hor. On dangers past, and pleasures to ensue.

Bal. [*Above.*] On pleasures past, and dangers to ensue.

Bel. What dangers and what pleasures dost thou mean?

Hor. Dangers of war, and pleasures of our love.

Lor. [*Above.*] Dangers of death, but pleasures none at all.

Bel. Let dangers go, thy war shall be with me,
But such a war as breaks no bond of peace.
Speak thou fair words, I'll cross them with fair words,
Send thou sweet looks, I'll meet them with sweet looks,
Write loving lines, I'll answer loving lines,
Give me a kiss, I'll countercheck thy kiss,
Be this our warring peace, or peaceful war.

Hor. But, gracious Madam, then appoint the field
Where trial of this war shall first be made.

Bal. [*Above.*] Ambitious villain, how his boldness grows!

Bel. Then be thy father's pleasant bower the field,
Where first we vowed a mutual amity.
The court were dangerous, that place is safe.
Our hour shall be when Vesper 'gins to rise,
That summons home distressful travelers.
There none shall hear us but the harmless birds.
Happily the gentle nightingale
Shall carol us asleep ere we be ware,
And singing with the prickle at her breast,
Tell our delight and mirthful dalliance.
Till then each hour will seem a year and more.

Hor. But, honey sweet, and honorable love,
Return we now into your father's sight.
Dangerous suspicion waits on our delight.

Lor. [*Above.*] Aye, danger mixed with jealious despite
Shall send thy soul into eternal night.

Exeunt.

[II.iii]

Enter King of Spain, Portingale Ambassador, Don Cyprian, *&c.*

King. Brother of Castile, to the Prince's love
What says your daughter Bel-imperia?

Cast. Although she coy it as becomes her kind,
And yet dissemble that she loves the Prince,
I doubt not, I, but she will stoop in time.
And were she froward, which she will not be,
Yet herein shall she follow my advice,
Which is to love him or forgo my love.

King. Then, Lord Ambassador of Portingale,
Advise thy King to make this marriage up,
For strengthening of our late-confirmed league.
I know no better means to make us friends.
Her dowry shall be large and liberal:
Besides that, she is daughter and half-heir
Unto our brother here, Don Cyprian,
And shall enjoy the moiety of his land.
I'll grace her marriage with an uncle's gift,
And this it is: in case the match go forward,
The tribute which you pay shall be released,
And if by Balthazar she have a son,
He shall enjoy the kingdom after us.

Amb. I'll make the motion to my sovereign Liege,
And work it if my counsel may prevail.

King. Do so, my Lord, and if he give consent,
I hope his presence here will honor us

---

15 **joys** enjoys
23 **fond** foolish
34 **cross** complement
37 **countercheck** oppose
42 **bower** arbor
45 **Vesper** (the evening star); **gins** begins (indicates dusk)
46 **distressful travelers** weary laborers (*travail*)
48–51 **Happily . . . dalliance** (according to classical myth, Philomela turned into a nightingale after avenging herself on her brother-in-law for raping her; she thrust a thorn in her breast to remember her suffering; proverbial for the proximity of artistic beauty to terror and violence; a forewarning)
48 **Happily** haply, perhaps
50 **prickle** thorn
56 **jealious** jealous, watchful, suspicious
II.iii.3 **coy it** affects disinterest; **kind** woman's nature
4 **dissemble** appears
5 **stoop** become obedient
6 **froward** perverse
10 **make . . . up** arrange the marriage
11 **league** union
16 **moiety** half-share
19 **released** canceled
22 **make the motion** put this proposal

In celebration of the nuptial day.
And let himself determine of the time.
Amb. Will't please your grace command me aught beside?
King. Commend me to the King, and so farewell.
But where's Prince Balthazar to take his leave?
Amb. That is performed already, my good Lord.
King. Among the rest of what you have in charge,
The Prince's ransom must not be forgot:
That's none of mine, but his that took him prisoner,
And well his forwardness deserves reward.
It was Horatio, our Knight Marshal's son
Amb. Between us there's a price already pitched,
And shall be sent with all convenient speed.
King. Then once again, farewell, my Lord.
Amb. Farewell, my Lord of Castile and the rest.
Exit.
King. Now brother, you must take some little pains
To win fair Bel-imperia from her will.
Young virgins must be ruled by their friends.
The Prince is amiable and loves her well.
If she neglect him and forgo his love,
She both will wrong her own estate and ours.
Therefore, whiles I do entertain the Prince
With greatest pleasure that our court affords,
Endeavor you to win your daughter's thought.
If she give back, all this will come to naught.
Exeunt.

[II.iv]

Enter Horatio, Bel-imperia, *and* Pedringano.

Hor. Now that the night begins with sable wings
To overcloud the brightness of the sun,
And that in darkness pleasures may be done,
Come, Bel-imperia, let us to the bower,
And there in safety pass a pleasant hour.
Bel. I follow thee, my love, and will not back,
Although my fainting heart controls my soul.
Hor. Why, make you doubt of Pedringano's faith?
Bel. No, he is as trusty as my second self.
Go, Pedringano, watch without the gate,
And let us know if any make approach.
Ped. [*Aside.*] Instead of watching, I'll deserve more gold
By fetching Don Lorenzo to this match.
Exit Pedringano.
Hor. What means my love?
Bel. I know not what myself:
And yet my heart foretells me some mischance.
Hor. Sweet, say not so; fair fortune is our friend,
And Heavens have shut up day to pleasure us.
The stars, thou seest, hold back their twinkling shine,
And Luna hides herself to pleasure us.
Bel. Thou hast prevailed, I'll conquer my misdoubt,
And in thy love and counsel drown my fear.
I fear no more. Love now is all my thoughts.
Why sit we not? for pleasure asketh ease.
Hor. The more thou sit'st within these leafy bowers,
The more will Flora deck it with her flowers.
Bel. Aye, but if Flora spy Horatio here,
Her jealous eye will think I sit too near.
Hor. Hark, madam, how the birds record by night,
For joy that Bel-imperia sits in sight.
Bel. No, Cupid counterfeits the nightingale,
To frame sweet music to Horatio's tale.
Hor. If Cupid sing, then Venus is not far.
Aye, thou art Venus or some fairer star.
Bel. If I be Venus thou must needs be Mars,
And where Mars reigneth there must needs be wars.
Hor. Then thus begin our wars. Put forth thy hand,
That it may combat with my ruder hand.
Bel. Set forth thy foot to try the push of mine.
Hor. But first my looks shall combat against thine.
Bel. Then ward thyself, I dart this kiss at thee.
Hor. Thus I retort the dart thou threw'st at me.
Bel. Nay, then, to gain the glory of the field,
My twining arms shall yoke and make thee yield.
Hor. Nay, then, my arms are large and strong withal:

35 **forwardness** zeal
37 **pitched** agreed
42 **will** willfulness
II.iv.1 **night** (an invocation to night conventionally presages evil); **sable** black
7 **controls** oppresses (in foreboding)
10 **without** outside
13 **match** meeting
15 **mischance** misfortune
19 **Luna** the moon
23 **asketh** requires
25 **Flora** Roman goddess of flowers
28 **record** sing
31 **frame** compose, accompany
34 **Venus . . . Mars** (Venus's love for Mars betrayed her husband Hephaestus)
37 **combat** encumber; **ruder** rougher
40 **ward** shield, guard
43 **yoke** join

Thus elms by vines are compassed till they fall.
Bel. Oh, let me go, for in my troubled eyes
Now may'st thou read that life in passion dies.
Hor. Oh stay awhile and I will die with thee,
So shalt thou yield and yet have conquered me.
Bel. Who's there? Pedringano! We are betrayed!

Enter Lorenzo, Balthazar, Serberine, Pedringano, *disguised.*

Lor. My Lord, away with her, take her aside.
Oh sir, forbear, your valor is already tried.
Quickly despatch, my masters.
They hang him in the arbor.
Hor. What, will you murder me?
Lor. Aye, thus, and thus, these are the fruits of love.
They stab him.
Bel. Oh, save his life and let me die for him! 56
Oh, save him brother, save him, Balthazar.
I loved Horatio but he loved not me.
Bal. But Balthazar loves Bel-imperia.
Lor. Although his life were still ambitious proud,
Yet is he at the highest now he is dead.
Bel. Murder! murder! Help, Hieronimo, help!
Lor. Come, stop her mouth, away with her.
Exeunt [, *leaving Horatio's body*].

[II.v]

Enter Hieronimo *in his shirt, &c.*

Hier. What outcries pluck me from my naked bed,
And chill my throbbing heart with trembling fear,
Which never danger yet could daunt before?
Who calls Hieronimo? Speak, here I am.
I did not slumber; therefore, 'twas no dream,
No, no, it was some woman cried for help,
And here within this garden did she cry,
And in this garden must I rescue her.
But stay, what murd'rous spectacle is this?
A man hanged up and all the murderers gone,
And in my bower, to lay the guilt on me.
This place was made for pleasure, not for death.
He cuts him down.
Those garments that he wears I oft have seen –
Alas, it is Horatio, my sweet son!
Oh, no, but he that whilom was my son.
Oh, was it thou that call'dst me from my bed?
Oh, speak, if any spark of life remain:
I am thy father. Who hath slain my son?
What savage monster, not of human kind,
Hath here been glutted with thy harmless blood?
And left thy bloody corpse dishonored here,
For me amid this dark and deathful shades,
To drown thee with an ocean of my tears?
Oh, heavens, why made you night to cover sin?
By day this deed of darkness had not been.
Oh, earth, why didst thou not in time devour
The vile profaner of this sacred bower?
Oh, poor Horatio, what hadst thou misdone,
To leese thy life ere life was new begun?
Oh wicked butcher, whatsoe'er thou wert,
How could thou strangle virtue and desert?
Aye, me most wretched, that have lost my joy,
In leesing my Horatio, my sweet boy!

Enter Isabella.

Isab. My husband's absence makes my heart to throb.
Hieronimo!
Hier. Here Isabella, help me to lament,
For sighs are stopped, and all my tears are spent.
Isab. What world of grief – my son Horatio!
Oh, where's the author of this endless woe?
Hier. To know the author were some ease of grief,
For in revenge my heart would find relief.
Isab. Then is he gone? and is my son gone too?
Oh, gush out, tears, fountains and floods of tears,
Blow, sighs, and raise an everlasting storm,
For outrage fits our cursèd wretchedness.
Hier. Sweet lovely rose, ill-plucked before thy time,
Fair worthy son, not conquered but betrayed.
I'll kiss thee now, for words with tears are stayed.

45 **elms . . . vines** (traditional symbols of Venus); **compassed** encircled
48 **die** (with pun on sexual orgasm)
52 **tried** tested, proven
60 **ambitious proud** (ambitious to satisfy his pride)
61 **highest** (deliberate pun on natural and social height)
II.v s.d. **shirt** nightshirt
1 **naked bed** (proverbial)
14 **it . . . son** (dramatically simple for effect)
15 **whilom** once, in the past
21 **dishonored** (1) disgraced; (2) violated
22 **shades** (connects night to death)
25 **deed of darkness** (puns on commonplace for sexual intercourse)
26 **in time** at the proper moment
29 **leese** lose; **was new begun** had entered a new phase
33 **leesing** losing
39 **author** one responsible
41 **revenge** (his first desire repeats that of Andrea's ghost)
45 **outrage** extreme passion

Isab. And I'll close up the glasses of his sight,
For once these eyes were only my delight.
Hier. Seest thou this handkercher besmeared with blood?
It shall not from me till I take revenge.
Seest thou those wounds that yet are bleeding fresh?
I'll not entomb them till I have revenged
Then will I joy amid my discontent,
Till then my sorrow never shall be spent.
Isab. The heavens are just. Murder cannot be hid.
Time is the author both of truth and right,
And time will bring this treachery to light.
Hier. Meanwhile, good Isabella, cease thy plaints,
Or at the least dissemble them awhile,
So shall we sooner find the practice out,
And learn by whom all this was brought about.
Come, Isabel, now let us take him up,
They take him up.
And bear him in from out this cursed place.
I'll say his dirge; singing fits not this case.
O aliquis mihi quas pulchrum ver educat herbas
Hieronimo *sets his breast unto his sword.*
Misceat, et nostor detur medicina dolori;
Aut, si qui faciunt animis oblivia, succos
Praebeat; ipse metam magnum quaecunque per orbem
Gramina Sol pulchras effert in luminis oras;
Ipse bibam quicquid meditatur saga veneni,
Quicquid et herbarum vi caeca nenia nectit:
Omnia perpetiar, lethum quoque, dum semel omnis
Noster in extincto moriatur pectore sensus.
Ergo tuos oculos nunquam, mea vita, videbo,
Et tua perpetuus sepelivit lumina somnus?
Emoriar tecum, sic, sic juvat ire sub umbras.
At tamen absistam properato cedere letho,
Ne mortem vindicta tuam tum nulla sequatur.
Here he throws it from him and bears the body away.

[II.vi]

Ghost. Brought'st thou me hither to increase my pain?
I looked that Balthazar should have been slain,
But 'tis my friend Horatio that is slain,
And they abuse fair Bel-imperia,
On whom I doted more than all the world,
Because she loved me more than all the world.
Revenge. Thou talk'st of harvest when the corn is green.
The end is crown of every work well done.
The sickle comes not till the corn be ripe.
Be still, and ere I lead thee from this place,
I'll show thee Balthazar in heavy case.

Act III

[III.i]

Enter Viceroy of Portingale, Nobles, Villuppo.

Vice. Infortunate condition of kings,
Seated amid so many helpless doubts!
First we are placed upon extremest height,
And oft supplanted with exceeding heat,
But ever subject to the wheel of chance.
And at our highest never joy we so,
As we both doubt and dread our overthrow.
So striveth not the waves with sundry winds
As fortune toileth in the affairs of kings,
That would be feared, yet fear to be beloved,
Sith fear or love to kings is flattery.
For instance, Lordings, look upon your King,
By hate deprived of his dearest son,
The only hope of our successive line.
I Nob. I had not thought that Alexandro's heart
Had been envenomed with such extreme hate.
But now I see that words have several works,

---

49 **glasses . . . sight** (i.e., her eyes)
51 **handkercher** (1) handkerchief; (2) small scarf
54 **entomb** bury
60 **plaints** complaints, sorrowing
62 **find . . . out** learn what happened and who was involved; **practice** plot
66 **dirge** funeral hymn
67–80 ***O . . . sequatur*** "Let someone bind for me the herbs which beautiful spring fosters, and let a salve be given for our grief; or let him apply juices, if there are any that bring forgetfulness to men's minds. I myself shall gather anywhere in the great world whatever plants the sun draws forth into the fair regions of light; I myself that drink whatever drug the wise-woman devises, and whatever herbs incantation assembles by its secret power. I shall face all things, death even, until the moment our every feeling dies in this dead breast. And so shall I never again, my life, see those eyes of yours, and has everlasting slumber sealed up your light of life? I shall perish with you; thus, thus would it please me to go to the shades below. But none the less I shall keep myself from yielding to a hastened death, lest in that case no revenge should follow your death" (Kyd's combination of passages from Lucretius, Virgil, and Ovid)
II.vi.2 looked hoped, expected
9 **sickle** as sign for (1) death; (2) harvest
11 **heavy case** sorrowful state
III.i.1 Infortunate unfortunate
2 **Seated** placed; **helpless** beyond help; **doubts** fears
4 **heat** fury
5 **chance** (the Wheel of Fortune was the most common portrayal of one's rise and fall)
7 **doubt** suspect
10 **That . . . beloved** (paraphrase of Machiavelli who thought rulers were better off if feared than if loved)
11 **Sith** since
12 **Lordings** Lords
14 **successive line** line of succession to rule
17 **words . . . works** (i.e., man may not always mean what he says)

And there's no credit in the countenance.
Vill. No; for, my Lord, had you beheld the train
That feigned love had colored in his looks,
When he in camp consorted Balthazar,
Far more inconstant had you thought the sun,
That hourly coasts the center of the earth,
Than Alexandro's purpose to the Prince.
Vice. No more, Villuppo, thou hast said enough,
And with thy words thou slay'st our wounded thoughts.
Nor shall I longer dally with the world,
Procrastinating Alexandro's death.
Go some of you and fetch the traitor forth,
That as he is condemned he may die.

Enter Alexandro *with a* Nobleman *and* Halberts.

2 Nob. In such extremes will naught but patience serve.
Alex. But in extremes what patience shall I use?
Nor discontents it me to leave the world,
With whom there nothing can prevail but wrong.
2 Nob. Yet hope the best.
Alex. 'Tis Heaven is my hope.
As for the earth, it is too much infect
To yield me hope of any of her mold.
Vice. Why linger ye? Bring forth that daring fiend
And let him die for his accursèd deed.
Alex. Not that I fear the extremity of death,
For nobles cannot stoop to servile fear,
Do I, Oh, King, thus discontented live.
But this, Oh, this, torments my laboring soul,
That thus I die suspected of a sin,
Whereof, as Heavens have known my secret thoughts,
So am I free from this suggestion.
Vice. No more, I say! to the tortures! when!
Bind him, and burn his body in those flames
They bind him to the stake.
That shall prefigure those unquenchèd fires
Of Phlegethon prepared for his soul.
Alex. My guiltless death will be avenged on thee,
On thee, Villuppo, that hath maliced thus,
Or for thy meed hast falsely me accused.
Vill. Nay, Alexandro, if thou menace me,
I'll lend a hand to send thee to the lake
Where those thy words shall perish with thy works,
Injurious traitor, monstrous homicide!

Enter Ambassador.

Amb. Stay, hold a while, and here,
With pardon of his Majesty,
Lay hands upon Villuppo.
Vice. Ambassador,
What news hath urged this sudden entrance?
Amb. Know, sovereign Lord, that Balthazar doth live.
Vice. What say'st thou? liveth Balthazar our son?
Amb. Your Highness' son, Lord Balthazar, doth live;
And, well entreated in the court of Spain,
Humbly commends him to your Majesty.
These eyes beheld, and these my followers,
With these, the letters of the King's commends,
Gives him letters.
Are happy witnesses of his highness' health.
The Viceroy looks on the letters, and proceeds.
Vice. "Thy son doth live, your tribute is received,
Thy peace is made, and we are satisfied:
The rest resolve upon as things proposed
For both our honors and thy benefit."
Amb. These are his Highness' farther articles.
He gives him more letters.
Vice. [*To Villupo.*] Accursed wretch, to intimate these ills
Against the life and reputation
Of noble Alexandro! – Come, my Lord,
Let him unbind thee that is bound to death,
To make a quital for thy discontent.
They unbind him.

---

18 credit necessary truth
19 train treachery
20 colored disguised
21 consorted keep company with
23 hourly coasts regularly encircles (Ptolemaic cosmology that measured time by the sun's orbit around the earth; symbol of regularity and constancy)
24 purpose attitude
31 s.d. Halberts (i.e., halberdiers)
32–4 But . . . wrong (Alexandro's discouragement anticipates Hieronimo's and sets tone for entire act)
34 With . . . wrong since all I ever see is wrong
36 infect infected
37 any . . . mold inhabitants born there
43 laboring belabored
46 suggestion false accusation
47 when! (exclamation of impatience)
49–50 unquenchèd . . . Phlegethon (Phlegethon was the river of fire in Hades)
52 maliced performed maliciously
53 meed (1) reward; (2) advantage
55 lake Acheron, into which the Phlegethon flows
66 commends sends greetings
75 intimate falsely accuse in public
79 quital requital, recompense
79 s.d. *They* (but the Viceroy has ordered only Villuppo to do so, as partial admission of his own mendacity)

Alex. Dread Lord, in kindness you could do no less,
Upon report of such a damned fact:
But thus we see our innocence hath saved
The hopeless life which thou, Villuppo, sought
By thy suggestions to have massacred.
Vice. Say, false Villuppo! wherefore didst thou thus
Falsely betray Lord Alexandro's life?
Him whom thou know'st that no unkindness else,
But even the slaughter of our dearest son,
Could once have moved us to have misconceived?
Alex. Say, treacherous Villuppo, tell the King,
Or wherein hath Alexandro used thee ill?
Vill. Rent with remembrance of so foul a deed,
My guilty soul submits me to thy doom:
For, not for Alexandro's injuries,
But for reward, and hope to be preferred,
Thus have I shamelessly hazarded his life.
Vice. Which, villain, shall be ransomed with thy death,
And not so mean a torment as we here
Devised for him, who thou said'st slew our son,
But with the bitterest torments and extremes
That may be yet invented for thine end.

Alexandro *seems to entreat.*

Entreat me not, go take the traitor hence.

Exit Villuppo [*guarded*].

And, Alexandro, let us honor thee
With public notice of thy loyalty.
To end those things articulated here
By our great lord, the mighty King of Spain,
We with our council will deliberate.
Come, Alexandro, keep us company.

Exeunt.

[III.ii]

Enter Hieronimo.

Hier. Oh, eyes, no eyes, but fountains fraught with tears;
Oh, life, no life, but lively form of death;
Oh, world, no world, but mass of public wrongs,
Confused and filled with murder and misdeeds;
Oh, sacred Heavens! if this unhallowed deed,
If this inhuman and barbarous attempt,
If this incomparable murder thus
Of mine, but now no more my son,
Shall unrevealed and unrevengèd pass,
How should we term your dealings to be just,
If you unjustly deal with those that in your justice trust?
The night, sad secretary to my moans,
With direful visions wake my vexed soul,
And with the wounds of my distressful son
Solicit me for notice of his death.
The ugly fiends do sally forth of hell,
And frame my steps to unfrequented paths,
And fear my heart with fierce inflamèd thoughts.
The cloudy day my discontents records,
Early begins to register my dreams
And drive me forth to seek the murderer.
Eyes, life, world, heavens, hell, night, and day,
See, search, show, send some man, some mean, that may –

A letter falleth.

What's here? a letter? tush, it is not so!
A letter written to Hieronimo!

Red ink.

"For want of ink, receive this bloody writ.
Me hath my hapless brother hid from thee.
Revenge thyself on Balthazar and him,
For these were they that murdered thy son.
Hieronimo, revenge Horatio's death,
And better fare than Bel-imperia doth."
What means this unexpected miracle?
My son slain by Lorenzo and the Prince!
What cause had they Horatio to malign?
Or what might move thee, Bel-imperia,
To accuse thy brother, had he been the mean?

---

80 **kindness** i.e., nature (of a viceroy)
81 **fact** deed
82 **our** my
84 **suggestions** false accusations
89 **misconceived** doubted
92 **Rent** torn
97 **ransomed** repaid
98 **mean** moderate
105 **articulated here** (in the written proposal sent by the King)
III.ii.1 **fraught** filled
2 **lively . . . death** looking alive although dead
4 **Confused** disordered, confounded
5 **unhallowed** unsanctified
12 **secretary** confidant
14 **distressful** i.e., causing distress
15 **notice** public announcement
18 **fear** frighten
23 **mean** method, way
23 **s.d.** ***letter falleth*** (1) accidentally; (2) Bel-imperia is overhearing him; (3) Revenge is at work with Andrea's ghost (cf. I.iv.100 s.d.)
26 **writ** writing, document
27 **hapless** unfortunate
34 **malign** (1) hate; (2) attack; (3) punish
36 **mean** means

Hieronimo, beware, thou art betrayed,
And to entrap thy life this train is laid.
Advise thee, therefore, be not credulous.
This is devised to endanger thee,
That thou by this Lorenzo shouldst accuse,
And he, for thy dishonor done, should draw
Thy life in question, and thy name in hate.
Dear was the life of my beloved son,
And of his death behooves me be revenged:
Then hazard not thine own, Hieronimo,
But live t' effect thy resolution.
I therefore will by circumstances try
What I can gather to confirm this writ,
And, heark'ning near the Duke of Castile's house,
Close if I can with Bel-imperia,
To listen more, but nothing to bewray.

Enter Pedringano.

Now, Pedringano!
Ped. Now, Hieronimo!
Hier. Where's thy Lady?
Ped. I know not; here's my Lord.

Enter Lorenzo.

Lor. How now, who's this? Hieronimo?
Hier. My Lord.
Ped. He asketh for my Lady Bel-imperia.
Lor. What to do, Hieronimo? The Duke my father hath
Upon some disgrace awhile removed her hence,
But if it be aught I may inform her of,
Tell me, Hieronimo, and I'll let her know it.
Hier. Nay, nay, my Lord, I thank you, it shall not need,
I had a suit unto her, but too late,
And her disgrace makes me unfortunate.
Lor. Why so, Hieronimo? Use me.
Hier. Oh, no, my Lord, I dare not, it must not be.
I humbly thank your Lordship.
Lor. Why then, farewell.
Hier. My grief no heart, my thoughts no tongue can tell.

Exit.

Lor. Come hither, Pedringano, seest thou this?
Ped. My Lord, I see it, and suspect it too.
Lor. This is that damned villain Serberine,
That hath, I fear, revealed Horatio's death.
Ped. My Lord, he could not, 'twas so lately done,
And since, he hath not left my company.
Lor. Admit he have not, his condition's such,
As fear or flattering words may make him false.
I know his humor, and therewith repent
That e'er I used him in this enterprise.
But Pedringano, to prevent the worst,
And 'cause I know thee secret as my soul,
Here, for thy further satisfaction, take thou this,

Gives him more gold,

And hearken to me – thus it is devised:
This night thou must, and prithee so resolve,
Meet Serberine at Saint Luigi's Park –
Thou know'st 'tis here hard by behind the house;
There take thy stand, and see thou strike him sure,
For die he must, if we do mean to live.
Ped. But how shall Serberine be there, my Lord?
Lor. Let me alone, I'll send to him to meet
The Prince and me, where thou must do this deed.
Ped. It shall be done, my Lord, it shall be done,
And I'll go arm myself to meet him there.
Lor. When things shall alter, as I hope they will,
Then shalt thou mount for this. Thou know'st my mind.

Exit Pedringano.

Che le Ieron!

Enter Page.

Page. My Lord?
Lor. Go, sirrah, to Serberine,
And bid him forthwith meet the Prince and me
At Saint Luigi's Park, behind the house.
This evening, boy!
Page. I go, my Lord.

---

37 **betrayed** deceived (i.e., why should he trust this accusation?)
38 **train** plot, trap
42–3 **draw . . . question** be able to accuse you of false charges and so endanger your own life
47 **resolution** (i.e., decision to avenge Horatio's death successfully)
48 **by circumstances** (1) by collected evidence; (2) indirect means
51 **Close** meet; reach an understanding
52 **bewray** disclose
62 **suit** request
64 **Use** employ
69 **see** observe (Hieronimo's behavior and remarks)
73 **since** ever since that moment
74 **condition's** nature's
76 **humor** disposition, temperament
79 **secret** (1) as secretive; (2) as reliable; (3) as a fellow conspirator with
85 **sure** mortally
88 **Let . . . alone** Leave that part to me
93 **mount** (1) rise socially; (2) advance by my rewards; (3) get your just deserts (ironically)
94 ***Che . . . Ieron*** (nonsense; perhaps, "Who is there? Ieron [the page]?")

Lor. But, sirrah, let the hour be eight o'clock.
Bid him not fail.
Page. I fly, my Lord.
Exit.
Lor. Now to confirm the complot thou hast cast
Of all these practices, I'll spread the watch,
Upon precise commandment from the King,
Strongly to guard the place where Pedringano
This night shall murder hapless Serberine.
Thus must we work that will avoid distrust,
Thus must we practice to prevent mishap,
And thus one ill another must expulse.
This sly inquiry of Hieronimo
For Bel-imperia breeds suspicion,
And this suspicion bodes a further ill.
As for myself, I know my secret fault,
And so do they, but I have dealt for them.
They that for coin their souls endangered
To save my life, for coin shall venture theirs:
And better it's that base companions die,
Than by their life to hazard our good haps.
Nor shall they live, for me to fear their faith.
I'll trust myself, myself shall be my friend,
For die they shall, slaves are ordained to no other end.
Exit.

[III.iii]

Enter Pedringano *with a pistol.*

Ped. Now, Pedringano, bid thy pistol hold,
And hold on, Fortune! once more favor me,
Give but success to mine attempting spirit,
And let me shift for taking of mine aim!
Here is the gold, this is the gold proposed:
It is no dream that I adventure for,
But Pedringano is possessed thereof.
And he that would not strain his conscience
For him that thus his liberal purse hath stretched,
Unworthy such a favor may he fail,
And, wishing, want, when such as I prevail.
As for the fear of apprehension,
I know, if need should be, my noble Lord
Will stand between me and ensuing harms:
Besides, this place is free from all suspect.
Here therefore will I stay and take my stand.

Enter the Watch.

1. I wonder much to what intent it is
That we are thus expressly charged to watch.
2. 'Tis by commandment in the King's own name.
3. But we were never wont to watch and ward
So near the Duke his brother's house before.
2. Content yourself, stand close, there's somewhat in't.

Enter Serberine.

Ser. Here, Serberine, attend and stay thy pace,
For here did Don Lorenzo's page appoint
That thou by his command shouldst meet with him.
How fit a place, if one were so disposed,
Methinks this corner is to close with one.
Ped. Here comes the bird that I must seize upon.
Now, Pedringano, or never play the man!
Ser. I wonder that his Lordship stays so long,
Or wherefore should he send for me so late?
Ped. For this, Serberine, and thou shalt ha't.
Shoots the dag.
So, there he lies, my promise is performed.

The Watch.

1. Hark, gentlemen, this is a pistol shot.
2. And here's one slain; stay the murderer.
Ped. Now by the sorrows of the souls in hell,
He strives with the Watch.
Who first lays hand on me, I'll be his priest.
3. Sirrah, confess, and therein play the priest,
Why hast thou thus unkindly killed the man?

---

100 **complot** scheme; conspiracy; **cast** (1) devised; (2) put into operation
101 **practices** deceits; **spread the watch** place the constables
102 **Upon** pretending to be the
105 **distrust** suspicion
106 **practice** scheme; **mishap** unforeseen obstructions
107 **expulse** expel
108 **sly** (1) clever; (2) significant
113 **for coin** (i.e., for monetary reward)
115 **base** low-bred; **companions** associates, conspirators
116 **good haps** (1) good fortune; (2) security
117 **faith** loyalty
119 **slaves** worthless (lower-class) villains
III.iii.1 **hold** function accurately
2 **hold on** continue
3 **attempting spirit** attempted design
4 **let me shift** hold me responsible
8 **not strain** not be too particular about
10 **fail** (1) be unsuccessful; (2) suffer poverty
15 **suspect** suspicion
20 **wont** accustomed; **watch and ward** keep patrol, act as sentinels
22 **close** (1) near; (2) concealed
23 **stay . . . pace** stop walking about
27 **to . . . one** to grapple with an adversary
28 **bird** quarry
32 **ha't** have it
32 s.d. ***dag*** heavy pistol
33 **promise** appointed task
35 **stay** arrest
37 **I'll . . . priest** I shall celebrate his own death
39 **unkindly** inhumanly, unnaturally

Ped. Why? because he walked abroad so late.
3. Come, sir, you had been better kept your bed,
Than have committed this misdeed so late.
2. Come, to the Marshal's with the murderer!
1. On to Hieronimo's! help me here
To bring the murdered body with us too.
Ped. Hieronimo! Carry me before whom you will.
Whate'er he be, I'll answer him and you,
And do your worst, for I defy you all.

Exeunt.

[III.iv]

Enter Lorenzo *and* Balthazar.

Bal. How now my Lord, what makes you rise so soon?
Lor. Fear of preventing our mishaps too late.
Bal. What mischief is it that we not mistrust?
Lor. Our greatest ills we least mistrust, my Lord,
And inexpected harms do hurt us most.
Bal. Why, tell me, Don Lorenzo, tell me, man,
If aught concerns our honor and your own.
Lor. Nor you nor me, my Lord, but both in one,
For I suspect, and the presumption's great,
That by those base confederates in our fault
Touching the death of Don Horatio,
We are betrayed to old Hieronimo.
Bal. Betrayed, Lorenzo? Tush. It cannot be.
Lor. A guilty conscience, urged with the thought
Of former evils, easily cannot err:
I am persuaded, and dissuade me not,
That all's revealed to Hieronimo.
And therefore know that I have cast it thus –

[*Enter* Page.]

But here's the page. How now, what news with thee?
Page. My Lord, Serberine is slain.
Bal. Who? Serberine, my man?
Page. Your Highness' man, my Lord.
Lor. Speak, page, who murdered him?
Page. He that is apprehended for the fact.
Lor. Who?
Page. Pedringano.
Bal. Is Serberine slain, that loved his Lord so well?
Injurious villain, murderer of his friend!
Lor. Hath Pedringano murdered Serberine?
My Lord, let me entreat you to take the pains
To exasperate and hasten his revenge
With your complaints unto my Lord the King.
This their dissension breeds a greater doubt.
Bal. Assure thee, Don Lorenzo, he shall die,
Or else His Highness hardly shall deny.
Meanwhile, I'll haste the marshall-sessions.
For die he shall for this his damned deed.

Exit Balthazar.

Lor. Why so, this fits our former policy,
And thus experience bids the wise to deal.
I lay the plot, he prosecutes the point,
I set the trap, he breaks the worthless twigs
And sees not that wherewith the bird was limed.
Thus hopeful men, that mean to hold their own,
Must look like fowlers to their dearest friends.
He runs to kill whom I have help to catch,
And no man knows it was my reaching fatch.
'Tis hard to trust unto a multitude,
Or anyone, in mine opinion,
When men themselves their secrets will reveal.

Enter a Messenger *with a letter.*

Boy!
Page. My Lord.
Lor. What's he?
Mes. I have a letter to your Lordship.
Lor. From whence?
Mes. From Pedringano that's imprisoned.
Lor. So, he is in prison then?
Mes. Aye, my good Lord.
Lor. What would he with us? He writes us here
To stand good Lord and help him in distress.
Tell him I have his letters, know his mind,
And what we may, let him assure him of.
Fellow, begone: my boy shall follow thee.

Exit Messenger.

40 **abroad** out of doors (criminals were known to break curfews and roam at night in England)
III.iv.2 **preventing** attempting to forestall
3 **mischief** evil, crime; **not mistrust** anticipate
8 **Nor** neither
10 **confederates . . . fault** partners in our plan
18 **cast it thus** laid these plans
24 **fact** deed, crime
31 **exasperate** make harsh
32 **complaints** outcries (so that Pedringano is punished and we are not implicated)
33 **doubt** (1) suspicion; (2) fear
35 **hardly shall** i.e., can hardly
36 **marshal-sessions** court of Marshalsea in England
38 **policy** (Machiavellian term for amoral strategies of self-interest)
40 **prosecutes the point** executes my desires for me
41 **worthless twigs** i.e., the victims
42 **limed** trapped (caught in birdlime)
46 **reaching** (1) far-reaching; (2) designing; **fatch** contrivance, stratagem
56 **stand . . . Lord** stand as good lord and protector on his behalf

This works like wax, yet once more try thy wits.
Boy, go convey this purse to Pedringano:
Thou know'st the prison, closely give it him,
And be advised that none be thereabout.
Bid him be merry still, but secret.
And though the marshal-sessions be today,
Bid him not doubt of his delivery.
Tell him his pardon is already signed,
And thereon bid him boldly be resolved:
For were he ready to be turned off
(As 'tis my will the uttermost be tried),
Thou with his pardon shalt attend him still.
Show him this box, tell him his pardon's in't,
But open't not, and if thou lov'st thy life,
But let him wisely keep his hopes unknown;
He shall not want while Don Lorenzo lives.
Away!

Page. I go my Lord, I run.

Lor. But sirrah, see that this be cleanly done.

Exit Page.

Now stands our fortune on a tickle point,
And now or never ends Lorenzo's doubts.
One only thing is uneffected yet,
And that's to see the executioner.
But to what end? I list not trust the air
With utterance of our pretense therein,
For fear the privy whisp'ring of the wind
Convey our words among unfriendly ears
That lie too open to advantages.
E quel che voglio io, nessun lo sa,
Intendo io: quel mi basterà.

Exit.

[III.v]

Enter Boy *with the box.*

Page. My master hath forbidden me to look in this box, and by my troth 'tis likely, if he had not warned me, I should not have had so much idle time: for we men's-kind in our minority are like women in their uncertainty: that they are most forbidden, they will soonest attempt. So I now. By my bare honesty, here's nothing but the bare empty box. Were it not sin against secrecy, I would say it were a piece of gentlemanlike knavery. I must go to Pedringano, and tell him his pardon is in this box – nay, I would have sworn it, had I not seen the contrary. I cannot choose but smile to think how the villain will flout the gallows, scorn the audience, and descant on the hangman, and all presuming of his pardon from hence. Will 't not be an odd jest, for me to stand and grace every jest he makes, pointing my finger at this box, as who would say, "Mock on, here's thy warrant." Is't not a scurvy jest, that a man should jest himself to death? Alas, poor Pedringano, I am in a sort sorry for thee, but if I should be hanged with thee, I cannot weep.

Exit.

[III.vi]

Enter Hieronimo *and the* Deputy.

Hier. Thus must we toil in other men's extremes,
That know not how to remedy our own,
And do them justice, when unjustly we,
For all our wrongs, can compass no redress.
But shall I never live to see the day
That I may come, by justice of the Heavens,
To know the cause that may my cares allay?
This toils my body, this consumeth age,
That only I to all men just must be,
And neither gods nor men be just to me.

Dep. Worthy Hieronimo, your office asks
A care to punish such as do transgress.

Hier. So is't my duty to regard his death
Who, when he lived, deserved my dearest blood.

60 **works like wax** follows my pattern
62 **closely** secretly
63 **be advised** take precaution
64 **secret** silent
68 **boldly be resolved** feel absolutely confident
69 **turned off** hanged
77 **cleanly** efficiently
78 **tickle** (1) delicate; (2) precarious
79 **doubts** fears
82 **list not** have no desire to
83 **pretense** plan, intention
84 **privy** private
87–8 ***E... basterà*** "And what I wish, no one knows; I understand; that suffices me"
III.v.2 s.d. *box* (one critic has suggested an allusion to the well-known Pandora's box in which only hope remained after every good and ill had been dispersed)
2 **troth** truth (a common oath)
5 **minority** boyhood; **uncertainty** fearfulness
7 **bare** naked, exposed
16 **descant** hold forth; comment
21 **warrant** license
22 **scurvy** bitter, base
III.vi s.d. Deputy the official title of the Spanish Knight Marshal's assistant
1–10 **Thus... me** (Hieronimo's concern here is justice, not revenge)
1 **extremes** hardships
4 **compass** locate
8 **toils** burdens, exhausts; **consumeth age** makes me grow old
14 **dearest blood** loyalty, support

But come, for that we came for, let's begin,
For here lies that which bids me to be gone.

Enter Officers, Boy, *and* Pedringano, *with a letter in his hand, bound.*

Dep. Bring forth the prisoner, for the court is set.
Ped. Gramercy boy, but it was time to come,
For I had written to my Lord anew
A nearer matter that concerneth him,
For fear his Lordship had forgotten me;
But sith he hath remembered me so well –
Come, come, come on, when shall we to this gear?
Hier. Stand forth, thou monster, murderer of men,
And here, for satisfaction of the world,
Confess thy folly and repent thy fault,
For there's thy place of execution.
Ped. This is short work. Well, to your marshalship.
First I confess, nor fear I death. Therefore,
I am the man, 'twas I slew Serberine.
But sir, then you think this shall be the place
Where we shall satisfy you for this gear?
Dep. Aye, Pedringano.
Ped. Now I think not so.
Hier. Peace, impudent, for thou shalt find it so.
For blood with blood shall, while I sit as judge,
Be satisfied, and the law discharged;
And though myself cannot receive the like,
Yet will I see that others have their right.
Despatch! the fault's approved and confessed,
And by our law he is condemned to die.
Hangman. Come on, sir, are you ready?
Ped. To do what, my fine officious knave?
Hangm. To go to this gear.
Ped. Oh, sir, you are too forward; thou wouldst fain furnish me with a halter, to disfurnish me of my habit, so I should go out of this gear, my raiment, into that gear, the rope; but hangman, now I spy your knavery, I'll not change without boot, that's flat.
Hangm. Come, sir.
Ped. So then, I must up?
Hangm. No remedy.
Ped. Yes, but there shall be for my coming down.
Hangm. Indeed, here's a remedy for that.
Ped. How? Be turned off?
Hangm. Aye, truly. Come, are you ready? I pray sir, despatch.
The day goes away.
Ped. What, do you hang by the hour? If you do, I may chance to break your old custom.
Hangm. Faith, you have reason, for I am like to break your young neck.
Ped. Dost thou mock me, hangman? Pray God I be not preserved to break your knave's pate for this!
Hangm. Alas sir, you are a foot too low to reach it, and I hope you will never grow so high while I am in the office.
Ped. Sirrah, dost see yonder boy with the box in his hand?
Hangm. What, he that points to it with his finger?
Ped. Aye, that companion.
Hangm. I know him not, but what of him?
Ped. Dost thou think to live till his old doublet will make thee a new truss?
Hangm. Aye, and many a fair year after, to truss up many an honester man than either thou or he.
Ped. What hath he in his box, as thou think'st?
Hangm. Faith, I cannot tell, nor I care not greatly. Methinks you should rather hearken to your soul's health.
Ped. Why, sirrah hangman? I take it, that that is good for the body is likewise good for the soul: and it may be, in that box is balm for both.
Hangm. Well, thou art even the merriest piece of man's flesh that e'er groaned at my office door.
Ped. Is your roguery become an office, with a knave's name?
Hangm. Aye, and that shall all they witness that see you seal it with a thief's name.
Ped. I prithee, request this good company to pray with me.

---

18 **Gramercy** (expression of relief)
20 **nearer** more serious
23 **gear** business
32 **gear** (1) action; (2) behavior
33 **think . . . so** I don't intend to satisfy you; I will get off anyway
43 **this gear** (i.e., to the gallows)
44 **forward** presumptuous
45 **halter** noose; **disfurnish . . . habit** (refers to the practice of those executed to give their clothing to the hangman in recompense for his task)
46 **habit** clothing
49 **boot** compensation; **flat** certain
55 **turned off** thrust off the support of the platform
59 **by the hour** (1) on the hour; (2) for hourly wages
65 **pate** head
72 **companion** fellow
75 **truss** close-fitting jacket (i.e., long enough to get my clothes and have them remade for you; he is descanting here)
76–7 **truss up** hang
81 **hearken** pay attention
90 **roguery** (in mockery of "office," line 89)
94 **prithee** pray thee (puns on *pray* later in line; Pedringano is still enjoying himself)

Hangm. Aye, marry, sir, this is a good motion. My masters, you see here's a good fellow.

Ped. Nay, nay, now I remember me, let them alone till some other time, for now I have no great need.

Hier. I have not seen a wretch so impudent!
Oh, monstrous times, where murder's set so light,
And where the soul that should be shrined in Heaven,
Solely delights in interdicted things,
Still wand'ring in the thorny passages
That intercepts itself of happiness.
Murder, Oh, bloody monster – God forbid
A fault so foul should 'scape unpunished.
Despatch, and see this execution done.
This makes me to remember thee, my son.

Exit Hieronimo.

Ped. Nay, soft, no haste.

Dep. Why, wherefore stay you? Have you hope of life?

Ped. Why, aye.

Hangm. As how?

Ped. Why, rascal, by my pardon from the King.

Hangm. Stand you on that? Then you shall off with this.

He turns him off.

Dep. So, executioner; convey him hence,
But let his body be unburied.
Let not the earth be choked or infect
With that which Heaven contemns and men neglect.

Exeunt.

[III.vii]

Enter Hieronimo.

Hier. Where shall I run to breathe abroad my woes,
My woes, whose weight hath wearied the earth?
Or mine exclaims, that have surcharged the air
With ceaseless plaints for my deceased son?
The blust'ring winds, conspiring with my words,
At my lament have moved the leaveless trees,
Disrobed the meadows of their flowered green,
Made mountains marsh with spring-tides of my tears,
And broken through the brazen gates of hell.
Yet still tormented is my tortured soul
With broken sighs and restless passions,
That winged mount, and, hovering in the air,
Beat at the windows of the brightest Heavens,
Soliciting for justice and revenge.
But they are placed in those empyreal heights
Where, counter-mured with walls of diamond,
I find the place impregnable, and they
Resist my woes, and give my words no way.

Enter Hangman *with a letter.*

Hangm. Oh, Lord, sir, God bless you sir, the man, sir, Petergade, sir, he that was so full of merry conceits –

Hier. Well, what of him?

Hangm. Oh, Lord, sir, he went the wrong way. The fellow had a fair commission to the contrary. Sir, here is his passport; I pray you, sir, we have done him wrong.

Hier. I warrant thee, give it me.

Hangm. You will stand between the gallows and me?

Hier. Aye, aye.

Hangm. I thank your lord-worship.

Exit Hangman.

Hier. And yet, though somewhat nearer me concerns,
I will, to ease the grief that I sustain,
Take truce with sorrow while I read on this.
"My lord, I writ as mine extremes required,
That you would labor my delivery.
If you neglect, my life is desperate,
And in my death I shall reveal the troth.
You know, my Lord, I slew him for your sake,
And was confederate with the Prince and you,
Won by rewards and hopeful promises,
I helped to murder Don Horatio, too."
Helped he to murder mine Horatio?
And actors in th' accursed tragedy
Wast thou, Lorenzo, Balthazar and thou,
Of whom my son, my son, deserved so well?

---

96 **motion** suggestion, idea
103 **shrined** enshrined
104 **interdicted** (1) prohibited; (2) censured
105 **Still** always
106 **intercepts . . . of** prevents its own
111 **soft** wait a moment
117 **Stand** delay
117 **s.d.** ***turns him off*** (it is possible the wooden frame used for the arbor reappears as a gallows, visually joining Horatio's death with Pedringano's)
122 **contemns** condemns

III.vii.1 **breathe abroad** give expression to
3 **exclaims** cries
11 **passions** sufferings
15 **empyreal heights** highest heavens, closest to God
16 **counter-mured** having two walls, one within the other
20 **Petergade** (mispronunciation of Pedringano)
21 **conceits** jests
24 **fair commission** proper written authority
27 **warrant** (1) assure; (2) protect
35 **extremes** dire predicament
37 **desperate** despaired of, without hope

What have I heard, what have mine eyes beheld?
Oh, sacred Heavens, may it come to pass
That such a monstrous and detested deed,
So closely smothered, and so long concealed,
Shall thus by this be venged or revealed?
Now see I what I durst not then suspect,
That Bel-imperia's letter was not feigned,
Nor feigned she, though falsely they have wronged
Both her, myself, Horatio and themselves.
Now may I make compare, 'twixt hers and this,
Of every accident. I ne'er could find
Till now, and now I feelingly perceive,
They did what Heaven unpunish'd would not leave.
O false Lorenzo, are these thy flattering looks?
Is this the honor that thou didst my son?
And Balthazar, bane to thy soul and me,
Was this the ransom he reserved thee for?
Woe to the cause of these constrained wars,
Woe to thy baseness and captivity,
Woe to thy birth, thy body and thy soul,
Thy cursèd father, and thy conquered self!
And banned with bitter execrations be
The day and place where he did pity thee!
But wherefore waste I mine unfruitful words,
When naught but blood will satisfy my woes?
I will go plain me to my Lord the King,
And cry aloud for justice through the court,
Wearing the flints with these my withered feet,
And either purchase justice by entreats
Or tire them all with my revenging threats.

Exit.

[III.viii]

Enter Isabella *and her* Maid.

Isab. So that you say this herb will purge the eye,
And this the head?
Ah, but none of them will purge the heart.
No, there's no medicine left for my disease,
Nor any physic to recure the dead.

She runs lunatic.

Horatio! Oh, where's Horatio?

Maid. Good madam, affright not thus yourself
With outrage for your son Horatio.
He sleeps in quiet in the Elysian fields.

Isab. Why, did I not give you gowns and goodly things,
Bought you a whistle and a whipstalk too,
To be revenged on their villainies?

Maid. Madam, these humors do torment my soul.

Isab. My soul? Poor soul, thou talks of things
Thou know'st not what – my soul hath silver wings,
That mounts me up unto the highest Heavens,
To Heaven, aye, there sits my Horatio,
Backed with a troop of fiery cherubins,
Dancing about his newly-healèd wounds,
Singing sweet hymns and chanting heavenly notes,
Rare harmony to greet his innocence,
That died, aye, died, a mirror in our days.
But say, where shall I find the men, the murderers,
That slew Horatio? Whither shall I run
To find them out that murdered my son?

Exeunt.

[III.ix]

Bel-imperia *at a window.*

Bel. What means this outrage that is offered me?
Why am I thus sequestered from the court?
No notice? Shall I not know the cause
Of this my secret and suspicious ills?
Accursed brother, unkind murderer,
Why bends thou thus thy mind to martyr me?

---

50 closely smothered carefully kept secret
52 durst dared
56 compare (details of the letters, one corroborating the other)
57 accident circumstances; **find** understand, determine
59 leave dismiss
62 bane (1) poison; (2) cause of ruin
64 constrained (1) forced; (2) unnecessary
68 banned cursed
71 blood justice
72 plain plead
73 through the court by means of law
III.viii s.d. Isabella . . . Maid (an intensely private scene, like the one preceding, although Isabella is here probably in her night-clothes)
1 purge (1) cleanse; (2) heal
5 recure restore, recover
8 outrage great passion

10–11 gowns . . . whipstalk (confusing combination illustrates her distracted mind)
11 whipstalk whip, presumably like that used to spin a top
13 humors uncontrolled behavior
14–22 Poor . . . days (Christian references here are sharply disjunctive to the pagan allusions elsewhere)
18 troop . . . cherubins second order of angels who guarded souls newly arrived in Heaven
19 newly-healèd (Isabella has "recured" Horatio herself)
21 greet honor
22 mirror model of excellence; exemplar
III.ix.1 outrage (repetition of III.viii.8 forces comparisons of the two scenes)
2 sequestered kept
3 No notice no information
4 suspicious ills suspect behavior
5 unkind unnatural

Hieronimo, why writ I of thy wrongs,
Or why art thou so slack in thy revenge?
Andrea, O Andrea, that thou sawest
Me for thy friend Horatio handled thus,
And him for me thus causeless murdered.
Well, force perforce, I must constrain myself
To patience, and apply me to the time,
Till heaven, as I have hoped, shall set me free.

Enter Christophil.

Chris. Come, Madam Bel-imperia, this may not be.

Exeunt.

[III.x]

Enter Lorenzo, Balthazar, *and the* Page.

Lor. Boy, talk no further, thus far things go well.
Thou art assured that thou sawest him dead?
Page. Or else, my Lord, I live not.
Lor. That's enough.
As for his resolution in his end,
Leave that to him with whom he sojourns now.
Here, take my ring, and give it Christophil,
And bid him let my sister be enlarged,
And bring her hither straight.

Exit Page.

This that I did was for a policy
To smooth and keep the murder secret,
Which as a nine-days' wonder being o'er-blown,
My gentle sister will I now enlarge.
Bal. And time, Lorenzo, for my Lord the Duke,
You heard, inquired for her yester-night.
Lor. Why, and, my Lord, I hope you heard me say
Sufficient reason why she kept away:
But that's all one. My Lord, you love her?
Bal. Aye.
Lor. Then in your love beware, deal cunningly,
Salve all suspicions, only soothe me up;
And if she hap to stand on terms with us,
As for her sweetheart, and concealment so,
Jest with her gently. Under feigned jest
Are things concealed that else would breed unrest.
But here she comes.

Enter Bel-imperia.

Now, sister –
Bel. Sister? No,
Thou art no brother, but an enemy;
Else wouldst thou not have used thy sister so:
First, to affright me with thy weapons drawn,
And with extremes abuse my company:
And then to hurry me, like whirlwind's rage,
Amid a crew of thy confederates,
And clap me up where none might come at me,
Nor I at any to reveal my wrongs.
What madding fury did possess thy wits?
Or wherein is't that I offended thee?
Lor. Advise you better, Bel-imperia,
For I have done you no disparagement,
Unless, by more discretion than deserved,
I sought to save your honor and mine own.
Bel. Mine honor! why Lorenzo, wherein is't
That I neglect my reputation so,
As you, or any, need to rescue it?
Lor. His Highness and my father were resolved
To come confer with old Hieronimo,
Concerning certain matters of estate
That by the Viceroy was determined.
Bel. And wherein was mine honor touched in that?
Bal. Have patience, Bel-imperia; hear the rest.
Lor. Me next in sight as messenger they sent,
To give him notice that they were so nigh.
Now when I came, consorted with the Prince,
And unexpected in an arbor there
Found Bel-imperia with Horatio –
Bel. How then?
Lor. Why then, remembering that old disgrace
Which you for Don Andrea had endured,
And now were likely longer to sustain,
By being found so meanly accompanied,
Thought rather, for I knew no readier mean,
To thrust Horatio forth my father's way.

---

12 **force perforce** of necessity
13 **apply . . . time** accept things as they are for the time being
III.x.4 **resolution** resolve, courage
7 **enlarged** freed
9 **policy** strategy, plot
10 **smooth** avoid difficulties
11 **a . . . wonder** (proverbial for strange events); **o'er-blown** past and forgotten
13 **time** just in time
19 **Salve** allay; **soothe me up** agree with me
20 **hap . . . terms** proves difficult
28 **extremes** harsh actions
31 **clap** unceremoniously lock; **at** to
36 **disparagement** dishonor, embarrassment
44 **estate** state, government (perhaps after the uprising)
48 **next in sight** standing near
50 **consorted** associated
54 **old disgrace** (deliberately unclear, but he suggests a relationship considered illicit)
57 **meanly accompanied** seen with someone of low rank
58 **mean** method
59 **forth** forth from

Bal. And carry you obscurely somewhere else,
Lest that His Highness should have found you there.
Bel. Even so, my Lord? And you are witness
That this is true which he entreateth of?
You, gentle brother, forged this for my sake,
And you, my Lord, were made his instrument.
A work of worth, worthy the noting too!
But what's the cause that you concealed me since?
Lor. Your melancholy, sister, since the news
Of your first favorite Don Andrea's death,
My father's old wrath hath exasperate.
Bal. And better was't for you, being in disgrace,
To absent yourself and give his fury place.
Bel. But why had I no notice of his ire?
Lor. That were to add more fuel to your fire,
Who burned like Aetna for Andrea's loss.
Bel. Hath not my father then enquired for me?
Lor. Sister, he hath, and thus excused I thee.

He whispereth in her ear.

But, Bel-imperia, see the gentle prince,
Look on thy love, behold young Balthazar,
Whose passions by thy presence are increased,
And in whose melancholy thou mayst see
Thy hate, his love; thy flight, his following thee.
Bel. Brother, you are become an orator,
I know not, I, by what experience,
Too politic for me, past all compare,
Since last I saw you. But content yourself,
The Prince is meditating higher things.
Bal. 'Tis of thy beauty then, that conquers kings:
Of those thy tresses, Ariadne's twines,
Wherewith my liberty thou hast surprised.
Of that thine ivory front, my sorrow's map,
Wherein I see no haven to rest my hope.
Bel. To love, and fear, and both at once, my Lord,
In my conceit, are things of more import
Than women's wits are to be busied with.
Bal. 'Tis I that love.
Bel. Whom?
Bal. Bel-imperia.
Bel. But I that fear.
Bal. Whom?
Bel. Bel-imperia.
Lor. Fear yourself?
Bel. Aye, brother.
Lor. How?
Bel. As those
That what they love are loath and fear to lose.
Bal. Then, fair, let Balthazar your keeper be.
Bel. No, Balthazar doth fear as well as we.
Et tremulo metui pavidum junxere timorem,
Et vanum stolidae proditionis opus.

Exit.

Lor. Nay, and you argue things so cunningly,
We'll go continue this discourse at court.
Bal. Led by the loadstar of her heavenly looks,
Wends poor oppressed Balthazar,
As o'er the mountains walks the wanderer,
Incertain to effect his pilgrimage.

Exeunt.

[III.xi]

Enter two Portingales, *and* Hieronimo *meets them.*

1. By your leave, sir.
Hier. Good leave have you, nay, I pray you go,
For I'll leave you, if you can leave me, so.
2. Pray you, which is the next way to my Lord the Duke's?
Hier. The next way from me.
1. To his house, we mean.
Hier. Oh, hard by, 'tis yon house that you see.
2. You could not tell us if his son were there?
Hier. Who, my Lord Lorenzo?
1. Aye, sir.

He goeth in at one door and comes out at another.

Hier. Oh, forbear,
For other talk for us far fitter were.
But if you be importunate to know
The way to him, and where to find him out,
Then list to me, and I'll resolve your doubt.
There is a path upon your left-hand side,
That leadeth from a guilty conscience

---

64 **forged** (1) executed; (2) fabricated
68 **melancholy** (as illness needing treatment)
70 **exasperate** made worse
72 **place** room to abate
75 **Aetna** a volcano in Italy
85 **politic** cunning
89 **Ariadne** (1) the Lydian weaver whom Athena transformed into a spider; (2) the daughter of King Minos of Crete who guided Theseus through a labyrinth by unwinding a thread; **twines** threads, cords
90 **surprised** conquered
91 **front** forehead; **map** (forehead was thought to convey feelings and reactions)
94 **In . . . conceit** to my mind
102–3 ***Et . . . opus*** "They yoked craven fear to trembling dread: and that a fruitless work of doltish treason"
104 **cunningly** shrewdly, subtly
106 **loadstar** star used to navigate by
110 **Incertain . . . effect** with no guarantee of success in
III.xi.5 **next** nearest
6 **hard** near
9 **other . . . were** (used to show Hieronimo's increasingly distracted mind)
10 **be . . . know** insist on knowing
13–29 **There . . . innocents** (1) his mind is on Hades where Horatio is; (2) this world is like Hades and I will prove it

Unto a forest of distrust and fear,
A darksome place and dangerous to pass.
There shall you meet with melancholy thoughts,
Whose baleful humors if you but uphold,
It will conduct you to despair and death.
Whose rocky cliffs when you have once beheld,
Within a hugy dale of lasting night,
That, kindled with the world's iniquities,
Doth cast up filthy and detested fumes.
Not far from thence, where murderers have built
A habitation for their cursèd souls,
There, in a brazen cauldron fixed by Jove
In his fell wrath upon a sulfur flame,
Yourselves shall find Lorenzo bathing him
In boiling lead and blood of innocents.
1. Ha, ha, ha!
Hier. Ha, ha, ha!
Why, ha, ha, ha! Farewell, good, ha, ha, ha!
Exit.
2. Doubtless this man is passing lunatic,
Or imperfection of his age doth make him dote.
Come, let's away to seek my Lord the Duke.
[*Exeunt.*]

[III.xii]

Enter Hieronimo *with a poniard in one hand, and a rope in the other.*

Hier. Now sir, perhaps I come and see the King,
The King sees me, and fain would hear my suit.
Why, is not this a strange and seld-seen thing,
That standers-by with toys should strike me mute?
Go to, I see their shifts, and say no more.
Hieronimo, 'tis time for thee to trudge.
Down by the dale that flows with purple gore,
Standeth a fiery tower. There sits a judge
Upon a seat of steel and molten brass,
And 'twixt his teeth he holds a firebrand,
That leads unto the lake where hell doth stand.
Away, Hieronimo, to him be gone.
He'll do thee justice for Horatio's death.
Turn down this path, thou shalt be with him straight,
Or this, and then thou need'st not take thy breath.
This way, or that way? Soft and fair, not so.
For if I hang or kill myself, let's know
Who will revenge Horatio's murder then?
No, no! fie, no! pardon me, I'll none of that:
He flings away the dagger and halter.
This way I'll take, and this way comes the King,
He takes them up again.
And here I'll have a fling at him, that's flat.
And, Balthazar, I'll be with thee to bring,
And thee, Lorenzo! Here's the King, nay, stay,
And here, aye, here, there goes the hare away.

Enter King, Ambassador, Castile, *and* Lorenzo.

King. Now show, Ambassador, what our Viceroy saith:
Hath he received the articles we sent?
Hier. Justice, Oh justice to Hieronimo!
Lor. Back! seest thou not the King is busy?
Hier. Oh, is he so?
King. Who is he that interrupts our business?
Hier. Not I. Hieronimo, beware: go by, go by.
Amb. Renowned King, he hath received and read
Thy kingly proffers, and thy promised league,
And, as a man extremely overjoyed
To hear his son so princely entertained,
Whose death he had so solemnly bewailed,
This, for thy further satisfaction
And kingly love, he kindly lets thee know:
First, for the marriage of his princely son
With Bel-imperia, thy belovèd niece,

---

18 baleful humors evil tendencies; evil habits of thought; **uphold** persist in
21 hugy profound
26 brazen brass
27 fell cruel
28 him himself
32 passing exceedingly
33 imperfection weakening
III.xii s.d. *poniard* dagger (traditional sign of the stage suicide)
2 fain gladly
3 seld seldom
4 toys trifles, trivialities
5 shifts tricks
6 trudge get along; do something
7–15 Down . . . breath (his projected, hellish landscape parallels Andrea's in I.i)
7 purple blood-red
11 leads shows the way to
14 straight directly
16 This . . . way? (i.e., rope or poniard)
17 kill stab
21 flat certain
22 be be even
24 here, there (King passes by not noticing Hieronimo as he stands ruminating)
31 go by, go by pretend nothing; don't get involved
33 league negotiated union

The news are more delightful to his soul,
Than myrrh or incense to the offended Heavens.
In person therefore will he come himself,
To see the marriage rites solemnized,
And, in the presence of the court of Spain,
To knit a sure, inexplicable band
Of kingly love, and everlasting league,
Betwixt the crowns of Spain and Portingale.
There will he give his crown to Balthazar,
And make a queen of Bel-imperia.

King. Brother, how like you this our Viceroy's love?

Cast. No doubt, my Lord, it is an argument
Of honorable care to keep his friend,
And wondrous zeal to Balthazar his son.
Nor am I least indebted to his grace,
That bends his liking to my daughter thus.

Amb. Now last, dread Lord, here hath His Highness sent
(Although he send not that his son return)
His ransom due to Don Horatio.

Hier. Horatio? Who calls Horatio?

King. And well remembered, thank His Majesty.
Here, see it given to Horatio.

Hier. Justice, oh justice, justice, gentle King!

King. Who is that? Hieronimo?

Hier. Justice, oh justice! Oh my son, my son,
My son, whom naught can ransom or redeem!

Lor. Hieronimo, you are not well-advised.

Hier. Away, Lorenzo, hinder me no more,
For thou hast made me bankrupt of my bliss.
Give me my son! You shall not ransom him.
Away! I'll rip the bowels of the earth,

He diggeth with his dagger.

And ferry over to th'Elysian plains,
And bring my son to show his deadly wounds.
Stand from about me!
I'll make a pickaxe of my poniard,
And here surrender up my marshalship.
For I'll go marshal up the fiends in hell,
To be avenged on you all for this.

King. What means this outrage?
Will none of you restrain his fury?

Hier. Nay, soft and fair. You shall not need to strive,
Needs must he go that the devils drive.

Exit.

King. What accident hath happed Hieronimo?
I have not seen him to demean him so.

Lor. My gracious Lord, he is with extreme pride,
Conceived of young Horatio his son,
And covetous of having to himself
The ransom of the young Prince Balthazar,
Distract, and in a manner lunatic.

King. Believe me, nephew, we are sorry for't:
This is the love that fathers bear their sons.
But, gentle brother, go give to him this gold,
The Prince's ransom. Let him have his due,
For what he hath Horatio shall not want.
Haply Hieronimo hath need thereof.

Lor. But if he be thus helplessly distract,
'Tis requisite his office be resigned,
And given to one of more discretion.

King. We shall increase his melancholy so.
'Tis best that we see further in it first:
Till when, ourself will not exempt the place.
And brother, now bring in the Ambassador,
That he may be a witness of the match
'Twixt Balthazar and Bel-imperia,
And that we may prefix a certain time,
Wherein the marriage shall be solemnized,
That we may have thy Lord the Viceroy here.

Amb. Therein Your Highness highly shall content
His Majesty, that longs to hear from hence.

King. On then, and hear you, Lord Ambassador.

Exeunt.

[III.xiii]

Enter Hieronimo *with a book in his hand.*

Hier. *Vindicta mihi!*
Aye, Heaven will be revenged of every ill,
Nor will they suffer murder unrepaid.
Then stay, Hieronimo, attend their will,
For mortal men may not appoint their time.

---

46 **inexplicable** unbreakable, indivisible
52 **an argument** a proposition
56 **bends** directs
57 **dread** awe-inspiring
58 **that** in order that
70 **shall not** cannot (apparently the King thinks Horatio is alive as a captive of the Portuguese)
71 **rip . . . earth** (to supply an Horatio who can yet be ransomed, his first overt act of madness)
79 **outrage** (1) outburst; (2) madness
83 **accident** event; **happed** happened to
84 **demean** underestimate
95 **Haply** perhaps
100 **see . . . it** examine it more deeply
101 **exempt** make vacant
102 **bring in** escort to an inner room
III.xiii s.d. ***book*** (by Seneca, from whom he will later quote for directions)
1 ***Vindicta mihi!*** "Vengeance is mine [,saith the Lord]" (Rom. 12: 19)
4 **attend their will** await Heaven's pleasure

Per scelus semper tutum est sceleribus iter. Strike, and strike home, where wrong is offered thee,
For evils unto ills conductors be,
And death's the worst of resolution.
For he that thinks with patience to contend
To quiet life, his life shall easily end.
Fata si miseros juvant, habes salutem;
Fata si vitam negant, habes sepulchrum.
If destiny thy miseries do ease,
Then hast thou health, and happy shalt thou be.
If destiny deny thee life, Hieronimo,
Yet shalt thou be assured of a tomb.
If neither, yet let this thy comfort be,
Heaven covereth him that hath no burial.
And to conclude, I will revenge his death!
But how? not as the vulgar wits of men,
With open, but inevitable ills,
As by a secret, yet a certain mean,
Which under kindship will be cloaked best.
Wise men will take their opportunity,
Closely and safely fitting things to time.
But in extremes advantage hath no time,
And therefore all times fit not for revenge.
Thus therefore will I rest me in unrest,
Dissembling quiet in unquietness,
Not seeming that I know their villainies,
That my simplicity may make them think
That ignorantly I will let all slip:
For ignorance, I wot, and well they know,
Remedium malorum iners est.
Nor aught avails it me to menace them,
Who, as a wintry storm upon a plain,
Will bear me down with their nobility.
No, no, Hieronimo, thou must enjoin
Thine eyes to observation, and thy tongue
To milder speeches than thy spirit affords,
Thy heart to patience, and thy hands to rest,
Thy cap to courtesy, and thy knee to bow,
Till to revenge thou know, when, where, and how.

A noise within.

How now, what noise? what coil is that you keep?

Enter a Servant.

Ser. Here are a sort of poor petitioners,
That are importunate, and it shall please you, sir,
That you should plead their cases to the King.
Hier. That I should plead their several actions?
Why, let them enter, and let me see them.

Enter three Citizens *and an* Old Man.

1. So I tell you this, for learning and for law,
There's not any advocate in Spain
That can prevail, or will take half the pain
That he will, in pursuit of equity.
Hier. Come near, you men that thus importune me.
[*Aside.*] Now must I bear a face of gravity,
For thus I used, before my Marshalship,
To plead in causes as corregidor.
Come on, sirs, what's the matter?
2. Sir, an action.
Hier. Of battery?
1. Mine of debt.
Hier. Give place.
2. No sir, mine is an action of the case.
3. Mine an *ejectione firmae* by a lease.
Hier. Content you sirs, are you determined
That I should plead your several actions?
1. Aye, sir, and here's my declaration.
2. And here is my band.
3. And here is my lease.

They give him papers.

Hier. But wherefore stands yon silly man so mute,

---

6 ***Per...iter*** "The safe way for crimes is through (further) crimes" (Seneca, *Agamemnon*, line 115)
7 **strike home** (Hieronimo thinks Lorenzo will perform a crime against himself as a decoy)
9 **of resolution** that follows bold action
10 **contend** strive
12–13 ***Fata...sepulchrum*** (translated in lines 14–17; Seneca, *Troades*, lines 511–12)
18 **neither** (health or tomb)
21 **vulgar** common
22 **open** obvious; **inevitable** inevitably successful; **ills** ill practices
23–4 **secret...best** (he prefers more subtle means)
24 **kindship** kindness
26 **time** opportunity
27 **But** i.e., only
29 **rest me in unrest** anxiously await the most opportune time
31 **Not seeming that** pretending not to
32 **simplicity** unawareness
34 **wot** know
35 ***Remedium...est*** "is an unskillful remedy to evils" (Seneca, cf. *Oedipus*, line 515)
38 **nobility** noble rank and influence
45 **coil** noise; **keep** make
46 **sort** company, group
49 **actions** claims by law
58 **corregidor** advocate (chief magistrate of a Spanish town)
61 **action...case** exceptional kind of cases needing special writs
62 ***ejectione firmae*** (a writ to remove a tenant before his lease expires)
65 **declaration** plaintiff's statement of claim
66 **band** bond (see line 61)
67 **silly** simple, pitiable

With mournful eyes and hands to Heaven upreared?
Come hither, father, let me know thy cause.
Senex. Oh, worthy sir, my cause but slightly known
May move the hearts of warlike Myrmidons
And melt the Corsic rocks with ruthful tears.
Hier. Say, father, tell me what's thy suit?
Senex. No sir, could my woes
Give way unto my most distressful words,
Then should I not in paper, as you see,
With ink bewray what blood began in me.
Hier. What's here? "The humble supplication
Of Don Bazulto for his murdered son."
Senex. Aye, sir.
Hier. No, sir, it was my murdered son,
Oh my son, my son, Oh my son Horatio!
But mine, or thine, Bazulto, be content.
Here, take my handkercher and wipe thine eyes,
Whiles wretched I in thy mishaps may see
The lively portrait of my dying self.

He draweth out a bloody napkin.

Oh no, not this. Horatio, this was thine,
And when I dyed it in thy dearest blood,
This was a token 'twixt thy soul and me
That of thy death revenged I should be.
But here, take this, and this – what, my purse? –
Aye, this and that, and all of them are thine,
For all as one are our extremities.
1. Oh, see the kindness of Hieronimo!
2. This gentleness shows him a gentleman.
Hier. See, see, oh, see thy shame, Hieronimo,
See here a loving father to his son!
Behold the sorrows and the sad laments
That he delivereth for his son's decease!
If love's effects so strives in lesser things,
If love enforce such moods in meaner wits,
If love express such power in poor estates:
Hieronimo, whenas a raging sea,
Tossed with the wind and tide, o'erturneth then
The upper billows, course of waves to keep,
Whilst lesser waters labor in the deep.
Then sham'st thou not, Hieronimo, to neglect
The sweet revenge of thy Horatio?
Though on this earth justice will not be found,
I'll down to hell, and in this passion
Knock at the dismal gates of Pluto's court,
Getting by force, as once Alcides did,
A troop of Furies and tormenting hags
To torture Don Lorenzo and the rest.
Yet lest the triple-headed porter should
Deny my passage to the slimy strond,
The Thracian poet thou shalt counterfeit.
Come on, old father, be my Orpheus,
And if thou canst no notes upon the harp,
Then sound the burden of thy sore heart's grief,
Till we do gain that Proserpine may grant
Revenge on them that murdered my son.
Then will I rent and tear them thus and thus,
Shivering their limbs in pieces with my teeth.

Tear the papers.

1. O sir, my declaration!

Exit Hieronimo *and they after.*

2. Save my bond!

Enter Hieronimo.

Save my bond!
3. Alas, my lease! it cost me ten pounds,
And you, my Lord, have torn the same.
Hier. That cannot be, I gave it never a wound,
Shew me one drop of blood fall from the same.
How is it possible I should slay it then?
Tush, no; run after, catch me if you can.

Exeunt all but the Old Man.

Bazulto *remains till* Hieronimo *enters again, who, staring him in the face, speaks.*

Hier. And art thou come, Horatio, from the depth,
To ask for justice in this upper earth?
To tell thy father thou art unrevenged,
To wring more tears from Isabella's eyes,

71 **Myrmidons** a Thessalian tribe with reputation for fierceness
72 **Corsic** of Corsica; **ruthful** compassionate
77 **bewray** disclose; **blood** passion
85 **lively** living
90 **this** (this coin)
92 **extremities** extreme sufferings
100 **meaner** (1) less elevated; (2) those of a lower class
102–7 **whenas . . . Horatio?** when those of lower status present claims, why do you, of higher status, withhold yours?
109 **passion** suffering
110 **Pluto's court** the court in the underworld (as opposed to his, which has failed him)
111 **Alcides** Hercules, who for his twelfth labor descended into the underworld and conquered Cerberus
114 **triple-headed porter** Cerberus (cf. I.i.30)
115 **strond** strand (cf. I.i.27–9)
116 **Thracian poet** Orpheus
117–21 **Come . . . son** Orpheus followed his dead wife Eurydice to the underworld and with his music won Persephone's (Proserpine's) help to let her go
119–23 **Then . . . teeth** (contrasts Orpheus's sweet music with the Bacchantes' dismemberment of him; this myth divorces art from real life)
122 **rent** rend

Whose lights are dimmed with over-long laments?
Go back, my son, complain to Aeacus,
For here's no justice. Gentle boy, be gone,
For justice is exiled from the earth.
Hieronimo will bear thee company.
Thy mother cries on righteous Rhadamanth
For just revenge against the murderers.

Senex. Alas my Lord, whence springs this troubled speech?

Hier. But let me look on my Horatio.
Sweet boy, how art thou changed in death's black shade!
Had Proserpine no pity on thy youth?
But suffered thy fair crimson-colored spring
With withered winter to be blasted thus?
Horatio, thou art older than thy father.
Ah ruthless fate, that favor thus transforms!

Senex. Ah my good Lord, I am not your young son.

Hier. What, not my son? thou, then, a Fury art,
Sent from the empty kingdom of black night
To summon me to make appearance
Before grim Minos and just Rhadamanth,
To plague Hieronimo that is remiss
And seeks not vengeance for Horatio's death.

Senex. I am a grieved man, and not a ghost,
That came for justice for my murdered son.

Hier. Aye, now I know thee, now thou nam'st thy son,
Thou art the lively image of my grief.
Within thy face, my sorrows I may see.
Thy eyes are gummed with tears, thy cheeks are wan,
Thy forehead troubled, and thy mutt'ring lips
Murmur sad words abruptly broken off,
By force of windy sighs thy spirit breathes,
And all this sorrow riseth for thy son.
And selfsame sorrow feel I for my son.
Come in, old man, thou shalt to Isabel.
Lean on my arm. I thee, thou me shalt stay,
And thou, and I, and she, will sing a song,
Three parts in one, but all of discords framed –
Talk not of cords, but let us now be gone,
For with a cord Horatio was slain.

Exeunt.

[III.xiv]

Enter King of Spain, *the* Duke, Viceroy, *and* Lorenzo, Balthazar, Don Pedro, *and* Bel-imperia.

King. Go brother, it is the Duke of Castile's cause,
Salute the Viceroy in our name.

Cast. I go.

Vice. Go forth, Don Pedro, for thy nephew's sake,
And greet the Duke of Castile.

Pedro. It shall be so.

King. And now to meet these Portuguese,
For as we now are, so sometimes were these,
Kings and commanders of the western Indies.
Welcome, brave Viceroy, to the court of Spain,
And welcome, all his honorable train.
'Tis not unknown to us, for why you come,
Or have so kingly crossed the seas:
Sufficeth it, in this we note the troth
And more than common love you lend to us.
So is it that mine honorable niece
(For it beseems us now that it be known)
Already is betrothed to Balthazar:
And by appointment and our condescent
To-morrow are they to be married.
To this intent we entertain thyself,
Thy followers, their pleasure and our peace.
Speak, men of Portingale, shall it be so?
If aye, say so. If not, say flatly no.

Vice. Renowned King, I come not as thou think'st,
With doubtful followers, unresolved men,
But such as have upon thine articles
Confirmed thy motion and contented me.
Know, Sovereign, I come to solemnize
The marriage of thy beloved niece,
Fair Bel-imperia, with my Balthazar –
With thee, my son, whom sith I live to see,
Here take my crown, I give it her and thee,
And let me live a solitary life,

---

137 lights (1) eyes; (2) more generally the senses
138 Aeacus judge in the underworld (cf. I.i.33)
142 cries on pleads to; **Rhadamanth** judge in the underworld (cf. I.i.33)
149 blasted blighted
151 favor appearance
153 Fury avenging spirit (cf. I.i.65)
156 Minos judge in the underworld (cf. I.i.33)
162 lively living
171 stay sustain
172 song dirge
174 cords (puns on *chords* and *rope*)
III.xiv.7 western Indies (perhaps a reference to Portuguese Brazil taken by Spain in the late sixteenth century)
9 train accompanying retinue and attendants
11 crossed the seas (possible only if the Spanish court is sitting in Seville, which it occasionally did)
12 troth loyalty
17 condescent agreement
20 their Balthazar's and Bel-imperia's
26 motion (1) proposal; (2) intention
32 solitary retired

In ceaseless prayers,
To think how strangely Heaven hath thee preserved.
King. See brother, see, how nature strives in him!
Come, worthy Viceroy, and accompany
Thy friend with thine extremities.
A place more private fits this princely mood.
Vice. Or here or where Your Highness thinks it good.

Exeunt all but Castile *and* Lorenzo.

Cast. Nay, stay, Lorenzo, let me talk with you.
Seest thou this entertainment of these Kings?
Lor. I do, my Lord, and joy to see the same.
Cast. And knowest thou why this meeting is?
Lor. For her, my Lord, whom Balthazar doth love,
And to confirm their promised marriage.
Cast. She is thy sister?
Lor. Who, Bel-imperia?
Aye, my gracious Lord, and this is the day
That I have longed so happily to see.
Cast. Thou wouldst be loath that any fault of thine
Should intercept her in her happiness.
Lor. Heavens will not let Lorenzo err so much.
Cast. Why then, Lorenzo, listen to my words:
It is suspected and reported too,
That thou, Lorenzo, wrong'st Hieronimo,
And in his suits towards His Majesty
Still keep'st him back, and seeks to cross his suit.
Lor. That I, my Lord –?
Cast. I tell thee son, myself have heard it said,
When to my sorrow I have been ashamed
To answer for thee, though thou art my son.
Lorenzo, know'st thou not the common love
And kindness that Hieronimo hath won
By his deserts within the court of Spain?
Or seest thou not the King my brother's care
In his behalf, and to procure his health?
Lorenzo, shouldst thou thwart his passions,
And he exclaim against thee to the King,
What honor were't in this assembly,
Or what a scandal were't among the Kings
To hear Hieronimo exclaim on thee?
Tell me, and look thou tell me truly too,
Whence grows the ground of this report in court?
Lor. My Lord, it lies not in Lorenzo's power
To stop the vulgar, liberal of their tongues.
A small advantage makes a water-breach,
And no man lives that long contenteth all.
Cast. Myself have seen thee busy to keep back
Him and his supplications from the King.
Lor. Yourself, my Lord, hath seen his passions,
That ill-beseemed the presence of a King,
And for I pitied him in his distress,
I held him thence with kind and courteous words,
As free from malice to Hieronimo
As to my soul, my Lord.
Cast. Hieronimo, my son, mistakes thee then.
Lor. My gracious father, believe me so he doth.
But what's a silly man, distract in mind,
To think upon the murder of his son?
Alas, how easy is it for him to err!
But for his satisfaction and the world's,
'Twere good, my Lord, that Hieronimo and I
Were reconciled, if he misconster me.
Cast. Lorenzo thou hast said, it shall be so,
Go one of you and call Hieronimo.

Enter Balthazar *and* Bel-imperia.

Bal. Come, Bel-imperia, Balthazar's content,
My sorrow's ease and sovereign of my bliss,
Sith heaven hath ordained thee to be mine:
Disperse those clouds and melancholy looks,
And clear them up with those thy sun-bright eyes
Wherein my hope and Heaven's fair beauty lies.
Bel. My looks, my Lord, are fitting for my love,
Which, new begun, can show brighter yet.
Bal. New-kindled flames should burn as morning sun.
Bel. But not too fast, lest heat and all be done.
I see my Lord my father.
Bal. Truce, my love,
I will go salute him.
Cast. Welcome Balthazar,
Welcome brave Prince, the pledge of Castile's peace.
And welcome Bel-imperia. How now, girl?
Why com'st thou sadly to salute us thus?

---

34 **strangely** wonderfully
35 **nature . . . him** he weeps for joy
37 **extremities** extreme emotions
41 **entertainment** welcoming meeting
50 **intercept** interrupt, obstruct
56 **cross** prevent
61 **common** widespread
63 **deserts** deservings
66 **passions** laments, complaints
67 **exclaim against** denounce
74 **vulgar** common people; **liberal** loose, free
75 **advantage** opportunity; **makes** allows; **water-breach** a gap caused by water-pressure
80 **ill-beseemed** ill-fitted, was unsuitable in
87 **silly** foolish; **distract** wandering
92 **misconster** misconstrue, misunderstand (perhaps willfully)
109 **sadly** i.e., seriously, gravely

Content thyself, for I am satisfied,
It is not now as when Andrea lived,
We have forgotten and forgiven that,
And thou art graced with a happier love.
But Balthazar, here comes Hieronimo,
I'll have a word with him.

Enter Hieronimo *and a* Servant.

Hier. And where's the Duke?
Ser. Yonder.
Hier. Even so:
What new device have they devised, trow?
Pocas palabras, mild as the lamb,
Is't I will be revenged? No, I am not the man.
Cast. Welcome, Hieronimo.
Lor. Welcome, Hieronimo.
Bal. Welcome, Hieronimo.
Hier. My Lords, I thank you for Horatio.
Cast. Hieronimo, the reason that I sent
To speak with you, is this.
Hier. What, so short?
Then I'll be gone, I thank you for't.
Cast. Nay, stay, Hieronimo! Go call him, son.
Lor. Hieronimo, my father craves a word with you.
Hier. With me, sir? Why my Lord, I thought you had done.
Lor. [*aside.*] No, would he had.
Cast. Hieronimo, I hear
You find yourself aggrieved at my son
Because you have not access unto the King,
And say 'tis he that intercepts your suits.
Hier. Why, is not this a miserable thing, my Lord?
Cast. Hieronimo, I hope you have no cause,
And would be loath that one of your deserts
Should once have reason to suspect my son,
Considering how I think of you myself.
Hier. Your son Lorenzo? Whom, my noble lord?
The hope of Spain, mine honorable friend?
Grant me the combat of them, if they dare.

Draws out his sword.

I'll meet him face to face to tell me so.
These be the scandalous reports of such
As love not me, and hate my Lord too much.
Should I suspect Lorenzo would prevent
Or cross my suit, that loved my son so well?
My Lord, I am ashamed it should be said.
Lor. Hieronimo, I never gave you cause.
Hier. My good Lord, I know you did not.
Cast. There then pause,
And for the satisfaction of the world,
Hieronimo, frequent my homely house,
The Duke of Castile, Cyprian's ancient seat,
And when thou wilt, use me, my son, and it.
But here, before Prince Balthazar and me,
Embrace each other, and be perfect friends.
Hier. Aye, marry, my Lord, and shall:
Friends, quoth he? see, I'll be friends with you all:
Specially with you, my lovely Lord;
For divers causes it is fit for us
That we be friends, the world is suspicious,
And men may think what we imagine not.
Bal. Why, this is friendly done, Hieronimo.
Lor. And thus, I hope, old grudges are forgot.
Hier. What else? It were a shame it should not be so.
Cast. Come on, Hieronimo, at my request;
Let us entreat your company today.

Exeunt [*all but* Hieronimo].

Hier. Your Lordship's to command. – Pha! keep your way.
Chi mi fa più carezze che non suole,
Tradito mi ha, o tradir mi vuole.

Exit.

[III.xv]

Ghost [*of* Andrea] *and* Revenge.

Ghost. Awake, Erichtho! Cerberus, awake!
Solicit Pluto, gentle Proserpine,
To combat, Acheron and Erebus in hell!
For ne'er by Styx and Phlegethon in hell
. . . .
Nor ferried Charon to the fiery lakes 6
Such fearful sights as poor Andrea sees!
Revenge, awake!
Revenge. Awake? for why?
Ghost. Awake, Revenge, for thou art ill-advised
To sleep away! What, thou art warned to watch!
Revenge. Content thyself, and do not trouble me.
Ghost. Awake, Revenge, if love, as love hath had,

117 **device** (1) plot; (2) trick; **trow?** do you think?
118 ***Pocas palabras*** "few words"
141 **the combat of them** right to meet them in hand-to-hand combat
145 **prevent** forestall, obstruct
146 **cross** thwart
151 **homely** welcoming, homey
153 **use** make use of
167 **Pha!** (sign of contempt or disgust)

168–9 ***Chi . . . vuole*** "He who gives me more caresses than usual has betrayed me or wishes to betray me"
III.xv.1 **Erichtho** the Thessalian sorceress
3 **Erebus** primeval darkness; the child of chaos
4 **Styx and Phlegethon** rivers in the underworld
6 **Charon** ferryman over the Styx (cf. I.i.20)
8 **awake** (Revenge falling asleep when it seems revenge will never come is conventional)
11 **sleep away** sleep out

Have yet the power or prevalence in hell!
Hieronimo with Lorenzo is joined in league
And intercepts our passage to revenge.
Awake, Revenge, or we are woe-begone!

Revenge. Thus worldlings ground, what they have dreamed, upon.
Content thyself, Andrea; though I sleep,
Yet is my mood soliciting their souls.
Sufficeth thee that poor Hieronimo
Cannot forget his son Horatio.
Nor dies Revenge although he sleep awhile,
For in unquiet, quietness is feigned,
And slumb'ring is a common worldly wile.
Behold, Andrea, for an instance how
Revenge hath slept, and then imagine thou
What 'tis to be subject to destiny.

Enter a Dumb Show.

Ghost. Awake, Revenge, reveal this mystery.

Revenge. The two first, the nuptial torches bore,
As brightly burning as the mid-day's sun:
But after them doth Hymen hie as fast,
Clothed in sable, and a saffron robe,
And blows them out and quencheth them with blood,
As discontent that things continue so.

Ghost. Sufficeth me, thy meaning's understood,
And thanks to thee and those infernal powers
That will not tolerate a lover's woe.
Rest thee, for I will sit to see the rest.

Revenge. Then argue not, for thou hast thy request.
[*Exeunt.*]

Act IV

[IV.i]

Enter Bel-imperia *and* Hieronimo.

Bel. Is this the love thou bear'st Horatio?
Is this the kindness that thou counterfeits?
Are these the fruits of thine incessant tears?
Hieronimo, are these thy passions,
Thy protestations and thy deep laments,
That thou wert wont to weary men withal?
Oh, unkind father, oh, deceitful world!
With what excuses canst thou show thyself,
With what . . . .
From this dishonor and the hate of men? –
Thus to neglect the loss and life of him
Whom both my letters and thine own belief
Assures thee to be causeless slaughtered.
Hieronimo, for shame, Hieronimo,
Be not a history to after-times
Of such ingratitude unto thy son.
Unhappy mothers of such children then,
But monstrous fathers, to forget so soon
The death of those whom they with care and cost
Have tendered so, thus careless should be lost.
Myself, a stranger in respect of thee,
So loved his life, as still I wish their deaths,
Nor shall his death be unrevenged by me,
Although I bear it out for fashion's sake.
For here I swear in sight of Heaven and earth,
Shouldst thou neglect the love thou shouldst retain
And give it over and devise no more,
Myself should send their hateful souls to hell
That wrought his downfall with extremest death.

Hier. But may it be that Bel-imperia
Vows such revenge as she hath deigned to say?
Why then, I see that Heaven applies our drift,
And all the saints do sit soliciting
For vengeance on those cursed murderers.
Madam, 'tis true, and now I find it so,
I found a letter, written in your name,
And in that letter, how Horatio died.
Pardon, oh, pardon, Bel-imperia,
My fear and care in not believing it,
Nor think I thoughtless think upon a mean
To let his death be unrevenged at full.
And here I vow (so you but give consent,
And will conceal my resolution)
I will ere long determine of their deaths,
That causeless thus have murdered my son.

Bel. Hieronimo, I will consent, conceal,
And aught that may effect for thine avail,
Join with thee to revenge Horatio's death.

Hier. On then, whatsoever I devise,

18 **ground** (1) realize; (2) base beliefs
25 **wile** (1) device; (2) trick
29 **reveal . . . mystery** explain this dumb show
32 **Hymen** god of marriage; **hie** run
33 **saffron** yellow (the usual color but here covered with *sable* or black)
IV.i.2 **counterfeits** pretends
4 **passions** strong exclamations
7 **unkind** unnatural
15 **history** (1) example; (2) story, narrative
20 **tendered** (1) nurtured; (2) cherished
21 **in respect of** in comparison to (his father)
24 **bear . . . sake** endure it for the sake of appearances
27 **devise** plot
29 **extremest** most cruel
31 **deigned** (1) vouchsafed; (2) condescended
32 **applies our drift** blesses our plan, our enterprise
39 **care** caution, hesitation
40 **thoughtless think** unconcerned
44 **determine of** bring about
47 **avail** assistance

Let me entreat you grace my practices;
For why, the plot's already in mine head.
Here they are.

Enter Balthazar *and* Lorenzo.

Bal. How now, Hieronimo?
What, courting Bel-imperia?
Hier. Aye, my Lord,
Such courting as, I promise you,
She hath my heart, but you, my Lord, have hers.
Lor. But now, Hieronimo, or never,
We are to entreat your help.
Hier. My help?
Why, my good Lords, assure yourselves of me,
For you have given me cause,
Aye, by my faith have you.
Bal. It pleased you
At the entertainment of the Ambassador
To grace the King so much as with a show.
Now were your study so well furnished,
As for the passing of the first night's sport
To entertain my father with the like,
Or any such-like pleasing motion,
Assure yourself it would content them well.
Hier. Is this all?
Bal. Aye, this is all.
Hier. Why, then, I'll fit you, say no more.
When I was young, I gave my mind
And plied myself to fruitless poetry
Which though it profit the professor naught,
Yet is it passing pleasing to the world.
Lor. And how for that?
Hier. Marry, my good lord, thus –
And yet methinks you are too quick with us –
When in Toledo there I studied,
It was my chance to write a tragedy,
See here, my Lords,

He shows them a book.

Which long forgot, I found this other day.
Now would your Lordships favor me so much
As but to grace me with your acting it.
I mean each one of you to play a part;
Assure you it will prove most passing strange
And wondrous plausible to that assembly.
Bal. What, would you have us play a tragedy?
Hier. Why, Nero thought it no disparagement,
And kings and emperors have ta'en delight
To make experience of their wits in plays!
Lor. Nay, be not angry, good Hieronimo,
The Prince but asked a question.
Bal. In faith, Hieronimo, and you be in earnest,
I'll make one.
Lor. And I another.
Hier. Now, my good Lord, could you entreat
Your sister Bel-imperia to make one –
For what's a play without a woman in it?
Bel. Little entreaty shall serve me, Hieronimo,
For I must needs be employed in your play.
Hier. Why, this is well; I tell you, Lordings,
It was determined to have been acted
By gentlemen and scholars too,
Such as could tell what to speak.
Bal. And now it shall be played by princes and courtiers,
Such as can tell how to speak,
If, as it is our country manner,
You will but let us know the argument.
Hier. That shall I roundly. The chronicles of Spain
Record this written of a knight of Rhodes:
He was betrothed and wedded at the length
To one Perseda, an Italian dame,
Whose beauty ravished all that her beheld,
Especially the soul of Soliman,
Who at the marriage was the chiefest guest.
By sundry means sought Soliman to win
Perseda's love, and could not gain the same.
Then gan he break his passions to a friend,
One of his bashaws whom he held full dear;
Her had this bashaw long solicited,
And saw she was not otherwise to be won

50 **grace** aid, support
51 **For why** because
55 **heart** intentions; **hers** heart (in presumed love)
59–60 **For . . . have you** (said ironically)
62 **grace** honor
63 **furnished** stocked
66 **motion** entertainment
70 **I'll fit you** (1) I'll provide you; (2) I'll give you what you deserve
72 **fruitlesss** unsuccessful
73 **professor** he who practices or professes it
76 **quick** (1) swift in repartee and questioning; (2) insistent
84 **most . . . strange** seem most remarkable
85 **plausible** (1) agreeable; (2) fitting
86 **What . . . tragedy** (Balthazar is becoming apprehensive, having second thoughts now that a tragedy is suggested)
87 **Nero** Roman emperor who patronized and acted in plays
92 **and** if
101 **determined** (1) intended; (2) arranged
103 **could tell** (1) knew; (2) had the skill to perform
103–5 **what . . . how** (i.e., scholars know the words but courtiers know best how to express or enact them)
107 **argument** plot
108 **roundly** at once, fully; **chronicles** the play of Soliman and Perseda parallels much in Kyd's play (as in later Renaissance drama the underplot will comment on the overplot)
117 **break** divulge
118 **bashaws** pashas; Turkish officers of high rank

But by her husband's death, this knight of Rhodes,
Whom presently by treachery he slew.
She, stirred with an exceeding hate therefore,
As cause of this slew Soliman,
And to escape the bashaw's tyranny
Did stab herself: and this the tragedy.
Lor. Oh, excellent!
Bal. But say, Hieronimo,
What then became of him that was the bashaw?
Hier. Marry thus, moved with remorse of his misdeeds,
Ran to a mountain top and hung himself.
Bal. But which of us is to perform that part?
Hier. Oh, that will I, my Lords, make no doubt of it:
I'll play the murderer, I warrant you,
For I already have conceited that.
Bal. And what shall I?
Hier. Great Soliman, the Turkish emperor.
Lor. And I?
Hier. Erastus, the knight of Rhodes.
Bel. And I?
Hier. Perseda, chaste and resolute.
And here, my Lords, are several abstracts drawn,
For each of you to note your parts,
And act it as occasion's offered you.
You must provide a Turkish cap,
A black mustachio and a fauchion;
Gives a paper to Balthazar.
You with a cross like to a knight of Rhodes;
Gives another to Lorenzo.
And Madam, you must attire yourself
He giveth Bel-imperia another.
Like Phoebe, Flora, or the Huntress,
Which to your discretion shall seem best.
And as for me, my Lords, I'll look to one,
And with the ransom that the Viceroy sent
So furnish and perform this tragedy,
As all the world shall say Hieronimo
Was liberal in gracing of it so.
Bal. Hieronimo, methinks a comedy were better.
Hier. A comedy?
Fie, comedies are fit for common wits:
But to present a kingly troop withal,
Give me a stately-written tragedy,
Tragedia cothurnata, fitting kings,
Containing matter, and not common things.
My Lords, all this must be performed
As fitting for the first night's reveling.
The Italian tragedians were so sharp of wit,
That in one hour's meditation
They would perform anything in action.
Lor. And well it may, for I have seen the like
In Paris, 'mongst the French tragedians.
Hier. In Paris? Mass, and well remembered!
There's one thing more that rests for us to do.
Bal. What's that, Hieronimo? forget not anything.
Hier. Each one of us must act his part
In unknown languages,
That it may breed the more variety.
As you, my Lord, in Latin, I in Greek,
You in Italian, and for because I know
That Bel-imperia hath practiced the French,
In courtly French shall all her phrases be.
Bel. You mean to try my cunning then, Hieronimo.
Bal. But this will be a mere confusion,
And hardly shall we all be understood.
Hier. It must be so, for the conclusion
Shall prove the invention and all was good:
And I myself in an oration,
And with a strange and wondrous show besides,
That I will have there behind a curtain,
Assure yourself shall make the matter known.
And all shall be concluded in one scene,
For there's no pleasure ta'en in tediousness.
Bal. [*Aside to Lorenzo.*] How like you this?
Lor. Why thus, my Lord,
We must resolve to soothe his humors up.
Bal. On then, Hieronimo, farewell till soon.
Hier. You'll ply this gear?
Lor. I warrant you.
Exeunt all but Hieronimo.
Hier. Why, so.

---

134 **conceited** (1) envisaged, imagined; (2) planned
141 **abstracts** outlines; **drawn** written out
144 **Turkish cap** fez
145 **fauchion** broad curved Turkish sword
148 **Huntress** Diana, goddess of the hunt
150 **look to** prepare
154 **gracing** adorning, presenting
158 **kingly troop** royal audience
160 ***Tragedia cothurnata*** the most serious Athenian tragedy (in which actors wear buskins, or cothurnata, thick-soled boots)
161 **matter** substance
165–6 **one . . . action** (refers to improvisational *commedia dell'arte*)
170 **rests** remains
173 **unknown** foreign (it is unclear that other languages were actually used; they could be, since the plot has already been given. Either way, the audience needs to exercise imagination since the plot is conveyed through other languages or the plot is clear but the other languages imagined)
179 **cunning** skill
183 **invention** basic idea
185 **strange . . . show** (i.e., Horatio's body)
192 **soothe . . . up** indulge his whims
194 **ply . . . gear** carry out this business; **warrant** assure

Now shall I see the fall of Babylon,
Wrought by the Heavens in this confusion.
And if the world like not this tragedy,
Hard is the hap of old Hieronimo.

Exit.

[IV.ii]

Enter Isabella *with a weapon.*

Isab. Tell me no more! Oh, monstrous homicides!
Since neither piety nor pity moves
The king to justice or compassion,
I will revenge myself upon this place
Where thus they murdered my beloved son.

She cuts down the arbor.

Down with these branches and these loathsome boughs
Of this unfortunate and fatal pine:
Down with them Isabella, rent them up
And burn the roots from whence the rest is sprung.
I will not leave a root, a stalk, a tree,
A bough, a branch, a blossom, nor a leaf,
No, not an herb within this garden plot –
Accursed complot of my misery.
Fruitless forever may this garden be,
Barren the earth, and blissless whosoever
Imagines not to keep it unmanured!
An eastern wind commixed with noisome airs
Shall blast the plants and the young saplings,
The earth with serpents shall be pestered,
And passengers, for fear to be infect,
Shall stand aloof, and looking at it, tell,
"There, murdered, died the son of Isabel."
Aye, here he died, and here I him embrace.
See where his ghost solicits with his wounds
Revenge on her that should revenge his death.
Hieronimo, make haste to see thy son,
For sorrow and despair hath cited me
To hear Horatio plead with Rhadamanth.
Make haste, Hieronimo, to hold excused
Thy negligence in pursuit of their deaths,
Whose hateful wrath bereaved him of his breath.
Ah nay, thou dost delay their deaths,
Forgives the murderers of thy noble son,
And none but I bestir me – to no end.
And as I curse this tree from further fruit,
So shall my womb be cursed for his sake,
And with this weapon will I wound the breast,

She stabs herself.

The hapless breast, that gave Horatio suck.

[*Exit.*]

[IV.iii]

Enter Hieronimo; *he knocks up the curtain. Enter the* Duke of Castile.

Cast. How now, Hieronimo, where's your fellows,
That you take all this pain?
Hier. Oh, sir, it is for the author's credit
To look that all things may go well:
But good my Lord, let me entreat your Grace
To give the King the copy of the play:
This is the argument of what we show.
Cast. I will, Hieronimo.
Hier. One thing more, my good Lord.
Cast. What's that?
Hier. Let me entreat your Grace,
That when the train are passed into the gallery
You would vouchsafe to throw me down the key.
Cast. I will, Hieronimo.

Exit Castile.

Hier. What, are you ready, Balthazar?
Bring a chair and a cushion for the King.

Enter Balthazar *with a chair.*

Well done Balthazar, hang up the title,
Our scene is Rhodes; what, is your beard on?
Bal. Half on, the other is in my hand.
Hier. Despatch for shame, are you so long?

Exit Balthazar.

195 Babylon (1) confusion with Babel; (2) as Babylon, city of sin punished by God (Isaiah 13; Jeremiah 2); (3) Babylon proverbial for Rome (the papacy) to which Spain paid allegiance and the unity of which caused Spain to be the enemy of Protestant England
198 hap fortune
IV.ii.7 unfortunate ominous
8 rent tear
13 complot conspiracy
16 unmanured uncultivated
17 noisome (1) annoying; (2) poisonous
18 blast kill
19 pestered destroyed
20 passengers passers-by; **infect** infected
27 cited summoned
32–3 delay... Forgives (Hieronimo's craftiness has eluded her)
IV.iii s.d. *knocks* hangs (to allow tableau with Horatio's body to be set up)
1 fellows (i.e., fellow actors)
12 gallery (perhaps in the long or great hall used for staging plays in country houses)
17 hang up (Elizabethan theaters probably used signboards to indicate settings otherwise only stated; Sidney complains of this in his *Defense of Poetry*)
18 beard (perhaps a line to distract the actors; the normalcy of the remark is at odds with Hieronimo's actual purpose for the staging)
20 Despatch hurry up

Bethink thyself, Hieronimo,
Recall thy wits, recompt thy former wrongs
Thou hast received by murder of thy son,
And lastly, not least, how Isabel,
Once his mother and thy dearest wife,
All woe-begone for him hath slain herself.
Behooves thee then, Hieronimo, to be revenged.
The plot is laid of dire revenge.
On, then, Hieronimo, pursue revenge,
For nothing wants but acting of revenge.
Exit Hieronimo.

[IV.iv]

Enter Spanish King, Viceroy, *the* Duke of Castile, *and their train.*

King. Now, Viceroy, shall we see the tragedy
Of Soliman the Turkish Emperor,
Performed of pleasure by your son the Prince,
My nephew, Don Lorenzo, and my niece.
Vice. Who, Bel-imperia?
King. Aye, and Hieronimo our Marshal,
At whose request they deign to do't themselves:
These be our pastimes in the court of Spain.
Here, brother, you shall be the book-keeper:
This is the argument of that they show.
He giveth him a book.

Gentlemen, this play of Hieronimo in sundry languages, was thought good to be set down in English more largely, for the easier understanding to every public reader.

Enter Balthazar, Bel-imperia, *and* Hieronimo.

Bal. *Bashaw, that Rhodes is ours, yield heavens the honor,*
And holy Mahomet, our sacred prophet:
And be thou graced with every excellence
That Soliman can give, or thou desire.
But thy desert in conquering Rhodes is less
Than in reserving this fair Christian nymph,
Perseda, blissful lamp of excellence,
Whose eyes compel, like powerful adamant,
The warlike heart of Soliman to wait.
King. See, Viceroy, that is Balthazar your son
That represents the emperor Soliman:
How well he acts his amorous passion.
Vice. Aye, Bel-imperia hath taught him that.
Cast. That's because his mind runs all on Bel-imperia.
Hier. *Whatever joy earth yields betide your Majesty.*
Bal. *Earth yields no joy without Perseda's love.*
Hier. *Let then Perseda on your grace attend.*
Bal. *She shall not wait on me, but I on her.*
Drawn by the influence of her lights, I yield.
But let my friend, the Rhodian knight, come forth,
Erasto, dearer than my life to me,
That he may see Perseda, my beloved.

Enter Erasto.

King. Here comes Lorenzo; look upon the plot,
And tell me, brother, what part plays he?
Bel. *Ah my Erasto, welcome to Perseda.*
Lor. *Thrice happy is Erasto that thou liv'st,*
Rhodes' loss is nothing to Erasto's joy.
Sith his Perseda lives, his life survives.
Bal. *Ah, Bashaw, here is love between Erasto*
And fair Perseda, sovereign of my soul.
Hier. *Remove Erasto, mighty Soliman,*
And then Perseda will be quickly won.
Bal. *Erasto is my friend, and while he lives*
Perseda never will remove her love.
Hier. *Let not Erasto live to grieve great Soliman.*
Bal. *Dear is Erasto in our princely eye.*
Hier. *But if he be your rival, let him die.*
Bal. *Why, let him die, so love commandeth me.*
Yet grieve I that Erasto should so die.
Hier. *Erasto, Soliman saluteth thee,*
And lets thee wit by me His Highness' will,
Which is, thou shouldst be thus employed.
Stab him.
Bel. *Aye, me,*
Erasto! see, Soliman, Erasto's slain!
Bal. *Yet liveth Soliman to comfort thee.*
Fair queen of beauty, let not favor die,
But with a gracious eye behold his grief,
That with Perseda's beauty is increased,
If by Perseda grief be not released.
Bel. *Tyrant, desist soliciting vain suits,*
Relentless are mine ears to thy laments,
As thy butcher is pitiless and base,

22 recompt recall to mind
30 wants is lacking
IV.iv.3 of at their
9 book-keeper prompter (who kept the only copy of the entire book, or playscript, in the Elizabethan theater)
10 s.d. *book* (cf. the other book on stage – Seneca's *Works* in III.xiii)
16 *reserving* protecting, preserving
18 *adamant* magnetic loadstone
19 *wait* attend on her
20–2 See . . . passion (Hieronimo's audience sees both the actors and their parts – the parallels he wishes them to see)
25 *betide* befall
29 *lights* eyes
33 plot i.e., the argument already distributed
37 *to* i.e., compared to
55 *favor* i.e., your love; your special attention

Which seized on my Erasto, harmless knight.
Yet by thy power thou thinkest to command,
And to thy power Perseda doth obey.
But were she able, thus she would revenge
Thy treacheries on thee, ignoble Prince.
Stab him.
And on herself she would be thus revenged.
Stab herself.
King. Well said, old Marshal, this was bravely done!
Hier. But Bel-imperia plays Perseda well.
Vice. Were this in earnest, Bel-imperia,
You would be better to my son than so.
King. But now what follows for Hieronimo?
Hier. Marry, this follows for Hieronimo:
Here break we off our sundry languages
And thus conclude I in our vulgar tongue.
Haply you think, but bootless are your thoughts,
That this is fabulously counterfeit,
And that we do as all tragedians do:
To die today, for fashioning our scene,
The death of Ajax, or some Roman peer,
And in a minute starting up again,
Revive to please tomorrow's audience.
No, Princes, know I am Hieronimo,
The hopeless father of a hapless son,
Whose tongue is tuned to tell his latest tale,
Not to excuse gross errors in the play.
I see your looks urge instance of these words,
Behold the reason urging me to this:
Shows his dead son.
See here my show, look on this spectacle.
Here lay my hope, and here my hope hath end.
Here lay my heart, and here my heart was slain.
Here lay my treasure, here my treasure lost.
Here lay my bliss, and here my bliss bereft.
But hope, heart, treasure, joy and bliss,
All fled, failed, died, yea, all decayed with this.
From forth these wounds came breath that gave me life,
They murdered me that made these fatal marks.
The cause was love, whence grew this mortal hate.
The hate, Lorenzo and young Balthazar,
The love, my son to Bel-imperia.
But night, the coverer of accursed crimes,
With pitchy silence hushed these traitors' harms
And lent them leave, for they had sorted leisure
To take advantage in my garden plot
Upon my son, my dear Horatio.
There merciless they butchered up my boy,
In black dark night, to pale dim cruel death.
He shrieks, I heard, and yet methinks I hear,
His dismal outcry echo in the air.
With soonest speed I hasted to the noise,
Where hanging on a tree I found my son,
Through-girt with wounds, and slaughtered as you see.
And grieved I, think you, at this spectacle?
Speak, Portuguese, whose loss resembles mine:
If thou canst weep upon thy Balthazar,
'Tis like I wailed for my Horatio.
And you, my Lord, whose reconciled son
Marched in a net, and thought himself unseen,
And rated me for brainsick lunacy,
With "God amend that mad Hieronimo!" –
How can you brook our play's catastrophe?
And here behold this bloody handkercher,
Which at Horatio's death I weeping dipped
Within the river of his bleeding wounds.
It as propitious, see, I have reserved,
And never hath it left my bloody heart,
Soliciting remembrance of my vow,
With these, oh, these accursèd murderers,
Which now performed, my heart is satisfied.
And to this end the bashaw I became
That might revenge me on Lorenzo's life,
Who therefore was appointed to the part
And was to represent the knight of Rhodes,
That I might kill him more conveniently.
So, Viceroy, was this Balthazar, thy son,
That Soliman which Bel-imperia
In person of Perseda murdered:
Solely appointed to that tragic part,

68 **Well said** (compliment to Hieronimo for his script)
75 **vulgar** vernacular
76 **Haply** perhaps; **bootless** unavailing
77 **fabulously counterfeit** fictionally presented
79 **for . . . scene** for enacting our play
85 **latest** i.e., last
87 **instance** explanation
89 **show** tableau
96 **From . . . life** my life's breath left me when wounds were made on his body
102 **harms** evil acts
103 **sorted** sought out
107 **pale** hide
112 **Through-girt** pierced through
117 **reconciled son** Balthazar (who is reconciled to the Viceroy his father)
118 **Marched . . . net** kept himself concealed (proverbial)
119 **rated** berated
120 **"God . . . Hieronimo"** (cf. Lorenzo's advice to the King at III.xii.85–9, 96–8)
125 **propitious** good omen

That she might slay him that offended her.
Poor Bel-imperia missed her part in this,
For though the story saith she should have died,
Yet I of kindness, and of care to her,
Did otherwise determine of her end.
But love of him whom they did hate too much
Did urge her resolution to be such.
And Princes, now behold Hieronimo,
Author and actor in this tragedy,
Bearing his latest fortune in his fist:
And will as resolute conclude his part
As any of the actors gone before.
And gentles, thus I end my play:
Urge no more words, I have no more to say.

He runs to hang himself.

King. Oh, hearken, Viceroy! Hold, Hieronimo!
Brother, my nephew and thy son are slain!
Vice. We are betrayed! My Balthazar is slain!
Break ope the doors, run, save Hieronimo!

[*They break in, and hold* Hieronimo.]

Hieronimo, do but inform the King of these events,
Upon mine honor thou shalt have no harm.
Hier. Viceroy, I will not trust thee with my life,
Which I this day have offered to my son.
Accursed wretch,
Why stayest thou him that was resolved to die?
King. Speak, traitor; damned, bloody murderer, speak!
For now I have thee I will make thee speak:
Why hast thou done this undeserving deed?
Vice. Why hast thou murdered my Balthazar?
Cast. Why hast thou butchered both my children thus?
Hier. Oh, good words!
As dear to me was my Horatio
As yours, or yours, or yours, my Lord, to you.
My guiltless son was by Lorenzo slain,
And by Lorenzo and that Balthazar
Am I at last revenged thoroughly,
Upon whose souls may Heavens be yet avenged
With greater far than these afflictions.
Cast. But who were thy confederates in this?
Vice. That was thy daughter Bel-imperia,
For by her hand my Balthazar was slain.
I saw her stab him.
King. Why speak'st thou not?
Hier. What lesser liberty can Kings afford
Than harmless silence? then afford it me:
Sufficeth I may not, nor I will not tell thee.
King. Fetch forth the tortures.
Traitor as thou art, I'll make thee tell.
Hier. Indeed,
Thou may'st torment me, as his wretched son
Hath done in murdering my Horatio,
But never shalt thou force me to reveal
The thing which I have vowed inviolate.
And therefore, in despite of all thy threats,
Pleased with their deaths, and eased with their revenge,
First take my tongue, and afterwards my heart.

[*He bites out his tongue.*]

King. Oh, monstrous resolution of a wretch!
See, Viceroy, he hath bitten forth his tongue
Rather than to reveal what we required.
Cast. Yet can he write.
King. And if in this he satisfy us not,
We will devise th' extremest kind of death
That ever was invented for a wretch.

Then he makes signs for a knife to mend his pen.

Cast. Oh, he would have a knife to mend his pen.
Vice. Here, and advise thee that thou write the troth.
King. Look to my brother! save Hieronimo.

He with a knife stabs the Duke and himself.

What age hath ever heard such monstrous deeds?
My brother, and the whole succeeding hope
That Spain expected after my decease!
Go bear his body hence, that we may mourn
The loss of our beloved brother's death,
That he may be entombed whate'er befall:
I am the next, the nearest, last of all.
Vice. And thou, Don Pedro, do the like for us,
Take up our hapless son, untimely slain:
Set me with him, and he with woeful me,
Upon the mainmast of a ship unmanned,
And let the wind and tide haul me along
To Scylla's barking and untamed gulf,
Or to the loathsome pool of Acheron,
To weep my want for my sweet Balthazar:
Spain hath no refuge for a Portingale.

The trumpets sound a dead march, the King of Spain *mourning after his brother's body, and the* Viceroy of Portingale *bearing the body of his son.*

140 **missed her part** strayed from the script
153 **Hold** (1) stop; (2) arrest
155 **betrayed** (ironic; his own son had already betrayed him)
156 **Break ope** (Hieronimo had requested the doors be locked); **save** (cf. line 153)
157 **inform** issue testimony
200 **troth** truth
213 **haul** drive
214 **Scylla's . . . gulf** (Scylla and Charybdis were rocks between Italy and Sicily; Scylla was thought to be accompanied by barking dogs)
215 **Acheron** (cf. I.i.19)
216 **my want for** my loss of

[IV.v]

Ghost [*of* Andrea] *and* Revenge.

Ghost. Aye, now my hopes have end in their effects,
When blood and sorrow finish my desires:
Horatio murdered in his father's bower,
Vild Serberine by Pedringano slain,
False Pedringano hanged by quaint device,
Fair Isabella by herself misdone,
Prince Balthazar by Bel-imperia stabbed,
The Duke of Castile and his wicked son
Both done to death by old Hieronimo,
My Bel-imperia fall'n as Dido fell,
And good Hieronimo slain by himself:
Aye, these were spectacles to please my soul.
Now will I beg at lovely Proserpine,
That by the virtue of her princely doom
I may consort my friends in pleasing sort,
And on my foes work just and sharp revenge.
I'll lead my friend Horatio through those fields
Where never-dying wars are still inured.
I'll lead fair Isabella to that train
Where pity weeps but never feeleth pain.
I'll lead my Bel-imperia to those joys
That vestal virgins and fair queens possess.
I'll lead Hieronimo where Orpheus plays,
Adding sweet pleasure to eternal days.
But say, Revenge, for thou must help or none,
Against the rest how shall my hate be shown?
Revenge. This hand shall haul them down to deepest hell,
Where none but Furies, bugs and tortures dwell.
Ghost. Then, sweet Revenge, do this at my request,
Let me be judge, and doom them to unrest.
Let loose poor Tityus from the vulture's gripe,
And let Don Cyprian supply his room.
Place Don Lorenzo on Ixion's wheel,
And let the lover's endless pains surcease
(Juno forgets old wrath and grants him ease).
Hang Balthazar about Chimaera's neck,
And let him there bewail his bloody love,
Repining at our joys that are above.
Let Serberine go roll the fatal stone,
And take from Sisyphus his endless moan.
False Pedringano, for his treachery,
Let him be dragged through boiling Acheron,
And there live, dying still in endless flames,
Blaspheming gods and all their holy names.
Revenge. Then haste we down to meet thy friends and foes,
To place thy friends in ease, the rest in woes:
For here, though death hath end their misery,
I'll there begin their endless tragedy.

Exeunt.

IV.v.4 **Vild** vile
5 **quaint** cunning, shrewd
6 **misdone** slain
10 **as Dido fell** Dido committed suicide after losing Aeneas (*Aeneid* IV)
14 **doom** judgment
15 **consort** accompany
18 **inured** carried on
19 **train** company
22 **vestal virgins** (consecrated to Vesta, they took a vow of chastity)
23 **Orpheus** (cf. III.xiii.117)
28 **bugs** bugbears, imagined horrors
30 **doom** sentence
31 **Tityus** a giant whose sins were punished by two vultures devouring his liver; **gripe** grip
32 **Don Cyprian** Duke of Castile (see II.i.45–8; II.iii.15); **supply his room** take his place
33 **Ixion's wheel** of perpetual punishment (cf. I.i.66)
36 **Chimaera's** (Greek mythological monster, with a lion's head, goat's body, and dragon's tail)
40 **Sisyphus** legendary King of Crete condemned to roll a large stone uphill eternally
43 **still** continually, forever
47 **end** ended

Arden of Faversham

Anonymous

Frontispiece to the 1633 Quarto, illustrating the murder of Arden at the "game of tables."

The bloody killing of Thomas Arden as he played backgammon in his parlor, situated on lands once belonging to the Abbey of Faversham, was one of the most famous – and most enduring – crimes of all Tudor England. The incident was variously interpreted. The first extant account is recorded in the *Breviat Chronicle* for 1551:

> This year on S[aint] Valentine's day at Faversham in Kent was committed a shameful murder, for one Arden a gentleman was by the consent of his wife murdered, wherefore she was burned at Canterbury, and there was hanged in chains for that murder and at Faversham (two) hanged in chains [one of them Arden's man-servant Michael Saunderson, who was hanged, drawn, and quartered], and a woman burned [Elizabeth Stafford, Alice Arden's day-servant], and in Smithfield [in London] was hanged one Mosby and his sister [Susan] for the murder also.

Six people were executed to even the score. The goods of the criminals in this cause célèbre, valued at £184.10s.4½d. along with some jewels, were forfeited to the Faversham treasury; the city of Canterbury was paid 43 shillings for executing George Bradshaw and for burning Alice Arden alive. Only two of the accomplices, the painter William Blackbourne and the hired assassin Shakebag, who probably actually did the killing, escaped.

A quarter-century later, in 1577, Edward White entered in the Stationers' Register the right to print the second book he would sell in St. Paul's Churchyard. Entitled *A Cruel Murder done in Kent*, it was probably based on the Arden crime. This seems to have led in turn to a play, *Murderous Michael*, staged at Elizabeth's court in 1579. Both works are now lost, but they were a part of a wave of plays based on actual and often sensational murders such as *A Warning for Fair Women*, in which actors in the allegorical roles of History, Tragedy, Comedy, Chastity, Lust, and Divine Providence played alongside a second cast enacting the 1573 murder of George Saunders by his wife, her lover, another woman, and her servant. Indeed, the *Arden* play (whose author has never been identified) was so potentially lucrative that Abel Jeffes rushed a pirated text into print before White and the Stationers' Company had to confiscate all the copies and destroy them. White's *Arden of Faversham* follows so closely the account of the crime and the marginalia in Holinshed's *Chronicles* (1587) that the play may well have been written (and performed) around 1588; the fact that neither Jeffes nor White published the play until 1592 suggests that it was so popular it was only then being cycled out of the repertory of the playing company that owned the script – a number of such companies, including Pembroke's Men, were then breaking up due to increased competition and increased epidemics of plague. The play was printed again in 1599, during a flurry of play publication in the wake of a government crackdown subsequent to the insurrection of the Earl of Essex, and again in 1633 to coincide with a ballad claiming to be Alice Arden's confession. But the story was by then commonplace: it could be found in the Faversham Wardmote Book, Thomas Southhouse's survey, Edward Hasted's history of Kent, Edward Jacob's *History of the Town and Port of Faversham*, Henry Machyn's diary, and Thomas Heywood's pageant *Troia Britannica.* It illustrated justice in works by Thomas Beard in 1597 and John Taylor in 1630. It was included in a list of such casualties as fire and plague and such wonders as Siamese twins and dolphins by Richard Baker in 1643. In the early eighteenth century the story was in a chapbook; in 1736 it became a puppet show; by 1799 it was performed as a ballet at Sadler's Wells. And as recently as 1969 it was the basis of a novel.

As a play, *Arden of Faversham* is thoroughly grounded in the actual, the local, and the domestic although by implication it deals also with politics, society, the economy, and religion – it spreads out to incorporate all phases of Tudor life. In fact, even as the play is based on a real event, it blurs the authenticity of its account with artful representation; it isolates and then confounds what Roger Chartier has called the two main branches of cultural history. By complicating events, it problematizes them. Thomas Arden, for instance, is portrayed as a greedy and avaricious landlord; yet he is also called gentle and harmless. He seems by turns to be aggressively cruel, deliberately self-isolated, and even suicidal. His initial journey to London suggests a kind of evasiveness and even willed absence which in the end is undermined by the ineradicable power of his presence, in his home and through the imprint his corpse makes in the ground long after his death. While his submissiveness and his wife's forceful strategies upset any traditional hierarchies of gender relations, Alice Arden's determination often wavers and her lust alternates with indecision. Her lover Mosby meanwhile is divided between his love of Alice and his intention to use marriage to her only to seize her inheritance. Together these two characters raise fundamental questions about social injustice as well as questions about individual misjudgment. Not only are their motives questioned, but also the very capacity – or ineptitude – of ordinary people to resolve their concerns in extraordinary circumstances, sometimes of their own making.

The action of the play centers on nine different attempts to take Arden's life: Mosby and Alice employing a counterfeit portrait and poisoned broth; attacks by assassins on a London street, in a London lodging, on the road to Rochester, and in the fog; Mosby and Alice provoking violence through a display of affection; Black Will's attempt to stab Arden at the fair; and the final descent of the conspirators at Arden's home. Arden is everyone's target, but he is thereby made the unifying device of an intricate network of relationships: of Alice and Mosby; of Michael and Clark for Susan (who is serving Mosby); of Alice with Greene and Arden; of Arden and Franklin and Michael; of Greene with Black Will and Shakebag but also with Mosby and Michael – the would-be killers spin their own webs of deceit, frustration, and failure. For the playwright does not seem interested so much in the bungling attempts to kill Arden – nor even, until the end, in his actual death – as in the psychology of those who want or need to kill. Their conspiracies and counter-conspiracies are creative, foolish, violent, intimidating, and always full of distrust. Even as they team up, they split apart and, with them, both the household and the merchant community fragment as well. Like the plans and oaths that are continually made and just as continually broken, theirs is a disintegrating world. What the playwright probes, then, through their thoughts and actions – which are never consonant – is the unstable culture they represent.

How much playhouse audiences knew of the real Thomas Arden (or Ardern) is not now known, but his actual life can establish one guide to measuring and interpreting events in the play and their significance. He was born in 1508 in Norwich where his mother went begging daily; but because the authorities were lenient with her, she must have come from a family of some means. Such a heritage may have caused young Thomas to become quickly a man on the make. By 1537 he was in London as one of the clerks for Edward North, Clerk of the Parliament, where he was copying out Parliamentary acts for Henry VIII; by 1539 he was under-steward to Sir Thomas Cheyne, Lord Warden of the Cinque Ports, and married to North's stepdaughter Alice. At the time of their marriage, he was forty; she was sixteen (she was thirty when Arden was murdered). Arden began styling himself gentleman and when Alice took Thomas Morsby as her lover, he began mocking the cuckold's humble origins, no doubt to overcome his own similar ambitions as a fortune-hunter through marriage. Why the three remained friends may be explained by John Stow:

> Arden perceiving right well their familiarity to be much greater than their honesty, was yet so greatly given to seek his advantage, and cared so little how he came by it that in hope of attaining some benefit of the Lord North by means of this Morsby who could do so much with him, he winked at that shameful disorder and both permitted and also invited him very often to be in his house.

Around 1540 Arden was appointed the King's Collector of Customs for Faversham; by September 1543 he was also appointed the King's Comptroller for the nearby port of Sandwich. Both were important towns; Archbishop Cranmer visited Faversham in 1540, the year of Cranmer's Bible, and in 1545 Henry VIII spent the night there. Arden concentrated all his efforts on Kent and, it would seem, on buying land. In 1540 he acquired the five-acre site of the Carmelite friary in Sandwich; at the end of 1544 he bought the site of the virtually demolished Faversham Abbey from Cheyne (and moved into the gatehouse, still standing at 80 Abbey Street). He bought another nine acres from the former abbot, ten acres in Thornmead, the manor of Ellenden, and some land in Hernhill in 1543. By 1545 he owned the manor of Otterpool in Lympne and Sellindge, formerly held by Sir Thomas Wyatt, and land in the parish of Saltwood and property in the suburbs of Canterbury that belonged to the Archbishop. At some point along the way he purchased Flood Mill and Surrenden Croft. He also intimidated Walter Morleyn into handing over to him 300 acres of land. He became mayor of Faversham in 1548 but then, on December 22, 1550, he was disenfranchised as a jurat. Two days before that, he had drawn up his will; two months later, he was murdered. Alice Arden argued that his evil practices would cause no one to inquire after his death, while others in Faversham thought that providence itself insured that his death could not be hidden for long. Many reports circulated about Arden during his life in Faversham: that he served North and the Privy Council as their *agent provocateur*; that he amassed wealth by shady dealing; that he acquired property through smuggling. It was also said that he had taken from a poor widow the field in which his body was eventually found and that she had predicted he would come to a violent end. Holinshed records all these strains, seeing Arden as a mercenary husband, a grasping landlord, and the King's man in Faversham.

Thomas Arden is thus for the playwright a ready-made way to examine not only a complicated personality from multiple perspectives – as hero, agent, villain, and victim – but as a means to survey contemporary cultural practices as well. The idea of land as a commodity subject to sale rather than preserved for farming was something new, for instance. So was the dissolution of the abbey, which had owned perhaps a quarter of the countryside, permitting nobility and gentlemen to increase their landholdings and with it social and economic stature. Debasement of coinage, rising prices, bad harvests, and widespread enclosures of common land for pasturage also radically shifted economic practices and allowed "new men" to invest in the new land market. Anxiety among those who had farmed the land could reach a high pitch; the *Book of Private Prayer* in 1553 even included a "Prayer for Landlords": "We heartily pray thee, to send thy holy Spirit into the hearts of them that possess the grounds, pastures, and dwelling places of the earth, that they... may not rack and stretch out the rents of their houses and lands... after the manner of covetous worldlings." In language strikingly similar to that Reede offers in the play, Robert Crowley writes of landlords in *An Information and Petición* (1548) that "if any of [the poor] perish through your default, know then for certain that the blood of them shall be required at your hands. If the impotent creatures perish for lack of necessaries, you are the murderers, for you have their inheritance and do not minister unto them," while in 1551 – the year of Arden's death – the author of *The Way to Wealth* condemned such "Men without conscience. Men utterly void of God's favor."

The play consistently raises such pressing concerns: drawing heavily on the spirit of the reign of Edward II, both the recycling of Church property and rack renting are central concerns. Greene collaborates in Arden's death because "My living is my life." Michael's courtship of Susan is linked with his brother's farm at Bolton. Arden establishes his self-worth to Franklin by his property even as Mosby tells Arden that Greene contests it. Arden sees his wife too as his property, both in the earlier sense of the conditions that establish welfare and place and in the emergent capitalist sense of ownership and investment; his behavior seems natural in a play which continually commodifies people by estimating their worth. Mosby, in turn, is seen by Arden as a man who can prevent him from building his estate. The playwright underscores this by having Arden killed on his own property, blood staining his home, and by harboring the assassins in his countinghouse. The world of *Arden of Faversham* is often a world of selfish entrepreneurs. This new sense of realigning society along monetary lines, rather than inherited social rank that had long characterized England, is seen to deconstruct that society. Everyone, like everything, is for sale. Michael joins the conspiracy in return for Susan, just as Clarke provides poison in return for her. Greene gets £10 and a promise of more for killing Arden and he hires others to do it. Mosby is more interested in Alice's inheritance than Alice, and he constantly quarrels with her in terms of "credit," "advantages," and "wealth." Such deconstructing personal relationships foreshadow the deconstruction of the community of Faversham and the very fabric of Tudor society. Alice sees only gossipy "narrow-prying neighbors" and "the biting speech of men," while Arden notes that men "mangle credit with their wounding words" and warns Mosby of "common talk" about his affair with Alice. In the traditional hierarchical and stratified society he would restore by having achieved financial success – in a play highly conscious of rank from Lord Cheyne at the apex to Reede at the bottom – Arden fails to recognize how his own actions compromise, subvert, and destroy the system he means only to reinforce (and on which he relies). All the others follow suit. While Franklin lures Arden because he resides on London's highly fashionable Aldersgate Street, the playwright clearly sees him as smug with his "most bounteous and liberal" hospitality and his blindness causes us to question the wisdom of his Epilogue. Reede's helplessness, moreover, is only a step ahead of such dangerous masterless men as Black Will and Shakebag for whom society also no longer provides, and all of them underscore the consequences of Arden's greed and Franklin's willed innocence. Indeed, men of amoral ambition and complacent selfishness were just as frightening to the first audiences of this play as those in the underworld.

This disintegration of public matters foreshadows private ones. There is a way in which the intense passion of Alice's love for Mosby is transferred into her passion for killing Arden; one consummation overtakes and substitutes for the other. Her lust for Mosby is similar in degree but not in kind to his lust for her money and position. Yet both feign otherwise: "what is life but love?" she asks Mosby in their hypocritical exchange; "And love shall last as long as life remains, And life shall end before my love depart" and he replies in kind: "Why, what's love, without true constancy?" What both react *against* is Arden: she would kill him because he "hinder[s] Mosby's love and mine"; Mosby kills Arden in revenge for "the pressing iron you told me of" – reminding him of his lower social status while (in a play of ironies) he is caught because of a stolen purse (mirroring his victim). The thoughts and speeches of both Alice and Mosby destabilize and their conversations often result in their speaking past each other, their minds (for different reasons) alike caught up in pride, despair, and guilt.

Such a potentially sensitive portrayal of Alice seems to have little to do with the proclamation on the play's title-page that she is meant primarily to display "the great malice and dissimulation of a wicked woman, the unsatiable desire of filthy lust." For viewed another way, Alice is the victim of an enforced marriage and the inability to seek divorce. Whereas the Catholic church had once permitted separation *a mensa et thoro* (from bed and board) for reason of cruelty, the newly Established Church under Edward VI made marriage indissoluble and forced partners to remain together despite any disharmony. Puritans, too, argued that man could not put asunder a coupling performed with the blessing of God; in the words of the well-known London preacher Henry Smith,

> If [man and wife] might be separated for discord, some would make a commodity of strife; but now they are not best to be contentious, for this law will hold their noses together, till weariness make them leave struggling, like two spaniels which are coupled in a chain, at last they learn to go together, because they may not go asunder.

Martin Bucer, Professor of Divinity at Cambridge, addressed Edward VI in *De Regno Christi* remarking that to deny the possibility of divorce would result in "whoredoms and adulteries, and worse things than these," "throwing men headlong into these evils."

A further result of such restrictions was the fear of murder as a way out of a bad marriage. In 1574 a man from Barnston complained his wife repeatedly tried to kill him. In 1590 one Philpott reported that the man living with his wife, John Chandler, had hired Rowland Gryffyth to murder him. In 1591 a Mistress Page of Plymouth was executed with her lover and two other men for the murder of her husband. In the county of Kent, about twenty women were convicted of murder in the surviving assize records extant from the whole of Elizabeth's reign, although only four of them involved a woman accused of murdering her husband. Clearly, however, this was not unknown, and Essex county records show the fear of many men who did not bring their cases to trial. According to Edwardian statute, such an act was petty treason – "when a servant slayeth his master, or a wife her husband" – linking Alice not only with Mosby but with Michael. That such behavior was condemned as treason became even more apparent between the time of Arden's death and the play, for Mary Stuart was accused of killing her husband Lord Darnley and then, in England, pursuing Elizabeth I much as Alice pursues Arden: "the Scottish Queen conspired with her Majesty's subjects to have her murdered in the field, in the chamber, in her bed, with daggers, with pistols, with poison, or any other way." Mary Stuart did not succeed as Alice does, but that did not lessen the fear or danger of such behavior – nor the accusation of treason for which she was finally beheaded. In a lesser sense, and metaphorically, the social, political, and economic activities displayed throughout *Arden of Faversham* are, at some level, potentially treasonous to the inherited, hierarchical regime enforced by Tudor rule.

There is a way in which such potentially treasonous acts are denied in the play by a kind of providentialism that, for at least eight attempts, prevents Arden's death. Some force intervenes to prevent the poisonous food from killing, the crucifix intended to kill from succeeding, and the prayerbook used as a repository for adulterous love letters to be destroyed. Even when the murderers are successful, they overlook damaging evidence and are victims of a coincidental snowstorm and a miraculous imprint of Arden's broken body. Such supernatural events are countered by a savage and ruthless human world, filled with the theatrical imagery of animals, of hunting and snaring, of the dismembered human body and the unweeded land. Theatrically, such occurrences and such visual effects raise real questions about the efficacy of human behavior, just as the play persistently interrogates man's fallen nature in a society under frightening duress.

Further Reading

Attwell, David, "Property, Status, and the Subject in a Middle-class Tragedy: *Arden of Faversham*," *English Literary Renaissance* 21 (1991): 328–48.

Belsey, Catherine, "Alice Arden's Crime," *Renaissance Drama* n.s. 13 (1982): 83–102.

Helgerson, Richard, "Murder in Faversham: Holinshed's Impertinent History," in *The Historical Imagination in Early Modern Britain*, ed. Donald R. Kelley and David Harris Sacks (Cambridge: Cambridge University Press, 1997), pp. 133–58.

Hyde, Patricia, *Thomas Arden in Faversham: The Man Behind the Myth*. Faversham: The Faversham Society, 1996.

Lake, Peter, "Deeds against Nature: Cheap Print, Protestantism and Murder in Early Seventeenth Century England," in *Culture and Poetics in Early Stuart England*, ed. Kevin Sharpe and Peter Lake (London: Macmillan, 1994), pp. 257–84.

Leggatt, Alexander, "'Arden of Faversham,'" *Shakespeare Survey* 36 (1983): 121–33.

Orlin, Lena Cowen, "Man's House as His Castle in *Arden of Faversham*," *Medieval and Renaissance Drama* 3 (1985): 57–89.

The Tragedy of Master Arden of Faversham

[*LIST OF CHARACTERS*
in order of appearance
Thomas Arden, *a Gentleman of Faversham.*
Franklin, *his friend.*
Alice, *Arden's wife.*
Adam Fowle, *landlord of the Flower-de-Luce.*
Michael, *Arden's servant.*
Mosby, *lover of Arden's wife.*
Clarke, *a painter.*
Greene, *a tenant.*
Susan, *Mosby's sister and Alice's servingmaid.*
Bradshaw, *a goldsmith.*
Black Will } *hired murderers*
Shakebag }
A Prentice.
Lord Cheyne *and his* Men.
A Ferryman.
Dick Reede, *sailor and inhabitant of Faversham.*
A Sailor, *his friend.*
Mayor of Faversham *and the* Watch.]

[Sc. i]

(*Enter* Arden [*at home,*] *and* Franklin [*his friend*].)

Franklin. Arden, cheer up thy spirits and droop no more.
My gracious Lord, the Duke of Somerset,
Hath freely given to thee and to thy heirs,
By letters patents from his Majesty,
All the lands of the Abbey of Faversham.
Here are the deeds, sealed and subscribed
With his name and the King's.
[*Presents papers.*]
Read them, and leave this melancholy mood.
Arden. Franklin, thy love prolongs my weary life,
And, but for thee, how odious were this life,
That shows me nothing but torments my soul,
And those foul objects that offend mine eyes
Which makes me wish that for this veil of heaven
The earth hung over my head and covered me.
Love letters passed 'twixt Mosby and my wife,
And they have privy meetings in the town.
Nay, on his finger did I spy the ring
Which at our marriage day the priest put on.
Can any grief be half so great as this?
Franklin. Comfort thyself, sweet friend; it is not strange
That women will be false and wavering.
Arden. Aye, but to dote on such a one as he
Is monstrous, Franklin, and intolerable.
Franklin. Why, what is he?
Arden. A botcher, and no better at the first,

TEXTUAL VARIANTS

Title Faversham] Q Feuersham **List of Characters**] not in Q **i.5** Faversham] Q Fevershame **83** than] Q there **135** narrow-prying] Q marrow-prying (but *marrow* means "sexual provocation") **353** my faith] Q faith my **ii.4**] Q sets speeches by Black Will and Shakebag inconsistently in prose and verse; here they are consistently in prose, although later speeches by both often scan as poetry **Black Will**] Q Will (throughout the speech prefixes and stage directions) **24** curtsy] Q cursy **iii.62 s.d.** Exit [P]rentice] Q s.d. at line 64 **98** curtsy] Q cursy **139** [Michael]] Q has no speech prefix, giving line to Greene **iv.38 s.d.**] Q s.d. at line 37 **50** wife's] Q wives **58 s.d.**] Q s.d. at line 57 **75** thee] Q there **v.s.d.**] in Q following line 1 **vi.27** shivers] Q shewers **vii.27** plot] Q plat **33** accept] Q except **viii.12** Though] Q Thought **19** whither] Q whether **24** ear] Q erre **133** fount once troubled] Q fence of trouble **156 s.d.** Exit [Bradshaw]] Q s.d. at line 155 **ix.35–7**] Q sets as prose **157** plot] Q plat **x.9** go to] Q go to the Isle of Sheppey (line is irremediably irregular) **17** desires] Q deserves **36–9, 43–70**] Q sets as prose **93** cement] Q semell **xi**] (entire scene is playwright's addition) **2 et seq.**] (Q sets Ferryman's lines as poetry) **xii**] (entire scene is playwright's invention and is set as poetry) **32** companions] Q companies **43** hocked] Q houghed **44** Hock] Q Hough **xiii**] (entire scene is playwright's invention) **41** shooter's] Q suitor's **90** thee] Q thy **112** until] Q while **xiv.21** tallies] Q tales **28** their] Q his **82** crammed] Q cram **122 s.d.**] Q has s.d. at line 110 **133** sieve] Q sine **141** whither] Q whether **162** snatch] Q snath **302–5**] (Q sets speech as prose) **323 s.d.**] Q s.d. at line 314 **333 s.d.**] Q s.d. at line 322 **343** whither] Q whether **366** them] Q then **xviii.16** woo] Q woe

Playsource

Arden of Faversham closely follows the account of the murder of Thomas Arden by his wife in Holinshed's *Chronicles* (1577; 1587), including the marginal glosses to the 1587 text, augmented by the account of John Stow in his *Annals.*

i s.d. according to common law, a franklin was a man who owned land
2 Duke of Somerset Edward Seymour, named Lord Protector for Edward VI on his accession in 1547; he was widely reputed to profit from selling church lands
4 letters patents open letters, usually from the monarch, conferring rights or title, property or office; **his Majesty** Edward VI (reigned 1547–53)
5 All the lands Sir Thomas Cheyne, who was awarded the Abbey lands by Henry VIII on March 16, 1540, with his dissolution of the monastery, sold or transferred the lands to Arden ca. 1545
11 shows grants
13 veil of heaven sky
19 grief Holinshed reports otherwise – that Arden encouraged Alice's adultery
25 botcher mender of old clothes

Who, by base brokage getting some small stock,
Crept into service of a nobleman,
And, by his servile flattery and fawning,
Is now become the steward of his house,
And bravely jets it in his silken gown.
Franklin. No nobleman will count'nance such a peasant.
Arden. Yes, the Lord Clifford, he that loves not me.
But through his favor let not him grow proud,
For, were he by the Lord Protector backed,
He should not make me to be pointed at.
I am by birth a gentleman of blood,
And that injurious ribald that attempts
To violate my dear wife's chastity
(For dear I hold her love, as dear as heaven)
Shall on the bed which he thinks to defile
See his dissevered joints and sinews torn,
While, on the planchers, pants his weary body,
Smeared in the channels of his lustful blood.
Franklin. Be patient, gentle friend, and learn of me
To ease thy grief and save her chastity.
Entreat her fair; sweet words are fittest engines
To raze the flint walls of a woman's breast.
In any case, be not too jealous,
Nor make no question of her love to thee,
But, as securely, presently take horse,
And lie with me at London all this term;
For women when they may, will not,
But, being kept back, straight grow outrageous.
Arden. Though this abhors from reason yet I'll try it,
And call her forth, and presently take leave. –
How, Alice!

Here enters Alice.

Alice. Husband, what mean you to get up so early?
Summer nights are short, and yet you rise ere day.
Had I been wake, you had not rise so soon.
Arden. Sweet love, thou know'st that we two, Ovid-like,
Have often chid the morning, when it 'gan to peep,
And often wished that dark Night's purblind steeds
Would pull her by the purple mantle back
And cast her in the ocean to her love.
But this night, sweet Alice, thou hast killed my heart;
I heard thee call on Mosby in thy sleep.
Alice. 'Tis like I was asleep when I named him,
For being awake he comes not in my thoughts.
Arden. Aye, but you started up, and suddenly,
Instead of him, caught me about the neck.
Alice. Instead of him? Why, who was there but you?
And, where but one is, how can I mistake?
Franklin. Arden, leave to urge her overfar.
Arden. Nay, love, there is no credit in a dream.
Let it suffice I know thou lovest me well.
Alice. Now I remember whereupon it came.
Had we no talk of Mosby yesternight?
Franklin. Mistress Alice, I heard you name him once or twice.
Alice. And thereof came it, and therefore blame not me.
Arden. I know it did, and therefore let it pass.
I must to London, sweet Alice, presently.
Alice. But tell me, do you mean to stay there long?
Arden. No longer than till my affairs be done.
Franklin. He will not stay above a month at most.
Alice. A month! Aye, me! Sweet Arden, come again
Within a day or two or else I die.
Arden. I cannot long be from thee, gentle Alice.
While Michael fetch our horses from the field,
Franklin and I will down unto the quay,
For I have certain goods there to unload.
Meanwhile, prepare our breakfast, gentle Alice,
For yet, ere noon, we'll take horse and away.

Exeunt Arden *and* Franklin.

---

26 **base brokage** shady dealing; later, means pimping
29 **steward** servant in charge of household arrangements and expenditures
30 **jets** swaggers; **silken gown** emblem of steward's office
32 **Lord Clifford** a fictional person; the historical Mosby served Sir Edward (eventually Lord) North, Alice's stepfather and Arden's former master. The playwright may be avoiding censorship here
33 **him** Mosby
36 **gentleman of blood** one entitled to bear arms but not of the nobility
37 **injurious ribald** insulting base fellow
42 **planchers** floorboards
46 **engines** instruments
48 **jealous** suspicious
50 **as securely** confidently; **presently** at once
51 **lie** lodge; **term** law term; the year was divided into four such terms
53 **outrageous** angry
60 **Ovid-like** as poet of love; cf. *Amores* 1; Elegy 13
62 **purblind** totally blind
73 **leave** forebear
74 **no credit in a dream** (proverbial)
90 **certain goods** Arden was chief King's Comptroller of the port of Faversham (and later Sandwich)
s.d. 92 ***Exeunt*** They leave (Latin)

Alice. Ere noon he means to take horse and away!
Sweet news is this! Oh, that some airy spirit
Would in the shape and likeness of a horse
Gallop with Arden 'cross the ocean
And throw him from his back into the waves!
Sweet Mosby is the man that hath my heart;
And he usurps it, having nought but this –
That I am tied to him by marriage.
Love is a god, and marriage is but words;
And therefore Mosby's title is the best.
Tush! Whether it be or no, he shall be mine
In spite of him, of Hymen, and of rites.

Here enters Adam *of the Flower-de-Luce.*

And here comes Adam of the Flower-de-Luce.
I hope he brings me tidings of my love.
How now, Adam, what is the news with you?
Be not afraid; my husband is now from home.
Adam. He whom you wot of, Mosby, Mistress Alice,
Is come to town and sends you word by me;
In any case, you may not visit him.
Alice. Not visit him?
Adam. No, nor take no knowledge of his being here.
Alice. But tell me, is he angry or displeased?
Adam. Should seem so, for he is wondrous sad.
Alice. Were he as mad as raving Hercules,
I'll see him. Aye, and were thy house of force,
These hands of mine should raze it to the ground
Unless that thou wouldst bring me to my love.
Adam. Nay; and you be so impatient, I'll be gone.
Alice. Stay, Adam, stay; thou wert wont to be my friend.
Ask Mosby how I have incurred his wrath;
Bear him from me these pair of silver dice
With which we played for kisses many a time,
And when I lost I won, and so did he –
Such winning and such losing Jove send me –
And bid him, if his love do not decline,
Come this morning but along my door,
And as a stranger, but salute me there.
This may he do without suspect or fear.
Adam. I'll tell him what you say, and so farewell.
Exit Adam.

Alice. [*Alone.*] Do, and one day I'll make amends for all.
I know he loves me well, but dares not come
Because my husband is so jealous,
And these my narrow-prying neighbors blab,
Hinder our meetings when we would confer.
But if I live, that block shall be removed;
And Mosby, thou that comes to me by stealth,
Shalt neither fear the biting speech of men
Nor Arden's looks. As surely shall he die
As I abhor him, and love only thee.

Here enters Michael.

How now, Michael, whither are you going?
Michael. To fetch my master's nag. I hope you'll think on me.
Alice. Aye. But Michael, see you keep your oath,
And be as secret as you are resolute.
Michael. I'll see he shall not live above a week.
Alice. On that condition, Michael, here is my hand;
None shall have Mosby's sister but thyself.
Michael. I understand the painter here hard by
Hath made report that he and Sue is sure.
Alice. There's no such matter, Michael, believe it not.
Michael. But he hath sent a dagger sticking in a heart,
With a verse or two stolen from a painted cloth,
The which I hear the wench keeps in her chest.
Well, let her keep it! I shall find a fellow
That can both write and read and make rhyme too;
And, if I do – well, I say no more.
I'll send from London such a taunting letter
As shall eat the heart he sent with salt
And fling the dagger at the painter's head.
Alice. What needs all this? I say that Susan's thine.
Michael. Why, then I say that I will kill my master
Or anything that you will have me do.
Alice. But, Michael, see you do it cunningly.
Michael. Why, say I should be took, I'll ne'er confess

93 **he** Arden
104 **Hymen** god of marriage
104 **s.d.** ***Flower-de-Luce*** an actual tavern in Hugh Place in Faversham just past the Guild Hall and several blocks from Arden's house (some half-timbered walls remain)
109 **wot** know
116 **mad as raving Hercules** Hercules was driven to madness and suicide by wearing a shirt given him by his wife Deianeira, who thought it would again make him faithful to her
117 **of force** fortified
120 **and** if
137 **block** obstruction
149 **hard** near
150 **is sure** are betrayed
153 **painted cloth** a cheap substitute for a woven tapestry with a picture (and perhaps a motto)

That you know anything; and Susan, being a maid,
May beg me from the gallows of the shrieve.
Alice. Trust not to that, Michael.
Michael. You cannot tell me; I have seen it, I.
But, mistress, tell her whether I live or die
I'll make her more worth than twenty painters can;
For I will rid mine elder brother away,
And then the farm of Bolton is mine own.
Who would not venture upon house and land
When he may have it for a right-down blow?

Here enters Mosby.

Alice. Yonder comes Mosby. Michael, get thee gone,
And let not him nor any know thy drifts.
Exit Michael.
Mosby, my love!
Mosby. Away, I say, and talk not to me now.
Alice. A word or two, sweetheart, and then I will.
'Tis yet but early days; thou need'st not fear.
Mosby. Where is your husband?
Alice. 'Tis now high water, and he is at the quay.
Mosby. There let him be; henceforward know me not.
Alice. Is this the end of all thy solemn oaths?
Is this the fruit thy reconcilement buds?
Have I for this given thee so many favors,
Incurred my husband's hate, and – out, alas! –
Made shipwreck of mine honor for thy sake?
And dost thou say, "Henceforward know me not?"
Remember when I locked thee in my closet,
What were thy words and mine? Did we not both
Decree to murder Arden in the night?
The heavens can witness, and the world can tell,
Before I saw that falsehood look of thine,
'Fore I was tangled with thy 'ticing speech,
Arden to me was dearer than my soul,
And shall be still. Base peasant, get thee gone.
And boast not of thy conquest over me,
Gotten by witchcraft and mere sorcery.
For what hast thou to countenance my love,
Being descended of a noble house
And matched already with a gentleman
Whose servant thou may'st be? And so farewell.
Mosby. Ungentle and unkind Alice, now I see
That which I ever feared and find too true:
A woman's love is as the lightning flame
Which, even in bursting forth, consumes itself.
To try thy constancy have I been strange.
Would I had never tried, but lived in hope!
Alice. What needs thou try me, whom thou never found false?
Mosby. Yet pardon me, for love is jealous.
Alice. So lists the sailor to the mermaid's song;
So looks the traveler to the basilisk.
I am content for to be reconciled
And that, I know, will be mine overthrow.
Mosby. Thine overthrow? First let the world dissolve!
Alice. Nay, Mosby, let me still enjoy thy love;
And, happen what will, I am resolute.
My saving husband hoards up bags of gold
To make our children rich, and now is he
Gone to unload the goods that shall be thine,
And he and Franklin will to London straight.
Mosby. To London, Alice? If thou'lt be ruled by me,
We'll make him sure enough for coming there.
Alice. Ah, would we could!
Mosby. I happened on a painter yesternight,
The only cunning man of Christendom,
For he can temper poison with his oil,
That whoso looks upon the work he draws
Shall, with the beams that issue from his sight,
Suck venom to his breast and slay himself.
Sweet Alice, he shall draw thy counterfeit,
That Arden may, by gazing on it, perish.
Alice. Aye, but Mosby, that is dangerous;

167 **May beg me** refers to the cultural belief that a virgin could save a man's life by offering to marry him; **shrieve** sheriff
171 **worth** wealthy
172 **rid . . . away** kill
173 **Bolton** Bolton-under-Blean, a village in Kent between Faversham and Canterbury
175 **right-down** downright
177 **drifts** schemes
181 **early days** early in the day
183 **water** tide
191 **closet** private room
196 **'ticing** enticing
200 **mere** pure, simple
209 **strange** distant
213 **lists** listens; **mermaid's song** refers to the mythic Siren whose song was seductive and deadly
214 **basilisk** a mythic serpent whose look was fatal
218 **still** always
221 **our children** Alice had a daughter by Arden who historically was present at his death. Since no children appear in the play, Alice is using the possibility to remind Mosby of Arden's wealth
223 **straight** directly
225 **make . . . for** prevent him from
228 **only** most; **cunning** possessing special or magical skills
229 **temper** mix
233 **counterfeit** likeness

For thou or I, or any other else,
Coming into the chamber where it hangs, may die.
Mosby. Aye, but we'll have it covered with a cloth,
And hung up in the study for himself.
Alice. It may not be; for, when the picture's drawn,
Arden, I know, will come and show it me.
Mosby. Fear not; we'll have that shall serve the turn.
[*They walk across the stage.*]
This is the painter's house. I'll call him forth.
Alice. But Mosby, I'll have no such picture, I.
Mosby. I pray thee, leave it to my discretion.
How, Clarke!

Here enters Clarke.

Oh, you are an honest man of your word; you served me well.
Clarke. Why, sir, I'll do it for you at any time,
Provided, as you have given your word,
I may have Susan Mosby to my wife.
For as sharp-witted poets, whose sweet verse
Make heavenly gods break off their nectar draughts
And lay their ears down to the lowly earth,
Use humble promise to their sacred Muse,
So we that are the poets' favorites
Must have a love. Aye, Love is the painter's Muse,
That makes him frame a speaking countenance,
A weeping eye that witnesses heart's grief.
Then tell me, Master Mosby, shall I have her?
Alice. 'Tis pity but he should. He'll use her well.
Mosby. Clarke, here's my hand; my sister shall be thine.
Clarke. Then, brother, to requite this courtesy,
You shall command my life, my skill, and all.
Alice. Ah, that thou couldst be secret!
Mosby. Fear him not. Leave, I have talked sufficient.
Clarke. You know not me that ask such questions.
Let it suffice I know you love him well
And fain would have your husband made away,
Wherein, trust me, you show a noble mind,
That rather than you'll live with him you hate,
You'll venture life and die with him you love.
The like will I do for my Susan's sake.
Alice. Yet nothing could enforce me to the deed
But Mosby's love. Might I without control
Enjoy thee still, then Arden should not die;
But seeing I cannot, therefore let him die.
Mosby. Enough, sweet Alice; thy kind words make me melt.
[*To Clarke.*] Your trick of poisoned pictures we dislike;
Some other poison would do better far.
Alice. Aye, such as might be put into his broth,
And yet in taste not to be found at all.
Clarke. I know your mind, and here I have it for you.
Put but a dram of this into his drink,
Or any kind of broth that he shall eat,
And he shall die within an hour after.
Alice. As I am a gentlewoman, Clarke, next day
Thou and Susan shall be marrièd.
Mosby. And I'll make her dowry more than I'll talk of, Clarke.
Clarke. Yonder's your husband. Mosby, I'll be gone.

Here enters Arden *and* Franklin.

Alice. In good time. See where my husband comes.
Master Mosby, ask him the question yourself.
Exit Clarke.
Mosby. Master Arden, being at London yesternight,
The Abbey lands whereof you are now possessed
Were offered me on some occasion
By Greene, one of Sir Antony Ager's men.
I pray you, Sir, tell me, are not the lands yours?
Hath any other interest herein?
Arden. Mosby, that question we'll decide anon.
Alice, make ready my breakfast; I must hence.
Exit Alice.
As for the lands, Mosby, they are mine

---

243 painter's house probably refers to a door at the rear of the stage

246 Clarke a fictional name; the Faversham Wardmote Book identifies him as William Blackborne

257 frame fashion

260 but unless

265 Leave cease; leave off

268 fain willingly

274 control constraint

283 dram in Holinshed Alice is directed to put poison at the bottom of the cup to obscure taste

290 In good time Alice addresses the departing Clarke; **See . . . comes** (Alice warns Mosby)

294 occasion pretext

295 Sir Antony Ager historically, Sir Anthony Aucher, a knight from Hautsbourne, Kent

298 anon presently

By letters patents from his Majesty.
But I must have a mandate for my wife;
They say you seek to rob me of her love.
Villain, what makes thou in her company?
She's no companion for so base a groom.
Mosby. Arden, I thought not on her. I came to thee,
But rather than I pocket up this wrong –
Franklin. What will you do, sir?
Mosby. Revenge it on the proudest of you both.
Then Arden draws forth Mosby's sword.
Arden. So, sirrah, you may not wear a sword!
The statute makes against artificers.
I warrant that I do. Now use your bodkin,
Your Spanish needle, and your pressing iron,
For this shall go with me. And mark my words –
You goodman botcher, 'tis to you I speak –
The next time that I take thee near my house,
Instead of legs I'll make thee crawl on stumps.
Mosby. Ah, Master Arden, you have injured me;
I do appeal to God and to the world.
Franklin. Why, canst thou deny thou wert a botcher once?
Mosby. Measure me what I am, not what I was.
Arden. Why, what art thou now but a velvet drudge,
A cheating steward, and base-minded peasant?
Mosby. Arden, now thou hast belched and vomited
The rancorous venom of thy mis-swoll'n heart.
Hear me but speak. As I intend to live
With God and His elected saints in heaven,
I never meant more to solicit her;
And that she knows, and all the world shall see.
I loved her once – sweet Arden, pardon me.
I could not choose; her beauty fired my heart.
But time hath quenched these overraging coals;
And, Arden, though I now frequent thy house,
'Tis for my sister's sake, her waiting-maid,
And not for hers. Mayest thou enjoy her long!
Hell-fire and wrathful vengeance light on me
If I dishonor her or injure thee.
Arden. Mosby, with these thy protestations,
The deadly hatred of my heart is appeased,
And thou and I'll be friends if this prove true.
As for the base terms I gave thee late,
Forget them, Mosby; I had cause to speak
When all the knights and gentlemen of Kent
Make common table-talk of her and thee.
Mosby. Who lives that is not touched with slanderous tongues?
Franklin. Then, Mosby, to eschew the speech of men,
Upon whose general bruit all honor hangs,
Forbear his house.
Arden. Forbear it! Nay, rather frequent it more.
The world shall see that I distrust her not.
To warn him on the sudden from my house
Were to confirm the rumor that is grown.
Mosby. By my faith, sir, you say true.
And therefore will I sojourn here awhile
Until our enemies have talked their fill;
And then, I hope, they'll cease and at last confess
How causeless they have injured her and me.
Arden. And I will lie at London at this term
To let them see how light I weigh their words.

Here enters Alice [*and* Michael].

Alice. Husband, sit down; your breakfast will be cold.
Arden. Come, Master Mosby, will you sit with us?
Mosby. I cannot eat, but I'll sit for company.
Arden. Sirrah Michael, see our horse be ready.
[*Exit* Michael.]
Alice. Husband, why pause ye? Why eat you not?
Arden. I am not well. There's something in this broth
That is not wholesome. Didst thou make it, Alice?
Alice. I did, and that's the cause it likes not you.
Then she throws down the broth on the ground.
There's nothing that I do can please your taste.
You were best to say I would have poisoned you.
I cannot speak or cast aside my eye
But he imagines I have stepped awry.
Here's he that you cast in my teeth so oft.
Now will I be convinced or purge myself.
I charge thee, speak to this mistrustful man,
Thou that wouldst see me hang, thou, Mosby, thou.

302 **mandate** deed of ownership
305 **groom** serving-man
307 **pocket up** submit to
310 **sirrah** (here as a term of contempt)
311 **statute** passed under Edward VI, forbidding those under the rank of gentleman (which Arden is) from wearing a sword; **makes** decrees; **artificers** (1) craftsmen; (2) tricksters
341 **late** just now
347 **bruit** report
360 **Husband** (some editors begin scene ii here, but stage was probably set with table and stools throughout)
367 **likes not** displeases
373 **convinced** proven guilty

What favor hast thou had more than a kiss
At coming or departing from the town?
Mosby. You wrong yourself and me to cast these doubts;
Your loving husband is not jealous.
Arden. Why, gentle Mistress Alice, cannot I be ill
But you'll accuse yourself? –
Franklin, thou hast a box of mithridate;
I'll take a little to prevent the worst.
Franklin. Do so, and let us presently take horse.
My life for yours, ye shall do well enough.
Alice. Give me a spoon. I'll eat of it myself.
Would it were full of poison to the brim,
Then should my cares and troubles have an end!
Was ever silly woman so tormented?
Arden. Be patient, sweet love; I mistrust not thee.
Alice. God will revenge it, Arden, if thou dost;
For never woman loved her husband better
Than I do thee.
Arden. I know it, sweet Alice. Cease to complain,
Lest that in tears I answer thee again.
[*Reenter* Michael.]
Franklin. Come, leave this dallying, and let us away.
Alice. Forbear to wound me with that bitter word;
Arden shall go to London in my arms.
Arden. Loath am I to depart, yet I must go.
Alice. Wilt thou to London then, and leave me here?
Ah, if thou love me, gentle Arden, stay.
Yet, if thy business be of great import,
Go if thou wilt; I'll bear it as I may.
But write from London to me every week,
Nay, every day, and stay no longer there
Than thou must needs, lest that I die for sorrow.
Arden. I'll write unto thee every other tide,
And so farewell, sweet Alice, till we meet next.
Alice. Farewell, husband, seeing you'll have it so.
And, Master Franklin, seeing you take him hence,
In hope you'll hasten him home I'll give you this.
And then she kisses him.
Franklin. And, if he stay, the fault shall not be mine.
Mosby, farewell, and see you keep your oath.
Mosby. I hope he is not jealous of me now.
Arden. No, Mosby, no. Hereafter think of me
As of your dearest friend, and so farewell.
Exeunt Arden, Franklin, *and* Michael.
Alice. I am glad he is gone. He was about to stay,
But did you mark me then how I brake off?
Mosby. Aye, Alice, and it was cunningly performed.
But what a villain is this painter Clarke!
Alice. Was it not a goodly poison that he gave!
Why, he's as well now as he was before.
It should have been some fine confection
That might have given the broth some dainty taste.
This powder was too gross and populous.
Mosby. But had he eaten but three spoonfuls more,
Then had he died and our love continued.
Alice. Why, so it shall, Mosby, albeit he live.
Mosby. It is unpossible, for I have sworn
Never hereafter to solicit thee
Or, whilst he lives, once more importune thee.
Alice. Thou shalt not need. I will importune thee!
What? Shall an oath make thee forsake my love?
As if I have not sworn as much myself
And given my hand unto him in the church!
Tush, Mosby! Oaths are words, and words is wind,
And wind is mutable. Then, I conclude,
'Tis childishness to stand upon an oath.
Mosby. Well proved, Mistress Alice; yet, by your leave,
I'll keep mine unbroken while he lives.
Alice. Aye, do, and spare not. His time is but short,
For, if thou beest as resolute as I,
We'll have him murdered as he walks the streets.
In London many alehouse ruffians keep,
Which, as I hear, will murder men for gold.
They shall be soundly fee'd to pay him home.

Here enters Greene.

Mosby. Alice, what's he that comes yonder? Knowest thou him?
Alice. Mosby, begone! I hope 'tis one that comes
To put in practice our intended drifts.
Exit Mosby.
Greene. Mistress Arden, you are well met.

382 **mithidrate** an antidote
389 **silly** helpless
408 **farewell** the customary route was from Faversham through Sittingbourne, Rainham, and Rochester, to Gravesend, then by boat along the Thames to London
425 **gross** indigestible; **populous** apparent
429 **unpossible** impossible
444 **keep** live
446 **pay him home** murder him

I am sorry that your husband is from home
Whenas my purposed journey was to him.
Yet all my labor is not spent in vain,
For I suppose that you can full discourse
And flat resolve me of the thing I seek.
Alice. What is it, Master Greene? If that I may
Or can with safety, I will answer you.
Greene. I heard your husband hath the grant of late,
Confirmed by letters patents from the King,
Of all the lands of the Abbey of Faversham
Generally entitled, so that all former grants
Are cut off, whereof I myself had one;
But now my interest by that is void.
This is all, Mistress Arden. Is it true nor no?
Alice. True, Master Greene, the lands are his in state.
And whatsoever leases were before
Are void for term of Master Arden's life.
He hath the grant under the Chancery seal.
Greene. Pardon me, Mistress Arden, I must speak,
For I am touched. Your husband doth me wrong
To wring me from the little land I have.
My living is my life; only that
Resteth remainder of my portion.
Desire of wealth is endless in his mind,
And he is greedy-gaping still for gain;
Nor cares he though young gentlemen do beg,
So he may scrape and hoard up in his pouch.
But seeing he hath taken my lands, I'll value life
As careless as he is careful for to get;
And tell him this from me: I'll be revenged,
And so as he shall wish the Abbey lands
Had rested still within their former state.
Alice. Alas, poor gentleman, I pity you,
And woe is me that any man should want.
God knows, 'tis not my fault. But wonder not
Though he be hard to others when to me –
Ah, Master Greene, God knows how I am used!
Greene. Why, Mistress Arden, can the crabbèd churl
Use you unkindly? Respects he not your birth,
Your honorable friends, nor what you brought?
Why, all Kent knows your parentage and what you are.
Alice. Ah, Master Greene, be it spoken in secret here,
I never live good day with him alone.
When he is at home, then have I froward looks,
Hard words, and blows to mend the match withal.
And though I might content as good a man,
Yet doth he keep in every corner trulls;
And, weary with his trugs at home,
Then rides he straight to London. There, forsooth,
He revels it among such filthy ones
As counsels him to make away his wife.
Thus live I daily in continual fear,
In sorrow, so despairing of redress
As every day I wish with hearty prayer
That he or I were taken forth the world.
Greene. Now trust me, Mistress Alice, it grieveth me
So fair a creature should be so abused.
Why, who would have thought the civil sir so sullen?
He looks so smoothly. Now, fie upon him, churl!
And if he live a day he lives too long.
But frolic, woman, I shall be the man
Shall set you free from all this discontent.
And if the churl deny my interest
And will not yield my lease into my hand,
I'll pay him home, whatever hap to me.
Alice. But speak you as you think?
Greene. Aye, God's my witness, I mean plain dealing,
For I had rather die than lose my land.
Alice. Then, Master Greene, be counselèd by me:
Endanger not yourself for such a churl,
But hire some cutter for to cut him short.
And here's ten pound to wager them withal.

---

452 **Whenas** whereas
454 **full discourse** completely explain
455 **flat resolve** make absolutely clear to
461 **Generally entitled** deeded without exception
465 **in state** by law
468 **Chancery seal** the court of the Lord Chancellor was highest next to the House of Lords
470 **touched** affected
472 **living** land
473 **portion** inheritance
475 **still** always
488 **crabbèd** ill-natured
489 **unkindly** unnaturally
490 **what you brought** that is, her dowry
494 **froward** bad-tempered
495 **mend** insure
497 **trulls** whores
498 **trugs** prostitutes
509 **smoothy** courteous
511 **frolic** be cheerful
513 **interest** legal property right
521 **cutter** thug, cut-throat
522 **wager** pay

When he is dead, you shall have twenty more;
And the lands whereof my husband is possessed
Shall be entitled as they were before.
Greene. Will you keep promise with me?
Alice. Or count me false and perjured while I live!
Greene. Then here's my hand; I'll have him so dispatched.
I'll up to London straight. I'll thither post
And never rest till I have compassed it;
Till then, farewell.
Alice. Good fortune follow all your forward thoughts.
And whosoever doth attempt the deed,
A happy hand I wish; and so farewell.
[*Exit* Greene.]
All this goes well. Mosby, I long for thee
To let thee know all that I have contrived.

Here enters Mosby *and* Clarke.

Mosby. How now, Alice, what's the news?
Alice. Such as will content thee well, sweetheart.
Mosby. Well, let them pass awhile, and tell me, Alice,
How have you dealt and tempered with my sister?
What, will she have my neighbor Clarke or no?
Alice. What, Master Mosby, let him woo himself.
Think you that maids look not for fair words?
Go to her, Clarke; she's all alone within.
Michael, my man, is clean out of her books.
Clarke. I thank you, Mistress Arden. I will in;
And, if fair Susan and I can make agree,
You shall command me to the uttermost
As far as either goods or life may stretch.
Exit Clarke.
Mosby. Now, Alice, let's hear thy news.
Alice. They be so good that I must laugh for joy
Before I can begin to tell my tale.
Mosby. Let's hear them, that I may laugh for company.
Alice. This morning, Master Greene – Dick Greene, I mean,
From whom my husband had the Abbey land –
Came hither railing, for to know the truth
Whether my husband had the lands by grant.
I told him all, whereat he stormed amain
And swore he would cry quittance with the churl
And, if he did deny his interest,
Stab him whatsoever did befall himself.
When as I saw his choler thus to rise,
I whetted on the gentleman with words.
And to conclude, Mosby, at last we grew
To composition for my husband's death.
I gave him ten pound to hire knaves,
By some device to make away the churl.
When he is dead, he should have twenty more
And repossess his former lands again.
On this we 'greed, and he is ridden straight
To London to bring his death about.
Mosby. But call you this good news?
Alice. Aye, sweetheart, be they not?
Mosby. 'Twere cheerful news to hear the churl were dead;
But trust me, Alice, I take it passing ill
You would be so forgetful of our state
To make recount of it to every groom.
What! to acquaint each stranger with our drifts,
Chiefly in case of murder – why, 'tis the way
To make it open unto Arden's self
And bring thyself and me to ruin both.
Forewarned, forearmed; who threats his enemy
Lends him a sword to guard himself withal.
Alice. I did it for the best.
Mosby. Well, seeing 'tis done, cheerly let it pass.
You know this Greene; is he not religious?
A man, I guess, of great devotion?
Alice. He is.
Mosby. Then, sweet Alice, let it pass. I have a drift
Will quiet all, whatever is amiss.

Here enters Clarke *and* Susan.

Alice. How now, Clarke? Have you found me false?
Did I not plead the matter hard for you?
Clarke. You did.
Mosby. And what? Will't be a match?
Clarke. A match, i'faith, sir. Aye, the day is mine.
The painter lays his colors to the life;
His pencil draws no shadows in his love.
Susan is mine.
Alice. You make her blush.

528 dispatched killed
532 forward eager
540 tempered with prepared
547 agree an agreement
558 amain mightily; violently
559 cry quittance get even
563 whetted on encouraged
565 composition agreed payment
575 passing extremely
580 make it open disclose it
585 cheerly cheerfully
595 shadows uncertainties

Mosby. What, sister? Is it Clarke must be the man?
Susan. It resteth in your grant. Some words are passed,
And haply we be grown unto a match
If you be willing that it shall be so.
Mosby. Ah, Master Clarke, it resteth at my grant;
You see my sister's yet at my dispose.
But, so you'll grant me one thing I shall ask,
I am content my sister shall be yours.
Clarke. What is it, Master Mosby?
Mosby. I do remember once in secret talk
You told me how you could compound by art
A crucifix impoisonèd,
That whoso look upon it should wax blind
And with the scent be stifled, that ere long
He should die poisoned that did view it well.
I would have you make me such a crucifix,
And then I'll grant my sister shall be yours.
Clarke. Though I am loath, because it toucheth life,
Yet rather or I'll leave sweet Susan's love,
I'll do it, and with all the haste I may.
But for whom is it?
Alice. Leave that to us. Why, Clarke, is it possible
That you should paint and draw it out yourself,
The colors being baleful and impoisoned,
And no ways prejudice yourself withal?
Mosby. Well questioned, Alice. Clarke, how answer you that?
Clarke. Very easily. I'll tell you straight
How I do work of these impoisoned drugs:
I fasten on my spectacles so close
As nothing can any way offend my sight;
Then, as I put a leaf within my nose,
So put I rhubarb to avoid the smell,
And softly, as another work, I paint.
Mosby. 'Tis very well, but against when shall I have it?
Clarke. Within this ten days.
Mosby. 'Twill serve the turn. –
Now, Alice, let's in and see what cheer you keep.
I hope, now Master Arden is from home,
You'll give me leave to play your husband's part.
Alice. Mosby, you know who's master of my heart
He well may be the master of the house.
Exeunt.

[Sc. ii]

Here enters Greene *and* Bradshaw.

Bradshaw. See you them that comes yonder, Master Greene?
Greene. Aye, very well. Do you know them?

Here enters Black Will *and* Shakebag.

Bradshaw. The one I know not, but he seems a knave,
Chiefly for bearing the other company;
For such a slave, so vile a rogue as he,
Lives not again upon the earth.
Black Will is his name. I tell you, Master Greene,
At Boulogne he and I were fellow soldiers,
Where he played such pranks
As all the camp feared him for his villainy.
I warrant you he bears so bad a mind
That for a crown he'll murder any man.
Greene. [*Aside.*] The fitter is he for my purpose, marry.
Black Will. How now, fellow Bradshaw, whither away so early?
Bradshaw. Oh, Will, times are changed. No fellows now,
Though we were once together in the field;
Yet thy friend to do thee any good I can.
Black Will. Why, Bradshaw, was not thou and I fellow soldiers at Boulogne, where I was a corporal and thou but a base mercenary groom? No fellows now because you are a goldsmith and have a little plate in your shop? You were glad to call me "fellow Will" and, with a curtsy to the earth, "One snatch, good corporal" when I stole the half ox from John the victualer and domineered with it among good fellows in one night.
Bradshaw. Aye, Will, those days are past with me.
Black Will. Aye, but they be not past with me, for I keep that same honorable mind still, good neighbor Bradshaw. You are too proud to be my fellow; but, were it not that I see more company coming down the hill, I would be

599 haply perhaps
609 wax grow
615 or than
620 baleful noxious
621 prejudice implicate
629 softly as as easily as
632 cheer hospitality; refreshment

ii.8 Boulogne a French port on the English Channel captured by Henry VIII in 1544 and returned to France by Edward VI in 1550
11 warrant assure
12 crown coin worth five shillings
13 marry an oath (corruption of "by the Virgin Mary")
24 snatch morsel
26 domineered celebrated

fellows with you once more, and share crowns with you too. But let that pass, and tell me whither you go.

Bradshaw. To London, Will, about a piece of service
Wherein haply thou mayst pleasure me.

Black Will. What is it?

Bradshaw. Of late Lord Cheyne lost some plate
Which one did bring and sold it at my shop,
Saying he served Sir Anthony Cooke.
A search was made, the plate was found with me,
And I am bound to answer at the 'size.
Now Lord Cheyne solemnly vows,
If law will serve him, he'll hang me for his plate.
Now I am going to London upon hope
To find the fellow. Now, Will, I know
Thou art acquainted with such companions.

Black Will. What manner of man was he?

Bradshaw. A lean-faced, writhen knave,
Hawk-nosed and very hollow-eyed,
With mighty furrows in his stormy brows,
Long hair down his shoulders curled;
His chin was bare, but on his upper lip
A mutchado, which he wound about his ear.

Black Will. What apparel had he?

Bradshaw. A watchet satin doublet all to-torn
(The inner side did bear the greater show),
A pair of threadbare velvet hose, seam rent,
A worsted stocking rent above the shoe,
A livery cloak, but all the lace was off –
'Twas bad, but yet it served to hide the plate.

Black Will. Sirrah Shakebag, canst thou remember since we trolled the bowl at Sittingburgh, where I broke the tapster's head of the Lion with a cudgel-stick?

Shakebag. Aye, very well, Will.

Black Will. Why, it was with the money that the plate was sold for. Sirrah Bradshaw, what wilt thou give him that can tell thee who sold thy plate?

Bradshaw. Who, I pray thee, good Will?

Black Will. Why, 'twas one Jack Fitten. He's now in Newgate for stealing a horse, and shall be arraigned the next 'size.

Bradshaw. Why then, let Lord Cheyne seek Jack Fitten forth,
For I'll back and tell him who robbed him of his plate.
This cheers my heart. Master Greene, I'll leave you,
For I must to the Isle of Sheppey with speed.

Greene. Before you go, let me entreat you
To carry this letter to Mistress Arden of Faversham
And humbly recommend me to herself.
[*He gives a letter to Bradshaw.*]

Bradshaw. That will I, Master Greene, and so farewell. –
Here, Will, there's a crown for thy good news.

Black Will. Farewell, Bradshaw; I'll drink no water for thy sake while this lasts. Now, gentleman, shall we have your company to London?

Greene. Nay, stay, sirs.
A little more I needs must use your help,
And in a matter of great consequence,
Wherein, if you'll be secret and profound,
I'll give you twenty angels for your pains.

Black Will. How? Twenty angels? Give my fellow George Shakebag and me twenty angels, and, if thou'lt have thy own father slain that thou mayst inherit his land, we'll kill him.

Shakebag. Aye, thy mother, thy sister, thy brother, or all thy kin.

Greene. Well, this it is: Arden of Faversham
Hath highly wronged me about the Abbey land,
That no revenge but death will serve the turn.
Will you two kill him? Here's the angels down,
And I will lay the platform of his death.

Black Will. Plat me no platforms! Give me the money, and I'll stab him as he stands pissing against a wall, but I'll kill him.

34–5 **share crowns with you** rob

40 **Lord Cheyne** Sir (never Lord) Thomas Cheyne, Lord Warden of the Cinque Ports and Lord Lieutenant of Kent, who entertained Henry VIII and Anne Boleyn on the Isle of Sheppey near Faversham in 1532

42 **Sir Anthony Cooke** tutor to Edward VI

44 **'size** court of assizes, circuit court representing the national government and making a circuit each law term

51 **writhen** pinched

56 **mutchado** moustache

58 **watchet** pale blue; **all to-torn** completely torn

59 **inner side** lining; **bear the greater show** was the more greatly seen

60 **seam rent** torn at the seams

65 **trolled** passed; **bowl** drinking vessel; **Sittingburgh** Sittingbourne, a town nine miles E of Faversham in Kent

66 **of the Lion** i.e., at the Lion Inn

75 **Newgate** London's chief prison

80 **Isle of Sheppey** an island opposite Faversham on the N coast of Kent, separated by a branch of the Medway River

92 **profound** cunning

93 **angels** coins worth about ten shillings that depicted the Archangel Michael slaying the dragon

103 **lay the platform** devise the plan

Shakebag. Where is he?
Greene. He is now at London, in Aldersgate Street.
Shakebag. He's dead as if he had been condemned by an Act of Parliament if once Black Will and I swear his death.
Greene. Here is ten pound; and, when he is dead,
Ye shall have twenty more.
Black Will. My fingers itches to be at the peasant. Ah, that I might be set awork thus through the year and that murder would grow to an occupation, that a man might without danger of law – Zounds, I warrant I should be warden of the company! Come, let us be going, and we'll bait at Rochester, where I'll give thee a gallon of sack to handsel the match withal.

Exeunt.

[Sc. iii]

Here enters Michael.

Michael. I have gotten such a letter as will touch the painter, and thus it is:

Here enters Arden *and* Franklin *who hear* Michael *read this letter.*

"My duty remembered, Mistress Susan, hoping in God you be in good health as I, Michael, was at the making hereof. This is to certify you that, as the turtle true when she hath lost her mate sitteth alone, so I, mourning for your absence, do walk up and down Paul's, till one day I fell asleep and lost my master's pantofles. Ah, Mistress Susan, abolish that paltry painter, cut him off by the shins with a frowning look of your crabbed countenance, and think upon Michael, who, drunk with the dregs of your favor, will cleave as fast to your love as a plaster of pitch to a galled horseback. Thus hoping you will let my passions penetrate, or rather impetrate, mercy of your meek hands, I end.

Yours,
Michael, or else not Michael."

Arden. Why, you paltry knave,
Stand you here loitering, knowing my affairs,
What haste my business craves to send to Kent?
Franklin. Faith, friend Michael, this is very ill,
Knowing your master hath no more but you.
And do ye slack his business for your own?
Arden. Where is the letter, sirrah? Let me see it. –

Then he [Michael] *gives him the letter.*

See, Master Franklin, here's proper stuff:
Susan my maid, the painter, and my man,
A crew of harlots, all in love, forsooth.
Sirrah, let me hear no more of this.
Now, for thy life, once write to her a word.

Here enters Greene, Black Will, *and* Shakebag.

Wilt thou be married to so base a trull?
'Tis Mosby's sister. Come I once at home,
I'll rouse her from remaining in my house.
Now, Master Franklin, let us go walk in Paul's.
Come but a turn or two, and then away.

Exeunt [Arden, Franklin, *and* Michael].

Greene. The first is Arden, and that's his man;
The other is Franklin, Arden's dearest friend.
Black Will. Zounds, I'll kill them all three.
Greene. Nay, sirs, touch not his man in any case.
But stand close, and take you fittest standing,
and, at his coming forth, speed him
To the Nag's Head. There is this coward's haunt .
But now I'll leave you till the deed be done.

Exit Greene.

Shakebag. If he be not paid his own, ne'er trust Shakebag.
Black Will. Sirrah Shakebag, at his coming forth I'll run him through, and then to the Blackfriars and there take water and away.
Shakebag. Why, that's the best; but see thou miss him not.

---

108 **Aldersgate Street** street running from Aldersgate to the w side of Cheapside where earls and a marquis had townhouses
115 **might** could practice
118 **Zounds** an oath (corruption of "by God's wounds" on the cross)
119 **company** an imaginary livery company dealing in murder and extortion
120 **bait** stop for food and rest [abate]; **Rochester** an episcopal city in Kent between London and Faversham
121 **sack** white wine imported from Spain and the Canary Islands; **handsel** confirm
iii.1 **touch** (1) implicate; (2) irritate
5 **certify** assure; **turtle** turtle-dove, a bird associated with love
7 **Paul's** Paul's Walk, the middle aisle of St. Paul's Cathedral, was a crowded meeting place and market for merchants, gossips, and petty criminals on weekdays
9 **pantofles** overshoes
14 **plaster of pitch** remedy for galled (chafed) horses
16 **impetrate** beseech
27 **harlots** lewd men and women
39 **close** concealed; **fittest standing** (1) best position to observe; (2) position next to (and so hidden by) a standing or stall
40 **speed** kill, dispatch
41 **Nag's Head** London tavern on the E corner of Cheapside and Friday Street
43 **paid his own** received his just deserts – i.e., killed
45 **Blackfriars** still a London sanctuary despite the dissolution in 1538 of the monastery there
46 **take water** take a boat across the Thames; **away** escape

Black Will. How can I miss him? When I think on the forty angels I must have more.

Here enters a Prentice.

Prentice. 'Tis very late. I were best shut up my stall, for here will be old filching when the press comes forth of Paul's.

Then lets he down his window, and it breaks Black Will's head.

Black Will. Zounds! Draw, Shakebag, draw! I am almost killed.

Prentice. We'll tame you, I warrant.

Black Will. Zounds, I am tame enough already.

Here enters Arden, Fran[klin], *and* Michael.

Arden. What troublesome fray or mutiny is this?

Franklin. 'Tis nothing but some brabbling, paltry fray,
Devised to pick men's pockets in the throng.

Arden. Is't nothing else? Come, Franklin, let us away.

Exeunt [Arden, Franklin, *and* Michael].

Black Will. What 'mends shall I have for my broken head?

Prentice. Marry, this 'mends, that, if you get you not away all the sooner, you shall be well beaten and sent to the Counter.

Exit [P]rentice.

Black Will. Well, I'll be gone; but look to your signs, for I'll pull them down all. Shakebag, my broken head grieves me not so much as by this means Arden hath escaped.

Here enters Greene.

I had a glimpse of him and his companion.

Greene. Why, sirs, Arden's as well as I.
I met him and Franklin going merrily to the ordinary.
What, dare you not do it?

Black Will. Yes, sir, we dare do it; but, were my consent to give again, we would not do it under ten pound more. I value every drop of my blood at a French crown. I have had ten pound to steal a dog, and we have no more here to kill a man. But that a bargain is a bargain and so forth, you should do it yourself.

Greene. I pray thee, how came thy head broke?

Black Will. Why, thou seest it is broke, dost thou not?

Shakebag. Standing against a stall, watching Arden's coming, a boy let down his shop window and broke his head. Whereupon arose a brawl, and in the tumult Arden escaped us and passed by unthought on. But forbearance is no acquittance. Another time we'll do it, I warrant thee.

Greene. I pray thee, Will, make clean thy bloody brow,
And let us bethink us on some other place
Where Arden may be met with handsomely.
Remember how devoutly thou hast sworn
To kill the villain. Think upon thine oath.

Black Will. Tush, I have broken five hundred oaths! But wouldst thou charm me to effect this deed, tell me of gold, my resolution's fee; say thou seest Mosby kneeling at my knees, off'ring me service for my high attempt; and sweet Alice Arden, with a lap of crowns, comes with a lowly curtsy to the earth, saying, "Take this but for thy quarterage; such yearly tribute will I answer thee." Why, this would steel soft-mettled cowardice, with which Black Will was never tainted with. I tell thee, Greene, the forlorn traveler whose lips are glued with summer's parching heat ne'er longed so much to see a running brook as I to finish Arden's tragedy. Seest thou this gore that cleaveth to my face? From hence ne'er will I wash this bloody stain till Arden's heart be panting in my hand.

Greene. Why, that's well said, but what saith Shakebag?

Shakebag. I cannot paint my valor out with words; but give me place and opportunity, such mercy as the starven lioness, when she is dry-sucked of her eager young, shows to the prey that next encounters her, on Arden so much pity would I take.

Greene. So should it fare with men of firm resolve.
And now, sirs, seeing this accident
Of meeting him in Paul's hath no success,
Let us bethink us on some other place

49 s.d. **Prentice** apprentice
50 **stall** book stall; St. Paul's Churchyard was the center of the London book trade; **old filching** much pilfering
51 **press** crowd
51 s.d. ***breaks*** bruises
53 **tame** hurt
56 **brabbling** brawling
59 **'mends** amends; relief
62 **Counter** a London prison for debtors
69 **ordinary** tavern that serves meals
74 **French crown** the ecu, then worth slightly less than five shillings
84 **on** of
89 **handsomely** conveniently
99 **quarterage** quarterly payment
100 **answer** guarantee
113 **starven** starved
114 **of** by

Whose earth may swallow up this Arden's blood.

Here enters Michael.

See, yonder comes his man and wot you what? The foolish knave is in love with Mosby's sister, and for her sake, whose love he cannot get unless Mosby solicit his suit, the villain hath sworn the slaughter of his master.
We'll question him, for he may stead us much.
How now, Michael, whither are you going?

Michael. My master hath new supped,
And I am going to prepare his chamber.

Greene. Where supped Master Arden?

Michael. At the Nag's Head, at the eighteenpence ordinary.
How now, Master Shakebag? What, Black Will!
God's dear Lady, how chance your face is so bloody?

Black Will. Go to, sirrah; there is a chance in it. This sauciness in you will make you be knocked.

Michael. Nay, and you be offended, I'll be gone.

Greene. Stay, Michael; you may not 'scape us so.
Michael, I know you love your master well.

Michael. Why, so I do; but wherefore urge you that?

Greene. Because I think you love your mistress better.

[*Michael.*] So think not I. But say, i'faith, what if I should?

Shakebag. Come to the purpose, Michael. We hear you have a pretty love in Faversham.

Michael. Why, have I two or three, what's that to thee?

Black Will. You deal too mildly with the peasant. Thus it is: 'tis known to us you love Mosby's sister; we know besides that you have ta'en your oath to further Mosby to your mistress' bed and kill your master for his sister's sake. Now, sir, a poorer coward than yourself was never fostered in the coast of Kent. How comes it then that such a knave as you dare swear a matter of such consequence?

Greene. Ah, Will –

Black Will. Tush, give me leave. There's no more but this: sith thou hast sworn, we dare discover all, and, hadst thou or shouldst thou utter it, we have devised a complot underhand, whatever shall betide to any of us, to send thee roundly to the devil of hell. And therefore, thus: I am the very man, marked in my birth-hour by the Destinies, to give an end to Arden's life on earth. Thou but a member but to whet the knife whose edge must search the closet of his breast. Thy office is but to appoint the place, and train thy master to his tragedy; mine to perform it when occasion serves. Then be not nice, but here devise with us how and what way we may conclude his death.

Shakebag. So shalt thou purchase Mosby for thy friend, and by his friendship gain his sister's love.

Greene. So shall thy mistress be thy favorer,
And thou disburdened of the oath thou made.

Michael. Well, gentlemen, I cannot but confess,
Sith you have urged me so apparently,
That I have vowed my Master Arden's death.
And he whose kindly love and liberal hand
Doth challenge nought but good deserts of me,
I will deliver over to your hands.
This night come to his house at Aldersgate;
The doors I'll leave unlocked against you come.
No sooner shall ye enter through the latch,
Over the threshold to the inner court,
But on your left hand shall you see the stairs
That leads directly to my master's chamber.
There take him and dispose him as ye please.
Now it were good we parted company.
What I have promisèd I will perform.

Black Will. Should you deceive us, 'twould go wrong with you.

Michael. I will accomplish all I have revealed.

Black Will. Come, let's go drink. Choler makes me as dry as a dog.

Exeunt Will, Greene, *and* Shakebag. *Manet* Michael.

---

122 wot know
127 stead us much give us useful information
132 eighteenpence ordinary tavern with meals at a fixed price of eighteen pence
135 Go to common phrase of protest; **a chance in it** i.e., your impertinence is risky
136 make cause
137 knocked beaten up
141 urge introduce
158 sith since;
158–9 discover disclose
160 complot conspiracy
162 roundly directly
164 Destinies the goddesses of Fate
165 member helper
168 train lure
170 nice squeamish
179 apparently plainly
182 challenge claim; **deserts** rewards, favors in return
185 against anticipating; in preparation that
195 Choler anger
195 s.d. *Manet* stays (Latin)

Michael. Thus feeds the lamb securely on the down
While through the thicket of an arbor brake
The hunger-bitten wolf o'erpries his haunt
And takes advantage to eat him up.
Ah, harmless Arden, how, how hast thou misdone
That thus thy gentle life is leveled at?
The many good turns that thou hast done to me
Now must I quittance with betraying thee.
I, that should take the weapon in my hand,
And buckler thee from ill-intending foes,
Do lead thee with a wicked, fraudful smile,
As unsuspected, to the slaughterhouse.
So have I sworn to Mosby and my mistress.
So have I promised to the slaughtermen.
And, should I not deal currently with them,
Their lawless rage would take revenge on me.
Tush, I will spurn at mercy for this once.
Let pity lodge where feeble women lie;
I am resolved, and Arden needs must die.
Exit Michael.

[Sc. iv]

Here enters Arden *and* Fran[klin].

Arden. No, Franklin, no. If fear or stormy threats,
If love of me or care of womanhood,
If fear of God, or common speech of men
Who mangle credit with their wounding words
And couch dishonor as dishonor buds
Might 'join repentance in her wanton thoughts,
No question then but she would turn the leaf
And sorrow for her dissolution.
But she is rooted in her wickedness,
Perverse and stubborn, not to be reclaimed.
Good counsel is to her as rain to weeds,
And reprehension makes her vice to grow
As Hydra's head that plenished by decay.
Her faults, methink, are painted in my face
For every searching eye to overread;
And Mosby's name, a scandal unto mine,
Is deeply trenchèd in my blushing brow.
Ah, Franklin, Franklin, when I think on this,
My heart's grief rends my other powers
Worse than the conflict at the hour of death.
Franklin. Gentle Arden, leave this sad lament.
She will amend, and so your griefs will cease;
Or else she'll die, and so your sorrows end.
If neither of these two do haply fall,
Yet let your comfort be that others bear
Your woes twice doubled all with patience.
Arden. My house is irksome; there I cannot rest.
Franklin. Then stay with me in London; go not hôme.
Arden. Then that base Mosby doth usurp my room
And makes his triumph of my being thence.
At home or not at home, where'er I be,
Here, here it lies [*He points to his heart.*], ah, Franklin, here it lies,
That will not out till wretched Arden dies.

Here enters Michael.

Franklin. Forget your griefs awhile. Here comes your man.
Arden. What o'clock is't, sirrah?
Michael. Almost ten.
Arden. See, see, how runs away the weary time!
Come, Master Franklin, shall we go to bed?
Franklin. I pray you, go before; I'll follow you.
Exeunt Arden *and* Michael. *Manet* Franklin.
Ah, what a hell is fretful jealousy!
What pity-moaning words, what deep-fetched sighs,
What grievous groans and overlading woes
Accompanies this gentle gentleman!
Now will he shake his care-oppressèd head,
Then fix his sad eyes on the sullen earth,
Ashamed to gaze upon the open world.
Now will he cast his eyes up towards the heavens,
Looking that ways for redress of wrong.
Sometimes he seeketh to beguile his grief
And tells a story with his careful tongue;

198 **o'erpries** looks upon
200 **harmless** innocent
201 **leveled** aimed
203 **quittance** reward
205 **buckler** shield
210 **currently** honestly
iv.4 **credit** reputation
5 **couch** contain
6 **'join** enjoin; introduce
8 **dissolution** dissolute behavior
12 **reprehension** rebuke
13 **Hydra's head . . . plenished** when Hercules attempted to kill the many-headed hydra (a large serpent), two heads replenished the beast each time one was cut off
17 **trenchèd** entrenched
21 **leave** cease
24 **haply fall** occur
29 **room** place
30 **thence** absent
48 **beguile** divert attention away from
49 **careful** full of care

Then comes his wife's dishonor in his thoughts
And in the middle cutteth off his tale,
Pouring fresh sorrow on his weary limbs.
So woe-begone, so inly charged with woe,
Was never any lived and bore it so.

Here enters Michael.

Michael. My master would desire you come to bed.
Franklin. Is he himself already in his bed?
Michael. He is and fain would have the light away.
Exit Franklin. *Manet* Michael.
Conflicting thoughts encampèd in my breast
Awake me with the echo of their strokes;
And I, a judge to censure either side,
Can give to neither wishèd victory.
My master's kindness pleads to me for life,
With just demand, and I must grant it him;
My mistress, she hath forced me with an oath
For Susan's sake, the which I may not break,
For that is nearer than a master's love,
That grim-faced fellow, pitiless Black Will,
And Shakebag, stern in bloody stratagem –
Two rougher ruffians never lived in Kent –
Have sworn my death if I infringe my vow,
A dreadful thing to be considered of.
Methinks I see them with their bolstered hair,
Staring and grinning in thy gentle face,
And in their ruthless hands their daggers drawn,
Insulting o'er thee with a peck of oaths
While thou, submissive, pleading for relief,
Art mangled by their ireful instruments.
Methinks I hear them ask where Michael is,
And pitiless Black Will cries, "Stab the slave!
The peasant will detect the tragedy."
The wrinkles in his foul, death-threat'ning face
Gapes open wide, like graves to swallow men.
My death to him is but a merriment,
And he will murder me to make him sport.
He comes, he comes! Ah, Master Franklin, help!
Call up the neighbors, or we are but dead!

Here enters Fran[klin] *and* Arden.

Franklin. What dismal outcry calls me from my rest?
Arden. What hath occasioned such a fearful cry?
Speak, Michael! Hath any injured thee?
Michael. Nothing, sir; but, as I fell asleep
Upon the threshold, leaning to the stairs,
I had a fearful dream that troubled me,
And in my slumber thought I was beset
With murderer thieves that came to rifle me.
My trembling joints witness my inward fear.
I crave your pardons for disturbing you.
Arden. So great a cry for nothing I ne'er heard.
What, are the doors fast locked and all things safe?
Michael. I cannot tell; I think I locked the doors.
Arden. I like not this, but I'll go see myself.
[*He tests the doors.*]
Ne'er trust me but the doors were all unlocked.
This negligence not half contenteth me.
Get you to bed; and if you love my favor,
Let me have no more such pranks as these.
Come, Master Franklin, let us go to bed.
Franklin. Aye, by my faith; the air is very cold.
Michael, farewell; I pray thee, dream no more.
Exeunt.

[Sc. v]

Here enters [Black] Will, Gre[ene], *and* Shak[ebag].

Shakebag. Black night hath hid the pleasures of the day, and sheeting darkness overhangs the earth, and with the black fold of her cloudy robe obscures us from the eyesight of the world, in which sweet silence such as we triumph. The lazy minutes linger on their time, loath to give due audit to the hour, till in the watch our purpose be complete and Arden sent to everlasting night. Greene, get you gone and linger here about, and at some hour hence come to us again, where we will give you instance of his death.

Greene. Speed to my wish whose will soe'er says no;
And so I'll leave you for an hour or two.
Exit Greene.

Black Will. I tell thee, Shakebag, would this thing were done; I am so heavy that I can scarce go. This drowsiness in me bodes little good.

58–63 Conflicting . . . him Holinshed notes "the force of fear and a troubled conscience"
60 censure pronounce judgment on
72 bolstered knotted (by blood)
73 thy i.e., Arden's
75 Insulting exulting; **peck** i.e., a great many
80 detect reveal
91 to against
94 rifle rob
v.2 sheeting covering
8 watch (1) one of the periods into which night hours were divided; (2) looked for Arden
12 instance evidence
13 Speed success

Shakebag. How now, Will, become a Precisian? Nay, then, let's go sleep when bugs and fears shall kill our courages with their fancy's work.

Black Will. Why, Shakebag, thou mistakes me much and wrongs me too in telling me of fear. Were't not a serious thing we go about, it should be slipped till I had fought with thee to let thee know I am no coward, I. I tell thee, Shakebag, thou abusest me.

Shakebag. Why, thy speech bewrayed an inly kind of fear and savored of a weak, relenting spirit. Go forward now in that we have begun, and afterwards attempt me when thou darest.

Black Will. And if I do not, heaven cut me off! But let that pass, and show me to this house where thou shalt see I'll do as much as Shakebag.

Shakebag. This is the door – but soft, methinks, 'tis shut. The villain Michael hath deceivèd us.

Black Will. Soft, let me see. Shakebag, 'tis shut indeed. Knock with thy sword; perhaps the slave will hear.

Shakebag. It will not be; the white-livered peasant is gone to bed and laughs us both to scorn.

Black Will. And he shall buy his merriment as dear as ever coistrel bought so little sport. Ne'er let this sword assist me when I need, but rust and canker after I have sworn, if I, the next time that I meet the hind, lop not away his leg, his arm, or both.

Shakebag. And let me never draw a sword again, nor prosper in the twilight, cockshut light, when I would fleece the wealthy passenger, but lie and languish in a loathsome den, hated and spit at by the goers-by, and in that death may die, unpitièd, if I, the next time that I meet the slave, cut not the nose from off the coward's face and trample on it for this villainy.

Black Will. Come, let's go seek out Greene; I know he'll swear.

Shakebag. He were a villain and he would not swear. 'Twould make a peasant swear among his boys, that ne'er durst say before but "yea" and "no," to be thus flouted of a coisterel.

Black Will. Shakebag, let's seek out Greene, and in the morning at the alehouse 'butting Arden's house watch the outcoming of that prick-eared cur, and then let me alone to handle him.

Exeunt.

[Sc. vi]

Here enters Ar[den], Fra[nklin], *and* Michael.

Arden. [*To Michael.*] Sirrah, get you back to Billingsgate
And learn what time the tide will serve our turn.
Come to us in Paul's. First go make the bed,
And afterwards go hearken for the flood.

Exit Michael.

Come, Master Franklin, you shall go with me.
This night I dreamed that, being in a park,
A toil was pitched to overthrow the deer,
And I upon a little rising hill,
Stood whistly watching for the herd's approach.
Even there, methoughts, a gentle slumber took me
And summoned all my parts to sweet repose.
But in the pleasure of this golden rest,
An ill-thewed foster had removed the toil
And rounded me with that beguiling home
Which late, methought, was pitched to cast the deer.
With that he blew an evil-sounding horn;
And at the noise another herdman came
With falchion drawn, and bent it at my breast,
Crying aloud, "Thou art the game we seek."
With this I waked and trembled every joint,
Like one obscurèd in a little bush
That sees a lion foraging about,

---

18 Precisian Puritan
19 bugs bugbears, imaginary terrors
20 fancy's work imagination's effects
22 telling accusing
24 slipped put off
27 bewrayed revealed
30 attempt engage
40 white-livered cowardly
44 coistrel knave (bird imagery)
47 hind fellow (animal imagery)
50 cockshut light dusk (when poultry roost)
51 passenger foot-traveler
60 and if
65 'butting abutting
67 prick pointed
vi.1 Billingsgate (1) the watergate of London on the N side of the Thames; (2) the famous fishmarket there
2 tide flood-tide or high tide
7 toil net; **pitched** fastened in place
9 whistly silently
13 ill-thewed ill-natured; **foster** forester
14 rounded surrounded
15 late but now; **cast** overthrow
18 falchion a curved broadsword; **bent** aimed

And, when the dreadful forest king is gone,
He pries about with timorous suspect
Throughout the thorny casements of the brake,
And will not think his person dangerless
But quakes and shivers though the cause be gone.
So, trust me, Franklin, when I did awake,
I stood in doubt whether I waked or no,
Such great impression took this fond surprise.
God grant this vision bedeem me any good!

Franklin. This fantasy doth rise from Michael's fear,
Who being awakèd with the noise he made,
His troubled senses yet could take no rest;
And this, I warrant you, procured your dream.

Arden. It may be so; God frame it to the best!
But oftentimes my dreams presage too true.

Franklin. To such as note their nightly fantasies,
Some one in twenty may incur belief.
But use it not; 'tis but a mockery.

Arden. Come, Master Franklin, we'll now walk in Paul's,
And dine together at the ordinary,
And by my man's direction draw to the quay,
And with the tide go down to Faversham.
Say, Master Franklin, shall it not be so?

Franklin. At your good pleasure, sir, I'll bear you company.

Exeunt.

[Sc. vii]

Here enters Michael *at one door. Here enters* Greene, [Black] Will, *and* Shakebag *at another door.*

Black Will. Draw, Shakebag, for here's that villain Michael.

Greene. First, Will, let's hear what he can say.

Black Will. Speak, milksop slave, and never after speak.

Michael. For God's sake, sirs, let me excuse myself.
For here I swear by heaven and earth and all,
I did perform the outmost of my task
And left the doors unbolted and unlocked.
But see the chance: Franklin and my master
Were very late conferring in the porch,
And Franklin left his napkin where he sat,
With certain gold knit in it, as he said.
Being in bed, he did bethink himself,
And coming down he found the doors unshut.
He locked the gates and brought away the keys,
For which offence my master rated me.
But now I am going to see what flood it is;
For with the tide my master will away,
Where you may front him well on Rainham Down,
A place well fitting such a stratagem.

Black Will. Your excuse hath somewhat mollified my choler. Why now, Greene, 'tis better now nor e'er it was.

Greene. But, Michael, is this true?

Michael. As true as I report it to be true.

Shakebag. Then, Michael, this shall be your penance: to feast us all at the Salutation, where we will plot our purpose thoroughly.

Greene. And, Michael, you shall bear no news of this tide
Because they two may be in Rainham Down
Before your master.

Michael. Why, I'll agree to anything you'll have me,
So you will accept of my company.

Exeunt.

[Sc. viii]

Here enters Mosby.

Mosby. Disturbed thoughts drive me from company
And dries my marrow with their watchfulness.
Continual trouble of my moody brain
Feebles my body by excess of drink
And nips me as the bitter northeast wind
Doth check the tender blossoms in the spring.

---

23 **forest king** lion
24 **suspect** apprehension
25 **brake** thicket
30 **took . . . surprise** this foolish terror made upon me
31 **bedeem . . . good** foretells no danger for me
36 **frame** makes
40 **use it not** do not believe it
42 **ordinary** tavern that serves meals
43 **quay** the wharf at Billingsgate (from which a barge left for Gravesend)
vii.3 **milksop** cowardly

6 **outmost** utmost
8 **chance** mischance; outcome
10 **napkin** handkerchief
11 **knit** tied up
15 **rated** berated
18 **front** confront; **Rainham Down** the open country around the village of Rainham in Kent, between Rochester and Faversham
22 **nor** than
26 **Salutation** a tavern in Newgate Street, possibly named for Gabriel's visit to Mary

Well fares the man, howe'er his cates do taste,
That tables not with foul suspicion;
And he but pines amongst his delicates
Whose troubled mind is stuffed with
discontent.
My golden time was when I had no gold;
Though then I wanted, yet I slept secure;
My daily toil begat me night's repose;
My night's repose made daylight fresh to me.
But since I climbed the top bough of the tree
And sought to build my nest among the
clouds,
Each gentle starry gale doth shake my bed
And makes me dread my downfall to the earth.
But whither doth contemplation carry me?
The way I seek to find where pleasure dwells
Is hedged behind me that I cannot back
But needs must on although to danger's gate.
Then, Arden, perish thou by that decree,
For Greene doth ear the land and weed thee
up
To make my harvest nothing but pure corn.
And for his pains I'll heave him up awhile
And, after, smother him to have his wax;
Such bees as Greene must never live to sting.
Then is there Michael and the painter too,
Chief actors to Arden's overthrow,
Who, when they shall see me sit in Arden's
seat,
They will insult upon me for my meed
Or fright me by detecting of his end.
I'll none of that, for I can cast a bone
To make these curs pluck out each other's
throat,
And then am I sole ruler of mine own.
Yet Mistress Arden lives; but she's myself,
And holy church rites makes us two but
one.
But what for that I may not trust you,
Alice?
You have supplanted Arden for my sake,
And will extirpen me to plant another.
'Tis fearful sleeping in a serpent's bed,
And I will cleanly rid my hands of her.

Here enters Alice [*holding a prayerbook*].

But here she comes, and I must flatter her.
How now, Alice? What, sad and passionate?
Make me partaker of thy pensiveness;
Fire divided burns with lesser force.

Alice. But I will dam that fire in my breast
Till by the force thereof my part consume.
[*Sighing.*] Ah, Mosby!

Mosby. Such deep pathaires, like to a cannon's
burst,
Discharged against a ruinated wall,
Breaks my relenting heart in thousand pieces.
Ungentle Alice, thy sorrow is my sore;
Thou know'st it well, and 'tis thy policy
To forge distressful looks to wound a breast
Where lies a heart that dies when thou art sad.
It is not love that loves to anger love.

Alice. It is not love that loves to murder love.

Mosby. How mean you that?

Alice. Thou knowest how dearly Arden loved me.

Mosby. And then?

Alice. And then – conceal the rest, for 'tis too bad,
Lest that my words be carried with the wind
And published in the world to both our
shames.
I pray thee, Mosby, let our springtime wither;
Our harvest else will yield but loathsome
weeds.
Forget, I pray thee, what hath passed betwixt
us,
For now I blush and tremble at the thoughts.

Mosby. What, are you changed?

Alice. Aye, to my former happy life again,
From title of an odious strumpet's name
To honest Arden's wife, not Arden's honest
wife.
Ha, Mosby, 'tis thou hast rifled me of that,
And made me sland'rous to all my kin.
Even in my forehead is thy name engraven,
A mean artificer, that low-born name.
I was bewitched. Woe worth the hapless hour

---

viii.7 **cates** delicacies
8 **tables** dines
9 **delicates** delights
24 **ear** plow
25 **nothing but pure corn** pure pleasure with Arden out of the way
26 **heave him up** extol him
27 **smother . . . wax** referring to the practice of smoking out bees to obtain honey from the hive
32 **insult upon** scornfully abuse; **meed** reward
33 **detecting** disclosing
34 **a bone** i.e., Susan
38 **holy church rites** Holinshed reports that Alice and Mosby performed the sacrament of marriage openly in church "on a Sunday," but this is omitted from the play
41 **extirpen** root out; destroy
43 **cleanly** completely
45 **passionate** sorrowful
51 **pathaires** sad and passionate outbursts
52 **ruinated** about to be ruined
55 **policy** scheme
56 **forge** contrive
73 **honest** chaste
78 **Woe worth** a curse upon; **hapless** unfortunate

And all the causes that enchanted me!
Mosby. Nay, if thou ban, let me breathe curses forth;
And if you stand so nicely at your fame,
Let me repent the credit I have lost.
I have neglected matters of import
That would have stated me above thy state,
Forslowed advantages, and spurned at time.
Aye, Fortune's right hand Mosby hath forsook
To take a wanton giglot by the left.
I left the marriage of an honest maid,
Whose dowry would have weighed down all thy wealth,
Whose beauty and demeanor far exceeded thee.
This certain good I lost for changing bad,
And wrapped my credit in thy company.
I was bewitched – that is no theme of thine –
And thou unhallowed hast enchanted me.
But I will break thy spells and exorcisms
And put another sight upon these eyes
That showed my heart a raven for a dove.
Thou art not fair; I viewed thee not till now.
Thou art not kind; till now I knew thee not.
And now the rain hath beaten off thy gilt
Thy worthless copper shows thee counterfeit.
It grieves me not to see how foul thou art,
But mads me that ever I thought thee fair.
Go, get thee gone, a copesmate for thy hinds!
I am too good to be thy favorite.
Alice. Aye, now I see, and too soon find it true,
Which often hath been told me by my friends,
That Mosby loves me not but for my wealth,
Which, too incredulous, I ne'er believed.
Nay, hear me speak, Mosby, a word or two;
I'll bite my tongue if it speak bitterly.
Look on me, Mosby, or I'll kill myself;
Nothing shall hide me from thy stormy look.
If thou cry war, there is no peace for me;
I will do penance for offending thee
And burn this prayerbook, where I here use
The holy word that had converted me.
See, Mosby, I will tear away the leaves,
And all the leaves, and in this golden cover
Shall thy sweet phrases and thy letters dwell;
And thereon will I chiefly meditate,
And hold no other sect but such devotion.
Wilt thou not look? Is all thy love overwhelmed?
Wilt thou not hear? What malice stops thine ears?
Why speaks thou not? What silence ties thy tongue?
Thou hast been sighted as the eagle is,
And heard as quickly as the fearful hare,
And spoke as smoothly as an orator,
When I have bid thee hear or see or speak.
And art thou sensible in none of these?
Weigh all thy good turns with this little fault
And I deserve not Mosby's muddy looks.
A fount once troubled is not thickened still;
Be clear again, I'll ne'er more trouble thee.
Mosby. Oh no, I am a base artificer;
My wings are feathered for a lowly flight.
Mosby? Fie, no! not for a thousand pound.
Make love to you? Why, 'tis unpardonable;
We beggars must not breathe where gentles are.
Alice. Sweet Mosby is as gentle as a king,
And I too blind to judge him otherwise.
Flowers do sometimes spring in fallow lands,
Weeds in gardens, roses grow on thorns;
So, whatsoe'er my Mosby's father was,
Himself valued gentle by his worth.
Mosby. Ah, how you women can insinuate
And clear a trespass with your sweet-set tongue!
I will forget this quarrel, gentle Alice,
Provided I'll be tempted so no more.

Here enters Bradshaw.

Alice. Then with thy lips seal up this new-made match.
[*They kiss.*]
Mosby. Soft, Alice, for here comes somebody.
Alice. How now, Bradshaw, what's the news with you?
Bradshaw. I have little news, but here's a letter

80 **ban** curse
81 **stand so nicely** insist so fastidiously on; **fame** reputation
84 **stated** raised; **state** rank
85 **Forslowed** wasted
87 **giglot** worthless woman
88 **honest** chaste
92 **wrapped** involved; compromised
94 **unhallowed** wicked
104 **copesmate** companion (with contempt); **hinds** servants
110 **Nay, hear me speak** (the sudden change in Alice's speech suggests Mosby prepares to leave her)
116 **where** wherein; **use** follow
122 **sect** religious belief
126 **eagle** reference is to the eagle's superior sight
127 **quickly** keenly
130 **sensible** capable of using the senses
133 **still** forever
139 **gentles** those of gentle birth or rank
140 **gentle** noble
147 **clear a trespass** acquit

That Master Greene importuned me to give you.

Alice. Go in, Bradshaw; call for a cup of beer. 'Tis almost supper time; thou shalt stay with us.

Exit [Bradshaw].

Then she reads the letter.

"We have missed of our purpose at London, but shall perform it by the way. We thank our neighbor Bradshaw.

Yours,
Richard Greene."

How likes my love the tenor of this letter?

Mosby. Well, were his date complete and expired!

Alice. Ah, would it were! Then comes my happy hour.
Till then my bliss is mixed with bitter gall.
Come, let us in to shun suspicion.

Mosby. Aye, to the gates of death to follow thee.

Exeunt.

[Sc. ix]

Here enters Greene, [Black] Will, *and* Shakebag.

Shakebag. Come, Will, see thy tools be in a readiness. Is not thy powder dank, or will thy flint strike fire?

Black Will. Then ask me if my nose be on my face, or whether my tongue be frozen in my mouth. Zounds, here's a coil! You were best swear me on the intergatories how many pistols I have took in hand, or whether I love the smell of gunpowder, or dare abide the noise the dag will make, or will not wink at flashing of the fire. I pray thee, Shakebag, let this answer thee, that I have took more purses in this Down than e'er thou handledst pistols in thy life.

Shakebag. Aye, haply thou hast picked more in a throng; but, should I brag what booties I have took, I think the overplus that's more than thine would mount to a greater sum of money than either thou or all thy kin are worth. Zounds, I hate them as I hate a toad that carry a muscado in their tongue and scarce a hurting weapon in their hand.

Black Will. Oh, Greene, intolerable! It is not for mine honor to bear this. Why, Shakebag, I did serve the king at Boulogne, and thou canst brag of nothing that thou hast done.

Shakebag. Why, so can Jack of Faversham that sounded for a fillip on the nose when he that gave it him holloed in his ear and he supposed a cannon-bullet hit him.

Then they fight.

Greene. [*Separating them.*] I pray you, sirs, list to Æsop's talk:
While two stout dogs were striving for a bone
There comes a cur and stole it from them both;
So, while you stand striving on these terms of manhood,
Arden escapes us and deceives us all.

Shakebag. Why, he begun.

Black Will. And thou shalt find I'll end.
I do but slip it until better time.
But, if I do forget –

Then he kneels down and holds up his hands to heaven.

Greene. Well, take your fittest standings, and once more
Lime your twigs to catch this weary bird.
I'll leave you, and at your dag's discharge
Make towards, like the longing water-dog
That coucheth till the fowling-piece be off,
Then seizeth on the prey with eager mood.
Ah, might I see him stretching forth his limbs
As I have seen them beat their wings ere now.

Shakebag. Why, that thou shalt see if he come this way.

Greene. Yes, that he doth, Shakebag, I warrant thee.
But brawl not when I am gone in any case,
But, sirs, be sure to speed him when he comes;
And in that hope I'll leave you for an hour.

Exit Gre[ene].

[Black Will *and* Shakebag *withdraw*]

Here enters Arden, Franklin, *and* Michael.

Michael. 'Twere best that I went back to Rochester.

---

ix.6 coil fuss
7 intergatories interrogatories
10 dag pistol; **wink** blink
21 muscado musket
28 sounded swooned; **fillip** sharp blows with the fist
29 holloed called
31 list listen
32 stout valiant
38 slip postpone
40 standings positions to catch quarry
41 Lime bird-lime, a sticky substance that was spread on branches to catch birds; **weary** wearisome, irksome
44 coucheth lies down; **fowling-piece** a light gun used for hunting wildfowl
47 them waterfowl

The horse halts downright; it were not good
He traveled in such pain to Faversham.
Removing of a shoe may haply help it.

Arden. Well, get you back to Rochester; but, sirrah, see
Ye overtake us ere we come to Rainham Down,
For it will be very late ere we get home.

Michael. [*Aside.*] Aye, God he knows, and so doth Will and Shakebag,
That thou shalt never go further than that Down;
And therefore have I pricked the horse on purpose
Because I would not view the massacre.

Exit Michael.

Arden. Come, Master Franklin, onwards with your tale.

Franklin. I assure you, sir, you task me much.
A heavy blood is gathered at my heart,
And on the sudden is my wind so short
As hindereth the passage of my speech.
So fierce a qualm yet ne'er assailed me.

Arden. Come, Master Franklin, let us go on softly.
The annoyance of the dust, or else some meat
You ate at dinner, cannot brook you.
I have been often so and soon amended.

Franklin. Do you remember where my tale did leave?

Arden. Aye, where the gentleman did check his wife.

Franklin. She being reprehended for the fact,
Witness produced that took her with the deed,
Her glove brought in which there she left behind,
And many other assured arguments,
Her husband asked her whether it were not so.

Arden. Her answer then? I wonder how she looked,
Having forsworn it with such vehement oaths,
And at the instant so approved upon her.

Franklin. First did she cast her eyes down to the earth,
Watching the drops that fell amain from thence;
Then softly draws she forth her handkercher,
And modestly she wipes her tear-stained face.
Then hemmed she out, to clear her voice should seem,
And with a majesty addressed herself
To encounter all their accusations.
Pardon me, Master Arden, I can no more;
This fighting at my heart makes short my wind.

Arden. Come, we are almost now at Rainham Down.
Your pretty tale beguiles the weary way;
I would you were in state to tell it out.

Shakebag.[*Aside.*] Stand close, Will; I hear them coming.

Here enters Lord Cheyne *with his* Men.

Black Will. [*Aside.*] Stand to it, Shakebag, and be resolute.

Lord Cheyne. Is it so near night as it seems,
Or will this black-faced evening have a shower?
What, Master Arden? You are well met.
I have longed this fortnight's day to speak with you.
You are a stranger, man, in the Isle of Sheppey.

Arden. Your honor's. Always bound to do you service!

Lord Cheyne. Come you from London and ne'er a man with you?

Arden. My man's coming after,
But here's my honest friend that came along with me.

Lord Cheyne. [*To Franklin.*] My Lord Protector's man, I take you to be.

Franklin. Aye, my good lord, and highly bound to you.

Lord Cheyne. You and your friend come home and sup with me.

Arden. I beseech your honor, pardon me;
I have made a promise to a gentleman,
My honest friend, to meet him at my house.
The occasion is great, or else would I wait on you.

Lord Cheyne. Will you come tomorrow and dine with me,
And bring your honest friend along with you?
I have divers matters to talk with you about.

Arden. Tomorrow we'll wait upon your honor.

---

54 **halts downright** limps badly
62 **pricked the horse** pierced the horse's feet so as to make the horse lame
69 **qualm** fit of illness
70 **softly** slowly, gently
72 **brook** digest
74 **leave** leave off
75 **check** reprimand
77 **took** caught; **with the deed** i.e., in the act
79 **arguments** evidence
83 **approved upon** proved against
85 **amain** with full force
95 **state** condition
115 **your honest friend** i.e., Franklin

Lord Cheyne. One of you stay my horse at the top of the hill.
[*Seeing Black Will.*] What, Black Will! For whose purse wait you?
Thou wilt be hanged in Kent when all is done.

Black Will. Not hanged, God save your honor. I am your beadsman, bound to pray for you.

Lord Cheyne. I think thou ne'er said prayer in all thy life.
One of you give him a crown.
And, sirrah, leave this kind of life.
If thou beest 'tainted for a penny matter
And come in question, surely thou wilt truss.
Come, Master Arden, let us be going;
Your way and mine lies four mile together.

Exeunt. Manet Black Will *and* Shakebag.

Black Will. The devil break all your necks at four miles' end! Zounds, I could kill myself for very anger! His lordship chops me in even when my dag was leveled at his heart. I would his crown were molten down his throat.

Shakebag. Arden, thou hast wondrous holy luck. Did ever man escape as thou hast done? Well, I'll discharge my pistol at the sky, for by this bullet Arden might not die. [*He fires.*]

Here enters Greene.

Greene. What, is he down? Is he dispatched?

Shakebag. Ay, in health towards Faversham to shame us all.

Greene. The devil he is! Why, sirs, how escaped he?

Shakebag. When we were ready to shoot, comes my Lord Cheyne to prevent his death.

Greene. The Lord of Heaven hath preserved him.

Black Will. Preserved, a fig! The Lord Cheyne hath preservèd him and bids him to a feast to his house at Shorlow. But by the way once more I'll meet with him; and if all the Cheynes in the world say no, I'll have a bullet in his breast tomorrow. Therefore come, Greene, and let us to Faversham.

Greene. Ay, and excuse ourselves to Mistress Arden.
Oh, how she'll chafe when she hears of this!

Shakebag. Why, I'll warrant you she'll think we dare not do it.

Black Will. Why, then let us go, and tell her all the matter, and plot the news to cut him off tomorrow.

Exeunt.

[Sc. x]

Here enters Arden *and* Alice, Franklin, *and* Michael.

Arden. See how the Hours, the guardant of heaven's gate,
Have by their toil removed the darksome clouds,
That Sol may well discern the trampled pace
Wherein he wont to guide his golden car.
The season fits. Come, Franklin, let's away.

Alice. I thought you did pretend some special hunt
That made you thus cut short the time of rest.

Arden. It was no chase that made me rise so early
But, as I told thee yesternight, to go to
The Isle of Sheppey, there to dine with my Lord Cheyne;
For so his honor late commanded me.

Alice. Aye, such kind husbands seldom want excuses;
Home is a wild cat to a wand'ring wit.
The time hath been – would God it were not past –
That honor's title nor a lord's command
Could once have drawn you from these arms of mine.
But my deserts, or your desires decay,
Or both; yet if true love may seem desert,
I merit still to have thy company.

Franklin. Why, I pray you, sir, let her go along with us.
I am sure his honor will welcome her,
And us the more for bringing her along.

Arden. Content. [*To Michael.*] Sirrah, saddle your mistress' nag.

[*Exit* Michael.]

Alice. No, begged favor merits little thanks.
If I should go, our house would run away
Or else be stol'n; therefore I'll stay behind.

---

122 **beadsman** one paid to pray for others
126–7 **If . . . truss** "if you are accused of anything, and brought to trial, you'll hang for certain"
127 **truss** hang
132 **chops me in** suddenly intervenes
134 **his** Lord Cheyne's
147 **Shorlow** Shurland, Lord Cheyne's house on the Isle of Sheppey
157 **plot the news** devise a new plan; **cut him off** kill him

x.1 **Hours** daughters of Zeus and Themis, guards of the gates of Olympus, who also directed changes in the seasons and weather
3 **Sol** the sun; **pace** path
5 **The . . . fits** the weather is suitable
6 **pretend** (1) intend; (2) use as pretext
11 **late** recently
12 **want** need; lack
17 **deserts** merits
18 **desert** deserving

Arden. Nay, see how mistaking you are.
I pray thee, go.
Alice. No, no, not now.
Arden. Then let me leave thee satisfied in this,
That time nor place nor persons alter me
But that I hold thee dearer than my life.
Alice. That will be seen by your quick return.
Arden. And that shall be ere night and if I live.
Farewell, sweet Alice; we mind to sup with thee.

Exit A[lice].

Franklin. Come, Michael, are our horses ready?

[*Enter* Michael.]

Michael. Aye, your horse are ready, but I am not ready
For I have lost my purse
With six-and-thirty shillings in it
With taking up of my master's nag.
Franklin. Why, I pray you, let us go before
While he stays behind to seek his purse.
Arden. Go to, sirrah! See you follow us to the Isle of Sheppey,
To my Lord Cheyne's, where we mean to dine.

Exeunt Arden *and* Franklin. *Manet* Michael.

Michael. So, fair weather after you; for before you lies
Black Will and Shakebag in the broom close,
Too close for you. They'll be your ferrymen to long home.

Here enters the Painter [Clarke].

But who is this? The painter, my corrival,
That would needs win Mistress Susan.
Clarke. How now, Michael? How doth my mistress
And all at home?
Michael. Who? Susan Mosby? She is your mistress, too?
Clarke. Aye, How doth she and all the rest?
Michael. All's well but Susan; she is sick.
Clarke. Sick? Of what disease?
Michael. Of a great fear.
Clarke. A fear of what?
Michael. A great fever.
Clarke. A fever? God forbid!
Michael. Yes, faith,
And of a lurdan, too, as big as yourself.
Clarke. Oh Michael, the spleen prickles you. Go to; you carry an eye over Mistress Susan.
Michael. Ay, faith, to keep her from the painter.
Clarke. Why more from a painter than from
A serving-creature like yourself?
Michael. Because you painters make but a painting-table
Of a pretty wench and spoil her beauty with blotting.
Clarke. What mean you by that?
Michael. Why, that you painters
Paint lambs in the lining of wenches' petticoats,
And we servingmen put horns to them
To make them become sheep.
Clarke. Such another word will cost you a cuff or a knock.
Michael. What, with a dagger made of a pencil?
Faith, 'tis too weak, and therefore
Thou too weak to win Susan.
Clarke. Would Susan's love lay upon this stroke!

Then he breaks Michael's head.

Here enters Mosby, Greene, *and* Alice.

Alice. I'll lay my life, this is for Susan's love.
[*To Michael.*] Stayed you behind your master to this end?
Have you no other time to brabble in
But now when serious matters are in hand?

[*Exit* Michael.]

Say, Clarke, hast thou done the thing thou promised?
Clarke. Aye, here it is: the very touch is death.

[*Exit* Clarke.]

Alice. Then this, I hope, if all the rest do fail,
Will catch Master Arden
And make him wise in death that lived a fool.
Why should he thrust his sickle in our corn,
Or what hath he to do with thee, my love,
Or govern me that am to rule myself?
Forsooth, for credit sake, I must leave thee!

---

33 **and if** if
45 **broom close** enclosed field with shrubbery
46 **ferrymen** acting like Charon, who was the boatman taking dead souls across the River Styx to Hades; **long home** permanent rest
57 **lurdan** rogue; loafer (fever-lurdan was the disease of laziness)
58 **spleen** organ associated with sudden passion such as a quick temper; **prickles** goads; **carry an eye over** are attracted to; have designs on
62 **painting-table** portrait (from the flat table on which it was painted)
63 **blotting** (1) making an error; (2) painting badly
65 **Paint** decorating (petticoats) by painting
66 **put horns** engage sexually
67 **sheep** (metaphor, as sexual objects)
72 **s.d.** ***breaks*** strikes
73 **lay** wager
75 **brabble** brawl
78 **it** i.e., poisoned crucifix
85 **Forsooth** in truth

Nay, he must leave to live that we may love,
May live, may love; for what is life but love?
And love shall last as long as life remains,
And life shall end before my love depart.

Mosby. Why, what's love without true constancy?
Like to a pillar built of many stones,
Yet neither with good mortar well compact
Nor cement to fasten it in the joints
But that it shakes with every blast of wind
And, being touched, straight falls unto the earth
And buries all his haughty pride in dust.
No, let our love be rocks of adamant,
Which time nor place nor tempest can asunder.

Greene. Mosby, leave protestations now,
And let us bethink us what we have to do.
Black Will and Shakebag I have placed
In the broom close, watching Arden's coming.
Let's to them and see what they have done.

Exeunt.

[Sc. xi]

Here enters Ard[en] *and* Fra[nklin.]

Arden. Oh, ferryman, where art thou?

Here enters the Ferryman.

Ferryman. Here, here! Go before to the boat, and I will follow you.

Arden. We have great haste; I pray thee, come away.

Ferryman. Fie, what a mist is here!

Arden. This mist, my friend, is mystical,
Like to a good companion's smoky brain,
That was half-drowned with new ale overnight.

Ferryman. 'Twere pity but his skull were opened to make more chimney room.

Franklin. Friend, what's thy opinion of this mist?

Ferryman. I think 'tis like to a curst wife in a little house that never leaves her husband till she have driven him out at doors with a wet pair of eyes. Then looks he as if his house were afire, or some of his friends dead.

Arden. Speaks thou this of thine own experience?

Ferryman. Perhaps aye; perhaps no; for my wife is as other women are, that is to say, governed by the moon.

Franklin. By the moon? How, I pray thee?

Ferryman. Nay, thereby lies a bargain, and you shall not have it fresh and fasting.

Arden. Yes, I pray thee, good ferryman.

Ferryman. Then for this once let it be midsummer moon, but yet my wife has another moon.

Franklin. Another moon?

Ferryman. Aye, and it hath influences and eclipses.

Arden. Why, then, by this reckoning you sometimes
Play the man in the moon.

Ferryman. Aye, but you had not best to meddle with that moon lest I scratch you by the face with my bramble- bush.

Arden. I am almost stifled with this fog. Come, let's away.

Franklin. And, sirrah, as we go, let us have
Some more of your bold yeomanry.

Ferryman. Nay, by my troth, sir, but flat knavery.

Exeunt.

[Sc. xii]

Here enters Black Will *at one door and* Shakebag *at another.*

Shakebag. Oh, Will, where art thou?

Black Will. Here, Shakebag, almost in hell's mouth, where I cannot see my way for smoke.

Shakebag. I pray thee, speak still, that we may meet by the sound, for I shall fall into some ditch or other unless my feet see better than my eyes.

Black Will. Didst thou ever see better weather to run away with another man's wife or play with a wench at potfinger?

Shakebag. No; this were a fine world for chandlers if this weather would last, for then a man should

---

86 leave cease
96 his its
99 leave leave off
xi.8 good suitable; i.e., one who likes to drink
10 but unless
13 curst shrewish; incited by the devil
15 at of
20–1 governed by the moon (1) changeable (the moon waxes and wanes); (2) susceptible to the menstrual cycle, thought to be caused by the moon
24 fresh and fasting for nothing
26 for this once as a single exception
26–7 midsummer moon Midsummer Night, June 24, a time of madness and unexpected behavior
27 another moon (reference to her sexual organs)
31 man in the moon (with sexual reference)
35 stifled (talk comes close to cuckoldry and Arden breaks off conversation)
37 bold yeomanry blunt humor
38 troth truth; **flat knavery** crude jesting
xii.4 speak still go on speaking
5 sound the river that runs between Faversham and the Isle of Sheppey and on out to the Thames, making Faversham a minor port
10 potfinger colloquialism for sexual act
11 chandlers candlemakers

never dine nor sup without candlelight. But, sirrah Will, what horses are those that passed?

Black Will. Why, didst thou hear any?

Shakebag. Aye, that I did.

Black Will. My life for thine, 'twas Arden and his companion, and then all our labor's lost.

Shakebag. Nay, say not so; for, if it be they, they may haply lose their way as we have done, and then we may chance meet with them.

Black Will. Come, let us go like a couple of blind pilgrims.

Then Shakebag *falls into a ditch.*

Shakebag. Help, Will, help! I am almost drowned.

Here enters the Ferryman.

Ferryman. Who's that, that calls for help?

Black Will. 'Twas none here; 'twas thou thyself.

Ferryman. I came to help him that called for help. Why, how now? Who is this that's in the ditch? [*He helps Shakebag out.*] You are well enough served to go without a guide such weather as this!

Black Will. Sirrah, what companions hath passed your ferry this morning?

Ferryman. None but a couple of gentlemen that went to dine at my Lord Cheyne's.

Black Will. Shakebag, did not I tell thee as much?

Ferryman. Why, sir, will you have any letters carried to them?

Black Will. No, sir; get you gone.

Ferryman. Did you ever see such a mist as this?

Black Will. No, nor such a fool as will rather be hocked than get his way.

Ferryman. Why, sir, this is no Hock Monday; you are deceived. What's his name, I pray you, sir?

Shakebag. His name is Black Will.

Ferryman. I hope to see him one day hanged upon a hill.

Exit Ferryman.

Shakebag. See how the sun hath cleared the foggy mist?
Now we have missed the mark of our intent.

Here enters Greene, Mosby, *and* Alice.

Mosby. Black Will and Shakebag, what make you here? What, is the deed done? Is Arden dead?

Black Will. What could a blinded man perform in arms? Saw you not how till now the sky was dark, that neither horse nor man could be discerned? Yet did we hear their horses as they passed.

Greene. Have they escaped you then and passed the ferry?

Shakebag. Aye, for a while; but here we two will stay and at their coming back meet with them once more. Zounds, I was ne'er so toiled in all my life in following so slight a task as this.

Mosby.[*To Shakebag.*] How cam'st thou so berayed?

Black Will. With making false footing in the dark. He needs would follow them without a guide.

Alice. [*Giving money.*] Here's to pay for a fire and good cheer.
Get you to Faversham to the Flower-de-Luce,
And rest yourselves until some other time.

Greene. Let me alone; it most concerns my state.

Black Will. Aye, Mistress Arden, this will serve the turn in case we fall into a second fog.

Exeunt Greene, Will, *and* Shakebag.

Mosby. These knaves will never do it. Let us give it over.

Alice. First tell me how you like my new device?
Soon, when my husband is returning back,
You and I both marching arm in arm,
Like loving friends, we'll meet him on the way
And boldly beard and brave him to his teeth.
When words grow hot and blows begin to rise,
I'll call those cutters forth your tenement,
Who, in a manner to take up the fray,
Shall wound my husband Hornsby to the death.

Mosby. Ah, fine device! Why, this deserves a kiss.

[*He kisses her.*] *Exeunt.*

[Sc. xiii]

Here enters Dick Reede *and* a Sailor.

Sailor. Faith, Dick Reede, it is to little end. His conscience is too liberal and he too niggardly to part from anything may do thee good.

Reede. He is coming from Shorlow as I understand. Here I'll intercept him, for at his house he never will vouchsafe to speak with me. If prayers and fair entreaties will not serve or make no batt'ry in his flinty breast,

---

43 **hocked** caught and controlled by a woman

44 **Hock Monday** a festival on the second Monday (and Tuesday) after Easter when women caught men and made them pay for their restored freedom

51 **make you** are you doing

61 **toiled** exhausted

64 **berayed** covered in mud

70 **Let** leave; **Let me alone** Let me decide what to do

74 **device** plan

78 **beard and brave** confront and affront; defy stoutly

80 **cutters** cut-throats; **forth** forth from; **tenement** dwelling; according to Holinshed, Mosby's sister lived in a tenement in Faversham belonging to Arden

82 **Hornsby** (slang for cuckold)

Here enters Fra[nklin], Ar[den], *and* Michael.

I'll curse the carl and see what that will do. See where he comes to further my intent. Master Arden, I am now bound to the sea. My coming to you was about the plot of ground which wrongfully you detain from me. Although the rent of it be very small, yet will it help my wife and children, which here I leave in Faversham, God knows, needy and bare. For Christ's sake, let them have it!

Arden. Franklin, hearest thou this fellow speak?
That which he craves I dearly bought of him
Although the rent of it was ever mine.
Sirrah, you that ask these questions,
If with thy clamorous impeaching tongue
Thou rail on me, as I have heard thou dost,
I'll lay thee up so close a twelvemonth's day
As thou shalt neither see the sun nor moon.
Look to it; for, as surely as I live,
I'll banish pity if thou use me thus.

Reede. What, wilt thou do me wrong and threat me too? Nay, then, I'll tempt thee, Arden, do thy worst. God, I beseech thee, show some miracle on thee or thine in plaguing thee for this. That plot of ground which thou detains from me – I speak it in an agony of spirit – be ruinous and fatal unto thee! Either there be butchered by thy dearest friends, or else be brought for men to wonder at, or thou or thine miscarry in that place, or there run mad and end thy cursèd days.

Franklin. Fie, bitter knave, bridle thine envious tongue;
For curses are like arrows shot upright,
Which, falling down, light on the shooter's head.

Reede. Light where they will! Were I upon the sea, as oft I have in many a bitter storm, and saw a dreadful southern flaw at hand, the pilot quaking at the doubtful storm, and all the sailors praying on their knees, even in that fearful time would I fall down and ask of God, whate'er betide of me, vengeance on Arden or some misevent to show the world what wrong the carl hath done. This charge I'll leave with my distressful wife; my children shall be taught such prayers as these. And thus I go but leave my curse with thee.

Exeunt Reede *and* Sailor.

Arden. It is the railingest knave in Christendom,
And oftentimes the villain will be mad.
It greatly matters not what he says,
But I assure you I ne'er did him wrong.

Franklin. I think so, Master Arden.

Arden. Now that our horses are gone home before,
My wife may haply meet me on the way;
For God knows she is grown passing kind of late
And greatly changèd from the old humor
Of her wonted frowardness,
And seeks by fair means to redeem old faults.

Franklin. Happy the change that alters for the best.
But see in any case you make no speech
Of the cheer we had at my Lord Cheyne's
Although most bounteous and liberal,
For that will make her think herself more wronged
In that we did not carry her along;
For sure she grieved that she was left behind.

Arden. Come, Franklin, let us strain to mend our pace
And take her unawares playing the cook;

Here enters Alice *and* Mosby [*arm in arm*].

For I believe she'll strive to mend our cheer.

Franklin. Why, there's no better creatures in the world
Than women are when they are in good humors.

Arden. Who is that? Mosby, what so familiar?
Injurious strumpet and thou ribald knave,
Untwine those arms.

Alice. Aye, with a sugared kiss let them untwine.

[*She kisses Mosby.*]

Arden. Ah, Mosby, perjured beast! Bear this and all!

Mosby. And yet no horned beast; the horns are thine.

---

xiii.9 carl villain; miser
22 impeaching accusing
24 lay . . . close imprison thee; put thee in close confinement
25 As that
29 tempt provoke
32 detains withholds
37 miscarry come to harm
39 envious malicious
44 flaw squall
45 doubtful dreaded
49 misevent ill fortune
61 passing exceedingly
62 humor temperament
63 frowardness ill humor
67 cheer hospitality
72 mend increase
78 Injurious insulting; **ribald** riotous; ill-mannered
82 horned beast i.e., cuckold

Franklin. Oh monstrous! Nay, then, 'tis time to draw.

[Arden, Franklin, *and* Mosby *draw.*]

Alice. Help! help! They murder my husband.

Here enters Black Will *and* Shakebag.

Shakebag. Zounds, who injures Master Mosby?

[*They fight.* Franklin *wounds Shakebag;* Arden *wounds Mosby.*]

Help, Will! I am hurt.

Mosby. I may thank you, Mistress Arden, for this wound.

Exeunt Mosby, Black Will, *and* Shakebag.

Alice. Ah, Arden, what folly blinded thee?
Ah, jealous harebrain man, what hast thou done?
When we, to welcome thee, intended sport,
Came lovingly to meet thee on thy way,
Thou drew'st thy sword, enraged with jealousy,
And hurt thy friend whose thoughts were free from harm.
All for a worthless kiss and joining arms,
Both done but merrily to try thy patience.
And me unhappy that devised the jest,
Which, though begun in sport, yet ends in blood.

Franklin. Marry, God defend me from such a jest!

Alice. Couldst thou not see us friendly smile on thee
When we joined arms and when I kissed his cheek?
Hast thou not lately found me overkind?
Didst thou not hear me cry "they murder thee?"
Called I not "Help" to set my husband free?
No, ears and all were 'witched. Ah, me, accursed,
To link in liking with a frantic man.
Henceforth I'll be thy slave, no more thy wife;
For with that name I never shall content thee.
If I be merry, thou straightways thinks me light;
If sad, thou sayest the sullens trouble me;
If well attired, thou thinks I will be gadding;
If homely, I seem sluttish in thine eye.
Thus am I still, and shall be until I die,
Poor wench abused by thy misgovernment.

Arden. But is it for truth that neither thou nor he
Intendedst malice in your misdemeanor?

Alice. The heavens can witness of our harmless thoughts.

Arden. Then pardon me, sweet Alice, and forgive this fault.
Forget but this and never see the like.
Impose me penance, and I will perform it,
For in thy discontent I find a death,
A death tormenting more than death itself.

Alice. Nay, hadst thou loved me as thou dost pretend,
Thou wouldst have marked the speeches of thy friend,
Who going wounded from the place, he said
His skin was pierced only through my device.
And if sad sorrow taint thee for this fault,
Thou wouldst have followed him, and seen him dressed,
And cried him mercy whom thou hast misdone.
Ne'er shall my heart be eased till this be done.

Arden. Content thee, sweet Alice, thou shalt have thy will,
Whate'er it be. For that I injured thee
And wronged my friend, shame scourgeth my offense.
Come thou thyself, and go along with me,
And be a mediator 'twixt us two.

Franklin. Why, Master Arden, know you what you do?
Will you follow him that hath dishonored you?

Alice. Why, canst thou prove I have been disloyal?

Franklin. Why, Mosby taunts your husband with the horn.

Alice. Aye, after he had reviled him
By the injurious name of perjured beast.
He knew no wrong could spite a jealous man
More than the hateful naming of the horn.

Franklin. Suppose 'tis true, yet is it dangerous
To follow him whom he hath lately hurt.

Alice. A fault confessed is more than half amends,
But men of such ill spirit as yourself
Work crosses and debates 'twixt man and wife.

Arden. I pray thee, gentle Franklin, hold thy peace;
I know my wife counsels me for the best.
I'll seek out Mosby where his wound is dressed
And salve his hapless quarrel if I may.

Exeunt Arden *and* Alice.

90 **intended** pretended
95 **merrily** in jest
104 **'witched** bewitched
109 **sullens** fit of sulking
111 **homely** plainly attired
112 **still** always
113 **misgovernment** misconduct
127 **him** i.e., his wounds
128 **misdone** wronged
131 **For that** because
151 **hapless** unfortunate

Franklin. He whom the devil drives must go perforce.
Poor gentleman, how soon he is bewitched!
And yet, because his wife is the instrument,
His friends must not be lavish in their speech.
Exit Franklin.

[Sc. xiv]

Here enters [Black] Will, Shakebag, *and* Greene.

Black Will. Sirrah Greene, when was I so long in killing a man?

Greene. I think we shall never do it; let us give it over.

Shakebag. Nay, zounds! We'll kill him though we be hanged at his door for our labor.

Black Will. Thou knowest, Greene, that I have lived in London this twelve years, where I have made some go upon wooden legs for taking the wall on me; divers with silver noses for saying, "There goes Black Will." I have cracked as many blades as thou hast done nuts.

Greene. Oh monstrous lie!

Black Will. Faith, in a manner I have. The bawdy-houses have paid me tribute; there durst not a whore set up unless she have agreed with me first for op'ning her shop windows. For a cross word of a tapster, I have pierced one barrel after another with my dagger and held him by the ears till all his beer hath run out. In Thames Street a brewer's cart was like to have run over me; I made no more ado but went to the clerk and cut all the notches off his tallies and beat them about his head. I and my company have taken the constable from his watch and carried him about the fields on a coltstaff. I have broken a sergeant's head with his own mace, and bailed whom I list with my sword and buckler. All the tenpenny alehouses would stand every morning with a quart pot in their hand, saying, "Will it please your worship drink?" He that had not done so had been sure to have had his sign pulled down and his lattice borne away the next night. To conclude, what have I not done? Yet cannot do this! Doubtless he is preserved by miracle.

Here enters Alice *and* Michael.

Greene. Hence, Will, here comes Mistress Arden.

Alice. Ah, gentle Michael, art thou sure they're friends?

Michael. Why, I saw them when they both shook hands.
When Mosby bled, he even wept for sorrow
And railed on Franklin that was cause of all.
No sooner came the surgeon in at doors,
But my master took to his purse and gave him money,
And, to conclude, sent me to bring you word
That Mosby, Franklin, Bradshaw, Adam Fowle,
With divers of his neighbors and his friends,
Will come and sup with you at our house this night.

Alice. Ah, gentle Michael, run thou back again;
And, when my husband walks into the fair,
Bid Mosby steal from him and come to me;
And this night shall thou and Susan be made sure.

Michael. I'll go tell him.

Alice. And, as thou goest, tell John, cook of our guests,
And bid him lay it on. Spare for no cost.
Exit Michael.

Black Will. Nay, and there be such cheer, we will bid ourselves, Mistress Arden. Dick Greene and I do mean to sup with you.

Alice. And welcome shall you be. Ah, gentlemen,
How missed you of your purpose yesternight?

Greene. 'Twas long of Shakebag, that unlucky villain.

Shakebag. Thou dost me wrong. I did as much as any.

Black Will. Nay then, Mistress Alice, I'll tell you how it was. When he should have locked with both his hilts, he in a bravery flourished over his head. With that comes Franklin at him lustily and hurts the slave. With that he slinks

---

152 perforce necessarily
xiv.8 taking the wall going along the wall and forcing Black Will into the muddy center of the street; **divers** some, several; **silver** false
14 set up establish her business
21 tallies sticks of wood with notches to mark debts or payments
24 coltstaff cowlstaff, a pole used by two people for carrying a cowl (or tub)
25 sergeant officer responsible for arresting offenders and summoning them to court
26 mace staff of office; **list** wished; pleased
27 tenpenny alehouses i.e., alehouse keepers who sold ale for tenpence a quart
32 lattice window (with latticework painted red or green to denote an alehouse)
47 fair i.e., of St. Valentine
51 cook of the cook for
53 and if;
54 bid invite
58 long account
61 locked attacked
62 hilts sword and dagger; **bravery** show of bravado
64 lustily vigorously

away. Now his way had been to have come hand and feet, one and two round at his costard. He like a fool bears his swordpoint half a yard out of danger. I lie here for my life. [*He takes a position of defense.*] If the devil come and he have no more strength than fence, he shall never beat me from this ward. I'll stand to it, a buckler in a skillful hand is as good as a castle; nay, 'tis better than a sconce, for I have tried it. Mosby, perceiving this, began to faint. With that comes Arden with his arming-sword and thrust him through the shoulder in a trice.

Alice. Aye, but I wonder why you both stood still.

Black Will. Faith, I was so amazed I could not strike.

Alice. Ah, sirs, had he yesternight been slain,
For every drop of his detested blood
I would have crammed in angels in thy fist,
And kissed thee, too, and hugged thee in my arms.

Black Will. Patient yourself; we cannot help it now. Greene and we two will dog him through the fair, and stab him in the crowd and steal away.

Here enters Mosby [*, his arm bandaged*].

Alice. It is unpossible. But here comes he
That will, I hope, invent some surer means.
Sweet Mosby, hide thy arm; it kills my heart.

Mosby. Aye, Mistress Arden, this is your favor.

Alice. Ah, say not so; for, when I saw thee hurt,
I could have took the weapon thou lett'st fall
And run at Arden, for I have sworn
That these mine eyes, offended with his sight,
Shall never close till Arden's be shut up.
This night I rose and walked about the chamber,
And twice or thrice I thought to have murdered him.

Mosby. What, in the night? Then had we been undone.

Alice. Why, how long shall he live?

Mosby. Faith, Alice, no longer than this night.
Black Will and Shakebag, will you two
Perform the complot that I have laid?

Black Will. Aye, or else think me as a villain.

Greene. And rather than you shall want, I'll help myself.

Mosby. You, Master Greene, shall single Franklin forth
And hold him with a long tale of strange news,
That he may not come home till suppertime.
I'll fetch Master Arden home; and we, like friends,
Will play a game or two at tables here.

Alice. But what of all this? How shall he be slain?

Mosby. Why, Black Will and Shakebag, locked within the countinghouse,
Shall, at a certain watchword given, rush forth.

Black Will. What shall the watchword be?

Mosby. "Now I take you" – that shall be the word.
But come not forth before in any case.

Black Will. I warrant you. But who shall lock me in?

Alice. That will I do; thou'st keep the key thyself.

Mosby. Come, Master Greene, go you along with me.
See all things ready, Alice, against we come.

Alice. Take no care for that; send you him home.
And, if he e'er go forth again, blame me.

Exeunt Mosby *and* Greene.

Come, Black Will, that in mine eyes art fair;
Next unto Mosby do I honor thee.
Instead of fair words and large promises
My hands shall play you golden harmony.
How like you this? Say, will you do it, sirs?

Black Will. Aye, and that bravely, too. Mark my device: place Mosby, being a stranger, in a chair, and let your husband sit upon a stool, that I may come behind him cunningly and with a towel pull him to the ground, then stab him till his flesh be as a sieve. That done, bear him behind the Abbey, that those that find him murdered may suppose some slave or other killed him for his gold.

---

65 **come** thrust
66 **round** directly; **costard** head
70 **fence** fencing skill
71 **ward** defensive stance
72 **buckler** small round shield
73 **sconce** small fort
74 **this** i.e., Shakebag's injury and defeat
75 **faint** lose his courage
76 **arming-sword** (1) broadsword; (2) sword he carried as a weapon
82 **angels** coins
84 **Patient** calm
91 **favor** love-token
95 **his sight** the sight of him
97 **This** i.e., last
103 **complot** plot
104 **as** also
105 **want** fall
110 **tables** backgammon (then a gentleman's game)
112 **countinghouse** (1) private office; (2) pun on accountability
115 **"Now I take you"** (1) to capture the opponent's pieces and win the game; (2) to take Arden's life
120 **against** before
121 **Take . . . that** i.e., leave it to me
126 **golden harmony** gold crowns (see iii. 91–7)
128 **bravely** extremely well

Alice. A fine device! You shall have twenty pound,
And, when he is dead, you shall have forty more;
And, lest you might be suspected staying here,
Michael shall saddle you two lusty geldings.
Ride whither you will – to Scotland or to Wales;
I'll see you shall not lack where'er you be.
Black Will. Such words would make one kill a thousand men!
Give me the key. Which is the countinghouse?
Alice. Here would I stay and still encourage you
But that I know how resolute you are.
Shakebag. Tush! You are too faint-hearted; we must do it.
Alice. But Mosby will be there, whose very looks
Will add unwonted courage to my thought
And make me the first that shall adventure on him.
Black Will. Tush, get you gone! 'Tis we must do the deed.
When this door opens next, look for his death.
[*Exeunt* Black Will *and* Shakebag.]
Alice. Ah, would he now were here, that it might open!
I shall no more be closed in Arden's arms,
That like the snakes of black Tisiphone
Sting me with their embracings. Mosby's arms
Shall compass me; and, were I made a star,
I would have none other spheres but those.
There is no nectar but in Mosby's lips!
Had chaste Diana kissed him, she like me
Would grow lovesick and from her wat'ry bower
Fling down Endymion and snatch him up.
Then blame not me that slay a silly man
Not half so lovely as Endymion.

Here enters Michael.

Michael. Mistress, my master is coming hard by.
Alice. Who comes with him?
Michael. Nobody but Mosby.
Alice. That's well, Michael. Fetch in the tables;
And, when thou hast done, stand before
The countinghouse door.
Michael. Why so?
Alice. Black Will is locked within to do the deed.
Michael. What? Shall he die tonight?
Alice. Aye, Michael.
Michael. But shall not Susan know it?
Alice. Yes, for she'll be as secret as ourselves.
Michael. That's brave! I'll go fetch the tables.
Alice. But, Michael, hark to me a word or two:
When my husband is come in, lock the street door;
He shall be murdered or the guests come in.
Exit Michael [*and reenters shortly with the tables*].

Here enters Arden *and* Mosby.

Husband, what mean you to bring Mosby home?
Although I wished you to be reconciled,
'Twas more for fear of you than love of him.
Black Will and Greene are his companions,
And they are cutters and may cut you short;
Therefore, I thought it good to make you friends.
But wherefore do you bring him hither now?
You have given me my supper with his sight.
Mosby. Master Arden, methinks your wife would have me gone.
Arden. No, good Master Mosby, women will be prating.
Alice, bid him welcome; he and I are friends.
Alice. You may enforce me to it if you will,
But I had rather die than bid him welcome.
His company hath purchased me ill friends,
And therefore will I ne'er frequent it more.
Mosby. [*Aside.*] Oh, how cunningly she can dissemble!
Arden. Now he is here, you will not serve me so.
Alice. I pray you be not angry or displeased;
I'll bid him welcome, seeing you'll have it so.
You are welcome, Master Mosby. Will you sit down?
[*Mosby sits down in chair facing the countinghouse door.*]
Mosby. I know I am welcome to your loving husband,
But for yourself you speak not from your heart.
Alice. And if I do not, sir, think I have cause.

---

150 **adventure** venture; attack
155 **Tisiphone** the Fury who punished those committing crimes against their kin; her hair and arms were encircled with snakes; she carried a whip and torch to sting the consciences of the guilty
157 **compass** encircle
162 **Endymion** mortal beloved by Diana, goddess of the moon
163 **silly** foolish
165 **hard by** close to hand
174 **brave** excellent
177 **or** ere; before
180 **of** for
181 **Greene** (Alice must mean Shakebag – cf. scene xiii – but rather than the playwright's error, this may be deliberately meant to show Alice's confusion, fear, or growing inability to see reality)
185 **You . . . sight** simply the sight of Mosby takes away my appetite
189 **enforce** compel
200 **And if** if

Mosby. Pardon me, Master Arden; I'll away.
Arden. No, good Master Mosby.
Alice. We shall have guests enough though you go hence.
Mosby. I pray you, Master Arden, let me go.
Arden. I pray thee, Mosby, let her prate her fill.
Alice. The doors are open, sir; you may be gone.
Michael. [*Aside.*] Nay, that's a lie, for I have locked the doors.
Arden. Sirrah, fetch me a cup of wine; I'll make them friends.

[*Exit* Michael.]

And, gentle Mistress Alice, seeing you are so stout,
You shall begin. Frown not; I'll have it so.
Alice. I pray you meddle with that you have to do.
Arden. Why, Alice, how can I do too much for him
Whose life I have endangered without cause?

[*Reenter* Michael *with wine.*]

Alice. 'Tis true; and, seeing 'twas partly through my means,
I am content to drink to him for this once.
Here, Master Mosby! And, I pray you, henceforth
Be you as strange to me as I to you.
Your company hath purchased me ill friends,
And I for you, God knows, have undeserved
Been ill spoken of in every place;
Therefore, henceforth frequent my house no more.
Mosby. I'll see your husband in despite of you.
Yet, Arden, I protest to thee by heaven,
Thou ne'er shalt see me more after this night.
I'll go to Rome rather than be forsworn.
Arden. Tush, I'll have no such vows made in my house.
Alice. Yes, I pray you, husband, let him swear;
And, on that condition, Mosby, pledge me here.
Mosby. Aye, as willingly as I mean to live.

[*He and Alice drink.*]

Arden. Come, Alice, is our supper ready yet?
Alice. It will by then you have played a game at tables.
Arden. Come, Master Mosby, what shall we play for?
Mosby. Three games for a French crown, sir, and please you.
Arden. Content.

[*He sits down on stool opposite Mosby.*]
Then they play at the tables.

[*Reenter* Black Will *and* Shakebag *from behind Arden.*]

Black Will. [*Aside.*] Can he not take him yet? What a spite is that!
Alice. [*Aside.*] Not yet, Will. Take heed he see thee not.
Black Will. [*Aside.*] I fear he will spy me as I am coming.
Michael. [*Aside.*] To prevent that, creep betwixt my legs.
Mosby. One ace, or else I lose the game. [*He throws the dice.*]
Arden. Marry, sir, there's two for failing.
Mosby. Ah, Master Arden, "Now I can take you."

Then Black Will *pulls him down with a towel.*

Arden. Mosby! Michael! Alice! What will you do?
Black Will. Nothing but take you up, sir, nothing else.
Mosby. There's for the pressing iron you told me of.

[*He stabs Arden.*]

Shakebag. And there's for the ten pound in my sleeve.

[*He stabs him.*]

Alice. What, groans thou? Nay, then give me the weapon!
Take this for hind'ring Mosby's love and mine.

[*She stabs him.*]

Michael. Oh, mistress!

[*Arden dies.*]

Black Will. Ah, that villain will betray us all.
Mosby. Tush, fear him not; he will be secret.
Michael. Why, dost thou think I will betray myself?
Shakebag. In Southwark dwells a bonny northern lass, the widow Chambley. I'll to her house now; and, if she will not give me harborough, I'll make booty of the quean even to her smock.

---

209 **stout** stubborn
210 **begin** make the first toast
225 **go to Rome** convert to Catholicism
228 **pledge** drink to (for assurance)
231 **by then** by the time
234 **s.d. from behind** Holinshed reports Michael stood behind Arden holding a candle and keeping the entrance of Black Will and Shakebag in shadow
239 **ace** side of die with one spot
240 **for failing** in case one is not enough
243 **take you up** deal with you
244 **pressing iron** (Holinshed reports that Mosby carried a pressing iron weighing fourteen pounds at his girdle)
246 **weapon** i.e., Shakebag's dagger
247 **s.d.** (according to Holinshed, Alice stabbed Arden seven or eight times; according to the Faversham Wardcote Book, she did not)
252 **Southwark** borough s of the Thames, outside the jurisdiction of London, and the area where most public playhouses stood, was known for crime
254 **harborough** harbor; shelter
255 **quean** prostitute; harlot

Black Will. Shift for yourselves; we two will leave you now.
Alice. First lay the body in the countinghouse.
Then they lay the body in the countinghouse.
Black Will. We have our gold. Mistress Alice, adieu; Mosby, farewell; and, Michael, farewell too.
Exeunt [Black Will *and* Shakebag].

Enter Susan.

Susan. Mistress, the guests are at the doors.
[*Knocking.*]
Hearken! They knock. What, shall I let them in?
Alice. Mosby, go thou and bear them company.
Exit M[osby.]
And, Susan, fetch water and wash away this blood.
[*Exit* Susan, *returning with pail of water begins washing the floor.*]
Susan. The blood cleaveth to the ground and will not out.
Alice. But with my nails I'll scrape away the blood.
[*She tries to scrape away the stain with increasing anxiety.*]
The more I strive, the more the blood appears.
Susan. What's the reason, Mistress. Can you tell?
Alice. Because I blush not at my husband's death.

Here enters Mosby.

Mosby. How now, what's the matter? Is all well?
Alice. Aye, well, if Arden were alive again.
In vain we strive, for here his blood remains.
Mosby. Why, strew rushes on it, can you not?
[*To Susan.*] This wench doth nothing. Fall unto the work.
Alice. 'Twas thou that made me murder him.
Mosby. What of that?
Alice. Nay, nothing, Mosby, so it be not known.
Mosby. Keep thou it close, and 'tis unpossible.
Alice. Ah, but I cannot. Was he not slain by me?
My husband's death torments me at the heart.
Mosby. It shall not long torment thee, gentle Alice.
I am thy husband; think no more of him.

Here enters Adam Fowle *and* Bradshaw.

Bradshaw. How now, Mistress Arden? What ail you weep?
Mosby. Because her husband is abroad so late.
A couple of ruffians threat'ned him yesternight,
And she, poor soul, is afraid he should be hurt.
Adam. Is't nothing else? Tush, he'll be here anon.

Here enters Greene.

Greene. Now, Mistress Arden, lack you any guests?
Alice. Ah, Master Greene, did you see my husband lately?
Greene. I saw him walking behind the Abbey even now.

Here enters Franklin.

Alice. I do not like this being out so late. –
Master Franklin, where did you leave my husband?
Franklin. Believe me, I saw him not since morning.
Fear you not; he'll come anon. Meantime,
You may do well to bid his guests sit down.
Alice. Aye, so they shall. Master Bradshaw, sit you there;
I pray you be content, I'll have my will.
Master Mosby, sit you in my husband's seat.
[*Mosby sits down on the chair, the guests on stools.*]
Michael. [*Aside.*] Susan, shall thou and I wait on them?
Or, and thou say'st the word, let us sit down too.
Susan. [*Aside.*] Peace, we have other matters now in hand.
I fear me, Michael, all will be bewrayed.
Michael. [*Aside.*] Tush, so it be known that I shall marry
Thee in the morning, I care not
Though I be hanged ere night. But
To prevent the worst, I'll buy some ratsbane.
Susan. [*Aside.*] Why, Michael, wilt thou poison thyself?
Michael. [*Aside.*] No, but my mistress, for I fear she'll tell.
Susan. [*Aside.*] Tush, Michael, fear not her; she's wise enough.
Mosby. Sirrah Michael, give's a cup of beer.
Mistress Arden, here's to your husband.
Alice. My husband?

---

273 rushes commonly used for floor matting
277 close secret
282 What ail you weep? why are you weeping?
296–300 I . . . hand (according to Holinshed, Alice asked her daughter to play the virginal, and she and the others danced while waiting for Arden to arrive)
299 and if
301 bewrayed revealed
305 ratsbane poison for rats; arsenic

Franklin. What ails you, woman, to cry so suddenly?
Alice. Ah, neighbors, a sudden qualm came over my heart;
My husband's being forth torments my mind.
I know something's amiss; he is not well,
Or else I should have heard of him ere now.
Mosby. [*Aside.*] She will undo us through her foolishness.
Greene. Fear not, Mistress Arden; he's well enough.
Alice. Tell not me; I know he is not well.
He was not wont for to stay thus late.
Good Master Franklin, go and seek him forth,
And, if you find him, send him home to me
And tell him what a fear he hath put me in.
Franklin. [*Aside.*] I like not this; I pray God all be well.
I'll seek him out and find him if I can.

Exeunt Fra[nklin], Mos[by], [*and* Greene]

Alice. [*Aside.*] Michael, how shall I do to rid the rest away?
Michael. [*Aside.*] Leave that to my charge; let me alone.
'Tis very late, Master Bradshaw,
And there are many false knaves abroad,
And you have many narrow lanes to pass.
Bradshaw. Faith, friend Michael, and thou sayest true.
Therefore I pray thee, light's forth and lend's a link.
Alice. Michael, bring them to the doors, but do not stay;
You know I do not love to be alone.

Exeunt Bradshaw, Adam, *and* Michael.

Go, Susan, and bid thy brother come.
But wherefore should he come? Here is nought but fear.
Stay, Susan, stay, and help to counsel me.
Susan. Alas, I counsel! Fear frights away my wits.

Then they open the countinghouse door and look upon Arden.

Alice. See, Susan, where thy quondam master lies.
Sweet Arden, smeared in blood and filthy gore.
Susan. My brother, you, and I shall rue this deed.
Alice. Come, Susan, help to lift his body forth,
And let our salt tears be his obsequies.

[*They bring forth his body.*]

Here enters Mosby *and* Greene.

Mosby. How now, Alice, whither will you bear him?
Alice. Sweet Mosby, art thou come? Them weep that will;
I have my wish in that I joy thy sight.
Greene. Well, it 'hooves us to be circumspect.
Mosby. Aye, for Franklin thinks that we have murdered him.
Alice. Aye, but he cannot prove it for his life.
We'll spend this night in dalliance and in sport.

Here enters Michael.

Michael. Oh mistress, the mayor and all the watch
Are coming towards our house with glaives and bills.
Alice. Make the door fast; let them not come in.
Mosby. Tell me, sweet Alice, how shall I escape?
Alice. Out at the back door, over the pile of wood,
And for one night lie at the Flower-de-Luce.
Mosby. That is the next way to betray myself.
Greene. Alas, Mistress Arden, the watch will take me here
And cause suspicion where else would be none.
Alice. Why, take that way that Master Mosby doth;
But first convey the body to the fields.

Then they [Mosby, Greene, Susan, *and* Michael] *bear the body into the fields* [*and return*].

Mosby. Until tomorrow, sweet Alice, now farewell;
And see you confess nothing in any case.
Greene. Be resolute, Mistress Alice; betray us not,
But cleave to us as we will stick to you.

Exeunt Mosby *and* Greene.

Alice. Now let the judge and juries do their worst;
My house is clear, and now I fear them not.
Susan. As we went, it snowed all the way,
Which makes me fear our footsteps will be spied.
Alice. Peace, fool! The snow will cover them again.
Susan. But it had done before we came back again.

[*Knocking.*]

Alice. Hark, hark, they knock! Go, Michael, let them in.

[Michael *opens the door.*]

331 **lend's a link** lend us a torch
338 **quondam** former
345 **joy** take pleasure in
346 **'hooves** behooves
350–2 (according to Holinshed, Alice's loud lamentations first alerted and summoned the mayor)
351 **glaives** swords; **bills** halberds
355 **lie** lodge
356 **next** quickest
360 **s.d.** (Alice is left alone on stage, presumably to take complete charge of the crime by cleaning up)
370 **done** stopped snowing

Here enters the Mayor *and the* Watch.

How now, Master Mayor, have you brought my husband home?

Mayor. I saw him come into your house an hour ago.

Alice. You are deceived; it was a Londoner.

Mayor. Mistress Arden, know you not one that is called Black Will?

Alice. I know none such. What mean these questions?

Mayor. I have the Council's warrant to apprehend him.

Alice. [*Aside.*] I am glad it is no worse.
Why, Master Mayor, think you I harbor any such?

Mayor. We are informed that here he is;
And, therefore, pardon us, for we must search.

Alice. Aye, search, and spare you not, through every room.
Were my husband at home, you would not offer this.

Here enters Franklin.

Master Franklin, what mean you come so sad?

Franklin. Arden, thy husband and my friend, is slain.

Alice. Ah, by whom? Master Franklin, can you tell?

Franklin. I know not, but behind the Abbey
There he lies murdered in most piteous case.

Mayor. But, Master Franklin, are you sure 'tis he?

Franklin. I am too sure; would God I were deceived!

Alice. Find out the murderers! Let them be known!

Franklin. Aye, so they shall. Come you along with us.

Alice. Wherefore?

Franklin. Know you this hand-towel and this knife?

Susan. [*Aside.*] Ah, Michael, through this, thy negligence,
Thou hast betrayed and undone us all.

Michael. [*Aside.*] I was so afraid I knew not what I did.
I thought I had thrown them both into the well.

Alice. [*To Franklin.*] It is the pig's blood we had to supper.
But wherefore stay you? Find out the murderers.

Mayor. I fear me you'll prove one of them yourself.

Alice. I one of them? What mean such questions?

Franklin. I fear me he was murdered in this house
And carried to the fields, for from that place
Backwards and forwards may you see
The print of many feet within the snow.
And look about this chamber where we are,
And you shall find part of his guiltless blood;
For in his slipshoe did I find some rushes
Which argueth he was murdered in this room.

Mayor. Look in the place where he was wont to sit.
See, see! His blood! It is too manifest.

Alice. It is a cup of wine that Michael shed.

Michael. Aye, truly.

Franklin. It is his blood, which, strumpet, thou hast shed.
But, if I live, thou and thy complices
Which have conspired and wrought his death
Shall rue it.

Alice. [*Pauses, looking for a reply.*] Ah, Master Franklin, God and heaven can tell
I loved him more than all the world beside.
But bring me to him; let me see his body.

Franklin. [*Pointing to Michael and Susan.*] Bring that villain and Mosby's sister too;
And one of you go to the Flower-de-Luce
And seek for Mosby, and apprehend him too.

Exeunt.

[Sc. xv]

Here enters Shakebag *solus.*

Shakebag. The widow Chambley in her husband's days I kept; and, now he's dead, she is grown so stout, she will not know her old companions. I came thither, thinking to have had, harbor as I was wont, and she was ready to thrust me out at doors. But, whether she would or no, I got me up, and, as she followed

374 a Londoner (Holinshed reports that after the murder Alice sent to London for two grocers, Prune and Cole, to join her for supper; here, it is used as Alice's hallucination)

383 offer this treat me this way

383 s.d. (Holinshed says the mayor and watch, not Franklin, discover Arden's body and the incriminating evidence)

388 piteous case pitiful condition

393 Know . . . knife? (so Holinshed; neither the towel nor knife is mentioned in the official Wardmote Book account)

398 to for

408 slipshoe slipper

xv.1 s.d. ***solus*** alone (on stage)

2 kept (as a mistress)

3 stout proud

me, I spurned her down the stairs, and broke her neck, and cut her tapster's throat. And now I am going to fling them in the Thames. I have the gold; what care I though it be known? I'll cross the water and take sanctuary.

Exit Shakebag.

[Sc. xvi]

Here enters the Mayor, Mosby, Alice, Franklin, Michael, *and* Susan [, *guarded by the* Watch].

Mayor. See, Mistress Arden, where your husband lies.
Confess this foul fault and be penitent.

Alice. [*Leaning over the body.*] Arden, sweet husband, what shall I say?
The more I sound his name, the more he bleeds.
This blood condemns me, and in gushing forth
Speaks as it falls and asks me why I did it.
Forgive me, Arden; I repent me now;
And, would my death save thine, thou shouldst not die.
Rise up, sweet Arden, and enjoy thy love,
And frown not on me when we meet in heaven.
In heaven I love thee, though on earth I did not.

Mayor. Say, Mosby, what made thee murder him?

Franklin. Study not for an answer; look not down.
His purse and girdle found at thy bed's head
Witness sufficiently thou didst the deed.
It bootless is to swear thou didst it not.

Mosby. I hired Black Will and Shakebag, ruffians both,
And they and I have done this murd'rous deed.
But wherefore stay we? Come and bear me hence.

Franklin. Those ruffians shall not escape. I will up to London
And get the Council's warrant to apprehend them.

Exeunt.

[Sc. xvii]

Here enters [Black] Will.

Black Will. Shakebag, I hear, hath taken sanctuary; but I am so pursued with hues and cries for petty robberies that I have done that I can come unto no sanctuary. Therefore must I in some oyster-boat at last be fain to go abroad some hoy, and so to Flushing. There is no staying here. At Sittingburgh the Watch was like to take me; and, had I not with my buckler covered my head and run full blank at all adventures, I am sure I had ne'er gone further than that place, for the constable had twenty warrants to apprehend me; besides that, I robbed him and his man once at Gadshill. Farewell, England; I'll to Flushing now.

Exit Black Will.

[Sc. xviii]

Here enters the Mayor, Mosby, Alice, Michael, Susan, *and* Bradshaw, [*led by the* Watch].

Mayor. [*To the Watch.*] Come, make haste and bring away the prisoners.

Bradshaw. Mistress Arden, you are now going to God,
And I am by the law condemned to die,
About a letter I brought from Master Greene,
I pray you, Mistress Arden, speak the truth:
Was I ever privy to your intent or no?

Alice. What should I say? You brought me such a letter,
But I dare swear thou knewest not the contents.

---

8 spurned kicked; pushed
12 take sanctuary seek refuge in a place made safe by the church or by local regulation; Holinshed says Widow Chambley lived in Southwark where the sanctuary was called the Mint and where Shakebag was eventually murdered
xvi.3–4 Arden . . . bleeds according to popular belief, a murdered person bled when the killer was present
11 In . . . not (Alice seems certain of her salvation because of her stated repentance)
13 Study not for do not invent
14 girdle belt (which held the purse)
16 bootless pointless
17 I (actually, Greene hired Black Will and Shakebag; Mosby may be confused, covering up, or deeply aware they are all caught)
xvii.5–6 oyster-boat . . . Flushing Faversham was widely known for its oyster beds and for trade with the Low Countries (Flushing)
5 fain obliged
6 hoy small boat
8 like likely
9 full blank headlong
10 at all adventures whatever the consequences
13 Gadshill a hill on the London–Rochester road popularly known as a site of frequent robberies
xviii.1 s.d. (The Wardmote Book records that sentencing took place in "the Abbey Hall which the said Arden purchased" abutting his own house)
4 About because of
6 privy informed

Leave now to trouble me with worldly things
And let me meditate upon my saviour Christ
Whose blood must save me for the blood I shed.

Mosby. How long shall I live in this hell of grief?
Convey me from the presence of that strumpet.

Alice. Ah, but for thee I had never been strumpet.
What cannot oaths and protestations do
When men have opportunity to woo?
I was too young to sound thy villainies,
But now I find it and repent too late.

Susan. [*To Mosby.*] Ah, gentle brother, wherefore should I die?
I knew not of it till the deed was done.

Mosby. For thee I mourn more than for myself,
But let it suffice I cannot save thee now.

Michael. [*To Susan.*] And if your brother and my mistress
Had not promised me you in marriage,
I had ne'er given consent to this foul deed.

Mayor. Leave to accuse each other now
And listen to the sentence I shall give:
Bear Mosby and his sister to London straight,
Where they in Smithfield must be executed.
Bear Mistress Arden unto Canterbury
Where her sentence is she must be burnt.
Michael and Bradshaw in Faversham must suffer death.

Alice. Let my death make amends for all my sins.

Mosby. Fie upon women: this shall be my song.
But bear me hence, for I have lived too long.

Susan. Seeing no hope on earth, in heaven is my hope.

Michael. Faith, I care not, seeing I die with Susan.

Bradshaw. My blood be on his head that gave the sentence!

Mayor. To speedy execution with them all.

Exeunt.

[Epilogue]

Here enters Franklin.

Franklin. Thus have you seen the truth of Arden's death.
As for the ruffians, Shakebag and Black Will,
The one took sanctuary and, being sent for out,
Was murdered in Southwark as he passed
To Greenwich, where the Lord Protector lay.
Black Will was burned in Flushing on a stage;
Greene was hanged at Osbridge in Kent;
The painter fled, and how he died we know not.
But this above the rest is to be noted:
Arden lay murdered in that plot of ground
Which he by force and violence held from Reede,
And in the grass his body's print was seen
Two years and more after the deed was done.
Gentlemen, we hope you'll pardon this naked tragedy
Wherein no filed points are foisted in
To make it gracious to the ear or eye;
For simple truth is gracious enough
And needs no other points of glozing stuff.

[*Exit.*]

---

9 **Leave** cease
17 **sound** fathom; comprehend
28 **straight** at once
29 **Smithfield** open land E of the Tower of London and outside the city walls where thieves were often executed

Epilogue

3 **one** former
6 **stage** scaffold
7 **Osbridge** a village in Kent about a mile SW of Faversham
14 **naked** plain; unadorned
15 **filed points** sophisticated rhetorical techniques (or points as sharp and memorable as a dagger); **foisted** thrust
16 **gracious** favorable
18 **glozing** specious

The Honorable Entertainment Given to the Queen's Majesty in Progress, at Elvetham in Hampshire

Anonymous

The crescent-shaped pond at the pageant at Elvetham in 1591, from John Nichols, *Progresses of Elizabeth I*, vol. II. Reproduced from David M. Bergeron, *English Civic Pageantry 1558–1642* (Columbia: University of South Carolina Press, 1971).

Throughout the decade of the 1590s the aging Queen Elizabeth clearly felt her powers waning, if not her authority. Despite the defeat of the Spanish Armada in 1588, the Spaniards were building a new force to set out against her. She could also measure her losses by the deaths of others: Leicester died in 1588 and Sir Francis Walsingham, Lord Treasurer and the efficient manager of foreign relations and espionage, who had helped to keep Spain in check and the alliance with the Low Countries as strong as possible, died in 1590. Her Principal Secretary and chief representative on her Privy Council, Lord Burghley, was also beginning to fail. She needed, therefore, to reassert herself and her rule symbolically and materially. One such means, which had been successful from the very first day she made her coronation passage through London, was to go on progresses to reacquaint herself with her people – and reacquaint them with her – in ways she could stagemanage. In 1559 the Venetian ambassador was already hearing in France that Elizabeth established and maintained power by "frequently showing herself in public, giving audience to all who wish for it, and using every mark of great graciousness towards everyone." Ten years later the Spanish ambassador reported home that "She was received everywhere with great acclamations and signs of joy as is customary in this country whereat she was exceedingly pleased." She knew the value and the effects of dramatic performance.

The grand European tradition of magnificence had been translated in her reign into the various entertainments and shows presented to her on her progresses throughout the counties near London. But there were other reasons for such progresses: health, for one thing, for such journeys permitted her to escape the bad air and sanitation of London in summer and possible epidemics of plague. Rest, for another: she could visit her country homes, like Odiham, as well as relatives and nobility that she liked (such as the Norrises) or might wish to keep in line (like the Seymours). Additional loyalty and support, for a third: those in the towns and villages through which she passed were honored to share her presence and she could use that allegiance when it came time to levy taxes or raise an army. Moreover, her presence tended to identify and subdue any sentiment that might be rising against her government. Still, such travel was not easy. The maintenance of roadways – often little more than tracks – was since 1555 the responsibility of the parishes, but they were required to spend only four (later, six) days a year working on them and they did little more than fill potholes with loose stone and cut away underbrush; drainage was almost never attended to. Although a swift man on horse might travel up to four miles an hour, the Queen, who found coaches and litters too uncomfortable on such roads, went much slower; she and her attendants might make ten to twelve miles a day, accompanied by an immense train of members of court and of servants – some 200 to 300 of them – who brought in carts drawn by teams of four or six horses all that the Queen's household and the Queen's Council would need: bedding, clothing, furniture, hangings, plate and kitchen utensils, and documents and office supplies. The Lord Steward, in charge of the household, supervised each department that went with them, including the bakehouse, the larder, the spicery, the cellar, the buttery, and the laundry. The Lord Chamberlain, in charge of court matters, brought along ushers, grooms, and pages; the Queen's companions and their maids; chaplains and court musicians and other entertainers. To insure a successful itinerary, some of her men would precede her, warning the houses she chose to visit of her impending arrival and seeing to it that the accommodations were sufficient for the court (although servants often slept under tents in the fields). Normally, the Queen would arrive in the early afternoon, in time for a welcoming entertainment and a long evening of food and festivity, leaving late the next morning unless, as in the instance described here, she stayed several days.

This too is the way Elizabeth arrived at Elvetham on Monday, September 20, 1591. Elvetham was one of the smaller estates of Sir Edward Seymour, ninth Earl of Hertford, whose title she had restored upon becoming Queen. She was not particularly close to Seymour, but he was the nephew of her father's third wife and so one of the family. The account that follows suggests that all her hosts had considerable warning of her visit because the entertainments described here are the most spectacular of her later years, and they employ all sorts of symbolic meanings and encode all sorts of messages which those in attendance at the performances will witness and to which the Queen herself must respond. She is first welcomed, for instance, by one of the *vates* or inspired poets whose green costume suggests joy, spring, and fertility, whose laurel wreath suggests his authority, and whose olive branch suggests peace. He speaks first in Latin but then, as if to extend his message to the widest possible audience, immediately translates it into English: all present, he says, "gaze on Thy perfections," although "Their eyes' desire is never satisfied," so infinite is her very being. She is more than a queen, she is an empress whose wide empire is not only space but time: "draw forth these days to years, Years to an age, ages to eternity." Each guarantees the authority of the other, and it might thus be argued that each needs the other. Indeed, as the Poet speaks, six Virgins clear away impediments placed in the Queen's path by Envy, suggesting that her welcome is sincere but also that Envy continues to lurk near by. When the Hours and Graces accompany her across the park to the manor house where the Seymours await her and then on to her lodgings, she is given the handmaidens traditionally associated with Venus. Joining them, she knowledgeably takes the part of Venus, so that perfection has now become redefined: she is the empress of love.

This is a sophisticated and subtle, if also traditional, move. "Thy presence," the Poet has said (in two languages) "frees each thing that lived in doubt," but having said that, the Virgins and the Poet free Elizabeth. Her beauty has won their respect. It has, moreover, turned the Poet into a kind of medieval troubadour, whose courtly love of this beautiful lady enables him to write such splendid poetry; it also makes her, as the beloved in the courtly love tradition, a superior who is, though beautiful, unattainable. It offers the Queen an honorable, and a dominant, role. It invites the Poet to serve her; as she came as his sovereign and he was her subject, she is now his beloved and he is her liege lord. At the same time, her very position rests on the fiction which the Poet is establishing and the role she must play, as Venus, is precisely the one that others have scripted for her. Such theater – such spectacle and drama – thus assigns the Queen a role by employing precisely those measures which the Queen herself would use at court. Handy dandy, who is the ruler and who is the subject? In due course, such tensions of expectation and enactment will allow political remarks to be embedded in the actions – such as the anti-Hapsburg remarks that both congratulate the Queen on the Armada victory and warn her that Spain still threatens – and more local comments that, through transfers in the poetic and symbolic registers from courtly love to pastoral to the antique, draw out roles for the Queen that describe her accomplishments and prescribe her behavior.

Tuesday's entertainment follows the template established on Monday. The action takes place at a specially created crescent-shaped pond that honors the Queen as Diana, goddess of the moon, and then turns the pond into a scene of treachery and warfare. The moon is itself a symbol of mutability. Yet – as if to suggest the power of poetry and of the poet – the sea gods represent virtue and Sylvanus' forces, from the woods, represent vengeance: there is considerable reason for Nereus to distrust Sylvanus' promises about the well-being of Neaera. While the beautiful sea nymph is protected and saved by the end of the performance, the enactment – with all of its action, comedy, and surprises – also underlines her vulnerability: her life, like that of Diana's, has a certain mutability about it that contests the previous day's description of the Queen as an empress who controls all time and space. "At the last," we are told, "Nereus parted the fray with a line or two, grounded on the excellence of Her Majesty's presence as being always friend to peace and enemy to war." The Queen is, then, not a spectator in the drama, but an actor in it; she is cause and consequence. Her very presence, simply her presence, is cited as reason for the outcome; and yet, of course, her very presence started the fray to provide entertainment: she may contain, but she does not prevent, conflict.

Often in such entertainments during the Queen's progress there is a shifting or even a merging of various mythical, historical, allegorical, and symbolic roles: Elizabeth might be reflected as Deborah or Phoebe or Chastity or Peace or the Fortress of Perfect Beauty as she is here made Venus and Diana. Identities are not necessarily fixed, as they might be in a more popular and public drama which is less allusive, and in the Elvetham entertainment the classical world is every bit as important as the courtly and pastoral ones. On the third day, the Poet's green costume – which could also represent hope or faith – takes on the color of verdure to suggest eternal springtime and the Queen is invited to insure crops through her association, in the scripts, with spring when crops are planted and autumn when they are harvested. She is meant to embody the Golden Age and the place she visits Paradise. The earthly Venus of the first day becomes the heavenly Venus of the final day. Since, in so emblematic a drama as the pageantry of royal progresses, there is always a chance of misinterpretation as well as multiple interpretation, there is some effort in the closing scenes to make clear the Queen's continuing vitality. But this is also accomplished through emblems. There is, for instance, the appearance of the Fairy Queen – surely a material transformation of the Gloriana of Edmund Spenser's epic poem, which had appeared just the year before. This plays once more to the Queen's centrality, beauty, and authority and to the adoration of her citizenry; yet Spenser's *Faerie Queene* is an epic which remained unfinished in 1591: only three books had been published of the twelve that were promised. By insisting, at the departure of the Queen, that she is the Sun that alone can make her land fruitful and allow it to multiply, there may be a more knowing and specialized reference to Elizabeth's position as the center of the universe: not Gloriana but the Sun for which Gloriana, basking in a reflected light, is a new sign of the moon. The Ditchley portrait of the Queen, painted the following year by Marcus Gheeraerts the Younger, has a motto that reads, in part, "The prince of light. The Sonne [Sun]." Here Elizabeth stands on a map of all England (her feet are on Oxfordshire, neighboring Hampshire) but she stands between earth and sky, reaching (as the Elvetham entertainment has it) towards the stars themselves. Her fertility catches up the May Lady of the plowman's song as well as the desires of shepherds, woodsmen, and sea gods – and the citizenry too of Elvetham and the surrounding countryside. Yet the renewed life given by the Queen's presence only augurs privation at her absence; the shows at Elvetham (and the pamphlet) end on a long, elegiac note.

In all this, the Queen is not only the thematic but the dramatic center; she is unable, finally, to step outside the spectacles that were created because she chose to visit Elvetham. There can be no doubt that she has honored Lord and Lady Seymour by her visit, just as there can be no doubt that they give her a gift in all sincerity and there is genuine sadness when she departs. Yet the Seymours pay a price: hosts of the Queen on progress could spend up to £2,000 and more on entertainment, and perhaps again as much on clothing for themselves and their household and for the household they needed to erect temporarily to house the Queen and her train. Parks could be denuded; gardens trampled down; plate and linen stolen. Lord Keeper Puckering would say in 1595 with a certain sourness, "To grace his lordship the more, she of herself took from him a salt, a spoon, and a fork, of fair agate." As the Queen leaves Elvetham, then, what have the Seymours managed to convey and what have they gained? How genuine is the Queen's persistent tribute to the actors of these entertainments? Even at its most emblematic and referential, the entertainments at Elvetham are Renaissance state drama at its most direct.

FURTHER READING

Bergeron, David M., *English Civic Pageantry 1558–1642*. Columbia: University of South Carolina Press, 1971.

Brennecke, Ernest, "The Entertainment at Elvetham, 1591," in *Music in English Renaissance Drama*, ed. John H. Long (Lexington: University of Kentucky Press, 1968), pp. 32–56.

Dovey, Zillah, *An Elizabethan Progress*. Madison: Fairleigh Dickinson University Press, 1997.

Frye, Susan, *Elizabeth I: The Competition for Representation*. New York: Oxford University Press, 1993.

Montrose, Louis, *The Purpose of Playing: Shakespeare and the Cultural Politics of the Elizabethan Theatre*. Chicago: University of Chicago Press, 1996.

Strong, Roy, *Gloriana: The Portraits of Queen Elizabeth I*. New York: Thames and Hudson, 1987.

Wilson, Jean, *Entertainments for Elizabeth I*. Woodbridge: D. S. Brewer-Rowman and Littlefield, 1980.

The Honorable Entertainment Given to the Queen's Majesty in Progress, at Elvetham in Hampshire

The Proëme

Before I declare the just time or manner of Her Majesty's arrival and entertainment at Elvetham, it is needful for the reader's better understanding of every part and process in my discourse that I set down as well the conveniency of the place, as also the sufficing, by art and labor, of what the place in itself could not afford on the sudden, for receiving of so great a Majesty and so honorable a train.

Elvetham House, being situated in a park but of two miles in compass or thereabouts, and of no great receipt, as being none of the Earl's chief mansion houses, yet for the desire he had to show his unfeigned love and loyal duty to Her Most Gracious Highness, purposing to visit him in this her late progress, whereof he had to understand by the ordinary guess as also by his honorable good friends at Court nearer to Her Majesty, his honor with all expedition set artificers to work, to the number of three hundred, many days before Her Majesty's arrival, to enlarge his house with new rooms and offices. Whereof I omit to speak how many were destined to the officers of the Queen's household, and will only make mention of other such buildings as were raised on the sudden, fourteen score off from the house on a hillside, within the said park, for entertainment of nobles, gentlemen, and others whatsoever.

Textual Variants

Title] Q continues "by the right honorable the Earl of Hertford. 1591" **8** receiving] Q receipt **10** situated] Q scituate **56** Pantry] Q Pastery **82** the other] Q other **89** Q3 adds: Here follows a description of the Great Pond in Elvetham and of the properties which it contained, at such time as Her Majesty was there presented with fair shows and pastimes:

A. Her Majesty's presence-seat and train.
B. Nereus and his followers.
C. The pinnace of Neaera and her music.
D. The Ship Isle.
E. A boat with music attending the pinnace of Neaera.
F. The Fort Mount.
G. The Snail Mount.
H. The Room of Estate.
I. Her Majesty's Court.
K. Her Majesty's wardrop [wardrobe].
L. The place whence Sylvanus and his company issued.

165 Cannae] Q Cannea **204** cassem] Q casses **212** famulae] Q famile **334** Q3 adds: and Her Majesty alighted from horseback at the Hall door; the Countess of Hertford, accompanied with diverse honorable ladies and gentlewomen, most humbly on her knees welcomed Her Highness to that place Who, most graciously embracing her, took her up and kissed her using many comfortable and princely speeches as well to her as to the Earl of Hertford standing hard [near] by, to the great rejoicing of many beholders. And after Her Majesty's entrance, **339** chambers discharged] Q3 chambers and two brass pieces discharged **370** Festival, the] Q3 Festival, there was in the morning presented to Her Majesty a fair and rich gift from the Countess of Hertford which greatly pleased and contented Her Highness. The **377** built] Q builded **382** dinner.] Q3 dinner, a variety of consorted music at dinner time. **394** four... gentlemen] Q3 four worthy knights, Sir Henry Greie, Sir Walter Hungerford, Sir James Marvin, and Lord George Caro; **411** Neptune and Oceanus] Q3 Neptune and Oceanus, Phorcus and Glaucus, **412** spoke] Q spake **447** escutcheon] Q scutcheon **476** leaped] Q lept **491** haul] Q hale **498** spoke] Q spake **511–14**] Q3 has different song:

Dem. What heavenly lamp with holy light
Doth so increase our climes delight?
Resp. A lamp whose beams are ever bright,
And never fears approaching Night.
Echo. Approaching Night.

Dem. Why sing we not eternal praise
To that fair shine of lasting days?
Resp. He shames himself that once assays
To fold such wonder in sweet lays.
Echo. In sweet lays.

Dem. Oh, yet devoid of envious blame,
Thou may'st unfold Her Sacred Name.
Resp. 'Tis dread Eliza, that fair name
Who fills the golden trump of Fame.
Echo. Trump of Fame.

Dem. Oh, never may so sweet a Queen
See dismal days or deadly teene [sorrow].
Resp. Grant Heavens Her days may still be green
For like to Her was never seen.
Echo. Was never seen.

525 spoke] Q spake **527** approach] Q reproach **528** spoke] Q spake **582** began] Q begun **592** spoke] Q spake **614** Now] Q I now

1 Proëme introductory discourse; preface
2 just precise
6 conveniency time and occasion; Elvetham is near the corner of Surrey and Berkshire
9 train attendants, retainers
11 compass measure; Hampshire was known for its woods and rivers
12 receipt income from rents and surrounding land; **Earl's** Sir Edward Seymour, ninth Earl, born October 12, 1537; he was created Baron Beauchamp and Earl of Hertford January 13, 1559; the largest landholding in Hampshire was Southampton's
26 score a measure equal to twenty paces

First there was made a room of estate for the nobles, and at the end thereof a withdrawing place for Her Majesty. The outsides of the walls were all covered with boughs and clusters of grapes or ripe hazelnuts, the insides with arras, the roof of the place with works of ivy leaves, the floor with sweet herbs and green rushes.

Near adjoining unto this were many offices new builded, as namely, spicery, larder, chandlery, wine cellar, ewery, and pantry, all of which were tiled. Not far off was erected a large hall for the entertainments of knights, ladies, and gentlemen of chief account. There was also a several place for Her Majesty's footmen and their friends.

Then was there a long bower for Her Majesty's guard.

Another for other servants of Her Majesty's house. Another to entertain all commoners, suitors, and such like.

Another for my Lord's Steward, to keep his table in.

Another for his Gentlemen that waited.

Most of these foresaid rooms were furnished with tables and the tables carried twenty-three yards in length. Moreover, on the same hill there was raised a great common buttery.

A pitcher-house.

A large Pantry with five ovens new built, some of them fourteen feet deep.

A great kitchen with four rooms, and a boiling place for small boiled meats.

Another kitchen with a very long range for the waste, to serve all the commoners.

A boiling-house for the great boiler.

A room for the scullery.

Another room for the cook's lodgings.

Some of these were covered with canvas and other some with boards.

Between my Lord's house and the foresaid hill where these rooms were raised, there had been made in the bottom, by hand labor, a pond, cut to the perfect figure of a half-moon. In this pond were three notable grounds where hence to present Her Majesty with sports and pastimes. The first was a Ship Isle, of a hundred feet in length and fourscore feet broad, bearing three trees orderly set for three masts. The second was a Fort twenty feet square every way, and overgrown with willows. The third and last was a Snail Mount rising to four circles of green privet hedges, the whole in height twenty feet and forty feet at the bottom. These three places were equally distant from the sides of the pond and every one, by a just measured proportion, distant from the other. In the said water were diverse boats prepared for music; but especially there was a pinnace full furnished with masts, yards, sails, anchors, cables, and all other ordinary tackling, and with iron pieces and, lastly, with flags, streamers, and pendants to the number of twelve, all painted with diverse colors and sundry devices.

To what use these particulars served, it shall evidently appear by that which followeth. And therefore I am to request the gentle reader that when any of these places are briefly specified in the sequel of this discourse, it will please him to have reference to this fore-description that, in avoiding tantilogies and reiterations, I may not seem to them obscure whom I study to please with my plainness. For proem, these may suffice. Now to the matter itself, that it may be *ultimum in executione* (to use the old phrase) *quod primum fuit in intentione*, as is usual to good carpenters who, intending to build a house, yet first lay their foundation and square many a post and fasten many a rafter before the house be set up: what they first purposed is last done. And thus much for excuse of a long foundation to a short building.

The First Day's Entertainment

On the twentieth day of September, being Monday, my Lord of Hertford joyfully expecting Her Majesty coming to Elvetham to supper, as Her

32–4 **boughs . . . ivy** the boughs and nuts may have been real or painted on the walls; the ivy leaves on the ceiling were carved or painted
33 **arras** rich colored tapestry into which were woven figures and scenes
35 **herbs . . . rushes** (for sanitation)
37 **chandlery** place for storing candles
38 **ewery** for storing ewers (pitchers) and towels for washing at table
41 **several** separate
45 **servants** officers
48 **Steward** official in charge of domestic affairs of a household
54 **buttery** place for storing liquor and provisions generally
55 **pitcher-house** room for storing ale and wine
60 **Another kitchen** where food not eaten by the court and its servants was dispersed to whomever came
63 **scullery** place for plates, dishes, and kitchen utensils
65–6 **Some . . . boards** i.e., they were temporary buildings
68 **raised** built
70 **figure . . . half-moon** with reference to Elizabeth I as Diana, goddess of the moon
74 **fourscore** (may be misprint for *forty*, which seems more probable)
83 **diverse** different, varied
84 **pinnace** a small double-banked boat
86–7 **iron pieces** guns
96 **tantilogies** tautologies
99–100 ***ultimum in executione*** the best in execution
100–1 ***quod . . . intentione*** finally in execution what it was first in conception

Highness had promised, after dinner when every other needful place of point of service was established for so great an entertainment, about three of the clock his Honor seeing all his retinue well mounted and ready to attend his pleasure, he drew them secretly into a chief thicket of the park where in few words, but well couched to the purpose, he put them in mind what quietness and what diligence or other duty they were to use at that present that their service might first work Her Majesty's content and thereby his honor; and lastly, their own credit with the increase of his love and favor towards them. This done, my Lord with his train amounting to the number of three hundred and most of them wearing chains of gold about their necks, and in their hats yellow and black feathers, met with Her Majesty two miles off, then coming to Elvetham from her own house of Odiham four miles from thence. As my Lord in this first action showed himself dutiful, so Her Majesty was to him and his most gracious; as also, in the sequel, between five and six of the clock, when Her Highness being most honorably attended entered into Elvetham Park and was more than half-way between the Park gate and the house, a poet saluted her with a Latin oration in heroical verse. I mean *veridcus vates*, a soothsaying poet, nothing inferior for truth and little for delivery of his mind to an ordinary orator. This poet was clad in green to signify the joy of his thoughts at her entrance, a laurel garland on his head to express that Apollo was patron of his studies, an olive branch in his hand to declare what continual peace and plenty he did both wish and abode Her Majesty, and, lastly, booted to betoken that he was *vates cothurnatus* and not a loose or low-creeping prophet as poets are interpreted by some idle or envious ignorants.

This poet's boy offered him a cushion at his first kneeling to Her Majesty, but he refused it, saying as followeth:

The Poet to his Boy offering him a Cushion.

Non iam pulvillis opus est, sed corde sereno:
Nam plusquam solitis istic advolvimur aris.

The Poet's Speech to Her Majesty

Nuper ad Aönium flexo dum poplite fontem
Indulsi placido, Phoebi sub pectine, somno,
Veridicos inter vates, quos Entheus ardor
Possidet, et virtus nullis offusa lituris,
Talia securo cantabant carmina Musae.
Aspicis insueto tingentem lumine coelum
Anglorum nostro maiorem nomine Nympham
Os, humerosque Deae similem, dum tuta Semeri
Tecta petit, qualis dilecta Philaermonis olim
Cannae Coelicolûm subiit magalia Rector?
Olli tu blandas humili dic ore salutes;
Nos dabimus numeros, numeros dabit ipsus
Apollo,
Sed metues tantae summas attingere laudes:
Nam specie solem, superos virtutibus aequans,
Maiestate locum, sacrisque timoribus implet.
Doctior est nobis, et nobis praesidet una:
Ditior est Ponto, Pontum quoque temperat una:
Pulchrior est nymphis, et nymphis imperat una:
Dignior est divis, et divos allicit una.
En supplex adsum, Musarum numine ductus,
Et meritis (Augusta) tuis, ô dulcis Elisa,
Fronte serenata modicum dignare poetam,
Né mea vernantem deponant tempora laurum,
Et miser in canto moriar. Se námque Semeri
Obsequiosa meis condit persona sub umbris:
Qui fert ore preces, oculo foecundat olivam;
Officium precibus, pacem designat oliva;
Affectum docet officiis, et pace quietem;
Mentes affectu mulcebit, membra quiete.
Hi mores, haec vera tui persona Semeri,
Cui laetum sine te nihil, illaetabile tecum
Est nihil. En rident ad vestros omnia vultus
Suaviter, immensum donec fulgoribus orbem
Elisabetha novis imples: nox invidet una:
Astra sed invidiae tollunt mala signa tenebras.
Caetera, qua possunt, sacrae gratantur Elisae
Laetitia, promptosque ferunt in gaudia vultus.
Limulus insultat per pictos hoedus agellos
Passibus obtoris; et torvum bucula taurum
Blanda petit; tremulus turgescit frondibus arbos,
Graminibus pratum, generosa pampinus uva:
Et tenui latices in arena dulce susurrant,
Insuetumque melos: Te, te, dulcissima princeps,
Terra, polus, fluvii, plantae, pecudesque salutant:
Dumque tuam cupide mirantur singula fornam,
Infixis haerent oculis, nequeuntque tuendo
Expleri; solitis sed nunc liberrima curis,
In placidos abeunt animos; non semina vermes,
Non cervi metuunt cassem, non herba calorem,
Non viscum volueres, non fruges grandinis ictum.
O istos (Augusta) dies, o profer in annos;
Et lustrum ex annis, è lustris saecula surgant;
E saeclis aevum, nullo numerabile motu:
Ut nostros dudum quotquot risere dolores,

---

125 chains of gold a common symbol of service in a noble or royal household indicating both allegiance and the wealth of the one who bestowed it

137 *veridcus vates* a poet who sees the inner truth through inspiration

145 abode presage; prophesy

146 *vates cothurnatus* i.e., he is wearing the high boots associated with the tragic actor

Gaudia iam numerent, intabescantque videndo.
En, iter obiecto qua clauserat obice livor,
Virtutis famulae charites, castrique superni
Custodes horae, blandissima numina, iunctim
Iam tollunt remoras, ut arenam floribus ornent.
Ergo age, supplicibus succede penatibus hospes,
Et nutu moderare tuo: tibi singula parent,
Et nisi parerent tibi singula, tota perirent.
Dicite Io Paean, et lo ter dicite Paean,
Spargite flore vias, et mollem cantibus auram.

Because all our countrymen are not Latinists, I think it not amiss to set this down in English, that all may be indifferently partakers of the poet's meaning.

The Poet's Speech to his Boy offering him a Cushion.

Now let us use no cushions, but fair hearts:
For now we kneel to more than usual saints.

The Poet's Speech to Her Majesty

While, at the fountain of the sacred hill,
Under Apollo's lute I sweetly slept,
'Mongst prophets full possessed with holy fury
And with true virtue void of all disdain,
The Muses sang, and waked me with these words:
Seest thou that English Nymph, in face and shape
Resembling some great Goddess, and whose beams
Do sprinkle Heaven with unacquainted light,
While She doth visit Semer's fraudless house,
As Jupiter did honor with his presence
The poor thatched cottage where Philaemon dwelt?
See thou salute Her with a humble voice;
Phoebus, and we, will let thee lack no verses.
But dare not once aspire to touch Her praise
Who, like the Sun for show, to Gods for virtue
Fills all with Majesty and holy fear.
More learned then ourselves She ruleth us.
More rich than seas she doth command the seas.
More fair than nymphs, she governs all the nymphs.
More worthy than the Gods, she wins the Gods.
Behold, Augusta, thy poor suppliant
Is here, at their desire, but thy desert.
Oh, sweet Eliza, grace me with a look
Or from my brows this laurel wreath will fall,
And I, unhappy, die amid my song.
Under my person Semer hides himself.
His mouth yields prayers; his eye, the olive branch;
His prayers betoken duty; th' olive, peace;
His duty argues love, his peace fair rest;
His love will smoothe your mind, fair rest your body.
This is your Semer's heart and quality.
To whom all things are joys, while Thou art present,
To whom nothing is pleasing in Thine absence.
Behold, on Thee how each thing sweetly smiles,
To see Thy brightness glad our hemisphere.
Night only envies whom fair stars do cross,
All other creatures strive to show their joys.
The crooked-winding kid trips over the lawns,
The milk-white heifer wantons with the bull;
The trees show pleasure with their quivering leaves,
The meadow with new grass, the vine with grapes,
The running brooks with sweet and silver sound.
Thee, Thee, sweet Princess, Heaven, and earth and floods
And plants and beasts salute with one accord.
And while they gaze on Thy perfections,
Their eyes' desire is never satisfied.
Thy presence frees each thing that lived in doubt.
No seeds now fear the biting of the worm,
Nor deer the toils, nor grass the parching heat,
Nor birds the snare, nor corn the storm of hail.
Oh, Empress, oh, draw forth these days to years,
Years to an age, ages to eternity,
That such as lately joyed to see our sorrows,
May sorrow now, to see our perfect joys.
Behold where all the Graces, Virtue's maids,
And light-foot Hours, the guardians of Heaven's gate,

---

221 set . . . English the author's attempt to widen the audience, perhaps to suggest this entertainment is as much popular as elitist

227 kneel . . . saints i.e., cushions or hassocks used for praying in church

229 sacred hill Mount Parnassus

237 Semer's play on Seymour; **fraudless house** simple dwelling

238–9 Jupiter . . . dwelt Philemon and Baucis were a poor couple but the only ones hospitable to Jupiter and Mercury, who visited them in disguise; the wonder of the gods was recognized when the winejug from which they drank was never empty

241 Phoebus another name for Apollo emphasizing his role as sun god

252 laurel wreath symbol of the state's honored poet

266 kid i.e., young goat

277 toils nets; traps or snares

282 May . . . joys the preceding catalogue refers to Elizabeth as a goddess of fertility and increase; there may be reference here also to Elizabeth as the goddess of autumn and plenty (when this visit takes place) who will also provide spring (the season of rebirth); both seasons are the moderate ones, neither too hot nor too cold, thus providing an annual climate for Elvetham that resembles Eden or Paradise

With joined forces do remove those blocks
Which Envy laid in Majesty's highway.
  Come, therefore, come under our humble roof,
And with a beck command what it contains.
For all is Thine; each part obeys Thy will;
Did not each part obey, the whole should perish.
  Sing songs, fair nymphs, sing sweet triumphal songs,
Fill ways with flowers and th' air with harmony.

While the poet was pronouncing this oration, six Virgins were behind him, busily removing blocks out of Her Majesty's way, which blocks were supposed to be laid there by the person of Envy, whose condition is to envy at every good thing, but especially to malice the proceedings of Virtue and the glory of true Majesty. Three of these Virgins represented the three Graces, and the other three the Hours, which by the poet are feigned to be the guardians of Heaven's gates. They were all attired in gowns of taffeta sarcenet of diverse colors, with flower garlands on their heads, and baskets full of sweet herbs and flowers upon their arms. When the poet's speech was happily ended, and in a scroll delivered to Her Majesty, for such was Her gracious acceptance that She deigned to receive it with her own hand. Then these six Virgins, after performance of their humble reverence to Her Highness, walked on before Her towards the house, strewing the way with flowers and singing a sweet song of six parts to this ditty which followeth.

The Ditty of the Six Virgins' Song

With fragrant flowers we strew the way,
And make this our chief holiday;
For though this clime were blessed of yore,
Yet was it never proud before.
  Oh, beauteous Queen of second Troy,
  Accept of our unfeigned joy.
Now th' air is sweeter than sweet balm,
And Satyrs dance about the palm;
Now earth, with verdure newly dight
Gives perfect sign of her delight.
  Oh, beauteous Queen of second Troy,
  Accept of our unfeigned joy.
Now birds record new harmony,
And trees do whistle melody;
Now everything that nature breeds
Doth clad itself in pleasant weeds.
  Oh, beauteous Queen of second Troy,
  Accept of our unfeigned joy.

This song ended with Her Majesty's entrance into the house where she had not rested her a quarter of an hour but from the Snail Mount and the Ship Isle in the pond (both being near under the prospect of Her gallery window) there was a long volley of chambers discharged. After this, supper was served us, first to Her Majesty, and then to the nobles and others. Were it not that I would not seem to flatter the honorable-minded Earl, or but that I fear to displease him, who rather desired to express his loyal duty in his liberal bounty than to hear of it again, I could here willingly particulate the store of his cheer and provision, as likewise the careful and kind diligence of his servants expressed in their quiet service to Her Majesty and the nobility, and by their loving entertainment to all other, friends or strangers. But I leave the bounty of the one, and the industry of the others, to the just report of such as beheld or tasted the plentiful abundance of that time and place.

After supper was ended, Her Majesty graciously admitted unto Her presence a notable consort of six musicians, which my Lord Hertford had provided to entertain Her Majesty withal, at Her will and pleasure, and when it should seem good to Her Highness. Their music so highly pleased her that in grace and favor thereof she gave a new name unto one of their pavans, made long since by Master Thomas Morley, then organist of Paul's Church.

These are the chief points which I noted in the first day's entertainment. Now therefore it followeth that I proceed to the second.

302 **Heaven's gates** continues fiction that Elizabeth's presence has turned Elvetham into Paradise

303 **sarcenet** a very fine and soft silk

314 **ditty** words (rather than music)

320 **second Troy** according to legend, London was built by Brutus, grandson of Aeneas, and other Trojans and named Troynovant

323 **Satyrs** (1) creatures of nature; (2) unrestrained celebrants

324 **dight** dressed

331 **weeds** garments

334 **song** assigned in *England's Helicon* (1600) to Thomas Watson, but the music may also have been by William Byrd or possibly Francis Pilkington

339 **chambers** small pieces of ordnance standing on the breech and used for salutes

346 **cheer** food and provisions

356 **consort** company of vocal or instrumental musicians

357 **six musicians** the implication is that they were neither of the Earl's nor the Queen's household but especially commissioned for this occasion

362 **pavans** grave and stately dances for which the dancers are usually elaborately dressed

363 **Master . . . Morley** one of the period's most distinguished composers

363–4 **Paul's Church** St. Paul's Cathedral, London

THE SECOND DAY'S ENTERTAINMENT

On the next day following, being Tuesday and Saint Matthew's Festival, the forenoon was so wet and stormy that nothing of pleasure could be presented Her Majesty. Yet it held up a little before dinner time and all the day after where, otherwise, fair sports would have been buried in foul weather.

This day Her Majesty dined with her nobles about her in the room of estate new built on the hillside above the pond's head. There sat below Her many lords, ladies, and knights. The manner of service, and abundance of dainties, I omit upon just consideration; as also the ordnance discharged in the beginning of dinner.

Presently, after dinner, my Lord of Hertford caused a large canopy of estate to be set at the pond's head for Her Majesty to sit under, and to view some sports prepared in the water. The canopy was of green satin, lined with green taffeta sarcenet; every seam covered with a broad silver lace; valenced about, and fringed with green silk and silver, more than a handbreadth in depth; supported with four silver pillars moveable; and decked above head with four white plumes spangled with silver. This canopy being upheld by four of my Lord's chief gentlemen, and tapestry spread all about the pond's head, Her Majesty, about four of the clock, came and sat under it, to expect the issue of some device, being advertised that there was some such thing towards.

At the further end of the pond, there was a bower, close built to the brink thereof; out of which there went a pompous array of seapersons, which waded breast-high or swam until they approached near the seat of Her Majesty. Nereus, the Prophet of the Sea, attired in red silk and having a cornered-cap on his curled head, did swim before the rest, as their pastor and guide. After him came five Tritons breast-high in the water, all with grizzly heads and beards of diverse colors and fashions, and all five cheerfully sounding their trumpets. After them went two other Gods of the Sea, Neptune and Oceanus, leading between them that pinnace whereof I spoke in the beginning of this treatise.

In the pinnace were three Virgins which, with their cornets, played Scottish jigs made three parts in one. There was also in the said pinnace another nymph of the sea named Neaera, the old supposed love of Sylvanus, a god of the woods. Near to her were placed three excellent voices to sing to one lute, and, in two other boats hard by, other lutes and voices to answer by manner of echo. After the pinnace, and two other boats which were drawn after it by other sea-gods; the rest of the train followed breast-high in the water, all attired in ugly marine suits and every one armed with a huge wooden squirt in his hand to what end it shall appear hereafter. In their marching towards the pond, all along the middle of the current, the Tritons sounded one half of the way; and then they ceasing, the cornets played their Scottish jigs. The melody was sweet and the show stately.

By the way, it is needful to touch here many things abruptly, for the better understanding of that which followeth.

First, that in the pinnace are two jewels to be presented Her Majesty, the one by Nereus, the other by Neaera.

Secondly, that the Fort in the pond is round environed with armed men.

Thirdly, that the Snail Mount now resembleth a monster, having horns full of wild fire, continually burning.

And lastly, that the god Sylvanus lieth with his train not far off in the woods and will shortly salute Her Majesty and present Her with a holy escutcheon wherein Apollo had long since written Her praises.

All this remembered and considered, I now return to the Sea gods who, having under the conduct of Nereus brought the pinnace near before Her Majesty, Nereus made his oration as followeth; but before he began, he made a privy sign unto one of his train which was gotten up

372 **held** kept
380 **dainties** delicacies
384 **canopy of estate** covering over the Queen's throne
397 **device** invention; entertainment; masque; **advertised** notified
401 **pompous** stately, splendid
403 **Nereus** in Greek mythology, a kind and gentle sea god
405 **cornered-cap** a three- or four-cornered cap associated with preachers (pastors)
406 **pastor** minister with special care of souls
407 **Tritons** minor sea gods
408 **grizzly** ugly
411 **Neptune** in Roman mythology the kind god of the sea associated with rain, growth, and vegetation; **Oceanus** in Greek mythology, the oldest of the Titans, represented as aged with bull's horns on his head and a garland of crab's claws
414 **Virgins** probably girls rather than boys dressed as girls
418 **Sylvanus** a common pastoral figure named for the ancient Roman god of untilled land
420 **hard** near
426 **squirt** an instrument to shoot water; a water-gun
447 **escutcheon** shield with a crest on it; badge
453 **privy** private, secret

into the Ship Isle directly before Her Majesty. And he presently did cast himself down, doing a somersault from the Isle into the water and then swam to his company.

The Oration of Nereus to Her Majesty

Fair Cynthia, the wide Ocean's Empress,
I, wat'ry Nereus, hovered on the coast,
To greet Your Majesty with this my train
Of dancing Tritons and shrill-singing Nymphs.
But all in vain. Eliza was not there.
For which our Neptune grieved, and blamed the star
Whose thwarting influence dashed our longing hope.
Therefore impatient, that this worthless earth
Should bear Your Highness's weight, and we Sea-gods
(Whose jealous waves have swallowed up your foes,
And to Your realm are walls impregnable),
With such large favor seldom time are graced.
I from the deeps have drawn this winding flood
Whose crescent form figures the rich increase
Of all that sweet Eliza holdeth dear.
And with me came gold-breasted India,
Who, daunted at Your sight, leaped to the shore
And, sprinkling endless treasure on this Isle,
Left me this jewel to present Your Grace.
For him, that under you doth hold this place,
See where her ship remains, whose silk-woven tackling
Is turned to twigs, and threefold mast to trees,
Receiving life from verdure of your looks
(For what cannot Your gracious looks effect?).
Yon ugly monsters creeping from the South
To spoil these blessed fields of Albion,
By self-same beams is changed into a snail,
Whose bulrush horns are not of force to hurt.
As this snail is, so be Thine enemies!
And never yet did Nereus wish in vain.
That fort did Neptune raise for your defense;
And, in this bark, which gods haul near the shore,
White-footed Thetis sends her music maids
To please Eliza's ears with harmony.
Hear them, fair Queen, and when their music ends,
My Triton shall awake the sylvan gods
To do their homage to Your Majesty.

This oration being delivered, and withal the present whereof he spoke, which was hidden in a purse of green rushes, cunningly woven together, immediately the three voices in the pinnace sang a song to the lute with excellent divisions, and the end of every verse was replied by lutes and voices in the other boat somewhat afar off, as if they had been echoes.

The Sea Nymph's Ditty

How haps it now when prime is done,
Another springtime is begun?
Our happy soil is overrun,
With beauty of a second Sun.
Echo. A second Sun.

What second Sun hath rays so bright
To cause this unacquainted light?
'Tis fair Eliza's matchless grace,
Who with her beames doth bless the place.
Echo. Doth bless the place.

This song being ended, Nereus commanded the five Tritons to sound. Then came Sylvanus with his attendants from the wood, himself attired from the middle downwards to the knee in kid's skins with the hair on his legs, body, and face naked but dyed over with saffron and his head hooded with a goat's skin and two little horns over his forehead, bearing in his right hand an olive tree and in his left an escutcheon, whereof I spoke somewhat before. His followers were all covered with ivy leaves and bore in their hands bows made like darts. At their approach near Her Majesty, Sylvanus spoke as followeth, and delivered up his escutcheon, engraven with golden characters, Nereus and all his train still continuing near Her Highness,

460 **Cynthia** goddess of the moon, another name for Diana; since the moon was thought to control the sea, Elizabeth is putatively in command of the sea gods in these devices

463 **shrill** high-pitched; but could also mean poignant

469–70 **swallowed . . . impregnable** with reference to the Spanish Armada of 1588

471–4 **With . . . dear** since the danger of Spanish invasion kept Elizabeth from the coast, Nereus is bringing the sea to her

475 **gold-breasted India** i.e., the India of the New World

478 **jewel** since it was left by India in the fiction, it must have been made of gold

482 **verdure** literally, green color supplying vegetation; here, fertilizing color

484 **South** i.e., Spain

485 **Albion** England; the passage appeals to Elizabeth as queen of the whole realm

486 **snail** proverbial for slowness and cowardice

487 **bulrush horns** deceptive horns, since bulrush although it appeared strong was actually quite pliant

491 **bark** small ship

492 **Thetis** female sea god, equivalent to Nereus

497 **withal** therewith

499 **cunningly** ingeniously

501–2 **divisions** parts

506 **haps** happens; fortunes; **prime** spring (as the first season)

521 **saffron** a meadow plant red-orange in color

The Oration of Sylvanus

Sylvanus comes from out the leavy groves,
To honor Her whom all the world adores,
Fair Cynthia, whom no sooner Nature framed
And decked with Fortune's and with Virtue's
  dower,
But straight admiring what her skill had wrought,
She broke the mold that never Sun might see,
The like to Albion's Queen for excellence.
'Twas not the Tritons air-enforcing shell,
As they perhaps would proudly make their vaunt,
But those fair beams that shoot from Majesty
Which drew our eyes to wonder at Thy worth.
That worth breeds wonder; wonder, holy fear,
And holy fear unfeigned reverence.
Among the wanton days of golden age,
Apollo playing in our pleasant shades,
And printing oracles in every leaf,
Let fall this sacred escutcheon from his breast;
Wherein is writ, "Detur dignissimae."
Oh, therefore hold what Heaven hath made thy
  right,
I but in duty yield desert her due.

Nereus.

But see, Sylvanus, where thy love doth sit.

Sylvanus.

My sweet Neaera, was her ear so near?
Oh, set my heart's delight upon this bank
That, in compassion of old sufferance,
She may relent in sight of Beauty's Queen.

Nereus.

On this condition shall she come on shore,
That with thy hand thou plight a solemn vow,
Not to prophane her undefiled state.

Sylvanus.

Here, take my hand, and therewithal I vow.

Nereus.

That water will extinguish wanton fire.

Nereus, in pronouncing this last line, did pluck Sylvanus over head and ears into the water, where all the sea-gods, laughing, did insult over him. In the meanwhile Her Majesty perused the verses written in the eschutcheon, which were these:

Adonis prior, et Divis es pulchrior alti
  Æquoris, ac Nymphis es prior Idaliis.
Idaliis prior es Nymphis, ac aequoris alti.
  Pulchrior et Divis, ac prior Adoniis.

Over these verses was this poesy written:

Detur dignissimae.

After that the sea-gods had sufficiently ducked Sylvanus, they suffered him to creep to the land, where he no sooner set footing but crying, "Revenge, Revenge," he and his began a skirmish with those of the water, the one side throwing their darts and the other using their squirts, and the Tritons sounding a point of war. At the last, Nereus parted the fray with a line or two, grounded on the excellence of Her Majesty's presence as being always friend to peace and enemy to war. Then Sylvanus with his followers retired to the woods; and Neaera, his fair love in the pinnace, presenting Her Majesty a sea-jewel bearing the form of a fan, spoke unto her as followeth:

The Oration of fair Neaera

When Neptune late bestowed on me this bark,
And sent by me this present to Your Grace,
Thus Nereus sang, who never sings but truth:
Thine eyes, Neaera, shall in time behold
A sea-borne Queen, worthy to govern Kings.
On her depends the fortune of thy boat.
If she but name it with a blissful word,
And view it with her life-inspiring beams,
Her beams yield gentle influence, like fair stars;
Her silver-sounding word is prophecy.
Speak, sacred Sibyl, give some prosperous name,
That it may dare attempt a golden fleece,
Or dive for pearls and lay them in thy lap.
For wind and waves, and all the world besides,
Will make her way, whom thou shalt doom to
  bliss,
For what is Sibyl's speech but oracle?

Here Her Majesty named the pinnace The Bonadventure and Neaera went on with her speech as followeth:

Now Neaera's bark is fortunate,
And in Thy service shall employ her sail,
And often make return to Thy avail.
Oh, live in endless joy, with glorious fame,
Sound trumpets, sound, in honor of Her name.

---

540 **air-enforcing shell** instruments in the shape of a shell
541 **vaunt** boast
547 **Apollo** as the god of music, poetry, and dance
550 **"Detur dignissimae"** "Let it be given to the most worthy"
563 **undefiled** a reference to the proverbial licentiousness of the satyrs, of whom Sylvanus was the leader
573–6 **Adonis . . . Adoniis** two antiphonal couplets saying "You take precedence over the Muses and the nymphs of Ida and are more beautiful than the goddesses of the deep sea"
605 **Sibyl** in ancient times woman with a special gift for prophecy
606 **golden fleece** an anti-Hapsburg reference to the Order of the Golden Fleece, founded in 1430 and the chief order of chivalry for Philip II of Spain, the equivalent of the English Order of the Garter
612 **Bonadventure** i.e., good venture; fortunate ship

Thus did Nereus retire back to his bower with all his train following him, in self-same order as they came forth before, the Tritons sounding their trumpets one-half of the way, and the cornets playing the other half. And here ended the second day's pastime, to the so great liking of Her Majesty, that Her gracious approbation thereof was to the actors more than a double reward; and yet withal Her Highness bestowed a largess upon them the next day after, before she departed.

The Third Day's Entertainment

On Wednesday morning about nine of the clock, as Her Majesty opened a casement of her gallery window, there were three excellent musicians who, being disguised in ancient country attire, did greet her with a pleasant song of Corydon and Phyllida, made in three parts of purpose. The song, as well for the worth of the ditty as for the aptness of the note thereto applied, it pleased Her Highness, after it had been once sung, to command it again, and highly to grace it with her cheerful acceptance and commendation.

The Plowman's Song

In the merry month of May,
In a morn by break of day,
Forth I walked by the woodside,
Where as May was in his pride.
There I spied, all alone,
Phyllida and Corydon.
Much ado there was, God wot,
He would love, and she would not.
She said, never man was true.
He said, none was false to you.
He said, he had loved her long.
She said, love should have no wrong.
Corydon would kiss her then.
She said, maids must kiss no men,
'Til they did for good and all.
Then she made the shepherd call
All the Heavens to witness truth,
Never loved a truer youth.
Thus with many a pretty oath,
Yea and nay, and faith and troth,
Such as silly shepherds use,
When they will not love abuse,
Love, which had been long deluded,
Was with kisses sweet concluded.
And Phyllida, with garlands gay,
Was made the Lady of the May.

The same day after dinner, about three of the clock, ten of my Lord of Hertford's servants, all Somersetshire men, in a square green court before Her Majesty's window did hang up lines, squaring out the form of a tennis court, and making a crossline in the middle. In this square they, being stripped of doublets, played five to five, with the handball, at bond and cord (as they term it) to so great liking of Her Highness that she graciously deigned to behold their pasttime more than an hour and a half.

After supper, there were two delights presented unto Her Majesty: curious fireworks and a sumptuous banquet; the first from the three islands in the pond, the second in a lower gallery in Her Majesty's privy garden. But I will first briefly speak of the fireworks.

First, there was a peal of a hundred chambers discharged from the Snail Mount, in counter whereof a like peal was discharged from the Ship Isle, and some great ordnance withal. Then was there a castle of fireworks of all sorts which played in the Fort. Answerable to that, there was in the Snail Mount a globe of all manner of fireworks, as big as a barrel. When these were spent on either side, there were many running rockets upon lines which passed between the Snail Mount and the castle in the Fort. On either side were many firewheels, pikes of pleasure, and balls of wild fire which burned in the water.

During the time of these fireworks in the water, there was a banquet served, all in glass and silver, into the low gallery in the garden from a hillside fourteen score off, by two hundred of my Lord of Hertford's gentlemen, every one carrying so many dishes that the whole number amounted to a thousand and there were to light them in their way a hundred torchbearers. To satisfy the curious, I will here set down some particulars in the banquet.

Her Majesty's arms in sugarwork.

The several arms of our nobility in sugarwork.

627 **largess** bountiful bestowal of gifts

635–6 **Corydon and Phyllida** traditional names for poetic shepherds

638 **note** music

668 **Lady of the May** as one who accepts the title, Phyllida accepts love; in *England's Helicon* (1600) Nicholas Breton is given as the author of this verse

675 **doublets** close-fitting upper garments with or without sleeves

676 **bond and cord** lawn tennis

697–8 **firewheels . . . fire** possibly Catherine wheels, golden rain, and Roman candles

700 **banquet** a dessert course, not a meal

709 **arms** state insignia; **sugarwork** confectionery

Many men and women in sugarwork and some enforced by hand.

Castles, forts, ordnance, drummers, trumpeters, and soldiers of all sorts in sugarwork.

Lions, unicorns, bears, horses, camels, bulls, rams, dogs, tigers, elephants, antelopes, dromedaries, apes, and all other beasts in sugarwork.

Eagles, falcons, franes, buzzards, heronshaws, bittern, pheasants, partridges, quails, larks, sparrows, pigeons, cocks, owls, and all that fly in sugarwork.

Snakes, adders, vipers, frogs, toads, and all kind of worms in sugarwork.

Mermaids, whales, dolphins, congers, sturgeons, pikes, carps, breams, and all sorts of fish in sugarwork.

All these were standing dishes of sugarwork. The self-same devices were also there in flatwork. Moreover, these particulars following, and many such-like, were in flat sugarwork and cinnamon.

Marchpane, grapes, oysters, mussels, cockles, periwinkles, crabs, lobsters.

Apples, pears, and plums, of all sorts.

Preserves, succades, jellies, leaches, marm lades, pasts comfits, of all sorts.

The Fourth Day's Entertainment

On Thursday morning, Her Majesty was no sooner ready and at her gallery window looking into the garden, but there began three cornets to play certain fantastic dances, at the measure whereof the Fairy Queen came into the garden, dancing with her maids about her. She brought with her a garland made in form of an imperial crown; within the sight of Her Majesty, she fixed open a silver staff and, sticking the staff into the ground, spoke as followeth:

The Speech of the Fairy Queen to Her Majesty

I that abide in places underground,
Aureola, the Queen of Fairy land,
That every night in rings of painted flowers
Turn around and carol out Eliza's name,
Hearing that Nereus and the Sylvan gods
Have lately welcomed your Imperial Grace,
Opened the earth with this enchanting wand,
To do my duty to Your Majesty,
And humbly to salute you with this chaplet,
Given me by Oberon, the Fairy King
Bright shining Phoebe, that in human shape,
Hid'st Heaven's perfection, vouchsafe t'accept it,
And I, Aureola, beloved in Heaven,
(For amorous stars fall nightly in my lap),
Will cause that Heavens enlarge Thy golden days,
And cut them short that envy at Thy praise.

After this speech, the Fairy Queen and her maids danced about the garden, singing a song of six parts, with the music of an exquisite consort, wherein was the lute, bandore, bass viol, cithern, treble-viol, and flute. And this was the Fairy's Song:

Eliza is the fairest Queen,
That ever trod upon this green.
Eliza's eyes are blessed stars,
Inducing peace, subduing wars.
Eliza's hand is crystal bright,
Her words are balm, her looks are light.
Eliza's breast is that fair hill
Where Virtue dwells, and sacred skill,
Oh, blessed be each day and hour
Where sweet Eliza builds her bower.

This spectacle and music so delighted Her Majesty that she desired to see and hear it twice over and then dismissed the actors with thanks and with a gracious largess which of Her exceeding goodness She bestowed upon them.

Within an hour after, Her Majesty departed, with her nobles, from Elvetham. On the one side of her way, as she passed through the park, there was placed, sitting on the pond side, Nereus and all the sea-gods, in their former attire; on her left hand, Sylvanus and all his company; in the way before her, the three Graces and the three Hours: all of them on every side, wringing their hands and showing sign of sorrow for her departure. While she beheld this dumb show, the poet made her a short oration as followeth:

716–17 dromedaries camels
718 heronshaws heron
724 congers eels
731 Marchpane marzipan
734 succades fruit preserved in sugar; **leaches** dishes containing sliced meat, eggs, fruit, and spices in jelly
735 pasts comfits sweetmeats in pastry
740 fantastic fanciful
750 Aureola perhaps Aurora, the dawn (see line 762)

757 chaplet garland of flowers or leaves
759 Phoebe goddess of the moon
767 exquisite consummate
768 bandore an instrument resembling a guitar or lute
769 cithern stringed instrument played with plectrum or quill
771–80 Eliza . . . bower the music has been identified as that by Edward Johnson
795 dumb show pantomime

The Poet's Speech at Her Majesty's Departure

Oh, see, sweet Cynthia, how the wat'ry gods
Which joined of late to view Thy glorious beams,
At this retire doe wail and wring their hands,
Distilling from their eyes salt showers of tears,
To bring in Winter with their wet lament.
For how can Summer stay, when Sun departs?
See where Sylvanus sits, and sadly mourns,
To think that Autumn, with his withered wings,
Will bring in tempest, when Thy beams are
hence.
For how can Summer stay, when Sun departs?
See where those Graces, and those Hours of
Heaven,
Which at Thy coming sang triumphal songs,
And smoothed the way and strewed it with sweet
flowers,
Now, if they durst, would stop it with green
boughs,
Least by Thine absence the year's pride decay.
For how can Summer stay, when Sun departs?
Leaves fall, grass dies, beasts of the wood hang
head,
Birds cease to sing and every creature wails
To see the season alter with this change.
For how can Summer stay, when Sun departs?
Oh, either stay, or soon return again,
For Summer's parting is the country's pain.

After this, as Her Majesty passed through the park gate, there was a consort of musicians hidden in a bower, to whose playing this ditty of "Come again" was sung, with excellent division, by two that were cunning.

Oh, come again, fair Nature's treasure,
Whose looks yield joys exceeding measure.
Oh, come again, Heaven's chief delight,
Thine absence makes eternal night.
Oh, come again, world's starbright eye,
Whose presence doth adorn the sky.
Oh, come again, sweet beauty's Sun,
When Thou art gone, our joys are done.

Her Majesty was so highly pleased with this and the rest that she openly protested to my Lord of Hertford that the beginning, process, and end of this his entertainment was so honorable as hereafter he should find the reward thereof in her especial favor.

Many and most happy years may Her Gracious Majesty continue to favor and foster him and all others which do truly love and honor Her.

---

804 Summer establishes Elizabeth as fruitful; **Sun** (1) that which fosters growth; (2) symbol of monarchy

812 durst dared; **stop** arrest

813 Least lest

The Tragical History of D. Faustus

Christopher Marlowe

The Tragicall Hiſtory of the Life and Death of Doctor FAVSTVS.

With new Additions.

Written by *Ch. Mar.*

Printed at London for *Iohn Wright*, and are to be ſold at his ſhop without Newgate, 1624.

Frontispiece, 1624.

The human drama of the fall of man and his possible redemption, first explored in medieval English mystery cycles and later in English morality plays, lies in one way or another at the heart of all Renaissance English drama; but Christopher Marlowe's *Dr. Faustus* is the quintessential example. According to the scholastic paradigm dominant in the West since Aquinas, devils approach man, visibly or invisibly, when he attracts them through his actions, his words, or his apparent proclivity to sin. As their affinity develops, his sins increase and he becomes hardened to them; seduced by promises of infernal rewards, man grows increasingly dependent on his wicked ways. Then at some personal crisis, usually near death, he confronts his life's history and according to his own self-judgment seeks and obtains grace or is eternally punished. No playwright, however, including Marlowe, was content with so bare an outline. To complicate the Chorus' presentation, Marlowe drew on Origen, another Church Father he studied at Cambridge, who proposed that each person is given not one but two guiding angels: "whenever good thoughts arise in our hearts they are suggested by the good angel, but when a contrary kind, they are the instigation of the evil angel," a belief fostered by Primaudaye in his *French Academy* and shared in the work of Marlowe's fellow Cambridge student, Thomas Nashe. Thus to scholastic theology Marlowe adds scholastic logic and disputation as the Good Angel and Evil Angel, later replaced by the Old Man and Mephastophilis, debate the Christian virtues of obedience, humility, and piety against the heroic values of power, glory, and pleasure. "Contrition, prayer, repentance: what of them," Faustus asks. "They are means to bring thee unto Heaven," replies the Good Angel; "Rather illusions," says the Evil Angel, "fruits of lunacy." What is at stake is a man's soul, all human souls, but also the very institution of Elizabeth I's Established Church, which is what the scholastic Faustus is citing. According to the prescribed "Homily of Repentance and True Reconciliation Unto God,"

> there be four parts of repentance, which being set together may be likened to an easy and short ladder, whereby we may climb from the bottomless pit of perdition, that we cast ourselves into by our daily offenses and grievous sins, up into the castle or tower of eternal and endless salvation. The first is contrition of the heart.... The second, an unfeigned confession and acknowledging of our sins unto God.... The third part of repentance is faith.... The fourth is amendment of life.

Marlowe's play, then, challenges part of the very backbone of Elizabethan culture by interrogating two of its fundamental institutions, the church and the university. *Dr. Faustus* questions the basis of faith and the purpose of education.

As the Elizabethan Everyman, Faustus yearns for what he does not have and all men at some point desire: joy, wealth, fame, and (most of all) immortality. His own advanced learning and intellectual stature are insufficient and unsatisfying; he wants literally to make the world his stage, to transcend his studies and the whole civilization they represent because they are too human, too confining, too limited. The question the play asks is whether that sense of uselessness is the fault of Faustus or the fault of the studies and beliefs that have been handed to him. The dialectic in which the subsequent narrative is grounded is that between Faustus' aspirations and his deprivation; it charts the increasing distance between his magical powers and his moral loss: at the play's center is the essential cost of his bargain with the Devil. Like the tradition of the *psychomachia* which it turns into a harrowing examination of Elizabethan life and thought, *Dr. Faustus* alternates between the serious and the comic, using the grotesque not merely to entertain the groundlings but to display what depravity looks like to those not yet depraved. Against Faustus' heightened if finally unformed vision of the future there is put the deplorable degeneracy of the present. Thus Marlowe in the end transforms the very morality play that inspires him: instead of dramatizing holy living or holy dying as, say, *Mankind* or *Everyman* does, he looks instead at evil living and desperate dying. *Dr. Faustus* is a drama about denial. This would be an easier matter for us, of course, if the play were about a remote and unrelated culture or simply a rousingly spectacular piece of theater, but that is not the case. The play asks tough questions: why God creates a Lucifer and permits evil; why Faustus is the one to be tested; whether there is ever any guarantee of grace. We are confronted with more specific problems, too: when the Good Angel proposes mercy, why does the Evil Angel get the last word? when the Old Man converts Faustus, why does he accept a dagger from Mephastophilis? when Faustus calls upon Christ's blood streaming in the firmament, why is it that Lucifer appears? This probing Elizabethan redaction of the English morality play, then, is not so much a narrative about the life of a fallen protagonist as it is an intense cultural analysis of the human soul.

Writing his play between 1589 and 1592, Marlowe found his protagonist complex but ready-made in the culture about him: there was a broadside ballad on Faustus, now lost, in 1589; later that year Faustus was mentioned by Gabriel Harvey in his *Advertisement for Papp-Hatchet* and in 1590 by Henry Holland in his *Treatise against Witchcraft.* But in fact the legend of Faust was already popular with the Protestant Reformers because it tested man's free will, the church's acculturation of the individual conscience, and the demonization of magic. The original Faust seems to have been Georgius of Helmstadt, a doctor and schoolmaster who became confused with Johannes Faust, an astrologer. Georgius was a showman, both embraced and dismissed by the learned and patronized by the Catholic middle classes; in time he was ostracized by civic authorities and banned from Ingolstadt in 1528 and Nuremberg in 1532. He then became "a vagabond, an empty babbler and a knave worthy to be whipped," "the Devil's brother-in-law" who was, from time to time, accused of sodomizing schoolboys. When after his death his reputation merged with that of Johannes Faustus, he became known as a black magician, practicing demonic arts, and under the influence of Martin Luther a Protestant Reformer named Johannes Gast reported that he had sold his soul to the Devil and had died from a broken neck, "the classic retribution for those who sell their souls." This culturally constructed biography was popularized in a German Faust-book that around 1592 was translated by P. F. Gent. into English, where Faust is described as "a worldly man" who "named himself an Astrologer, a Mathematician, and...a Physician [who] did great cures." To the church he was also a heretic.

For Marlowe, however, the initial heresy of Faustus is intellectual. He has been "ravished," he says, intellectually raped and brought to a kind of intellectual orgasm by Aristotle's *Analytics* and yet,

> Is to dispute well logic's chiefest end?
> Affords this art no greater miracle?
> Then read no more; thou hast attained the end.

Perhaps mastering logic takes away any challenge and so any desire to dominate; but "miracle" is a strange word to introduce into the syllogism, rendering it confused and invalid. Yet it seems to accord with the next subject in his curricular inventory:

> Be a physician, Faustus. Heap up gold,
> And be eternized for some wondrous cure:

Once again the metaphysical realm intervenes in the physical. Law, too, is mundane as "A pretty case of paltry legacies" when it is considered alongside other occupations where he might "make man to live eternally," or, "being dead, raise [him] to life again." Intellectual domination is thus confounded with religious domination, and his own ability conflated with God's, yet when he turns to God's scriptures, Faustus' reading and logic stop short at only half the passage before his eyes: "The reward of sin is death. That's hard." Faustus has reversed himself, for here the apparent premise to a syllogism admits the metaphysical as another premise in the rest of the verse that remains unvoiced: "but the gift of God is eternal life through Jesus Christ our Lord." It is as if Faustus wishes to withhold the miraculous, to reserve it for those "Lines, circles, signs, letters, and characters" that together make "necromatic books" that are, for him, "heavenly." The play asks us to determine whether Faustus' sophistry and moral blindness are caused by a blackened soul – one colored by intellectual pride, perhaps – or whether his soul, already misguided for reasons he chooses deliberately not to examine, have caused such moral blindness. When he goes on to mock the two sacred rites admitted from the Catholic faith to Elizabeth's Reformed Church, those of baptism and communion, he is urged on by Mephastophilis dressed in the robes of a Catholic friar: "the shortest cut for conjuring," Faustus is taught, "Is stoutly to abjure all godliness, And pray devoutly to the Prince of hell." He is asked to trade one metaphysics for another; and yet what he seems to want is not something abstract but joy of the concrete that his advanced studies have not given him: the raising of the dead, the fetching of grapes, the kissing of Helen of Troy – just those "miracles" which, because they seem more real, are more precious. What we need to determine is whether they seem more precious because they seem less abstract or, because they are conceived infernally, they are especially tempting and delicious because they are dangerous, because they flirt with rebellion against God. The power of his own new tutors is sharply circumscribed – Mephastophilis cannot give Faustus a wife; Lucifer will not name God – and even Faustus knows that the spirits he raises to show his power are "insubstantial." Why he would settle for such illusions when the mystery of grace can be manifested in congealed blood or in an inscription on his arm warning him to flee raises fundamental questions about Faustus' own nature and whether that depraved nature was his birthright, the result of his learning, or his sudden decision, by his own free will, to forsake the commonplaces of church and university for the tantalizing because still unknown world beyond the standard Elizabethan curriculum. The great pageant of the seven deadly sins he calls forth – so formulaic that they themselves mock intelligence – become his new premises as, through his subsequent travels, he too practices pride, lechery, gluttony, and sloth, covetousness and wrath. In such a singular pursuit, he denies the kind of scholastic training that Donne upholds in a sermon on Matt. 12:31 that cites Augustine alongside Aquinas:

> The first couple is *presumption* and *desperation*; for presumption takes away the fear of God, and desperation the love of God. And then, they name *Impenitence*, and *hardness of heart*; for Impenitence removes all sorrow for sins past, and hardness of heart all tenderness towards future temptations. And lastly, they name *The resisting of a truth acknowledged before*, and *the envying of other men, who have made better use of God's grace than we have done*, for this resisting of a Truth is a shutting up of ourselves against it, and this envying of others is a sorrow that that Truth should prevail upon them.

Nor does he acknowledge the unexpected and contrary arguments which a frank and informed Mephastophilis advances to provide a new disputation: he is, for instance, one of the "Unhappy spirits that fell with Lucifer, Conspired against our God with Lucifer, And are forever damned with Lucifer." Damnation, moreover, is not an act or moment in time but a perpetual condition:

> this is hell, nor am I out of it.
> Think'st thou that I, who saw the face of God
> And tasted the eternal joys of Heaven,
> Am not tormented with ten thousand hells
> In being deprived of everlasting bliss?

Lucifer is equally straightforward: "Christ cannot save thy soul," he tells Faustus, "for He is just" and adds in all candor, "There's none but I have int'rest in the same." Faustus' own teasing disputations with Mephastophilis may be a kind of parodying of church catechisms, but here he is surprisingly, yet consistently, deaf. It is as if his initial physical stabbing of his arm, drawing blood to sign his infernal pact with the Devil, already suggests a maimed soul as well, and the "Poison, guns, halters, and envenomed steel [that] Are laid before me to dispatch myself" are preparatory for the dagger he reaches out for at the end. For the pleasures that at first withhold this study in despair and suicide are only, in the end, momentary distractions, pastimes to divert his attention.

Why, then, does Faustus turn from Christianity and to what extent does he actually deny it? The very sense of despair which would seem to characterize Faustus only makes sense if there is a sense of lost opportunity, a tacit acknowledgment, that is, of God. Faustus' teasing of Mephastophilis in their initial discussions, when he is not hardened to sin through the pleasures his diabolical pact has granted him, suggests that he does not take either the pact or the possibility of damnation seriously but sees them only as a temporary learning experience on the way to an eventual pardon: "Who buzzeth in mine ears I am a spirit? Be I a devil, yet God may pity me; Aye, God will pity me if I repent." The impermanence of the pleasures Faustus enjoys argues for his nagging doubt of their worth; after the joke played on the horse-courser, he consoles himself by thinking, "Tush! Christ did call the thief upon the cross; Then rest thee, Faustus, quiet in conceit," oblivious, apparently, of the context of his citation. According to John Woolton's *Christian Manual* (1576), "That saying of the Hebrew is memorable, and never to be forgotten: 'Say not, Tush, the mercy of the Lord is great, he shall forgive me my sins, be they never so many: for like as He is merciful, so goeth wrath from Him also, and his indignation cometh down upon sinners.'" Faustus comes to see such possible wrath – or justice – as his life's end.

> The stars move still; time runs; the clock will strike,
> The devil will come, and Faustus must be damned.
> Oh, I'll leap up to my God! Who pulls me down?
> See, see where Christ's blood streams in the firmament!
> One drop would save my soul, half a drop. Ah, my Christ!
> Ah, rend not my heart for naming of my Christ!
> Yet will I call on him. Oh, spare me, Lucifer!

His mind, worn smooth with dialectic, cannot call on Christ without also calling on Lucifer. His dilemma is thus to know God and not to know Him; his training in divinity has taught him that unless he repents he cannot be saved, yet he seems unable to repent without the assurance of grace. The risk he first sought he now forbids. The Old Man argues for an angel "with a vial full of precious grace"; Faustus' vision is at once more concrete and bloodier. Near the end, at the moment he requests to see Helen of Troy, he makes not Christ but Mephastophilis-as-friar a father confessor, just as earlier Marlowe had made a father of lies the teller of truth. This is not the only remarkable feature about *Dr. Faustus*. In making his protagonist both the Everyman and the Vice of his Renaissance morality play, Marlowe seems now to subvert the whole tradition in turning his attention to the new diabolical pact between church tradition and higher learning.

This is a dangerous proposition, as the play itself continually navigates dangerous waters, in a nation deeply concerned with a rise in atheism. As early as 1549 Bishop Hugh Latimer was reporting to Elizabeth's brother, Edward VI, that "there be a great many in England that say there is no soul, that think it is not eternal, but like a dog's soul, that think there is neither heaven nor hell." By the time of Marlowe Richard Hooker was writing in his *Laws of Ecclesiastical Polity* that the rise of atheism fulfilled St. Peter's prophecy about conditions at the end of the world and urged the death penalty. Such a rise in disbelief took on unexpected range and force. In accepting Aristotle on a world without end, Robert Master of Woodchurch, Kent, was one of many who "denieth that God made the sun, the moon, the earth, the water." In December 1584 the priest John Hilton confessed at Westminster that he had preached a sermon at St. Martin-in-the-Fields in which he had claimed "that the Old and New Testaments are but Fables." John Boyce of Stock, Essex, likened the Trinity "to a football play." Such doubts as Faustus realizes were shared across the island kingdom and through all the professions and classes; the Earl of Oxford was accused in 1581 of declaring that the Trinity was a fable and adding that the scriptures were used for state policy. The surprising state of ignorance about Christianity shows how unsettling for the Elizabethans a play such as *Dr. Faustus* might be: during Bishop Hooper's visitation of Gloucester in 1551, for instance, he found that of the 311 parish priests he examined, 175 could not repeat the Ten Commandments, ten could not say the Lord's Prayer, and twenty-seven did not know its author. Confusion reigned under a Reformed Church that made salvation an unmediated relation between an individual and his God in a nation where between 1547 and 1558 the national faith had itself changed four times. Religion must have seemed to many more than Oxford not so much a matter of faith as one of instilling obedience to the state.

From the perspective of both state and church, then, we can understand why a strong faction of Elizabeth's Privy Council, including the Earl of Leicester and Francis Walsingham, pursued a policy of Calvinism in which a God of fearful majesty brought many of Elizabeth's people to submission. Calvin's *Institutes*, the dominant theological text during Marlowe's days at Cambridge, argued with the ruthlessness of scholastic logic that an omnipotent and omniscient God would necessarily know the election or damnation of any of His people; such a belief, in fact, was made state policy when it was inscribed into the Thirty-Nine Articles at the start of Elizabeth's reign: while election, according to Article 17, "is full of sweet, pleasant, and unspeakable comfort to godly persons," "for curious and carnal persons, lacking the spirit of Christ, ... God's predestination is a most dangerous downfall, whereby the Devil doth thrust them either into desperation, or into wretchedness of most unclean living, no less perilous than desperation." There was also the related Calvinist doctrine of total depravity where a fallen man's free will was always exercised in evil; God's grace from man's perspective was random, arbitrary, and past earning, either by the soul's inclination or by any human acts.

In the 1580s and 1590s the most famous, popular, and widely read Calvinist was William Perkins – first a student at Corpus Christi College, Cambridge, Marlowe's college, and then fellow of Christ's College and lecturer at Great St. Andrews in town. He was stunningly effective; according to his colleague Samuel Ward, Perkins was so forceful that when preaching he was "able almost to make his hearers' hearts fall down and hairs to stand upright." He preached that the sin of witchcraft, such as Marlowe's Faustus practices, was analogous to the sin of Eden since in both instances men "not satisfied with the measure of inward gifts received, as of knowledge, wit, understanding, memory and suchlike ... search out such things as God would have kept secret." Their very lives are a form of heresy and damnation; they are, in a word, reprobate. In his bestselling book found in many Elizabethan homes, *A Golden Chain or the Description of Theology* (1590), Perkins asserts that

> First, the reprobate is deceived by some sin. Secondly, his heart is hardened by the same sin. Thirdly, his heart being hardened, it becometh wicked and perverse. Fourthly, then followeth his incredulity and unbelief, whereby he consenteth not to God's word, when he hath heard and known it. Fifthly, an apostacy, or falling away from faith in Christ.... After apostacy followeth pollution, which is the very fullness of all iniquity, altogether contrary to sanctification,

followed by damnation "whereby the reprobates are delivered up to eternal punishment." Following Perkins, the reprobate is both hopeless and totally trapped, his capacity for fear always outweighing his capacity for trust. Such a sinner, Perkins preached in Cambridge in 1593

> hath a veil before his face so that he seeth nothing... but rusheth securely into all manner of sin, the night of impenitence and the mist of ignorance so blinding his eyes that he seeth not the narrow bridge of this life, from which if he slide he falls immediately into the bottomless pit of hell.

That pit, according to Perkins' *Foundation of Christian Religion* (also 1590), is precisely what Marlowe's Mephastophilis describes:

> first, a perpetual separation from God's presence; secondly, fellowship with the devil and his angels; thirdly, an horrible pang and torment both of body and soul

> arising of the feeling of the whole wrath of God, poured forth on the wicked forever, world without end.

That *Dr. Faustus* is just such a study of an Elizabethan reprobate seems clear in the play's final judgment, without pity or remorse, rendered on Faustus by Chorus 5:

> Faustus is gone. Regard his hellish fall,
> Whose fiendful fortune may exhort the wise
> Only to wonder at unlawful things,
> Whose deepness doth entice such forward wits
> To practice more than heavenly power permits.

Such a Chorus, taken at its word, likens the play to one of Perkins' own sermons. But in the drama itself we are never permitted to escape our own individual responses to Faustus, his condition, and his predicament and supply what the play openly, stoutly refuses: pity. By making a reprobate his protagonist, and quite possibly his hero, Marlowe may be *using* the morality play not only to expose the consequences of absolute Calvinism but to interrogate the theology of the newly reformed state church.

Knowledge is power, according to Francis Bacon – *nam et ipsa scientia potestas est* – but whose knowledge does the play emphasize? that of the Good or Evil Angel, the Old Man or Lucifer, Faustus or Marlowe? In a town like Cambridge saturated with Calvinism, and a nation like England, woefully ignorant and perilously atheistic, these too are dangerous matters. Little wonder, then, that the government prohibited those who "handle in their plays certain matters of Divinity and of State unfit to be suffered" by an act of the Privy Council on December 12, 1589 – the very time Marlowe was writing *Dr. Faustus* – and further proposed that the Archbishop of Canterbury and the Lord Mayor of London review each play through their representatives and instruct the government's Master of the Revels to "strike out or reform such parts and matters as they shall find unfit and indecent to be handled in plays, both for divinity and state." At such an incendiary time, the only way for the state to impose controls was censorship; the only way for Marlowe to get away with staging his own ideas may well have been the theatrical disguise of the morality play.

But then entertainment for Marlowe had always had something of the subversive about it. The "preachers of God's sacred word" in his native town of Canterbury condemned as pagan the town's shows throughout his childhood; English drama as a potential instrument of state propaganda and religious dogma was countered by May games, bonfires in the streets, and bell-ringing on saints' days. Four years before his birth, the town's most famous jester-minstrel, Richard Borrows, known as "Railing Dick," led one hundred town boys to a bonfire set at the Bull Stake in Burgate. He was "an unshameful ribald and common smell-feast," a parasite and greedy sponger known for his "bawdy songs at all banquets of the papists," and his provocative pagan acts must have set the stage, for Marlowe, for the atheism spawned by the performances of disputations he found on arriving at Cambridge. "The whole Scriptures," Henry Barrow complained, "must in these their schools and disputations, be unsufferably corrupted, abused, wrested, perverted" by those students learning rhetoric, logic, divinity, and law through debate and who "must handle, divide, utter and discuss according to their vain affected arts." Not only Faustus but his fellow scholars and students are trained in such potentially subversive tactics; to give just one example, the Agrippa whom Faustus cites was the author of two books widely taught at Cambridge which, paired, inform the opening scenes of the play: *De Vanitate*, a work of skepticism which emphasizes the emptiness of the traditional kinds of orthodox knowledge, and *De Occulta*, which supplies that absence with the presence of the perilous vanity of magic. But Marlowe, later state spy and double agent, would by the time of *Dr. Faustus* in 1592, "in table talk or otherwise," according to his chamber-fellow Thomas Kyd, "jest at the divine scriptures, jibe at prayers, and strive in argument to frustrate and confute what hath been spoken or written by prophets and such holy men."

Nature herself seems to have conspired: *Dr. Faustus* was first staged in 1592, in a year plague disrupted London. The play itself disrupts, especially in its sly remarks in passing and its short unfolding scenes that look at the ways in which power seems always to corrupt. There is the fireship at Antwerp, the wealth stolen from the New World by the Spanish, the tyranny of the Pope, and the pettiness of the Duchess of Vanholt, yet it is the urgent need for power, in other forms, that first motivates Faustus. He would "make man to live eternally," cause "whole cities" to escape the plague, "be eternized for some wondrous cure." Not merely fame, however, is what he wants, nor to be resolved "of all ambiguities," perhaps common ends for students at Cambridge, but a breathtaking sense of sheer power:

> All things that move between the quiet poles
> Shall be at my command. Emperors and kings
> Are but obeyed in their several provinces,
> Nor can they raise the wind or rend the clouds;
> But his dominion that exceeds in this
> Stretcheth as far as doth the mind of man.

In the event, he is able to countermand the Pope only through papist devices, and he is no more than a court entertainer when he visits the Emperor and the Duke. These may be pointed comments on the potential outcome of a disciplined, delimiting education of the mind that ends up warping intellectual and personal values; but when Faustus manages his life so that he is entirely ruled by another, he combines questions of religion with those of imperialism – another volatile concern for Elizabeth and her government. Faustus would rule the world, and much of the play is taken up with his travels, always degenerating into a parody of man's capacities, yet the final journey – in which the devils take Faustus off to hell – is serious, momentous, and final. Faustus' defeat is meant to serve God; but the real question for us must be this: how does it serve the playwright?

Faustus is a double loser: his servitude to the devils allows them to serve the purposes of God. To analyze such an outcome, Marlowe enlists all the phases of theater: dialogue, conflict, soliloquy, but, above all, spectacle. The demonic bride with fireworks (recalling Belial in *The Castle of Perseverance*), the stock grotesqueries of the seven deadly sins, the cheap tricks at the papal court and with the horse-courser all invite the parody of Wagner and the Clown, of Rafe and Robin. All seem to pale before that first, long-awaited appearance of Mephastophilis, which really begins the drama of the soul, and the last terrifying appearance of Lucifer and his fellow devils which ends it. Here sights and actions leave their imprint on the soul in the ways words cannot manage, nor perhaps ever sufficiently convey. In thus demonstrating the shortcoming of language, Marlowe once again questions the value of education; but more, he also questions the value of drama and of theater. The Privy Council never doubted the pressure of either, even in a play where the actors, like their magic tricks, are finally "but shadows, not substantial." Perhaps that is because the invasion of the consciousness by the conscience enables Marlowe to interrogate the very roots of his culture as it attempted to shape its citizenry. The play insists we do likewise.

FURTHER READING

Bartels, Emily C., *Spectacles of Strangeness: Imperialism, Alienation, and Marlowe*, esp. ch. 5. Philadelphia: University of Pennsylvania Press, 1993.

——, ed., *Critical Essays on Christopher Marlowe*, esp. essays by Riggs and Sinfield. New York: G. K. Hall and Co., 1997.

Blackburn, William, "Heavenly Words: Marlowe's Faustus as a Renaissance Magician," *English Studies in Canada* 4:1 (Spring 1978): 1–14.

Dollimore, Jonathan, *Radical Tragedy: Religion, Ideology, and Power in the Drama of Shakespeare and His Contemporaries*, 2nd edn. pp. 109–19. Chicago: University of Chicago Press, 1989.

Garber, Marjorie, "'Here's Nothing Writ' Scribe, Script, and Circumscription in Marlowe's Plays," *Theatre Journal* 36:3 (October 1984): 308–20.

Grantley, Darryll and, Peter Roberts, eds., *Christopher Marlowe and English Renaissance Culture*, esp. essays by Davidson, Gareth Roberts and Peter Roberts. Aldershot: Scolar Press, 1996.

Honderich, Pauline, "John Calvin and Doctor Faustus," *Modern Language Review* 68:1 (January 1973): 1–13.

McAlindon, T., "Classical Mythology and Christian Tradition in Marlowe's *Doctor Faustus*," *PMLA* 81:2 (June 1966): 214–23.

Manley, Frank, "The Nature of Faustus," *Modern Philology* 66:3 (February 1969): 218–31.

Westlund, Joseph, "The Orthodox Christian Framework of Marlowe's *Faustus*," *Studies in English Literature 1500–1900* 3:2 (Spring 1963): 191–205.

THE TRAGICAL HISTORY OF D. FAUSTUS

[*DRAMATIS PERSONAE*

The Chorus.
Doctor John Faustus.
Wagner.
Good Angel.
Evil Angel.
Valdes.
Cornelius.
Three Scholars.
Mephastophilis.
Robin, *the Clown.*
Devils.
Rafe.
Lucifer.
Beelzebub.

Pride.
Covetousness.
Wrath.
Envy.
Gluttony.
Sloth.
Lechery. } *The Seven Deadly Sins*
The Pope.
The Cardinal of Lorraine.
Friars.
A Vintner.
The Emperor of Germany, Charles V.
A Knight.
Attendants.
Alexander the Great.
His Paramour. } *Spirits*
A Horse-courser.
The Duke of Vanholt.
The Duchess of Vanholt.
Helen of Troy, *a spirit.*
An Old Man.]

[Chorus 1]

Enter Chorus.

Chorus. Not marching now in fields of Trasimene
Where Mars did mate the Carthaginians,
Nor sporting in the dalliance of love
In courts of kings where state is overturned,
Nor in the pomp of proud audacious deeds,
Intends our Muse to daunt his Heavenly verse.
Only this, gentlemen: we must perform
The form of Faustus' fortunes, good or bad.
To patient judgments we appeal our plaud,
And speak for Faustus in his infancy.
Now is he born, his parents base of stock,
In Germany, within a town called Rhodes.
Of riper years to Wittenberg he went,
Whereas his kinsmen chiefly brought him up.
So soon he profits in divinity,
The fruitful plot of scholarism graced,
That shortly he was graced with Doctor's name,

TEXTUAL VARIANTS

The textual situation of Marlowe's *Dr. Faustus* is one of the most vexed in all of Renaissance English drama, but the recent work of Roma Gill and especially Eric Rasmussen has overturned the preference for the "B-Text" of 1616 with compelling arguments for the "A-Text" of 1604. Still this is not without its difficulties. Only one extant copy of the A-Text survives, that at the Bodleian Library, which serves as the copy-text for that given here; but here there are two enduring passages that are troublesome. The location of the first scene between Rafe and Robin (here scene vi) may have divided a longer earlier scene v at line 180, although that is not what is recorded in our exemplar as the only early textual witness to what Rasmussen believes are the actual foul papers (manuscript) of Marlowe and a collaborator. In scene viii, some awkward lines beginning at line 29 may be a compositor's error, leaving in the extant copytext some lines of an earlier draft. In keeping with the practice of this anthology to edit from the earliest surviving quartos as testimony of early modern performances – as well as likeliest to be nearest to the author's intentions and work – the A-Text, with minor exceptions noted below, has been followed despite some questionable passages and placements of lines.

Chorus 1.12 Rhodes] Q Rhode **i.36** Too servile] Q The devil **52** signs] Q scenes **79** this!] Q this? **101 s.d.**] Q has s.d. at line 100 **130** the] Q their **131** From] Q For **iii.9** anagrammatized] Q Agramithist **35** Now] Q No **60** Beelzebub] Q Belsibub **iv.1 s.d.**] some editions identify Robin with Clown but there is no textual basis for this and the characterizations are somewhat different **v.31** he]: Q I **147–57**] Q sets this as prose **161** no more] Q more **175–81**] Q sets this as prose **234–8**] Q sets this as prose **245–9**] Q sets this as prose **292–300**] Q sets this as prose **374–8**] Q sets this as prose **vi**] In the Q of A-Text, the two scenes with Rafe and Robin are sequential as a single scene following Chorus 3, but that Chorus is meant to introduce the scene at the papal court. Thus the ordering of B-Text, but with the playtext of A, is given here **Chorus 2.6** yoked] Q yoky **vii.33–4**] Q omits these lines (taken here from B-Text) to provide a reference for line 35 (from A-Text) **42** pyramides] Q spelling has been retained for *pyramids* for the meter **63** spoke] Q spake **64–89**] Q sets as this as prose **ix.1–37**] Q sets this as prose **44–6**] Q sets this as prose **48–51**] Q sets this as prose **54–9**] Q sets this as prose **69–78**] Q sets this as prose **89–101**] Q sets this as prose **108 s.d.** *Exeunt*] Q Exit **x.1–38**] Q sets this entirely as prose **32 s.d.**] Q s.d. at line 29 **85–8**] Q sets this as prose **xi.2–38** Q sets this as prose **xii.11–19**] Q sets this as prose **xiii**] Q sets Faustus' lines as prose **54** to save Faustus] Q to Faustus

Playsource

Dr. Faustus takes its material on the life of Georg or Johannes Faustus, a scholar and reputed magician at Wittenberg earlier in the sixteenth century, from a partly mythical biography published in Germany in 1587 and translated into English by P. F. Gent. as *The Historie of the damnable life, and deserved death of Doctor John Faustus.* Because the unidentified P. F. had traveled in Europe and added details that Marlowe also used, it is clear that Marlowe turned to the English rather than the German text.

Dramatis Personae Q usually uses spelling of *Mephastophilis*, which has been regularized here to indicate what was likely the early modern pronunciation

Chorus 1.1–5 apparently references to plays in the company's repertory; line 1 probably alludes to a play about the victory of the Carthaginians under Hannibal at Lake Thrasymenus in 217 BC; line 3 is general but in time could include Marlowe's own *Edward II*

2 Mars Roman god of war; **mate** became ally with

3 dalliance frivolity; licentiousness (often ascribed to the Romans)

4 state government

6 Muse (1) inspiration; (2) the poet; (3) the acting company

9 appeal . . . plaud seek approval (applause)

13 Wittenberg historically true, the university was also associated in the popular mind with Martin Luther and with skepticism; university references usually refer to those at Marlowe's own Cambridge

14 kinsmen fellow scholars

17 graced the term of permission to the degree at Cambridge; Marlowe's name is in the University Grace Book for 1584 and 1587

Excelling all whose sweet delight disputes
In Heavenly matters of theology;
Till, swoll'n with cunning of a self-conceit,
His waxen wings did mount above his reach,
And melting Heavens conspired his overthrow.
For, falling to a devilish exercise,
And glutted more with learning's golden gifts,
He surfeits upon cursèd necromancy;
Nothing so sweet as magic is to him,
Which he prefers before his chiefest bliss.
And this the man that in his study sits.

Exit.

[Sc. i]

Enter Faustus *in his study.*

Faustus. Settle thy studies, Faustus, and begin
To sound the depth of that thou will profess.
Having commenced, be a Divine in show,
Yet level at the end of every art,
And live and die in Aristotle's works.
Sweet *Analytics*, 'tis thou hast ravished me!
[*He reads.*] *Bene disserere est finis logices*
Is to dispute well logic's chiefest end?
Affords this art no greater miracle?
Then read no more; thou hast attained the end.
A greater subject fitteth Faustus' wit.
Bid *On kai me on* farewell. Galen, come!
Seeing *ubi desinit philosophus, ibi incipit medicus*,
Be a physician, Faustus. Heap up gold,
And be eternized for some wondrous cure.
[*He reads.*] *Summum bonum medicinae sanitas*:
The end of physic is our body's health.
Why Faustus, hast thou not attained that end?
Is not thy common talk sound aphorisms?
Are not thy bills hung up as monuments,
Whereby whole cities have escaped the plague
And thousand desp'rate maladies been eased?
Yet art thou still but Faustus, and a man.
Wouldst thou make man to live eternally?
Or, being dead, raise them to life again?
Then this profession were to be esteemed.
Physic, farewell! Where is Justinian?
[*He reads.*] *Si una eademque res legatur duobus,*
Alter rem, alter valorem rei, etc.
A pretty case of paltry legacies!
[*He reads.*] *Exhaereditare filium non potest pater nisi* –
Such is the subject of the Institute
And universal body of the Church.
His study fits a mercenary drudge
Who aims at nothing but external trash –
Too servile and illiberal for me.
When all is done, divinity is best.
Jerome's Bible, Faustus, view it well.
[*He reads.*] *Stipendium peccati mors est.* Ha!
Stipendium, etc.
The reward of sin is death. That's hard!
[*He reads.*] *Si peccasse negamus, fallimur*
Et nulla est in nobis veritas.
If we say that we have no sin,

18–19 whose . . . theology who especially enjoy theological (scholastic) debates

20 cunning (1) ingenious; (2) shrewd; (3) false; **self-conceit** i.e., pride

21–2 waxen . . . overthrow allusion to Icarus, who flew near the sun with waxen wings which melted so that he drowned; proverbial for great pride and ambition

23 falling . . . exercise Faustus is compared to (1) Icarus; (2) Adam; (3) Lucifer

25 necromancy divination by means of communicating with the dead

27 bliss eternal life

28 this the man (1) Faustus walks on stage; (2) Faustus is revealed seated behind a curtain, perhaps on an inner stage

i.1 Settle determine

2 sound measure; **profess** (1) specialize in; (2) study; (3) teach

3 commenced graduated (a Cambridge term); **Divine** theologian; **show** appearance

4 level aim

6 Analytics Aristotle's works on the nature of argumentative proof

7 *Bene . . . logices* (translation, line 8) from Peter Ramus' *Dialecticae* (not Aristotle); Ramus' division of logic from rhetoric was radical at the time, but popular at Cambridge

12 *On kai me on* on being and not being; **Galen** Greek medical authority of the second century and a source of medical theory in early England that was being challenged by Paracelsus and others

13 *ubi . . . medicus* "since the doctor starts where the philosopher leaves off" (Aristotle, *De sensu* 436a)

14 gold profit, wealth

15 eternized immortalized

16–17 *Summun* . . . health (translation, line 17) from Aristotle, *Nicomachean Ethics* 1094a

19 aphorisms the name of a popular medical text by Hippocrates with whom Faustus associates himself

20 bills prescriptions

21 plague any infectious epidemic

24–5 Wouldst . . . again? Faustus compares himself to Christ raising Lazarus (John 2: 1–44)

27 Justinian as author of the *Institutionae*, part of his *Corpus Juri*, a popular textbook in law

28–9 *Si . . . rei* "if one and the same thing is bequeathed to two persons, one should have the thing itself, the other the value of the thing" (*Institutes* 2.20)

31 *Exhaereditare . . . nisi* "A father cannot disinherit his son unless . . ." (*Institutes* 2.13)

36 illiberal mercenary

38 Jerome's Bible the Vulgate, mainly but not entirely by St. Jerome

39 *Stipendium . . . est* "For the wages of sin is death" (Rom. 6:23, but not in Jerome's Latin); the rest of the verse reads, "but the free gift of God is eternal life in Christ Jesus our Lord"

41–2 *Si . . . veritas* "If we confess our sins, he is faithful and just to forgive our sins" (John 1:8); verse continues, "and to cleanse us from all unrighteousness"

We deceive ourselves, and there's no truth in us.
Why then belike we must sin,
And so consequently die.
Aye, we must die an everlasting death.
What doctrine call you this, *Che serà, serà*,
What will be, shall be? Divinity, adieu!
[*He picks up a book of magic.*]
These metaphysics of magicians
And necromantic books are Heavenly,
Lines, circles, signs, letters, and characters –
Aye, these are those that Faustus most desires.
Oh, what a world of profit and delight,
Of power, of honor, of omnipotence,
Is promised to the studious artisan!
All things that move between the quiet poles
Shall be at my command. Emperors and kings
Are but obeyed in their several provinces,
Nor can they raise the wind or rend the clouds;
But his dominion that exceeds in this
Stretcheth as far as doth the mind of man.
A sound magician is a mighty god.
Here, Faustus, try thy brains to gain a deity.
Wagner!

Enter Wagner.

Commend me to my dearest friends,
The German Valdes and Cornelius.
Request them earnestly to visit me.
Wagner. I will, sir.
Exit.
Faustus. Their conference will be a greater help to me
Than all my labors, plod I ne'er so fast.

Enter the Good Angel *and the* Evil Angel.

Good Angel. Oh, Faustus, lay that damnèd book aside
And gaze not on it, lest it tempt thy soul
And heap God's heavy wrath upon thy head!
Read, read the Scriptures. That is blasphemy.
Evil Angel. Go forward, Faustus, in that famous art
Wherein all nature's treasury is contained.
Be thou on earth as Jove is in the sky,
Lord and commander of these elements.
Exeunt [Angels].
Faustus. How am I glutted with conceit of this!
Shall I make spirits fetch me what I please,
Resolve me of all ambiguities,
Perform what desperate enterprise I will?
I'll have them fly to India for gold,
Ransack the ocean for orient pearl,
And search all corners of the new-found world
For pleasant fruits and princely delicates.
I'll have them read me strange philosophy
And tell the secrets of all foreign kings.
I'll have them wall all Germany with brass
And make swift Rhine circle fair Wittenberg.
I'll have them fill the public schools with silk,
Wherewith the students shall be bravely clad.
I'll levy soldiers with the coin they bring
And chase the Prince of Parma from our land,
And reign sole king of all our provinces;
Yea, stranger engines for the brunt of war
Than was the fiery keel at Antwerp's bridge
I'll make my servile spirits to invent.
Come, German Valdes and Cornelius,
And make me blessed with your sage conference!

Enter Valdes *and* Cornelius.

Valdes, sweet Valdes, and Cornelius,
Know that your words have won me at the last
To practice magic and concealèd arts.
Yet not your words only, but mine own fantasy,
That will receive no object, for my head
But ruminates on necromantic skill.

45 **belike** in all likelihood
48 ***Che serà, serà*** "Whatever will be, will be"
50 **metaphysics** speculative inquiry into the first principles of things; the metaphysics of magicians, however, would be occult lore
56 **artisan** craftsman, practitioner
57 **quiet poles** the poles of the universe are quiet because they do not move
59 **several** own, respective
61 **dominion** authority; **exceeds** excels; **this** i.e., necromancy, magic art
71 **damnèd book** (1) book of magic; (2) ungodly book
77 **Jove** (evil angel makes no Christian references)
78 **these elements** earth, air, fire, and water, which in some combination made all matter and served as basis for Galenic medicine
79 **glutted with conceit** drunk at the thought
80 **spirits** apparently evil spirits
82 **desperate** daring
84 **orient** (1) precious; (2) so named because they came from the Indian Ocean
85 **new-found** newly discovered (generally, but not exclusively, the Americas)
86 **delicates** delicacies
87 **read** teach
90 **Rhine** in fact, Wittenberg is on the Elbe River
91 **public schools** probably university lecture halls; **silk** (as in formal academic wear)
92 **bravely** smartly; handsomely
94–7 **Prince . . . bridge** the Prince of Parma, Spanish governor-general of the United Provinces of the Netherlands, 1579–92, built a bridge to protect Antwerp that was destroyed by a fireship in the Siege of Antwerp in 1585
96 **engines** machines
103 **concealèd** occult
104 **fantasy** imagination (often thought delusory or demonic as well as creative)
105 **That . . . object** which prevents my thinking of anything else

Philosophy is odious and obscure;
Both law and physic are for petty wits;
Divinity is basest of the three,
Unpleasant, harsh, contemptible, and vile.
'Tis magic, magic that hath ravished me.
Then, gentle friends, aid me in this attempt,
And I, that have with concise syllogisms
Graveled the pastors of the German Church
And made the flow'ring pride of Wittenberg
Swarm to my problems as the infernal spirits
On sweet Musaeus when he came to hell,
Will be as cunning as Agrippa was,
Whose shadows made all Europe honor him.
Valdes. Faustus, these books, thy wit, and our experience
Shall make all nations to canonize us.
As Indian Moors obey their Spanish lords,
So shall the subjects of every element
Be always serviceable to us three.
Like lions shall they guard us when we please,
Like Almaine rutters with their horsemen's staves,
Or Lapland giants, trotting by our sides;
Sometimes like women, or unwedded maids,
Shadowing more beauty in their airy brows
Than in the white breasts of the Queen of Love.
From Venice shall they drag huge argosies,
And from America the golden fleece
That yearly stuffs old Philip's treasury,
If learnèd Faustus will be resolute.
Faustus. Valdes, as resolute am I in this
As thou to live. Therefore object it not.
Cornelius. The miracles that magic will perform
Will make thee vow to study nothing else.
He that is grounded in astrology,
Enriched with tongues, well seen minerals,
Hath all the principles magic doth require.
Then doubt not, Faustus, but to be renowned,
And more frequented for this mystery
Than heretofore the Delphian oracle.
The spirits tell me they can dry the sea
And fetch the treasure of all foreign wrecks –
Aye, all the wealth that our forefathers hid
Within the massy entrails of the earth.
Then tell me, Faustus, what shall we three want?
Faustus. Nothing, Cornelius. Oh, this cheers my soul!
Come, show me some demonstrations magical,
That I may conjure in some lusty grove
And have these joys in full possession.
Valdes. Then haste thee to some solitary grove,
And bear wise Bacon's and Albanus' works,
The Hebrew Psalter, and New Testament;
And whatsoever else is requisite
We will inform thee ere our conference cease.
Cornelius. Valdes, first let him know the words of art,
And then, all other ceremonies learned,
Faustus may try his cunning by himself.
Valdes. First I'll instruct thee in the rudiments,
And then will thou be perfecter than I.
Faustus. Then come and dine with me, and after meat
We'll canvass every quiddity thereof,
For ere I sleep I'll try what I can do.
This night I'll conjure, though I die therefore.
Exeunt.

[Sc. ii]

Enter two Scholars.

First Scholar. I wonder what's become of Faustus, that was wont to make our schools ring with "*sic probo.*"
Second Scholar. That shall we know, for see, here comes his boy.

113 syllogisms deductive reasoning (from his own premises)
114 Graveled (1) confounded; (2) embarrassed
115 flow'ring pride of Wittenburg youth eager to know
116 problems types of academic disputations
117 Musaeus Homeric bard surrounded by spirits of priests and poets in Hades (Virgil, *Aeneid* vi.667–8)
118 Agrippa Henry Cornelius Agrippa van Nettesheim (1486–1535), famous necromancer known for calling up spirits from the dead (*shadows*)
122 Indian Moors American Indians
126 Almaine . . . staves German cavalry with lances
130 Queen of Love Venus
131 argosies merchant ships
132 golden fleece the precious treasure sought by Jason and the Argonauts
133 stuffs . . . treasury (reference is to the wealth of the New World taken home by the Spanish to Philip II in his plate-fleet)
136 object . . . not don't raise objections
139 grounded well instructed
140 tongues Greek and Hebrew (not Latin, which was commonplace); **well . . . minerals** knowledgeable in the properties studied in alchemy
143 frequented sought after; **mystery** (1) knowledge; (2) craft
144 Delphian oracle Apollo's oracle at Delphi
148 massy entrails solid inner core
152 lusty pleasant
155 Bacon's Roger Bacon (?1214–94), Oxford philosopher popularly known for practicing black magic; **Albanus'** Pietro d'Abano (?1250–1316), Italian humanist, physician, and conjuror
156 Psalter (for Ps. 22, 51 as invocations); **New Testament** (John 1:1 as incantatory)
159 words of art technical language for incantations
165 canvass explore; **quiddity** a scholastic term for the essence of a thing
ii.3 *"sic probo"* "thus I prove it" (term from scholastic disputations)

Enter Wagner, [*carrying wine*].

First Scholar. How now, sirrah, where's thy master?

Wagner. God in Heaven knows.

Second Scholar. Why, dost not thou know?

Wagner. Yes, I know, but that follows not.

First Scholar. Go to, sirrah! Leave your jesting, and tell us where he is.

Wagner. That follows not necessary by force of argument that you, being licentiate, should stand upon't. Therefore, acknowledge your error, and be attentive.

Second Scholar. Why, didst thou not say thou knew'st?

Wagner. Have you any witness on't?

First Scholar. Yes, sirrah, I heard you.

Wagner. Ask my fellow if I be a thief.

Second Scholar. Well, you will not tell us.

Wagner. Yes, sir, I will tell you. Yet if you were not dunces, you would never ask me such a question. For is not he *corpus naturale*? And is not that *mobile*? Then, wherefore should you ask me such a question? But that I am by nature phlegmatic, slow to wrath, and prone to lechery – to love, I would say – it were not for you to come within forty foot of the place of execution, although I do not doubt to see you both hanged the next sessions. Thus, having triumphed over you, I will set my countenance like a precisian and begin to speak thus: Truly, my dear brethren, my master is within at dinner with Valdes and Cornelius, as this wine, if it could speak, it would inform your worships. And so the Lord bless you, preserve you, and keep you, my dear brethren, my dear brethren. *Exit.*

First Scholar. Nay, then, I fear he is fall'n into that damned art for which they two are infamous through the world.

Second Scholar. Were he a stranger, and not allied to me, yet should I grieve for him. But come, let us go and inform the Rector, and see if he, by his grave counsel, can reclaim him.

First Scholar. Oh, but I fear me nothing can reclaim him.

Second Scholar. Yet let us try what we can do.

Exeunt.

[Sc. iii]

Enter Faustus *to conjure*, [*holding a book*].

Faustus. Now that the gloomy shadow of the earth,
Longing to view Orion's drizzling look,
Leaps from th'Antarctic world unto the sky
And dims the welkin with her pitchy breath,
Faustus, begin thine incantations,
And try if devils will obey thy hest,
Seeing thou hast prayed and sacrificed to them.

[*He draws a circle.*]

Within this circle is Jehovah's name,
Forward and backward anagrammatized,
The breviated names of holy saints,
Figures of every adjunct to the Heavens,
And characters of signs and erring stars,
By which the spirits are enforced to rise.
Then fear not, Faustus, but be resolute,
And try the uttermost magic can perform.
Sint mihi dei Acherontis propitii! Valeat numen triplex Jehovae! Ignei, aerii, aquatici, terreni, spiritus, salvete! Orientis princeps Lucifer, Beelzebub, inferni ardentis monarcha, et Demogorgon, propitiamus vos, ut appareat et surgat Mephastophilis! Quid tu mor-

---

13 licentiate i.e., graduate study

14 stand upon't understand

23 dunces fools (with play on Dunses, followers of Dun Scotus' logic thought to focus on quibbling)

24–5 *corpus . . . mobile* scholastic terms for the study of physics (as the study of moving bodies)

29–30 place of execution play on (1) the dining room where Faustus, Valdes, and Cornelius are eating and (2) the gallows

33 precisian Puritan (Wagner now parodies Puritan language)

45 Rector head of the university

iii.1 shadow . . . earth night (term is from La Primadaye's *The French Academy*)

2 Orion's . . . look the rainy constellation of Orion

3 Antarctic (Marlowe apparently believed night advances from the s)

4 welkin (1) sky; (2) firmament; **pitchy** (1) black; (2) stinking

6 hest behest; invitation

7 prayed and sacrificed preparatory exercises in conjuring

8–15 Within . . . perform (the conjuror first drew a circle around him, inscribing on the periphery signs [such as the zodiac] and the tetragrammaton [four Hebrew letters of the Divine Being, usually rendered in English as *Yahweh*] both as part of the invocation and as protection for as long as the circle remained unbroken)

11 adjunct heavenly body joined to the firmament

12 signs i.e., of the zodiac; **erring stars** planets

16–24 *Sint . . . Mephastophilis!* "May the gods of Acheron [river in Greek underworld, therefore pagan] look favorably upon me. Away with the spirit of the threefold Jehovah [Father, Son, and Spirit]. Welcome spirits of fire, air, water, and earth. We ask your favor, oh, Prince of the East [Lucifer; cf. Isa. 14:2], Beelzebub, the monarch of burning hell, and Demagorgon [in classical mythology one of the most terrifying gods] that Mephastophilis [Marlowe was the first to use this name] may appear and arise. Why do you delay? [Impatience is a common characteristic of invocations] By Jehovah, Gehenna [place of sacrifice], and the holy water which I now sprinkle [as an unholy parody of the rite of baptism], and the sign of the cross which I now form [as a charm to overcome diabolic disobedience and as protection for the conjuror], and by our vows, may Mephastophilis himself now rise, compelled to obey us"

aris? Per Jehovam, Gehennam, et consecratam aquam quam nunc spargo, signumque crucis quod nunc facio, et per vota nostra, ipse nunc surgat nobis dicatus Mephastophilis!
[*Faustus sprinkles holy water and makes a sign of the cross.*]

Enter a Devil [Mephastophilis].

I charge thee to return and change thy shape.
Thou art too ugly to attend on me.
Go, and return an old Franciscan friar;
That holy shape becomes a devil best.
Exit Devil [Mephastophilis].
I see there's virtue in my Heavenly words.
Who would not be proficient in this art?
How pliant is this Mephastophilis,
Full of obedience and humility!
Such is the force of magic and my spells.
Now, Faustus, thou art Conjurer Laureate,
That canst command great Mephastophilis.
Quin redis, Mephastophilis, fratris imagine!

Enter Mephastophilis [*disguised as a friar*].

Mephastophilis. Now, Faustus, what wouldst thou have me do?
Faustus. I charge thee wait upon me whilst I live,
To do whatever Faustus shall command,
Be it to make the moon drop from her sphere
Or the ocean to overwhelm the world.
Mephastophilis. I am a servant to great Lucifer
And may not follow thee without his leave;
No more than he commands must we perform.
Faustus. Did not he charge thee to appear to me?
Mephastophilis. No, I came now hither of mine own accord.
Faustus. Did not my conjuring speeches raise thee? Speak.
Mephastophilis. That was the cause, but yet *per accidens.*
For when we hear one rack the name of God,
Abjure the Scriptures and his Saviour Christ,
We fly in hope to get his glorious soul,
Nor will we come unless he use such means
Whereby he is in danger to be damned.
Therefore, the shortest cut for conjuring
Is stoutly to abjure the Trinity
And pray devoutly to the prince of hell.
Faustus. So Faustus hath already done,
And holds this principle:
There is no chief but only Beelzebub,
To whom Faustus doth dedicate himself.
This word "damnation" terrifies not him,
For he confounds hell in Elysium.
His ghost be with the old philosophers!
But leaving these vain trifles of men's souls,
Tell me, what is that Lucifer thy lord?
Mephastophilis. Arch-regent and commander of all spirits.
Faustus. Was not that Lucifer an angel once?
Mephastophilis. Yes, Faustus, and most dearly loved of God.
Faustus. How comes it then that he is prince of devils?
Mephastophilis. Oh, by aspiring pride and insolence,
For which God threw him from the face of Heaven.
Faustus. And what are you that live with Lucifer?
Mephastophilis. Unhappy spirits that fell with Lucifer,
Conspired against our God with Lucifer,
And are forever damned with Lucifer.
Faustus. Where are you damned?
Mephastophilis. In hell.
Faustus. How comes it then that thou art out of hell?
Mephastophilis. Why, this is hell, nor am I out of it.
Think'st thou that I, who saw the face of God
And tasted the eternal joys of Heaven,
Am not tormented with ten thousand hells
In being deprived of everlasting bliss?
Oh, Faustus, leave these frivolous demands,
Which strike a terror to my fainting soul!
Faustus. What, is great Mephastophilis so passionate
For being deprivèd of the joys of Heaven?
Learn thou of Faustus manly fortitude,
And scorn those joys thou never shalt possess.
Go bear these tidings to great Lucifer:

26 **change thy shape** (tradition had it that a creature of fire first appeared, gradually taking the shape of a man)
30 **virtue** supernatural power (Faustus takes Mephastophilis' eagerness to get a soul and hence obey him as a sign of his own authority)
32 **pliant** compliant
35 **Laureate** a title denoting preeminence, but here self-awarded
37 ***Quin... imagine!*** "Why do you not return, Mephastophilis, in the likeness of a friar?"
49 ***per accidens*** (1) only in appearance; the conjuring was the real cause; (2) fortuitously
50 **rack** (1) violate (take the name of the Lord in vain); (2) torture (for which the rack was a common if notorious means)
52 **glorious** (1) beautiful; (2) vainglorious
56 **stoutly** (1) resolutely; (2) arrogantly
60 **Beelzebub** chief prince of devils and servant to Lucifer
63 **confounds... Elysium** makes no distinction between Christian Hell and the pagan Elysium
64 **old philosophers** those who share his belief in eternal punishment (thought to be a saying of Averroës)
66 **Lucifer** (see Isa. 14: 12–15)
84 **deprived** (the torment of deprivation is taken from St. John Chrysostom)

Seeing Faustus hath incurred eternal death
By desp'rate thoughts against Jove's deity,
Say he surrenders up to him his soul,
So he will spare him four-and-twenty years,
Letting him live in all voluptuousness,
Having thee ever to attend on me,
To give me whatsoever I shall ask,
To tell me whatsoever I demand,
To slay mine enemies and aid my friends,
And always be obedient to my will.
Go, and return to mighty Lucifer,
And meet me in my study at midnight,
And then resolve me of thy master's mind.

Mephastophilis. I will, Faustus.

Exit.

Faustus. Had I as many souls as there be stars,
I'd give them all for Mephastophilis.
By him I'll be great Emperor of the world,
And make a bridge through the moving air
To pass the ocean with a band of men;
I'll join the hills that bind the Afric shore
And make that land continent to Spain,
And both contributory to my crown.
The Emp'ror shall not live but by my leave,
Nor any potentate of Germany.
Now that I have obtained what I desire,
I'll live in speculation of this art
Till Mephastophilis return again.

Exit.

[Sc. iv]

Enter Wagner *and the* Clown.

Wagner. Sirrah boy, come hither.

Clown. How, "boy"? 'Swounds, "boy"! I hope you have seen many boys with such pickedevants as I have. "Boy," quotha?

Wagner. Tell me, sirrah, hast thou any comings in?

Clown. Aye, and goings out too, you may see else.

Wagner. Alas, poor slave, see how poverty jesteth in his nakedness! The villain is bare and out of service, and so hungry that I know he would give his soul to the devil for a shoulder of mutton, though it were blood raw.

Clown. How? My soul to the devil for a shoulder of mutton, though 'twere blood raw? Not so, good friend. By'r Lady, I had need have it well roasted, and good sauce to it, if I pay so dear.

Wagner. Well, wilt thou serve me, and I'll make thee go like *Qui mihi discipulus*?

Clown. How, in verse?

Wagner. No, Sirrah, in beaten silk and stavesacre.

Clown. How, how, knave's acre? [*Aside.*] Aye, I thought that was all the land his father left him. [*To Wagner.*] Do ye hear? I would be sorry to rob you of your living.

Wagner. Sirrah, I say in stavesacre.

Clown. Oho, oho, "stavesacre"! Why then, belike, if I were your man, I should be full of vermin.

Wagner. So thou shalt, whether thou beest with me or no. But sirrah, leave your jesting, and bind yourself presently unto me for seven years, or I'll turn all the lice about thee into familiars, and they shall tear thee in pieces.

Clown. Do you hear, sir? You may save that labor. They are too familiar with me already. 'Swounds, they are as bold with my flesh as if they had paid for my meat and drink.

Wagner. Well, do you hear, sirrah? Hold, take these guilders.

[*Offering money.*]

Clown. Gridirons? What be they?

Wagner. Why, French crowns.

Clown. Mass, but for the name of French crowns a man were as good have as many English counters. And what should I do with these?

Wagner. Why now, sirrah, thou art at an hour's warning whensoever or wheresoever the devil shall fetch thee.

Clown. No, no, here, take your gridirons again.

[*He attempts to return the money.*]

---

95 **So** on condition that
104 **resolve me** explain; make clear
109–10 **make . . . men** like Xerxes, who built a bridge (with boats) across the Hellespont for his men to march over
111–12 **join . . . Spain** (uniting hills both sides of the Straits of Gibraltar would make Africa and Europe a single continent)
117 **speculation** (1) contemplation; (2) consideration
iv.3 **pickedevants** small, pointed beards (resembling a goat's)
5 **comings in** income
6 **goings out** (1) expenses; (2) torn clothing (customary in a clown's costume)
9 **service** employment
14 **By'r Lady** "By our Lady [Mary]" (a common Christian oath)
17 ***Qui . . . discipulus*** "you who are my pupil" (opening of a didactic Latin poem in Lily's standard grammarschool text; his low learning parodies Faustus' Latin and later garbled Latin in subsequent clown scenes)
19 **beaten** embroidered; **stavesacre** delphinium seeds used to kill vermin such as fleas and lice
25 **belike** probably
29 **bind** apprentice
31 **familiars** attendant spirits (with witches, they often appeared as dogs)
39 **French crowns** money with play on colloquialism for heads made bald by syphilis
40 **Mass** "By the holy Mass" (another common Christian oath)
42 **counters** tokens used to count money but themselves worthless
46 **gridirons** instruments of torture (here confused with Dutch guilders)

Wagner. Truly, I'll none of them.

Clown. Truly, but you shall.

Wagner. [*To the audience.*] Bear witness I gave them him.

Clown. Bear witness I give them you again.

Wagner. Well, I will cause two devils presently to fetch thee away. – Balioll and Belcher!

Clown. Let your Balio and your Belcher come here and I'll knock them. They were never so knocked since they were devils. Say I should kill one of them, what would folks say? "Do ye see yonder tall fellow in the round slop? He has killed the devil." So I should be called "Kill devil" all the parish over.

Enter two Devils, *and the Clown runs up and down crying.*

Wagner. Balioll and Belcher! Spirits, away!

Exeunt [Devils].

Clown. What, are they gone? A vengeance on them! They have vile long nails. There was a he-devil and a she-devil. I'll tell you how you shall know them: all he-devils has horns, and all she-devils has clefts and cloven feet.

Wagner. Well, sirrah, follow me.

Clown. But do you hear? If I should serve you, would you teach me to raise up Banios and Belcheos?

Wagner. I will teach thee to turn thyself to anything, to a dog, or a cat, or a mouse, or a rat, or anything.

Clown. How? A Christian fellow to a dog or a cat, a mouse or a rat? No, no, sir. If you turn me into anything, let it be in the likeness of a little, pretty, frisking flea, that I may be here and there and everywhere. Oh, I'll tickle the pretty wenches' plackets! I'll be among them, i'faith!

Wagner. Well, sirrah, come.

Clown. But do you hear, Wagner?

Wagner. How? Balioll and Belcher!

Clown. Oh Lord, I pray sir, let Banio and Belcher go sleep.

Wagner. Villain, call me Master Wagner, and let thy left eye be diametarily fixed upon my right heel, with *quasi vestigiis nostris insistere.*

Exit.

Clown. God forgive me, he speaks Dutch fustian. Well, I'll follow him, I'll serve him, that's flat.

Exit.

[Sc. v]

Enter Faustus *in his study.*

Faustus. Now, Faustus, must thou needs be damned,
And canst thou not be saved?
What boots it then to think of God or Heaven?
Away with such vain fancies and despair!
Despair in God, and trust in Beelzebub.
Now go not backward. No, Faustus, be resolute.
Why waverest thou? Oh, something soundeth in mine ears:
"Abjure this magic, turn to God again!"
Aye, and Faustus will turn to God again.
To God? He loves thee not.
The god thou servest is thine own appetite,
Wherein is fixed the love of Beelzebub.
To him I'll build an altar and a church,
And offer lukewarm blood of new-born babes.

Enter Good Angel *and* Evil [Angel].

Good Angel. Sweet Faustus, leave that execrable art.

Faustus. Contrition, prayer, repentance: what of them?

Good Angel. Oh, they are means to bring thee unto Heaven.

Evil Angel. Rather illusions, fruits of lunacy,
That makes men foolish that do trust them most.

Good Angel.
Sweet Faustus, think of Heaven and Heavenly things.

Evil Angel. No, Faustus, think of honor and wealth.

Exeunt [Angels].

---

52 **Balioll and Belcher** simple-minded corruptions of the devils Belial and Beelzebub

54 **knock** strike

57 **tall** fine; **round slop** loose-fitting trousers (common clown's costume)

58–9 **"Kill devil"** (1) reckless youth; (2) colloquialism for rum

64 **horns** (1) devil's horns; (2) cuckold's horns

65 **clefts** (1) cloven hoofs; (2) vulvas

68–9 **Banios and Belcheos** mistaken for earlier Balioll and Belcher

76 **frisking flea** i.e., a creature who has access to all of the woman's body (from a well-known poem by Ovid)

78 **plackets** (1) petticoats; (2) openings at top of petticoats; (3) colloquial for vagina

84 **diametarily** diametrically

85 ***quasi . . . insistere*** "as it were tread in our footsteps" (rightly *vestigiis nostris*)

86 **Dutch** gibberish; "double Dutch"; **fustian** bombast, rant

87 **flat** certain

v.3 **boots** avails

4 **fancies** fantasies

6 **backward** return to a previous life

15 **execrable** detestable

16 **Contrition** sorrow for wrongdoing

18 **lunacy** delusion

Faustus. Of wealth?
Why, the seigniory of Emden shall be mine.
When Mephastophilis shall stand by me,
What god can hurt thee, Faustus? Thou art safe;
Cast no more doubts. Come, Mephastophilis,
And bring glad tidings from great Lucifer.
Is't not midnight? Come, Mephastophilis!
Veni, veni, Mephastophiles!

Enter Mephastophilis.

Now tell, what says Lucifer thy lord?
Mephastophilis. That I shall wait on Faustus while he lives,
So he will buy my service with his soul.
Faustus. Already Faustus hath hazarded that for thee.
Mephastophilis. But, Faustus, thou must bequeath it solemnly
And write a deed of gift with thine own blood,
For that security craves great Lucifer.
If thou deny it, I will back to hell.
Faustus. Stay, Mephastophilis, and tell me,
What good will my soul do thy lord?
Mephastophilis. Enlarge his kingdom.
Faustus. Is that the reason he tempts us thus?
Mephastophilis. *Solamen miseris socios habuisse doloris.*
Faustus. Have you any pain, that tortures others?
Mephastophilis. As great as have the human souls of men.
But tell me, Faustus, shall I have thy soul?
And I will be thy slave, and wait on thee,
And give thee more than thou hast wit to ask.
Faustus. Aye, Mephastophilis, I give it thee.
Mephastophilis. Then stab thine arm courageously,
And bind thy soul that at some certain day
Great Lucifer may claim it as his own,
And then be thou as great as Lucifer.
Faustus. [*Cutting his arm.*]
Lo, Mephastophilis, for love of thee
I cut mine arm, and with my proper blood
Assure my soul to be great Lucifer's,
Chief lord and regent of perpetual night.
View here the blood that trickles from mine arm,
And let it be propitious for my wish.
Mephastophilis. But Faustus, thou must write it
In manner of a deed of gift.
Faustus. Aye, so I will. [*He writes.*] But Mephastophilis,
My blood congeals, and I can write no more.
Mephastophilis. I'll fetch thee fire to dissolve it straight.
Exit.
Faustus. What might the staying of my blood portend?
Is it unwilling I should write this bill?
Why streams it not, that I may write afresh?
"Faustus gives to thee his soul" – ah, there it stayed!
Why shouldst thou not? Is not thy soul thine own?
Then write again: "Faustus gives to thee his soul."

Enter Mephastophilis *with a chafer of coals.*

Mephastophilis. Here's fire. Come Faustus, set it on.
Faustus. So; now the blood begins to clear again,
Now will I make an end immediately.
[*He writes.*]
Mephastophilis. [*Aside.*]
Oh, what will not I do to obtain his soul?
Faustus. *Consummatum est.* This bill is ended,
And Faustus hath bequeathed his soul to Lucifer.
But what is this inscription on mine arm?
"*Homo, fuge!*" Whither should I fly?
If unto God, he'll throw thee down to hell.
My senses are deceived; here's nothing writ.

---

23 **seigniory** governorship; **Emden** a bustling seaport on the North Sea at the mouth of the Ems River known for heavy English trading
26 **Cast** (1) give birth to; (2) ponder; (3) reckon; **doubts** (1) suspicions; (2) hesitations
29 ***Veni*** "come"
32 **So** provided
33 **hazarded** jeopardized
35 **deed of gift** an act of a will and testament (Faustus is asked to be a client of an infernal law that parodies what he has just abjured)
40 **Enlarge . . . kingdom** (popularly thought Lucifer's chief and only objective)
42 ***Solamen . . . doloris*** "fellow-suffering is consolation to the wicked"
52 **as . . . Lucifer** (a fallacious argument; Lucifer's nature is to be the greatest devil and the most wretched; here Faustus is blind to logic and theology)
54 **proper** own
58 **propitious** (1) acceptable; (2) desirable (cf. Christ's sacrifice on the cross)
62 **congeals** (God's saving grace attempts to intervene to alert Faustus)
63 **fire** the Devil's chief element (whereas humans employ all four)
64 **staying** withholding
68 **Is . . . own?** (Faustus' moral blindness alone causes such a question)
70 **s.d. *chafer*** pan for carrying fire; portable grate
70 **set it on** put blood in saucer to use as ink
71 **blood . . . again** (in fact, fire will not liquefy congealed blood)
72 **make an end** sign the writ
74 ***Consummatum est*** "It is finished" (deliberate repetition of Christ's final words; cf. John 19: 30)
77 ***Homo, fuge*** "fly, O man" (another sign of grace)
77–8 **Whither . . . hell** (cf. Ps. 139: 7–8)
79 **senses** (but also his mind)

I see it plain. Here in this place is writ
"*Homo, fuge!*" Yet shall not Faustus fly.

Mephastophilis. [*Aside.*]
I'll fetch him somewhat to delight his mind.
Exit.

Enter [Mephastophilis] *with* Devils, *giving crowns and rich apparel to Faustus, and dance and then depart.*

Faustus. Speak, Mephastophilis. What means this show?

Mephastophilis.
Nothing, Faustus, but to delight thy mind withal
And to show thee what magic can perform.

Faustus. But may I raise up spirits when I please?

Mephastophilis. Aye, Faustus, and do greater things than these.

Faustus. Then there's enough for a thousand souls.
Here, Mephastophilis, receive this scroll,
A deed of gift of body and of soul
But yet conditionally that thou perform
All articles prescribed between us both.

Mephastophilis. Faustus, I swear by hell and Lucifer
To effect all promises between us made.

Faustus. Then hear me read them.
"On these conditions following:
First, that Faustus may be a spirit in form and substance.
Secondly, that Mephastophilis shall be his servant, and at his command.
Thirdly, that Mephastophilis shall do for him, and bring him whatsoever.
Fourthly, that he shall be in his chamber or house invisible.
Lastly, that he shall appear to the said John Faustus at all times in what form or shape soever he please.
I, John Faustus of Wittenberg, Doctor, by these presents, do give both body and soul to Lucifer, Prince of the East, and his minister Mephastophilis; and furthermore grant unto them that four-and-twenty years being expired, the articles above written inviolate, full power to fetch or carry the said John Faustus, body and soul, flesh, blood, or goods, into their habitation wheresoever.
By me, John Faustus."

Mephastophilis. Speak, Faustus. Do you deliver this as your deed?

Faustus. [*Giving the deed.*] Aye. Take it, and the devil give thee good on't.

Mephastophilis. Now, Faustus, ask what thou wilt.

Faustus. First will I question with thee about hell.
Tell me, where is the place that men call hell?

Mephastophilis. Under the Heavens.

Faustus. Aye, but whereabout?

Mephastophilis. Within the bowels of these elements,
Where we are tortured and remain for ever.
Hell hath no limits, nor is circumscribed
In one self place, for where we are is hell,
And where hell is must we ever be.
And, to conclude, when all the world dissolves,
And every creature shall be purified,
All places shall be hell that is not Heaven.

Faustus. Come, I think hell's a fable.

Mephastophilis. Aye, think so still, till experience change thy mind.

Faustus. Why, think'st thou then that Faustus shall be damned?

Mephastophilis. Aye, of necessity, for here's the scroll
Wherein thou hast given thy soul to Lucifer.

Faustus. Aye, and body too. But what of that?
Think'st thou that Faustus is so fond
To imagine that after this life there is any pain?
Tush, these are trifles and mere old wives' tales.

Mephastophilis. But, Faustus, I am an instance to prove the contrary,
For I am damned and am now in hell.

Faustus. How? Now in hell? Nay, and this *be* hell,
I'll willingly be damned here. What?
Walking, disputing, etc.? But leaving off this,
Let me have a wife, the fairest maid in Germany,
For I am wanton and lascivious and cannot live without a wife.

Mephastophilis. How, a wife? I prithee, Faustus,
Talk not of a wife.

Faustus. Nay, sweet Mephastophilis, fetch me one,
For I will have one.

---

82 **somewhat** something
88 **enough . . . souls** enough reward to be worth a thousand souls
97 **spirit** (for Elizabethans, spirits were usually damned past redemption)
102 **whatsoever** anything (he pleases)
109 **presents** legal articles
110 **Prince . . . East** (i.e., male counterpart to Venus, as the demonic morning star)
113 **inviolate** fully executed
126–7 **bowels . . . elements** below God's world of air, water, fire, and earth
129 **self** particular
131–2 **when . . . purified** (cf. 2 Pet. 3: 10–11; Dan. 12: 9–10)
134 **fable** (Faustus must be teasing, since this assumption opposes his recent thoughts and actions)
142 **fond** foolish
144 **old . . . tales** proverbial for fables or foolish beliefs
149 **disputing** (Chorus 1 claims this activity is what most delights Faustus)
151 **lascivious** lecherous
153 **talk . . . wife** (this requires the Christian ceremony of marriage)

Mephastophilis. Well, thou will have one. Sit there till I come.
I'll fetch thee a wife, in the devil's name.

[*Exit.*]

Enter [Mephastophilis] *with a* Devil *dressed like a woman, with fireworks.*

Mephastophilis. Tell, Faustus, how dost thou like thy wife?
Faustus. A plague on her for a hot whore!
Mephastophilis. Tut, Faustus, marriage is but a ceremonial toy.
If thou lovest me, think no more of it.

[*Exit* Devil.]

I'll cull thee out the fairest courtesans
And bring them ev'ry morning to thy bed.
She whom thine eye shall like, thy heart shall have,
Be she as chaste as was Penelope,
As wise as Saba, or as beautiful
As was bright Lucifer before his fall.

[*Presenting a book.*]

Hold, take this book. Peruse it thoroughly.
The iterating of these lines brings gold;
The framing of this circle on the ground
Brings whirlwinds, tempests, thunder, and lightning.
Pronounce this thrice devoutly to thyself,
And men in armor shall appear to thee,
Ready to execute what thou desir'st.
Faustus. Thanks, Mephastophilis. Yet fain would
I have a book wherein I might behold all spells
And incantations, that I might raise up spirits when I please.
Mephastophilis. Here they are in this book.

There turn to them.

Faustus. Now would I have a book
Where I might see all characters and planets of the Heavens,
That I might know their motions and dispositions.
Mephastophilis. Here they are, too.

Turn to them.

Faustus. Nay, let me have one book more, and then I have done, wherein I might see all plants, herbs, and trees that grow upon the earth.
Mephastophilis. Here they be.
Faustus. O, thou art deceived.
Mephastophilis. Tut, I warrant thee.

Turn to them.

Faustus. When I behold the Heavens, then I repent
And curse thee, wicked Mephastophilis,
Because thou hast deprived me of those joys.
Mephastophilis. Why Faustus,
Think'st thou Heaven is such a glorious thing?
I tell thee, 'tis not half so fair as thou
Or any man that breathes on earth.
Faustus. How provest thou that?
Mephastophilis. It was made for man; therefore is man more excellent.
Faustus. If it were made for man, 'twas made for me.
I will renounce this magic and repent.

Enter Good Angel *and* Evil Angel.

Good Angel. Faustus, repent yet, God will pity thee.
Evil Angel. Thou art a spirit. God cannot pity thee.
Faustus. Who buzzeth in mine ears I am a spirit?
Be I a devil, yet God may pity me;
Aye, God will pity me if I repent.
Evil Angel. Aye, but Faustus never shall repent.

Exeunt [Angels].

Faustus. My heart's so hardened I cannot repent.
Scarce can I name salvation, faith, or heaven
But fearful echoes thunder in mine ears:
"Faustus, thou art damned!" Then swords and knives,
Poison, guns, halters, and envenomed steel
Are laid before me to dispatch myself;
And long ere this I should have slain myself
Had not sweet pleasure conquered deep despair.

---

158 s.d. *fireworks* squibs, which ended in a slight explosion
160 toy trifle
161 If . . . me (Mephastophilis suggests an alternative marriage)
162 cull choose, select
165 chaste monogamous; **Penelope** Odysseus' wife renowned for her fidelity during her husband's twenty-year absence
166 Saba the Queen of Sheba who tested Solomon's wisdom (1 Kgs. 10)
167 bright Lucifer (for the infernal Mephastophilis, the brightest and therefore most desirable of all)
169 iterating repeating
175 fain gladly
180 characters signs, symbols
181 dispositions placements in the heavens
184 wherein . . . see (Faustus' earlier references to his studies should have taught him this)
190–2 When . . . joys (Faustus' sharply new line of reasoning has caused editors to start a new scene here, but it may simply represent his confused state of mind)
204 buzzeth whispers (i.e., Mephastophilis does not see or hear the angels)
205 Be I (1) if I were; (2) if I am
208 hardened (1) adamant; (2) blinded (in theological terminology)
212 halters (1) nooses; (2) hangman's ropes; **envenomed steel** poisoned sword
213–5 dispatch . . . despair suicide and despair were thought the greatest sins because they stem from the denial of God's power to create and His mercy

Have not I made blind Homer sing to me
Of Alexander's love and Oenone's death?
And hath not he that built the walls of Thebes
With ravishing sound of his melodious harp
Made music with my Mephastophilis?
Why should I die, then, or basely despair?
I am resolved Faustus shall ne'er repent.
Come, Mephastophilis, let us dispute again
And argue of divine astrology.
Tell me, are there many heavens above the moon?
Are all celestial bodies but one globe,
As is the substance of this centric earth?

Mephastophilis. As are the elements, such are the spheres,
Mutually folded in each others' orb;
And, Faustus, all jointly move upon one axle-tree,
Whose terminine is termed the world's wide pole.
Nor are the names of Saturn, Mars, or Jupiter
Feigned, but are erring stars.

Faustus. But tell me, have they all one motion,
Both *situ et tempore*?

Mephastophilis. All jointly move from east to west
In four-and-twenty hours upon the poles of the world,
But differ in their motion upon the poles of the zodiac.

Faustus. Tush, these slender trifles Wagner can decide.
Hath Mephastophilis no greater skill?
Who knows not the double motion of the planets?
The first is finished in a natural day,
The second thus, as Saturn in thirty years,
Jupiter in twelve, Mars in four,
The sun, Venus, and Mercury in a year,
The moon in twenty-eight days.
Tush, these are freshmen's suppositions.
But tell me, hath every sphere a dominion
Or *intelligentia*?

Mephastophilis. Aye.

Faustus. How many Heavens or spheres are there?

Mephastophilis. Nine: the seven planets, the firmament,
And the empyreal Heaven.

Faustus. Well, resolve me in this question:
Why have we not conjunctions, oppositions, aspects,
Eclipses all at one time, but in some years
We have more, in some less?

Mephastophilis. *Per inaequalem motum respectu totius.*

Faustus. Well, I am answered. Tell me who made the world.

Mephastophilis. I will not.

Faustus. Sweet Mephastophilis, tell me.

Mephastophilis. Move me not, for I will not tell thee.

Faustus. Villain, have I not bound thee to tell me anything?

Mephastophilis. Aye, that is not against our kingdom, but this is. Think thou on hell, Faustus, for thou art damned.

Faustus. Think, Faustus, upon God, that made the world.

Mephastophilis. Remember this. *Exit*

Faustus. Ay, go, accursèd spirit, to ugly hell!
'Tis thou hast damned distressèd Faustus' soul.
Is't not too late?

Enter Good Angel *and* Evil [Angel].

Evil Angel. Too late.

Good Angel. Never too late, if Faustus can repent.

---

216 **blind Homer** Greek poet legendarily thought to be blind

217 **Alexander's . . . death** Alexander (Homer's name for Paris) loved Oenone before Helen; wounded in the Trojan War, he was carried to Oenone and when he died at her feet, she stabbed herself

218 **he that built** Amphion, whose harp caused stones to move

225–56 (allusions are to the Ptolemaic cosmology then generally upheld in which the universe is composed of concentric spheres around the earth; closest was the Moon, while farther out the spheres were occupied by erring [as opposed to fixed] stars: Mercury, Venus, Sun, Mars, Jupiter, and Saturn. The eighth sphere was the firmament of fixed stars, then the primum mobile [or chief mover]; the farthest [tenth] sphere was the fixed empyrean [the empyrean orb]

228 **As . . . elements** analogous to the four elements enclosing one another, as water surrounds earth, air surrounds water, and fire surrounds air; these beliefs were commonly held in early modern England although challenged by Copernicus on the Continent

231 **terminine** astrological boundary

235 ***situ et tempore*** "in direction and time"; i.e., do all planets move in the same direction and at the same speed? The commonplace answer (which Faustus knows) is that planets are caused by the primum mobile to move on a W to E rotation around the earth every 24 hours, while their own nature (changing their relative dispositions) is W to E; thus the planets' complete orbits were thought to be: Saturn, $29\frac{1}{2}$ years; Jupiter, $11\frac{3}{4}$ years; Mars, 1 year, 11 months; Sun, 1 year; Venus $7\frac{1}{2}$ months; Mercury, 3 months (as closest to earth, with shortest orbit)

247 **freshmen's suppositions** elementary facts given first-year university undergraduates

248–9 **dominion or *intelligentia*** (belief, ultimately from Plato, that angelic spirit [intelligence] guides each planet)

254 **conjunctions** the appearance (from earth) of two planets joining together; **oppositions** planets at their farthest apart; **aspects** any medial relationship

257 ***Per . . . totius*** "through an irregular motion [that is, varying speeds] so far as the whole is concerned"

259 **I . . . not** (for he cannot name God)

261 **Move** (1) urge; (2) anger

264 **Think** concentrate only

Evil Angel. If thou repent, devils shall tear thee in pieces.

Good Angel. Repent, and they shall never raze thy, skin.

Exeunt [Angels].

Faustus. Ah, Christ, my Savior,
Seek to save distressèd Faustus' soul!

Enter Lucifer, Beelzebub, *and* Mephastophilis.

Lucifer. Christ cannot save thy soul, for He is just.
There's none but I have int'rest in the same.

Faustus. Oh, who art thou that look'st so terrible?

Lucifer. I am Lucifer,
And this is my companion prince in hell.

Faustus. Oh, Faustus, they are come to fetch away thy soul!

Lucifer. We come to tell thee thou dost injure us.
Thou talk'st of Christ, contrary to thy promise.
Thou shouldst not think of God. Think of the devil,
And of his dame, too.

Faustus. Nor will I henceforth. Pardon me in this,
And Faustus vows never to look to Heaven,
Never to name God or to pray to him,
To burn his Scriptures, slay his ministers,
And make my spirits pull his churches down.

Lucifer. Do so, and we will highly gratify thee.
Faustus, we are come from hell
To show thee some pastime. Sit down,
And thou shalt see all the Seven Deadly Sins
Appear in their proper shapes.

Faustus. That sight will be as pleasing unto me
As paradise was to Adam the first day of his creation.

Lucifer. Talk not of paradise nor creation,
But mark this show. Talk of the devil,
And nothing else. Come away

[*Calling offstage.*]
[*Faustus sits.*]

Enter the Seven Deadly Sins.

Now, Faustus, examine them of their several names
And dispositions.

Faustus. What art thou, the first?

Pride. I am Pride. I disdain to have any parents. I am like to Ovid's flea: I can creep into every corner of a wench. Sometimes like a periwig I sit upon her brow, or like a fan of feathers I kiss her lips. Indeed I do – what do I not? But fie, what a scent is here! I'll not speak another word, except the ground were perfumed and covered with cloth of arras.

Faustus. What art thou, the second?

Covetousness. I am Covetousness, begotten of an old churl in an old leathern bag; and might I have my wish, I would desire that this house and all the people in it were turned to gold, that I might lock you up in my good chest. Oh, my sweet gold!

Faustus. What art thou, the third?

Wrath. I am Wrath. I had neither father nor mother. I leaped out of a lion's mouth when I was scarce half an hour old, and ever since I have run up and down the world with this case of rapiers, wounding myself when I had nobody to fight withal. I was born in hell, [*Address audience.*] and look to it, for some of you shall be my father.

Faustus. What art thou, the fourth?

Envy. I am Envy, begotten of a chimney-sweeper and an oyster-wife. I cannot read, and therefore wish all books were burned. I am lean with seeing others eat. Oh, that there would come a famine through all the world, that all might die, and I live alone! Then thou shouldst see how fat I would be. But must thou sit and I stand? Come down, with a vengeance!

Faustus. Away, envious rascal! – What are thou, the fifth?

Gluttony. Who, I, sir? I am Gluttony. My parents are all dead, and the devil a penny they have left me but a bare pension, and that is thirty meals a day, and ten bevers – a small trifle to suffice nature. Oh, I come of a royal parentage. My grandfather was a gammon of bacon, my grandmother a hogshead of claret wine. My godfathers were these: Peter Pickle-herring and Martin Martlemas-beef. Oh, but my godmother, she was a jolly gentlewoman, and well

273 raze graze, scratch
277 int'rest in legal claim on
282 injure insult
301 several different
302 dispositions (1) natures; (2) accomplishments; (3) activities
305 periwig wig
310 cloth of arras fine Flemish tapestries
313 churl (1) peasant, or one of low status; (2) boor; (3) villain; **leathern bag** miser's moneybag, common to lechery in medieval iconology
322 case pair
324 withal with
328–9 chimney-sweeper . . . oyster-wife (i.e., Envy is dirty and stinks by nature)
341 bevers drinks; snacks
344 hogshead large cask holding 63 or 64 gallons
346 Martin Martlemas-beef beef slaughtered, salted, and hung around Martinmas (November 11) to preserve it throughout the winter

beloved in every good town and city; her name was Mistress Margery March-beer. Now, Faustus, thou hast heard all my progeny, wilt thou bid me to supper?

Faustus. No, I'll see thee hanged. Thou will eat up all my victuals.

Gluttony. Then the devil choke thee!

Faustus. Choke thyself, glutton! – What art thou, the sixth?

Sloth. I am Sloth. I was begotten on a sunny bank, where I have lain ever since, and you have done me great injury to bring me from thence. Let me be carried thither again by Gluttony and Lechery. I'll not speak another word for a king's ransom.

Faustus. What are you, Mistress Minx, the seventh and last?

Lechery. Who, I, sir? I am one that loves an inch of raw mutton better than an ell of fried stockfish, and the first letter of my name begins with lechery.

Lucifer. Away, to hell, to hell!

Exeunt the Sins.

Now, Faustus, how dost thou like this?

Faustus. Oh, this feeds my soul!

Lucifer. Tut, Faustus, in hell is all manner of delight.

Faustus. Oh, might I see hell and return again,
How happy were I then!

Lucifer. Thou shalt. I will send for thee at midnight.
[*Presenting a book.*] In meantime, take this book.
Peruse it throughly, and thou shalt
Turn thyself into what shape thou wilt.

Faustus. [*Taking the book.*] Great thanks, mighty Lucifer.
This will I keep as chary as my life.

Lucifer. Farewell, Faustus, and think on the devil.

Faustus. Farewell, great Lucifer. Come, Mephastophilis.

Exeunt omnes, [*different ways*].

[Sc. vi]

Enter Robin *the ostler with a book in his hand.*

Robin. Oh, this is admirable! Here I ha' stol'n one of Doctor Faustus' conjuring books, and, i'faith, I mean to search some circles for my own use. Now will I make all the maidens in our parish dance at my pleasure stark naked before me, and so by that means I shall see more than e'er I felt or saw yet.

Enter Rafe, *calling Robin.*

Rafe. Robin, prithee, come away. There's a gentleman tarries to have his horse, and he would have his things rubbed and made clean; he keeps such a chafing with my mistress about it, and she has sent me to look thee out. Prithee, come away.

Robin. Keep out, keep out, or else you are blown up, you are dismembered, Rafe! Keep out, for I am about a roaring piece of work.

Rafe. Come, what dost thou with that same book? Thou canst not read.

Robin. Yes, my master and mistress shall find that I can read, he for his forehead, she for her private study. She's born to bear with me, or else my art fails.

Rafe. Why, Robin, what book is that?

Robin. What book? Why the most intolerable book for conjuring that e'er was invented by any brimstone devil.

Rafe. Canst thou conjure with it?

Robin. I can do all these things easily with it: first, I can make thee drunk with hippocras at any tavern in Europe for nothing. That's one of my conjuring works.

Rafe. Our Master Parson says that's nothing.

Robin. True, Rafe; and more, Rafe, if thou hast any mind to Nan Spit, our kitchen maid, then turn her and wind her to thy own use as often as thou will, and at midnight.

---

349 **March-beer** a rich ale made in March and allowed to mature for two years

350 **progeny** i.e., ancestors, lineage

353 **victuals** food, provisions

363 **Mistress Minx** proverbial for wanton woman, a prostitute

366 **raw mutton** colloquialism for penis (from mutton, colloquialism for prostitute)

366 **ell** a variable measure: in England, 45 inches; in Scotland, 37.2 inches

367 **stockfish** dried cod; proverbial for impotence

380 **chary** (1) carefully; (2) preciously

vi.3 **circles** (1) magicians' circles; (2) (with sexual implications)

4 **maidens** unwed women

10 **his things rubbed** (with sexual implication for stroking; *things* means genitalia)

11 **chafing** (1) scolding; (2) sexual rubbing

13 **Prithee** "I pray thee" (standard form of requesting)

16 **roaring** (1) noisy; (2) dangerous; (3) exciting

20 **forehead** allusion to being cuckolded by Robin

20–1 **her . . . study** i.e. study of (or attention to dealing with) her private parts

21 **bear** (with sexual pun)

24 **intolerable** (he probably means incomparable)

26 **brimstone** sulfurous; but of fires of hell see Gen. 19:24 and Rev. 19:20

29 **hippocras** spiced wine

30 **nothing** i.e., useless; not to be used

34 **Nan Spit** (the name suggests her to be pliant, easily turned)

Rafe. O brave, Robin! Shall I have Nan Spit, and to mine own use? On that condition I'll feed thy devil with horse-bread as long as he lives, of free cost.

Robin. No more, sweet Rafe. Let's go and make clean our boots, which lie foul upon our hands, and then to our conjuring, in the devil's name.

Exeunt.

[Chorus 2]

Enter Wagner *solus.*

Wagner. Learnèd Faustus,
To know the secrets of astronomy
Graven in the book of Jove's high firmament,
Did mount himself to scale Olympus' top,
Being seated in a chariot burning bright
Drawn by the strength of yoked dragons' necks.
He now is gone to prove cosmography,
And, as I guess, will first arrive at Rome
To see the Pope and manner of his court
And take some part of holy Peter's feast
That to this day is highly solemnized.

Exit Wagner.

[Sc. vii]

Enter Faustus *and* Mephastophilis.

Faustus. Having now, my good Mephastophilis,
Passed with delight the stately town of Trier,
Environed round with airy mountain-tops,
With walls of flint and deep intrenchèd lakes,
Not to be won by any conquering prince;
From Paris next, coasting the realm of France,
We saw the river Maine fall into Rhine,
Whose banks are set with groves of fruitful vines.
Then up to Naples, rich Campania,
Whose buildings, fair and gorgeous to the eye,
The streets straight forth and paved with finest brick,
Quarters the town in four equivalents.
There saw we learnèd Maro's golden tomb,
The way he cut an English mile in length
Through a rock of stone in one night's space.
From thence to Venice, Padua, and the rest,
In midst of which a sumptuous temple stands
That threats the stars with her aspiring top.
Thus hitherto hath Faustus spent his time.
But, tell me now, what resting place is this?
Hast thou, as erst I did command,
Conducted me within the walls of Rome?

Mephastophilis. Faustus, I have. And because we will not be
Unprovided, I have taken up
His Holiness' privy chamber for our use.

Faustus. I hope His Holiness will bid us welcome.

Mephastophilis. Tut, 'tis no matter, man.
We'll be bold with his good cheer.
And now, my Faustus, that thou mayst perceive
What Rome containeth to delight thee with,
Know that this city stands upon seven hills
That underprops the groundwork of the same.
Just through the midst runs flowing Tiber's stream,
With winding banks that cut it in two parts,
Over the which four stately bridges lean,
That makes safe passage to each part of Rome.
Upon the bridge called Ponte Angelo
Erected is a castle passing strong,
Within whose walls such store of ordnance are,
And double cannons, framed of carvèd brass,

37 **brave** excellent (as in *bravo*)
39 **horse-bread** common horse fodder made of coarse grain and perhaps beans
40 **of** at
Chorus 2.3 Graven inscribed, engraven
4 **mount himself** ascend in his chariot; **Olympus** Mount Olympus was the mythological home of the Greek gods
7 **prove cosmography** explore the earth to confirm the accuracy (or inaccuracy) of maps
10 **holy . . . feast** St. Peter's feast day is June 29; the Pope is Peter's successor as earthly head of the Roman church
vii.2 Trier city in the Moselle valley of w Germany
3 **Environed** surrounded, encircled
4 **lakes** moats
5 **Not . . . prince** (i.e., the geography makes Trier impregnable)
6 **coasting** (1) exploring; (2) skirting
9 **Campania** region in which Naples lies
11 **straight** i.e., running straight
13 **learnèd Maro** Virgil, posthumously thought of as a magician; legend ascribes a tunnel leading to his magic art from his tomb in Naples
17 **a sumptuous temple** St. Mark's Cathedral, Venice, known for its gilded roof and mosaics
18 **aspiring top** perhaps a nearby campanile
21 **erst** earlier
23 **because** in order that
25 **privy** private
37–8 **Upon . . . strong** the Ponte Angelo built in 135 AD by Hadrian whose mausoleum (facing but not standing on the bridge) eventually became the Castle of St. Angelo
40 **double cannons** cannons of high caliber reputed to send seven bullets in a single charge

As match the days within one complete year,
Besides the gates and high pyramides
Which Julius Caesar brought from Africa.
Faustus. Now, by the kingdoms of infernal rule,
Of Styx, Acheron, and the fiery lake
Of ever-burning Phlegethon, I swear
That I do long to see the monuments
And situation of bright splendent Rome.
Come, therefore, let's away!
Mephastophilis.
Nay, Faustus, stay. I know you'd fain see the Pope
And take some part of holy Peter's feast,
Where thou shalt see a troupe of bald-pate friars
Whose *summum bonum* is in belly cheer.
Faustus. Well, I am content to compass then some sport,
And by their folly make us merriment.
Then charm me that I may be invisible,
To do what I please unseen of any
While I stay in Rome.
Mephastophilis. [*Placing a robe on Faustus.*] So, Faustus, now do what thou will,
Thou shalt not be discerned.

Sound a sennet. Enter the Pope *and the* Cardinal of Lorraine *to the banquet, with* Friars *attending.*

Pope. My lord of Lorraine, will't please you draw near?
Faustus. Fall to, and the devil choke you and you spare.
Pope. How now, who's that which spoke? Friars, look about.
Friar. Here's nobody, if it like your Holiness.
Pope. My lord, here is a dainty dish was sent me
From the Bishop of Milan.
[*He presents a dish.*]
Faustus. I thank you, sir.
Snatch it.
Pope. How now, who's that which snatched the meat
From me? Will no man look? My lord,
This dish was sent me from the Cardinal of Florence.
Faustus. [*Snatching the dish.*] You say true. I'll ha't.
Pope. What again? My lord, I'll drink to your Grace.
Faustus. [*Snatching the cup.*] I'll pledge your Grace.
Lorraine. My lord, it may be some ghost,
Newly crept out of purgatory, come to beg
A pardon of your Holiness.
Pope. It may be so. Friars, prepare a dirge
To lay the fury of this ghost.
Once again, my lord, fall to.
The Pope crosseth himself.
Faustus. What, are you crossing of yourself?
Well, use that trick no more, I would advise you.
[*The Pope*] *cross*[*es himself*] *again.*
Well, there's a second time. Aware the third,
I give you fair warning.

[*The Pope*] *cross*[*es himself*] *again, and Faustus hits him a box of the ear, and they all run away.*

Come on, Mephastophilis. What shall we do?
Mephastophilis. Nay, I know not. We shall be cursed
With bell, book, and candle.
Faustus. How? Bell, book, and candle, candle, book, and bell,
Forward and backward, to curse Faustus to hell.
Anon you shall hear a hog grunt, a calf bleat,
And an ass bray, because it is Saint Peter's holy day.

Enter all the Friars *to sing the dirge.*

Friar. Come, brethren, let's about our business with good devotion.
[*The Friars*] *sing this:*
Cursèd be he that stole away his Holiness' meat from the table.
Maledicat Dominus!
Cursèd be he that struck his Holiness a blow on the face.

41 As match are equal in number to
42–3 pyramides . . . Africa the obelisk standing in front of St. Peter's was brought from Africa by the Roman emperor Caligula
45–6 Styx . . . Phlegethon three of the four rivers in Hades, the Greek underworld
48 situation layout; **splendent** i.e., resplendent
50 fain like to; take pleasure in
53 *summum bonum* "greatest good" (in scholastic theology, a description of God)
54 compass contrive (usually in a bad sense)
56 charm put a spell on
62 Fall to begin; **and** if; **spare** falter
70 ha't have it (contracted for meter)
72 pledge toast
75 pardon papal indulgence
76 dirge antiphon for the Matins in the Office of the Dead, here made a curse
79 s.d. *crosseth* the Pope was said to ever be blessing and crossing his mouth in devotion
82 s.d. *box of* strike on
85 bell . . . candle (at the close of the Office of Excommunication [here cursing the evil spirits] the bell is tolled, the Bible closed, and the candle extinguished)
92 *Maledicat Dominus* "May the Lord curse him"

Maledicat Dominus!
Cursèd be he that took Friar Sandelo a blow on the pate.
Maledicat Dominus!
Cursèd be he that disturbeth our holy dirge.
Maledicat Dominus!
Cursèd be he that took away his Holiness' wine.
Maledicat Dominus!
Et omnes sancti. Amen.

[Faustus *and* Mephastophilis] *beat the* Friars, *and fling fireworks among them, and so exeunt.*

[Sc. viii]

Enter Robin [*with a conjuring book*] *and* Rafe *with a silver goblet.*

Robin. Come, Rafe, did not I tell thee we were forever made by this Doctor Faustus' book? *Ecce signum!* Here's a simple purchase for horse-keepers. Our horses shall eat no hay as long as this lasts.

Enter the Vintner.

Rafe. But Robin, here comes the Vintner.

Robin. Hush, I'll gull him supernaturally. Drawer, I hope all is paid. God be with you. Come, Rafe.

[*They start to go.*]

Vintner. [*To Robin.*] Soft, sir, a word with you. I must yet have a goblet paid from you ere you go.

Robin. I, a goblet? Rafe, I, a goblet? I scorn you, and you are but a etc. I, a goblet? Search me.

Vintner. I mean so, sir, with your favor.

[*The Vintner searches Robin.*]

Robin. How say you now?

Vintner. I must say somewhat to your fellow. You, sir.

Rafe. Me, sir? Me, sir? Search your fill. [*He gives the goblet to Robin; then the Vintner searches Rafe.*] Now, sir, you may be ashamed to burden honest men with a matter of truth.

Vintner. Well, t'one of you hath this goblet about you.

Robin. You lie, drawer, 'tis afore me. Sirrah, you, I'll teach ye to impeach honest men. Stand by. I'll scour you for a goblet. Stand aside, you had best, I charge you in the name of Beelzebub. [*Tossing the goblet to Rafe.*] Look to the goblet, Rafe.

Vintner. What mean you, sirrah?

Robin. I'll tell you what I mean.

He reads.

Sanctobulorum Periphrasticon! Nay, I'll tickle you, Vintner. Look to the goblet, Rafe. *Polypragmos Belseborams framanto pacostiphos tostu Mephastophilis!* etc.

Enter Mephastophilis: *sets squibs at their backs: they run about.*

Vintner. *Oh nomine Domine!* What mean'st thou, Robin? Thou has no goblet.

Rafe. *Peccatum peccatorum!* Here's thy goblet, good Vintner.

Robin. *Misericordia pro nobis!* What shall I do? Good devil, forgive me now, and I'll never rob thy library more.

Enter to them Mephastophilis.

Mephastophilis. Vanish, villains, th'one like an ape, another like a bear, the third an ass, for doing this enterprise.

[*Exit the* Vintner, *running.*]

Monarch of hell, under whose black survey
Great potentates do kneel with awful fear,
Upon whose altars thousand souls do lie,
How am I vexèd with these villains' charms!
From Constantinople am I hither come
Only for pleasure of these damnèd slaves.

Robin. How, from Constantinople? You have had a great journey. Will you take sixpence in your purse to pay for your supper and be gone?

Mephastophilis. Well, villains, for your presumption I transform thee [*To Robin.*] into an ape and thee [*To Rafe.*] into a dog. And so, begone!

Exit.

---

95 **took** gave; **Sandelo** (perhaps a jibe at the friar's use of sandals)
101 ***Et . . . sancti*** "and all the saints"
viii.3 ***Ecce signum!*** "behold the proof" (i.e., sign); **simple purchase** clear profit
4 **hay** ordinary food
7 **gull** trick; **Drawer** (1) tapster; (2) waiter
10 **Soft** wait a moment
11 **ere** before
14 **but a etc.** (a sign in the playtext for impromptu stage business and dialogue)
15 **with your favor** i.e., by your leave
26 **impeach** accuse
27 **scour** scourge, punish
33–6 ***Sanctobulorum . . . Mephastophilis!*** (imitation Latin); **tickle** beat, chastize
37–46 **Vintner . . . enterprise** (editors often omit these lines as a rough draft of the scene accidentally kept in type and printed)
37 ***nomine Domine*** "In the name of the Lord"
39 ***Peccatum peccatorum*** "sin of sins"
41 ***Misericordia . . . nobis*** "have mercy on us"
44 **villains** stupid practitioners; neophytes

Robin. How, into an ape? That's brave. I'll have fine sport with the boys; I'll get nuts and apples enough.
Rafe. And I must be a dog.
Robin. I'faith, thy head will never be out of the pottage pot.
Exeunt.

[Chorus 3]

Enter Chorus.

Chorus. When Faustus had with pleasure ta'en the view
Of rarest things and royal courts of kings,
He stayed his course and so returnèd home,
Where such as bear his absence but with grief –
I mean his friends and nearest companions –
Did gratulate his safety with kind words.
And in their conference of what befell,
Touching his journey through the world and air,
They put forth questions of astrology,
Which Faustus answered with such learnèd skill
As they admired and wondered at his wit.
Now is his fame spread forth in every land.
Among the rest the Emperor is one,
Carolus the Fifth, at whose palace now
Faustus is feasted 'mongst his noblemen.
What there he did in trial of his art
I leave untold, your eyes shall see performed.
Exit.

[Sc. ix]

Enter Emperor, Faustus, [Mephastophilis,] *and a* Knight, *with* Attendants.

Emperor. Master Doctor Faustus, I have heard
Strange report of thy knowledge in the black art –
How that none in my empire, nor in the whole world,
Can compare with thee for the rare effects of magic.
They say thou hast a familiar spirit by whom
Thou canst accomplish what thou list. This, therefore,
Is my request: that thou let me see some proof of thy skill,
That mine eyes may be witnesses to confirm
What mine ears have heard reported.
And here I swear to thee, by the honor
Of mine imperial crown, that whatever thou dost
Thou shalt be no ways prejudiced or endamaged.
Knight. [*Aside.*] I'faith, he looks much like a conjurer.
Faustus. My gracious Sovereign, though I must confess myself
Far inferior to the report men have published,
And nothing answerable to the honor
Of your Imperial Majesty, yet, for that love
And duty binds me thereunto, I am content to do
Whatsoever your Majesty shall command me.
Emperor. Then, Doctor Faustus, mark what I shall say.
As I was sometime solitary set
Within my closet, sundry thoughts arose
About the honor of mine ancestors –
How they had won by prowess such exploits,
Got such riches, subdued so many kingdoms
As we that do succeed or they that shall
Hereafter possess our throne shall,
I fear me, never attain to that degree
Of high renown and great authority.
Among which kings is Alexander the Great,
Chief spectacle of the world's preeminence,
The bright shining of whose glorious acts
Lightens the world with his reflecting beams,
As when I hear but motion made of him,
It grieves my soul I never saw the man.
If, therefore, thou by cunning of thine art
Canst raise this man from hollow vaults below,
Where lies entombed this famous conqueror,
And bring with him his beauteous paramour,
Both in their right shapes, gesture, and attire

63 pottage pot porridge or soup pot
Chorus 3.3 stayed ended
6 gratulate express joy at
7 conference discussion
14 Carolus the Fifth Charles V (1519–56), who held court at Innsbruck
ix.2 black devils'; diabolical
6 list pleased
12 prejudiced or endamaged scorned or punished
16 nothing answerable to nothing in the least approaching
21 set sitting
22 closet private room or study; **sundry** various
26 succeed inherit
30 Alexander the Great Alexander III of Macedon (356–323 BC)
34 motion mention
39 paramour (normally *mistress*, but in this case perhaps Alexander's wife Roxana)

They used to wear during their time of life,
Thou shalt both satisfy my just desire
And give me cause to praise thee while I live.

Faustus. My gracious Lord, I am ready to accomplish
Your request, so far forth as by art and power
Of my spirit I am able to perform.

Knight. [*Aside.*] I'faith, that's just nothing at all.

Faustus. But if it like your Grace, it is not
In my ability to present before your eyes
The true substantial bodies of those two deceased princes
Which long since are consumed to dust.

Knight. [*Aside.*] Aye, marry, Master Doctor, now there's a sign of grace in you, when you will confess the truth.

Faustus. But such spirits as can lively resemble Alexander
And his paramour shall appear before your Grace
In that manner that they best lived in,
In their most flourishing estate – which I doubt not
Shall sufficiently content your Imperial Majesty.

Emperor. Go to, Master Doctor. Let me see them presently.

Knight. Do you hear, Master Doctor? You bring
Alexander and his paramour before the Emperor?

Faustus. How then, sir?

Knight. I'faith, that's as true as Diana turned me to a stag.

Faustus. No, sir, but when Actaeon died,
He left the horns for you. [*Aside to Mephastophilis.*] Mephastophilis, begone!

Exit Mephastophilis.

Knight. Nay, and you go to conjuring, I'll be gone.

Exit Knight.

Faustus. [*Aside.*] I'll meet with you anon for
Interrupting me so. Here they are, my gracious Lord.

Enter Mephastophilis *with* Alexander *and his* Paramour.

Emperor. Master Doctor, I heard this lady
While she lived had a wart or mole in her neck.
How shall I know whether it be so or no?

Faustus. Your Highness may boldly go and see.

[*The Emperor makes an inspection, and then*]
Exeunt Alexander [*and his* Paramour].

Emperor. Sure these are no spirits, but the true
Substantial bodies of those two deceased princes.

Faustus. Will't please your Highness now to send
For the knight that was so pleasant with me here of late?

Emperor. One of you call him forth.

[*An* Attendant *goes to summon the Knight.*]

Enter the Knight *with a pair of horns on his head.*

How now, sir Knight? Why, I had thought thou hadst been a bachelor, but now I see thou hast a wife that not only gives thee horns but makes thee wear them. Feel on thy head.

Knight. [*To Faustus.*] Thou damnèd wretch and execrable dog,
Bred in the concave of some monstrous rock,
How dar'st thou thus abuse a gentleman?
Villain, I say, undo what thou hast done.

Faustus. O, not so fast, sir. There's no haste but good.
Are you remembered how you crossed me
In my conference with the Emperor?
I think I have met with you for it.

Emperor. Good Master Doctor, at my entreaty release him.
He hath done penance sufficient.

Faustus. My gracious Lord, not so much
For the injury he offered me here in your presence
As to delight you with some mirth hath Faustus
Worthily requited this injurious knight;
Which being all I desire, I am content
To release him of his horns.
And, sir Knight, hereafter speak well of scholars. [*Aside to Mephastophilis.*]
Mephastophilis, transform him straight. [*The horns are removed.*] Now, my good Lord, having done my duty, I humbly take my leave.

---

46 my spirit i.e., Mephastophilis

58 estate condition, situation

64–5 Diana . . . died Diana transformed Actaeon into a stag as punishment for seeing her bathe naked; his own hounds tore him to pieces

66 horns (normally sign of a cuckold, but here of a fool who is easily deceived)

69 anon forthwith; shortly

78 pleasant (said sardonically)

81 bachelor (puns on bachelor knight as rank and unmarried man)

86 concave hollow cavity

89 but that produces any (haste makes waste)

90 Are . . . remembered have you forgotten

Emperor. Farewell, Master Doctor. Yet, ere you go,
Expect from me a bounteous reward.

Exeunt Emperor, [Knight, *and* Attendants].

Faustus. Now, Mephastophilis, the restless course
That time doth run with calm and silent foot,
Short'ning my days and thread of vital life,
Calls for the payment of my latest years.
Therefore, sweet Mephastophilis, let us make haste
To Wittenberg.

Mephastophilis. What, will you go on horseback or on foot?

Faustus. Nay, till I am past this fair and pleasant green,
I'll walk on foot.

[Sc. x]

Enter a Horse-courser.

Horse-courser. I have been all this day seeking one Master Fustian. Mass, see where he is. God save you, Master Doctor.

Faustus. What, Horse-courser! You are well met.

Horse-courser. [*Offering money.*] Do you hear, sir? I have brought you forty dollars for your horse.

Faustus. I cannot sell him so. If thou lik'st him
For fifty, take him.

Horse-courser. Alas, sir, I have no more.

[*To Mephastophilis.*]

I pray you, speak for me.

Mephastophilis. [*To Faustus.*] I pray you, let him have him.
He is an honest fellow, and he has a great charge,
Neither wife nor child.

Faustus. Well, come, give me your money. [*He takes the money.*]
My boy will deliver him to you. But I must tell you
One thing before you have him: ride him
Not into the water, at any hand.

Horse-courser. Why, sir, will he not drink of all waters?

Faustus. Oh, yes, he will drink of all waters, but ride him not
Into the water. Ride him over hedge,
Or ditch, or where thou will, but not into the water.

Horse-courser. Well, sir. [*Aside.*] Now am I made man for ever. I'll not leave my horse for forty. If he had but the quality of hey, ding, ding, hey, ding, ding, I'd make a brave living on him; he has a buttock as slick as an eel. [*To Faustus.*] Well, goodbye, sir. Your boy will deliver him me? But hark ye, sir: if my horse be sick or ill at ease, if I bring his water to you, you'll tell *me* what it is?

Faustus. Away, you villain! What, dost think
I am a horse-doctor?

Exit Horse-courser.

What art thou, Faustus, but a man condemned to die?
Thy fatal time doth draw to final end.
Despair doth drive distrust unto my thoughts.
Confound these passions with a quiet sleep.
Tush! Christ did call the thief upon the cross;
Then rest thee, Faustus, quiet in conceit.

Sleep in his chair.

Enter Horse-courser *all wet, crying.*

Horse-courser. Alas, alas! "Doctor" Fustian, quotha! Mass, Doctor Lopus was never such a doctor. H'as given me a purgation, h'as purged me of forty dollars. I shall never see them more. But yet, like an ass as I was, I would not be ruled by

109 **thread of vital life** (image of life as a single thread is taken from Greek mythology; his life hangs by a thread)

110 **payment** debt (by terms of his compact with Lucifer and Mephastophilis); **latest** last (Marlowe shows swift passage of time and prepares for his conclusion here)

x.1 **s.d. Horse-courser** horse-dealer, often thought dishonest as dealers

2 **Fustian** (1) mispronunciation of Faustus; (2) bombast, rank (since the Clown also uses this word, some critics think the two parts were doubled)

9 **s.d.** ***To Mephastophilis*** (i.e., he has now made himself visible)

12 **charge** burden (because he has no one else to share it with)

17 **Not . . . water** (alludes to common belief that running water dissolves a witch's spell [water as the enemy of witchcraft was used in testing them]); **at any hand** under any circumstances

18 **drink . . . waters** go anywhere

22–3 **made man** (i.e., he is a man whose fortune has suddenly been made)

23 **leave** part with

24 **forty** (used to mean any amount of money; a common term biblically)

24–5 **quality . . . ding** were the horse a stallion (with obscene overtones) and not a gelding

29 **water** urine (for analysis)

34 **fatal** allotted

36 **Confound** (1) allay; (2) disperse

37 **Christ** (His words of comfort to the thieves on the cross beside him at the hour of His death is what Faustus needs now)

38 **conceit** thought, reflection

40 **Doctor Lopus** Dr. Roderigo Lopez, personal physician to Elizabeth I who in 1594 was accused of poisoning her (no one has accounted for this late interpolation)

41 **purgation** (usually by bleeding or evacuation, but here to mean purged of money)

him, for he bade me I should ride him into no water. Now I, thinking my horse had had some rare quality that he would not have had me known of, I, like a venturous youth, rid him into the deep pond at the town's end. I was no sooner in the middle of the pond but my horse vanished away and I sat upon a bottle of hay, never so near drowning in my life. But I'll seek out my Doctor and have my forty dollars again, or I'll make it the dearest horse! O, yonder is his snipper-snapper. Do you hear? You, hey-pass, where's your master?

Mephastophilis. Why, sir, what would you? You cannot speak with him.

Horse-courser. But I will speak with him.

Mephastophilis. Why, he's fast asleep. Come some other time.

Horse-courser. I'll speak with him now, or I'll break his glass windows about his ears.

Mephastophilis. I tell thee he has not slept this eight nights.

Horse-courser. And he have not slept this eight weeks, I'll speak with him.

Mephastophilis. See where he is, fast asleep.

Horse-courser. Aye, this is he. God save ye, Master Doctor. Master Doctor, Master Doctor Fustian! Forty dollars, forty dollars for a bottle of hay!

Mephastophilis. Why, thou seest he hears thee not.

Horse-courser. (*Holler in his ear.*) So-ho, ho! So-ho, ho!
No, will you not wake? I'll make you wake ere I go.

Pull him by the leg, and pull it away.

Alas, I am undone! What shall I do?

Faustus. O my leg, my leg! Help, Mephastophilis! Call the officers! My leg, my leg!

Mephastophilis. [*Seizing the Horse-courser.*] Come, villain, to the constable.

Horse-courser. Oh, Lord, sir, let me go, and I'll give you forty dollars more.

Mephastophilis. Where be they?

Horse-courser. I have none about me. Come to my hostry, and I'll give them you.

Mephastophilis. Begone, quickly.

Horse-courser *runs away.*

Faustus. What, is he gone? Farewell, he! Faustus has his leg again, and the Horse-courser, I take it, a bottle of hay for his labor. Well, this trick shall cost him forty dollars more.

Enter Wagner.

How now, Wagner, what's the news with thee?

Wagner. Sir, the Duke of Vanholt doth earnestly entreat your company.

Faustus. The Duke of Vanholt! An honorable gentleman,
To whom I must be no niggard of my cunning.
Come, Mephastophilis, let's away to him.

Exeunt.

[Sc. xi]

[*Enter* Faustus *with* Mephastophilis.] *Enter to them the* Duke [of Vanholt] *and the* [*pregnant*] Duchess. *The* Duke *speaks.*

Duke. Believe me, Master Doctor, this merriment hath much pleased me.

Faustus. My gracious Lord, I am glad it contents you
So well. But it may be, madam,
You take no delight in this. I have heard
That great-bellied women do long for some dainties or other.
What is it, madam? Tell me, and you shall have it.

Duchess. Thanks, good Master Doctor. And,
For I see your courteous intent to pleasure me,
I will not hide from you the thing my heart desires.
And were it now summer, as it is January
And the dead time of the winter,
I would desire no better meat than
A dish of ripe grapes.

Faustus. Alas, madam, that's nothing.
[*Aside to Mephastophilis.*] Mephastophilis, begone!

Exit Mephastophilis.

Were it a greater thing than this,
So it would content you, you should have it.

---

47 venturous inexperienced
51 bottle bundle
53 dearest costliest
54 snipper-snapper impudent person; "wise guy"
55 hey-pass (a conjuror's catchphrase)
62 glass windows eyeglasses
72 So-ho a huntman's cry when he sees the quarry
81 they (the dollars)
83 hostry hostelry, inn (as a trader who has no fixed abode)
93 no niggard not stingy; **cunning** (1) ability; (2) ledgerdemain
xi.1 s.d. Vanholt Anhalt, a German duchy near Wittenberg
6 great-bellied . . . other (refers to hunger common to pregnant women)
13 meat food
15 s.d. *Aside* (Mephastophilis is assumed to be invisible in this scene)

Enter Mephastophilis *with the grapes.*

Here they be, madam. Will't please you taste on them?

[*The Duchess tastes the grapes.*]

Duke. Believe me, Master Doctor, this makes me wonder
Above the rest, that, being in the dead time of winter
And in the month of January, how you
Should come by these grapes.

Faustus. If it like your Grace, the year is divided
Into two circles over the whole world
That when it is here winter with us, in the contrary circle
It is summer with them, as in India, Saba, and farther countries
In the East; and by means of a swift spirit that I have
I had them brought hither, as ye see.
How do you like them, madam? Be they good?

Duchess. Believe me, Master Doctor, they be
The best grapes that e'er I tasted in my life before.

Faustus. I am glad they content you so, madam.

Duke. Come, madam, let us in,
Where you must well reward this learnèd man
For the great kindness he hath showed to you.

Duchess. And so I will, my Lord, and whilst I live
Rest beholding for this courtesy.

Faustus. I humbly thank your Grace.

Duke. Come, Master Doctor, follow us and receive your reward.

Exeunt.

[Chorus 4]

Enter Wagner *solus.*

Wagner. I think my master means to die shortly,
For he hath given to me all his goods.
And yet methinks if that death were near
He would not banquet and carouse and swill
Among the students, as even now he doth,
Who are at supper with such belly-cheer
As Wagner ne'er beheld in all his life.
See where they come. Belike the feast is ended.

[*Exit.*]

[Sc. xii]

Enter Faustus *with two or three* Scholars [*and* Mephastophilis].

First Scholar. Master Doctor Faustus, since our conference about fair ladies – which was the beautifull'st in all the world – we have determined with ourselves that Helen of Greece was the admirablest lady that ever lived. Therefore, Master Doctor, if you will do us that favor as to let us see that peerless dame of Greece, whom all the world admires for majesty, we should think ourselves much beholding unto you.

Faustus. Gentlemen,
For that I know your friendship is unfeigned,
And Faustus' custom is not to deny
The just requests of those that wish him well,
You shall behold that peerless dame of Greece
No otherways for pomp and majesty
Than when Sir Paris crossed the seas with her
And brought the spoils to rich Dardania.
Be silent then, for danger is in words.

[Mephastophilis *goes to the door.*]

Music sounds. [Mephastophilis *returns,*] *and* Helen *passeth over the stage.*

Second Scholar. Too simple is my wit to tell her praise,
Whom all the world admires for majesty.

Third Scholar. No marvel though the angry Greeks pursued
With ten years' war the rape of such a queen,
Whose heavenly beauty passeth all compare.

First Scholar. Since we have seen the pride of nature's works
And only paragon of excellence,

Enter an Old Man.

Let us depart; and for this glorious deed

---

24 circles hemispheres (although the reference to the E would make Marlowe seem to be thinking of E and W rather than, properly, N and S)
26 Saba Sheba, now the Yemen
Chorus 4.4 swill drink heavily or riotously
6 belly-cheer abandon
8 Belike apparently
xii.4 Helen of Greece Helen of Troy, given to Paris as a reward for judging the contest of three goddesses renowned for their beauty
18 spoils booty (including Helen); **Dardania** i.e., Troy (given by transfer from Dardania built by Dardanus on the Hellespont)
20 s.d. ***passeth over*** (apparently crossing the stage by entering on one side and exiting on the other, or coming on and off the stage in an innyard or hall)
23 rape (Menelaus' abduction of Helen was the initial cause of the Trojan War)
25 pride most excellent

Happy and blest be Faustus evermore.
Faustus. Gentlemen, farewell. The same I wish to you.
Exeunt Scholars.
Old Man. Ah, Doctor Faustus, that I might prevail
To guide thy steps unto the way of life
By which sweet path thou mayst attain the goal
That shall conduct thee to celestial rest.
Break heart, drop blood, and mingle it with tears,
Tears falling from repentant heaviness
Of thy most vile and loathsome filthiness,
The stench whereof corrupts the inward soul
With such flagitious crimes of heinous sins
As no commiseration may expel
But mercy, Faustus, of thy Savior sweet,
Whose blood alone must wash away thy guilt.
Faustus. Where art thou, Faustus? Wretch, what hast thou done?
Damned art thou, Faustus, damned! Despair and die!
Hell calls for right, and with a roaring voice
Says, "Faustus, come! Thine hour is come."
Mephastophilis gives him a dagger.
And Faustus will come to do thee right.
[*Faustus prepares to stab himself.*]
Old Man. Ah, stay, good Faustus, stay thy desperate steps!
I see an angel hovers o'er thy head,
And with a vial full of precious grace
Offers to pour the same into thy soul.
Then call for mercy and avoid despair.
Faustus. Ah, my sweet friend, I feel thy words
To comfort my distressèd soul.
Leave me a while to ponder on my sins
Old Man. I go, sweet Faustus, but with heavy cheer,
Fearing the ruin of thy hopeless soul.
[*Exit.*]
Faustus. Accursèd Faustus, where is mercy now?
I do repent, and yet I do despair.
Hell strives with grace for conquest in my breast.
What shall I do to shun the snares of death?
Mephistophilis. Thou traitor, Faustus, I arrest thy soul
For disobedience to my sovereign lord.
Revolt, or I'll in piecemeal tear thy flesh.
Faustus. Sweet Mephastophilis, entreat thy lord
To pardon my unjust presumption,
And with my blood again I will confirm
My former vow I made to Lucifer.
Mephastophilis. Do it then quickly, with unfeignèd heart,
Lest greater danger do attend thy drift.
[*Faustus cuts his arm and writes with his blood.*]
Faustus. Torment, sweet friend, that base and crooked age
That durst dissuade me from thy Lucifer,
With greatest torments that our hell affords.
Mephastophilis. His faith is great. I cannot touch his soul.
But what I may afflict his body with
I will attempt, which is but little worth.
Faustus. One thing, good servant, let me crave of thee
To glut the longing of my heart's desire:
That I might have unto my paramour
That heavenly Helen which I saw of late,
Whose sweet embracings may extinguish clean
These thoughts that do dissuade me from my vow,
And keep mine oath I made to Lucifer.
Mephastophilis. Faustus, this, or what else thou shalt desire,
Shall be performed in twinkling of an eye.

Enter Helen [*brought in by* Mephastophilis].

Faustus. Was this the face that launched a thousand ships
And burned the topless towers of Ilium?
Sweet Helen, make me immortal with a kiss.
[*They kiss.*]
Her lips sucks forth my soul. See where it flies!
Come, Helen, come, give me my soul again.
[*They kiss again.*]
Here will I dwell, for Heaven be in these lips,
And all is dross that is not Helena.

Enter Old Man.

I will be Paris, and for love of thee
Instead of Troy shall Wittenberg be sacked,

32 goal (apparently a textual error; he means pathway)
38 flagitious extremely wicked; atrocious
39 commiseration (apparently another textual error; he means contrition)
42 Where . . . thou? (cf. God to Adam, Gen. 3: 9)
44 roaring (cf. 1 Pet. 5: 8)
45 Thine . . . come (cf. Christ at His death, John 13: 1)
46 s.d. *stab himself* (suicide, the greatest and final sin against God, the giver of life)
55 cheer disposition, mood
63 Revolt return to your allegiance (to Lucifer)
69 drift (1) drifting waywardness; (2) purpose
70 crooked age (i.e., the Old Man)
71 durst (1) dared; (2) tried
80 extinguish (to embrace a sinner or devil, such as the pagan Helen brought up by Mephastophilis, is to insure damnation); **clean** entirely
86 Ilium Troy

And I will combat with weak Menelaus,
And wear thy colors on my plumèd crest.
Yea, I will wound Achilles in the heel
And then return to Helen for a kiss.
Oh, thou art fairer than the evening air,
Clad in the beauty of a thousand stars.
Brighter art thou than flaming Jupiter
When he appeared to hapless Semele,
More lovely than the monarch of the sky
In wanton Arethusa's azured arms;
And none but thou shalt be my paramour.
Exeunt [Faustus *and* Helen].

Old Man. Accursèd Faustus, miserable man,
That from thy soul exclud'st the grace of Heaven
And fliest the throne of His tribunal seat!

Enter the Devils. [*They menace the Old Man.*]

Satan begins to sift me with his pride.
As in this furnace God shall try my faith,
My faith, vile hell, shall triumph over thee.
Ambitious fiends, see how the Heavens smiles
At your repulse and laughs your state to scorn!
Hence, hell! For hence I fly unto my God.
Exeunt [*different ways*].

[Sc. xiii]

Enter Faustus *with the* Scholars.

Faustus. Ah, gentlemen!
First Scholar. What ails Faustus?
Faustus. Ah, my sweet chamber-fellow! Had I
Lived with thee, then had I lived still,
But now I die eternally. Look, comes he not?
Comes he not?
Second Scholar. What means Faustus?
Third Scholar. Belike he is grown into some sickness by being over-solitary.
First Scholar. If it be so, we'll have physicians to cure him.
[*To Faustus.*] 'Tis but a surfeit. Never fear, man.
Faustus. A surfeit of deadly sin that hath damned both body and soul.
Second Scholar. Yet, Faustus, look up to Heaven. Remember God's mercies are infinite.
Faustus. But Faustus' offense can ne'er be pardoned.
The serpent that tempted Eve may be saved,
But not Faustus. Ah, gentlemen, hear me with patience,
And tremble not at my speeches. Though my heart pants
And quivers to remember that I have been a student here
These thirty years, oh, would I had never seen Wittenberg,
Never read book! And what wonders I have done,
All Germany can witness, yea, all the world,
For which Faustus hath lost both Germany and the world,
Yea, Heaven itself – Heaven, the seat of God,
The throne of the blessed, the kingdom of joy
And must remain in hell forever.
Hell, ah, hell forever! Sweet friends,
What shall become of Faustus, being in hell forever?
Third Scholar. Yet, Faustus, call on God.
Faustus. On God, whom Faustus hath abjured?
On God, whom Faustus hath blasphemed?
Ah, my God, I would weep, but the devil draws in my tears.
Gush forth blood instead of tears, yea, life and soul
Oh, he stays my tongue! I would lift up my hands, but see,
They hold them, they hold them.
All. Who, Faustus?
Faustus. Lucifer and Mephastophilis. Ah, gentlemen! I gave them my soul for my cunning.
All. God forbid!

---

96 **wound . . . heel** the only vulnerable part of Achilles' body as a result of a shot by Paris
100–1 **flaming . . . Semele** the human Semele was consumed by Jupiter's divine splendor, too bright for human eyes
101 **hapless** unfortunate
102–3 **monarch . . . arms** the nymph Arethusa was changed into a fountain when, bathing, she excited Alpheus (said to be related to the sun)
103 **azured** reflecting the blue of the sky
107 **throne** i.e., Heaven; **tribunal seat** God's throne of heavenly judgment (cf. Rev.)
108 **s.d. *menace*** (perhaps with pitchforks or obscene gestures; the Old Man's faith renders them harmless); **sift** make trial of (cf. Luke 22: 3)
109 **furnace** (i.e., the fiery furnace of Dan. 3)
111 **Heavens smiles** the joy of celestial being
111–12 **smiles . . . scorn** (cf. Ps. 2: 4)
xiii.3 **chamber-fellow** scholars shared quarters at the university
9 **sickness** (extended solitude could produce melancholy or depression, according to Galenic medicine)
11 **surfeit** indigestion, temporary excess
23 **all the world** (cf. Mark 8: 36; what does it profit a man to win the world and lose his soul?)
35 **stays** stops, holds back
39 **cunning** (1) special knowledge; (2) special talents

Faustus. God forbade it indeed, but Faustus hath done it.
For vain pleasure of four-and-twenty years
Hath Faustus lost eternal joy and felicity. I writ them a bill
With mine own blood. The date is expired,
The time will come, and he will fetch me.

First Scholar. Why did not Faustus tell us of this before, that divines might have prayed for thee?

Faustus. Oft have I thought to have done so,
But the devil threatened to tear me in pieces
If I named God, to fetch both body and soul
If I once gave ear to divinity. And now 'tis too late.
Gentlemen, away, lest you perish with me.

Second Scholar. Oh, what shall we do to save Faustus?

Faustus. Talk not of me, but save yourselves and depart.

Third Scholar. God will strengthen me. I will stay with Faustus.

First Scholar. [*To the Third Scholar.*] Tempt not God, sweet friend, but let us into the next room and there pray for him.

Faustus. Aye, pray for me, pray for me!
And what noise soever ye hear, come not unto me
For nothing can rescue me.

Second Scholar. Pray thou, and we will pray that God may have mercy upon thee.

Faustus. Gentlemen, farewell. If I live till morning,
I'll visit you; if not, Faustus is gone to hell.

All. Faustus, farewell.

Exeunt Scholars.
The clock strikes eleven.

Faustus. Ah, Faustus,
Now hast thou but one bare hour to live,
And then thou must be damned perpetually.
Stand still, you ever-moving spheres of heaven,
That time may cease and midnight never come!
Fair nature's eye, rise, rise again, and make
Perpetual day; or let this hour be but
A year, a month, a week, a natural day,
That Faustus may repent and save his soul!
O lente, lente currite noctis equi!
The stars move still; time runs; the clock will strike;
The devil will come, and Faustus must be damned.
Oh, I'll leap up to my God! Who pulls me down?
See, see where Christ's blood streams in the firmament!
One drop would save my soul, half a drop. Ah, my Christ!
Ah, rend not my heart for naming of my Christ!
Yet will I call on him. Oh, spare me, Lucifer!
Where is it now? 'Tis gone; and see where God
Stretcheth out his arm and bends his ireful brows!
Mountains and hills, come, come and fall on me,
And hide me from the heavy wrath of God!
No, no! Then will I headlong run into the earth.
Earth, gape! Oh, no, it will not harbor me.
You stars that reigned at my nativity,
Whose influence hath allotted death and hell,
Now draw up Faustus like a foggy mist
Into the entrails of yon laboring cloud,
That when you vomit forth into the air,
My limbs may issue from your smoky mouths,
So that my soul may but ascend to heaven.

The watch strikes.

Ah, half the hour is past!
'Twill all be past anon.
O God,
If thou wilt not have mercy on my soul,
Yet for Christ's sake, whose blood hath ransomed me.
Impose some end to my incessant pain.
Let Faustus live in hell a thousand years,
A hundred thousand, and at last be saved.
O, no end is limited to damnèd souls.
Why wert thou not a creature wanting soul?
Or why is this immortal that thou hast?
Ah, Pythagoras' metempsychosis, were that true,

47 **divines** preachers
73 **Fair nature's eye** the sun
77 ***O... equi!*** "Go slowly, slowly, you horses of the night" (from Ovid, where the poet yearns for eternal night of lovemaking; a thoroughly pagan reference combined with the horsemen of the Apocalypse that pronounce doom)
80 **leap... down** (man's divided soul can pull in opposite directions; cf. the emblem on the title-page of the 1604 quarto)
85 **it** i.e., the vision of Christ's blood of mercy
87–8 **Mountains... God!** (cf. Hos. 10; Rev. 6: 16; Luke 23: 3)
91–2 **stars... hell** (reference is to astrological relations at the hour of birth that provide his life's horoscope; once again Faustus has turned to pagan belief)
93–6 **draw... mouths** (as an act of purgation)
99 **anon** at once (or so it seems to the surely damned)
106 **no end is limited** i.e., the state of damnation is eternal
109 **metempsychosis** the belief in the transmigration of souls attributed to Pythagoras by which the human soul at a body's death took on another form of life

This soul should fly from me and I be changed
Unto some brutish beast.
All beasts are happy, for, when they die,
Their souls are soon dissolved in elements;
But mine must live still to be plagued in hell.
Cursed be the parents that engendered me!
No, Faustus, curse thyself. Curse Lucifer,
That hath deprived thee of the joys of heaven.

The clock striketh twelve.

Oh, it strikes, it strikes! Now, body, turn to air,
Or Lucifer will bear thee quick to hell.

Thunder and lightning.

Oh, soul, be changed into little waterdrops,
And fall into the ocean, ne'er be found!
My God, my God, look not so fierce on me!

Enter [Lucifer, Mephastophilis, *and other*] Devils.

Adders and serpents, let me breathe a while!
Ugly hell, gape not. Come not, Lucifer!
I'll burn my books. Ah, Mephastophilis!

[*The* Devils] *exeunt with him.*

[Chorus 5]

Enter Chorus.

Chorus. Cut is the branch that might have grown full straight,
And burnèd is Apollo's laurel bough
That sometime grew within this learnèd man.
Faustus is gone. Regard his hellish fall,
Whose fiendful fortune may exhort the wise
Only to wonder at unlawful things,
Whose deepness doth entice such forward wits
To practice more than Heavenly power permits.

[*Exit.*]

Terminat hora diem; terminat author opus.

---

114 still ever

119 quick living

125 burn my books (renunciation of magic and evil by destroying the works of necromancy is formulaic here)

Chorus 5.2 laurel bough (reference is to iii. 33)

3 sometime formerly

6 wonder at i.e., not perform

7 forward aggressive, eager

9 *Terminat . . . opus* "The hour ends the day; the author ends his work" (this may be an insertion by the printer and not authorial)

The Troublesome Reign and Lamentable Death of Edward the Second

Christopher Marlowe

The execution of Piers Gaveston, from Raphael Holinshed, *The Chronicles of England, Scotland, and Ireland* (London: Lucas Harrison, 1577). Folger Shakespeare Library.

Throughout the staunchly patriotic and nationalistic decade of the 1590s, between the defeat of the Spanish Armada in 1588 and the downfall of Essex in 1601, between Marlowe's groundbreaking portrayal of *Tamburlaine* and Shakespeare's culminating portrait of *Henry V*, the chronicle history play as a dramatic form was not only in vogue; it was at the zenith of its development. Indeed, by 1612 Thomas Heywood could claim that there was "no notable thing recorded even from William the Conqueror, nay from the landing of Brut, until this day" that was not common knowledge because of English drama. Much of this was due to Raphael Holinshed's massive chronicle of English history first published in 1577, drawing on the work of Edward Hall, Robert Fabyan, and others, that, expanded and revised, was republished in 1587, nearly on the eve of the significant naval victory over Spain; to that, Francis Thynne added a history of Scotland. But there were others, too, including the works by Richard Grafton and John Stow. From such multiple resources Marlowe found ample material on the life of England's Edward II, and by the time his play appeared in 1592 Shakespeare's own initial efforts, the three parts of *Henry VI* and perhaps *Richard III*, were already being acted. So was George Peele's play on Edward I, filled with the progresses and pageants that Marlowe's Gaveston would bring to the court of Edward II. These three playwrights, and many others in their wake, did not follow the chronicles rigorously, however; instead, they digested, selected, and rearranged their material for thematic and dramatic effectiveness – and it is this history that England came best to know. Thus when a character in Ben Jonson's *The Devil Is an Ass* is praised for his "cunning in the Chronicle," he replies, in all modesty and truthfulness, "No, I confess I ha't from the Play-books, And think they are more authentic." His ready distinction is apparent in the play on Edward II, in which Marlowe transforms events, scrambles the dates, and invents certain characters and facts to achieve a much deeper understanding of English political life and to provide playgoers with a much richer emotional experience: he has, from his perspective, turned recorded facts into enacted truths. And there is much of Marlowe in this play, too: not simply the portrait of Baldock as a frustrated university scholar nor the penetrating recreation of homosexual longing and passion that critics commonly see, but also matters equally fundamental and at least as pervasive: the factious barons which Marlowe must have seen almost daily in Elizabeth's divided court, and the way in which government rested on personal ambitions and self-interest that, full of distrust, played out in continued surveillance, bribery, constant gossip, and deliberate rumor. Elizabeth's troubled regime – the unsettled policies and desires of the Elizabethan Settlement – are always being insinuated in this play, while something more uncomfortable cuts even nearer to the bone of reality: Marlowe's refined and insightful analysis of personal rule in which the portrait of Edward II and the methods of his governance can dangerously approach Elizabeth's own.

In collapsing and rearranging historical events over a twenty-three-year period, from Edward II's accession in 1307 to Roger Mortimer's execution three years after Edward's death in 1330, Marlowe tells the story of a king whose personal passions and whose indulgence in flattery led to dissension with the nobility and worked against the good of the country. But such a story is only the narrative way of getting at something far more important: the historic confrontation between Edward and his nobility is not simply a collision of personalities and styles of life but incompatible ways of governance. What is at stake is the integrity and survival of the nation itself. And the confrontation is precisely that which Marlowe saw at the heart of the politics of his day: the repeated oaths of allegiance to tradition alongside the fact that Elizabeth's Privy Council and bureaucracy were increasingly made up of new men, like Burghley, whose ambition matched their qualifications so that they invented a lineage that would make them acceptable. That Gaveston – and later Spencer and Baldock – do not invent backgrounds for themselves, and that Edward does not invent them, either, is only Marlowe's stark way of questioning government by inheritance by conveniently using the accommodating historical facts from the chronicles.

Edward II inherits a kingdom which is grounded on feudal law and practice. It is based in mutual and cooperative trust between the King and his lords. The hierarchy of birth provides the ruler with peers who support him in time of need and of war (such as that period in which the play is set) and in turn receive from him ongoing privilege and respect: it is the foundation of the English state. The enormous differentiation in status between those of noble birth and inherited power and landholdings and parvenus like Gaveston, Spencer, or Baldock (as Marlowe portrays them, not to mention Marlowe himself) ruptures the nation.

Edward's brother Edmund recalls what such a stable government was like:

I do remember, in my father's days,
Lord Percy of the north, being highly moved,
Braved Mowbray in presence of the King,
For which, had not His Highness loved him well,
He should have lost his head; but with his look
The undaunted spirit of Percy was appeased,
And Mowbray and he were reconciled.

The barons constantly refer to title and position and lineage not because they are suspicious of their King's intentions or because Gaveston as a person is so disagreeable – Mortimer Senior and others think he represents a stage in Edward's maturity and nothing more – but that the titles he is given freely undermine the entire operations of the state. Moreover, Gaveston's recall from France reverses a political decision made by Edward I who had exiled him, and so directly opposes royal decree. As Mortimer Junior puts it,

Mine uncle here, this earl, and I myself
Were sworn to your father at his death
That he should ne'er return into the realm;
And know, my Lord, ere I will break my oath,
This sword of mine that should offend your foes
Shall sleep within the scabbard at thy need,
And underneath thy banners march who will,
For Mortimer will hang his armor up.

Lancaster would do even more – he would surrender and sell his estates "Ere Gaveston shall stay within the realm." Warnings that English stability and rule rest alone on traditional privilege become choric. "If you love us, my Lord," says Mortimer Senior, "hate Gaveston," to which the Archbishop adds, "Either banish him... Or I will presently discharge these Lords Of duty and allegiance to thee."

Edward's flagrant disregard for age-old customs and practices of governance is even further disrupted when he imprisons the Bishop of Coventry, at least in part to give his lands to the recalled Gaveston. By weakening the church as well as the state he challenges both institutions. Such matters of personal desire and mismanagement then lead to greater consequences. Soon Lancaster admonishes Edward of what his self-indulgent distractions may bring about.

Look for rebellion. Look to be deposed.
Thy garrisons are beaten out of France,
And, lame and poor, lie groaning at the gates;
The wild O'Neil, with swarms of Irish kerns,
Lives uncontrolled within the English pale;
Unto the walls of York the Scots made road,
And unresisted drive away such spoils.

Moreover, the "haughty Dane" controls the seas; the "northern borderers" are in revolt; and the country is denied foreign aid. In every way imaginable, Marlowe shows us, Edward's England is bankrupt: when Mortimer Junior demands that the King provide ransom money for his uncle, Edward hands him the Great Seal and orders him to wander throughout the land to collect the money for himself. The anxiety of the barons reflects the words of an anonymous chronicler in early modern England concerning Edward II: "For want of good government he lost the realm of Scotland, and other lands and seignoiries in Gascony, and elsewhere, which his father had left him in peace." It also forewarns of the Elizabethan John Stow's dreadful account of interior decay: "Horseflesh was counted great delicates; the poor stole fat dogs to eat. Some (as it was said), compelled through famine, in hidden places, did eat the flesh of their own children, and some stole others' which they devoured." As Mortimer Junior sums,

Thy court is naked, being bereft of those
That makes a king seem glorious to the world –
I mean the peers whom thou shouldst dearly love;
Libels are cast against thee in the street,
Ballads and rhymes made of thy overthrow.

Nor are these the only results of misguided personal rule. To maintain his slender hold on the state, Edward exiles Gaveston; then, in sharp reversal, negotiates his almost immediate return, vowing as well a new commitment to the Queen. When Gaveston is nevertheless ambushed and murdered, he grows tyrannical.

By this right hand and by my father's sword,
And all the honors 'longing to my crown,
I will have heads and lives for him – as many
As I have manors, castles, towns, and towers.
Treacherous Warwick! Traitorous Mortimer!
If I be England's King, in lakes of gore
Your headless trunks, your bodies will I trail,
That you may drink your fill and quaff in blood,

following hard on the urging of Young Spencer, his new favorite, whose own fierce political strategies become an even more dangerous substitute for the elaborate and ornate prodding of his predecessor Gaveston. There is never any appeal (as there would be with Elizabeth I) to the divine right of kings, and its very absence darkens the play. Mortimer and the other barons become equally resolute, turning upside down the Elizabethans' central homily on obedience: "You must be proud, bold, pleasant, resolute – And now and then, stab, as occasion serves." Edward's England implodes, the story of Actaeon which is recalled extending beyond Gaveston and the barons to the King and the Queen themselves; thus Marlowe imbeds in his text that also of another church homily, this one on disobedience and willful rebellion. According to this frequent church lesson, even when God "maketh a wicked man to reign," no one had the right to rebel "were they never so great or noble, so many, so stout, so witty and politic" nor would they ever succeed but "always they came by the overthrow, and to a shameful, end." In such an unrelenting and escalating dissolution of church and state, Pembroke's initial offer of refuge for Gaveston makes even salvation seem ominous. (This tribute, in fact, may be inserted since it was his descendant who patronized the company that acted Marlowe's play.) In such an unrelenting and escalating dissolution of church and state, Edmund's own indecision is not only understandable but perhaps unavoidable. When the barons sentence him to death before the opposition of both Edward II and Edward III he is reduced to bafflement: "Where is the court but here?" Edward's even greater suffering provides an answer, although not directly, to his well-intentioned brother. "What are kings, when regiment is gone," he asks himself rhetorically, "But perfect shadows in a sunshine day?" This remains one of the play's most haunting lines because it too is interrogative: it forces us to reexamine the play's arguments about the premises and conditions of right rule – and, when we do, the astonishing range of positions dramatized makes any answer difficult.

Elizabethan historians believed the past they recorded was a looking glass or mirror of the present which held within it both the lessons and the costs of governance. The government agreed that the lessons, and the plays, of history were not innocent matters. On November 12, 1589, the Privy Council wrote to the Archbishop of Canterbury that players were offering their own interpretations of political and theological matters. Surely *Edward II* is a case in point. For one thing, it is one of the first visual stagings of the murder of an English monarch. For another, it supplies arguments for opposing the state. For a third, it interjects into a wholly masculinist history the portrait of a Queen who, like Elizabeth I, needs to establish and tailor a regime that is personally satisfying. From Isabella's first clandestine remarks to Mortimer – we are never told what they are – and his consequent resolve to eliminate Gaveston, she is quietly in control through much of this play, instigating the death of Gaveston, inviting revolt against Edward, and finally inciting Mortimer to kill the King. Initially she is lonely, frustrated, ignored, and largely sympathetic, but the adultery first caused by her own personal needs for recognition and love becomes hardened as the play advances. Even the denial of her brother in France to aid her will not stop her.

When force to force is knit and sword and glaive
In civil broils makes kin and countrymen
Slaughter themselves in others, and their sides
With their own weapons gored. But what's the help?
Misgoverned kings are cause of all this wrack;
And Edward, Thou art one among them all,
Whose looseness hath betrayed thy land to spoil
And made the channels overflow with blood.

Her open admission of Edward's own infidelity drives her punishment of the King and gives her a vitality that outlasts the lives of Gaveston, Spencer, Baldock, Edmund, Edward, and even (the play hints) Mortimer; in the end, her only mistake is to misgauge the loyalty of her son. Gaveston, who first seduced the King and so the state, dies more innocently than the Queen, who was his first apparent victim. Under a queen like Elizabeth, this portrait of Isabella, which demonstrates how regimes must be made to fit rulers, is searching, provocative – and telling.

Harboring as it does a dual world of visual splendor and covert hypocrisy, *Edward II* is an intensely political play that is nevertheless about the intensely personal. Edward finds himself at the start trapped in a dilemma: to remain the King, he must give up Gaveston, but to give up Gaveston robs him of being a man. From the start, the King's two bodies are at irreconcilable odds. We know from recorded remarks of Marlowe that man's private preferences were a recurring and important concern: "all they that love not tobacco and boys were fools," the Baines Libel ascribes to him; further, "That St. John the Evangelist was bedfellow to Christ and leaned always in his bosom that he used him as the sinners of Sodom." Even if these remarks are untrue and merely libelous, there is no denying that Edward's passion for Gaveston is the crucial private premise of the play. Their remarks about each other testify to their love; so do their embraces on stage. And like all maturing passions, it has many sides to it: Gaveston's opening lines imagine a kingdom that embodies Edward's own dream, while Edward's response is more tangible, supplying Gaveston with a host of titles and gifts, showering him long before Spencer Junior applies the myth of Danae. Yet it is just as true that Gaveston does not ask for titles or wealth, just as Edward does not stage pageants; what they yearn for is the presence of each other. Thus they extend the original suggestion of Holinshed: "A wonderful matter that the king should be so enchanted with the said earl, and so addict himself, or rather fix his heart upon a man of such a corrupt humor, against whom the heads of the noblest houses in the land were bent to devise his overthrow." By not initially narrowing his charge to one of sodomy, Holinshed suggests the consequences were more widespread, although they extend from this single source; he notes Edward gave himself "to wantonness, passing his time in voluptuous pleasure, and riotous excess: and to help them forward in that kind of life, the foresaid Piers." Indeed, same-sex relationships were relatively frequent in Elizabethan England and far more complicated than our single word *homosexuality* or our single term *gay* might suggest. Embraces and protestations of love between men, from courtiers to soldiers, were commonplace; in crowded quarters men often shared the same bed without necessarily any physical intimacy. The widespread rhetoric of friendship, with its classical pedigree, was transferred to networks of patrons and clients, and even fellow playwrights and actors. Whole vocabularies treating neoplatonism, companionship, marriage, or sodomy, as well as classical history and myth, provided interchangeable metaphors. Even the suggestion of sodomy does not disturb Mortimer Senior: if Edward's "mind so dotes on Gaveston," he says, "Let him without controlment have his will." Nor is it a matter of mind alone: he will in due course list for his nephew a number of classical rulers and heroes whose love of their minions – notoriously a French word, allowing a later reference to a French strumpet to mean Gaveston or Isabella – has not interfered with their historic accomplishments.

Still, as the contentious Marlowe knew in advocating tobacco and boys, sodomy was an especially charged word in early modern England. Elizabethan law, renewed from Henrician times with an Act of Parliament in 1563, made sodomy a capital offense in which "diverse evil disposed persons have been the more bold to commit the said most horrible and detestable Vice of Buggery," against the polity, against society and decency, and "to the high displeasure of Almighty God." Legislators traced their authority back to Leviticus and renewed it specifically in a church homily; the Cambridge divinity student like Marlowe would also know, from Aquinas and Justinian, that it was diabolical. "*Diablo*," exclaims Lancaster of Edward and Gaveston, "what passions call you these?" and in due course even Mortimer Senior fears Edward is "bewitched." Sodomy in England in Marlowe's time was a capital offense, yet even here it was treated more lightly than we might think; in the combined forty-five years under Elizabeth and James, only six men were indicted simply on charges of sodomy in the home countries, and only one was convicted; by illuminating contrast, Catholics and others thought traitors to the state were freely accused of it. In neighboring Scotland, however, it seems to have been a different matter. A contemporary history there notes that in 1570,

> There [were] enormities in the country [such as civil war], as there were against policy and reason, so Sathan had also possessed the minds of two men to commit the abhominable sin of Sodomy within Edinburgh, for the which they were punished in this manner: first, they were detained in prison for the space of 8 days, upon bread and water; then they were placed at the market place, with the inscription of their fault written on their forehead; after that they were placed in the kirk, to repent before the people there several sundays; fourthly, they were ducked in a deep loch over the head three several times; and last of all bound to a stake and fire kindled about them where their bodies were burned to ashes to the death.

Marlowe's reference to tobacco, which James VI of Scotland was defending, and this concern in stricter Calvinist Scotland with sodomy, are also relevant to *Edward II*, since James's own love of his minion, the Duke of Lennox, was widely known, especially to those who, like Marlowe, might see James as Elizabeth's successor. Of Lennox, the Englishman Sir Henry Widdrington had written, James was "in such love . . . as in the open sight of the people, oftentimes he will clasp him about the neck with his arms and kiss him." The Presbyterian leader James Melville added that "his Majesty took the matter [of caressing men] further to heart than any man would have believed," and Lennox, writing to James on the day he died, promises to send the King his embalmed heart. As for Edward II, historians disagreed. The Scottish writer John Major argued that he was mistaken only in "that he followed the counsel of bad men"; the Englishman John Ponet, however, saw Edward's behavior as unjustified but inevitable because "without law he killed his subjects, spoiled them of their goods, and wasted the treasure of the realm." Against such a collocation of early modern attitudes, we are asked to interpret and evaluate the "Elysium" where as soulmate to Edward ("a new-come soul") Gaveston will jet about in Italian clothes. Such clothing, which is not only effeminate but to which Gaveston is unentitled by rank, challenges Elizabethan dress code and sumptuary law and turns royal troops into a pageant of mockery: "thy soldiers marched like players," Mortimer Junior says,

> With garish robes, not armor, and thyself,
> Bedaubed with gold, rode laughing at the rest,
> Nodding and shaking of thy spangled crest,
> Where women's favors hung like labels down,

just as elsewhere Edward and Gaveston are seen looking out an upper window at the street below as a kind of disguising.

It is in just such a setting as this, however, where Edward wails at Gaveston's second exile and stands tiptoe in excitement at his return, that we are to see beneath their outrageous actions a deeper passion that is far more human and sincere. "Thou shalt not hence," says Edward, learning of the barons' threatened banishment; "I'll hide thee, Gaveston." Elsewhere, he offers up his kingdom for a mere corner of it alone with his minion. If we question such deep affection, the play makes it clear why we should not. When the two exchange pictures upon their forced parting, Gaveston says spontaneously, " 'Tis something to be pitied of a king"; there is here an innocence of awe and respect and devotion. Edward entertains similar thoughts; confronted by Mortimer's interrogations concerning Gaveston, Edward answers straightforwardly, disarmingly, "Because he loves me more than all the world." Both remarks resonate again and again throughout a play that knows little of true love and devotion and much of passionate self-interest and slaughter; there are ways that even the cold and embittered Mortimer, who uses Isabella to gain power not love, seems jealous – almost intimately jealous – of the untainted caring Gaveston gives to Edward. As the play develops, it may be possible to see Mortimer as partly motivated by a rivalry with Gaveston and Spencer for recognition from Edward.

Matters of power and love, public and private, the state's governance and the individual's basic human needs and hungers, are never divorced in *Edward II*. Even the act of regicide at the end is also an act of rape; Mortimer is deliberate in instigating an execution that, it turns out, is also an act of sodomy. The playtext provides no details, but those who knew their Holinshed would know what to expect on stage:

> They came suddenly one night into the chamber where he lay in bed fast asleep, and with heavy featherbeds or a table (as some write) being cast upon him, they kept him down and withal put into his fundament an horn, and through the same they thrust up into his body an hot spit, or (as others have) through the pipe of a trumpet a plumbers instrument of iron made very hot, the which passing up into his entrails, and being rolled to and fro, burned the same, but so as no appearance of any wound or hurt outwardly might be once perceived. His cry did move many within the castle and town of Berkeley to compassion, plainly hearing him utter a wailful noise, as the tormentors were about to murder him, so that diverse being awakened therewith (as they themselves confessed) prayed heartily to God to receive his soul, when they understood by his cry what the matter meant.

Marlowe had also gone to Stow, where he found the puddle-shaving – and where he also found, and chose not to use, a mock crowning of Edward with hay as if to engender some reference to the betrayal of Christ. That is omitted because the emphasis is otherwise: on the courtship between Lightborn and Edward where the executioner displays false affection and pity, provides a bed on which Edward can take rest from the stench of the sewer, and for which Edward gives him a jewel – as he had given jewels to Gaveston on whom his thoughts dwell. This extraordinary violation of the King's two bodies is thus a violation too of love, of humanity itself. Such a scene, cheek by jowl with Mortimer's glee and Isabella's proud disdain, force us to ask what love is and where love may be found.

Sexual orientation, then, like political, social, material, and marital orientation, is a matter neither easily evaluated nor even, perhaps, finally capable of resolution. The Protestant Reformer John Calvin saw theater as stunning, dazzling, and even blinding in the face of worldly activity and allurement. No character here – not even the three poor men, the Mower, or Lightborn – is, finally, one-dimensional in this mosaic of early modern England; when Edmund raises the notion of "this unnatural revolt" and Edward of "that unnatural Queen," we realize that what is natural and what unnatural is not easily resolved either. In showing the multidimensionality of people and events – and thus ways in which the medieval past was his very present time – Marlowe provides no final clue through satire, philosophy, or even a concluding sentiment: Edward III's final lines seem to trail off until they simply cease and he falls silent. It is the way of theater, of course, and what the antitheatricalists of Marlowe's time proclaimed; plays, wrote Stephen Gosson, are as "ratsbane to the government of commonweals." They functioned only by moving the senses, delighting the affections, tickling the ear, leading men to waste time and money, provoking men to lasciviousness and utter wantonness, and making them effeminate. Awaking all these senses, risking all these responses, Marlowe's *Edward II* may be most provocative, in the end, by interrogating the purpose, the legality, the morality, and the ends of theater itself: using drama to test its nature and its very validity. To a man like Marlowe, quick of temper and joyous in a good fight, this is the play's most daring risk, and, for us, another matter we cannot avoid addressing. At the start, the play is full of speeches as it makes its comprehensive way from the end of a kingly father to the end of his kingly son. When Edward demands of the scurrying Bishop of Coventry "Whither goes my Lord of Coventry so fast?" he is told, bluntly, "To celebrate your father's exequies," but the Bishop complicates the matter by adding, "But is that wicked Gaveston returned?" At the close, words slowly meld into, perhaps surrender to, spectacle. The young Edward III becomes the Bishop: "Go fetch my father's hearse, where it shall lie, And bring my funeral robes." But we see neither: what we see is the bloody head of Mortimer that at the same time he holds, dripping, in his fists. What finally speaks to us in Marlowe's *Edward II* is spectacle – in our mind's eye and in our heart's soul – and, going beyond the approximations of words, it asks us to decipher what this history means as it mirrors the England of Elizabeth I.

FURTHER READING

Belt, Debra, "Anti-Theatricalism and Rhetoric in Marlowe's *Edward II*," *English Literary Renaissance* 21:2 (Spring 1991): 134–60.

Bredbeck, Gregory W., *Sodomy and Interpretation: Marlowe to Milton*. Ithaca, NY: Cornell University Press, 1991.

Cole, Douglas, *Suffering and Evil in the Plays of Christopher Marlowe*. Princeton: Princeton University Press, 1962.

Comensoli, Viviana, "Homophobia and the Regulation of Desire: A Psychoanalytic Reading of Marlowe's *Edward II*," *Journal of the History of Sexuality* 4:2 (October 1993): 175–200.

Friedenreich, Kenneth, Roma Gill, and Constance B. Kuriyama, eds., *"A Poet and a Filthy Play-maker": New Essays on Christopher Marlowe*, esp. essays by Deats and Summers. New York: AMS Press, 1988.

Grantley, Darryll and Peter Roberts, eds., *Christopher Marlowe and English Renaissance Culture*. Aldershot: Scolar Press, 1996.

McElroy, John F., "Repetition, Contrariety, and Individualization in *Edward II*," *Studies in English Literature 1500–1900* 24:2 (Spring 1984): 205–24.

Thurn, David H., "Sovereignty, Disorder, and Fetishism in Marlowe's *Edward II*," *Renaissance Drama* n.s. 21 (1990): 115–41.

Voss, James, "*Edward II*: Marlowe's Historical Tragedy," *English Studies* 63:6 (December 1982): 517–30.

The Troublesome Reign and Lamentable Death of Edward the Second

[*DRAMATIS PERSONAE*

King Edward the Second
Prince Edward, *his son, afterwards* King Edward the Third
Edmund, Earl of Kent, *brother of* King Edward the Second
Pierce of Gaveston, Earl of Cornwall
Guy, Earl of Warwick
Thomas, Earl of Lancaster
Aymer de Valence, Earl of Pembroke
Edmund Fitzalan, Earl of Arundel
Henry, Earl of Leicester
Sir Thomas Berkeley
Mortimer Senior (Roger Mortimer of Chirke)
Mortimer Junior (Roger Mortimer of Wigmore), *nephew of* Mortimer Senior, *afterwards Lord Protector over* Edward the Third
Spencer Senior (Hugh le Despenser), Earl of Winchester
Spencer Junior (Hugh le Despenser), Earl of Wiltshire, *later* Earl of Gloucester, *son of* Spencer Senior
The Archbishop of Canterbury (Walter Reynolds)
The Bishop of Coventry (Walter Langton)
The Bishop of Winchester (John Stratford)
Robert Baldock, *a clerk, attendant on* Lady Margaret de Clare
Henry de Beaumont, *a follower of the King*
Sir William Trussel
Sir Thomas Gurney (Gournay), Sir John Matrevis (Maltravers) } *henchmen of* Mortimer Junior
Lightborn, *a murderer*
Sir John of Hainault, *brother of the* Marquis of Hainault
Levune, *a Frenchman*
Rice ap Howell
The Abbot (of Neath)
James, *one of* Pembroke's *men*
Three Poor Men
A Chaplain
The Clerk of the Crown
A Guard

A Post from Scotland
A Post from France
The Mayor of Bristol
A Messenger
A Horse-Boy
A Herald
A Mower
The King's Champion

Queen Isabella, *wife of* Edward the Second, *daughter (and now sister) of the* King of France (Philip IV; Charles IV)
Lady Margaret de Clare, *daughter of the* Earl of Gloucester, *niece of* King Edward the Second, *betrothed to* Gaveston
Lords, Ladies in Waiting, Soldiers, Attendants, Monks, Servants

The Scene: *England, France*.]

Act I

[I.i]

Enter Gaveston *reading on a letter that was brought him from the King.*

Gaveston. "My father is deceased; come, Gaveston,
And share the kingdom with thy dearest friend."
Ah, words that make me surfeit with delight!
What greater bliss can hap to Gaveston
Than live and be the favorite of a king?
Sweet Prince, I come. These, these thy amorous lines
Might have enforced me to have swum from France,
And, like Leander, gasped upon the sand,
So thou wouldst smile and take me in thy arms.
The sight of London to my exiled eyes
Is as Elysium to a new-come soul;
Not that I love the city or the men,
But that it harbors him I hold so dear –
The King, upon whose bosom let me die,
And with the world be still at enmity.
What need the arctic people love star-light
To whom the sun shines both by day and night?
Farewell, base stooping to the lordly peers;
My knee shall bow to none but to the King.
As for the multitude, that are but sparks
Raked up in embers of their poverty,
Tanti! I'll fan first on the wind

TEXTUAL VARIANTS

Title] Q adds "King of England, with the Tragical Fall of Proud Mortimer, as it was sundry times publicly acted in the honorable city of London by the right honorable the Earl of Pembroke his servants" ***Dramatis Personae*** Berkeley] spelled "Bartley" in Q Archbishop of Canterbury] "Bishop" of Canterbury in Q **I.i.199** accursed] Q accurst **I.ii.29** We'd] Q We'ld haul] Q hale **77–8**] Q gives these lines to Mortimer Junior **I.iv.71** among] Q amongst **102** make] Q may **144 s.d.**] Q reads "Enter Edmund and Queen Isabella" **205** shipwrecked] Q shipwrack **237** aye] Q I **284** mushroom] Q mushrump **392** Hylas] Q Hercules **II.i.1**] Q has a six-foot line here **38** closed] Q close **72 s.d.**] Q s.d. at line 71 **II.ii.2** wrecked] Q wracked **69** Edmund] Q assigns line to Edward **82** Edward] Q assigns line to Pembroke **91** haul] Q hale **115** pounds] Q pound **143** thoroughout] throughout **162** drove] Q drave **174** burned] Q burnt **200** life's] Q lives **203** Edward] Q changes prefix to Kent **234** while] Q whilst **II.iii**] Q uses speech prefix of Kent for Edmund throughout **II.iv.1 s.d.**] Q adds "and to them, Gaveston" **16 s.d.**] Q adds "Exeunt omnes manet Isabella" **26** hauling] Q haling **III.i.58 s.d.** Levune] Q reads Lewne throughout **89 s.d.** Arundel] Q Matre (continues throughout scene) **106** Spoke] Q Spake **108** bespoke] Q bespake **120** Strike] Q Strake **151, 156** Herald] Q uses prefix "Messenger" **IV.iii.10 s.d.** Arundel] Q Matre (continues throughout scene) **11**] Later editors have inserted a nonauthorial passage ultimately from Holinshed as phrased by Leo Kirschbaum to give Spencer Junior something to read, as follows:

[*Spencer Junior.* "The Lord William Tuchet, the Lord William Fitzwilliam, the Lord Warren de Lisle, the Lord Henry Bradborne, and the Lord William Chenie, Barons, with John Page, an esquire, were drawn and hanged at Pomfret.

"And then shortly after, Roger Lord Clifford, John Lord Mowbray, and Sir Gosein d'Eevill, Barons, were drawn and hanged at York.

"At Bristol in like manner were executed Sir Henry de Willington and Sir Henry Montford, Baronets.

"And at Gloucester, the Lord John Gifford and Sir William Elmebridge, Knight.

"And at London, the Lord Henry Teies, Baron.

"At Winchelsea, Sir Thomas Culpepper, Knight.

"At Windsor, the Lord Francis de Aldham, Baron.

"And at Canterbury, the Lord Bartholomew de Badelismere and the Lord Bartholomew de Ashbornham, Barons.

"Also at Cardiff, in Wales, Sir William Fleming, Knight, was executed.

"Divers were executed in their counties, as Sir Thomas Mandit and others."]

IV.iv.22 wreak] Q wrack **IV.vii.63** glower] Q lower **V.i.32** While] Q Whilst **86** while] Q whilst **112**] Q has s.d. "Enter Berkeley" Bishop] Q reads Berkeley **V.ii.9** grip] Q gripe gripped] Q griped **62** cursedly] Q curstly **V.iii.57** grip] Q gripe **V.iv.33** while] Q whilst **104** haul] Q hale **105 s.d.** haul] Q hale

Playsource

Edward II relies principally on the account of the reign of Edward II in Holinshed's *Chronicle*, with some additional material from Robert Fabyan's *Chronicle* (1559), from which Marlowe took the Scottish "jig" quoted by Lancaster; John Stow's *Chronicles of England* (1580), which tells about Edward washed and shaved in puddle water; and Richard Grafton's *Chronicle* (1569). In addition, the murderer at the conclusion of the play *Thomas of Woodstock* may have suggested Marlowe's creation of Lightborn. The central concern with the ability of rule is similar to that of other chronicle history plays popular at the time of *Edward II*, while the idea of homosexuality may have been suggested by the career of Henry III of France, who was assassinated in 1587, shortly before Marlowe's play.

I.i.1 My father Edward I
3 surfeit indulge
4 hap befall
7 France Gaveston had been exiled to his home in Gascony by Edward I
8 Leander tragic hero in Marlowe's poem "Hero and Leander" who swam across the Hellespont to Sestos each night to see his beloved. "I come" (line 6) is from the poem
11 Elysium classical islands of the blessed equivalent to Heaven
14 die (1) swoon; (2) enjoy sexual orgasm
16 love i.e., to love
18 lordly peers nobility
20–1 multitude . . . poverty as opposed to the King who represents the sun to Gaveston
22 *Tanti* "So much for them"; **I'll** I would as soon; **fan . . . wind** to stir the embers or the poor whom he thinks he can thus easily control

That glanceth at my lips and flieth away.
But how now, what are these?

Enter three Poor Men.

Poor Men. Such as desire your worship's service.
Gaveston. What canst thou do?
1 Poor Man. I can ride.
Gaveston. But I have no horses. What art thou?
2 Poor Man. A traveler.
Gaveston. Let me see; thou wouldst do well
To wait at my trencher and tell me lies
At dinner time, and, as I like your discoursing,
I'll have you. And what art thou?
3 Poor Man. A soldier that hath served against the Scot.
Gaveston. Why, there are hospitals for such as you.
I have no war, and therefore, sir, be gone.
3 Poor Man. Farewell, and perish by a soldier's hand, [*Offers to leave.*]
That wouldst reward them with a hospital.
Gaveston. [*Aside.*] Aye, aye. These words of his move me as much
As if a goose should play the porcupine,
And dart her plumes, thinking to pierce my breast;
But yet it is no pain to speak men fair.
I'll flatter these and make them live in hope.
[*To them.*] You know that I came lately out of France,
And yet I have not viewed my Lord the King.
If I speed well, I'll entertain you all.
Poor Men. We thank your worship.
Gaveston. I have some business; leave me to myself.
Poor Men. We will wait here about the court. *Exeunt.*
Gaveston. Do. These are not men for me;
I must have wanton poets, pleasant wits,
Musicians that, with touching of a string,
May draw the pliant King which way I please.
Music and poetry is his delight;
Therefore, I'll have Italian masques by night,
Sweet speeches, comedies, and pleasing shows;
And in the day, when he shall walk abroad,
Like sylvan nymphs my pages shall be clad,
My men, like satyrs grazing on the lawns,
Shall with their goat-feet dance an antic hay.
Sometime a lovely boy in Dian's shape,
With hair that gilds the water as it glides,
Crownets of pearl about his naked arms,
And in his sportful hands an olive tree
To hide those parts which men delight to see,
Shall bathe him in a spring; and there, hard by,
One like Actaeon, peeping through the grove,
Shall by the angry goddess be transformed,
And, running in the likeness of an hart,
By yelping hounds pulled down, and seem to die.
Such things as these best please His Majesty,
My Lord. Here comes the King and the nobles
From the Parliament. I'll stand aside. [*Walks apart.*]

Enter [Edward] *the* King, [*the* Earl of] Lancaster, Mortimer Senior, Mortimer Junior, Edmund Earl of Kent, Guy Earl of Warwick, [*and others*].

Edward. Lancaster.
Lancaster. My Lord?
Gaveston. [*Aside.*] That Earl of Lancaster do I abhor.
Edward. Will you not grant me this? [*Aside.*] In spite of them
I'll have my will; and these two Mortimers
That cross me thus shall know I am displeased.
Mortimer Senior. If you love us, my Lord, hate Gaveston.
Gaveston. [*Aside.*] That villain Mortimer! I'll be his death.
Mortimer Junior. Mine uncle here, this earl, and I myself

25 **s.d. three Poor Men** Marlowe is attracted to characters both realistic and emblematic; cf. the Mower at IV.vii.29
31 **trencher** wooden plate; **lies** i.e., exaggerated travelers' tales
32 **as** if
34 **soldier . . . Scot** the English under Edward I were fighting the Scots army led by Robert the Bruce
35 **hospitals** workhouses
41 **dart . . . plumes** refers to common belief that porcupines shot their quills against the enemy in self-defense
46 **speed** succeed; **entertain** take into service
51 **wanton** lascivious; **pleasant wits** enjoyable companions
53 **pliant** easily influenced
55 **Italian masques** anachronistic; elaborate Elizabethan entertainments with music and dance thought to originate in Italy
57 **abroad** outdoors
58 **sylvan nymphs** female wood spirits
59 **satyrs** reveling creatures of Bacchus part-human and part-goat
60 **antic** grotesque, possibly obscene; **hay** country dance with a serpent-like movement
61 **Dian's** Diana as goddess of the moon was associated with chastity
62 **gilds** makes golden in color
63 **Crownets** bracelets
64 **sportful** playful
66 **hard** near
67–70 **Actaeon . . . die** in classical mythology Diana caught Actaeon watching her as she bathed naked and punished him by transforming him into a stag who was hunted down and killed by his own dogs
70 **die** pun on sexual orgasm
79 **cross** oppose

Were sworn to your father at his death
That he should ne'er return into the realm;
And know, my Lord, ere I will break my oath,
This sword of mine that should offend your foes
Shall sleep within the scabbard at thy need,
And underneath thy banners march who will,
For Mortimer will hang his armor up.

Gaveston. [*Aside.*] *Mort Dieu!*

Edward. Well, Mortimer, I'll make thee rue these words.
Beseems it thee to contradict thy King?
Frown'st thou thereat, aspiring Lancaster?
The sword shall plane the furrows of thy brows
And hew these knees that now are grown so stiff.
I will have Gaveston, and you shall know
What danger 'tis to stand against your King.

Gaveston. [*Aside.*] Well done, Ned.

Lancaster. My Lord, why do you thus incense your peers,
That naturally would love and honor you
But for that base and obscure Gaveston?
Four earldoms have I besides Lancaster –
Derby, Salisbury, Lincoln, Leicester;
These will I sell to give my soldiers pay
Ere Gaveston shall stay within the realm.
Therefore, if he be come, expel him straight.

Edmund. Barons and Earls, your pride hath made me mute,
But now I'll speak – and to the proof, I hope:
I do remember, in my father's days,
Lord Percy of the north, being highly moved,
Braved Mowbray in presence of the King,
For which, had not His Highness loved him well,
He should have lost his head; but with his look
The undaunted spirit of Percy was appeased,
And Mowbray and he were reconciled.
Yet dare you brave the King unto his face?
Brother, revenge it; and let these their heads
Preach upon poles for trespass of their tongues.

Warwick. Oh, our heads!

Edward. Aye, yours; and therefore I would wish you grant –

Warwick. Bridle thy anger, gentle Mortimer.

Mortimer Junior. I cannot nor I will not; I must speak.
Cousin, our hands, I hope, shall fence our heads,
And strike off his that makes you threaten us.
Come, uncle, let us leave the brainsick King,
And henceforth parley with our naked swords.

Mortimer Senior. Wiltshire hath men enough to save our heads.

Warwick. [*Sarcastically.*] All Warwickshire will love him for my sake.

Lancaster. [*With like irony.*] And northward Gaveston hath many friends.
Adieu, my Lord, and either change your mind,
Or look to see the throne where you should sit
To float in blood, and at thy wanton head
The glozing head of thy base minion thrown.

Exeunt Nobles [*except* Edmund].

Edward. I cannot brook these haughty menaces;
Am I a king and must be overruled?
Brother, display my ensigns in the field.
I'll bandy with the Barons and the Earls,
And either die, or live with Gaveston.

Gaveston. [*Coming forward.*] I can no longer keep me from my Lord.

[*Kneels.*]

Edward. What, Gaveston! Welcome! Kiss not my hand;
Embrace me, Gaveston, as I do thee.
Why shouldst thou kneel? Knowest thou not who I am?
Thy friend, thy self, another Gaveston!
Not Hylas was more mourned of Hercules
Than thou hast been of me since thy exile.

---

90 ***Mort Dieu*** "by God's death" (a common French oath referring to the crucifixion, perhaps to note Gaveston's foreignness; later Latin is used to characterize English nobility)

91 **rue** regret

92 **Beseems it** is it fitting for

98 **Ned** affectionate, familiar name for King Edward

101 **base** low-born; **obscure** lowly

108 **to the proof** irrefutably

110 **moved** angry

111 **Braved** challenged

118 **Preach . . . poles** traitors' heads were publicly displayed after their execution as a warning to others

120 **grant** assent

123 **Cousin** contemptuous use of a common term of familiarity and relationship or close friendship; **fence** protect

126 **parley** speak; negotiate; determine

127 **Wiltshire** perhaps a misreading of Welschery; Mortimer Senior was Lieutenant and Justice of Wales; the older Mortimer was "of Chirk" in Denbeigh, the younger Mortimer "of Wigmore" in Hereford

129 **many friends** Lancaster's point is that Gaveston is friendless

133 **glozing** flattering; **minion** (1) servant; (2) homosexual favorite

134 **brook** endure

136 **ensigns** military banners; **the field** field of battle

137 **bandy** take and give blows

144 **Hylas . . . Hercules** close companions on the journey with the Argonauts, Hercules remained on Mysia to find Hylas after he was abducted by water nymphs

Gaveston. And since I went from hence, no soul in hell
Hath felt more torment than poor Gaveston.
Edward. I know it. [*To Edmund.*] Brother, welcome home my friend.
[*To Gaveston.*] Now let the treacherous Mortimers conspire,
And that high-minded Earl of Lancaster.
I have my wish in that I joy thy sight,
And sooner shall the sea o'erwhelm my land
Than bear the ship that shall transport thee hence.
I here create thee Lord High Chamberlain,
Chief Secretary to the state and me,
Earl of Cornwall, King and Lord of Man.
Gaveston. My Lord, these titles far exceed my worth.
Edmund. Brother, the least of these may well suffice
For one of greater birth than Gaveston.
Edward. Cease, brother, for I cannot brook these words.
[*To Gaveston.*] Thy worth, sweet friend, is far above my gifts;
Therefore to equal it, receive my heart.
If for these dignities thou be envied,
I'll give thee more; for but to honor thee
Is Edward pleased with kingly regiment.
Fear'st thou thy person? Thou shalt have a guard.
Wants thou gold? Go to my treasury.
Wouldst thou be loved and feared? Receive my seal.
Save or condemn, and in our name command
Whatso thy mind affects or fancy likes.
Gaveston. It shall suffice me to enjoy your love,
Which whiles I have, I think myself as great
As Caesar riding in the Roman street
With captive kings at his triumphant car.

Enter the Bishop of Coventry.

Edward. Whither goes my Lord of Coventry so fast?
Bishop. To celebrate your father's exequies.
But is that wicked Gaveston returned?
Edward. Aye, priest, and lives to be revenged on thee
That were the only cause of his exile.
Gaveston. 'Tis true; and but for reverence of these robes
Thou should'st not plod one foot beyond this place.
Bishop. I did no more than I was bound to do,
And Gaveston, unless thou be reclaimed,
As then I did incense the Parliament,
So will I now, and thou shalt back to France.
Gaveston. Saving your reverence, you must pardon me.
[*Manhandles Bishop.*]
Edward. Throw off his golden miter, rend his stole
And in the channel christen him anew.
Edmund. Ah brother, lay not violent hands on him,
For he'll complain unto the See of Rome.
Gaveston. Let him complain unto the see of hell;
I'll be revenged on him for my exile.
Edward. [*To Gaveston.*] No, spare his life, but seize upon his goods.
Be thou Lord Bishop and receive his rents,
And make him serve thee as thy chaplain.
I give him thee; here, use him as thou wilt.
Gaveston. He shall to prison, and there die in bolts.
Edward. Aye, to the Tower, the Fleet, or where thou wilt.
Bishop. For this offense be thou accursed of God.
Edward. Who's there?
[*Calls attendants offstage.*]
Convey this priest to the Tower.
Bishop. True, true!
[*Exit guarded.*]
Edward. But in the meantime, Gaveston, away,
And take possession of his house and goods.
Come, follow me, and thou shalt have my guard
To see it done and bring thee safe again.

---

150 **high-minded** arrogant
154 **Lord High Chamberlain** chief officer of government
156 **King . . . Man** rulers of the Isle of Man were called kings
163 **dignities** titles
165 **regiment** rules
168 **seal** sign of royal authority, often on a ring; this could visually resemble a marriage ceremony
170 **affects** desires
174 **triumphant car** chariot
176 **exequies** funeral rights
177 **wicked** evil
183 **reclaimed** reformed morally
184 **incense** incite
186 **Saving . . . me** (formula of obedience here used sarcastically)
187 **golden miter** church symbol of office uncommon after the Reformation; **stole** ecclesiastical vestment
188 **channel** gutter; open drain (cf. Edward at V.v.3); **christen . . . anew** give him a new name (since he is no longer a bishop)
190 **See of Rome** i.e., the Pope
194 **rents** (1) revenues from church property; (2) taxes levied by the church
197 **bolts** fetters
198 **Fleet** London prison then used exclusively for debtors
199 **accursed** damned
200 **Tower** Tower of London where traitors were incarcerated; **True, true** ironic; the Bishop assigns the common meaning of "steal" to Edward's "convey"
203 **guard** (1) soldiers; (2) protection

Gaveston. What should a priest do with so fair a house?
A prison may beseem His Holiness.
[*Exeunt.*]

[I.ii]

Enter both the Mortimers [*on one side*], Warwick *and* Lancaster [*on the other*].

Warwick. 'Tis true, the Bishop is in the Tower,
And goods and body given to Gaveston.
Lancaster. What! Will they tyrannize upon the Church?
Ah, wicked King! Accursèd Gaveston!
This ground which is corrupted with their steps
Shall be their timeless sepulcher, or mine.
Mortimer Junior. Well, let that peevish Frenchman guard him sure;
Unless his breast be sword-proof, he shall die.
Mortimer Senior. How now, why droops the Earl of Lancaster?
Mortimer Junior. Wherefore is Guy of Warwick discontent?
Lancaster. That villain Gaveston is made an earl.
Mortimer Senior. An earl!
Warwick. Aye, and besides Lord Chamberlain of the realm,
And Secretary too, and Lord of Man.
Mortimer Senior. We may not, nor we will not suffer this.
Mortimer Junior. Why post we not from hence to levy men?
Lancaster. "My Lord of Cornwall" now at every word;
And happy is the man whom he vouchsafes,
For vailing of his bonnet, one good look.
Thus, arm in arm, the King and he doth march –
Nay, more, the guard upon his Lordship waits,
And all the court begins to flatter him.
Warwick. Thus, leaning on the shoulder of the King,
He nods, and scorns, and smiles at those that pass.
Mortimer Senior. Doth no man take exceptions at the slave?
Lancaster. All stomach him, but none dare speak a word.
Mortimer Junior. Ah, that bewrays their baseness, Lancaster.
Were all the Earls and Barons of my mind,
We'd haul him from the bosom of the King,
And at the court gate hang the peasant up,
Who, swol'n with venom of ambitious pride,
Will be the ruin of the realm and us.

Enter the [Arch]bishop of Canterbury [*talking to a* Chaplain].

Warwick. Here comes my Lord of Canterbury's Grace.
Lancaster. His countenance bewrays he is displeased.
[*Arch*]*bishop.* [*To Chaplain.*] First were his sacred garments rent and torn;
Then laid they violent hands upon him, next
Himself imprisoned and his goods asseized;
This certify the Pope. Away, take horse!
[*Exit* Chaplain.]
Lancaster. My Lord, will you take arms against the King?
[*Arch*]*bishop.* What need I? God himself is up in arms
When violence is offered to the Church.
Mortimer Junior. Then will you join with us that be his peers
To banish or behead that Gaveston?
[*Arch*]*bishop.* What else, my Lords? for it concerns me near;
The bishopric of Coventry is his.

Enter [Isabella] *the* Queen.

Mortimer Junior. Madam, whither walks Your Majesty so fast?
Queen. Unto the forest, gentle Mortimer,
To live in grief and baleful discontent;
For now my Lord the King regards me not,
But dotes upon the love of Gaveston.
He claps his cheeks and hangs about his neck,
Smiles in his face and whispers in his ears,

205 **fair** fine; Elizabethans would appreciate this anti-papist jibe
206 **beseem** be more suitable to
I.ii.3 **tyrannize** by imprisoning the Bishop, Edward usurps church authority
6 **timeless** (1) eternal; (2) untimely, early
7 **peevish** foolish; **him** i.e., himself
11 **villain** (1) scoundrel; (2) pun on *villein*, serf or bondman
14 **Lord of Man** i.e., of the Isle of Man
15 **suffer** tolerate
16 **post** hasten; **men** soldiers
19 **vailing** doffing, tipping
26 **stomach** resent
27 **bewrays** reveals
37 **asseized** taken forcefully
38 **certify** inform
44 **near** (1) deeply; (2) personally; as a Bishop, Gaveston is a direct concern of the Archbishop
45 **bishopric** diocese
47 **forest** wastelands (metaphorically)
48 **baleful** wretched
51 **claps** pats affectionately

And when I come, he frowns, as who should say
"Go whither thou wilt, seeing I have Gaveston."

Mortimer Senior. Is it not strange that he is thus bewitched?

Mortimer Junior. Madam, return unto the court again.
That sly inveigling Frenchman we'll exile,
Or lose our lives; and yet, ere that day come,
The King shall lose his crown, for we have power,
And courage too, to be revenged at full.

[Arch]bishop. But yet lift not your swords against the King.

Lancaster. No, but we'll lift Gaveston from hence.

Warwick. And war must be the means, or he'll stay still.

Queen. Then let him stay; for rather than my Lord
Shall be oppressed by civil mutinies,
I will endure a melancholy life,
And let him frolic with his minion.

[Arch]bishop. My Lords, to ease all this, but hear me speak:
We and the rest that are his counselors
Will meet, and with a general consent
Confirm his banishment with our hands and seals.

Lancaster. What we confirm the King will frustrate.

Mortimer Junior. Then may we lawfully revolt from him.

Warwick. But say, my Lord, where shall this meeting be?

[Arch]bishop. At the New Temple.

Mortimer Junior. Content.

Canterbury. And in the meantime I'll entreat you all
To cross to Lambeth, and there stay with me.

Lancaster. Come then, let's away.

Mortimer Junior. Madam, farewell.

Queen. Farewell, sweet Mortimer; and, for my sake,
Forbear to levy arms against the King.

Mortimer Junior. Aye, if words will serve; if not, I must.

[*Exeunt severally.*]

[I.iii]

Enter Gaveston *and* [Edmund] *the* Earl of Kent.

Gaveston. Edmund, the mighty prince of Lancaster,
That hath more earldoms than an ass can bear,
And both the Mortimers, two goodly men,
With Guy of Warwick, that redoubted knight,
Are gone towards Lambeth. There let them remain.

Exeunt.

[I.iv]

Enter Nobles [Lancaster, Warwick, Pembroke, Mortimer Senior, Mortimer Junior, *and the* Archbishop of Canterbury, *attended*].

Lancaster. Here is the form of Gaveston's exile;
May it please your Lordship to subscribe your name.

[Arch]bishop. Give me the paper.

Lancaster. Quick, quick, my lord;
I long to write my name.

[*Canterbury and the others after him subscribe.*]

Warwick. But I long more to see him banished hence.

Mortimer Junior. The name of Mortimer shall fright the King,
Unless he be declined from that base peasant.

Enter [Edward] *the* King, *and* Gaveston [*and* Edmund. Edward *seats* Gaveston *beside him on the throne*].

Edward. What? Are you moved that Gaveston sits here?
It is our pleasure; we will have it so.

Lancaster. Your Grace doth well to place him by your side,
For nowhere else the new Earl is so safe.

Mortimer Senior. What man of noble birth can brook this sight?
Quam male conveniunt!

---

57 **inveigling** deceiving
62 **lift** (1) steal; (2) raise by hanging
63 **still** forever
66 **melancholy** (1) sad; (2) solitary
67 **frolic . . . minion** (implication is sexual with one he has procured)
72 **frustrate** annul, defeat
75 **New Temple** quarters of the Knights Templar in Holborn; Edward II gave it to Spencer in 1324 according to Holinshed; in Edward II's time, the site of frequent disputes between the crown and wealthy subjects
78 **Lambeth** Lambeth Palace, the London house of the Archbishop of Canterbury
I.iii.4 redoubted feared
I.iv.s.d. Nobles and **Barons** are used interchangeably throughout the play
1 **form** document
7 **declined** turned aside
8 **s.d. *beside*** i.e., in the position reserved for the Queen
8 **moved** (1) surprised; (2) shocked
9 **pleasure** (1) will; (2) joy with erotic overtones
13 ***Quam . . . conveniunt!*** "How badly they go together!"

See what a scornful look the peasant casts.
Pembroke. Can kingly lions fawn on creeping ants?
Warwick. Ignoble vassal, that like Phaethon
Aspir'st unto the guidance of the sun.
Mortimer Junior. Their downfall is at hand, their forces down.
We will not thus be faced and over-peered.
Edward. Lay hands on that traitor Mortimer!
Mortimer Senior. Lay hands on that traitor Gaveston!
[*They draw their swords.*]
Edmund. Is this the duty that you owe your King?
Warwick. We know our duties; let him know his peers.
[*They seize Gaveston.*]
Edward. Whither will you bear him? Stay, or ye shall die.
Mortimer Senior. We are no traitors; therefore, threaten not.
Gaveston. No, threaten not, my Lord, but pay them home.
Were I a king –
Mortimer Junior. Thou villain, wherefore talks thou of a king,
That hardly art a gentleman by birth?
Edward. Were he a peasant, being my minion,
I'll make the proudest of you stoop to him.
Lancaster. My Lord, you may not thus disparage us.
Away, I say, with hateful Gaveston.
Mortimer Senior. And with the Earl of Kent that favors him.
[*Exeunt* Edmund *and* Gaveston *guarded.*]
Edward. Nay, then, lay violent hands upon your King.
Here, Mortimer, sit thou in Edward's throne;
Warwick and Lancaster, wear you my crown.
Was ever king thus overruled as I?
Lancaster. Learn then to rule us better and the realm.
Mortimer Junior. What we have done, our heart-blood shall maintain.
Warwick. Think you that we can brook this upstart pride?
Edward. Anger and wrathful fury stops my speech.
[*Arch*]*bishop.* Why are you moved? Be patient, my Lord,
And see what we your counselors have done.
[*Gives Edward the document of Gaveston's exile.*]
Mortimer Junior. My Lords, now let us all be resolute,
And either have our wills or lose our lives.
Edward. Meet you for this, proud overdaring peers?
Ere my sweet Gaveston shall part from me,
This isle shall fleet upon the ocean
And wander to the unfrequented Inde.
[*Arch*]*bishop.* You know that I am legate to the Pope;
On your allegiance to the see of Rome,
Subscribe as we have done to his exile.
Mortimer Junior. [*To Archbishop.*] Curse him if he refuse, and then may we
Depose him and elect another king.
Edward. Aye, there it goes; but yet I will not yield.
Curse me. Depose me. Do the worst you can.
Lancaster. Then linger not, my Lord, but do it straight.
[*Arch*]*bishop.* Remember how the Bishop was abused;
Either banish him that was the cause thereof,
Or I will presently discharge these Lords
Of duty and allegiance due to thee.
Edward. [*Aside.*] It boots me not to threat; I must speak fair.
The legate of the Pope will be obeyed.
[*To Archbishop.*] My Lord, you shall be Chancellor of the realm;
Thou, Lancaster, High Admiral of our fleet.
Young Mortimer and his uncle shall be Earls,
And you, Lord Warwick, President of the North,
[*To Pembroke.*] And thou of Wales. If this content you not,
Make several kingdoms of this monarchy,
And share it equally among you all,
So I may have some nook or corner left
To frolic with my dearest Gaveston.
[*Arch*]*bishop.* Nothing shall alter us; we are resolved.
Lancaster. Come, come, subscribe.

---

14 scornful contemptuous; superior
16 vassal slave; **Phaethon** in classical mythology, the son of Apollo who against commands drove his father's chariot too near the sun and caused much destruction on earth before being destroyed by Jupiter; proverbial for overweening ambition
19 faced outfaced, bullied; **over-peered** be given superiors; Marlowe is fond of compounds, often neologisms of his own making
24 bear take
26 pay them home chastize them
32 disparage degrade, vilify
50 Inde (1) India; (2) East Indies (metaphorically, to the ends of the earth)
51 legate official representative
54 Curse excommunicate
58 straight at once
61–2 discharge . . . thee subjects of excommunicated rulers were absolved of obedience to them
63 boots avails

Mortimer Junior. Why should you love him whom the world hates so?
Edward. Because he loves me more than all the world.
Ah, none but rude and savage-minded men
Would seek the ruin of my Gaveston.
You that be noble-born should pity him.
Warwick. You that are princely born should shake him off.
For shame subscribe, and let the lown depart.
Mortimer Senior. Urge him, my Lord.
[Arch]bishop. Are you content to banish him the realm?
Edward. I see I must, and therefore am content;
Instead of ink, I'll write it with my tears.
[*Subscribes.*]
Mortimer Junior. The King is lovesick for his minion.
Edward. 'Tis done, and now, accursèd hand, fall off.
Lancaster. Give it me; I'll have it published in the streets.
Mortimer Junior. I'll see him presently dispatched away.
[Arch]bishop. Now is my heart at ease.
Warwick. And so is mine.
Pembroke. This will be good news to the common sort.
Mortimer Senior. Be it or no, he shall not linger here.
Exeunt Nobles [*and all except* Edward].
Edward. How fast they run to banish him I love!
They would not stir, were it to do me good.
Why should a king be subject to a priest?
Proud Rome, that hatchest such imperial grooms,
For these thy superstitious taper-lights,
Wherewith thy antichristian churches blaze,
I'll fire thy crazèd buildings and enforce
The papal towers to kiss the lowly ground,
With slaughtered priests make Tiber's channel swell,
And banks raised higher with their sepulchers.
As for the peers that back the clergy thus,
If I be King, not one of them shall live.

Enter Gaveston.

Gaveston. My Lord, I hear it whispered everywhere
That I am banished and must fly the land.
Edward. 'Tis true, sweet Gaveston. Oh, were it false!
The legate of the Pope will have it so,
And thou must hence, or I shall be deposed.
But I will reign to be revenged of them,
And therefore, sweet friend, take it patiently.
Live where thou wilt. I'll send thee gold enough.
And long thou shalt not stay; or if thou dost,
I'll come to thee. My love shall ne'er decline.
Gaveston. Is all my hope turned to this hell of grief?
Edward. Rend not my heart with thy too-piercing words.
Thou from this land, I from my self am banished.
Gaveston. To go from hence grieves not poor Gaveston,
But to forsake you, in whose gracious looks
The blessedness of Gaveston remains,
For nowhere else seeks he felicity.
Edward. And only this torments my wretched soul
That, whether I will or no, thou must depart.
Be governor of Ireland in my stead,
And there abide till fortune call thee home.
Here, take my picture, and let me wear thine;
[*They exchange miniature portraits.*]
Oh, might I keep thee here, as I do this,
Happy were I – but now, most miserable!
Gaveston. 'Tis something to be pitied of a king.
Edward. [*Suddenly decisive.*] Thou shalt not hence;
I'll hide thee, Gaveston.
Gaveston. I shall be found, and then 'twill grieve me more.
Edward. Kind words and mutual talk makes our grief greater;
Therefore, with dumb embracement, let us part –
Stay, Gaveston, I cannot leave thee thus.
Gaveston. For every look my Lord drops down a tear;
Seeing I must go, do not renew my sorrow.
Edward. The time is little that thou hast to stay,
And, therefore, give me leave to look my fill.
But come, sweet friend, I'll bear thee on thy way.

78 rude uncivilized
82 lown peasant
89 published proclaimed
90 presently immediately
92 sort people
97 imperial imperious; **grooms** servants
98 taper-lights (1) vigil candles; (2) candles used for penitential prayers; the attack on the church is anachronistic but consonant with Elizabethan thought and prejudice
100 crazèd (1) cracked; (2) unsound
102 Tiber's channel river in Rome
121 blessedness special happiness
131 hence go
134 dumb silent
140 bear accompany

Gaveston. The peers will frown.
Edward. I pass not for their anger. Come, let's go.
Oh, that we might as well return as go.

Enter Queen Isabella.

Queen. Whither goes my Lord?
Edward. Fawn not on me, French strumpet; get thee gone.
Queen. On whom but on my husband should I fawn?
Gaveston. On Mortimer; with whom, ungentle Queen –
I say no more; judge you the rest, my Lord.
Queen. In saying this, thou wrongst me, Gaveston.
Is't not enough that thou corrupts my Lord,
And art a bawd to his affections,
But thou must call mine honor thus in question?
Gaveston. I mean not so; Your Grace must pardon me.
Edward. Thou art too familiar with that Mortimer,
And by thy means is Gaveston exiled;
But I would wish thee reconcile the Lords,
Or thou shalt ne'er be reconciled to me.
Queen. Your Highness knows it lies not in my power.
Edward. Away then; touch me not. Come, Gaveston.
Queen. [*To Gaveston.*] Villain, 'tis thou that robb'st me of my Lord.
Gaveston. Madam, 'tis you that rob me of my Lord.
Edward. Speak not unto her; let her droop and pine.
Queen. Wherein, my Lord, have I deserved these words?
Witness the tears that Isabella sheds,
Witness this heart, that sighing for thee breaks,
How dear my Lord is to poor Isabel.
Edward. And witness Heaven how dear thou art to me.
There weep; for till my Gaveston be repealed,
Assure thyself thou com'st not in my sight.
Exeunt Edward *and* Gaveston.

Queen. Oh, miserable and distressèd Queen!
Would, when I left sweet France and was embarked,
That charming Circe, walking on the waves,
Had changed my shape, or at the marriage-day
The cup of Hymen had been full of poison,
Or with those arms that twined about my neck
I had been stifled, and not lived to see
The King my Lord thus to abandon me.
Like frantic Juno will I fill the earth
With ghastly murmur of my sighs and cries,
For never doted Jove on Ganymede
So much as he on cursèd Gaveston.
But that will more exasperate his wrath;
I must entreat him, I must speak him fair,
And be a means to call home Gaveston.
And yet he'll ever dote on Gaveston,
And so am I for ever miserable.

Enter the Nobles [Lancaster, Warwick, Pembroke, Mortimer Senior, *and* Mortimer Junior] *to* [Isabella] *the* Queen.

Lancaster. Look where the sister of the King of France
Sits wringing of her hands and beats her breast.
Warwick. The King, I fear, hath ill entreated her.
Pembroke. Hard is the heart that injures such a saint.
Mortimer Junior. I know 'tis 'long of Gaveston she weeps.
Mortimer Senior. Why? He is gone.
Mortimer Junior. Madam, how fares Your Grace?
Queen. Ah, Mortimer, now breaks the King's hate forth,
And he confesseth that he loves me not.
Mortimer Junior. Cry quittance, madam, then; and love not him.
Queen. No, rather will I die a thousand deaths.
And yet, I love in vain. He'll ne'er love me.
Lancaster. Fear ye not, Madam; now his minion's gone,
His wanton humor will be quickly left.
Queen. O never, Lancaster! I am enjoined

142 pass care
144 s.d. Edmund has no lines and so may not enter; but, if he does, what he observes will help to motivate his later acts
145 strumpet loose woman, harlot
147 On Mortimer Gaveston is the first to accuse the Queen of adultery
151 bawd procurer
159 touch (1) come not near me; (2) do not meddle in my affairs
168 repealed recalled from exile
172 Circe witch who transformed men into pigs
174 Hymen as god of marriage
175 those . . . neck (the implication is that Edward here embraces Gaveston)
178–80 Juno . . . Ganymede in classical mythology, Juno became jealous when her husband Jove chose Ganymede as his cupbearer because of the boy's beauty
179 murmur (1) rumor; (2) report
182 exasperate aggravate
183 entreat (1) negotiate; (2) beg; **fair** courteously
185 ever always
189 entreated treated
191 'long of on account of
195 Cry quittance (1) retaliate; (2) renounce the marriage
199 humor mood, disposition
200 enjoined (1) obliged; (2) requested

To sue unto you all for his repeal.
This wills my Lord; and this must I perform,
Or else be banished from His Highess' presence.

Lancaster. For his repeal! Madam, he comes not back,
Unless the sea cast up his shipwrecked body.

Warwick. And to behold so sweet a sight as that
There's none here but would run his horse to death.

Mortimer Junior. But Madam, would you have us call him home?

Queen. Aye, Mortimer, for till he be restored,
The angry King hath banished me the court;
And therefore, as thou lovest and tend'rest me,
Be thou my advocate unto these peers.

Mortimer Junior. What, would ye have me plead for Gaveston?

Mortimer Senior. Plead for him he that will, I am resolved.

Lancaster. And so am I, my Lord; dissuade the Queen.

Queen. Oh, Lancaster, let him dissuade the King,
For 'tis against my will he should return.

Warwick. Then speak not for him. Let the peasant go.

Queen. 'Tis for myself I speak, and not for him.

Pembroke. No speaking will prevail, and therefore cease.

Mortimer Junior. Fair Queen, forbear to angle for the fish
Which, being caught, strikes him that takes it dead –
I mean that vile torpedo, Gaveston,
That now, I hope, floats on the Irish seas.

Queen. Sweet Mortimer, sit down by me awhile,
And I will tell thee reasons of such weight
As thou wilt soon subscribe to his repeal.

Mortimer Junior. It is impossible. But – speak your mind.

Queen. Then thus – but none shall hear it but ourselves.

[*Draws* Mortimer Junior *to a seat apart.*]

Lancaster. My Lords, albeit the Queen with Mortimer,
Will you be resolute and hold with me?

Mortimer Senior. Not I, against my nephew.

Pembroke. Fear not; the Queen's words cannot alter him.

Warwick. No? Do but mark how earnestly she pleads.

Lancaster. And see how coldly his looks make denial.

Warwick. She smiles! Now, for my life, his mind is changed.

Lancaster. I'll rather lose his friendship, aye, than grant.

Mortimer Junior. [*Coming forward.*] Well, of necessity, it must be so.
My Lords, that I abhor base Gaveston
I hope your honors make no question;
And therefore, though I plead for his repeal,
'Tis not for his sake, but for our avail –
Nay, for the realm's behoof and for the King's.

Lancaster. Fie Mortimer, dishonor not thyself!
Can this be true, 'twas good to banish him?
And is this true, to call him home again?
Such reasons make white black and dark night day.

Mortimer Junior. My Lord of Lancaster, mark the respect.

Lancaster. In no respect can contraries be true.

Queen. Yet, good my Lord, hear what he can allege.

Warwick. All that he speaks is nothing. We are resolved.

Mortimer Junior. Do you not wish that Gaveston were dead?

Pembroke. I would he were.

Mortimer Junior. Why then, my Lord, give me but leave to speak.

Mortimer Senior. But nephew, do not play the sophister.

Mortimer Junior. This which I urge is of a burning zeal
To mend the King and do our country good.
Know you not Gaveston hath store of gold
Which may, in Ireland, purchase him such friends
As he will front the mightiest of us all?
And whereas he shall live and be beloved,
'Tis hard for us to work his overthrow.

Warwick. Mark you but that, my Lord of Lancaster.

211 tend'rest care for
223 torpedo sting-ray, a fish known for its wiliness and numbing effect
224 floats sails
226 weight importance
234 mark observe
237 grant assent (to Gaveston's return)
242 avail advantage
243 behoof benefit; welfare
248 respect (1) considerations; (2) circumstances
250 allege urge as reason
255 sophister philosopher who uses fallacious or specious arguments
257 mend reform
260 front confront
262 work effect

Mortimer Junior. But were he here, detested as he is,
How easily might some base slave be suborned
To greet his Lordship with a poniard,
And none so much as blame the murderer,
But rather praise him for that brave attempt,
And in the chronicle enroll his name
For purging of the realm of such a plague.
Pembroke. He saith true.
Lancaster. Aye, but how chance this was not done before?
Mortimer Junior. Because, my Lords, it was not thought upon.
Nay, more, when he shall know it lies in us
To banish him, and then to call him home,
'Twill make him vail the topflag of his pride
And fear to offend the meanest nobleman.
Mortimer Senior. But how if he do not, nephew?
Mortimer Junior. Then may we with some color rise in arms,
For howsoever we have borne it out,
'Tis treason to be up against the King.
So shall we have the people of our side,
Which, for his father's sake, lean to the King
But cannot brook a night-grown mushroom –
Such a one as my Lord of Cornwall is –
Should bear us down of the nobility;
And when the commons and the nobles join,
'Tis not the King can buckler Gaveston;
We'll pull him from the strongest hold he hath.
My Lords, if to perform this I be slack,
Think me as base a groom as Gaveston.
Lancaster. On that condition Lancaster will grant.
Pembroke. And so will Pembroke.
Warwick. And I.
Mortimer Senior. And I.
Mortimer Junior. In this I count me highly gratified,
And Mortimer will rest at your command.
Queen. And when this favor Isabel forgets,
Then let her live abandoned and forlorn.
But see, in happy time, my Lord the King,
Having brought the Earl of Cornwall on his way,
Is new returned. This news will glad him much,
Yet not so much as me. I love him more
Than he can Gaveston; would he loved me
But half so much, then were I treble blessed.

Enter King Edward *mourning, [attended, with* Beaumont *and the* Clerk *of the Crown*].

Edward. He's gone, and for his absence thus I mourn.
Did never sorrow go so near my heart
As doth the want of my sweet Gaveston;
And could my crown's revénue bring him back,
I would freely give it to his enemies
And think I gained, having bought so dear a friend.
Queen. Hark! How he harps upon his minion.
Edward. My heart is as an anvil unto sorrow,
Which beats upon it like the Cyclops' hammers,
And with the noise turns up my giddy brain
And makes me frantic for my Gaveston.
Ah, had some bloodless Fury rose from hell,
And with my kingly scepter struck me dead
When I was forced to leave my Gaveston!
Lancaster. Diablo! What passions call you these?
Queen. My gracious Lord, I come to bring you news.
Edward. That you have parlied with your Mortimer.
Queen. That Gaveston, my Lord, shall be repealed.
Edward. Repealed? The news is too sweet to be true.
Queen. But will you love me if you find it so?
Edward. If it be so, what will not Edward do?
Queen. For Gaveston, but not for Isabel.
Edward. For thee, fair Queen, if thou lov'st Gaveston;
I'll hang a golden tongue about thy neck,
Seeing thou hast pleaded with so good success.
[*Embraces her.*]
Queen. No other jewels hang about my neck
Than these, my Lord; nor let me have more wealth
Than I may fetch from this rich treasury.
[*They kiss.*]

265 **suborned** bribed
266 **poniard** dagger
268 **brave attempt** worthy assault
269 **the chronicle** history
276 **vail the topflag** lower the colors in a naval salute of submitting with respect
277 **meanest** lowest-ranked
279 **color** pretext
280 **borne it out** pretended
282 **of** on
284 **mushroom** upstart (proverbial since mushrooms were thought to spring up overnight)
286 **Should . . . down** overwhelm us
288 **buckler** shield
289 **hold** castle, fortification
291 **groom** servant
312 **Cyclops' hammers** in classical mythology he forged thunderbolts for Vulcan under Mount Etna
313 **up** upside down
315 **Fury** in classical mythology the Furies, who lived in the underworld, punished wrongdoers
318 ***Diablo!*** "The devil!" (Spanish)
320 **parlied** negotiated
330 **these** i.e., Edward's arms (in embrace)

Oh, how a kiss revives poor Isabel!
Edward. Once more receive my hand, and let this be
A second marriage 'twixt thyself and me.
Queen. And may it prove more happy than the first.
My gentle Lord, bespeak these nobles fair
That wait attendance for a gracious look
And on their knees salute Your Majesty.
[*Nobles kneel.*]
Edward. Courageous Lancaster, embrace thy King,
And as gross vapors perish by the sun,
Even so let hatred with Thy Sovereign's smile:
Live thou with me as my companion.
Lancaster. This salutation overjoys my heart.
Edward. Warwick shall be my chiefest counselor:
These silver hairs will more adorn my court
Than gaudy silks or rich embroidery.
Chide me, sweet Warwick, if I go astray.
Warwick. Slay me, my Lord, when I offend Your Grace.
Edward. In solemn triumphs and in public shows
Pembroke shall bear the sword before the King.
Pembroke. And with this sword Pembroke will fight for you.
Edward. But wherefore walks young Mortimer aside?
Be thou commander of our royal fleet,
Or if that lofty office like thee not,
I make thee here Lord Marshal of the realm.
Mortimer Junior. My Lord, I'll marshal so your enemies
As England shall be quiet and you safe.
Edward. And as for you, Lord Mortimer of Chirke,
Whose great achievements in our foreign war
Deserves no common place nor mean reward,
Be you the general of the levied troops
That now are ready to assail the Scots.
Mortimer Senior. In this Your Grace hath highly honored me,
For with my nature war doth best agree.
Queen. Now is the King of England rich and strong,
Having the love of his renownèd peers.
Edward. Aye, Isabel, ne'er was my heart so light.
Clerk of the Crown, direct our warrant forth
For Gaveston to Ireland; Beaumont, fly
As fast as Iris or Jove's Mercury.
Beaumont. It shall be done, my gracious Lord.
[*Exit, with* Clerk.]
Edward. [*To Mortimer Junior.*] Lord Mortimer, we leave you to your charge.
Now let us in and feast it royally.
Against our friend the Earl of Cornwall comes
We'll have a general tilt and tournament,
And then his marriage shall be solemnized;
For wot you not that I have made him sure
Unto our cousin, the Earl of Gloucester's heir?
Lancaster. Such news we hear, my Lord.
Edward. That day, if not for him, yet for my sake,
Who in the triumph will be challenger,
Spare for no cost; we will requite your love.
Warwick. In this, or aught, Your Highness shall command us.
Edward. Thanks, gentle Warwick; come, let's in and revel.
Exeunt. [*The* Mortimers *remain.*]
Mortimer Senior. Nephew, I must to Scotland; thou stay'st here.
Leave now to oppose thyself against the King;
Thou seest by nature he is mild and calm,
And seeing his mind so dotes on Gaveston,
Let him without controlment have his will.
The mightiest kings have had their minions:
Great Alexander loved Hephestion;
The conquering Hercules for Hylas wept;
And for Patroclus stern Achilles drooped.
And not kings only, but the wisest men:
The Roman Tully loved Octavius,
Grave Socrates, wild Alcibiades.
Then let His Grace, whose youth is flexible
And promiseth as much as we can wish,
Freely enjoy that vain light-headed Earl,

336 **bespeak** speak to
340 **gross vapors** fog, thick mists
346 **gaudy** ornate
349 **triumphs . . . shows** pageants, processionals
350 **sword** i.e., sword of state
352 **aside** apart
354 **like** please
358 **Chirke** i.e., Mortimer Senior whose estate bordered Shropshire and Wales
360 **mean** stingy
368 **Clerk of the Crown** a chancery office that framed and issued writs
370 **Iris . . . Mercury** messengers for Juno and Jupiter, respectively
374 **Against** until
375 **tilt** joust
377 **wot** know; **sure** betrothed (to distract him from Edward)
378 **Earl . . . heir** i.e., Lady Margaret de Clare
389 **controlment** restraint
391–3 **Alexander . . . Achilles** famous male companions and couples sometimes portrayed as homosexual unions
395 **Tully** Cicero; there is no recorded relationship with Octavius
396 **Socrates . . . Alcibiades** in Plato's *Symposium*, where Socrates argues for homosexual love, as does Alcibiades (who has just enjoyed a liaison)

For riper years will wean him from such toys.
Mortimer Junior. Uncle, his wanton humor grieves not me,
But this I scorn – that one so basely born
Should by his Sovereign's favor grow so pert
And riot it with the treasure of the realm
While soldiers mutiny for want of pay.
He wears a lord's revénue on his back,
And, Midas-like, he jets it in the court
With base outlandish cullions at his heels,
Whose proud fantastic liveries make such show
As if that Proteus, god of shapes, appeared.
I have not seen a dapper jack so brisk;
He wears a short Italian hooded cloak
Larded with pearl, and in his Tuscan cap
A jewel of more value than the crown.
Whiles other walk below, the King and he
From out a window laugh at such as we,
And flout our train and jest at our attire.
Uncle, 'tis this that makes me impatient.
Mortimer Senior. But, nephew, now you see the King is changed.
Mortimer Junior. Then so am I, and live to do him service;
But whiles I have a sword, a hand, a heart,
I will not yield to any such upstart.
You know my mind. Come, uncle, let's away.
Exeunt

Act II

[II.i]

Enter Spencer [Junior] *and* Baldock.

Baldock. Spencer, seeing that our Lord th' Earl of Gloucester's
Dead, Which of the nobles dost thou mean to serve?
Spencer Junior. Not Mortimer, nor any of his side,
Because the King and he are enemies.
Baldock, learn this of me: a factious lord
Shall hardly do himself good, much less us;
But he that hath the favor of a king
May with one word advance us while we live.
The liberal Earl of Cornwall is the man
On whose good fortune Spencer's hope depends.
Baldock. What, mean you then to be his follower?
Spencer Junior. No, his companion; for he loves me well
And would have once preferred me to the King.
Baldock. But he is banished; there's small hope of him.
Spencer Junior. Aye, for a while; but Baldock, mark the end:
A friend of mine told me in secrecy
That he's repealed and sent for back again;
And even now, a post came from the court
With letters to our Lady from the King,
And as she read, she smiled, which makes me think
It is about her lover, Gaveston.
Baldock. 'Tis like enough, for since he was exiled,
She neither walks abroad nor comes in sight.
But I had thought the match had been broke off
And that his banishment had changed her mind.
Spencer Junior. Our Lady's first love is not wavering;
My life for thine, she will have Gaveston.
Baldock. Then hope I by her means to be preferred,
Having read unto her since she was a child.
Spencer Junior. Then, Baldock, you must cast the scholar off
And learn to court it like a gentleman.
'Tis not a black coat and a little band,
A velvet-caped cloak, faced before with serge,
And smelling to a nosegay all the day,

400 **toys** trifles, pastimes
403 **pert** impudent
406 **revénue** annual income
407 **Midas-like** as if made of gold; Midas, King of Phrygia, found everything he touched turned to gold; **jets** struts
408 **outlandish** foreign; **cullions** low fellows
409 **fantastic liveries** extravagant uniforms
410 **Proteus** sea god who could change shapes
411 **dapper jack** fashionable gentleman; **brisk** smartly dressed
412–15 **short . . . below** these Italian fashions were often thought to be effeminate and worn especially by homosexuals
413 **Larded** encrusted
417 **flout** mock; **train** attendants
II.i.1 **Earl of Gloucester** Gilbert de Clare, ninth earl, historically killed at the battle of Bannockburn (1314) two years after Gaveston's death

5 **factious** seditious
9 **liberal** (1) gentle; (2) licentious
11 **follower** retainer
12 **companion** (1) ally; (2) lover
15 **end** conclusion
19 **our Lady** i.e., Margaret de Clare; betrothed to Gaveston in the play, she was historically married to him in 1307
29 **Having . . . child** Baldock suggests he was Margaret's tutor
30 **cast . . . off** stop playing the academic
31 **court it** behave like a courtier
32–3 **black . . . serge** academic dress
33 **faced** trimmed; **serge** cheap woollen cloth
34 **nosegay** bunch of flowers (for Elizabethans, a conventional feminine act)

Or holding of a napkin in your hand,
Or saying a long grace at a table's end,
Or making low legs to a nobleman,
Or looking downward with your eyelids closed,
And saying "truly, an't may please your honor,"
Can get you any favor with great men.
You must be proud, bold, pleasant, resolute –
And, now and then, stab as occasion serves.

Baldock. Spencer, thou knowest I hate such formal toys,
And use them but of mere hypocrisy.
Mine old Lord, whiles he lived, was so precise
That he would take exceptions at my buttons,
And, being like pins' heads, blame me for the bigness,
Which made me curate-like in mine attire,
Though inwardly licentious enough,
And apt for any kind of villainy.
I am none of these common pedants, I,
That cannot speak without "*propterea quod.*"

Spencer Junior. But one of those that saith "*quandoquidem*"
And hath a special gift to form a verb.

Baldock. Leave off this jesting – here my Lady comes.

[*They draw aside.*]

Enter the Lady [Margaret de Clare].

Lady Margaret. The grief for his exile was not so much
As is the joy of his returning home.
This letter came from my sweet Gaveston.

[*Reads a letter.*]

What needst thou, love, thus to excuse thyself?
I know thou couldst not come and visit me.
"I will not long be from thee, though I die";
This argues the entire love of my Lord.
"When I forsake thee, death seize on my heart";
But rest thee here where Gaveston shall sleep.

[*Puts the letter into her bosom.*]

Now to the letter of my Lord the King.

[*Reads another letter.*]

He wills me to repair unto the court
And meet my Gaveston. Why do I stay,
Seeing that he talks thus of my marriage-day?
Who's there? Baldock,

[Baldock *and* Spencer Junior *come forward.*]

See that my coach be ready; I must hence.

Baldock. It shall be done, Madam.

Lady Margaret. And meet me at the park pale presently.

Exit [Baldock].

Spencer, stay you and bear me company,
For I have joyful news to tell thee of;
My Lord of Cornwall is a-coming over
And will be at the court as soon as we.

Spencer Junior. I knew the King would have him home again.

Lady Margaret. If all things sort out as I hope they will,
Thy service, Spencer, shall be thought upon.

Spencer Junior. I humbly thank your Ladyship.

Lady Margaret. Come, lead the way; I long till I am there.

[*Exeunt.*]

[II.ii]

Enter Edward, [Isabella] *the* Queen, Lancaster, Mortimer [Junior], Warwick, Pembroke, [Edmund Earl of] Kent, Attendants.

Edward. The wind is good; I wonder why he stays.
I fear me he is wrecked upon the sea.

Queen. Look, Lancaster, how passionate he is,
And still his mind runs on his minion.

Lancaster. My Lord –

Edward. How now, what news? Is Gaveston arrived?

Mortimer Junior. Nothing but Gaveston! What means Your Grace?
You have matters of more weight to think upon;
The King of France sets foot in Normandy.

Edward. A trifle! We'll expel him when we please.

---

35 napkin handkerchief
36 table's end i.e., bottom end, denoting low social rank
37 making low legs i.e., bowing
41 pleasant jocular
42 stab (1) quick repartee; (2) sexual thrust
43 formal toys conventions
44 mere simple
45 old former; **precise** puritanical
46 take exceptions at fault
48 curate-like (1) plain; (2) religious (religious figures were a favorite butt of homosexual remarks)
49 licentious (1) unrestrained; (2) sexually active
51 common pedants ordinary schoolmasters
52 *"propterea quod"* prosaic way to say "because"
53 *"quandoquidem"* learned way to say "because"
54 form conjugate
66 repair come
70 coach (anachronistic)
72 pale fence; **presently** directly
73 bear keep
81 long am anxious
II.ii.2 the sea Gaveston is sailing across the North Sea from Ireland to Tynemouth Castle in Durham (geographically impossible) since Marlowe here combines two exiles, the first to Ireland and the second to Flanders
9 Normandy (then English territory)

But tell me, Mortimer, what's thy device
Against the stately triumph we decreed?
Mortimer Junior. A homely one, my Lord, not worth the telling.
Edward. Prithee, let me know it.
Mortimer Junior. But seeing you are so desirous, thus it is:
A lofty cedar tree fair flourishing,
On whose top branches kingly eagles perch,
And by the bark a canker creeps me up
And gets unto the highest bough of all;
The motto: *Æque tandem.*
Edward. And what is yours, my Lord of Lancaster?
Lancaster. My Lord, mine's more obscure than Mortimer's:
Pliny reports there is a flying fish
Which all the other fishes deadly hate,
And therefore, being pursued, it takes the air;
No sooner is it up, but there's a fowl
That seizeth it; this fish, my Lord, I bear;
The motto this: *Undique mors est.*
Edward. Proud Mortimer! Ungentle Lancaster!
Is this the love you bear your Sovereign?
Is this the fruit your reconcilement bears?
Can you in words make show of amity
And in your shields display your rancorous minds?
What call you this but private libeling
Against the Earl of Cornwall and my brother?
Queen. Sweet husband, be content; they all love you.
Edward. They love me not that hate my Gaveston.
I am that cedar (shake me not too much!)
And you the eagles; soar ye ne'er so high,
I have the jesses that will pull you down,
And *Æque tandem* shall that canker cry
Unto the proudest peer of Britainy.
Though thou compar'st him to a flying fish,
And threat'nest death whether he rise or fall,
'Tis not the hugest monster of the sea
Nor foulest harpy that shall swallow him.
Mortimer Junior. [*To Nobles.*] If in his absence thus he favors him,
What will he do whenas he shall be present?
Lancaster. That shall we see. Look where his Lordship comes.

Enter Gaveston.

Edward. My Gaveston!
Welcome to Tynemouth, welcome to thy friend.
Thy absence made me droop and pine away,
For as the lovers of fair Danaë,
When she was locked up in a brazen tower,
Desired her more and waxed outrageous,
So did it sure with me; and now thy sight
Is sweeter far than was thy parting hence
Bitter and irksome to my sobbing heart.
Gaveston. Sweet Lord and King, your speech preventeth mine,
Yet have I words left to express my joy:
The shepherd nipped with biting winter's rage
Frolics not more to see the painted spring
Than I do to behold Your Majesty.
Edward. Will none of you salute my Gaveston?
Lancaster. Salute him? Yes! Welcome, Lord Chamberlain.
Mortimer Junior. Welcome is the good Earl of Cornwall.
Warwick. Welcome, Lord Governor of the Isle of Man.
Pembroke. Welcome, Master Secretary.
Edmund. Brother, do you hear them?
Edward. Still will these Earls and Barons use me thus!
Gaveston. My Lord, I cannot brook these injuries.
Queen. [*Aside.*] Aye me, poor soul, when these begin to jar.
Edward. Return it to their throats; I'll be thy warrant.
Gaveston. Base leaden Earls that glory in your birth,
Go sit at home and eat your tenants' beef,
And come not here to scoff at Gaveston,

11 **device** heraldic emblem
12 **Against** prepared for; **stately triumph** public state entertainment
14 **Prithee** I pray thee (a common expression)
18 **canker** worm
20 ***Æque tandem*** equal in height (Latin) (Gaveston as a lowly worm would make his way to the political and social treetop)
22 **obscure** difficult to understand
23 **Pliny** classical author of unnatural natural history
28 ***Undique mors est*** "Death is on all sides" (Latin)
35 **my brother** i.e., Gaveston
40 **jesses** straps used to fasten the legs of hawks
42 **Britainy** i.e., England and Scotland; an alternative form of Britain
46 **harpy** bird-like creatures with female faces and breasts who harassed their victims
53 **Danaë** in classical mythology, Danae was incarcerated in a bronze tower when an oracle prophesied her son would kill her father
55 **waxed outrageous** grew unrestrained
59 **preventeth** forestalls
62 **painted** colorful
70 **use** treat
72 **jar** quarrel
73 **Return . . . throats** turn back their abuse; **warrant** protection, surety
75 **beef** (beef-witted was proverbial for stupid)

Whose mounting thoughts did never creep so low
As to bestow a look on such as you.

Lancaster. Yet I disdain not to do this for you.
[*Draws his sword.*]

Edward. Treason, treason! Where's the traitor?

Pembroke. [*Pointing to Gaveston.*] Here, here!

Edward. Convey hence, Gaveston; [*To no one in particular.*] they'll murder him.

Gaveston. [*To Lancaster.*] The life of thee shall salve this foul disgrace.

Mortimer Junior. Villain, thy life, unless I miss mine aim.
[*Wounds Gaveston.*]

Queen. Ah, furious Mortimer, what hast thou done?

Mortimer Junior. No more than I would answer were he slain.
[*Exit* Gaveston *with* Attendants.]

Edward. Yes, more than thou canst answer though he live.
Dear shall you both aby this riotous deed.
Out of my presence! Come not near the court.

Mortimer Junior. I'll not be barred the court for Gaveston.

Lancaster. We'll haul him by the ears unto the block.

Edward. Look to your own heads; his is sure enough.

Warwick. Look to your own crown, if you back him thus.

Edmund. Warwick, these words do ill beseem thy years.

Edward. Nay all of them conspire to cross me thus;
But if I live, I'll tread upon their heads
That think with high looks thus to tread me down.
Come Edmund, let's away and levy men;
'Tis war that must abate these Barons' pride.
Exit [Edward] *the* King [*with* Queen Isabella *and* Edmund].

Warwick. Let's to our castles, for the King is moved.

Mortimer Junior. Moved may he be and perish in his wrath.

Lancaster. [*To Mortimer Junior.*] Cousin, it is no dealing with him now;
He means to make us stoop by force of arms,
And therefore let us jointly here protest
To prosecute that Gaveston to the death.

Mortimer Junior. By Heaven, the abject villain shall not live.

Warwick. I'll have his blood or die in seeking it.

Pembroke. The like oath Pembroke takes.

Lancaster. And so doth Lancaster.
Now send our heralds to defy the King
And make the people swear to put him down.

Enter a Post.

Mortimer Junior. Letters? From whence?

Post. From Scotland, my lord.

Lancaster. Why how now, cousin, how fares all our friends?

Mortimer Junior. [*Reading letter.*] My uncle's taken prisoner by the Scots.

Lancaster. We'll have him ransomed, man; be of good cheer.

Mortimer Junior. They rate his ransom at five thousand pounds.
Who should defray the money but the King,
Seeing he is taken prisoner in his wars?
I'll to the King.

Lancaster. Do cousin, and I'll bear thee company.

Warwick. Meantime, my Lord of Pembroke and myself
Will to Newcastle here and gather head.

Mortimer Junior. About it, then, and we will follow you.

Lancaster. Be resolute and full of secrecy.

Warwick. I warrant you.
[*Exeunt all but* Mortimer Junior *and* Lancaster.]

Mortimer Junior. Cousin, an if he will not ransom him,
I'll thunder such a peal into his ears
As never subject did unto his King.

Lancaster. Content, I'll bear my part. [*Calling.*] Holla! Who's there?

---

80 s.d. ***Draws . . . sword*** it was an offense to draw a weapon in the King's presence

83 **life . . . disgrace** I'll have your life for humiliating me

86 **answer** answer for

88 **both** i.e., Lancaster and Mortimer Junior; **aby** pay for; **riotous** (1) mutinous; (2) wanton

91 **block** place of execution

92 **sure** safe

94 **words . . . years** your age should teach you more wisdom (Warwick is a senior peer)

102 **Cousin** broad term for any kin or ally

103 **stoop** submit

104 **protest** vow

105 **prosecute** pursue

106 **abject** most contemptible

111 s.d. **Post** messenger

116 **defray** pay for

121 **gather head** raise forces

123 **warrant** give assurance

127 **Content** agreed

[*Enter* Guard.]

Mortimer Junior. Aye, marry, such a guard as this doth well.
Lancaster. Lead on the way!
Guard. Whither will your lordships?
Mortimer Junior. Whither else but to the King?
Guard. His Highness is disposed to be alone.
Lancaster. Why, so he may, but we will speak to him.
Guard. You may not in, my Lord.
Mortimer Junior. May we not?

[*Enter* King Edward *and* Edmund.]

Edward. How now, what noise is this?
Who have we there? Is't you?
[*Offers to go back.*]
Mortimer Junior. Nay, stay my Lord; I come to bring you news:
Mine uncle's taken prisoner by the Scots.
Edward. Then ransom him.
Lancaster. 'Twas in your wars; you should ransom him.
Mortimer Junior. And you shall ransom him, or else –
Edmund. What, Mortimer, you will not threaten him?
Edward. Quiet yourself; you shall have the broad seal
To gather for him thoroughout the realm.
Lancaster. Your minion Gaveston hath taught you this.
Mortimer Junior. My Lord, the family of the Mortimers
Are not so poor but, would they sell their land,
Would levy men enough to anger you.
We never beg, but use such prayers as these.
[*Grasps his sword.*]
Edward. Shall I still be haunted thus?
Mortimer Junior. Nay, now you are here alone, I'll speak my mind.
Lancaster. And so will I, and then, my Lord, farewell.
Mortimer Junior. The idle triumphs, masques, lascivious shows,
And prodigal gifts bestowed on Gaveston
Have drawn thy treasure dry and made thee weak;
The murmuring commons overstretchèd hath.
Lancaster. Look for rebellion. Look to be deposed.
Thy garrisons are beaten out of France,
And, lame and poor, lie groaning at the gates;
The wild O'Neil, with swarms of Irish kerns,
Lives uncontrolled within the English pale;
Unto the walls of York the Scots made road,
And unresisted drove away rich spoils.
Mortimer Junior. The haughty Dane commands the narrow seas,
While in the harbor ride thy ships unrigged.
Lancaster. What foreign prince sends thee ambassadors?
Mortimer Junior. Who loves thee, but a sort of flatterers?
Lancaster. Thy gentle Queen, sole sister to Valois,
Complains that thou hast left her all forlorn.
Mortimer Junior. Thy court is naked, being bereft of those
That makes a king seem glorious to the world –
I mean the peers whom thou shouldst dearly love;
Libels are cast against thee in the street,
Ballads and rhymes made of thy overthrow.
Lancaster. The northern borderers, seeing their houses burned,
Their wives and children slain, run up and down
Cursing the name of thee and Gaveston.
Mortimer Junior. When wert thou in the field with banner spread?
But once! And then thy soldiers marched like players,
With garish robes, not armor. And thyself,
Bedaubed with gold, rode laughing at the rest,
Nodding and shaking of thy spangled crest,
Where women's favors hung like labels down.

128 marry to be sure (contraction of "By Mary," a common oath)
133 in enter
142 broad seal i.e., the Great Seal, letters patent giving the bearer the right to raise money for a specific cause without being accused of begging
149 haunted threatened
152 idle worthless
153 prodigal extravagant
154 treasure treasury
155 murmuring discontented
159 wild O'Neil anachronistic; Ulster chieftain whom Elizabeth could not subdue; **kerns** lightly armed Irish footsoldiers, drawn from the poorer class
160 English pale area around Dublin preserved for English settlers in Ireland
161 made road raided
163 narrow seas the English Channel
164 ride lie at anchor
166 sort group
167 Valois i.e., Philip Valois, King of Spain
169 naked destitute
170 seem appear
178 players i.e., actors
181 crest plume at the top of the helmet
182 favors tokens; **labels** strips of parchment used to affix a seal to a document

Lancaster. And thereof came it that the fleering Scots,
To England's high disgrace, have made this jig:
"Maids of England, sore may you mourn,
For your lemans you have lost at Bannocks bourne.
With a heave and a ho.
What weeneth the King of England,
So soon to have won Scotland?
With a rombelow."
Mortimer Junior. Wigmore shall fly, to set my uncle free.
Lancaster. And when 'tis gone, our swords shall purchase more.
If ye be moved, revenge it as you can;
Look next to see us with our ensigns spread.
Exeunt Nobles [Lancaster *and* Mortimer Junior].
Edward. My swelling heart for very anger breaks!
How oft have I been baited by these peers
And dare not be revenged, for their power is great?
Yet, shall the crowing of these cockerels
Affright a lion? Edward, unfold thy paws
And let their life's blood slake thy fury's hunger.
If I be cruel and grow tyrannous,
Now let them thank themselves and rue too late.
Edmund. My Lord, I see your love to Gaveston
Will be the ruin of the realm and you,
For now the wrathful Nobles threaten wars;
And therefore, brother, banish him forever.
Edward. Art thou an enemy to my Gaveston?
Edmund. Aye, and it grieves me that I favored him.
Edward. Traitor, be gone; whine thou with Mortimer.
Edmund. So will I, rather than with Gaveston.
Edward. Out of my sight and trouble me no more.
Edmund. No marvel though thou scorn thy noble peers,
When I thy brother am rejected thus.
Edward. Away!
Exit [Edmund].
Poor Gaveston, that hast no friend but me –
Do what they can, we'll live in Tynemouth here.
And, so I walk with him about the walls,
What care I though the Earls begirt us round?
Here comes she that's cause of all these jars.

Enter [Isabella] *the* Queen, *three* Ladies [Margaret de Clare *and* Ladies in Waiting], Baldock, *and* Spencer [Junior, *and* Gaveston].

Queen. My Lord, 'tis thought the Earls are up in arms.
Edward. Aye, and 'tis likewise thought you favor him.
Queen. Thus do you still suspect me without cause.
Lady Margaret. Sweet uncle, speak more kindly to the Queen.
Gaveston. [*Aside to Edward.*] My Lord, dissemble with her, speak her fair.
Edward. Pardon me, sweet, I forgot myself.
Queen. Your pardon is quickly got of Isabel.
Edward. The younger Mortimer is grown so brave
That to my face he threatens civil wars.
Gaveston. Why do you not commit him to the Tower?
Edward. I dare not, for the people love him well.
Gaveston. Why, then, we'll have him privily made away.
Edward. Would Lancaster and he had both caroused
A bowl of poison to each other's health.
But let them go, and tell me what are these.
[*Indicates Baldock and Spencer Junior.*]
Lady Margaret. Two of my father's servants while he lived.
May't please your Grace to entertain them now.
Edward. [*To Baldock.*] Tell me, where wast thou born? What is thine arms?
Baldock. My name is Baldock, and my gentry
I fetched from Oxford, not from heraldry.
Edward. The fitter art thou, Baldock, for my turn.

183 **fleering** sneering
184 **jig** jingle (often scurrilous)
186 **lemans** sweethearts; **Bannocks bourne** the battle of Bannockburn (June 1314) ended in the defeat of Edward's forces
188 **weeneth** hopes
190 **rombelow** (nonsense word)
191 **Wigmore** Wigmore Castle, Mortimer Junior's estate in Herefordshire; **fly** be sold
192 **purchase** acquire
198–9 **cockerels . . . lion** proverbially, lions feared a cock's crowing (lions were the animal associated with the monarch)
217 **begirt** enclose
220 **him** e.g., Mortimer Junior
223 **fair** courteously
226 **brave** defiant
228 **Tower** Tower of London where traitors were imprisoned
230 **privily . . . away** secretly murdered
231 **caroused** reveled with
235 **entertain** (1) give hospitality; (2) give employment
236 **arms** coat of arms
237 **gentry** rank of gentleman
238 **fetched from** acquired through education at; **Oxford** Robert Baldock held a doctorate from Oxford; in 1332 the Spencers appointed him Chancellor; **heraldry** rank

Wait on me, and I'll see thou shalt not want.
Baldock. I humbly thank Your Majesty.
Edward. Knowest thou him, Gaveston?
[*Points to Spencer Junior.*]
Gaveston. Ay, my Lord.
His name is Spencer; he is well allied.
For my sake let him wait upon Your Grace.
Scarce shall you find a man of more desert.
Edward. Then, Spencer, wait upon me; for his sake
I'll grace thee with a higher style ere long.
Spencer Junior. No greater titles happen unto me
Than to be favored of Your Majesty.
Edward. [*To Lady Margaret.*] Cousin, this day shall be your marriage feast;
And Gaveston, think that I love thee well
To wed thee to our niece, the only heir
Unto the Earl of Gloucester late deceased.
Gaveston. I know, my Lord, many will stomach me,
But I respect neither their love nor hate.
Edward. The headstrong Barons shall not limit me;
He that I list to favor shall be great.
Come, let's away; and when the marriage ends,
Have at the rebels and their complices.
Exeunt.

[II.iii]

Enter Lancaster, Mortimer [Junior], Warwick, Pembroke, [Edmund Earl of] Kent [*and others*].

Edmund. My Lords, of love to this our native land
I come to join with you and leave the King,
And in your quarrel and the realm's behoof
Will be the first that shall adventure life.
Lancaster. I fear me you are sent of policy
To undermine us with a show of love.
Warwick. He is your brother; therefore have we cause
To cast the worst, and doubt of your revolt.
Edmund. Mine honor shall be hostage of my truth;
If that will not suffice, farewell, my Lords.
Mortimer Junior. Stay, Edmund; never was Plantagenet
False of his word, and therefore trust we thee.
[*Lancaster and Edmund converse apart.*]
Pembroke. But what's the reason you should leave him now?
Edmund. I have informed the Earl of Lancaster.
Lancaster. And it sufficeth. Now, my Lords, know this,
That Gaveston is secretly arrived,
And here in Tynemouth frolics with the King.
Let us with these our followers scale the walls
And suddenly surprise them unawares.
Mortimer Junior. I'll give the onset.
Warwick. And I'll follow thee.
Mortimer Junior. This tattered ensign of my ancestors,
Which swept the desert shore of that dead sea
Whereof we got the name of Mortimer,
Will I advance upon these castle walls;
Drums strike alarum, raise them from their sport,
And ring aloud the knell of Gaveston.
Lancaster. None be so hardy as to touch the King,
But neither spare you Gaveston nor his friends.
Exeunt.

[II.iv]

[*Alarums.*] *Enter,* [*at opposite doors,* Edward] *the* King *and* Spencer [Junior].

Edward. Oh, tell me, Spencer, where is Gaveston?
Spencer. I fear me he is slain, my gracious Lord.
Edward. No, here he comes! Now let them spoil and kill.

[*Enter to them* Gaveston *and others*: Queen Isabella, Lady Margaret de Clare, Lords].

Fly, fly, my Lords; the Earls have got the hold.
Take shipping and away to Scarborough;
Spencer, and I will post away by land.
Gaveston. Oh, stay, my Lord; they will not injure you.
Edward. I will not trust them, Gaveston. Away!
Gaveston. Farewell, my Lord.
Edward. [*To Lady Margaret.*] Lady, farewell.

243 allied connected
247 style title
248 happen befall
254 stomach resent
257 list please (to give)
259 Have at attack
II.iii.4 adventure risk
5 of policy as a trick
8 doubt suspicion
17 frolics enjoys himself (with sexual implications)
22–3 Which . . . Mortimer a false genealogy; the Mortimers came from Mortemer, Normandy, and never took part in the Crusades and the Dead Sea (*Mortum Mare* in Latin)
25 alarum battle-cry
26 knell i.e., death knell normally announced with a peal of church bells
27 hardy bold, presumptuous
II.iv.3 spoil plunder
4 hold fortress

Lady Margaret. Farewell, sweet uncle, till we meet again.
Edward. Farewell, sweet Gaveston, and farewell, niece.
Queen. No farewell to poor Isabel, thy queen?
Edward. Yes, yes – for Mortimer your lover's sake.
Queen. Heavens can witness I love none but you.
Exeunt all except [Queen] Isabella.
From my embracements thus he breaks away;
Oh, that mine arms could close this isle about,
That I might pull him to me where I would,
Or that these tears that drizzle from mine eyes
Had power to mollify his stony heart
That, when I had him, we might never part.

Enter the Barons [Lancaster, Warwick, Mortimer Junior]. *Alarums* [*within*].

Lancaster. I wonder how he scaped.
Mortimer Junior. Who's this? The Queen!
Queen. Aye, Mortimer, the miserable Queen,
Whose pining heart her inward sighs have blasted,
And body with continual mourning wasted;
These hands are tired with hauling of my Lord
From Gaveston, from wicked Gaveston –
And all in vain, for when I speak him fair,
He turns away and smiles upon his minion.
Mortimer Junior. Cease to lament, and tell us where's the King.
Queen. What would you with the King? Is't him you seek?
Lancaster. No, madam, but that cursèd Gaveston.
Far be it from the thought of Lancaster
To offer violence to his Sovereign.
We would but rid the realm of Gaveston;
Tell us where he remains, and he shall die.
Queen. He's gone by water unto Scarborough:
Pursue him quickly and he cannot 'scape;
The King hath left him, and his train is small.
Warwick. Forslow no time; sweet Lancaster, let's march.
Mortimer Junior. How comes it that the King and he is parted?
Queen. That this your army, going several ways,
Might be of lesser force, and with the power
That he intendeth presently to raise
Be easily suppressed; and therefore be gone.
Mortimer Junior. Here in the river rides a Flemish hoy;
Let's all aboard and follow him amain.
Lancaster. The wind that bears him hence will fill our sails.
Come, come aboard; 'tis but an hour's sailing.
Mortimer Junior. Madam, stay you within this castle here.
Queen. No, Mortimer, I'll to my Lord the King.
Mortimer Junior. Nay, rather sail with us to Scarborough.
Queen. You know the King is so suspicious,
As if he hear I have but talked with you,
Mine honor will be called in question,
And therefore, gentle Mortimer, be gone.
Mortimer Junior. Madam, I cannot stay to answer you,
But think of Mortimer as he deserves.
[*Exeunt* Lancaster, Warwick, *and* Mortimer Junior.]
Queen. So well hast thou deserved, sweet Mortimer,
As Isabel could live with thee forever.
In vain I look for love at Edward's hand,
Whose eyes are fixed on none but Gaveston.
Yet once more I'll importune him with prayers;
If he be strange and not regard my words,
My son and I will over into France,
And to the King, my brother, there complain
How Gaveston hath robbed me of his love.
But yet I hope my sorrows will have end
And Gaveston this blessèd day be slain.
[*Exit.*]

[II.v]

Enter Gaveston, *pursued.*

Gaveston. Yet, lusty Lords, I have escaped your hands,
Your threats, your 'larums, and your hot pursuits,
And though divorcèd from King Edward's eyes,
Yet liveth Pierce of Gaveston unsurprised,
Breathing, in hope (*malgrado* all your beards
That muster rebels thus against your King)
To see His royal Sovereign once again.

24 blasted wasted
39 train retinue
40 Forslow waste
46 hoy small fishing ship used by Flemings in the North Sea
47 amain at full speed
64 strange (1) unresponsive; (2) estranged

II.v.1 s.d. presumably in the vicinity of Scarborough, an immense castle in Yorkshire
1 lusty insolent
4 unsurprised unambushed, uncaught
5 *malgrado* in defense of (Italian)

Enter the Nobles [Lancaster, Warwick, Pembroke, Mortimer Junior, Soldiers, James, Horse-Boy, *and* Servants of Pembroke].

Warwick. Upon him, soldiers! Take away his weapons!
Mortimer Junior. Thou proud disturber of thy country's peace,
Corrupter of thy King, cause of these broils,
Base flatterer, yield! And were it not for shame,
Shame and dishonor to a soldier's name,
Upon my weapon's point here shouldst thou fall,
And welter in thy gore.
Lancaster. Monster of men,
That, like the Greekish strumpet, trained to arms
And bloody wars so many valiant knights,
Look for no other fortune, wretch, than death;
King Edward is not here to buckler thee.
Warwick. Lancaster, why talkst thou to the slave?
Go, soldiers, take him hence; for, by my sword,
His head shall off. Gaveston, short warning
Shall serve thy turn; it is our country's cause
That here severely we will execute
Upon thy person: hang him at a bough!
Gaveston. My Lord –
Warwick. Soldiers, have him away.
But for thou wert the favorite of a King,
Thou shalt have so much honor at our hands.
[*Gestures to indicate beheading.*]
Gaveston. I thank you all, my Lords. Then I perceive
That heading is one, and hanging is the other,
And death is all.

Enter Earl of Arundel.

Lancaster. How now, my Lord of Arundel?
Arundel. My Lords, King Edward greets you all by me.
Warwick. Arundel, say your message.
Arundel. His Majesty,
Hearing that you had taken Gaveston,
Entreateth you by me, yet but He may
See him before he dies; for why, He says,
And sends you word, He knows that die He shall;
And if you gratify His Grace so far,
He will be mindful of the courtesy.
Warwick. How now?
Gaveston. [*Aside.*] Renownèd Edward, how thy name
Revives poor Gaveston!
Warwick. No, it needeth not,
Arundel; we will gratify the King
In other matters; he must pardon us in this.
Soldiers, away with him.
Gaveston. [*Sarcastically.*] Why, my Lord of Warwick,
Will not these delays beget my hopes?
I know it, Lords, it is this life you aim at;
Yet grant King Edward this.
Mortimer Junior. Shalt thou appoint
What we shall grant? Soldiers, away with him!
[*To Arundel.*] Thus we'll gratify the King:
We'll send his head by thee; let him bestow
His tears on that, for that is all he gets
Of Gaveston, or else his senseless trunk.
Lancaster. Not so, my Lord, lest he bestow more cost
In burying him than he hath ever earned.
Arundel. My Lords, it is His Majesty's request,
And in the honor of a king he swears
He will but talk with him and send him back.
Warwick. When, can you tell? Arundel, no; we wot
He that the care of realm remits,
And drives his nobles to these exigents
For Gaveston, will, if he seize him once,
Violate any promise to possess him.
Arundel. Then if you will not trust His Grace in keep,
My Lords, I will be pledge for his return.
Mortimer Junior. It is honorable in thee to offer this,
But for we know thou art a noble gentleman,
We will not wrong thee so,
To make away a true man for a thief.
Gaveston. How meanst thou, Mortimer? That is over-base!
Mortimer Junior. Away, base groom, robber of Kings' renown.

10 **broils** disturbances
15 **Greekish strumpet** Helen of Troy whose abduction by Paris began the Trojan War against her native Greeks
18 **buckler** protect
21 **short warning** i.e., quick execution with no time for penitence (suggesting he is unredeemable in their eyes)
26 **But for** even though
27 **honor** true nobility were exempt from hanging
29 **heading . . . other** I will be either beheaded or hanged (punishments for treason)
36 **for why** because
39 **be mindful of** take into consideration
45 **beget** engender
47 **appoint** dictate
59 **remits** surrenders
60 **exigents** extreme measures
61 **seize** have possession of
63 **in keep** with this temporary situation
64 **pledge** security
68 **make away** murder (Arundel would be executed in substitution)

Question with thy companions and thy mates.
Pembroke. My Lord Mortimer, and you my Lords each one,
To gratify the King's request therein,
Touching the sending of this Gaveston,
Because His Majesty so earnestly
Desires to see the man before his death,
I will upon mine honor undertake
To carry him and bring him back again,
Provided this, that you, my Lord of Arundel,
Will join with me.
Warwick. Pembroke, what wilt thou do?
Cause yet more bloodshed? Is it not enough
That we have taken him, but must we now
Leave him on "had I wist" and let him go?
Pembroke. My Lords, I will not over-woo your honors,
But if you dare trust Pembroke with the prisoner,
Upon mine oath I will return him back.
Arundel. My Lord of Lancaster, what say you in this?
Lancaster. Why I say, let him go on Pembroke's word.
Pembroke. And you, Lord Mortimer?
Mortimer Junior. How say you, my Lord of Warwick?
Warwick. Nay, do your pleasures; I know how 'twill prove.
Pembroke. Then give him me.
Gaveston. Sweet Sovereign, yet I come
To see thee ere I die.
Warwick. [*Aside.*] Yet not perhaps,
If Warwick's wit and policy prevail.
Mortimer Junior. My Lord of Pembroke, we deliver him you;
Return him on your honor, Sound away!

Exeunt [Mortimer Junior, Lancaster, Warwick]. [Pembroke, Arundel, Gaveston, *and* Pembroke's Men (*including* Horse-Boy), *four* Soldiers (*including* James) *remain*].

Pembroke. [*To Arundel.*] My Lord, you shall go with me;
My house is not far hence – out of the way
A little, but our men shall go along.
We that have pretty wenches to our wives,
Sir, must not come so near and balk their lips.
Arundel. 'Tis very kindly spoke, my Lord of Pembroke;
Your honor hath an adamant of power
To draw a Prince.
Pembroke. So, my Lord. Come hither, James.
I do commit this Gaveston to thee;
Be thou this night his keeper. In the morning
We will discharge thee of thy charge; be gone.
Gaveston. Unhappy Gaveston, whither goest thou now?

Exit [Gaveston] *with* Servants of Pembroke [*including* James].

Horse-Boy. [*To Arundel.*] My Lord, we'll quickly be at Cobham.

Exeunt [Pembroke *and* Arundel, *attended*].

[II.vi]

Enter Gaveston *mourning, and the* Earl of Pembroke's Men [*four* Soldiers *including* James].

Gaveston. Oh, treacherous Warwick, thus to wrong thy friend!
James. I see it is your life these arms pursue.
Gaveston. Weaponless must I fall and die in bands.
Oh, must this day be period of my life,
Center of all my bliss? An' ye be men,
Speed to the King.

Enter Warwick *and his company.*

Warwick. My Lord of Pembroke's men,
Strive you no longer; I will have that Gaveston.
James. Your Lordship doth dishonor to yourself
And wrong our Lord, your honorable friend.
Warwick. No, James, it is my country's cause I follow.
[*To his Men.*] Go, take the villain; soldiers, come away,
We'll make quick work. [*To James.*] Commend me to your master,
My friend, and tell him that I watched it well.

71 **Question** debate
83 **"had I wist"** had I known (proverbial)
91 **your pleasures** whatever you will
94 **wit** cunning; **policy** strategy
96 **Sound away!** trumpet call signifying departure
97 **go with me** (this may have had parodic overtones; while Marlowe suggests male bonding here, in fact the Elizabethan claimants were notorious enemies)
101 **balk** neglect, ignore
102 **kindly** spoken in the nature of a husband
103 **adamant** magnet
109 **Cobham** name of towns in Surrey and in Kent near Gravesend (geographically nonsensical and perhaps randomly chosen as a place-name by Marlowe; Pembroke's house was at Deddington, Oxfordshire)
II.vi.1 friend i.e., Pembroke
2 **arms** soldiers
3 **bands** bonds
4 **period** i.e., the end
5 **Center . . . bliss** (1) day when he was to be reunited with Edward; (2) nadir as center of the earth, man at his lowest condition
7 **Strive** struggle
13 **watched** guarded

[*To Gaveston.*] Come, let thy shadow parley with
King Edward.
Gaveston. Treacherous Earl! Shall I not see the
King?
Warwick. The King of Heaven perhaps, no other
king. Away!
Exeunt Warwick *and his* Men, *with* Gaveston. [James
remains with the others.]
James. Come, fellows, it booted not for us to
strive.
We will in haste go certify our Lord.
Exeunt.

Act III

[III.i]

Enter King Edward *and* Spencer [Junior, *and* Baldock], *with drums and fifes.*

Edward. I long to hear an answer from the Barons
Touching my friend, my dearest Gaveston.
Ah, Spencer, not the riches of my realm
Can ransom him; ah, he is marked to die.
I know the malice of the younger Mortimer;
Warwick, I know, is rough, and Lancaster
Inexorable; and I shall never see
My lovely Pierce, my Gaveston, again.
The Barons overbear me with their pride.
Spencer Junior. Were I King Edward, England's
Sovereign,
Son to the lovely Eleanor of Spain,
Great Edward Longshanks' issue, would I bear
These braves, this rage, and suffer uncontrolled
These Barons thus to beard me in my land,
In mine own realm? My Lord, pardon my
speech.
Did you retain your father's magnanimity,
Did you regard the honor of your name,
You would not suffer thus Your Majesty
Be counterbuffed of your nobility.
Strike off their heads, and let them preach on
poles;
No doubt such lessons they will teach the rest,
As by their preachments they will profit much
And learn obedience to their lawful King.
Edward. Yea, gentle Spencer, we have been too
mild,
Too kind to them, but now have drawn our
sword,
And if they send me not my Gaveston,
We'll steel it on their crest and poll their tops.
Baldock. This haught resolve becomes Your
Majesty,
Not to be tied to their affection
As though Your Highness were a schoolboy
still,
And must be awed and governed like a child.

Enter Hugh Spencer [Senior,] *an old man, father to the young* Spencer [Junior], *with his truncheon, and* Soldiers.

Spencer Senior. Long live my Sovereign, the noble
Edward,
In peace triumphant, fortunate in wars.
Edward. Welcome old man; com'st thou in
Edward's aid?
Then tell thy Prince of whence and what thou
art.
Spencer Senior. Lo, with a band of bowman and of
pikes,
Brown bills and targeteers, four hundred
strong,
Sworn to defend King Edward's royal right,
I come in person to Your Majesty –
Spencer, the father of Hugh Spencer there,
Bound to Your Highness everlastingly
For favors done in him unto us all.
Edward. Thy father, Spencer?
Spencer Junior. True, an it like Your Grace,
That pours in lieu of all your goodness shown
His life, my Lord, before your princely feet.
Edward. Welcome ten thousand times, old man,
again;
[*To Spencer Junior.*] Spencer, this love, this
kindness to thy King,
Argues thy noble mind and disposition.
Spencer, I here create thee Earl of Wiltshire,

---

14 shadow ghost
17 booted not was useless
18 certify inform
III.i.11 Eleanor of Spain Eleanor of Castile, first wife of Edward I
12 Edward Longshanks Edward I, known for his long legs
13 braves insults
14 beard defy
16 magnanimity fortitude
19 counterbuffed opposed
27 steel it sharpen his sword; **poll their tops** cut off their heads (punning on line 20)
28 haught haughty
29 affection support
31 awed deeply impressed, made fearful
32 s.d. *truncheon* short staff or club; cudgel
36 bowman archer; **pikes** lances with sharp metal tips at both ends driven into the ground in front of the archers for protection
37 Brown bills footsoldiers carrying bronzed halberds; **targeteers** infantrymen carrying shields
43 an it like if it please
48 Argues demonstrates (ironically, Edward is again offered help by men lower than the nobility)
49 create not true historically, but in Elizabethan times the eldest son of the Marquess of Winchester was styled Earl of Wiltshire

And daily will enrich thee with our favor
That, as the sunshine, shall reflect o'er thee.
Beside, the more to manifest our love,
Because we hear Lord Bruce doth sell his land,
And that the Mortimers are in hand withal,
Thou shalt have crowns of us t'outbid the Barons;
And, Spencer, spare them not, but lay it on.
Soldiers, a largess, and thrice welcome all.

Spencer Junior. My Lord, here comes the Queen.

Enter [Isabella] *the* Queen *and* [Prince Edward] *her son, and* Levune, *a Frenchman.*

Edward. Madam, what news?

Queen. News of dishonor, Lord, and discontent:
Our friend Levune, faithful and full of trust,
Informeth us by letters and by words
That Lord Valois our brother, King of France,
Because Your Highness hath been slack in homage,
Hath seizèd Normandy into his hands;
These be the letters, this the messenger.

Edward. Welcome Levune. [*To the Queen.*] Tush, Sib, if this be all,
Valois and I will soon be friends again.
But to my Gaveston – shall I never see,
Never behold thee now? Madam, in this matter
We will employ you and your little son;
You shall go parley with the King of France.
Boy, see you bear you bravely to the King
And do your message with a majesty.

Prince Edward. Commit not to my youth things of more weight
Than fits a Prince so young as I to bear.
And fear not, Lord and father; Heaven's great beams
On Atlas' shoulder shall not lie more safe
Than shall your charge committed to my trust.

Queen. Ah, boy, this towardness makes thy mother fear
Thou art not marked to many days on earth.

Edward. Madam, we will that you with speed be shipped,
And this our son. Levune shall follow you
With all the haste we can dispatch him hence.
Choose of our Lords to bear you company,
And go in peace; leave us in wars at home.

Queen. Unnatural wars, where subjects brave their King –
God end them once. My Lord, I take my leave
To make my preparation for France.
[*Exit* Queen *and* Prince Edward.]

Enter Lord Arundel.

Edward. What, Lord Arundel, dost thou come alone?

Arundel. Yea, my good Lord, for Gaveston is dead.

Edward. Ah traitors, have they put my friend to death?
Tell me, Arundel, died he ere thou cam'st,
Or didst thou see my friend to take his death?

Arundel. Neither, my Lord, for as he was surprised,
Begirt with weapons and with enemies round,
I did Your Highness' message to them all,
Demanding him of them – entreating rather –
And said, upon the honor of my name,
That I would undertake to carry him
Unto Your Highness, and to bring him back.

Edward. And tell me, would the rebels deny me that?

Spencer Junior. Proud recreants!

Edward. Yea Spencer, traitors all.

Arundel. I found them at the first inexorable;
The Earl of Warwick would not bide the hearing,
Mortimer hardly; Pembroke and Lancaster
Spoke least. And when they flatly had denied,
Refusing to receive me pledge for him,
The Earl of Pembroke mildly thus bespoke:
"My Lords, because our sovereign sends for him,
And promiseth he shall be safe returned,
I will this undertake, to have him hence
And see him re-delivered to your hands."

Edward. Well, and how fortunes that he came not?

Spencer Junior. Some treason or some villainy was cause.

Arundel. The Earl of Warwick seized him on his way,
For, being delivered unto Pembroke's men,
Their Lord rode home, thinking his prisoner safe;
But ere he came, Warwick in ambush lay,
And bare him to his death, and in a trench
Strike off his head, and marched unto the camp.

---

54 are in hand withal bargaining for it
55 crowns money
56 lay it on be extravagant in your counteroffer
57 largess bounty
66 Sib affectionate diminutive of Isabella
77 Atlas in classical mythology Atlas carried the sky on his shoulder
79 towardness boldness
87 once once and for all; finally
102 recreants breakers of loyalty
104 bide abide, endure

Spencer Junior. A bloody part, flatly against law of arms.
Edward. O, shall I speak, or shall I sigh and die?
Spencer Junior. My Lord, refer your vengeance to the sword
Upon these Barons; hearten up your men.
Let them not unrevenged murder your friends.
Advance your standard, Edward, in the field,
And march to fire them from their starting holes.
Edward (kneels and saith). By earth, the common mother of us all,
By Heaven and all the moving orbs thereof,
By this right hand, and by my father's sword,
And all the honors 'longing to my crown,
I will have heads and lives for him – as many
As I have manors, castles, towns, and towers.
[*Rises.*]
Treacherous Warwick! Traitorous Mortimer!
If I be England's King, in lakes of gore
Your headless trunks, your bodies will I trail,
That you may drink your fill and quaff in blood,
And stain my royal standard with the same,
That so my bloody colors may suggest
Remembrance of revenge immortally
On your accursèd traitorous progeny –
You villains that have slain my Gaveston.
[*To Spencer Junior.*] And in this place of honor and of trust,
Spencer, sweet Spencer, I adopt thee here;
And merely of our love we do create thee
Earl of Gloucester and Lord Chamberlain,
Despite of times, despite of enemies.
Spencer Junior. My Lord, here is a messenger from the Barons
Desires access unto Your Majesty.
Edward. Admit him near.

Enter the Herald *from the* Barons, *with his coat of arms.*

Herald. Long live King Edward, England's lawful Lord.
Edward. So wish not they, I wis, that sent thee hither.
Thou com'st from Mortimer and his complices –
A ranker rout of rebels never was.
Well, say thy message.
Herald. The Barons up in arms by me salute
Your Highness with long life and happiness,
And bid me say as plainer to Your Grace,
That if without effusion of blood
You will this grief have ease and remedy,
That from your princely person you remove
This Spencer [*Indicating Spencer Junior.*] as a putrifying branch
That deads the royal vine, whose golden leaves
Empale your princely head, your diadem,
Whose brightness such pernicious upstarts dim;
Say they – and lovingly advise Your Grace
To cherish virtue and nobility,
And have old servitors in high esteem,
And shake off smooth dissembling flatterers –
This granted, they, their honors, and their lives
Are to Your Highness vowed and consecrate.
Spencer Junior. Ah, traitors, will they still display their pride?
Edward. Away! Tarry no answer, but be gone.
Rebels! Will they appoint their Sovereign
His sports, his pleasures, and his company?
Yet ere thou go, see how I do divorce
Spencer from me.
Embraces Spencer [*Junior*].
Now get thee to thy Lords,
And tell them I will come to chastise them
For murdering Gaveston. Hie thee, get thee gone;
Edward with fire and sword follows at thy heels.
[*Exit* Herald.]
My Lords, perceive you how these rebels swell?
Soldiers, good hearts, defend your Sovereign's right,

121 **part** act
123 **refer** assign
127 **fire . . . holes** smoke them out from refuge (refers to Barons as animals seeking home in the ground)
129 **orbs** heavenly bodies moving in their orbs
131 **'longing** belonging
137 **quaff** drink
145 **merely** by command rather than right of succession
146 **Earl of Gloucester** historically, Spencer's brother-in-law; **Lord Chamberlain** head of government
152 **wis** know
153 **complices** conspirators
154 **rout** band
158 **plainer** complainant
159 **effusion** shedding
163 **deads . . . vine** kills the crown decorated with four large and four small strawberry leaves (anachronistic; Marlowe is thinking of a later crown which had vine leaves)
164 **Empale** encircle; **diadem** crown
167 **virtue** worth
168 **old servitors** long-standing supporters (as opposed to a Gaveston or a Spencer)
171 **consecrate** made sacred
173 **Tarry** await
179 **Hie** hasten
181 **swell** grow increasingly proud and dominant

For now, even now, we march to make them stoop.
Away!

Exeunt.

[III.ii]

Alarums, excursions, a great fight, and a retreat [*sounded*]. *Enter* [Edward] *the* King, Spencer [Senior] (*the father*), Spencer [Junior] (*the son*), *and the* Noblemen *of the* King's *side.*

Edward. Why do we sound retreat? Upon them, Lords!
This day I shall pour vengeance with my sword
On those proud rebels that are up in arms,
And do confront and countermand their King.
Spencer Junior. I doubt it not, my Lord; right will prevail.
Spencer Senior. 'Tis not amiss, my Liege, for either part
To breathe a while; our men, with sweat and dust
All choked well near, begin to faint for heat,
And this retire refresheth horse and man.
Spencer Junior. Here come the rebels.

Enter the Barons, Mortimer [Junior], Lancaster, [Edmund,] Warwick, Pembroke, [*with others*].

Mortimer Junior. Look, Lancaster,
Yonder is Edward among his flatterers.
Lancaster. And there let him be,
Till he pay dearly for their company.
Warwick. And shall, or Warwick's sword shall smite in vain.
Edward. What, rebels, do you shrink and sound retreat?
Mortimer Junior. No, Edward, no; thy flatterers faint and fly.
Lancaster. Th'ad best betimes forsake them and their trains,
For they'll betray thee, traitors as they are.
Spencer Junior. Traitor on thy face, rebellious Lancaster.
Pembroke. Away, base upstart; brav'st thou nobles thus?
Spencer Senior. A noble attempt and honorable deed
Is it not, trow ye, to assemble aid
And levy arms against your lawful King?
Edward. For which ere long their heads shall satisfy
T'appease the wrath of their offended King.
Mortimer Junior. Then, Edward, thou wilt fight it to the last,
And rather bathe thy sword in subjects' blood
Than banish that pernicious company.
Edward. Aye, traitors all! Rather than thus be braved,
Make England's civil towns huge heaps of stones
And ploughs to go about our palace gates.
Warwick. A desperate and unnatural resolution.
Alarum to the fight!
Saint George for England and the Barons' right!
Edward. Saint George for England and King Edward's right.

[*Exeunt severally. Alarums.*]

Enter Edward, [Spencer Senior, Spencer Junior, Baldock, Levune, *and* Soldiers] *with the* Barons [Edmund, Warwick, Lancaster, *and* Mortimer Junior,] *captives.*

Edward. Now, lusty, Lords, now, not by chance of war
But justice of the quarrel and the cause,
Vailed is your pride. Methinks you hang the heads,
But we'll advance them, traitors! Now 'tis time
To be avenged on you for all your braves
And for the murder of my dearest friend,
To whom right well you knew our soul was knit,
Good Pierce of Gaveston, my sweet favorite.
Ah, rebels, recreants, you made him away.
Edmund. Brother, in regard of thee and of thy land
Did they remove that flatterer from thy throne.
Edward. So sir, you have spoke. Away, avoid our presence.

[*Exit* Edmund.]

Accursed wretches, was't in regard of us,
When we had sent our messenger to request
He might be spared to come to speak with us,
And Pembroke undertook for his return,
That thou, proud Warwick, watched the prisoner,

183 make them stoop humiliate them
III.ii.1 s.d. *excursions* rush of soldiers across the stage; the battle occurred near Boroughbridge, Yorkshire
9 retire (1) break; (2) retreat
18 Th'ad thou had; **betimes** in good time; **trains** tricks, devices
23 trow think
30 braved (1) opposed; (2) denied
35 Saint George anachronistic; he became patron saint of England in the reign of Edward III
39 Vailed lowered
40 advance raise the enemy's heads on pikes
48 avoid depart

Poor Pierce, and headed him against law of arms?
For which thy head shall overlook the rest
As much as thou in rage outwent'st the rest!

Warwick. Tyrant, I scorn thy threats and menaces;
'Tis but temporal that thou canst inflict.

Lancaster. The worst is death, and better die to live,
Than live in infamy under such a King.

Edward. [*To Spencer Senior.*] Away with them, my Lord of Winchester!
These lusty leaders, Warwick and Lancaster –
I charge you roundly, off with both their heads.
Away!

Warwick. Farewell, vain world.

Lancaster. Sweet Mortimer, farewell.

[*Exeunt* Warwick *and* Lancaster, *guarded, with* Spencer Senior.]

Mortimer Junior. England, unkind to thy nobility,
Groan for this grief; behold how thou art maimed.

Edward. Go, take that haughty Mortimer to the Tower;
There see him safe bestowed. And for the rest,
Do speedy execution on them all. Be gone!

Mortimer Junior. What, Mortimer! Can ragged stony walls
Immure thy virtue that aspires to Heaven?
No, Edward, England's scourge, it may not be;
Mortimer's hope surmounts his fortune far.

[*Exit guarded.*]

Edward. Sound drums and trumpets! March with me, my friends;
Edward this day hath crowned him King anew.

Exit [*attended*].

[Spencer Junior, Levune, *and* Baldock *remain.*]

Spencer Junior. Levune, the trust that we repose in thee
Begets the quiet of King Edward's land;
Therefore be gone in haste, and with advice
Bestow that treasure on the Lords of France,
That therewith all enchanted, like the guard
That suffered Jove to pass in showers of gold
To Danaë, all aid may be denied
To Isabel the Queen, that now in France
Makes friends to cross the seas with her young son
And step into his father's regiment.

Levune. That's it these Barons and the subtle Queen
Long leveled at.

Baldock. Yea, but Levune, thou seest
These Barons lay their heads on blocks together;
What they intend, the hangman frustrates clean.

Levune. Have you no doubts, my Lords; I'll clap so close
Among the Lords of France with England's gold
That Isabel shall make her plaints in vain,
And France shall be obdurate with her tears.

Spencer Junior. Then make for France amain; Levune, away!
Proclaim King Edward's wars and victories.

Exeunt.

Act IV

[IV.i]

Enter Edmund [Earl of Kent].

Edmund. Fair blows the wind for France. Blow, gentle gale,
Till Edmund be arrived for England's good.
Nature, yield to my country's cause in this.
A brother – no, a butcher of thy friends –
Proud Edward, dost thou banish me Thy presence?
But I'll to France and cheer the wrongèd Queen,
And certify what Edward's looseness is.
Unnatural King, to slaughter noblemen
And cherish flatterers. Mortimer,
I stay thy sweet escape.
Stand gracious gloomy night to his device.

Enter Mortimer [Junior] *disguised.*

54 **headed** i.e., beheaded
55 **overlook** be mounted higher on a pole than
58 **temporal** earthly suffering
61 **Lord of Winchester** i.e., Spencer Senior
63 **roundly** without hesitating
65 **vain** futile
71 **ragged** rugged
72 **Immure** enclose; **virtue** noble power
73 **scourge** one who lays waste a nation
78 **Begets** obtains
86 **regiment** authority, regime
87 **subtle** cunning
88 **leveled** aimed
90 **clean** absolutely
91 **clap** strike as in "strike a bargain" (such arrangements were announced by the clapping of hands); **close** secretly
IV.i.7 **looseness** (1) lax authority; (2) loose sexual behavior (implying a new love in Spencer)
10 **stay** await; **escape** historically, Mortimer's escape had no connection with Edmund
11 **gracious** in grace; Edmund will use night's darkness to free Mortimer; **device** plan, intent

Mortimer Junior. Holla! Who walketh there? Is't
you, my Lord?
Edmund. Mortimer, 'tis I; But hath thy potion
Wrought so happily?
Mortimer Junior. It hath, my Lord;
The warders all asleep,
I thank them,
Gave me leave to pass in peace.
But hath Your Grace got shipping unto France?
Edmund. Fear it not.

Exeunt.

[IV.ii]

Enter [Isabella] *the* Queen *and her son* [Prince Edward].

Queen. Ah, boy, our friends do fail us all in France.
The Lords are cruel and the King unkind.
What shall we do?
Prince Edward. Madam, return to England
And please my father well, and then a fig
For all my uncle's friendship here in France.
I warrant you, I'll win His Highness quickly;
'A loves me better than a thousand Spencers.
Queen. Ah boy, thou art deceived at least in this,
To think that we can yet be tuned together.
No, no, we jar too far. Unkind Valois!
Unhappy Isabel, when France rejects!
Whither, oh, whither dost thou bend thy steps?

Enter Sir John of Hainault.

Sir John. Madam, what cheer?
Queen. Ah, good Sir John of Hainault,
Never so cheerless, nor so far distressed.
Sir John. I hear, sweet Lady, of the King's
unkindness,
But droop not, Madam; noble minds contemn
Despair. Will Your Grace with me to Hainault,
And there stay time's advantage with your son?
How say you, my Lord, will you go with your
friends,
And shake off all our fortunes equally?
Prince Edward. So pleaseth the Queen, my mother,
me it likes.
The King of England, nor the court of France
Shall have me from my gracious mother's side,
'Till I be strong enough to break a staff,
And then have at the proudest Spencer's head.
Sir John. Well said, my Lord.
Queen. Oh, my sweetheart, how do I moan thy
wrongs,
Yet triumph in the hope of thee, my joy.
Ah sweet Sir John, even to the utmost verge
Of Europe, or the shore of Tanaïs,
Will we with thee; to Hainault, so we will.
The Marquis is a noble gentleman;
His grace, I dare presume, will welcome me.
But who are these?

Enter Edmund [Earl of Kent] *and* Mortimer [Junior].

Edmund. Madam, long may you live
Much happier than your friends in England do.
Queen. Lord Edmund and Lord Mortimer alive!
Welcome to France. [*To Mortimer Junior.*] The
news was here, my Lord,
That you were dead, or very near your death.
Mortimer Junior. Lady, the last was truest of the
twain;
But Mortimer, reserved for better hap,
Hath shaken off the thraldom of the Tower,
[*To Prince Edward.*] And lives t'advance your
standard, good my Lord.
Prince Edward. How mean you, an the King my
father lives?
No, my Lord Mortimer, not I, I trow.
Queen. Not, son! Why not? I would it were no
worse.
But gentle Lords, friendless we are in France.
Mortimer Junior. Monsieur le Grand, a noble friend
of yours,
Told us at our arrival all the news –
How hard the nobles, how unkind the King
Hath showed himself. But, Madam, right
makes room
Where weapons want; and though a many
friends
Are made away (as Warwick, Lancaster,

13 potion drug (to use on Mortimer's guards)
IV.ii.4 a fig obscene expression of contempt accompanied by thrusting the thumb into the mouth or through two closed fingers
6 warrant assure
7 'A he
9 yet still
10 jar upset the tune
11 Unhappy unfortunate
12 Whither . . . steps what shall I do now?
13 cheer is your mood
16 contemn despise
17 Hainault Flemish county in the Low Countries, bordering France
20 shake cast
24 staff i.e., lance (in battle)
25 have at attack
29 utmost verge farthest limit
30 Tanaïs the River Don, then thought the boundary between Europe and Asia
32 Marquis Sir John's brother, William, Count of Hainault
41 thraldom bondage
42 standard banner (in war)
44 trow reckon, trust
47 Monsieur le Grand Marlowe's invention
49 King i.e., of France
51 want are required; **a** (for emphasis)
52 made away executed, killed

And others of our party and faction),
Yet have we friends, assure Your Grace, in England
Would cast up caps and clap their hands for joy
To see us there, appointed for our foes.
Edmund. Would all were well and Edward well reclaimed,
For England's honor, peace, and quietness.
Mortimer Junior. But by the sword, my Lord, it must be deserved;
The King will ne'er forsake his flatterers.
Sir John. My Lords of England, sith the ungentle King
Of France refuseth to give aid of arms
To this distressèd Queen his sister here,
Go you with her to Hainault. Doubt ye not,
We will find comfort, money, men, and friends
Ere long, to bid the English King a base.
How say, young Prince? What think you of the match?
Prince Edward. I think King Edward will outrun us all.
Queen. Nay, son, not so; and you must not discourage
Your friends that are so forward in your aid.
Edmund. Sir John of Hainault, pardon us, I pray;
These comforts that you give our woeful Queen
Bind us in kindness all at your command.
Queen. Yea, gentle brother, and the God of Heaven
Prosper your happy motion, good Sir John.
Mortimer Junior. This noble gentleman, forward in arms,
Was born, I see, to be our anchor-hold.
Sir John of Hainault, be it thy renown
That England's Queen and nobles in distress
Have been by thee restored and comforted.
Sir John. Madam, along, [*To Prince Edward.*] and you, my Lord, with me,
That England's peers may Hainault's welcome see.

[*Exeunt.*]

[IV.iii]

Enter [Edward] *the* King, [Arundel], *the two* Spencers [Junior *and* Senior], *with others.*

Edward. Thus after many threats of wrathful war,
Triumpheth England's Edward with his friends;
And triumph Edward with his friends uncontrolled.
[*To Spencer Junior.*] My Lord of Gloucester, do you hear the news?
Spencer Junior. What news, my Lord?
Edward. Why man, they say there is great execution
Done through the realm. My Lord of Arundel,
You have the note, have you not?
Arundel. From the lieutenant of the Tower, my Lord.
Edward. I pray, let us see it.

[*He takes the note from Arundel, then hands it to Spencer Junior.*]

What have we there?
Read it, Spencer.

Spencer [Junior] *reads their names.*

Edward. Why so. They barked apace a month ago;
Now, on my life, they'll neither bark nor bite.
Now, sirs, the news from France; Gloucester, I trow
The Lords of France love England's gold so well
As Isabella gets no aid from thence.
What now remains? Have you proclaimed, my Lord,
Reward for them can bring in Mortimer?
Spencer Junior. My Lord, we have; and if he be in England,
'A will be had ere long, I doubt it not.
Edward. If, dost thou say? Spencer, as true as death,
He is in England's ground; our port-masters
Are not so careless of their King's command.

Enter a Post.

How now, what news with thee? From whence come these?
Post. Letters, my Lord, and tidings forth of France

56 appointed armed
57 reclaimed (1) subdued; (2) taken back
61 sith since
66 base challenge (from "prisoner's base," a children's game)
67 match competition
74 brother i.e., brother-in-law
75 motion proposal
76 forward eager
IV.iii.3 uncontrolled without censure
8 note official list of those dead
12 barked embarked
15 love . . . well i.e., Edward's bribe has been successful
20 'A he (i.e., Mortimer); **had** captured

To you, my Lord of Gloucester, from Levune.
[*He gives letters to Spencer Junior.*]

Edward. Read.

Spencer Junior (reads the letter). "My duty to your honor promised, *et cetera*, I have, according to instructions in that behalf, dealt with the King of France his Lords, and effected that the Queen, all discontented and discomforted, is gone. Whither, if you ask, with Sir John of Hainault, brother to the Marquis, into Flanders. With them are gone Lord Edmund and the Lord Mortimer, having in their company divers of your nation, and others; and as constant report goeth, they intend to give King Edward battle in England sooner than he can look for them. This is all the news of import.
Your Honor's in all service, Levune."

Edward. Ah, villains, hath that Mortimer escaped?
With him is Edmund gone associate?
And will Sir John of Hainault lead the round?
Welcome, a God's name, Madam, and your son;
England shall welcome you and all your rout.
Gallop apace bright Phoebus through the sky,
And dusky night, in rusty iron car,
Between you both shorten the time, I pray,
That I may see that most desirèd day
When we may meet these traitors in the field.
Ah, nothing grieves me but my little boy
Is thus misled to countenance their ills.
Come, friends, to Bristol, there to make us strong;
And, winds, as equal be to bring them in
As you injurious were to bear them forth.
[*Exeunt.*]

[IV.iv]

Enter [Isabella] *the* Queen, her son [Prince Edward], Edmund [Earl of Kent], Mortimer [Junior], *and* Sir John [of Hainault, *with* Soldiers].

Queen. Now Lords, our loving friends and countrymen,
Welcome to England all; with prosperous winds
Our kindest friends in Belgia have we left,
To cope with friends at home – a heavy case,
When force to force is knit and sword and glaive
In civil broils makes kin and countrymen
Slaughter themselves in others, and their sides
With their own weapons gored. But what's the help?
Misgoverned Kings are cause of all this wrack;
And Edward, Thou art one among them all,
Whose looseness hath betrayed thy land to spoil
And made the channels overflow with blood.
Of Thine own people patron shouldst thou be,
But Thou –

Mortimer Junior. Nay Madam, if you be a warrior,
Ye must not grow so passionate in speeches.
Lords, sith that we are by sufferance of Heaven
Arrived and armèd in this Prince's right,
Here for our country's cause swear we to him
All homage, fealty, and forwardness.
And for the open wrongs and injuries
Edward hath done to us, his Queen, and land,
We come in arms to wreak it with the sword,
That England's Queen in peace may repossess
Her dignities and honors, and withal
We may remove these flatterers from the King,
That havocs England's wealth and treasury.

Sir John. Sound trumpets, my Lord, and forward let us march;
Edward will think we come to flatter him.

Edmund. I would he never had been flattered more.
[*Trumpets sound. Exeunt.*]

[IV.v]

[*Alarums and excursions.*] *Enter* [Edward] *the* King, Baldock, *and* Spencer [Junior] (*the son*), *flying about the stage.*

Spencer Junior. Fly, fly, my Lord; the Queen is over-strong,
Her friends do multiply, and yours do fail.

---

31 **effected** have brought about
32 **discomforted** discouraged
37–8 **constant** repeated
44 **round** (1) dance; (2) next stage
47 **Phoebus** the sun god
53 **countenance** (1) observe; (2) support
54 **strong** (1) prepared; (2) resolute
IV.iv.3 Belgia i.e., the Low Countries (Gallia Belgica); Hainault is in Flanders (modern Belgium)
4 **cope** battle; **friends** (1) relatives; (2) allies; **heavy** sad
5 **glaive** (1) spear; (2) broadsword; (3) halberd
8 **help** remedy
9 **Misgoverned** (1) unruly; (2) those who govern poorly or improperly; **wrack** (1) misfortune; (2) destruction
13 **patron** (1) benefactor; (2) father; (3) exemplary
17 **sufferance** permission
20 **fealty** loyalty; **forwardness** readiness
23 **wreak** avenge
27 **havocs** misuses
IV.v.1 Fly run
2 **fail** (1) grow faint; (2) fall, die; (3) decline numerically

Shape we our course to Ireland, there to breathe.
Edward. What, was I born to fly and run away,
And leave the Mortimers conquerors behind?
Give me my horse, and let's r'enforce our troops
And in this bed of honor die with fame.
Baldock. Oh, no, my Lord, this princely resolution
Fits not the time. Away! We are pursued.
[*Exeunt.*]

[IV.vi]

[*Enter*] Edmund [Earl of Kent] *alone with a sword and target.*

Edmund. This way he fled, but I am come too late.
Edward, alas, my heart relents for thee.
Proud traitor Mortimer, why dost thou chase
Thy lawful King, thy Sovereign, with thy sword?
[*Addressing himself.*] Vile wretch, and why hast thou, of all unkind,
Borne arms against thy brother and thy King?
Rain showers of vengeance on my cursèd head,
Thou God, to whom in justice it belongs
To punish this unnatural revolt.
Edward, this Mortimer aims at thy life;
Oh, fly him, then! But, Edmund, calm this rage;
Dissemble or thou diest, for Mortimer
And Isabel do kiss while they conspire;
And yet she bears a face of love, forsooth.
Fie on that love that hatcheth death and hate.
Edmund, away! Bristol to Longshanks' blood
Is false; be not found single for suspect;
Proud Mortimer pries near into thy walks.

Enter [Isabella] *the* Queen, Mortimer [Junior], *the young* Prince [Edward,] *and* Sir John of Hainault [*with* Soldiers].

Queen. Successful battles gives the God of Kings
To them that fight in right and fear His wrath.
Since then successfully we have prevailed,
Thanks be Heaven's great architect and you.
Ere farther we proceed, my noble Lords,
We here create our well belovèd son,
Of love and care unto His royal Person,
Lord Warden of the realm; and sith the fates
Have made his father so infortunate,
Deal you, my Lords, in this, my loving Lords,
As to your wisdoms fittest seems in all.
Edmund. Madam, without offense, if I may ask,
How will you deal with Edward in his fall?
Prince Edward. Tell me, good uncle, what Edward do you mean?
Edmund. Nephew, your father – I dare not call him King.
Mortimer Junior. My Lord of Kent, what needs these questions?
'Tis not in her controlment, nor in ours;
But as the realm and Parliament shall please,
So shall your brother be disposèd of.
[*Aside to the Queen.*] I like not this relenting mood in Edmund;
Madam, 'tis good to look to him betimes.
Queen. [*Aside to Mortimer Junior.*] My Lord, the Mayor of Bristol knows our mind?
Mortimer Junior. [*Aside.*] Yea, Madam, and they scape not easily
That fled the field.
Queen. Baldock is with the King;
A goodly chancellor, is he not, my Lord?
Sir John. So are the Spencers, the father and the son.
Edmund. [*Aside, despairingly.*] This, Edward, is the ruin of the realm.

Enter Rice ap Howell *and the* Mayor of Bristol, *with* Spencer [Senior] (*the father*), [*prisoner, with* Attendants].

Rice ap Howell. God save Queen Isabel and her princely son.
[*Pointing to the Mayor.*] Madam, the mayor and citizens of Bristol,
In sign of love and duty to this presence,
Present by me this traitor to the state –
Spencer, the father to that wanton Spencer,
That, like the lawless Catiline of Rome,

3 **Ireland** Holinshed says that Edward fled to Bristol en route to Wales for support; Ireland was considered an alternate escape route if things went badly
5 **the Mortimers** Marlowe nods; the elder Mortimer is now dead, not having survived his imprisonment in the Tower
7 **bed of honor** England
IV.vi.5 unkind unnatural (as Edward's brother he seeks fratricide)
12 **Dissemble** be deceptive; change motive
14 **forsooth** in truth
16–17 **Bristol . . . false** the Mayor of Bristol has joined the rebellion
17 **single** alone (for Mortimer will surely kill him)
18 **pries** (1) peers; (2) spies; **walks** movements
22 **architect** God; **you** Isabella's earthly supporters
26 **Lord Warden** viceroy (customary position of a king during his minority)
28 **Deal** proceed
32 **what . . . mean** (1) attempt to secure position as Lord Warden; (2) reprimand for not referring to Edward by his title; (3) for clarity and Edmund's declaration of allegiance (since he has wavered in the past)
38 **relenting** (1) sympathetic; (2) change of heart
48 **presence** i.e., royal presence
51 **Catiline of Rome** a corrupt Roman, then proverbial for political disorder

Reveled in England's wealth and treasury.
Queen. We thank you all.
Mortimer Junior. Your loving care in this
Deserveth princely favors and rewards.
But where's the King and the other Spencer fled?
Rice ap Howell. Spencer the son, created Earl of Gloucester,
Is with that smooth-tongued scholar Baldock gone,
And shipped but late for Ireland with the King.
Mortimer Junior. [*Aside.*] Some whirlwind fetch them back, or sink them all!
They shall be started thence, I doubt it not.
Prince Edward. Shall I not see the King my father yet?
Edmund. [*Aside.*] Unhappy Edward, chased from England's bounds.
Sir John. Madam, what resteth? Why stand ye in a muse?
Queen. I rue my Lord's ill fortune, but, alas,
Care of my country called me to this war.
Mortimer Junior. Madam, have done with care and sad complaint;
Your King hath wronged your country and himself,
And we must seek to right it as we may.
Meanwhile, have hence this rebel to the block.
[*To Spencer Senior, sarcastically.*] Your Lordship cannot privilege your head!
Spencer Senior. Rebel is he that fights against his Prince;
So fought not they that fought in Edward's right.
Mortimer Junior. Take him away; he prates.
[*Exit* Spencer Senior, *guarded.*]
You, Rice ap Howell,
Shall do good service to Her Majesty,
Being of countenance in your country here,
To follow these rebellious runagates.
We in meanwhile, Madam, must take advice
How Baldock, Spencer, and their 'complices
May in their fall be followed to their end.
Exeunt.

[IV.vii]

Enter the Abbot [*and*] Monks [*of Neath Abbey in Wales,* King] Edward, Spencer [Junior], *and* Baldock, [*the latter three disguised*].

Abbot. Have you no doubt, my Lord, have you no fear;
As silent and as careful will we be
To keep Your royal Person safe with us,
Free from suspect and fell invasion
Of such as have Your Majesty in chase –
Yourself and those your chosen company –
As danger of this stormy time requires.
Edward. Father, thy face should harbor no deceit;
Oh, hadst thou ever been a king, thy heart
Pierced deeply with sense of my distress,
Could not but take compassion of my state.
Stately and proud, in riches and in train,
Whilom I was, powerful and full of pomp;
But what is he whom rule and empery
Have not in life or death made miserable?
Come, Spencer; come, Baldock, come sit down by me;
Make trial now of that philosophy,
That in our famous nurseries of arts
Thou sucked'st from Plato and from Aristotle.
Father, this life contemplative is Heaven –
Oh, that I might this life in quiet lead!
But we, alas, are chased; and you, my friends,
Your lives and my dishonor they pursue.
Yet, gentle monks, for treasure, gold, nor fee,
Do you betray us and our company.
Monk. Your Grace may sit secure, if none but we
Do wot of your abode.
Spencer Junior. Not one alive; but shrewdly I suspect
A gloomy fellow in a mead below;
'A gave a long look after us, my Lord,
And all the land, I know, is up in arms –
Arms that pursue our lives with deadly hate.
Baldock. We were embarked for Ireland, wretched we,
With awkward winds and sore tempests driven,
To fall on shore and here to pine in fear

58 but late just lately
60 started forced out
61 yet again
63 resteth remains to be done; **a muse** thought, reflection
70 privilege your head your new rank will not prevent beheading
71 Prince legitimate ruler
73 prates talks nonsense
75 countenance authority
76 runagates (1) renegades; (2) fugitives
77 take advice consider, deliberate
79 end death
IV.vii.4 fell cruel
5 chase pursuit
13 Whilom formerly; **pomp** magnificence
14 empery empire
18 nurseries Oxford and Cambridge universities
28 shrewdly intuitively
29 gloomy fellow the Mower, a figure of death (cf. the Grim Reaper); **mead** meadow; **below** outside the Abbey walls
34 sore harsh

Of Mortimer and his confederates.
Edward. Mortimer! Who talks of Mortimer?
Who wounds me with the name of Mortimer,
That bloody man? [*Kneeling.*] Good father, on thy lap
Lay I this head, laden with mickle care.
Oh, might I never open these eyes again,
Never again lift up this drooping head,
Oh, never more lift up this dying heart!
Spencer Junior. Look up, my Lord. Baldock, this drowsiness
Betides no good. Here even we are betrayed!

Enter, with Welsh hooks, Rice ap Howell [*and* Soldiers], *a* Mower, *and the* Earl of Leicester. [*They remain temporarily upstage.*]

Mower. [*To Rice ap Howell, pointing.*] Upon my life, those be the men ye seek.
Rice ap Howell. Fellow, enough. [*To Leicester.*] My Lord, I pray be short;
A fair commission warrants what we do.
Leicester. [*Aside, with irony.*] The Queen's commission, urged by Mortimer!
What cannot gallant Mortimer with the Queen?
Alas, see where he sits and hopes unseen
T'escape their hands that seek to reave his life.
Too true it is: *quem dies vidit veniens superbum,*
Hunc dies vidit fugiens iacentem.
But Leicester, leave to grow so passionate.
[*Coming forward with his party.*] Spencer and Baldock – by no other names –
I arrest you of high treason here.
Stand not on titles, but obey th'arrest;
'Tis in the name of Isabel the Queen.
[*To King Edward.*] My Lord, why droop you thus?
Edward. Oh, day! The last of all my bliss on earth,
Center of all misfortune. Oh, my stars!
Why do you glower unkindly on a king?
Comes Leicester, then, in Isabella's name
To take my life, my company, from me?
Here, man, rip up this panting breast of mine,
And take my heart in rescue of my friends!
Rice ap Howell. Away with them.
Spencer Junior. It may become thee yet
To let us take our farewell of His Grace.
Abbot. [*Aside.*] My heart with pity earns to see this sight;
A king to bear these words and proud commands!
Edward. Spencer,
Ah sweet Spencer, thus then must we part?
Spencer Junior. We must, my Lord; so will the angry Heavens.
Edward. Nay, so will hell and cruel Mortimer;
The gentle Heavens have not to do in this.
Baldock. My Lord, it is in vain to grieve or storm.
Here humbly of Your Grace we take our leaves;
Our lots are cast. I fear me, so is thine.
Edward. In Heaven we may, in earth never shall we meet.
And Leicester, say, what shall become of us?
Leicester. Your Majesty must go to Killingworth.
Edward. Must! 'Tis somewhat hard when Kings must go.
Leicester. Here is a litter ready for Your Grace
That waits your pleasure. And the day grows old.
Rice ap Howell. As good be gone as stay and be benighted.
Edward. A litter hast thou? Lay me in a hearse,
And to the gates of hell convey me hence;
Let Pluto's bells ring out my fatal knell
And hags howl for my death at Charon's shore,
For friends hath Edward none but these, and these,
And these must die under a tyrant's sword.
Rice ap Howell. My Lord, be going; care not for these,
For we shall see them shorter by the heads.
Edward. Well, that shall be shall be; part we must.
Sweet Spencer, gentle Baldock, part we must.
Hence feignèd weeds, unfeignèd are my woes!
[*He throws off his disguise.*]

---

39 **bloody** i.e., bloodthirsty
40 **mickle** much
44 **drowsiness** (often considered a dangerous omen)
45 **Betides** bodes
46 **s.d. *hooks*** bill-hooks, agricultural tools with hooked ends for moving or cutting brush
48 **fair** legal
50 **gallant** (1) bold; (2) as her lover
52 **reave** take away by force
53–4 ***quem . . . iacentem*** whom dawn has seen to reign in pride the late evening sees overthrown
56 **no other names** i.e., they have now lost their new titles from Edward
67 **rescue** (1) ransom; (2) release
69 **let . . . Grace** an apparent genuine fondness for Edward II here similar to that displayed by Gaveston for the King
70 **earns** grieves
81 **Killingworth** Kenilworth castle in Warwickshire (spelling, taken directly from Holinshed, may be a play on *killing*)
83 **litter** coach carried by men
84 **day grows old** i.e., night is coming
88 **Pluto** in classical mythology the keeper of the underworld and ruler of the dead; he was not associated with bells
89 **Charon** ferryman who took the dead into hell across the River Styx
93 **shorter . . . heads** i.e., they will be beheaded
96 **feignèd weeds** fake clothes; disguise

Father, farewell. Leicester, thou stay'st for me,
And go I must. Life, farewell, with my friends!
Exeunt [King] Edward *and* Leicester.

Spencer Junior. Oh, is he gone? Is noble Edward gone?
Parted from hence, never to see us more?
Rend, sphere of Heaven, and fire, forsake thy orb,
Earth, melt to air; gone is my Sovereign,
Gone, gone alas, never to make return.

Baldock. Spencer, I see our souls are fleeted hence;
We are deprived the sunshine of our life.
Make for a new life, man; throw up thy eyes,
And heart and hand to Heaven's immortal throne,
Pay nature's debt with cheerful countenance.
Reduce we all our lessons unto this:
To die, sweet Spencer, therefore live we all;
Spencer, all live to die, and rise to fall.

Rice ap Howell. Come, come, keep these preachments till you come to the place appointed. You, and such as you are, have made wise work in England. [*Sardonically.*] Will your Lordships away?

Mower. [*To Rice ap Howell.*] Your worship, I trust, will remember me?

Rice ap Howell. Remember thee, fellow? What else? Follow me to the town.

[*Exeunt.*]

Act V

[V.i]

Enter [Edward] *the* King, Leicester, *with a* Bishop [of Winchester] *for the crown,* [*and* Trussel].

Leicester. Be patient, good my Lord, cease to lament.
Imagine Killingworth Castle were your court,
And that you lay for pleasure here a space,
Not of compulsion or necessity.

Edward. Leicester, if gentle words might comfort me,
Thy speeches long ago had eased my sorrows,
For kind and loving hast thou always been.
The griefs of private men are soon allayed,
But not of Kings. The forest deer, being struck,
Runs to an herb that closeth up the wounds;
But when the imperial lion's flesh is gored,
He rends and tears it with his wrathful paw;
Highly scorning that the lowly earth
Should drink his blood, mounts up into the air.
And so it fares with me, whose dauntless mind
The ambitious Mortimer would seek to curb,
And that unnatural Queen, false Isabel,
That thus hath pent and mewed me in a prison;
For such outrageous passions cloy my soul,
As with the wings of rancor and disdain
Full often am I soaring up to Heaven
To plain me to the gods against them both.
But when I call to mind I am a King,
Methinks I should revenge me of the wrongs
That Mortimer and Isabel have done.
But what are Kings when regiment is gone
But perfect shadows in a sunshine day?
My nobles rule, I bear the name of King;
I wear the crown, but am controlled by them,
By Mortimer, and my unconstant Queen,
Who spots my nuptial bed with infamy
While I am lodged within this cave of care,
Where sorrow at my elbow still attends
To company my heart with sad laments,
That bleeds within me for this strange exchange.
But tell me, must I now resign my crown
To make usurping Mortimer a king?

Bishop. Your Grace mistakes; it is for England's good
And princely Edward's right we crave the crown.

Edward. No, 'tis for Mortimer, not Edward's head,
For he's a lamb, encompassèd by wolves,
Which in a moment will abridge his life.
But if proud Mortimer do wear this crown,
Heavens turn it to a blaze of quenchless fire,
Or, like the snaky wreath of Tisiphon,
Engirt the temples of his hateful head;

---

101 forsake thy orb some astronomers believed in a sphere or orb of fire (*cœlum igneum*)
104 fleeted hence have left our bodies
105 sunshine the King
108 Pay . . . debt die (proverbial)
109 Reduce summarize
113 appointed the gallows where those about to be executed made speeches telling others not to follow their evil example
114 made wise work created great difficulties
117 What else? of course!
V.i.3 lay resided; **space** period of time
10 herb dittany, supposedly a herb that healed the wounds of arrows to stags
18 pent shut up; **mewed** caged
19 outrageous excessive
22 plain complain, plead
27 perfect mere, simple
30 unconstant unfaithful
35 strange exchange change of circumstances unnatural to a king
44 blaze . . . fire a crown that will burn the head of the wearer as Medea prepared for Jason when he deserted her for Creusa
45 Tisiphon one of the Furies who had snakes for hair

So shall not England's vine be perishèd,
But Edward's name survive though Edward dies.

Leicester. My Lord, why waste you thus the time away?
They stay your answer; will you yield your crown?

Edward. Ah, Leicester, weigh how hardly I can brook
To lose my crown and kingdom without cause.
To give ambitious Mortimer my right
That like a mountain overwhelms my bliss
In which extreme my mind here murdered is.
But, what the Heavens appoint I must obey.
Here, take my crown – the life of Edward too.
[*Takes off crown.*]
Two Kings in England cannot reign at once.
But stay awhile; let me be King till night,
That I may gaze upon this glittering crown;
So shall my eyes receive their last content,
My head, the latest honor due to it,
And jointly both yield up their wishèd right.
Continue ever thou celestial sun;
Let never silent night possess this clime.
Stand still you watches of the element;
All times and seasons rest you at a stay,
That Edward may be still fair England's King.
But day's bright beams doth vanish fast away,
And needs I must resign my wishèd crown.
Inhuman creatures, nursed with tiger's milk,
Why gape you for your Sovereign's overthrow –
My diadem, I mean, and guiltless life?
See, monsters, see, I'll wear my crown again.
[*Puts on crown.*]
What, fear you not the fury of your King?
But hapless Edward, thou art fondly led.
They pass not for thy frowns as late they did,
But seek to make a new-elected King,
Which fills my mind with strange despairing thoughts,
Which thoughts are martyrèd with endless torments;
And in this torment comfort find I none
But that I feel the crown upon my head;
And therefore let me wear it yet a while.

Trussel. My Lord, the Parliament must have present news,
And therefore say, will you resign or no?
The King rageth.

Edward. I'll not resign, but while I live, be King!
Traitors, be gone. And join you with Mortimer.
Elect, conspire, install, do what you will;
Their blood and yours shall seal these treacheries.

Bishop. This answer we'll return, and so farewell.
[*Bishop and Trussel offer to leave.*]

Leicester. [*Aside to Edward.*] Call them again, my Lord, and speak them fair,
For if they go, the Prince shall lose his right.

Edward. Call thou them back; I have no power to speak.

Leicester. [*To Bishop.*] My Lord, the king is willing to resign.

Bishop. If he be not, let him choose –

Edward. Oh, would I might! But Heavens and earth conspire
To make me miserable. Here, receive my crown.
Receive it? No, these innocent hands of mine
Shall not be guilty of so foul a crime.
He of you all that most desires my blood
And will be called the murderer of a King,
Take it. What, are you moved? Pity you me?
Then send for unrelenting Mortimer
And Isabel, whose eyes, being turned to steel,
Will sooner sparkle fire than shed a tear.
Yet, stay, for rather than I will look on them,
Here, here!
[*He resigns the crown.*]
Now, sweet God of heaven,
Make me despise this transitory pomp,
And sit for aye enthronizèd in Heaven.
Come, death, and with thy fingers close my eyes,
Or, if I live, let me forget myself.

Bishop. My Lord –

Edward. Call me not Lord! Away, out of my sight!
Ah, pardon me; grief makes me lunatic.
Let not that Mortimer protect my son.
More safety is there in a tiger's jaws
Than his embracements. Bear this to the Queen,
Wet with my tears and dried again with sighs.
[*Gives a handkerchief.*]
If with the sight thereof she be not moved,

47 **vine** royal lineage
50 **stay** await
51 **weigh** consider; **brook** afford
66 **watches of the element** stars and planets (days and nights were divided into periods known as watches)
71 **nursed . . . milk** nursed with cruelty
76 **fondly** foolishly
77 **pass** care
84 **present news** a prompt report
88 **install** place someone in authority
92 **right** inheritance (out of revenge on Edward II)
109 **for aye** forever; **enthronizèd** enthroned
115 **protect** become Protector of the realm for

Return it back and dip it in my blood.
Commend me to my son, and bid him rule
Better than I. Yet how have I transgressed
Unless it be with too much clemency?
Trussel. And thus most humbly do we take our leave.
[*Exeunt* Bishop *and* Trussel *with the crown.*]
Edward. Farewell. I know the next news that they bring
Will be my death, and welcome shall it be;
To wretched men death is felicity.

[*Enter* Berkeley *to* Leicester *with a letter.*]

Leicester. Another post. What news brings he?
Edward. Such news as I expect. Come, Berkeley, come,
And tell thy message to my naked breast.
Berkeley. My Lord, think not a thought so villainous
Can harbor in a man of noble birth.
To do Your Highness service and devoir
And save you from your foes, Berkeley would die.
Leicester. [*Reading letter.*] My Lord, the council of the Queen commands
That I resign my charge.
Edward. And who must keep me now? [*To Berkeley.*] Must you, my Lord?
Berkeley. Aye, my most gracious Lord, so 'tis decreed.
Edward. [*Taking the letter.*] By Mortimer, whose name is written here.
Well may I rend his name that rends my heart!
[*Tears the paper.*]
This poor revenge hath something eased my mind.
So may his limbs be torn, as is this paper!
Hear me, immortal Jove, and grant it too.
Berkeley. Your Grace must hence with me to Berkeley straight.
Edward. Whither you will; all places are alike,
And every earth is fit for burial.
Leicester. [*To Berkeley.*] Favor him, my Lord, as much as lieth in you.
Berkeley. Even so betide my soul as I use him.
Edward. Mine enemy hath pitied my estate,
And that's the cause that I am now removed.
Berkeley. And thinks Your Grace that Berkeley will be cruel?
Edward. I know not; but of this am I assured,
That death ends all, and I can die but once.
Leicester, farewell.
Leicester. Not yet, my Lord; I'll bear you on your way.
Exeunt.

[V.ii]

Enter Mortimer [Junior] *and* Queen Isabella.

Mortimer Junior. Fair Isabel, now have we our desire.
The proud corrupters of the light-brained King
Have done their homage to the lofty gallows,
And he himself lies in captivity.
Be ruled by me, and we will rule the realm.
In any case, take heed of childish fear,
For now we hold an old wolf by the ears,
That, if he slip, will seize upon us both,
And grip the sorer, being gripped himself.
Think therefore, Madam, that imports us much
To erect your son with all the speed we may,
And that I be Protector over him,
For our behoof will bear the greater sway
Whenas a King's name shall be underwrit.
Queen. Sweet Mortimer, the life of Isabel,
Be thou persuaded that I love thee well,
And therefore, so the Prince my son be safe,
Whom I esteem as dear as these mine eyes,
Conclude against his father what thou wilt,
And I myself will willingly subscribe.
Mortimer Junior. First would I hear news that he were deposed,
And then let me alone to handle him.

Enter Messenger [*and then the* Bishop of Winchester *with the crown*].

Letters! From whence?
Messenger. From Killingworth, my Lord.
Queen. How fares my Lord the King?
Messenger. In health, madam, but full of pensiveness.
Queen. Alas, poor soul. Would I could ease his grief.

---

133 **devoir** duty (French)
144 **straight** directly
149 **Mine enemy** i.e., Leicester; **estate** condition
V.ii.2 **light-brained** frivolous, wanton, foolish
7 **old wolf** (proverbial)
9 **grip . . . gripped** will seize us more grievously
10 **imports . . . much** is to our distinct advantage
11 **erect** place in office
12 **Protector** actual ruler with authority to sign papers on behalf of the King; Edward VI, Elizabeth's younger brother, had ruled under Protector Somerset
19 **Conclude** bring a final verdict
22 **let me alone** trust me
25 **pensiveness** melancholy

[*Acknowledging the arrival of the crown.*] Thanks, gentle Winchester. [*To the Messenger.*] Sirrah, be gone.

[*Exit* Messenger.]

Bishop. [*Presenting the document of abdication.*] The King hath willingly resigned his crown.

Queen. Oh, happy news! Send for the Prince, my son.

Bishop. Further, ere this letter was sealed, Lord Berkeley came,
So that he now is gone from Killingworth,
And we have heard that Edmund laid a plot
To set his brother free; no more but so.
The Lord of Berkeley is so pitiful
As Leicester that had charge of him before.

Queen. Then let some other be his guardian.

[*Exit* Bishop.]

Mortimer Junior. Let me alone – here is the privy seal.
Who's there? [*To Attendants within.*] Call hither Gurney and Matrevis.
To dash the heavy-headed Edmund's drift,
Berkeley shall be discharged, the King removed,
And none but we shall know where he lieth.

Queen. But Mortimer, as long as he survives,
What safety rests for us, or for my son?

Mortimer Junior. Speak, shall he presently be dispatched and die?

Queen. I would he were, so it were not by my means.

Enter Matrevis *and* Gurney. [Mortimer Junior *confers with them apart.*]

Mortimer Junior. Enough. Matrevis, write a letter presently
Unto the Lord of Berkeley from ourself
That he resign the King to thee and Gurney;
And when 'tis done, we will subscribe our name.

Matrevis. It shall be done, my Lord.

[*He writes.*]

Mortimer Junior. Gurney.

Gurney. My Lord?

Mortimer Junior. As thou intendest to rise by Mortimer,
Who now makes Fortune's wheel turn as he please,
Seek all the means thou canst to make him droop,
And neither give him kind word nor good look.

Gurney. I warrant you, my Lord.

Mortimer Junior. And this above the rest, because we hear
That Edmund casts to work his liberty,
Remove him still from place to place by night,
And at the last he come to Killingworth,
And then from thence to Berkeley back again;
And by the way to make him fret the more,
Speak cursedly to him; and in any case
Let no man comfort him if he chance to weep,
But amplify his grief with bitter words.

Matrevis. Fear not, my Lord, we'll do as you command.

Mortimer Junior. So now away. Post thitherwards amain.

Queen. Whither goes this letter? To my Lord the King?
Commend me humbly to his Majesty,
And tell him that I labor all in vain
To ease his grief and work his liberty.
And bear him this, as witness of my love.

[*Gives a jewel.*]

Matrevis. I will, Madam.

Exeunt Matrevis *and* Gurney.
[Queen Isabella *and* Mortimer Junior *remain.*]

Enter the young Prince [Edward], *and* [Edmund] *the* Earl of Kent *talking with him.*

Mortimer Junior. [*Aside to the Queen.*] Finely dissembled; do so still, sweet Queen.
Here comes the young Prince with the Earl of Kent.

Queen. [*Aside to Mortimer Junior.*] Something he whispers in his childish ears.

Mortimer Junior. [*Aside.*] If he have such access unto the Prince,
Our plots and stratagems will soon be dashed.

Queen. [*Aside.*] Use Edmund friendly, as if all were well.

Mortimer Junior. [*To Edmund.*] How fares my honorable Lord of Kent?

---

34 **pitiful** sympathetic (to Edward's plight)
37 **privy seal** symbol and means of enforcing royal authority
38 **Gurney and Matrevis** historically, a knight (Sir Thomas Gourney) and a peer (the lord Matreuers) according to Holinshed
39 **dash** frustrate; **heavy-headed** dull; **drift** plot
43 **rests** is guaranteed
44 **dispatched** killed (i.e., dare they risk regicide)
48 **resign** surrender
52 **Fortune's wheel** a perspective of Fortune as cyclic
57 **casts** plans
62 **cursedly** (1) meanly; (2) threateningly; (3) virulently; in Elizabethan times, this word was usually associated with women (shrews and witches)
66 **post thitherwards** go there
73 **dissembled** acted with deceit; **still** continually

Edmund. In health, sweet Mortimer. [*To the Queen.*] How fares Your Grace?
Queen. Well – if my Lord your brother were enlargèd.
Edmund. I hear of late he hath deposed himself.
Queen. The more my grief.
Mortimer Junior. And mine.
Edmund. [*Aside.*] Ah, they do dissemble.
Queen. Sweet son, come hither; I must talk with thee.
Mortimer Junior. [*To Edmund.*] Thou, being his uncle and the next of blood,
Do look to be Protector over the Prince.
Edmund. Not I, my Lord; who should protect the son
But she that gave him life – I mean the Queen?
Prince Edward. Mother, persuade me not to wear the crown.
Let him be King; I am too young to reign.
Queen. But be content, seeing it His Highness' pleasure.
Prince Edward. Let me but see him first, and then I will.
Edmund. Aye, do, sweet nephew.
Queen. Brother, you know it is impossible.
Prince Edward. Why, is he dead?
Queen. No, God forbid.
Edmund. I would those words proceeded from your heart.
Mortimer Junior. Inconstant Edmund, dost thou favor him
That wast a cause of his imprisonment?
Edmund. The more cause have I now to make amends.
Mortimer Junior. I tell thee 'tis not meet that one so false
Should come about the person of a Prince.
[*To Prince Edward.*] My Lord, he hath betrayed the King, his brother,
And therefore trust him not.
Prince Edward. But he repents and sorrows for it now.
Queen. Come son, and go with this gentle Lord and me.
Prince Edward. With you I will, but not with Mortimer.
Mortimer Junior. Why youngling, 'sdain'st thou so of Mortimer?
Then I will carry thee by force away.
Prince Edward. Help, uncle Kent, Mortimer will wrong me.
[*Mortimer Junior grasps Prince Edward; Edmund tries to intervene.*]
Queen. Brother Edmund, strive not; we are his friends.
Isabel is nearer than the Earl of Kent.
Edmund. Sister, Edward is my charge. Redeem him.
Queen. [*Leaving*] Edward is my son, and I will keep him.
Edmund. [*To the Queen.*] Mortimer shall know that he hath wronged me.
[*Aside.*] Hence will I haste to Killingworth Castle
And rescue agèd Edward from his foes,
To be revenged on Mortimer and thee.
Exeunt [*on one side* Queen Isabella, Prince Edward, *and* Mortimer Junior; *on the other* Edmund].

[V.iii]

Enter Matrevis *and* Gurney *with* [Edward] *the* King [*and* Soldiers].

Matrevis. My Lord, be not pensive; we are your friends.
Men are ordained to live in misery;
Therefore, come; dalliance dangereth our lives.
Edward. Friends, whither must unhappy Edward go?
Will hateful Mortimer appoint no rest?
Must I be vexèd like the nightly bird
Whose sight is loathsome to all wingèd fowls?
When will the fury of his mind assuage?
When will his heart be satisfied with blood?
If mine will serve, unbowel straight this breast,
And give my heart to Isabel and him;
It is the chiefest mark they level at.
Gurney. Not so, my Liege; the Queen hath given this charge
To keep Your Grace in safety.
Your passions make your dolors to increase.
Edward. This usage makes my misery increase.
But can my air of life continue long

---

81 enlarged freed; given liberty
92 him i.e., his father
98 cause (by freeing Mortimer and renewing the rebellion)
100 meet proper
107 youngling novice; stripling (a contemptuous term); **'sdain'st** disdain'st
112 charge responsibility; **Redeem** release
116 agèd historically, Edward II was 43 at his death

V.iii.4 unhappy unfortunate
6–7 nightly bird . . . fowls the owl (omen of death); traditionally, thought to be persecuted by birds of the day
9 with blood simply to kill me
10 unbowel cut open; **straight** at once
12 mark target
15 dolors habitual sorrows
17 air of life breath

When all my senses are annoyed with stench?
Within a dungeon England's King is kept,
Where I am starved for want of sustenance.
My daily diet is heart-breaking sobs,
That almost rends the closet of my heart.
Thus lives old Edward, not relieved by any,
And so must die, though pitièd by many.
Oh, water, gentle friends, to cool my thirst
And clear my body from foul excrements.

Matrevis. Here's channel water, as our charge is given.
Sit down, for we'll be barbers to Your Grace.

Edward. [*Struggling.*] Traitors, away! What, will you murder me,
Or choke your Sovereign with puddle water?

Gurney. No, but wash your face and shave away your beard,
Lest you be known and so be rescuèd.

Matrevis. Why strive you thus? Your labor is in vain.

Edward. The wren may strive against the lion's strength,
But all in vain; so vainly do I strive
To seek for mercy at a tyrant's hand.

They wash him with puddle water, and shave his beard away.

Immortal powers, that knows the painful cares
That waits upon my poor distressèd soul,
Oh, level all your looks upon these daring men,
That wrongs their Liege and Sovereign, England's King.
Oh, Gaveston, it is for thee that I am wronged;
For me, both thou and both the Spencers died,
And for your sakes a thousand wrongs I'll take.
The Spencers' ghosts, wherever they remain,
Wish well to mine; then tush, for them I'll die.

Matrevis. 'Twixt theirs and yours shall be no enmity.
Come, come away. [*To Soldiers.*] Now put the torches out;
We'll enter in by darkness to Killingworth.

Enter Edmund [Earl of Kent].

Gurney. How now, who comes there?

Matrevis. Guard the King sure; it is the Earl of Kent.

Edward. Oh, gentle brother, help to rescue me.

Matrevis. Keep them asunder; thrust in the King.

Edmund. Soldiers, let me but talk to him one word.

Gurney. Lay hands upon the Earl for this assault.

Edmund. Lay down your weapons; traitors, yield the King!

[*Soldiers seize Edmund.*]

Matrevis. Edmund, yield thou thyself or thou shalt die.

Edmund. Base villains, wherefore do you grip me thus?

Gurney. Bind him, and so convey him to the court.

Edmund. Where is the court but here? Here is the King,
And I will visit him. Why stay you me?

Matrevis. The court is where Lord Mortimer remains.
Thither shall your honor go; and so, farewell.

Exeunt Matrevis *and* Gurney *with* [Edward] *the* King.
[Edmund Earl of Kent *and the* Soldiers *remain.*]

Edmund. Oh, miserable is that commonweal, where Lords
Keep courts and Kings are locked in prison!

Soldier. Wherefore stay we? On, sirs, to the court.

Edmund. Aye, lead me whither you will, even to my death,
Seeing that my brother cannot be released.

Exeunt.

[V.iv]

Enter Mortimer [Junior] *alone.*

Mortimer Junior. The King must die, or Mortimer goes down;
The commons now begin to pity him.
Yet he that is the cause of Edward's death
Is sure to pay for it when his son is of age,
And therefore will I do it cunningly.
This letter, written by a friend of ours,
Contains his death, yet bids them save his life.

[*He reads.*]

"*Edwardum occidere nolite timere, bonum est*;
Fear not to kill the King, 'tis good he die."
But read it thus, and that's another sense:
"*Edwardum occidere nolite, timere bonum est;*
Kill not the King, 'tis good to fear the worst."
Unpointed as it is, thus shall it go,
That, being dead, if it chance to be found,
Matrevis and the rest may bear the blame,

---

22 **closet** private chamber
27 **channel** sewer; **charge** command
31–2 **shave . . . rescuèd** (not in Holinshed but in John Stow's *Annals of England*)
44 **remain** exist
59 **Where . . . here?** in early modern thought, the court was wherever the King or Queen was
63 **commonweal** state
V.iv.2 **commons** (1) common people; (2) House of Commons, Parliament (while this is less likely, the possible pun underscores Mortimer's growing anxiety)
7 **death** i.e., death warrant
13 **Unpointed** unpunctuated
14 **being dead** once Edward is murdered

And we be quit that caused it to be done.
Within this room is locked the messenger
That shall convey it and perform the rest.
And by a secret token that he bears
Shall he be murdered when the deed is done.
[*Calling.*] Lightborn, come forth.

[*Enter* Lightborn.]

Art thou as resolute as thou wast?
Lightborn. What else, my Lord? And far more resolute.
Mortimer Junior. And hast thou cast how to accomplish it?
Lightborn. Aye, aye, and none shall know which way he died.
Mortimer Junior. But at his looks, Lightborn, thou wilt relent.
Lightborn. Relent? Ha, ha! I use much to relent.
Mortimer Junior. Well, do it bravely, and be secret.
Lightborn. You shall not need to give instructions;
'Tis not the first time I have killed a man.
I learned in Naples how to poison flowers,
To strangle with a lawn thrust through the throat,
To pierce the windpipe with a needle's point,
Or while one is asleep, to take a quill
And blow a little powder in his ears.
Or open his mouth and pour quicksilver down.
But yet I have a braver way than these.
Mortimer Junior. What's that?
Lightborn. Nay, you shall pardon me; none shall know my tricks.
Mortimer Junior. I care not how it is, so it be not spied.
Deliver this to Gurney and Matrevis.
[*He gives the letter.*]
At every ten miles' end thou hast a horse.
[*Giving a token.*] Take this. Away, and never see me more.
Lighborn. No?
Mortimer Junior. No, unless thou bring me news of Edward's death.
Lightborn. That will I quickly do. Farewell, my Lord.
[*Exit.*]
Mortimer Junior. The Prince I rule, the Queen do I command,
And with a lowly congé to the ground
The proudest Lords salute me as I pass;
I seal, I cancel, I do what I will.
Feared am I more than loved; let me be feared,
And when I frown, make all the court look pale.
I view the Prince with Aristarchus' eyes,
Whose looks were as a breeching to a boy.
They thrust upon me the Protectorship
And sue to me for that that I desire.
While at the council table, grave enough,
And not unlike a bashful Puritan,
First I complain of imbecility,
Saying it is *onus quam gravissimum*,
Till being interrupted by my friends,
Suscepi that *provinciam*, as they term it,
And to conclude, I am Protector now.
Now is all sure; the Queen and Mortimer
Shall rule the realm, the King, and none rule us.
Mine enemies will I plague, my friends advance,
And what I list command who dare control?
Maior sum quam cui possit fortuna nocere.
And that this be the coronation day,
It pleaseth me, and Isabel the Queen.
[*Trumpets sound within.*]
The trumpets sound; I must go take my place.

---

16 **quit** acquitted
21 **s.d. Lightborn** English name for Lucifer, the biblical devil in the popular mystery plays in England
26 **use much** much accustomed (sardonically)
27 **bravely** (1) boldly; (2) skillfully; (3) forcefully
30–5 **I...down** Naples as a dangerous city; in 1591 it was widely believed a hired Italian assassin attempted to poison Queen Elizabeth
31 **strangle** choke; **lawn** fine linen
32 **pierce** block
34 **powder** arsenic
35 **quicksilver** another poison
36 **braver** more cunning
38 **tricks** professional methods
42 **Take this** the secret death warrant on Lightborn
47 **congé** bow
49 **seal** authorize official documents
50 **Feared...feared** following the well-known rule in Machiavelli's *The Prince* that to retain power it is better to be feared than loved
52 **Aristarchus' eyes** proverbially harsh schoolmaster in second century BC
53 **breeching** whipping; flogging
55 **sue** petition
57 **Puritan** one strictly religious, at least in outward behavior; proverbial for hypocrisy
58 **imbecility** weakness
59 ***onus...gravissimum*** "a very heavy burden" (Latin)
61 ***Suscepi...provinciam*** "I have undertaken that office" (Latin)
66 **list** am pleased to
67 ***Maior...nocere*** "I am so great that Fortune cannot harm me" (Latin)
68 **coronation day** historically, Edward III was crowned on Candlemas Day 1327

Enter the young King [Edward III, *the* Arch]bishop [*of* Canterbury], Champion, Nobles, [*and*] Queen [Isabella].

[Arch]bishop. Long live King Edward, by the grace of God,
King of England and Lord of Ireland.
Champion. If any Christian, Heathen, Turk, or Jew
Dares but affirm that Edward's not true King,
And will avouch his saying with the sword,
I am the Champion that will combat him.
Mortimer Junior. None comes. Sound trumpets.
[*Trumpets sound.*]
King Edward III. Champion, here's to thee.
[*Drinks a toast and gives Champion the goblet.*]
Queen. Lord Mortimer, now take him to your charge.

Enter Soldiers *with* [Edmund,] *the* Earl of Kent, *prisoner.*

Mortimer Junior. What traitor have we there with blades and bills?
Soldier. Edmund, the Earl of Kent.
King Edward III. What hath he done?
Soldier. 'A would have taken the King away perforce,
As we were bringing him to Killingworth.
Mortimer Junior. Did you attempt his rescue, Edmund? Speak.
Edmund. Mortimer, I did; he is our King,
And thou compell'st this Prince to wear the crown.
Mortimer Junior. Strike off his head! He shall have martial law.
Edmund. Strike off my head? Base traitor, I defy thee.
King Edward III. [*To Mortimer Junior.*] My Lord, he is my uncle and shall live.
Mortimer Junior. My Lord, he is your enemy and shall die.
Edmund. Stay, villains.
King Edward III. Sweet mother, if I cannot pardon him,
Entreat my Lord Protector for his life.
Queen. Son, be content; I dare not speak a word.
King Edward III. Nor I, and yet methinks I should command;
But, seeing I cannot, I'll entreat for him.
[*To Mortimer Junior.*] My Lord, if you will let my uncle live,
I will requite it when I come to age.
Mortimer Junior. 'Tis for Your Highness' good and for the realm's.
[*To Soldiers.*] How often shall I bid you bear him hence?
Edmund [*To Mortimer Junior.*] Art thou King? Must I die at thy command?
Mortimer Junior. At our command. Once more, away with him.
Edmund. [*Struggling.*] Let me but stay and speak; I will not go.
Either my brother or his son is King,
And none of both them thirst for Edmund's blood.
And therefore, soldiers, whither will you haul me?
They haul Edmund [Earl of Kent] *away, and carry him to be beheaded.*
King Edward III. [*To the Queen.*] What safety may I look for at his hands,
If that my uncle shall be murdered thus?
Queen. Fear not, sweet boy, I'll guard thee from thy foes.
Had Edmund lived, he would have sought thy death.
Come son, we'll ride a-hunting in the park.
King Edward III. And shall my uncle Edmund ride with us?
Queen. He is a traitor; think not on him. Come.
Exeunt.

[V.v]

Enter Matrevis *and* Gurney.

Matrevis. Gurney, I wonder the King dies not,
Being in a vault up to the knees in water,
To which the channels of the castle run,
From whence a damp continually ariseth
That were enough to poison any man,
Much more a King brought up so tenderly.
Gurney. And so do I, Matrevis. Yesternight
I opened but the door to throw him meat,
And I was almost stifled with the savor.
Matrevis. He hath a body able to endure
More than we can inflict, and therefore now
Let us assail his mind another while.
Gurney. Send for him out thence, and I will anger him.
Matrevis. But stay, who's this?

79 blades and bills swords and halberds
81 perforce by force, violently
85 martial law summary execution without trial
100 our (1) as ruler, the royal *we*; (2) in partnership with the Queen; (3) on behalf of Edward III
103 none neither
V.v.4 damp mist
8 meat food
9 savor stench

Enter Lightborn [*bearing a letter.*]

Lightborn. My Lord Protector greets you. [*Gives the letter.*]

Gurney. What's here? I know not how to conster it.

Matrevis. Gurney, it was left unpointed for the nonce:
[*Reading.*] "*Edwardum occidere nolite timere* –";
That's his meaning.

Lightborn. Know you this token? [*Shows the token*].
I must have the King.

Matrevis. Aye, stay a while; thou shalt have answer straight.
[*Aside to Gurney.*] This villain's sent to make away the King.

Gurney [*Aside.*] I thought as much.

Matrevis. [*Aside.*] And when the murder's done,
See how he must be handled for his labor.
Pereat iste! Let him have the King.
[*To Lightborn.*] What else? Here is the keys; this is the lake.
Do as you are commanded by my Lord.

Lightborn. I know what I must do. Get you away.
Yet be not far off; I shall need your help.
See that in the next room I have a fire,
And get me a spit, and let it be red hot.

Matrevis. Very well.

Gurney. Need you anything besides?

Lightborn. What else? A table and a featherbed.

Gurney. That's all?

Lightborn. Aye, aye; so, when I call you, bring it in.

Matrevis. Fear not you that.

Gurney. Here's a light to go into the dungeon.
[*He gives a light, then exit with* Matrevis.]

Lightborn. So now, must I about this gear; ne'er was there any
So finely handled as this King shall be.
[*Opens the dungeon.*]
Foh! Here's a place indeed with all my heart.

[Edward *comes up from below, or is discovered.*]

Edward. Who's there? What light is that? Wherefore comes thou?

Lightborn. To comfort you and bring you joyful news.

Edward. Small comfort finds poor Edward in thy looks.
Villain, I know thou com'st to murder me.

Lightborn. To murder you, my most Gracious Lord?
Far is it from my heart to do you harm.
The Queen sent me to see how you were used,
For she relents at this your misery.
And what eyes can refrain from shedding tears
To see a King in this most piteous state?

Edward. Weepst thou already? List awhile to me,
And then thy heart, were it as Gurney's is,
Or as Matrevis', hewn from the Caucasus,
Yet will it melt ere I have done my tale.
This dungeon where they keep me is the sink
Wherein the filth of all the castle falls.

Lightborn. Oh, villains!

Edward. And there in mire and puddle have I stood
This ten days' space; and lest that I should sleep,
One plays continually upon a drum.
They give me bread and water, being a King,
So that for want of sleep and sustenance
My mind's distempered, and my body's numbed,
And whether I have limbs or no I know not.
Oh, would my blood dropped out from every vein,
As doth this water from my tattered robes.
Tell Isabel, the Queen, I looked not thus
When for her sake I ran at tilt in France
And there unhorsed the Duke of Cleremont.

Lightborn. Oh, speak no more, my Lord; this breaks my heart.
[*A bed is thrust out or brought onstage.*]
Lie on this bed and rest yourself awhile.

Edward. These looks of thine can harbor nought but death.
I see my tragedy written in thy brows.
Yet stay a while; forbear thy bloody hand,
And let me see the stroke before it comes,
That and even then when I shall lose my life,
My mind may be more steadfast on my God.

Lightborn. What means Your Highness to mistrust me thus?

---

15 **conster** interpret, construe

16 **for the nonce** on purpose

21 **make away** murder

24 ***Pereat iste!*** "Let him die!" (Latin)

25 **lake** dungeon (by association with hell)

30 **spit** presumably put red-hot up Edward's anus, perhaps kept from view by the table or featherbed or Lightborn himself (whose name is connected to the spit)

40 **Foh!** (reaction to the stench)

51 **List** hear

53 **Caucasus** mountain range between Black and Caspian Seas known for its harsh terrain and bitterly cold weather

55 **sink** cesspool

56 **filth** sewage

63 **distempered** deranged

68 **ran at tilt** jousted

73 **tragedy** fatal end

Edward. What means thou to dissemble with me thus?
Lightborn. These hands were never stained with innocent blood,
Nor shall they now be tainted with a King's.
Edward. Forgive my thought for having such a thought.
One jewel have I left; receive thou this.
[*Gives a jewel.*]
Still fear I, and I know not what's the cause,
But every joint shakes as I give it thee.
Oh, if thou harbor'st murder in thy heart,
Let this gift change thy mind and save thy soul.
Know that I am a King. Oh, at that name,
I feel a hell of grief. Where is my crown?
Gone, gone! And do I remain alive?
Lightborn. You're overwatched, my Lord. Lie down and rest.
Edward. But that grief keeps me waking, I should sleep;
For not these ten days have these eyes' lids closed.
Now as I speak they fall, and yet with fear
Open again. Oh, wherefore sits thou here?
[*Lies on the bed.*]
Lightborn. If you mistrust me, I'll be gone, my Lord.
Edward. No, no, for if thou mean'st to murder me,
Thou wilt return again, and therefore stay.
[*Edward falls asleep.*]
Lightborn. [*Aside.*] He sleeps.
Edward. [*Waking.*] Oh let me not die! Yet stay, Oh, stay a while.
Lightborn. How now, my Lord?
Edward. Something still buzzeth in mine ears
And tells me if I sleep I never wake.
This fear is that which makes me tremble thus;
And therefore tell me, wherefore art thou come?
Lightborn. To rid thee of thy life. Matrevis, come!

[*Enter* Matrevis.]

Edward. I am too weak and feeble to resist.
Assist me, sweet God, and receive my soul.
Lightborn. Run for the table.
[*Exit* Matrevis.]

[*Reenter* Matrevis *with* Gurney, *bringing the table and spit.*]

Edward. O spare me! Or dispatch me in a trice!
Lightborn. So, lay the table down, and stamp on it,
But not too hard, lest that you bruise his body.
[*Using the table and featherbed to hold him down, they murder Edward, who screams as the spit penetrates him.*]
Matrevis. I fear me that this cry will raise the town,
And therefore let us take horse and away.
Lightborn. Tell me, sirs, was it not bravely done?
Gurney. Excellent well. Take this for thy reward.
Then Gurney stabs Lightborn, [*who dies*].
Come, let us cast the body in the moat,
And bear the King's to Mortimer, our Lord.
Away!
Exeunt [*with the bodies*].

[V.vi]

Enter Mortimer [Junior] *and* Matrevis [*at different doors*].

Mortimer Junior. Is't done, Matrevis, and the murderer dead?
Matrevis. Aye, my good Lord; I would it were undone.
Mortimer Junior. Matrevis, if thou now growest penitent
I'll be thy ghostly father; therefore choose
Whether thou wilt be secret in this
Or else die by the hand of Mortimer.
Matrevis. Gurney, my Lord, is fled, and will, I fear,
Betray us both; therefore let me fly.
Mortimer Junior. Fly to the savages.
Matrevis. I humbly thank your honor.
[*Exit.*]
Mortimer Junior. As for myself, I stand as Jove's huge tree,
And others are but shrubs compared to me.
All tremble at my name, and I fear none;
Let's see who dare impeach me for his death.

Enter [Isabella] *the* Queen.

Queen. Ah, Mortimer, the King my son hath news
His father's dead, and we have murdered him.
Mortimer Junior. What if he have? The King is yet a child.

---

83 **jewel** (if this was the Queen's gift, it is the King's last act of betrayal)
90 **Gone** (an uncrowned king is already tantamount to being dead)
91 **overwatched** overtired (watching out for yourself)
92 **grief** anxiety, fear
102 **buzzeth** murmurs, whispers
110 **in a trice** quickly
113 **raise** arouse; according to Holinshed, his scream at inflicted pain became legendary
115 **bravely** skillfully
V.vi.4 **ghostly father** priest who performs last rites (here as euphemism for murderer)
9 **to the savages** i.e., beyond the bounds of civilization
11 **Jove's huge tree** the oak, known for strength and steadfastness
17 **yet** still; only

Queen. Aye, aye, but he tears his hair and wrings his hands,
And vows to be revenged upon us both.
Into the council chamber he is gone
To crave the aid and succor of his peers.
Aye, me, see where he comes, and they with him.
Now, Mortimer, begins our tragedy.

Enter the King [Edward III] *with the* Lords [*and* Attendants].

First Lord. Fear not, my Lord; know that you are a King.
King Edward III. [*To Mortimer Junior.*] Villain!
Mortimer Junior. How now, my Lord?
King Edward III. Think not that I am frighted with thy words.
My father's murdered through thy treachery,
And thou shalt die; and on his mournful hearse
Thy hateful and accursèd head shall lie
To witness to the world that by thy means
His kingly body was too soon interred.
Queen. Weep not, sweet son.
King Edward III. Forbid not me to weep; he was my father;
And had you loved him half so well as I,
You could not bear his death thus patiently.
But you, I fear, conspired with Mortimer.
First Lord. [*To Mortimer Junior.*] Why speak you not unto my lord the King?
Mortimer Junior. Because I think it scorn to be accused.
Who is the man dare say I murdered him?
King Edward III. Traitor, in me my loving father speaks
And plainly saith, 'twas thou that murd'redst him.
Mortimer Junior. But hath Your Grace no other proof than this?
King Edward III. Yes, if this be the hand of Mortimer.
[*Shows a letter.*]
Mortimer Junior. [*Aside to the Queen.*] False Gurney hath betrayed me and himself.
Queen. [*Aside.*] I feared as much; murder cannot be hid.
Mortimer Junior. 'Tis my hand; what gather you by this?
King Edward III. That thither thou didst send a murderer.
Mortimer Junior. What murderer? Bring forth the man I sent.
King Edward III. Ah, Mortimer, thou knowest that he is slain;
And so shalt thou be too. [*To Attendants.*] Why stays he here?
Bring him unto a hurdle, drag him forth;
Hang him, I say, and set his quarters up!
But bring his head back presently to me.
Queen. For my sake, sweet son, pity Mortimer.
Mortimer Junior. Madam, entreat not; I will rather die
Than sue for life unto a paltry boy.
King Edward III. Hence with the traitor, with the murderer!
Mortimer Junior. Base Fortune, now I see that in thy wheel
There is a point to which, when men aspire,
They tumble headlong down. That point I touched,
And, seeing there was no place to mount up higher,
Why should I grieve at my declining fall?
Farewell, fair Queen; weep not for Mortimer,
That scorns the world, and, as a traveler,
Goes to discover countries yet unknown.
King Edward III. What! Suffer you the traitor to delay?
[*Exit* Mortimer Junior *with* First Lord, *attended.*]
Queen. As thou receivèd'st thy life from me,
Spill not the blood of gentle Mortimer.
King Edward III. This argues that you spilt my father's blood,
Else would you not entreat for Mortimer.
Queen. I spill his blood? No!
King Edward III. Aye, Madam, you; for so the rumor runs.
Queen. That rumor is untrue; for loving thee
Is this report raised on poor Isabel.
King Edward III. I do not think her so unnatural.
Second Lord. My Lord, I fear me it will prove too true.
King Edward III. Mother, you are suspected for his death,

21 succor support
35 patiently calmly
43 hand handwriting
51 hurdle frame on which traitors were carried through public streets to their execution
52 Hang...quarters Mortimer is to be hanged, drawn, and quartered (rather than beheaded, the customary means of death accorded nobility)
58 Fortune refers to Fortune's wheel
65 countries yet unknown i.e., before death
72 rumor common report
75 unnatural opposed to human nature

And therefore we commit you to the Tower
Till further trial may be made thereof;
If you be guilty, though I be your son,
Think not to find me slack or pitiful.

Queen. Nay, to my death, for too long have I lived
Whenas my son thinks to abridge my days.

King Edward III. Away with her. Her words enforce these tears,
And I shall pity her if she speak again.

[*Second Lord, attended, arrests the Queen.*]

Queen. Shall I not mourn for my belovèd Lord,
And with the rest accompany him to his grave?

Second Lord. Thus, Madam, 'tis the King's will you shall hence.

Queen. He hath forgotten me; [*To Attendants.*] stay, I am his mother.

Second Lord. That boots not; therefore, gentle Madam, go.

Queen. Then come, sweet death, and rid me of this grief.

[*Exit* Queen *with* Second Lord, *attended.*]

[*Reenter* First Lord *with the head of Mortimer Junior.*]

First Lord. My Lord, here is the head of Mortimer.

King Edward III. Go fetch my father's hearse, where it shall lie,
And bring my funeral robes.

[*Exeunt* Attendants.]

Accursèd head!
Could I have ruled thee then, as I do now,
Thou hadst not hatched this monstrous treachery.
Here comes the hearse.

[*Reenter* Attendants *with the hearse and funeral robes.*]

Help me to mourn, my Lords.
Sweet father, here unto thy murdered ghost,
I offer up this wicked traitor's head,
And let these tears, distilling from mine eyes,
Be witness of my grief and innocency.

[*Exeunt.*]

78 **commit . . . Tower** historically, Isabella was not imprisoned but placed under house arrest at Castle Rising, Norfolk; Holinshed says her land and revenues were confiscated but she was given a thousand pounds and Edward III occasionally visited her

79 **trial** investigation

83 **abridge** cut short

84 **enforce** bring about

90 **boots** matters

The Shoemakers' Holiday

Thomas Dekker

Leadenhall Market, from Hugh Alley's Caveat: The Markets of London in 1598 (Folger Shakespeare Library, MS V.a.318).

For centuries Thomas Dekker has been praised, sometimes lavishly, for *The Shoemakers' Holiday* as a romantic comedy, the first important play about Elizabethan citizen life, and one notably marked with ebullient high spirits. Little is actually known about Dekker. He was born sometime around 1570, presumably of Dutch ancestry (and so somewhat younger than Shakespeare), and by 1599, when this play was written, he was supplying parts of up to sixteen plays a year under contract to Philip Henslowe for the Lord Admiral's Company. He knew London intimately and lovingly; as he writes in *The Seven Deadly Sins of London* (1606), "from thy womb received I my being, from thy breasts my nourishment." He never writes of his parents or his family, but he writes a great deal, in drama and prose, about his city:

> In every street, carts and coaches make such a thundering as if the world ran upon wheels; at every corner men, women and children meet in such shoals that posts are set up of purpose to strengthen the houses, lest with jostling one another they should shoulder them down. Besides, hammers are beating in one place, tubs hooping in another, pots clinking in a third, water tankards running at tilt in a fourth: here are porters sweating under burdens, there merchants' men bearing bags of money, chapmen (as if they were at leap-frog) skip out of one shop into another, tradesmen (as if they were dancing galliards) are lusty at legs and never stand still. All are as busy as country attorneys at Assizes. How then can Idleness think to inhabit here?

Nor could he ever imagine a world elsewhere: even during the dreadful plague of 1603, he remained in the city to record its horrors in a pamphlet he ironically entitled *The Wonderful Year*. Although in his lifetime, and for all his hard work, he would know debtors' prison as well as performances before the Queen and Lord Mayor's shows by commission, his easy reach for similes and metaphors, often as concrete and graphic as the facts they allude to, pays tribute to London. It is not so much that he wrote about London, as one critic has put it, as that he collaborated with it.

Yet for all the reality portrayed in *The Shoemakers' Holiday* about dawn at a shoemaker's shop and a pancake breakfast on Shrove Tuesday, there is a great deal of fantasy too: a country gentleman falls in love with a seamstress; a nobleman successfully disguises himself as a Dutch journeyman to court a citizen's daughter; and a hard-working, clever craftsman makes his way speedily to sheriff, alderman, and Lord Mayor of London, inviting the King himself to join a pancake breakfast with the laborers of his guild. Simon Eyre's career here, in fact, is the kind of rags-to-riches story that all of us can appreciate and may at times yearn for. It seems only natural in Dekker's celebratory tribute to the community and fraternity of the guild system which promotes family and friendship, love and loyalty and sacrifice: *The Shoemakers' Holiday* provides a reminiscent appreciation for an earlier medieval time (in which the play is presumably set) that catches up the romance supplied by Hammond's pursuit of Jane and Lacy's courtship of Rose. If at times this all seems highly improbable, there is a way in which the upside-down world of Shrove Tuesday permitted just such liberty, like the other holidays of misrule when social customs and regulations are loosened, and role-playing naturally thrives.

This is the customary way of reading Dekker's play, but the playwright himself is much too honest to settle for simply praising the past or taking unquestioned joy in the present. Even if we wish to see this play as one of dreams coming true and loves fulfilled, where morality and just deserts predominate, we are constantly reminded that matters are otherwise: Rafe returns from war permanently maimed; the shoemakers attempt a kind of vigilante justice armed with cudgels and ready for fighting and riot; and the play begins and ends with the grim reminder of an ongoing military engagement with France for which no end is in sight. A merchant finds his ship's cargo threatened with confiscation; a young nobleman is charged with treason; Lincoln and Oatley seem doomed to enmity; military conscription hangs over the city; aldermen die without warning or cause. Such serious matters are made inescapable by Dekker through juxtaposition: just as Lacy plans to desert the English army where he is an officer, he recruits the luckless and newly married Rafe. Just as Firk announces with considerable excitement that Simon Eyre has been elected a sheriff of London, Rafe returns home from the war, discharged because he has been crippled for life. Even Simon Eyre's own glorious rise depends on his exploitation of a luckless merchant and his false disguise in the robes of an alderman. Such harsh realities do not disappear in this play; they keep returning, unexpectedly, to interrupt, trouble, and question any easy reading that would entertain by way of ignorance or innocence the real cost of social mobility and fluidity that is necessary in a class-ridden society to allow such dreams to succeed, however much its very repressiveness might nourish them.

Take the matter of social rank. The romance of Lacy and Rose with which the play opens seems the very stuff of romantic comedy, where a nobleman falls in love with a woman of a lower rank, faces family opposition, and must choose to turn his back either on his family or the one he loves. Either way victory involves loss: he can be ethically responsible by marrying the woman beneath him or he can be socially responsible by upholding family and social loyalty, but he cannot do both – and in a world of reinforced social hierarchy where he (and perhaps his wife and surely his family) will live out the consequences. At the same time, those who object to such a match face similarly difficult problems, for they must relax standards and expectations and thereby betray their own past behavior, or they must remain constant and so be uncaring and even tyrannical. There is no easy victory and no escape from subsequent relationships whatever choice is made. Such gross problems are transformed by Dekker with extraordinary subtlety in the conversation between the aristocratic Earl of Lincoln and the citizen Lord Mayor. While both achieve a kind of coded conversation that harbors hypocrisy in its refusal to be open, Lincoln demonstrates that he sees citizen blood as base and intermarriage between ranks as a kind of bastardy, whereas Oatley sees the nobility as idle, fiscally irresponsible, luxurious, and harmful. Both see the other as inherently exploitative of the society that has allowed them to function in a kind of freedom without bounds. Such tension is palpable; and it introduces, and frames, Simon Eyre's inexhaustible ambition to rise in a society which the guild system, through quite another set of means, sought firmly to regulate. Just as Lincoln and Oatley maintain a patina of civility, so Simon, even in his comradely blustering, maintains a kind of paternalism that underlies what are for all of them strong personal desires and motives often in divisive conflict with those around them. Such matters dramatize a deeper realism of Dekker's time. The portrait of Oatley can represent John Spencer, the Lord Mayor of London in 1594–5, who opposed the marriage of his daughter to an aristocrat and who, in 1599, the year Dekker's play was written, was imprisoned in the Fleet for financial difficulties while his daughter, an heiress, had eloped with the courtier after all, the latter disguising himself as a baker's boy to make away with her.

But there are strong social markers throughout Dekker's play, in nearly every speech and nearly every gesture. Often social distinctions are unquestioningly upheld, as when Simon welcomes Hans with suspicion, attempts to protect Rafe from recruitment but quickly gives in to his superiors, or degrades his wife as he never does his men. Lincoln's extreme behavior in charging his own nephew with treason at the play's end, then, resonates with other socially correct actions in the play and on all levels – social, political, economic, military, legal. Conversely, a gentleman like Hammon, accustomed to hunting on country estates, is perplexed at his lack of appeal for a woman so simple and comparatively deprived as Jane. Dekker follows through on such matters with images like the wine Simon serves on Shrove Tuesday (repeating Oatley's actions while Lord Mayor) instead of the beer to which his men are accustomed. Indeed, the very spaces of this play – Old Ford, Cornhill, Tower Street, Eastcheap, the shoemakers' shop, Guildhall – all seem in good measure to dictate events as well as attitudes and values. This concern with proper status is something Dekker seems to share, for his manuscript as reflected in the first quarto uses speech prefixes like *Lord Mayor* and *Wife*, demoting individuals to class markers – a distinction that later quartos and editors tend to erase. (Such speech prefixes have all been restored here.) Thus the only way in which someone like Lacy can even converse with a merchant's daughter is by disguising himself as an alien journeyman; the only way Simon can advance his capitalist interests is by pretending to be an alderman; and the only way Hammon can even see his Jane is by muffling his face and watching her from a distance. *The Shoemakers' Holiday* keeps asking us what we are to make of such disguises: of the society that forces them; of the people who choose them; and even of those who do not manage to see through them.

Such matters come naturally, of course, to a play that means to examine the new world of the merchant, whose own rising prominence and power threatens to undermine the old aristocracy as well as national traditions and inherited patterns of life. Within London during Elizabeth's reign – during all the years of Dekker's life there – the merchant class had been increasing in size and wealth so that by the time of *The Shoemakers' Holiday*, the richest aldermen had become, in fortune, equal to some of the nation's peers, with most of that newly accumulated wealth concentrated in London. In fact, the twelve main livery companies that ran the city government did not hesitate, whenever the occasion arose, to take issue over matters of governance with the Queen's Privy Council, composed of men of means as well as nobility. Yet at the same time that Elizabeth attempted to regulate her people along the lines of her predecessors, holding to the old ways, she was also, through her support of capitalist investment, international trade, and even piracy, ardently supporting a kind of entrepreneurialism that threatened the long-established codes of conduct. The success of commercial trading – what permits Simon to surpass his destined position at the shoemakers' shop – was slowly separating the craftsmen who continued to make goods with little advance in profit from the tradesmen who were using such goods by sending them to a variety of new foreign markets at large profits. This disproportionate advantage for the trader set off a number of ongoing disputes and promised continuing disruptions in the expanding Elizabethan economy: in places like Eastcheap, where Simon lives and works, nearly 70 percent were employed in the production of hand goods in 1599; while in Fleet Street, a minority of men grew increasingly affluent. Such unequal distribution of work and income led to stronger and stronger rivalry, one which Simon attempts to overcome by leaving the laborers in his shop to join forces with a luckless merchant's ship – his entry into the trading market to which the socially superior Lacy (in the disguise of Hans) alone can help him.

But then the Company of Cordwainers, to which Simon apprentices and owes his primary identity, was accustomed to skirmishes and even outright battles to survive from nearly the beginning. Founded in the thirteenth century and taking its name from Cordova (Corduba), a Spanish town that produced the goatskins from which the finest shoes and boots were fashioned, the Cordwainers' Company had stood opposed to the cobblers, whose job was to repair and resell old shoes. Cobblers were seen as parasites; their success in recycling shoes, moreover, diminished the potential market of the Cordwainers. Although the Cordwainers continued to expand because of their excellent materials and workmanship, they never became one of the Twelve Great City Companies that supplied aldermen to the City Council and candidates for Lord Mayor. Simon himself is keenly aware of this distinction. He never uses the word "cobbler," but instead refers to himself and his men as "the gentlemen shoemakers, the courageous cordwainers." At the same time (as Dekker knows), as a Cordwainer he is ineligible to become Lord Mayor; that he does so stands as an implicit comment on the stratification of the shoemakers. (The historic Simon Eyre, who did become Lord Mayor, was a draper.)

Still, this is not the only economic problem facing the guilds to which Dekker alludes. By referring to the expulsion of the Hanseatic League in 1597 (vii. 18), he hints at the new threat of alien trade and, in the presence of Hans (who is saved from condemnation because he is really the Englishman Lacy), he underscores the potential disruption which such alien laborers presented to the very foundation of the London guild system. During the reign of Elizabeth, the wardens of the Cordwainers' Company complained to her Principal Secretary, Lord Burghley, that aliens were producing faulty work at lower prices and seriously threatened their market. They demanded concessions from the foreign leatherworkers citing 3 Henry VIII c. 10 and 21 Henry VIII c. 16, although these statutes had in fact been overturned by Elizabeth. The aliens contested such pleas, arguing that Cordwainers had no right to enforce such regulations, especially in the wards of the liberties where the aliens had set up their own shops. Burghley did not act on behalf of either side, and in 1593 the shoemakers made unauthorized "searches" through the precinct of St. Martin's-le-Grand. This time when the alien workforce protested, the English craftsmen rioted. They rioted again in 1595, when sharply rising prices for rents and food left half the urban laborers, according to one report, living "in direst poverty and squalor, on the edge of destitution and starvation." For the shoemakers, the Dutch were especially egregious: by 1599, the year of Dekker's play, there were 131 Dutch shoemakers in London – more than one quarter of those making the required payments to the Cordwainers' Company – and about the same number as the Company's 152 yeomen. If "Hans" *were* actually Dutch, then, he would represent a real and present danger of sizeable proportions, and Dekker may be softening this grim reminder in part by having Firk parody his language. Thomas Deloney, the author of *The Gentle Craft* which Dekker used as a source for his play, was neither so guarded nor so lucky: with others he protested the alien workforce in 1596 and was imprisoned by the city authorities for asking church parishes to hang out notices about their alleged unfair labor practices.

Dekker may also have been more guarded because for him the problem was more complex, as he indicates in the recruitment of Lacy and Rafe and in the presence of war that hangs over *The Shoemakers' Holiday*. Both the practices of conscription and the lists of mounting casualties were a great concern in the London of 1599. Since 1596 an increasing number of men had been forced into the army to serve on several fronts: in Ireland, in the Low Countries, and at home as a preventive force against another Armada being mounted by Spain, still hoping to return Protestant England to the Catholicism known under Mary Tudor and Philip II. Spanish invasion, in fact, seemed especially imminent in the summer of 1599; on August 1, John Chamberlain, in London, wrote to Dudley Carelton, in Ostend, that

> the alarm whereof begins to ring in our ears here at home as shrill as in your besieged town: for upon what grounds of good intelligence I know not but we are all in a hurl as though the enemy were at our doors. The Queen's ships are all making ready, but this town is commanded to furnish 16 of their best ships to defend the river and 10,000 men, whereof 6,000 to be

trained presently and every man else to have his arms ready.

The difficulty the government faced was that the crucial allies in the international causes of Protestantism and peace were those same Dutch that, as an alien workforce, were causing disturbances in London; they were the "strangers" who had been granted asylum and religious freedom earlier by the Elizabethan government. Thus even as Londoners were posting angry libels in the city streets and on the walls of the Dutch church of the Austin Friars, accusing the alien workers from the Low Countries of being "beastly brutes" and "Drunken Drones" and "faint-hearted Flemings" as early as 1596, shortly after, in 1597, Essex was writing Elizabeth that if she wished to be "commandress of the seas" and safe from Spanish invasion, she would need to augment her naval forces with those from the Netherlands: "Your confederates of the Low Countries will furnish you with better ships of war than any the King of Spain can hire or draw... for the Low Country ships are better of sail, nimbler and carry as good pieces." This dilemma between siding with the Dutch in the cause of peace and admitting Dutch workers who were disrupting the guild system by undermining it was one Burghley continually faced, and which Dekker clearly understands. For Dekker confronts this dilemma directly in the figure of Hans, who combines in Lacy a nobleman who is upsetting the social order with a disguised Dutchman who reminds the playwright's audiences at the Rose Theater of the alien workforce that is threatening the economic order of the realm. The issue is likewise confronted in the Dutch skipper whom Hans introduces to Simon; he is at once a providential agent for Simon, who needs to make an investment in the skipper's lost goods (pointedly with a loan from Hans) at the same time Simon disguises himself as a social and political superior in order to undertake the transaction.

This continuing conflict between native and alien workforces is again represented in Dekker's play when the Cordwainers take their cudgels off to a Protestant church to protest Hammon's enforced marriage to Jane. The fight is quickly resolved but only in a temporary way – through intimidation of superior force – and the play moves forward to another time of traditional riots by workers, that of Shrove Tuesday, the day before Lent. Traditionally, this was society's built-in day of release, a kind of social safety-valve, when young men, particularly apprentices, raided brothels and carted prostitutes through the streets, stormed storehouses of grain in Southwark, vandalized theaters, executed skimmingtons, and tortured performing animals in a kind of penitential sacrifice: they took freedom in hand and used their liberty aggressively, but in ways that might argue to right wrongs and long-standing grievances. Given such potential danger on a day of permitted misrule, Dekker redraws the liberty of Shrove Tuesday into Simon Eyre's celebration in which he brings together royalty and commoner. Perhaps more than a wish, it is meant to be a crucial and exemplary tactic. Simon tells the King that his men celebrate "Saint Hugh's holiday" by substituting food and plenty for dearth and poverty, but he also points out that "Sim Eyre and my brethren the Gentleman Shoemakers shall set your sweet Majesty's image cheek by jowl by Saint Hugh for this honor you have done poor Simon Eyre." Whether or not Dekker means this as an encoded plea for the plight of native workers, it has been argued that this strange juxtaposition of St. Hugh with royalty suggests a similar banqueting on another holiday, that of the Queen's Accession Day each November 17. At that time, rioting was displaced by another bell-ringing throughout London, by feasting, dancing, torch-lit processions, and bonfires – but also, this time, by special sermons in Protestant churches that united state and church in the causes of Protestantism and peace. In this context, the Catholic St. Hugh – deliberately, it would seem, reflected in Hugh Lacy's name – and Lincoln – where he enjoys his earldom – would stand out as Catholic references. Lincoln, representative of the old aristocracy overthrown in the instance of young Lacy's marriage (his protests to the King fall on deaf ears and the King divorces Lacy and Rose only to perform the marriage again himself), also then represents the old Catholicism that is overthrown by the leveling effect of the new Protestant ethic, an ethic, moreover, that admitted a certain kind of independent spirit and even entrepreneurship.

Indeed, in the issues raised in the final lines of his play which put Shrove Tuesday (and possibly Accession Day) alongside the threat of France and of Spain, Dekker may also be returning to John Spencer. The most unpopular and notorious Lord Mayor in the living memory of Dekker, his actors, and his audiences, Spencer was known not only for his spectacular wealth, his stinginess, his tyrannical behavior, and his continual harassment of apprentices, but also for his outspoken opposition to the theaters of London. He wrote at least two letters to Burghley and to the Privy Council demanding the total suppression of theatrical performances where "profane fables, lascivious matters, cozening devices, and other unseemly and scurrilous matters" were, in his view, the main cause of "disorders and lewd demeanors which appear of late in young people of all degrees." He challenged, that is, Dekker's own livelihood (as, in other ways, he had challenged Deloney's).

We know little about Dekker's ancestry but there may be a crucial clue in his name: *dekker* is Dutch for thatcher, and it is likely he was descended from a line of craftsmen himself. If so, he had traded in work of the hands for work of the mind, and the life of a craftsman for that of a merchant. "The theater," Dekker would soon write in *The Gull's Horn Book* (published in 1609), "is your poet's Royal Exchange." He himself was trading in words and ideas. With time he hoped to turn a profit, make his own living among the company of fellow playwrights that formed its own new kind of guild. Still later, with *Dekker His Dream* in 1619, he would write, "There is a Hell named in our Creed, and a Heaven, and the Hell comes before. If we look not into the first, we shall never live in the last." Just what equivalents we might find for temptation in *The Shoemakers' Holiday* (or, as a later quarto retitles the play, *The Shoemakers' Holy Day*), and whether those temptations are (or can be) contained or resolved, is a task Dekker sets for us in what turns out to be a complicated and complex play.

Further Reading

Gasper, Julia, *The Dragon and the Dove: The Plays of Thomas Dekker*. Oxford: Clarendon Press, 1990.

Kaplan, Joel H., "Virtue's Holiday: Thomas Dekker and Simon Eyre," *Renaissance Drama* n.s. 2 (1969): 103–22.

Kastan, David Scott, "Workshop and/as Playhouse: Comedy and Commerce in *The Shoemaker's Holiday*," *Studies in Philology* 84:3 (1987): 324–7.

Mortenson, Peter, "The Economics of Joy in *The Shoemakers' Holiday*," *Studies in English Literature 1500–1900* 16:2 (Spring 1976): 241–52.

Novarr, David, "Dekker's Gentle Craft and the Lord Mayor of London," *Modern Philology* 57 (1960): 233–9.

Straznicky, Marta, "The End(s) of Discord in *The Shoemaker's Holiday*," *Studies in English Literature 1500–1900* 36 (1996): 357–72.

Wiles, David, " 'That Day Are you Free': *The Shoemaker's Holiday*," *Cahiers Elisabethains* 38 (October 1990): 49–60.

The Shoemakers' Holiday

[*DRAMATIS PERSONAE*]

The King of England.
The courtiers:
Sir Hugh Lacy, Earl of Lincoln.
Rowland Lacy, *Lincoln's nephew; afterwards disguised as* Hans Meulter.
Askew, *Lacy's cousin.*
Cornwall.
Lovell.
Dodger, *a "parasite" of the Earl of Lincoln.*

The citizens:
Sir Roger Oatley, *Lord Mayor of London.*
Rose, *Oatley's daughter.*
Sybil, *Rose's maid.*
Master Hammon, *a City gentleman.*
Master Warner, *Hammon's brother-in-law.*
Master Scott, *a friend of Oatley's.*

The shoemakers:
Simon Eyre.
Margery, *Eyre's wife.*

Textual Variants

Title-page] Since no apostrophe appears on the title-page of the Q, it is unclear whether the reference to shoemakers is singular or plural **Title**] Q adds "A Pleasant Comedy of the Gentle Craft" **i.50 s.d.**] Q s.d. at line 51 **207 s.d.**] Q s.d. at line 206 **ii.17 s.d.**] Q s.d. at line 15 **viii.11** *Lincoln*] Q the line is given to Dodger **45** is it] Q it is **ix.77 s.d.**] Q s.d. at line 78 **95** Lurks] Q Lurch **102 s.d.**] Q s.d. at line 101 **x. 121 s.d.**] Q s.d. at line 120 **186** Master] Q Mistress **xii.110–12**] Q sets as prose **xiii.70** *edle* (for needle)] Q egle **xv.41 s.d.**] Q s.d. at line 40 **xvi.145** Restrain] Q Refrain **xviii.130** saw] Q see **xxi.77ff**] Q prefix for the remainder of the scene is *Hans* **160** Majesty!] Q majesty all shoemaker. **192–204**] Q Simon Eyre breaks into poetry to conclude his speech

Playsource

The Shoemakers' Holiday is taken largely from Part One of Thomas Deloney's *The Gentle Craft* (1597), a collection of stories praising shoemakers. He combines three tales – that of St. Hugh, the patron saint of shoemakers; the adventures of the royal brothers Crispine and Crispianus; and the career of Simon Eyre. The blending of the various stories into the multiple plotting of his relatively unified play is Dekker's own contribution.

Dramatis Personae

1 The King In Simon Eyre's day Henry VI was King, but the characterization in the play is far more similar to the contemporary characterization of Henry V

2 Sir Hugh Lacy there was no Earl of Lincoln in Eyre's time

4 Hans Meulter common stage name for a Dutch character

8 Sir Roger Oatley historically, Robert Oteley, a grocer

14 Simon Eyre historically a draper, not a shoemaker, who became sheriff of London in 1434, Lord Mayor in 1445. He died in 1458. Stow gives him partial credit for building Leadenhall

Roger Hodge, *Eyre's foreman.*
Rafe Damport, *a journeyman of Eyre's.*
Jane, *Rafe's wife.*
Firk, *a journeyman of Eyre's.*

A Dutch Skipper.

A Boy, *working for Eyre.*
A Boy, *with the hunters.*
A Prentice, *working for Oatley.*

Noblemen, Soldiers, Huntsmen, Shoemakers, Apprentices, Servants.

[The Epistle]

To all good fellows, professors of the Gentle Craft, of what degree soever.

Kind gentlemen and honest boon companions, I present you here with a merry conceited comedy called *The Shoemakers' Holiday*, acted by my Lord Admiral's Players this present Christmas before the Queen's most excellent Majesty for the mirth and pleasant matter by her Highness graciously accepted, being indeed no way offensive. The argument of the play I will set down in this epistle: Sir Hugh Lacy, Earl of Lincoln, had a young gentleman of his own name, his near kinsman, that loved the Lord Mayor's daughter of London; to prevent and cross which love the Earl caused his kinsman to be sent colonel of a company into France, who resigned his place to another gentleman his friend, and came disguised like a Dutch shoemaker to the house of Simon Eyre in Tower Street, who served the Mayor and his household with shoes: the merriments that passed in Eyre's house, his coming to be Mayor of London, Lacy's getting his love, and other accidents; with two merry three-man's songs. Take all in good worth that is well intended, for nothing is purposed but mirth. Mirth lengtheneth long life, which with all other blessings I heartily wish you.

Farewell.

The First Three-Man's Song

Oh, the month of May, the merry month of May,
So frolic, so gay, and so green, so green, so green;
Oh and then did I unto my true love say,
"Sweet Peg, thou shalt be my Summer's Queen."
Now the nightingale, the pretty nightingale,
The sweetest singer in all the forest's choir,
Entreats thee, sweet Peggy, to hear thy true love's tale,
Lo, yonder she sitteth, her breast against a briar.
But Oh, I spy the cuckoo, the cuckoo, the cuckoo;
See where she sitteth – come away, my joy.
Come away, I prithee, I do not like the cuckoo
Should sing where my Peggy and I kiss and toy.
Oh, the month of May, the merry month of May,
So frolic, so gay, and so green, so green, so green;
And then did I unto my true love say,
"Sweet Peg, thou shalt be my Summer's Queen."

The Second Three-Man's Song
(This is to be sung at the latter end.)

Cold's the wind, and wet's the rain,
Saint Hugh be our good speed.
Ill is the weather that bringeth no gain,
Nor helps good hearts in need.
Troll the bowl, the jolly nut-brown bowl,
And here, kind mate, to thee.
Let's sing a dirge for Saint Hugh's soul,
And down it merrily.
Down-a-down, hey down-a-down,
Hey-derry-derry down-a-down
(*Close with the tenor boy*)

[The Epistle]

1 **Title** ***professors*** members; ***Gentle Craft*** common name for shoemaking trade; according to legend the founder, St. Hugh, was visited in prison by shoemakers: they "never left him, but yielded him great relief continually, so that he wanted nothing was necessary for him; in requital of which kindness he called them Gentlemen of the Gentle Craft" (Thomas Deloney, *The Gentle Craft*)
2 **conceited** ingenious, contrived
3–4 **Lord Admiral's Players** professional company that was chief rival to Shakespeare's company, the Chamberlain's Men
4 **present Christmas** title-page claims a court performance on New Year's Day (January 1), 1600
8 **argument** outline
20 **accidents** events
21 **three-man's songs** songs with parts for three male voices

The First Three-Man's Song

1 Placement unknown; perhaps (1) before the play; (2) at the morris dance at xi; or (3) as a jig following the play
4 **Summer's Queen** i.e., Lady of May
8 **breast . . . briar** the pain from a thorn in the nightingale's side was supposedly the cause of its sweet song
9 **cuckoo** bird of promiscuity; symbol of cuckoldry
12 **toy** dally

Second Three-Man's Song

2 **Saint Hugh** patron saint of shoemakers
5 **Troll** pass; **nut-brown** color of the ale it contains

Ho, well done, to me let come,
Ring compass, gentle joy.
Troll the bowl, the nut-brown bowl,
And here, kind *etc.*
(*as often as there be men to drink*)

At last when all have drunk, this verse:

Cold's the wind, and wet's the rain,
Saint Hugh be our good speed.
Ill is the weather that bringeth no gain,
Nor helps good hearts in need.

The Prologue

as it was pronounced before the Queen's Majesty.

As wretches in a storm, expecting day,
With trembling hands and eyes cast up to heaven,
Make prayers the anchor of their conquered hopes,
So we, dear Goddess, wonder of all eyes,
Your meanest vassals, through mistrust and fear
To sink into the bottom of disgrace
By our imperfect pastimes, prostrate thus
On bended knees our sails of hope do strike,
Dreading the bitter storms of your dislike.
Since then, unhappy men, our hap is such
That to ourselves ourselves no help can bring,
But needs must perish if your saint-like ears,
Locking the temple where all mercy sits,
Refuse the tribute of our begging tongues.
Oh, grant, bright mirror of true chastity,
From those life-breathing stars your sun-like eyes
One gracious smile; for your celestial breath
Must send us life, or sentence us to death.

[Sc. i]

Enter [Sir Roger Oatley, *the*] Lord Mayor, [*and the* Earl of] Lincoln.

Lincoln. My Lord Mayor, you have sundry times
Feasted myself and many courtiers more.
Seldom or never can we be so kind
To make requital of your courtesy.
But leaving this, I hear my cousin Lacy
Is much affected to your daughter Rose.

Lord Mayor. True, my good lord; and she loves him so well
That I mislike her boldness in the chase.

Lincoln. Why, my Lord Mayor, think you it then a shame
To join a Lacy with an Oatley's name?

Lord Mayor. Too mean is my poor girl for his high birth.
Poor citizens must not with courtiers wed,
Who will in silks and gay apparel spend
More in one year than I am worth by far.
Therefore your honor need not doubt my girl.

Lincoln. Take heed, my lord; advise you what you do.
A verier unthrift lives not in the world
Than is my cousin; for, I'll tell you what,
'Tis now almost a year since he requested
To travel countries for experience.
I furnished him with coin, bills of exchange,
Letters of credit, men to wait on him,
Solicited my friends in Italy
Well to respect him. But to see the end:
Scant had he journeyed through half Germany
But all his coin was spent, his men cast off,
His bills embezzled, and my jolly coz,
Ashamed to show his bankrupt presence here,
Became a shoemaker in Wittenberg –
A goodly science for a gentleman
Of such descent! Now judge the rest by this:
Suppose your daughter have a thousand pound,
He did consume me more in one half-year;
And make him heir to all the wealth you have,
One twelve-month's rioting will waste it all.

12 **Ring compass** full range of sound

The Prologue

before the Queen's Majesty written especially for the January 1, 1600 performance before Elizabeth I
5 **vassals** (with pun on *vessels*)
8 **strike** lower
10 **hap** fortune

i.1 **s.d. Roger Oatley** according to Stow's *Survey of London*, a Robert Oteley, grocer, was Lord Mayor of London in 1434
1 **sundry** several

5 **cousin** common term of kinship; he is actually Lacy's nephew
6 **affected** attracted
11 **mean** low in social and economic status
15 **doubt** worry over
17 **verier** truer
21 **bills of exchange** promissory notes
25 **Scant** scarcely
27 **embezzled** wasted
29 **Wittenberg** German university town on the Elbe with popular connections to Protestantism through Martin Luther and to Dr. Faustus; it had no known connection with shoemaking
33 **me** i.e., at my expenses
35 **rioting** excessive high spirits or good times

Then seek, my lord, some honest citizen
To wed your daughter to.
Lord Mayor. I thank your lordship.
[*Aside.*] Well, fox, I understand your subtlety.
[*To Lincoln.*] As for your nephew, let your lordship's eye
But watch his actions and you need not fear;
For I have sent my daughter far enough.
And yet your cousin Rowland might do well
Now he hath learned an occupation.
[*Aside.*] And yet I scorn to call him son-in-law.
Lincoln. Aye, but I have a better trade for him.
I thank His Grace, he hath appointed him
Chief colonel of all those companies
Mustered in London and the shires about
To serve His Highness in those wars of France.
See where he comes.

Enter Lovell, Lacy, *and* Askew.

Lovell, what news with you?
Lovell. My Lord of Lincoln, 'tis His Highness' will
That presently your cousin ship for France
With all his powers. He would not for a million
But they should land at Dieppe within four days.
Lincoln. Go certify His Grace it shall be done.

Exit Lovell.

Now, cousin Lacy, in what forwardness
Are all your companies?
Lacy. All well prepared.
The men of Hertfordshire lie at Mile End;
Suffolk and Essex train in Tothill Fields;
The Londoners, and those of Middlesex,
All gallantly prepared in Finsbury,
With frolic spirits long for their parting hour.
Lord Mayor. They have their imprest, coats, and furniture,
And if it please your cousin Lacy come
To the Guildhall, he shall receive his pay,
And twenty pounds besides my brethren
Will freely give him to approve our loves
We bear unto my lord your uncle here.
Lacy. I thank your honor.
Lincoln. Thanks, my good Lord Mayor.
Lord Mayor. At the Guildhall we will expect your coming.

Exit.

Lincoln. To approve your loves to me? No, subtlety!
Nephew, that twenty pound he doth bestow
For joy to rid you from his daughter Rose.
But, cousins both, now here are none but friends,
I would not have you cast an amorous eye
Upon so mean a project as the love
Of a gay, wanton, painted citizen.
I know this churl even in the height of scorn
Doth hate the mixture of his blood with thine.
I pray thee, do thou so. Remember, coz,
What honorable fortunes wait on thee.
Increase the King's love which so brightly shines
And gilds thy hopes. I have no heir but thee,
And yet not thee if with a wayward spirit
Thou start from the true bias of my love.
Lacy. My lord, I will for honor (not desire
Of land or livings, or to be your heir)
So guide my actions in pursuit of France
As shall add glory to the Lacy's name.
Lincoln. Coz, for those words here's thirty portagues;
And, nephew Askew, there's a few for you.
Fair honor in her loftiest eminence
Stays in France for you till you fetch her thence.
Then, nephews, clap swift wings on your designs.
Begone, begone; make haste to the Guildhall.
There presently I'll meet you. Do not stay.
Where honor becomes, shame attends delay.

Exit.

Askew. How gladly would your uncle have you gone!

38 **fox** sly creature
46 **His Grace** the King
47 **companies** militia
48 **shires** counties
49 **those wars of France** French–English wars continued from the accession of Henry V in 1413 until after Eyre's mayoralty
52 **presently** without delay
53 **powers** forces
56 **forwardness** preparation
58 **Mile End** common land NE of London used for military training and for mustering troops
59 **Tothill Fields** a mustering area in Westminster
61 **Finsbury** fields N of London usually the site of archery
63 **imprest** recruitment pay; **furniture** equipment
65 **Guildhall** center of local London government and corporation of guilds on Catte Street
67 **approve** demonstrate
77 **painted** (1) with cosmetics; (2) made to look of higher status
78 **churl** fellow (a contemptuous usage)
85 **start . . . bias** deviate from the proper course (taken from game of bowls)
90 **portagues** Portuguese gold coins worth about £5

Lacy. True, coz; but I'll o'er-reach his policies.
I have some serious business for three days,
Which nothing but my presence can dispatch.
You, therefore, cousin, with the companies,
Shall haste to Dover. There I'll meet with you,
Or if I stay past my prefixèd time,
Away for France; we'll meet in Normandy.
The twenty pounds my Lord Mayor gives to me
You shall receive, and these ten portagues,
Part of mine uncle's thirty. Gentle coz,
Have care to our great charge. I know your wisdom
Hath tried itself in higher consequence.

Askew. Coz, all myself am yours. Yet have this care,
To lodge in London with all secrecy.
Our uncle Lincoln hath (besides his own)
Many a jealous eye that in your face
Stares only to watch means for your disgrace.

Lacy. Stay, cousin, who be these?

Enter Simon Eyre, [Margery] *his wife*, Hodge, Firk, Jane, *and* Rafe *with a piece.*

Eyre. Leave whining, leave whining. Away with this whimpering, this puling, these blubbering tears, and these wet eyes! I'll get thy husband discharged, I warrant thee, sweet Jane. Go to!

Hodge. Master, Here be the captains.

Eyre. Peace, Hodge; hush, ye knave, hush.

Firk. Here be the cavaliers and the colonels, master.

Eyre. Peace, Firk; peace, my fine Firk. Stand by, with your pishery-pashery, away! I am a man of the best presence. I'll speak to them an' they were popes. [*To Lacy and Askew.*] Gentlemen, captains, colonels, commanders; brave men, brave leaders, may it please you to give me audience. I am Simon Eyre, the mad shoemaker of Tower Street. This wench with the mealy mouth that will never tire is my wife, I can tell you. Here's Hodge, my man and my foreman. Here's Firk, my fine firking journeyman; and this is blubbered Jane. All we come to be suitors for this honest Rafe. Keep him at home and, as I am a true shoemaker and a gentleman of the Gentle Craft, buy spurs yourself and I'll find ye boots these seven years.

Wife. Seven years, husband?

Eyre. Peace, midriff, peace. I know what I do. Peace.

Firk. Truly, Master Cormorant, you shall do God good service to let Rafe and his wife stay together. She's a young, new-married woman. If you take her husband away from her a night, you undo her; she may beg in the daytime; for he's as good a workman at a prick and an awl as any is in our trade.

Jane. Oh, let him stay, else I shall be undone.

Firk. Aye, truly, she shall be laid at one side like a pair of old shoes else, and be occupied for no use.

Lacy. Truly, my friends, it lies not in my power.
The Londoners are pressed, paid, and set forth
By the Lord Mayor. I cannot change a man.

Hodge. Why, then, you were as good be a corporal as a colonel, if you cannot discharge one good fellow. And I tell you true, I think you do more than you can answer, to press a man within a year and a day of his marriage.

Eyre. Well said, melancholy Hodge! Gramercy, my fine foreman!

Wife. Truly, gentlemen, it were ill done for such as you to stand so stiffly against a poor young wife, considering her case. She is new-married. But let that pass. I pray, deal not roughly with her. Her husband is a young man and but newly entered. But let that pass.

---

99 **o'er-reach his policies** outmaneuver him
105 **Normandy** scene of battles between English and French forces under both Henry V and Henry VI
110 **higher consequence** more crucial situations
114 **jealous** vigilant
117 **s.d. *piece*** firearm (probably a musket)
118 **puling** whining
123 **cavaliers** horse soldiers
125 **pishery-pashery** nonsense; fuss
126 **an'** as if
130 **mad** exuberant, carefree, madcap
131 **Tower Street** major street leading from Tower Hill to Eastcheap where Eyre has his shop; **wench** working-class woman
132 **mealy mouth** voluble tongue; one who minces matters
134 **firking** (a bawdy term for copulating); Firk can also mean (1) brisk; (2) trickster;
134–5 **journeyman** a craftsman who has served his apprenticeship and is now qualified to work for daily; (*journée*) wages
135 **blubbered** weeping
141 **midriff** (may refer to Margery's gaining weight)
143 **Cormorant** corruption of "colonel"
148 **awl** hole (with bawdy overtones in connection with *prick*, *our trade*, *undone*, and *occupied*)
152 **shoes** (often used for bawdy jokes)
155 **pressed** conscripted
155–6 **set . . . Lord Mayor** the Lord Mayor was responsible for recruiting soldiers from London
162 **melancholy** thoughtful; **Gramercy** "Thanks" (corruption of *grant you mercy*)
165 **stand so stiffly** behave so inflexibly
169 **entered** i.e., into marriage

Eyre. Away with your pishery-pashery, your pols and your edepols. Peace, midriff. Silence, Cicely Bumtrinket. Let your head speak.

Firk. Yea and the horns too, master.

Eyre. Tawsoone, my fine Firk, tawsoone. Peace, scoundrels. See you this man? Captains, you will not release him? Well, let him go. He's a proper shot. Let him vanish. Peace, Jane. Dry up thy tears, they'll make his powder dankish. Take him, brave men. Hector of Troy was an hackney to him, Hercules and Termagant scoundrels. Prince Arthur's Round Table, by the Lord of Ludgate, ne'er fed such a tall, such a dapper swordman. By the life of Pharaoh, a brave, resolute swordman. Peace, Jane. I say no more, mad knaves.

Firk. See, see, Hodge, how my master raves in commendation of Rafe.

Hodge. Rafe, thou'rt a gull, by this hand, an thou goest not.

Askew. I am glad, good Master Eyre, it is my hap
To meet so resolute a soldier.
Trust me, for your report and love to him
A common slight regard shall not respect him.

Lacy. Is thy name Rafe?

Rafe. Yes, sir.

Lacy. Give me thy hand.
Thou shalt not want, as I am a gentleman.
[*To Jane.*] Woman, be patient. God, no doubt, will send
Thy husband safe again. But he must go,
His country's quarrel says it shall be so.

Hodge. Thou'rt a gull, by my stirrup, if thou dost not go. I will not have thee strike thy gimlet into these weak vessels. Prick thine enemies, Rafe.

Enter Dodger.

Dodger. [*To Lacy.*] My lord, your uncle on the Tower Hill
Stays with the Lord Mayor and the Aldermen,
And doth request you with all speed you may
To hasten thither.

Askew. Cousin, let's go.

Lacy. Dodger, run you before. Tell them we come.

Exit Dodger.

This Dodger is mine uncle's parasite,
The arrant's varlet that e'er breathed on earth.
He sets more discord in a noble house
By one day's broaching of his pickthank tales
Than can be salved again in twenty years;
And he, I fear, shall go with us to France
To pry into our actions.

Askew. Therefore, coz,
It shall behoove you to be circumspect.

Lacy. Fear not, good cousin. Rafe, hie to your colors.

[*Exeunt* Lacy *and* Askew.]

Rafe. I must, because there is no remedy.
But, gentle master and my loving dame,
As you have always been a friend to me,
So in mine absence think upon my wife.

Jane. Alas, my Rafe.

Wife. She cannot speak for weeping.

Eyre. Peace, you cracked groats, you mustard tokens, disquiet not the brave soldier. Go thy ways, Rafe.

Jane. Aye, aye, you bid him go; what shall I do when he is gone?

Firk. Why, be doing with me, or my fellow Hodge. Be not idle.

Eyre. Let me see thy hand, Jane. [*He takes her hand.*] This fine hand, this white hand, these pretty fingers must spin, must card, must work. Work, you bombast-cotton-candle quean, work for your living. With a pox to you. Hold thee, Rafe, here's five sixpences for thee. Fight for the honor of the Gentle Craft, for the Gentlemen Shoemakers, the courageous cordwainers, the flower of

170 **pols** pleadings;
171 **edepols** protestations
172 **Cicely Bumtrinket** later (iv.45–6) identified as Margery's personal maidservant
172 **head** Eyre as head of household
173 **horns** of the cuckold
174 **Tawsoone** "Be quiet" (Welsh)
176 **Well . . . go** Eyre's bribery and persuasion fail; from now on, he will double his assertion of authority
178 **powder** gunpowder
180 **hackney** drudge; **Termagant** violent god of the Saracens (seen in mystery plays)
182 **Lord of Ludgate** King Lud, legendary founder of London, whose statue stood on the E side of Ludgate
183 **By . . . Pharaoh** a common oath (ultimately from Gen. 42:15)
188 **gull** fool
193–4 **A . . . him** he will get more consideration than ordinary recruits
199 **stirrup** shoemaker's strap
200 **gimlet** a boring tool
201 **weak vessels** women (a bawdy pun)
207 **parasite** servant
208 **arrant'st varlet** most complete rascal
210 **broaching** introduction; **pickthank** sycophantic
215 **colors** regimental standard
221 **cracked groats** fourpenny coins not circulated when damaged
221–2 **mustard tokens** substitute coins used as small change
230 **card** comb wool for spinning
231–2 **bombast-cotton-candle quean** delicate wench (bombast for cotton wool; candles had cotton wicks)
232–3 **With . . . you** oath of vengeance (pox = syphilis)
236 **cordwainers** shoemakers (from Cordova, Spain, known for leather)

Saint Martin's, the mad knaves of Bedlam, Fleet Street, Tower Street, and Whitechapel. Crack me the crowns of the French knaves, a pox on them; crack them. Fight, by the Lord of Ludgate, fight, my fine boy.

Firk. Here, Rafe, here's three twopences. Two carry into France; the third shall wash our souls at parting (for sorrow is dry). For my sake, firk the *baisez-mon-culs.*

Hodge. Rafe, I am heavy at parting, but here's a shilling for thee. God send thee to cram thy slops with French crowns, and thy enemies' bellies with bullets.

Rafe. I thank you, Master; and I thank you all.
Now, gentle wife, my loving, lovely Jane,
Rich men at parting give their wives rich gifts,
Jewels and rings to grace their lily hands.
Thou know'st our trade makes rings for
women's heels.
Here, take this pair of shoes cut out by Hodge,
Stitched by my fellow, Firk, seamed by myself,
Made up and pinked with letters for thy name.
Wear them, my dear Jane, for thy husband's sake,
And every morning, when thou pull'st them on,
Remember me, and pray for my return.
Make much of them, for I have made them so
That I can know them from a thousand moe.

Sound drum. Enter [Sir Roger Oatley, *the*] Lord Mayor, [*the* Earl of] Lincoln, Lacy, Askew, Dodger, *and soldiers. They pass over the stage.* Rafe *falls in amongst them.* Firk *and the rest cry "Farewell," etc., and so exeunt.*

[Sc. ii]

Enter Rose *alone, making a garland.*

[*Rose.*] Here sit thou down upon this flow'ry
bank,
And make a garland for thy Lacy's head.
These pinks, these roses, and these violets,
These blushing gilliflowers, these marigolds,
The fair embroidery of his coronet,
Carry not half such beauty in their cheeks
As the sweet countenance of my Lacy doth.
Oh, my most unkind father! Oh, my stars!
Why loured you so at my nativity
To make me love, yet live robbed of my love?
Here as a thief am I imprisoned
(For my dear Lacy's sake) within those walls
Which by my father's cost were builded up
For better purposes. Here must I languish
For him that doth as much lament (I know)
Mine absence, as for him I pine in woe.

Enter Sybil.

Sybil. Good morrow, young mistress. I am sure you make that garland for me, against I shall be Lady of the Harvest.

Rose. Sybil, what news at London?

Sybil. None but good. My Lord Mayor your father, and Master Philpot your uncle, and Master Scott your cousin, and Mistress Frigbottom, by Doctors' Commons, do all, by my troth, send you most hearty commendations.

Rose. Did Lacy send kind greetings to his love?

Sybil. Oh, yes, out of cry. By my troth, I scant knew him. Here 'a wore a scarf, and here a scarf, here a bunch of feathers, and here precious stones and jewels, and a pair of garters – Oh, monstrous! – like one of our yellow silk curtains at home here in Old Ford House, here in Master Bellymount's chamber. I stood at our door in Cornhill, looked at him, he at me indeed; spake to him, but he not to me, not a word. "Marry gup," thought I, "with a

---

237 **Saint Martin's** St. Martin's-le-Grand parish, center of the shoemaking trade; **Bedlam** Bethlehem Hospital, main asylum for madmen just outside Bishopsgate;
238 **Fleet Street** known for its exhibitions of freaks and oddities; **Whitechapel** E of London, known as an overcrowded and crimeridden suburb
239 **crowns** heads
243–4 **wash our souls** buy us a drink
245 ***baisez-mon-culs*** "kiss-my-arses"
246 **heavy** sad
248 **slops** loose breeches (or tunics); **French crowns** money or bald heads (from syphilis, the "French disease")
257 **pinked** pricked; decorated
262 **moe** more
1 **s.d. *pass over the stage*** processional movement from the audience to the stage and back or across an upper stage or balcony
ii.3 **pinks** common garden flowers
4 **gilliflowers** wallflowers
5 **coronet** wreath, small crown
9 **loured** scowled
18 **against** when
19 **Lady of the Harvest** chosen queen for Harvest Home celebrations
24 **by** lives by; **Doctors' Commons** lodgings for lawyers at the corner of Saint Bennett's Hill and Knightrider Street, a new building and a gathering place for idlers in Dekker's time
25 **troth** truth
28 **out of cry** beyond all saying
29 **'a** he
33 **Old Ford House** the Oatley country house in Old Ford, a village NE of London
35 **Cornhill** i.e., the Oatley town house; Cornhill Street, named for the cornmarket there, ran SW from Leadenhall to Lombard Street
37 **"Marry gup"** "My, aren't we getting uppity"

wanion!" He passed by me as proud – "marry, foh, are you grown humorous?" thought I – and so shut the door, and in I came.

Rose. Oh, Sybil, how dost thou my Lacy wrong!
My Rowland is as gentle as a lamb;
No dove was ever half so mild as he.

Sybil. Mild? Yea, as a bushel of stamped crabs. He looked upon me as sour as verjuice. "Go thy ways," thought I, "thou mayest be much in my gaskins, but nothing in my netherstocks." This is your fault, mistress, to love him that loves not you. He thinks scorn to do as he's done to; but if I were as you, I'd cry "Go by, Jeronimo, go by!"
I'ld set mine old debts against my new driblets, and the hare's foot against the goose giblets; for if ever I sigh when sleep I should take, pray God I may lose my maidenhead when I wake.

Rose. Will my love leave me then, and go to France?

Sybil. I know not that, but I am sure I see him stalk before the soldiers. By my troth, he is a proper man – but he is proper that proper doth. Let him go snick up, young mistress.

Rose. Get thee to London, and learn perfectly
Whether my Lacy go to France or no.
Do this, and I will give thee for thy pains
My cambric apron, and my Romish gloves,
My purple stockings, and a stomacher.
Say, wilt thou do this, Sybil, for my sake?

Sybil. Will I, quoth 'a! At whose suit? By my troth, yes, I'll go. A cambric apron, gloves, a pair of purple stockings, and a stomacher! I'll sweat in purple, mistress, for you; I'll take anything that comes a' God's name. Oh, rich, a cambric apron! Faith, then, have at uptails all, I'll go jiggy- joggy to London and be here in a trice, young mistress.

Exit.

Rose. Do so, good Sybil. Meantime wretched I
Will sit and sigh for his lost company.

Exit.

[Sc. iii]

Enter Rowland Lacy *like a Dutch shoemaker.*

Lacy. How many shapes have gods and kings devised
Thereby to compass their desirèd loves!
It is no shame for Rowland Lacy, then,
To clothe his cunning with the Gentle Craft,
That, thus disguised, I may unknown possess
The only happy presence of my Rose.
For her have I forsook my charge in France,
Incurred the King's displeasure, and stirred up
Rough hatred in mine uncle Lincoln's breast.
Oh, love, how powerful art thou that canst change
High birth to bareness, and a noble mind
To the mean semblance of a shoemaker!
But thus it must be; for her cruel father,
Hating the single union of our souls,
Hath secretly conveyed my Rose from London
To bar me of her presence. But I trust
Fortune and this disguise will further me
Once more to view her beauty, gain her sight.
Here in Tower Street, with Eyre the shoemaker,
Mean I a while to work. I know the trade;
I learnt it when I was in Wittenberg.
Then cheer thy drooping sprites. Be not dismayed.
Thou canst not want. Do Fortune what she can,
The Gentle Craft is living for a man!

Exit.

---

38 **wanion** vengeance
39 **humorous** moody, capricious
44 **bushel** eight gallons; **stamped crabs** crabapples crushed for their sour juice
45 **verjuice** juice of unripe fruit used for cooking
47 **gaskins** [breeches] ... **netherstocks** [stockings] "though I may act civilly, don't presume intimacy"
50 **"Go by, Jeronimo"** "Be off with you" (colloquialism from Kyd's play)
52–6 **I'ld ... wake** proverbial expressions urging awareness; **driblets** petty debts
55 **maidenhead** virginity
61 **proper** headstrong
62 **snick up** hang
64 **perfectly** exactly
67 **cambric** fine linen; **Romish** Roman
68 **stomacher** ornamental chest covering
70 **At ... suit?** "Need you ask?"
72–3 **sweat in purple** i.e., damned for wearing rich clothes
74 **a' God's name** free; for nothing
75 **have ... all** "Let's get moving"
iii.1 **s.d. like** disguised as; ***Dutch shoemaker*** traditional Dutch stage clothing included baggy breeches and a large felt hat
1 **shapes** disguises
2 **compass** encompass; win
11 **bareness** poverty
22 **sprites** spirits

[Sc. iv]

Enter Eyre, *making himself ready.*

Eyre. Where be these boys, these girls, these drabs, these scoundrels? They wallow in the fat brewis of my bounty, and lick up the crumbs of my table, yet will not rise to see my walks cleansed. Come out, you powder-beef queans! What, Nan! What, Madge Mumblecrust! Come out, you fat midriff-swag-belly whores, and sweep me these kennels, that the noisome stench offend not the nose of my neighbors. What, Firk, I say! What, Hodge! Open my shop windows! What, Firk, I say!

Enter Firk.

Firk. Oh, master, is't you that speak bandog and bedlam this morning? I was in a dream, and mused what madman was got into the street so early. Have you drunk this morning, that your throat is so clear?

Eyre. Ah, well said, Firk; well said. Firk, to work, my fine knave, to work! Wash thy face, and thou'lt be more blessed.

Firk. Let them wash my face that will eat it. Good master, send for a souse-wife if you'll have my face cleaner.

Enter Hodge.

Eyre. Away, sloven! Avaunt, scoundrel! Good morrow,
Hodge; good morrow, my fine foreman.

Hodge. Oh, master, good morrow. You're an early stirrer. Here's a fair morning. Good morrow, Firk. I could have slept this hour. Here's brave day towards.

Eyre. Oh, haste to work, my fine foreman, haste to work.

Firk. Master, I am dry as dust to hear my fellow Roger talk of fair weather. Let us pray for good leather, and let clowns and ploughboys, and those that work in the fields, pray for brave days. We work in a dry shop – what care I if it rain?

Enter [Margery,] *Eyre's wife.*

Eyre. How now, Dame Margery, can you see to rise? Trip and go, call up the drabs your maids.

Wife. See to rise? I hope 'tis time enough; 'tis early enough for any woman to be seen abroad. I marvel how many wives in Tower Street are up so soon. God's me, 'tis not noon! Here's a yawling.

Eyre. Peace, Margery, peace. Where's Cicely Bumtrinket, your maid? She has a privy fault: she farts in her sleep. Call the quean up. If my men want shoethread, I'll swinge her in a stirrup.

Firk. Yet that's but a dry beating. Here's still a sign of drought.

Enter Lacy [*as* Hans], *singing.*

Lacy [*as Hans*]. *Der was een bore van Gelderland,*
Frolick sie byen;
He was als dronck he could niet stand,
Upsoke sie byen;
Tap eens de canneken,
Drincke, schone mannekin.

Firk. Master, for my life, yonder's a brother of the Gentle Craft! If he bear not Saint Hugh's bones, I'll forfeit my bones. He's some uplandish workman. Hire him, good master, that I may learn some gibble-gabble. 'Twill make us work the faster.

---

iv.1 s.d. *making himself ready* dressing himself
2 drabs dirty and untidy women
3 brewis broth
5–6 powder-beef queans women who sell salted beef (or perhaps are old and tough like the beef); generally Eyre abuses women but not men verbally
6–7 Madge Mumblecrust a toothless character in Nicholas Udall's play *Ralph Roister Doister*
8 kennels gutters; drains
9 noisome annoying
11 Open my shop windows Elizabethan shop windows had shutters that let down to form counters for trading
12 bandog savage watchdog
13 bedlam loud madness
20 Let . . . it as one washes a pig's head for cooking
21 souse-wife one who cleans and pickles offal
23 Avaunt "Forward"
28 brave fine
29 towards ahead
34 clowns laborers, peasants
38 see "Is it light enough for you?" (sarcastic)
39 Trip hasten
44 yawling howling
46 privy private, secret
47 quean wanton, prostitute
48 want are without (her job is apparently to spin and wax thread)
48–9 swinge . . . stirrup beat her with a strap
50 dry beating one that draws no blood (Firk reminds others of his thirst)
52–7 *Der . . . mannekin* "There was a boor from Gelderland, Merry they be. He was so drunk he could not stand; Pissed they all be. Fill up the cannikin; Drink, my fine mannikin." The Dutch were legendary drinkers; Dutch "boer" had become English "boor," bore
59–60 Saint Hugh's bones shoemakers' tools; according to legend, St. Hugh was a shoemaker martyred for his love of St. Winifred; after his death his bones were discovered and used by shoemakers
61 uplandish foreign

Eyre. Peace, Firk. A hard world; let him pass, let him vanish. We have journeymen enough. Peace, my fine Firk.

Wife. Nay, nay, you are best follow your man's counsel. You shall see what will come on't. We have not men enough but we must entertain every butter-box. But let that pass.

Hodge. Dame, 'fore God, if my master follow your counsel he'll consume little beef. He shall be glad of men an he can catch them.

Firk. Aye, that he shall.

Hodge. 'Fore God, a proper man and, I warrant, a fine workman. Master, farewell. Dame, adieu. If such a man as he cannot find work, Hodge is not for you.

Offer[s] to go.

Eyre. Stay, my fine Hodge.

Firk. Faith, and your foreman go, dame, you must take a journey to seek a new journeyman. If Roger remove, Firk follows. If Saint Hugh's bones shall not be set a-work, I may prick mine awl in the walls, and go play. Fare ye well, master. Goodbye, dame.

Eyre. Tarry, my fine Hodge, my brisk foreman. Stay, Firk. Peace, pudding-broth. By the Lord of Ludgate, I love my men as my life. Peace, you gallimaufry. Hodge, if he want work, I'll hire him. One of you to him – stay, he comes to us.

Lacy [as Hans]. Goeden dach, meester, end you fro, auch.

Firk. 'Nails, if I should speak after him without drinking, I should choke! And you, friend Auch, are you of the Gentle Craft?

Lacy [as Hans]. Yaw, yaw; ik bin den skomawker.

Firk. "*Den skomawker,*" quoth 'a; and hark you, skomawker, have you all your tools – a good rubbing-pin, a good stopper, a good dresser, your four sorts of awls, and your two balls of wax, your paring-knife, your hand- and thumb-leathers, and good Saint Hugh's bones to smooth up your work?

Lacy [as Hans]. Yaw, yaw, be niet vorveard. Ik hab all de dingen voour mack skoes groot end klene.

Firk. Ha, ha! Good master, hire him. He'll make me laugh so that I shall work more in mirth than I can in earnest.

Eyre. Hear ye, friend: have ye any skill in the mystery of cordwainers?

Lacy [as Hans]. Ik weet niet wat you seg; ik verstaw you niet.

Firk. Why thus, man! [*He mimes the actions of a shoemaker.*] "*Ik verste you niet,*" quoth 'a.

Lacy [as Hans]. Yaw, yaw, yaw; ik can dat wel doen.

Firk. "*Yaw, yaw*" – he speaks yawing like a jackdaw that gapes to be fed with cheese curds. O, he'll give a villainous pull at a can of double beer. But Hodge and I have the vantage; we must drink first, because we are the eldest journeymen.

Eyre. What is thy name?

Lacy [as Hans]. Hans; Hans Meulter.

Eyre. Give me thy hand: thou'rt welcome. Hodge, entertain him. Firk, bid him welcome. Come, Hans. Run, wife; bid your maids, your trullibubs, make ready my fine men's breakfasts. To him, Hodge.

Hodge. Hans, thou'rt welcome. Use thyself friendly, for we are good fellows; if not, thou shalt be fought with, wert thou bigger than a giant.

Firk. Yea, and drunk with, wert thou Gargantua. My master keeps no cowards, I tell thee. Ho, boy, bring him an heelblock. Here's a new journeyman.

Enter Boy.

Lacy [as Hans]. O, ik verstaw you. Ik moet een halve dossen cans betaelen. Here, boy, *nempt dis skilling, tap eens freelick.*

Exit Boy.

Eyre. Quick, snipper-snapper, away! Firk, scour thy throat; thou shalt wash it with Castilian liquor. Come, my last of the fives,

70 **butter-box** addicted to butter (a common nickname for the Dutch)
72 **consume little beef** i.e., not prosper
82 **Roger** apparently Hodge's first name (showing familiarity)
87 **pudding-broth** fat person (apparently Margery)
89 **gallimaufry** ragbag
92 ***Goeden . . . auch*** "Good day, master, and you mistress also"
93 **'Nails** common oath derived from "God's nails" (referring to the crucifixion)
96 ***Yaw . . . skomawker*** "Yes, yes, I am a shoemaker"
104–5 ***Yaw . . . klene*** "Yes, yes, never fear. I have everything for making shoes large and small"
110 **mystery** craft (with allusion to the secrets of the trade)
111–12 ***Ik . . . niet*** "I don't know what you say; I cannot understand you"
115 ***Yaw . . . doen*** "Yes, yes, yes; I can do that well"
116 **jackdaw** birds caught as pets and taught to talk
118 **double** extra strong
125–6 **trullibubs** literally, fat guts; a slut
128 **Use thyself** be
132 **Gargantua** giant from French folklore
134 **heelblock** small wooden block used to fasten a heel to a shoe; perhaps here also used to tally rounds of drink
136–8 ***O . . . freelick*** "Oh, I understand you: I must pay for half a dozen cans. Here, boy, take this shilling, fill up once all around"
139 **snipper-snapper** whippersnapper; cheeky young fellow
140–1 **Castilian liquor** drink from Castile;
141 **last . . . fives** little one (last = wooden model for small feet)

Enter Boy.

give me a can. Have to thee, Hans! Here, Hodge; here, Firk. Drink, you mad Greeks, and work like true Trojans, and pray for Simon Eyre the shoemaker. Here, Hans; and thou'rt welcome.

Firk. Lo, dame, you would have lost a good fellow that will teach us to laugh. This beer came hopping in well.

Wife. Simon, it is almost seven.

Eyre. Is't so, Dame Clapperdudgeon? Is't seven o'clock and my men's breakfast not ready? Trip and go, you soused conger, away. Come, you mad Hyperboreans. Follow me, Hodge. Follow me, Hans. Come after, my fine Firk. To work, to work a while, and then to breakfast.

Exit.

Firk. Soft, yaw, yaw, good Hans. Though my master have no more wit but to call you afore me, I am not so foolish to go behind you, I being the elder journeyman.

Exeunt.

[Sc. v]

Holloaing within. Enter Warner *and* Hammon, *like hunters.*

Hammon. Cousin, beat every brake. The game's not far.
This way with wingèd feet he fled from death
While the pursuing hounds, scenting his steps,
Find out his highway to destruction.
Besides, the miller's boy told me even now
He saw him take soil, and he holloaed him,
Affirming him so embossed that
Long he could not hold.

Warner. If it be so,
'Tis best we trace these meadows by Old Ford.

A noise of hunters within. Enter a Boy.

Hammon. How now, boy, where's the deer? Speak. Sawst thou him?

Boy. O yea, I saw him leap through a hedge, and then over a ditch, then at my Lord Mayor's pale. Over he skipped me and in he went me, and "Holloa" the hunters cried, and "There, boy, there, boy," but there he is, 'a mine honesty.

Hammon. Boy, godamercy. Cousin, let's away.
I hope we shall find better sport today.

Exeunt.

[Sc. vi]

Hunting within. Enter Rose *and* Sybil.

Rose. Why, Sybil, wilt thou prove a forester?

Sybil. Upon some, no! Forester, go by. No, faith, mistress, the deer came running into the barn through the orchard and over the pale. I wot well I looked as pale as a new cheese to see him, but "Whip!" says Goodman Pinclose, up with his flail, and our Nick with a prong, and down he fell, and they upon him, and I upon them. By my troth, we had such sport; and in the end we ended him; his throat we cut, flayed him, unhorned him, and my Lord Mayor shall eat of him anon when he comes.

Horns sound within.

Rose. Hark, hark, the hunters come. You're best take heed. They'll have a saying to you for this deed.

Enter Hammon, Warner, Huntsmen, *and* Boy.

Hammon. God save you, fair ladies.

Sybil. Ladies! Oh, gross!

Warner. Came not a buck this way?

Rose. No, but two does.

Hammon. And which way went they? Faith, we'll hunt at those.

Sybil. At those? Upon some, no! When, can you tell?

---

144 **work...Trojans** (1) Trojans were hard fighters; (2) Trojans meaning Greek suggests they are merry and boisterous
151 **Clapperdudgeon** beggar (after wooden clapdishes used by beggars and lepers)
153 **soused** pickled; **conger** eel
154 **Hyperboreans** mythical people who lived beyond the N wind
160 **elder** senior
v.1 **brake** thicket
6 **soil** refuge
7 **embossed** exhausted; foaming or panting
13 **pale** fence
vi.1 **prove** become
2 **Upon...no!** "Never!"
4 **wot** know
11 **flayed** skinned
12 **anon** soon
15 **saying** rebuke
17 **gross** stupid (Sybil is not a lady)
18 **does** i.e., Sybil and herself; the following play of homonyms is commonplace

Warner. Upon some, aye!
Sybil. Good Lord!
Warner. 'Wounds, then farewell.
Hammon. Boy, which way went he?
Boy. This way, sir, he ran.
Hammon. This way he ran indeed. Fair Mistress Rose,
Our game was lately in your orchard seen.
Warner. Can you advise which way he took his flight?
Sybil. Follow your nose, his horns will guide you right.
Warner. Thou'rt a mad wench.
Sybil. Oh, rich!
Rose. Trust me, not I.
It is not like the wild forest deer
Would come so near to places of resort.
You are deceived. He fled some other way.
Warner. Which way, my sugar candy; can you show?
Sybil. Come up, good honey-sops; upon some, no!
Rose. Why do you stay, and not pursue your game?
Sybil. I'll hold my life their hunting nags be lame.
Hammon. A deer more dear is found within this place.
Rose. But not the deer, sir, which you had in chase.
Hammon. I chased the deer; but this dear chaseth me.
Rose. The strangest hunting that ever I see.
But where's your park?
She offers to go away.
Hammon. 'Tis here. Oh, stay!
Rose. Impale me, and then I will not stray.
Warner. They wrangle, wench. We are more kind than they.
Sybil. What kind of hart is that dear hart you seek?
Warner. A heart, dear heart.
Sybil. Whoever saw the like?
Rose. To lose your hart? Is't possible you can?
Hammon. My heart is lost.
Rose. Alack, good gentleman.
Hammon. This poor lost heart would I wish you might find.
Rose. You by such luck might prove your hart a hind.
Hammon. Why, luck had horns, so have I heard some say.
Rose. Now God an't be His will send luck into your way.

Enter Lord Mayor *and* Servants.

Lord Mayor. What, Master Hammon! Welcome to Old Ford!
Sybil. God's pitikins, hands off, sir, here's my lord.
Lord Mayor. I hear you had ill luck and lost your game.
Hammon. 'Tis true, my lord.
Lord Mayor. I am sorry for the same.
What gentleman is this?
Hammon. My brother-in-law.
Lord Mayor. You're welcome, both. Sith Fortune offers you
Into my hands, you shall not part from hence
Until you have refreshed your wearied limbs.
Go, Sybil: cover the board. You shall be guest
To no good cheer, but even a hunters' feast.
Hammon. I thank your lordship. [*Aside to Warner.*]
Cousin, on my life,
For our lost venison, I shall find a wife.
Lord Mayor. In, gentlemen. I'll not be absent long.
Exeunt [*all except the Lord Mayor*].
This Hammon is a proper gentleman,
A citizen by birth, fairly allied.
How fit an husband were he for my girl!
Well, I will in, and do the best I can
To match my daughter to this gentleman.
Exit.

[Sc. vii]

Enter Lacy [*as* Hans], Skipper, Hodge, *and* Firk.

Skipper. Ik sal you wat seggen, Hans; dis skip dat comen from Candy is wel, by Got's sacrament, van sugar, civet, almonds, cambric, end alle dingen – tousand tousand ding. Nempt it, Hans, nempt it vor your meester. Daer be de bils van laden. Your meester Simon Eyre sal hae good copen. Wat seggen you, Hans?

21 **'Wounds** common oath (God's wounds)
26 **nose** Sybil refers to the fact that they have already killed the deer; **horns** play on another sense of cuckoldry in that they have taken the hunters' prey
32 **honey-sops** bread soaked in honey (satiric response to *sugar candy*)
39 **s.d.** ***away*** (to the suggested deer park)
40 **Impale me** fence me in
47 **hind** female deer
51 **God's pitikins** by God's pity (mild oath)
55 **Sith** since
58 **cover the board** lay the table
59 **hunters' feast** impromptu meal
vii.1–6 ***Ik . . . Hans?*** "I'll tell you what, Hans; this ship that came from Candy [Candia, now Crete] is absolutely full, by God's sacrament, of sugar, civet [animal extract to make perfume], almonds, cambric, and all things – a thousand, thousand things. Take it, Hans, take it for your master. There are the bills of lading. Your master Simon Eyre will have a good bargain. What do you say, Hans?"

Firk. *Wat seggen de reggen de copen, slopen*. Laugh, Hodge, laugh!

Lacy [*as Hans*]. *Mine liever broder Firk, bringt Meester Eyre lot den signe un swannekin. Daer sal you find dis skipper end me. Wat seggen you, broder Firk? Doot it, Hodge!* Come, skipper!

Exeunt [Lacy *as* Hans *and* Skipper].

Firk. "Bring him," quoth you? Here's no knavery, to bring my master to buy a ship worth the lading of two or three hundred thousand pounds. Alas, that's nothing. A trifle, a bauble, Hodge.

Hodge. The truth is, Firk, that the merchant owner of the ship dares not show his head, and therefore this skipper that deals for him, for the love he bears to Hans, offers my master Eyre a bargain in the commodities. He shall have a reasonable day of payment. He may sell the wares by that time, and be an huge gainer himself.

Firk. Yea, but can my fellow Hans lend my master twenty porpentines as an earnest-penny?

Hodge. "Portagues" thou wouldst say. Here they be, Firk. Hark! They jingle in my pocket like Saint Mary Overy's bells.

Enter Eyre *and* [Margery] *his wife* [*and a* Boy].

Firk. Mum, here comes my dame and my master. She'll scold, on my life, for loitering this Monday. But all's one. Let them all say what they can, Monday's our holiday.

Wife. You sing, Sir Sauce, but I beshrew your heart,
I fear for this your singing we shall smart.

Firk. Smart for me, dame? Why, dame, why?

Hodge. Master, I hope you'll not suffer my dame to take down your journeymen.

Firk. If she take me down, I'll take her up – yea, and take her down, too, a buttonhole lower.

Eyre. Peace, Firk. Not I, Hodge. By the life of Pharaoh, by the Lord of Ludgate, by this beard, every hair whereof I value at a king's ransom, she shall not meddle with you. Peace, you bombast-cotton-candle quean. Away, Queen of Clubs, quarrel not with me and my men, with me and my fine Firk. I'll firk you if you do.

Wife. Yea, yea, man, you may use me as you please. But let that pass.

Eyre. Let it pass, let it vanish away. Peace, am I not Simon Eyre? Are not these my brave men, brave shoemakers, all gentlemen of the Gentle Craft? Prince am I none, yet am I nobly born, as being the sole son of a shoemaker. Away, rubbish. Vanish, melt, melt like kitchen-stuff.

Wife. Yea, yea, 'tis well. I must be called rubbish, kitchen-stuff, for a sort of knaves.

Firk. Nay, dame, you shall not weep and wail in woe for me. Master, I'll stay no longer. Here's a venentory of my shop tools. Adieu, master. Hodge, farewell.

Hodge. Nay, stay, Firk, thou shalt not go alone.

Wife. I pray, let them go. There be more maids than Malkin, more men than Hodge, and more fools than Firk.

Firk. Fools? 'Nails, if I tarry now, I would my guts might be turned to shoe-thread.

Hodge. And if I stay, I pray God I may be turned to a Turk and set in Finsbury for boys to shoot at. Come, Firk.

Eyre. Stay, my fine knaves, you arms of my trade, you pillars of my profession. What, shall a tittle-tattle's words make you forsake Simon Eyre? Avaunt, kitchen-stuff. Rip, you brown-bread Tannikin, out of my sight! Move me not. Have not I ta'en you from selling tripes in Eastcheap, and set you in my shop, and made you hail-fellow with Simon Eyre the shoemaker? And now do you deal thus with my journeymen? Look, you powder-beef quean, on the face of Hodge. Here's a face for a lord.

---

7 ***Wat . . . slopen*** (nonsense)

9–12 ***Mine . . . Hodge!*** "My dear brother Firk, bring Master Eyre to the sign of the Swan. There you shall find this skipper and me. What do you say, brother Firk? Do it, Hodge!" (The Dutch frequented a tavern called the Swan)

14–15 **worth the lading** with a cargo

15 **hundred thousand** (apparently a textual error or perhaps a revision; "hundred hundred" is more likely)

18 **dares not show his head** perhaps a reference to the expulsion of Hanseatic merchants from England in 1597, who were thus forced to a quick sale of their goods

21 **commodities** merchandise

22 **day** period

26 **porpentines** porcupines; **earnest-penny** down payment

29 **Saint Mary Overy's** so called as "over" the Thames (presently the cathedral of St. Saviour in Southwark)

33 **Monday's** the traditional day off for shoemakers (Firk may sing this phrase)

34 **Sir Sauce** ironic way to say saucy; **beshrew** curse

38 **take down** admonish

40 **buttonhole lower** down a peg or two (with bawdy wordplay)

46 **Queen of Clubs** troublemaker

56 **kitchen-stuff** drippings from cooking

58 **sort** gang

61 **venentory** inventory

64–5 **more maids than Malkin** more virtuous women than bad

69–71 **turned . . . at** effigies of Turks were then used for target practice

75 **Rip** get out; **brown-bread** a bread despised for its coarseness

76 **Tannikin** diminutive form of "Anne" applied to Dutch or German girls (mildly abusive)

77 **tripes** stomachs or entrails of ox, swine, or fish; **Eastcheap** London district famous for its butchers and taverns

Firk. And here's a face for any lady in Christendom.

Eyre. Rip, you chitterling, avaunt! Boy, bid the tapster of the Boar's Head fill me a dozen cans of beer for my journeymen.

Firk. A dozen cans! Oh, brave, Hodge, now I'll stay!

Eyre. [*Aside to the Boy.*] And the knave fills any more than two, he pays for them.

[*Exit* Boy.]

[*Aloud.*] A dozen cans of beer for my journeymen!

[*Enter the* Boy *with two cans, and exit.*]

Here, you mad Mesopotamians, wash your livers with this liquor. Where be the odd ten? No more, Madge; no more. Well said, drink and to work. What work dost thou, Hodge, what work?

Hodge. I am a-making a pair of shoes for my Lord Mayor's daughter, Mistress Rose.

Firk. And I a pair of shoes for Sybil, my Lord's maid. I deal with her.

Eyre. Sybil? Fie, defile not thy fine, workmanly fingers with the feet of kitchen-stuff and basting-ladles. Ladies of the Court, fine ladies, my lads, commit their feet to our appareling. Put gross work to Hans. Yerk and seam, yerk and seam.

Firk. For yerking and seaming let me alone, an I come to't.

Hodge. Well, master, all this is from the bias. Do you remember the ship my fellow Hans told you of? The skipper and he are both drinking at the Swan. Here be the Portagues to give earnest. If you go through with it, you cannot choose but be a lord at least.

Firk. Nay, dame, if my master prove not a lord, and you a lady, hang me.

Wife. Yea, like enough, if you may loiter and tipple thus.

Firk. Tipple, dame? No, we have been bargaining with Skellum-Skanderbag-can-you-Dutch-spreaken for a ship of silk cypress, laden with sugar candy.

Enter the Boy *with a velvet coat and an Alderman's gown. Eyre puts it on.*

Eyre. Peace, Firk. Silence, tittle-tattle. Hodge, I'll go through with it. Here's a seal ring, and I have sent for a guarded gown and a damask cassock. See where it comes. Look here, Maggy. Help me, Firk. Apparel me, Hodge. Silk and satin, you mad Philistines, silk and satin!

Firk. Ha, ha! My master will be as proud as a dog in a doublet, all in beaten damask and velvet.

Eyre. Softly, Firk, for rearing of the nap and wearing threadbare my garments. How dost thou like me, Firk? How do I look, my fine Hodge?

Hodge. Why, now you look like yourself, master. I warrant you, there's few in the City but will give you the wall, and come upon you with the "Right Worshipful."

Firk. 'Nails, my master looks like a threadbare cloak new turned and dressed. Lord, Lord, to see what good raiment doth. Dame, dame, are you not enamored?

Eyre. How sayst thou, Maggy; am I not brisk? Am I not fine?

Wife. Fine? By my troth, sweetheart, very fine. By my troth, I never liked thee so well in my life, sweetheart. But let that pass. I warrant there be many women in the City have not such handsome husbands, but only for their apparel. But let that pass, too.

[*Lacy as*] *Hans. Godden day, mester; dis be de skipper dat heb de skip van marchandice. De commodity ben good. Nempt it, master; nempt it.*

Eyre. Godamercy, Hans. Welcome, skipper. Where lies this ship of merchandise?

Skipper. De skip ben in rovere. Dor be van sugar, civet, almonds, cambric, and a tousand tousand tings, Got's sacrament! Nempt it, meester; you sal heb good copen.

---

85 **chitterling** sausage

86 **Boar's Head** perhaps the tavern in Eastcheap between Small Alley and St. Michael's Alley, but that is a considerable distance; another tavern by that name may be meant

105 **Yerk** stitch

109 **from the bias** off the main point

112 **the Swan** Old Swan tavern on Upper Thames Street near London Bridge

120 **Skellum** thief, rogue; **Skanderbag** colloquial name for John Castriota (1403–67), the Albanian hero who freed his country from the Turks

121–2 **silk . . . candy** Firk parodies the skipper at vii.1–3

125 **guarded** braided

130 **beaten** inlaid, embroidered

132 **rearing of the nap** i.e., making a fuss

138 **give you the wall** allow you to pass on the inside (give you preference)

139 **"Right Worshipful"** proper form of address for an alderman

144 **brisk** sartorial; smart

152–4 ***Godden . . . it*** "Good day, master. This is the skipper who owns the ship of merchandise. The commodity is good; take it, master, take it"

157–9 ***De . . . copen*** "The ship is in the river. There are sugar, civet, almonds, cambric, and a thousand things, by God's sacrament! Take it, master, you shall have a good bargain"

Firk. To him, master. Oh, sweet master! Oh sweet wares! Prunes, almonds, sugar candy, carrot-roots, turnips. Oh, brave fatting meat! Let not a man buy a nutmeg but yourself.

Eyre. Peace, Firk. Come, skipper, I'll go aboard with you. Hans, have you made him drink?

Skipper. Yaw, yaw. Ik heb veale gedrunck.

Eyre. Come, Hans, follow me. Skipper, thou shalt have my countenance in the City.

Exeunt [Eyre, Skipper, *and* Lacy *as* Hans].

Firk. "*Yaw heb veale gedrunck*," quoth 'a! They may well be called butter-boxes when they drink fat veal, and thick beer too. But come, dame; I hope you'll chide us no more.

Wife. No, faith, Firk. No, perdie, Hodge. I do feel honor creep upon me, and, which is more, a certain rising in my flesh. But let that pass.

Firk. Rising in your flesh do you feel, say you? Aye, you may be with child; but why should not my master feel a rising in his flesh, having a gown and a gold ring on! But you are such a shrew, you'll soon pull him down.

Wife. Ha, ha! Prithee, peace, thou makest my worship laugh. But let that pass. Come, I'll go in. Hodge, prithee, go before me. Firk, follow me!

Firk. Firk doth follow. Hodge, pass out in state!

Exeunt.

[Sc. viii]

Enter [*the* Earl of] Lincoln *and* Dodger.

Lincoln. How now, good Dodger, what's the news in France?
Dodger. My lord, upon the eighteen day of May
The French and English were prepared to fight.
Each side with eager fury gave the sign
Of a most hot encounter. Five long hours
Both armies fought together. At the length
The lot of victory fell on our sides.
Twelve thousand of the Frenchmen that day died,
Four thousand English, and no man of name
But Captain Hyam and young Ardington,
Lincoln. Two gallant gentlemen; I knew them well.
But, Dodger, prithee tell me, in this fight
How did my cousin Lacy bear himself?
Dodger. My lord, your cousin Lacy was not there.
Lincoln. Not there?
Dodger. No, my good lord.
Lincoln. Sure, thou mistakest.
I saw him shipped, and a thousand eyes beside
Were witnesses of the farewells which he gave
When I with weeping eyes bid him adieu.
Dodger, take heed.
Dodger. My lord, I am advised
That what I spake is true. To prove it so,
His cousin Askew, that supplied his place,
Sent me for him from France that secretly
He might convey himself thither.
Lincoln. Is't even so?
Dares he so carelessly venture his life
Upon the indignation of a King?
Hath he despised my love, and spurned those favors
Which I with prodigal hand poured on his head?
He shall repent his rashness with his soul.
Since of my love he makes no estimate,
I'll make him wish he had not known my hate.
Thou hast no other news?
Dodger. None else, my lord.
Lincoln. None worse I know thou hast. Procure the King
To crown his giddy brows with ample honors,
Send him chief colonel, and all my hope
Thus to be dashed? But 'tis in vain to grieve.
One evil cannot a worse relieve.
Upon my life, I have found out his plot.
That old dog love that fawned upon him so,
Love to that puling girl, his fair-cheeked Rose,
The Lord Mayor's daughter, hath distracted him,
And in the fire of that love's lunacy
Hath he burned up himself, consumed his credit,
Lost the King's love, yea and, I fear, his life,
Only to get a wanton to his wife.
Dodger, is it so.
Dodger. I fear so, my good lord.
Lincoln. It is so. Nay, sure it cannot be.
I am at my wits' end. Dodger –
Dodger. Yea, my lord?
Lincoln. Thou art acquainted with my nephew's haunts.

162 carrot-roots, turnips (1) a parody of Hans; (2) recent Dutch imports (like the contraband cargo itself)
163 nutmeg as the tiniest of purchases
166 *Yaw . . . gedrunck* "Yes, yes, I have drunk well"
168 countenance protection
175 rising in my flesh flushing red
180 pull him down humble him
181 Prithee "Pray thee"
viii.9 of name i.e., rank of gentleman or above
19 advised knowledgeable
21 supplied took
27 prodigal lavish

Spend this gold for thy pains. Go seek him out.
Watch at my Lord Mayor's. There if he live,
Dodger, thou shalt be sure to meet with him.
Prithee, be diligent. Lacy, thy name
Lived once in honor, now dead in shame!
Be circumspect.

Exit.

Dodger. I warrant you, my lord.

Exit.

[Sc. ix]

Enter Lord Mayor *and* Master Scott.

Lord Mayor. Good Master Scott, I have been bold with you
To be a witness to a wedding knot
Betwixt young Master Hammon and my daughter.
Oh, stand aside. See where the lovers come.

Enter Hammon *and* Rose.

Rose. Can it be possible you love me so?
No, no; within those eyeballs I espy
Apparent likelihoods of flattery.
Pray now, let go my hand.
Hammon. Sweet Mistress Rose,
Misconstrue not my words, nor misconceive
Of my affection, whose devoted soul
Swears that I love thee dearer than my heart.
Rose. As dear as your own heart? I judge it right:
Men love their hearts best when they're out of sight.
Hammon. I love you, by this hand.
Rose. Yet hands off, now.
If flesh be frail, how weak and frail's your vow!
Hammon. Then by my life I swear.
Rose. Then do not brawl.
One quarrel loseth wife and life and all.
Is not your meaning thus?
Hammon. In faith, you jest.
Rose. Love loves to sport; therefore leave love, you're best.
Lord Mayor. What, square they, Master Scott?
Scott. Sir, never doubt.
Lovers are quickly in and quickly out.
Hammon. Sweet Rose, be not so strange in fancying me.
Nay, never turn aside. Shun not my sight.
I am not grown so fond to fond my love
On any that shall quit it with disdain.
If you will love me, so. If not, farewell.
Lord Mayor. Why, how now, lovers; are you both agreed?
Hammon. Yes, faith, my lord.
Lord Mayor. 'Tis well. Give me your hand;
Give me yours, daughter. How now – both pull back! What means this, girl?
Rose. I mean to live a maid.
Hammon. (*Aside.*) But not to die one. Pause ere that be said.
Lord Mayor. Will you still cross me? Still be obstinate?
Hammon. Nay, chide her not, my lord, for doing well.
If she can live an happy virgin's life,
'Tis far more blessèd than to be a wife.
Rose. Say, sir, I cannot. I have made a vow:
Whoever be my husband, 'tis not you.
Lord Mayor. Your tongue is quick. But, Master Hammon, know I bade you welcome to another end.
Hammon. What, would you have me pule, and pine, and pray
With "lovely lady," "mistress of my heart,"
"Pardon your servant," and the rhymer play,
Railing on Cupid and his tyrant's dart?
Or shall I undertake some martial spoil,
Wearing your glove at tourney and at tilt,
And tell how many gallants I unhorsed?
Sweet, will this pleasure you?
Rose. Yea; when wilt begin?
What, love-rhymes, man? Fie on that deadly sin!
Lord Mayor. If you will have her, I'll make her agree.
Hammon. Enforcèd love is worse than hate to me.
[*Aside.*] There is a wench keeps shop in the Old Change.
To her will I. It is not wealth I seek;
I have enough, and will prefer her love

ix.2 wedding knot betrothal ceremony
16 brawl quarrel
20 square quarrel
22 strange perverse, remote
24 fond . . . fond foolish . . . bestow
25 quit requite
32 still insistently
40 end outcome
45 spoil adventure
46 tourney tournament; **tilt** combat between two men on horseback with lances
52 wench prostitute; **Old Change** street named for the Old Exchange, superseded by Thomas Gresham's Royal Exchange in 1566

Before the world. [*To the Lord Mayor.*] My good Lord Mayor, adieu.
[*Aside.*] Old love for me; I have no luck with new.

Exit.

Lord Mayor. [*To Rose.*] Now, mammet, you have well behaved yourself.
But you shall curse your coyness, if I live.
– Who's within, there? See you convey your mistress
Straight to th'Old Ford. [*To Rose.*] I'll keep you straight enough.
– Fore God, I would have sworn the puling girl
Would willingly accepted Hammon's love.
But banish him, my thoughts. – Go, minion, in.

Exit Rose.

Now tell me, Master Scott, would you have thought
That Master Simon Eyre, the shoemaker,
Had been of wealth to buy such merchandise?
Scott. 'Twas well, my lord, your honor and myself
Grew partners with him; for your bills of lading
Show that Eyre's gains in one commodity
Rise at the least to full three thousand pound,
Besides like gain in other merchandise.
Lord Mayor. Well, he shall spend some of his thousands now,
For I have sent for him to the Guildhall.

Enter Eyre.

See where he comes. Good morrow, Master Eyre.
Eyre. Poor Simon Eyre, my lord, your shoemaker.
Lord Mayor. Well, well, it likes yourself to term you so.

Enter Dodger.

Now, Master Dodger, what's the news with you?
Dodger. I'ld gladly speak in private to your honor.
Lord Mayor. You shall, you shall. Master Eyre, and Master Scott,
I have some business with this gentleman.
I pray, let me entreat you to walk before
To the Guildhall. I'll follow presently.
Master Eyre, I hope ere noon to call you sheriff.
Eyre. I would not care, my lord, if you might call me King of Spain. Come, Master Scott.

[*Exeunt* Eyre *and* Scott.]

Lord Mayor. Now, Master Dodger, what's the news you bring?
Dodger. The Earl of Lincoln by me greets your lordship
And earnestly requests you, if you can,
Inform him where his nephew Lacy keeps.
Lord Mayor. Is not his nephew Lacy now in France?
Dodger. No, I assure your lordship, but, disguised,
Lurks here in London.
Lord Mayor. London? Is't even so?
It may be, but upon my faith and soul,
I know not where he lives, or whether he lives.
So tell my Lord of Lincoln. – Lurks in London?
Well, Master Dodger, you perhaps may start him.
Be but the means to rid him into France,
I'll give you a dozen angels for your pains,
So much I love his honor, hate his nephew;
And, prithee, so inform thy lord from me.
Dodger. I take my leave.
Lord Mayor. Farewell, good Master Dodger.

Exit Dodger.

Lacy in London? I dare pawn my life
My daughter knows thereof, and for that cause
Denied young Master Hammon in his love.
Well, I am glad I sent her to Old Ford.
God's Lord, 'tis late; to Guildhall I must hie.
I know my brethren stay my company.

Exit

[Sc. x]

Enter Firk *Eyre's wife*, [Lacy *as*] Hans, *and* Roger [Hodge].

Wife. Thou goest too fast for me, Roger.
Firk. Aye, forsooth.
Wife. I pray thee, run – do you hear – run to Guildhall, and learn if my husband, Master

57 **mammet** puppet (from false images of Mohammed)

60 **Old Ford** a village $3\frac{1}{2}$ miles NE of St. Paul's Cathedral where the Essex–London road forded the Lea River

74 **Master Eyre** the new title of address indicates Eyre's financial advance

82 **presently** immediately

85 **King of Spain** a strong insult, since Spain was the chief enemy of England at the time of the play

96 **start** flush him out (term from hunting)

98 **dozen angels** gold coins worth ten shillings each with the Archangel Michael on one side; the sum equals a customary three-month salary for Dodger

106 **hie** go

Eyre, will take that worshipful vocation of Master Sheriff upon him. Hie thee, good Firk.

Firk. Take it? Well, I go. And he should not take it, Firk swears to forswear him. [*To Wife.*] Yes, forsooth, I go to Guildhall.

Wife. Nay, when! Thou art too compendious and tedious.

Firk. Oh, rare. Your excellence is full of eloquence.

[*Aside.*]

How like a new cartwheel my dame speaks; and she looks like an old musty ale-bottle going to scalding.

Wife. Nay, when! Thou wilt make me melancholy.

Firk. God forbid your worship should fall into that humor. I run.

Exit.

Wife. Let me see now, Roger and Hans.

Roger [*Hodge*]. Aye, forsooth, dame – mistress, I should say, but the old term so sticks to the roof of my mouth; I can hardly lick it off.

Wife. Even what thou wilt, good Roger. Dame is a fair name for any honest Christian. But let that pass. How dost thou, Hans?

[*Lacy as*] *Hans. Me tank you, fro.*

Wife. Well, Hans and Roger, you see God hath blessed your master; and, perdie, if ever he comes to be Master Sheriff of London – as we are all mortal – you shall see I will have some odd thing or other in a corner for you. I will not be your back friend. But let that pass. Hans, pray thee, tie my shoe.

[*Lacy as*] *Hans. Yaw, ik sal, fro.*

Wife. Roger, thou knowest the length of my foot. As it is none of the biggest, so I thank God it is handsome enough. Prithee, let me have a pair of shoes made; cork, good Roger; wooden heel, too.

Roger [*Hodge*]. You shall.

Wife. Art thou acquainted with never a farthingale-maker, nor a French-hood-maker? I must enlarge my bum. Ha, ha! How shall I look in a hood, I wonder? Perdie, oddly, I think.

Roger [*Hodge*]. [*Aside.*] As a cat out of a pillory. [*To wife.*] Very well, I warrant you, mistress.

Wife. Indeed, all flesh is grass. And Roger, canst thou tell where I may buy a good hair?

Roger [*Hodge*]. Yes, forsooth; at the poulterer's in Gracious Street.

Wife. Thou art an ungracious wag. Perdie, I mean a false hair for my periwig.

Roger [*Hodge*]. Why, mistress, the next time I cut my beard you shall have the shavings of it. But they are all true hairs.

Wife. It is very hot. I must get me a fan, or else a mask.

Roger [*Hodge*]. [*Aside.*] So you had need, to hide your wicked face.

Wife. Fie upon it, how costly this world's calling is! Perdie, but that it is one of the wonderful works of God, I would not deal with it. Is not Firk come yet? Hans, be not so sad. Let it pass and vanish, as my husband's worship says.

[*Lacy as*] *Hans. Ik bin frolick; lot see you so.*

Roger [*Hodge*]. Mistress, will you drink a pipe of tobacco?

Wife. O, fie upon it, Roger! Perdie, these filthy tobacco pipes are the most idle, slavering baubles that ever I felt. Out upon it, God bless us; men look not like men that use them.

Enter Rafe, *being lame.*

Roger [*Hodge*]. What, fellow Rafe! Mistress, look here! Jane's husband! Why, how now, lame? Hans, make much of him. He's a brother of our trade, a good workman, and a tall soldier.

[*Lacy as*] *Hans.* You be welcome, *broder.*

Wife. Perdie, I knew him not. How dost thou, good Rafe? I am glad to see thee well.

---

x.8 **forswear** renounce
10 **Nay, when!** "What's stopping you?" **compendious** brief (she means the opposite)
14 **like a new cartwheel** i.e., with a squeaky voice
15 **musty ale-bottle** ale was put in leather bottles
16 **scalding** cleaning of bottle compared to common treatment of venereal disease
24 **Dame** then women of lower rank
27 ***Me . . . fro*** "I thank you, mistress"
29 **perdie** "By God" (common oath from French *par dieu*)
33 **back friend** false friend
35 ***Yaw . . . fro*** "Yes, I will, mistress"
39 **cork** used to line and raise shoes; these and following fashions designate Margery's elevation to a citizen's wife
42–3 **farthingale** hooped underskirt
43 **French-hood** close-fitting pleated hood with flaps on each side
46 **cat . . . pillory** reference is colloquial to a prostitute looking out of a head-hole in the pillory
49 **hair** hairpiece
51 **Gracious Street** corruption of Gracechurch Street leading from London Bridge to the city, sometimes (as in Hodge's pun) called "Grass Street"
56 **hairs** (with pun on *heirs*)
57–8 **fan . . . mask** items for fashionable citizens' wives; some, including the fan, were new to Dekker's England
60 **wicked** ugly
66 ***Ik . . . so*** "I am cheerful; let's see you so"
67 **drink** smoke
70 **slavering baubles** slobbering useless trinkets
76 **tall** brave

Rafe. I would God you saw me, dame, as well
As when I went from London into France.

Wife. Trust me, I am sorry, Rafe, to see thee impotent. Lord, how the wars have made him sunburned! The left leg is not well. 'T was a fair gift of God the infirmity took not hold a little higher, considering thou came from France. But let that pass.

Rafe. I am glad to see you well, and I rejoice
To hear that God hath blessed my master so
Since my departure.

Wife. Yea, truly, Rafe, I thank my maker. But let that pass.

Roger [*Hodge*]. And, sirrah Rafe, what news, what news in France?

Rafe. Tell me, good Roger, first, what news in England?
How does my Jane? When didst thou see my wife?
Where lives my poor heart? She'll be poor indeed
Now I want limbs to get whereon to feed.

Roger [*Hodge*]. Limbs? Hast thou not hands, man? Thou shalt never see a shoemaker want bread though he have but three fingers on a hand.

Rafe. Yet all this while I hear not of my Jane.

Wife. O Rafe, your wife! Perdie, we know not what's become of her. She was here a while, and because she was married grew more stately than became her. I checked her, and so forth. Away she flung, never returned, nor said "bye" nor "bah." And, Rafe, you know "ka me, ka thee." And so as I tell ye. Roger, is not Firk come yet?

Roger [*Hodge*]. No, forsooth.

Wife. And so, indeed, we heard not of her; but I hear she lives in London. But let that pass. If she had wanted, she might have opened her case to me or my husband or to any of my men; I am sure there's not any of them, perdie, but would have done her good to his power. Hans, look if Firk be come.

[*Lacy as*] *Hans. Yaw, ik sal, fro.*

Exit [Lacy *as*] Hans.

Wife. And so as I said. But Rafe, why dost thou weep? Thou knowest that naked we came out of our mother's womb, and naked we must return; and therefore thank God for all things.

Roger [*Hodge*]. No, faith, Jane is a stranger here. But, Rafe, pull up a good heart; I know thou hast one. Thy wife, man, is in London. One told me he saw her a while ago very brave and neat. We'll ferret her out, an London hold her.

Wife. Alas, poor soul, he's overcome with sorrow. He does but as I do, weep for the loss of any good thing. But, Rafe, get thee in. Call for some meat and drink. Thou shalt find me worshipful towards thee.

Rafe. I thank you, dame, Since I want limbs and lands,
I'll to God, my good friends, and to these my hands.

Exit.

Enter [Lacy *as*] Hans, *and* Firk, *running.*

Firk. Run, good Hans. Oh, Hodge, Oh, mistress! Hodge, heave up thine ears. Mistress, smug up your looks, on with your best apparel. My master is chosen, my master is called, nay, condemned, by the cry of the country to be sheriff of the City for this famous year now to come and time now being. A great many men in black gowns were asked for their voices and their hands, and my master had all their fists about his ears presently, and they cried "Aye, aye, aye, aye"; and so I came away.
Wherefore without all other grieve, I do salute you, Mistress Shrieve.

[*Lacy as*] *Hans. Yaw, my meester is de groot man, de shrieve.*

Roger [*Hodge*]. Did not I tell you, mistress? Now I may boldly say, "Good morrow to your worship."

Wife. Good morrow, good Roger. I thank you, my good people all. Firk, hold up thy hand. Here's a threepenny piece for thy tidings.

Firk. 'Tis but three halfpence, I think. Yes, 'tis threepence. I smell the rose.

83 **impotent** lame
84 **sunburned** maimed
86 **a little higher** reference is to genitals; France was known for venereal diseases
99 **hands** i.e., able to work again as a shoemaker
107 **stately** proud; **checked** reproached
110 **ka me, ka thee** one good turn deserves another
115–16 **opened her case** revealed her predicament (with a bawdy pun)

120 ***Yaw...fro*** "Yes, I shall, mistress"
129 **brave** fashionably dressed
136 **worshipful** beneficent
140 **smug up** prepare
143 **condemned** Firk means confirmed (elected)
146 **voices** approval
152 ***Yaw...shrieve*** "Yes, my master is the great man, the sheriff"
160 **smell** discern; **rose** (1) reward; (2) trick; (3) name of a neighboring tavern where he might spend his coin

Roger [*Hodge*]. But, mistress, be ruled by me, and do not speak so pulingly.

Firk. 'Tis her worship speaks so, and not she. No, faith, mistress, speak me in the old key. "To it, Firk," "There, good Firk," "Ply your business, Hodge" – "Hodge," with a full mouth, "I'll fill your bellies with good cheer till they cry twang."

Enter Simon Eyre *wearing a gold chain.*

[*Lacy as*] *Hans. See, myn liever broder, heer compt my meester.*

Wife. Welcome home, Master Shrieve. I pray God continue you in health and wealth.

Eyre. See here, my Maggy, a chain, a gold chain for Simon Eyre! I shall make thee a lady. Here's a French hood for thee. On with it, on with it. Dress thy brows with this flap of a shoulder of mutton, to make thee look lovely. Where be my fine men? Roger, I'll make over my shop and tools to thee. Firk, thou shalt be the foreman. Hans, thou shalt have an hundred for twenty. Be as mad knaves as your master Sim Eyre hath been, and you shall live to be sheriffs of London. How dost thou like me, Margery? Prince am I none, yet am I princely born! Firk, Hodge, and Hans!

All three. Aye, forsooth; what says your worship Master Sheriff?

Eyre. Worship and honor, you Babylonian knaves, for the Gentle Craft! But I forgot myself. I am bidden by my Lord Mayor to dinner to Old Ford. He's gone before, I must after. Come, Madge, on with your trinkets. Now, my true Trojans, my fine Firk, my dapper Hodge, my honest Hans, some device, some odd crotchets, some morris or suchlike for the honor of the gentle shoemakers. Meet me at Old Ford. You know my mind. Come, Madge, away; shut up the shop, knaves, and make holiday.

Exeunt [Eyre *and* Wife]

Firk. O, rare! O, brave! Come, Hodge. Follow me, Hans;
We'll be with them for a morris dance.

Exeunt.

[Sc. xi]

Enter Lord Mayor, Eyre, *his wife in a French hood,* [Rose], Sybil, *and other* Servants.

Lord Mayor. [*To Eyre and his wife.*] Trust me, you are as welcome to Old Ford
As I myself.

Wife. Truly, I thank your lordship.

Lord Mayor. Would our bad cheer were worth the thanks you give.

Eyre. Good cheer, my Lord Mayor, fine cheer; a fine house, fine walls, all fine and neat.

Lord Mayor. Now, by my troth, I'll tell thee, Master Eyre,
It does me good, and all my brethren,
That such a madcap fellow as thyself
Is entered into our society.

Wife. Aye, but, my lord, he must learn now to put on gravity.

Eyre. Peace, Maggy; a fig for gravity. When I go to Guildhall in my scarlet gown I'll look as demurely as a saint, and speak as gravely as a Justice of Peace; but now I am here at Old Ford, at my good Lord Mayor's house, let it go by, vanish, Maggy; I'll be merry. Away with flip-flap, these fooleries, these gulleries. What, honey – prince am I none, yet am I princely born! What says my Lord Mayor?

Lord Mayor. Ha, ha, ha! I had rather than a thousand pound I had an heart but half so light as yours.

Eyre. Why, what should I do, my lord? A pound of care pays not a dram of debt. Hum, let's be merry whiles we are young. Old age, sack, and sugar will steal upon us ere we be aware.

Lord Mayor. It's well done. Mistress Eyre, pray give good counsel to my daughter.

Wife. I hope Mistress Rose will have the grace to take nothing that's bad.

Lord Mayor. Pray God she do; for i' faith, Mistress Eyre,
I would bestow upon that peevish girl
A thousand marks more than I mean to give her

162 pulingly with affectation
169 s.d. *gold chain* the emblem of sheriff's office
169 *See . . . meester* "See, my dear brother, here comes my master"
175 flap the French hood
179–80 an hundred for twenty a fivefold return on his loan to Eyre at vii.25–6
193–4 device . . . crotchets entertainment with music and dance
194 morris a ring dance with costumes and bells
195 gentle i.e., gentlemen (again, he thinks of social rank)
xi.12 scarlet gown ceremonial gown worn by aldermen and Lord Mayors
18 gulleries deceptions
27 sack sweet wine to which the elderly commonly added sugar
34 marks coins worth $\frac{2}{3}$ pound

Upon condition she'ld be ruled by me.
The ape still crosseth me. There came of late
A proper gentleman of fair revenues
Whom gladly I would call son-in-law.
But my fine cockney would have none of him.
You'll prove a coxcomb for it ere you die.
A courtier or no man must please your eye.

Eyre. Be ruled, sweet Rose; thou'rt ripe for a man. Marry not with a boy that has no more hair on his face than thou hast on thy cheeks. A courtier – wash, go by! Stand not upon pishery-pashery. Those silken fellows are but painted images. Outsides, outsides, Rose, their inner linings are torn. No, my fine mouse, marry me with a Gentleman Grocer like my Lord Mayor your father. A grocer is a sweet trade; plums, plums! Had I a son or daughter should marry out of the generation and blood of the shoemakers, he should pack. What! the Gentle Trade is a living for a man through Europe, through the world.

A noise within of a tabor and a pipe.

Lord Mayor. What noise is this?

Eyre. O, my Lord Mayor, a crew of good fellows that, for love to your honor, are come hither with a morris dance. Come in, my Mesopotamians, cheerly.

Enter Hodge, [Lacy *as*] Hans, Rafe, Firk, *and other* Shoemakers *in a morris. After a little dancing, the* Lord Mayor *speaks.*

Lord Mayor. Master Eyre, are all these shoemakers?

Eyre. All cordwainers, my good Lord Mayor.

Rose. [*Aside.*] How like my Lacy looks yond shoemaker!

[*Lacy as*] *Hans.* [*Aside.*] O, that I durst but speak unto my love!

Lord Mayor. Sybil, go fetch some wine to make these drink.
You are all welcome.

All [*the Shoemakers*]. We thank your lordship.

Rose *takes a cup of wine and goes to* [Lacy *as*] Hans.

Rose. For his sake whose fair shape thou represent'st,
Good friend, I drink to thee.

Lacy [*as Hans*]. Ik be dancke, good frister.

Wife. I see, Mistress Rose, you do not want judgment. You have drunk to the properest man I keep.

Firk. Here be some have done their parts to be as proper as he.

Lord Mayor. Well, urgent business calls me back to London.
Good fellows, first go in and taste our cheer,
And to make merry as you homeward go,
Spend these two angels in beer at Stratford Bow.

Eyre. To these two, my mad lads, Sim Eyre adds another. Then cheerly, Firk, tickle it, Hans, and all for the honor of shoemakers.

All [*the* Shoemakers] *go dancing out.*

Lord Mayor. Come, Master Eyre, let's have your company.

Exeunt [Lord Mayor, Eyre, *and Eyre's wife*].

Rose. Sybil, what shall I do?

Sybil. Why, what's the matter?

Rose. That Hans the shoemaker is my love, Lacy,
Disguised in that attire to find me out.
How should I find the means to speak with him?

Sybil. What, mistress, never fear! I dare venture my maidenhead to nothing, and that's great odds, that Hans the Dutchman, when we come to London, shall not only see and speak with you, but, in spite of all your father's policies, steal you away and marry you. Will not this please you?

Rose. Do this, and ever be assured of my love.

Sybil. Away, then, and follow your father to London, lest your absence cause him to suspect something. Tomorrow, if my counsel be obeyed, I'll bind you prentice to the Gentle Trade.

[*Exeunt.*]

---

40 **cockney** spoiled child
41 **coxcomb** fool
46 **wash** rubbish (colloquial)
46–7 **pishery-pashery** gaudy rags
49 **mouse** (common term of endearment)
54 **he should pack** I'd throw him out
57 **s.d.** ***tabor and a pipe*** small drum often played with a pipe by a single musician
62 **s.d.** ***dancing*** if Rafe dances, he would fall down; the scene invites possible pathos
69 **represent'st** resemble
71 ***Ik . . . frister*** "I thank you, good maid"
72 **want** lack
75 **parts** (Firk's usual obscenity)
79 **beer** a class marker; the Lord Mayor offers wine; **Stratford Bow** a small village between Old Ford and London, one mile N of Mile End
81 **tickle** enliven

[Sc. xii]

Enter Jane *in a sempster's shop, working, and* Hammon, *muffled, at another door. He stands aloof.*

Hammon. Yonder's the shop, and there my fair love sits.
She's fair and lovely, but she is not mine.
Oh, would she were! Thrice have I courted her,
Thrice hath my hand been moistened with her hand
While my poor famished eyes do feed on that
Which made them famish. I am infortunate.
I still love one, yet nobody loves me.
I muse in other men what women see
That I so want. Fine Mistress Rose was coy,
And this too curious. O no, she is chaste,
And, for she thinks me wanton, she denies
To cheer my cold heart with her sunny eyes.
How prettily she works! Oh, pretty hand!
Oh, happy work! It doth me good to stand
Unseen to see her. Thus I oft have stood
In frosty evenings, a light burning by her,
Enduring biting cold only to eye her.
One only look hath seemed as rich to me
As a king's crown, such is love's lunacy.
Muffled I'll pass along, and by that try
Whether she know me.
Jane. Sir, what is't you buy?
What is't you lack, sir? Calico, or lawn,
Fine cambric shirts, or bands? what will you buy?
Hammon. [*Aside.*] That which thou will not sell. Faith, yet I'll try.
[*To Jane.*] How do you sell this handkercher?
Jane. Good cheap.
Hammon. And how these ruffs?
Jane. Cheap, too.
Hammon. And how this band?
Jane. Cheap too.
Hammon. All cheap. How sell you then this hand?
Jane. My hands are not to be sold.
Hammon. To be given, then.
Nay, faith, I come to buy.
Jane. But none knows when.
Hammon. Good sweet, leave work a little while. Let's play.
Jane. I cannot live by keeping holiday.
Hammon. I'll pay you for the time which shall be lost.
Jane. With me you shall not be at so much cost.
Hammon. Look how you wound this cloth, so you wound me.
Jane. It may be so.
Hammon. 'Tis so.
Jane. What remedy?
Hammon. Nay, faith; you are too coy.
Jane. Let go my hand.
Hammon. I will do any task at your command.
I would let go this beauty, were I not
In mind to disobey you by a power
That controls kings. I love you.
Jane. So. Now part.
Hammon. With hands I may, but never with my heart.
In faith, I love you.
Jane. I believe you do.
Hammon. Shall a true love in me breed hate in you?
Jane. I hate you not.
Hammon. Then you must love.
Jane. I do.
What, are you better now? I love not you.
Hammon. All this, I hope, is but a woman's fray,
That means "Come to me!" when she cries "Away!"
In earnest, mistress, I do not jest;
A true chaste love hath entered in my breast.
I love you dearly as I love my life.
I love you as a husband loves a wife.
That, and no other love, my love requires.
Thy wealth, I know, is little. My desires
Thirst not for gold. Sweet beauteous Jane, what's mine
Shall, if thou make myself thine, all be thine.
Say, judge, what is thy sentence – life or death?
Mercy or cruelty lies in thy breath.
Jane. Good sir, I do believe you love me well.
For 'tis a silly conquest, silly pride,
For one like you (I mean, a gentleman)
To boast that by his love tricks he hath brought
Such and such women to his amorous lure.

---

xii.1 s.d. ***sempster's*** seamstress's; Hammon's behavior may stem from the proverb "as stale [i.e., whore] as an Exchange Sempster"; ***muffled*** (1) wrapped up against the cold; (2) hidden; (3) disguised
9 want lack
10 curious fastidious; bewildering; *difficult* to woo
22 What . . . lack common market cry; **Calico** cotton cloth imported from the East; **lawn** fine linen
23 cambric fine white linen; **bands** collars, ruffs
34 wound . . . wound with a needle . . . prick my heart
46 fray trick
59 silly . . . silly unworthy . . . foolish

I think you do not so, yet many do,
And make it even a very trade to woo.
I could be coy, as many women be;
Feed you with sunshine smiles and wanton looks.
But I detest witchcraft. Say that I
Do constantly believe you constant have –

Hammon. Why dost thou not believe me?

Jane. I believe you.
But yet, good sir, because I will not grieve you
With hopes to taste fruit which will never fall,
In simple truth, this is the sum of all:
My husband lives – at least, I hope he lives.
Pressed was he to these bitter wars in France;
Bitter they are to me by wanting him.
I have but one heart, and that heart's his due.
How can I then bestow the same on you?
While he lives, his I live, be it ne'er so poor;
And rather be his wife than a king's whore.

Hammon. Chaste and dear woman, I will not abuse thee,
Although it cost my life if thou refuse me.
Thy husband pressed for France – what was his name?

Jane. Rafe Damport.

Hammon. Damport. Here's a letter sent
From France to me from a dear friend of mine,
A gentleman of place. Here he doth write
Their names that have been slain in every fight.

Jane. I hope death's scroll contains not my love's name.

Hammon. Cannot you read?

Jane. I can.

Hammon. Peruse the same.
To my remembrance such a name I read
Among the rest. See here.

Jane. Aye, me, he's dead.
He's dead. If this be true, my dear heart's slain.

Hammon. Have patience, dear love.

Jane. Hence, hence!

Hammon. Nay, sweet Jane,
Make not poor sorrow proud with these rich tears.
I mourn thy husband's death because thou mournest.

Jane. That bill is forged. 'Tis signed by forgery.

Hammon. I'll bring thee letters sent besides to many
Carrying the like report. Jane, 'tis too true.
Come, weep not. Mourning, though it rise from love,
Helps not the mournèd, yet hurts them that mourn.

Jane. For God's sake, leave me.

Hammon. Whither dost thou turn?
Forget the dead; love them that are alive.
His love is faded. Try how mine will thrive.

Jane. 'Tis now no time for me to think on love.

Hammon. 'Tis now best time for you to think on love,
Because your love lives not.

Jane. Though he be dead,
My love to him shall not be buried.
For God's sake, leave me to myself alone.

Hammon. 'Twould kill my soul to leave thee drowned in moan.
Answer me to my suit, and I am gone.
Say to me yea or no.

Jane. No.

Hammon. Then farewell.
One farewell will not serve. I come again.
Come, dry these wet cheeks. Tell me, faith, sweet Jane,
Yea, or no, once more.

Jane. Once more I say no.
Once more, be gone, I pray, else will I go.

Hammon. Nay, then, I will grow rude. By this white hand,
Until you change that cold no, here I'll stand
Till by your hard heart –

Jane. Nay, for God's love, peace.
My sorrows by your presence more increase.
Not that you thus are present; but all grief
Desires to be alone. Therefore in brief
Thus much I say, and saying bid adieu:
If ever I wed man it shall be you.

Hammon. O blessèd voice. Dear Jane, I'll urge no more.
Thy breath hath made me rich.

Jane. Death makes me poor.

Exeunt.

[Sc. xiii]

Enter Hodge *at his shop board*, Rafe, Firk, [Lacy *as*] Hans, *and a* Boy, *at work.*

All. [*Singing.*] Hey down, a-down, down-derry.

Hodge. Well said, my hearts! Ply your work today; we loitered yesterday. To it, pell-mell, that we may live to be Lord Mayors, or Aldermen at least.

75 wanting missing
85 of place in rank
86 names 4,000 were killed; Jane is easily deceived

95 bill bill of mortality (common in London as lists of plague victims)
115 rude firm

Firk. [*Singing.*] Hey down a-down derry.

Hodge. Well said, i'faith! How sayst thou, Hans? Doth not Firk tickle it?

[*Lacy as*] *Hans. Yaw, meester.*

Firk. Not so, neither. My organ-pipe squeaks this morning for want of liquoring. [*Sings.*] Hey down a-down derry.

[*Lacy as*] *Hans. Forware, Firk, tow best un jolly youngster. Hort, aye, meester, ik bid you cut me un pair vampies vor Meester Jeffrey's boots.*

Hodge. Thou shalt, Hans.

Firk. Master.

Hodge. How now, boy?

Firk. Pray, now you are in the cutting vein, cut me out a pair of counterfeits, or else my work will not pass current. [*Sings.*] Hey down a-down.

Hodge. Tell me, sirs, are my cousin Mistress Priscilla's shoes done?

Firk. Your cousin? No, master, one of your aunts. Hang her; let them alone.

Rafe. I am in hand with them. She gave charge that none but I should do them for her.

Firk. Thou do for her? Then 'twill be a lame doing, and that she loves not. Rafe, thou mightest have sent her to me. In faith, I would have yerked and firked your Priscilla. [*Sings.*] Hey down a-down derry. [*Speaks.*] This gear will not hold.

Hodge. How sayst thou, Firk? Were we not merry at Old Ford?

Firk. How, merry? Why, our buttocks went jiggy-joggy like a quagmire. Well, Sir Roger Oatmeal, if I thought all meal of that nature I would eat nothing but bagpuddings.

Rafe. Of all good fortunes, my fellow Hans had the best.

Firk. 'Tis true, because Mistress Rose drank to him.

Hodge. Well, well, work apace. They say seven of the Aldermen be dead, or very sick.

Firk. I care not, I'll be none.

Rafe. No, nor I; but then my Master Eyre will come quickly to be Lord Mayor.

Enter Sybil.

Firk. Whoop, yonder comes Sybil!

Hodge. Sybil! Welcome, i'faith; and how dost thou, mad wench?

Firk. Syb-whore, welcome to London.

Sybil. Godamercy, sweet Firk. Good Lord, Hodge, what a delicious shop you have got! You tickle it, i'faith.

Rafe. Godamercy, Sybil, for our good cheer at Old Ford.

Sybil. That you shall have, Rafe.

Firk. Nay, by the Mass, we had tickling cheer, Sybil. And how the plague dost thou and Mistress Rose, and my Lord Mayor? (I put the women in first.)

Sybil. Well, godamercy. But God's me, I forget myself. Where's Hans the Fleming?

Firk. Hark, butter-box, now you must yelp out some *spreaken.*

[*Lacy as*] *Hans. Vat begey gon, vat vod you, Frister.*

Sybil. Marry, you must come to my young mistress, to pull on her shoes you made last.

[*Lacy as*] *Hans. Vare ben your edle fro? Vare ben your mistress?*

Sybil. Marry, here at our London house in Cornwall.

Firk. Will nobody serve her turn but Hans?

Sybil. No, sir. Come, Hans, I stand upon needles.

Hodge. Why then, Sybil, take heed of pricking.

Sybil. For that, let me alone. I have a trick in my budget. Come, Hans.

[*Lacy as*] *Hans. Yaw, yaw; ik sal mit you gane.*

Exit [Lacy *as*] Hans *and* Sybil.

Hodge. Go, Hans, make haste again. Come, who lacks work?

Firk. I, master; for I lack my breakfast. 'Tis munching time, and past.

Hodge. Is't so? Why then, leave work, Rafe. To breakfast.
Boy, look to the tools. Come, Rafe. Come, Firk.

Exeunt.

---

xiii.13–15 ***Forware... boots*** "Indeed, Firk, you are a jolly youth. Listen, master, I bid you cut me a pair of vamps [the upper front of the shoe] for Mr. Jeffrey's boots"

18 **boy** term for one of inferior class

20 **counterfeits** (1) copies; (2) replacements; (3) as counterforts, stiff back portions around the heel

21 **pass current** be sound

25 **aunts** whores

33 **gear** (1) tools; (2) shoe; (3) voice

39 **bagpuddings** oatmeal

45 **dead, or very sick** reflective of suddenness of plague epidemics (the suddenness is casual, random, and brutal)

53 **Godamercy** "Thanks"

58 **That you shall have** i.e., come again

66 ***spreaken*** double-Dutch

67 ***Vat... Frister*** "What do you want? What would you, girl?"

70–1 ***Vare... mistress?*** "Where is your noble lady? Where is your mistress?"

72–3 **Cornwall** alternative name for Cornhill Street

77 **pricking** (bawdy)

78–9 **trick in my budget** I can compete

80 ***Yaw... gane*** "Yes, yes, I will go with you"

[Sc. xiv]

Enter a Servingman.

Servingman. Let me see, now, the Sign of the Last in Tower Street. Mass, yonder's the house. What, haw! Who's within?

Enter Rafe.

Rafe. Who calls, there? What want you, sir?

Servingman. Marry, I would have a pair of shoes made for a gentlewoman against tomorrow morning. What, can you do them?

Rafe. Yes, sir; you shall have them. But what length's her foot?

Servingman. Why, you must make them in all parts like this shoe. But at any hand, fail not to do them, for the gentlewoman is to be married very early in the morning.

Rafe. How? By this shoe must it be made? By this? Are you sure, sir, by this?

Servingman. How, "by this" am I sure, "by this"! Art thou in thy wits? I tell thee, I must have a pair of shoes. Dost thou mark me? A pair of shoes, two shoes, made by this very shoe, this same shoe, against tomorrow morning by four o'clock. Dost understand me? Canst thou do't?

Rafe. Yes, sir, yes. Aye, aye, I can do't. By this shoe, you say? I should know this shoe. Yes, sir, yes, by this shoe. I can do't. Four o'clock. Well, whither shall I bring them?

Servingman. To the Sign of the Golden Ball, in Watling Street. Inquire for one Master Hammon, a gentleman, my master.

Rafe. Yea, sir. By this shoe, you say.

Servingman. I say Master Hammon at the Golden Ball. He's the bridegroom, and those shoes are for his bride.

Rafe. They shall be done, by this shoe. Well, well, Master Hammon at the Golden Shoe – I would say, the Golden Ball. Very well, very well; but, I pray you, sir, where must Master Hammon be married?

Servingman. At Saint Faith's Church, under Paul's. But what's that to thee? Prithee, dispatch those shoes; and so, farewell.

Exit.

Rafe. By this shoe, said he? How am I amazed
At this strange accident! Upon my life,
This was the very shoe I gave my wife
When I was pressed for France; since when, alas,
I never could hear of her. It is the same,
And Hammon's bride no other but my Jane.

Enter Firk.

Firk. 'Snails, Rafe, thou hast lost thy part of three pots a countryman of mine gave me to breakfast.

Rafe. I care not. I have found a better thing.

Firk. A thing? Away! Is it a man's thing, or a woman's thing?

Rafe. Firk, dost thou know this shoe?

Firk. No, by my troth. Neither doth that know me. I have no acquaintance with it. 'Tis a mere stranger to me.

Rafe. Why, then, I do. This shoe, I durst be sworn,
Once coverèd the instep of my Jane.
This is her size, her breadth. Thus trod my love.
These true-love knots I pricked. I hold my life,
By this old shoe I shall find out my wife.

Firk. Ha, ha! Old shoe, that wert new. How a murrain came this ague-fit of foolishness upon thee?

Rafe. Thus, Firk: even now here came a servingman;
By this shoe would he have a new pair made
Against tomorrow morning for his mistress,
That's to be married to a gentleman.
And why may not this be my sweet Jane?

Firk. And why mayst not thou be my sweet ass? Ha, ha!

Rafe. Well, laugh and spare not. But the truth is this.
Against tomorrow morning I'll provide
A lusty crew of honest shoemakers
To watch the going of the bride to church.
If she prove Jane, I'll take her in despite
From Hammon and the devil, were he by.
If it be not my Jane, what remedy?

---

xiv.1 **Sign of the Last** sign of a shoemaker's shop
6 **against** by
11 **at any hand** in any event
26 **Sign of the Golden Ball** presumably the sign of an inn
27 **Watling Street** a wealthy district for shops, especially those of drapers, running E from St. Paul's Cathedral
38 **Saint Faith's Church** a parish church for London residents in the crypt of the old St. Paul's Cathedral
42 **accident** coincidence
48 **countryman of mine** i.e., neighbor
50 **thing** bawdy reference to the genitalia
55 **mere** absolute
57 **durst** dare
60 **love knots** decorations
63 **murrain** plague; **ague-fit** sudden fever

Hereof am I sure, I shall live till I die,
Although I never with a woman lie.

Exit.

Firk. Thou lie with a woman – to build nothing but Cripplegates! Well, God sends fools fortune, and it may be he may light upon his matrimony by such a device; for wedding and hanging goes by destiny.

Exit.

[Sc. xv]

Enter [Lacy *dressed as*] Hans *and* Rose, *arm in arm.*

[*Lacy as*] *Hans.* How happy am I by embracing thee!
Oh, I did fear such cross mishaps did reign
That I should never see my Rose again.

Rose. Sweet Lacy, since fair opportunity
Offers herself to further our escape,
Let not too over-fond esteem of me
Hinder that happy hour. Invent the means,
And Rose will follow thee through all the world.

[*Lacy as*] *Hans.* Oh, how I surfeit with excess of joy,
Made happy by thy rich perfection!
But since thou payest sweet interest to my hopes,
Redoubling love on love, let me once more,
Like to a bold-faced debtor, crave of thee
This night to steal abroad, and at Eyre's house,
Who now by death of certain aldermen
Is Mayor of London, and my master once,
Meet thou thy Lacy, where, in spite of change,
Your father's anger, and mine uncle's hate,
Our happy nuptials will we consummate.

Enter Sybil.

Sybil. Oh, God, what will you do, mistress? Shift for yourself. Your father is at hand. He's coming, he's coming. Master Lacy, hide yourself. In, my mistress! For God's sake, shift for yourselves.

Lacy [*as Hans*]. Your father come! Sweet Rose, what shall I do?
Where shall I hide me? How shall I escape?

Rose. A man, and want wit in extremity?
Come, come: be Hans still; play the shoemaker.
Pull on my shoe.

Enter [Sir Roger Oatley, *the former*] Lord Mayor.

[*Lacy as*] *Hans.* Mass, and that's well remembered.

Sybil. Here comes your father.

[*Lacy as*] *Hans. Forware, metress, 'tis un good skoe, it sal vel dute, or ye sal neit betaelen.*

Rose. Oh, God, it pincheth me! What will you do?

[*Lacy*] *as Hans.* [*Aside.*] Your father's presence pincheth, not the shoe.

Lord Mayor. Well done. Fit my daughter well, and she shall please thee well.

[*Lacy as*] *Hans. Yaw, yaw, ik weit dat well. Forware, 'tis un good skoe, 'tis gi-mait van neat's leather; se ever, mine heer.*

Lord Mayor. I do believe it.

Enter a Prentice.

What's the news with you?

Prentice. Please you, the Earl of Lincoln at the gate
Is newly lighted, and would speak with you.

Lord Mayor. The Earl of Lincoln come to speak with me?
Well, well, I know his errand. Daughter Rose,
Send hence your shoemaker. Dispatch, have done.
Syb, make things handsome. Sir boy, follow me.

Exeunt [Lord Mayor, Sybil, *and* Prentice].

Lacy. Mine uncle come! Oh, what may this portend?
Sweet Rose, this of our love threatens an end.

Rose. Be not dismayed at this. Whate'er befall,
Rose is thine own. To witness I speak truth,
Where thou appoints the place I'll meet with thee.
I will not fix a day to follow thee,
But presently steal hence. Do not reply.
Love which gave strength to bear my father's hate
Shall now add wings to further our escape.

Exeunt.

81 Cripplegates one of the seven city gates where the disabled (including soldiers) habitually gathered (a crude joke)
83–4 wedding . . . destiny (proverbial)
xv.2 cross adverse
6 over-fond excessive
26 want wit lack initiative; **extremity** crisis
31–2 *Forware . . . betaelen* "Indeed, mistress, 'tis a good shoe; it will do well, or you shall not pay for it"
38–40 *Yaw . . . heer* "Yes, yes, I know that well. Indeed, 'tis a good shoe, 'tis made of neat's [cow's] leather – just look, my lord"

[Sc. xvi]

Enter Lord Mayor *and* [*the* Earl of] Lincoln.

Lord Mayor. Believe me, on my credit I speak truth,
Since first your nephew Lacy went to France
I have not seen him. It seemed strange to me
When Dodger told me that he stayed behind,
Neglecting the high charge the King imposed.
Lincoln. Trust me, Sir Roger Oatley, I did think
Your counsel had given head to this attempt,
Drawn to it by the love he bears your child.
Here I did hope to find him in your house;
But now I see mine error, and confess
My judgment wronged you by conceiving so.
Lord Mayor. Lodge in my house, say you? Trust me, my lord,
I love your nephew Lacy too too dearly
So much to wrong his honor; and he hath done so
That first gave him advice to stay from France.
To witness I speak truth, I let you know
How careful I have been to keep my daughter
Free from all conference or speech of him –
Not that I scorn your nephew, but in love
I bear your honor, lest your noble blood
Should by my mean worth be dishonourèd.
Lincoln. [*Aside.*] How far the churl's tongue wanders from his heart!
[*To Lord Mayor.*] Well, well, Sir Roger Oatley, I believe you,
With more than many thanks for the kind love,
So much you seem to bear me. But, my lord,
Let me request your help to seek my nephew,
Whom if I find, I'll straight embark for France.
So shall your Rose be free, my thoughts at rest,
And much care die which now lives in my breast.

Enter Sybil.

Sybil. O Lord, help, for God's sake. My mistress, Oh, my young mistress!
Lord Mayor. Where is thy mistress? What's become of her?
Sybil. She's gone! She's fled!
Lord Mayor. Gone? Whither is she fled?
Sybil. I know not, forsooth. She's fled out of doors with Hans the shoemaker. I saw them scud, scud, scud, apace, apace.
Lord Mayor. Which way? What, John, where be my men? Which way?
Sybil. I know not, and it please your worship.
Lord Mayor. Fled with a shoemaker? Can this be true?
Sybil. Oh, Lord, sir, as true as God's in heaven.
Lincoln. [*Aside.*] Her love turned shoemaker? I am glad of this.
Lord Mayor. A Fleming butter-box, a shoemaker!
Will she forget her birth? Requite my care
With such ingratitude? Scorned she young Hammon
To love a honnikin, a needy knave?
Well, let her fly. I'll not fly after her.
Let her starve if she will. She's none of mine.
Lincoln. Be not so cruel, sir.

Enter Firk *with shoes.*

Sybil. [*Aside.*] I am glad she's 'scaped.
Lord Mayor. I'll not account of her as of my child.
Was there no better object for her eyes
But a foul drunken lubber, swill-belly,
A shoemaker? That's brave!
Firk. Yea, forsooth, 'tis a very brave shoe, and as fit as a pudding.
Lord Mayor. How now, what knave is this? From whence comest thou?
Firk. No knave, sir. I am Firk, the shoemaker, lusty Roger's chief lusty journey man, and I come hither to take up the pretty leg of sweet Mistress Rose, and thus hoping your worship is in as good health as I was at the making hereof, I bid you farewell, Yours, Firk.
Lord Mayor. Stay, stay, sir knave.
Lincoln. Come hither, shoemaker.
Firk. 'Tis happy the knave is put before the shoemaker, or else I would not have vouchsafed to come back to you. I am moved, for I stir.
Lord Mayor. My lord, this villain calls us knaves by craft.
Firk. Then 'tis by the Gentle Craft, and to call one "knave" gently is no harm. Sit your worship merry. [*Aside.*] Syb, your young mistress, I'll so bob them, now my master, Master Eyre, is Lord Mayor of London!

---

xvi.1 **credit** reputation
7 **head** encouragement
14 **he** the culprit who actually misled Lacy
35 **forsooth** in truth
37 **scud** scuttle off
42 **I ... this** Lincoln has been successfully deceived
46 **honnikin** boor
53 **brave** splendid (sarcastic)
65 **vouchsafed** condescended
72 **bob** make fools of

Lord Mayor. Tell me, sirrah, whose man are you?

Firk. I am glad to see your worship so merry. I have no maw to this gear, no stomach as yet to a red petticoat (*pointing to Sybil*).

Lincoln. He means not, sir, to woo you to his maid,
But only doth demand whose man you are.

Firk. I sing now to the tune of Rogero. Roger, my fellow, is now my master.

Lincoln. Sirrah, knowest thou one Hans, a shoemaker?

Firk. Hans shoemaker? Oh, yes, stay, yes, I have him. I tell you what – I speak it in secret – Mistress Rose and he are by this time – no, not so, but shortly are to come over one another with "Can you dance the shaking of the sheets?" It is that Hans – [*Aside.*] I'll so gull these diggers.

Lord Mayor. Knowest thou then where he is?

Firk. Yes, forsooth. Yea, marry.

Lincoln. Canst thou in sadness?

Firk. No, forsooth. No, marry.

Lord Mayor. Tell me, good, honest fellow, where he is,
And thou shalt see what I'll bestow of thee.

Firk. "Honest fellow?" No, sir, not so, sir. My profession is the Gentle Craft. I care not for seeing, I love feeling. Let me feel it here, *aurium tenus*, ten pieces of gold, *genuum tenus*, ten pieces of silver, and then Firk is your man in a new pair of stretchers.

Lord Mayor. Here is an angel, part of thy reward,
Which I will give thee. Tell me where he is.

Firk. No point. Shall I betray my brother? No. Shall I prove Judas to Hans? No. Shall I cry treason to my corporation? No. I shall be firked and yerked then. But give me your angel. Your angel shall tell you.

Lincoln. Do so, good fellow. 'Tis no hurt to thee.

Firk. Send simpering Syb away.

Lord Mayor. Huswife, get you in.

Exit Sybil.

Firk. Pitchers have ears, and maids have wide mouths. But for Hauns Prauns, upon my word, tomorrow morning he and young Mistress Rose go to this gear. They shall be married together, by this rush, or else turn Firk to a firkin of butter to tan leather withal.

Lord Mayor. But art thou sure of this?

Firk. Am I sure that Paul's Steeple is a handful higher than London Stone? Or that the Pissing Conduit leaks nothing but pure Mother Bunch? Am I sure I am lusty Firk? God's nails, do you think I am so base to gull you?

Lincoln. Where are they married? Dost thou know the church?

Firk. I never go to church, but I know the name of it. It is a swearing church. Stay a while, 'tis "Aye, by the Mass" – no, no, 'tis "Aye, by my troth" – no, nor that, 'tis "Aye, by my faith" – that, that, 'tis "Aye by my Faith's" Church under Paul's Cross. There they shall be knit like a pair of stockings in matrimony. There they'll be incony.

Lincoln. Upon my life, my nephew Lacy walks
In the disguise of this Dutch shoemaker.

Firk. Yes, forsooth.

Lincoln. Doth he not, honest fellow?

Firk. No, forsooth, I think Hans is nobody but Hans, no spirit.

Lord Mayor. My mind misgives me now 'tis so indeed.

Lincoln. My cousin speaks the language, knows the trade.

Lord Mayor. Let me request your company, my lord.
Your honorable presence may, no doubt,
Restrain their headstrong rashness, when myself,
Going alone, perchance may be o'erborne.
Shall I request this favor?

Lincoln. This or what else.

---

76 **maw** appetite; **gear** (1) task; (2) conversation
80 **Rogero** a popular song
88–9 **"Can . . . sheets?"** opening line of a popular bawdy ballad
89 **gull** deceive
90 **diggers** those who desire information
93 **in sadness** in all seriousness
99 **feeling** a bribe (colloquial)
100 ***aurium tenus*** up to the ears; ***genuum tenus*** up to the knees
102 **stretchers** (1) stretchers for shoes; (2) stretched truth or lies; exaggerated stories
105 **No point** absolutely not
107 **corporation** governors of the guild
112 **Huswife** (1) housewife; (2) slut
116 **gear** business
117 **by this rush** Firk swears on rushes covering the floor
118 **firkin** small bag
120 **Paul's Steeple** the steeple of St. Paul's Cathedral burned down in 1561 and was not repaired
121 **London Stone** a well-known stone landmark on Candlewick Street from which all original Roman roads in London radiated (now part of the wall of St. Swithin's Church in Cannon Street)
122 **Pissing Conduit** small stone water cistern at the intersection of Cornhill, Threadneedle, and Lombard Streets near the present site of Mansion House
123 **Mother Bunch** famous tavern hostess
128 **swearing church** a church whose name was part of an oath
134 **incony** well in
147 **what else** anything you wish

Firk. Then you must rise betimes, for they mean to fall to their "hey-pass-and-repass, pindy-pandy, which hand will you have?" very early.

Lord Mayor. My care shall every way equal their haste.
This night accept your lodging in my house.
The earlier shall we stir, and at Saint Faith's
Prevent this giddy, hare-brained nuptial.
This traffic of hot love shall yield cold gains.
They ban our loves, and we'll forbid their banns.

Exit.

Lincoln. At Saint Faith's Church, thou sayst?

Firk. Yes, by their troth.

Lincoln. Be secret, on thy life.

[*Exit.*]

Firk. Yes, when I kiss your wife! Ha, ha, here's no craft in the Gentle Craft. I came hither of purpose with shoes to Sir Roger's worship, while Rose his daughter be coneycatched by Hans. Soft, now, these two gulls will be at Saint Faith's Church tomorrow morning to take Master Bridegroom and Mistress Bride napping, and they in the meantime shall chop up the matter at the Savoy. But the best sport is, Sir Roger Oatley will find my fellow, lame Rafe's wife, going to marry a gentleman, and then he'll stop her instead of his daughter. Oh, brave, there will be fine tickling sport. Soft now, what have I to do? Oh, I know – now a mess of shoemakers meet at the Woolsack in Ivy Lane to cozen my gentleman of lame Rafe's wife, that's true.

Alack, alack,
Girls, hold out tack,
For now smocks for this jumbling
Shall go to wrack.

[*Exeunt.*]

148 **betimes** very early
149–50 **"hey . . . have?"** magician's patter
157 **ban** curse; **banns** public nuptial announcements
164 **coneycatched** cheated (as in a confidence game; cony was also a bawdy term for the female genitalia)
168 **chop up** divide
169 **Savoy** a pauper's hospital between the Thames and the Strand; the chapel there was frequently a site for clandestine marriages
175 **mess** group
175 **Woolsack** a tavern
176 **Ivy Lane** small street running from Paternoster Row to Newgate Street; **cozen** trick
179 **hold out tack** be on guard
180 **smocks for this jumbling** maidenheads for this foolery

[Sc. xvii]

Enter Eyre, *his wife*, [Lacy *dressed as*] Hans, *and* Rose.

Eyre. This is the morning, then – say, my bully, my honest Hans – is it not?

[*Lacy as*] *Hans.* This is the morning that must make us two
Happy or miserable; therefore if you –

Eyre. A way with these "ifs" and "ands," Hans, and these "etceteras." By mine honor, Rowland Lacy, none but the King shall wrong thee. Come, fear nothing. Am not I Sim Eyre? Is not Sim Eyre Lord Mayor of London? Fear nothing, Rose. Let them all say what they can. "Dainty, come thou to me." Laughest thou?

Wife. Good my lord, stand her friend in what thing you may.

Eyre. Why, my sweet Lady Madgy, think you Simon Eyre can forget his fine Dutch journeyman? No, vah! Fie! I scorn it! It shall never be cast in my teeth that I was unthankful. Lady Madgy, thou hadst never covered thy Saracen's head with this French flap, nor loaded thy bum with this farthingale – 'tis trash, trumpery, vanity. Simon Eyre had never walked in a red petticoat, nor wore a chain of gold, but for my fine journeyman's portagues; and shall I leave him? No. Prince am I none, yet bear a princely mind.

[*Lacy as*] *Hans.* My lord, 'tis time for us to part from hence.

Eyre. Lady Madgy, Lady Madgy, take two or three of my piecrust eaters, my buff-jerkin varlets, that do walk in black gowns at Simon Eyre's heels. Take them, good Lady Madgy; trip and go, my brown Queen of Periwigs, with my delicate Rose and my jolly Rowland to the Savoy, see them linked, countenance the marriage, and when it is done, cling, cling together, you Hamborow turtle-doves. I'll bear you out. Come to Simon Eyre, come dwell with me, Hans, thou shalt eat

xvii s.d. **Hans** Lacy is still dressed as Hans but no longer disguised
1 **bully** companion
11 **"Dainty . . . me"** a popular ballad tune
13 **stand** act
19–20 **Saracen's head** an ugly caricature on an inn sign outside Newgate
20 **French flap** French hood
22–3 **red petticoat** the scarlet gown that identifies the Lord Mayor
29 **buff-jerkin varlets** city servants at his direction
30 **black gowns** denoting office
32 **brown** lusty
34 **countenance** witness
36 **turtle-doves** birds associated with love

minced-pies and marchpane. Rose, a way, cricket. Trip and go, my Lady Madgy, to the Savoy. Hans, wed and to bed; kiss and away; go; vanish.

Wife. Farewell, my lord.

Rose. Make haste, sweet love.

Wife. She'd fain the deed were done.

[*Lacy as*] *Hans.* Come, my sweet Rose, faster than deer we'll run.

They go out.

Eyre. Go, vanish, vanish, avaunt, I say. By the Lord of Ludgate, it's a mad life to be a Lord Mayor. It's a stirring life, a fine life, a velvet life, a careful life. Well, Simon Eyre, yet set a good face on it, in the honor of Saint Hugh. Soft, the King this day comes to dine with me, to see my new buildings. His Majesty is welcome. He shall have good cheer, delicate cheer, princely cheer. This day my fellow prentices of London come to dine with me too. They shall have fine cheer, gentlemanlike cheer. I promised the mad Cappadocians, when we all served at the conduit together, that if ever I came to be Mayor of London, I would feast them all; and I'll do't, I'll do't. By the life of Pharaoh, by this beard, Sim Eyre will be no flincher. Besides, I have procured that upon every Shrove Tuesday, at the sound of the pancake bell, my fine dapper Assyrian lads shall clap up their shop windows and away. This is the day, and this day they shall do't, they shall do't. Boys, that day are you free. Let masters care, and prentices shall pray for Simon Eyre.

Exit.

[Sc. xviii]

Enter Hodge, Firk, Rafe, *and five or six* Shoemakers, *all with cudgels, or such weapons.*

Hodge. Come, Rafe. Stand to it, Firk. My masters, as we are the brave bloods of the shoemakers, heirs apparent to Saint Hugh, and perpetual benefactors to all good fellows, thou shalt have no wrong. Were Hammon a king of spades, he should not delve in thy close without thy sufferance. But tell me, Rafe, art thou sure 'tis thy wife?

Rafe. Am I sure this is Firk? This morning, when I stroked on her shoes, I looked upon her, and she upon me, and sighed, asked me if ever I knew one Rafe. "Yes," said I. "For his sake," said she, tears standing in her eyes, "and for thou art somewhat like him, spend this piece of gold." I took it. My lame leg and my travel beyond sea made me unknown. All is one for that. I know she's mine.

Firk. Did she give thee this gold? Oh, glorious, glittering gold. She's thine own. 'Tis thy wife, and she loves thee; for, I'll stand to't, there's no woman will give gold to any man but she thinks better of him than she thinks of them she gives silver to. And for Hammon, neither Hammon nor hangman shall wrong thee in London. Is not our old master, Eyre, Lord Mayor? Speak, my hearts.

All. Yes, and Hammon shall know it to his cost.

Enter Hammon, [a Servant] *his man*, Jane, *and others.*

Hodge. Peace, my bullies; yonder they come.

Rafe. Stand to't, my hearts. Firk, let me speak first.

Hodge. No, Rafe, let me. Hammon, whither away so early?

Hammon. Unmannerly rude slave, what's that to thee?

Firk. To him, sir? Yes, sir, and to me, and others. Good morrow, Jane, how dost thou? Good Lord, how the world is changed with you, God be thanked.

Hammon. Villains, hands off! How dare you touch my love?

All [*the Shoemakers*]. Villains? Down with them. Cry "Clubs for prentices!"

Hodge. Hold, my hearts. Touch her, Hammon? Yea, and more than that, we'll carry her away with us. My masters and gentlemen, never draw your bird-spits. Shoemakers are steel to the back, men every inch of them, all spirit.

---

38 marchpane marzipan (a delicacy)

39 cricket term of endearment

47–8 velvet . . . careful Eyre already enjoys the luxury of a higher class status

56–7 served . . . together as apprentices fetching water for their respective shops

60 flincher pennypincher

62 pancake bell originally a bell rung at church to remind people to make confession before Lent, transformed by shoemakers to announce Shrove Tuesday (a traditional apprentices' holiday)

63 clap shut; **shop windows** wooden shutters

xviii.2 bloods brothers

6 close patch (bawdy)

7 sufferance permission

24 Hammon nor hangman play on Haman who is hanged on the gallows he built for his enemy (Esther, 3–5)

38 "Clubs for prentices!" a common cry, especially during Shrovetide

42 bird-spits rapiers

All of Hammon's side. Well, and what of all this?

Hodge. I'll show you. Jane, dost thou know this man? 'Tis Rafe, I can tell thee. Nay, 'tis he, in faith. Though he be lamed by the wars, yet look not strange, but run to him; fold him about the neck, and kiss him.

Jane. Lives then my husband? Oh, God, let me go!
Let me embrace my Rafe!

Hammon. What means my Jane?

Jane. Nay, what meant you to tell me he was slain?

Hammon. Pardon me, dear love, for being misled.
[*To Rafe.*] 'Twas rumored here in London thou wert dead.

Firk. Thou seest he lives. Lass, go, pack home with him. Now, Master Hammon, where's your mistress your wife?

Servant. 'Swounds, master, fight for her. Will you thus lose her?

All [*the Shoemakers*]. Down with that creature! Clubs! Down with him!

Hodge. Hold, hold!

Hammon. Hold, fool! Sirs, he shall do no wrong.
Will my Jane leave me thus, and break her faith?

Firk. Yea, sir, she must, sir, she shall, sir. What then? Mend it.

Hodge. Hark, fellow Rafe. Follow my counsel. Set the wench in the midst, and let her choose her man, and let her be his woman.

Jane. Whom should I choose? Whom should my thoughts affect
But him whom heaven hath made to be my love?
[*To Rafe.*] Thou art my husband, and these humble weeds
Makes thee more beautiful than all his wealth.
Therefore I will but put off his attire,
Returning it into the owner's hand,
And after ever be thy constant wife.

Hodge. Not a rag, Jane. The law's on our side. He that sows in another man's ground forfeits his harvest. Get thee home, Rafe. Follow him, Jane. He shall not have so much as a busk point from thee.

Firk. Stand to that, Rafe. The appurtenances are thine own. Hammon, look not at her.

Servant. Oh, swounds, no.

Firk. Bluecoat, be quiet. We'll give you a new livery else. We'll make Shrove Tuesday Saint George's Day for you. Look not, Hammon. Leer not. I'll firk you. For thy head now, one glance, one sheep's eye, anything at her. Touch not a rag, lest I and my brethren beat you to clouts.

Servant. Come, Master Hammon, there's no striving here.

Hammon. Good fellows, hear me speak. And, honest Rafe,
Whom I have injured most by loving Jane,
Mark what I offer thee. Here in fair gold
Is twenty pound. I'll give it for thy Jane.
If this content thee not, thou shalt have more.

Hodge. Sell not thy wife, Rafe. Make her not a whore.

Hammon. Say, wilt thou freely cease thy claim in her,
And let her be my wife?

All [*the Shoemakers*]. No, do not, Rafe!

Rafe. Sirrah Hammon, Hammon, dost thou think a shoemaker is so base to be a bawd to his own wife for commodity? Take thy gold, choke with it! Were I not lame, I would make thee eat thy words.

Firk. A shoemaker sell his flesh and blood? Oh, indignity!

Hodge. Sirrah, take up your pelf, and be packing.

Hammon. I will not touch one penny. But in lieu
Of that great wrong I offerèd thy Jane,
To Jane and thee I give that twenty pound.
Since I have failed of her, during my life
I vow no woman else shall be my wife.
Farewell, good fellows of the Gentle Trade.
Your morning's mirth my mourning day hath made.

Exeunt [Hammon *and* Servants].

Firk. [*To Servant going out.*] Touch the gold, creature, if you dare. You're best be trudging. Here, Jane, take thou it.
Now let's home, my hearts.

---

60 **creature** miserable person
69 **affect** find affection in
71 **weeds** clothes
73 **his attire** his gift of her wedding gown
79–80 **busk point** corset-lace
84 **Bluecoat** livery worn by servants
85 **livery** regulation clothing denoting position
85–6 **Saint George's Day** named for the legendary patron saint of England who slew the dragon attacking the country, it was the day servants traditionally changed jobs
87 **For** If you value
88 **sheep's eye** amorous glance
90 **clouts** rags
107 **pelf** spoils

Hodge. Stay, who comes here? Jane, on again with thy mask.

Enter Lincoln, Lord Mayor, *and* Servants.

Lincoln. Yonder's the lying varlet mocked us so.
Lord Mayor. Come hither, sirrah.
Firk. Aye, sir, I am sirrah. You mean me, do you not?
Lincoln. Where is my nephew married?
Firk. Is he married? God give him joy, I am glad of it. They have a fair day, and the sign is in a good planet, Mars in Venus.
Lord Mayor. Villain, thou told'st me that my daughter Rose
This morning should be married at Saint Faith's.
We have watched there these three hours at the least,
Yet saw we no such thing.
Firk. Truly, I am sorry for't. A bride's a pretty thing.
Hodge. Come to the purpose. Yonder's the bride and bridegroom you look for, I hope. Though you be lords, you are not to bar by your authority men from women, are you?
Lord Mayor. See, see, my daughter's masked.
Lincoln. True, and my nephew,
To hide his guilt, counterfeits him lame.
Firk. Yea, truly, God help the poor couple; they are lame and blind.
Lord Mayor. I'll ease her blindness.
Lincoln. I'll his lameness cure.
Firk. [*Aside, to the Shoemakers.*] Lie down, sirs, and laugh! My fellow, Rafe, is taken for Rowland Lacy, and Jane for Mistress Damask Rose – this is all my knavery!
Lord Mayor. [*To Jane.*] What, have I found you, minion!
Lincoln. [*To Rafe.*] Oh, base wretch!
Nay, hide thy face; the horror of thy guilt
Can hardly be washed off. Where are thy powers?
What battles have you made? Oh, yes, I see
Thou fought'st with shame, and shame
Hath conquered thee. This lameness will not serve.
Lord Mayor. Unmask yourself.
Lincoln. [*To Lord Mayor.*] Lead home your daughter.
Lord Mayor. [*To Lincoln.*] Take your nephew hence.
Rafe. Hence? 'Swounds, what mean you? Are you mad? I hope you cannot enforce my wife from me. Where's Hammon?
Lord Mayor. Your wife?
Lincoln. What Hammon?
Rafe. Yea, my wife. And therefore the proudest of you that lays hands on her first, I'll lay my crutch cross his pate.
Firk. To him, lame Rafe! Here's brave sport!
Rafe. Rose, call you her? Why, her name is Jane. Look here else. [*He unmasks her.*] Do you know her now?
Lincoln. Is this your daughter?
Lord Mayor. No, nor this your nephew.
My Lord of Lincoln, we are both abused
By this base crafty varlet.
Firk. Yea, forsooth, no "varlet," forsooth, no "base," forsooth, I am but mean. No "crafty" neither, but of the Gentle Craft.
Lord Mayor. Where is my daughter Rose? Where is my child?
Lincoln. Where is my nephew Lacy marrièd?
Firk. Why, here is good laced mutton, as I promised you.
Lincoln. Villain, I'll have thee punished for this wrong.
Firk. Punish the journeyman villain, but not the journeyman shoemaker.

Enter Dodger.

Dodger. My lord, I come to bring unwelcome news.
Your nephew Lacy and [*To Lord Mayor.*] your daughter Rose
Early this morning wedded at the Savoy,
None being present but the Lady Mayoress.
Besides, I learned among the officers
The Lord Mayor vows to stand in their defense
'Gainst any that shall seek to cross the match.
Lincoln. Dares Eyre the shoemaker uphold the deed?
Firk. Yes, sir, shoemakers dare stand in a woman's quarrel, I warrant you, as deep as another, and deeper, too.

---

119 mask women commonly wore masks outdoors as protection against sunburn (as well as modesty)
120 varlet knave, rascal
126 Mars in Venus i.e., the planets of war and love in conjunction
140 his lameness cure presumably Lincoln pulls away Rafe's crutch
145 minion dragon
147 powers troops
159 pate head
168 "base" . . . mean (musical analogy to two parts of a two-part song)
172 mutton prostitute (punning on Lacy's use of Rose)
174 journeyman villain i.e., journeyman villein, an itinerant day-laborer

Dodger. Besides, His Grace today dines with the Mayor,
Who on his knees humbly intends to fall
And beg a pardon for your nephew's fault.

Lincoln. But I'll prevent him. Come, Sir Roger Oatley,
The King will do us justice in this cause.
Howe'er their hands have made them man and wife,
I will disjoin the match, or lose my life.

Exeunt [the Earl of Lincoln, Lord Mayor, *and* Dodger].

Firk. Adieu, Monsieur Dodger! Farewell, fools! Ha, ha! Oh, if they had stayed, I would have so lammed them with flouts! Oh, heart, my codpiece point is ready to fly in pieces every time I think upon Mistress Rose. But let that pass, as my Lady Mayoress says.

Hodge. This matter is answered. Come, Rafe, home with thy wife. Come, my fine shoemakers, let's to our master's the new Lord Mayor, and there swagger this Shrove Tuesday. I'll promise you wine enough, for Madge keeps the cellar.

All. Oh, rare! Madge is a good wench.

Firk. And I'll promise you meat enough, for simpering Susan keeps the larder. I'll lead you to victuals, my brave soldiers. Follow your captain. Oh, brave! Hark hark!

Bell rings.

All. The pancake bell rings, the pancake bell. Trilill, my hearts!

Firk. Oh, brave! Oh, sweet bell! Oh, delicate pancakes! Open the doors, my hearts, and shut up the windows. Keep in the house, let out the pancakes. Oh, rare, my hearts! Let's march together for the honor of Saint Hugh to the great new hall in Gracious Street corner, which our master the new Lord Mayor hath built.

Rafe. Oh, the crew of good fellows that will dine at my Lord Mayor's cost today!

Hodge. By the Lord, my Lord Mayor is a most brave man. How shall prentices be bound to pray for him and the honor of the Gentlemen Shoemakers! Let's feed and be fat with my lord's bounty.

Firk. Oh, musical bell still! Oh, Hodge, Oh, my brethren! There's cheer for the heavens – venison pasties walk up and down piping hot like sergeants; beef and brewis comes marching in dry fats; fritters and pancakes comes trolling in in wheelbarrows, hens and oranges hopping in porters' baskets, collops and eggs in scuttles, and tarts and custards comes quavering in in malt shovels.

Enter more Prentices.

All. Whoop, look here, look here!

Hodge. How now, mad lads, whither away so fast?

First Prentice. Whither? Why, to the great new hall! Know you not why? The Lord Mayor hath bidden all the prentices in London to breakfast this morning.

All. Oh, brave shoemaker! Oh, brave lord of incomprehensible good fellowship! Hoo, hark you, the pancake bell rings!

Cast up caps.

Firk. Nay, more, my hearts, every Shrove Tuesday is our year of jubilee; and when the pancake bell rings, we are as free as my Lord Mayor. We may shut up our shops and make holiday. I'll have it called "Saint Hugh's Holiday."

All. Agreed, agreed – "Saint Hugh's Holiday!"

Hodge. And this shall continue forever.

All. Oh, brave! Come, come, my hearts; away, away.

Firk. Oh, eternal credit to us of the Gentle Craft! March fair, my hearts. Oh, rare!

Exeunt.

[Sc. xix]

Enter King *and his train over the stage.*

King. Is our Lord Mayor of London such a gallant?

Nobleman. One of the merriest madcaps in your land.
Your Grace will think, when you behold the man,

187 **His Grace** the King
196 **lammed** wounded; **flouts** jibes
197 **codpiece** threads on clothing covering male genitalia
200 **answered** concluded
204 **Madge** a servant (not Margery Eyre)
207 **meat** i.e., food or refreshment generally
208 **larder** pantry
209 **victuals** provisions, food
215 **Keep in** lock up
218 **great new hall** Leadenhall, for which Eyre was historically given some credit
224 **brave** impressive
230 **pasties** pies
231 **brewis** broth
232 **dry fats** barrels
234 **collops** bacon
235 **scuttles** dishes
247 **year of jubilee** special holiday in the year

He's rather a wild ruffian than a Mayor.
Yet thus much I'll insure your Majesty:
In all his actions that concern his state
He is as serious, provident, and wise,
As full of gravity among the grave,
As any Mayor hath been these many years.

King. I am with child till I behold this huffcap.
But all my doubt is, when we come in presence,
His madness will be dashed clean out of countenance.

Nobleman. It may be so, my liege.

King. Which to prevent,
Let someone give him notice 'tis our pleasure
That he put on his wonted merriment.
Set forward.

All. On afore!

Exeunt.

[Sc. xx]

Enter Eyre, Hodge, Firk, Rafe, *and other* Shoemakers, *all with napkins on their shoulders.*

Eyre. Come, my fine Hodge, my jolly Gentlemen Shoemakers. Soft, where be these cannibals, these varlets my officers? Let them all walk and wait upon my brethren; for my meaning is that none but shoemakers, none but the livery of my company shall in their satin hoods wait upon the trencher of my sovereign.

Firk. Oh, my lord, it will be rare.

Eyre. No more, Firk. Come, lively. Let your fellow prentices want no cheer. Let wine be plentiful as beer and beer as water. Hang these penny-pinching fathers, that cram wealth in innocent lamb-skins. Rip, knaves! Avaunt! Look to my guests.

Hodge. My lord, we are at our wits' end for room. Those hundred tables will not feast the fourth part of them.

Eyre. Then cover me those hundred tables again, and again, till all my jolly prentices be feasted. Avoid, Hodge; run, Rafe; frisk about, my nimble Firk; carouse me fathom healths to the honor of the shoemakers. Do they drink lively, Hodge? Do they tickle it, Firk?

Firk. Tickle it? Some of them have taken their liquor standing so long that they can stand no longer. But for meat, they would eat it and they had it.

Eyre. Want they meat? Where's this swag-belly, this greasy kitchen-stuff cook? Call the varlet to me. Want meat! Firk, Hodge, lame Rafe, run, my tall men, beleaguer the shambles, beggar all Eastcheap, serve me whole oxen in chargers, and let sheep whine upon the tables like pigs for want of good fellows to eat them. Want meat! Vanish, Firk! Avaunt, Hodge!

Hodge. Your lordship mistakes my man Firk. He means their bellies want meat, not the boards; for they have drunk so much they can eat nothing.

Enter [Lacy *dressed as*] Hans, Rose, *and* [Eyre's] *wife.*

Wife. Where is my lord?

Eyre. How now, Lady Madgy?

Margery. The King's most excellent Majesty is new come; he sends me for Thy Honor. One of his most worshipful peers bade me tell thou must be merry, and so forth. But let that pass.

Eyre. Is my sovereign come? Vanish, my tall shoemakers, my nimble brethren. Look to my guests, the prentices. Yet stay a little. How now, Hans? how looks my little Rose?

[*Lacy as*] *Hans.* Let me request you to remember me.
I know your honor easily may obtain
Free pardon of the King for me and Rose,
And reconcile me to my uncle's grace.

Eyre. Have done, my good Hans, my honest journeyman. Look cheerly. I'll fall upon both my knees till they be as hard as horn, but I'll get thy pardon.

Wife. Good my lord, have a care what you speak to His Grace.

---

xix.6 **state** official position
10 **with child** greatly anxious
11 **all my doubt** what I suspect
15 **wonted** customary
xx.2 **cannibals** cf. xvii.29 (they are about to feast on pancakes)
5 **livery** livery men; retainers
6 **satin hoods** distinguishing livery of the shoemakers' guild
12 **penny-pinching fathers** pennyfathers (i.e., misers)
13 **lamb-skins** purses (with play on wineskins)
20 **Avoid** hurry
21 **carouse . . . healths** drink deep
23 **tickle it** have a good time
31 **beleaguer** besiege; **shambles** butchers' stalls
33 **chargers** large serving dishes
34 **want** lack (not desire)
55 **grace** favor

Eyre. Away, you Islington whitepot. Hence, you hopperarse, you barley pudding full of maggots, you broiled carbonado. Avaunt, avaunt! Avoid, Mephistophilus! Shall Sim Eyre learn to speak of you, Lady Madgy? Vanish, Mother Miniver-Cap, vanish! Go, trip and go, meddle with your partlets and your pishery-pashery, your flews and your whirligigs! Go, rub, out of mine alley! Sim Eyre knows how to speak to a Pope, to Sultan Soliman, to Tamburlaine an he were here. And shall I melt? Shall I droop before my sovereign? No! Come, my Lady Madgy; follow me, Hans; about your business, my frolic freebooters. Firk, frisk about, and about, and about, for the honor of mad Simon Eyre, Lord Mayor of London.

Firk. Hey, for the honor of the shoemakers!

Exeunt.

[Sc. xxi]

A long flourish or two. Enter King, Nobles, Eyre, *his wife,* Lacy [*dressed as himself*], Rose. Lacy *and* Rose *kneel.*

King. Well, Lacy, though the fact was very foul
Of your revolting from our kingly love
And your own duty, yet we pardon you.
Rise, both; and, Mistress Lacy, thank my Lord Mayor
For your young bridegroom here.

Eyre. So, my dear liege, Sim Eyre and my brethren the Gentlemen Shoemakers shall set your sweet Majesty's image cheek by jowl by Saint Hugh for this honor you have done poor Simon Eyre. I beseech your Grace pardon my rude behavior. I am a handicraftsman, yet my heart is without craft. I would be sorry at my soul that my boldness should offend my King.

King. Nay, I pray thee, good Lord Mayor, be even as merry
As if thou wert among thy shoemakers.
It does me good to see thee in this humor.

Eyre. Sayst thou me so, my sweet Diocletian? Then, hump! Prince am I none, yet am I princely born! By the Lord of Ludgate, my liege, I'll be as merry as a pie.

King. Tell me, in faith, mad Eyre, how old thou art.

Eyre. My liege, a very boy, a stripling, a yonker. You see not a white hair on my head, not a grey in this beard. Every hair, I assure thy Majesty, that sticks in this beard Sim Eyre values at the King of Babylon's ransom. Tamar Cham's beard was a rubbing-brush to't. Yet I'll shave it off and stuff tennis balls with it to please my bully King.

King. But all this while I do not know your age.

Eyre. My liege, I am six-and-fifty year old; yet I can cry "hump" with a sound heart for the honor of Saint Hugh. Mark this old wench, my King. I danced the shaking of the sheets with her six-and-thirty years ago, and yet I hope to get two or three young Lord Mayors ere I die. I am lusty still, Sim Eyre still. Care and cold lodging brings white hairs. My sweet Majesty, let care vanish. Cast it upon thy nobles. It will make thee look always young, like Apollo, and cry "Hump!" – Prince am I none, yet am I princely born.

King. Ha, ha! Say, Cornwall, didst thou ever see his like?

Nobleman. Not I, my Lord.

Enter Lincoln *and* Lord Mayor.

King. Lincoln, what news with you?

Lincoln. My gracious Lord, have care unto yourself,

62 **Islington whitepot** a favorite dish of milk or cream boiled with eggs, flour, and spices
63 **hopperarse** big bum
63 **barley pudding** sausage
64 **broiled carbonado** meat, fish, or fowl scored and then grilled
65 **Avoid, Mephistophilus!** a colloquialism from Marlowe's *Dr. Faustus*
67 **Miniver-Cap** cap trimmed with miniver (ermine) (Margery has dressed up for the occasion)
68 **partlets** collars
69 **flews . . . whirligigs** special bits of fine fashion
71 **Sultan . . . Tamburlaine** conquerors of the Middle East (and rulers in popular contemporary plays by Kyd and Marlowe)
75 **freebooters** pirates
xxi.1 **fact** i.e., his desertion from the army
4 **thank my Lord Mayor** Eyre has already pleaded Lacy's cause to the King
6 **liege** lord (to whom obedience and service are owed)
12 **craft** guile
18 **Diocletian** a Roman emperor
19 **hump** perhaps a toast
21 **pie** magpie (proverbial)
23 **yonker** Dutch for young gentleman
28 **Tamar Cham** famous Chinese ruler and character in a play of 1596 now lost
29 **stuff tennis balls** tennis balls of white leather were stuffed with dog's hair; tennis was a royal game especially identified with Henry VIII
35 **danced . . . sheets** colloquialism for wedding night
37 **get** beget
41 **Apollo** handsome young god of medicine

For there are traitors here.
All. Traitors? Where? Who?
Eyre. Traitors in my house? God forbid! Where be my officers? I'll spend my soul ere my King feel harm.
King. Where is the traitor, Lincoln?
Lincoln. [*Indicating Lacy.*] Here he stands.
King. Cornwall, lay hold on Lacy. Lincoln, speak.
What canst thou lay unto thy nephew's charge?
Lincoln. This, my dear liege; Your Grace to do me honor
Heaped on the head of this degenerous boy
Desertless favors. You made choice of him
To be commander over powers in France;
But he –
King. Good Lincoln, prithee, pause a while.
Even in thine eyes I read what thou wouldst speak.
I know how Lacy did neglect our love,
Ran himself deeply, in the highest degree,
Into vile treason.
Lincoln. Is he not a traitor?
King. Lincoln, he was. Now have we pardoned him.
'Twas not a base want of true valor's fire
That held him out of France, but love's desire.
Lincoln. I will not bear his shame upon my back.
King. Nor shalt thou, Lincoln. I forgive you both.
Lincoln. Then, good my liege, forbid the boy to wed
One whose mean birth will much disgrace his bed.
King. Are they not married?
Lincoln. No, my liege.
Both. We are.
King. Shall I divorce them, then? Oh, be it far
That any hand on earth should dare untie
The sacred knot knit by God's majesty.
I would not for my crown disjoin their hands
That are conjoined in holy nuptial bands.
How sayst thou, Lacy? Wouldst thou lose thy Rose?
Lacy. Not for all India's wealth, my sovereign.
King. But Rose, I am sure, her Lacy would forgo.
Rose. If Rose were asked that question, she'd say no.
King. You hear them, Lincoln?
Lincoln. Yea, my liege, I do.
King. Yet canst thou find i'the heart to part these two?
Who seeks, besides you, to divorce these lovers?
Lord Mayor. I do, my gracious Lord. I am her father.
King. Sir Roger Oatley, our last Mayor, I think?
Nobleman. The same, my liege.
King. Would you offend love's laws?
Well, you shall have your wills. You sue to me
To prohibit the match. Soft, let me see,
You both are married, Lacy, art thou not?
Lacy. I am, dread sovereign.
King. Then, upon thy life,
I charge thee not to call this woman wife.
Lord Mayor. I thank Your Grace.
Rose. O my most gracious Lord!
Kneel.
King. Nay, Rose, never woo me. I tell you true,
Although as yet I am a bachelor,
Yet I believe I shall not marry you.
Rose. Can you divide the body from the soul,
Yet make the body live?
King. Yea, so profound?
I cannot, Rose, but you I must divide.
Fair maid, this bridegroom cannot be your bride.
Are you pleased, Lincoln? Oatley, are you pleased?
Both. Yes, my Lord.
King. Then must my heart be eased;
For, credit me, my conscience lives in pain
Till these whom I divorced be joined again.
Lacy, give me thy hand. Rose, lend me thine.
Be what you would be. Kiss now. So, that's fine.
At night, lovers, to bed. Now, let me see,
Which of you all mislikes this harmony?
Lord Mayor. Will you then take from me my child perforce?
King. Why, tell me, Oatley, shines not Lacy's name
As bright in the world's eye as the gay beams
Of any citizen?
Lincoln. Yea, but, my gracious Lord,
I do mislike the match far more than he.
Her blood is too, too base.
King. Lincoln, no more.
Dost thou not know that love respects no blood,

49 spend give
55 degenerous ungrateful, degenerate
60 our love i.e., love of King and country
64 want lacking
84 last former, preceding
89 dread most respected; awesome
98 bride spouse
109 gay joyful

Cares not for difference of birth or state?
The maid is young, well born, fair, virtuous,
A worthy bride for any gentleman.
Besides, your nephew for her sake did stoop
To bare necessity and, as I hear,
Forgetting honors and all courtly pleasures,
To gain her love became a shoemaker.
As for the honor which he lost in France,
Thus I redeem it. Lacy, kneel thee down.
Arise, Sir Rowland Lacy. Tell me now,
Tell me in earnest, Oatley, canst thou chide,
Seeing thy Rose a lady and a bride?

Lord Mayor. I am content with what your Grace hath done.

Lincoln. And I, my liege, since there's no remedy.

King. Come on, then, all shake hands. I'll have you friends.
Where there is much love, all discord ends.
What says my mad Lord Mayor to all this love?

Eyre. O, my liege, this honor you have done to my fine journeyman here, Rowland Lacy, and all these favors which you have shown to me this day in my poor house, will make Simon Eyre live longer by one dozen of warm summers more than he should.

King. Nay, my mad Lord Mayor – that shall be thy name –
If any grace of mine can length thy life,
One honor more I'll do thee. That new building
Which at thy cost in Cornhill is erected
Shall take a name from us. We'll have it called
The Leaden Hall, because in digging it
You found the lead that covereth the same.

Eyre. I thank your Majesty.

Wife. God bless your Grace.

King. Lincoln, a word with you.

Enter Hodge, Firk, Rafe, *and more* Shoemakers.

Eyre. How now, my mad knaves! Peace, speak softly.
Yonder is the King.

King. With the old troop which there we keep in pay
We will incorporate a new supply.
Before one summer more pass o'er my head,
France shall repent England was injurèd.
What are all those?

Lacy. All shoemakers, my liege,
Sometimes my fellows. In their companies
I lived as merry as an emperor.

King. My mad Lord Mayor, are all these shoemakers?

Eyre. All shoemakers, my liege; all gentlemen of the Gentle Craft, true Trojans, courageous cordwainers. They all kneel to the shrine of holy Saint Hugh.

All [*the Shoemakers*]. God save your Majesty!

King. Mad Simon, would they anything with us?

Eyre. [*To the Shoemakers.*] Mum, mad knaves, not a word. I'll do't, I warrant you. [*To the King.*] They are all beggars, my liege, all for themselves; and I for them all, on both my knees do entreat that for the honor of poor Simon Eyre and the good of his brethren, these mad knaves, your Grace would vouchsafe some privilege to my new Leaden Hall, that it may be lawful for us to buy and sell leather there two days a week.

King. Mad Sim, I grant your suit. You shall have patent
To hold two market days in Leaden Hall,
Mondays and Fridays, those shall be the times.
Will this content you?

All [*the Shoemakers*]. Jesus bless your Grace!

Eyre. In the name of these my poor brethren shoemakers, I most humbly thank your Grace. But before I rise, seeing you are in the giving vein, and we in the begging, grant Sim Eyre one boon more.

King. What is it, my Lord Mayor?

Eyre. Vouchsafe to taste of a poor banquet that stands sweetly waiting for your sweet presence.

King. I shall undo thee, Eyre, only with feasts.
Already have I been too troublesome;
Say, have I not?

Eyre. O my dear King, Sim Eyre was taken unawares upon a day of shroving which I promised long ago to the prentices of London. For, an't please your Highness, in time past I bare the water-tankard, and my coat sits not a whit the worse upon my back. And then upon a morning some mad boys – it was Shrove Tuesday even as 'tis now – gave me my breakfast, and I swore then by the stopple of my tankard if ever I came to be Lord Mayor of London, I would feast all the prentices. This day, my liege, I did it, and the slaves had an hundred tables five times covered. They are

---

125 lady proper title for the wife of a knight
142 Leaden Hall a central building in Dekker's London
153 Sometimes formerly
172 patent letters patent; royal license
181 boon favor
183 banquet i.e., sweet or dessert
186 undo bankrupt
197 stopple bung-hole

gone home and vanished. Yet add more honor to the Gentle Trade: taste of Eyre's banquet, Simon's happy made.

King. Eyre, I will taste of thy banquet, and will say
I have not met more pleasure on a day.
Friends of the Gentle Craft, thanks to you all.
Thanks, my kind Lady Mayoress, for our cheer.
Come, lords, a while let's revel it at home.
When all our sports and banquetings are done,
Wars must right wrongs which Frenchmen have begun.

Exeunt.

A Woman Killed with Kindness

Thomas Heywood

A

WOMAN

KILDE

with Kindnesse.

Written by Tho: Heywood.

LONDON

Printed by William Iaggard dwelling in Barbican, and
are to be sold in Paules Church-yard.
by Iohn Hodgets. 1607.

Title-page of the 1607 edition, reproduced from the unique copy in the British Museum. A sixteenth-century couple being married. Reprinted from Alison Sim, *The Tudor Housewife* (Montreal: McGill-Queen's University Press, 1996), p. I.

Thomas Heywood's masterpiece about the precarious conditions of a private and public life during the transitional years of Tudor–Stuart rule both opens and ends with marriage. It begins just after the wedding of John Frankford and Anne Acton and stops just short of Susan Mountford's wedding to Anne's brother Sir Francis. But the spontaneous joy of marriage comes in the second scene where household servants compete to name the country measure they intend to dance, not in the first where the gentry are at deeper odds with one another: when Sir Francis tells the bridegroom "This marriage music hoists me from the ground," Frankford replies, "Aye, you may caper, you are light and free; Marriage hath yoked my heels, pray then pardon me." Even the other knight at the wedding chides Frankford – "You are a happy man, sir" – to no avail. The next time we see these two knights, in the play's third scene, they too have become fractious in a hawking competition with a quarrel that becomes so uncontrolled that two servants are killed. Thus Heywood's "Muse," "bent," as the Prologue tells us, "Upon a barren subject, a bare scene," moves swiftly toward yet another competition – this time a semi-private evening of cards in which all the conversation is riddled with accusations and boasts of adultery – which will lead ultimately to still another death. Yet it is Sir Charles Mountford, in the play's second line, who sets these possibilities in motion by requesting as appropriate music an old ballad entitled "The Shaking of the Sheets," with its sly references to the nuptial bed but with an even grimmer conclusion: "Can you dance the shaking of the sheets A dance that every man must do? Can you trim it up with dainty sweets And everything that longs thereto? Make ready then your winding sheet And see how you can bestir your feet For death is the man that all must meet." For Heywood's tightly organized, even spare, play is a play full of premonitions, anticipations, and fears: in the space between the first and second weddings he focuses, with penetrating cultural analysis and rich psychological portraiture, on spoken and unspoken intersections between public and private life. This deeply troubled, and deeply troubling, play confronts the moral issues of revenge and in that it resembles *The Spanish Tragedy*; but it also is concerned with the possibilities of salvation as *Dr. Faustus* is. By bringing such larger concerns into the private gentry household, however, Heywood at once narrows his focus and broadens its relevance.

Marital relations which necessitate complete trust and surrender are always a risky business, and the unsettled marriage patterns of the early modern period did not help matters. Theoretically, the husband ruled his wife and she obeyed him in all things; as he provided wise governing of the household and the fundamental needs of life, so she managed the daily supervision and operation of their household, including the care of children and servants, and even guests. But such tasks modified, if they did not actually ignore, a sense of subordination. As Dorothy Leigh writes in *The Mother's Blessing* (1616), "if she be thy wife, she is always too good to be thy servant, and worthy to be thy fellow." Nor were household manuals then coming into wide circulation of much help, either. In *A Bride-bush, or A Direction for Married Persons* (1623), William Whately contends that a husband could beat his wife "if she give just cause, after much bearing and forbearing, and trying all other ways, in case of utmost necessity," although he should restrain when a wife's weaknesses "are incident even to virtuous women." Conversely, in his collection of sermons entitled *Of Domestical Duties* (1620), William Gouge, preacher at Blackfriars, claims that as one flesh, a husband beating his wife would be beating himself and that he should instead refer contentious matters "to a public magistrate." Rather than define marriage as one partner dominant over the other, Gouge proposes that marriages should be companionate:

> There may not only be a fellowship but also an equality in some things betwixt those that in other things are one of them inferior and subject as betwixt man and wife in the power of one another's bodies, for the wife (as well as the husband) is therein both a servant and a mistress, a servant to yield her body, a mistress to have the power of his.

The normal rules of patriarchy, then, did not extend into the household.

> When I came to deliver the husband's duties, I showed that he ought not to exact whatsoever his wife was bound unto (in case it were exacted by him) but that he ought to make her a joint governor of the family with himself, and refer the ordering of many things to her discretion, and with all honorable and kind respect to carry himself toward her.... That which maketh a wife's yoke heavy and hard is a husband's abuse of

his authority, and more pressing his own wife's duty, than performing his own.

Just such a view of a marriage of equals is what Sir Charles tells Frankford when he lists Anne's "ornaments Both of the mind and body": her pedigree, he argues,

> Is noble, and her education such
> As might become the daughter of a prince.
> Her own tongue speaks all tongues, and her own hand
> Can teach all strings to speak in their best grace,
> From the shrill treble to the hoarsest bass.
> To end her many praises in one word,
> She's beauty and perfection's eldest daughter,
> Only found by yours, though many a heart hath sought her.

Later, alone in his study, Frankford assesses the same relationship but with a difference:

> I am a gentleman, and by my birth
> Companion with a king; a king's no more.
> I am possessed of many fair revenues,
> Sufficient to maintain a gentleman.
> Touching my mind, I am studied in all arts,
> The riches of my thoughts, and of my time
> Have been a good proficient. But the chief
> Of all the sweet felicities on earth,
> I have a fair, a chaste, and loving wife,
> Perfection all, all truth, all ornament.
> If man on earth may truly happy be,
> Of these at once possessed, sure I am he.

Meditating, his mind subtly shifts from a position of equality to one of dominance in which his own qualifications, separately listed, must outweigh those of his wife and her "perfection" becomes his to "possess." In doing so, he melds his friend's first description of Frankford's marriage with a second:

> This lady is no clog, as many are;
> She doth become you like a well-made suit
> In which the tailor hath used all his art,
> Not like a thick coat of unseasoned frieze,
> Forced on your back in summer; she's no chain
> To tie your neck and curb you to the yoke,
> But she's a chain of gold to adorn your neck.

By thus comparing the partners to this marriage, both men compromise the notion of a companionate marriage only, finally, to ignore and deny it, in opposition to Heywood's own attitude, published in 1624 in *Gunaikeion*, that "the sacred institution of marriage, was not only for procreation, but that man should make choice of a woman, and a woman to make election of a man, as companions and comforters one of another as well in adversity as prosperity."

Indeed, Frankford moves rather promptly to fulfill the role of companion not with Anne but with Wendoll. This substitution comes at an important psychological moment, just as he meditates on Anne as mere "ornament." Ignoring the possible motivation for Wendoll's abrupt appearance or his mud-splattered condition, Frankford says to himself,

> This Wendoll I have noted, and his carriage
> Hath pleased me much. By observation
> I have noted many good deserts in him:
> He's affable and seen in many things,
> Discourses well, a good companion,
> And though of small means, yet a gentleman
> Of a good house, somewhat pressed by want.
> I have preferred him to a second place
> In my opinion and my best regard.

Thus Anne is displaced by Wendoll. Indeed, this man of little means is made an equal insofar as Frankford is able to sustain one; first given his own room, horse, and manservant, Wendoll receives Frankford's full range and authority. "Choose of my men which shall attend on you, And he is yours," Frankford promises, "Be my companion." In his only deeply troubled soliloquy, Wendoll himself notices the strangeness of all this: "He cannot eat without me, Nor laugh without me. I am to his body As necessary as his digestion, And equally do make him whole or sick." In time, Frankford insists that Wendoll become his deputy, and in managing his household and his wife in his absence, finally to displace Frankford as he had displaced Anne. We must consider Frankford's intentions, even if he does not; he uses Anne, it might seem, as a stalking-horse to promote his own relationship with Wendoll, to insure he stays, to maintain his dominance. Before such a startling transition Anne stands confused, helpless, and without guidance. One of Heywood's great sources of power as a playwright here is that in presenting the development of a marital triangle he spends no time in supplying succinct statements of motivation, but instead shows us how people react when caught in the sudden strengths of their own passions, made vulnerable by the unexpected conditions in which they find themselves.

From quite another perspective, Frankford should have known better – should have realized the erotic and tragic possibilities of such privileged access. As John Dod and Robert Cleaver warn in *A Godly Form of Household Government* (1598), "the wise husband shall never set himself so far in love that he forget that he is a man, the ruler and governor of the house and of his wife, and that he is set (as it were) in a station to watch and diligently to take heed what is done in his house, and to see who goeth out and in"; and Thomas Gainsford adds, in *The Rich Cabinet Furnished with Variety of Excellent Descriptions* (1616), "Oeconomic instructeth the husbands that they bring no suspicious person to their houses." But Frankford, not questioning his own motivations or behavior, never questions Wendoll's arrival, either, nor its possible effect on his wife. Rather, Wendoll, notably marginalized both at the Frankfords' wedding and at the Acton–Mountford hunt, is brought center-stage in the Frankford household. There, Wendoll observes in the tortured soliloquy that opens scene vi how endangered he has become: "I am a villain if I apprehend But such a thought; then to attempt the deed – Slave, thou art damned without redemption." Unable to examine his motivation as he is unable to name the deed – adultery – Wendoll is instead plagued by a desire which seems dictated by the commands of an absent Frankford and by his own passions and yet denied by his sense of Anne's social unavailability and by the pains of moral guilt over a potential act that would threaten their very salvation. Unlike Frankford – who seems never to look forward to the consequences of his actions, much less his intentions – Wendoll is well aware that choices always exact a cost. Moreover, unlike Nicholas – whose name is that of the Devil himself, and whose own vicarious pleasures in Anne's adultery and his ability to judge and condemn stem from motives he is, like Frankford, unwilling to confront – Wendoll is honest with himself, however despicable his thoughts and illicit his behavior.

In the late sixteenth and early seventeenth centuries in England, however, the attitude toward adultery and proper punishment for it were no more settled than the matter of marital relationships. At one end of the spectrum were those who cited penalties prescribed by the Old Testament, the death of both parties in the case of adultery by a married woman; at the other end, there were those who cited Christ from the New Testament: "He that is without sin among you, let him cast first a stone at her." Adultery was not considered a legal offense but an ecclesiastical one. If discovered by the church, it could mean public humiliation for the woman, as in the case of Elizabeth Hood who, according to the Ely Diocesan Records, had "to stand at the Bull Ring in Cambridge clothed in a white sheet down to the ground, holding a white rod or wand in her hand and having a paper written with great letters pinned upon her breast and the like paper upon her back declaring her offense." She stood there, on a market Saturday, from 10 a.m. until 2 p.m., and then repeated the act at her parish church for three consecutive Sundays. But the vast majority of cases of adultery were discovered instead by the husbands, who never reported them to church authorities for fear of their own public humiliation for cuckoldry; like Frankford, they took matters into their own hands and kept the matter within the household. Although Frankford is tempted to revenge his wife's and friend's betrayal with murder – defending his honor as Mountford defended his at the hunt – he in fact chooses the common legal recourse of grounds for divorce *a mensa et thoro*, that is, a judicial separation from bed and board which nevertheless did not mean a dissolution of the marriage. This was meant – by early modern law and practice – to allow a possible reconciliation; it denied the right of either partner to remarry. History has recorded few suits for separation from bed and board for this period, but informal separations seem to have been quite common. The rationale behind divorce *a mensa et thoro* was the Roman Catholic belief in marriage as a holy sacrament terminated only by God; after the Reformation, Elizabeth's Established Church upheld the indissolubility of wedlock, arguing that "What therefore God hath joined together, let not man put asunder" (Matt. 19:6). As for the conduct books, Whately acknowledges that "the party so transgressing hath . . . laid himself open (if the Magistrate did as God's law commands) to the bloody stroke of a violent death," but adds,

> in case the man or woman have offended once or so, through infirmity, and yet being convicted, shall by manifest outward tokens, testify his or her repentance, and sure desire of amendment, then it is meet and convenient that this offense be by the yoke-fellow passed by: for the love of the married couple should be very fervent and abundant, and therefore able to pass by great, yea by the greatest wrongs, so far as it may with safe conscience be done.

The popular Puritan theologian William Perkins went even further, urging that the repenting couple seek the public aid and counsel of their local parish. Heywood seems to have had a mind divided; he urges the welfare of both partners – the "vices of the wife are either to be corrected, or endured; he that chastiseth her makes her the more conformable, he that suffers her, makes himself the better by it" and then adds, "yet are not their insolencies anyway to be encouraged, because it is a duty exacted from all men, to have a respect to the honor of their houses and families." The second time Frankford withdraws into his private study to meditate, he too is transformed into an excessive self-awareness that considers all these possibilities. He is torn not only between public exposure and private humiliation in his own honorable household – now no longer honorable no matter what he says or does – but also between accepting Anne's repentance and dismissing her.

Whatever we may think of Frankford's initial smugness and self-indulgence, of his intentions conscious or not, this particular moment is enacted with considerable sympathy; and it is up to us, measuring it against the careful attempt to accuse and arraign the adulterers during the card game and the subsequent sly attempt to catch them in the act by making waxen molds of the doorlocks and sneaking back at night under an elaborate ruse, to come to our own judgment on him.

If Heywood is at great pains to show us Wendoll's and Frankford's conditions, and the dilemmas they embody, he is no less concerned with Anne. She seems aware from the beginning of her marriage that the qualities most highly and frequently recommended for wives in her culture are obedience, chastity, silence, discretion, and modesty, and her initial behavior shows her to be exemplary in all of them. It is her husband who must seem to her unconventional and unpredictable, and who therefore seems to redefine her role in their partnership. At the same time he is disinterested in her, Wendoll provides in their household the kind of passion she must have expected: he treats her not as an adornment but as a real woman. If she needs and appreciates that, however, she can draw the line at sexual innuendo and provocation; and even on the night her adulterous relationship is revealed, she cries out for her husband's protection and tries to prevent an encounter with Wendoll: "I hope your business craves no such dispatch That you must ride to-night"; "I'll call you up by five o'clock to-morrow"; "Then if you needs must go This dangerous evening, Master Wendoll, Let me entreat you bear him company." Again ignored by Frankford, who refuses to share their bed, she seems mightily distracted:

> You have tempted me to mischief, Master Wendoll;
> I have done I know not what. Well, you plead custom;
> That which for want of wit I granted erst
> I now must yield through fear. Come, come, let's in.
> Once o'ershoes, we are straight o'er head in sin.

He has tempted her; but the custom she pleads may be that of prescribed abstinence or continued involvement with him sexually. Her motives include, she says, both fear and resignation. She seems overburdened by the thought and the fear of adultery that Gouge prescribed ought always to command all her being:

> A diligent keeping of the heart (that lustful thoughts proceed not from thence); of the eyes (that they wander not on the beauty or properness of any one's person, or on lascivious pictures, or any like allurements); of the ears (that they harken not to any enticements of others); of the tongue (that it utter not unchaste and corrupt communication); of the lips (that they delight not in wanton kisses); of the hands (that they use no wanton dalliance); of the feet (that they carry thee not to the place where adultery may be committed); of thy company (that thou be not defiled with others' wantonness and uncleanness); of thy diet (that it be not immoderate); of thine apparel (that it be not garish and lascivious); of thy time (that it be not vainly and idly spent).

Yet Gouge's immediate remedy is beyond her: "One of the best remedies that can be prescribed to married persons . . . is that husband and wife mutually delight in each other." In her characteristically Puritan thought, she takes full responsibility for the mischief, the sin: she "sees the justice of her punishment"; "He cannot be so base as to forgive me," Anne says of Frankford, "Nor I so shameless to accept his pardon." Rather, she would commit suicide if it would protect his honor and that of their children: "Nay, to whip but this scandal out, I would hazard The rich and dear redemption of my soul." Yet so reprobate is she, that she has no other choice; so acculturated is she to the position and honor of her husband that she sees his forgiveness alone as the possibility for any salvation for herself: "My fault so heinous is That if you in this world forgive it not, Heaven will not clear it in the world to come." Seeing herself damned, she tells her husband, he too damns her. But for Heywood, and for us, this question of responsibility for adultery is not so simple. For who, in the end, is at fault here? Frankford, out of blind ignorance and self-absorption? Wendoll, out of the inability to control his own passions? Anne, out of her loneliness and "fear," even a possible love of Wendoll as Frankford's closest companion? Nicholas, Jenkin, and Sisly, who seeing what is about to happen, do nothing to discourage it and seem even to enjoy knowing of it? Sir Charles Mountford and Sir Francis Acton, who suggest and then support Frankford's sense of his wife as just another possession and accouterment of his household, an ornamental furnishing? Like murder, adultery, once discovered, cannot be amended or erased. The risk is always high; the cost, perhaps intolerable.

Another masterful stroke of dramaturgy is Heywood's construction of the underplot to *A Woman Killed with Kindness.* Both Frankford and Mountford suffer acts of betrayal of their honor, and both become wholly preoccupied with their own integrity and the integrity of their family lines. Both are endangered by their acts of spontaneous passions that destroy their contentment, which they had thought to be their natural right, and indestructible. In each plot, man's honor is secured only by ignoring or sacrificing a woman's honor. Thus Sir Charles transfers his sister's chastity and potential violation to his house –

Where he the first of all our house begun,
I now the last will end and keep this house,
This virgin title never yet deflowered,
By any unthrift of the Mountfords' line.
In brief, I will not sell it for more gold
Than you could hide or pave the ground withal,

although he will, in the end, sell his sister Susan in order to keep it. His own honor will come before hers, the unspoiled house will remain after her spoliation. She too, like Anne, would thus be "killed" with the "kindness" of his decision, kindness here referring to the Mountford nature in bloodline and in possessions as well as kindness meaning kin. Sir Charles's sudden passion to kill and his long trial and recovery are, in a way, another aftermath that Frankford might face (and would perhaps face if he had killed Anne and Wendoll); it is as if the play were starting over again, within itself, spinning out past the play itself the inherent dangers in the concepts of male and female honor. Yet Heywood knows, as we must by play's end, that honor alone is what the whole early modern culture was grounded on. *A Woman Killed with Kindness* means not to question early modern marriage and adultery alone, but the entire society of which they remain a vital part.

Heywood's play takes place in England's period of the "Great Rebuilding," which placed new and heavy premium on "Every Man's proper Mansion House and Home, being the Theater of his Hospitality, the Seat of Self-fruition, the Comfortablest part of his own Life, the Noblest of his Son's Inheritance, a kind of private Princedom; nay, to the Possessors thereof, an Epitome of the whole World," as Henry Wotton puts it in *The Elements of Architecture* (1624). Frankford takes considerable pride and pleasure in his mansion house and home, as Sir Charles learns to enjoy his summerhouse amidst a chastened life of husbandry; but Frankford defiles his property when he stalks toward his "polluted bedchamber," his thoughts singularly focused on discovering adultery, and Sir Charles defiles his by keeping it pure at the cost of his sister's purity. Defilement, common to them both, is thus the outcome of more public rituals – wedding, hunting, even cardplaying – that contain but do not alleviate private needs and fears. What *A Woman Killed with Kindness* keeps reminding us is how troubled life can become because of a complacent society that refuses to allow for unaccountable human passions; and whether, given such potentially incendiary conditions, human salvation is even possible. This "bare" play, like the play of *Othello* with which it has much in common, is rich with unspoken motivation and need, as full and its presentation as abbreviated as opera. But in its stout refusal to separate public and private, this play moves social and religious issues into a contemporary gentrified life, testing the theological in the everyday, and making the material ethical. Such invasive concerns, Heywood finally argues, are inescapable.

Further Reading

Bach, Rebecca Ann, "The Homosocial Imaginary of *A Woman Killed with Kindness*," *Textual Practice* 12:3 (Winter 1998): 503–24.

Baines, Barbara J., *Thomas Heywood*. Boston: Twayne Publishers, 1984.

Bromley, Laura G., "Domestic Conduct in *A Woman Killed with Kindness*," *Studies in English Literature 1500–1900* 26 (1986): 259–76.

Cary, Cecile Williamson, "'Go Breake This Lute': Music in Heywood's *A Woman Killed with Kindness*," *Huntington Library Quarterly* 37:2 (February 1974): 111–22.

Cook, David, "*A Woman Killed with Kindness*: An Unshakespearian Tragedy," *English Studies* 45:5 (October 1964): 353–72.

Kiefer, Frederick, "Heywood as Moralist in *A Woman Killed with Kindness*," *Medieval and Renaissance Drama* 3 (1986): 83–98.

Orlin, Lena Cowen, *Private Matters and Public Culture in Post-Reformation England*, ch. 2. Ithaca: Cornell University Press, 1994.

Panek, Jennifer, "Punishing Adultery in *A Woman Killed with Kindness*," *Studies in English Literature 1500–1900* 34:2 (1994): 337–78.

A Woman Killed with Kindness

[DRAMATIS PERSONAE

Sir Francis Acton.
Sir Charles Mountford.
John Frankford.
Wendoll, } *his friends.*
Cranwell, }
Malby, *friend to Sir Francis.*
Old Mountford, *uncle to Sir Charles.*
Tydy, *cousin to Sir Charles.*
Sandy, *former friend to Sir Charles.*
Roder, *former tenant to Sir Charles.*
Shafton, *false friend to Frankford.*
Nicholas, } *servants to Frankford.*
Jenkin, }
Spiggot, *butler to Frankford.*
Roger Brickbat, } *country fellows.*
Jack Slime, }
Sheriff.
Keeper of the Prison.
Sergeant.
Officers, Falconers, Huntsmen, Coachman, Carters, Musicians, Servants, Frankford's Children.

Anne, *wife to Frankford and sister to Sir Francis.*
Susan, *sister to Sir Charles.*
Sisly Milk-pail, *servingwoman to Frankford.*
Joan Miniver, } *country wenches.*
Jane Trubkin, }
Isbel Motley, }
Servingwomen
The Scene: Yorkshire.]

THE PROLOGUE

I come but like a harbinger, being sent
To tell you what these preparations mean:
Look for no glorious state, our Muse is bent
Upon a barren subject, a bare scene.
We could afford this twig a timber-tree,
Whose strength might boldly on your favors build;
Our russet, tissue; drone, a honey-bee;
Our barren plot, a large and spacious field;
Our coarse fare, banquets; our thin water, wine;
Our brook, a sea; our bat's eyes, eagle's sight;
Our Poet's dull and earthy Muse, divine;
Our ravens, doves; our crow's black feathers, white.
But gentle thoughts, when they may give the foil,
Save them that yield, and spare where they may spoil.

TEXTUAL VARIANTS

i.64 adorn] Q adore **iii.42 s.d.** both] Q one **44** innocents] Q innocent **57 s.d.**] Charles's sister Susan is named Jane throughout this scene in Q **99** many] Q man **iv.23** rode] Q rid **36 s.d.** Anne] Q Master Frankford **40** hawks] Q hawks? **42** wife's] Q wives **66** it.] Q it? **85** not] Q nor **v.10 s.d.** Sir Charles] Q Sir Francis **vi.9** thoughts] Q thoughts? **35** me] Q be **70 s.d.** Anne] Q Mistress Frankford **75** kind] Q kinds **87** so!] Q so? **102** not.] Q not? **107** countenance] Q countenance? **110** me] we **119** your] Q you **157** my] Q has omitted the word **169** just in the nick] Q puts this at line 170 **185** whore] Q &c. **vii.36** names] Q means **78** Lord's] Q Lord **91** Oh,] Q Or **94** struck] Q stroke **95 s.d.** *Runs*] Q Run **viii.5**] in this scene Q uses But[ler] as the speech prefix rather than Spiggot **ix.1 s.d.** Susan, Old Mountford] Q Sir Charles, his sister **4** my] Q me **26** were] Q was **27** on] Q in **60** rapt] Q wrapt **x.1 s.d.** *feet*] Q face **91** Acton] Q action **xi.1 s.d.**] Q reads "Enter Frankford and Nick with keys, and a letter in his hand." **5**] Q makes "The letter, sir" a separate speech by Nick **10** struck] Q stroke **34** Mistress] Q Master **98** injure] Q injury **106** do] Q to **108** Puritan] Q Puritant **xii.26** this] Q his **xiii.1–3**] Q sets as prose **79** swoons] Q sounds **109** my] Q thy **113** neither] Q either **xiv.8** ruffian] Q ruffin **59** sister] Q Jane **xv.4** wife's] Q wives **xvi.26** lay claim to] Q claim to lay **75** upon] Q omits word **93** naught] Q nought **128** have] Q ha' **xvii.26–30**] Q sets this as poetry **34–9**] Q sets this as poetry **56** brother Acton?] Q master Frankford? **61**] Q assigns this line to Charles **63** arrival] Q arrive **64–7**] Q assigns these lines to Charles

Playsource

A Woman Killed with Kindness is apparently based on Heywood's observations and ideas about married life following the conventional classical three-part structuring of rising action, climax, and falling action with Anne's fall, Frankford's judgment, and their reconciliation. No source has ever been identified.

The Prologue

3 **glorious state** ostentatious presentation (possibly referring to a history play as play of state)
4 **barren** (1) sterile; (2) meager
5 **afford** put forward; precedent; **timber-tree** full-grown tree
7 **russet** coarse homespun cloth; **tissue** rich cloth with gold or silver threads
13 **gentle** i.e., gentlemen and gentlewomen; **give . . . foil** bring the defeat (from wrestling)
14 **spoil** destroy

[Sc. i]

Enter Master John Frankford, Sir Francis Acton, Mistress Anne, Sir Charles Mountford, Master Malby, Master Wendoll, Master Cranwell [,*and* Musicians].

Sir Fra. Some music there! None lead the bride a dance?
Sir Cha. Yes, would she dance "The Shaking of the Sheets:"
But that's the dance her husband means to lead her.
Wen. That's not the dance that every man must dance,
According to the ballad.
Sir Fra. Music, ho!
By your leave, sister – by your husband's leave
I should have said – the hand that but this day
Was given you in the church I'll borrow. [*To the Musicians.*] Sound!
This marriage music hoists me from the ground.
Frank. Aye, you may caper, you are light and free;
Marriage hath yoked my heels, pray then pardon me.
Sir Fra. I'll have you dance, too, brother.
Sir Cha. Master Frankford,
You are a happy man, sir; and much joy
Succeed your marriage mirth, you have a wife
So qualified and with such ornaments
Both of the mind and body. First, her birth
Is noble, and her education such
As might become the daughter of a prince.
Her own tongue speaks all tongues, and her own hand
Can teach all strings to speak in their best grace,
From the shrill treble to the hoarsest bass.
To end her many praises in one word,
She's beauty and perfection's eldest daughter,
Only found by yours, though many a heart hath sought her.
Frank. But that I know your virtues and chaste thoughts,
I should be jealous of your praise, Sir Charles.
Cran. He speaks no more than you approve.
Mal. Nor flatters he that gives to her her due.
Anne. I would your praise could find a fitter theme
Than my imperfect beauty to speak on.
Such as they be, if they my husband please,
They suffice me now I am married.
His sweet content is like a flattering glass,
To make my face seem fairer to mine eye:
But the least wrinkle from his stormy brow
Will blast the roses in my cheeks that grow.
Sir Fra. A perfect wife already, meek and patient.
How strangely the word "husband" fits your mouth,
Not married three hours since, sister. 'Tis good;
You that begin betimes thus, must needs prove
Pliant and duteous in your husband's love.
Godamercies, brother, wrought her to it already?
"Sweet husband," and a curtsey the first day.
Mark this, mark this, you that are bachelors,
And never took the grace of honest man,
Mark this against you marry, this one phrase:
"In a good time that man both wins and woos
That takes his wife down in her wedding shoes."
Frank. Your sister takes not after you, Sir Francis.
All his wild blood your father spent on you;
He got her in his age when he grew civil.
All his mad tricks were to his land entailed,
And you are heir to all; your sister, she
Hath to her dower her mother's modesty.
Sir Cha. Lord, sir, in what a happy state live you;
This morning, which to many seems a burden
Too heavy to bear, is unto you a pleasure.
This lady is no clog, as many are;
She doth become you like a well-made suit
In which the tailor hath used all his art,
Not like a thick coat of unseasoned frieze,
Forced on your back in summer; she's no chain
To tie your neck and curb you to the yoke,

---

i.2 **"The Shaking of the Sheets"** a bawdy ballad about the nuptial bed and the dance of death
5 **according . . . ballad** "Can you dance the shaking of the sheets A dance that every man must do? Can you trim it up with dainty sweets And everything that longs thereto? Make ready then your winding sheet And see how you can bestir your feet For death is the man that all must meet."
15 **qualified** endowed
25 **But** were it not
27 **approve** agree to (by marrying her)
36 **blast** blight, wither
38 **strangely** unaccustomed
40 **betimes** early
42 **Godamercies** "God have mercy" (mild oath); **wrought** shaped
45 **took . . . man** i.e., married
47 **In . . . time** at the right moment
48 **takes . . . shoes** asserts superiority from the first moment
50 **spent on** (1) expended; (2) bequeathed
51 **got** begot; **civil** civilized, refined
52 **his . . . entailed** bestowed inseparably with the land
58 **clog** impediment (attached to hands or necks of prisoners to prevent their escape)
61 **unseasoned frieze** coarse woollen cloth worn out of season

But she's a chain of gold to adorn your neck.
You both adorn each other, and your hands
Methinks are matches. There's equality
In this fair combination; you are both scholars,
Both young, both being descended nobly.
There's music in this sympathy, it carries
Consort and expectation of much joy,
Which God bestow on you, from this first day,
Until your dissolution – that's for aye.

Sir Fra. We keep you here too long, good brother Frankford.
Into the hall! Away, go, cheer your guests!
What, bride and bridegroom both withdrawn at once?
If you be missed, the guests will doubt their welcome,
And charge you with unkindness.

Frank. To prevent it,
I'll leave you here, to see the dance within.

Anne. And so will I.

[*Exeunt* Frankford *and* Anne.]

Sir Fra. To part you it were sin.
Now gallants, while the town musicians
Finger their frets within, and the mad lads
And country lasses, every mother's child
With nosegays and bride-laces in their hats,
Dance all their country measures, rounds, and jigs,
What shall we do? Hark, they are all on the hoigh,
They toil like mill-horses, and turn as round –
Marry, not on the toe. Aye, and they caper,
But without cutting. You shall see to-morrow
The hall floor pecked and dinted like a millstone,
Made with their high shoes; though their skill be small,
Yet they tread heavy where their hobnails fall.

Sir Cha. Well, leave them to their sports. Sir Francis Acton,
I'll make a match with you: meet me to-morrow
At Chevy Chase, I'll fly my hawk with yours.

Sir Fra. For what? for what?

Sir Cha. Why, for a hundred pounds.

Sir Fra. Pawn me some gold of that.

Sir Cha. Here are ten angels;
I'll make them good a hundred pounds to-morrow
Upon my hawk's wing.

Sir Fra. 'Tis a match, 'tis done.
Another hundred pounds upon your dogs,
Dare you, Sir Charles?

Sir Cha. I dare. Were I sure to lose
I durst do more than that. Here's my hand,
The first course for a hundred pounds.

Sir Fra. A match.

Wen. Ten angels on Sir Francis Acton's hawk;
As much upon his dogs.

Cran. I am for Sir Charles Mountford; I have seen
His hawk and dog both tried. What, clap you hands?
Or is't no bargain?

Wen. Yes, and stake them down.
Were they five hundred they were all my own.

Sir Fra. Be stirring early with the lark to-morrow;
I'll rise into my saddle ere the sun
Rise from his bed.

Sir Cha. If there you miss me, say
I am no gentleman; I'll hold my day.

Sir Fra. It holds on all sides; come, to-night let's dance.
Early to-morrow let's prepare to ride;
We had need be three hours up before the bride.

[*Exeunt.*]

[Sc. ii]

Enter Nicholas *and* Jenkin, Jack Slime, Roger Brickbat, *with country* Wenches, *and two or three* Musicians.

Jenk. Come, Nick, take you Joan Miniver to trace withal; Jack Slime, traverse you with Sisly Milk-pail; I will take Jane Trubkin, and Roger Brickbat shall have Isbel Motley; and now that they

66 **matches** matched for each other
69 **sympathy** concord
70 **Consort** (1) accord; (2) companionship
74 **cheer** entertain
77 **unkindness** unnaturalness, discourtesy (Frankford will pride himself on his kindness to others)
80 **gallants** men of pleasure and fashion
83 **nosegays** bunches of flowers; **bride-laces** traditional laces of gold silk
84 **country measures** stately court dances; **rounds** country circle dances; **jigs** lively country dances
85 **on the hoigh** excited
87 **caper** exuberant dance
88 **cutting** leaping
94 **Chevy Chase** here a field for hawking but with possible reference to a ballad of that name about a border skirmish
96 **Pawn me** put down a deposit; **angels** gold coins (picturing the Archangel Michael on one side)
101 **durst** dare
102 **course** race between two hounds after game
106 **clap** shake
107 **stake . . . down** deposit as a pledge
112 **hold my day** keep my appointment
ii.1 **trace** dance
2 **traverse** (1) to march up and down; (2) to keep time

are busy in the parlor. Come, strike up; we'll have a crash here in the yard.

Nich. My humor is not compendious. Dancing I possess not, though I can foot it; yet, since I am fallen into the hands of Sisly Milk-pail, I assent.

Jack. Truly, Nick, though we were never brought up like serving courtiers, yet we have been brought up with serving creatures, aye, and God's creatures, too, for we have been brought up to serve sheep, oxen, horses, and hogs, and such like; and though we be but country fellows, it may be in the way of dancing we can do the horse-trick as well as servingmen.

Roger. Aye, and the crosspoint, too.

Jenk. Oh, Slime, Oh, Brickbat, do not you know that comparisons are odious? Now we are odious ourselves, too; therefore, there are no comparisons to be made betwixt us.

Nich. I am sudden, and not superfluous;
I am quarrelsome, and not seditious;
I am peaceable, and not contentious;
I am brief, and not compendious.
Slime, foot it quickly. If the music overcome not my melancholy, I shall quarrel; and if they suddenly do not strike up, I shall presently strike thee down.

Jenk. No quarreling, for God's sake! Truly, if you do, I shall set a knave between you.

Jack. I come to dance, not to quarrel. Come, what shall it be? "Rogero"?

Jenk. "Rogero"? No. We will dance "The Beginning of the World."

Sisly. I love no dance so well as "John, Come Kiss Me Now."

Nich. I, that have ere now deserved a cushion, call for "The Cushion Dance."

Roger. For my part, I like nothing so well as "Tom Tyler."

Jenk. No, we'll have "The Hunting of the Fox."

Jack. "The Hay," "The Hay," there's nothing like "The Hay."

Nich. I have said, I do say, and I will say again –

Jenk. Every man agree to have it as Nick says.

All. Content.

Nich. It hath been, it now is, and it shall be –

Sisly. What, Master Nicholas, what?

Nich. "Put on Your Smock a Monday."

Jenk. So the dance will come cleanly off. Come, for God's sake, agree of something. If you like not that, put it to the musicians, or let me speak for all, and we'll have "Sellenger's Round."

All. That, that, that!

Nich. No, I am resolved thus it shall be:
First take hands, then take you to your heels.

Jenk. Why, would you have us run away?

Nich. No, but I would have you shake your heels.
Music, strike up.

They dance; Nicholas, *dancing, speaks stately and scurvily, the rest after the country fashion.*

Jenk. Hey! Lively, my lasses! Here's a turn for thee!
[*Exeunt.*]

[Sc. iii]

Wind horns. Enter Sir Charles, Sir Francis, Malby, Cranwell, Wendoll, Falconers, *and* Huntsmen.

Sir Cha. So! Well cast off! Aloft, aloft! Well flown!
Oh, now she takes her at the souse, and strikes her
Down to the earth, like a swift thunder clap.

Wen. She hath stroke ten angels out of my way.

Sir Fra. A hundred pounds from me.

Sir Cha. What! Falconer?

Falc. At hand, sir.

Sir Cha. Now she hath seized the fowl, and 'gins to plume her.
Rebeck her not; rather stand still and cherk her.

---

6 **crash** bout of revelry
7 **humor** temperament; **compendious** (probably he means comprehensive)
12 **serving courtiers** gentlemen
18 **horse-trick** (pun on homonym *whores*)
20 **crosspoint** dance step (with bawdy reference)
22 **comparisons** i.e., between masters and servants
25 **sudden** peremptory
26 **seditious** troublesome
31 **suddenly** immediately
34 **knave** (1) male servant; (2) rogue
36 **"Rogero"** a popular tune
37–8 **"The . . . World"** as "Sellenger's Round," another popular tune
41 **deserved a cushion** earned the right to some luxury
46 **"The Hay"** an especially physical and noisy dance
53 **"Put on Your Smock [woman's undergarment] a Monday"** also known as "Pretty Nancy"
54 **cleanly** adroitly (with a bawdy pun)
64 **s.d. *scurvily*** impolitely
iii.1 **s.d. *Wind*** blow
2 **at the souse** as the prey was rising from the ground
7 **plume her** pluck the feathers of its prey
8 **Rebeck** recall; **cherk** incite

So! seize her gets, her jesses, and her bells.
Away!
Sir Fra. My hawk killed, too.
Sir Cha. Aye, but 'twas at the querre,
Not at the mount like mine.
Sir Fra. Judgment, my masters.
Cran. Yours missed her at the ferre.
Wen. Ay, but our merlin first had plumed the fowl,
And twice renewed her from the river, too.
Her bells, Sir Francis, had not both one weight,
Nor was one semitune above the other;
Methinks these Milan bells do sound too full,
And spoil the mounting of your hawk.
Sir Cha. 'Tis lost.
Sir Fra. I grant it not. Mine likewise seized a fowl
Within her talents, and you saw her paws
Full of the feathers; both her petty singles
And her long singles gripped her more than other.
The terrials of her legs were stained with blood;
Not of the fowl only she did discomfit
Some of her feathers, but she broke away.
Come, come, your hawk is but a rifler.
Sir Cha. How?
Sir Fra. Aye, and your dogs are trindle-tails and curs.
Sir Cha. You stir my blood.
You keep not a good hound in all your kennel,
Nor one good hawk upon your perch.
Sir Fra. How, knight?
Sir Cha. So, knight? You will not swagger, sir?
Sir Fra. Why, say I did?
Sir Cha. Why, sir, I say you would gain as much by swagg'ring
As you have got by wagers on your dogs;
You will come short in all things.
Sir Fra. Not in this!
Now I'll strike home.
Sir Cha. Thou shalt to thy long home,
Or I will want my will.
Sir Fra. All they that love Sir Francis follow me.
Sir Cha. All that affect Sir Charles draw on my part.
Cran. On this side heaves my hand.
Wen. Here goes my heart.
They divide themselves.

Sir Charles, Cranwell, Falconer, *and* Huntsman *fight against* Sir Francis, Wendoll, *his* Falconer, *and* Huntsman, *and* Sir Charles *hath the better, and beats them away, killing both of* Sir Francis *his men.* [*Exeunt all except* Sir Charles.]

Sir Cha. My God! what have I done? what have I done?
My rage hath plunged into a sea of blood,
In which my soul lies drowned. Poor innocents,
For whom we are to answer. Well, 'tis done,
And I remain the victor. A great conquest,
When I would give this right hand, nay, this head,
To breathe in them new life whom I have slain.
Forgive me, God, 'twas in the heat of blood,
And anger quite removes me from myself;
It was not I, but rage, did this vile murder.
Yet I, and not my rage, must answer it.
Sir Francis Acton he is fled the field,
With him, all those that did partake his quarrel,
And I am left alone, with sorrow dumb,
And in my height of conquest, overcome.

Enter Susan.

Susan. Oh, God, my brother wounded among the dead;
Unhappy jest that in such earnest ends.
The rumor of this fear stretched to my ears,
And I am come to know if you be wounded.
Sir Cha. Oh, sister, sister, wounded at the heart.
Susan. My God forbid!
Sir Cha. In doing that thing which he forbade,
I am wounded, sister.
Susan. I hope not at the heart.
Sir Cha. Yes, at the heart.
Susan. Oh, God! A surgeon there!
Sir Cha. Call me a surgeon, sister, for my soul;
The sin of murder it hath pierced my heart,

9 **gets . . . jesses** leather straps attached to the hawk's legs
11 **at the querre** on the ground
12 **the mount** ascending
13 **ferre** opposite riverbank
14 **merlin** small falcon
15 **renewed** drove out by attack
17 **one . . . other** the bells were properly pitched a semitone apart
18 **Milan** city known for metalwork
21 **talents** talons
22 **petty singles** short claws
24 **terrials** probably *terrets*, rings enabling the jesses to be attached in the leash
24–6 **blood . . . away** our hawk drew blood, not just feathers, but the prey escaped
27 **rifler** hawk that only seizes feathers
28 **trindle-tails** low-bred dogs known by their curly tails
32 **swagger** pick a quarrel
37 **long home** grave
58 **jest** exploit; **earnest** (1) serious battle; (2) single combat
59 **rumor** news; **fear** feared happening; **stretched** reached

And made a wide wound there. But for these scratches,
They are nothing, nothing.
Susan. Charles, what have you done?
Sir Francis hath great friends, and will pursue you
Unto the utmost danger of the law.
Sir Cha. My conscience is become my enemy,
And will pursue me more than Acton can.
Susan. Oh, fly, sweet brother.
Sir Cha. Shall I fly from thee?
What, Sue, art weary of my company?
Susan. Fly from your foe.
Sir Cha. You, sister, are my friend,
And flying you, I shall pursue my end.
Susan. Your company is as my eyeball dear;
Being far from you, no comfort can be near.
Yet fly to save your life; what would I care
To spend my future age in black despair,
So you were safe? And yet to live one week
Without my brother Charles, through every cheek
My streaming tears would downwards run so rank
Till they could set on either side a bank,
And in the midst a channel; so my face
For two salt water brooks shall still find place.
Sir Cha. Thou shalt not weep so much, for I will stay
In spite of danger's teeth. I'll live with thee,
Or I'll not live at all. I will not sell
My country and my father's patrimony,
No, thy sweet sight, for a vain hope of life.

Enter Sheriff *with* Officers.

Sher. Sir Charles, I am made the unwilling instrument
Of your attach and apprehension.
I am sorry that the blood of innocent men
Should be of you exacted. It was told me
That you were guarded with a troop of friends,
And therefore I come armed.
Sir Cha. Oh, master Sheriff,
I came into the field with many friends,
But, see, they all have left me; only one
Clings to my sad misfortune, my dear sister.
I know you for an honest gentleman;
I yield my weapons and submit to you.
Convey me where you please.
Sher. To prison then,
To answer for the lives of these dead men.
Susan. Oh, God! Oh, God!
Sir Cha. Sweet sister, every strain
Of sorrow from your heart augments my pain.
Your grief abounds and hits against my breast.
Sher. Sir, will you go?
Sir Cha. Even where it likes you best.
[*Exeunt.*]

[Sc. iv]

Enter Master Frankford *in a study.*

Frank. How happy am I among other men
That in my mean estate embrace content.
I am a gentleman, and by my birth
Companion with a king; a king's no more.
I am possessed of many fair revenues,
Sufficient to maintain a gentleman.
Touching my mind, I am studied in all arts,
The riches of my thoughts, and of my time
Have been a good proficient. But the chief
Of all the sweet felicities on earth,
I have a fair, a chaste, and loving wife,
Perfection all, all truth, all ornament.
If man on earth may truly happy be,
Of these at once possessed, sure I am he.

Enter Nicholas.

Nich. Sir, there's a gentleman attends without to speak with you.
Frank. On horseback?
Nich. Aye, on horseback.
Frank. Entreat him to alight; I will attend him.
Knowest thou him, Nick?
Nich. I know him; his name's Wendoll.
It seems he comes in haste – his horse is booted
Up to the flank in mire, himself all spotted
And stained with plashing. Sure he rode in fear
Or for a wager: horse and man both sweat.
I ne'er saw two in such a smoking heat.

---

71 utmost danger full extent of punishment
77 end death
84 rank abundantly
87 still always
94 attach arrest
96 exacted shed
97 guarded protected
108 abounds overflows
iv.1 s.d. ***in a study*** in deep thought

2 mean modest
9 a good proficient i.e., put to good use
11 chaste virtuous
12 ornament qualities that confer beauty, grace, or honor
14 once i.e., the same time
21 booted covered
23 plashing splashing

Frank. Entreat him in; about it instantly.
[*Exit* Nicholas.]
This Wendoll I have noted, and his carriage
Hath pleased me much. By observation
I have noted many good deserts in him:
He's affable and seen in many things,
Discourses well, a good companion,
And though of small means, yet a gentleman
Of a good house, somewhat pressed by want.
I have preferred him to a second place
In my opinion and my best regard.

Enter Wendoll, Anne, *and* Nicholas.

Anne. Oh, Master Frankford, Master Wendoll here
Brings you the strangest news that e'er you heard.
Frank. What news, sweet wife? What news, good Master Wendoll?
Wen. You knew the match made 'twixt Sir Francis Acton
And Sir Charles Mountford.
Frank. True, with their hounds and hawks.
Wen. The matches were both played.
Frank. Ha! and which won?
Wen. Sir Francis, your wife's brother, had the worst
And lost the wager.
Frank. Why, the worse his chance;
Perhaps the fortune of some other day
Will change his luck.
Anne. Oh, but you hear not all.
Sir Francis lost, and yet was loath to yield;
In brief, the two knights grew to difference,
From words to blows, and so to banding sides,
Where valorous Sir Charles slew in his spleen
Two of your brother's men – his falconer
And his good huntsman, whom he loved so well.
More men were wounded, no more slain outright.
Frank. Now trust me, I am sorry for the knight;
But is my brother safe?
Wen. All whole and sound,
His body not being blemished with one wound.
But poor Sir Charles is to the prison led,
To answer at th' assize for them that's dead.
Frank. I thank your pains, sir; had the news been better,
Your will was to have brought it, Master Wendoll.
Sir Charles will find hard friends; his case is heinous,
And will be most severely censured on.
I am sorry for him. [*To Wendoll.*] Sir, a word with you:
I know you, sir, to be a gentleman
In all things, your possibilities but mean;
Please you to use my table and my purse.
They are yours.
Wen. Oh, Lord, sir, I shall never deserve it.
Frank. Oh, sir, disparage not your worth too much;
You are full of quality and fair desert.
Choose of my men which shall attend on you,
And he is yours. I will allow you, sir,
Your man, your gelding, and your table, all
At my own charge. Be my companion.
Wen. Master Frankford, I have oft been bound to you
By many favors; this exceeds them all
That I shall never merit your least favor.
But when your last remembrance I forget,
Heaven at my soul exact that weighty debt.
Frank. There needs no protestation, for I know you
Virtuous, and therefore grateful. Prithee, Nan,
Use him with all thy lovingest courtesy.
Anne. As far as modesty may well extend,
It is my duty to receive your friend.
Frank. To dinner. Come, sir, from this present day
Welcome to me for ever. Come, away.
[*Exeunt* Master Frankford, Wendoll, *and* Anne.]
Nich. I do not like this fellow by no means;
I never see him but my heart still earns.
'Zounds! I could fight with him, yet know not why;
The Devil and he are all one in my eye.

Enter Jenkin.

Jenk. Oh, Nick, what gentleman is that comes to lie at our house? My master allows him one to wait on him, and I believe it will fall to thy lot.

27 carriage conduct
30 seen accomplished
34 preferred promoted
48 banding forming
49 Where whereupon
57 assize county court (held periodically)
59 Your . . . it you would have chosen to bring us that
60 hard friends find support difficult to come by
61 censured on judged
64 possibilities resources
71 gelding horse; **table** meals
76 your last remembrance i.e., this latest kindness
79 Nan fond nickname for Anne (cf. use at xi.84, 101)
80 Use treat
86 earns curdles
87 'Zounds God's wounds (on the cross; a common oath)
90 lie lodge

Nich. I love my master – by these hilts I do –
But rather than I'll ever come to serve him,
I'll turn away my master.

Enter Sisly.

Sisly. Nicholas, where are you, Nicholas? You must come in, Nicholas, and help the young gentleman off with his boots.

Nich. If I pluck off his boots, I'll eat the spurs,
And they shall stick fast in my throat like burrs.

Exit.

Sisly. Then, Jenkin, come you.

Jenk. 'Tis no boot for me to deny it. My master hath given me a coat here, but he takes pains himself to brush it once or twice a day with a holly wand.

Sisly. Come, come, make haste, that you may wash your hands again and help to serve in dinner.

[*Exit.*]

Jenk. [*To the audience.*] You may see, my masters, though it be afternoon with you, 'tis but early days with us, for we have not dined yet. Stay but a little, I'll but go in and help to bear up the first course and come to you again presently.

Exit.

[Sc. v]

Enter Malby *and* Cranwell.

Mal. This is the sessions day; pray, can you tell me
How young Sir Charles hath sped? Is he acquit,
Or must he try the law's strict penalty?

Cran. He's cleared of all, 'spite of his enemies,
Whose earnest labors was to take his life;
But in this suit of pardon he hath spent
All the revenues that his father left him,
And he is now turned a plain countryman,
Reformed in all things. See, sir, here he comes.

Enter Sir Charles *and his* Keeper.

Keep. Discharge your fees, and you are then at freedom.

Sir Cha. Here, master Keeper, take the poor remainder
Of all the wealth I have. My heavy foes
Have made my purse light, but, alas, to me,
'Tis wealth enough that you have set me free.

Mal. God give you joy of your delivery;
I am glad to see you abroad, Sir Charles.

Sir Cha. The poorest knight in England, Master Malby.
My life hath cost me all the patrimony
My father left his son. Well, God forgive them
That are the authors of my penury.

Enter Shafton.

Shaf. Sir Charles, a hand, a hand – at liberty.
Now by the faith I owe, I am glad to see it.
What want you? Wherein may I pleasure you?

Sir Cha. Oh, me! Oh, most unhappy gentleman!
I am not worthy to have friends stirred up
Whose hands may help me in this plunge of want.
I would I were in Heaven, to inherit there
Th' immortal birthright which my Savior keeps,
And by no unthrift can be bought and sold;
For here on earth, what pleasures should we trust?

Shaf. To rid you from these contemplations,
Three hundred pounds you shall receive of me.
Nay, five for fail. Come, sir, the sight of gold
Is the most sweet receipt for melancholy
And will revive your spirits. You shall hold law
With your proud adversaries. Tush, let Frank Acton
Wage with knighthood-like expense with me,
And he will sink, he will. Nay, good Sir Charles,
Applaud your fortune, and your fair escape
From all these perils.

Sir Cha. Oh, sir, they have undone me.
Two thousand and five hundred pounds a year
My father at his death possessed me of,

92 **hilts** i.e., of the daggers he wears
93 **him** i.e., Wendoll
102 **boot** avail
103 **coat** his servant's livery
104–5 **to . . . holly wand** i.e., to give me a beating
113 **presently** after a short time
v.1 **sessions** i.e., the day the assizes meets
2 **sped** fared
3 **try** suffer
8 **turned a plain countryman** is no longer a landlord
9 **Reformed . . . things** changed in all circumstances
16 **abroad** at liberty
22 **owe** profess
26 **plunge of want** crisis of impoverishment
28 **immortal birthright** promise of eternal life (bliss)
29 **unthrift** (1) spendthrift; (2) unthriftiness
33 **for fail** (1) for security; (2) for good measure
34 **receipt** antidote
35 **hold law** engage in litigation
37 **wage** wager

All which the envious Acton made me spend,
And notwithstanding all this large expense,
I had much ado to gain my liberty;
And I have now only a house of pleasure,
With some five hundred pounds reserved
Both to maintain me and my loving sister.

Shaf. [*Aside.*] That must I have; it lies convenient for me.
If I can fasten but one finger on him,
With my full hand I'll grip him to the heart.
'Tis not for love I proffered him this coin,
But for my gain and pleasure. [*To Sir Charles.*] Come, Sir Charles,
I know you have need of money; take my offer.

Sir Cha. Sir, I accept it, and remain indebted
Even to the best of my unable power.
Come, gentlemen, and see it tendered down.

Exeunt.

[Sc. vi]

Enter Wendoll *melancholy.*

Wen. I am a villain if I apprehend
But such a thought; then to attempt the deed –
Slave, thou art damned without redemption.
I'll drive away this passion with a song.
A song! Ha, ha! A song, as if, fond man,
Thy eyes could swim in laughter, when thy soul
Lies drenched and drowned in red tears of blood.
I'll pray, and see if God within my heart
Plant better thoughts. Why, prayers are meditations,
And when I meditate – Oh, God, forgive me –
It is on her divine perfections.
I will forget her; I will arm myself
Not to entertain a thought of love to her;
And when I come by chance into her presence,
I'll hale these balls until my eyestrings crack
From being pulled and drawn to look that way.

Enter over the stage Frankford, Anne, *and* Nicholas.

Oh, God! Oh, God! with what a violence
I am hurried to my own destruction.
There goest thou the most perfectest man
That ever England bred a gentleman;
And shall I wrong his bed? Thou God of thunder,
Stay in Thy thoughts of vengeance and of wrath
Thy great almighty and all-judging hand
From speedy execution on a villain,
A villain and a traitor to his friend.

Enter Jenkin [*behind*].

Jenk. Did your worship call?

Wen. [*Not noticing Jenkin.*] He doth maintain me, he allows me largely
Money to spend –

Jenk. [*Aside.*] By my faith, so do not you me; I cannot get a cross of you.

Wen. My gelding and my man.

Jenk. [*Aside.*] That's Sorrel and I.

Wen. This kindness grows of no alliance 'twixt us.

Jenk. [*Aside.*] Nor is my service of any great acquaintance.

Wen. I never bound him to me by desert,
Of a mere stranger, a poor gentleman,
A man by whom in no kind he could gain!
He hath placed me in the height of all his thoughts,
Made me companion with the best and chiefest
In Yorkshire. He cannot eat without me,
Nor laugh without me. I am to his body
As necessary as his digestion,
And equally do make him whole or sick.
And shall I wrong this man? Base man! Ingrate!
Hast thou the power straight with thy gory hands
To rip thy image from his bleeding heart?
To scratch thy name from out the holy book
Of his remembrance, and to wound his name
That holds thy name so dear, or rend his heart
To whom thy heart was joined and knit together?
And yet I must. Then, Wendoll, be content;

43 **envious** malicious
46 **house of pleasure** a secondary or summer-house (i.e., not the manor house)
48 **Both to maintain** to maintain both
56 **unable** weakened
57 **tendered down** paid according to legal form
vi.1 s.d. ***melancholy*** thoughtful
1 **apprehend** conceive
5 **fond** foolish
15 **balls** eyeballs
27 **largely** generously
30 **cross** a coin (picturing a cross)
35 **desert** deserving
36 **Of** from; **mere** absolute
37 **kind** way
46 **thy** i.e., my
47 **thy name** my reputation

Thus villains, when they would, cannot repent.
Jenk. [*Aside.*] What a strange humor is my new master in. Pray God he be not mad. If he should be so, I should never have any mind to serve him in Bedlam. It may be he is mad for missing of me.
Wen. [*Seeing Jenkin.*] What, Jenkin? Where's your mistress?
Jenk. Is your worship married?
Wen. Why dost thou ask?
Jenk. Because you are my master, and if I have a mistress, I would be glad like a good servant to do my duty to her.
Wen. I mean, where's Mistress Frankford?
Jenk. Marry, sir, her husband is riding out of town, and she went very lovingly to bring him on his way to horse. Do you see, sir, here she comes, and here I go.
Wen. Vanish.

[*Exit* Jenkin.]

Enter Anne.

Anne. You are well met, sir. Now in troth my husband
Before he took horse had a great desire
To speak with you. We sought about the house,
Halloed into the fields, sent every way,
But could not meet you; therefore he enjoined me
To do unto you his most kind commends.
Nay, more, he wills you as you prize his love,
Or hold in estimation his kind friendship,
To make bold in his absence and command
Even as himself were present in the house;
For you must keep his table, use his servants,
And be a present Frankford in his absence.
Wen. I thank him for his love.
[*Aside.*] Give me a name, you, whose infectious tongues
Are tipped with gall and poison. As you would
Think on a man that had your father slain,
Murd'red thy children, made your wives base strumpets,
So call me, call me so! Print in my face
The most stigmatic title of a villain
For hatching treason to so true a friend.
Anne. Sir, you are much beholding to my husband;
You are a man most dear in his regard.
Wen. I am bound unto your husband and you too.
[*Aside.*] I will not speak to wrong a gentleman
Of that good estimation, my kind friend.
I will not! 'Zounds, I will not! I may choose,
And I will choose. Shall I be so misled?
Or shall I purchase to my father's crest
The motto of a villain? If I say
I will not do it, what thing can enforce me?
Who can compel me? What sad destiny
Hath such command upon my yielding thoughts?
I will not. Ha! some fury pricks me on;
The swift Fates drag me at their chariot wheel
And hurry me to mischief. Speak I must –
Injure myself, wrong her, deceive his trust.
Anne. Are you not well, sir, that you seem thus troubled?
There is sedition in your countenance.
Wen. And in my heart, fair angel, chaste and wise.
I love you. Start not, speak not, answer not.
I love you. Nay, let me speak the rest.
Bid me to swear, and I will call to record
The host of Heaven.
Anne. The host of Heaven forbid
Wendoll should hatch such a disloyal thought.
Wen. Such is my fate; to this suit I was born,
To wear rich Pleasure's crown, or Fortune's scorn.
Anne. My husband loves you.
Wen. I know it.
Anne. He esteems you
Even as his brain, his eyeball, or his heart.
Wen. I have tried it.
Anne. His purse is your exchequer, and his table
Doth freely serve you.
Wen. So I have found it.
Anne. Oh, with what face of brass, what brow of steel,
Can you unblushing speak this to the face
Of the espoused wife of so dear a friend?
It is my husband that maintains your state;
Will you dishonor him? I am his wife
That in your power hath left his whole affairs;
It is to me you speak?

56 Bedlam Bethlehem, the London hospital for the insane
65 Marry from reference to the Virgin; a common expletive
66 bring accompany
70 troth truth
73 Halloed called
74 meet i.e., meet with
75 commends compliments
80 keep i.e., preside over
88 stigmatic infamous
90 beholding indebted
98 villain i.e., villein, a serf whose family bore no crest
100 sad distressing
104 mischief evil
107 sedition internal strife
118 tried tested

Wen. Oh, speak no more,
For more than this I know and have recorded
Within the red-leaved table of my heart.
Fair, and of all beloved, I was not fearful
Bluntly to give my life into your hand,
And at one hazard all my earthly means.
Go, tell your husband; he will turn me off,
And I am then undone. I care not, I.
'Twas for your sake. Perchance in rage he'll kill me.
I care not; 'twas for you. Say I incur
The general name of villain through the world,
Of traitor to my friend. I care not, I.
Beggary, shame, death, scandal, and reproach –
For you I'll hazard all. What care I?
For you I'll live, and in your love I'll die.

Anne. You move me, sir, to passion and to pity;
The love I bear my husband is as precious
As my soul's health.

Wen. I love your husband, too,
And for his love I will engage my life.
Mistake me not, the augmentation
Of my sincere affection borne to you
Doth no whit lessen my regard of him.
I will be secret, lady, close as night,
And not the light of one small glorious star
Shall shine here in my forehead to bewray
That act of night.

Anne. [*Aside.*] What shall I say?
My soul is wand'ring and hath lost her way.
[*To him.*] Oh, Master Wendoll, Oh!

Wen. Sigh not, sweet saint,
For every sigh you breathe draws from my heart
A drop of blood.

Anne. [*Aside.*] I ne'er offended yet;
My fault, I fear, will in my brow be writ.
Women that fall not quite bereft of grace
Have their offenses noted in their face.
I blush and am ashamed. [*To him.*] O Master Wendoll,
Pray God I be not born to curse your tongue,
That hath enchanted me. This maze I am in
I fear will prove the labyrinth of sin.

Enter Nicholas [*behind*].

Wen. The path of pleasure and the gate to bliss,
Which on your lips I knock at with a kiss.
[*Kisses her.*]

Nich. [*Aside.*] I'll kill the rogue.

Wen. Your husband is from home, your bed's no blab –
Nay, look not down and blush.

[*Exeunt* Wendoll *and* Anne.]

Nich. 'Zounds, I'll stab.
Aye, Nick, was it thy chance to come just in the nick?
I love my master, and I hate that slave;
I love my mistress, but these tricks I like not.
My master shall not pocket up this wrong;
I'll eat my fingers first. [*Drawing his dagger.*]
What sayest thou, metal?
Does not the rascal Wendoll go on legs
That thou must cut off? Hath he not hamstrings
That thou must hock? Nay, metal, thou shalt stand
To all I say. I'll henceforth turn a spy,
And watch them in their close conveyances.
I never looked for better of that rascal
Since he came miching first into our house.
It is that Satan hath corrupted her,
For she was fair and chaste. I'll have an eye
In all their gestures. Thus I think of them:
If they proceed as they have done before,
Wendoll's a knave, my mistress is a whore.
Exit.

[Sc. vii]

Enter Sir Charles *and* Susan.

Sir Cha. Sister, you see we are driven to hard shift
To keep this poor house we have left unsold;
I am now enforced to follow husbandry,
And you to milk; and do we not live well?
Well, I thank God.

Susan. Oh, brother, here's a change,

129 table i.e., tablet, notebook
132 at one hazard put at all risk
142 passion anger
149 close secret
150 glorious boastful
151 bewray betray, expose
152 act of night adultery
155–6 every . . . blood a popular belief held that each sigh cost one's heart a drop of blood
162 maze (1) bewilderment; (2) dilemma
167 blab tell-tale
169 in the nick just in time
172 pocket up submit to
173 metal (1) dagger; (2) courage (mettle)
176 hock cut off
178 close conveyances secret communications
180 miching skulking
182 chaste monogamous; loyal
183 In for; **gestures** movements
vii.1 hard shift difficult expedients
3 husbandry farming

Since old Sir Charles died in our father's house.
Sir Cha. All things on earth thus change, some up, some down;
Content's a kingdom, and I wear that crown.

Enter Shafton *with a* Sergeant.

Shaf. Good morrow, good morrow, Sir Charles; what, with your sister
Plying your husbandry? Sergeant, stand off.
You have a pretty house here, and a garden,
And goodly ground about it. Since it lies
So near a lordship that I lately bought,
I would fain buy it of you. I will give you –
Sir Cha. Oh, pardon me; this house successively
Hath 'longed to me and my progenitors
Three hundred years. My great-great-grandfather,
He in whom first our gentle style began,
Dwelt here, and in this ground increased this molehill
Unto that mountain which my father left me.
Where he the first of all our house begun,
I now the last will end and keep this house,
This virgin title never yet deflowered
By any unthrift of the Mountfords' line.
In brief, I will not sell it for more gold
Than you could hide or pave the ground withal.
Shaf. Ha, ha! A proud mind and a beggar's purse.
Where's my three hundred pounds, beside the use?
I have brought it to an execution
By course of law. What, is my money ready?
Sir Cha. An execution, sir, and never tell me
You put my bond in suit? You deal extremely.
Shaf. Sell me the land and I'll acquit you straight.
Sir Cha. Alas, alas! 'Tis all trouble hath left me
To cherish me and my poor sister's life.
If this were sold, our names should then be quite
Razed from the bead-roll of gentility.
You see what hard shift we have made to keep it
Allied still to our own name. This palm you see
Labor hath gloved within; her silver brow,
That never tasted a rough winter's blast
Without a mask or fan, doth with a grace
Defy cold winter and his storms outface.
Susan. Sir, we feed sparing, and we labor hard,
We lie uneasy, to reserve to us
And our succession this small plot of ground.
Sir Cha. I have so bent my thoughts to husbandry
That I protest I scarcely can remember
What a new fashion is, how silk or satin
Feels in my hand. Why, pride is grown to us
A mere, mere stranger. I have quite forgot
The names of all that ever waited on me;
I cannot name ye any of my hounds,
Once from whose echoing mouths I heard all the music
That e'er my heart desired. What should I say?
To keep this place I have changed myself away.
Shaf. [*To the Sergeant.*] Arrest him at my suit. [*To Sir Charles.*]
Actions and actions
Shall keep thee in perpetual bondage fast.
Nay, more, I'll sue thee by a late appeal
And call thy former life in question.
The Keeper is my friend; thou shalt have irons,
And usage such as I'll deny to dogs.
Away with him!
Sir Cha. You are too timorous. But trouble is my master,
And I will serve him truly. My kind sister,
Thy tears are of no force to mollify
This flinty man. Go to my father's brother,
My kinsmen and allies; entreat them from me
To ransom me from this injurious man
That seeks my ruin.
Shaf. Come, irons, irons, away!
I'll see thee lodged far from the sight of day.
Exeunt. [*Manet* Susan.]

Enter Acton *and* Malby [*behind*].

Susan. My heart's so hardened with the frost of grief

8 **Content . . . crown** (proverbial)
9 **s.d. Sergeant** an officer charged with the arrest of offenders and summoning persons before court
13 **lordship** i.e., estate
14 **fain** like to
16 **'longed** belonged
18 **gentle style** rank of gentleman
23 **title** claim; legal right of possession
28 **use** interest (on the principal)
29 **execution** legal seizure of goods (or of person defaulting his bond with Shafton)
32 **put . . . suit** set law in motion for foreclosure; **extremely** severely
35 **cherish** support
37 **Razed** erased; **bead-roll** list
44 **sparing** i.e., sparingly
45 **reserve** preserve
46 **succession** descendants
57 **Actions** i.e., legal actions
59 **late appeal** revived charge (of killing Sir Francis's men)
61 **irons** chains and locks
64 **timorous** fearful (of my resisting you)

Death cannot pierce it through. Tyrant too fell!
So lead the fiends condemned souls to Hell.
Sir Fra. Again to prison! Malby, hast thou seen
A poor slave better tortured? Shall we hear
The music of his voice cry from the grate
"Meat for the Lord's sake"? No, no, yet I am not
Throughly revenged. They say he hath a pretty wench
Unto his sister. Shall I, in mercy sake
To him and to his kindred, bribe the fool
To shame herself by lewd, dishonest lust?
I'll proffer largely, but, the deed being done,
I'll smile to see her base confusion.
Mal. Methinks, Sir Francis, you are full revenged
For greater wrongs than he can proffer you.
See where the poor sad gentlewoman stands.
Sir Fra. Ha, ha! Now I will flout her poverty,
Deride her fortunes, scoff her base estate;
My very soul the name of Mountford hates.
But stay, my heart. Oh, what a look did fly
To strike my soul through with thy piercing eye.
I am enchanted, all my spirits are fled,
And with one glance my envious spleen struck dead.
Susan. [*Seeing them.*] Acton, that seeks our blood! *Runs away.*
Sir Fra. Oh, chaste and fair!
Mal. Sir Francis! Why, Sir Francis; 'zounds, in a trance?
Sir Francis, what cheer, man? Come, come, how is't?
Sir Fra. Was she not fair? Or else this judging eye
Cannot distinguish beauty.
Mal. She was fair.
Sir Fra. She was an angel in a mortal's shape,
And ne'er descended from old Mountford's line.
But soft, soft, let me call my wits together.
A poor, poor wench, to my great adversary
Sister, whose very souls denounce stern war
One against other. How now, Frank, turned fool
Or madman, whether? But no master of
My perfect senses and directest wits.
Then why should I be in this violent humor
Of passion and of love? and with a person
So different every way, and so opposed
In all contractions and still-warring actions?
Fie, fie, how I dispute against my soul.
Come, come, I'll gain her, or in her fair quest
Purchase my soul free and immortal rest.
Exeunt.

[Sc. viii]

Enter 3 or 4 Servingmen [*including* Spiggot *the* Butler *and* Nicholas], *one with a voider and a wooden knife to take away all; another the salt and bread; another the tablecloth and napkins; another the carpet.* Jenkin *with two lights after them.*

Jenk. So, march in order and retire in battle 'ray. My master and the guests have supped already. All's taken away. Here, now spread for the servingmen in the hall. Butler, it belongs to your office.

Spig. I know it, Jenkin. What do you call the gentleman that supped there to-night?

Jenk. Who, my master?

Spig. No, no, Master Wendoll, he is a daily guest; I mean the gentleman that came but this afternoon.

Jenk. His name is Master Cranwell. God's light! Hark, within there, my master calls to lay more billets on the fire. Come, come! Lord, how we that are in office here in the house are troubled! One spread the carpet in the parlor and stand ready to snuff the lights; the rest be ready to prepare their stomachs. More lights in the hall there. Come, Nicholas.

[*Exeunt. Manet* Nicholas.]

Nich. I cannot eat, but had I Wendoll's heart
I would eat that; the rogue grows impudent.
Oh, I have seen such vild, notorious tricks

---

73 **fell** cruel, ruthless
77 **grate** prison bars
79 **wench** maiden
82 **dishonest** dishonorable, unchaste
83 **largely** generously, attractively
84 **base confusion** degrading reason
94 **envious spleen** malicious anger
102 **soft, soft** i.e., wait a moment
104 **denounce** declare
106 **whether** which
111 **contractions** dealings
viii.1 s.d. ***voider*** receptacle for wastes
1 **'ray** array
11 **God's light!** (common oath)
13 **billets** thick pieces of wood
14 **office** service
15 **spread the carpet** (as a table covering)
17 **stomachs** appetites
21 **vild** vile

Ready to make my eyes dart from my head.
I'll tell my master, by this air I will;
Fall what may fall, I'll tell him. Here he comes.

Enter Frankford, *as it were brushing the crumbs from his clothes with a napkin, and newly risen from supper.*

Frank. Nicholas, what make you here? Why are not you
At supper in the hall there with your fellows?
Nich. Master, I stayed your rising from the board
To speak with you.
Frank. Be brief, then, gentle Nicholas,
My wife and guests attend me in the parlor.
Why dost thou pause? Now, Nicholas, you want money,
And unthrift-like would eat into your wages
Ere you have earned it. Here's, sir, half a crown;
Play the good husband, and away to supper.
Nich. [*Aside.*] By this hand, an honorable gentleman. I will not see him wronged. [*To him.*] Sir, I have served you long; you entertained me seven years before your beard.
You knew me, sir, before you knew my mistress.
Frank. What of this, good Nicholas?
Nich. I never was a make-bate or a knave;
I have no fault but one – I am given to quarrel,
But not with women. I will tell you, master,
That which will make your heart leap from your breast,
Your hair to startle from your head, your ears to tingle.
Frank. What preparation's this to dismal news?
Nich. 'Sblood, sir, I love you better than your wife –
[*Frankford threatens him.*] I'll make it good.
Frank. Thou art a knave, and I have much ado
With wonted patience to contain my rage
And not to break thy pate. Thou art a knave.
I'll turn you with your base comparisons
Out of my doors.
Nich. Do, do. There's not room for Wendoll and me too
Both in one house. Oh, master, master
That Wendoll is a villain.
Frank. [*Striking him.*] Aye, saucy!
Nich. Strike, strike,
Do strike; yet hear me. I am no fool;
I know a villain when I see him act
Deeds of a villain. Master, master, that base slave
Enjoys my mistress and dishonors you.
Frank. Thou hast killed me with a weapon
Whose sharp'ned point hath pricked quite
Through and through my shivering heart.
Drops of cold sweat sit dangling on my hairs
Like morning's dew upon the golden flowers,
And I am plunged into a strange agony.
What didst thou say? If any word that touched
His credit or her reputation,
It is as hard to enter my belief
As Dives into Heaven.
Nich. I can gain nothing.
They are two that never wronged me.
I knew before 'twas but a thankless office,
And perhaps as much as is my service or my life
Is worth. All this I know, but this and more,
More by a thousand dangers could not hire me
To smother such a heinous wrong from you.
I saw, and I have said.
Frank. [*Aside.*] 'Tis probable;
Though blunt, yet he is honest.
Though I durst pawn my life, and on their faith
Hazard the dear salvation of my soul,
Yet in my trust I may be too secure.
May this be true? Oh, may it? Can it be?
Is it by any wonder possible?
Man, woman, what thing mortal may we trust
When friends and bosom wives prove so unjust?
[*To him.*] What instance hast thou of this strange report?
Nich. Eyes, eyes.
Frank. Thy eyes may be deceived I tell thee,
For should an angel from the heavens drop down
And preach this to me that thyself hast told,

25 **make** do
27 **stayed** waited until
29 **attend** await
30 **want** lack
31 **unthrift** spendthrift; **eat into** borrow against
32 **Ere** before
33 **husband** i.e., husband (save or manage) your money
36 **entertained** employed
41 **make-bate** mischief-maker; **knave** rascal
45 **startle** start, stand up
47 **'Sblood** God's blood (at the crucifixion; a common oath)
48 **I'll . . . good** I can justify what I say
50 **wonted** accustomed
51 **pate** head
60 **Enjoys** has sexual relations with
68 **credit** good name, honor
70 **Dives** popular name for a rich man (cf. Luke 16)
81 **too secure** overconfident
85 **unjust** faithless
86 **instance** evidence

He should have much ado to win belief,
In both their loves I am so confident.
Nich. Shall I discourse the same by circumstance?
Frank. No more; to supper, and command your fellows
To attend us and the strangers. Not a word;
I charge thee on thy life, be secret then,
For I know nothing.
Nich. I am dumb,
And now that I have eased my stomach,
I will go fill my stomach. [*Exit.*]
Frank. Away, be gone.
She is well born, descended nobly;
Virtuous her education; her repute
Is in the general voice of all the country.
Honest and fair; her carriage, her demeanor
In all her actions that concern the love
To me her husband, modest, chaste, and godly.
Is all this seeming gold plain copper?
But he, that Judas that hath borne my purse,
And sold me for a sin – oh, God, oh, God,
Shall I put up these wrongs? No. Shall I trust
The bare report of this suspicious groom
Before the double guilt, the well-hatched ore
Of their two hearts? No, I will loose these thoughts;
Distraction I will banish from my brow
And from my looks exile sad discontent.
Their wonted favors in my tongue shall flow;
Till I know all, I'll nothing seem to know.
Lights and a table there. Wife, Master Wendoll,
And gentle Master Cranwell –

Enter Anne, Master Wendoll, Master Cranwell, Nicholas, *and* Jenkin, *with cards, carpet, stools, and other necessaries.*

Frank. Oh, you are a stranger, Master Cranwell, you,
And often balk my house; faith, you are a churl.
Now we have supped, a table and to cards.
Jenk. A pair of cards, Nicholas, and a carpet to cover the table.
Where's Sisly with her counters and her box? Candles and candlesticks there! [*Enter* Sisly *and a* Servingman *with counters and candles.*] Fie, we have such a household of serving creatures! Unless it be Nick and I, there's not one among them all can say "bo" to a goose. [*To Nicholas.*] Well said, Nick.

They spread a carpet, set down lights and cards. [*Exeunt all the* Servants *except* Nicholas.]

Anne. Come, Master Frankford, who shall take my part?
Frank. Marry, that will I, sweet wife.
Wen. No, by my faith, sir, when you are together
I sit out; it must be Mistress Frankford
And I, or else it is no match.
Frank. I do not like that match.
Nich. [*Aside.*] You have no reason, marry, knowing all.
Frank. 'Tis no great matter, neither. Come, Master Cranwell.
Shall you and I take them up?
Cran. At your pleasure, sir.
Frank. I must look to you, Master Wendoll,
For you will be playing false. Nay,
So will my wife, too.
Nich. [*Aside.*] Aye, I will be sworn she will.
Anne. Let them that are taken playing false forfeit the set.
Frank. Content. [*Aside.*] It shall go hard, but I'll take you.
Cran. Gentlemen, what shall our game be?
Wen. Master Frankford, you play best at noddy.
Frank. You shall not find it so; [*Aside.*] indeed you shall not!
Anne. I can play at nothing so well as double ruff.
Frank. If Master Wendoll and my wife be together,

---

92 **discourse** relate; **by circumstance** in detail
94 **strangers** guests
97 **eased my stomach** got this matter out
107 **Judas . . . purse** John claims Judas held the money-bag (cf. John 13: 29); cf. xiii.72
109 **put up** accept, submit to
110 **groom** personal servant
111 **ore** golden behavior (play on guilt/gilt)
112 **loose** be free of
115 **wonted favors** usual kindnesses
120 **balk** pass by; **churl** base fellow (in behavior, not rank)
122 **pair** pack
123 **counters . . . box** means with which to keep score
128 **say "bo" to a goose** are capable of the simplest task (proverbial)
129 **said** done
130 **take my part** be my partner
138 **take them up** play against them
140 **playing false** (1) at cards; (2) with my wife
142 **set** game
143 **take you** find you out
145 **noddy** (1) the card game; (2) fool, cuckold
147 **double ruff** (1) a different card game similar to whist; (2) *double* as deceitful

There's no playing against them at double hand.
Nich. I can tell you, sir, the game that
Master Wendoll is best at.
Wen. What game is that, Nick?
Nich. Marry, sir, knave out of doors.
Wen. She and I will take you at lodam.
Anne. Husband, shall we play at saint?
Frank. [*Aside.*] My saint's turned devil;
[*To her.*] No, we'll none of saint. You're best at new-cut, Wife; [*Aside.*] you'll play at that!
Wen. If you play at new-cut,
I am soonest hitter of any here, for a wager.
Frank. [*Aside.*] 'Tis me they play on. Well, you may draw out,
For all your cunning; 'twill be to your shame.
I'll teach you at your new-cut a new game. [*To them.*] Come, come.
Cran. If you cannot agree upon the game, to post and pair.
Wen. We shall be soonest pairs, and my good host,
When he comes late home, he must kiss the post.
Frank. Whoever wins, it shall be to thy cost.
Cran. Faith, let it be vide-ruff, and let's make honors.
Frank. If you make honors, one thing let me crave:
Honor the king and queen; except the knave.
Wen. Well, as you please for that. Lift who shall deal.
Anne. The least in sight. What are you, Master Wendoll?
Wen. [*Cutting the cards.*] I am a knave.
Nich. [*Aside.*] I'll swear it.
Anne. [*Cutting.*] I a queen?
Frank. [*Aside.*] A quean thou should'st say; [*To them.*] well, the cards are mine.
They are the grossest pair that e'er I felt.
Anne. Shuffle, I'll cut. [*Aside.*] Would I had never dealt!
Frank. [*Deals.*] I have lost my dealing.
Wen. Sir, the fault's in me.
This queen I have more than my own, you see
Give me the stock. [*Deals.*]
Frank. My mind's not on my game;
[*Aside.*] Many a deal I have lost, the more's your shame.
[*To them.*] You have served me a bad trick, Master Wendoll.
Wen. Sir, you must take your lot. To end this strife,
I know I have dealt better with your wife.
Frank. [*Aside.*] Thou hast dealt falsely, then.
Anne. What's trumps?
Wen. Hearts. Partner, I rub.
Frank. [*Aside.*] Thou robbest me of my soul, of her chaste love;
In thy false dealing thou hast robbed my heart.
Booty you play; I like a loser stand,
Having no heart, or here or in my hand.
[*To them.*] I will give o'er the set; I am not well
Come, who will hold my cards?
Anne. Not well, sweet Master Frankford?
Alas, what ail you? 'Tis some sudden qualm.
Wen. How long have you been so, Master Frankford?
Frank. Sir, I was lusty and I had my health,
But I grew ill when you began to deal.
Take hence this table.
[*The* Servants *enter and remove the table, cards, &c.*]
Gentle Master Cranwell,

---

149 double hand (1) when partners; (2) at duplicity
151 knave out of doors (1) a card game; (2) a reference to Wendoll; **lodam** (1) a card game; (2) translates (from the Italian) "load the ass"
152 saint (1) cent, a card game in which the winner is the first to reach 100 points; (2) pun
153 new-cut (1) card game; (2) bawdy pun
155 hitter scorer
156 draw out (1) their cards; (2) Frankford's suspicions
159 post and pair a card game with three cards for each player (with reference to the sexual triangle)
161 kiss the post [doorpost] i.e., to be left out
163 vide-ruff variant game of ruff with vying or backing trump; perhaps a sense also of vying for Anne (who is presumably wearing a ruff); **honors** the four highest trumps (ace and face cards)
165 except exclude
166 Lift cut; **deal** (with a sexual pun)
167 least in sight person with lowest card deals (puns on Wendoll as from the lowest class at the table)
169 quean harlot; adulteress
170 grossest pair crudest pack (of cards, but also of remarks); **felt** (1) handled; (2) tested
171 dealt (1) the cards; (2) sexually
172 lost my dealing made a mistake in my dealing
173 stock part of pack that remains undealt
175 trick (1) a turn in cards; (2) with his wife
180 rub (1) take all the cards of a single suit; (2) annoy, irritate; (3) sexual contact
183 Booty falsely (to play booty is to play with the intention of losing)
185 give . . . set give up the game
188 qualm (1) illness; (2) sinking feeling of certainty
190 lusty strong
191 deal (1) cards; (2) adultery

You are welcome; see your chamber at your pleasure.
I am sorry that this megrim takes me so
I cannot sit and bear you company.
Jenkin, some lights, and show him to his chamber.

[*Exeunt* Cranwell *and* Jenkin.]

Anne. A night gown for my husband, quickly there.

[*Enter a* Servant *with a gown, and exit.*]

It is some rheum or cold.
Wen. Now, in good faith,
This illness you have got by sitting late
Without your gown.
Frank. I know it, Master Wendoll.
Go, go to bed, lest you complain like me.
Wife, prithee wife, into my bedchamber.
The night is raw and cold and rheumatic.
Leave me my gown and light; I'll walk away my fit.
Wen. Sweet sir, good night.
Frank. Myself good night.

[*Exit* Wendoll.]

Anne. Shall I attend you, husband?
Frank. No, gentle wife.
Thou'lt catch cold in thy head; prithee, begone, sweet,
I'll make haste to bed.
Anne. No sleep will fasten
On mine eyes, you know, until you come.
Frank. Sweet Nan, I prithee, go.

[*Exit* Anne.]

[*To Nicholas.*] I have bethought me; get me by degrees
The keys of all my doors, which I will mold
In wax, and take their fair impression,
To have by them new keys. This being compassed,
At a set hour a letter shall be brought me,
And when they think they may securely play,
They are nearest to danger. Nick, I must rely
Upon thy trust and faithful secrecy.
Nich. Build on my faith.
Frank. To bed then, not to rest;
Care lodges in my brain, grief in my breast.

Exeunt.

[Sc. ix]

Enter Susan, Old Mountford, Sandy, Roder, *and* Tydy.

[*Old*]*Mount.* You say my nephew is in great distress –
Who brought it to him but his own lewd life?
I cannot spare a cross. I must confess
He was my brother's son; why, niece, what then?
This is no world in which to pity men.
Susan. I was not born a beggar, though his extremes
Enforce this language from me; I protest
No fortune of mine could lead my tongue
To this base key. I do beseech you, uncle,
For the name's sake, for Christianity,
Nay, for God's sake, to pity his distress.
He is denied the freedom of the prison,
And in the hole is laid with men condemned;
Plenty he hath of nothing but of irons,
And it remains in you to free him thence.
[*Old*]*Mount.* Money I cannot spare; men should take heed.
He lost my kindred when he fell to need.

Exit.

Susan. Gold is but earth; thou earth enough shalt have
When thou hast once took measure of thy grave.
You know me, Master Sandy, and my suit.
Sandy. I knew you, lady, when the old man lived;
I knew you ere your brother sold his land.
Then you were Mistress Sue, tricked up in jewels;
Then you sung well, played sweetly on the flute;
But now I neither know you nor your suit.

[*Exit.*]

Susan. You, Master Roder, were my brother's tenant:
Rent-free he placed you on that wealthy farm
Of which you are possessed.
Roder. True, he did;
And have I not there dwelt still for his sake?
I have some business now, but without doubt

---

194 megrim migraine headache
198 rheum headcold; chill
203 rheumatic likely to cause headcolds
205 Myself my dear (intimate) friend; both a pun and sarcasm
214 compassed accomplished
ix.2 lewd wicked
3 cross small coin
10 name's family name's
12 freedom of the prison right to roam within prison walls
13 hole dungeon
17 kindred kindness; relationship
21 old man her father
23 tricked fashionably wearing

They that have hurled him in will help him out.
Exit.

Susan. Cold comfort still. What say you, cousin Tydy?

Tydy. I say this comes of roisting, swagg'ring.
Call me not cousin; each man for himself!
Some men are born to mirth and some to sorrow;
I am no cousin unto them that borrow.
Exit.

Susan. Oh, Charity, why art thou fled to Heaven,
And left all things on this earth uneven?
Their scoffing answers I will ne'er return,
But to myself his grief in silence mourn.

Enter Sir Francis *and* Malby.

Sir Fra. She is poor; I'll therefore tempt her
With this gold.
Go, Malby, in my name deliver it,
And I will stay thy answer.

Mal. Fair Mistress, as I understand your grief
Doth grow from want, so I have here in store
A means to furnish you, a bag of gold
Which to your hands I freely tender you.

Susan. I thank you, Heavens; I thank you, gentle sir!
God make me able to requite this favor.

Mal. This gold Sir Francis Acton sends by me,
And prays you &c.

Susan. Acton!
Oh, God, that name I am born to curse.
Hence, bawd; hence, broker! See, I spurn his gold;
My honor never shall for gain be sold.

Sir Fra. Stay, lady, stay!

Susan. From you I'll posting hie,
Even as the doves from feathered eagles fly.
[*Exit.*]

Sir Fra. She hates my name, my face. How should I woo?
I am disgraced in everything I do.
The more she hates me and disdains my love,
The more I am rapt in admiration
Of her divine and chaste perfections.
Woo her with gifts I cannot, for all gifts
Sent in my name she spurns. With looks I cannot,
For she abhors my sight. Nor yet with letters,
For none she will receive. How then? how then?
Well, I will fasten such a kindness on her
As shall o'ercome her hate and conquer it.
Sir Charles, her brother, lies in execution
For a great sum of money; and, besides,
The appeal is sued still for my huntsmen's death,
Which only I have power to reverse.
In her I'll bury all my hate of him.
Go seek the Keeper, Malby; bring me to him.
To save his body, I his debts will pay;
To save his life, I his appeal will stay.
Exeunt.

[Sc. x]

Enter Sir Charles *in prison, with irons; his feet bare, his garments all ragged and torn.*

Sir Cha. Of all on the earth's face most miserable,
Breathe in the hellish dungeon thy laments.
Thus like a slave ragged, like a felon gyved –
That hurls thee headlong to this base estate.
Oh, unkind uncle! Oh, my friends ingrate!
Unthankful kinsmen! Mountfords all too base,
To let thy name lie fettered in disgrace.
A thousand deaths here in this grave I die.
Fear, hunger, sorrow, cold – all threat my death
And join together to deprive my breath.
But that which most torments me, my dear sister,
Hath left to visit me, and from my friends
Hath brought no hopeful answer; therefore I
Divine they will not help my misery.
If it be so, shame, scandal, and contempt
Attend their covetous thoughts, need make their graves.
Usurers they live, and may they die like slaves.

---

32 **Cold comfort** little relief (proverbial)
33 **roisting** reveling
34 **cousin** close friend or relation
38 **uneven** unjust
39 **return** (1) tell her brother; (2) respond to
43 **stay** wait for
45 **store** plentiful supply
51 **&c** (may indicate stage business, such as whispering)
53 **broker** procurer, pander
55 **posting hie** leaving in haste
68 **in execution** imprisoned
70 **appeal . . . death** (he has still levied charges against Charles for the deaths during the hunting)
75 **stay** withhold; remove
x.3 **gyved** shackled
5 **unkind** (1) unnatural; (2) denying kinship; **ingrate** ungrateful
9 **threat** threaten
12 **left** ceased

Enter Keeper.

Keep. Knight, be of comfort, for I bring thee freedom
From all thy troubles.
Sir Cha. Then I am doomed to die;
Death is th'end of all calamity.
Keep. Live!
Your appeal is stayed, the execution
Of all your debts discharged, your creditors
Even to the utmost penny satisfied,
In sign whereof your shackles I knock off.
You are not left so much indebted to us
As for your fees; all is discharged, all paid.
Go freely to your house or where you please;
After long miseries embrace your ease.
Sir Cha. Thou grumblest out the sweetest music to me
That ever organ played. Is this a dream?
Or do my waking senses apprehend
The pleasing taste of these applausive news?
Slave that I was, to wrong such honest friends,
My loving kinsmen and my near allies.
Tongue, I will bite thee for the scandal breath
Against such faithful kinsmen; they are all
Composed of pity and compassion,
Of melting charity, and of moving ruth.
That which I spake before was in my rage;
They are my friends, the mirrors of this age,
Bounteous and free. The noble Mountfords' race
Ne'er bred a covetous thought or humor base.

Enter Susan.

Susan. I can no longer stay from visiting
My woeful brother; while I could I kept
My hapless tidings from his hopeful ear.
Sir Cha. Sister, how much am I indebted to thee
And to thy travail!
Susan. What, at liberty?
Sir Cha. Thou seest I am, thanks to thy industry.
Oh, unto which of all my courteous friends
Am I thus bound? My uncle Mountford, he
Even of an infant loved me; was it he?
So did my cousin Tydy; was it he?
So Master Roder; Master Sandy, too.
Which of all these did this high kindness do?
Susan. Charles, can you mock me in your poverty,
Knowing your friends deride your misery?
Now I protest I stand so much amazed
To see your bonds free and your irons knocked off
That I am rapt into a maze of wonder,
The rather for I know not by what means
This happiness hath chanced.
Sir Cha. Why, by my uncle,
My cousins, and my friends; who else, I pray,
Would take upon them all my debts to pay?
Susan. Oh, brother, they are men all of flint,
Pictures of marble, and as void of pity
As chased bears. I begged, I sued, I kneeled,
Laid open all your griefs and miseries,
Which they derided. More than that, denied us
A part in their alliance, but in pride
Said that our kindred with our plenty died.
Sir Cha. Drudges! Too much! What, did they? Oh, known evil:
Rich fly the poor as good men shun the Devil.
Whence should my freedom come? Of whom alive,
Saving of those, have I deserved so well?
Guess, sister, call to mind, remember me.
These I have raised, these follow the world's guise,
Whom, rich in honor, they in woe despise.
Susan. My wits have lost themselves; let's ask the Keeper.
Sir Cha. Jailer!!
Keep. At hand, sir.
Sir Cha. Of courtesy resolve me one demand –
What was he took the burden of my debts
From off my back, stayed my appeal to death,
Discharged my fees, and brought me liberty?
Keep. A courteous knight, one called Sir Francis Acton.
Susan. Acton!
Sir Cha. Ha! Acton! Oh, me, more distressed in this
Than all my troubles. Hale me back,
Double my irons, and my sparing meals
Put into halves, and lodge me in a dungeon

21 **stayed** lifted
32 **applausive** agreeable
35 **scandal breath** scandalous talk
38 **ruth** compassion
40 **mirrors** models, exemplars
41 **free** i.e., generous
42 **humor** disposition
45 **hapless** unfortunate
47 **travail** labor
65 **Pictures** statues
66 **chased** (1) hunted; (2) tormented (as in bearbaiting)
69 **alliance** kinship
71 **Drudges** slaves
75 **remember** remind
76 **guise** manner
80 **resolve . . . demand** answer me one question
87 **Hale** haul

More deep, more dark, more cold, more comfortless.
By Acton freed! Not all thy manacles
Could fetter so my heels as this one word
Hath thralled my heart, and it must now lie bound
In more strict prison than thy stony jail.
I am not free. I go but under bail.

Keep. My charge is done, sir, now I have my fees;
As we get little, we will nothing leese.

Exit.

Sir Cha. By Acton freed, my dangerous opposite.
Why, to what end? or what occasion? Ha!
Let me forget the name of enemy
And with indifference balance this high favor. Ha!

Susan. [*Aside.*] His love to me, upon my soul 'tis so;
That is the root from whence these strange things grow.

Sir Cha. [*Aside.*] Had this proceeded from my father, he
That by the law of nature is most bound
In offices of love, it had deserved
My best employment to requite that grace.
Had it proceeded from my friends, or him,
From them this action had deserved my life.
And from a stranger more, because from such
There is less execution of good deeds.
But he, nor father, nor ally, nor friend,
More than a stranger, both remote in blood
And in his heart opposed my enemy,
That this high bounty should proceed from him –
Oh, there I lose myself. What should I say?
What think, what do, his bounty to repay?

Susan. You wonder, I am sure, whence this strange kindness
Proceeds in Acton. I will tell you, brother:
He dotes on me and oft hath sent me gifts,
Letters, and tokens; I refused them all.

Sir Cha. I have enough; though poor, my heart is set
In one rich gift to pay back all my debt.

Exeunt.

[Sc. xi]

Enter Frankford *with a letter in his hand, and* Nicholas *with keys.*

Frank. This is the night, and I must play the touch,
To try two seeming angels. Where's my keys?

Nich. They are made according to your mold in wax.
I bade the smith be secret, gave him money,
And there they are. [*Reminding Frankford.*] The letter, sir.

Frank. True, take it; there it is.
And when thou seest me in my pleasantest vein
Ready to sit to supper, bring it me.

Nich. I'll do't; make no more question but I'll do't.

Exit.

Enter Anne, Cranwell, Wendoll, *and* Jenkin.

Anne. Sirra, 'tis six o'clock already struck;
Go bid them spread the cloth and serve in supper.

Jenk. It shall be done forsooth, mistress. Where is Spiggot the butler to give us out salt and trenchers?

[*Exit.*]

Wen. We that have been a-hunting all the day
Come with prepared stomachs, Master Frankford;
We wish'd you at our sport.

Frank. My heart
Was with you, and my mind was on you;
Fie, Master Cranwell, you are still thus sad.
A stool, a stool! Where's Jenkin, and where's Nick?
'Tis supper time at least an hour ago.
What's the best news abroad?

Wen. I know none good.

Frank. [*Aside.*] But I know too much bad.

Enter [Spiggot *the*] Butler *and* Jenkin *with a tablecloth, bread, trenchers, and salt* [, *then exeunt*].

Cran. Methinks, sir, you might have that interest

---

93 thralled held captive
97 leese lose, be deprived of
98 opposite enemy
99 occasion (1) opportunity; (2) purpose
101 indifference impartiality; **balance** weigh
107 employment endeavor
108 him i.e., his father
111 execution performance
118 strange kindness (theme that here links underplot to overplot; in both, men's passions seem unaccountable)

xi.1 touch (1) tester; (2) touchstone to determine gold or lack of it in angels as coins
2 seeming apparent
4 smith locksmith
12 forsooth in truth
13 trenchers wooden plates
15 prepared stomachs good appetites
18 Fie (expression of reproach)
23 interest (1) concern; (2) influence

In your wife's brother to be more remiss
In this hard dealing against poor Sir Charles,
Who, as I hear, lies in York Castle, needy,
And in great want.
Frank. Did not more weighty business of my own
Hold me away, I would have labored peace
Betwixt them, with all care; indeed I would, sir.
Anne. I'll write unto my brother earnestly
In that behalf.
Wen. A charitable deed,
And will beget the good opinion of all
Your friends that love you, Mistress Frankford.
Frank. That's you for one; I know you love Sir Charles.
[*Aside.*] And my wife too well.
Wen. He deserves the love
Of all true gentlemen; be yourselves judge.
Frank. But supper, ho! Now as thou lovest me, Wendoll,
Which I am sure thou dost, be merry, pleasant,
And frolic it to-night. Sweet Master Cranwell,
Do you the like. Wife, I protest, my heart
Was ne'er more bent on sweet alacrity.
Where be those lazy knaves to serve in supper?

Enter Nicholas.

Nich. Sir, here's a letter.
Frank. Whence comes it? and who brought it?
Nich. A stripling that below attends your answer,
And as he tells me it is sent from York.
Frank. Have him into the cellar; let him taste a cup of
Our March beer. Go, make him drink.
[*Reads the letter.*]
Nich. I'll make him drunk, if he be a Trojan.
[*Exit.*]
Frank. My boots and spurs! Where's Jenkin? God forgive me,
How I neglect my business. Wife, look here;
I have a matter to be tried to-morrow
By eight o'clock, and my attorney writes me
I must be there betimes with evidence,
Or it will go against me. Where's my boots?

Enter Jenkin *with boots and spurs.*

Anne. I hope your business craves no such dispatch
That you must ride to-night.
Wen. [*Aside.*] I hope it doth.
Frank. God's me! No such dispatch?
Jenkin, my boots. Where's Nick? Saddle my roan,
And the gray dapple for himself. Content ye,
It much concerns me. [*Exit* Jenkin.] Gentle Master Cranwell
And Master Wendoll, in my absence use
The very ripest pleasure of my house.
Wen. Lord, Master Frankford, will you ride to-night?
The ways are dangerous.
Frank. Therefore will I ride
Appointed well, and so shall Nick, my man.
Anne. I'll call you up by five o'clock to-morrow.
Frank. No, by my faith, wife, I'll not trust to that;
'Tis not such easy rising in a morning
From one I love so dearly. No, by my faith,
I shall not leave so sweet a bedfellow
But with much pain. You have made me a sluggard
Since I first knew you.
Anne. Then if you needs will go
This dangerous evening, Master Wendoll,
Let me entreat you bear him company.
Wen. With all my heart, sweet mistress. My boots there!
Frank. Fie, fie, that for my private business
I should disease my friend and be a trouble
To the whole house. Nick!
Nich. [*Off stage.*] Anon, sir.
Frank. Bring forth my gelding. [*To Wendoll.*] As you love me, sir,
Use no more words; a hand, good Master Cranwell.
Cran. Sir, God be your good speed.
Frank. Good night, sweet Nan. Nay, nay, a kiss and part.
[*Aside.*] Dissembling lips, you suit not with my heart.
[*Exit.*]
Wen. [*Aside.*] How business, time, and hours all gracious proves
And are the furtherers to my newborn love.
I am husband now in Master Frankford's place

24 remiss lenient
42 alacrity lively enjoyment
46 stripling youth
48 into the cellar offer him a drink from our supply
49 March beer an especially strong beer
50 Trojan (1) roisterer; (2) drunkard (colloquialisms)
59 God's me! "God save me" (common oath); **dispatch** haste
61 Content ye be assured
64 ripest fullest
66 ways are dangerous highwaymen were common threats in the country
67 Appointed armed
68 call you up awaken you
79 disease disturb
85 suit match

And must command the house. [*To Anne.*] My pleasure is
We will not sup abroad so publicly,
But in your private chamber, Mistress Frankford.

Anne. [*To Wendoll.*] Oh, sir, you are too public in your love,
And Master Frankford's wife –

Cran. Might I crave favor,
I would entreat you I might see my chamber;
I am on the sudden grown exceeding ill
And would be spared from supper.

Wen. Light there, ho!
See you want nothing, sir, for if you do,
You injure that good man, and wrong me too.

Cran. I will make bold. Good night.

[*Exit.*]

Wen. How all conspire
To make our bosom sweet and full entire.
Come, Nan, I prithee let us sup within.

Anne. Oh, what a clog unto the soul is sin.
We pale offenders are still full of fear;
Every suspicious eye brings danger near,
When they whose clear heart from offense are free,
Despise report, base scandals do outface,
And stand at mere defiance with disgrace.

Wen. Fie, fie, you talk too like a Puritan.

Anne. You have tempted me to mischief, Master Wendoll;
I have done I know not what. Well, you plead custom;
That which for want of wit I granted erst
I now must yield through fear. Come, come, let's in.
Once o'er shoes, we are straight o'er head in sin.

Wen. My jocund soul is joyful above measure;
I'll be profuse in Frankford's richest treasure.

Exeunt.

[Sc. xii]

Enter Sisly, Jenkin, [Spiggot *the*] Butler, *and other* Servingmen.

Jenk. My mistress and Master Wendoll, my master, sup in her chamber to-night; Sisly, you are preferred from being the cook to be chambermaid. Of all the loves betwixt thee and me, tell me what thou thinkest of this.

Sisly. Mum; there's an old proverb, "When the cat's away the mouse may play."

Jenk. Now you talk of a cat, Sisly, I smell a rat.

Sisly. Good words, Jenkin, lest you be called to answer them.

Jenk. Why, "God make my mistress an honest woman." Are not these good words? "Pray God my new master play not the knave with my old master." Is there any hurt in this? "God send no villainy intended, and if they do sup together, pray God they do not lie together. God keep my mistress chaste and make us all His servants." What harm is there in all this? Nay, more, here is my hand; thou shalt never have my heart unless thou say "Amen."

Sisly. "Amen, I pray God," I say.

Enter Servingman.

Ser. My mistress sends that you should make less noise, to lock up the doors, and see the household all got to bed; you, Jenkin, for this night are made the porter, to see the gates shut in.

Jenk. Thus by little and little I creep into office. Come to kennel, my masters, to kennel; 'tis eleven o'clock already.

Ser. When you have locked the gates in, you must send up the keys to my mistress.

Sisly. Quickly, for God's sake, Jenkin; for I must carry them. I am neither pillow nor bolster, but I know more than both.

Jenk. To bed, good Spiggot; to bed, good honest serving creatures, and let us sleep as snug as pigs in pease-straw.

Exeunt.

[Sc. xiii]

Enter Frankford *and* Nicholas.

Frank. Soft, soft. We have tied our geldings to a tree

---

100 **bosom** desires
103 **pale** white (from fear)
105 **When** while
106 **report** rumor; common talk
108 **Puritan** prude
110 **custom** habitual practice
111 **erst** earliest; first
113 **o'er shoes** in deep (colloquialism)
114 **jocund** cheerful
xii.3 **preferred** promoted
6 **Mum** silence
9 **Good words** i.e., be careful what you say
28 **office** i.e., of bawd or pander
29 **to kennel** as though a pack of hounds
38 **pigs in pease-straw** straw from the pea plant ("as snug as pigs in pease-straw" is proverbial)

Two flight-shoot off, lest by their thund'ring hooves
They blab our coming back. Hearest thou no noise?
Nich. Hear? I hear nothing but the owl and you.
Frank. So; now my watch's hand points upon twelve,
And it is dead midnight. Where are my keys?
Nich. Here, sir.
Frank. This is the key that opes my outward gate,
This is the hall door, this my withdrawing chamber.
But this, that door that's bawd unto my shame,
Fountain and spring of all my bleeding thoughts,
Where the most hallowed order and true knot
Of nuptial sanctity hath been profaned.
It leads to my polluted bedchamber,
Once my terrestrial heaven, now my earth's hell,
The place where sins in all their ripeness dwell,
But I forget myself; now to my gate.
Nich. It must ope with far less noise
Than Cripple-gate, or your plot's dashed.
Frank. So, reach me my dark-lantern to the rest.
Tread softly, softly.
Nich. I will walk on eggs this pace.
Frank. A general silence hath surprised the house,
And this is the last door. Astonishment,
Fear, and amazement play against my heart,
Even as a madman beats upon a drum.
Oh, keep my eyes, you Heavens, before I enter,
From any sight that may transfix my soul;
Or if there be so black a spectacle,
Oh, strike mine eyes stark blind; or if not so,
Lend me such patience to digest my grief
That I may keep this white and virgin hand
From any violent outrage or red murder.
And with that prayer I enter.
Nich. Here's a circumstance!
[*Exit.*]
A man may be made cuckold in the time
That he's about it. And the case were mine
As 'tis my master's – 'sblood, that he makes me swear –
I would have placed his action, entered there.
I would, I would.

[*Enter* Frankford.]

Frank. Oh, Oh!
Nich. Master, 'sblood, master, master!
Frank. O me unhappy! I have found them lying
Close in each other's arms, and fast asleep.
But that I would not damn two precious souls
Bought with my Savior's blood and send them laden
With all their scarlet sins upon their backs
Unto a fearful Judgment, their two lives
Had met upon my rapier.
Nich. 'Sblood, master,
Have you left them sleeping still?
Let me go wake them.
Frank. Stay, let me pause awhile.
Oh, God, oh, God, that it were possible
To undo things done, to call back yesterday!
That Time could turn up his swift sandy glass
To untell the days and to redeem these hours!
Or that the Sun could, rising from the west
Draw his coach backward, take from
The account of time so many minutes,
Till he had all these seasons called again,
Those minutes and those actions done in them,
Even from her first offense. That I might take her
As spotless as an angel in my arms.
But oh, I talk of things impossible,
And cast beyond the moon. God give me patience,
For I will in to wake them.
Nich. Here's patience perforce;
Exit.
He needs must trot afoot that tires his horse.

Enter Wendoll, *running over the stage in a night gown, he* [Frankford] *after him with his sword drawn; the* Maid *in her smock stays his hand and clasps hold on him. He pauses awhile.*

Frank. I thank thee, maid; thou like the angel's hand

---

xiii.2 **flight-shoot** distance twice the maximum range of bow and arrow
3 **blab** reveal
9 **withdrawing chamber** i.e., parlor
19 **Cripple-gate** London city gate near the Red Bull Theater where this play may have been staged
20 **dark-lantern** lantern with a slide that can conceal the light
21 **walk . . . pace** (proverbial)
22 **surprised** overtaken
33 **And** if
37 **placed his action** discovered him (Wendoll)
44–5 **all . . . Judgment** without potential prayers at death
51 **sandy glass** hourglass filled with sand
52 **untell** undo
61 **cast . . . moon** speculate wildly
62 **perforce** of necessity
64–5 **angel's . . . stayed** as Abraham's hand was stayed (Gen. 22:11–12)

Hast stayed me from a bloody sacrifice.
Go, villain, and my wrongs sit on thy soul
As heavy as this grief doth upon mine.
When thou recordest my many courtesies
And shalt compare them with thy treacherous heart,
Lay them together, weigh them equally,
'Twill be revenge enough. Go, to thy friend
A Judas. Pray, pray, lest I live to see
Thee, Judas-like, hanged on an elder tree.

Enter Mistress Frankford *in her smock, night gown, and night attire.*

Anne. Oh, by what word, what title, or what name
Shall I entreat your pardon? Pardon! Oh,
I am as far from hoping such sweet grace
As Lucifer from Heaven. To call you husband –
Oh, me most wretched, I have lost that name;
I am no more your wife.
Nich. 'Sblood, sir, she swoons.
Frank. Spare thou thy tears, for I will weep for thee;
And keep thy countenance, for I'll blush for thee.
Now I protest I think 'tis I am tainted,
For I am most ashamed, and 'tis more hard
For me to look upon thy guilty face
Than on the sun's clear brow. What wouldst thou speak?
Anne. I would I had no tongue, no ears, no eyes,
No apprehension, no capacity.
When do you spurn me like a dog? When tread me
Under your feet? When drag me by the hair?
Though I deserve a thousand, thousand fold
More than you can inflict, yet, once my husband,
For womanhood – to which I am ashamed,
Though once an ornament – even for His sake
That hath redeemed our souls, mark not my face
Nor hack me with your sword. But let me go
Perfect and undeformed to my tomb.
I am not worthy that I should prevail
In the least suit, no, not to speak to you,
Nor look on you, nor to be in your presence;
Yet, as an abject, this one suit I crave,
This granted I am ready for my grave.
Frank. My God with patience arm me. Rise, nay, rise,
And I'll debate with thee. Was it for want
Thou play'dst the strumpet? Wast thou not supplied
With every pleasure, fashion, and new toy,
Nay, even beyond my calling?
Anne. I was.
Frank. Was it then disability in me,
Or in thine eye seem'd he a properer man?
Anne. Oh, no.
Frank. Did I not lodge thee in my bosom?
Wear thee here in my heart?
Anne. You did.
Frank. I did indeed; witness my tears I did.
Go bring my infants hither.
[*Exit* Maid *and return with two* Children.]
Oh, Nan, oh, Nan,
If neither fear of shame, regard of honor,
The blemish of my house, nor my dear love
Could have withheld thee from so lewd a fact,
Yet for these infants, these young harmless souls,
On whose white brows thy shame is charactered,
And grows in greatness as they wax in years –
Look but on them, and melt away in tears.
Away with them, lest as her spotted body
Hath stained their names with stripe of bastardy,
So her adult'rous breath may blast their spirits
With her infectious thoughts. Away with them!
[*Exeunt* Maid *and* Children.]
Anne. In this one life I die ten thousand deaths.
Frank. Stand up, stand up. I will do nothing rashly.
I will retire awhile into my study,
And thou shalt hear thy sentence presently.
Exit.
Anne. 'Tis welcome, be it death. Oh, me, base strumpet,
That having such a husband, such sweet children,
Must enjoy neither. Oh, to redeem my honor
I would have this hand cut off, these my breasts seared,

---

87 **apprehension . . . capacity** active and passive powers of the mind
100 **an abject** one who is cast aside
105 **toy** trinket, bauble
106 **calling** rank, station
108 **properer** more handsome; worthier
115 **fact** action, deed
117 **charactered** written
118 **wax** increase
120 **spotted** morally stained
121 **stripe** i.e., badge
122 **blast** blight
127 **presently** shortly
131 **seared** (as with hot irons)

Be racked, strappadoed, put to any torment;
Nay, to whip but this scandal out, I would hazard
The rich and dear redemption of my soul.
He cannot be so base as to forgive me,
Nor I so shameless to accept his pardon.
[*To the audience.*] Oh, women, women, you that have yet kept
Your holy matrimonial vow unstained,
Make me your instance. When you tread awry,
Your sins like mine will on your conscience lie.

Enter Sisly, Spiggot, *all the* Servingmen, *and* Jenkin, *as newly come out of bed.*

All. Oh, mistress, mistress, what have you done, mistress?
Nich. 'Sblood, what a caterwauling keep you here!
Jenk. Oh, Lord, mistress, how comes this to pass? My master is run away in his shirt, and never so much as called me to bring his clothes after him.
Anne. See what guilt is. Here stand I in this place,
Ashamed to look my servants in the face.

Enter Master Frankford *and* Cranwell, *whom seeing she falls on her knees.*

Frank. My words are registered in Heaven already.
With patience hear me. I'll not martyr thee
Nor mark thee for a strumpet, but with usage
Of more humility torment thy soul
And kill thee even with kindness.
Cran. Master Frankford –
Frank. Good Master Cranwell. Woman, hear thy judgment:
Go make thee ready in thy best attire,
Take with thee all thy gowns, all thy apparel;
Leave nothing that did ever call thee mistress,
Or by whose sight being left here in the house
I may remember such a woman by.
Choose thee a bed and hangings for a chamber,
Take with thee everything that hath thy mark,
And get thee to my manor seven mile off,
Where live. 'Tis thine; I freely give it thee.
My tenants by shall furnish thee with wains
To carry all thy stuff within two hours;
No longer will I limit thee my sight.
Choose which of all my servants thou likest best,
And they are thine to attend thee.
Anne. A mild sentence.
Frank. But as thou hopest for Heaven, as thou believest
Thy name's recorded in the Book of Life,
I charge thee never after this sad day
To see me, or to meet me, or to send
By word, or writing, gift, or otherwise
To move me, by thyself or by thy friends,
Nor challenge any part in my two children.
So farewell, Nan, for we will henceforth be
As we had never seen, ne'er more shall see.
Anne. How full my heart is in my eyes appears;
What wants in words, I will supply in tears.
Frank. Come, take your coach, your stuff; all must along.
Servants and all make ready, all be gone.
It was thy hand cut two hearts out of one.
[*Exeunt.*]

[Sc. xiv]

Enter Sir Charles, *gentlemanlike, and* [Susan] *his Sister, gentlewomanlike.*

Susan. Brother, why have you tricked me like a bride?
Bought me this gay attire, these ornaments?
Forget you our estate, our poverty?
Sir Cha. Call me not brother, but imagine me
Some barbarous outlaw or uncivil kern,
For if thou shutest thy eye and only hearest
The words that I shall utter, thou shalt judge me
Some staring ruffian, not thy brother Charles.
Oh, Susan!
Susan. Oh, brother, what
Doth this strange language mean?
Sir Cha. Dost love me, sister? Wouldst thou see me live
A bankrupt beggar in the world's disgrace
And die indebted to my enemies?

132 **racked** stretched out by pulleys on a rack; **strappadoed** lifted in a harness and then dropped suddenly and jerked
139 **instance** example, lesson
142 **caterwauling** loud cries like that of cats in heat
144 **shirt** nightshirt
164 **wains** wagons
166 **limit thee my sight** will I allow you in my sight
170 **Book of Life** record of the names of those who shall inherit eternal life (Phil. 4:3; Rev. 20:12)
177 **seen** seen each other
xiv.1 **s.d.** ***gentlemanlike . . . gentlewomanlike*** Charles and Susan have been restored to their proper rank and status
3 **estate** financial situation
5 **kern** peasant
8 **staring** frantic

Wouldst thou behold me stand like a huge
beam
In the world's eye, a byword and a scorn?
It lies in thee of these to acquit me free,
And all my debt I may outstrip by thee.
Susan. By me? Why? I have nothing, nothing left;
I owe even for the clothes upon my back;
I am not worth, &c.
Sir Cha. Oh, sister, say not so.
It lies in you my downcast state to raise,
To make me stand on even points with the
world.
Come, sister, you are rich! Indeed, you are,
And in your power you have without delay
Acton's five hundred pounds back to repay.
Susan. Till now I had thought you loved me. By
mine honor,
Which I had kept as spotless as the moon,
I ne'er was mistress of that single doit
Which I reserved not to supply your wants.
And do you think that I would hoard from
you?
Now by my hopes in Heaven, knew I the
means
To buy you from the slavery of your debts,
Especially from Acton, whom I hate,
I would redeem it with my life or blood.
Sir Cha. I challenge it, and kindred set apart
Thus ruffian-like I lay siege to your heart.
What do I owe to Acton?
Susan. Why, some
Five hundred pounds, toward which I swear
In all the world I have not one denier.
Sir Cha. It will not prove so. Sister, now resolve
me:
What do you think – and speak your
conscience –
Would Acton give might he enjoy your bed?
Susan. He would not shrink to spend a thousand
pounds
To give the Mountfords' name so deep a
wound.
Sir Cha. A thousand pounds! I but five hundred
owe.
Grant him your bed; he's paid with interest so.
Susan. Oh, brother!
Sir Cha. Oh, sister! only this one way,
With that rich jewel you my debts may pay.
In speaking this my cold heart shakes with
shame,
Nor do I woo you in a brother's name,
But in a stranger's. Shall I die in debt
To Acton, my grand foe, and you still wear
The precious jewel that he holds so dear?
Susan. My honor I esteem as dear and precious
As my redemption.
Sir Cha. I esteem you, sister,
As dear for so dear prizing it.
Susan. Will Charles
Have me cut off my hands and send them
Acton?
Rip up my breast, and with my bleeding heart
Present him as a token?
Sir Cha. Neither, sister,
But hear me in my strange assertion:
Thy honor and my soul are equal in my regard,
Nor will thy brother Charles survive thy shame.
His kindness like a burden hath surcharged me,
And under his good deeds I stooping go,
Not with an upright soul. Had I remained
In prison still, there doubtless I had died
Then unto him that freed me from that prison,
Still do I owe that life. What moved my foe
To enfranchise me? 'Twas, sister, for your love!
With full five hundred pounds he bought your
love,
And shall he not enjoy it? Shall the weight
Of all this heavy burden lean on me,
And will not you bear part? You did partake
The joy of my release; will you not stand
In joint-bond bound to satisfy the debt?
Shall I be only charged?
Susan. But that I know
These arguments come from an honored mind,
As in your most extremity of need,
Scorning to stand in debt to one you hate.
Nay, rather would engage your unstained
honor
Than to be held ingrate, I should condemn you.
I see your resolution and assent.
So Charles will have me, and I am content.
Sir Cha. For this I tricked you up.
Susan. But here's a knife,
To save mine honor shall slice out my life.

14 beam conspicuous sight (Matt. 7:3)
15 byword colloquial object of scorn
20 &c. (suggests interruption)
22 points terms
28 doit small amount (from Dutch coin of little value)
39 denier coin of little value (from French coin worth one-twelfth of a sou)
40 resolve tell
48 that rich jewel i.e., her maidenhead, her virginity
52 grand arch
59 token present, keepsake
63 surcharged overburdened
69 enfranchise release (from jail and the bond)
75 In ... bound bound with me jointly
80 engage compromise
84 tricked you up provided you fashionable clothes and trinkets

Sir Cha. I know thou pleasest me a thousand times
More in that resolution than thy grant.
[*Aside.*] Observe her love: to soothe them in my suit
Her honor she will hazard though not lose;
To bring me out of debt, her rigorous hand
Will pierce her heart. Oh, wonder, that will choose,
Rather than stain her blood, her life to lose.
[*To her.*] Come you, sad sister to a woeful brother,
This is the gate. I'll bear him such a present,
Such an acquittance for the knight to seal,
As will amaze his senses, and surprise
With admiration all his phantasies.

Enter Sir Francis *and* Malby.

Susan. Before his unchaste thoughts shall seize on me,
'Tis here shall my imprisoned soul set free.
Sir Fra. How! Mountford with his sister hand in hand!
What miracle's afoot?
Mal. It is a sight
Begets in me much admiration.
Sir Cha. Stand not amazed to see me thus attended.
Acton, I owe thee money, and being unable
To bring thee the full sum in ready coin,
Lo! for thy more assurance here's a pawn,
My sister, my dear sister, whose chaste honor
I prize above a million. Here – nay, take her;
She's worth your money, man; do not forsake her.
Sir Fra. [*Aside.*] I would he were in earnest.
Susan. Impute it not to my immodesty.
My brother being rich in nothing else
But in his interest that he hath in me,
According to his poverty hath brought you
Me, all his store, whom howsoevr you prize
As forfeit to your hand, he values highly,
And would not sell but to acquit your debt
For any emperor's ransom.
Sir Fra. [*Aside.*] Stern heart, relent;
Thy former cruelty at length repent.
Was ever known in any former age
Such honorable wrested courtesy?
Lands, honors, lives, and all the world forgo
Rather than stand engaged to such a foe.
Sir Cha. Acton, she is too poor to be thy bride,
And I too much opposed to be thy brother.
There, take her to thee. If thou hast the heart
To seize her as a rape or lustful prey,
To blur our house that never yet was stained,
To murder her that never meant thee harm,
To kill me now whom once thou savedst from death,
Do them at once on her. All these rely
And perish with her spotted chastity.
Sir Fra. You overcome me in your love, Sir Charles.
I cannot be so cruel to a lady
I love so dearly. Since you have not spared
To engage your reputation to the world,
Your sister's honor which you prize so dear,
Nay, all the comforts which you hold on earth,
To grow out of my debt, being your foe,
Your honored thoughts, lo, thus I recompense.
Your metamorphosed foe receives your gift
In satisfaction of all former wrongs.
This jewel I will wear here in my heart,
And where before I thought her for her wants
Too base to be my bride, to end all strife,
I seal you my dear brother, her my wife.
Susan. You still exceed us. I will yield to fate
And learn to love where I till now did hate.
Sir Cha. With that enchantment you have charmed my soul
And made me rich even in those very words.
I pay no debt but am indebted more;
Rich in your love I never can be poor.
Sir Fra. All's mine is yours; we are alike in state.
Let's knit in love what was opposed in hate.
Come, for our nuptials we will straight provide,
Blessed only in our brother and fair bride.

[*Exeunt.*]

[Sc. xv]

Enter Cranwell, Frankford, *and* Nicholas.

Cran. Why do you search each room about your house,
Now that you have dispatched your wife away?

88 **soothe . . . suit** to appease those who are pursuing me
95 **acquittance . . . seal** document discharging Sir Charles's debt
97 **admiration** astonishment; **phantasies** powers of imagination
99 **'Tis here** the knife which will release her
106 **pawn** a pledge of security for the debt
113 **interest** (1) emotional; (2) financial
121 **wrested** strained
127 **lustful prey** victim of your lust
128 **blur** defile
131 **at once** simultaneously
139 **To grow out of** to disburden yourself
144 **where** whereas; **her wants** poverty and lack of status
156 **Blessed only** i.e., with the blessing of a dowry

Frank. Oh, sir, to see that nothing may be left
That ever was my wife's. I loved her dearly,
And when I do but think of her unkindness,
My thoughts are all in Hell, to avoid which torment,
I would not have a bodkin or a cuff,
A bracelet, necklace, or rebato wire,
Nor anything that ever was hers,
Left me, by which I might remember her.
Seek round about.

Nich. 'Sblood, master, here's her lute flung in a corner.

Frank. Her lute! Oh, God, upon this instrument
Her fingers have run quick division,
Sweeter than that which now divides our hearts.
These frets have made me pleasant, that have now
Frets of my heartstrings made. Oh, Master Cranwell,
Oft hath she made this melancholy wood,
Now mute and dumb for her disastrous chance,
Speak sweetly many a note, sound many a strain
To her own ravishing voice, which being well strung,
What pleasant, strange airs have they jointly sung.
Post with it after her. Now nothing's left;
Of her and hers I am at once bereft.

Nich. I'll ride and overtake her, do my message,
And come back again.

[*Exit.*]

Cran. Meantime, sir, if you please,
I'll to Sir Francis Acton and inform him
Of what hath passed betwixt you and his sister.

Frank. Do as you please. How ill am I bestead
To be a widower ere my wife be dead.

[*Exeunt.*]

[Sc. xvi]

Enter Anne, *with* Jenkin, *her maid* Sisly, *her* Coachman, *and three* Carters.

Anne. Bid my coach stay. Why should I ride in state,
Being hurled so low down by the hand of fate?
A seat like to my fortunes let me have,
Earth for my chair, and for my bed a grave.

Jenk. Comfort, good mistress; you have watered your coach with tears already. You have but two miles now to go to your manor. A man cannot say by my old Master Frankford as he may say by me, that he wants manors, for he hath three or four, of which this is one that we are going to.

Sisly. Good mistress, be of good cheer. Sorrow you see hurts you, but helps you not; we all mourn to see you so sad.

Carter. Mistress, I spy one of my landlord's men
Come riding post; 'tis like he brings some news.

Anne. Comes he from Master Frankford, he is welcome;
So are his news, because they come from him.

Enter Nicholas.

Nich. [*Handing her the lute.*] There.

Anne. I know the lute. Oft have I sung to thee;
We both are out of tune, both out of time.

Nich. Would that had been the worst instrument
That e'er you played on. My master
Commends him to ye; there's all he can find
That was ever yours. He hath nothing left
That ever you could lay claim to but his own heart,
And he could afford you that.
All that I have to deliver you is this:
He prays you to forget him, and so he bids you farewell.

Anne. I thank him; he is kind and ever was.
All you that have true feeling of my grief,
That know my loss, and have relenting hearts,
Gird me about, and help me with your tears
To wash my spotted sins. My lute shall groan;
It cannot weep, but shall lament my moan.

[*She plays.*]

Enter Wendoll [*behind*].

Wen. Pursued with horror of a guilty soul
And with the sharp scourge of repentance lashed,
I fly from my own shadow. Oh, my stars!

---

xvi.7 bodkin long pin used to fasten hair; **cuff** ornamental cuff
8 rebato wire collar made of wire to support a ruff
14 division (1) melodic passage in music; (2) a run rapidly executed
16 frets . . . now (1) divisions of the lute fingerboard; (2) fretting sores, cankers; **pleasant** merry
19 chance fortune
21 which . . . strung i.e., Anne's own voice
22 strange wonderful
29 bestead situated
xvi.8 by with respect to
9 manors (with pun on *manners*)
16 post in haste
22 worst instrument (bawdy pun on her sexual instrument)
33 Gird gather

What have my parents in their lives deserved
That you should lay this penance on their son?
When I but think of Master Frankford's love
And lay it to my treason, or compare
My murdering him for his relieving me,
It strikes a terror like a lightning's flash
To scorch my blood up. Thus I like the owl,
Ashamed of day, live in these shadowy woods
Afraid of every leaf or murmuring blast,
Yet longing to receive some perfect knowledge
How he hath dealt with her. [*Sees Anne.*] Oh, my sad fate!
Here, and so far from home, and thus attended!
Oh, God, I have divorced the truest turtles
That ever lived together, and being divided
In several places, make their several moan;
She in the fields laments and he at home.
So poets write that Orpheus made the trees
And stones to dance to his melodious harp,
Meaning the rustic and the barbarous hinds,
That had no understanding part in them;
So she from these rude carters tears extracts,
Making their flinty hearts with grief to rise
And draw rivers from their rocky eyes.

Anne. [*To Nicholas.*] If you return unto your master, say –
Though not from me, for I am all unworthy
To blast his name with a strumpet's tongue –
That you have seen me weep, wish myself dead.
Nay, you may say too – for my vow is passed –
Last night you saw me eat and drink my last.
This to your master you may say and swear,
For it is writ in Heaven and decreed here.

Nich. I'll say you wept; I'll swear you made me sad.
Why, how now, eyes? what now? what's here to do?
I am gone, or I shall straight turn baby too.

Wen. [*Aside.*] I cannot weep; my heart is all on fire.
Cursed be the fruits of my unchaste desire.

Anne. Go break this lute upon my coach's wheel,
As the last music that I e'er shall make –
Not as my husband's gift, but my farewell
To all earth's joy; and so your master tell.

Nich. If I can for crying.

Wen. [*Aside.*] Grief, have done,
Or like a madman I shall frantic run.

Anne. You have beheld the woefullest wretch on earth,
A woman made of tears. Would you had words
To express but what you see; my inward grief
No tongue can utter, yet unto your power
You may describe my sorrow and disclose
To thy sad master my abundant woes.

Nich. I'll do your commendations.

Anne. Oh, no.
I dare not so presume; nor to my children.
I am disclaimed in both; alas, I am.
Oh, never teach them, when they come to speak,
To name the name of mother. Chide their tongue
If they by chance light on that hated word.
Tell them 'tis naught, for when that word they name,
Poor pretty souls, they harp on their own shame.

Wen. [*Aside.*] To recompense her wrongs, what canst thou do?
Thou hast made her husbandless and childless too.

Anne. I have no more to say. Speak not for me,
Yet you may tell your master what you see.

Nich. I'll do't.

Exit.

Wen. [*Aside.*] I'll speak to her and comfort her in grief.
Oh, but her wound cannot be cured with words.
No matter, though, I'll do my best good will
To work a cure on her whom I did kill.

Anne. So now unto my coach, then to my home,
So to my deathbed, for from this sad hour
I never will nor eat, nor drink, nor taste
Of any cates that may preserve my life.
I never will nor smile, nor sleep, nor rest,
But when my tears have washed my black soul white,
Sweet Savior, to Thy hands I yield my sprite.

Wen. [*Coming forward.*] Oh, Mistress Frankford –

Anne. Oh, for God's sake fly!
The Devil doth come to tempt me ere I die.

---

42 **lay** compare
48 **perfect** reliable
51 **turtles** turtle-doves, birds proverbial for their fidelity
53 **several** separate
55 **Orpheus** commonplace reference to legendary Greek poet who could move inanimate objects by his music
57 **hinds** farm servants
64 **blast** dull
66 **passed** made
84 **unto your power** as far as you can
87 **do your commendations** give your remembrances
93 **naught** (1) nothing; (2) wicked
107 **cates** food
110 **sprite** spirit

My coach! This sin that with an angel's face
Courted mine honor till he sought my wrack,
In my repentant eyes seems ugly black.

Exeunt all [*except* Wendoll *and* Jenkin], *the* Carters *whistling.*

Jenk. What, my young master that fled in his shirt! How come you by your clothes again? You have made our house in a sweet pickle, have you not, think you? What, shall I serve you still or cleave to the old house?

Wen. Hence, slave! Away with thy unseasoned mirth;
Unless thou canst shed tears, and sigh, and howl,
Curse thy sad fortunes, and exclaim on fate,
Thou art not for my turn.

Jenk. Marry, and you will not, another will; farewell and be hanged. Would you had never come to have kept this coil within our doors. We shall have you run away like a sprite again. [*Exit.*]

Wen. She's gone to death. I live to want and woe.
Her life, her sins, and all upon my head,
And I must now go wander like a Cain
In foreign countries and remoted climes,
Where the report of my ingratitude
Cannot be heard. I'll over, first to France,
And so to Germany, and Italy,
Where, when I have recovered, and by travel
Gotten those perfect tongues, and that these rumors
May in their height abate, I will return;
And I divine, however now dejected,
My worth and parts being by some great man praised,
At my return I may in court be raised.
Exit.

[Sc. xvii]

Enter Sir Francis, Sir Charles, Cranwell, [Malby,] *and* Susan.

Sir Fra. Brother, and now my wife, I think these troubles
Fall on my head by justice of the Heavens,
For being so strict to you in your extremities,
But we are now atoned. I would my sister
Could with like happiness o'ercome her griefs
As we have ours.

Susan. You tell us, Master Cranwell, wondrous things
Touching the patience of that gentleman,
With what strange virtue he demeans his grief.

Cran. I told you what I was witness of;
It was my fortune to lodge there that night.

Sir Fra. Oh, that same villain Wendoll! 'Twas his tongue
That did corrupt her; she was of herself
Chaste and devoted well. Is this the house?

Cran. Yes, sir, I take it here your sister lies.

Sir Fra. My brother Frankford showed too mild a spirit
In the revenge of such a loathed crime;
Less than he did, no man of spirit could do.
I am so far from blaming his revenge
That I commend it; had it been my case,
Their souls at once had from their breasts been freed;
Death to such deeds of shame is the due meed.

Enter Jenkin *and* Sisly.

Jenk. Oh, my mistress, my mistress, my poor mistress!

Sisly. Alas, that ever I was born! What shall I do for my poor mistress?

Sir Cha. Why, what of her?

Jenk. O Lord, sir, she no sooner heard that her brother and his friends were come to see how she did, but she for very shame of her guilty conscience fell into a swoon, and we had much ado to get life into her.

Susan. Alas, that she should bear so hard a fate;
Pity it is repentance comes too late.

Sir Fra. Is she so weak in body?

Jenk. Oh, sir, I can assure you there's no help of life in her, for she will take no sustenance. She hath plainly starved herself, and now she is as lean as a lath. She ever looks for the good

---

114 wrack ruin
121 unseasoned untimely, inappropriate
123 exclaim on make an outcry against
124 for my turn suitable to my purpose
127 coil confusion, disturbance
131 Cain one condemned to wander as punishment for murdering his brother (Gen. 4:8–14)
132 remoted distant
134 over travel
137 Gotten those perfect tongues learned those languages completely
139 divine predict
xvii.4 atoned reconciled
9 demeans governs
14 devoted well very faithful
15 lies lives
22 meed reward, desert
37 lath narrow strip of wood
37–8 good hour i.e., hour of death (as release to eternal life)

hour. Many gentlemen and gentlewomen of the country are come to comfort her.

Enter Mistress Frankford *in her bed.*

Mal. How fare you, Mistress Frankford?
Anne. Sick, sick, Oh, sick! Give me some air, I pray you.
Tell me, Oh, tell me, where's Master Frankford?
Will not he deign to see me ere I die?
Mal. Yes, Mistress Frankford; divers gentlemen,
Your loving neighbors, with that just request
Have moved and told him of your weak estate,
Who, though with much ado to get belief,
Examining of the general circumstance,
Seeing your sorrow and your penitence,
And hearing therewithal the great desire
You have to see him ere you left the world,
He gave to us his faith to follow us,
And sure he will be here immediately.
Anne. You half revived me with those pleasing news.
Raise me a little higher in my bed.
Blush I not, brother Acton? Blush I not, Sir Charles?
Can you not read my fault writ in my cheek?
Is not my crime there? Tell me, gentlemen.
Sir Cha. Alas, good mistress, sickness hath not left you
Blood in your face enough to make you blush.
Anne. Then sickness like a friend my fault would hide.
Is my husband come? My soul but tarries
His arrival and I am fit for Heaven.
Sir Fra. I came to chide you, but my words of hate
Are turned to pity and compassionate grief;
I came to rate you, but my brawls, you see,
Melt into tears, and I must weep by thee.

Enter Frankford.

Here's Master Frankford now.
Frank. Good morrow, brother; good morrow, gentlemen.
God, that hath laid this cross upon our heads,
Might had He pleased have made our cause of meeting
On a more fair and a more contented ground;
But He that made us, made us to this woe.
Anne. And is he come? Methinks that voice I know.
Frank. How do you, woman?
Anne. Well, Master Frankford, well; but shall be better,
I hope, within this hour. Will you vouchsafe,
Out of your grace and your humanity,
To take a spotted strumpet by the hand?
Frank. That hand once held my heart in faster bonds
Than now 'tis gripped by me. God pardon them
That made us first break hold.
Anne. Amen, amen.
Out of my zeal to Heaven, whither I am now bound,
I was so impudent to wish you here,
And once more beg your pardon. Oh, good man,
And father to my children, pardon me.
Pardon, Oh, pardon me! My fault so heinous is
That if you in this world forgive it not,
Heaven will not clear it in the world to come.
Faintness hath so usurped upon my knees
That kneel I cannot; but on my heart's knees,
My prostrate soul lies thrown down at your feet
To beg your gracious pardon. Pardon, Oh, pardon me!
Frank. As freely from the low depth of my soul
As my Redeemer hath forgiven His death,
I pardon thee. I will shed tears for thee,
Pray with thee, and in mere pity
Of thy weak state I'll wish to die with thee.
All. So do we all.
Nich. [*Aside.*] So will not I;
I'll sigh and sob, but, by my faith, not die.
Sir Fra. Oh, Master Frankford, all the near alliance
I lose by her shall be supplied in thee.
You are my brother by the nearest way;
Her kindred hath fallen off, but yours doth stay.
Frank. Even as I hope for pardon at that day
When the Great Judge of Heaven in scarlet sits,
So be thou pardoned. Though thy rash offense

43 **deign** condescend
44 **divers** different, several
46 **moved** taken action
47 **to get belief** to convince him
52 **faith** pledge
66 **rate** berate; **brawls** scoldings
72 **more contented** ground for happier reasons
73 **to this** i.e., to suffer this
76 **better** i.e., in Heaven
79 **spotted** morally blemished
90 **usurped** taken possession of
94 **low depth** i.e., bottom
101 **near alliance** close kinship
104 **kindred . . . off** i.e., after her death, she will no longer be my sister
106 **in scarlet** i.e., in the robes of a judge

Divorced our bodies, thy repentant tears
Unite our souls.

Sir Cha. Then comfort, Mistress Frankford;
You see your husband hath forgiven your fall;
Then rouse your spirits and cheer your fainting soul.

Susan. How is it with you?

Sir Fra. How do you feel yourself?

Anne. Not of this world.

Frank. I see you are not, and I weep to see it.
My wife, the mother to my pretty babes,
Both those lost names I do restore thee back,
And with this kiss I wed thee once again.
Though thou art wounded in thy honored name,
And with that grief upon thy deathbed liest,
Honest in heart, upon my soul, thou diest.

Anne. Pardoned on earth, soul, thou in Heaven art free;
Once more thy wife dies thus embracing thee.
[*Dies.*]

Frank. New married and new widowed! Oh, she's dead,
And a cold grave must be our nuptial bed.

Sir Cha. Sir, be of good comfort, and your heavy sorrow
Part equally among us. Storms divided
Abate their force, and with less rage are guided.

Cran. Do, Master Frankford; he that hath least part
Will find enough to drown one troubled heart.

Sir Fra. Peace with thee, Nan. Brothers and gentlemen,
All we that can plead interest in her grief
Bestow upon her body funeral tears.
Brother, had you with threats and usage bad
Punished her sin, the grief of her offense
Had not with such true sorrow touched her heart.

Frank. I see it had not; therefore on her grave
I will bestow this funeral epitaph,
Which on her marble tomb shall be engraved.
In golden letters shall these words be filled:
"Here lies she whom her husband's kindness killed."

FINIS.

THE EPILOGUE

An honest crew, disposed to be merry,
Came to a tavern by and called for wine.
The drawer brought it, smiling like a cherry,
And told them it was pleasant, neat, and fine.
"Taste it," quoth one. He did so. "Fie!" quoth he,
"This wine was good; now't runs too near the lee."
Another sipped, to give the wine his due,
And said unto the rest, it drunk too flat.
The third said it was old, the fourth, too new.
"Nay," quoth the fifth, "the sharpness likes me not."
Thus, gentlemen, you see how in one hour
The wine was new, old, flat, sharp, sweet, and sour.
Unto this wine we do allude our play,
Which some will judge too trivial, some too grave.
You as our guests we entertain this day
And bid you welcome to the best we have.
Excuse us, then; good wine may be disgraced
When every several mouth hath sundry taste.

---

118 honored name reputation
122 Once . . . wife restored as your wife
139 golden . . . filled engraved letters should be filled with gold

The Epilogue

2 by nearby
4 neat pure
6 lee dregs, sediment
13 allude compare
18 sundry individual

The Magnificent Entertainment

Thomas Dekker

THE

MAGNIFICENT

Entertainment:

Giuen to King *Iames*, Queene *Anne* his wife, and *Henry Frederick* the Prince, vpon the day of his Maiesties Trvumphant Passage (from the Tower) through his Honourable Citie (and Chamber) of *London*, being the 15. of March. 1603.

As well by the English as by the Strangers: VVith the speeches and Songes, deliuered in the seuerall Pageants.

Mart. *Templa Deis, mores populis dedit, otia ferro, Astra suis, Calo sydera, serta Ioui.*

Tho. Dekker.

Imprinted at London by T. C. for Tho. Man the yonger. 1604.

Frontispiece, 1604.

Londinium arch at Fenchurch, 1604 royal entry in London. From Stephen Harrison's *Arches of Triumph* (London, 1604), reproduced by courtesy of the Trustees of the British Library.

Long before he ascended the English throne in 1603, King James understood the potentially powerful relationship between politics and theater – that politics was, in fact, often a kind of theater. "A King," he wrote to his son Prince Henry in the *Basilikon Doron*, "is as one set on a stage, whose smallest actions and gestures, all the people gazingly do behold"; he could, therefore, through spectacle and display promote his own political agenda. Elizabeth I had known this, too, as her staged coronation progress of 1558 makes clear; but James had had the advantage of participating in two similar pageants before the one in London in 1604 documented here by Thomas Dekker. First, there was his own earlier coronation pageant in Edinburgh in October 1579 as James VI. There, at the West Port, he had witnessed a tableau which likened him to Solomon for his learning and wisdom, a portrait he would reinforce during his rule in England. At the Over Bow "a bonny boy" came out of a globe to hand him the keys to the city; at the old Tolbooth four women connected him to a realignment of the four virtues as justice, peace, plenty, and policy – a particular Jacobean mix – before Bacchus concluded the celebrations at the Nether Bow by dispensing wine. James VI participated in the entry of Queen Anne into Edinburgh in May 1590, too, where again the device of the globe was introduced (this time at the West Port where it opened to reveal a boy as an angel to give the silver keys of the city to the new Queen), the four virtues reappeared but more traditionally correct as justice, temperance, prudence, and fortitude at the old Tolbooth, and the nine Muses were introduced on a scaffold at the Butter Trone to establish the importance of the arts and sciences. Both King James and Queen Anne, then, were prepared for the symbolic pageantry – some of it deliberately resonating that of the past – when on March 15, 1604, James passed officially through the city of London as the new British King James I *and* VI. "The people is full of expectation," John Manningham confided in his *Diary*, "and great with hope of his worthiness."

Still, such a hope was a long time coming. Elizabeth I died in the early morning hours of March 24, 1603, after months of steadily declining health, and by that afternoon James was being proclaimed King in London while a messenger rode without rest to Edinburgh with the news. The city of London began, almost at once, to lay plans for the official welcome and the coronation pageantry, scheduling it appropriately, they thought, for St. James's Day, July 25. The city aldermen required £2,500 from the Twelve Great Livery Companies to help finance the King's reception and coronation, and the construction of elaborate sets began when, in the summer, plague interrupted their plans. Although King James was crowned, the celebrations were put off indefinitely while the epidemic claimed over 30,000 lives. Early the following year, when James announced his intention to ride ceremonially through London on March 15 to open Parliament, work began again in earnest. Seven Roman arches, unprecedented and huge, were completed as stages for the various shows and, announcing James's own imperial theme – his first major proposal was to reunite England with Scotland and Wales to form Great Britain – painters set about to embellish them with iconography that would stress wisdom, fortitude, might, peace, and policy. Gilbert Dugdale records in *The Time Triumphant* (1604) that before the day arrived, James and Anne visited the Exchange to see the preparations for his royal entry, but the "hurly burly" of the crowd was so great that the King and Queen took refuge inside the Exchange. Three days before the ceremony, he came with his wife, son, and attendants to the Tower of London to await the occasion as Elizabeth I had done before him. The evening of the royal entry, Dugdale tells us, there was a spectacle of fireworks on the Thames that was "pass pleasing"; in addition, there was a show on the water: a castle or fort, built on two barges and "planted with much munition" was attacked by two pinnaces; although the boats were initially repulsed, they eventually succeeded in taking the castle. It was a show, says Dugdale, "worthy the sight of many Princes being there placed at the cost of the Cinque Ports." They also managed to relate that to James: "all pleased made answer that their love was like the wildfire unquenchable."

Four works published in 1604 report the day itself: Dugdale's eyewitness account, hampered in part because he could not see or hear it all in the noisy crowds; the architect Stephen Harrison's record, given with his designs of the great royal arches in engravings by William Kip; and Ben Jonson and Thomas Dekker, who wrote the shows and may have had a hand in directing them. Of these two, Jonson's work – *His Part of the Magnificent Entertainment* – came out a few weeks before Dekker's but it recounts only the two shows, at Fenchurch and Temple Bar, which Jonson had written. The fullest report of *The Magnificent Entertainment* was that given here, by Thomas Dekker, first as we have it, and later, in a corrected second edition which incorporated some of Jonson's material after a dispute between the two writers was settled in Dekker's favor.

Dekker's detailed account shows us how this coronation pageant aims for far different effects than that of Elizabeth's, but it is Harrison's *Arches of Triumph* that initially sets the scene:

> Between the hours of 11 and 12 and before 5 [the King] had made his royal passage through the City, having a canopy borne over him by 8 knights. The first object that His Majesty's eye encountered (after his entrance into London) was part of the children of Christs Church Hospital, to the number of 300 who were placed on a scaffold, erected for that purpose in Barking Churchyard by the Tower. The way from the Tower to Temple Bar was not only sufficiently graveled, but all the streets (lying between those two places) were on both sides (where the breadth would permit) railed in at the charges of the City, Paul's Churchyard excepted. The Liveries of the Companies (having their streamers, ensigns, and bannerets spread on the tops of their rails before them) reached from the middle of Mark Lane to the pegme [framework for the stage; Jonson's learned term] at Temple Bar. Two Marshals were chosen for the day to clear the passage, both of them being well mounted, and attended on by six men (suitably attired) to each Marshal. The conduits of Cornhill, of Cheap, and of Fleetstreet, that day ran claret wine very plenteously: which (by reason of so much excellent music, that sounded forth not only from each several pegme, but also from diverse other places) ran the faster and more merrily down into somebodies' bellies.

Around and above them the royal arches and the eagle were constant reminders that their new King, like the Romans and like Brute to whom he would be made analogous, was also a new emperor. Jonson, in fact, is quick to make such parallels evident and both visually and dramatically effective.

Dekker, too, begins his most detailed section of *The Magnificent Entertainment* by noting that the arch which featured the Italian merchants at Gracechurch Street depicted Henry VII seated "in his imperial robes, to whom King James (mounted on horseback) approaches and receives a scepter, over both their heads these words being written, HIC VIR, HIC EST [This is the man, this is he]." The new imperial King who would unite England with Scotland as a Stuart is made the counterpart of his Tudor imperial predecessor, who had united the Houses of Lancaster and York and would claim rule too over France and Ireland. Near the Royal Exchange Dekker locates another of the great arches, where the Dutch merchants place at the top a woman holding a warder in one hand while pointing heavenward with the other: she reflects James in the person of Divine Providence, making visible and public James's more private writings on the divine right of kings. Dekker, responsible for the next arch in Cheapside at Soper-lane End called Nova Faelix Arabia, places as his central icon "a woman attired all in white, a rich mantle of green cast about her, an imperial crown on her head, and a scepter in one hand" who is called Arabia Britannica. A chorister from St. Paul's in the role of Circumspection comes forth to liken James I to Brute and makes the King complicit by appropriating him into the playlet as the one who can bring light to darkness and quicken Virtue back to life. At the Little Conduit in Cheap, Sylvanus comes forth from earlier pastoral pageantry, such as the one staged for Elizabeth at Elvetham, to welcome the new King to a reign of peace and plenty while at the last arch Dekker reports in detail, at Fleetstreet, a globe is opened to show all the estates and conditions of man presided over by Justice: the globe, borrowed from the Edinburgh pageants of 1579 and 1590, now incorporates the elements, the four cardinal virtues (likened to James's four countries), and, from Elizabeth's coronation pageant, virtues trampling on vices. In this triumphal ending, James embodies all that was identified with his predecessors – and more.

Just how much of this deliberate propaganda was recognized and understood is what we must try to judge based on how evident the issues are and how effectively they are presented. We learn of the general joy. We also know, from Dugdale, that Queen Anne greeted her new subjects "so humbly and with mildness... never leaving to bend her body to them, this way and that" and, as a consequence, "women and men in my sight wept with joy." Prince Henry, "smiling as overjoyed to the peoples' eternal comfort, salute[s] them with many a bend" [bow]. But James's reaction was much different. According to an historian later in the seventeenth century,

> the city and suburbs being one great pageant, wherein he must give his ears leave to suck in their gilded oratory, though never so nauseous to the stomach. He was not like his predecessor, the late Queen of famous memory, that with a well-pleased affection met her peoples' acclamations.... He endured the day's brunt with patience, being assured he should never have such another.... But afterwards in his public appearances... the accesses of the people made him so impatient that he often dispersed them with frowns that we may not say with curses.

He was at once public in his disapproval, if not outright scorn. He refused the bid of the chorister to accept freedom in the Mercers' Company; worse, within months of the Dutch plea to protect their Protestant provinces from Catholic incursion, he did just the reverse: in August 1604 he signed the Treaty of London, making peace with England's long-time enemy, Spain.

Were such decisive acts directly or indirectly caused by the presentations in which the Italians, Dutch, and English of London argued their positions as well as what they presumed might be the King's? There is a sense in which Elizabeth I's pageantry is always looking backward, toward the age of medieval hierarchy and chivalry and pastoralism, so that common elements in the pageantry of both reigns become strikingly out of place. They deny what may be serious ideological divisions. In an imperial age that James was now introducing so conspicuously, what place does Sylvanus have – and why introduce him? Why emphasize and valorize "another Tower of Pleasure" that has "all the states of the land from the nobleman to the plowman"? How "new" *is* Dekker's "New World," and how timely? One of the most provocative observations about Dekker's magnificent entertainment – in which the King's magnificence is meant to come from magnanimity – is (especially in light of Elizabeth's coronation pageant) the noticeable absence of Christian references. At a few places, Christianity is hinted at; but, for the most part, morality is subjected to pagan beliefs and pagan myths. Understanding why this is so is one way into exploring how this costly work of spectacle and celebration is, at heart, political theater with urgent voiced and unvoiced issues always at the margins – and sometimes at the center – of the drama.

Further Reading

Bergeron, David M., *English Civic Pageantry 1558–1642*. Columbia: University of South Carolina Press, 1971.

——, "Gilbert Dugdale and the Royal Entry of James I (1604)," *Journal of Medieval and Renaissance Studies* 13:1 (Spring 1983): 111–25.

——, "Stuart Civic Pageants and Textual Performance," *Renaissance Quarterly* 51:1 (Spring 1998): 163–83.

Gasper, Julia, *The Dragon and the Dove: The Plays of Thomas Dekker*. Oxford: Clarendon Press, 1990.

Goldberg, Jonathan, *James I and the Politics of Literature*. Baltimore: The Johns Hopkins University Press, 1988.

Knowles, James, "The Spectacle of the Realm: Civic Consciousness, Rhetoric and Ritual in Early Modern London," in *Theatre and Government under the Early Stuarts*, ed. J. R. Mulryne and M. Shewring (Cambridge: Cambridge University Press, 1993), pp. 157–89.

Orgel, Stephen, "Making Greatness Familiar," in *Pageantry in the Shakespearean Theater*, ed. David M. Bergeron (Athens: University of Georgia Press, 1985), pp. 19–25.

The Magnificent Entertainment

The sorrow and amazement, that like an earthquake began to shake the distempered body of this island (by reason of our late sovereign's departure) being wisely and miraculously prevented, and the feared wounds of a civil sword (as Alexander's fury was with music) being stopped from bursting forth, by the sound of trumpets that proclaimed King James: all men's eyes were presently turned to the north, standing even stone-still in their circles, like the points of so many geometrical needles, through a fixed and adamantine desire to behold this forty-five years' wonder now brought forth by Time: their tongues neglecting all language else, save that which spake zealous prayers, and unceasable wishes, for his most speedy and longed-for arrival. Insomuch that the night was thought unworthy to be crowned with sleep, and the day not fit to be looked upon by the sun, which brought not some fresh tidings of His Majesty's more near and nearer approach.

At length Expectation (who is ever waking) and that so long was great, grew near the time of her delivery, Rumor coming all in a sweat to play the midwife, whose first comfortable words were, that this treasure of a kingdom (a man-ruler) hid so many years from us, was now brought to light, and at hand.

Martial. *Et populi vox erat una, Venit.*

And that he was to be conducted through some outer part of this his City, to his royal castle the Tower, that in the age of a man (till this very minute) had not been acquainted nor borne the name of a King's Court. Which entrance of his (in this manner) being famed abroad, because his loving subjects the citizens would give a taste of their duty and affection: the device following was suddenly made up, as the first service, to a more royal and serious ensuing entertainment; and this (as it was then purposed) should have been performed about the bars beyond Bishopsgate.

The Device.

Saint George, Saint Andrew (the patrons of both kingdoms) having a long time looked upon each other, with countenances rather of mere strangers, than of such near neighbors, upon the present aspect of His Majesty's approach toward London, were (in his sight) to issue from two several places on horseback, and in complete armor, their breasts and caparisons suited with the arms of England and Scotland (as now they are quartered) to testify their leagued combination, and new-sworn brotherhood. These two armed knights, encountering one another on the way, were to

Textual variants

Title-page reads in full: The magnificent Entertainment Given to King James, Queen Anne his wife, and Henry Frederick the Prince, upon the day of his Majesty's Triumphant Passage (from the Tower) through the Honorable City (and Chamber) of London, being the 15. of March. 1603. As well by the English as by the Strangers: With the speeches and Songs, delivered in the several Pageants. Martial: Templa Deis, mores populi dedit, otia ferro Astra suis, caelo sydera, serta jovi ["He gave temples to the gods, morals to the people, rest to the sword, immortality to his own kind, to heaven stars, wreaths to Jove," Martial, *Epigrams* IX.101. 21–2] Tho[mas] Dekker. **Preceding 1**] A Device [never actually presented; see lines 42–165] (projected down [drafted], but till now not published), that should have served at His Majesty's first access to the City. **31** outer] Q utter **46** than] Q then **407** spoke] Q spake **545** spoke] Q spake **663** spoke] Q spake **974** Forget] Q Forgat **1200** 18] Q 16 (Q2 corrects to 18) **1201** 12] Q 10 (Q2 corrects to 12) **1210** 25] Q 20 (Q2 corrects to 25) **1219** 44] Q4 **1275** sang] Q sung **1395** he!] Q had! **1399** Chorus] Q omits **1406** !] Q ? **1407** Had still he stayed!] Q Here stayed had still! **1410** he] Q had **1077** he] Q had **1510** rose] Q riz **1529** since] Q sithence **1570** engine] Q Eronie **1580** praters] Q parts **1598** other) being at first] Q other being at first) **1742** born] Q borne **1789** *summa*] Q summa summa **1835** correction.] Q corrections. As in F. 2. For *From his own clear strength*. Read clear, straight, &c. And within few lines beneath that: Instead of (*Because alluring this triumph*) Read because that during these, &c. In the *Cant.* likewise, beginning thus, *Shine Titan Shine*, Instead of, *O this is Had*, read O this is He. And in the sixth staff: For, *Here stayd*, Had still. But here *Had* list not to tarry. Read for every *Had*, he. [Table of errors at end may show last-minute proofing and a desire to match Jonson for accuracy]

4–5 prevented forestalled
9 north James was proceeding to London from Edinburgh
10 circles sockets
11 needles (as on a compass)
12–13 forty-five years' wonder Elizabeth I reigned from 1558 to 1603
26 man-ruler (England's previous male king was Edward VI, reigned 1547–52)
29 *Et . . . Venit* "And the voice of the people was all one: 'He comes'" (Martial, *Epigrams* X.6)
32 age . . . man in living memory
40–1 should . . . Bishopsgate (the first pageant was not staged; rather, Ben Jonson's pageant at Fenchurch was made first)
45 mere perfect
48 several different
50 caparisons trappings on a horse's saddle and harness

ride hand in hand, till they met His Majesty. But the strangeness of this newly-begotten amity, flying over the earth, it calls up the Genius of the City, who (not so much amazed, as wondering at the novelty) intercepts their passage.

And most aptly (in our judgment) might this *domesticum numen* (the Genius of place) lay just claim to this preminence of first bestowing salutations and welcomes on His Majesty, Genius being held (*inter fictos deos*), to be god of hospitality and pleasure: and none but such a one was meet to receive so excellent and princely a guest.

Or if not worthy, for those two former respects: yet being *deus generationis*, and having a power as well over countries, herbs and trees, as over men, and the City having now put on a regeneration, or new birth; the induction of such a person, might (without a warrant from the court of critists) pass very current.

To make a false flourish here with the borrowed weapons of all the old masters of the noble science of poesy, and to keep a tyrannical coil, in anatomizing Genius, from head to foot (only to show how nimbly we can carve up the whole mess of the poets) were to play the executioner, and to lay our City's household god on the rack, to make him confess, how many pair of Latin sheets, we have shaken and cut into shreds to make him a garment. Such feats of activity are stale, and common among scholars (before whom it is protested we come not now (in a pageant) to play a master's prize) for *Nunc ego ventosae plebis suffragia venor.*

The multitude is now to be our audience, whose heads would miserably run a-wool-gathering, if we do but offer to break them with hard words. But suppose (by the way) contrary to the opinion of all the doctors that our Genius (in regard the place is feminine, and the person itself, drawn *figura humana, sed ambiguo sexu*) should at this time be thrust into woman's apparel. It is no schism: be it so: our Genius is then a female; antique, and reverend both in years and habit: a chaplet of mingled flowers, (inter-woven with branches of the plane tree) crowning her temples: her hair long and white: her vesture a loose robe, changeable and powdered with stars: and being (on horseback likewise) thus furnished, this was the tune of her voice.

Genius Loci. Stay: we conjure you, by that potent name,
Of which each letter's (now) a triple charm:
Stay; and deliver us, of whence you are,
And why you bear (alone) th'ostent of war,
When all hands else rear olive-boughs and palm:
And Halcyonean days assure all's calm.
When every tongue speaks music: when each pen
(Dulled and dyed black in gall) is white again,
And dipped in nectar, which by delphic-fire
Being heated, melts into an Orphean-choir.
When Troy's proud buildings show like fairy-bowers,
And streets (like gardens) are perfumed like flowers:
And windows glazed only with wond'ring eyes;
(In a King's look such admiration lies!)
And when soft-handed Peace, so sweetly thrives,
That bees in soldiers' helmets build their hives.
When Joy a-tip-toe stands on Fortune's wheel,
In silken robes, how dare you shine in steel?

Saint George. Lady, what are you that so question us?

Genius. I am the place's Genius, whence now springs
A vine, whose youngest branch shall produce kings.

64 ***inter . . . deos*** among the fictitious gods

65 **meet** appropriate

73 **critists** critics (an allusion to Ben Jonson's character Criticus in *Cynthia's Revels* [1600]; **pass . . . current** win general acceptance

76–7 **keep . . . foot** make a dreadful fuss with scholarly apparatus (a comment on Jonson's earlier publication of *His Part* of the entertainment that year – a far shorter work but one larded with notes)

79 **mess** portion (here of food)

86 **master's prize** from the degree of fencing match for which prizes were awarded (master's, provost's, scholar's)

86–7 ***Nunc . . . venor*** "Now I chase the votes of the fickle masses" (Horace, *Epistles* I.19.37)

89–90 **a-wool-gathering** i.e., daydreaming

93 **feminine** (Jonson's Genius is male in the first pageant)

94 ***figura . . . sexu*** "a human figure but sexually ambiguous" (Latin)

97 **antique** ancient (like that of the classical period)

101 **changeable** shot; showing different colors under different aspects

106 **deliver** i.e., tell

107 **ostent** vainglorious display

111 **dyed . . . gall** insect deposits used to make ink and thought to be intensely bitter

112 **delphic** from the home of Apollo's oracle at Delphi

114 **Troy's** i.e., London's (reference is to Troynovant; see Munday's *Triumphs*)

119 **bees . . . hives** (a commonplace image for peace, hence the unused helmet)

124 **vine . . . kings** (refers to James as a father whereas Elizabeth never married)

This little world of men; this precious stone,
That sets out Europe: this (the glass alone),
Where the neat sun each morn himself attires,
And gilds it with his repercussive fires.
This jewel of the land; England's right eye;
Altar of love; and sphere of majesty;
Green Neptune's minion, 'bout whose virgin-waist,
Isis is like a crystal girdle cast.
Of this are we the Genius; here have I
Slept (by the favor of a deity)
Forty-four summers and as many springs,
Not frighted with the threats of foreign kings.
But held up in that gowned state I have,
By twice twelve fathers politic and grave:
Who with a sheathed sword, and silken law,
Do keep (within weak walls) millions in awe.

I charge you therefore say, for what you come?
What are you?

Both. Knights at arms.
St. George. St. George.
St. Andrew. St. Andrew.
For Scotland's honor I.
St. George. For England's I.
Both sworn into a League of Unity.
Genius. I clap my hands for joy, and seat you both
Next to my heart: in leaves of purest gold,
This most auspicious love shall be enrolled.
Be joined to us. And as to earth we bow,
So, to those royal feet, bend your steeled brow.
In name of all these senators (on whom
Virtue builds more than those of antique Rome)
Shouting a cheerful welcome. Since no clime,
Nor age that has gone o'er the head of Time,
Did e'er cast up such joys nor the like sum
(But here) shall stand in the world, years to come,
Dread King, our hearts make good what words do want,
To bid thee boldly enter Troynovant.

Rerum certa salus, terrarum gloria Caesar! Martial
Sospite quo, magnos credimus esse deos.
Dilexere prius pueri, juvenesque senesque, Idem.
At nunc infantes te quoque Caesar amant.

This should have been the first offering of the City's love. But His Majesty not making his entrance (according to expectation) it was (not utterly thrown from the altar) but laid by.

Martial. *Iam crescunt media Paegmata celsa via.*

By this time imagine that poets (who draw speaking pictures) and painters (who make dumb poesy) had their heads and hands full, the one for native and sweet invention; the other for lively illustration of what the former should devise. Both of them emulously contending (but not striving) with the properest and brightest colors of wit and art to set out the beauty of the great triumphant-day.

For more exact and formal managing of which business, a select number both of aldermen and commoners (like so many Roman aediles) were (*communi counsilio*) chosen forth, to whose discretion, the charge, contrivings, projects, and all other dependences, owing to so troublesome a work, was entirely and judicially committed.

Many days were thriftily consumed, to mold the bodies of these triumphs comely, and to the honor of the place; and at last, the stuff whereof to frame them was beaten out. The soul that should give life and a tongue to this Entertainment, being to breathe out of writers' pens. The limbs of it to lie at the hard-handed mercy of mechanicians.

---

126 out off; **glass** mirror
128 repercussive reflected
132 Isis i.e., the Thames
135 Forty-four . . . springs (referring to Elizabeth I's reign)
138 twice . . . grave (the London aldermen, who actually numbered twenty-six, one representing each of the city's twenty-six wards)
150 senators a Roman term here applied to the London aldermen (the triumphal arches give a Roman motif to the day's ceremonies, perhaps in part to emphasize James as emperor – that is, ruler of more than one country)
157 Troynovant (a reference to the mythic forerunner of London; see Munday's *Triumphs*)
158–9 *Rerum . . . deos* "Sure savior of the state, the glory of the world, Caesar, from whose safety we may believe that the great gods exist" (Martial, *Epigrams* II.91.1–2)
160–1 *Dilexere . . . amant* "Boys loved you before, and young men, and old men; but now even infants love you, Caesar" (Martial, *Epigrams* IX.9–10)
166 *Iam . . . via* "Now very tall stages grow up in the middle of the street" (Martial, *De spectaculis* II.2); this frequent, excessive, and unnecessary use of Martial is a parody of Jonson and Dekker's self-defense against Jonson's charge of his lack of learning)
167–9 poets . . . poesy (a commonplace of Renaissance poetics; cf. Sidney's *Defense of Poesie*)
176–83 For . . . committed on April 9, 1603, the Livery Companies were told they would provide £2,500 to the Guildhall for the costs of the King's reception and coronation
191 mechanicians skilled artisans at machinery; machinists

In a moment therefore of time are carpenters, joiners, carvers, and other artificers sweating at their chisels.

Virgil. *Accingunt omnes operi.*

Not a finger but had an office. He was held unworthy ever after to "suck the honey-dew of peace," that (against his coming, by whom our peace wears a triple wreath) would offer to play the drone. The streets are surveyed; heights, breadths, and distances taken, as it were to make fortifications, for the solemnities. Seven pieces of ground (like so many fields for a battle) are plotted forth, upon which these Arches of Triumph must show themselves in their glory: aloft, in the end do they advance their proud foreheads.

Virgil. *Circum pueri, innuptaeque puellae,*
Sacra canunt, funemque manu contingere gaudent.

Even children (might they have been suffered) would gladly have spent their little strength about the engines that mounted up the frames, such a fire of love and joy was kindled in every breast.

The day (for whose sake these wonders of wood climbed thus into the clouds) is now come; being so early up by reason of artificial lights, which wakened it, that the sun over-slept himself, and rose not in many hours after, yet bringing with it into the very bosom of the City, a world of people. The streets seemed to be paved with men. Stalls instead of rich wares were set out with children, open casements filled up with women.

All glass windows taken down, but in their places sparkled so many eyes that had it not been the day, the light which reflected from them was sufficient to have made one. He that should have compared the empty and untrodden walks of London which were to be seen in that late mortally-destroying deluge with the thronged streets now might have believed that upon this day began a new Creation, and that the City was the only workhouse wherein sundry nations were made.

A goodly and civil order was observed, in martialing all the companies according to their degrees, the first beginning at the upper end of Saint Mark's Lane, and the last reaching above the conduit in Fleet Street, their seats being double-railed: upon the upper part whereon they leaned, the streamers, ensigns and bannerets, of each particular company decently fixed, and directly against them (even quite through the body of the City, so high as to Temple Bar) a single rail (in fair distance from the other) was likewise erected to put off the multitude. Among whose tongues (which in such consorts never lie still) though there were no music, yet as the poet says:

(Martial). *Vox diversa sonat, populorum est vox tamen una.*

Nothing that they speak could be made anything, yet all that was spoken sounded to this purpose, that still His Majesty was coming. They have their longings and behold, afar off they spy him, richly mounted on a white jennet under a rich canopy sustained by eight Barons of the Cinque Ports. The Tower serving that morning but for his withdrawing chamber, wherein he made him ready and from thence stepped presently into his City of London, which for the time might worthily borrow the name of his Court Royal, his passage along that Court, offering itself (for more state) through seven gates, of which the first was erected at Fenchurch.

Thus presenting itself

It was an upright flat square (for it contained fifty foot in the perpendicular, and fifty foot in the ground-line) the upper roof thereof (on distinct

195 ***Accingunt . . . operi*** "They all make ready for the work" (Virgil, *Aeneid* II.233)

196 an office a designated job

200 drone sluggard

207–9 ***Circum . . . gaudent*** "Boys and girls sang hymns around it, and rejoiced to touch the ropes with their hands" (Virgil, *Aeneid* II.238–9)

210 suffered permitted

229–30 that . . . deluge the London plague of 1603

239–40 double-railed two parallel railings draped with cloth to the ground were placed near the pageants to provide a corridor of special seating for members of the Livery Companies who were responsible for the shows

249–50 ***Vox . . . una*** "Different voices speak, but the voice of the people is one" (Martial, *De spectaculis* III.2)

251–2 anything i.e., made out, understood

255 jennet small Spanish horse

257 Cinque Ports originally protective coastal ports of Dover, Sandwich, Hastings, Romney, and Hythe, and later, Rye and Winchelsea, but by the time of the Spanish Armada in 1588 it was clear the protection was more symbolic than real

262 Court Royal i.e., the court is wherever the king is; cf. *Edward II*

264 Fenchurch the pageant here was Jonson's and he more fully describes it in *His Part*, lines 1–371

grices) bore up the true models of all the notable houses, turrets, and steeples within the City. The gate under which His Majesty did pass, was 12 foot wide, and 18 foot high; a postern likewise (at one side of it) being four foot wide and 8 foot in height. On either side of the gate, stood a great French term of stone, advanced upon wooden pedestals; two half pilasters of rustic, standing over their heads. I could shoot more arrows at this mark, and teach you without the carpenter's rule how to measure all the proportions belonging to this fabric. But an excellent hand being at this instant curiously describing all the seven, and bestowing on them their fair prospective limbs, your eye shall hereafter rather be delighted in beholding those pictures, than now be wearied in looking upon mine.

The personages (as well mutes as speakers) in this pageant, were these: viz.

1. The highest person was *The Britain Monarchy.*
2. At her feet sat *Divine Wisdom.*
3. Beneath her stood *The Genius of the City*, a man.
4. At his right hand was placed a personage figuring *The Counsel of the City.*
5. Under all these lay a person representing *Thamesis the River.*

Six other persons (being daughters to Genius) were advanced above him, on a spreading ascent, of which the first was,

1. *Gladness.*
2. The second, *Veneration.*
3. The third, *Promptitude.*
4. The fourth, *Vigilance.*
5. The fifth, *Loving Affection.*
6. The sixth, *Unanimity.*

Of all which personages, Genius and Thamesis were the only speakers, Thamesis being presented by one of the Children of Her Majesty's Revels, Genius by Master Alleyn (servant to the young Prince); his gratulatory speech (which was delivered with excellent action, and a well-tuned audible voice) being to this effect:

That London may be proud to behold this day, and therefore in name of the Lord Mayor and Aldermen, the Council, Commoners and Multitude, the heartiest welcome is tendered to His Majesty, that ever was bestowed on any king, &c.

Which banquet being taken away with sound of music, there, ready for the purpose, His Majesty made his entrance into this his Court Royal: under this first gate, upon the battlements of the work, in great capitals was inscribed, thus:

LONDINIUM

And under that, in a smaller (but not different) character, was written,

CAMERA REGIA:
The King's Chamber.

Too short a time (in their opinions that were glued there together so many hours to behold him) did His Majesty dwell upon this first place; yet too long it seemed to other happy spirits, that higher up in these Elysian fields awaited for his presence. He sets on therefore (like the sun in his zodiac) bountifully dispersing his beams among particular nations: the brightness and warmth of which was now spent first upon the Italians, and next upon the Belgians. The space of ground on which their magnificent arches were builded, being not unworthy to bear the name of the Great Hall to this our Court Royal, wherein was to be heard and seen the sundry languages and habits of strangers, which under princes' roofs render excellent harmony.

In a pair of scales do I weigh these two nations and find them (neither in hearty love to His Majesty, in advancement of the City's honor, nor

---

274–5 a ... term an architectural word for a statue or bust representing the upper body (sometimes portrayed without arms)

276 rustic rough-hewn

280 an excellent hand Stephen Harrison, whose descriptions of his designs were published as *The Arches of Triumph* later in 1604 with engravings by William Kip

282 prospective perspective

292 *Counsel ... City* Dekker's summary omits here "the warlike forces of the City" which Jonson reports came next

306 Children ... Revels the Children of Queen Elizabeth's Chapel, a boys' company acting at Blackfriars in London who were taken under the patronage of Queen Anne on February 4, 1604

307 Master Alleyn Edward Alleyn, the leading actor of the Admiral's Company, which became Prince Henry's Company at least by February 19, 1604

311–12 London ... day Dekker's summary of Jonson's initial passage omitted in this account

318 music Jonson notes that music was supplied by waits (a small instrumental group of flutists) and haut-boys (oboes)

322 Londinium London (Latin)

326 King's Chamber a term for London, first used by Camden and then Jonson

336 Belgians a general name for those from any of the seventeen provinces of the Low Countries (the Netherlands)

in forwardness to glorify these triumphs) to differ one grain.

To dispute which have done best were to doubt that one had done well. Call their inventions therefore Twins: or if they themselves do not like that name (for happily they are emulous of one glory) yet thus we may speak of them.

> ...*Facies non omnibus una*, Ovid.
> *Nec diversa tamen, qualem decet esse sororum.*

Because, whosoever (*fixis oculis*) beholds their proportions),

> *Expleri mentem nequit, ardescitque tuendo.* Virgil.

The street, upon whose breast this Italian jewel was worn, was never worthy of that name which it carries till this hour. For here did the King's eye meet a second object, that enticed him by tarrying to give honor to the place. And thus did the quaintness of the engine seem to discover itself before him.

The Italians' Pageant.

The building took up the whole breadth of the street, of which the lower part was a square garnished with four great columns, in the midst of which square was cut out a fair and spacious high gate, arched, being twenty-seven foot in the perpendicular line, and eighteen at the ground line. Over the gate, in golden characters, these verses (in a long square) were inscribed:

> *Tu Regere Imperio populos Jacobe memento,*
> *Hae tibi erunt artes, pacique imponere morem,*
> *Parcere subjectis, et debellare superbos.*

And directly above this was advanced the arms of the Kingdom. The supporters fairly cut out to the life; over the Lion (some pretty distance from it) was written.

> JACOBO REGI MAGN.

And above the head of the Unicorn, at the like distance, this,

> HENRICI VII. ABNEP.

In a large square erected above all these King Henry the Seventh was royally seated in his imperial robes, to whom King James (mounted on horseback) approaches and receives a scepter, over both their heads these words being written,

> HIC VIR, HIC EST.

Between two of the columns (on the right hand) was fixed up a square table wherein, in lively and excellent colors, was limned a woman figuring Peace, her head securely leaning on her left hand, her body modestly bestowed (to the length) upon the earth. In her other hand, was held an olive branch, the ensign of Peace. Her word was out of Virgil, being thus,

> ...*Deus nobis haec otia fecit.*

Beneath that piece was another square table, reaching almost to the bases of the two columns in which two (seeming) sea personages were drawn to the life, both of them lying, or rather leaning on the bosom of the earth, naked; the one a woman, her back only seen; the other a man, his hand stretching and fastening itself upon her shoulder. The word that this dead body spoke, was this,

> *I Decus, I Nostrum.*

Upon the left-hand side of the gate, between the other two columns, were also two square tables. In the one of which were two persons portrayed to the life, naked, and wild in looks, the word,

---

346 forwardness i.e., eagerness

347 grain iota; the lightest of substances

353–4 *Facies...sororum* "They have not all the same appearance, and yet not altogether different; as it should be with sisters" (Ovid, *Metamorphoses* II.13.14)

355 *fixis oculis* "with fixed eyes" (Latin)

357 *Expleri...tuendo* "Her feelings could not be sated, and she burned with looking" (Virgil, *Aeneid* I.713)

358 street Gracechurch (Gracious) Street

374–6 *Tu...superbos* "Remember, James, that you have nations to govern under your command, and these shall be your skills, to make a tradition of peace, to spare the conquered and to subdue utterly the proud" (Virgil, *Aeneid* VI.851–3); this quotation is a compliment to James, who uses it at the close of his own book to his son, *Basilikon Doron*, printed in London in 1603

379 pretty considerable

381 JACOBO... MAGN[O] "To Great King James" (Latin)

384 HENRICI... ABNEP[OS] "Great, great grandson of Henry VII" (Latin)

390 HIC...EST "This is the man, this is he" (Latin)

392 table flat piece of wood used for paintings

399 *Deus...fecit* "God made the peace for us" (Virgil, *Eclogues* I.7)

409 *I...Nostrum* "Pass on, our glory and our friend" (from Ovid, *Ex Ponto* II.8.25)

Expectate solo Trinobanti.

and over that, in another square, carrying the same proportion, stood a woman upright, holding in her hand a shield, beneath whom was inscribed in golden characters,

. . . Spes o fidissima rerum.

And this was the shape and front of the first great square, whose top being flat was garnished with pilasters, and upon the roof was erected a great pedestal on which stood a person carved out to the life (a woman), her left hand leaning on a sword, with the point downward, and her right hand reaching forth a diadem, which she seemed by bowing of her knee and head to bestow upon His Majesty.

On the four corners of this upper part stood four naked portraitures (in great) with artificial trumpets in their hands.

In the arch of the gate was drawn (at one side) a company of palm trees, young and as it were but newly springing, over whose branches two naked winged angels, flying, held forth a scroll, which seemed to speak thus,

Spes altera.

On the contrary side was a vine, spreading itself into many branches and winding about olive and palm trees, two naked winged angels hanging likewise in the air over them, and holding a scroll between them, filled with this inscription,

Uxor tua, sicut vitis abundans,
Et filii tui, sicut palmites olivarum.

If your imaginations (after the beholding of these objects) will suppose that His Majesty is now gone to the other side of this Italian trophy, do but cast your eyes back and there you shall find just the same proportions which the fore-part or breast of our arch carrieth, with equal number of columns, pedestals, pilasters, limned pieces, and carved statues. Over the gate this distichon presents itself:

Nonne tuo imperio satis est Jacobe potiri?
Imperium in musas, aemule quaeris? Habes.

Under which verses a wreath of laurel seemed to be ready to be let fall on His Majesty's head, as he went under it, being held between two naked antique women, their bodies stretching (at the full length) to compass over the arch of the gate. And above those verses, in a fair azure table, this inscription was advanced in golden capitals:

EXPECTATIONI ORBIS TERRARUM
REGIB. GENITO NUMBEROSISS.
REGUM GENITORI FAELICISS.
REGI MARTIGENARUM AUGUSTISS.
REGI MUSARUM GLORIOSISS.
Itali statuerunt laetitiae & cultus signum.

On the right hand of this back part, between two of the columns was a square table, in which was drawn a woman, crowned with beautiful and fresh flowers, a caduceus in her hand, all the notes of a plenteous and lively spring being carried about her. The soul that gave life to this speaking picture, was:

. . . Omnis feret omnia tellus.

Above this piece, in another square, was portrayed a Triton, his trumpet at his mouth, seeming to utter thus much,

Dum coelum stellas.

Upon the left hand of this back part, in most excellent colors, antiquely attired stood the four kingdoms, England, Scotland, France and Ireland,

---

415 ***Expectate . . . Trinobanti*** "Wait for him alone, citizens of London"; ***Trinobanti*** citizens of London (from Stow's reference to citizens of Troynovant)

420 ***Spes . . . rerum*** "Oh surest hope of all things" (from Virgil, *Aeneid* II.280)

430 **in great** in large scale

437 ***Spes altera*** "Our next hope" (Latin; cf. John 12:24)

443–4 ***Uxor . . . olivarum*** "Your wife, like the overflowing vine, and your sons, like branches of olive-trees" (Latin)

447 **trophy** i.e., monument

452 **distichon** two lines of verse, often serving as epigraph or summary

453–4 ***Nonne . . . Habes*** "Surely, James, it is enough that you are master of your own empire? Do you seek likewise an empire among the Muses? You have it" (Latin)

459 **compass** circle

462–7 **EXPECTATIONI . . . *signum*** "To the expectation of the world, born of innumerable kings. To the most fortunate father of kings. To the most majestic king of the sons of Mars. To the most glorious king of the Muses. The Italians have erected this token of joy and honor" (Latin)

471 **caduceus** Mercury's winged staff with two serpents entwined around it

474 ***Omnis . . . tellus*** "The whole earth brings forth everything" (Virgil, *Eclogues* VI.39)

476 **Triton** a sea god

478 ***Dum . . . stellas*** "While the heavens, the stars" (Tibullus, I.4.66)

481 **England . . . Ireland** lands the Tudors had claimed fell under their rule

holding hands together, this being the language of them all,

Concordes stabili Fatorum numine.

The middle great square, that was advanced over the frieze of the gate, held Apollo, with all his ensigns and properties belonging unto him as a sphere, books, a caduceus, an octoedron, with other geometrical bodies, and a harp in his left hand, his right hand with a golden wand in it, pointing to the battle of Lepanto fought by the Turks (of which His Majesty hath written a poem) and to do him honor, Apollo himself doth here seem to take upon him to describe his word,

Fortunate puer.

These were the mutes, and properties that helped to furnish out this great Italian theater upon whose stage the sound of no voice was appointed to be heard, but of one (and that, in the presence of the Italians themselves) who in two little opposite galleries under and within the arch of the gate, very richly and neatly hung, delivered thus much Latin to His Majesty:

The Italian's Speech

Salve, Rex magne, salve. Salutem Majestati tuae Itali, faelicissimum adventum laeti, faelices sub Te futuri, precamur. Ecce hic omnes, exigui munere, pauculi numero: sed magni erga Majestatem tuam animi, multi obsequii. At nec Atlas, qui Coelum sustinet, nec ipsa coeli connexa, altitudinem attingant meritorum Regis optimi; Hoc est, eius, quem de Teipso expressisti doctissimo (Deus!) et admirabili penicillo: beatissimos populos, ubi et philosophus regnat, et Rex Philosophatur. Salve, Rex nobilissime, salve, vive, Rex potentissime, faeliciter. Regna, Rex sapientissime, faeliciter, Itali optamus omnes, Itali clamamus omnes: omnes, omnes.

Having hoisted up our sails, and taken leave of this Italian shore, let our next place of casting anchor be upon the land of the 17 Provinces where the Belgians (attired in the costly habits of their own native country, without the fantastic mixtures of other nations) but more richly furnished with love, stand ready to receive His Majesty, who (according to their expectation) does most graciously make himself and his royal train their princely guests. The house which these strangers have builded to entertain him in is thus contrived.

The Pageant of the Dutchmen, by the Royal Exchange

The foundation of this was (as it were by Fate) laid near unto a royal place, for it was a royal and magnificent labor. It was bounded in with the houses on both sides the street, so proudly (as all the rest also did) did this extend her body in breadth. The passage of state was a gate, large, ascending eighteen foot high, aptly proportioned to the other limbs, and twelve foot wide, arched; two lesser posterns were for common feet cut out and opened on the sides of the other.

Within a small frieze (and kissing the very forehead of the gate) the edifice spoke thus,

Unicus a Fato surgo non degener haeres.

While lifting up your eye to an upper larger frieze, you may there be enriched with these golden capitals,

484 ***Concordes . . . numine*** "United in the firm will of the Fates" (Virgil, *Eclogues* IV.47)

488 **octoedron** octahedron, an eight-sided object

491–3 **pointing . . . poem** "The Lepanto of James the sixth, King of Scotland," in *His Majesty's Poetical Exercises* (Edinburgh, 1571). Lepanto was an historic sea battle of that year in which Spain and Venice decisively defeated the Turks

496 ***Fortunate puer*** "Oh, blessed child" (Virgil, *Eclogues* V.49)

507–18 ***Salve . . . omnes*** Quarto 2, printed later in 1604, includes this translation: "The Italians speech in English. All hail, mighty Monarch! We (the Italians) full of joy to behold your most happy presence, and full of hopes to enjoy a felicity under your royal wing, do wish and pray for the health of Your Majesty. Behold, here we are all: mean in merit; few in number; but towards your Soverign Self, in our loves, great; in our duties, more. For neither Atlas, who bears up heaven; no, nor the arched roof itself of heaven, can by many many degrees reach to the top and glorious height of a good and virtuous King's deservings. And such a one is he whom (good God) most lively, most wisely and in wonderful colors, you did then pencil down in your own person, when you said that those people were blessed where a philosopher rules and where the ruler plays the philosopher. All hail, thou royallest of Kings. Live, thou mightiest of Princes, in all happiness. Reign, thou wisest of Monarchs, in all prosperity. These are the wishes of us Italians; the hearty wishes of us all. Thus we cry all, all, even all"

535 **royal place** the Royal Exchange, London's great burse, was built by Sir Thomas Gresham but officially opened by Elizabeth I (hence royal)

542 **posterns** any gates but those of the main entrance

546 ***Unicus . . . haeres*** "I arise by divine will, and no unworthy successor" (Latin)

JACOBO ANGL. SCOT. FRANC. HIBERN. REGI OPT.
PRINC. MAX. BELGAE ded.

But bestowing your sight upon a large azure table, lined quite through with characters of gold, likewise you may for your pains receive this inscription.

ORBIS RESTITUTOR. PACIS FUND. RELIG.
PROPUG. D. JAC. P.F. REGI. P.P.
D. ANNAE REGIAE CONIUG. SOR. FIL.
NEPTI, ET. D. HENRICO. I. FIL. PRINC.
IUVENT.
IN PUBL. URBIS ET ORBIS LAETITIA.
SECULIQUE FAELICITAT. XVII. BELGIAE
PROV. MERCATORES BENIGNE REGIA
HAC IN URBE EXCEPTI, ET
S. M. VESTRAE OB ANTIQ. SOCIALE FOEDUS,
ET D. ELIZ. BENEFICENT. DEVOTI.
FAUSTA OMNIA ET FOELICIA AD IMPERII
AETERNITAT. PRECANTUR.

Above which (being the heart of the trophy) was a spacious square room left open, silk curtains drawn before it, which (upon the approach of His Majesty) being put by, 17 young damsels (all of them sumptuously adorned, after their country fashion) sat as it were in so many chairs of state, and figuring in their persons the 17 provinces of Belgia, of which every one carried in a scutcheon (excellently penciled) the arms and coat of one.

Above the upper edge of this large square room, and over the first battlement, in another front, advanced for the purpose, a square table was fastened upright, in which was drawn the lively picture of the King in his imperial robes, a crown on his head, the sword and scepter in his hands. Upon his left side stood a woman, her face fixed upon his, a burning heart in her right hand, her left hanging by, a heron standing close unto her. Upon his other side stood upright (with her countenance directed likewise upon him) another woman, winged, and in a frieze beneath them, which took up the full length of this square, this inscription set out itself in golden words:

... *Utroque satellite tutus.*

Suffer your eyes to be wearied no longer with gazing up so high at those sunbeams, but turn them aside to look below through the little posterns whose state swelled quickly up to a greatness, by reason of two columns that supported them on either side. In a table, over the right-hand portal, was in perfect colors drawn a serpent, pursued by a lion. Between them adders and snakes, chasing one another, the lion scornfully casting his head back to behold the violence of a black storm that heaven poured down to overtake them. The sound that came from all this, was thus:

... *Sequitur gravis ira feroces.*

The opposite body to this (on the other side, and directly over the other portal, whose pomp did in like manner lean upon and uphold itself by two main columns) was a square piece, in which were to be seen sheep browsing, lambs nibbling, birds flying in the air, with other arguments of a serene and untroubled season, whose happiness was proclaimed in this manner.

... *Venit alma cicuribus aura.*

Directly above this, in a square table, were portrayed two kings, reverently and antiquely attired, who seemed to walk upon these golden lines,

Nascitur in nostro Regum par nobile Rege
Alter Iesiades, alter Amoniades.

From whom, lead but your eye in a straight line to the other side (over the contrary postern) and there in a second upper picture you may meet

550–1 JACOBO . . . ded. "The Belgians dedicate this to James, best King and mightiest Prince of England, Scotland, France, and Ireland" (Latin)

556–68 *Orbis . . . precantur* "To the restorer of the world, securer of peace, defender of the faith, our lord King James, father of the family, father of the country; to our lady Queen Anne, a wife, sister, daughter and granddaughter; and to the lord Henry, first son and prince: may they be happy. Among the public rejoicing of the city and the world, and the happiness of the age, the merchants of the seventeen Belgian provinces, kindly received in this royal city, devoted both to your Sacred Majesty on account of the ancient treaty of alliance, and to the lady Elizabeth for her kindness, pray for all things auspicious and fruitful to your eternal reign" (Latin)

573 country i.e., country's

592 *Utroque . . . tutus* "safe with an attendant on either side" (Latin)

605 *Sequitur . . . feroces* "Heavy wrath follows the warlike ones" (Latin)

611 arguments emblems

614 *Venit . . . aura* "A kindly breeze comes to the tame ones" (Latin)

618–19 *Nascitur . . . Amoniades* "There is born in our noble King the equal of other kings, a second Jesiades, a second Amoniades" (Latin); ***Iesiades*** Solomon, a common name given to James to denote his learning and his wisdom; ***Amoniades*** son of Ammon or Jupiter, possibly here Apollo

with two other kings, not fully so antique, but as rich in their ornaments; both of them, out of golden letters, composing these words,

Lucius ante alios, Edwardus, & inde JACOBUS
Sextus, & hic sanxit, sextus & ille fidem.

And these were the nerves, by which this great triumphal body was knit together; in the inferior parts of it, upon the shoulders whereof (which were garnished with rows of pilasters that supported lions rampant bearing up banners) there stood another lesser square, the head of which wore a coronet of pilasters also; and above them, upon a pedestal, curiously closed in between the tails of two dolphins, was advanced a woman, holding in one hand a golden warder, and pointing with the forefinger of the other hand up to heaven. She figured Divine Providence, for so at her feet was written,

Provida Mens Coeli.

Somewhat beneath which was to be seen an imperial crown, two scepters being fastened (cross-wise) unto it, and delivering this speech:

... *Sceptra haec concreditit uni.*

At the elbows of this upper square, stood upon the four corners of a great pedestal four pyramids, hollow, and so neatly contrived that in the night time (for anger that the sun would no longer look upon these earthly beauties) they gave light to themselves, and the whole place about them. The windows, from whence these artificial beams were thrown, being cut out in such a fashion, that (as Ovid, describing the Palace of the Sun, says)

Clara micante auro, flammasque imitante pyropo.

So did they shine afar off, like chrysolites, and sparkled like carbuncles: between those two pyramids that were lifted up on the right hand, stood Fortitude; her pillar resting itself upon this golden line,

Perfero curarum pondus, discrimina temno.

Between the two pyramids on the other side, Justice challenged her place, being known both by her habit and by her voice, that spoke thus,

Auspice me dextra solium regale perennat.

We have held His Majesty too long from entering this third gate of his Court Royal; it is now high time that those eyes, which on the other side ache with rolling up and down for his gladsome presence, should enjoy that happiness. Behold, he is in an instance passed through; the objects that there offer themselves before him, being these:

Our Belgic Statue of Triumph wears on her back as much riches as she carried upon her breast, being altogether as glorious in columns; standing on tip-toe, on as lofty and as proud pyramids; her walks encompassed with as strong and as neat pilasters. The colors of her garments are as bright, her adornments as many, for,

In the square field, next and lowest, over one of the portals were the Dutch country people toiling at their husbandry: women carding of their hemp, the men beating it, such excellent art being expressed in their faces, their stoopings, bendings, sweatings, &c. that nothing is wanting in them but life (which no colors can give) to make them be thought more than the works of painters.

Lift up your eyes a little above them, and behold their Exchange; the countenance of the merchants there being so lively that bargains seem to come from their lips.

But instead of other speech, this is only to be had,

PIO INVICTO
R. JACOBO.
QUOD FEL. EIUS AUSPICIIS UNIVERSUM
BRIT, IMPERIUM PACAT, MARE TUTUM
PORTUS APERIT.

626–7 ***Lucius . . . fidem*** a puzzling passage; literally, it translates, "Lucius before the others, Edward and then James the Sixth, and former, latter, and the sixth made sacred their trust" (Latin); it probably argues the sanctity of James's kingship following that of Lucius, a mythical king who introduced Christianity into early Britain, and Edward the Confessor

634 **coronet** crown

635 ***curiously*** artfully, ingeniously

637 **warder** staff of office

640 ***Provida . . . Coeli*** "The foreseeing mind of heaven" (Latin)

644 ***Sceptra . . . uni*** "He entrusts these scepters to one man" (Latin)

654 ***Clara . . . pyropo*** "with bright gold sparkling and bronze imitating flames" (Ovid, *Metamorphoses* II.2)

655 **chrysolites** precious stones greenish in color

656 **carbuncles** forms of garnet, precious stones red in color

660 ***Perfero . . . temno*** "I bear the weight of cares and look down on crises"

664 ***Auspice . . . perennat*** "The royal throne lasts forever with me as patron on its right hand"

681 **carding** combing and cleaning

692–6 **PIO . . . APERIT** "To the godly and invincible King James, because he has made the whole British Empire fortunate under his auspices and the sea safe, the harbor open" (Latin)

Over the other portal, in a square (proportioned to the bigness of those other) men, women and children (in Dutch habits) are busy at other works: the men weaving, the women spinning, the children at their hand-looms &c. Above whose heads you may with little labor walk into the Mart, where as well the froe as the burgher are buying and selling, the praise of whose industry (being worthy of it) stands published in gold, thus:

QUOD MUTUIS COMMERCIIS, ET ARTIFICUM,
NAUTARUMQUE SOLERTIA CRESCAT,
DESIDIA EXULAT, MUTUAQUE
AMICITIA CONSERVETUR.

Just in the midst of these four squares, and directly over the gate, in a larger table whose feet are fastened to the frieze, is their fishing and shipping lively and sweetly set down: the skipper (even though he be hard tugging at his net) loudly singing this:

Quod celebret hoc emporium prudenti industria suos,
Quovis terrarum negotiatores emittat, exteros
Humaniter admittat, foris famam, domi divitias
augeat.

Let us now climb up to the upper battlements where, at the right hand, Time stands: at the left (in a direct line) his daughter Truth; under her foot is written,

Sincera.

And under his,

Durant.
Sincera Durant.

In the midst of these two, three other persons are ranked together, Art, Sedulity, and Labor, beneath whom, in a frieze roving along the whole breadth of that square, you may find these words in gold,

Artes, Perfecit, Sedulitate, Labor.

As on the foreside, so on this and equal in height to that of Divine Providence, is the figure of a woman advanced beneath whom is an imperial crown with branches of olive fixed (crosswise) unto it, and gives you this word,

Sine caede et sanguine.

And thus have we bestowed upon you all the dead colors of this picture (wherein, notwithstanding, was left so much life) as can come from art. The speaking instrument was a boy, attired all in white silk, a wreath of laurel about his temples. From his voice came this sound:

Sermo ad Regem

Quae tot sceptra tenes forti, Rex maxime, dextra,
Provida Mens summi numinis illa dedit.
Aspice ridentem per gaudia plebis Olympum,
Reddentem et plausus ad sua verba suos,
Tantus honos paucis, primi post secula mundi
Obtigit, et paucis tantum onus incubuit,
Nam regere imperiis populum faelicibus unum,
Ardua res, magnis res tamen apta viris.
At non unanimes nutu compescere gentes,
Non hominis pensum, sed labor ille Dei,
Ille ideo ingentes qui temperat orbis habenas,
Adjungit longas ad tua fraena manus.
Et menti de mente sua praelucet, et artem
Regnandi, regnum qui dedit ille, docet.
Crescentes variis cumulat virtutibus annos,
Quas inter pietas, culmina summa tenet.
Hac proavos reddis patriae, qui barbara gentis
Flexere inducto numine corda ferae.
Hac animos tractas rigidos, subigisque rebelles,

698–701 **men . . . hand-looms** (weaving was a customary scene in civic pageantry)

703 **froe** Dutchwoman; **burgher** Dutchman

706–9 **QUOD . . . CONSERVETUR** "That by mutual trade the skill both of craftsmen and sailors may increase, idleness be banished and mutual friendship preserved" (Latin)

716–18 ***Quod . . . augeat*** "That this market may celebrate its own people for their prudent industry, it sends businessmen out anywhere in the world, and humanely admits foreigners. May it increase its fame abroad, its wealth at home" (Latin)

723–6 ***Sincera . . . Durant*** "Things honest endure" (Latin)

738 ***Sine . . . sanguine*** "Without murder and bloodshed" (Latin)

745 ***Sermo . . . Regem*** "Sermon to the King" (Latin)

746–83 ***Quae . . . decus*** Thus Q2: "Which Verses utter thus much in English Prose. Great KING, those so many scepters, which even fill thy right hand, are all thine own, only by the providence of heaven. Behold, heaven itself laughs to see how thy subjects smile, and thunders out loud plaudits to hear their *Avès.* This honor of sovereignty, being at the beginning of the world, bestowed but upon few; upon the heads of few were the cares of a crown set. For to sway only but one empire (happily) as it is a labor, hard; so none can undergo the weight, but such as are mighty. But (with a beck as it were) to control many nations (and those of different dispositions, too) oh, the arm of man can never do that, but the finger of GOD. God therefore (that guides the chariot of the world) holds the reins of thy kingdom in his own hand. It is he whose beams lend a light to thine. It is he that teaches thee the art of ruling, because none but he made thee a King. And therefore, as thou growest in years, thou waxest old in virtues, of all thy virtues, Religion sitting highest. And most

Et level persuades quod trahis ipse iugum,
Illi fida comes terram indignata profanam,
Aut nunc te tanto Rege reversa Themis.
Assidet et robusta soror, ingentibus ausis
Pro populo carum tradere prompta caput.
Quin et Regis amor, musae et dilectus Apollo,
Regali gaudent subdere plectra manu.
Aurea et ubertas solerti nata labore,
Exhibet aggestas ruris et urbis opes.
Sunt haec dona poli, certa quae prodita fama
Miratum ut veniat, venit uterque polus.
Venimus et Belgae, patriis gens exul ab oris
Quos fovit tenero mater Eliza sinu,
Matri sacratum, Patri duplicamus amorem,
Poscimus et simili posse favore frui.
Sic Deum Panthaici tibi proferat alitis oevum,
Sceptra per innumeros qui tibi tradit avos.
Sic Regina tui pars altera, et altera proles,
Spes populi longum det, capiatque decus.

While the tongues of the strangers were employed in extolling the gracious aspect of the King, and his princely behavior towards them, His Majesty (by the quickness of Time, and the earnestness of expectation, whose eyes ran a thousand ways to find him) had won more ground and was gotten so far as to Saint Mildred's Church in the Poultery close to the side of which a scaffold was erected where (at the City's cost) to delight the Queen with her own country music, nine trumpets, and a kettle drum, did very sprightly and actively sound the Danish March: whose cunning and quick stops, by that time they had touched the last lady's ear in the train. Behold, the King was advanced up so high as to Cheapside into which place (if Love himself had entered, and seen so many gallant gentlemen, so many ladies, and beautiful creatures, in whose eyes glances (mixed with modest looks) seemed to dance courtly measures in their motion) he could not have chosen to have given the room any other name than The Presence Chamber.

The stately entrance into which was a fair gate in height 18 foot, in breadth 12, the thickness of the passage under it being 24. Two posterns stood wide open on the two sides, either of them being 4 foot wide, and 8 foot high. The two portals that jetted out before these posterns had their sides open four several ways, and served as pedestals (of rustic) to support two pyramids which stood upon four great balls and four great lions: the pedestals, balls, and pyramids, devouring in their full upright height, from the ground line to the top, just 60 foot. But burying this mechanic body in silence, let us now take note in what fashion it stood attired. Thus then it went appareled.

The Device at Soper-Lane End

Within a large compartiment, mounted above the forehead of the gate, over the frieze, in capitals was inscribed this title:

NOVA FAELIX ARABIA

Under that shape of Arabia, this island being figured which two names of New and Happy the country could by no merit in itself challenge to be her due, but only by means of that secret influence accompanying His Majesty wheresoever he goes, and working such effects.

The most worthy personage advanced in this place was Arabia Britannica, a woman attired all in white, a rich mantle of green cast about her, an imperial crown on her head, and a scepter in one hand, a mound in the other upon which she sadly leaned: a rich veil (under the crown) shadowing

---

worthy, for by Religion, the hearts of barbarous nations are made soft. By Religion, Rebellion has a yoke cast about her neck and is brought to believe that those laws to which thou submittest even thy royal self, are most easy. With Religion, Justice keeps company, who once fled from this profane world but, hearing the name of KING JAMES, she is again returned. By her side sits her sister Fortitude, whose life is ready (in heroic actions) to be lavishly spent, for the safety of thy people. Besides, to make these virtues full, Apollo and the Muses resign, the one his golden lyre, the other their laurel, to thy royal hands while Plenty (daughter to Industry) lays the blessings both of country and city in heaps at thy feet. These are the gifts of heaven, the fame of them spreading itself so far that (to wonder at them) both the Poles seem to come together. We (the Belgians) likewise come to that intent: a nation banished from our own cradles, yet nursed and brought up in the tender bosom of princely Mother ELIZA. The love which we once dedicated to her (as a mother) doubly do we vow it to you, our Sovereign and Father, entreating we may be sheltered under your wings now as then under hers. Our prayers being that he who through the loins of so many grandfathers hath brought thee to so many kingdoms may likewise multiply thy years and lengthen them out to the age of a phoenix. And that thy Queen (who is one part of thyself) with thy progeny (who are the second hopes of thy people) may both give to, and receive from, thy kingdom immortal glory"

796 quick stops lively changes

804–5 Presence Chamber the center of the royal court where ceremonial business was conducted and the King might be seen by anyone admitted to the court

806 stately entrance (at Soper Lane)

822 compartiment subdivisions of the ornamental design

825 NOVA . . . ARABIA "New happy (fruitful) Arabia" (Latin); Arabia was emblematic for fertility

828 challenge claim

her eyes, by reason that her countenance (which till His Majesty's approach could by no worldly object be drawn to look up) was pensively dejected. Her ornaments were marks of Chastity and Youth: the crown, mound, and scepter, badges of sovereignty.

Directly under her in a cant by herself, Fame stood upright, a woman in a watchet robe, thickly set with open eyes and tongues, a pair of large golden wings at her back, a trumpet in her hand, a mantle of sundry colors traversing her body, all these ensigns displaying but the property of her swiftness, and aptness to disperse rumors.

In a descent beneath her, being a spacious concave room, were exalted five mounts, swelling up with different ascensions upon which sat the Five Senses drooping: viz.

1. *Auditus*, Hearing.
2. *Visus*, Sight.
3. *Tactus*, Feeling.
4. *Olfactus*, Smelling.
5. *Gustus*, Taste.

Appareled in robes of distinct colors, proper to their natures, and holding scutcheons in their hands upon which were drawn hieroglyphical bodies to express their qualities.

Some pretty distance from them (and as it were in the midst before them) an artificial laver or fount was erected called the Fount of Arete (Virtue). Sundry pipes (like veins) branching from the body of it the water receiving liberty but from one place, and that very slowly.

At the foot of this fount, two personages (in greater shapes than the rest) lay sleeping. Upon their breasts stuck their names, Detractio, Oblivio: the one holds an open cup about whose brim a wreath of curled snakes were winding, intimating that whatsoever his lips touched was poisoned. The other held a black cup covered, in token of an envious desire to drown the worth and memory of noble persons.

Upon an ascent, on the right hand of these, stood the three Charites or Graces, hand in hand, attired like three sisters.

Aglaia,		Brightness, or Majesty.
Thalia,	figuring	Youthfulness, or flourishing.
Euphrosyne		Cheerfulness, or gladness.

They were all three virgins their countenances laboring to smother an innated sweetness and cheerfulness that appareled their cheeks, yet hardly to be hid. Their garments were long robes of sundry colors, hanging loose; the one had a chaplet of sundry flowers on her head, clustered here and there with the fruits of the earth. The second, a garland of ears of corn. The third, a wreath of vine-branches, mixed with grapes and olives.

Their hair hung down over their shoulders loose, and of a bright color, for that epithet is properly bestowed upon them by Homer in his Hymn to Apollo.

PULCHRICOMAE CHARITES,
The Bright-Hair'd Graces.

They held in their hands penciled shields. Upon the first was drawn a rose: on the second, three dice; on the third, a branch of myrtle.

	Pleasantness
Figuring	Accord.
	Flourishing

In a direct line against them stood the three Hours, to whom in this place we give the names of Love, Justice, and Peace. They were attired in loose robes of light colors, painted with flowers, for so Ovid apparels them.

Conveniunt pictis incictae vestibus Horae.

Wings at their feet, expressing their swiftness, because they are lackeys to the sun: *Iungere equos Tytan velocibus imperat Horis.* Ovid.

Each of them held two goblets, the one full of flowers (as ensign of the spring), the other full of ripened figs, the cognizance of summer.

Upon the approach of His Majesty (sad and solemn music having beaten the air all the time of his absence, and now ceasing), Fame speaks.

---

844 **cant** niche

845 **watchet** pale blue, inclining toward green; often used to denote steadfastness

851 **descent** declivity

880 **three Charites** Aglaia (splendor), Thalia (bloom), and Euphrosyne (mirth), daughters of Zeus and Eurynome (popular figures in pageantry)

886 **innated** innate, inborn

898 **Hymn** "To Apollo," line 194

907–9 **direct . . . Peace** (from Hesiod's *Theogony*, lines 901–2)

912 ***Conveniunt . . . Horae*** "The Hours meet, girded in ornately-colored robes" (Ovid, *Fasti* V.217)

914–15 ***Iungere . . . Horis*** "Titan [the Sun] orders his horses to yoke together with the swift Hours" (Ovid, *Metamorphoses* II.118)

917 **ensign** sign

918 **cognizance** recognizable sign

Fama. Turn into ice mine eye-balls, whilst the sound
Flying through this brazen trump, may back rebound
To stop Fame's hundred tongues, leaving them mute
As in an untouched bell, or stringless lute,
For Virtue's Fount, which late ran deep and clear,
Dries, and melts all her body to a tear.
You Graces! and you Hours that each day run
On the quick errands of the golden sun,
O say! to Virtue's Fount what has befell,
That thus her veins shrink up.
Charites, Horae. We cannot tell.
Euphrosyne. Behold the five-fold guard of Sense, which keeps
The sacred stream, sit drooping: near them sleep
Two horrid monsters. Fame! summon each Sense,
To tell the cause of this strange accidence.

Hereupon Fame sounding her trumpet, Arabia Britannica looks cheerfully up. The Senses are startled. Detraction and Oblivion throw off their iron slumber, busily bestowing all their powers to fill their cups at the Fount with their old malicious intention to suck it dry, but a strange and heavenly music suddenly striking through their ears, which causing a wildness and quick motion in their looks, drew them to light upon the glorious presence of the King, they were suddenly thereby daunted and sunk down, the Fount in the same moment of time, flowing fresh and abundantly through several pipes, with milk, wine, and balm, while a person (figuring Circumspection) that had watched day and night to give note to the world of this blessed time, which he foresaw would happen, steps forth on a mounted stage extended 30 foot in length from the main building, to deliver to His Majesty the interpretation of this dumb mystery.

This presenter was a boy, one of the choristers, belonging to Paul's.

His speech

[*Circumspection*]. Great Monarch of the West, whose glorious stem,
Doth now support a triple diadem,
Weighing more than that of thy grand grandsire Brute,
Thou that may'st make a King thy substitute,
And dost besides the red-rose and the white,
With the rich flower of France thy garland dight,
Wearing above Kings now, or those of old,
A double crown of laurel and of gold.
Oh, let my voice pass through thy royal ear,
And whisper thus much, that we figure here:
A new Arabia, in whose spiced nest
A phoenix lived and died in the sun's breast.
Her loss, made Sight, in tears to drown her eyes,
The Ear grew deaf, Taste like a sick-man lies,
Finding no relish. Every other Sense
Forgot his office, worth and excellence,
Whereby this Fount of Virtue gan to freeze,
Threatened to be drunk up by two enemies,
Snakey Detraction, and Oblivion,
But at thy glorious presence, both are gone.
Thou being that sacred phoenix, that dost rise
From th'ashes of the first. Beams from thine eyes
So virtually shining that they bring
To England's new Arabia, a new spring.
For joy whereof, Nymphs, Senses, Hours, and Fame,
Echo loud hymns to his imperial name.

At the shutting up of this speech, His Majesty (being ready to go on), did most graciously feed the eyes of the beholders with his presence, till a song was spent, which to a loud and excellent music (composed of violins and another rare artificial instrument) wherein besides sundry several sounds effused (all at one time) were also sensibly distinguished the chirpings of birds, was by two boys (choristers of Paul's) delivered in sweet and ravishing voices.

Cantores

Troynovant is now no more a city.
Oh, great pity! is't not pity?
And yet her towers on tiptoe stand,
Like pageants built on fairy land,
And her marble arms,

936 accidence occurrence
939–42 Detraction . . . dry Harrison, in *Arches of Triumph*, declares the two attempted to beat down the fountain with clubs
945 light upon discover
957 Paul's St. Paul's School
959 stem lineage
960 triple (apparently Ireland is omitted)
961 Brute mythical founder of Britain; see Munday's *Triumphs*
962 Thou . . . substitute (since he is now an emperor)
963 red-rose emblem of the House of Lancaster; **white** white rose, emblem of the House of York
964 flower of France the fleur-de-lys; **dight** array
966 double . . . gold as king of poetry and of country
970 phoenix Elizabeth, from whose ashes James arises
981 virtually with virtue
995 *Cantores* singers (Latin)

Like to magic charms,
Bind thousands fast unto her,
That for her wealth and beauty daily woo her,
Yet for all this, is't not pity?
Troynovant is now no more a city.

2

Troynovant is now a summer arbor,
Or the nest wherein doth harbor,
The eagle, of all birds that fly
The sovereign, for his piercing eye.
If you wisely mark,
'Tis besides a park,
Where runs (being newly born)
With the fierce lion, the fair unicorn,
Or else it is a wedding hall,
Where four great Kingdoms hold a festival.

3

Troynovant is now a bridal chamber,
Whose roof is gold, floor is of amber,
By virtue of that holy light
That burns in Hymen's hand, more bright,
Than the silver moon,
Or the torch of noon.
Hark what the echoes say!
Britain till now ne'er kept a holiday
For Jove dwells here, and 'tis no pity,
If Troynovant be now no more a city.

Nor let the screw of any wresting comment upon these words,

Troynovant is now no more a city

enforce the author's invention away from his own clear, straight, and harmless meaning. All the scope of this fiction stretching only to this point, that London (to do honor to this day, wherein springs up all her happiness) being ravished with unutterable joys makes no account (for the present) of her ancient title, to be called a city (because that during these triumphs she puts off her formal habit of Trade and Commerce, treading even Thrift itself under foot), but now becomes a reveler and a courtier. So that, albeit in the end of the first stanza, 'tis said,

Yet for all this, is't not pity,
Troynovant is now no more a city.

by a figure called castigatio or the mender. Here follows presently a reproof, wherein titles of summer arbor, the eagle's nest, a wedding hall &c. are thrown upon her, the least of them being at this time by virtue of poetical heraldry, but especially in regard of the state that now upholds her, thought to be names of more honor than that of her own. And this short apology doth our verse make for itself, in regard that some (to whose settled judgment and authority the censure of these devices was referred) brought (though not bitterly) the life of those lines into question. But appealing with Machaetas to Philip, now these reasons have awakened him. Let us follow King James, who having passed under this our third gate, is by this time graciously receiving a gratulatory oration from the mouth of Sir Henry Montague, Recorder of the City, a square low gallery set around with pilasters being for that purpose erected some 4 foot from the ground, and joined to the front of the Cross in Cheap, where likewise stood all the Aldermen, the Chamberlain, Town Clerk, and Council of the City.

The Recorder's Speech

High Imperial Majesty, it is not yet a year in days since with acclamation of the people, citizens and nobles, auspiciously here at this Cross was proclaimed your true succession to the crown. If then it was joyous with hats, hands and hearts, lift up to heaven to cry King James, what is it now to see King James? Come, therefore, oh, worthiest of kings as a glorious bridegroom through your royal chamber: but to come nearer, *Adest quem querimus.* Twenty and more are the Sovereigns we have served since our conquest, but conqueror of hearts it is you and

1010 **piercing eye** the eagle was another symbol associated in the popular mind with the Roman Empire; here the sovereign shares the eagle's ability to see everything clearly at a distance (and, according to legend, even able to look directly into the sun)

1014 **lion . . . unicorn** the supports of the Stuart royal arms

1028 **wresting** perverse

1044 **castigatio** castigate in order to emend (?); there is no known reference to this term in the rhetorical books of the period

1055–6 **Machaetas to Philip** (may allude to the story of Philip of Macedon [Machaetas] in which he wrongly accused a foreign woman when drunk; she claimed she would appeal to him but only when he was sober)

1058 **third** (actually, the fourth, following Fenchurch, the Italians, and the Dutch)

1059–60 **Sir . . . City** Sir Henry Montague, grandson of the Lord Chief Justice and a member of Middle Temple, was MP for Higham Ferrers in 1601, knighted by James on July 23, 1603, and elected Recorder on James's recommendation to the Lord Mayor and aldermen in a letter dated May 25, 1603

1064 **the Chamberlain** Cornelius Fishe

1065 **Town Clerk** William Sebright

1067 **not yet a year** James was declared King by proclamation at 2 p.m. on March 24, 1603, the day Elizabeth died

1072 **lift** i.e., lifted

1075–6 **come nearer** proceed to the point

1076 ***Adest . . . querimus*** "He is present whom we seek" (Latin; cf. Matt. 28)

1077–8 **our conquest** the Norman Conquest

your posterity that we have vowed to love and wish to serve while London is a city. In pledge whereof my Lord Mayor, the Aldermen, and Commons of the City, wishing a golden reign unto you, present your greatness with a little cup of gold.

At the end of the oration three cups of gold were given (in the name of the Lord Mayor and the whole body of the city) to His Majesty, the young Prince, and the Queen.

All which but above all (being gifts of greater value) the loyal hearts of the citizens, being lovingly received, his Grace was (at least it was appointed he should have been) met on his way near to the Cross, by Sylvanus dressed up in green ivy, a cornet in his hand, being attended on by four other Sylvans in ivy likewise, their bows and quivers hanging on their shoulders and wind instruments in their hands.

Upon sight of His Majesty, they make a stand, Sylvanus breaking forth into this abrupt passion of joy.

Sylvanus. Stay Sylvans, and let the loudest voice of music proclaim it (even as high as heaven) that he is come.
Alter Apollo redit, novus en, iam regnat Apollo.

Which acclamation of his was borne up into the air, and there mingled with the breath of their musical instruments, whose sound being vanished to nothing, thus goes our speaker on:

Sylvanus. Most happy Prince, pardon me, that being mean in habit, and wild in appearance (for my richest livery is but leaves, and my stateliest dwelling but in the woods), thus rudely with piping Sylvans I presume to intercept your royal passage. These are my walks, yet stand I here, not to cut off your way, but to give it a full and a bounteous welcome, being a messenger sent from the Lady Irene my mistress, to deliver an errand to the best of all these worthies, your royal self. Many kingdoms hath the Lady sought out to abide in, but from them all hath she been most churlishly banished: not that her beauty did deserve such unkindness, but that (like the eye of heaven) hers were too bright, and there were no eagles breeding in those nests that could truly behold them.

At last here she arrived, Destiny subscribing to this warrant, that none but this land should be her inheritance. In contempt of which happiness, envy shoots his impoisoned stings at her heart, but his adders (being charmed) turn their dangerous heads upon his own bosom. Those that dwell far off pine away with vexing to see her prosper, because all the acquaintance which they have of her is this, that they know there is such a goodly creature as Irene in the world, yet her face they know not, while all those that here sleep under the warmth of her wings adore her by the sacred and celestial name of Peace, for number being (as her blessings are) infinite.

Her daughter *Euporia* (well known by the name of Plenty) is at this present with her (being indeed never from her side). Under yonder arbor they sit, which after the daughter's name is called *Hortus Euporiae* (Plenty's Bower) chaste are they both, and both maidens in memory of a virgin, to whom they were nurse children, for whose sake (because they were bound to her for their life) me have they charged to lay at your imperial feet (being your hereditary due) the tribute of their love, and with it thus to say.

That they have languished many heavy months for your presence, which to them would have been (and proud they are that it shall be so now) of the same operation and influence that the sun is to the spring, and the spring to the earth. Hearing therefore what treble preferment you have bestowed upon this day, wherein besides the beams of a glorious sun, two other clear and gracious stars shine cheerfully on these her homely buildings into which (because no duty should be wanting) she hath given leave even to strangers to be sharers in her happiness, by suffering them to bid you likewise welcome. By me (once hers, now your vassal) she entreats, and with a knee sinking lower than the ground on which you tread do I humbly

1085 **three cups** these cups, given in cases of crimson velvet at the order of the Court of Aldermen, cost £416.10s.5d.
1091–2 **at . . . been** (probably one of the speeches omitted; see below, line 1830–1)
1093 **Sylvanus** god of the woods, a traditional figure in pageantry (cf. the entertainment at Elvetham)
1094 **cornet** small wind instrument
1095 **Sylvans** woodland spirits
1098 **stand** a pageant at the Little Conduit
1104 ***Alter . . . Apollo*** "A second Apollo returns; see, he is new; now Apollo is king" (Virgil, *Eclogues* IV.10)
1117 **Irene** i.e., Peace
1149 **virgin** Elizabeth I
1163–4 **two . . . stars** Queen Anne and Prince Henry
1167 **strangers** foreigners (i.e., the Dutch and the Italians)

execute her pleasure, that ere you pass further you would deign to walk into yonder garden. The Hesperides live not there but the Muses, and the Muses no longer than under your protection. Thus far am I sent to conduct you thither, prostrately begging this grace (since I dare not, as being unworthy, lackey by your royal side) in that yet these my green followers and myself may be joyful fore-runners of your expected approach. Away, Sylvans.

And being (in this their return) come near to the arbor, they gave a sign with a short flourish from all their cornets that His Majesty was at hand, whose princely eye while it was delighting itself with the quaint object before it, a sweet pleasure likewise courted his ear in the shape of music, sent from the voices of nine boys (all of them Choristers of Paul's) who in that place presenting the nine Muses sang the ditty following to their viols and other instruments.

But, lest leaping too bluntly into the midst of our garden at first, we deface the beauty of it, let us send you round about it, and survey the walls, alleys, and quarters of it as they lie in order.

This being the fashion of it.

The passages through it were two gates, arched and grated arborwise, their height being 18 foot, their breadth 12: from the roof, and so on the sides down to the ground, cucumbers, pompions, grapes, and all other fruits growing in the land, hanging artificially in clusters. Between the two gates, a pair of stairs were mounted with some 20 ascents; at the bottom of them (on two pillars) were fixed two satyrs carved out in wood, the sides of both the gates, being strengthened with four great French frames standing upon pedestals, taking up in their full height 25 foot.

The upper part also carried the proportion of an arbor, being closed with their round tops, the midst whereof was exalted above the other two, Fortune standing on the top of it, the garnishments for the whole bower, being apples, pears, cherries, grapes, roses, lilies, and all other both fruits and flowers most artificially molded to the life. The whole frame of this summer banqueting house stood (at the ground line) upon 44 foot; the perpendicular stretching itself to 45. We might (that day) have called it The Music Room, by reason of the change of tunes that danced round about it; for in one place we heard a noise of cornets, in a second, a consort, the third (which sat in sight), a set of viols, to which the Muses sang.

The principal persons advanced in this bower, were Irene (Peace) and Euporia (Plenty) who sat together.

Irene.

Peace was richly attired, her upper garment of carnation, hanging loose, a robe of white under it, powdered with stars, and girt to her; her hair of a bright color, long, and hanging at her back, but interwoven with white ribbons and jewels; her brows were encompassed with a wreath compounded of the olive, the laurel, and the date tree. In one hand she held a caduceus (or Mercury's rod, the god of eloquence); in the other, ripe ears of corn gilded; on her lap sat a dove: all these being ensigns and furnitures of Peace.

Euporia.

Plenty, her daughter sat on the left hand, in changeable colors, a rich mantle of gold traversing her body; her hair large and loosely spreading over her shoulders; on her head a crown of poppy and mustard seed, the antique badges of Fertility and Abundance; in her right hand a cornucopia, filled with flowers, fruits &c.

Chrusos.

Directly under these sat Chrusos, a person figuring Gold, his dressing a tinsel robe of the color of gold.

Argurion.

And close by him, Argurion, Silver, all in white tinsel; both of them crowned, and both their hands supporting a globe between them, in token that they commanded over the world.

1174 Hesperides nymphs who guarded Hera's golden apples, which grew in a garden beyond the sea protected by a dragon
1178 lackey act as a running footman
1182 Sylvans i.e., Sylvanus
1196 alleys pathways that divided a garden into separate areas
1200 grated trellised
1202 pompions pumpkins
1207 satyrs woodland spirits, the upper half man, the lower half goat
1217 molded carved, shaped
1224 consort a company of musicians
1232 carnation light pink
1233 girt fastened
1241 furnitures i.e., furnishings
1249 cornucopia Horn of Plenty
1253 tinsel fine cloth, usually wool or silk, interwoven with gold or silver threads

Pomona.

Pomona, the goddess of garden fruits, sat at the one side of Gold and Silver, attired in green, a wreath of fruitages circling her temples; her arms naked; her hair beautiful, and long.

Ceres.

On the other side sat Ceres, crowned with ripened ears of wheat, in a loose straw-colored robe.

In two large descents (a little below them) were placed at one end,

The Nine Muses	Clio Euterpe Thalia Melpomene Terpsicore Erato Polymnia Urania Calliope	With musical instruments in their hands, to which they sang all the day.

At the other end.

The 7 liberal arts.	Grammar Logic Rhetoric Music Arithmetic Geometry Astrology	Holding shields in their hands, expressing their several offices.

Upon the very upper edge of a fair large frieze, running quite along the full breadth of the arbor, and just at their feet were planted ranks of artificial artichokes and roses.

To describe what apparel these Arts and Muses wore were a hard labor, and when it were done, all were but idle. Few tailors know how to cut out their garments: they have no wardrobe at all, not a mercer nor merchant, though they can all write and read very excellently well, will suffer them to be great in their books. But (as in other countries) so in this of ours, they go attired in such thin clothes, that the wind every minute is ready to blow through them. Happy was it for them, that they took up their lodging in a summer arbor, and that they had so much music to comfort them, their joys (of which they do not every day taste) being notwithstanding now infinitely multiplied in this, that where before they might have cried out till they grew hoarse, and none would hear them, now they sing.

Aderit que vocatus Apollo.

Chorus in full voices answering it thus:

Ergo alacris Sylvas, et caetera rura voluptas
Panaque pastoresque tenet, Dryadasque puellas,
Nec Lupus insidias pecori, nec retia cervis
Ulla dolum meditantur, amat bonus otia Daphnis;
Ipsi laetitia voces ad sidera iactant
Intonsi montes: ipsae iam carmina Rupes,
Ipsa sonant Arbusta, Deus, Deus ille!

Sylvanus (as you may perceive by his office before) was but sent of an errand; there was another of a higher calling, a travailer and one that had gone over much ground, appointed to speak to His Majesty, his name Vertumnus, the master gardener, and husband to Pomona. To tell you what clothes he had on his back were to do him wrong, for he had (to say truth) but one suit. Homely it was, yet meet and fit for a gardener. Instead of a hat, his brows were bound about with flowers, out of whose thick heaps here and there peeped a queen-apple, a cherry, or a pear; this boon-grace he made of purpose to keep his face from heat (because he desired to look lovely) yet the sun found him out, and by casting a continual eye at him, while the old man was dressing his arbors, his cheeks grew tawny, which color for the better grace he himself interpreted, blushing. A white head he had, and sun-burned hands. In the one he held a weeding hook, in the other a grafting knife. And this was the tenor of his speech. That he was bound to give thanks to heaven in that the arbor and the trees which growing in that

1265 Ceres goddess of the harvest

1274–5 Nine Muses daughters of Zeus and Mnemosyne who presided over (and helped to inspire) various arts and sciences

1283–7 . . . arts the trivium and quadrivium that was the basis for English grammar school and university curricula

1296 mercer dealer in textiles

1309 *Aderit . . . Apollo* "And he will come, the Apollo we call upon" (Latin)

1311–17 *Ergo . . . ille!* "Therefore pleasure grips the cheerful woods, and the rest of the countryside, both Pan and the shepherds, dryads and young girls, neither does the wolf plan to ambush the flock, nor does any net plot its trickery for the deer; good Daphnis loves the peace. The shaggy mountains themselves hurl their voices for joy to the stars; the very rocks and trees now sing songs – the god, the god, 'tis he" (Virgil, *Eclogues* V.58–64)

1319 of i.e., off

1320 travailer laborer

1322 Vertumnus god of the changing seasons and giver of fruit

1329 queen-apple a species of apple that ripens early

1330 boon-grace a sunshade worn on the front of a cap

fruitful Cynthian garden began to droop and hang down their green heads and to uncurl their crisped forelocks, as fearing and in some sort feeling the sharpness of autumnian malice, are now on the sudden by the divine influence appareled with a fresh and more lively verdure than ever they were before. The nine Muses that could expect no better entertainment than sad banishment, having now lovely and amiable faces: Arts that were threatened to be trod under foot by barbarism, now (even at sight of His Majesty, who is the Delian patron both of the Muses and Arts) being likewise advanced to most high preferment while the very rural and Sylvan troops danced for joy. The Lady therefore of the place, Irene (his mistress) in name of the Praetor, Consuls and Senators of the City, who carefully prune this garden (weeding out all hurtful and idle branches that hinder the growth of the good) and who are indeed, Ergatai Pistoi, faithful laborers in this piece of ground, she doth in all their names (and he in behalf of his Lady) offer themselves, this arbor, the bowers and walks, yea her children gold and silver, with the loving and loyal hearts of all those Sons of Peace, standing about him, to be disposed after his royal pleasure. And so wishing his happy arrival at a more glorious bower, to which he is now going, yet welcoming him to this, and praying His Majesty not to forget this poor arbor of his Lady, music is commanded to carry all their prayers for his happy reign, with the loud Amen of all his subjects, as high as heaven.

Cantor

Shine, Titan, shine.
Let thy sharp rays be hurled
Not on this under world,
For now 'tis none of thine.

These first four lines were sung by one alone, the single lines following by a Chorus in full voices.

Chorus. No, no, 'tis none of thine.

2

But in that sphere,
Where what thine arms enfold
Turns all to burnished gold,
Spend thy gilt arrows there,
Chorus. Do, do, shoot only there.

3

Earth needs thee not,
Her childbed days are done,
And she another sun,
Fair as thyself has got.
Chorus. A new new sun is got.

4

Oh, this is he!
Whose new beams make our spring,
Men glad and birds to sing,
Hymns of praise, joy, and glee.
Chorus. Sing, sing, oh, this is he!

5

That in the north
First rising shone (so far)
Bright as the morning star,
At his gay coming forth.
Chorus. See, see, he now comes forth.

6

How soon joys vary!
Had still he stayed! Oh, then
Happy both place and men,
But here he list not tarry.
Chorus. O grief! he list not tarry.

7

No, no, his beams,
Must equally divide,
Their heat to orbs beside,
Like nourishing silver streams.
Chorus. Joys slide away like streams.

8

Yet in this lies
Sweet hope; how far soever,
He bides, no clouds can sever
His glory from our eyes.
Chorus. Dry, dry, your weeping eyes.

9

And make heaven ring,
His welcomes shouted loudly,
For heaven itself looks proudly,
That earth has such a King.
Chorus. Earth has not such a King.

His Majesty dwelt here a reasonable long time, giving both good allowance to the song and music, and liberally bestowing his eye on the workmanship of the place, from whence at the

---

1341 **Cynthian** Elizabethan (Elizabeth was called Cynthia in reference to the goddess' chastity)
1342 **crisped** tightly curled
1344 **autumnian** i.e., autumnal
1352 **Delian** of Delos, home of Apollo, god of music and poetry
1356–7 **Praetor... Senators** another analogy to Rome; here the Praetor means Lord Mayor; the Consuls, sheriffs; the Senators, aldermen

1375 **Titan** the sun
1401 **north** i.e., Scotland
1403 **morning star** Venus
1411 **list not** choose not to
1415 **orbs beside** other orbs
1421 **bides** abides, stays

length departing, his next entrance was, as it were, into the closet or rather the privy chamber to this our Court Royal, through the windows of which he might behold the cathedral temple of Saint Paul upon whose lower battlements an anthem was sung by the Choristers of the church to the music of loud instruments. Which being finished, a Latin oration was viva voce delivered to His Grace, by one of Master Mulcaster's scholars at the door of the Free School founded by the Mercers.

Oratio Habita, et ad Regem, et coram Rege prae Schola Paulina.

Brevis ero, ne ingratus sim, Rex serenissime, licet, at plane, et plene putem Regem tam prudentem, in tam profusa suorum laetitia, ita se hodie patientia contra taedium armavisse, ne ullius taedii ipsum posset taedere. Aedificium hoc magno sumptu suo extructum Dominus Johannes Collettus Ecclesiae Paulinae Decanus, sub Henrico septimo, majestatis tuae prudentissimo abavo, erudiendae pueritiae consecravit, ut huius scholae infantia tuo in Regnum Anglicanum iure coetanea existat. Tanta magnificentia conditum parque magnificentia dotatum fidelissimae Mercerorum huius urbis primariae semper, hodie etiam Praetoriae societati tuendum testamento moriens commendavit. Quae societas, et de mortui fundatoris spe, et nostrae educationis studio fidem suam sanctissime exolvit. His nos cum multis aliis erudimur, qui communi nomine totius pueritiae Anglicanae, a Domino Rege, licet sponte sua ad omnia optima faris incitato, humillime tamen contendimus, ut quemadmodem sua aetatis ratione in omni re adultioribus prospicit, ita in summae spei Principis Henrici gratiam tenerioribus, parique cum ipso aetate pueris, in scholarum cura velit etiam consulere. Virgae enim obsequium, sceptri obedientiam et parit, et praeit, inquit preceptor meus. Quique metu didicit iuvenis parere puerque, grandibus imperiis officiosus erit. Habent scholae Anglicanae multa, in quibus Regiam majestatis correctionem efflagitant, ne inde in academias implumes evolent unde in Rempublicam implumiores etiam e prima nuditate emittuntur. Quod malum a Preceptore nostro accepimus: qui annos iam quatuor supra quinquaginta publice, privatimque eruiendae pueritiae praefuit, et haec

---

1435 privy chamber the King's private quarters where only those closest to him may be admitted

1441 viva voce spoken aloud

1442 Master Mulcaster Richard Mulcaster, from 1596 the Master of St. Paul's School; from 1561 to 1586 he was Master of the Merchant Taylors' School. He was also known for his books on pedagogy

1443–4 Free . . . Mercers (founded in 1541 on the N side of Cheap Street by St. Mary Cole Church)

1445–96 *Oratio . . . Dixi* Thus Q2: "The Oration delivered at Paul's School by one of Master Mulcaster's Scholars. Most Gracious Sovereign, my speech shall not be long for fear it appear loathsome; yet do I fully and freely believe that a king (so crowned with wisdom as yourself) hath (this day) put on such strong armor of patience to bear-off tediousness in this so main and universal meeting of joy in his subjects that the extension and stretching out of any part of time can by no means seem irksome unto him. This building received her foundation from the liberal purse of John Colet, Dean of Paul's Church under Henry VII, great-grandfather to Your Majesty, and was by him consecrated to learning for the erudition of youth, to the intent that the infancy of this school may now, by your right to the kingdom of England, grow up to a full and ripe age. Which work of his, so magnificent for the building, so commendable for the endowments, he by last will and testament bequeathed to the faithful Society and Brotherhood of the Mercers, always the chiefest and now this year by reason of a Lord Mayor (who is a member among them) more than the chiefest of the Companies of this city. Which Society have most religious performed all rites both due to the hopes of our deceased founder and to the ornaments of our education. Within these walls, we with many others suck the milk of learning, and in the general name of all the youth in England most humbly entreat of our Lord the King (who of himself, we know, is forward enough to advance all goodness) that, as by reason of his manly years, his chiefest care is spent about looking to, and governing men, so (notwithstanding) in favor of that his royal son Henry (Prince of unspeakable hopes) he would a little suffer his eye to descend and behold our school and therein to provide that those who are but green in years and of equal age with his Princely issue may likewise receive a virtuous education. For the obedience which is given to the rod brings along with it obedience to the scepter, nay (as our Master tells us) it goes even before it.
Quique metu didicis, iuuenis parere, puerque, Grandibus Imperijs officosus erit.
Our schools of England are in many limbs deformed whose crookedness requires the hands of a King to set them straight lest out of these young nests those that are there bred, flying without their feathers into universities, should afterward light upon the branches of the commonwealth more naked than at first, by reason they were not perfectly fledged. Which evil hath been discovered by the observation of our teacher who now, by the space of more than 54 years (both publicly and privately) hath instructed youth and with no little grief of his own hath both here and abroad sifted out these gross vices that are mingled among schools. Oh, how happy, therefore, should this our nursery of learning be if (after having first met with Colet a founder so religious, and, secondly, the Mercers our patrons, men so faithful and virtuous), our Lord the King would now at last also be pleased (considering many kings of England by doing so have won wonderful love from their subjects) to suffer his royal name to be enrolled among the citizens of London by vouchsafing to be free of that worthy and chiefest Society of Mercers! What glory should thereby rise up to the city? what dignity to that Society? to this our school what infinite benefit? what honor besides our Sovereign himself might acquire, he that makes this wish now wisheth rather (in fitter place and at fitter hours) to discover to his Prince, than now clean beyond his aim, to overshoot himself by tediousness. The Almighty &c."

1452 *Johannes Collettus* John Colet; in 1512 he founded the Free School at St. Paul's Churchyard for 153 poor men's children, later transferring the oversight of the school to the Mercers' Company

1457 *primariae* the Mercers' Company was reckoned to be the oldest, founded in 1172

scholarum errata, cum aliquo etiam dolore suo, et passim, et sparsim deprehendit. Nostra haec scholar fundatorem Colletum hominem tam pium, tutores Merceros homines tam fidos consequuta, quam esset foelix, si placeret, Domino etiam Regi, quod Regibus Angliae, ad summam apud suos charitatem saepissime profuit, huic Mercerorum principi societati, fratrem se, et concivem adscribere. Quantum huic urbi ornamentum, quantum societiati honestamentum, quantum scholae nostrae emolumentum? Quantus etiam Regi ipsi honos inde accederet, mavult, qui hoc vult alias inter alia per otium Regi suo apperire, quam hodie cum taedio et praeter aream eidem explicare. Omnipotens Deus Jesus Christus et cum eo, ac per eum noster, et Pater, et Deus serenissimum Regem Jacobum, honoratissimam Reginam Annam, nobilissimum Principem Henricum, reliquamque Regiae stirpis ad omnia summa natam sobolem diu nobis ita incolumes tueatur, ut cum huius vitae secundissimum curriculum confeceritis, beatissimam vitae caelestis aeternitatem consequamini. Dixi.

Our next arch of triumph was erected above the Conduit in Fleet Street, into which (as into the long and beauteous gallery of the City) His Majesty being entered, afar off (as if it had been some swelling promontory, or rather some enchanted castle guarded by ten thousand harmless spirits) did his eye encounter another Tower of Pleasure.

Presenting itself.

Fourscore and ten foot in height, and fifty in breadth; the gate twenty foot in the perpendicular line, and fourteen in the ground-line; the two posterns were answerable to these that are set down before. Over the posterns rose up in proportionable measures two turrets, with battlements on the tops. The middest of the building was laid open to the world, and great reason it should be so, for the globe of the world was there seen to move, being filled with all the degrees, and states that are in the land, and these were the mechanical and dead limbs of this carved body. As touching those that had the use of motion in it, and for a need durst have spoken, but that there was no stuff fit for their mouths.

The principal and worthiest was Astraea (Justice) sitting aloft, as being newly descended from heaven, gloriously attired; all her garments being thickly strewed with stars, a crown of stars on her head: a silver veil covering her eyes. Having told you that her name was Justice, I hope you will not put me to describe what properties she held in her hands since every painted cloth can inform you.

Directly under her, in a cant by herself, was Arete (Virtue) enthroned, her garments white, her head crowned, and under her Fortuna, her foot treading on the globe, that moved beneath her intimating that His Majesty's fortune was above the world, but his virtues above his fortune.

Invidia.

Envy, unhandsomely attired all in black, her hair of the same color, filleted about with snakes, stood in a dark and obscure place by herself, near unto Virtue, but making show of a fearfulness to approach her and the light, yet still and anon, casting her eyes, sometimes to the one side beneath, where on several greces sat the four Cardinal Virtues:

Viz. { Justitia
Fortitudo
Temperantia
Prudentia } In habiliments fitting to their natures.

And sometimes throwing a distorted and repining countenance to the other opposite seat on which His Majesty's four kingdoms were advanced.

Viz. { England
Scotland
France
Ireland }

All of them in rich robes and mantles, crowns on their heads, and scepters with penciled scutcheons in their hands, lined with the coats of the particular kingdoms. For very madness, that she beheld these glorious objects, she stood feeding on the heads of adders.

The four Elements in proper shapes (artificially and aptly expressing their qualities), upon the

1509 answerable corresponding
1510 before (in the description of Nova Faelix Arabia, lines 808–10)
1516 degrees ranks; **states** estates
1519 durst dared
1520–1 but ... mouths but no scripts were provided for them
1528 properties i.e., the sword and scales or balances
1529 filleted bound, as with a headband
1558 penciled painted with a fine brush
1559 coats i.e., coats of arms
1563 four Elements Harrison describes it this way: "over the gate, and just in the midst of the building (which was spacious and left open) a globe was seen to move being filled with all the estates that are in the land; and this engine was turned about by four persons, representing the four elements (earth, water, air, and fire) who were placed so quaintly that the globe seemed to have his motion even on the crowns of their heads"; **artificially** artfully

approach of His Majesty, went round in a proportionable and even circle, touching that cantle of the globe (which was open) to the full view of His Majesty, which being done, they bestowed themselves in such comely order, and stood so, as if the engine had been held up on the tops of their fingers.

Upon distinct ascensions (neatly raised within the hollow womb of the globe) were placed all the states of the land, from the nobleman to the plowman, among whom there was not one word to be heard, for you must imagine as Virgil saith:

Aegl.4. *Magnus ab integro seclorum nascitur ordo.*
Iam redit et virgo redeunt Saturnia Regna.*
*Astraea

That it was now the golden world, in which there were few praters.

All the tongues that went in this place was the tongue of Zeal, whose personage was put on by W. Bourne, one of the servants to the young prince.

And thus went his speech

[*Zeal*]. The populous globe of this our English isle,
Seemed to move backward, at the funeral pile
Of her dead female Majesty. All states
From nobles down to spirits of meaner fates,
Moved opposite to Nature and to Peace,
As if these men had been th'antipodes,
But see, the virtue of a regal eye,
Th'attractive wonder of man's Majesty,
Our globe is drawn in a right line again,
And now appear new faces, and new men.
The Elements, Earth, Water, Air, and Fire,
(Which ever clipped a natural desire,
To combat each with other) being at first
Created enemies to fight their worst,
See at the peaceful presence of their King,
How quietly they moved, without their sting.
Earth not devouring, Fire not defacing,
Water not drowning, and the Air not chasing,
But propping the quaint fabric that here stands,
Without the violence of their wrathful hands.
Mirror of times, lo where thy Fortune sits,
Above the world, and all our human wits,
But thy high Virtue above that. What pen,
Or art, or brain can reach thy virtue then?
At whose immortal brightness and true light,
Envy's infectious eyes have lost their sight,
Her snakes (not daring to shoot forth their stings
'Gainst such a glorious object) down she flings
Their forks of venom into her own maw,
While her rank teeth the glittering poisons chaw,
For 'tis the property of Envy's blood
To dry away at every kingdom's good,
Especially when she had eyes to view
These four main virtues figured all in you,
Justice in causes, Fortitude 'gainst foes,
Temp'rance in spleen, and Prudence in all those,
And then so rich an empire, whose fair breast
Contains four kingdoms by your entrance blest,
By Brute divided, but by you alone,
All are again united and made One,
Whose fruitful glories shine so far and even,
They touch not only earth, but they kiss heaven,
From whence Astraea is descended hither,
Who with our last Queen's spirit fled up thither,
Fore-knowing on the earth she could not rest,
Till you had locked her in your rightful breast.
And therefore all estates, whose proper arts
Live by the breath of Majesty, had hearts
Burning in holy Zeal's immaculate fires,
With quenchless ardors and unstained desires,
To see what they now see, your powerful Grace,

1565 went round (they revolved the globe by means of the "engine")
1565–6 proportionable well-proportioned
1566 cantle port
1572 ascensions gradations
1577–8 *Magnus . . . Regna* "Great order is born from the completion of the ages. And now the virgin [Astraea] returns, and Saturn's reign is come again" (Latin) (Astraea was also another name for Elizabeth I)
1579 golden world Saturn reigned during the Golden Age when Astraea lived on earth; man's impiety during the Bronze Age and Iron Age drove her back to heaven, but she will return when the Golden Age is restored
1580 praters foolish, idle talkers
1583 W. Bourne William Borne or Byrd, an actor with the Admiral's Men (and so by then Prince Henry's Men) since 1597; he began writing plays in 1601
1587 pile pyre (Elizabeth was buried in Westminster Abbey, not cremated)
1591 antipodes opposite end of the earth
1593 attractive i.e., able to attract
1597 clipped embraced
1604 quaint refined
1614 maw gullet
1615 chaw chew

Reflecting joys on every subject's face:
These painted flames and yellow burning stripes,
Upon this robe, being but as shows and types,
Of that great Zeal. And therefore in the name
Of this glad City, whither no prince ever came,
More loved, more longed for, lowly I entreat,
You'ld be to her as gracious as y'are great:
So with reverberate shouts our globe shall ring,
The music's close being thus: God save our King.

If there be any glory to be won by writing these lines, I do freely bestow it (as his due) on Tho[mas] Middleton, in whose brain they were begotten, though they were delivered here: *Quae nos non fecimus ipsi, vix ea nostra voco.*

But having pieced up our wings now again with our own feathers, suffer us awhile to be pruning them, and to lay them smooth, while this song, which went forth at the sound of haut-boys and other loud instruments, flies along with the train.

Cantor/ Cantores

Where are all these honors owing?
Why are seas of people flowing?
Tell me, tell me Rumor,
Though it be thy humor,
More often to be lying,
Than from thy breath to have truth flying
Yet alter, now, that fashion,
And without the stream of passion,
Let thy voice swim smooth and clear,
When words want gilding, then they are most dear.
Behold where Jove and all the states
Of heav'n, through heav'n's seven silver gates,
All in glory riding
(Backs of clouds bestriding)
The Milky Way do cover,
Which starry path being measur'd over,
The deities convent,
In Jove's high court of Parliament.
Rumor thou dost lose thine aims,
This is not Jove, but one as great, King JAMES.

And now take we our flight up to Temple Bar (the other end of this our gallery) where by this time, His Majesty is upon the point of giving a gracious and princely farewell to the Lord Mayor and the City. But that his eye meeting a seventh beautiful object is invited by that to delay awhile his (lamented) departure.

The building being set out thus.

The front or surface of it was proportioned in every respect like a temple, being dedicated to Janus, as by this inscription over the Janus head may appear.

Jano Quadrifronti Sacrum.

The height of the whole edifice, from the ground line to the top was 57 foot, the full breadth of it 18 foot: the thickness of the passage 12.

The personages that were in this temple, are these:

1. The principal person, Peace.
2. By her stood Wealth.
3. Beneath the feet of Peace lay Mars (War) groveling.
4. And upon her right hand (but with some little descent) was seated Quiet, the first hand-maid of Peace.
5. She had lying at her feet, Tumult.
6. On the other side was the second hand-maid, Liberty, at whose feet lay a cat.
7. This person trod upon Servitude.
8. The third hand-maid was Safety.
9. Beneath her was Danger.
10. The fourth attendant was Felicity.
11. At her feet, Unhappiness.

Within the temple was an altar to which, upon the approach of the King, a Flamen appears, and to him the former Genius of the City.

The effect of whose speech was that whereas the Flamen came to perform rites there, in honor of one Anna, a goddess of the Romans, the Genius vows that none shall do sacrifice there but himself, the offering that he makes being the heart of the City, &c.

And thus have we (lowly and aloof) followed our Sovereign through the seven triumphal gates of this his Court Royal, which name, as London received at the rising of the sun, so now at his

---

1647–8 Tho[mas] Middleton (Dekker's reference would seem to be intentional alongside his intentional omission of Jonson's name throughout this work)

1649–50 *Quae . . . voco* "I hardly call these things ours which we did not make ourselves" (Latin)

1651 pieced patched

1655 train procession

1666 want lack

1673 convent convene

1677 Temple Bar the pageant at Temple Bar, summarized here, was the work of Ben Jonson and printed in *His Part* (1604), lines 372–763

going from her (even in a moment) she lost that honor. And being (like an actor on a stage) stripped out of her borrowed majesty, she resigns her former shape and title of City; nor is it quite lost, considering it went along with him, to whom it is due. For such virtue is begotten in princes, that their very presence hath power to turn a village to a city, and to make a city appear great as a kingdom. Behold how glorious a flower happiness is, but how fading. The minutes (that lackey at the heels of Time) run not faster away than do our joys. What tongue could have expressed the raptures on which the soul of the City was carried beyond itself for the space of many hours? What wealth could have allured her to have closed her eyes, at the coming of her King, and yet see her bridegroom is but stepped from her, and in a minute (nay in shorter time than a thought can be born) is she made a widow. All her consolation being now to repeat over by rote those honors which lately she had perfectly by heart. And to tell of those joys, which but even now she really beheld; yet thus of her absent beloved do I hear her gladly and heartily speaking.

Virgi[il] *In freta dum fluvii current: dum montibus umbrae,*
Lustrabunt convexa, polus dum sidera pascit,
Semper honos, nomenque tuum, laudesque manebunt.

The Pageant in the Strand

The City of Westminster and Duchy of Lancaster, perceiving what preparation their neighbor city made to entertain her Sovereign; though in greatness they could not match her, yet in greatness of love and duty they gave testimony that both were equal. And in token they were so, hands and hearts went together, and in the Strand erected up a monument of their affection.

The invention was a rainbow, the moon, sun, and the seven stars, called the Pleiades, being advanced between two pyramids. Electra (one of those seven hanging in the air, in figure of a comet) was the speaker, her words carrying this effect.

That as His Majesty had left the City of London happy, by delivering it from the noise of tumult, so he would crown this place with the like joys; which being done, she reckons up a number of blessings that will follow upon it.

The work of this was thought upon begun and make perfect in xii. days.

As touching those five which the City builded, the arbor in Cheapside and the Temple of Janus at Temple Bar, were both of them begun, and finished in six weeks. The rest were taken in hand first in March last, after His Majesty was proclaimed, upon which at that time they wrought till a month after Saint James Day following, and then gave over by reason of the sickness; at this second setting upon them, six weeks more were spent.

The city elected sixteen committees to whom the managing of the whole business was absolutely referred of which number, four were aldermen, the other grave commoners.

There were also committees appointed as overseers, and surveyors of the works.

Artificum operariumque in hoc tam celebri apparatu, summa.

The city employed in the framing, building, and setting up of their five arches these officers and workmen.

A clerk that attended on the committees.
Two officers that gave summons for their meetings &c.
A clerk of the works.
Two master carpenters.
Painters.

Of which number, those that gave the main direction and undertook for the whole business, were only these seven:

1726 resigns returns to; submits to

1729 virtue power

1743–4 by rote routinely from memory

1748–50 *In . . . manebunt* "While rivers flow to the sea, while shadows drift over the slopes of mountains, and the poles cherish the stars, your honor, name and praises will always remain" (Virgil, *Aeneid* I.607–9)

1752 Westminster a separate town and government where Parliament sat; **Duchy of Lancaster** royal lands and properties kept apart from other crown lands and administered from the Savoy in Westminster

1779 Saint James Day July 25, the original date for James's coronation, postponed because of plague

1783 sixteen committees appointed by the Common Council of London on March 30, 1603, to prepare for the reception and coronation of the King

1786 grave commoners one representing each of the Twelve Great Livery Companies

1789 *Artificum . . . summa* "A summary of the craftsmen and workmen [employed] in this so famous preparation" (Latin; again unnecessary and a final jab at Jonson)

William Friselfield.
George Mosse.
John Knight.
Paul Isacson.
Samuell Goodrick.
Richard Wood
George Heron.

Carvers.	24

Over whom, Stephen Harrison, joiner, was appointed chief, who was the sole inventor of the architecture and from whom all directions, for so much as belonged to carving, joining, molding, and all other work in those five pageants of the City (painting excepted) were set down.

Joiners	80
Carpenters	60
Turners	6
Laborers to them	6
Sawyers.	12
Laborers during all the time and for the day of the triumph	70

Besides these, there were other artificers, as: plumbers, smiths, molders.

To the Reader.

Reader, you must understand, that a regard being had that His Majesty should not be wearied with tedious speeches, a great part of those which are in this book set down were left unspoken, so that thou dost here receive them as they should have been delivered, not as they were. Some errors wander up and down in these sheets, under the printer's warrant which notwithstanding may by thy authority be brought in, and receive their due correction. Other faults pardon, these I think are the grossest.

Finis

1815 Joiners furniture makers who joined rather than nailed parts

1817 Turners craftsmen who used lathes to form wooden parts

The Masque of Blackness

Ben Jonson

A daughter of Niger (Inigo Jones). From David Lindley, ed., *Court Masques* (Oxford: Oxford University Press, 1995).

The most sought-after commission for any performance in the reign of King James was that for the annual Twelfth Night masque staged before the court at Whitehall that ended each year's Christmas revels. The first such royal invitation, for January 6, 1605, went to the playwright Ben Jonson and the scenic designer Inigo Jones. The result, *The Masque of Blackness*, produced at a cost of £3,000, established a partnership, between a scholarly writer and an architect heavily influenced by the luxuriousness of Italian art, that would last for years. Throughout the Jacobean period, Jonson and Jones remained the undisputed leaders of the masque as a form of entertainment, as lavish spectacle, and as a means of symbolic meaning. Today, the masque is perhaps the most difficult English Renaissance performance to recreate; a few pages of script, embellished with Jonson's introduction and notes, is all that is extant of what would have been a three-hour performance of pageantry, formal speeches, music, extraordinary scenic effects, and dancing. Yet the script is what ties all of these features together, establishing one or more themes in a dialectic that, at the close of the masque, will find some kind of reconciliation of initially opposing forces. In the course of its development, the masquers will leave the stage and dance with members of the audience, the representational icons in partnership with the mimetic beholders. Indeed, by merging the masquer with the spectator, masques effectively transform the courtly audience into the idealized world of the poet's controlling vision, another way in which what begins dialectically ends in synthesis and unity. Moreover, Jonson's script, he tells us, registering "the honor and splendor of these spectacles" is what he publishes so that this "eminent celebration" will be "redeem[ed]" from "oblivion."

Jonson also notes, early on, that for the chief personages in his initial masque, "it was Her Majesty's will to have them blackamores at first"; this masque, then, as many to follow, was the Queen's doing. This may explain how Jonson received his commission: the Queen's closest companion, Lucy, Countess of Bedford, was Jonson's patron. Nor is the choice to portray Africans unprecedented. At his wedding in 1590 to Anne, Princess of Denmark, in Oslo, James had arranged for an entertainment featuring blacks: "By his orders four young Negroes danced naked in the snow in front of the royal carriage"; unfortunately, "the cold was so intense that they died a little later of pneumonia." That was the first spectacle staged for the royal couple; but it was followed by a wedding pageant featuring forty-two men dressed in white and silver, something like the women in *The Masque of Blackness*, all "wearing visors over blackened faces." At Queen Anne's subsequent reception in Scotland on May 1, 1590, performers in blackface greeted her in pageantry: "three score young men of the town, like Moors, and clothed in cloth of silver, with chains about their necks and bracelets about their arms," whom the poet John Burel called "savagely noble." Unlike these three presentations, however, or the English mummings, Christmas revels, street pageants, or royal Elizabethan entertainments out of which the masque grew on English soil, *The Masque of Blackness* centers on identifiable court women in blackface and on a central dance with mysterious hieroglyphics held up in explanation that is not only extraordinarily spectacular but just as extraordinarily abstruse – so much so that on printing the masque Jonson added a narrative introduction and his own notes (included here in the footnotes).

Nevertheless, like all masques the fundamental situation, or device, is fairly easily grasped. Oceanus, guardian of the realm of Albion, is approached by Niger "in form and color of an Ethiop," and twelve masquers, including the Queen herself, disguised as his daughters. They enter in a great shell, led by their lightbearers, the Oceaniae, seated on sea monsters who seem to bounce about in the "water." Niger tells Oceanus that his daughters have read poets who tell them how beautiful foreign women are and they have become dissatisfied with their dark skins. When they saw a face glowing with light in a lake they also saw the lines inscribed by an oracle who told them they could be made white if they sought a remedy in a land whose name ended in -TANIA, a land lit by a far greater light than the one that had burned their skins black. They travel west through lands such as Mauretania and Aquitania, until they arrive at Britannia, where the goddess of the moon, Aethiopia, appears to tell them they have found the land they were seeking. The masquers leave the shell to celebrate by dancing until they are interrupted by Aethiopia, who asks them to go perform certain rites which will transform them into being fair.

Critics have long pointed out that Jonson faces two problems with such a story: he must make blackness permissible for the ladies of the court even though, culturally, it meant ugliness, dirtiness, or even evil. And he must also find a way for the women to become white once again at the conclusion. The first problem takes most of his attention. The masquers are given colorful costumes that sparkle in the light that plays on them from the Oceaniae; their backdrop is a huge shell the color of mother of pearl. The first Song likewise directs the audience's response: "this beauteous race, Who, though but black in face, Yet are they bright, And full of life and light," perhaps acknowledging specifically the Queen herself, full of life because six months pregnant. Blacks, then, are people of energy and fertility. Moreover, as daughters of Oceanus, Jonson points out in a note, their father was "source of gods and things, because nothing is born or decays without moisture." Water serves as the basis, too, for a unifying element in the main dance where all the strange emblems and symbols are aligned both with water and with light: purity, truth, education, clarity, and divinity. Such ideas are further emphasized in the costuming. Niger and Oceanus both wear blue for water; the moon as light is in silver; and the masquers wear costumes of both "azure and silver." Jonson's notes also direct his readers, if not his original spectators, back to the Bible, reminding them quite possibly of the frontispiece of the Bishops' Bible printed in 1602 which shows Adam and Eve in a garden distinctively African. But then Genesis had already told them that the River Gihon, commonly glossed as the Nile, was a part of God's Creation. The other chief symbol, that of light, is first linked to the moon, perhaps to suggest its relationship to the biological cycles of women and so, once again, energy and fertility: but the moon, like the water, is ever changing and ever constant. The dialectic in the masque, then, is one of strangeness and diversity synthesized in the underlying constancy: the moon repeats her cycles; the water, through its waves, nevertheless is the same. Water and light, in the end, lead the searching masquers to "A world divided from the world," to the "blessèd isle" of "Britannia, whose new name makes all tongues sing," "A world divided from the world" that is "Ruled by a sun that to this height doth grace it, Whose beams shine day and night, and are of force To blanch an Ethiop, and revive a corpse." That, of course, is King James himself – who can perform such miracles with "His light sciential," an allusion to his Solomonic learning and wisdom. In Albion – literally, "white land" – the masquers meet James, "Neptune's son, who ruleth here," so that he too becomes complicit in the masque even before he joins others in dancing with the masquers. The whole entertainment, then, turns on the performance of the enlightenment, rule, and learning of James, who alone resolves the matter of race and allows the masquers' leader Aethiopia, as the white moon, to take them off to become white. Through the medial and miraculous power of James, Ethiopia joins Aethiopia, as Oceanus and the Oceaniae bring the women to rest happily in Albion. The matter of racial change will happen offstage, just after the masque. So James's decision, with Aethiopia's management, will "[form] all beauty" so that "this night, the year gone round, You do again salute this ground, And in the beams of yond' bright sun Your faces dry, and all is done." By Twelfth Night 1606, then, the dancers will reappear before the court in another entertainment cleansed, dried, purified, and white.

Not everyone at court, however, was appreciative of such costly and dazzling extravaganzas. For Francis Bacon, court masques were "but toys"; for a character in Beaumont and Fletcher's play *The Maid's Tragedy*, masques were "tied to rules of flattery" – they were obsequious and self-serving. For still others – who doubtless remembered seeing Shakespeare's *Othello* staged at court just a few months before, in the fall of 1604 – the whole matter of blackface must have been, at the least, distasteful. Othello, after all, had turned savage and murdered his white wife. For such spectators, Queen Anne had turned the revels into a grotesque mockery of court ideology and had made herself, at such a festivity, the Lady of Misrule. Instead of promoting the love and honor of the King, her decision to dress up as a blackamoor enacted a sexual lust and a spiritual depravity that made the Queen, not the King, the center of attention and wonder. As for the Queen, she may have been responding to her husband's own spectacle of blackamoors – who had died of the cold. But then, as this foreign Queen knew, blacks had not been treated well in her new country: in 1554 John Lok had abducted four Africans and taken them to England for display; and the Englishman John Hawkins had established a lucrative slave trade, buying Africans with English goods, selling them to the New World as slaves, and taking the goods thus received in the Americas back to England for sale. He had, just as *The Masque of Blackness* could seem to do, commodified Africans. Certainly Dudley Carleton was one spectator of the masque who was disgusted. "Apparel was rich," he wrote John Chamberlain, "but too light and Courtesan-like for such great ones. Instead of vizards [masks], their faces and arms up to the elbows were painted black... and you cannot imagine a more ugly sight than a troop of lean-cheeked Moors." In a later letter, he called it "a very loathsome sight."

At the court masque as at royal performances at court, the King had the best perspective, and he was always a second – and perhaps the main – focal point for the others in the audience. In *The Masque of Blackness*, Queen Anne has contrived things – no matter what the symbology of the "story" – to make herself the center. It could be seen as an act of subversion. It could be seen as the Queen seeking compensation for four African boys who died from dancing naked in the snow. The court was well aware that James's marriage was not a happy one; that he and his Catholic Queen often lived apart and seemed always to be quarreling. They had in fact fought over Prince Henry, each in turn attempting to hold him hostage as they made their initial way from Scotland to England. The Queen's blackface, setting herself and her women apart, might have been commenting on the homosocial King who even then was setting himself apart with his court favorites, all of them men and boys. If so, this very real struggle for attention, control, and sympathy, danced out before the court itself, ended with a general dance in which the white audience was required to dance with the black masquers. Enclosing the dance within the masque – for the final speeches came after the general dance of masquers and audience – means that James has, at least momentarily, surrendered to the strategies of the spectacle. We are left to determine who wins such a battle of will and whether, in his first outing at court, Jonson had the finesse – especially without his introduction and notes – to pull it off in a way that would please his Queen and not condemn his King.

Further Reading

Aasand, Hardin, "'To blanch an Ethiop, and revive a corse': Queen Anne and *The Masque of Blackness*," *Studies in English Literature 1500–1900* 32:2 (Spring 1992): 273–85.

Bevington, David, and Holbrook, Peter, eds., *The Politics of the Stuart Court Masque*. Cambridge: Cambridge University Press, 1998.

Gordon, D. J., "The Imagery of Ben Jonson's *Masques of Blacknesse and Beautie*," in *The Renaissance Imagination*, ed. Stephen Orgel (Berkeley: University of California Press, 1975), pp. 134–41.

Hall, Kim F., "Sexual Politics and Cultural Identity in *The Masque of Blackness*," in *The Performance of Power: Theatrical Discourse and Politics*, ed. Sue-Ellen Case and Janelle Reinelt (Iowa City: University of Iowa Press, 1991), pp. 3–18.

Kelly, Ann Cline, "The Challenge of the Impossible: Ben Jonson's *Masque of Blackness*," *CLA Journal* 20:3 (March 1977): 341–53.

Nicoll, Allardyce, *Stuart Masques and the Renaissance Stage*, esp. pp. 58–60. New York: Harcourt, Brace, and Company, 1938.

Orgel, Stephen, *The Illusion of Power: Political Theater in the English Renaissance*. Berkeley: University of California Press, 1975.

——, *The Jonsonian Masque*. Cambridge, Mass.: Harvard University Press, 1965.

Siddiqi, Yumna, "Dark Incontinents: The Discourses of Race and Gender in Three Renaissance Masques," *Renaissance Drama* n.s. 23 (1992): 139–63.

The Masque of Blackness

The honor and splendor of these spectacles was such in the performance as, could those hours have lasted, this of mine now had been a most unprofitable work. But when it is the fate even of the greatest and most absolute births to need and borrow a life of posterity, little had been done to the study of magnificence in these if presently with the rage of the people, who, as a part of greatness, are privileged by custom to deface their carcasses, the spirits had also perished. In duty, therefore, to that Majesty who gave them their authority and grace, and, no less than the most royal of predecessors, deserves eminent celebration for these solemnities, I add this later hand to redeem them as well from ignorance as envy, two common evils, the one of censure, the other of oblivion.

Pliny, Solinus, Ptolemy, and of late Leo the African, remember unto us a river in Ethiopia

Textual Variants

Title] the masque was first published in Q in 1608 in *The Characters of Two Royal Masques. The one of Blackness, The Other of Beauty. Personated by the most magnificent of Queens,* ANNE, *Queen of Great Britain* [*sic*] *with her honorable Ladies.* The heading to the text printed here reads: *The Queen's Masques.* The first of Blackness Personated at the Court at Whitehall on the Twelfth Night 1605. **12** than] Q then **25** blackamores] Q Blackmores **76** greces (from F)] Q graces **81** silver] Ms adds "their hair thick and curled upright in tresses, like pyramids" **260** corpse] Q cor's **276** (Which] Q Which **280** Ethopians.)] Q Æthiopians **306** 'em] Q 'hem **313** than] Q then

5 absolute noble (literally, perfect)

7 magnificence (the virtue Aristotle associated with monarchy; see the previous work by Dekker); **these** i.e., these masques (the Q also included the Masque of Beauty)

8–9 rage . . . carcasses viewers were traditionally permitted to take down the scenery and plunder the decorations at the end of the performance

14 them i.e., the spirits (line 10)

17 Pliny *Natural History* V.viii.[43–4]; **Solinus** [Julius Solinus] *Polyhistor* [or *Collectanea Rerum Memorabilium* xxvii.5 and xxx.I]; **Ptolemy** [Ptolemy of Alexandria, *Geography*] IV.vi.[4–5]; **Leo the African** [Joannes Leo Africanus] *Description of Africa* [I, "Division of Africa"]. [Jonson's note.]

17–18 Leo the African Leon Africanus whose *Description of Africa* was first published in 1526

18 remember recall; record

famous by the name of Niger, of which the people were called *Nigritae*, now Negroes, and are the blackest nation of the world. This river taketh spring out of a certain lake, eastward, and after a long race falleth into the western ocean. Hence, because it was Her Majesty's will to have them blackamores at first, the invention was derived by me, and presented thus.

First, for the scene, was drawn a Landtschap consisting of small woods, and here and there a void place filled with huntings; which falling, an artificial sea was seen to shoot forth, as if it flowed to the land, raised with waves which seemed to move, and in some places the billow to break, as imitating that orderly disorder which is common in nature. In front of this sea were placed six Tritons in moving and sprightly actions, their upper parts human, save that their hairs were blue, as partaking of the sea color, their desinent parts fish, mounted above their heads, and all varied in disposition. From their backs were borne out certain light pieces of taffeta as if carried by the wind, and their music made out of wreathed shells. Behind these a pair of sea-maids, for song, were as conspicuously seated; between which two great sea-horses, as big as the life, put forth themselves, the one mounting aloft and writhing his head from the other, which seemed to sink forwards (so intended for variation, and that the figure behind might come off better); upon their backs Oceanus and Niger were advanced.

Oceanus presented in a human form, the color of his flesh blue, and shadowed with a robe of sea-green; his head grey and horned, as he is described by the ancients; his beard of the like mixed color. He was garlanded with algae, or sea grass, and in his hand a trident.

Niger in form and color of an Ethiop, his hair and rare beard curled, shadowed with a blue and bright mantle; his front, neck and wrists adorned with pearl; and crowned with an artificial wreath of cane and paper-rush.

These induced the masquers, which were twelve nymphs, Negroes, and the daughters of Niger, attended by so many of the Oceaniae, which were their light-bearers.

The masquers were placed in a great concave shell like mother of pearl, curiously made to move on those waters and rise with the billow; the top thereof was stuck with a chevron of lights which, indented to the proportion of the shell, struck a glorious beam upon them as they were seated one above another; so that they were all seen, but in an extravagant order.

On sides of the shell did swim six huge sea-monsters, varied in their shape and dispositions, bearing on their backs the twelve torch-bearers, who were planted there in several greces, so as the backs of some were seen, some in purfle, or side, others in face; and all having their lights burning out of whelks or murex shells.

---

21 **river** Some take it to be the same with Nilus, which is by Lucan called *Melas*, signifying *niger* [black]. Howsoever, Pliny, in the place above noted, hath this: "The river Niger has the same nature as the Nile; it produces reeds, papyrus and the same animals." See Solinus above-mentioned. [Jonson's note.]

22 **lake** Lake Chad

24 **them** the performers

25 **invention** concept; device

27 **Landtschap** landscape-curtain (Dutch spelling of what was then a neologism)

29 **huntings** animals at prey; **falling** the landscape-curtain was dropped from above to the floor in front of the stage (not pulled open) to reveal the scene

30–2 **artificial ... break** (caused by turning a machine that raised and lowered colored cloths)

35 **Tritons** sea gods

35 **Tritons** The form of these tritons, with their trumpets, you may read lively described in Ovid, *Metamorphoses* I.[330ff.]: "He calls the sea-colored triton," etc., and in Virgil, *Aeneid* X.[209ff.]: "He sails upon the huge triton," *et seq.* [Jonson's note.]

36–7 **hairs ... blue** common to representations of sea gods

37 **desinent** terminal; lower

39 **disposition** placement

48–9 **upon ... backs** Lucian in *Rhetoron Didaskalos* [*The Professor of Public Speaking*, 6] presents Nilus so, "sitting on a hippopotamus." And Statius Neptune, in the *Thebaid* [II.45]. [Jonson's note.]

51 **shadowed** i.e., covered; shaded

52 **horned** The ancients induced Oceanus always with a bull's head, *on account of the violence of the winds by which he is stirred up and driven, or because he is borne against the shore raging like a bull.* Euripides in the *Orestes* [1376–9]: "The land, which bull-headed Ocean rolls round and encircles with his arms." And rivers sometimes were so called. Look Virgil on the Tiber and the Eridanus, *Georgics* IV. [369–72]; *Aeneid* VIII. [77]; Horace, *Odes* IV.xiv.[25]; and Euripides in *Ion* [untraced; not in *Ion*]. [Jonson's note.]

57 **rare** thin

58 **front** forehead

60 **paper-rush** papyrus

61 **induced** brought on

63 **Oceaniae** sea nymphs who are daughters of Oceanus and Tethys

63 **Oceaniae** The daughters of Oceanus and Tethys. See Hesiod in the *Theogony* [346–70], Orpheus in the *Hymns* [*Homeric Hymns* ii (*To Demeter*), 5], and Virgil in the *Georgics* [IV.382]. [Jonson's note.]

66 **curiously** ingeniously, artfully

72 **extravagant** (1) uncommon; (2) extraordinary

74 **dispositions** positions

76 **greces** steps

77 **purfle** profile

The attire of the masquers was alike in all, without difference: the colors, azure and silver; but returned on the top with a scroll and antique dressing of feathers and jewels interlaced with ropes of pearl. And for the front, ear, neck and wrists, the ornament was of the most choice and orient pearl, best setting off from the black.

For the light-bearers, sea-green, waved about the skirts with gold and silver; their hair loose and flowing, garlanded with sea-grass, and that stuck with branches of coral.

These thus presented, the scene behind seemed a vast sea, and united with this that flowed forth, from the termination or horizon of which (being the level of the state, which was placed in the upper end of the hall) was drawn, by the lines of perspective, the whole work shooting downwards from the eye; which decorum made it more conspicuous, and caught the eye afar off with a wandering beauty. To which was added an obscure and cloudy night-piece that made the whole set off. So much for the bodily part, which was of Master Inigo Jones his design and act.

By this, one of the Tritons, with the two sea-maids, began to sing to the others' loud music, their voices being a tenor and two trebles.

SONG

Sound, sound aloud
The welcome of the orient flood
Into the west;
Fair Niger, son to great Oceanus,
Now honored thus,
With all his beauteous race,
Who, though but black in face,
Yet are they bright,
And full of life and light,
To prove that beauty best
Which not the color but the feature
Assures unto the creature.

Oceanus. *Be silent now the ceremony's done,*
And Niger, say, how comes it, lovely son,
That thou, the Ethiop's river, so far east,
Art seen to fall into th'extremest west
Of me, the king of floods, Oceanus,
And in mine empire's heart salute me thus?
My ceaseless current now amazèd stands
To see thy labor through so many lands
Mix thy fresh billow with my brackish stream,
And in thy sweetness stretch thy diadem
To these far distant and unequaled skies,
This squarèd circle of celestial bodies.

Niger. *Divine Oceanus, 'tis not strange at all*
That, since the immortal souls of creatures mortal
Mix with their bodies, yet reserve forever
A power of separation, I should sever
My fresh streams from thy brackish, like things fixed,
Though with thy powerful saltness thus far mixed.
Virtue, though chained to earth, will still live free,
And hell itself must yield to industry.

Oceanus. *But what's the end of thy herculean labors*
Extended to these calm and blessèd shores?

Niger. *To do a kind and careful father's part,*
In satisfying every pensive heart
Of these my daughters, my most lovèd birth,
Who, though they were the first formed dames of earth,
And in whose sparkling and refulgent eyes
The glorious sun did still delight to rise;
Though he – the best judge and most formal cause
Of all dames' beauties – in their firm hues draws
Signs of his fervent'st love, and thereby shows
That in their black the perfect'st beauty grows,
Since the fixed color of their curlèd hair,
Which is the highest grace of dames most fair,

91–2 **seemed... sea** (effect of wave machine and moving back-cloth)

94 **level... state** the vanishing point of the ideal perspective as taken from the King's viewpoint; **level** height; **state** the royal throne

100 **night-piece** the upper part of the scenery through which the moon later descends

102 **Inigo Jones** the architect and stage designer (1573–1652) with whom Jonson collaborated throughout his career on works for the court

103 **this** this time

105 **trebles** sopranos

110 ***son*** All rivers are said to be the sons of the Ocean, for, as the ancients thought, out of the vapors exhaled by the heat of the sun, rivers and fountains were begotten. And both by Orpheus in the *Hymns* [*Orphica* LXXXIII] and Homer, *Iliad* XIV. [201, 246, 302], Oceanus is celebrated *as father and source of gods and things, because nothing is born or decays without moisture.* [Jonson's note.]

115 ***full of life*** (may refer to Queen Anne, who was six months pregnant at the time of her performance)

117 ***feature*** form

127 ***Mix*** There wants not enough in nature to authorize this part of our fiction in separating Niger from the Ocean (beside the fable of Alpheus, and that to which Virgil alludes of Arethusa in his tenth eclogue [4–5]: "When you glide beneath Sicilian waves, may the briny sea not mix her stream with yours"), examples of Nilus, Jordan and others, whereof see Nicanor, book I *De Fluminibus*, and Plutarch in the *Life of Sulla* [xx.4], even of this our river (as some think) by the name of Melas. [Jonson's note.]

130 ***This... bodies*** heavenly bodies perfectly transferred into the earthly realm

138 ***hell... industry*** "herculean effort overcame hell" (Horace, *Odes* I.3.36)

144 ***first formed*** Read Diodorus Siculus, [*The Library of History*] III. [ii.I]. It is a conjecture of the old ethnics that they which dwell under the south were the first begotten of the earth. [Jonson's note.]

147 ***formal cause*** one of four Aristotelian causes, this one of essence (form)

150 ***black*** (usually, although not always, used to signify ugliness)

No cares, no age can change, or there display
The fearful tincture of abhorrèd gray,
Since Death herself (herself being pale and blue)
Can never alter their most faithful hue;
All which are arguments to prove how far
Their beauties conquer in great beauty's war,
And more, how near divinity they be
That stand from passion or decay so free.
Yet since the fabulous voices of some few
Poor brainsick men, styled poets here with you,
Have with such envy of their graces sung
The painted beauties other empires sprung,
Letting their loose and wingèd fictions fly
To infect all climates, yea, our purity;
As of one Phaëton, that fired the world,
And that before his heedless flames were hurled
About the globe, the Ethiops were as fair
As other dames, now black with black despair;
And in respect of their complexions changed,
Are eachwhere since for luckless creatures ranged.
Which when my daughters heard, as women are
Most jealous of their beauties, fear and care
Possessed them whole; yea, and believing them,
They wept such ceaseless tears into my stream
That it hath thus far overflowed his shore
To seek them patience, who have since e'ermore
As the sun riseth charged his burning throne
With volleys of revilings, 'cause he shone
On their scorched cheeks with such intemperate fires,
And other dames made queens of all desires.
To frustrate which strange error oft I sought,
Though most in vain, against a settled thought
As women's are, till they confirmed at length
By miracle what I with so much strength
Of argument resisted, else they feigned.
For in the lake where their first spring they gained,
As they sat cooling their soft limbs one night,
Appeared a face all circumfused with light –
And sure they saw't, for Ethiops never dream –
Wherein they might decipher through the stream
These words:
That they a land must forthwith seek
Whose termination, of the Greek,
Sounds -tania; where bright Sol, that heat
Their bloods, doth never rise or set,
But in his journey passeth by,
And leaves that climate of the sky
To comfort of a greater light,
Who forms all beauty with his sight.
In search of this have we three princedoms passed
That speak out -tania in their accents last;
Black Mauretania first, and secondly
Swarth Lusitania; next we did descry
Rich Aquitania, and, yet, cannot find
The place unto these longing nymphs designed.
Instruct and aid me, great Oceanus,
What land is this that now appears to us?
Oceanus. *This land that lifts into the temperate air*
His snowy cliff is Albion the fair,
So called of Neptune's son, who ruleth here;
For whose dear guard, myself four thousand year,
Since old Deucalion's days, have walked the round
About his empire, proud to see him crowned
Above my waves.

At this the moon was discovered in the upper part of the house, triumphant in a silver throne made in figure of a *pyramis*. Her garments white and silver, the dressing of her head antique, and crowned with a luminary, or sphere of light, which striking on the clouds, and heightened with silver, reflected as natural clouds do by the splendor of the moon. The heaven about her was vaulted with blue silk and set with stars of silver which had in them their several lights burning. The sudden sight of which made Niger to interrupt Oceanus with this present passion.

---

167 ***Phaëton*** the son of Phoebus Apollo who drove the sun so close to the earth that Zeus destroyed him to prevent the earth from catching fire

167 ***Phaëton*** *The famous story*; Ovid, *Metamorphoses* II.[1ff.] [Jonson's note.]

172 ***luckless*** Alluding to that of Juvenal, *Satires* v.[54], "and whom you would rather not meet at midnight." [Jonson's note.]

175 ***believing them*** i.e., the poets

179 ***charged*** A custom of the Ethiops, notable in Herodotus [II.22] and Diodorus Siculus [III.ix.2]. See Pliny, *Natural History* V.viii.[45]. [Jonson's note.]

191 ***never dream*** Pliny, ibid. [Jonson's note.]

196 ***Sol*** the sun

197 ***rise or set*** Consult with Tacitus in the *Life of Agricola* [12], and the *Panegyric to Constantine* [anonymous; in *XII Panegyrici Latini*, ed. E. Baehrens (Leipzig, 1911), VI, 9 (p. 207)]. [Jonson's note.]

200 ***greater light*** King James

204 ***Mauretania*** the land of the Moors in northern Africa, now Morocco and part of Algeria

205 ***swarth*** swarthy, dark; sunburned; **Lusitania** Portugal and western Spain

206 ***Aquitania*** southwestern France

207 ***designed*** designated

211 ***Albion*** an early name for England; see the preceding and following entertainments by Dekker and Munday

211 ***Albion*** Orpheus in his *Argonautica* calls it "white land" [untraced; not in *Argonautica.* The reference is taken from Camden's *Britannia* (London, 1586), p. 20]. [Jonson's note.]

212 ***Neptune's son*** King James (as a consequence of the allusion to Albion)

212 ***Neptune's son*** Alluding to the rite of styling princes after the name of their princedoms; so is he still Albion and Neptune's son that governs. As also his being dear to Neptune in being so embraced by him. [Jonson's note.]

214 ***Deucalion*** a Greek survivor of the great flood (analogous to Noah)

219 ***pyramis*** i.e., pyramid

228 **present** sudden; immediate

Niger. *O see, our silver star!*
Whose pure, auspicious light greets us thus far!
Great Aethiopia, goddess of our shore,
Since with particular worship we adore
Thy general brightness, let particular grace
Shine on my zealous daughters. Show the place
Which long their longings urged their eyes to see.
Beautify them, which long have deified thee.
Aethiopia. *Niger, be glad; resume thy native cheer.*
Thy daughters' labors have their period here,
And so thy errors. I was that bright face
Reflected by the lake, in which thy race
Read mystic lines; which skill Pythagoras
First taught to men by a reverberate glass.
This blessèd isle doth with that -tania end,
Which there they saw inscribed, and shall extend
Wished satisfaction to their best desires.
Britannia, which the triple world admires,
This isle hath now recovered for her name,
Where reign those beauties that with so much fame
The sacred muses' sons have honorèd,
And from bright Hesperus to Eos spread.
With that great name Britannia, this blessed isle
Hath won her ancient dignity and style,
A world divided from the world, and tried
The abstract of it in his general pride.
For were the world with all his wealth a ring,
Britannia, whose new name makes all tongues sing,
Might be a diamond worthy to enchase it,
Ruled by a sun that to this height doth grace it,
Whose beams shine day and night, and are of force
To blanch an Ethiop, and revive a corpse.
His light sciential is, and, past mere nature,
Can salve the rude defects of every creature.
Call forth thy honored daughters, then,
And let them, 'fore the Britain men,
Indent the land with those pure traces
They flow with in their native graces.
Invite them boldly to the shore;
Their beauties shall be scorched no more;
This sun is temperate, and refines
All things on which his radiance shines.

Here the Tritons sounded, and they danced on shore, every couple as they advanced severally presenting their fans, in one of which were inscribed their mixed names, in the other a mute hieroglyphic expressing their mixed qualities. (Which manner of symbol I rather chose than *imprese*, as well for strangeness as relishing of antiquity, and more applying to that original doctrine of sculpture which the Egyptians are said first to have brought from the Ethiopians.)

	The names	The symbols
The Queen	*Euphoris*	A golden tree laden with fruit.
	1.	
Countess of Bedford	*Aglaia*	
Lady Herbert	*Diaphane*	The figure icosahedron of crystal.
	2.	
Countess of Derby	*Eucampse*	
Lady Rich	*Octye*	A pair of naked feet in a river.
	3.	
Countess of Suffolk	*Kathare*	

231 ***Aethiopia*** goddess of the moon

231 ***Aethiopia*** The Ethiopians worshipped the moon by that surname. See Stephanus [of Byzantium], *De Urbibus*, under the word *Aithiopion*, and his reasons. [Jonson's note.]

238 ***period*** end

241–2 ***Pythagoras . . . glass*** according to legend, Pythagoras was able to reflect messages onto the moon by writing on a mirror in blood; **reverberate** reflecting

246 ***triple world*** heaven, earth, and underworld that together admire James's triple world of Scotland, England, and Wales

250 ***Hesperus*** evening star; the west; **Eos** dawn; the east

252 ***style*** characterization

253 ***A . . . world*** refers to the commonplace that Britain was a distinct and fortunate world of its own

253–4 ***tried . . . pride*** i.e., experienced the ideal of it through England's own pride in it

256 ***new name*** James attempted to initiate the name of Great Britain (following the Britain of Brute) when he became King of both Scotland and England (see Munday's *Triumphs*); ***all tongues*** an overstatement; Parliament refused to adopt the new name and so did others who feared its imperial implications

257 ***enchase*** set in

260 ***To . . . corpse*** i.e., both are equally desirable and equally impossible

261 ***sciential*** having the powers of science

265 ***Indent the land*** making impressions by dancing; leaving footprints; ***traces*** footsteps

277 ***imprese*** emblems

280 ***from . . . Ethiopians*** Diodorus Siculus, [*The Library of History* III.iii.4]; Herodotus [*History* II.110]. [Jonson's note.]

282 ***Euphoris*** abundance; **golden tree** symbol of fertility

284 ***Countess of Bedford*** Lucy, wife of Edward, third Earl of Bedford and daughter of Lord John Harington; a patron of the arts, she was especially generous to Jonson; ***Aglaia*** splendor (the only name not invented here by Jonson)

285 ***Lady Herbert*** Anne Herbert, daughter of Sir William Herbert who married Sir Edward, later Lord Herbert of Cherbury; ***Diaphane*** transparent; **icosahedron** twenty-sided figure standing for water

287 ***Countess of Derby*** Alice, daughter of Sir John Spencer of Althorpe and widow of Ferdinando, fifth Earl of Derby; her second husband was Lord Keeper Egerton; ***Eucampse*** flexibility

288 ***Lady Rich*** Penelope Rich, then unmarried companion of Mountjoy, Earl of Devonshire; ***Octye*** swiftness

288–9 ***naked . . . river*** symbol of purity

290 ***Countess of Suffolk*** Catherine, the daughter of Sir Henry Knevit, married to Richard, Lord Rich before her marriage to Lord Thomas Howard, Earl of Suffolk; ***Kathare*** spotless (in this instance, perhaps satirical)

Lady Bevill	4.	*Notis*	The salamander simple.
Lady Effingham		*Psychrote*	
Lady Elizabeth Howard	5.	*Glycyte*	A cloud full of rain, dropping.
Lady Susan de Vere		*Malacia*	
Lady Wroth	6.	*Baryte*	An urn, sphered with wine.
Lady Walsingham		*Periphere*	

The names of the Oceaniae were

DORIS.	CYDIPPE.	BEROE.	IANTHE.
PETRAEA.	GLAUCE.	ACASTE.	LYCORIS.
OCYRHOE.	TYCHE.	CLYTIA.	PLEXAURE.

Their own single dance ended, as they were about to make choice of their men, one from the sea was heard to call 'em with this charm, sung by a tenor voice.

SONG

Come away, come away,
We grow jealous of your stay;
If you do not stop your ear,
We shall have more cause to fear
Sirens of the land, than they
To doubt the sirens of the sea.

Here they danced with their men several measures and corantos. All which ended, they were again accited to sea with a song of two trebles, whose cadences were iterated by a double echo from several parts of the land.

SONG

Daughters of the subtle flood,
Do not let earth longer entertain you;
1st Echo. *Let earth longer entertain you.*
2nd Echo. *Longer entertain you.*
'Tis to them enough of good
That you give this little hope to gain you.
1st Echo. *Give this little hope to gain you.*
2nd Echo. *Little hope to gain you.*
If they love,
You shall quickly see;
For when to flight you move,
They'll follow you, the more you flee.
1st Echo. *Follow you, the more you flee.*
2nd Echo. *The more you flee.*
If not, impute it each to other's matter;
They are but earth –
1st Echo. *But earth,*
2nd Echo. *Earth –*
And what you vowed was water.
1st Echo. *And what you vowed was water.*
2nd Echo. *You vowed was water.*
Aethiopia. *Enough, bright nymphs, the night grows old,*
And we are grieved we cannot hold
You longer light; but comfort take.
Your father only to the lake
Shall make return; yourselves, with feasts,
Must here remain the Ocean's guests.
Nor shall this veil the sun hath cast
Above your blood more summers last;
For which, you shall observe these rites:
Thirteen times thrice, on thirteen nights
(So often as I fill my sphere
With glorious light throughout the year),
You shall, when all things else do sleep
Save your chaste thoughts, with reverence steep
Your bodies in that purer brine
And wholesome dew called rosmarine;
Then with that soft and gentler foam,
Of which the ocean yet yields some,
Whereof bright Venus, beauty's queen,
Is said to have begotten been,
You shall your gentler limbs o'er-lave,
And for your pains perfection have;
So that, this night, the year gone round,
You do again salute this ground,
And in the beams of yond' bright sun
Your faces dry, and all is done.

At which, in a dance they returned to the sea, where they took their shell, and with this full song went out.

---

291 ***Lady Bevill*** Frances, sister of the Countess of Suffolk and wife of Sir William Bevill, a gentleman of Cornwall; ***Notis*** moisture; **salamander** a reptile that, impervious to fire, can extinguish it; symbol of constancy

293 ***Lady Effingham*** Anne, daughter of Lord St. John, married in 1597 to William, eldest son of Lord Howard of Effingham, Lord High Admiral during the Spanish Armada; ***Psychrote*** coldness

294 ***Lady Elizabeth Howard*** daughter of Lady Effingham who married Lord Mordaunt, afterwards Earl of Peterborough; ***Glycyte*** sweetness

294–5 ***cloud . . . dropping*** symbol of education

296 ***Lady Susan de Vere*** Susan Herbert, daughter of Edward, Earl of Oxford; about a week before this masque was performed she married Philip Herbert, afterwards Earl of Montgomery; ***Malacia*** delicacy

297 ***Lady Wroth*** Lady Mary Wroth, daughter of Robert, Earl of Leicester, niece of Sir Philip Sidney and wife of Sir Robert Wroth of Durants, Middlesex; herself a writer, Jonson later dedicated *The Alchemist* to her; ***Baryte*** weight; **urn . . . wine** symbol of the earth

299 ***Lady Walsingham*** wife of Sir Thomas Walsingham who had been sent to Scotland to accompany Queen Anne into England; **Periphere** revolving, circular

315 **measures** slow, stately dances

316 **corantos** dances with a running or gliding step, French in origin

317 **accited** summoned

357 ***rosmarine*** sea dew

SONG

Now Dian with her burning face
Declines apace,
By which our waters know
To ebb, that late did flow.
Back seas, back nymphs, but with a forward grace
Keep, still, your reverence to the place;
And shout with joy of favor you have won
In sight of Albion, Neptune's son.

So ended the first masque, which, beside the singular grace of music and dances, had that success in the nobility of performance as nothing needs to the illustration but the memory by whom it was personated.

371 ***Dian*** Diana, goddess of the moon

The Triumphs of Re-United Britannia

Anthony Munday

THE

TRIVMPHES of re-vnited *BRITANIA.*

Performed at the cost and charges of the Right Worship: Company of the Merchant-Taylors, in honor of Sir *Leonard Halliday* kni: to solemnize his entrance as Lorde Mayor of the City of *London*, on Tuesday the 29. of October. 1605.

Deuised and Written by A. Mundy, *Citizen and Draper of London.*

Printed in London by W. Jaggard. 1605.

Frontispiece, 1605. The Huntingdon Library, San Marino, CA.

Anthony Munday is for the London Lord Mayor's shows what Ben Jonson is to the Jacobean court masque: they dominate their forms. Eight of Munday's shows survive, but Guild records show that he had a hand in at least fifteen of them between 1602, as the author of the last Lord Mayor's show under Elizabeth I, and 1623. No other dramatist comes close. To this statistic we can add his responsibility, in 1610, for preparing the civic entertainment surrounding the investiture of Henry as Prince of Wales. Like the court masque, the Lord Mayor's show was occasional theater that used considerable amounts of money to stage spectacles to celebrate a particular event; but unlike the court masques, with their limited space for settings and machinery and their limited because elitist audience, the Lord Mayor's shows had the open streets of London at their disposal and the entire citizenry, of all ranks and incomes, as the potential audience. For any enterprising man of the theater like Munday, the invitation to stage memorable spectacles and at the same time make important celebratory, social, or political comments must have seemed extraordinary. Moreover, as a member himself of the Drapers' Company, who hired him again and again for their shows, he could honor the mercantile development which was already the backbone of London's political and economic life.

Henry Machyn's *Diary* for 1553 first reports a Lord Mayor's show, the name for a processional with dramatic entertainment staged annually to include and celebrate the installation of a new Lord Mayor for London that quickly displaced the earlier pageants celebrating Midsummer Watch on June 24 and 29. (These featured dramatic representations largely of biblical and allegorical subjects that recalled the medieval origins of the guilds that sponsored them.) The Lord Mayor was chosen from the governing elite of the aldermen representing the Twelve Great Companies or guilds, which included the Drapers, Haberdashers, Mercers, and, above all, the increasingly wealthy Merchant Taylors' Company, whose fortunes had soared in Tudor and Stuart years with the great expansion of the cloth trade, England's dominant export. The election was held on the eve of St. Simon and St. Jude's Day, October 29; the following morning, the brothers of the new Lord Mayor's livery escorted him to the London Guildhall for installation. Then they embarked at the Three Cranes in the Vintry for the state voyage down the Thames to Westminster where the new Lord Mayor took the oath of office before the Barons of the Exchequer. He returned to a landing below St. Paul's where he was met by a full procession, including a pageant, in the yard of the Bell Inn; then he proceeded by way of St. Paul's Churchyard and Cheapside to the Guildhall for a banquet. He returned to St. Paul's for a special evening service and some final speeches before being accompanied to the Lord Mayor's residence. Throughout, the route was cleared by fencers and men with fireworks, while others took down signs or other obstructions. The almsmen of the livery company to which the new Lord Mayor belonged were given new blue gowns for the parade, and the company's schoolboys received breakfast and took part in the banquet as compensation for reciting the speeches and performing in the shows that Munday and others wrote. The company members also had new gowns, half of the Bachelors furred with marten (or "foynes") and half with lambskin (or "budge"). Clearly it was the analogue, in power and display, to the magnificent entertainments that celebrated a new monarch taking his (or her) oath of office, and no expense was spared: while an early Elizabethan Lord Mayor's show might cost £151 in 1561, by the time Munday wrote his first show, in 1602, the bills amounted to £747 and more.

Despite the public shows, banquet, and communion service, however, the two key moments of the Lord Mayor's installation featured the Lord Mayor himself taking oaths. The first was in the Guildhall where he bound himself to service with his fraternity and with the aldermen of the city. The second was at Westminster where the oath of office was taken before the monarch and the court, accompanied by a speech from the Recorder of the City and sometimes by the monarch; here, at the seat of national government, the mayor swore himself into a hierarchy that formed a chain of government from God through the monarch to the mayor and bound country and city. Munday seems to have had these particular moments in mind by writing a Lord Mayor's show that focuses on the politics of history and uses this to make analogous the responsibility of both the King and the Lord Mayor in following the model of the nation's founder, Brute. The political theme, that James would reunite a divided country by reuniting England and Scotland into "Great Britain," was already a chief aim of the new King James. In the book of counsel to his son Prince Henry newly issued in England in 1603, the *Basilikon Doron*, James I advises that any division of the kingdom will "leave the seed of division and discord among your posterity: as befell to this Isle by the division and assignment thereof, to the three sons of Brutus, Locrine, Albanact, and Camber." This was James's bid to make himself a part of the "Tudor myth," to author his own genealogy so as to combine the two countries over which he was now sole ruler. According to this well-known mythic history, accepted by such historians of the time as Matthew Paris, Richard Grafton, John Stow, William Camden, and Raphael Holinshed, Brutus, the descendant of Aeneas, left Troy and settled a new land he called Albion. He established a new civilization by ridding the land of barbaric giants and tribes of men and by establishing on the banks of the Thames River the city of Troynovant (new Troy), later London. But before his death, Brutus divided the kingdom among his three sons, opening the way for the invasions of the Saxons and others. Henry VII, who claimed direct descent from Brutus, eliminated factionalism by uniting the houses of Lancaster and York through his marriage, and James sees that as history's precedent for him to follow suit by reuniting Scotland with Wales and England. The Succession Act of 1604, one year before Munday's *Triumphs*, praises the "inestimable and unspeakable blessings" that will come from

> a reuniting, of two mighty, famous, and ancient kingdoms (yet anciently but one) of England and Scotland under one Imperial Crown in your most Royal Person, who is lineally, rightfully, and lawfully descended of the body of the most excellent Lady Margaret, eldest daughter of the most renowned King Henry the Seventh and the high and noble Princess, Queen Elizabeth his wife, eldest daughter of King Edward the Fourth, the said Lady Margaret being eldest sister of King Henry the Eighth, father of the high and mighty Princess of famous memory, Elizabeth, late Queen of England.

This follows in subject and spirit the King's own early proclamation of May 19, 1603, in which he declares widespread support for such a beneficial union:

> That as his Majesty hath found in the hearts of all the best disposed Subjects of both the Realms of all qualities, a most earnest desire, that the said happy Union should be perfected, the memory of all preterite Discontentments abolished, and the Inhabitants of both the Realms to be the Subjects of one Kingdom: so his Highness will with all convenient diligence with the advice of the Estates and Parliament of both the Kingdoms make the same to be perfected.

Clearly this was the lynchpin of the new royal politics; the first year of his reign James also minted a new coin reading *Henricus rosas regna Jacobus*.

In Munday's show, Neptune and his wife Amphitrita, riding on a lion and a camel, the animals on the coat of arms of the Merchant Taylors' Company whose member, Sir Leonard Holiday, had just been installed as the Lord Mayor, witness the pageant in which two defeated giants, Corineus and Goemagot, in chains of gold, bring forth a triangular mount on which Britannia sits. She is displeased that Brute is dividing Albion and renaming her kingdom, but he reminds her that his warlike conquest has many benefits: he will tame the wilderness, banish the giants, and establish Troynovant. His sons, who historically inherited the divided kingdom, speak in praise of its unification, and the rivers that bound the three kingdoms (impersonated by boys as nymphs) sing songs in honor of their "second Brute": "Welcome King James, welcome Great Britain's King." Such a timely and open political statement, however, is turned to a particular purpose when it is joined with virtues impersonating seven former kings who are in some direct way associated with the history of the Merchant Taylors' Company. They pass in a chariot led by Fame with a vacant seat inviting King James to join them. The analogy is clear enough: the history of Brute which concludes with the plans of reunification by James is analogous to the earlier kings brought together by the Merchant Taylors and epitomized in turn by the new Lord Mayor: the pageantry moves directly from Brute to James to Sir Leonard Holliday. Each element of the show reinforces the other elements and in opening the techniques of the stage into the public streets makes politics a universal issue.

As it turned out, the pageant was prepared twice. A storm on October 29, 1605, curtailed performance and it was readied again for October 31, All Saints' Day, when "the same shows were new repaired, and carried abroad." The total cost to the company was recorded at £710.2s.5d. and two payments were given to Munday: £38 for providing clothing for the children in the "pageant, ship, lion, and camel, and for the chariot" and an additional £6 for "printing the books of the speeches in the pageant and the other shows." Mr. Hearne, a painter, received £75 for "making, painting, and gilding the pageant, chariot, lions, camel, and new painting and furnishing the ship, and for the furniture for both giants." In addition, the company paid £10 to "88 porters for carrying the pageant, ship, and beasts" – unlike the royal entry pageants, which were stationary, the Lord Mayor's show followed the streets of London, playing to the crowds. But in publishing the text, Munday may have taken his cue from Jonson, for he prefaces the actual show with the most comprehensive retelling of the story of Brute in all of the civic pageants and surrounds the margins of his text with learned citations as sidenotes. Thus he stages a political event as ceremonial and subsequently captures it, immortalizes it, for a potentially larger reading market who might have seen only a part of, or none of, the show.

By placing the new Lord Mayor analogously next to the founder and present monarch of England and Scotland, Munday suggests the importance not only of Sir Leonard but of his and the other livery companies. For as the new King was attempting to dominate Parliament and the people with his own personal project of Union, so the companies dominated the government, economy, and society of London. Through the Court of Common Council and the Court of Aldermen, in vestries and parishes, they fostered the local economy, were the basis of foreign trade, and through widespread acts of charity remained the city's chief almsgivers. The political system of aldermen which the livery companies solely controlled resembles the social system which their economic practices maintained; they also as a consequence maintained a firm status quo, a kind of stability through all the phases of London life. They were the chief agents of peace and prosperity in London – precisely what James was promising himself to be in the larger nation: it may well be that Munday is using James's own public posture to insist that the Merchant Taylors are his necessary counterpart. In that sense, a Lord Mayor's show which seems to be more about James than Sir Leonard may be, in the end, mostly about the livery companies and the guild system and what they represent: tradition, order, status, property, wealth. In 1617 the Irishman Fynes Moryson, reflecting on a display of civic pageantry in Dublin, remarked, "There is a secret mystery in these solemn pomps." There are secret mysteries – and some mysteries perhaps not so secret – in Anthony Munday's celebration of Sir Leonard Holliday and the Merchant Taylors' Company, and beginning with the first word of his title – "triumphs" – he insistently asks us to discover what the meaning and purpose of his entertainment may be.

FURTHER READING

Bergeron, David M., *English Civic Pageantry 1558–1642*. Columbia: University of South Carolina Press, 1971.

——, "Stuart Civic Pageants and Textual Performance," *Renaissance Quarterly* 51:1 (Spring 1998): 163–83.

Bradbrook, M.C., "The Politics of Pageantry: Social Implications in Jacobean London," in *Poetry and Drama 1570–1700: Essays in Honour of Harold F. Brooks*, ed. Anthony Coleman and Anthony Hammond (London: Methuen, 1981), pp. 60–75.

Leinwand, Theodore B., "London Triumphing: The Jacobean Lord Mayor's Show," *Clio* 11:2 (1982): 137–53.

Lobanov-Rostovsky, Sergei, "*The Triumphes of Golde*: Economic Authority in the Jacobean Lord Mayor's Show," *ELH* 60:4 (1993): 879–98.

Paster, Gail Kern, "The Idea of London in Masque and Pageant," in *Pageantry in the Shakespearean Theater*, ed. David M. Bergeron (Athens: University of Georgia Press, 1985), pp. 48–64.

Sayle, R. T. D., *Lord Mayors' Pageants of the Merchant Taylors Company in the 15th, 16th, and 17th Centuries*. London, 1931.

Wirthington Robert, *English Pageantry*, Vol. II. Cambridge, Mass.: Harvard University Press, 1920.

The Triumphs of Re-United Britannia

Because our present conceit reacheth unto the antiquity of Britain, which (in many minds) hath carried as many and variable opinions, I thought it not unnecessary (being thereto earnestly solicited) to speak somewhat concerning the estate of this our country, even from the very first original until her honorably attaining the name of Britannia, and then lastly how she came to be called England. Most writers do agree that after the Deluge Noah was the sole monarch of all the world, and that he divided the dominion of the whole earth to his three sons: all Europe with the isles thereto belonging (wherein this our Isle of Britain was one among the rest) fell to the lot and possession of Japhet his third son. Samothes the sixth son of Japhet, called by Moses Mesech, by others Dys, had for his portion the whole country lying between the river of Rhine and the Pyrenean Mountains, where he founded his kingdom of Celtica over his people called Celtae, which name, by the opinion of Bale our countryman, was indifferent to them of Gallia and us of this Isle of Britain. This Samothes being the first king over these people, of him came lineally these kings following: Magus, Sarron, Druis and Bardus, all ruling severally over the Celts and Britons, who were not then so called, but Samotheans, after the name of Samothes. Of Bardus, who according to Berosus was very famous for inventing of music and ditties, came an order of philosophical poets or heralds called Bardi after his own name, whose excellent qualities were of such power as they could enforce armies of enemies ready to fight fierce battle, to stand at a gaze and forbear their cruel intent, until these bards left singing, and went out of the battle. According to Lucan. Lib.1.:

Vos quoque qui fortes animas belloque peremptas,
Laudibus in longum vates dimittitis aevum,
Plurima securi fudistis carmina Bardi.

Many of these bards lived among the Britons before the birth of Christ, as Plenidius and Oro-

TEXTUAL VARIANTS

Title-page reads in full: The Triumphs of Re-United Britannia. Performed at the cost and charges of the Right Worship[ful] Company of the Merchant-Taylors, in honor of Sir Leonard Holliday, kni[ght], to solemnize his entrance as Lord Mayor of the City of London, on Tuesday the 29 of October, 1605. Devised and written by A[nthony] Munday, Citizen and Draper of London. **10** marginal sidenote in Q] "Annius de viterb. in coment.super 4 lib. Beros, de anti. **16** marginal sidenote in Q] Wolf[g]angus Lazius **19** marginal sidenote in Q] J. Bale cent. 1 **38** Laudibus] Q Laudius **40–5** marginal sidenote in Q] J. Bale script. Brit. cent. 2 J. Prise. defens hist. Brit. Caius de ant Cent lib. 1 John Leland filla. ant. dict. **49–55** marginal sidenote in Q] Neptune for his many ships, called king or god of the Seas, and in regard of his great skill in Navigation. **59** 900] Bodleian Q (only) reads 600 **89** Humphrey] Q Humfrey marginal sidenote in Q] Gal. Mon. [i.e., Golfridus Monemutensis, Geoffrey of Monmouth] **129** Germans] Q Germains **130** Goths] Q Gothes **130** Vandals] Q Vandales **152** indigo] Q indico **between 171 and 172**] Q has *Finis* at end of A gathering; the word is also set at the ends of B and C gatherings. While these come properly at the ends of shows, they are unusual and may indicate the end of work of each of three compositors who set the pamphlet simultaneously to hasten this timely event to the market **253** Gwendolyn's] Q Guendolenae's **276** marginal sidenote in Q] Albania in Greece **329–332** marginal sidenote in Q] Merlyn, who prophesied hereof long ago **388** Gwendolyn] Q Quendoline **between 400 and 401** Q has *Finis* at the end of B gathering; see note to between lines 171 and 172–4 above **536** Satan] Q Sathan

2 **antiquity of Britain** *Triumphs of a Re-United Britannia* is the only comprehensive treatment of the mythical Brute-Troy history in all Renaissance civic pageantry

9 **Most writers** Munday lists his sources in a sidenote (see Textual Variants); the primary one is Annius de Viterbo (1432–1502), esp. *Antiquitatu variam volumina* (Paris, 1512); this contains fragments of Berosus' *De Antiquitatibus* as well as Annius' commentary on Berosus, but throughout the sixteenth century there were several editions of Annius that contained commentary on the spurious works of Berosus the Chaldean (ca. 250 BC) and the lineage of Moses. A more available source on the presumed works of Berosus was Richard Lynche, *An Historical Treatise of the Travels of Noah into Europe* (1601)

14–16 **fell . . . Dys** Munday gives as a source Wolfgangus Lazius (1514–65) in a sidenote; Book III of Lazius' *De Gentium aliquot Migrationibus* (Frankfurt, 1600), a twelve-volume history beginning after the Flood, covers the history of Moses, Samothes, and others

16 **Mesech** (cf. Gen. 10:2)

21 **Bale** John Bale (1495–1563) was a popular Protestant Bishop, historian, and dramatist in the mid-sixteenth century; his *Illustrium Majoris Britanniae Scriptorum* (1548) is based on Berosus and Annius' commentary from which he constructs an elaborate history beginning with Noah

22 **indifferent** used interchangeably by and of the Gauls and the British

37–9 ***Vos . . . Bardi*** "You bards who by the praises of your verse transmit to distant ages the fame of heroes slain in battle, poured forth at ease your many lays" (Lucan, *Pharsalia* II. 447–9). Munday could have found this same passage many places, such as Price or Leland (see following note)

40–7 **Many . . . Bardhes** Bale is erroneously cited; the remarks are in centura prima, not as in the sidenote; other sources for this passage are said by the sidenote to be John Price (1502?–1555), *Historiae Brytannicae Defensio* (1573); John Caius (1510–73), *De antiquitate Cantebrigiensis Academiae* (1568); and John Leland (1506?–1552), *Syllabus, et interpretatio antiquarom dictionum* in *Genethliacon illustrissimi* (1543)

nius; since then, Thalestine, the two Merlins, Melkin, Elaskirion, and others. Among the Welshmen now of late days, David Die, Iollo Gough, David ap-Williams, and divers others remaining yet among them, and called in their own language Bardhes.

Thus continued the name of Samothes the space of 310 years, till Neptune put his son Albion the Giant in possession of this land, who subduing the Samotheans, called this island Albion after his own name. Concerning the coming hither of Danaus' 50 daughters, and that one of them should be called Albina, and so the land to be named by her: first, not any one of them was so named, neither do I think the story so authentical, but do hold Albion's name for the truest.

The country thus peopled with giants, and continuing after the name of Albion for 900 years, Brute (being directed by a vision in his sleep to find out a country situated in the west) with the remains of his Trojan followers, arrived and landed at the haven now called Totnes; the year of the world, 2850, after the destruction of Troy 66, before the building of Rome 368, and 1116 before Christ's nativity. He, searching the land over from side to side, found it to be very fertile and inhabited by uncivil, monstrous huge men of stature, termed giants, whom he with his bold and resolved companions slew and destroyed. One of them named Goemagot or Goemagog, exceeding the rest in strength and courage, Brute caused Corineus, one of his confederates, to wrestle with the said Goemagot at a place beside Dover, where the giant happened to break a rib in the side of Corineus which so sharply incensed him that redoubling his power to win the victory, he threw him headlong down from off one of the rocks, which place was after called Gogmagog's Leap. The giant being thus dispatched, in reward of this honorable piece of service Brute gave unto Corineus a part of his land, which according to his name was, and yet is unto this day, called Cornwall.

Brute thus having the whole land in his own quiet possession, began to build a city near to the side of the River Thamesis, in the second year of his reign, which he named Troynovant, or as Humphrey Lloyd saith, Troinewith; which is New Troy in remembrance of that famous city Troy whence he and his people (for the greater part) were descended. Now began he to alter the name of the island, and according to his own name called it Britain and caused all the inhabitants to be named Britons for a perpetual memory that he was the first bringer of them into this land. In this time he had by his wife fair Innogen, daughter to King Pandrasus, King of the Greeks, three worthy sons, the first named Locrine, the second Camber, and the third Albanact to which three (not long before his death) he divided his whole kingdom in several partitions, giving to Locrine all that part which we know best by the name of England, then termed by him Loegria or Logres. To Camber he limited the country of Wales, called Cambria after his name, and divided from Loegria by the river of Severn. To Albanact his third son, he appointed all the north part of the isle lying beyond the river of Humber, then called Albania, now Scotland; and to that river then Albania did reach. But since that time the limits of Loegria were enlarged, first by the prowess of the Romans, then by our own conquests, that the Tweed on the one side, and the Solve on the other, were taken for the principal bounds between us and Scotland.

After Brute, I find not any other alternation of our country's name until the reign of King Ecbert, who about the year of grace 800 and the first of his reign, gave forth an especial edict, dated at Winchester that it should be named Angles' Land, or Angellandt, for which (in our time) we do pronounce it England. Nor can Hengist the Saxon be the father of this latter name, for Ecbert, because of his ancestors descended from the Angles, one of the six nations that came with the Saxons into Britain (for they were not all of one, but of divers countries viz. Angles, Saxons, Germans, Switzers, Norwegians, Jutes, otherwise termed Jutons, Vites, Goths, or Getes, and Vandals, and all comprehended under the name of

53 **Danaus** King of Argos

60 **Brute** descendant of Aeneas who settled the British island and after his period of rule passed it on to his sons; this mythical history was first told by Geoffrey of Monmouth in his *Historia Regum Britanniae* (printed in London in 1508), but the story was commonplace among English chronicle writers

88 **Troynovant** an erroneous chronology; Troynovant is actually a back-formation of Trinovantes, an early British tribe living N and E of London

89 **Humphrey Lloyd** Lloyd (or more properly Llwyd, 1527–68), physician and antiquary, was translated by Thomas Twyne in *The Breviary of Britayne* (1573)

99 **Locrine** Munday may be influenced by a relatively recent play of *Locrine* (1595)

114 **Solve** Solway Firth

118 **King Ecbert** King of the West Saxons (Wessex) who ruled from 802 to 859

123 **Hengist** the earliest Anglo-Saxon invader who, as prince, founded the kingdom of Kent (historically, he was a Jute, not a Saxon)

Saxons because of Hengist the Saxon and his company that first arrived here before any of the other) and thereto having now the monarchy and pre-eminence, in manner of this whole island, called the same after the name of the country from whence he derived his original. So that neither Hengist, nor any qu(een) named Angla, or derivation ab Angulo, is to be allowed before this sound and sure authority. Thus much briefly concerning the names of our country, now come we to discourse the whole frame and body of our device in this solemn triumph of re-united Britannia.

The Ship Called the Royal Exchange

Master. All hail fair London, to behold thy towers,
After our voyage long and dangerous,
In seamen's comfort; thanks unto those powers,
That in all perils have preserved us.
Our Royal Exchange hath made a rich return,
Laden with spices, silks, and indigo;
Our wives that for our absence long did mourn,
Now find release from all their former woe.
Mate. Master, good news. Our owner, as I hear,
Is this day sworn in London's Mayoralty:
Boy. Master 'tis true, for see what troupes appear,
Of citizens, to bear him company.
Hark how the drums and trumpets cheerly sound,
To solemnize the triumph of this day;
Shall we do nothing, but be idle found
On such a general mirthful holiday?
Master. Take of our pepper, of our cloves and mace,
And liberally bestow them round about,
'Tis our ship's luggage, and in such a case,
I know our owner means to bear us out.
Then, in his honor: and that company,
Whose love and bounty this day doth declare,
Hurl, boy; hurl, mate. And gunner, see you ply
Your ordnance, and of fireworks make no spare,
To add the very uttermost we may,
To make this up a cheerful Holi-day.

The Lion and the Camel

On the Lion and the Camel we do figuratively personate Neptune, and his Queen, Amphitrita, who first seated their son Albion in this land. And in them we figure poetically that as they then triumphed in their son's happy fortune, so now they cannot choose but do the like, seeing what happy success hath thereon ensued, to renown this country from time to time. And as times have altered former harsh incivilities, bringing the state to more perfect shape of majesty, so (as occasion serves) do they likewise lay their borrowed forms aside and speak according to the nature of the present business in hand, without any imputations of grossness or error, considering the laws of poesy grants such allowance and liberty. Corineus and Goemagot, appearing in the shape and proportion of huge giants, for the more grace and beauty of the show, we place as guides to Britanniae's Mount, and being fettered unto it in chains of gold, they seem (as it were) to draw the whole frame, showing much envy and contention who shall exceed most in duty and service.

The Pageant

On a mount triangular, as the Island of Britain itself is described to be, we seat in the supreme place, under the shape of a fair and beautiful nymph, Britannia herself accosted with Brute's divided kingdoms, in the like female representations, Loegria, Cambria, and Albania. Britannia speaking to Brute her conqueror, who is seated somewhat lower in the habit of an adventurous warlike Trojan, tells him that she had still continued her name of Albion but for his conquest of her virgin honor; which since it was by heaven so appointed, she reckons it to be the very best of her fortunes. Brute shows her what height of happiness she hath attained unto by his victory, being before a vast wilderness inhabited by giants and a mere den of monsters: Goemagot and his barbarous brood being quite subdued, his civil followers first taught her modest manners and the means how to reign as an imperial lady, building his *Troya nova* by the river Thamesis and beautifying his land with other cities beside. But then the three virgin kingdoms seem to reprove him,

145 **Royal Exchange** London's great burse, built by Sir Thomas Gresham in 1566 and opened by Elizabeth I
162 **mace** dried nutmeg husks used as a spice
169 **ordnance** cannon
172 **Lion ... Camel** the two animals on the coat of arms of the Merchant Taylors' Company
179 **renown** celebrate (with a show)
199 **accosted** placed side by side

for his overmuch love to his sons and dividing her (who was one sole monarchy) into three several estates, the hurt and inconvenience whereon ensuing, each one of them modestly delivered unto him. He stays their further progress in reproof, by his and their now present revived conditions, being raised again by the powerful virtue of poesy (after such length of time) to behold Britannia's former felicity again, and that the same Albania, where Humber slew his son Albanact, had bred a second Brute, by the blessed marriage of Margaret, eldest daughter to King Henry the Seventh, to James the Fourth, King of Scotland, of whom our second Brute (Royal King James) is truly and rightfully descended: by whose happy coming to the crown, England, Wales, and Scotland, by the first Brute severed and divided, is in our second Brute re-united and made one happy Britannia again, peace and quietness bringing that to pass which war nor any other means could attain unto. For joy of which sacred union and combination, Locrine, Camber, and Albanact, figured there also in their antique estates, deliver up their crowns and sceptres, applauding the day of this long-wished conjunction, and *Troya nova* (now London) incites fair Thamesis and the rivers that bounded the severed kingdoms (personated in fair and beautiful nymphs) to sing paeans and songs of triumph in honor of our second Brute, Royal King James. Thamesis, as Queen of all Britain's rivers, begins the triumphal course of solemn rejoicing. Next her, Severn, that took her name of Sabrina, begotten by Locrine on fair Elstrid, and both mother and daughter were drowned in that river, by Gwendolyn's command, the wife to Locrine doth the like. Lastly Humber, whose name was derived from Humber King of the Scythians, who being pursued by Locrine and Camber in revenge of their brother's death, was enforced to leap into that river, and there drowned himself, of whom I find these verses, written:

Dum fugite obstat ei flumen submergitur illic,
Deque suo tribuit nomine nomen aquae.

What further may be required to express Britannia's triumph more perfectly to the life with all the other personages, her servants and attendants, is more at large set down in the several speeches which I have hereto annexed as most meet and convenient.

The speeches delivered by the several children, according to their degrees of seating in the Pageant

Britannia. I that was sometime termed Albion,
After the name of Neptune's valiant son,
Albion the Giant, and so had still held on,
But that my conquest, first by thee begun,
Hath in fame's chronicle such honor won,
That thy first setting from Albania,
Crowned me thy virgin Queen Britannia.

Brute. Wherein recount thy height of happiness,
Thou that before my honored victory
Wert as a base and o'ergrown wilderness,
Peopled with men of incivility,
Huge and stern giants, keeping company
With savage monsters, thus was Albion then
Till I first furnished thee with civil men.
Goemagot, and all his barbarous brood,
(When he was foiled by Corineus' hand)
Were quite subdued and not one withstood
My quiet progress over all thy land,
But as sole conqueror I did command:
And then from Albion did I change thy name,
To Brute's Britannia, still to hold the same.
Then built I my New Troy, in memory
Of whence I came, by Thamesis' fair side,
And nature giving me posterity,
Three worthy sons, not long before I died,
My kingdom to them three I did divide.
And as in three parts I had set it down,
Each named his seat, and each did wear a crown.

Loegria. But she whom thou hadst made one monarchy
To be so severed, to thy sons might show
Some sign of love, to her small courtesy;
When three possess what one did solely owe,
It makes more ways to harm than many know.
And so proved that division of the land,
It brought in war, that hellish firebrand.

222 stays halts
223 his and their i.e., by pointing out
240 antique ancient
241 estates conditions
251 Elstrid i.e., Estrildis, recorded in Geoffrey of Monmouth as a German woman brought to England by King Humber; Locrine fell in love with her and they produced a daughter, Sabrina. This so enraged Queen Gwendolyn that she ordered the deaths of both mother and child
260–1 *Dum . . . aquae* Munday translates this below, lines 311–12
269 *degrees* formal orders of precedence
274 thee i.e., Brute
302 owe i.e., own

Cambria. The King of Huns entered Albania,
Slew Albanact thy son, and there bare sway,
Till Locrine rose with valiant Cambria,
And to revenge their brother's death made way,
Which instantly they did without delay,
And made that river bear the proud King's name,
That thus intruded, drowned him in the same.
Albania. Fair Elstrid taken in that fatal fight,
And Locrine's love to her, wrong to his wife,
Duke Corineus' daughter; dear delight,
That reft both her and Locrine of his life,
Opened a gap to much more dismal strife,
Of all which heavy haps there has been none,
Had Brute left me one governor alone.
Brute. See, after so long slumb'ring in our tombs,
Such multitudes of years, rich poesy,
That does revive us to fill up these rooms,
And tell our former ages' history,
(The better to record Brute's memory,)
Turns now our accents to another key,
To tell old Britain's new-born happy day.
That separation of her sinewed strength,
Weeping so many hundred years of woes,
Whereto that learned bard dated long length
Before those ulcered wounds again could close,
And reach unto their former first dispose,
Hath run his course through time's sandy glass,
And brought the former happiness that was.
Albania, Scotland, where my son was slain
And where my folly's wretchedness began,
Hath bred another Brute, that gives again
To Britain her first name, he is the man
On whose fair birth our elder wits did scan,
Which prophet-like seventh Henry did foresee,
Of whose fair child comes Britain's unity.
And what fierce war by no means could effect,
To re-unite those sundered lands in one,
The hand of heaven did peacefully elect
By mildest grace, to seat on Britain's throne
This second Brute, than whom there else was none.
Wales, England, Scotland, severed first by me
To knit again in blessed unity.
For this Britannia rides in triumph thus,
For this these sister-kingdoms now shake hands,
Brute's Troy (now London) looks most amorous
And stands on tiptoe, telling foreign lands,
So long as seas bear ships, or shores have sands,
So long shall we in true devotion pray,
And praise high heaven for that most happy day.
Locrine. England, that first was called Loegria,
After my name, when I commanded here,
Gives back her due unto Britannia
And doth her true-born son in right prefer,
Before divided rule, irregular,
Wishing my brethren in like sort resign,
A sacred union once more to combine.
Camber. I yielded long ago, and did in heart,
Allow Britanniae's first created name,
My true-born Brutes have ever took her part
And to their last hour will maintain the same.
Albanact. It is no marvel though you gladly yield,
When the all-ruling power doth so command;
I bring that monarch now into the field,
With peace and plenty in his sacred hand,
To make Britannia one united land.
And when I brought him, after times will say
It was Britannia's happy Holi-day.
Troya Nova. Then you fair swans in Thamesis that swim,
And you choice nymphs that do delight to play
On Humber and fair Severn, welcome him
In canzons, jigs, and many a roundelay
That from the north brought you this blessed day.
And in one tuneful harmony let's sing,
Welcome King James, welcome bright Britain's king.
Thamesis. I that am Queen of all Britannia's streams,
The ocean's darling and endeared delight,
That wanton daily with the sun's gilt beams
And o'er my bosom suffer day and night,
Fair floats of ships to sail in goodly sight.
Unto my second Brute shall homely sing,
Welcome King James, welcome Great Britain's King.

306 King of Huns an alternate name for King Humber
329 that learned bard Merlin (in Geoffrey of Monmouth, VII.iii)
336 another Brute James I of England
364 true-born Brutes the Welsh, considered the true descendants of the ancient British tribes
372 It . . . Holi-day (this line may deliberately echo *The Magnificent Entertainment*)
382 gilt golden
386 Great Britain's King James's title by his own proclamation in October 1604 – as a first step to the Union of England and Scotland since he was King of both countries – after the House of Commons demurred in bestowing that title on him

Saverne. Fair Elfrid's and Sabrinae's fatal grave,
(Whereby the name of Saverne fell to me)
When Locrine's Gwendolyn in anger gave
My womb to be their dismal tragedy,
Whereof my nymphs (as yet) talk mournfully,
Unto my second Brute do likewise sing,
Welcome King James, welcome Great Britain's King.
Humber. Proud Scythians' Humber that slew Albanact,
Whose brethren forced him to a shameful flight,
When in my wat'ry arms his life I wracked,
I took his name, and kept it as my right,
For which my nymphs still dancing in delight,
With these paeans and canzons sing,
Welcome King James, our second Brute and King.

The Chariot: Pheme riding before it

[*Pheme*]. Fame that attends on Britain's monarchy,
Thus re-united to one state again,
Ushers this chariot of true dignity,
Wherein seven king that did in England reign,
These royal virtues in their shields contain,
Expressing what great grace each Majesty
Gave to the Merchant-Taylors' Company.
When they were first a guild, and bare the style
Of Tailors, and of Armorers beside
Of the linen armory: for no little while
Were they so known and daily did provide
Those coats of arms that quailed our foemen's pride,
When England's bent-bow, and the grey-goose wing
Our many victories abroad did sing.
From this employment for the state's defense,
Their ancient title first unto them came,
And then their following care and diligence,
Squared them the way to order well and frame
All means to keep their guild in honest fame.
Now gracious Virtues unto you I leave
What further fortunes Time did them bequeath.
Tapeinotes. Edward the Third, whose royal name I bear,
Hearing the love and royal amity
That good report gave of them everywhere,
Preserving peace and kind society,
In his first year unto this Company,
He gave this charter to confirm their guild:
And they enjoyed it, as His Highness willed.
Eros. To build this body on a stronger frame,
Richard the Second gave authority,
A Master and four Keepers they should name.
And full elect to sway their mystery,
Granting them power to have a livery,
And hold a feast on Saint John Baptist day,
Yearly forever, as they do and may.
Eleutheriotes. To fortify a work so well begun,
Henry the Fourth did liberally create
(Beside the former favors to them done)
Their guild a Brotherhood incorporate,
And thought it no disgrace to his high state
To wear the clothing of the Company,
A most majestic royal courtesy.
Sophrosyne. Henry the Fifth my war-like lord maintained
His father's love to this society.
Agnites. Of my sixth Henry they as freely gained
All former grants in self-same quality.
He wore their clothing, mild and graciously.
For princes lose no part of dignity
In being affable, it adds to majesty.
Hypomone. Thus long a Master and four Keepers stood,
Till my fourth Edward changed the Keepers' name
To Wardens, for the strength of brotherhood,
And thus at first Master and Wardens came.
Epimeleia. And for they traded, as no men did more,
With foreign realms, by clothes and merchandise,
Returning hither other countries' store,
Of what might best be our commodities.

---

388 **Saverne** i.e., Severn

401 **Pheme** Greek for fame

409 **bare** bore

411 **linen armory** i.e., they made non-metallic adjuncts to armor

414 **grey-goose wing** (feathers of the gray goose were used for arrows shot from longbows)

423 ***Tapeinotes*** Greek for lowness of spirit or meanness; perhaps Munday means humility

430 ***Eros*** Greek for love

433 **mystery** guild or company (which taught secret techniques to apprentices)

434 **livery** regulation clothing worn on special occasions

435 **feast . . . day** June 24; the Merchant Taylors' guild, initially incorporated as the Fraternity of St. John the Baptist, took John as their patron saint

437 ***Eleutheriotes*** Greek for freedom, liberality

444 ***Sophrosyne*** Greek for prudence, temperance

446 ***Agnites*** Greek for purity, chastity

451 ***Hypomone*** Greek for patience

455 ***Epimeleia*** Greek for care, diligence

Henry the Seventh, a gracious king, and wise,
To Merchant-Taylors did exchange their name
Since when, with credit they have kept the same.
Pheme. But sacred Lady, deign me so much grace,
As tell me why that seat is unsupplied,
Being the most eminent and chiefest place,
With state, with crown, and scepter dignified?
Epimeleia. Have our discourses (Pheme) let thee know,
That seven Kings have borne Free Brethren's name
Of this society, and may not Time bestow
An eighth, when heaven shall so appoint the same?
Pheme. I find recorded in my register,
Seven Kings have honoured this society:
Fourteen great Dukes did willingly prefer
Their love and kindness to this Company,
Three score eight Lords declared like amity,
Terming themselves all Brethren of this band,
The very worthiest Lords of all the land.
Three Dukes, three Earls, four Lords of noble name
All in one year did join in Brother-hood:

(In the year 1390 Edward Duke of York; Thomas Duke of Gloucester; Henry Duke of Hereford and Earl of Derby, who afterward was K. Henry the Fourth; Edward Earl of Rutland; Thomas Earl of Warwick; John Holland, Earl of Huntingdon; John, Lord Ros; Rafe, Lord Nevill; Thomas, Lord Furnivall; Reignald, Lord Gray of Rithin.)

I find beside great Lords from France there came
To hold like league, and do them any good.

(Gaylard, Lord Danvers. Barard, Lord Delamote. Barard, Lord Montferrant, &c)

Yet no embasing to their height in blood,
For they accounted honor then most high,
When it was held up by community.
Of Bishops, Knights and Deans, to those before
(Not spoke in vaunt, or any spirit of pride),
My records could afford as many more,
All Brethren, Merchant-Taylors signified
That lived in love with them, and when they died
Left me their names, to after times to tell,
Thus then they died, and thought it good and well.

Neptune on the Lion

My borrowed name of Neptune now I leave,
The like doth Amphitrita my fair Queen,
And worthy Lord, grant favor to receive
What in these mysteries we seem to mean.
Britanniae's glory hath been heard and seen
Revived from her old chaos of distress,
And now united in firm happiness.
Blest be that second Brute, James our dread King,
That set this wreath of union on her head,
Whose very name did heavenly comfort bring,
When in despair our hopes lay drooping dead,
When comfort from most hearts was gone and fled,
Immediately the trumpet's tongue did say,
God save King James: oh, 'twas a happy day!
Amphitrita. Our latest Phoenix whose dead cinders shine,
In angels' spheres, she, like a mother mild,
Yielding to nature, did her right resign
To Time's true heir, her godson, and loved child,
When giddy expectation was beguiled.
And Scotland yielded out of Tudor's race,
A true-born bud, to sit in Tudor's place,
Which seat to him and his, heaven ever bless,
That we ne'er want a rose of Tudor's tree,
To maintain Britain's future happiness,
To the world's end in true tranquility.

468–9 **Time . . . eighth** James I, who accepted the freedom of the Cordwainers' Company, did not become free of the Merchant Taylors' Company, but he did attend a dinner at the Guildhall in 1607 with Prince Henry where the major speech was by Ben Jonson (Prince Henry did become a member of the Merchant Taylors' guild)

490 **embasing** lowering in rank or position, humbling

492 **community** i.e., the mystic elements of brotherhood in the guild system

500 **Neptune** (an appropriate guide for a Lord Mayor representing the sea trade of the Merchant Taylors)

504 **seem** think appropriate, seemly; **mean** convey

508 **dread** wondrous

511 **despair** mourning at the death of Elizabeth I, who left no heirs

515 **Our . . . Phoenix** Elizabeth I

518 **Time's true heir** James I, whom Elizabeth named her successor on her deathbed; **godson** Elizabeth, represented by proxy, was godparent at James's baptism

519 **giddy** thoughtless, anxious; **beguiled** cheated, deceived

520 **Tudor's race** (as descended from Margaret Tudor, eldest daughter of Henry VII)

Neptune

Sir Leonard Holliday, now unto thee,
My love in some mean measure let me show;
Since heaven hath called thee to his dignity,
Which (than myself) far better thou dost know,
I make no doubt thou wilt thy time bestow,
As fits so great a subject's place as this,
To govern greatly, and amend each miss.

Bethink thee how on that high holyday,
Which bears God's champion, th'archangel's name,
When conquering Satan in a glorious fray,
Michael hell's monster nobly overcame,
And now a sacred sabbath being the same,
A free and full election on all parts,
Made choice of thee, both with their hands and hearts.
Albeit this day is usual every year
For new election of a magistrate,
Yet, now to me some instance doth appear,
Worth note, which to myself I thus relate,
Holiday called on holyday to state,
Requires methinks a year of holidays,
To be disposed in good and virtuous ways.
For I account 'tis a Lord's holiday,
When justice shines in perfect majesty,
When as the poor can to the rich may say,
The magistrate hath given us equity,
And lent no ear to partiality,
When sin is punished, lewdness bears no sway:
All that day long, each day is Holyday.

When good provision for the poor is made,
Sloth set to labor, vice curbed everywhere,
When through the city every honest trade,
Stands not of might or insolence in fear,
But justice in their goodness does them bear.
Then, as before, in safety I may say,
All that year long, each day is Holliday.
Now in behalf of that society,
Whereof thou bear'st a loving brother's name,
What hath been done this day to dignify
They pray thee kindly to accept the same.
More circumstance I shall not need to frame,
But from the Merchant-Taylors this I say:
They wish all good to Leonard Holliday.

FINIS

527 **Sir . . . Holliday** (Holliday was sheriff of the city of London in 1598; knighted by James I on July 26, 1603. The subsequent pun on holiday–holy day was commonplace)

533 **miss** wrong

534 **high holyday** Michaelmas, September 29

545 **Holliday . . . holyday** Holliday's election fell on Sunday and on Michaelmas that year

The Knight of the Burning Pestle

Francis Beaumont

THE KNIGHT OF the Burning Peſtle.

—— —— —— —— *Quod ſi*
Iudicium ſubtile, videndis artibus illud
Ad libros & ad hæc Muſarum dona vocares:
Bœotum in craſſo iurares aëre natos.
Horat. in Epiſt. ad Oct. Aug.

Aut prodesse volunt aut delectare poetæ.

LONDON,
Printed for *Walter Burre*, and are to be ſold at the ſigne of the Crane in Paules Church-yard.
1613.

Frontispiece, 1613.

In an age when culture was reflected in plays which could in turn explore culture, the boundaries between art and reality – between the worlds of the plays and the worlds they played to – could become porous, permeable, and might even disappear altogether. Nor were plays themselves sacrosanct. In the infectious burlesque that initiates and energizes much of Francis Beaumont's *Knight of the Burning Pestle*, he questions the very form he practices. By asking his audience to become actors and his mimetic actors to stand back and view their own theatricality, Beaumont is able to parody – even satirize – recent London plays: George and Nell, his grocer and grocer's wife, are meant to recall Simon and Margery Eyre, the shoemaker who would be Lord Mayor of London and his wife who would dress like a Lord Mayor's wife, just as Beaumont's Rafe and his call to the militia at Mile-End deliberately resonates with Dekker's Rafe, who reluctantly leaves Jane for the army. The entire rising gentry, in fact, with their personal ambitions and insecurities, their interest in commerce, and their anxiety over public and private morality, like the characters of *Arden of Faversham* and *A Woman Killed with Kindness*, are also the subject of Beaumont's metadramatic interrogations. But *The Knight of the Burning Pestle* is not merely a play about shortcomings; it is also very much a play about *be*comings – about the magic power of the stage that liberates his characters so that a hard-headed grocer like George can not only find a capacity to dream but to dream publicly, while his wife Nell, at first hardly able to climb onto the stage at the Blackfriars Theater where the gentlemen gallants sit watching the play while the playgoers watch them, winds up inviting those same gentlemen back home for a drink and even a pipe of tobacco. This stage-struck, wide-eyed couple, at once full of common sense and full of dreams, manage to become a sort of artist themselves as they both create and destroy the work around them once upon a time called "The London Merchant." They are playgoers who become actors, actors who remain playgoers, and like us expose the basic human hunger for fiction. Indeed, this very will *for* fiction – its causes, its desirability, its inspiration, and its pitfalls – brings to its complicity with all phases of early Jacobean culture a buoyant probity that sets it apart, raising issues not only fundamental but very nearly infinite. The sudden twists and turns of perspective and plot in this merry, multilayered play continually investigate the nature of reality and the nature of the self by stepping in and out of its own drama – and then asking if even that is possible.

At the same time it poses such far-reaching questions, there is also something decidedly intimate about Beaumont's play, a premise of familiarity that makes it far more appropriate for the newer private theaters in London than for the older public playhouses that were staging the works of Dekker and Heywood, or the pageantry of the streets which they also composed. Indeed, the play was specifically written for the second Blackfriars Theater built by Richard Burbage in 1596 in a hall of the Upper Frater building of the dissolved Dominican Priory within the city walls but, because of its religious foundation, outside the city's jurisdiction. It provided a kind of opulence, since the theater was constructed to resemble physically the great halls such as Kenilworth or Whitehall; by charging higher prices – a minimum of sixpence or six times the admission to the public playhouse – and reducing the seating – to 600 or 700 instead of 2,000 or more – it also promoted a kind of exclusivity. All the playgoers at Blackfriars could sit level with (or even on) the stage and be adjacent to it. Such surroundings were conducive to the children's companies, whose voices need not project so far; to music and dancing that resembled court entertainments rather than mummings; and invited topical allusions, social satire, and even personal ridicule. The appeal, in short, was one of flattering the audience, so that it is quite likely a place George and Nell would want to visit (and where they would want to be seen); it was the perfect environment for the socially mobile and for the socially and politically ambitious. In *The Knight of the Burning Pestle* such concerns are not only those of the playgoers, however, but of the players as well.

Still, this should not imply homogeneity. The Children of the Revels for whom Beaumont wrote *The Knight*, for instance, even though it refers to adult companies as the other companies, had children of all ages and adults, or those nearly adult, too: the year after *The Knight* opened, in fact, in 1608, two of their company, William Ostler and John Underwood, left the Blackfriars to join the King's Men, Shakespeare's company, as members of that adult company playing at the Globe. Nor was the audience easily categorized. Ben Jonson describes the audience at Blackfriars in 1608, in a poem for Beaumont's future partner John Fletcher, as varied and judgmental, even censorious:

The wise and many-headed bench that sits
  Upon the life and death of plays, and wits,
(Composed of gamester, captain, knight, knight's man,
  Lady or pusil [child], that wears mask or fan,
Velvet or taffeta cap, ranked in the dark
  With the shop's foreman, or some such brave spark,
That may judge for his sixpence) had, before
  They saw it half, damned the whole play, and more;
Their motives were, since it had not to do
  With vices, which they looked for, and came to –

having paid top price to see a show, each playgoer, no matter what his or her predisposition, wanted only to see the show each thought he had paid to see. Just the year before *The Knight*, in 1606, John Day's play for Blackfriars, *The Isle of Gulls*, portrays a similarly divided audience where three gallants each demand a different play – one wants satire, a second prefers bawdy, and a third insists on chronicle history – and one even threatens to leave the play before it is finished. In still another instance of audience dissatisfaction and demand, a moral drama entitled *Spectrum* was replaced at the last moment by a comedy pointedly entitled *Wily Beguiled*. *The Knight of the Burning Pestle* opens with just such a suspicious and angry citizen in the grocer George, who is certain that the play he has come to see, like all the other plays in the theater's seven-year history, will be full of sneers at merchant citizens like himself.

Beaumont, however, seems to have relished such a challenge rather than to falter before it, with what seems like a workable premise: to provide a traditional kind of play, like the prodigal-son play, and to give it a traditional title, like *The London Merchant*, and then to parody it in the course of the performance. The prodigal-son play was a cautionary moral tale, a staple of Dutch and German schoolmasters who originated it and the Tudor humanist schoolmasters who perpetuated it, based on the parable in Luke (15:11–32). Typically in these plays, used to teach Latin and rhetoric, schoolboys would revolt against their lessons and hard work, turn to riot and disobedience, suffer, and repent; it was a lesson that worked simultaneously on several levels. With the coming of the public playhouses, the story moved from the life of students to the life of gallants, and the rather simple plot turned into increasingly complicated analyses of the prodigal and of the society he disowned as well as the society he temporarily chose; with the coming of the private playhouses, such analyses became more topical and more daring. In *The Knight of the Burning Pestle*, such a conventional narrative is reshaped through a mercenary outlook and deliberate bias of rank. In Beaumont's *London Merchant*, Venturewell sees his manager Jasper rebelling against his lower status in courting Venturewell's daughter; Jasper's mother dismisses him as a typical prodigal, a runaway, a "wastethrift," an "ungracious child" who would "[chop] logic with his mother." As the play progresses, however, it becomes clear that the formula has been turned upside-down: it is Jasper's father, the happy-go-lucky old Master Merrythought, who is the prodigal spendthrift, not his son; and it is his wife, Jasper's mother, who leaves home to experience the misfortunes that cause her to repent and return. Moreover, Mistress Merrythought's treatment of her son is likened to Venturewell's treatment of his daughter Luce – one of thoughtless dismissal – and his blindness to the idiocy of his chosen prospect for son-in-law Humphrey is similar to Mistress Merrythought's blind support of her foolish younger son Michael. But prodigality, Beaumont would seem to argue, is entirely perspectival. When George and his wife Nell side automatically with the merchant Venturewell as one of their kind and against Jasper, they ignore Jasper's credible self-defense, are unable to appreciate Luce's desire for him, and overlook Humphrey's failings. They not only judge badly; they intervene foolishly when they insist their apprentice Rafe enter the fray by taking on Jasper in a hand-to-hand combat in which Rafe is sorely defeated. For them the prodigal situation is unconventionally and undeservedly overturned, but they also overlook the fact that, in revolting against the play they have come to see, and threatening it, they have become prodigal themselves.

By thus making one plot intervene in another plot in his larger play, Beaumont keeps audience and play, life and art, perpetually entangled and our perspective, unless we are careful, tends to slip into that of George and Nell. We can be careful because George and Nell embody the bad qualities gallants had come to place on rising merchants: smugness, social climbing, self-satisfaction and pride, prudence and conventionality; with George, and Nell especially, the self-assured sense of propriety they enact is embarrassing: they interrupt the play they have come to see; they make silly comments as well as foolish demands; they fail to understand what is unfolding before them; Nell particularly makes obscene remarks; and they make a spectacle of private affection. Yet nothing in this play is that simple, and neither are George and Nell. George is full of admiration for his apprentice Rafe, never once doubting or scorning him, and he has a great (if sadly misplaced) faith in Rafe's abilities as actor, knight, Lord of the May, and even a master of the trained bands he remembers so fondly from his own earlier days; although any of these roles would take Rafe from the grocer's shop perhaps never to return, George is quite willing to see how instead Rafe's adventures will do honor to his own guild – one of London's Twelve Great Companies. Nell, for all her complacency and pride, shows instant and often indiscriminate compassion for those she is watching, following up her concern with words of advice and a purseful of licorice, green ginger, and other quack remedies that she is happy to share wherever she sees the need for them. In addition, they share what seems to be an unlimited capacity for romanticism. Their romantic reading is apparently largely limited to the Iberian romances of chivalry – especially *Don Quixote* – then so popular with the gentry and they, like Rafe, take deep pleasure in all of its formulaic moments. Rafe's investiture, his visit to the enchanted castle and the host of the Bell, and his vanquishing of Barbaroso are heavily conventional and disjointedly episodic – unlike good art or even good romance – but George and Nell find such moments deeply fulfilling because they bring an ideal way of lost life that invests their mundane world with values at the same time they transform their mundane world, through Rafe, into the more glamorous and altogether uncommercial world of chivalry. They are, in this sense, perfect readers and wonderfully appreciative of art. Thus formed, their minds also want to create art.

But at the same time George and Nell seem to want to destroy art. George opens the play by bullying the actors and threatening them; the objections of the Prologue and the Boy are brutally pushed aside. When George demands that the Prologue "let the grocer do rare things" and the Prologue objects that "we have never a boy to play him; everyone hath a part already," he supplies Rafe. When George and Nell insist that their play of the knight of the burning pestle revenge Humphrey by combatting Rafe, the Boy objects: "you must pardon us; the plot of our play lies contrary, and 'twill hazard the spoiling of our play." George is emphatic: "Plot me no plots. I'll ha' Rafe come out. I'll make your house too hot for you else." Even when the comedy draws to a close, George insists that the knight's tragedy also draw to its natural close, in the knight's death. Reality succumbs to the conventions of art, but then art in the battle of wills between the actors and George and Nell has become a reality. Nell continually makes this point by taking each episode of each play literally. Yet in this she is not always predictable. While her greatest affection is for Rafe, she also has compassion for Humphrey – whom she sees as one of her own – and, at one point, for Jasper – whom she does not. She defends Jasper before his mother, who accuses him of lying about his dismissal from Venturewell's service: "No, indeed, Mistress Merrythought, though he be a notable gallows, yet I'll assure you his master did turn him away; even in this place 'twas, i'faith, within this half hour, about his daughter, my husband was by," and when George objects to her defense – "Hang him, rogue. He served him well enough. Love his master's daughter!" – she counters this denial of rank with a higher platitude: "Aye, George, but yet truth is truth." Later, when Jasper confesses the real truth of his love for Luce – in the play's most romantic, if sentimental, lines – and pulls a sword on her to test her constancy alongside his, Nell forgets the speech at once and sees (and hears) only the danger to Luce: "Away, George, away; raise the watch at Ludgate, and bring a mittimus from the justice for this desperate villain." And George is equally concerned: "I warrant thee, sweetheart, we'll have him hampered [imprisoned]." While such interventions threaten the play of *The London Merchant*, they also extend and confirm it.

Indeed, alongside *The London Merchant* and the play we might call *Rafe* or *The Knight*, a third play, *George and Nell*, as traced especially in the interludes that demarcate each act with song or dance and commentary, shows the possible if not necessary effects of the desired suspension of disbelief on which all art and all dramatic performances rest. At the end of the first act, the boy dances, but for George it is a "scurvy boy" and he demands "bid the players send Rafe"; they respond by starting their play up again with Venturewell and Humphrey. When the "scurvy music" returns at the end of Act II – "I gave the whoreson gallows money, and I think he has not got me the waits of Southwark" – Nell too longs "that we might see our Rafe again," and, on cue, the players respond adversely with the love scene between Jasper and Luce, hoping the romantic side of their merchant's tale will calm George and Nell. The third time the music is attempted, George and Nell no longer request; they demand; their authority takes over, at least momentarily, as the Boy dances "Fading," both a common jig and an obscene gesture. Thus successful, at the final interlude, at the end of Act IV, George and Nell demand Rafe's appearance, and his long appearance as the Lord of May *becomes* the interlude. Act V ends not with a final interlude but with an epilogue in which Nell displaces the Prologue by insinuating herself as the hostess inviting all of the gentlemen on stage to leave the stage and come to her home: "I would have a pottle of wine and a pipe of tobacco for you; for truly I hope you do like the youth, but I would be glad to know the truth." She (like George) has no trouble once the play is completed continuing with her own play; at the same time she knows that the play they have come to Blackfriars to see is over, finished. In fact, it is Nell along with George who has made the play classical art – their presence alone has turned the ranging adventures of both *The London Merchant* and *Rafe*, with its passage of time and transformations into the unities of time, place, and action that Sidney had required in his *Defense of Poesie* and that Ben Jonson was attempting, almost singlehandedly, to return to the playhouses as the most perfect form of art.

In light of Thomas Dekker's Eyres or Thomas Heywood's Frankfords, both Venturewell and George seem likely enough as dramatic characters representing and so interrogating the very culture that produces them. Rafe's disparate throwback to a medieval culture of knight errantry is what seems out of place. As long before as 1570, the humanist Roger Ascham had inveighed in *The Schoolmaster* against the "books of feigned chivalry" that led to "manslaughter and bawdry." But in fact, as a contemporary show like Anthony Munday's Lord Mayor's pageant here suggests, the Arthurian legend with all of its chivalric trappings was the very stuff of British nationalism, chauvinism, and patriotism; and they found in it all the codes of hierarchical responsibility and all the manners of courtly and civic ceremony that might model Jacobean England; even in the face of Ascham, Sir Philip Sidney had admitted in his *Defense* to his strong approval for memorable ballads of Percy and Douglas. George Clifford, Earl of Cumberland, in fact, fought for Queen Elizabeth as her champion under the title of "Knight of Pendragon Castle" and in 1572 armed Skipton Castle with some fourteen cannon. James fostered such activities, in part to strengthen his interest in his connections with Brute spelled out in *The Magnificent Entertainment* and *The Triumphs of Re-united Britannia*. In 1606, the third Earl of Pembroke, his brother Philip, the Earl of Southampton, and the Duke of Lenox, all called themselves "The Knights Errant" and with "sound of trumpet before the Palace-gate of Greenwich" challenged "all honorable Men of Arms and Knights Adventurers of hereditary note and exemplary nobleness, that for most maintainable actions do wield their swords or lances in the quest for glory." Sir Edmund Verney, in a report issued on a battle in Ireland, concludes "after we put some four score men to the sword, but like valiant knights errant, gave quarter and liberty to all the women." Edward Herbert, in 1603, according to his *Autobiography*, was inducted into the Knights of Bath where he vowed throughout his life "never to sit in place where injustice should be done, but they shall right to the uttermost of their power; and particularly ladies and gentlewomen that shall be wronged in their honor, if they demand assistance . . . not unlike the romances of knight errantry." We recall that Jonson found knights in the audiences at Blackfriars and that the adventures of Don Quixote were being read admiringly; in becoming a knight errant, even the Knight of the Burning Pestle named by a Prologue (but as a play) who does not even know him, Rafe is doing King James's work. "Rafe plays a stately part and he must needs have shawms," notes George; and he is right: if the costume ill fits him – as it might well have done – Rafe's language does not: he has all the words and all the manners of a true knight errant. Given his own reputed craving for theater – he could play Mucedorus or Hieronimo if necessary – Rafe displays the power of imagination and demonstrates how, in seeking its own visions and ideals, the human imagination in any social rank can soar. Moreover, what comes naturally to Rafe are the admirable sides of knight errantry: magnanimity, courage, service, and compassion. If the body sometimes falters, as it does before Jasper, the mind never weakens. It is as if Rafe were born to play the part with the script already in his head: he needs only a cue from his employer and the magic of his inventiveness takes charge. We may laugh at that imagination, too – when he thinks an inn a castle or the anxious Jasper a caitiff or the barber a giant – but our laughter at such escapades, as with their similar models in *Don Quixote*, cannot carry the scorn Sidney says all laughter must, because we would not deny the intentions or values behind such beliefs. Just as the very goodness of Rafe redeems him, so, to some degree, does it redeem his begetters, George and Nell. What, then, are we to make of their surrender, after the defeat at the hands of Jasper, to other roles? In playing Lord of the May or a muster-master, does Rafe settle for a lesser style of life or, in more realistically playing out the visions or hopes of each merchant of each of the Twelve Great Companies, does he rise in the end to redeem not himself but the entire merchant class? It has been argued that this is not at all a diminution of roles, but that a willed dysfunctional life of knight errantry has prepared him to become, instead, a representative of the new world of commerce and a hero of the new working class. What Beaumont may well be asking is this: does Rafe come to represent a brave new world or a world well lost? or is he himself the loser?

At some metaphoric level, of course, Rafe's real vision is that of a freeman roaming his playworld universe, not that of an indentured servant. But the play keeps reminding us that is what he really is: all the roles he takes on he assumes at the direction of his master and his master's wife. They never fear losing him; he seems never to regret serving them; *The Knight of the Burning Pestle* tests hierarchy and convention by stretching them without seriously threatening them. Indeed, in what might be considered still a fourth play – Beaumont's own metadrama that we write by pulling all three of his plots into a singular narrative – there is a way in which Venturewell mirrors George in his insistence on rank-dictated behavior (except when a promising match will socially advance his daughter and himself!). Jasper in turn mirrors Rafe, for despite their departures from their respective masters, both find themselves enclosed in other stock dramatic roles. Jasper can switch roles as Rafe can – from prodigal son to young courting lover to a man at combat – but he cannot escape them altogether. The sincere protest on his part when he is accused by Venturewell of disobedience is put in Beaumont's larger design alongside Rafe's rhetorical sincerity in becoming a knight at arms; and it seems clear that Beaumont wants each speech to reflect on the other. Rafe's attempt to act out his ideals is matched in turn by Jasper's attempt to live out the commitments of his genuine feelings for Luce; and there are ways in which Rafe's knightly honor and magnanimity come to characterize both of them. Just as both prosper through adversity, both in the end feign their own deaths as their greatest and final achievements: by acting a part that is clearly theatrical, they win their ways back to lives that are truly authentic – as the husband of Luce, forgiven by Venturewell and the Merrythoughts, and the apprentice of George and Nell who repays every bit of their pride in him. But what do such parallels mean? that only smart ingenuity will win reward? that life without fantasy is not worth living? or that life with fantasy does not permit life to go on? Beaumont's Jasper challenges rigid hierarchy of rank determined by birth and escapes it only to surrender to it, we would suppose, after his marriage to Luce; Rafe never even tries and his fair Susan of Milk Street, who never appears to this man concerned with his grocer's pestle, may in the end only be yet another figment of his lively and supportive imagination. The very essence of Jacobean gentry life is being tested in the careers of these characters.

And what, in the end, are we to make of Master Merryweather in this nation of shopkeepers? A man of mirth and song – not really of riotousness, despite his wife's charges – it is he who can sense the truth and honor in Jasper and share part of his last bit of money with his elder son; it is he who must forgive his erring wife; he brings about the reconciliation between Venturewell and Jasper, and so the play's marriage of Jasper and Luce. In the final act, everybody willingly resigns to his world of song. Is this meant to suggest that without revelry, life is not worth living? or that life is incomplete without art? Merrythought, after all, is forever genial, yet that very geniality depends on the willingness of others to support him – he survives on the legacy from others. He can also carry his one-dimensional philosophy to an excess we would consider *in*human: "If both my sons were on the gallows, I would sing." He is just as insensitive to Venturewell's grief over the loss of his daughter. He stands at the end as a successor to Rafe as May Lord, as a Lord of Misrule, a King of Carnival coming after, rather than before, a long Lenten period of trial and tribulation. But he can hardly be the resolution to the play's concerns even as, momentarily, he seems to be to the plot. *Merry-thought* may itself be an irreconcilable paradox. In 1632, Jonson dramatized a poetics in a work called *The Magnetic Lady*, which seems resonant of *The Knight of the Burning Pestle*:

> *Boy*. . . . So if a child could be born in a play and grow up to a man in the first scene, before he went off the stage, and then after to come forth a squire and be made a knight, and that knight to travel between the Acts and do wonders in the holy land, or elsewhere; kill pagans, wild boars, dun cows, and other monsters; beget him a reputation, and marry an emperor's daughter for his mistress; convert her father's country and at the last come home, lame, and all to be laden with miracles.
>
> *Damplay*. These miracles would please, I assure you, and take the People! For there be of the People that will expect miracles, and more than miracles from this pen.
>
> *Boy*. Do they think this pen can juggle? . . . who expect what is impossible, or beyond nature, defraud themselves.

Yet at the dead center of this play, voluntarily defrauded without any urging from George or Nell, the boys of the Blackfriars Company, acting *The London Merchant*, turn all their talents to extemporizing the scenes at the Bell Inn and Barbaroso's shop, and even the kingdom of Cracovia. In their world, they play many parts – that *is* their world – just as we play many parts in our own.

And what of us, at the end? Merrythought thinks singing is a universal panacea, and we feel he must surely be wrong. Nell thinks the gentlemen, having heard her throughout the play, will now be quick to join her at home, and we feel that is very doubtful. In such responses, we take this play just as seriously as, for a time, the boys' company takes Rafe. In such responses, we take this play seriously without being deluded – or defrauded – by it. But such questions would not arise, and all that they signify would not be on our minds if, at least temporarily, we had *not* believed in this play and been defrauded by it. For all of its high spirits and contagious joy, *The Knight of the Burning Pestle* asks us whether this play or any other play or entertainment in this collection is, finally, an act of fraud.

Further Reading

Bliss, Lee, *Francis Beaumont*. Boston: Twayne Publishers, 1987.

Bristol, Michael D., *Carnival and Theater*. London: Methuen, 1985.

Finkelpearl, Philip J., *Court and Country Politics in the Plays of Beaumont and Fletcher.* Princeton: Princeton University Press, 1990.

Miller, Ronald F., "Dramatic Form and Dramatic Imagination in Beaumont's *The Knight of the Burning Pestle*," *English Literary Renaissance* 8:1 (Winter 1978): 67–84.

Osborne, Laurie E., "Female Audiences and Female Authority in *The Knight of the Burning Pestle*," *Exemplaria* 3:2 (Fall 1991): 491–517.

Samuelson, David A., "The Order in Beaumont's *Knight of the Burning Pestle*," *English Literary Renaissance* 9:2 (Spring 1979): 302–18.

Shapiro, Michael, *Children of the Revels: The Boy Companies of Shakespeare's Time and Their Plays.* New York: Columbia University Press, 1977.

Steinberg, Glenn A., "'You Know the Plot / We Both Agreed On?': Plot, Self-Consciousness, and *The London Merchant* in Beaumont's *The Knight of the Burning Pestle*," *Medieval and Renaissance Drama in England* 5 (1991): 211–24.

The Knight of the Burning Pestle

To his many ways endeared friend, Master Robert Keysar

Sir,

This unfortunate child, who in eight days (as lately I have learned) was begot and born, soon after was by his parents (perhaps because he was so unlike his brethren) exposed to the wide world, who for want of judgment, or not understanding the privy mark of irony about it (which showed it was no offspring of any vulgar brain) utterly rejected it; so that for want of acceptance it was even ready to give up the ghost, and was in danger to have been smothered in perpetual oblivion, if you (out of your direct antipathy to ingratitude) had not been moved both to relieve and cherish it, wherein I must needs commend both your judgment, understanding, and singular love to good wits. You afterwards sent it to me, yet being an infant and somewhat ragged, I have fostered it privately in my bosom these two years, and now to show my love return it to you, clad in good lasting clothes, which scarce memory will wear out, and able to speak for itself; and withal, as it telleth me, desirous to try his fortune in the world, where if yet it be welcome, both father and foster-father, nurse and child, have their desired end. If it be slighted or traduced, it hopes his father will beget him a younger brother, who shall revenge his quarrel, and challenge the world either of fond and merely literal interpretation or illiterate misprision.

TEXTUAL VARIANTS

I.O] Q reads "Actus primi, Scoena prima." **117 s.d.**] Q has s.d. at line 116 **156** shoot] Q sute **212** of] Q omits **214** me] Q men **231** struck] Q stroke **351 s.d.**] Q has s.d. at line 353 **391** list] Q lust **442 s.d.**] Q has s.d. at line 440 **472** no] Q now **491**] Q reads "finis Actus primi" **II.o**] Q reads "Actus Secundi scoena prima." **51** swore] Q sweare **56** swore] Q sweare **206** pounds] Q pound **206** pounds] Q pound **276** thing] Q things **341** thou] Q thou thou **344** of] Q off **366** than] Q then **372** shrewdly] Q shrodly **412** hight] Q high **415** Tapstero] Q Tastero **450** errand] Q errant **521** lungs] Q longs **553** wi'] Q wee **564** cares] Q cares cares **585**] Q reads "Musicke. Finis Actus secundi." **Interlude II.8** 'em] Q him **III.o**] Q reads "Actus tertius, Scoena prima." **1** dear] Q deer deer **5** this] Q these **17** wear] Q were **69** than] Q then **160** true] Q truery true **fair**] Q fair fair **226** knight] Q knights **284** swoops] Q soopes **313** dispatched] Q dispatch **331 s.d.**] Q has s.d. at line 330 **398** give him] Q give **405** ribbons] Q ribbands **465** *3. Knight*] Q Man **481** *3. Knight*] Q Man **620** Come . . . aloft] Q prints third line of song fragment as prose; many of the remaining songs are printed as prose if they are sung by Merrythought (indicated in this text by roman rather than italic type) **Interlude III.7**] Q reads "Finis Actus tertij. Musicke. Actus quartus, Scoena prima." **IV.63 s.d.**] Q has s.d. at line 65 **82** Strand] Q strond **148** *Exeunt*] Q Exit **179** He] Q ha **252** hope] Q hopt **275** These] Q There **287** *Ribbons*] Q Ribbands **289** *moaning*] Q mourning **308** than] Q then **Interlude IV.29 s.d.**] Q has s.d. at line 31 **66**] Q reads "Finis Act.4." Act **V.o**] Q reads "Actus 5. Scoena prima." **89** struck] Q stroke **208** minion] Q mimon **209** long] Q long long **308** 'em] Q ham **309** said] Q sad **316** Make an end] Q Make **Epilogue. 3** than] Q then

Playsource

The Knight of the Burning Pestle seems to have been Beaumont's own invention, although it relies on such preceding romantic dramas as Robert Greene's *Orlando Furioso* (1591–2), Dekker's *Old Fortunatus* (1599), Thomas Heywood's *The Four Prentices of London* (1600), and *The Travels of the Three English Brothers* (1607) by John Day, William Rowley, and George Wilkins, as well as the perennially popular *Mucedorus* (1588). Heroic extravagance had previously been parodied in George Peele's *Old Wives' Tale* (1590), but clear references point as well to the prose romance by Cervantes of *Don Quixote*, available in Spanish and in English translation in manuscript.

Dedicatory Epistle

Robert Keysar a wealthy London goldsmith who from about 1606 financed the Children of the Revels at the Blackfriars Theater in London

2 eight days (those spent in composition has been taken literally)

5 brethren other plays by Beaumont and John Fletcher

8 offspring . . . brain (not just an ordinary citizen comedy)

8–9 utterly rejected possibly means (1) unperformed; (2) unappreciated

17 ragged (the author's foul papers of manuscript)

23–4 father . . . child i.e., author, dedicatee, publisher, play

28 misprision misunderstanding

Perhaps it will be thought to be of the race of *Don Quixote*. We both may confidently swear it is his elder above a year, and therefore may (by virtue of his birthright) challenge the wall of him. I doubt not but they will meet in their adventures, and I hope the breaking of one staff will make them friends; and perhaps they will combine themselves, and travel through the world to seek their adventures. So I commit him to his good fortune, and myself to your love.

Your assured friend,
W.B.

THE SPEAKERS' NAMES

The Prologue
Then a Citizen
The Citizen's Wife, and Rafe, her Man, sitting below amidst
the Spectators
[Venturewell,] A rich Merchant
Jasper, his Apprentice
Master Humphrey, a friend to the Merchant
Luce, the Merchant's daughter
Mistress Merrythought, Jasper's mother
Michael, a second son of Mistress Merrythought
Old Master Merrythought
[Tim,] A Squire } [Apprentices]
[George,] A Dwarf }
A Tapster
A Boy that dances and sings
An Host
A Barber
[Three Captive] Knights
[Captive Woman]
A Sergeant
Soldiers
[Boys
William Hammerton, pewterer
George Greengoose, poulterer
Pompiona, daughter to the King of Moldavia]

[Induction]

Enter Prologue. [Gentlemen *seated on stage*, Citizen, Wife, *and* Rafe *in the audience below.*]

Prologue. From all that's near the court, from all that's great
Within the compass of the city walls,
We now have brought our scene.

Enter Citizen, [*climbing to the stage.*]

Citizen. Hold your peace, goodman boy.

Prologue. What do you mean, sir?

Citizen. That you have no good meaning. This seven years there hath been plays at this house; I have observed it, you have still girds at citizens, and now you call your play *The London Merchant*. Down with your title, boy; down with your title!

Prologue. Are you a member of the noble city?

Citizen. I am.

Prologue. And a freeman?

Citizen. Yea, and a grocer.

Prologue. So, grocer, then by your sweet favor, we intend no abuse to the city.

Citizen. No, sir? Yes, sir! If you were not resolved to play the jacks, what need you study for new subjects purposely to abuse your betters? Why could not you be contented as well as others with *The Legend of Whittington*; or *The Life and*

29–30 *Don Quixote* the original (1605) and Shelton's translation (1612) were both in circulation by the time of the printing; Shelton could have been known to Beaumont by 1607 in manuscript

31–2 virtue . . . birthright i.e., claim precedence

40 W.B. Walter Burre, the publisher

Induction

1 s.d. Gentlemen gallants who paid for seats on the stage so as to be seen; Nell will address them throughout the play

1 court at Westminster

2 city walls medieval city walls enclosing London except along the Thames

4 Hold . . . boy (Beaumont's first parody; here of John Day's *Isle of Gulls* [1606] at Blackfriars, where three gentlemen playgoers interrupt the Prologue to tell him what play they want to see)

6–7 This . . . house the Children of the Revels played at Blackfriars from 1600 to 1608

8 still always; **girds** sneers

9–10 *The . . . Merchant* probably the play here about Venturewell and the courtship of Luce

10 title (name of the play was given on a stage placard)

12 member citizen; inhabitant

14 freeman rank admitting persons to the privileges of the city after apprenticeship

15 grocer (the Grocers were one of the city's Twelve Great Livery Companies; the others were the Mercers, Drapers, Fishmongers, Goldsmiths, Skinners, Merchant Taylors, Haberdashers, Salters, Ironmongers, Vintners, and Clothworkers)

19 play . . . jacks play a knave; play tricks

20 betters adult companies

22–25 *Legend . . . Woolsacks* all plays glorifying London and stressing merchants and commerce put on at public playhouses; (1) Dick Whittington was a legendary Lord Mayor who rose from low to high estate; a play about him is entered in the Stationers' Register for 1605; (2) Thomas Gresham is in Thomas Heywood's *If You Know Not Me, You Know Nobody*, Part II (1606); the Royal Exchange was London's great burse opened by Elizabeth I and featured in Dekker's play in this collection; (3) Queen Elenor is in George Peele's *Edward I* (1593, but possibly revived on stage); (4) "The Building of London Bridge upon Wool Pack" was a popular dance song referring to the levy placed upon wool to build the bridge

Death of Sir Thomas Gresham, with the Building of the Royal Exchange; or *The Story of Queen Elenor, with the Rearing of London Bridge upon Woolsacks*?

Prologue. You seem to be an understanding man. What would you have us do, sir?

Citizen. Why, present something notably in honor of the commons of the city.

Prologue. Why, what do you say to *The Life and Death of Fat Drake, or The Repairing of Fleet-privies*?

Citizen. I do not like that, but I will have a citizen, and he shall be of my own trade.

Prologue. Oh, you should have told us your mind a month since. Our play is ready to begin now.

Citizen. 'Tis all one for that. I will have a grocer and he shall do admirable things.

Prologue. What will you have him do?

Citizen. Marry, I will have him ——

Wife. [*Below.*] Husband, husband!

Rafe. [*Below.*] Peace, mistress.

Wife. Hold thy peace, Rafe; I know what I do, I warrant thee. Husband, husband!

Citizen. What sayest thou, cony?

Wife. Let him kill a lion with a pestle, husband; let him kill a lion with a pestle.

Citizen. So he shall. I'll have him kill a lion with a pestle.

Wife. Husband, shall I come up, husband?

Citizen. Aye, cony. Rafe, help your mistress this way. Pray, gentlemen, make her a little room. I pray you, sir, lend me your hand to help up my wife. I thank you, sir. So.

[*They help* Wife *to stage.*]

Wife. By your leave, gentlemen all, I'm something troublesome; I'm a stranger here. I was ne'er at one of these plays, as they say, before; but I should have seen *Jane Shore* once, and my husband hath promised me any time this twelvemonth to carry me to *The Bold Beauchamps*; but in truth he did not. I pray you, bear with me.

Citizen. Boy, let my wife and I have a couple stools, and then begin, and let the grocer do rare things.

Prologue. But, sir, we have never a boy to play him; everyone hath a part already.

Wife. Husband, husband, for God's sake, let Rafe play him. Beshrew me if I do not think he will go beyond them all.

Citizen. Well remembered, wife. Come up, Rafe. I'll tell you, gentlemen, let them but lend him a suit of reparel and necessaries and, by Gad, if any of them all blow wind in the tail on him, I'll be hanged.

[Rafe *climbs to stage.*]

Wife. I pray you, youth, let him have a suit of reparel. I'll be sworn, gentlemen, my husband tells you true. He will act you sometimes at our house that all the neighbors cry out on him. He will fetch you up a couraging part so in the garret that we are all as feared, I warrant you, that we quake again. We'll fear our children with him if they be never so unruly. Do but cry, "Rafe comes, Rafe comes," to them, and they'll be as quiet as lambs. Hold up thy head, Rafe; show the gentlemen what thou canst do; speak a huffing part. I warrant you, the gentlemen will accept of it.

Citizen. Do, Rafe, do.

Rafe. By heaven, methinks it were an easy leap
To pluck bright honor from the pale-faced moon,
Or dive into the bottom of the sea,
Where never fathom line touched any ground,
And pluck up drowned honor from the lake of hell.

Citizen. How say you, gentlemen? Is it not as I told you?

Wife. Nay, gentlemen; he hath played before, my husband says, Mucedorus before the wardens of our company.

Citizen. Aye, and he should have played Jeronimo with a shoemaker for a wager.

---

26 **understanding** (pun on those standing on the ground below and in front of the stage for the lowest admission price)
29 **commons** the freemen
31–2 ***Fleet-privies*** (Fleet Ditch was used as a sewer)
38 **admirable** wonderful
45 **cony** rabbit; a common term of endearment
50 **Husband . . . up** (it was unusual and immodest for a woman to sit on the stage)
60 ***The Bold Beauchamps*** a lost play assigned to Thomas Heywood
68 **Beshrew me** "the devil take me" (a commonplace expression)
72 **reparel** apparel (archaic form)
73 **blow . . . him** (1) come near (from horseracing); (2) disparage
78 **cry out on** complain of
79 **couraging** spirited
86 **huffing** swaggering; bombastic
89–92 **By . . . hell** Hotspur's speech in *1 Henry IV* I.iii.201ff, substituting "from the lake of hell" for "by the locks"
96 **Mucedorus** a popular but extravagant play (1578) that mixed romantic adventures and buffoonery; **before the wardens** livery companies played at the London Guildhall and at court; the companies were directed by wardens
98 **Jeronimo** protagonist of Thomas Kyd's *Spanish Tragedy* in this collection

Prologue. He shall have a suit of apparel if he will go in.

Citizen. In, Rafe; in, Rafe, and set out the Grocery in their kind, if thou lovest me.

[*Exit* Rafe.]

Wife. I warrant our Rafe will look finely when he's dressed.

Prologue. But what will you have it called?

Citizen. *The Grocer's Honor.*

Prologue. Methinks *The Knight of the Burning Pestle* were better.

Wife. I'll be sworn, husband, that's as good a name as can be.

Citizen. Let it be so. Begin, begin; my wife and I will sit down.

Prologue. I pray you, do.

Citizen. What stately music have you? You have shawms?

Prologue. Shawms? No.

Citizen. No? I'm a thief if my mind did not give me so. Rafe plays a stately part and he must needs have shawms. I'll be at the charge of them myself, rather than we'll be without them.

Prologue. So you are like to be.

Citizen. Why, and so I will be. There's two shillings. Let's have the waits of Southwark. They are as rare fellows as any are in England, and that will fetch them all o'er the water with a vengeance, as if they were mad.

Prologue. You shall have them. Will you sit down then?

Citizen. Aye. Come, wife.

Wife. Sit you merry all, gentlemen. I'm bold to sit among you for my ease.

[*They sit.*]

Prologue. From all that's near the court, from all that's great
Within the compass of the city walls,
We now have brought our scene. Fly far from hence
All private taxes, immodest phrases,
Whate'er may but show like vicious.
For wicked mirth never true pleasure brings,
But honest minds are pleased with honest things.
Thus much for that we do, but for Rafe's part
– You must answer for yourself.

Citizen. Take you no care for Rafe. He'll discharge himself, I warrant you.

Wife. I'faith, gentlemen, I'll give my word for Rafe.

[*Exit* Prologue.]

Act I

Enter Merchant [*i.e.* Venturewell], *and* Jasper, *his prentice.*

Merchant. Sirrah, I'll make you know you are my prentice,
And whom my charitable love redeemed
Even from the fall of fortune; gave thee heat
And growth to be what now thou art; new cast thee,
Adding the trust of all I have at home,
In foreign staples, or upon the sea
To thy direction; tied the good opinions
Both of myself and friends to thy endeavors,
So fair were thy beginnings. But with these,
As I remember, you had never charge
To love your master's daughter; and even then,
When I had found a wealthy husband for her,
I take it, sir, you had not. But, however,
I'll break the neck of that commission,
And make you know you are but a merchant's factor.

Jasper. Sir, I do liberally confess I am yours,
Bound both by love and duty to your service,

---

101 go in i.e., to the tiring (attiring) house behind the stage where costumes were kept

103 in . . . kind (each London company had its distinctive livery worn by regulation)

108 *Burning Pestle* pestle (or club) was appropriate for a representative of the Grocers, for they used pestles to prepare medicines for sale, but this also is a phallic allusion; ***Burning*** alludes to the effects of syphilis, often referred to in this play

116 shawms forerunners of oboes

124–5 two shillings (a modest if fair daily wage)

125 waits town musicians

127 o'er . . . water the Thames River separated London from Southwark, site of most public theaters

137 private taxes attacks on individuals; personal ridicule; **immodest phrases** (such as obscenities by boys' companies, here both an indication of what is to come and self-defense against such potential charges)

143 discharge (1) acquit; (2) ejaculate

Act I

1 Sirrah a common form of address to an inferior; **prentice** i.e., bound in terms of service

3 fall of fortune (rank-conscious phrasing to mean *poverty*)

3–4 heat . . . growth room and board

4 new cast reformed; instructed

5 trust use

6 staples (1) commercial centers; (2) warehouses

9 fair promising

13 you had not i.e., given up your love for someone above you in class

14 commission pun: (1) committed act of courting; (2) not within the warrant of his job

15 factor agent; manager

16 liberally willingly

In which my labor hath been all my profit.
I have not lost in bargain, nor delighted
To wear your honest gains upon my back,
Nor have I given a pension to my blood,
Or lavishly in play consumed your stock.
These and the miseries that do attend them,
I dare with innocence proclaim are strangers
To all my temperate actions. For your daughter,
If there be any love to my deservings
Borne by her virtuous self, I cannot stop it;
Nor am I able to refrain her wishes.
She's private to herself and best of knowledge
Whom she'll make so happy as to sigh for.
Besides, I cannot think you mean to match her
Unto a fellow of so lame a presence,
One that hath little left of nature in him.

Merchant. 'Tis very well, sir. I can tell your wisdom
How all this shall be cured.

Jasper. Your care becomes you.

Merchant. And thus it must be, sir. I here discharge you
My house and service. Take your liberty,
And when I want a son, I'll send for you.

Exit.

Jasper. These be the fair rewards of them that love.
Oh, you that live in freedom, never prove
The travail of a mind led by desire.

Enter Luce.

Luce. Why, how now, friend, struck with my father's thunder?

Jasper. Struck and struck dead unless the remedy
Be full of speed and virtue. I am now
What I expected long, no more your father's.

Luce. But mine.

Jasper. But yours and only yours I am;
That's all I have to keep me from the statute.
You dare be constant still?

Luce. Oh, fear me not.
In this I dare be better than a woman,
Nor shall his anger nor his offers move me,
Were they both equal to a prince's power.

Jasper. You know my rival?

Luce. Yes, and love him dearly,
Even as I love an ague or foul weather.
I prithee, Jasper, fear him not.

Jasper. Oh, no,
I do not mean to do him so much kindness.
But to our own desires; you know the plot
We both agreed on?

Luce. Yes, and will perform
My part exactly.

Jasper. I desire no more.
Farewell, and keep my heart; 'tis yours.

Luce. I take it;
He must do miracles makes me forsake it.

Exeunt.

Citizen. Fie upon 'em, little infidels. What a matter's here now? Well, I'll be hanged for a halfpenny if there be not some abomination knavery in this play. Well, let 'em look to't. Rafe must come, and if there be any tricks a-brewing –

[*Enter* Boy.]

Wife. Let 'em brew and bake too, husband, a'God's name. Rafe will find all out, I warrant you, and they were older than they are. I pray, my pretty youth, is Rafe ready?

Boy. He will be presently.

Wife. Now, I pray you, make my commendations unto him, and withal carry him this stick of licorice. Tell him his mistress sent it him, and bid him bite a piece; 'twill open his pipes the better, say.

[*Exit* Boy.]

Enter Merchant *and* Master Humphrey.

Merchant. Come, sir, she's yours; upon my faith, she's yours.

---

18 **labor . . . profit** (the irony here responds to line 14)
20 **your** (heavily ironic)
21 **pension** precise market value; **blood** sexual drive
22 **play** gambling
28 **refrain** prevent
29 **private to herself** free to decide
32 **lame a presence** feeble a personality
33 **little . . . nature** vitality and endowment (the first indication of Humphrey's general idiocy)
38 **son** i.e., son-in-law
40 **prove** (1) comprehend; (2) experience
41 **travail** suffering; grief
42 **friend** i.e., sweetheart
44 **virtue** power; determination
47 **statute** (1) that pertaining to vagabonds and masterless men for those unemployed; (2) that pertaining to apprenticeship by which those in service were not allowed to leave the parish; both these statutes provided punishment by imprisonment
49 **better . . . woman** (women were known for inconstancy)
53 **ague** acute fever, often a result of cold, damp weather
54 **prithee** pray thee
56 **plot** plan
61 **infidels** (George's natural and class loyalty is to the merchant)
65 **Rafe** (ironic, for Rafe is the citizen's Jasper)
70 **pretty** clever
74 **licorice** home remedy for loosening phlegm and clearing the throat (line 75); Nell will have a continuing simple wisdom (and supply) of such quack remedies

You have my hand. For other idle lets
Between your hopes and her, thus with a wind
They are scattered and no more. My wanton prentice,
That like a bladder blew himself with love,
I have let out, and sent him to discover
New masters yet unknown.

Humphrey. I thank you, sir.
Indeed, I thank you, sir; and ere I stir
It shall be known, however you do deem,
I am of gentle blood and gentle seem.

Merchant. Oh, sir, I know it certain.

Humphrey. Sir, my friend,
Although, as writers say, all things have end,
And that we call a pudding hath his two,
Oh, let it not seem strange, I pray, to you,
If in this bloody simile I put
My love, more endless than frail things or gut.

Wife. Husband, I prithee, sweet lamb, tell me one thing, but tell me truly. – Stay, youths, I beseech you, till I question my husband.

Citizen. What is it, mouse?

Wife. Sirrah, didst thou ever see a prettier child? How it behaves itself, I warrant ye, and speaks, and looks, and perts up the head! [*To Master Humphrey.*] I pray you, brother, with your favor, were you never none of Master Monkester's scholars?

Citizen. Chicken, I prithee heartily, contain thyself. The childer are pretty childer, but when Rafe comes, lamb –

Wife. Aye, when Rafe comes, cony. [*To* Merchant.] – Well, my youth, you may proceed.

Merchant. Well, sir, you know my love, and rest, I hope,
Assured of my consent. Get but my daughter's,
And wed her when you please. You must be bold
And clap in close unto her. Come, I know
You have language good enough to win a wench.

Wife. A whoreson tyrant; h'as been an old stringer in's days, I warrant him!

Humphrey. I take your gentle offer, and withal
Yield love again for love reciprocal.

Merchant. [*Calls.*] What, Luce, within there?

Enter Luce.

Luce. Called you, sir?

Merchant. I did.
Give entertainment to this gentleman
And see you be not froward. To her, sir;
My presence will but be an eyesore to you. *Exit.*

Humphrey. Fair Mistress Luce, how do you? Are you well?
Give me your hand, and then, I pray you, tell
How doth your little sister and your brother?
And whether you love me or any other.

Luce. Sir, these are quickly answered.

Humphrey. So they are,
Where women are not cruel. But how far
Is it now distant from this place we are in
Unto that blessèd place, your father's warren?

Luce. What makes you think of that, sir?

Humphrey. Even that face;
For, stealing rabbits whilom in that place,
God Cupid, or the keeper, I know not whether,
Unto my cost and charges brought you thither,
And there began –

Luce. Your game, sir?

Humphrey. Let no game,
Or anything that tendeth to the same,
Be evermore remembered, thou fair killer,
For whom I sat me down and broke my tiller.

---

78 hand confirmation; **lets** obstacles
80 wanton promiscuous; undisciplined
81 bladder (with obscene overtones)
86 gentle gentility (a term of social rank implying some money)
89 pudding blood sausage (cf. line 91; gut in line 92); this is an indication of Humphrey's ability with words (cf. Rafe's vocabulary and usage)
94 youths the actors, all boys in this private theater company
96 mouse common term of affection (similarly *Chicken*, line 103; *lamb*, line 105)
97 prettier more clever; better endowed
99 perts perks
101–2 Master Monkester Richard Mulcaster (d. 1611), from 1596 to 1608 the popular and respected master of St. Paul's School; the remark is both ignorant and tactless since the boys' company for this play is at the rival Blackfriars Theater (in 1608); Paul's Boys played at Whitefriars, although they were occasionally hired at Blackfriars. When headmaster at Merchant Taylors' School in London (1561–86) Mulcaster had sponsored one of the city's first boys' troupes
104 childer children (dialectical)
111 clap . . . unto embrace
112 wench (1) maid, unmarried woman; (2) working-class girl; (3) prostitute
113 whoreson tyrant (Nell sides with Luce in the absence of Venturewell's wife); **stringer** fornicator
115 withal also; as well
117 s.d. Luce throughout the play, (1) loose sexually; (2) disobedient of her father's wishes
118 entertainment hospitality
119 froward perverse
128 warren game preserve for rabbits
130 whilom while (archaic)
136 tiller (1) crossbeam of the crossbow; (2) sexual quibble; (3) an unacknowledged obscenity

Wife. There's kind gentleman, I warrant you.
When will you do as much for me, George?
Luce. Beshrew me, sir, I am sorry for your losses.
But, as the proverb says, I cannot cry.
I would you had not seen me.
Humphrey. So would I,
Unless you had more maw to do me good.
Luce. Why, cannot this strange passion be withstood?
Send for a constable and raise the town.
Humphrey. Oh, no, my valiant love will batter down
Millions of constables, and put to flight
Even that great watch of Midsummer Day at night.
Luce. Beshrew me, sir, 'twere good I yielded then;
Weak women cannot hope where valiant men
Have no resistance.
Humphrey. Yield, then. I am full
Of pity, though I say it, and can pull
Out of my pocket, thus, a pair of gloves.
Look, Lucy, look; the dog's tooth nor the dove's
Are not so white as these, and sweet they be,
And whipped about with silk, as you may see.
If you desire the price, shoot from your eye
A beam to this place, and you shall espy
"*F.S.*," which is to say, my sweetest honey,
They cost me three and two pence, or no money.
Luce. Well, sir, I take them kindly, and I thank you.
What would you more?
Humphrey. Nothing.
Luce. Why then, farewell.
Humphrey. Nor so, nor so; for, lady, I must tell,
Before we part, for what we met together.
God grant me time and patience and fair weather.
Luce. Speak, and declare your mind in terms so brief.
Humphrey. I shall. Then first and foremost, for relief
I call to you, aye, if that you can afford it,
I care not at what price; for, on my word, it
Shall be repaid again, although it cost me
More than I'll speak of now. For love hath tossed me
In furious blanket, like a tennis ball;
And now I rise aloft, and now I fall.
Luce. Alas, good gentleman, alas the day.
Humphrey. I thank you heartily and, as I say,
Thus do I still continue without rest,
I'th' morning like a man, at night a beast,
Roaring and bellowing mine own disquiet,
That much I fear forsaking of my diet
Will bring me presently to that quandàry,
I shall bid all adieu.
Luce. Now, by Saint Mary,
That were great pity.
Humphrey. So it were, beshrew me.
Then ease me, lusty Luce, and pity show me.
Luce. Why, sir, you know my will is nothing worth
Without my father's grant. Get his consent,
And then you may with assurance try me.
Humphrey. The worshipful your sire will not deny me;
For I have asked him, and he hath replied,
"Sweet Master Humphrey, Luce shall be thy bride."
Luce. Sweet Master Humphrey, then I am content.
Humphrey. And so am I, in truth.
Luce. Yet take me with you;
There is another clause must be annexed,
And this it is – I swore and will perform it –
No man shall ever joy me as his wife
But he that stole me hence. If you dare venture,
I am yours – you need not fear; my father loves you –
If not, farewell forever.
Humphrey. Stay, nymph, stay.
I have a double gelding, colored bay,
Sprung by his father from Barbarian kind;
Another for myself, though somewhat blind,

---

140 proverb "I am sorry for you, but I cannot cry for you"
142 maw craving (from *mouth*)
144 Send . . . town (on charges of harassment)
147 that great watch an annual elaborate pageant at which the city and livery companies mustered militia and constabulary to serve for the following year; **Midsummer Day** June 24
152 gloves common token at a betrothal
155 whipped embroidered
156–8 shoot . . . "*F.S.*" it was believed that light beams from the eyes returned with images they struck
158 "*F.S.*" (1) merchant's mark; (2) Humphrey had bought them for someone else; (3) Humphrey inherited them (the point is their inappropriateness)
159 three i.e., three shillings and twopence – very expensive for gloves
165 so brief i.e., as transient as time or weather
170–1 love . . . blanket an unknowing allusion to Don Quixote's humiliation, linking Humphrey once again to Rafe
178 diet a common treatment for venereal disease
180 bid all adieu i.e., die (for love); again, he is embarrassingly prosaic
182 lusty (intended to mean *pretty*)
185 try (with probable sexual overtones)
190 take . . . you let me make this clear
193 joy enjoy
197 double gelding horse for two riders
198 Barbarian Barbary, a famous breed of Saracen horses

Yet true as trusty tree.

Luce. I am satisfied,
And so I give my hand. Our course must lie
Through Waltham Forest, where I have a friend
Will entertain us. So farewell, Sir Humphrey,
And think upon your business.

Exit Luce.

Humphrey. Though I die,
I am resolved to venture life and limb
For one so young, so fair, so kind, so trim.

Exit Humphrey.

Wife. By my faith and troth, George, and, as I am virtuous, it is e'en the kindest young man that ever trod on shoe leather. Well, go thy ways; if thou hast her not, 'tis not thy fault, 'faith.

Citizen. I prithee, mouse, be patient; 'a shall have her, or I'll make some of 'em smoke for't.

Wife. That's my good lamb, George. Fie, this stinking tobacco kills me. Would there were none in England. Now, I pray, gentlemen, what good does this stinking tobacco do you? Nothing, I warrant; you make chimneys o' your faces! Oh, husband, husband, now, now, there's Rafe; there's Rafe.

Enter Rafe, *like a grocer in's shop, with two prentices* [Tim *and* George,] *reading Palmerin of England.*

Citizen. Peace, fool. Let Rafe alone. Hark you, Rafe, do not strain yourself too much at the first. Peace! Begin, Rafe.

Rafe. [*Reads.*] "Then Palmerin and Trineus, snatching their lances from their dwarfs and clasping their helmets, galloped amain after the giant; and Palmerin, having gotten a sight of him, came posting amain, saying, 'Stay, traitorous thief, for thou may'st not so carry away her that is worth the greatest lord in the world.' And with these words gave him a blow on the shoulder, that he struck him besides his elephant; and Trineus, coming to the knight that had Agricola behind him, set him soon besides his horse, with his neck broken in the fall, so that the princess, getting out of the throng, between joy and grief, said, 'All-happy knight, the mirror of all such as follow arms, now may I be well assured of the love thou bearest me.'" – I wonder why the kings do not raise an army of fourteen or fifteen hundred thousand men, as big as the army that the Prince of Portigo brought against Rosicleer, and destroy these giants. They do much hurt to wandering damsels that go in quest of their knights.

Wife. Faith, husband, and Rafe says true; for they say the King of Portugal cannot sit at his meat, but the giants and the ettins will come and snatch it from him.

Citizen. Hold thy tongue. On, Rafe.

Rafe. And certainly those knights are much to be commended who, neglecting their possessions, wander with a squire and a dwarf through the deserts to relieve poor ladies.

Wife. Aye, by my faith, are they, Rafe. Let 'em say what they will, they are indeed. Our knights neglect their possessions well enough, but they do not the rest.

Rafe. There are no such courteous and fair well-spoken knights in this age. They will call one "the son of a whore" that Palmerin of England would have called "fair sir"; and one that Rosicleer would have called "right beauteous damsel," they will call "damned bitch."

Wife. I'll be sworn will they, Rafe; they have called me so an hundred times about a scurvy pipe of tobacco.

Rafe. But what brave spirit could be content to sit in his shop, with a flappet of wood and a blue

---

202 Waltham Forest (then 12 miles N of London in Hertfordshire)
203 entertain (she returns his word ironically, since she means Jasper)
204 die (metaphorically to have a sexual orgasm)
207 troth truth
208 it he
211 'a he
213 smoke suffer
214 tobacco a popular habit for gallants, introduced by Ralegh from the New World and condemned by King James in a prose pamphlet (1602)
220 s.d. *like a grocer* (wearing the blue livery of the apprentice); ***Palmerin of England*** (actually, *Palmerin d'Olivia* I.51, for which *Palmerin of England* is the sequel; both were recently translated from the Spanish by Anthony Munday)
232 elephant actually, "horse"; Beaumont means to parody both book and reader
233 Agricola known as a rhetorician for the humanists; Rafe means Agriola, the princess Palmerin is rescuing (throughout the play Rafe has no real romance, like Don Quixote, although he claims to serve Susan, counterpart to the Don's Dulcinea)
234–5 set...horse i.e., unhorsed him
237 mirror model; paragon
242 Portigo Portugal
243 Rosicleer hero of a romance owned by Don Quixote by Ortuñez de Calahorra, translated into English as *The Mirror of Knighthood* by Margaret Tyler (1578–1601)
244–5 wandering... knights (mistaken reversal of romance conventions)
248 ettins giants (from German folklore)
257 neglect...possessions (refers to King James's notorious sale of knighthoods)
259–64 There... "bitch." a parody of Gertrude's speech in Jonson, Marston, and Chapman's *Eastward Ho!* (1605)
269 flappet shop's hinged counter or shutter

apron before him, selling mithridatum and dragon's water to visited houses, that might pursue feats of arms, and through his noble achievements procure such a famous history to be written of his heroic prowess?

Citizen. Well said, Rafe; some more of those words, Rafe.

Wife. They go finely, by my troth.

Rafe. Why should not I then pursue this course, both for the credit of myself and our company? For among all the worthy books of achievements, I do not call to mind that I yet read of a grocer errant. I will be the said knight. Have you heard of any that hath wandered unfurnished of his squire and dwarf? My elder prentice Tim shall be my trusty squire, and little George my dwarf. Hence, my blue apron! Yet in remembrance of my former trade, upon my shield shall be portrayed a burning pestle, and I will be called the Knight o'th' Burning Pestle.

Wife. Nay, I dare swear thou wilt not forget thy old trade; thou wert ever meek.

Rafe. Tim.

Tim. Anon.

Rafe. My beloved squire, and George my dwarf, I charge you that from henceforth you never call me by any other name but the "Right, Courteous and Valiant Knight of the Burning Pestle," and that you never call any female by the name of a woman or wench, but "Fair Lady," if she have her desires, if not, "Distressed Damsel"; that you call all forests and heaths "deserts," and all horses "palfreys."

Wife. This is very fine, faith. Do the gentlemen like Rafe, think you, husband?

Citizen. Aye, I warrant thee, the players would give all the shoes in their shop for him.

Rafe. My beloved squire Tim, stand out. Admit this were a desert, and over it a knight errant pricking, and I should bid you inquire of his intents, what would you say?

Tim. Sir, my master sent me to know whither you are riding?

Rafe. No, thus: "Fair sir, the Right Courteous and Valiant Knight of the Burning Pestle commanded me to inquire upon what adventure you are bound, whether to relieve some distressed damsels, or otherwise."

Citizen. Whoreson blockhead cannot remember!

Wife. I'faith, and Rafe told him on't before. All the gentlemen heard him. Did he not, gentlemen; did not Rafe tell him on't?

George. Right Courteous and Valiant Knight of the Burning Pestle, here is a distressed damsel to have a halfpenny-worth of pepper.

Wife. That's a good boy. See, the little boy can hit it; by my troth, it's a fine child.

Rafe. Relieve her with all courteous language. Now shut up shop; no more my prentice, but my trusty squire and dwarf. I must bespeak my shield and arming pestle.

[*Exeunt* Tim *and* George.]

Citizen. Go thy ways, Rafe. As I'm a true man, thou art the best on 'em all.

Wife. Rafe, Rafe.

Rafe. What say you, mistress?

Wife. I prithee, come again quickly, sweet Rafe.

Rafe. By and by.

Exit Rafe.

Enter Jasper *and his mother,* Mistress Merrythought.

Mrs Merrythought. Give thee my blessing? No, I'll ne'er give thee my blessing; I'll see thee hanged first. It shall ne'er be said I gave thee my blessing. Th'art thy father's own son, of the right blood of the Merrythoughts. I may curse the time that e'er I knew thy father. He hath spent all his own, and mine too, and when I tell him of it, he laughs and dances and sings and cries, "*A merry heart lives long-a.*" And thou art a wastethrift and art run away from thy master that loved thee well, and art come to me; and I have laid up a little for my younger son, Michael; and thou think'st to bezzle that, but thou shalt never be able to do it.

Enter Michael.

Come hither, Michael; come, Michael, down on thy knees. Thou shalt have my blessing.

270 **mithridatum** herbal medicine for poison and illness (named for King Mithridates)

271 **dragon's water** used against agues and plagues; **visited** i.e., by the plague

282 **grocer errant** (actually, there was a precedent in Eustace of Heywood's *Four Prentices of London*)

305–6 **players . . . shop** (boys' costumes were costly and precious)

309 **pricking** spurring on the horse (with a possible pun; cf. lines 316–17)

318 **Whoreson blockhead** (it is George's own servants who are being led astray by Rafe's reading)

320–1 **gentlemen** the other playgoers onstage

330 **arming** armorial; as a part of his shield and crest

341 **right** legitimate

345 ***"A . . . long-a"*** (sung by Autolycus in *Winter's Tale* IV.iii; cf. Silence in *2 Henry IV* V.iii)

346 **wastethrift** spendthrift

349 **bezzle** squander (from embezzle, to violate a trust; cf. line 5 above)

Michael. I pray you, mother, pray to God to bless me.

Mrs Merrythought. God bless thee; but Jasper shall never have my blessing. He shall be hanged first, shall he not, Michael? How say'st thou?

Michael. Yes, forsooth, mother, and grace of God.

Mrs Merrythought. That's a good boy.

Wife. I'faith, it's a fine-spoken child.

Jasper. Mother, though you forget a parent's love,
I must preserve the duty of a child.
I ran not from my master, nor return
To have your stock maintain my idleness.

Wife. Ungracious child, I warrant him. Hark how he chops logic with his mother. – Thou hadst best tell her she lies; do, tell her she lies.

Citizen. If he were my son, I would hang him up by the heels and flay him and salt him, whoreson haltersack.

Jasper. My coming only is to beg your love,
Which I must ever, though I never gain it.
And howsoever you esteem of me,
There is no drop of blood hid in these veins
But I remember well belongs to you
That brought me forth, and would be glad for you
To rip them all again, and let it out.

Mrs Merrythought. I'faith, I had sorrow enough for thee, God knows; but I'll hamper thee well enough! Get thee in, thou vagabond; get thee in, and learn of thy brother Michael.

[*Exeunt* Jasper *and* Michael.]

Old Merrythought. [*Sings.*] *within.*
Nose, nose, jolly red nose,
And who gave thee this jolly red nose?

Mrs Merrythought. Hark, my husband; he's singing and hoiting, and I'm fain to cark and care, and all little enough. – Husband, Charles, Charles Merrythought.

Enter Old Merrythought.

Old Merrythought. [*Sings.*]
Nutmegs and ginger, cinnamon and cloves,
And they gave thee this jolly red nose.

Mrs Merrythought. If you would consider your state, you would have little list to sing, iwis.

Old Merrythought. It should never be considered while it were an estate, if I thought it would spoil my singing.

Mrs Merrythought. But how wilt thou do, Charles? Thou art an old man, and thou canst not work, and thou hast not forty shillings left, and thou eatest good meat and drinkest good drink and laughest?

Old Merrythought. And will do.

Mrs Merrythought. But how wilt thou come by it, Charles?

Old Merrythought. How? Why, how have I done hitherto this forty years? I never came into my dining room but at eleven and six o'clock I found excellent meat and drink a'th'table; my clothes were never worn out but next morning a tailor brought me a new suit; and without question it will be so ever. Use makes perfectness. If all should fail, it is but a little straining myself extraordinary, and laugh myself to death.

Wife. It's a foolish old man this; is not he, George?

Citizen. Yes, cony.

Wife. Give me a penny i'th' purse while I live, George.

Citizen. Aye, by Lady, cony; hold thee there.

Mrs Merrythought. Well, Charles, you promised to provide for Jasper, and I have laid up for Michael. I pray you, pay Jasper his portion. He's come home, and he shall not consume Michael's stock. He says his master turned him away, but I promise you truly, I think he ran away.

Wife. No, indeed, Mistress Merrythought, though he be a notable gallows, yet I'll assure you his master did turn him away; even in this place 'twas, i'faith, within this half hour, about his daughter; my husband was by.

Citizen. Hang him, rogue. He served him well enough. Love his master's daughter! By my troth, cony, if there were a thousand boys,

---

358 forsooth truly
364 stock (1) provisions; (2) money
366 chops logic formulates sophistical or specious arguments
370 haltersack gallows-bird
378 sorrow enough (i.e., in childbirth with him)
379 hamper (1) basket for infants; (2) prison fetters (for masterless men like Jasper)
382 Nose . . . nose (refrain from Thomas Ravenscroft, *Deuteronmelia* 7 [1609]
385 hoiting reveling; loud laughing; **cark** fret, carp
391 state (1) estate or financial condition; (2) carefree mood; **list** desire; **iwis** for certain
405 eleven . . . o'clock the normal time for the main meals (dinner; supper)
409–10 Use . . . perfectness proverbial for practice guarantees performance
416 Give . . . purse i.e., never leave me penniless (destitute)
418 by Lady "by Our Lady the Virgin Mary" (a common oath); **hold thee there** i.e., rest assured
421 portion inheritance
423 stock inheritance
427 notable gallows deserving of hanging

thou wouldst spoil them all with taking their parts. Let his mother alone with him.

Wife. Aye, George, but yet truth is truth.

Old Merrythought. Where is Jasper? He's welcome how ever. Call him in. He shall have his portion. Is he merry?

Mrs Merrythought. Aye, foul chive him, he is too merry. Jasper! Michael!

Enter Jasper *and* Michael.

Old Merrythought. Welcome Jasper, though thou run'st away, welcome; God bless thee. 'Tis thy mother's mind thou shouldst receive thy portion. Thou hast been abroad, and I hope hast learned experience enough to govern it. Thou art of sufficient years. Hold thy hand: one, two, three, four, five, six, seven, eight, nine; there's ten shillings for thee. Thrust thyself into the world with that, and take some settled course. If fortune cross thee, thou hast a retiring place. Come home to me; I have twenty shillings left. Be a good husband, that is, wear ordinary clothes, eat the best meat, and drink the best drink; be merry and give to the poor and, believe me, thou hast no end of thy goods.

Jasper. Long may you live free from all thought of ill,
And long have cause to be thus merry still.
But, father –

Old Merrythought. No more words, Jasper. Get thee gone; thou hast my blessing. Thy father's spirit upon thee.
Farewell, Jasper. [*Sings.*]
But yet, or ere you part, Oh, cruel,
Kiss me, kiss me, sweeting, mine own dear jewel.
So, now begone; no words.

Exit Jasper.

Mrs Merrythought. So, Michael, now get thee gone too.

Michael. Yes, forsooth, mother, but I'll have my father's blessing first.

Mrs Merrythought. No, Michael, 'tis no matter for his blessing; thou hast my blessing; begone I'll fetch my money and jewels, and follow thee. I'll stay no longer with him, I warrant thee.

[*Exit* Michael.]

– Truly, Charles, I'll be gone, too.

Old Merrythought. What! You will not?

Mrs Merrythought. Yes, indeed will I.

Old Merrythought. [*Sings.*]
Hey-ho, farewell, Nan.
I'll never trust wench more again, if I can.

Mrs Merrythought. You shall not think, when all your own is gone, to spend that I have been scraping up for Michael.

Old Merrythought. Farewell, good wife, I expect it not. All I have to do in this world is to be merry, which I shall if the ground be not taken from me, and if it be, [*Sings.*]
When earth and seas from me are reft,
The skies aloft for me are left.

Exeunt.

[Interlude I]

[*Enter*] Boy, *danceth. Music.*

Wife. I'll be sworn he's a merry old gentleman for all that. Hark, hark, husband, hark, fiddles, fiddles! Now, surely, they go finely. They say 'tis present death for these fiddlers to tune their rebecks before the great Turk's grace, is't not, George? But look, look, here's a youth dances. – Now, good youth, do a turn o'th' toe. – Sweetheart, i'faith, I'll have Rafe come and do some of his gambols. – He'll ride the wild mare, gentlemen, 'twould do your hearts good to see him. – I thank you, kind youth. Pray, bid Rafe come.

Citizen. Peace, cony. – Sirrah, you scurvy boy, bid the players send Rafe, or by God's – and they do not, I'll tear some of their periwigs beside their heads. This is all riff-raff.

[*Exit* Boy.]

434–5 **taking... parts** (1) support them; (2) play on sexual organs
438 **how ever** whatever the circumstances
440 **foul chive** ill betide
445–57 **Thou... goods** (a parody of Dekker's *Old Fortunatus* [1599])
451 **cross** oppose
453 **a... husband** thrifty (i.e., husband thy goods)
465–6 **But... jewel** from Song xv in John Dowland's *First Book of Songs or Airs* (1597)
482 **think** i.e., stop to think, but
489 **reft** taken away

Interlude I

1 s.d. ***danceth. Music.*** common to interludes between acts of a play
4 **present** instant
5 **rebecks** early form of fiddle, having three strings; **Turk's** sultans were notorious for impatience and fearsome tempers
9 **gambols** leaping; frolicking
10 **wild mare** she means see-saw, also proverbial for sexual intercourse
14 **God's –** probably "God's [i.e., Christ's] body" on the cross, considered sacrilegious and disallowed by statute; Beaumont's use may be satirical here
15 **periwigs** boys frequently wore wigs in performance

Act II

Enter Merchant *and* Humphrey.

Merchant. And how, faith, how goes it now, son Humphrey?

Humphrey. Right worshipful, and my beloved friend
And father dear, this matter's at an end.

Merchant. 'Tis well it should be so. I'm glad the girl
Is found so tractable.

Humphrey. Nay, she must whirl
From hence – and you must wink; for so, I say,
The story tells – tomorrow before day.

Wife. George, dost thou think in thy conscience now 'twill be a match? Tell me but what thou thinkst, sweet rogue. Thou seest the poor gentleman, dear heart, how it labors and throbs, I warrant you, to be at rest. I'll go move the father for't.

Citizen. No, no, I prithee, sit still, honeysuckle. Thou'lt spoil all. If he deny him, I'll bring half a dozen good fellows myself, and in the shutting of an evening knock't up, and there's an end.

Wife. I'll buss thee for that, i'faith, boy. Well, George, well, you have been a wag in your days, I warrant you; but God forgive you, and I do with all my heart.

Merchant. How was it, son? You told me that tomorrow
Before daybreak you must convey her hence.

Humphrey. I must, I must, and thus it is agreed:
Your daughter rides upon a brown-bay steed,
I on a sorrel, which I bought of Brian,
The honest host of the Red Roaring Lion,
In Waltham situate. Then, if you may,
Consent in seemly sort, lest by delay
The fatal sisters come and do the office,
And then you'll sing another song.

Merchant. Alas,
Why should you be thus full of grief to me,
That do as willing as yourself agree
To anything, so it be good and fair?
Then steal her when you will, if such a pleasure
Content you both. I'll sleep and never see it,
To make your joys more full. But tell me why
You may not here perform your marriage?

Wife. God's blessing o' thy soul, old man. I'faith, thou art loath to part true hearts, I see. 'A has her, George, and I'm as glad on't. Well, go thy ways, Humphrey, for a fair-spoken man. I believe thou hast not thy fellow within the walls of London; and I should say the suburbs too I should not lie. Why dost not rejoice with me, George?

Citizen. If I could but see Rafe again, I were as merry as mine host, i'faith.

Humphrey. The cause you seem to ask, I thus declare:
– Help me, O Muses Nine! – your daughter swore
A foolish oath, the more it was the pity;
Yet none but myself within this city
Shall dare to say so, but a bold defiance
Shall meet him, were he of the noble science.
And yet she swore, and yet why did she swear?
Truly, I cannot tell, unless it were
For her own ease; for sure sometimes an oath,
Being sworn, thereafter is like cordial broth.
And this it was she swore: never to marry
But such a one whose mighty arm could carry
(As meaning me, for I am such a one)
Her bodily away through stick and stone,
Till both of us arrive, at her request,
Some ten miles off in the wild Waltham Forest.

Merchant. If this be all, you shall not need to fear
Any denial in your love. Proceed;
I'll neither follow nor repent the deed.

Humphrey. Good night, twenty good nights, and twenty more,
And twenty more good nights; that makes threescore.

Exeunt.

Act II

6 **wink** turn a blind eye
16–17 **shutting... evening** dusk
17 **knock't up** put an end to this
19 **buss** kiss
20 **wag** youth who is (1) mischievous; (2) merry (cf. Merrythought)
27 **sorrel** chestnut-colored horse
28 **host** publican
29 **situate** located (twisted syntax suggests Humphrey's attempts to be a gentleman)
31 **fatal sisters** the Three Furies who control man's life; **the office** cause him to die
33 **grief to** complain about
45 **suburbs** (a joke; outside city jurisdiction, they were best known for illicit behavior)
51 **Muses** (a joke; they do not inspire pledges and oaths)
55 **noble science** i.e., fencing
59 **cordial** i.e., restorative
69–70 **Good... threescore** (a parody of many famous speeches, including those in the balcony scenes of *Romeo and Juliet*; Humphrey is thus compared to Rafe's mimicking chivalric romances)

Enter Mistress Merrythought [*with jewel casket and purse of money*], *and her son* Michael.

Mrs Merrythought. Come, Michael, art thou not weary, boy?

Michael. No, forsooth, mother, not I.

Mrs Merrythought. Where be we now, child?

Michael. Indeed, forsooth, mother, I cannot tell, unless we be at Mile-End. Is not all the world Mile-End, mother?

Mrs Merrythought. No, Michael, not all the world, boy; but I can assure thee, Michael, Mile-End is a goodly matter. There has been a pitch-field, my child, between the naughty Spaniels and the Englishmen, and the Spaniels ran away, Michael, and the Englishmen followed. My neighbor Coxstone was there, boy, and killed them all with a birding-piece.

Michael. Mother, forsooth –

Mrs Merrythought. What says my white boy?

Michael. Shall not my father go with us too?

Mrs Merrythought. No, Michael, let thy father go snick-up. He shall never come between a pair of sheets with me again while he lives. Let him stay at home and sing for his supper, boy. Come, child, sit down, and I'll show my boy fine knacks indeed. [*Opens casket.*] Look here, Michael, here's a ring, and here's a brooch, and here's a bracelet, and here's two rings more, and here's money and gold by th' eye, my boy.

Michael. Shall I have all this, mother?

Mrs Merrythought. Aye, Michael, thou shalt have all, Michael.

Citizen. How likest thou this, wench?

Wife. I cannot tell. I would have Rafe, George; I'll see no more else indeed, la; and I pray you let the youths understand so much by word of mouth, for I tell you truly, I'm afraid o' my boy. Come, come, George, let's be merry and wise. The child's a fatherless child; and say they should put him into a strait pair of gaskins, 'twere worse than knot-grass; he would never grow after it.

Enter Rafe, Squire [Tim], *and* Dwarf [George].

Citizen. Here's Rafe, here's Rafe.

Wife. How do you, Rafe? You are welcome, Rafe, as I may say. It's a good boy. Hold up thy head and be not afraid. We are thy friends, Rafe. The gentlemen will praise thee, Rafe, if thou playst thy part with audacity. Begin, Rafe, o' God's name.

Rafe. My trusty squire, unlace my helm; give me my hat.
Where are we, or what desert may this be?

Dwarf. Mirror of knighthood, this is, as I take it, the perilous Waltham Down, in whose bottom stands the enchanted valley.

Mrs Merrythought. Oh, Michael, we are betrayed; we are betrayed! Here be giants. Fly, boy; fly, boy; fly!

Exeunt Mother *and* Michael [*dropping purse and casket*].

Rafe. Lace on my helm again. What noise is this?
A gentle lady flying the embrace
Of some uncourteous knight? I will relieve her.
Go, squire, and say, the knight that wears this pestle
In honor of all ladies, swears revenge
Upon that recreant coward that pursues her.
Go comfort her, and that same gentle squire
That bears her company.

Squire. I go, brave knight.

[*Exit* Time.]

Rafe. My trusty dwarf and friend, reach me my shield,
And hold it while I swear. First by my knighthood;
Then by the soul of Amadis de Gaul,
My famous ancestor; then by my sword
The beauteous Brionella girt about me;
By this bright burning pestle, of mine honor
The living trophy; and by all respect
Due to distressèd damsels: here I vow
Never to end the quest of this fair lady
And that forsaken squire, till by my valor
I gain their liberty.

Dwarf. Heaven bless the knight
That thus relieves poor errant gentlewomen.

Exit [Rafe *and* George].

---

77 **Mile-End** a hamlet one mile from Aldersgate, used as a training ground for the city militia and for mustering troops as well as for entertainment (at the end of this play they will become the same thing)

80–1 **pitch-field** sham battle

81 **naughty** wicked; **Spaniels** (for Spanish)

87 **white** darling (*white boy* could mean favorite son)

90 **snick-up** hang himself

94 **knacks** trinkets (as in knick-knacks)

97 **by . . . eye** unlimited in view

104 **youths** child actors

108 **strait** tight

109 **gaskins** breeches; **knot-grass** (a common weed supposed to stunt growth; she is dwelling on sexual hindrances)

124 **giants** (she is unaccustomed to boys in costumes of knights, squires, and dwarfs)

131 **recreant** (1) dishonorable; (2) traitorous

136 **Amadis de Gaul** a famous Spanish knight; his romance was translated by Munday in parts (1590–1618)

138 **Brionella** mistress of Palmerin's friend Ptolome; **girt** fastened

Wife. Aye, marry, Rafe, this has some savor in't. I would see the proudest of them all offer to carry his books after him. But, George, I will not have him go away so soon. I shall be sick if he go away, that I shall. Call Rafe again, George, call Rafe again. I prithee, sweetheart, let him come fight before me, and let's ha' some drums and some trumpets, and let him kill all that comes near him, and thou lovest me, George.

Citizen. Peace a little, bird; he shall kill them all, and they were twenty more on 'em than there are.

Enter Jasper.

Jasper. Now, Fortune, if thou be'st not only ill,
Show me thy better face, and bring about
Thy desperate wheel, that I may climb at length
And stand. This is our place of meeting,
If love have any constancy. Oh, age!
Where only wealthy men are counted happy!
How shall I please thee? how deserve thy smiles?
When I am only rich in misery?
My father's blessing, and this little coin
Is my inheritance, a strong revènue.
From earth thou art, and to the earth I give thee.
[*Throws away the money.*]
There grow and multiply whilst fresher air
Breeds me a fresher fortune. *Spies the casket.* How, illusion!
What, hath the devil coined himself before me?
'Tis metal good; it rings well. I am waking,
And taking too, I hope. Now God's dear blessing
Upon his heart that left it here. 'Tis mine;
These pearls, I take it, were not left for swine.
Exit.

Wife. I do not like that this unthrifty youth should embezzle away the money. The poor gentlewoman, his mother, will have a heavy heart for it, God knows.

Citizen. And reason good, sweetheart.

Wife. But let him go. I'll tell Rafe a tale in's ear shall fetch him again with a wanion, I warrant him, if he be above ground; and besides, George, here are a number of sufficient gentlemen can witness, and myself, and yourself, and the musicians, if we be called in question. But here comes Rafe, George. Thou shalt hear him speak an he were an emperal.

Enter Rafe *and* Dwarf [George].

Rafe. Comes not Sir Squire again?
Dwarf. Right courteous knight,
Your squire doth come and with him comes the lady,

Enter Mistress Merrythought *and* Michael *and* Squire [Tim].

For and the Squire of Damsels, as I take it.

Rafe. Madam, if any service or devoir
Of a poor errant knight may right your wrongs,
Command it. I am prest to give you succor,
For to that holy end I bear my armor.

Mrs Merrythought. Alas, sir, I am a poor gentlewoman, and I have lost my money in this forest.

Rafe. Desert, you would say, lady, and not lost
Whilst I have sword and lance. Dry up your tears,
Which ill befits the beauty of that face,
And tell the story, if I may request it,
Of your disastrous fortune.

Mrs Merrythought. Out, alas! I left a thousand pounds, a thousand pounds, e'en all the money I had laid up for this youth upon the sight of your mastership, you looked so grim; and, as I may say it, saving your presence, more like a giant than a mortal man.

Rafe. I am as you are, lady; so are they,
All mortal. But why weeps this gentle squire?

147–8 offer . . . him i.e., be eager to serve him (she is unintentionally agreeing with his sexual puns)
160–1 better . . . wheel the wheel of Fortune should raise rather than lower him (show its happier side or face)
169 From . . . thee i.e., from dust to dust (meditating on Fortune's wheel)
170 grow and multiply (parody of the parable of the talents; Matt. 25:14–30)
172 coined created (as a trick)
174 God's . . . blessing (Jasper unknowingly blesses the mother who would not bless him)
183 wanion vengeance (to seek retribution)
185 sufficient able
189 an as if; **emperal** emperor (were imperial)
192 For and as well as; **Squire of Damsels** (cf. Spenser's *Faerie Queene* III.vii.51ff)
193 devoir knight's duty
195 prest prepared
198 lost my money (cf. "How Palmerin and Ptolome met with a Damasel, who made great moan for a casket which two knights had forcibly taken from her, and what happened to them," *Palmerin d'Olivia* I.21)
212 All wholly

Mrs Merrythought. Has he not cause to weep, do you think, when he hath lost his inheritance?

Rafe. Young hope of valor, weep not. I am here
That will confound thy foe and pay it dear
Upon his coward head, that dares deny
Distressèd squires and ladies' equity.
I have but one horse, on which shall ride
This lady fair behind me, and before
This courteous squire; fortune will give us more
Upon our next adventure. Fairly speed
Beside us, squire and dwarf, to do us need.

Exeunt.

Citizen. Did not I tell you, Nell, what your man would do? By the faith of my body, wench, for clean action and good delivery, they may all cast their caps at him.

Wife. And so they may, i'faith, for, I dare speak it boldly, the twelve Companies of London cannot match him, timber for timber. Well, George, and he be not inveigled by some of these paltry players, I ha' much marvel; but, George, we ha' done our parts, if the boy have any grace to be thankful.

Citizen. Yes, I warrant thee, duckling.

Enter Humphrey *and* Luce.

Humphrey. Good Mistress Luce, however I in fault am
For your lame horse, you're welcome unto Waltham.
But which way now to go or what to say
I know not truly till it be broad day.

Luce. Oh, fear not, Master Humphrey, I am guide
For this place good enough.

Humphrey. Then up and ride,
Or, if it please you, walk for your repose,
Or sit, or, if you will, go pluck a rose;
Either of which shall be indifferent
To your good friend and Humphrey, whose consent
Is so entangled ever to your will
As the poor harmless horse is to the mill.

Luce. Faith, and you say the word, we'll e'en sit down
And take a nap.

Humphrey. 'Tis better in the town,
Where we may nap together; for, believe me,
To sleep without a snatch would mickle grieve me.

Luce. You're merry, Master Humphrey.

Humphrey. So I am,
And have been ever merry from my dam.

Luce. Your nurse had the less labor.

Humphrey. Faith, it may be,
Unless it were by chance I did beray me.

Enter Jasper.

Jasper. Luce, dear friend, Luce.

Luce. Here, Jasper.

Jasper. You are mine.

Humphrey. If it be so, my friend, you use me fine.
What do you think I am?

Jasper. An arrant noddy.

Humphrey. A word of obloquy! Now, by God's body,
I'll tell thy master, for I know thee well.

Jasper. Nay, and you be so forward for to tell,
Take that, and that, and tell him, sir, I gave it, [*Beats him.*]
And say I paid you well.

Humphrey. Oh, sir, I have it,
And do confess the payment. Pray be quiet.

Jasper. Go, get to your nightcap and the diet
To cure your beaten bones.

Luce. Alas, poor Humphrey.
Get thee some wholesome broth with sage and comfrey;
A little oil of roses and a feather
To 'noint thy back withal.

Humphrey. When I came hither,
Would I had gone to Paris with John Dory.

Luce. Farewell, my pretty Nump; I am very sorry
I cannot bear thee company.

Humphrey. Farewell;
The devil's dam was ne'er so banged in hell.

Exeunt [Luce *and* Jasper]; *Manet* Humphrey.

218 equity individual justice
226 clean adroit
227 cast . . . at give up trying to imitate
230 timber for timber limb for limb
231 inveigled (masters of boys' companies occasionally kidnapped possible actors)
243 go . . . rose (euphemism for) defecate
249 nap (1) sleep; (2) drink
251 snatch snack; **mickle** much
253 dam mother
255 beray me befoul myself (he means *bewray*, reveal)
258 arrant itinerant; **noddy** simpleton, fool
259 God's body (but cf. Interlude I, line 14n.)
264 confess admit; acknowledge; **quiet** at peace
265 get . . . nightcap get you to bed to rest up (nightcaps could signify ill health)
267 comfrey medicinal plant common to ditches and streams
270 John Dory a hero captured by English highwaymen on his way to visit the King of France according to a song by Thomas Ravenscroft (1609)
271 Nump (1) nickname for Humphrey; (2) common term for fool
273 devil's . . . hell morality plays in which the Devil and his crew were belabored by vices

Wife. This young Jasper will prove me another thing, o' my conscience, and he may be suffered. George, dost not see, George, how 'a swaggers and flies at the very heads o'folks as he were a dragon? Well, if I do not do his lesson for wronging the poor gentleman, I am no true woman. His friends that brought him up might have been better occupied, iwis, than ha' taught him these fegaries. He's e'en in the highway to the gallows, God bless him.

Citizen. You're too bitter, cony; the young man may do well enough for all this.

Wife. Come hither, Master Humphrey. Has he hurt you? Now beshrew his fingers for't. Here, sweetheart, here's some green ginger for thee. Now beshrew my heart, but 'a has peppernel in's head as big as a pullet's egg. Alas, sweet lamb, how thy temples beat. Take the peace on him, sweetheart; take the peace on him.

Enter a Boy.

Citizen. No, no, you talk like a foolish woman. I'll ha' Rafe fight with him, and swinge him up well-favoredly. Sirrah boy, come hither. Let Rafe come in and fight with Jasper.

Wife. Aye, and beat him well; he's an unhappy boy.

Boy. Sir, you must pardon us; the plot of our play lies contrary, and 'twill hazard the spoiling of our play.

Citizen. Plot me no plots. I'll ha' Rafe come out. I'll make your house too hot for you else.

Boy. Why, sir, he shall; but if anything fall out of order, the gentlemen must pardon us.

Citizen. Go your ways, goodman boy.

[*Exit* Boy.]

I'll hold him a penny he shall have his bellyful of fighting now. Ho, here comes Rafe; no more.

Enter Rafe, Mistress Merrythought, Michael, Squire [Tim], *and* Dwarf [George].

Rafe. What knight is that, squire? Ask him if he keep
The passage, bound by love of lady fair,
Or else but prickant.

Humphrey. Sir, I am no knight,
But a poor gentleman, that this same night
Had stolen from me on yonder green
My lovely wife, and suffered (to be seen
Yet extant on my shoulders) such a greeting
That whilst I live I shall think of that meeting.

Wife. Aye, Rafe, he beat him unmercifully, Rafe; and thou sparest him, Rafe, I would thou wert hanged.

Citizen. No more, wife, no more.

Rafe. Where is the caitiff wretch hath done this deed?
Lady, your pardon, that I may proceed
Upon the quest of this injurious knight.
And thou, fair squire, repute me not the worse,
In leaving the great venture of the purse
And the rich casket till some better leisure.

Enter Jasper *and* Luce.

Humphrey. Here comes the broker hath purloined my treasure.

Rafe. Go, squire, and tell him I am here,
An errant knight-at-arms, to crave delivery
Of that fair lady to her own knight's arms.
If he deny, bid him take choice of ground,
And so defy him.

Squire. From the knight that bears
The golden pestle, I defy thee, knight,
Unless thou make fair restitution
Of that bright lady.

Jasper. Tell the knight that sent thee
He is an ass, and I will keep the wench
And knock his head-piece.

Rafe. Knight, thou art but dead,
If thou recall not thy uncourteous terms.

Wife. Break's pate, Rafe; break's pate, Rafe, soundly.

Jasper. Come, knight, I am ready for you. Now your pestle

Snatches away his pestle.

Shall try what temper, sir, your mortar's of.

---

283 fegaries vagaries, pranks
289 green ginger medicine to relieve aches and pains
291 peppernel lump; swelling
292–3 Take...peace obtain sureties for his safe conduct
296 with for; on his behalf; **swinge** thrash
297 well-favoredly thoroughly
299 unhappy good-for-nothing
302 spoiling (George and Nell have attempted to redo the play by adding Rafe; now they attempt to rewrite it; eventually they will want to displace it)
309 hold bet
310–11 no more silence; let the play with Rafe go on
312–13 keep...passage guard the castle entrance
314 prickant riding fast (with sexual pun)
317 wife i.e., betrothed
324 caitiff wicked
326 injurious malicious, injuring
330 broker pimp
342 pate head
343 s.d. *Snatches... pestle* (i.e., renders Rafe impotent)

[*Recites.*] "With that he stood upright in his stirrups, and gave the Knight of the Calfskin such a knock

[*Knocks Rafe down.*]

that he forsook his horse and down he fell, and then he leaped upon him, and plucking off his helmet –"

Humphrey. Nay, and my noble knight be down so soon,
Though I can scarcely go, I needs must run.

Exit Humphrey *and* Rafe [*with* Squire *and* Dwarf].

Wife. Run, Rafe; run, Rafe; run for thy life, boy; Jasper comes, Jasper comes.

Jasper. Come, Luce, we must have other arms for you.
Humphrey and Golden Pestle, both adieu.

Exeunt [Jasper *and* Luce].

Wife. Sure the devil, God bless us, is in this springald. Why, George, didst ever see such a fire-drake? I am afraid my boy's miscarried. If he be, though he were Master Merrythought's son a thousand times, if there be any law in England, I'll make some of them smart for't.

Citizen. No, no, I have found out the matter, sweetheart; Jasper is enchanted. As sure as we are here, he is enchanted. He could no more have stood in Rafe's hands than I can stand in my Lord Mayor's. I'll have a ring to discover all enchantments, and Rafe shall beat him yet. Be no more vexed, for it shall be so.

Enter Rafe, Squire [Tim], Dwarf [George], Mistress Merrythought *and* Michael.

Wife. Oh, husband, here's Rafe again. Stay, Rafe, let me speak with thee. How dost thou, Rafe? Art thou not shrewdly hurt? The foul great lungies laid unmercifully on thee. There's some sugar-candy for thee. Proceed; thou shalt have another bout with him.

Citizen. If Rafe had him at the fencing-school, if he did not make a puppy of him and drive him up and down the school, he should ne'er come in my shop more.

Mrs Merrythought. Truly, Master Knight of the Burning Pestle, I am weary.

Michael. Indeed, la, mother, and I am very hungry.

Rafe. Take comfort, gentle dame, and you, fair squire,
For in this desert there must needs be placed
Many strong castles held by courteous knights;
And till I bring you safe to one of those,
I swear by this my order ne'er to leave you.

Wife. Well said, Rafe. George, Rafe was ever comfortable, was he not?

Citizen. Yes, duck.

Wife. I shall ne'er forget him, when we had lost our child. You know it was strayed almost, alone, to Puddle Wharf, and the criers were abroad for it, and there it had drowned itself but for a sculler; Rafe was the most comfortablest to me. "Peace, mistress," says he, "Let it go; I'll get you another as good." Did he not, George; did he not say so?

Citizen. Yes indeed did he, mouse.

Dwarf. I would we had a mess of pottage and a pot of drink, squire, and were going to bed.

Squire. Why, we are at Waltham Town's end, and that's the Bell Inn.

Dwarf. Take courage, valiant knight, damsel, and squire.
I have discovered, not a stone's cast off,
An ancient castle, held by the old knight
Of the most holy order of the Bell,
Who gives to all knights-errant entertain.
There plenty is of food, and all prepared
By the white hands of his own lady dear.
He hath three squires that welcome all his guests:
The first, hight Chamberlino, who will see
Our beds prepared, and bring us snowy sheets,
Where never footman stretched his buttered hams;
The second, hight Tapstero, who will see

---

346 Calfskin (alludes to vellum, on which old manuscripts were written)
352 go walk
358 springald stripling
359 fire-drake firebird or dragon; **miscarried** came to harm
366 have stood in withstand
372 shrewdly severely
373 lungies skinny louts
377 puppy coward
387 my order (i.e., the order of knighthood)
388–9 comfortable helpful
393 Puddle Wharf landing place at the foot of St. Andrew's Hill (now Puddle Duck); **criers** one of the functions of town criers was to advertise for lost children
395 sculler (1) an oarsman; (2) a light boat for rowing
397 get (obscene pun on *beget*)
400 pottage a boiled dish of vegetables, sometimes with meat
405 discovered (this whole episode of mistaking an inn for a castle is taken from the beginning of Book I of *Don Quixote*)
412 hight called; named
414 Where . . . hams footmen who ran with their master's carriage greased their calves to prevent cramps; **hams** the back of the knees or thighs

Our pots full fillèd and no froth therein;
The third, a gentle squire, Ostlero hight,
Who will our palfreys slick with wisps of straw,
And in the manger put them oats enough,
And never grease their teeth with candle-snuff.

Wife. That same dwarf's a pretty boy, but the squire's a groutnoll.

Rafe. Knock at the gates, my squire, with stately lance.

Enter Tapster.

Tapster. Who's there? You're welcome, gentlemen. Will you see a room?

Dwarf. Right courteous and valiant Knight of the Burning Pestle, this is the squire Tapstero.

Rafe. Fair squire Tapstero, I, a wandering knight,
Hight of the Burning Pestle, in the quest
Of this fair lady's casket and wrought purse,
Losing myself in this vast wilderness,
Am to this castle well by fortune brought;
Where, hearing of the goodly entertain
Your knight of holy order of the Bell
Gives to all damsels and all errant knights,
I thought to knock, and now am bold to enter.

Tapster. An't please you see a chamber, you are very welcome.

Exeunt.

Wife. George, I would have something done, and I cannot tell what it is.

Citizen. What is it, Nell?

Wife. Why, George, shall Rafe beat nobody again? Prithee, sweetheart, let him.

Citizen. So he shall, Nell, and if I join with him, we'll knock them all.

Enter Humphrey *and* Merchant.

Wife. Oh, George, here's Master Humphrey again now, that lost Mistress Luce, and Mistress Luce's father. Master Humphrey will do somebody's errand, I warrant him.

Humphrey. Father, it's true in arms I ne'er shall clasp her,
For she is stolen away by your man Jasper.

Wife. I thought he would tell him.

Merchant. Unhappy that I am to lose my child!
Now I begin to think on Jasper's words,
Who oft hath urged to me thy foolishness.
Why didst thou let her go? Thou lovest her not,
That wouldst bring home thy life, and not bring her.

Humphrey. Father, forgive me. Shall I tell you true?
Look on my shoulders; they are black and blue.
Whilst to and fro fair Luce and I were winding,
He came and basted me with a hedge-binding.

Merchant. Get men and horses straight. We will be there
Within this hour. You know the place again?

Humphrey. I know the place where he my loins did swaddle. I'll get six horses, and to each a saddle.

Merchant. Meantime I'll go talk with Jasper's father.

Exeunt.

Wife. George, what wilt thou lay with me now that Master Humphrey has not Mistress Luce yet? Speak, George, what wilt thou lay with me?

Citizen. No, Nell, I warrant thee Jasper is at Puckeridge with her by this.

Wife. Nay, George, you must consider Mistress Luce's feet are tender, and besides, 'tis dark; and I promise you truly, I do not see how he should get out of Waltham Forest with her yet.

Citizen. Nay, cony, what wilt thou lay with me that Rafe has her not yet?

Wife. I will not lay against Rafe, honey, because I have not spoken with him. But look, George, peace; here comes the merry old gentleman again.

Enter Old Merrythought.

Old Merrythought. [*Sings*.]
When it was grown to dark midnight,
And all were fast asleep,
In came Margaret's grimly ghost,
And stood at William's feet.

I have money and meat and drink beforehand till tomorrow at noon; why should I be sad? Methinks I have half a dozen jovial spirits within me. [*Sings*.]
I am three merry men, and three merry men.

---

418 slick make sleek
420 never . . . candle-snuff a common trick to prevent horses from eating
422 groutnoll blockhead
431 wrought embroidered
449–50 do . . . errand perform a worthy deed
451 in arms pun on (1) embracing Luce; (2) defending Luce in combat
462 basted beat
463 straight immediately
466 swaddle beat soundly
469 lay wager (with obscene pun)
473–4 Puckeridge a village 23 miles N of London and 16 miles N of Waltham Forest in Hertfordshire
485–8 When . . . feet a version of "Fair Margaret and Sweet William"
487 grimly grim-looking
493 I . . . men from a song in Peele's *Old Wives' Tale*

To what end should any man be sad in this world? Give me a man that when he goes to hanging cries: [*Sings.*]

Troll the black bowl to me!

And a woman that will sing a catch in her travail. I have seen a man come by my door with a serious face, in a black cloak, without a hatband, carrying his head as if he looked for pins in the street. I have looked out of my window half a year after, and have spied that man's head upon London Bridge. 'Tis vile. Never trust a tailor that does not sing at his work; his mind is of nothing but filching.

Wife. Mark this, George; 'tis worth noting. Godfrey, my tailor, you know, never sings, and he had fourteen yards to make this gown; and I'll be sworn, Mistress Pennistone, the draper's wife, had one made with twelve.

Old Merrythought. [*Sings.*]

'Tis mirth that fills the veins with blood,
More than wine, or sleep, or food.
Let each man keep his heart at ease;
No man dies of that disease.
He that would his body keep
From diseases must not weep,
But whoever laughs and sings
Never he his body brings
Into fevers, gouts, or rheums,
Or ling'ringly his lungs consumes,
Or meets with achès in the bone,
Or catarrhs or griping stone,
But contented lives for aye,
The more he laughs, the more he may.

Wife. Look, George how sayst thou by this, George? Is't not a fine old man? Now God's blessing o' thy sweet lips. When wilt thou be so merry, George? Faith, thou art the frowning'st little thing, when thou art angry, in a country.

Enter Merchant.

Citizen. Peace, cony; thou shalt see him taken down too, I warrant thee. Here's Luce's father come now.

Old Merrythought. [*Sings.*]

As you came from Walsingham,
From that holy land,
There met you not with my true love
By the way as you came?

Merchant. O, Master Merrythought, my daughter's gone.
This mirth becomes you not; my daughter's gone.

Old Merrythought. [*Sings.*]

Why, an if she be, what care I?
Or let her come, or go, or tarry.

Merchant. Mock not my misery. It is your son,
Whom I have made my own when all forsook him,
Has stolen my only joy, my child, away.

Old Merrythought. [*Sings.*]

He set her on a milk-white steed,
And himself upon a gray.
He never turned his face again,
But he bore her quite away.

Merchant. Unworthy of the kindness I have shown
To thee and thine! Too late I well perceive
Thou art consenting to my daughter's loss.

Old Merrythought. Your daughter! what a stir's here wi' your daughter! Let her go. Think no more on her, but sing loud. If both my sons were on the gallows, I would sing, [*Sings.*]

Down, down, down, they fall
Down, and arise they never shall.

Merchant. Oh, might I behold her once again,
And she once more embrace her agèd sire.

Old Merrythought. Fie, how scurvily this goes! "And she once more embrace her agèd sire?" You'll make a dog on her, will ye? She cares much for her agèd sire, I warrant you. [*Sings.*]

She cares not for her daddy, nor
She cares not for her mammy;
For she is, she is, she is, she is
My Lord of Lowgave's lassy.

Merchant. For this thy scorn, I will pursue that son of thine to death.

---

497 ***Troll . . . me!*** from a harvest song in Thomas Nashe's *Summers Last Will and Testament*; but cf. song at the end of *Shoemakers' Holiday*; ***Troll*** pass; ***black bowl*** customary drinking bowl nut-brown from the color of ale

498 **catch** (1) short, usually bawdy, song sung in three or more parts; (2) sudden shortness of breath (as *travail* = labor in pregnancy)

500–1 **without a hatband** (the sign of a Puritan)

504 **head . . . Bridge** as a traitor whose head after execution was displayed on a pole on London Bridge as a deterrent and warning to others

506 **filching** stealing; trickery

508 **tailor** (proverbially, they were thought dishonest merchants)

523 **catarrhs** inflammation of the nose and throat; **griping stone** sharply painful gallstone

534–7 **As . . . came?** popular ballad; Walsingham was a village in Norfolk and in earlier years a major European shrine for Catholic pilgrims, since its relic was said to be milk from the Virgin Mary

540–1 **Why . . . tarry** from "Farewell, Dear Love," in Robert Jones's *First Book of Songs and Airs* (1600); (cf. *Twelfth Night* II.iii.97)

545–8 **He . . . away** (cf. "The Ballad of the Knight and the Shepherd's Daughter")

556–7 **Down . . . shall** from "Sorrow's Story" in John Dowland's *Second Book of Songs and Airs* (1600)

562 **dog** (response to Venturewell as Luce's sire [line 559])

Old Merrythought. Do, and when you ha' killed him: [*Sings.*]

Give him flowers enow, palmer; give him flowers enow.
Give him red, and white, and blue, green, and yellow.

Merchant. I'll fetch my daughter.

Old Merrythought. I'll hear no more o'your daughter; it spoils my mirth.

Merchant. I say, I'll fetch my daughter.

Old Merrythought. [*Sings.*]

Was never man for lady's sake,
Down, down,
Tormented as I, poor Sir Guy,
De derry down,
For Lucy's sake, that lady bright,
Down, down,
As ever men beheld with eye,
De derry down.

Merchant. I'll be revenged, by Heaven.

Exeunt.

[Interlude II]

Music.

Wife. How dost thou like this, George?

Citizen. Why, this is well, cony; but if Rafe were hot once, thou shouldst see more.

Wife. The fiddlers go again, husband.

Citizen. Aye, Nell, but this is scurvy music. I gave the whoreson gallows money, and I think he has not got me the waits of Southwark. If I hear 'em not anon, I'll twinge him by the ears. You musicians, play "Baloo."

Wife. No, good George, let's ha "Lachrymae."

Citizen. Why, this is it, cony.

Wife. It's all the better, George. Now, sweet lamb, what story is that painted upon the cloth? The Confutation of Saint Paul?

Citizen. No, lamb, that's Rafe and Lucrece.

Wife. Rafe and Lucrece? Which Rafe? Our Rafe?

Citizen. No, mouse, that was a Tartarian.

Wife. A Tartarian? Well, I would the fiddlers had done, that we might see our Rafe again.

Act III

Enter Jasper *and* Luce.

Jasper. Come, my dear; though we have lost our way,
We have not lost ourselves. Are you not weary
With this night's wand'ring; broken from your rest?
And frighted with the terror that attends
The darkness of this wild, unpeopled place?

Luce. No, my best friend, I cannot either fear
Or entertain a weary thought whilst you,
The end of all my full desires, stand by me.
Let them that lose their hopes, and live to languish
Among the number of forsaken lovers,
Tell the long weary steps, and number time,
Start at a shadow, and shrink up their blood,
Whilst I, possessed with all content and quiet,
Thus take my pretty love, and thus embrace him.

Jasper. You have caught me, Luce, so fast, that whilst I live
I shall become your faithful prisoner,
And wear these chains forever. Come, sit down,
And rest your body, too, too delicate
For these disturbances. So, will you sleep?
Come, do not be more able than you are.
I know you are not skillful in these watches,
For women are no soldiers. Be not nice,
But take it; sleep, I say.

Luce. I cannot sleep.
Indeed, I cannot, friend.

Jasper. Why, then, we'll sing,
And try how that will work upon our senses.

---

571 ***enow*** enough; ***palmer*** pilgrim
577–84 **Was . . . down** from the legend of Sir Guy
579 **Sir Guy** Guy of Warwick, popular hero of romance and ballads

Interlude II

3 **hot** aroused
8 **twinge** tweak
9 **"Baloo"** (a common word in the refrains of lullabies; perhaps here an allusion to "Lady Bothwell's Lamentation")
10 **"Lachrymae"** a set of pavans – stately dances – by John Dowland (1605)
13 **story . . . cloth** painted cloths, imitating tapestries, were used as backdrops at the rear of stages
14 **Confutation . . . Paul** (bawdy confusion for "The Conversion of St. Paul")
16 **Rafe and Lucrece** bawdy pun on "The Rape of Lucrece" (Shakespeare's poem and a play by Thomas Heywood in 1608)
17 **Tartarian** (1) again, mispronunciation of Tarquin, who raped Lucrece; (2) proverbial cruelty of the inhabitants of Tatary (N of the Himalayas) toward their women; (3) cant term for thief

Act III

3 **broken** roused
11 **Tell** count
12 **shrink . . . blood** fear was thought to diminish the vital spirits and bodily elements
20 **able** capable of endurance
21 **watches** vigils
22 **nice** reluctant, fastidious, foolish
23 **take it** yield

Luce. I'll sing, or say, or anything but sleep.
Jasper. Come, little mermaid, rob me of my heart
With that enchanting voice.
Luce. You mock me, Jasper.

Song

Jasper. *Tell me, dearest, what is love?*
Luce. *'Tis a lightning from above,*
'Tis an arrow, 'tis a fire,
'Tis a boy they call Desire,
'Tis a smile
Doth beguile.
Jasper. *The poor hearts of men that prove.*
Tell me more, are women true?
Luce. *Some love change, and so do you.*
Jasper. *Are they fair, and never kind?*
Luce. *Yes, when men turn with the wind.*
Jasper. *Are they froward?*
Luce. *Ever toward*
Those that love, to love anew.
Jasper. Dissemble it no more; I see the god
Of heavy sleep lay on his heavy mace
Upon your eyelids.
Luce. I am very heavy.
[*Sleeps.*]
Jasper. Sleep, sleep, and quiet rest crown thy sweet thoughts.
Keep from her fair blood distempers, startings,
Horrors, and fearful shapes. Let all her dreams
Be joys and chaste delights, embraces, wishes,
And such new pleasures as the ravished soul
Gives to the senses. So, my charms have took.
Keep her, you powers divine, whilst I contèmplate
Upon the wealth and beauty of her mind.
She is only fair and constant, only kind,
And only to thee, Jasper. Oh, my joys,
Whither will you transport me? Let not fullness
Of my poor buried hopes come up together
And overcharge my spirits. I am weak.
Some say, however ill, the sea and women
Are governed by the moon: both ebb and flow,
Both full of changes. Yet to them that know
And truly judge, these but opinions are,
And heresies to bring on pleasing war
Between our tempers, that without these were
Both void of after-love and present fear,
Which are the best of Cupid. Oh, thou child!
Bred from despair, I dare not entertain thee,
Having a love without the faults of women,
And greater in her perfect goods than men;
Which to make good, and please myself the stronger,
Though certainly I am certain of her love,
I'll try her, that the world and memory
May sing to aftertimes her constancy.
[*Draws his sword.*]
Luce, Luce, awake.
Luce. Why do you fright me, friend,
With those distempered looks? What makes your sword
Drawn in your hand? Who hath offended you?
I prithee, Jasper, sleep; thou art wild with watching.
Jasper. Come, make your way to heaven, and bid the world,
With all the villainies that stick upon it,
Farewell. You're for another life.
Luce. Oh, Jasper!
How have my tender years committed evil,
Especially against the man I love,
Thus to be cropped untimely?
Jasper. Foolish girl,
Canst thou imagine I could love his daughter
That flung me from my fortune into nothing,
Dischargèd me his service, shut the doors
Upon my poverty, and scorned my prayers,
Sending me, like a boat without a mast,
To sink or swim? Come, by this hand you die;
I must have life and blood to satisfy
Your father's wrongs.
Wife. Away, George, away, raise the watch at Ludgate, and bring a mittimus from the justice for this desperate villain. Now, I charge you, gentlemen, see the King's peace kept! Oh, my

---

26 **say** recite
27 **mermaid** a teasing reference to the Sirens who tempted Odysseus (Ulysses) with their singing
29–42 ***Tell . . . anew*** a song in several of Fletcher's plays including *The Captain*
35 ***prove*** strive
43 **Dissemble it** pretend
43–4 **god . . . sleep** Morpheus (his symbol was the mace)
44 **heavy** drowsy (the repetition here seems almost hypnotically suggestive)
47 **distempers** mental or physical ailments
50 **ravished** transported from the body
54 **is only** alone is
63–4 **heresies . . . tempers** pleasant if false notions about love
65 **void . . . fear** love's pleasures including present anxiety and retrospective joy
66 **Cupid** (as god of love); best of Cupid means the greatest pleasures
70 **make good** demonstrate
72 **try** test
77 **wild . . . watching** mad with anxiety
83 **cropped** cut off from life; **untimely** before my normal life span
93 **Ludgate** a station for the night watch as well as a prison; Nell is in London, not in Waltham Forest; **mittimus** warrant for arrest

heart, what a varlet's this to offer manslaughter upon the harmless gentlewoman!

Citizen. I warrant thee, sweetheart, we'll have him hampered.

Luce. Oh, Jasper, be not cruel;
If thou wilt kill me, smile and do it quickly,
And let not many deaths appear before me.
I am a woman, made of fear and love,
A weak, weak woman. Kill not with thy eyes;
They shoot me through and through. Strike, I am ready,
And, dying, still I love thee.

Enter Merchant, Humphrey, *and his* men.

Merchant. Whereabouts?

Jasper. [*Aside.*] No more of this; now to myself again.

Humphrey. There, there he stands with sword, like martial knight,
Drawn in his hand. Therefore beware the fight,
You that be wise; for were I good Sir Bevis,
I would not stay his coming, by your leaves.

Merchant. Sirrah, restore my daughter.

Jasper. Sirrah, no.

Merchant. Upon him, then.

[*They strike at Jasper, wounding him.*]

Wife. So, down with him; down with him; down with him. Cut him i'th' leg, boys; cut him i'th' leg!

Merchant. [*Takes hold of Luce.*] Come your ways, minion. I'll provide a cage
For you, you're grown so tame. Horse her away.

Humphrey. Truly I'm glad your forces have the day.

Exeunt, manet Jasper.

Jasper. They are gone, and I am hurt; my love is lost,
Never to get again. Oh, me unhappy!
Bleed, bleed, and die, I cannot. Oh, my folly,
Thou hast betrayed me. Hope, where art thou fled?
Tell me if thou be'st anywhere remaining.
Shall I but see my love again? Oh, no!
She will not deign to look upon her butcher,
Nor is it fit she should; yet I must venture.
Oh Chance, or Fortune, or whate'er thou art
That men adore for powerful, hear my cry,
And let me loving live, or losing die.

Exit.

Wife. Is 'a gone, George?

Citizen. Aye, cony.

Wife. Marry, and let him go, sweetheart. By the faith o' my body, 'a has put me into such a fright that I tremble, as they say, as 'twere an aspen leaf. Look o' my little finger, George, how it shakes. Now i'truth, every member of my body is the worse for't.

Citizen. Come, hug in mine arms, sweet mouse. He shall not fright thee any more. Alas, mine own dear heart, how it quivers.

Enter Mistress Merrythought, Rafe, Michael, Squire [Tim], Dwarf [George], Host *and a* Tapster.

Wife. Oh, Rafe, how dost thou, Rafe? How hast thou slept tonight? Has the knight used thee well?

Citizen. Peace, Nell; let Rafe alone.

Tapster. Master, the reckoning is not paid.

Rafe. Right courteous knight, who, for the order's sake
Which thou hast ta'en, hangst out the holy bell,
As I this flaming pestle bear about,
We render thanks to your puissant self,
Your beauteous lady, and your gentle squires,
For thus refreshing of our wearied limbs,
Stiffened with hard achievements in wild desert.

Tapster. Sir, there is twelve shillings to pay.

Rafe. Thou merry squire Tapstero, thanks to thee
For comforting our souls with double jug;
And if advent'rous fortune prick thee forth,
Thou jovial squire, to follow feats of arms,
Take heed thou tender every lady's cause,

99 **hampered** chained; confined
110 **Sir Bevis** hero of the famous medieval romance of Sir Bevis of Hampton
111 **stay** wait for
112 **restore** i.e., return (to her father)
117 **minion** hussy
118 **you're** until you are; **tame** submissive
121 **unhappy** reprehensible
122–3 **folly . . . betrayed** (presumably for overstepping social boundaries)
126 **deign** condescend; **her butcher** (since he had no time to explain his actions to Luce she will mistake them)
130 **loving** (in soliloquy; here love, not money, is his sole reason for living)
144 **tonight** i.e., last night
146 **reckoning** tavern bill for bed, food, and drink
150 **puissant** powerful, admirable
154 **twelve shillings** a modest amount for the three guests and their horse
156 **double jug** a large vessel holding about two pints
157 **advent'rous** hazardous, dangerous; **prick thee forth** spur you on
159 **tender** honor; have a care for

Every true knight and every damsel fair;
But spill the blood of treacherous Saracens
And false enchanters, that with magic spells
Have done to death full many a noble knight.

Host. Thou valiant Knight of the Burning Pestle, give ear to me; there is twelve shillings to pay, and, as I am a true knight, I will not bate a penny.

Wife. George, I pray thee tell me, must Rafe pay twelve shillings now?

Citizen. No, Nell, no; nothing but the old knight is merry with Rafe.

Wife. Oh, is't nothing else? Rafe will be as merry as he.

Rafe. Sir knight, this mirth of yours becomes you well;
But, to requite this liberal courtesy,
If any of your squires will follow arms,
He shall receive from my heroic hand
A knighthood, by the virtue of this pestle.

Host. Fair knight, I thank you for your noble offer.
Therefore, gentle knight,
Twelve shillings you must pay, or I must cap you.

Wife. Look, George, did not I tell thee as much; the Knight of the Bell is in earnest. Rafe shall not be beholding to him. Give him his money, George, and let him go snick-up.

Citizen. Cap Rafe? No. [*Rises and goes to Host.*] – Hold your hand, Sir Knight of the Bell; there's your money. Have you anything to say to Rafe now? Cap Rafe?

[*Returns to seat.*]

Wife. I would you should know it. Rafe has friends that will not suffer him to be capped for ten times so much, and ten times to the end of that. Now take thy course, Rafe.

Mrs Merrythought. Come, Michael, thou and I will go home to thy father. He hath enough left to keep us a day or two, and we'll set fellows abroad to cry our purse and our casket. Shall we, Michael?

Michael. Aye, I pray, mother. In truth my feet are full of chilblains with traveling.

Wife. Faith, and those chilblains are a foul trouble. Mistress Merrythought, when your youth comes home, let him rub all the soles of his feet and the heels and his ankles with a mouse skin; or if none of your people can catch a mouse, when he goes to bed let him roll his feet in the warm embers, and I warrant you he shall be well; and you may make him put his fingers between his toes and smell to them. It's very sovereign for his head if he be costive.

Mrs Merrythought. Master Knight of the Burning Pestle, my son Michael and I bid you farewell. I thank your worship heartily for your kindness.

Rafe. Farewell, fair lady, and your tender squire.
If, pricking through these deserts, I do hear
Of any traitorous knight who through his guile
Hath light upon your casket and your purse,
I will despoil him of them and restore them.

Mrs Merrythought. I thank your worship.

Exit with Michael.

Rafe. Dwarf, bear my shield; squire, elevate my lance.
And now farewell, you Knight of holy Bell.

Citizen. Aye, aye, Rafe, all is paid.

Rafe. But yet before I go, speak, worthy knight,
If aught you do of sad adventures know,
Where errant knight may through his prowess win
Eternal fame and free some gentle souls
From endless bonds of steel and ling'ring pain.

Host. [*To Tapster.*] Sirrah, go to Nick the Barber and bid him prepare himself, as I told you before, quickly.

Tapster. I am gone, sir.

Exit Tapster.

Host. Sir knight, this wilderness affordeth none
But the great venture, where full many a knight
Hath tried his prowess and come off with shame,
And where I would not have you lose your life
Against no man but furious fiend of hell.

---

161 Saracens the Muslim enemies of the Crusaders, Moors who are the enemy of Don Quixote and, by extension, villains in the romances

162 false enchanters according to Don Quixote, enchanters turn inns into castles and back again to victimize knights errant

166 bate rebate; deduct

170–1 knight is merry (George is caught up in the same romance as his apprentice); **merry** teasing; jesting

178 knighthood (Rafe is as free with the honor as King James – or freer, since with Rafe the honor costs nothing); **virtue . . . pestle** (with obscene reference)

181 cap seize, arrest

184 beholding indebted

196 cry proclaim the loss of (like town criers)

200 chilblains inflammation and irritation

210 sovereign good, beneficial; **costive** constipated

219 despoil deprive by force

225 sad grave, serious

229 Nick (Don Quixote's barber is Master Nicholas [1.5], but surely the play here is on the barber's job of cutting)

Rafe. Speak on, sir knight; tell what he is and where;
For here I vow upon my blazing badge,
Never to blaze a day in quietness;
But bread and water will I only eat,
And the green herb and rock shall be my couch,
Till I have quelled that man or beast, or fiend,
That works such damage to all errant knights.

Host. Not far from hence, near to a craggy cliff,
At the north end of this distressèd town,
There doth stand a lowly house
Ruggedly builded, and in it a cave
In which an ugly giant now doth won,
Yclepèd Barbaroso. In his hand
He shakes a naked lance of purest steel,
With sleeves turned up, and him before he wears
A motley garment to preserve his clothes
From blood of those knights which he massacres,
And ladies gent. Without his door doth hang
A copper basin on a prickant spear,
At which no sooner gentle knights can knock
But the shrill sound fierce Barbaroso hears,
And rushing forth, brings in the errant knight
And sets him down in an enchanted chair.
Then with an engine which he hath prepared
With forty teeth, he claws his courtly crown;
Next makes him wink, and underneath his chin
He plants a brazen pece of mighty bord,
And knocks his bullets round about his cheeks,
Whilst with his fingers and an instrument
With which he snaps his hair off, he doth fill
The wretch's ears with a most hideous noise.
Thus every knight adventurer he doth trim,
And now no creature dares encounter him.

Rafe. In God's name, I will fight with him. Kind sir,
Go but before me to this dismal cave
Where this huge giant, Barbaroso, dwells,
And by that virtue that brave Rosicleer
That damnèd brood of ugly giants slew,
And Palmerin Frannarco overthrew,
I doubt not but to curb this traitor foul,
And to the devil send his guilty soul.

Host. Brave-sprighted knight, thus far I will perform
This your request: I'll bring you within sight
Of this most loathsome place, inhabited
By a more loathsome man; but dare not stay,
For his main force swoops all he sees away.

Rafe. Saint George, set on before! March, squire and page.

Exeunt.

Wife. George, dost think Rafe will confound the giant?

Citizen. I hold my cap to a farthing he does. Why, Nell, I saw him wrastle with the great Dutchman and hurl him.

Wife. Faith, and that Dutchman was a goodly man, if all things were answerable to his bigness; and yet they say there was a Scotchman higher than he, and that they two and a knight met and saw one another for nothing; but of all the sights that ever were in London since I was married, methinks the little child that was so fair grown about the members was the prettiest, that and the hermaphrodite.

Citizen. Nay, by your leave, Nell, Ninivie was better.

Wife. Ninivie? Oh, that was the story of Joan and the wall, was it not, George?

Citizen. Yes, lamb.

Enter Mistress Merrythought.

Wife. Look, George, here comes Mistress Merrythought again, and I would have Rafe come and fight with the giant. I tell you true, I long to see't.

243 quelled slain
249 ugly fearsome
250 Yelepèd named; called; **Barbaroso** (1) barbarian; (2) barber
251 lance razor
254 massacres cuts hair
255 gent (1) fair; (2) gentle (rank of gentility)
256 copper . . . spear the traditional sign of the barber-surgeon who was permitted to cut hair, draw teeth, and let blood (the pole was painted red and white); the bowl signified the bloodletting; **prickant** pointing upward
257 can do
261 engine comb
262 crown head
263 wink (cleansing eyes afterward; see line 406 below)
264 pece cup; **bord** rim; circumference
265 bullets small balls of soap
267–8 snaps . . . ears (refers to the long hair of knights frequently satirized)
269 trim (with additional meaning of *trounce*)
275 damnèd . . . slew refers to Rosicleer's adventure with the giant Brandagedeon and his thirty knights (*The Mirror of Knighthood* I.36)
276 Frannarco a giant slain by Palmerin (*Palmerin d'Olivia* I.51; the same chapter Rafe is reading at I.223ff above)
283 main full
284 Saint George . . . before! a battle – cry (St. George was the patron saint of England who as a knight slayed the dragon that was threatening the country)
288 hold pledge
299 hermaphrodite (a satire on the citizens' taste for freaks)
300 Ninivie (a contemporary puppet show about Jonah and the whale; he sees this as an analogous entertainment)

Citizen. Good Mistress Merrythought, be gone, I pray you, for my sake. I pray you, forbear a little. You shall have audience presently. I have a little business.

Wife. Mistress Merrythought, if it please you to refrain your passion a little till Rafe have dispatched the giant out of the way, we shall think ourselves much bound to you. I thank you, good Mistress Merrythought.

Exit Mistress Merrythought.

Enter a Boy.

Citizen. Boy, come hither; send away Rafe and this whoreson giant quickly.

Boy. In good faith, sir, we cannot. You'll utterly spoil our play and make it to be hissed, and it cost money. You will not suffer us to go on with our plot. I pray, gentlemen, rule him.

Citizen. Let him come now and dispatch this, and I'll trouble you no more.

Boy. Will you give me your hand of that?

Wife. Give him thy hand, George, do, and I'll kiss him. I warrant thee, the youth means plainly.

Boy. [*Shakes hands with Citizen.*] I'll send him to you presently.

Wife. I thank you, little youth. [*Kisses Boy.*]

Exit Boy.

Faith, the child hath a sweet breath, George, but I think it be troubled with the worms. *Carduus benedictus* and mare's milk were the only thing in the world for't.

Enter Rafe, Host, Squire [Tim], *and* Dwarf [George].

Oh, Rafe's here, George. God send thee good luck, Rafe.

Host. Puissant knight, yonder his mansion is;
Lo, where the spear and copper basin are;
Behold that string on which hangs many a tooth
Drawn from the gentle jaw of wand'ring knights.
I dare not stay to sound; he will appear.

Exit Host.

Rafe. Oh, faint not, heart, Susan, my lady dear,
The cobbler's maid in Milk Street, for whose sake
I take these arms, oh, let the thought of thee
Carry thy knight through all adventurous deeds;
And in the honor of thy beauteous self
May I destroy this monster, Barbaroso.
Knock, squire, upon the basin, till it break
With the shrill strokes, or till the giant speak.

Enter Barber.

Wife. Oh, George, the giant, the giant! – Now, Rafe, for thy life.

Barber. What fond unknowing wight is this that dares
So rudely knock at Barbaroso's cell,
Where no man comes but leaves his fleece behind?

Rafe. I, traitorous caitiff, who am sent by fate
To punish all the sad enormities
Thou hast committed against ladies gent
And errant knights. Traitor to God and men,
Prepare thyself; this is the dismal hour
Appointed for thee to give strict account
Of all thy beastly treacherous villainies.

Barber. Foolhardy knight, full soon thou shalt aby
This fond reproach. Thy body will I bang,

He takes down his pole.

And, lo, upon that string thy teeth shall hang.
Prepare thyself, for dead soon shalt thou be.

Rafe. Saint George for me!

They fight.

Barber. Gargantua for me!

Wife. To him, Rafe, to him. Hold up the giant. Set out thy leg before, Rafe.

Citizen. Falsify a blow, Rafe; falsify a blow. The giant lies open on the left side.

Wife. Bear't off, bear't off still. There, boy. Oh, Rafe's almost down, Rafe's almost down.

Rafe. Susan, inspire me. Now have up again.

Wife. Up, up, up, up, up! So, Rafe, down with him, down with him, Rafe.

Citizen. Fetch him o'er the hip, boy.

Wife. There, boy. Kill, kill, kill, kill, kill, Rafe.

---

317 **away** along
321 **suffer** permit
322 **rule** overrule
327 **plainly** honestly
329 **presently** at once
333 ***Carduus benedictus*** the blessed thistle, used as a cure-all; **mare's milk** thought a good purgative
340 **sound** blow a horn
341–77 **Oh, . . . first** (a parody of chivalric romance known to readers of the *Quixote*; the invocation to the lady, the formal challenge, the hero's magnanimity, and the battle or contest)
342 **Milk Street** (ran N from Cheapside to Gresham Street, originally the milk market of London)
350 **fond** foolish; **wight** man
352 **fleece** (1) beard; (2) money
353 **caitiff** wretch
360 **aby** pay for
362 **string . . . teeth** a common sight outside a barber-surgeon's shop
365 **Gargantua** the hero of folk tale (Rabelais' giant was not yet translated)
368 **Falsify** pretend, feign
376 **Kill . . . kill** (a parody of *King Lear* V.iii)

Citizen. No, Rafe, get all out of him first.

[Rafe *knocks down Barber, and disarms him.*]

Rafe. Presumptuous man, see to what desperate end
Thy treachery hath brought thee. The just gods,
Who never prosper those that do despise them,
For all the villainies which thou hast done
To knights and ladies, now have paid thee home
By my stiff arm, a knight adventurous.
But say, vile wretch, before I send thy soul
To sad Avernus, whither it must go,
What captives holdst thou in thy sable cave.

Barber. Go in and free them all; thou hast the day.

Rafe. Go, squire and dwarf, search in this dreadful cave
And free the wretched prisoners from their bonds.

Exit Squire [Tim] *and* Dwarf [George].

Barber. [*Kneels.*] I crave for mercy, as thou art a knight,
And scornst to spill the blood of those that beg.

Rafe. Thou show'dst no mercy, nor shalt thou have any;
Prepare thyself, for thou shalt surely die.

Enter Squire [Tim], *leading one winking, with a basin under his chin.*

Squire. Behold, brave knight, here is one prisoner,
Whom this wild man hath usèd as you see.

Wife. This is the first wise word I heard the squire speak.

Rafe. Speak what thou art and how thou hast been used,
That I may give him condign punishment.

1. Knight. I am a knight that took my journey post
Northward from London, and in courteous wise
This giant trained me to his loathsome den
Under pretense of killing of the itch,
And all my body with a powder strewed,
That smarts and stings, and cut away my beard,
And my curled locks wherein were ribbons tied,
And with a water washed my tender eyes
(Whilst up and down about me still he skipped),
Whose virtue is that till mine eyes be wiped
With a dry cloth, for this my foul disgrace
I shall not dare to look a dog i'th' face.

Wife. Alas, poor knight. Relieve him, Rafe; relieve poor knights whilst you live.

Rafe. My trusty squire, convey him to the town,
Where he may find relief. Adieu, fair knight.

Exit Knight [*with* Tim, *who reenters*].

Enter Dwarf [George,] *leading one with a patch o'er his nose.*

Dwarf. Puissant Knight of the Burning Pestle hight,
See here another wretch whom this foul beast
Hath scorched and scored in this inhuman wise.

Rafe. Speak me thy name and eke thy place of birth,
And what hath been thy usage in this cave.

2. Knight. I am a knight, Sir Pockhole is my name,
And by my birth I am a Londoner,
Free by my copy; but my ancestors
Were Frenchmen all; and riding hard this way
Upon a trotting horse, my bones did ache;
And I, faint knight, to ease my weary limbs,
Light at this cave, when straight this furious fiend,
With sharpest instrument of purest steel
Did cut the gristle of my nose away,
And in the place this velvet plaster stands.
Relieve me, gentle knight, out of his hands.

Wife. Good Rafe, relieve Sir Pockhole and send him away, for in truth, his breath stinks.

Rafe. Convey him straight after the other knight.
Sir Pockhole, fare you well.

2. Knight. Kind sir, good night.

Exit [Knight *with* George, *who reenters*].
Cries within.

379–80 **just . . . them** (another parody, of Gloucester, in *King Lear*)
382 **home** in full
385 **Avernus** a gloomy lake near Naples believed to be the entrance to the underworld
386 **sable** black; hence funereal
387 **day** victory
394 **s.d. *winking*** i.e., with his eyes shut; ***basin*** (1) to catch lather and gristle after shaving; (2) to catch blood from tooth extractions; the entire parade of Barbaroso's freed customers may parody the galley slaves Don Quixote frees in Book I
398 **condign** suitable
399 **post** hastily
402 **itch** (from venereal disease)
405 **ribbons** (foppish knights thought them fashionable for their hair)
415 **s.d. *patch . . . nose*** as suffering from an advanced case of syphilis
417 **scorched** slashed (with a knife); **scored** cut or carved
418 **eke** also
422 **copy** certificate of admission to freedom of the city
423 **Frenchmen** pox (syphilis) was popularly called "the French disease"
424 **bones . . . ache** symptoms of advanced syphilis
429 **velvet plaster** a typical covering for any kind of incision
432 **breath stinks** effect of mercury used to treat syphilis

3. Knight. [*Within.*] Deliver us.
Woman. [*Within.*] Deliver us.
Wife. Hark, George, what a woeful cry there is. I think some woman lies in there.
3. Knight. [*Within.*] Deliver us.
Woman. [*Within.*] Deliver us.
Rafe. What ghastly noise is this? Speak, Barbaroso,
Or by this blazing steel thy head goes off.
Barber. Prisoners of mine, whom I in diet keep.
Send lower down into the cave,
And in a tub that's heated smoking hot,
There may they find them and deliver them.
Rafe. Run, squire and dwarf; deliver them with speed.

Exeunt Squire [Tim] *and* Dwarf [George].

Wife. But will not Rafe kill this giant? Surely, I am afeared if he let him go he will do as much hurt as ever he did.

Citizen. Not so, mouse, neither, if he could convert him.

Wife. Aye, George, if he could convert him; but a giant is not so soon converted as one of us ordinary people. There's a pretty tale of a witch that had the devil's mark about her, God bless us, that had a giant to her son, that was called Lob-lie-by-the-fire. Didst never hear it, George?

Enter Squire [Tim], *leading a* Man [3. Knight] *with a glass of lotion in his hand, and the* Dwarf [George], *leading a* Woman *with diet-bread and drink.*

Citizen. Peace, Nell, here comes the prisoners.
Dwarf. Here be these pinèd wretches, manful knight,
That for these six weeks have not seen a wight.
Rafe. Deliver what you are, and how you came
To this sad cave, and what your usage was.
3. Knight. I am an errant knight that followed arms
With spear and shield, and in my tender years
I stricken was with Cupid's fiery shaft
And fell in love with this my lady dear,
And stole her from her friends in Turnbull Street,
And bore her up and down from town to town,
Where we did eat and drink and music hear,
Till at the length, at this unhappy town
We did arrive, and coming to this cave
This beast us caught and put us in a tub
Where we this two months sweat, and should have done
Another month if you had not relieved us.
Woman. This bread and water hath our diet been,
Together with a rib cut from a neck
Of burnèd mutton. Hard hath been our fare.
Release us from this ugly giant's snare.
3. Knight. This hath been all the food we have received;
But only twice a day, for novelty,
He gave a spoonful of this hearty broth

Pulls out a syringe.

To each of us, through this same slender quill.
Rafe. From this infernal monster you shall go,
That useth knights and gentle ladies so.
Convey them hence.

Exeunt Man[3. Knight] *and* Woman [*with* Tim *and* George, *who reenters*].

Citizen. Cony, I can tell thee the gentlemen like Rafe.

Wife. Aye, George, I see it well enough. Gentlemen, I thank you all heartily for gracing my man Rafe, and I promise you you shall see him oft'ner.

Barber. Mercy, great knight, I do recant my ill,
And henceforth never gentle blood will spill.
Rafe. I give thee mercy, but yet shalt thou swear
Upon my burning pestle to perform
Thy promise uttered.
Barber. I swear and kiss.

[*Kisses pestle.*]

Rafe. Depart, then, and amend.
Come, squire and dwarf, the sun grows towards his set,
And we have many more adventures yet.

Exeunt.

Citizen. Now Rafe is in this humor, I know he would ha' beaten all the boys in the house if they had been set on him.

Wife. Aye, George, but it is well as it is. I warrant you the gentlemen do consider what it is to overthrow a giant. But look, George, here comes Mistress Merrythought and her son Michael. Now you are welcome, Mistress

435–40 Deliver . . . us (parodies Litany for General Supplication in the Book of Common Prayer)
445 tub (sweating-tubs were thought to cure the pox)
453 convert him (converting heathens was a customary part of chivalric romance)
456 devil's mark (certain spots or toothmarks taken as sure identification of a witch)
459 s.d. ***diet-bread*** special bread for syphilitics
461 pinèd wasted, starved
463 Deliver tell
469 Turnbull Street originally Turnmill Street, notorious for prostitution
478 rib . . . neck portion of the inferior end of the neck of mutton
479 mutton common term for prostitute
483 hearty nourishing
502 humor mood

Merrythought. Now Rafe has done, you may go on.

Enter Mistress Merrythought *and* Michael.

Mrs Merrythought. Mick, my boy.

Michael. Aye, forsooth, mother.

Mrs Merrythought. Be merry, Mick; we are at home now, where, I warrant you, you shall find the house flung out at the windows. [*Music within.*] Hark, hey dogs, hey, this is the old world, i'faith, with my husband. If I get in among 'em, I'll play 'em such a lesson that they shall have little list to come scraping hither again. [*Calls.*] Why, Master Merrythought, husband, Charles Merrythought.

Old Merrythought. [*Sings*] *within.*

If you will sing and dance and laugh
And hollo and laugh again,
And they cry "There, boys, there," why then,
One, two, three, and four,
We shall be merry within this hour.

Mrs Merrythought. Why, Charles, do you not know your own natural wife? I say, open the door and turn me out those mangy companions. 'Tis more than time that they were fellow and fellow-like with you. You are a gentleman, Charles, and an old man, and father of two children; and I myself (though I say it) by my mother's side niece to a worshipful gentleman, and a conductor. He has been three times in His Majesty's service at Chester, and is now the fourth time, God bless him and his charge, upon his journey.

Old Merrythought. [*Sings at the window.*]

Go from my window, love, go;
Go from my window, my dear.
The wind and the rain
Will drive you back again.
You cannot be lodgèd here.

Hark you, Mistress Merrythought, you that walk upon adventures and forsake your husband because he sings with never a penny in his purse. What, shall I think myself the worse? Faith, no, I'll be merry. You come not here; here's none but lads of mettle, lives of a hundred years and upwards. Care never drunk their bloods, nor want made 'em warble: [*Sings.*]

Heigh-ho, my heart is heavy.

[*Leaves the window.*]

Mrs Merrythought. Why, Master Merrythought, what am I that you should laugh me to scorn thus abruptly? Am I not your fellow-feeler, as we may say, in all our miseries, your comforter in health and sickness? Have I not brought you children? Are they not like you, Charles? Look upon thine own image, hard-hearted man. And yet for all this –

Old Merrythought. [*Sings*] *within.*

Begone, begone, my Juggy, my puggy,
Begone, my love, my dear.
The weather is warm;
'Twill do thee no harm.
Thou canst not be lodgèd here.

Be merry, boys; some light music and more wine.

Wife. He's not in earnest, I hope, George, is he?

Citizen. What if he be, sweetheart?

Wife. Marry, if he be, George, I'll make bold to tell him he's an ingrant old man to use his bedfellow so scurvily.

Citizen. What, how does he use her, honey?

Wife. Marry, come up, Sir Saucebox, I think you'll take his part, will you not? Lord, how hot you are grown. You are a fine man, an' you had a fine dog; it becomes you sweetly.

Citizen. Nay, prithee, Nell, chide not; for as I am an honest man and a true Christian grocer, I do not like his doings.

Wife. I cry you mercy, then, George. You know we are all frail and full of infirmities. D'ye hear, Master Merrythought, may I crave a word with you?

Old Merrythought. Within. Strike up lively, lads.

Wife. I had not thought, in truth, Master Merrythought, that a man of your age and discretion, as I may say, being a gentleman, and therefore known by your gentle conditions, could have used so little respect to the weakness of his wife. For your wife is your own

---

516 **house . . . windows** (as signs of undisciplined living; rioting)
517 **world** behavior, habit
520 **list** desire; **scraping** playing (bowing) the fiddle
525 **hollo** shout
530 **companions** ne'er-do-wells
535 **worshipful** honorable
536 **conductor** captain
537 **Chester** port of embarkation for Ireland with reputation for military corruption
540–4 **Go . . . here** a popular song in many contemporary works including Heywood's *Rape of Lucrece*
550 **mettle** courage
550–1 **lives . . . upwards** (their merry lives have kept them young)
562 **Juggy** diminutive of Joan; **puggy** term of endearment
570 **Marry** indeed
571 **ingrant** ill-mannered; ignorant; ungracious
574 **Marry, come up** "now, now" (a taunt)
581 **cry you mercy** beg your pardon
589 **conditions** qualities; characteristics

flesh, the staff of your age, your yoke-fellow, with whose help you draw through the mire of this transitory world. Nay, she's your own rib. And again –

Old Merrythought. [*Sings at window.*]

I come not hither for thee to teach;
I have no pulpit for thee to preach;
I would thou hadst kissed me under the breech,
As thou art a lady gay.

[*Leaves window.*]

Wife. Marry, with a vengeance! I am heartily sorry for the poor gentlewoman, but if I were thy wife, i'faith, graybeard, i'faith –

Citizen. I prithee, sweet honeysuckle, be content.

Wife. Give me such words that am a gentlewoman born! Hang him, hoary rascal! Get me some drink, George, I am almost molten with fretting; now beshrew his knave's heart for it!

[*Exit* Citizen.]

Old Merrythought. [*Within.*] Play me a light lavolta. Come, be frolic. Fill the good fellows wine.

Mrs Merrythought. Why, Master Merrythought, are you disposed to make me wait here? You'll open, I hope; I'll fetch them that shall open else.

Old Merrythought. [*At window.*] Good woman, if you will sing I'll give you something; if not –

Song

You are no love for me, Marg'ret.
I am no love for you.

[*Leaves window.*]

[*Within.*] – Come aloft, boys, aloft.

Mrs Merrythought. Now a churl's fart in your teeth, sir. Come, Mick, we'll not trouble him. 'A shall not ding us i'th' teeth with his bread and his broth, that he shall not. Come, boy, I'll provide for thee, I warrant thee. We'll go to Master Venturewell's, the merchant. I'll get his letter to mine host of the Bell in Waltham; there I'll place thee with the tapster. Will not that do well for thee, Mick? And let me alone for that old cuckoldly knave, your father. I'll use him in his kind, I warrant ye.

[*Exeunt.*]

[Interlude III]

Music. [*Enter* Citizen.]

Wife. Come George, where's the beer?

Citizen. Here, love.

Wife. This old fornicating fellow will not out of my mind yet. – Gentlemen, I'll begin to you all, and I desire more of your acquaintance, with all my heart. [*Drinks.*] Fill the gentlemen some beer, George.

[*Enter*] Boy, *danceth.*

Look, George, the little boy's come again. Methinks he looks something like the Prince of Orange in his long stocking, if he had a little harness about his neck. George, I will have him dance "Fading." "Fading" is a fine jig, I'll assure you, gentlemen. Begin, brother. Now 'a capers, sweetheart. Now a turn o'th' toe, and then tumble. Cannot you tumble, youth?

Boy. No, indeed, forsooth.

Wife. Nor eat fire?

Boy. Neither.

Wife. Why then, I thank you heartily. There's twopence to buy you points withal.

[*Exit* Boy.]

Act IV

Enter Jasper *and* [*a*] Boy.

Jasper. [*Gives a letter.*] There, boy, deliver this, but do it well.
Hast thou provided me four lusty fellows
Able to carry me? And art thou perfect
In all thy business?

Boy. Sir, you need not fear;

---

592 yoke-fellow companion (reference to oxen at a plow)
594 rib (see Gen. 2:22)
610 lavolta dance for couples; **frolic** merry
618–19 You . . . you (thought to belong to a ballad about Fair Margaret and Sweet William; see II.485–8)
621 churl man; husband
623 ding strike (taunt)
630 cuckoldly adulterous
631 in his kind (1) according to his nature; (2) just deserts

Interlude III

4 begin toast
9–10 Prince of Orange Prince Maurice of Nassau, whose picture in "long stocking" was widely circulated
11 harness armor
12 "Fading" (1) an Irish dance; (2) a sexual orgasm
14 capers lively dancing
15 tumble (with sexual overtones)
20 points tagged laces for tying hose to doublet

Act IV

2 lusty vigorous
3 perfect perfected; i.e., instructed

I have my lesson here and cannot miss it.
The men are ready for you, and what else
Pertains to this employment.

Jasper. [*Gives money.*] There, my boy,
Take it, but buy no land.

Boy. Faith, sir, 'twere rare
To see so young a purchaser. I fly,
And on my wings carry your destiny.

Exit.

Jasper. Go, and be happy. Now, my latest hope,
Forsake me not, but fling thy anchor out
And let it hold. Stand fixed, thou rolling stone,
Till I enjoy my dearest. Hear me, all
You powers that rule in men celestial.

Exit.

Wife. Go thy ways; thou art as crooked a sprig as ever grew in London. I warrant him he'll come to some naughty end or other, for his looks say no less. Besides, his father (you know, George) is none of the best. You heard him take me up like a flirt-gill, and sing bawdy songs upon me; but, i'faith, if I live, George –

Citizen. Let me alone, sweetheart; I have a trick in my head shall lodge him in the Arches for one year, and make him sing *peccavi* ere I leave him, and yet he shall never know who hurt him neither.

Wife. Do, my good George, do.

[*Enter a* Boy.]

Citizen. What shall we have Rafe do now, boy?

Boy. You shall have what you will, sir.

Citizen. Why, so, sir, go and fetch me him then, and let the Sophy of Persia come and christen him a child.

Boy. Believe me, sir, that will not do so well. 'Tis stale. It has been had before at the Red Bull.

Wife. George, let Rafe travel over great hills, and let him be very weary, and come to the King of Cracovia's house, covered with velvet, and there let the King's daughter stand in her window, all in beaten gold, combing her golden locks with a comb of ivory, and let her spy Rafe and fall in love with him, and come down to him and carry him into her father's house, and then let Rafe talk with her.

Citizen. Well said, Nell, it shall be so. Boy, let's ha't done quickly.

Boy. Sir, if you will imagine all this to be done already, you shall hear them talk together. But we cannot present a house covered with black velvet, and a lady in beaten gold.

Citizen. Sir boy, let's ha't as you can, then.

Boy. Besides, it will show ill-favoredly to have a grocer's prentice to court a king's daughter.

Citizen. Will it so, sir? You are well read in histories! I pray you, what was Sir Dagonet? Was not he prentice to a grocer in London? Read the play of *The Four Prentices of London*, where they toss their pikes so. I pray you, fetch him in, sir; fetch him in.

Boy. It shall be done. It is not our fault, gentlemen.

Exit.

Wife. Now we shall see fine doings, I warrant'ee, George.

Enter Rafe *and the* Lady [Pompiona], Squire [Tim], *and* Dwarf [George].

Oh, here they come. How prettily the King of Cracovia's daughter is dressed.

Citizen. Aye, Nell, it is the fashion of that country, I warrant'ee.

Lady. Welcome, sir knight, unto my father's court,
King of Moldavia; unto me, Pompiona,
His daughter dear. But sure you do not like
Your entertainment, that will stay with us
No longer but a night.

Rafe. Damsel right fair,

---

8 **buy no land** (proverbial: "He that buys land buys many stones")
12 **anchor** an emblem associated with hope
13 **rolling stone** (1) the earth; (2) uncertain fortune (metaphorical)
15 **powers ... celestial** Venus Coelestis (Heavenly Love) who possesses the minds whose intellects go beyond the sensible to the heavenly (neoplatonic)
16 **sprig** youth
18 **naughty** mischievous, evil
21 **flirt-gill** promiscuous woman
24 **Arches** the ecclesiastical court of appeal that heard cases breaking church law and practices
25 ***peccavi*** "I have sinned" (Latin); i.e., pay penance
30 **You ... sir** i.e., we've given up trying to perform *our* play
32–3 **Sophy ... child** reference to the Sophy of Persia standing godfather to Robert Sherley's child in Day, Rowley, and Wilkins's *The Travels of the Three English Brothers* (1607)
35 **stale** (plays of sheer spectacle were considered of little value); **Red Bull** a popular theater in Clerkenwell built around 1605 where *Travels* had been acted
38 **Cracovia** i.e., Cracow, capital of Poland until 1609
40 **beaten gold** (cf. elaborate costumes for *The Masque of Blackness*)
52 **ill-favoredly** inappropriately
55 **Sir Dagonet** (probably as part of Arthur's Show, an archery exhibition at Mile-End, but actually King Arthur's fool)
57 ***The ... London*** (in this play by Heywood [printed 1615] Eustace and Guy toss their pikes back and forth to demonstrate their strength of arms before their combat)
68 **Moldavia** a Danubian province, now Romania, sometimes confused with Poland; in November 1607 the Prince of Moldavia was Turkish ambassador to the English court

I am on many sad adventures bound,
That call me forth into the wilderness;
Besides, my horse's back is something galled,
Which will enforce me ride a sober pace.
But many thanks, fair lady, be to you,
For using errant knight with courtesy.

Lady. But say, brave knight, what is your name and birth?

Rafe. My name is Rafe; I am an Englishman,
As true as steel, a hearty Englishman,
And prentice to a grocer in the Strand
By deed indent, of which I have one part.
But Fortune calling me to follow arms,
On me this holy order I did take
Of Burning Pestle, which in all men's eyes
I bear, confounding ladies' enemies.

Lady. Oft have I heard of your brave countrymen,
And fertile soil and store of wholesome food.
My father oft will tell me of a drink
In England found, and nipitato called,
Which driveth all the sorrow from your hearts.

Rafe. Lady, 'tis true; you need not lay your lips
To better nipitato than there is.

Lady. And of a wild fowl he will often speak,
Which powdered beef and mustard callèd is,
For there have been great wars 'twixt us and you;
But truly, Rafe, it was not long of me.
Tell me then, Rafe, could you contented be
To wear a lady's favor in your shield?

Rafe. I am a knight of religious order,
And will not wear a favor of a lady's
That trusts in Antichrist and false traditions.

Citizen. Well said, Rafe; convert her if thou canst.

Rafe. Besides, I have a lady of my own
In merry England, for whose virtuous sake
I took these arms; and Susan is her name,
A cobbler's maid in Milk Street, whom I vow
Ne'er to forsake whilst life and pestle last.

Lady. Happy that cobbling dame, whoe'er she be,
That for her own, dear Rafe, hath gotten thee;
Unhappy I, that ne'er shall see the day
To see thee more, that bearst my heart away.

Rafe. Lady, farewell, I needs must take my leave.

Lady. Hard-hearted Rafe, that ladies dost deceive.

Citizen. Hark thee, Rafe, there's money for thee. Give something in the King of Cracovia's house; be not beholding to him.

Rafe. Lady, before I go, I must remember
Your father's officers, who, truth to tell,
Have been about me very diligent.
Hold up thy snowy hand, thou princely maid.
There's twelve pence for your father's chamberlain;
And another shilling for his cook,
For, by my troth, the goose was roasted well;
And twelve pence for your father's horse-keeper,
For 'nointing my horse back; and for his butter,
There is another shilling. To the maid
That washed my boot-hose, there's an English groat;
And twopence to the boy that wiped my boots;
And last, fair lady, there is for yourself
Threepence to buy you pins at Bumbo Fair.

Lady. Full many thanks, and I will keep them safe
Till all the heads be off, for thy sake, Rafe.

Rafe. Advance, my squire and dwarf; I cannot stay.

Lady. Thou killst my heart in parting thus away.

Exeunt.

Wife. I commend Rafe yet that he will not stoop to a Cracovian. There's properer women in London than any are there, iwis. But here comes Master Humphrey and his love again now, George.

Citizen. Aye, cony, peace.

Enter Merchant, Humphrey, Luce, *and a* Boy.

Merchant. Go, get you up; I will not be entreated.
And, gossip mine, I'll keep you sure hereafter
From gadding out again with boys and unthrifts.
Come, they are women's tears. I know your fashion.
Go, sirrah, lock her in, and keep the key
Safe as you love your life.

Exeunt Luce *and* Boy.

74 **galled** sore (from chafing)
82 **Strand** one of the great streets for fashionable mansions
83 **deed indent** agreement of indenture between master and servant
87 **confounding** deliberate pun: (1) bewildering; (2) defeating
91 **nipitato** prime ale
96 **powdered** salted
98 **long** on account
103 **Antichrist** (because Turkish)
110 **cobbling** bungling
129 **boot-hose** often elaborately embroidered stockings covering the calf; they were made without feet
130 **boots** attire of gallants and aspiring gentlemen
132 **pins** (if elaborate, a fashionable gift); **Bumbo** a drink made from rum, sugar, nutmeg, and water and sold at fairs
137 **stoop** submit
138 **properer** (1) more suitable; (2) more handsome
143 **up** (1) from kneeling; (2) to your own bedchamber
144 **gossip** female friend
145 **unthrifts** i.e., prodigals
146 **women's tears** i.e., not to be taken seriously

Now, my son Humphrey,
You may both rest assurèd of my love
In this, and reap your own desire.

Humphrey. I see this love you speak of, through your daughter,
Although the hole be little; and hereafter
Will yield the like in all I may or can,
Fitting a Christian and a gentleman.

Merchant. I do believe you, my good son, and thank you;
For 'twere an impudence to think you flattered.

Humphrey. It were indeed, but shall I tell you why?
I have been beaten twice about the lie.

Merchant. Well, son, no more of compliment; my daughter
Is yours again. Appoint the time and take her;
We'll have no stealing for it. I myself
And some few of our friends will see you married.

Humphrey. I would you would, i'faith, for be it known,
I ever was afraid to lie alone.

Merchant. Some three days hence, then.

Humphrey. Three days, let me see,
'Tis somewhat of the most; yet I agree,
Because I mean against the appointed day
To visit all my friends in new array.

Enter Servant.

Servant. Sir, there's a gentlewoman without would speak with your worship.

Merchant. What is she?

Servant. Sir, I asked her not.

Merchant. Bid her come in.

[*Exit* Servant.]

Enter Mistress Merrythought *and* Michael.

Mrs Merrythought. Peace be to your worship. I come as a poor suitor to you, sir, in the behalf of this child.

Merchant. Are you not wife to Merrythought?

Mrs Merrythought. Yes, truly, would I had ne'er seen his eyes. He has undone me and himself and his children, and there he lives at home and sings, and hoits, and revels among his drunken companions; but, I warrant you, where to get a penny to put bread in his mouth, he knows not; and therefore, if it like your worship, I would entreat your letter to the honest host of the Bell in Waltham, that I may place my child under the protection of his tapster in some settled course of life.

Merchant. I'm glad the heavens have heard my prayers. Thy husband,
When I was ripe in sorrows, laughed at me.
Thy son, like an unthankful wretch, I having
Redeemed him from his fall and made him mine,
To show his love again, first stole my daughter,
Then wronged this gentleman, and last of all,
Gave me that grief had almost brought me down
Unto my grave, had not a stronger hand
Relieved my sorrows. Go and weep, as I did,
And be unpitied; for I here profess
An everlasting hate to all thy name.

Mrs Merrythought. Will you so, sir? How say you by that? Come, Mick, let him keep his wind to cool his porridge. We'll go to thy nurse's, Mick. She knits silk stockings, boy, and we'll knit too, boy, and be beholding to none of them all.

Exeunt Michael *and* Mother.

Enter a Boy *with a letter.*

Boy. Sir, I take it you are the master of this house.

Merchant. How then, boy?

Boy. Then to yourself, sir, comes this letter.

Merchant. From whom, my pretty boy?

Boy. From him that was your servant, but no more
Shall that name ever be, for he is dead.
Grief of your purchased anger broke his heart.
I saw him die, and from his hand received
This paper, with a charge to bring it hither;
Read it, and satisfy yourself in all.

Letter

Merchant. [*Reads.*] "*Sir, That I have wronged your love, I must confess, in which I have purchased to myself, besides mine own undoing, the ill opinion of my friends. Let not your anger, good sir, outlive me, but suffer me to rest in peace with your forgiveness. Let my body (if a dying man may so much prevail with you) be brought to your daughter, that she may truly know my hot flames are now buried, and, withal, receive a testimony of the zeal I bore her virtue. Farewell forever, and be ever happy.* Jasper."
God's hand is great in this. I do forgive him;
Yet I am glad he's quiet, where I hope
He will not bite again. Boy, bring the body

161 We'll . . . it we shall not have another elopement
166 of . . . most overlong
167 against in expectation of
181 hoits laughs riotously
201–2 keep . . . porridge (proverbial)
212 purchased incurred by his behavior
226 great evident

And let him have his will, if that be all.
Boy. 'Tis here without, sir.
Merchant. So, sir, if you please,
You may conduct it in; I do not fear it.
Humphrey. I'll be your usher, boy; for, though I say it,
He owed me something once and well did pay it.

Exeunt.

Enter Luce, *alone.*

Luce. If there be any punishment inflicted
Upon the miserable, more than yet I feel,
Let it together seize me, and at once
Press down my soul. I cannot bear the pain
Of these delaying tortures. Thou that art
The end of all and the sweet rest of all,
Come, come, oh, Death; bring me to thy peace
And blot out all the memory I nourish,
Both of my father and my cruel friend.
Oh, wretched maid, still living to be wretched,
To be a say to Fortune in her changes
And grow to number times and woes together!
How happy had I been, if being born
My grave had been my cradle.

Enter Servant.

Servant. By your leave,
Young mistress, here's a boy hath brought a coffin.
What 'a would say, I know not, but your father
Charged me to give you notice. Here they come.

Enter two [Carrier *and* Boy] *bearing a coffin,* Jasper *in it.*

Luce. For me I hope 'tis come, and 'tis most welcome.
Boy. Fair mistress, let me not add greater grief
To that great store you have already. Jasper,
That whilst he lived was yours, now dead
And here enclosed, commanded me to bring
His body hither, and to crave a tear
From those fair eyes, though he deserved not pity,
To deck his funeral; for so he bid me
Tell her for whom he died.
Luce. He shall have many.
Good friends, depart a little, whilst I take
My leave of this dead man, that once I loved.

Exeunt Coffin-carrier *and* Boy [*and* Servant].

Hold yet a little, life, and then I give thee
To thy first heavenly being. Oh, my friend,
Hast thou deceived me thus, and got before me?
I shall not long be after, but, believe me,
Thou wert too cruel, Jasper, 'gainst thyself
In punishing the fault I could have pardoned,
With so untimely death. Thou didst not wrong me
But ever wert most kind, most true, most loving;
And I the most unkind, most false, most cruel.
Didst thou but ask a tear? I'll give thee all,
Even all my eyes can pour down, all my sighs,
And all myself. Before thou goest from me
These are but sparing rites. But if thy soul
Be yet about this place and can behold
And see what I prepare to deck thee with,
It shall go up, borne on the wings of peace,
And satisfied. First will I sing thy dirge,
Then kiss thy pale lips, and then die myself,
And fill one coffin and one grave together.

Song.

Come, you whose loves are dead,
And, whiles I sing,
Weep, and wring
Every hand; and every head
Bind with cypress and sad yew;
Ribbons black and candles blue
For him that was of men most true.

Come with heavy moaning,
And on his grave
Let him have
Sacrifice of sighs and groaning.
Let him have fair flowers enow,
White and purple, green and yellow,
For him that was of men most true.

Thou sable cloth, sad cover of my joys,
I lift thee up, and thus I meet with death.
Jasper. [*Rising out of the coffin.*] And thus you meet the living.
Luce. Save me, heaven!
Jasper. Nay, do not fly me, fair. I am no spirit;
Look better on me. Do you know me yet?
Luce. Oh thou dear shadow of my friend.
Jasper. Dear substance.

---

232 **usher** (1) doorkeeper; (2) assistant
244 **say** assay; i.e., touchstone, test
275 **sparing** meager; minimal
279 **dirge** funeral hymn
286 ***cypress and sad yew*** traditional emblems of mourning; cf. *Twelfth Night* II.iv.50ff
287 ***blue*** (color of constancy)
294 ***White . . . yellow*** white symbolized purity; purple, sorrow and patience; green, regeneration of the soul; yellow, divinity
301 **shadow** spirit

I swear I am no shadow. Feel my hand;
It is the same it was. I am your Jasper,
Your Jasper, that's yet living and yet loving.
Pardon my rash attempt, my foolish proof
I put in practice of your constancy;
For sooner should my sword have drunk my blood
And set my soul at liberty, than drawn
The least drop from that body; for which boldness
Doom me to anything. If death, I take it,
And willingly.

Luce. This death I'll give you for it. [*Kisses him.*]
So, now I am satisfied. You are no spirit,
But my own truest, truest, truest friend.
Why do you come thus to me?

Jasper. First to see you,
Then to convey you hence.

Luce. It cannot be,
For I am locked up here and watched at all hours,
That 'tis impossible for me to 'scape.

Jasper. Nothing more possible. Within this coffin
Do you convey yourself. Let me alone;
I have the wits of twenty men about me.
Only I crave the shelter of your closet
A little, and then fear me not. Creep in
That they may presently convey you hence.
Fear nothing, dearest love; I'll be your second.

[Luce *lies in the coffin;* Jasper *covers her with the cloth.*]

Lie close, so. All goes well yet. – Boy!

[*Enter* Coffin-Carrier *and* Boy.]

Boy. At hand, sir.

Jasper. Convey away the coffin, and be wary.

Boy. 'Tis done already.

Jasper. Now must I go conjure.

Exit.

Enter Merchant.

Merchant. Boy, boy.

Boy. Your servant, sir.

Merchant. Do me this kindness, boy (hold, here's a crown). Before thou bury the body of this fellow, carry it to his old merry father and salute him from me, and bid him sing. He hath cause.

Boy. I will, sir.

Merchant. And then bring me word what tune he is in, and have another crown; but do it truly. I have fitted him a bargain now will vex him.

Boy. God bless your worship's health, sir.

Merchant. Farewell, boy.

Exeunt.

Enter Master Merrythought.

Wife. Ah, old Merrythought, art thou there again? Let's hear some of thy songs.

Old Merrythought. [*Sings.*]
Who can sing a merrier note
Than he that cannot change a groat?

Not a denier left, and yet my heart leaps. I do wonder yet, as old as I am, that any man will follow a trade or serve, that may sing and laugh, and walk the streets. My wife and both my sons are I know not where. I have nothing left, nor know I how to come by meat to supper, yet am I merry still; for I know I shall find it upon the table at six o'clock. Therefore, hang thought. [*Sings.*]

I would not be a serving-man
To carry the cloak-bag still,
Nor would I be a falconer
The greedy hawks to fill;
But I would be in a good house,
And have a good master too,
But I would eat and drink of the best,
And no work would I do.

This is it that keeps life and soul together: mirth. This is the philosopher's stone that they write so much on, that keeps a man ever young.

Enter a Boy.

Boy. Sir, they say they know all your money is gone, and they will trust you for no more drink.

Old Merrythought. Will they not? Let 'em choose. The best is, I have mirth at home, and need not send abroad for that; let them keep their drink to themselves.

[*Sings.*]

310 death (i.e., the kiss momentarily prevents breathing)
321 closet private room
322 fear me not do not have fear for me
324 second support
325 close hidden
327 conjure perform my trick
336 tune mood
338 fitted furnished
343–4 Who . . . groat? a catch in Ravenscroft's *Pammelia* (1609)
344 groat fourpenny coin
345 denier French coin worth very little (one-twelfth of a sou)
353 hang dismiss all
355 cloak-bag portmanteau
363 philosopher's stone (as his panacea; in alchemy, this transmutes base metals into gold, heals wounds, and prolongs life)

For Jillian of Berry, she dwells on a hill,
And she hath good beer and ale to sell,
And of good fellows she thinks no ill;
And thither will we go now, now, now, now,
And thither will we go now.
And when you have made a little stay,
You need not ask what is to pay,
But kiss your hostess and go your way,
And thither &c.

Enter another Boy.

2. *Boy.* Sir, I can get no bread for supper.

Old Merrythought. Hang bread and supper! Let's preserve our mirth, and we shall never feel hunger, I'll warrant you. Let's have a catch; boy, follow me; come.

[*Sing this catch.*]

Ho, ho, nobody at home!
Meat, nor drink, nor money ha' we none.
Fill the pot, Eedy,
Never more need I.

So, boys, enough; follow me. Let's change our place and we shall laugh afresh.

Exeunt.

[Interlude IV]

Wife. Let him go, George. 'A shall not have any countenance from us, nor a good word from any i'th' company, if I may strike stroke in't.

Citizen. No more 'a sha'not, love; but, Nell, I will have Rafe do a very notable matter now, to the eternal honor and glory of all grocers. Sirrah, you there, boy! Can none of you hear?

[*Enter* Boy.]

Boy. Sir, your pleasure?

Citizen. Let Rafe come out on May Day in the morning and speak upon a conduit, with all his scarfs about him, and his feathers and his rings and his knacks.

Boy. Why, sir, you do not think of our plot. What will become of that, then?

Citizen. Why, sir, I care not what become on't. I'll have him come out, or I'll fetch him out myself. I'll have something done in honor of the City. Besides, he hath been long enough upon adventures. Bring him out quickly, or if I come in among you –

Boy. Well, sir, he shall come out. But if our play miscarry, sir, you are like to pay for't.

Citizen. Bring him away, then.

Exit Boy.

Wife. This will be brave, i'faith; George, shall not he dance the morris too, for the credit of the Strand?

Citizen. No, sweetheart, it will be too much for the boy.

Enter Rafe.

Oh, there he is, Nell. He's reasonable well in reparel, but he has not rings enough.

Rafe. London, to thee I do present the merry month of May.
Let each true subject be content to hear me what I say:
For from the top of conduit head, as plainly may appear,
I will both tell my name to you and wherefore I came here.
My name is Rafe, by due descent though not ignoble, I,
Yet far inferior to the flock of gracious grocery;
And by the Common Council of my fellows in the Strand,
With gilded staff and crossèd scarf, the May Lord here I stand.
Rejoice, oh, English hearts, rejoice; rejoice, oh, lovers dear;
Rejoice, oh, city, town, and country; rejoice, eke every shire.
For now the fragrant flowers do spring and sprout in seemly sort;
The little birds do sit and sing, the lambs do make fine sport.
And now the birchen tree doth bud, that makes the school-boy cry.
The morris rings while hobby-horse doth foot it feateously.
The lords and ladies now abroad for their disport and play,

385 **catch** song sung as a round
387–90 **Ho . . . I** another catch in *Pammelia*

Interlude IV

2 **countenance** favor
3 **strike stroke** have my say
9 **May Day** the bringing home of May (hawthorn) signified spring's renewal of nature; festivities included serious and parodic speeches, bonfires, shows, and dances
10 **conduit** fountain
11 **scarfs** as part of the dress for Morris dancing on May Day

31–66 ***London . . . cease*** the use of wooden "fourteeners" as the measure here parodies May Lords' banality and perhaps hymn-books as well
35 ***My . . . ignoble*** (probably deliberate parody of Revenge at the start of Kyd's *Spanish Tragedy*)
38 ***gilded . . . scarf*** symbols of the May Lord's office
43 ***birchen . . . cry*** branches of the birch tree were used for flogging
44 ***hobby-horse*** a feature of the Morris dance; a wooden frame and costume allowed one dancer to be the horse; it was considered a sexual symbol because of its rocking motion; **feateously** nimbly

Do kiss sometimes upon the grass, and sometimes in the hay.
Now butter with a leaf of sage is good to purge the blood;
Fly Venus and phlebotomy, for they are neither good.
Now little fish on tender stone begin to cast their bellies,
And sluggish snails, that erst were mute, do creep out of their shellies.
The rumbling rivers now do warm for little boys to paddle;
The sturdy steed now goes to grass, and up they hang his saddle.
The heavy hart, the bellowing buck, the rascal, and the pricket,
Are now among the yeoman's peas, and leave the fearful thicket.
And be like them, oh, you, I say, of this same noble town,
And lift aloft your velvet heads, and slipping off your gown,
With bells on legs, and napkins clean unto your shoulders tied,
With scarfs and garters as you please, and "Hey for our town" cried,
March out and show your willing minds, by twenty and by twenty,
To Hogsdon or to Newington, where ale and cakes are plenty.
And let it ne'er be said for shame, that we the youths of London
Lay thrumming of our caps at home, and left our custom undone.
Up then, I say, both young and old, both man and maid a-Maying,
With drums and guns that bounce aloud, and merry tabor playing!
Which to prolong, God save our king, and send his country peace,
And root out treason from the land, and so, my friends, I cease.

[*Exit.*]

Act V

Enter Merchant, *solus.*

Merchant. I will have no great store of company at the wedding: a couple of neighbors and their wives, and we will have a capon in stewed broth, with marrow, and a good piece of beef stuck with rosemary.

Enter Jasper, *his face mealed.*

Jasper. Forbear thy pains, fond man; it is too late.
Merchant. Heaven bless me? Jasper?
Jasper. Aye, I am his ghost,
Whom thou hast injured for his constant love,
Fond worldly wretch, who dost not understand
In death that true hearts cannot parted be.
First, know thy daughter is quite borne away
On wings of angels through the liquid air
To far out of thy reach, and never more
Shalt thou behold her face. But she and I
Will in another world enjoy our loves,
Where neither father's anger, poverty,
Nor any cross that troubles earthly men
Shall make us sever our united hearts.
And never shalt thou sit or be alone
In any place, but I will visit thee
With ghastly looks, and put into thy mind
The great offenses which thou didst to me.
When thou art at thy table with thy friends,
Merry in heart and filled with swelling wine,
I'll come in midst of all thy pride and mirth,
Invisible to all men but thyself,
And whisper such a sad tale in thine ear
Shall make thee let the cup fall from thy hand,
And stand as mute and pale as Death itself.
Merchant. Forgive me, Jasper. Oh, what might I do,
Tell me, to satisfy thy troubled ghost?
Jasper. There is no means; too late thou thinkst of this.
Merchant. But tell me what were best for me to do?
Jasper. Repent thy deed, and satisfy my father,

47 ***butter*** (was thought to take on medicinal properties in May)
48 ***Venus and phlebotomy*** (sexual intercourse and bloodletting were both thought to weaken the body)
49 ***cast . . . bellies*** spawn
50 ***snails . . . shellies*** crawling on the hearth, snails were said to leave the initials of the lover's name in the ashes; ***erst*** formerly
53 ***rascal*** the young or inferior deer in the herd; ***pricket*** two-year-old buck
56 ***velvet heads*** (perhaps alluding to new, velvety horns of the new cuckold)
57–8 ***bells . . . garters*** part of the Morris dancers' dress
60 ***Hogsdon*** district N of London; ***Newington*** suburb S of Southwark and London
62 ***thrumming . . . caps*** decorating caps with tassels; i.e., wasting time; ***custom*** wenching
64 ***tabor*** small drum

Act V

3–5 **capon . . . rosemary** traditional wedding meal (rosemary symbolizes remembrance)
6 s.d. ***mealed*** whitened with flour
6 **pains** preparations (for the wedding)
12 **liquid** clear
17 **cross** difficulty
21–9 **With . . . itself** (parodies *Macbeth* III.iv)
35 **satisfy** compensate

And beat fond Humphrey out of thy doors.

Exit Jasper.

Enter Humphrey.

Wife. Look, George, his very ghost would have folks beaten.

Humphrey. Father, my bride is gone, fair Mistress Luce.
My soul's the fount of vengeance, mischief's sluice.

Merchant. Hence, fool, out of my sight with thy fond passion! Thou hast undone me.

[*Beats him.*]

Humphrey. Hold, my father dear,
For Luce thy daughter's sake, that had no peer.

Merchant. Thy father, fool? There's some blows more, begone!
Jasper, I hope thy ghost be well appeased
To see thy will performed. Now will I go
To satisfy thy father for thy wrongs.

Exit.

Humphrey. What shall I do? I have been beaten twice,
And Mistress Luce is gone. Help me, device!
Since my true love is gone, I never more,
Whilst I do live, upon the sky will pore;
But in the dark will wear out my shoe-soles
In passion in Saint Faith's Church under Paul's.

Exit.

Wife. George, call Rafe hither; if you love me, call Rafe hither.
I have the bravest thing for him to do, George; prithee, call him quickly.

Citizen. Rafe, why Rafe, boy!

Enter Rafe.

Rafe. Here, sir.

Citizen. Come hither, Rafe; come to thy mistress, boy.

Wife. Rafe, I would have thee call all the youths together in battle-ray, with drums and guns and flags, and march to Mile End in pompous fashion, and there exhort your soldiers to be merry and wise, and to keep their beards from burning, Rafe; and then skirmish, and let your flags fly, and cry, "Kill, kill, kill." My husband shall lend you his jerkin, Rafe, and there's a scarf. For the rest, the house shall furnish you, and we'll pay for't. Do it bravely, Rafe, and think before whom you perform, and what person you represent.

Rafe. I warrant you, mistress, if I do it not for the honor of the city and the credit of my master, let me never hope for freedom.

Wife. 'Tis well spoken, i'faith. Go thy ways; thou art a spark indeed.

Citizen. Rafe, Rafe, double your files bravely, Rafe.

Rafe. I warrant you, sir.

Exit Rafe.

Citizen. Let him look narrowly to his service. I shall take him else. I was there myself a pikeman once in the hottest of the day, wench; had my feather shot sheer away, the fringe of my pike burned off with powder, my pate broken with a scouring-stick, and yet I thank God I am here.

Drum within.

Wife. Hark, George, the drums.

Citizen. Ran, tan, tan, tan; ran, tan. Oh, wench, an thou hadst but seen little Ned of Aldgate, Drum Ned, how he made it roar again, and laid on like a tyrant, and then struck softly till the ward came up, and then thundered again, and together we go. "Sa, sa, sa, bounce," quoth the guns. "Courage, my hearts," quoth the captains. "Saint George," quoth the pikemen; and withal here they lay, and there they lay; and yet for all this, I am here, wench.

Wife. Be thankful for it, George, for indeed 'tis wonderful.

Enter Rafe *and his company, with drums and colors.*

Rafe. March fair, my hearts. Lieutenant, beat the rear up. Ancient, let your colors fly; but have a great care of the butchers' hook at Whitechapel; they have been the death of many a fair

40 **fount** source; **mischief's sluice** may pun on (1) mischief's loose; (2) mischief's Luce; *sluice* gate holding back the power of water (i.e., of vengeance)
42 **passion** grief
49 **device** contrivance
53 **Saint . . . Paul's** parish church in the crypt of St. Paul's under the choir of the cathedral (gallants would parade in the aisles overhead)
55 **bravest** most splendid
62 **pompous** ceremonial
64–5 **keep . . . burning** (a real danger of fire because of the mechanism that exploded the charge)
67 **jerkin** close-fitting jacket or short coat
68 **house** theater
74 **freedom** rank of freeman in the Grocers' Company
77 **double . . . files** combine your two ranks
79 **narrowly** closely; precisely; **service** maneuvers
80 **take** reprehend; **pikeman** soldier who carries a steel-headed spear on a wooden lance; with musketeers they constituted infantry forces
84 **scouring-stick** stock used to clean the barrel of a gun (with obscene pun)
90 **ward** detachment of militia
98–9 **beat . . . up** round up with a drum-roll
99 **Ancient** ensign-bearer
100–1 **Whitechapel** parish E of Aldgate known for its butcher shops

ancient. Open your files that I may take a view both of your persons and munition. Sergeant, call a muster.

Sergeant. A stand! William Hammerton, pewterer!

Hammerton. Here, Captain.

Rafe. A corslet and a Spanish pike; 'tis well. Can you shake it with a terror?

Hammerton. I hope so, Captain.

Rafe. Charge upon me! [*He charges at Rafe.*] 'Tis with the weakest. Put more strength, William Hammerton, more strength! As you were again. Proceed, Sergeant.

Sergeant. George Greengoose, poulterer!

Greengoose. Here.

Rafe. Let me see your piece, neighbor Greengoose. When was she shot in?

Greengoose. An't like you, Master Captain, I made a shot even now, partly to scour her, and partly for audacity.

Rafe. It should seem so certainly, for her breath is yet inflamed. Besides, there is a main fault in the touch-hole; it runs and stinketh; and I tell you, moreover, and believe it, ten such touch-holes would breed the pox in the army. Get you a feather, neighbor; get you a feather, sweet oil, and paper, and your piece may do well enough yet. Where's your powder?

Greengoose. Here.

Rafe. What, in a paper? As I am a soldier and a gentleman, it craves a martial court. You ought to die for't. Where's your horn? Answer me to that.

Greengoose. An't like you, sir, I was oblivious.

Rafe. It likes me not you should be so. 'Tis a shame for you and a scandal to all our neighbors, being a man of worth and estimation, to leave your horn behind you; I am afraid 'twill breed example. But let me tell you no more on't. Stand, till I view you all. What's become o'th'nose of your flask?

1 Soldier. Indeed, la, Captain, 'twas blown away with powder.

Rafe. Put on a new one at the city's charge. Where's the stone of this piece?

2 Soldier. The drummer took it out to light tobacco.

Rafe. 'Tis a fault, my friend; put it in again. You want a nose, and you a stone. Sergeant, take a note on't, for I mean to stop it in the pay. Remove and march. Soft and fair, gentlemen, soft and fair! Double your files! As you were! Faces about. Now, you with the sodden face, keep in there. Look to your match, sirrah, it will be in your fellow's flask anon. So, make a crescent now; advance your pikes; stand, and give ear! Gentlemen, countrymen, friends, and my fellow-soldiers, I have brought you this day from the shops of security and the counters of content to measure out in these furious fields honor by the ell, and prowess by the pound. Let it not, Oh, let it not, I say, be told hereafter the noble issue of this city fainted, but bear yourselves in this fair action like men, valiant men and freemen. Fear not the face of the enemy, nor the noise of the guns. For believe me, brethren, the rude rumbling of a brewer's car is far more terrible, of which you have a daily experience. Neither let the stink of powder offend you, since a more valiant stink is nightly with you. To a resolved mind his home is everywhere. I speak not this to take away the hope of your return; for you shall see, I do not doubt it, and that very shortly, your loving wives again, and your sweet children, whose care doth bear you company in baskets. Remember, then, whose cause you have in hand and, like a sort of true-born scavengers, scour me this famous realm of enemies. I have no more to say but this: stand to your tacklings, lads, and show to the world you can as

---

104 muster roll
105 A stand! "Attention!"
107 corslet armor covering the body; **Spanish pike** (probably superior to the English)
108 shake it (with obscene pun)
110 Charge (with obscene pun)
116 piece firearm (and obscene pun)
123 touch-hole (1) a small hole in the breech of a firearm through which the charge is ignited; (2) bawdy anatomical reference
125 pox syphilis
126–7 feather . . . paper (used to keep the gun clean)
132 horn (1) powder horn, to hold powder; (2) cuckold's horns
134 oblivious forgetful
135 It . . . me I prefer
141 nose (cf. III.415 s.d.)
145 stone (1) flint; (2) testicles
149 want lack
153 sodden (1) drunken; (2) stewed from the sweating-tub used for syphilis
154 match match-lock on the muskets
156 crescent common military formation; **advance . . . pikes** training maneuver in which the pike was shifted from the "trail" position to the hip
157 Gentlemen (the following lines parody *Richard III* V.iii.313ff)
161 ell a measurement of 45 inches
170 valiant stink (another allusion to syphilis)
176 baskets (or provisions)
178 sort company
180–1 tacklings weapons

well brandish a sword as shake an apron. Saint George, and on, my hearts!

Omnes. Saint George, Saint George!

Exeunt.

Wife. 'Twas well done, Rafe. I'll send thee a cold capon a-field, and a bottle of March beer; and it may be, come myself to see thee.

Citizen. Nell, the boy has deceived me much; I did not think it had been in him. He has performed such a matter, wench, that if I live, next year I'll have him captain of the galley-foist, or I'll want my will.

Enter Old Merrythought.

Old Merrythought. Yet, I thank God, I break not a wrinkle more than I had. Not a stoup, boys? Care, live with cats; I defy thee. My heart is as sound as an oak; and though I want drink to wet my whistle, I can sing:

Come no more there, boys, come no more there;
For we shall never whilst we live come any more there.

Enter a Boy [*and* Coffin-carriers] *with a coffin.*

Boy. God save you, sir.

Old Merrythought. It's a brave boy. Canst thou sing?

Boy. Yes, sir, I can sing, but 'tis not so necessary at this time.

Old Merrythought. [*Sings.*]
Sing we and chant it,
Whilst love doth grant it.

Boy. Sir, sir, if you knew what I have brought you, you would have little list to sing.

Old Merrythought. [*Sings.*]
Oh, the minion round,
Full long I have thee sought,
And now I have thee found,
And what hast thou here brought?

Boy. A coffin, sir, and your dead son Jasper in it.

Old Merrythought. Dead? [*Sings.*]
Why, farewell he.
Thou wast a bonny boy,
And I did love thee.

Enter Jasper.

Jasper. Then, I pray you, sir, do so still.

Old Merrythought. Jasper's ghost? [*Sings.*]
Thou art welcome from Stygian lake so soon;
Declare to me what wondrous things in Pluto's court are done.

Jasper. By my troth, sir, I ne'er came there; 'tis too hot for me, sir.

Old Merrythought. A merry ghost, a very merry ghost. [*Sings.*]
And where is your true love? Oh, where is yours?

Jasper. Marry, look you, sir.
Heaves up the coffin [*and* Luce, *up-ended, scrambles out*].

Old Merrythought. Ah, ha! Art thou good at that, i'faith? [*Sings.*]
With hey, trixy, terlery-whiskin,
The world it runs on wheels.
When the young man's———,
Up goes the maiden's heels.

Mistress Merrythought *and* Michael *within.*

Mrs Merrythought. What, Master Merrythought, will you not let's in? What do you think shall become of us?

Old Merrythought. What voice is that that calleth at our door?

Mrs Merrythought. [*Within.*] You know me well enough. I am sure I have not been such a stranger to you.

Old Merrythought. [*Sings.*]
And some they whistled, and some they sung,
Hey, down, down!
And some did loudly say,
Ever as the Lord Barnet's horn blew,
Away, Musgrave, away!

Mrs Merrythought. [*Within.*] You will not have us starve here, will you, Master Merrythought?

Jasper. Nay, good sir, be persuaded; she is my mother.
If her offenses have been great against you,
Let your own love remember she is yours,
And so forgive her.

Luce. Good Master Merrythought,
Let me entreat you; I will not be denied.

---

186 March beer early beer known for its strength
191–2 galley-foist Lord Mayor's state barge
193 break show
194 stoup drinking vessel holding two quarts
195 Care . . . cats "Care will kill a cat" (proverbial)
204 Sing . . . it from Thomas Morley's *Ballets to Five Voices* (1595; 1600)
208 minion saucy wench
218 Stygian lake the river Styx in the underworld (Hades)
220 Pluto King of Hades
230 world . . . wheels (proverbial)
231 ——— frisking (perhaps omitted from the printed text because of the new statute on swearing and obscenity; perhaps a parody of that)
241–5 And . . . away! from the ballad of Little Musgrave and Lady Barnard
250 own love self-love

Mrs Merrythought. [*Within.*] Why, Master Merrythought, will you be a vexed thing still?

Old Merrythought. Woman, I take you to my love again, but you shall sing before you enter; therefore, dispatch your song and so come in.

Mrs Merrythought. [*Within.*] Well, you must have your will, when all's done. Mick, what song canst thou sing, boy?

Michael. [*Within.*] I can sing none, forsooth, but "A Lady's Daughter of Paris" properly.

Mrs Merrythought. [*and Michael.*] [*Within.*]

Song

It was a lady's daughter, &c.

[Old Merrythought *admits* Mistress Merrythought *and* Michael.]

Old Merrythought. Come, you're welcome home again. [*Sings.*]
If such danger be in playing,
And jest must to earnest turn,
You shall go no more a-maying.

Merchant. [*Within.*] Are you within, sir? Master Merrythought!

Jasper. It is my master's voice. Good sir, go hold him in talk, whilst we convey ourselves into some inward room.

[*Exit with* Luce.]

Old Merrythought. What are you? Are you merry?
You must be very merry if you enter.

Merchant. [*Within.*] I am, sir.

Old Merrythought. Sing, then.

Merchant. [*Within.*] Nay, good sir, open to me.

Old Merrythought. Sing, I say, or, by the merry heart, you come not in.

Merchant. [*Within.*] Well, sir, I'll sing:
Fortune my foe, &c.

[Old Merrythought *admits* Merchant.]

Old Merrythought. You are welcome, sir; you are welcome.
You see your entertainment. Pray you, be merry.

Merchant. Oh, Master Merrythought, I am come to ask you
Forgiveness for the wrongs I offered you
And your most virtuous son. They're infinite;
Yet my contrition shall be more than they.
I do confess my hardness broke his heart,
For which just heaven hath given me punishment
More than my age can carry. His wand'ring spirit,
Not yet at rest, pursues me everywhere,
Crying, "I'll haunt thee for thy cruelty."
My daughter, she is gone, I know not how,
Taken invisible, and whether living
Or in grave, 'tis yet uncertain to me.
O Master Merrythought, these are the weights
Will sink me to my grave. Forgive me, sir.

Old Merrythought. Why, sir, I do forgive you, and be merry;
And if the wag in's lifetime played the knave,
Can you forgive him too?

Merchant. With all my heart, sir.

Old Merrythought. Speak it again, and heartily.

Merchant. I do, sir.
Now, by my soul, I do.

Old Merrythought. [*Sings.*]
With that came out his paramour.
She was as white as the lily flower.
Hey troll, trollie, lollie.

Enter Luce *and* Jasper.

With that came out her own dear knight.
He was as true as ever did fight. &c.
Sir, if you will forgive 'em, clap their hands together.
There's no more to be said i'th' matter.

Merchant. I do, I do.

Citizen. I do not like this. Peace, boys; hear me, one of you! Everybody's part is come to an end but Rafe's and he's left out.

Boy. 'Tis long of yourself, sir; we have nothing to do with his part.

---

254 vexed cantankerous

263 It...&c. From a broadside ballad that begins:

It was a lady's daughter,
Of Paris properly,
Her mother her commanded
To mass that she should hie:
Oh, pardon me, dear mother,
Her daughter dear did say,
Unto that filthy idol
I never can obey.

265–7 If...a-maying the refrain of "My Love Hath Vowed" in Philip Rosseter's *Book of Airs* (1601)

265 playing flirtation

281 Fortune...&c. One of the period's most popular songs. The first stanza is this:

Fortune, my foe, why dost thou frown on me?
And will thy favors never better be?
Wilt thou, I say, forever breed my pain?
And wilt thou not restore my joys again?

299 wag mischievous boy

308 clap...together as sign of betrothal

314 long on account

Citizen. Rafe, come away. Make an end on him as you have done of the rest, boys; come.

Wife. Now, good husband, let him come out and die.

Citizen. He shall, Nell. Rafe, come away quickly and die, boy.

Boy. 'Twill be very unfit he should die, sir, upon no occasion, and in a comedy too.

Citizen. Take you no care of that, sir boy. Is not his part at an end, think you, when he's dead? Come away, Rafe.

Enter Rafe, *with a forked arrow through his head.*

Rafe. When I was mortal, this my costive corpse
Did lap up figs and raisins in the Strand,
Where sitting, I espied a lovely dame,
Whose master wrought with lingel and with awl,
And under ground he vampied many a boot.
Straight did her love prick forth me, tender sprig,
To follow feats of arms in warlike wise,
Through Waltham Desert, where I did perform
Many achievements, and did lay on ground
Huge Barbaroso, that insulting giant,
And all his captives soon set at liberty.
Then honor pricked me from my native soil
Into Moldavia, where I gained the love
Of Pompiona, his beloved daughter,
But yet proved constant to the black-thumbed maid,
Susan, and scorned Pompiona's love.
Yet liberal I was, and gave her pins,
And money for her father's officers.
I then returnèd home, and thrust myself
In action, and by all men chosen was
Lord of the May, where I did flourish it,
With scarfs and rings, and posy in my hand.
After this action, I preferrèd was
And chosen city captain at Mile End,
With hat and feather, and with leading-staff,
And trained my men, and brought them all off clear
Save one man that berayed him with the noise.
But all these things I, Rafe, did undertake
Only for my beloved Susan's sake.
Then coming home, and sitting in my shop
With apron blue, Death came unto my stall
To cheapen *aqua vitae*; but ere I
Could take the bottle down and fill a taste,
Death caught a pound of pepper in his hand
And sprinkled all my face and body o'er,
And in an instant vanishèd away.

Citizen. 'Tis a pretty fiction, i'faith.

Rafe. Then took I up my bow and shaft in hand,
And walked into Moorfields to cool myself;
But there grim cruel Death met me again,
And shot this forkèd arrow through my head,
And now I faint. Therefore be warned by me,
My fellows every one, of forkèd heads.
Farewell, all you good boys in merry London;
Ne'er shall we more upon Shrove Tuesday meet
And pluck down houses of iniquity.
My pain increaseth. I shall never more
Hold open, whilst another pumps both legs,
Nor daub a satin gown with rotten eggs;
Set up a stake, oh, never more I shall.
I die; fly, fly, my soul, to Grocers' Hall.
Oh, oh, oh, *&c.*

Wife. Well said, Rafe. Do your obeisance to the gentlemen and go your ways. Well said, Rafe.

Exit Rafe.

Old Merrythought. Methinks all we, thus kindly and unexpectedly reconciled, should not depart without a song.

Merchant. A good motion.

Old Merrythought. Strike up, then.

Song.

Better music ne'er was known
Than a choir of hearts in one.
Let each other that hath been

---

326 s.d. *forked* barbed (cf. Clifford with an arrow in his neck in *The True Tragedy of Richard Duke of York* [1595])
327–62 When . . . away (parodies ghost scenes in *The Spanish Tragedy*, *Richard III*, *Eastward Ho!*, and elsewhere)
327 costive reluctant (plays on constipated)
328 figs and raisins (as laxatives)
330 lingel waxed or rosined thread used by shoemakers
331 vampied renewed the upper parts of
332 prick (1) spur; (2) obscene pun
336 insulting bragging
340 his the King's (as metonym for the country)
348 posy bouquet
349 preferrèd promoted
350 city captain i.e., of the trained bands
351 leading-staff officer's baton (with obscene pun)
353 berayed befouled
358 cheapen bargain for
365 Moorfields summer resort neighboring Finsbury Fields N of London between Bishopsgate and Cripplegate
369 forkèd heads cuckolds
371–2 Shrove . . . iniquity Shrove Tuesday (the last day before Lent and a traditional day for confession) was also a time of revelry for apprentices, who sometimes attacked playhouses and brothels
375 satin gown dress of gallants as dandies
376 Set . . . stake (1) for a sport where cockerels were tied to a stake as targets; (2) obscene pun
382 depart i.e., leave one another

Troubled with the gall or spleen,
Learn of us to keep his brow
Smooth and plain as ours are now.
Sing, though before the hour of dying;
He shall rise, and then be crying,
"Hey, ho, 'tis nought but mirth
That keeps the body from the earth."

Exeunt omnes.

EPILOGUE

Citizen. Come, Nell, shall we go? The play's done.

Wife. Nay, by my faith, George, I have more manners than so; I'll speak to these gentlemen first. I thank you all, gentlemen, for your patience and countenance to Rafe, a poor fatherless child; and if I might see you at my house, it should go hard but I would have a pottle of wine and a pipe of tobacco for you; for truly I hope you do like the youth, but I would be glad to know the truth. I refer it to your own discretions whether you will applaud him or no; for I will wink, and whilst you shall do what you will. I thank you with all my heart. God give you good night. Come, George.

[*Exeunt.*]

FINIS.

Epilogue

8 pottle measure of two quarts; **tobacco** (but cf. I.213–18)

12 wink close my eyes; look aside; **whilst** meanwhile

A Chaste Maid in Cheapside

Thomas Middleton

A CHAST MAYD IN CHEAPE SIDE.

A Pleaſant conceited Comedy neuer before printed.

As it hath beene often acted at the Swan on the Banke-ſide, by the Lady ELIZABETH her *Seruants.*

By THOMAS MIDELTON Gent.

LONDON,
Printed for *Francis Conſtable* dwelling at the ſigne of the *Crane* in *Pauls* Church-yard.
1630.

Frontispiece, 1630.

"Our scene is London," Ben Jonson writes in the Prologue to *The Alchemist* (1612),

> 'cause we would make known
> No country's mirth is better than our own.
> No clime breeds better matter, for your whore,
> Bawd, squire, imposter, many persons more,
> Whose manners, now called humors, feed the stage
> And which have still been subject for the rage
> Or spleen of comic writers,

concluding, "The vices that she breeds, above their cure." A year later, with *A Chaste Maid in Cheapside*, Thomas Middleton provided, in his most accomplished city comedy, the same troubled perspective on the vitality and venality of a city that had grown too fast to keep morality and discipline firmly in check. London had housed 20,000 under Henry VIII; it now housed 200,000 and was still growing. The warm geniality of Thomas Dekker's London, even the exuberant inquiries of Francis Beaumont, give way in Middleton as in Jonson to a complexity that invites drama but defies easy comprehension.

In fact, it can be argued that London is the chief character as well as the setting of *Chaste Maid*: most of the action centers in Cheapside, the wide street that remained the old market of the city, stretching from St. Paul's churchyard to the Poultry, from the meat markets at Smithfield to the Little Pissing Conduit. Along the way side streets were named for the trades – Bread Street; Milk Street; Goldsmiths Row. But contemporary maps show us that even this is too neat. St. Paul's stood between Newgate prison and Blackfriars Theater and not far from Bridewell; the Poultry was surrounded by the Counter (also a jail), the stock market, and the Royal Exchange. Even Goldsmiths Row, where the Yellowhammers have their shop and residence, is between St. Paul's School, where young Tim Yellowhammer first learned Latin, and Goose Lane, which would more accurately measure his accomplishments (since "goose" was the cant term for fool). For the unofficial city historian and recorder John Stow, Goldsmiths Row held ineluctable joy: there he found "the most beautiful frame of fair houses and shops that be within the walls of London, or elsewhere in England .... It containeth in number ten fair dwelling-houses and fourteen shops, all in one frame, uniformly built four storys high," adding that Cheapside "is worthily called, the Beauty of London." It is also highly emblematic, as Middleton unfailingly points out, since the pleasures of living were the pleasures of getting, both in the bedchambers and in the shops; equally emblematic is the fact that both the Allwits and the Touchwoods convert their households into business partnerships and their families into thriving enterprises – it is often difficult to tell, in this play, where family life shades off into commercial venture. The world of Cheapside is clearly one in which the characters seem to know the price of everything but the value of nothing: when Tim finds his sister Moll has escaped close confinement, he calls out,

> Thieves, thieves! My sister's stol'n!
> Some thief hath got her.
> Oh, how miraculously did my father's plate 'scape!
> 'Twas all left out, tutor.

Tim's attitude towards his sister and towards the family's silver plate is indistinguishable. Both are commercial: investments, property, goods to be owned or traded. In Cheapside, everything (and everyone) is potentially marketable, even (perhaps especially) chastity, so that the title of Middleton's play is oxymoronic. It is highly unlikely, from the perspective of every Yellowhammer but Moll (whose name means prostitute), that chastity, despite its high value, could still be found there. On the other hand, as the center of city life, Cheapside was the broad thoroughfare down which whores were publicly punished and humiliated, either displayed in an open cart or, following it, being whipped as they walked. Thus the title's bitter pun: the "chased" maids of Cheapside were no maids (virgins) at all. It is just this hard-headed, open-eyed view of London life that lies at the heart of Middleton's comedy. The brilliant cameo scene of the Promoters, or informers, ripples out to the play as a whole – their "pricking up their ears, And snuffing up their noses, like rich men's dogs When the first course goes in" is also Middleton's technique. Only his attitude is more dispassionate as this anatomy of London life transforms a kind of investigative journalism into high but hyperbolic art.

At least five plots compete for attention in *Chaste Maid* involving the Yellowhammers, the Allwits, the Kixes, the Touchwoods, and Sir Walter Whorehound, and the network of confusion they engender reflects the broader confusion of Jacobean city life. The explosive London population was varied and unsettled: members of the older aristocracy jostled alongside the new money of merchants and tradesmen and the poverty of vagrants and beggars as well as sporadic groups of demobilized soldiers and sailors. A city government controlled by the guilds tried to establish order and preserve peace, but it was susceptible to the older traditions embedded in the rules and regulations coming from the royal government seated in neighboring Westminster. Social ranks were also breaking down. The landed aristocracy and inherited wealth in many cases suffered from reduced holdings (like the Touchwoods) at the same time James I readily sold new knighthoods and honors, lending uncertainty to the titles themselves. Thus Sir Walter Whorehound insists on landholdings in Wales to support his entitlement; and Sir Oliver Kix and his wife worry about his impotency and ability to maintain their family line. Indeed, their unspoken contest for having families has high stakes: if the Kixes don't conceive, Sir Walter will inherit a fortune. The very economic foundation of this play, then, is problematic for us: should the Kixes, who seem deserving enough, be disinherited because of Sir Oliver's physical shortcoming? And should Sir Walter – a lecher who has no lands at all and lives on borrowed money – be allowed to take their inheritance? How are we to judge such a social system and the economics in which it is so firmly rooted?

The rising number of ambitious merchants and tradesmen can easily answer this, so attracted are they by Sir Walter's title and money. Yellowhammer, for instance, the successful goldsmith, is willing to purchase Sir Walter as a son-in-law with a £2,000 dowry and his daughter Moll; as for his son Tim, "the Cambridge boy" with the silver spoon, he is a suitable match for Sir Walter's "landed niece brought out of Wales," and, moreover, "'Tis a match of Sir Walter's own making To bind us to him, and our heirs forever." As parents, they will hear of nothing else. "You fit for a knight's bed!" Maudline Yellowhammer tells her daughter, bullying her for being "Drowsy-browed, dull-eyed, drossy-spirited" because of her secret and preferred courtship with Touchwood Jr.; when Moll tries to elope, Mistress Yellowhammer chases her in a smelt boat. "I'll tug thee home by the hair," she tells her daughter; "You are a cruel mother," comment the watermen. Nor is Yellowhammer himself any more sympathetic. When told that Sir Walter is "an arrant whoremaster," the father, granting "his deeds are black," replies,

> The knight is rich; he shall be my son-in-law.
> No matter, so the whore he keeps be wholesome.
> My daughter takes no hurt then, so let them wed;
> I'll have him sweat well [in case of syphilis] e'er they go to bed.

Nor does Tim fare any better. Maudline bullies him too, even before his tutor, speaking of her son's early foolishness, and before her fellow gossips at the christening of Mistress Allwit's new child (by Sir Walter), for he is ill-at-ease among such a horde of women and inexperienced: "This is intolerable," he tells his tutor; "This woman has a villainous sweet breath, did she not stink of comfits. Help me, sweet tutor." Even Yellowhammer, at the moment of Tim's match with Sir Walter's niece – no landed Welsh gentlewoman, but a whore who has come to London as Sir Walter's mistress – even Yellowhammer decries it as an "unfortunate marriage." It is easy to judge such behavior from our perspective, but Middleton will not give us such luxury. From the perspective of the London of *Chaste Maid*, what opportunities are there for Moll and Tim – and what alternatives are open to their parents?

Against such gross misconduct, the Yellowhammers' competitor is the willing cuckold Allwit, who is supported by Sir Walter's money (so long as only Sir Walter sleeps with his wife) and does not wish – cannot afford, it might seem – to lose it. To Yellowhammer, Allwit presents himself as a tradesman, living much as they do, thriving as they thrive, "butchers by selling flesh, Poulters by venting conies." In the London he knows, this is true enough: the city breeds just such venality. As Yellowhammer would sell his daughter, Allwit has sold his wife. He has learned to live with such economic conditions, in fact, with what might at first seem to us a charming insouciance.

> I see these things, but like a happy man,
> I pay for none at all, yet fools think's mine;
> I have the name, and in his gold I shine;
> And where some merchants would in soul kiss Hell
> To buy a paradise for their wives, and dye
> Their conscience in the bloods of prodigal heirs
> To deck their night-piece, yet all this being done,
> Eaten with jealousy to the inmost bone...
> These torments stand I freed of, I am as clear
> From jealousy of a wife as from the charge.

Indeed, he has turned economic and social corruption not only to his advantage, but in his good nature to a kind of religious significance – "two miraculous blessings" by which his wife is physically satisfied and he is economically fulfilled without economic cost or worry. But his easy confession is belied by the refrain: "*La dildo, dildo, la dildo*," and by the very shabbiness of his life that forces us to measure his personal compromise against Yellowhammer's. This ability to judge them may become more difficult, rather than less so, when the two men finally confront each other in Act IV. For Allwit has *become* a Yellowhammer by disguising himself as a lost cousin, while in excusing Sir Walter and consenting to an actual whorehound as son-in-law, the goldsmith becomes a complacent wittol like Allwit. It is in fact Sir Walter who, in judging Allwit, may be judging Yellowhammer just as incisively:

> When man turns base, out goes his soul's pure flame;
> The fat of ease o'erthrows the eyes of shame.

Yet Sir Walter's condemnation may only be bravado. For Sir Walter is not at all sure of Mistress Allwit – "What entertainment has lain open here? No strangers in my absence?" – nor is he even sure of Allwit himself: "Yet, by your leave, I heard you were once off'ring to go to bed to her," possibly making her pregnant and so, at least for a time, frustrating Sir Walter's liaison. In a world of such uncertainty – Sir Walter's own uneasiness in courting Moll, for instance – the economic, social, and moral slippage can, it would seem, unmoor anybody. Is it possible that Yellowhammer, Allwit, and Sir Walter are not so much the determinants as the victims of the world of Cheapside?

To shore up London life, as well as English life generally, the state with and through the church attempted to resurrect the family as a stable unit. Thus Thomas Becon writes that

> Matrimony is a high, holy, and blessed order of life... wherein one man and one woman are coupled and knit together in one flesh and body in the fear and love of God, and by the free, loving, hearty, and good consent of them both to the intent that they two may dwell together, as one flesh and body of one will and mind in all honesty, virtue and godliness, and spend their lives in the equal partaking of all such things.

Quite possibly, yet as Middleton was writing *Chaste Maid*, certain events intruded into London life. There was, for instance, the recent birthing of the Countess of Salisbury reported by John Chamberlain on February 4, 1613, which makes the "little countess" born to the Allwits and their christening ceremony look tame: "About this day... the Countess of Salisbury was brought abed of a daughter, and lies in very richly, for the hangings of her chamber, being white satin, embroidered with gold (or silver) pearl is valued at fourteen thousand pounds." Then there was the Essex affair. By early 1613 it was common talk that the Countess of Essex wanted a divorce – perhaps because in the royal favorite Carr she had taken a new lover – but what would resonate among the playgoers at the Swan was that both Essexes, like the Kixes, accused each other of impotency. Even Maudline Yellowhammer's treatment of Tim has its analogue; in a letter of February 12, 1612, Chamberlain reports of "a son of the bishop of Bristol his eldest, of 19 or 20 years killed himself, with a knife to avoid the disgrace of breeching, which his mother or mother-in-law (I know not whether) would needs have put him to for losing his money at tennis." In such an environment, there would be little surprise in Yellowhammer's wife calling Moll "a plumber's daughter," or in Tim whimpering over a treat of six sugarplums, or even, perhaps, at Allwit taking credit for his wife's newborn child while inviting the father to attend as godparent, or Whorehound, when presented his own sons Wat and Nick, who are noticeably frightened of him, cursing them as bastards. Put against such situations, Touchwood Senior's concern for the support of his ever-growing family may seem touching. "Some only can get riches and no children," he says, bringing the Kixes to mind; "We only can get children and no riches!" Consequently, he tells his wife, "we must give way to need And live awhile asunder. Our desires Are both too fruitful for our barren fortunes." Family life in *Chaste Maid*, even at its most disarming, appears dysfunctional.

What Middleton persistently interrogates in this play, however, is whether given the economic pressures and social uncertainty of London life, the very institution of marriage will in time corrupt the partners or the partners bring corruption to the marriage. The affable Touchwood Sr., alone on stage, confesses that "I must forth with't, chiefly for country wenches, For every harvest I shall hinder hay-making. I had no less than seven lay-in last progress." Mistress Yellowhammer tells Moll of her indiscretions and at Moll's age: "When I was of your youth, I was lightsome, and quick, two years before I was married"; later, she will seduce Tim's tutor. Yellowhammer tells the disguised Allwit, "I have kept a whore myself, and had a bastard, By Mistress Anne." Even the Country Wench who brings her newborn to Touchwood Sr., claiming to have been a virgin when she met him, remarks later that the bastard is her fifth child. All the other babies in the play, in fact, the putative heirs of the next generation – the Country Wench's, Mistress Allwit's, Lady Kix's – are bastards; even the Promoter's whore is pregnant. There is plenty of new life in *Chaste Maid* – yet all of it (without exception) undermines patrilineal descent, which was the very backbone of early modern English culture. There is a way in which every comic moment is, therefore, a chilling challenge to the society it gives birth to on stage.

That such destructive possibilities for the self and society result from unbridled appetites is reinforced by setting the play in Lent. This liturgical season emphasized limitation and even deprivation, and put a strong limit on the use of meat with regulations that combined the church's interest in preparing souls for the glory of Easter and the economic needs of the fishing industry.

A proclamation in January 1608 permitted only eight butchers in Eastcheap, four in St. Nicholas Shambles and ten in the London suburbs; the number was lowered in 1610 and restrictions were further tightened in 1612. As for 1613, John Stow notes that

> The last summer through want of rain, both grain and hay waxed very scant in most shires of this kingdom, so as such persons as had not extraordinary means of provision of winters food for their cattle were extremely dismayed and perplexed, lest the ensuing winter should prove hard like as did this summer.... Also the King in his prudent care for the better prevention of the great feared famine... to command his subjects in general that all the time of Lent should utterly abstain from eating all manner of butchers' flesh, and that no butcher should be suffered to kill flesh within London nor near the city, as had been used in many late years (which restraint... had not been in the memory of man)... by this means all sorts of cattle were preserved and increased, and at Easter all manner of flesh very plenteous.... The Lords of the Privy Council incessantly sent word to the Lord Mayor and sheriffs to look and search diligently that no flesh should be killed or sold within London and their liberties: in which service they used all diligence and strictness, committing the offenders to the jail, and gave their meat to prisoners.

Continuing "abuse and contempt" of such orders of the Privy Council caused the Council to write the Lord Mayor on February 13, "to resolve now absolutely to prohibit the killing and uttering of flesh by any butcher or other person in the city of London or in any other parts of the kingdom during Lent," and to issue a warrant to "messengers of His Majesty's Chamber" on November 16 to "make diligent search and inquiry ... for all such butchers and graziers [who grazed or fed cattle for the market] as kill or sell flesh... and to bring them and every of them forthwith and in your company before us, to answer their contempts." The corrupt Promoters of *Chaste Maid*, then, taking bribes and left with babies, are nevertheless grim reminders of national rule and the state of the economy – as well as the religious significance of Lent. In light of such scarcity and sacrifice, Middleton provides a play which deals with a bastard as "this half yard of flesh" and with cuckoldry as the selling of meat. The play's two great set pieces at dead center, the Promoters and the christening, are focused on the withholding and dispensing of meat and drink. Men and women, in such an environment, become the new flesh for hire and sale. Sir Walter brings his "ewe-mutton to find A ram at London." Touchwood Sr. keeps a few gulls "in pickle" to take chewed country "mutton" off his plate; Tim delights in his new "Welsh mutton" and the Promoters "lard their whores with lamb-stones." Perhaps most perversely in the world of the play as one vast meat market, the Country Wench passes her bastard child off as a joint of lamb in the season celebrating the loss of the Lamb of God. Fish are also at issue; when Mistress Yellowhammer goes "a-fishing" for Moll, Tim describes her catch as a "mermaid": "she's but half my sister now, as far as the flesh goes; the rest may be sold to fishwives." It is, at the least, a grotesque image, but so are moments when in the play Lent seems to promote renewed breeding: not only does Sir Walter bring the Welsh Gentlewoman to London, but Mistress Allwit gives birth, grunting and wallowing like a sow, and the Promoter's bawds are described as witch cows.

Events in *A Chaste Maid* are, in fact, measured by the entire liturgical season of the national church and its Protestant offshoots: baptism, penance, the passion, and the resurrection, at moments which may give renewed life or a kind of parodic death knell to another tradition meant to supply order and morality. As Puritan women gather for the Allwit christening, we learn that the baptism was performed "Without idolatry or superstition" but instead "After the pure manner of Amsterdam," which the Jacobean church was trying to rein in, and to it they welcome young Tim, fresh from Puritan Cambridge, "the wellspring of discipline, that waters all the brethren" when together they echo the Yellowhammers' parson who considers all Latin "papistry." But in the celebratory feast that follows – in which the gossips eagerly gobble up phallic sweetmeats and drink too much wine before urinating and staggering off to Little Pissing Conduit – they mock and perhaps desecrate the eucharist for which Lent should prepare them. Later, the seriousness of the season returns unexpectedly with the confession of Sir Walter, seriously seeking to salvage his soul on the way to death. What at first seems like a horrible parody of the Passion soon takes on a remarkable linguistic coloring: "Thou know'st me to be wicked," he tells Allwit,

> for thy baseness
> Kept the eyes open still on all my sins;
> None knew the dear account my soul stood charged with
> So well as thou, yet like Hell's flattering angel
> Would'st never tell me on't, let'st me go on,
> And join with death in sleep. That if I had not wak'd
> Now by chance, even by a stranger's pity,
> I had everlastingly slept out all hope
> Of grace and mercy.

What are we to make of this sudden recoiling from the past and admission of mortal error? And are we to judge it differently in Sir Walter's subsequent last will and testament filled with cursing those who, he said, cursed him? Might Middleton suggest that this calling to account is meant as a call to the Allwits and, beyond them, to the Yellowhammers? Or is it Sir Walter's last great rise to cloak his disinheritance (with the announcement of Lady Kix's pregnancy) and his bankruptcy? And then, are we to judge these moments still differently once we see the Allwits reunite with the ill-gotten gains from Sir Walter to make their ambitious way out of Cheapside and on up to the Strand where, with the help of bay windows, they may open a truly fashionable brothel? The last liturgically inspired moment comes with the presumed death and the wondrous resurrection of Touchwood Jr. and Moll. Touchwood Sr.'s eulogy drives home the point: "Never could death boast of a richer prize From the first parent... The true, chaste monument of her living name, Which no time can deface," adding,

I say of her
The full truth freely, without fear of censure.
What nature could there shine, that might redeem
Perfection home to woman, but in her
Was fully glorious; beauty set in goodness
Speaks what she was, that jewel so infixed;
There was no want of anything of life
To make these virtuous precedents man and wife.

Lest we dismiss such sentiment too quickly, this solemn moment and Touchwood Sr.'s stirring speech bring the Cheapside community together as one voice at the only point in the play. When the two coffins at the double funeral open, then, so that Touchwood Jr. and Moll can turn their winding-sheets into wedding-sheets, does this confirm a trust in, or merely provide, a mockery of the Easter passion towards which all of *A Chaste Maid* seems to have been heading? Would it, at this moment, be churlish to recall that despite the chastity of these two lovers, their courtship and wedding was a product of their own deception and hypocrisy? And what of the feast to follow at Goldsmiths Hall with Yellowhammer as host – how significant is it that the play moves finally out of the church and back to the site of commerce?

But this may be only the last set of conundrums *A Chaste Maid* requires us to resolve. In Middleton's topsy-turvy world, the cuckolding father of the Allwit child attends the christening as godfather to his own baby, while the titular father wears the cuckolder's suit. Before they were cozened, the Promoters were calculating how they might dispose of the meat they have confiscated; after, they are left to determine how to nourish the live meat they have been given freely. Sir Oliver, with a child at last, invites Touchwood Sr. to join his family, and the Kixes – knights this time, and not mere tradesmen of flesh – become the new wittols. And what of them all, congregating at Moll's wedding, asked to reject the very actions which they have spent each day indulging? The marriage would not have occurred if Touchwood Sr. had not impregnated Lady Kix and so disinherited Whorehound; those acts of adultery and cuckoldry have permitted the play's only chaste union. Cuckolding Sir Oliver, in fact, allows Touchwood Sr. himself to renew living with his wife and so reestablish another chaste union. It may be that in this play's world of deception, with its parents, Promoters, Puritans, and gossips, people triumph in the end not because they are just, good, or deserving, and not just because they are lucky, but because they are clever at deception in a world which seems only to foster it. In the unexpected and unequaled chiaroscuro effect of the play's final scene, we may recall that, near the play's beginning, Tim announced that the fruits of a Cambridge education were to know how to prove a fool rational and a whore honest. By the play's end, he has enacted just that with his own marriage. *A Chaste Maid in Cheapside* interrogates its culture by interrogating its playgoers and readers: where now do we begin to probe London life and what, in the end, are we to make of it?

FURTHER READING

Altieri, Joanne, "Against Moralizing Jacobean Comedy: Middleton's *Chaste Maid*," *Criticism* 30:2 (Spring 1988): 171–87.

Chakravorty, Swapan, *Society and Politics in the Plays of Thomas Middleton*. Oxford: Clarendon Press, 1996.

Chatterji, Ruby, "Theme, Imagery, and Unity in *A Chaste Maid in Cheapside*," *Renaissance Drama* 8 (1965): 105–26.

Covatta, Anthony, *Thomas Middleton's City Comedies*. Lewisburg: Bucknell University Press, 1973.

Farr, Dorothy M., *Thomas Middleton and the Drama of Realism*. Edinburgh: Oliver and Boyd, 1973.

Gibbons, Brian, *Jacobean City Comedy*. Cambridge, Mass.: Harvard University Press, 1968.

Levin, Richard, "The Four Plots of *A Chaste Maid in Cheapside*," *Review of English Studies* n.s. 16:61 (Fall 1965): 14–24.

Wigler, Stephen, "Thomas Middleton's *A Chaste Maid in Cheapside*: The Delicious and the Disgusting," *American Imago* 33:2 (Summer 1976): 197–215.

A Chaste Maid in Cheapside

[DRAMATIS PERSONAE]

The Names of the Principal Persons.

Master Yellowhammer, *a goldsmith.*
Maudline, *his wife.*
Tim, *their son.*
Moll, *their daughter* [*sometimes called* Mary].
Tutor *to* Tim.
Sir Walter Whorehound, *a suitor to* Moll.
Sir Oliver Kix, *and his Wife* [Lady], *kin to* Sir Walter.
Master Allwit, *and his Wife* [Wife], *whom* Sir Walter *keeps.*
Welsh Gentlewoman, Sir Walter's *whore.*
Wat *and* Nick, *his bastards* [*by* Mistress Allwit].
Davy Dahumma, *his man.*
Touchwood Senior, *and his Wife* [Wife], *a decayed gentleman.*
Touchwood Junior, *another suitor to* Moll.
[Parson.]
2 Promoters.
Servants.
Watermen.
[Porter.]
[Gentleman.]
[2 Men, *with baskets.*]
[Country Wench, *with a child.*]
[Jugg, a *maid to* Lady Kix.]
[Dry Nurse.]
[Wet Nurse.]
[Mistress Underman, *a Puritan.*]
[Puritans *and* Gossips.]
[Midwife.]
[Susan, *maid to* Moll.]
[Scene: Cheapside]

TEXTUAL VARIANTS
I.i.24 pounds] Q pound **87** *carissimis*] Q charissimis **137** pounds] Q pound **139** Whorehound!] Q Whorehound? **145 s.d.** *Reenter Moll*] Q Enter Mary **204** than] Q then **250** wear] Q were **264 s.d.** *Exeunt*] Q Exit **I.ii.4** In to] Q Into **48** Than] Q Then **79** a'faith] Q a faith **II.i.23** Than] Q Then **33** Than] Q Then **45** desires] Q desire **58** than] Q then **62** than] Q then **94** broke] brake **119** than] Q then **149** pounds] Q pound **200** years] Q year **207** pounds] Q pound **209–10**] lines reversed in Q and all given to Lady Kix **210 s.d.** *Exeunt*] Q Exit **II.ii.13** pounds] Q pound **16 s.d.**]Q has s.d. at line 14 **63** corpse] Q corps **181** Now] Q Not **II.iii.25 s.d.** *Exeunt*] Q Exit **59 s.d.** *Exeunt*] Q Exit **III.i.27** were you] Q were **III.ii.13** Eyed] Q Ey's **220 s.d.** *Exeunt*] Q Exit **221 s.d.** *Exeunt*] Q Exit **223** than] Q then **III.iii.5** I enjoy] Q enjoy **17** eryngoes] Q Oringoes **18** Hartichokes] Q Hartechokes **95** than] Q then **147** broke] Q brake **155** pounds] Q pound **158** wife] Q wifes **181 s.d.** *Exeunt*] Q Exit **IV.i.16** *disputas*] Q disputus **213** quickly, quickly] Q quickly **216**]entire line missing from Q **217** lose] Q loose **245** Than] Q Then **255** passed] Q past **IV.iv.28 s.d.** *Exeunt*] Q Exit **67** pounds] Q pound **93 s.d.** *Exeunt*] Q Exit **V.i.45** than] Q then **46** parts] Q part **49** Than] Q Then **73** he] Q ho **153** Than] Q Then **V.ii.17** your] Q you **63** sprang] Q sprung **V.iii.11** pounds] Q pound **38 s.d.** *Exeunt*] Q Exit **V.iv.7** Than] Q Then **35** *Touchwood Junior*] Q Touchwood Senior **44** Than] Q Then **89** saw] Q say **103** a bout] Q about **105** *nequeo*] Q neguro

Playsource

A Chaste Maid in Cheapside is largely invented by Thomas Middleton, but he may have found suggestions in an epigram to Thomas Campion's *Art of English Poesie* (1602) for the Allwit–Whorehound plot; the anonymous ballad, "Who Would Not Be a Cuckold?" for Allwit; and Thomas Dekker's *Bachelor's Banquet* (1603) for the christening scene. The character of Yellowhammer may be indebted to a suit brought against Middleton and others by Robert Keysar, a goldsmith of Cheapside, in 1609 for indebtedness.

Title (1) chaste maid as oxymoron; (2) Cheapside suggests maids for sale

The Names of the Principal Persons

1 **Yellowhammer** indicates his trade as goldsmith but also colloquial for (1) gold coin; (2) fool
2 **Maudline** Magdalen (presumably after Mary Magdalen, a reformed prostitute)
4 **Moll** diminutive for Mary (colloquial nickname for prostitutes and associates of criminals)
7 **Oliver** fruitful; **Kix** a dry hollow stalk; hence sterile
8 **Allwit** pun on wittol, or fool
11 **Dahumma** from Welsh "dwech yma," "come here"
12 **Touchwood** tinder (hence quickly passionate); **decayed** reduced in property
15 **Promoters** informers; courts required two when submitting evidence
17 **Watermen** boatmen hired to take people across the Thames
26 **Gossips** literally, godparents; colloquial for female friends who attend births and christenings
29 **Cheapside** i.e., Westcheap, running E from St. Paul's Cathedral to the Poultry; both a commercial center and the route for publicly humiliating prostitutes and shrews by whipping and/or carting them

Act I

[I.i]

Enter Maudline *and* Moll, *a shop being discovered.*

Maudline. Have you played over all your old lessons o'the virginals?

Moll. Yes.

Maudline. Yes! You are a dull maid a' late, methinks you had need have somewhat to quicken your green sickness (do you weep?) – a husband! Had not such a piece of flesh been ordained, what had us wives been good for? To make sallets, or else cried up and down for sampier. To see the difference of these seasons! When I was of your youth, I was lightsome, and quick two years before I was married. You fit for a knight's bed! Drowsy-browed, dull-eyed, drossy-spirited – I hold my life you have forgot your dancing. When was the dancer with you?

Moll. The last week.

Maudline. Last week? When I was of your bord, he missed me not a night. I was kept at it; I took delight to learn, and he to teach me, pretty brown gentleman, he took pleasure in my company; but you are dull. Nothing comes nimbly from you; you dance like a plumber's daughter; and deserve two thousand pounds in lead to your marriage, and not in goldsmith's ware.

Enter Yellowhammer.

Yellowhammer. Now what's the din betwixt mother and daughter, ha?

Maudline. Faith, small, telling your daughter Mary of her errors.

Yellowhammer. Errors! Nay, the city cannot hold you, wife, but you must needs fetch words from Westminster, I ha' done, i'faith. Has no attorney's clerk been here a' late and changed his half-crown-piece his mother sent him, or rather cozened you with a gilded twopence, to bring the word in fashion for her faults or cracks in duty and obedience? Term 'em e'en so, sweet wife. As there is no woman made without a flaw, your purest lawns have frays, and cambrics bracks.

Maudline. But 'tis a husband sowders up all cracks.

Moll. What, is he come, sir?

Yellowhammer. Sir Walter's come.
He was met at Holborn Bridge, and in his company
A proper fair young gentlewoman, which I guess
By her red hair, and other rank descriptions,
To be his landed niece brought out of Wales,
Which Tim our son (the Cambridge boy) must marry.
'Tis a match of Sir Walter's own making
To bind us to him, and our heirs forever.

Maudline. We are honored then, if this baggage would be humble,
And kiss him with devotion when he enters.
I cannot get her for my life
To instruct her hand thus, before and after,
Which a knight will look for, before and after.
I have told her still, 'tis the waving of a woman
Does often move a man, and prevails strongly.
But sweet, ha' you sent to Cambridge,
Has Tim word on't?

I.i.1 s.d. *discovered* (perhaps by drawing back a curtain on a recessed stage); Goldsmith's Row was on the s side of Cheap

2 **virginals** keyboard instruments precedent to harpsichord and pianoforte, but also here the basis of several puns

4 **dull** dispirited; **maid** unmarried woman

6 **quicken** (1) be more energetic; (2) become pregnant;; **green sickness** (1) chlorosis, anemia in young women which could lead to a greenish complexion; (2) love-sickness

9 **sallets** salads; **cried . . . down** hawked (as street vendors)

10 **sampier** marsh-sampier, a green for salads (as a medicine, it provoked urination and aroused an appetite for meat)

12 **quick** (1) spirited; (2) pregnant (literally, with life)

15 **dancing** (1) as a lady's skill; (2) colloquial for intercourse (London was then known for its dancing as well as its fencing schools)

18 **bord** (1) caliber, or age; (2) quality or condition

23 **plumber's daughter** (presumably heavy-footed)

27 **din** quarrel

29 **Mary** (her father uses the respectable name, which carries associations with purity)

32 **fetch words** borrow terms (of Law French)

33 **Westminster** the law courts (Common Pleas, King's Bench, Chancery)

35 **half-crown-piece** worth 2s.6d. and made of 22-carat gold (colloquialism for difficult terms or words)

36 **cozened** tricked; **gilded twopence** (counterfeit, since twopence were silver; they were similar in size to half-crowns)

40 **lawns** fine white linens

41 **cambrics** fine dress linen, initially imported from France; **bracks** flaws, openings (with sexual pun)

42 **sowders** solders; repairs; **cracks** (referring to female pudenda)

45 **Holborn Bridge** bridge over Fleet Ditch that served as main entrance to London from w through Newgate

47 **red hair** (thought to indicate especially passionate people); **rank** (1) class; (2) overabundance; (3) coarse; (4) corrupt, lecherous

52 **baggage** (a term of derision)

55 **before and after** (1) affected way of walking with one hand at the waist, the other at the small of the back; (2) sexual pun

57 **still** constantly; **waving** body or hand movements

Yellowhammer. Had word just the day after when you sent him the silver spoon to eat his broth in the hall among the gentlemen commoners.

Maudline. Oh, 'twas timely.

Enter Porter.

Yellowhammer. How now?

Porter. A letter from a gentleman in Cambridge.

Yellowhammer. Oh, one of Hobson's porters, thou art welcome. I told thee, Maud, we should hear from Tim. [*He reads the letter.*] *Amantissimis carissimisque ambobus parentibus patri et matri.*

Maudline. What's the matter?

Yellowhammer. Nay, by my troth, I know not, ask not me, he's grown too verbal. This learning is a great witch.

Maudline. Pray let me see it, I was wont to understand him. [*She reads.*] *Amantissimus carissimus,* he has sent the carrier's man, he says; *ambobus parentibus,* for a pair of boots; *patri et matri,* pay the porter, or it makes no matter.

Porter. Yes, by my faith! Mistress, there's no true construction in that; I have took a great deal of pains, and come from the Bell sweating. Let me come to't, for I was a scholar forty years ago. 'Tis thus, I warrant you: [*He takes the letter and reads.*] *Matri,* it makes no matter; *ambobus parentibus,* for a pair of boots; *patri,* pay the porter; *amantissimis carissimis,* he's the carrier's man, and his name is Sims. And there he says true, forsooth, my name is Sims indeed; I have not forgot all my learning. A money matter, I thought I should hit on't.

Yellowhammer. Go, thou art an old fox, there's a tester for thee. [*Gives money.*]

Porter. If I see your worship at Goose Fair, I have a dish of birds for you.

Yellowhammer. Why, dost dwell at Bow?

Porter. All my lifetime, sir, I could ever say Bo, to a goose.
Farewell to your worship.

Exit Porter.

Yellowhammer. A merry porter!

Maudline. How can he choose but be so, coming with Cambridge letters from our son Tim?

Yellowhammer. What's here? [*Reads.*] *Maximus diligo.* Faith, I must to my learned counsel with this gear, 'twill ne'er be discerned else.

Maudline. Go to my cousin then, at Inns of Court.

Yellowhammer. Fie, they are all for French; they speak no Latin.

Maudline. The parson then will do it.

Enter a Gentleman *with a chain.*

Yellowhammer. Nay, he disclaims it, calls Latin "Papistry": he will not deal with it. What is't you lack, gentleman?

Gentleman. Pray weigh this chain.

[*Yellowhammer weighs it.*]

Enter Sir Walter Whorehound, Welsh Gentlewoman *and* Davy Dahumma.

Sir Walter. Now, wench, thou art welcome to the heart of the city of London.

Welsh Gentlewoman. *Dugat a whee.*

Sir Walter. You can thank me in English, if you list.

Welsh Gentlewoman. I can, sir, simply.

Sir Walter. 'Twill serve to pass, wench; 'twas strange that I should lie with thee so often, to leave thee without English; that were unnatural.
I bring thee up to turn thee into gold, wench,
And make thy fortune shine like your bright trade;

63 **hall** dining hall for students and members of college; **gentlemen commoners** wealthy undergraduates who purchased special privileges, including a table separate from poorer scholars (Tim is socially ambitious)

67 **Hobson** Thomas Hobson, famous Cambridge carrier with stables at the present site of St. Catharine's College chapel; his large wagons carried mail and goods between London and Cambridge

69–70 ***Amantissimis . . . matri*** "To my two most loving and dearest parents, father and mother" (deliberately parodic)

71 **matter** substance; meaning

80–1 **true construction** accurate translation

82 **the Bell** an inn in Coleman Street off Moorgate; Cambridge carriers also used the Black Bull in Bishopsgate Street (and this has been argued to be a compositor's error)

92 **fox** schemer

93 **tester** sixpence

94 **Goose Fair** fair on Whitsun (Thursday following Pentecost) at Stratford-le-Bow, 4½ miles N of London where young "green" geese were roasted and sold; goose also cant for (1) fool; (2) harlot (cf. dish of birds)

97 **Bo, to a goose** (1) bow to a goose (proverbial); (2) female pudenda

102 ***Maximus diligo*** "I am the greatest and I owe (you)"; presumably he means, "I esteem you most highly"

104 **gear** business; matter; **discerned** understood

105 **Inns of Court** fourteen collegial bodies of lawyers and law students in London

106 **French** Law French, a mongrel Latin, was practiced widely at the Inns of Court and favored by students as easier than classical Latin

107 **s.d. *chain*** gold chains were frequently worn by gentlemen as class markers

110 **"Papistry"** (Catholic Mass was celebrated in Latin)

115 ***Dugat a whee*** Welsh for "God keep you" (phonetic spelling)

117 **list** please; prefer

119 **wench** (1) woman; (2) prostitute; **'twas** would be

124 **your** one's

A goldsmith's shop sets out a city maid.
Davy Dahumma, not a word!

Davy. Mum, mum, sir.

Sir Walter. Here you must pass for a pure virgin.

Davy. [*Aside.*] Pure Welsh virgin! She lost her maidenhead in Brecknockshire.

Sir Walter. I hear you mumble, Davy.

Davy. I have teeth, sir, I need not mumble yet this forty years.

Sir Walter. [*Aside.*] The knave bites plaguily.

Yellowhammer. [*To Gentleman.*] What's your price, sir?

Gentleman. A hundred pounds, sir.

Yellowhammer. A hundred marks the utmost, 'tis not for me else.
What, Sir Walter Whorehound!

[*Exit* Gentleman.]

Moll. Oh, death!

Exit Moll.

Maudline. Why, daughter! Faith, the baggage!
A bashful girl, sir; these young things are shamefast;
Besides you have a presence, sweet Sir Walter,
Able to daunt a maid brought up i'the city:

Reenter Moll.

A brave Court spirit makes our virgins quiver,
And kiss with trembling thighs. Yet see, she comes, sir.

Sir Walter. Why, how now, pretty mistress, now I have caught you. [*Catches Moll by the hand.*] What, can you injure so your time to stray thus from your faithful servant?

Yellowhammer. Pish, stop your words, good knight, 'twill make her blush else, which wound too high for the daughters of the Freedom. "Honor," and "faithful servant," they are compliments for the worthies of Whitehall, or Greenwich. E'en plain, sufficient, subsidy words serves us, sir. And is this gentlewoman your worthy niece?

Sir Walter. You may be bold with her on these terms, 'tis she, sir, heir to some nineteen mountains.

Yellowhammer. Bless us all! You overwhelm me, sir, with love and riches.

Sir Walter. And all as high as Paul's.

Davy. [*Aside.*] Here's work, i'faith.

Sir Walter. How sayest thou, Davy?

Davy. Higher, sir, by far; you cannot see the top of 'em.

Yellowhammer. What, man? Maudline, salute this gentlewoman – our daughter, if things hit right.

[*Maudline kisses Welsh Gentlewoman.*]

Enter Touchwood Junior.

Touchwood Junior. [*Aside.*] My knight with a brace of footmen
Is come and brought up his ewe mutton
To find a ram at London; I must hasten it,
Or else pick a famine; her blood's mine,
And that's the surest. Well, knight, that choice spoil
Is only kept for me.

[*He attracts Moll's attention from behind.*]

Moll. Sir?

Touchwood Junior. Turn not to me till thou may'st lawfully, it but whets my stomach, which is too sharp set already. [*Gives her a letter.*] Read that note carefully, keep me from suspicion still, nor know my zeal but in thy heart; read and send but thy liking in three words, I'll be at hand to take it.

Yellowhammer. Oh, turn, sir, turn.
A poor plain boy, an university man,
Proceeds next Lent to a Bachelor of Art;

---

125 sets out displays advantageously; **maid** unmarried woman
127 Mum silence (about the Welsh gentlewoman's relationship to Sir Walter)
128 pure virginal, chaste
130 maidenhead virginity; **Brecknockshire** in SE Wales, with pun on "break nock," nock meaning pudendum
132 need do
134 plaguily (1) confoundedly; (2) vexatiously (presumably Sir Walter lacks teeth, a possible sign of venereal disease)
138 marks a mark was equal to two-thirds of a pound (13s.4d.)
142 shamefast modest; bashful
146 trembling thighs (reference to sexual intercourse in a standing position)
152 wound proceed
153 Freedom (i.e., London citizens who had freeman status in one of the guilds, or license to practice their trade)
155 worthies courtiers (as opposed to freemen)
155–6 Whitehall . . . Greenwich royal palaces near London
156 subsidy commercial; bourgeois
164 as . . . Paul's (proverbial; the tower of old St. Paul's before the fire of 1666 was 245 feet; before 1561, it was 450 feet)
169 salute i.e., kiss
173 ewe mutton prostitute
174 ram husband (Touchwood Junior, true to his name, is quick to respond); **hasten it** act quickly
175 pick a famine choose to starve; **blood** (suggests sexual arousal)
180 stomach sexual appetite
181 sharp set keen
184 liking consent
188 Proceeds graduates

He will be called Sir Yellowhammer, then,
Over all Cambridge, and that's half a knight.
Maudline. Please you draw near, and taste the welcome of the city, sir?
Yellowhammer. Come, good Sir Walter, and your virtuous niece here.
Sir Walter. 'Tis manners to take kindness.
Yellowhammer. Lead 'em in, wife.
Sir Walter. Your company, sir.
Yellowhammer. I'll give't you instantly.
[*Exeunt* Maudline, Sir Walter, Davy *and* Welsh Gentlewoman; Moll *is unwilling to follow.*]
Touchwood Junior. [*Aside.*] How strangely busy is the devil and riches;
Poor soul kept in too hard, her mother's eye
Is cruel toward her, being to him.
'Twere a good mirth now to set him a-work
To make her wedding ring; I must about it.
Rather than the gain should fall to a stranger.
'Twas honesty in me to enrich my father.
Yellowhammer. [*Aside.*] The girl is wondrous peevish; I fear nothing
But that she's taken with some other love;
Then all's quite dashed. That must be narrowly looked to;
We cannot be too wary in our children.
What is't you lack?
Touchwood Junior. [*Aside.*] Oh, nothing now, all that I wish is present.
I would have a wedding ring made for a gentlewoman
With all speed that may be.
Yellowhammer. Of what weight, sir?
Touchwood Junior. Of some half ounce,
Stand fair and comely with the spark of a diamond.
Sir, 'twere pity to lose the least grace.
Yellowhammer. Pray let's see it; [*He takes the stone.*] indeed, sir, 'tis a pure one.
Touchwood. So is the mistress.
Yellowhammer. Have you the wideness of her finger, sir?
Touchwood Junior. Yes, sure, I think I have her measure about me.
Good faith, 'tis down. I cannot show't you;
I must pull too many things out to be certain.
Let me see: long, and slender, and neatly jointed;
Just such another gentlewoman that's your daughter, sir.
Yellowhammer. And therefore, sir, no gentlewoman.
Touchwood Junior. I protest I never saw two maids handed more alike;
I'll ne'er seek farther, if you'll give me leave, sir.
Yellowhammer. If you dare venture by her finger, sir.
Touchwood Junior. Aye, and I'll bide all loss, sir.
Yellowhammer. Say you so, sir? Let's see hither, girl.
Touchwood Junior. Shall I make bold with your finger, gentlewoman?
Moll. Your pleasure, sir.
Touchwood Junior. [*Trying the ring on Moll's finger.*]
That fits her to a hair, sir.
Yellowhammer. What's your posy now, sir?
Touchwood. Mass, that's true, posy, i'faith. E'en thus, sir:
Love that's wise, blinds parents' eyes.
Yellowhammer. How, how? If I may speak without offense, sir,
I hold my life –
Touchwood Junior. What, sir?
Yellowhammer. Go to, you'll pardon me?
Touchwood Junior. Pardon you? Aye, sir.
Yellowhammer. Will you, i'faith?
Touchwood Junior. Yes, faith, I will.
Yellowhammer. You'll steal away some man's daughter, am I near you?
Do you turn aside? You gentlemen are mad wags!
I wonder things can be so warily carried.

189–90 Sir... knight title (from translation of "Dominus") given to graduates of Oxford and Cambridge but used only with surname (hence half-knight)
195 take accept
201 being... him (i.e., her mother's interest in Sir Walter)
202 him Yellowhammer
205 'Twas it would be
206 the girl Moll; **peevish** (1) foolish; (2) perverse (Moll has not responded to Sir Walter's advances)
208 dashed ended; **narrowly** closely
215 Stand that would stand; **spark ... diamond** (wedding rings were bands with small gems or hands clasping a heart set with a larger jewel); **spark** small stone
222 measure (1) size; (2) capacity (for penis)
223 down (1) lost; (2) at the bottom of his pocket; (3) detumescent
225 long... jointed (comparison of finger and penis)
226 that's as is
227 no gentlewoman (Yellowhammer insists she is not gentry)
232 bide... loss pay for any mistakes
233 hither here
236 to a hair (1) exactly; (2) with reference to pubic hair
237 posy motto in the ring
238 Mass "By the Mass" (a common oath)
247 near understand (found out your secret)
248 wags merry or mischievous men

And parents blinded so; but they're served right
That have two eyes, and wear so dull a sight.

Touchwood Junior. [*Aside.*] Thy doom take hold of thee.

Yellowhammer. Tomorrow noon shall show your ring well done.

Touchwood Junior. Being so, 'tis soon. Thanks – and your leave, sweet gentlewoman.

Exit.

Moll. Sir, you are welcome.
[*Aside.*] Oh, were I made of wishes, I went with thee.

Yellowhammer. Come now, we'll see how the rules go within.

Moll. [*Aside.*] That robs my joy; there I lose all I win.

Exeunt.

[I.ii]

Enter Davy *and* Allwit *severally.*

Davy. Honesty wash my eyes, I have spied a wittol.

Allwit. What, Davy Dahumma? Welcome from North Wales,
I'faith; and is Sir Walter come?

Davy. New come to town, sir.

Allwit. In to the maids, sweet Davy, and give order
His chamber be made ready instantly;
My wife's as great as she can wallow, Davy,
And longs for nothing but pickled cucumbers,
And his coming, and now she shall ha't, boy.

Davy. She's sure of them, sir.

Allwit. Thy very sight will hold my wife in pleasure,
Till the knight come himself. Go in, in, in, Davy.

Exit [Davy].

The founder's come to town! I am like a man
Finding a table furnished to his hand,
As mine is still to me, prays for the founder:
"Bless the right worshipful, the good founder's life."
I thank him, h'as maintained my house this ten years.
Not only keeps my wife, but a keeps me,
And all my family; I am at his table,
He gets me all my children, and pays the nurse,
Monthly, or weekly, puts me to nothing,
Rent, nor church duties, not so much as the scavenger:
The happiest state that ever man was born to.
I walk out in a morning, come to breakfast,
Find excellent cheer, a good fire in winter;
Look in my coal house about midsummer eve,
That's full, five or six chaldron, new laid up.
Look in my back yard, I shall find a steeple
Made up with Kentish faggots, which o'erlooks
The waterhouse and the windmills; I say nothing,
But smile, and pin the door. When she lies in,
And now she's even upon the point of grunting,
A lady lies not in like her. There's her embossings,
Embroid'rings, spanglings, and I know not what,
As if she lay with all the gaudy shops
In Gresham's Burse about her. Then her restoratives,
Able to set up a young 'pothecary,
And richly stock the foreman of a drug shop;

252 doom fate
261 rules revels; unruly events
I.ii.1 s.d. *severally* from different directions
1 wittol (1) complacent cuckold; (2) transposition of the name "Allwit"
6 great pregnant; **wallow** walk with a rolling gait
7 pickled cucumbers made with a sharp cider, not vinegar (to suggest the strange cravings of those pregnant)
8 coming arrival (of Sir Walter), not birth of child
12 founder Sir Walter, as his employer (literally, one who endows an institution)
13 furnished (with provisions)
17 keeps provides for; **a** he
19 gets me (1) receives from me; (2) pays me for supplying
21 church duties parish dues paid in service or money; **scavenger** official who supervises streets and pavements and keeps them and chimneys clean
24 cheer provisions
25 midsummer eve June 21
26 chaldron a dry measure of 32 bushels (of coal)
28 Kentish faggots kindling; bundles of brushwood about 8 feet long and 1 foot thick
29 waterhouse the cistern at the head of the New River in Islington completed in 1613 and supplying London with fresh water; **windmills** the six windmills on Windmill Hill in Finsbury Fields, NE of London
30 pin bolt; **lies in** (awaiting childbirth; for Allwit, a regular event)
32 embossings ornamental reliefs (here on cloth)
33 spanglings material decorated with spangles
34 gaudy trinkets; fine silks and draperies
35 Gresham's Burse the Royal Exchange, a meeting place for merchants built by Sir Thomas Gresham and opened in 1568; **restoratives** (1) medicines; (2) cordials
36 'pothecary druggist

Her sugar by whole loaves, her wines by rundlets.
I see these things, but like a happy man,
I pay for none at all, yet fools think's mine;
I have the name, and in his gold I shine.
And where some merchants would in soul kiss Hell
To buy a paradise for their wives, and dye
Their conscience in the bloods of prodigal heirs
To deck their night-piece, yet all this being done,
Eaten with jealousy to the inmost bone
(As what affliction nature more constrains
Than feed the wife plump for another's veins?)
These torments stand I freed of, I am as clear
From jealousy of a wife as from the charge.
Oh, two miraculous blessings! 'Tis the knight
Hath took that labor all out of my hands.
I may sit still and play; he's jealous for me,
Watches her steps, sets spies. I live at ease,
He has both the cost and torment. When the strings
Of his heart frets, I feed, laugh, or sing.
La dildo, dildo la dildo, la dildo dildo de dildo.

Enter two Servants.

1 [*Servant*]. What has he got a-singing in his head now?

2 [*Servant*]. Now's out of work he falls to making dildoes.

Allwit. Now, sirs, Sir Walter's come.

1 [*Servant*]. Is our master come?

Allwit. Your master? What am I?

1 [*Servant*]. Do not you know, sir?

Allwit. Pray, am not I your master?

1 [*Servant*]. Oh, you are but our mistress's husband.

Enter Sir Walter *and* Davy.

Allwit. *Ergo* knave, your master.

1 [*Servant*]. *Negatur argumentum.* – Here comes Sir Walter. [*Aside to 2 Servant.*] Now a stands bare as well as we; make the most of him, he's but one peep above a servingman, and so much his horns make him.

Sir Walter. How dost, Jack?

Allwit. Proud of your worship's health, sir.

Sir Walter. How does your wife?

Allwit. E'en after your own making, sir;
She's a tumbler, a' faith, the nose and belly meets.

Sir Walter. They'll part in time again.

Allwit. At the good hour, they will, and please your worship.

Sir Walter. [*To 1 Servant*]. Here, sirrah, pull off my boots. [*To Allwit.*] Put on, put on, Jack.

Allwit. I thank your kind worship, sir.

Sir Walter. Slippers! [*2 Servant brings slippers.*] Heart, you are sleepy.

Allwit. [*Aside.*] The game begins already.

Sir Walter. Pish, put on, Jack.

Allwit. [*To audience.*] Now I must do it, or he'll be as angry now as if I had put it on at first bidding, 'tis but observing, [*He puts on his hat.*] 'tis but observing a man's humor once, and he may ha' him by the nose all his life.

Sir Walter. What entertainment has lain open here?
No strangers in my absence?

1 Servant. Sure, sir, not any.

Allwit. [*Aside.*] His jealously begins. Am not I happy now
That can laugh inward whilst his marrow melts?

Sir Walter. How do you satisfy me?

1 Servant Good sir, be patient.

Sir Walter. For two months' absence I'll be satisfied.

1 Servant. No living creature entered.

Sir Walter. Entered? Come, swear –

---

38 **rundlets** large barrels holding $18\frac{1}{2}$ gallons
43–4 **dye . . . heirs** extort money from spendthrift sons to buy trinkets for mistresses
45 **night-piece** mistress; bedfellow
47 **nature . . . constrains** more oppresses nature
48 **veins** i.e., blood, sexual desire or pleasure
50 **charge** cost
55 **strings** (the heart was thought to be braced with strings that frayed or broke under emotional stress; hence heartbreak)
57 ***La dildo*** (1) nonsense refrain of a song; (2) artificial penis
58 **a-singing . . . head** sign of cuckoldry
60 **out of work** (1) unemployed; (2) sexually deprived
69–70 ***Ergo . . . argumentum*** "Therefore . . . I deny your proof" (standard formula in disputations)
71 **bare** hatless
73 **peep** degree (from "pip" on playing cards)
74 **horns** sign of a cuckold
78 **making** (with play on *mating*)
79 **tumbler** (1) acrobat; (2) sexually agile; **nose and belly meets** (i.e., the pregnancy is far along)
83 **sirrah** (form of address to an inferior)
84 **Put on** (i.e., his hat; hats were worn indoors and taken off to show respect, then replaced)
86 **Heart** "God's heart" (common exclamation)
93 **observing** (deference paid to superior); **humor** mood, disposition
94 **by . . . nose** at his mercy
96 **strangers** rivals (someone other than mistress's husband)
98 **marrow melts** (heat of jealousy was thought to dry up the blood)
99 **satisfy** content with convincing proof

1 Servant. You will not hear me out, sir –
Sir Walter. Yes, I'll hear't out, sir.
1 Servant. Sir, he can tell himself.
Sir Walter. Heart, he can tell!
Do you think I'll trust him? – as a usurer
With forfeited lordships? Him? Oh, monstrous injury!
Believe him? Can the devil speak ill of darkness?
What can you say, sir?
Allwit. Of my soul and conscience sir, she's a wife as honest of her body to me as any lord's proud lady can be.
Sir Walter. Yet, by your leave, I heard you were once off'ring to go to bed to her.
Allwit. No, I protest, sir.
Sir Walter. Heart if you do, you shall take all. I'll marry!
Allwit. Oh, I beseech you, sir –
Sir Walter. [*Aside.*] That wakes the slave, and keeps his flesh in awe.
Allwit. [*Aside.*] I'll stop that gap
Where e'er I find it open, I have poisoned
His hopes in marriage already –
Some old rich widows, and some landèd virgins,

Enter two Children [Wat *and* Nick].

And I'll fall to work still before I'll lose him;
He's yet too sweet to part from.
1 Boy [*Wat*]. God-den, father.
Allwit. Ha, villain, peace!
2 Boy [*Nick*]. God-den, father.
Allwit. Peace, bastard! [*Aside.*] Should he hear 'em!
[*Aloud.*] These are two foolish children, they do not know the gentleman that sits there.
Sir Walter. Oh, Wat! How dost, Nick? Go to school, ply your books, boys, ha?
Allwit. [*To the boys.*] Where's your legs, whoresons?
[*Aside.*] They should kneel indeed if they could say their prayers.
Sir Walter. [*Aside.*] Let me see, stay;
How shall I dispose of these two brats now
When I am married? For they must not mingle
Among my children that I get in wedlock;
'Twill make foul work that, and raise many storms.
I'll bind Wat 'prentice to a goldsmith – my father Yellowhammer.
As fit as can be! Nick with some vintner; good!
Goldsmith and vintner; there will be wine in bowls, i'faith.

Enter Allwit's Wife.

Wife. Sweet knight,
Welcome; I have all my longings now in town,
Now well-come the good hour. [*She embraces him.*]
Sir Walter. How cheers my mistress?
Wife. Made lightsome, e'en by him that made me heavy.
Sir Walter. Methinks she shows gallantly, like a moon at full, sir.
Allwit. True, and if she bear a male child, there's the man in the moon, sir.
Sir Walter. 'Tis but the boy in the moon yet, goodman calf.
Allwit. There was a man, the boy had never been there else.
Sir Walter. It shall be yours, sir.
Allwit. No, by my troth, I'll swear it's none of mine.
Let him that got it keep it! [*Aside.*] Thus do I rid myself of fear,
Lie soft, sleep hard, drink wine, and eat good cheer.

[*Exeunt.*]

Act II

[II.i]

Enter Touchwood Senior *and his* Wife.

Wife. 'Twill be so tedious, sir, to live from you,
But that necessity must be obeyed.
Touchwood Senior. I would it might not, wife, the tediousness
Will be the most part mine, that understand
The blessings I have in thee; so to part,

102 hear me out let me finish
104 usurer money lender
105 forfeited lordships mortgaged estates forfeit on failure to repay loan
118 awe (1) respect; (2) subjection
119 gap rumor; wrong belief
125 God-den "Good evening" from "God give ye good evening" (but actually any time after noon)
126 villain (perhaps as his child now his charge)
130 do not know (they are not aware Sir Walter is their father; they think Allwit is)
133 legs bows out of courtesy and respect
141 my i.e., the
148 heavy (1) sad in his absence; (2) pregnant
150 moon (full moon was mythically time of greatest fertility)
154 calf fool (play on "mooncalf" as false pregnancy)
158 troth truth
II.i.5 blessings (1) favors; (2) children

That drives the torment to a knowing heart.
But as thou say'st, we must give way to need
And live awhile asunder. Our desires
Are both too fruitful for our barren fortunes.
How adverse runs the destiny of some
creatures!
Some only can get riches and no children,
We only can get children and no riches!
Then 'tis the prudent'st part to check our wills
And, till our state rise, make our bloods lie still.
Life, every year a child, and some years two,
Besides drinkings abroad, that's never
reckoned;
This gear will not hold out.

Wife. Sir, for a time, I'll take the courtesy of my
uncle's house,
If you be pleased to like on't, till prosperity
Look with a friendly eye upon our states.

Touchwood Senior. Honest wife, I thank thee; I ne'er
knew
The perfect treasure thou brought'st with thee
more
Than at this instant minute. A man's happy
When he's at poorest that has matched his
soul
As rightly as his body. Had I married
A sensual fool now, as 'tis hard to 'scape it
'Mongst gentlewomen of our time, she would
ha' hanged
About my neck, and never left her hold
Till she had kissed me into wanton businesses,
Which, at the waking of my better judgment,
I should have cursed most bitterly,
And laid a thicker vengeance on my act
Than misery of the birth; which were enough
If it were born to greatness, whereas mine
Is sure of beggary, though it were got in
wine.
Fulness of joy showeth the goodness in thee;
Thou art a matchless wife. Farewell, my joy.

Wife. I shall not want your sight?

Touchwood Senior. I'll see thee often,
Talk in mirth, and play at kisses with thee.
Anything, wench, but what may beget beggars;
There I give o'er the set, throw down the cards,
And dare not take them up.

Wife. Your will be mine, sir.
Exit.

Touchwood Senior. This does not only make her
honesty perfect,
But her discretion, and approves her
judgment.
Had her desires been wanton, they'd been
blameless
In being lawful ever, but of all creatures
I hold that wife a most unmatched treasure
That can unto her fortunes fix her pleasure.
And not unto her blood; this is like wedlock;
The feast of marriage is not lust but love,
And care of the estate. When I please blood,
Merely I sing, and suck out others'; then,
'Tis many a wise man's fault; but of all men
I am the most unfortunate in that game
That ever pleased both genders. I ne'er played
yet
Under a bastard; the poor wenches curse me
To the Pit where e'er I come; they were ne'er
served so.
But used to have more words than one to a
bargain.
I have such a fatal finger in such business
I must forth with't, chiefly for country
wenches,
For every harvest I shall hinder hay-making.

Enter a Wench *with a child.*

I had no less than seven lay-in last progress.
Within three weeks of one another's time.

Wench. Oh, Snaphance, have I found you?

Touchwood Senior. How "Snaphance"?

---

6 **knowing** appreciating my loss
13 **wills** sexual drives
14 **bloods** sexual passions
15 **Life** "By God's life" (a common oath)
16 **drinkings abroad** adulteries; **abroad** away from home; **reckoned** (he has never counted up the number of children he conceived)
17 **gear** (1) business; (2) genitals
18 **courtesy** hospitality; shelter
32 **thicker vengeance** (i.e., by cursing it)
32–3 **thicker . . . birth** (i.e., pain of birth into life is worse when subjected to poverty)
35 **got in wine** (1) conceived when inebriated; (2) conceived by parents full of joy
37 **matchless** (1) peerless; (2) without a husband
38 **want** lack, foresake (sight of you)
41 **give . . . set** abandon this game (of separation)
44 **approves** attests to
45 **wanton** undisciplined
46 **lawful** (marriage makes sexual desire legitimate)
52 **sing** copulate; **suck out** arouse
55–6 **I . . . bastard** i.e., I'm always left with a bastard at least (term is from card playing, where bastard is a card left in the hand giving a penalty)
57 **Pit** (1) Hell; (2) pudendum; **served** (1) treated; (2) serviced sexually
58 **But . . . bargain** i.e., expected several sexual acts before a single pregnancy
59 **finger** (with play on penis)
61 **For . . . hay-making** i.e., every pregnancy limits workforce
62 **lay-in** confinement during pregnancy; **progress** time of royal progresses (usually July and August)
64 **Snaphance** (1) bandit; (2) flintlock of gun (with touchhole or pudendum)

Wench. [*Showing the child.*] Do you see your workmanship? Nay, turn not from it, nor offer to escape, for if you do, I'll cry it through the streets, and follow you. Your name may well be called Touchwood. A pox on you. You do but touch and take. Thou hast undone me; I was a maid before, I can bring a certificate for it, from both the churchwardens.

Touchwood Senior. I'll have the parson's hand too, or I'll not yield to't.

Wench. Thou shalt have more, thou villain! Nothing grieves me but Ellen, my poor cousin in Derbyshire. Thou hast cracked her marriage quite: she'll have a bout with thee.

Touchwood Senior. Faith, when she will, I'll have a bout with her.

Wench. A law bout, sir, I mean.

Touchwood Senior. True, lawyers use such bouts as other men do.
And if that be all thy grief, I'll tender her a husband;
I keep of purpose two or three gulls in pickle
To eat such mutton with, and she shall choose one.
Do but in courtesy, faith, wench, excuse me
Of this half yard of flesh, in which I think it wants
A nail or two.

Wench. No, thou shalt find, villain, it hath right shape, and all the nails it should have.

Touchwood Senior. Faith, I am poor; do a charitable deed, wench;
I am a younger brother, and have nothing.

Wench. Nothing! Thou hast too much, thou lying villain, unless thou were more thankful.

Touchwood Senior. I have no dwelling,
I broke up house but this morning. Pray thee, pity me;
I am a good fellow, faith, have been too kind
To people of your gender: if I ha't
Without my belly, none of your sex shall want it.
[*Aside.*] That word has been of force to move a woman.
[*To her.*] There's tricks enough to rid thy hand on't, wench:
Some rich man's porch, tomorrow before day,
Or else anon i'th evening; twenty devices.
[*Gives money.*] Here's all I have, i'faith, take purse and all,
[*Aside.*] And would I were rid of all the ware i'the shop so.

Wench. Where I find manly dealings, I am pitiful. [*She gestures towards the child.*] This shall not trouble you.

Touchwood Senior. And I protest, wench, the next I'll keep myself.

Wench. Soft, let it be got first. [*Aside.*] This is the fifth; if e'er I venture more, where I now go for a maid, may I ride for a whore.

Exit.

Touchwood Senior. What shift she'll make now with this piece of flesh
In this strict time of Lent, I cannot imagine;
Flesh dare not peep abroad now, I have known
This city now above this seven years,
But I protest in better state of government
I never knew it yet, nor ever heard of;
There has been more religious, wholesome laws
In the half circle of a year erected

---

69 **pox** venereal disease; syphilis

70 **touch and take** i.e., speedily in touching (proverbial); quick to make contact and impregnate

71 **certificate** document establishing chastity and allowing bearer to leave parish; they were notoriously unreliable and often forged

72 **churchwardens** lay church officers who helped the incumbent in his duties

73 **hand** signature

76 **cracked** broken

77 **bout** (1) quarrel; (2) lawsuit; (3) sexual encounter

81 **tender** provide, offer

82 **gulls** fools; victims of cheaters; **pickle** (1) preserve; (2) sweating-tub as a treatment for syphilis

83 **mutton** whore

85 **this . . . flesh** (1) the baby measured by the length of cloth (it is smaller than normal); (2) the penis

86 **nail** (1) cloth measure of $2\frac{1}{4}$ inches (children of syphilitics were often stunted in growth); (2) fingernail (which syphilitic babies sometimes lacked)

90 **younger . . . nothing** i.e., because of primogeniture he had no inheritance

91 **too much** (sexual pun)

95 **good fellow** (1) kind man; (2) roisterer

97 **without . . . it** (puzzling; perhaps "If I were starving, none of you would find me sexually desirable")

98 **That word** it (line 97; presumably the penis)

99 **on't** of it

100 **rich . . . porch** (where to deposit the baby)

101 **anon** quickly

103 **ware** (1) bastards; (2) dissolute woman (in Middleton's special use)

109 **go** walk

110 **maid** woman who passes for a virgin; **ride . . . whore** be publicly humiliated as whores are by riding in the cart; **ride** (pun on straddling sexually)

111 **shift** expedient

111–12 **flesh . . . Lent** (by the statute of 1613 it was forbidden to kill or eat meat during Lent even for pregnant women and invalids, with some exceptions)

115 **better** stricter

118 **half . . . year** i.e., six months

For common good, than memory ever knew of,

Enter Sir Oliver Kix *and his* Lady.

Setting apart corruption of promoters,
And other poisonous officers that infect
And with a venomous breath, taint every goodness.

Lady. Oh, that e'er I was begot, or bred, or born!

Sir Oliver. Be content, sweet wife.

Touchwood Senior. [*Aside.*] What's here to do, now?
I hold my life she's in deep passion
For the imprisonment of veal and mutton
Now kept in garrets, weeps for some calf's head now;
Methinks her husband's head might serve, with bacon.

Enter Touchwood Junior.

Lady. Hist!

Sir Oliver. Patience, sweet wife. [*They walk aside.*]

Touchwood Junior. Brother, I have sought you strangely.

Touchwood Senior. Why, what's the business?

Touchwood Junior. With all speed thou canst, procure a license for me.

Touchwood Senior. How, a license?

Touchwood Junior. Cud's foot, she's lost else, I shall miss her ever.

Touchwood Senior. Nay, sure, thou shalt not miss so fair a mark
For thirteen shillings fourpence.

Touchwood Junior. Thanks by hundreds. *Exit.*

Sir Oliver. Nay, pray thee cease. I'll be at more cost yet;
Thou know'st we are rich enough.

Lady. All but in blessings,
And there the beggar goes beyond us. Oh, oh, oh!
To be seven years a wife and not a child, oh, not a child!

Sir Oliver. Sweet wife, have patience.

Lady. Can any woman have a greater cut?

Sir Oliver. I know 'tis great, but what of that, wife?
I cannot do withal: there's things making
By thine own doctor's advice at 'pothecary's;
I spare for nothing, wife; no, if the price
Were forty marks a spoonful,
I'd give a thousand pounds to purchase fruitfulness.
'Tis but bating so many good works
In the erecting of Bridewells and spital-houses,
And so fetch it up again; for, having none,
I mean to make good deeds my children.

Lady. Give me but those good deeds, and I'll find children.

[Touchwood Senior *smiles, and goes out.*]

Sir Oliver. Hang thee, thou hast had too many!

Lady. Thou liest, brevity!

Sir Oliver. Oh, horrible! Dar'st thou call me "brevity"?
Dar'st thou be so short with me?

Lady. Thou deservest worse.
Think but upon the goodly lands and livings
That's kept back through want on't.

Sir Oliver. Talk not on't, pray thee;
Thou'lt make me play the woman and weep too.

Lady. 'Tis our dry barrenness puffs up Sir Walter;
None gets by your not-getting, but that knight;
He's made by th'means, and fats his fortune shortly
In a great dowry with a goldsmith's daughter.

Sir Oliver. They may all be deceived;

120 **Setting apart** except for; **promoters** informers (in 1613 the Privy Council appointed them to spy and report any violation of Lenten regulations)

125 **deep passion** sexually starved

126–7 **imprisonment . . . garrets** meat secretly hidden for butchering during Lent

127 **garrets** attics; **calf's head** fool's phallus

131 **strangely** extremely (i.e., I've been looking all over for you)

133 **license** for marriage (necessary when banns have not been called; only the bishop could issue such a license for marriage outside a church or chapel)

135 **Cud's foot** "by God's foot" (an oath; by regulation playwrights were forbidden to use God or Christ on the stage, provoking Middleton to play with alternatives)

136 **mark** (1) target; (2) pudendum

137 **thirteen . . . fourpence** the cost of the special license

143 **cut** (1) humiliation; (2) misfortune; (3) pudendum; (4) gelding for a husband

145 **do** (1) help; (2) copulate

150 **bating** reducing; diminishing

151 **erecting** (pun on founding institutions and sexual activity); **Bridewells** houses of correction for prostitutes; **spital-houses** hospitals for treating venereal diseases

152 **fetch . . . again** make amends

153 **good deeds** charitable contributions as to the hospitals

154 **good deeds** sexual acts

157 **brevity** (attack on his sexual shortcomings)

159 **short** (as retort to *brevity*)

161–2 **Think . . . on't** (Sir Walter inherits if Lady Kix fails to produce an heir)

164 **play . . . woman** become emotional (proverbial)

167–8 **He's . . . daughter** Sir Walter has used his anticipated income to persuade Yellowhammer to permit him to marry Moll

169 **deceived** (1) feigned; (2) exposed; (3) overcome

Be but you patient, wife.
Lady. I have suff'red a long time.
Sir Oliver. Suffer thy heart out! A pox suffer thee!
Lady. Nay, thee, thou desertless slave!
Sir Oliver. Come, come. I ha' done.
You'll to the gossiping of Master Allwit's child?
Lady. Yes, to my much joy!
Everyone gets before me: there's my sister
Was married but at Barthol'mew eve last,
And she can have two children at a birth.
Oh, one of them, one of them would ha' serv'd my turn.
Sir Oliver. Sorrow consume thee, thou art still crossing me,
And know'st my nature –

Enter Maid.

Maid. Oh, mistress! [*Aside.*] Weeping or railing,
That's our house harmony.
Lady. What say'st, Jugg?
Maid. The sweetest news.
Lady. What is't, wench?
Maid. Throw down your doctor's drugs,
They're all but heretics; I bring certain remedy
That has been taught, and proved, and never failed.
Sir Oliver. Oh that, that, that or nothing.
Maid. There's a gentleman,
I haply have his name, too, that has got
Nine children by one water that he useth.
It never misses; they come so fast upon him,
He was fain to give it over.
Lady. His name, sweet Jugg?
Maid. One Master Touchwood, a fine gentleman,
But run behind hand much with getting children.
Sir Oliver. Is't possible?
Maid. Why, sir, he'll undertake,
Using that water, within fifteen years,
For all your wealth, to make you a poor man,
You shall so swarm with children.
Sir Oliver. I'll venture that, i'faith.
Lady. That shall you, husband.
Maid. But I must tell you first, he's very dear.
Sir Oliver. No matter, what serves wealth for?
Lady. True, sweet husband.
[*Sir Oliver*]. There's land to come. Put case his water stands me
In some five hundred pounds a pint,
'Twill fetch a thousand, and a Kersten soul.
[*Lady*]. And that's worth all, sweet husband.
[*Sir Oliver*]. I'll about it.
Ex[*eunt*].

[II.ii]

Enter Allwit.

Allwit. I'll go bid gossips presently myself,
That's all the work I'll do; nor need I stir,
But that it is my pleasure to walk forth
And air myself a little; I am tied to nothing
In this business, what I do is merely recreation.
Not constraint.
Here's running to and fro, nurse upon nurse,
Three charwomen, besides maids and neighbors' children.
Fie, what a trouble have I rid my hands on!
It makes me sweat to think on't.

Enter Sir Walter Whorehound.

Sir Walter. How now, Jack?
Allwit. I am going to bid gossips for your worship's child, sir.
A goodly girl, i'faith, give you joy on her;
She looks as if she had two thousand pounds to her portion
And run away with a tailor; a fine, plump, black-eyed slut;
Under correction, sir,
I take delight to see her. – Nurse!

Enter Dry Nurse.

Dry Nurse. Do you call, sir?
Allwit. I call not you, I call the wet nurse hither.
Exit [Dry Nurse].
Give me the wet nurse.

---

175 gossiping christening
178 Barthol'mew eve August 23; twins delivered during Lent means they were conceived before the marriage
185 Jugg Joan (a stereotypical name for a maidservant)
188 Throw . . . drugs (doctors were often accused of magical practices)
189 heretics (1) improper; (2) inadequate
193 haply by chance
194 water (1) special potion; (2) ejaculation
196 fain gladly
198 behind hand in debt
204 dear costly
206 Put case suppose
206–7 stands me In costs
208 Kersten Christian
II.ii.1 bid summon; **gossips** literally, godparents; here female friends attending a christening; **presently** shortly
10 sweat (with pun on treatment for venereal disease)
14 run . . . tailor (because his clothes are so fine)
15 Under correction I'm sorry
16 s.d. Dry Nurse one who cares for the child

Enter Wet Nurse [*carrying baby*].

Aye, 'tis thou.
Come hither, come hither,
Let's see her once again; I cannot choose
But buss her thrice an hour.

Wet Nurse. You may be proud on't, sir;
'Tis the best piece of work that e'er you did.

Allwit. Think'st thou so, nurse? What sayest to Wat and Nick?

Wet Nurse. They're pretty children both, but here's a wench
Will be a knocker.

Allwit. Pup! – Say'st thou me so? – Pup, little countess;
– Faith, sir, I thank your worship for this girl
Ten thousand times and upward.

Sir Walter. I am glad I have her for you, sir.

Allwit. Here, take her in, nurse; wipe her, and give her spoon-meat.

Wet Nurse. [*Aside.*] Wipe your mouth, sir.

Exit [*with child*].

Allwit. And now about these gossips.

Sir Walter. Get but two, I'll stand for one myself.

Allwit. To your own child, sir?

Sir Walter. The better policy; it prevents suspicion.
'Tis good to play with rumor at all weapons.

Allwit. Troth, I commend your care, sir; 'tis a thing
That I should ne'er have thought on.

Sir Walter. [*Aside.*] The more slave!
When man turns base, out goes his soul's pure flame;
The fat of ease o'erthrows the eyes of shame.

Allwit. I am studying who to get for godmother
Suitable to your worship. Now I ha' thought on't.

Sir Walter. I'll ease you of that care, and please myself in't.
[*Aside.*] My love, the goldsmith's daughter, if I send,
Her father will command her. – Davy Dahumma!

Enter Davy.

Allwit. I'll fit your worship then with a male partner.

Sir Walter. What is he?

Allwit. A kind, proper gentleman, brother to Master Touchwood.

Sir Walter. I know Touchwood. Has he a brother living?

Allwit. A neat bachelor.

Sir Walter. Now we know him, we'll make shift with him.
Dispatch, the time draws near. Come hither, Davy.

Exit [*with* Davy].

Allwit. In troth, I pity him, he ne'er stands still.
Poor knight, what pains he takes: sends this way one,
That way another, has not an hour's leisure.
I would not have thy toil, for all thy pleasure.

Enter two Promoters.

[*Aside.*] Ha, how now? What are these that stand so close
At the street corner, pricking up their ears,
And snuffing up their noses, like rich men's dogs
When the first course goes in? By the mass, promoters!
'Tis so, I hold my life; and planted there
To arrest the dead corpse of poor calves and sheep,
Like ravenous creditors that will not suffer
The bodies of their poor departed debtors
To go to th' grave, but e'en in death to vex
And stay the corpse, with bills of Middlesex.
This Lent will fat the whoresons up with sweetbreads
And lard their whores with lamb-stones; what their golls
Can clutch goes presently to their Molls and Dolls.
The bawds will be so fat with what they earn

---

18 s.d. **Wet Nurse** one who suckles the child
21 **buss** kiss
26 **knocker** (1) knockout, spectacular; (2) sexually active
27 **Pup** (nonsense term of affection)
31 **spoon-meat** soft food
32 **Wipe . . . mouth** (with possible pun on sign of an adulterous woman; see Prov. 30:20)
33 **gossips** (here meaning witnesses)
36 **suspicion** (that I, not you, are the father)
37 **play with** forestall; **weapons** means
39 **slave** (1) member of a lower class; (2) fool
40 **pure** holy
42 **studying** considering
47 **fit** match, complement
51 **neat** elegant, fine
61 **By the mass** (a common oath)
67 **bills of Middlesex** writs with false charges for offenses in Middlesex, extending the authority of King's Bench; once arrested, the real charges were issued
68 **whoresons** (common term of abuse); **sweetbreads** pancreas or thymus glands of animals regarded as aphrodisiacs
69 **golls** hands
70 **Molls and Dolls** common names for prostitutes and criminal companions
71 **bawds** whores

Their chins will hang like udders by Easter eve,
And, being stroked, will give the milk of witches.
How did the mongrels hear my wife lies in?
Well, I may baffle 'em gallantly. By your favor, gentlemen,
I am a stranger both unto the city
And to her carnal strictness.

1 Promoter. Good; your will, sir?

Allwit. Pray tell me where one dwells that kills this Lent.

1 Promoter. How, kills? [*Aside.*] Come hither, Dick; a bird, a bird!

2 Promoter. What is't that you would have?

Allwit. Faith, any flesh,
But I long especially for veal and green sauce.

1 Promoter. [*Aside.*] Green goose, you shall be sauced.

Allwit. I have half a scornful stomach; no fish will be admitted.

1 Promoter. Not this Lent, sir?

Allwit. Lent? What cares colon here for Lent?

1 Promoter. You say well, sir;
Good reason that the colon of a gentleman
(As you were lately pleased to term your worship, sir)
Should be fulfilled with answerable food,
To sharpen blood, delight health, and tickle nature.
Were you directed hither to this street, sir?

Allwit. That I was, aye, marry.

2 Promoter. And the butcher, belike,
Should kill and sell close in some upper room?

Allwit. Some apple loft, as I take it, or a coal house;
I know not which, i'faith.

2 Promoter. Either will serve;
[*Aside.*] This butcher shall kiss Newgate, 'less he turn up
The bottom of the pocket of his apron.
[*To Allwit*]. You go to seek him?

Allwit. Where you shall not find him;
I'll buy, walk by your noses with my flesh,
Sheep-biting mongrels, hand-basket freebooters!
My wife lies in; a foutra for promoters!
Exit.

1 Promoter. That shall not serve your turn. What a rogue's this! How cunningly he came over us!

Enter a Man *with meat in a basket.*

2 Promoter. Hush't, stand close.

Man. I have 'scap'd well thus far; they say the knaves are wondrous hot and busy.

1 Promoter. By your leave, sir.
We must see what you have under your cloak there.

Man. Have? I have nothing.

1 Promoter. No, do you tell us that? What makes this lump stick out then? We must see, sir.

Man. What will you see, sir? A pair of sheets, and two of my wife's foul smocks, going to the washers?

2 Promoter. Oh, we love that sight well, you cannot please us better!
[*He searches the basket.*]
What, do you gull us? Call you these "shirts and smocks"?

Man. Now a pox choke you!
You have cozened me and five of my wife's kin'red
Of a good dinner; we must make it up now
With herrings and milk-pottage.
Exit.

1 Promoter. 'Tis all veal.

2 Promoter. All veal? Pox, the worse luck! I promised faithfully to send this morning a fat quarter of lamb to a kind gentlewoman in Turnbull Street that longs; and how I'm crossed!

72 **chins** double chins were believed a feature of bawds
73 **milk of witches** witches nourished familiars by having them suck on teats made by the devil
75 **baffle** (1) silence; (2) outsmart; (3) disgrace (informers visited homes of pregnant women knowing they had strange tastes)
77 **carnal** (pertaining to flesh)
78 **kills . . . Lent** i.e., is a butcher
79 **bird** victim
81 **green sauce** spiced sauce made from vinegar often used to disguise the fact that the meat was undercooked; hence to eat veal and green sauce was proverbial for being cheated
82 **Green goose** naive fool; **be sauced** made to pay dearly
83 **I . . . stomach** I am selectively fasting for Lent
85 **colon** intestines; stomach (colloquial for hunger)
89 **fulfilled** satisfied; **answerable** accommodating
90 **sharpen . . . nature** sexually arouse
93 **close** secretly; **upper room** (1) attic; (2) pun on Christ's betrayal
96 **kiss Newgate** go to prison (Newgate imprisoned London freemen charged with criminal offenses)
96–7 **turn . . . apron** empty his pockets with a bribe
100 **Sheep-biting** cant for whoring; **freebooters** pirates (raiding baskets of passers-by)
101 **foutra** (obscene French oath)
102 **That . . . turn** that won't do (since pregnant women were not exempt)
103 **cunningly** deceitfully; skillfully
116 **gull** trick
118 **cozened** cheated
120 **milk-pottage** milk broth
125 **Turnbull Street** Turnmill Street near Clerkenwell Green, known for its brothels; **longs** desires because she is pregnant
126 **crossed** thwarted

1 Promoter. Let's share this, and see what hap comes next then.

Enter another [Man] *with a basket.*

2 Promoter. Agreed, Stand close again; another booty. What's he?
1 Promoter. Sir, by your favor.
[2] *Man.* Meaning me, sir?
1 Promoter. Good Master Oliver? Cry thee mercy, i'faith!
What hast thou there?
[2] *Man.* A rack of mutton, sir, and half a lamb;
You know my mistress's diet.
1 Promoter. Go, go, we see thee not; away, keep close!
Heart, let him pass! Thou'lt never have the wit
To know our benefactors.

[*Exit* 2 Man.]

2 Promoter. I have forgot him.
1 Promoter. 'Tis Master Beggarland's man, the wealthy merchant
That is in fee with us.
2 Promoter. Now I have a feeling of him.
1 Promoter. You know he purchased the whole Lent together,
Gave us ten groats a-piece on Ash Wednesday.
2 Promoter. True, true.

Enter a Wench *with a basket, and a child in it under a loin of mutton.*

1 Promoter. A wench.
2 Promoter. Why, then, stand close indeed.
Wench. [*Aside.*] Women had need of wit, if they'll shift here;
And she that hath wit may shift anywhere.
1 Promoter. Look, look! Poor fool,
She has left the rump uncovered, too,
More to betray her; this is like a murd'rer
That will outface the deed with a bloody band.
2 Promoter. What time of the year is't, sister?
Wench. Oh, sweet gentlemen, I am a poor servant,
Let me go.
1 Promoter. You shall, wench, but this must stay with us.
Wench. Oh, you undo me, sir!
'Tis for a wealthy gentlewoman that takes physic, sir;
The doctor does allow my mistress mutton.
Oh, as you tender the dear life of a gentlewoman!
I'll bring my master to you; he shall show you
A true authority from the higher powers,
And I'll run every foot.
2 Promoter. Well, leave your basket then,
And run and spare not.
Wench. Will you swear then to me
To keep it till I come?
1 Promoter. Now by this light, I will.
Wench. What say you, gentleman?
2 Promoter. What a strange wench 'tis!
Would we might perish else.
Wench. Nay, then I run, sir.

Exit.

1 Promoter. And ne'er return, I hope.
2 Promoter. A politic baggage,
She makes us swear to keep it;
I prithee, look what market she hath made.
1 Promoter. [*Unpacking the basket.*] *Imprimis*, sir, a good fat loin of mutton:
What comes next under this cloth?
Now for a quarter of lamb.
2 Promoter. Now for a shoulder of mutton.
1 Promoter. Done.
2 Promoter. Why, done, sir!
1 Promoter. [*Feeling in the basket.*] By the mass, I feel I have lost;
'Tis of more weight, i'faith.
2 Promoter. Some loin of veal?
1 Promoter. No, faith, here's a lamb's head,
I feel that plainly. Why yet [I'll] win my wager.

[*Takes out child.*]

2 Promoter. Ha?
1 Promoter. Swounds, what's here?
2 Promoter. A child!

---

127 hap chance
135 rack neck (considered a delicacy for invalids)
136 benefactors those who pay bribes
141 fee league, conspiracy
142 of for
143 purchased bought immunity from us for
144 groats originally, fourpenny pieces; by 1600 any small sum; **Ash Wednesday** the first day in Lent; in 1613 on February 21
146 s.d. Wench (probably the one who was dismissed by Touchwood Senior at II.i.111–12)
148 shift (1) catch me; (2) trick me
153 outface brazenly pretend innocence; **band** collar
159 physic medicine
161 tender attend
163 authority official certificate of exemption (given to some ambassadors and the sick)
175 politic crafty
177 market profit
178 *Imprimis* first (as in an inventory)
188 lamb's head fool's head (apparently the object of the wager)
191 Swounds "God's wounds" (a common oath)

1 Promoter. A pox of all dissembling cunning whores!
2 Promoter. Here's an unlucky breakfast!
1 Promoter. What shall's do?
2 Promoter. The quean made us swear to keep it, too.
1 Promoter. We might leave it else.
2 Promoter. Villainous strange!
Life, had she none to gull but poor promoters,
That watch hard for a living?
1 Promoter. Half our gettings must run in sugar-sops
And nurses' wages now, besides many a pound of soap,
And tallow; we have need to get loins of mutton still,
To save suet to change for candles.
2 Promoter. Nothing mads me but this was a lamb's head with you, you felt it. She has made calves' heads of us.
1 Promoter. Prithee, no more on't.
There's time to get it up; it is not come
To mid-Lent Sunday yet.
2 Promoter. I am so angry, I'll watch no more today.
1 Promoter. Faith, nor I neither.
2 Promoter. Why, then, I'll make a motion.
1 Promoter. Well, what is't?
2 Promoter. Let's e'en go to the Checker at Queenhive and roast the loin of mutton, till young flood; then send the child to Brainford.

[*Exeunt.*]

[II.iii]

Enter Allwit *in one of Sir Walter's suits, and* Davy *trussing him.*

Allwit. 'Tis a busy day at our house, Davy.
Davy. Always the kurs'ning day, sir.
Allwit. Truss, truss me, Davy.
Davy. [*Aside.*] No matter and you were hanged, sir.
Allwit. How does this suit fit me, Davy?
Davy. Excellent neatly; my master's things were ever fit for you, sir, e'en to a hair, you know.
Allwit. Thou has hit it right, Davy,
We ever jumped in one, this ten years, Davy.

Enter a Servant *with a box.*

So, well said. What art thou?
Servant. Your comfit-maker's man, sir.
Allwit. Oh, sweet youth, into the nurse quick,
Quick, 'tis time, i'faith;
Your mistress will be here?
Servant. She was setting forth, sir.

Enter two Puritans.

Allwit. Here comes our gossips now. Oh I shall have such kissing work today. Sweet Mistress Underman, welcome, i'faith.
1 Puritan. Give you joy of your fine girl, sir.
Grant that her education may be pure,
And become one of the faithful.
Allwit. Thanks to your sisterly wishes, Mistress Underman.
2 Puritan. Are any of the brethren's wives yet come?
Allwit. There are some wives within, and some at home.
1 Puritan. Verily, thanks, sir.

Exeunt [Puritans].

Allwit. "Verily," you are an ass, forsooth;
I must fit all these times, or there's no music.

Enter two Gossips.

Here comes a friendly and familiar pair;
Now I like these wenches well.
1 Gossip. How dost, sirrah?
Allwit. Faith, well, I thank you, neighbor; and how dost thou?
2 Gossip. Want nothing, but such getting, sir, as thine.
Allwit. My gettings, wench? They are poor.

---

196 quean whore
201 sugar-sops bread soaked in sugar water (for nourishment)
203 tallow (for cleaning the baby's rump)
204 To . . . candles (suet was used for cheap candles, presumably to care for the baby at night)
209 get it up redeem the loss (but with bawdy pun)
210 mid-Lent Sunday fourth Sunday in Lent
213 motion suggestion
215 Checker a famous inn; its sign was a checkerboard
215–16 Queenhive (Queenhithe) a large quay just W of Southwark Bridge where most London fish was caught, and so important during Lent
216–17 young flood incoming tide (the Thames is a tidal river)
217 Brainford Brentford, a Middlesex town opposite Kew on N side of the Thames known as a popular place for putting out children

II.iii.1 s.d. *trussing* (1) tying up laces; (2) preparing him for a hanging
2 Always (1) it always is; (2) pun on still (i.e., we are always having a christening here); **kurs'ning** christening
4 No . . . and it would not matter if
8 hit it guessed
9 jumped in one (1) agreed; (2) went for the same woman
11 comfit-maker confectioner; comfits are crystallized fruit
21 become suit
23 brethren's other Puritans (in this scene, Middleton mocks Puritan language)
25 Verily truly (further parody)
27 I . . . music I must play along or my easy life will cease
33 gettings (1) children; (2) earnings

1 Gossip. Fie that thou'lt say so!
Th'ast as fine children as a man can get.
Davy. [*Aside.*] Aye, as a man can get,
And that's my master.
Allwit. They are pretty, foolish things.
Put to making in minutes;
I ne'er stand long about 'em.
Will you walk in, wenches?
[*Exeunt* Gossips.]

Enter Touchwood Junior *and* Moll.

Touchwood Junior. The happiest meeting that our souls could wish for. Here's the ring ready; I am beholding unto your father's haste, h'as kept his hour.
Moll. He never kept it better.

Enter Sir Walter Whorehound.

Touchwood Junior. Back, be silent.
Sir Walter. Mistress and partner, I will put you both into one cup. [*Drinks to them.*]
Davy. [*Aside.*] Into one cup! Most proper;
A fitting compliment for a goldsmith's daughter.
Allwit. Yes, sir, that's he must be your worship's partner
In this day's business, Master Touchwood's brother.
Sir Walter. I embrace your acquaintance, sir.
Touchwood Junior. It vows your service, sir.
Sir Walter. It's near high time. Come, Master Allwit.
Allwit. Ready, sir.
Sir Walter. Will't please you walk?
Touchwood Junior. Sir, I obey your time.
Ex[*eunt*].

[II.iv]

Enter Midwife *with the child*, [Maudline, *two* Puritans] *and the* Gossips *to the kurs'ning.*

[*Exit* Midwife *with child.*]

1 Gossip. [*Offering precedence.*] Good Mistress Yellowhammer.
Maudline. In faith, I will not.
1 Gossip. Indeed, it shall be yours.
Maudline. I have sworn, i'faith.
1 Gossip. I'll stand still then.
Maudline. So will you let the child go without company
And make me forsworn.
1 Gossip. You are such another creature.
[*Exeunt* 1 Gossip *and* Maudline.]
2 Gossip. Before me? I pray come down a little.
3 Gossip. Not a whit; I hope I know my place.
2 Gossip. Your place? Great wonder, sure! Are you any better than a comfit-maker's wife?
3 Gossip. And that's as good at all times as a 'pothecary's.
2 Gossip. Ye lie. Yet I forbear you too.
[*Exeunt* 2 *and* 3 Gossips.]
1 Puritan. Come, sweet sister, we go in unity, and show the fruits of peace like children of the spirit.
2 Puritan. I love lowliness.
[*Exeunt* Puritans.]
4 Gossip. True, so say I: though they strive more,
There comes as proud behind, as goes before.
5 Gossip. Every inch, i'faith.
Exit [4 Gossip *and* 5 Gossip].

Act III

[III.i]

Enter Touchwood Junior *and a* Parson.

Touchwood Junior. Oh, sir, if ever you felt the force of love, pity it in me!
Parson. Yes, though I ne'er was married, sir,
I have felt the force of love from good men's daughters,
And some that will be maids yet three years hence.
Have you got a license?
Touchwood Junior. Here, 'tis, ready, sir.
Parson. That's well.
Touchwood Junior. The ring and all things perfect; she'll steal hither.
Parson. She shall be welcome, sir; I'll not be long
A-clapping you together.

Enter Moll *and* Touchwood Senior.

Touchwood Junior. Oh, here she's come, sir.
Parson. What's he?
Touchwood Junior. My honest brother.

---

39 Put...making conceived
40 stand (1) delay; (2) remain erect
48–9 put...cup join you both in a toast (ironically anticipatory)
51 goldsmith's daughter (perhaps punning on the ceremonial cup made for a wedding)
56 high time (1) the festive moment; (2) noon
59 obey...time follow your lead

II.iv.1 s.d. Gossips (this processional is one of squabbling over precedence; a mockery of the guilds)
5 stand witness
9 come...little be more humble
20 There... before (proverbial); with pun on *proud* as *erect*
21 inch (with sexual pun)
III.i.4–5 I...hence (the parson hints at his own sexual past)

Touchwood Senior. Quick, make haste, sirs!
Moll. You must dispatch with all the speed you can,
For I shall be missed straight; I made hard shift
For this small time I have.
Parson. Then I'll not linger;
Place that ring upon her finger:
[Touchwood Junior *places the ring on Moll's finger.*]
This the finger plays the part,
Whose master-vein shoots from the heart;
Now join hands –

Enter Yellowhammer *and* Sir Walter.

Yellowhammer. Which I will sever,
And so ne'er again meet never!
Moll. Oh, we are betrayed.
Touchwood Junior. Hard fate!
Sir Walter. I am struck with wonder.
Yellowhammer. Was this the politic fetch, thou mystical baggage,
Thou disobedient strumpet?
[*To Sir Walter.*] And were you so wise to send for her to such an end?
Sir Walter. Now I disclaim the end; you'll make me mad.
Yellowhammer. [*To Touchwood Junior.*] And what are you, sir?
Touchwood Junior. And you cannot see with those two glasses, put on a pair more.
Yellowhammer. I dreamt of anger still! Here, take your ring, sir;
[*Takes ring off Moll's finger.*]
Ha! This? Life, 'tis the same. Abominable!
Did not I sell this ring?
Touchwood Junior. I think you did, you received money for 't.
Yellowhammer. Heart, hark you, knight;
Here's no inconscionable villainy!
Set me a-work to make the wedding ring,
And come with an intent to steal my daughter!
Did ever runaway match it?
Sir Walter. [*To Touchwood Senior.*] This your brother, sir?
Touchwood Senior. He can tell that as well as I.
Yellowhammer. The very posy mocks me to my face:
"Love that's wise, blinds parents' eyes."
I thank your wisdom, sir, for blinding of us;
We have good hope to recover our sight shortly.
In the meantime, I will lock up this baggage
As carefully as my gold. She shall see as little sun,
If a close room or so can keep her from the light on't.
Moll. Oh, sweet father, for love's sake, pity me.
Yellowhammer. Away!
Moll. [*To Touchwood Junior.*] Farewell, sir, all content bless thee,
And take this for comfort.
Though violence keep me, thou canst lose me never;
I am ever thine although we part forever.
Yellowhammer. Aye, we shall part you, minx.
Exit [*with* Moll].
Sir Walter. [*To Touchwood Junior.*] Your acquaintance, sir, came very lately,
Yet it came too soon;
I must hereafter know you for no friend,
But one that I must shun like pestilence,
Or the disease of lust.
Touchwood Junior. Like enough, sir; you h' ta'en me at the worst time for words that e'er ye picked out; faith, do not wrong me, sir.
Exit [*with* Parson].
Touchwood Senior. Look after him and spare not. There he walks
That never yet received baffling; you're blessed
More than e'er I knew. Go take your rest.
Exit.
Sir Walter. I pardon you, you are both losers.
Exit.

[III.ii]

A bed thrust out upon the stage, Allwit's Wife *in it. Enter all the* Gossips [*including* Maudline, Lady Kix, *the* Puritans, *also* Dry Nurse *with the child*].

1 Gossip. How is't, woman? We have brought you home
A Kursen soul.

12 dispatch complete the ceremony
13 made . . . shift arranged with difficulty
16 finger (with pun on penis)
18 master-vein an artery believed to go directly from the heart to the third finger of the left hand
19 join hands (once they do, the service is completed; Yellowhammer intervenes at the last possible moment)
25 politic fetch cunning trick; **mystical** (1) secret; (2) mysterious; (3) concealed
32 glasses eyeglasses
39 inconscionable unconscionable; accidental
52 close confined; **so** something else
59 minx (1) pert girl; (2) lewd or wanton woman
60 lately recently
68 Look after watch out for
69 baffling (1) silencing; (2) public humiliation

Wife. Aye, I thank your pains.
[*1*] *Puritan.* And verily well kursened, i'the right way,
Without idolatry or superstition.
After the pure manner of Amsterdam.
Wife. Sit down, good neighbors. Nurse!
Nurse. At hand, forsooth.
Wife. Look they have all low stools.
Nurse. They have, forsooth.
2 Gossip. Bring the child hither, Nurse. How say you now,
Gossip, is't not a chopping girl, so like the father?
3 Gossip. As if it had been spit out of his mouth,
Eyed, nosed and browed as like a girl can be;
Only, indeed, it has the mother's mouth.
2 Gossip. The mother's mouth up and down, up and down!
3 Gossip. 'Tis a large child; she's but a little woman.
[*1*] *Puritan.* No believe me, a very spiny creature, but all heart,
Well mettled, like the faithful, to endure
Her tribulation here, and raise up seed.
2 Gossip. She had a sore labor on't, I warrant you.
You can tell, neighbor.
3 Gossip. Oh, she had great speed;
We were afraid once,
But she made us all have joyful hearts again;
'Tis a good soul, i'faith;
The midwife found her a most cheerful daughter.
[*1*] *Puritan.* 'Tis the Spirit; the sisters are all like her.

Enter Sir Walter *with two spoons and plate and* Allwit.

2 Gossip. Oh, here comes the chief gossip, neighbors.
[*Exit* Nurse *with child.*]
Sir Walter. The fatness of your wishes to you all, ladies.
3 Gossip. Oh, dear, sweet gentleman, what fine words he has:
"The fatness of our wishes."
2 Gossip. Calls us all "ladies"!
4 Gossip. I promise you, a fine gentleman, and a courteous.
2 Gossip. Methinks her husband shows like a clown to him.
3 Gossip. I would not care what clown my husband were too, so I had such fine children.
2 Gossip. She's all fine children, gossip.
3 Gossip. Aye, and see how fast they come.
[*1*] *Puritan.* Children are blessings, if they be got with zeal,
By the brethren, as I have five at home.
Sir Walter. [*To Mistress Allwit.*] The worst is past, I hope now, gossip.
Mistress Allwit. So I hope too, good sir.
Allwit. [*Aside.*] Why then, so hope I too, for company!
I have nothing to do else.
Sir Walter. [*Giving cup and spoons.*] A poor remembrance, lady,
To the love of the babe; I pray accept of it.
Mistress Allwit. Oh, you are at too much charge, sir.
2 Gossip. Look, look, what has he given her? What is't, gossip?
3 Gossip. Now, by my faith, a fair high standing cup, and two great 'postle spoons, one of them gilt.
1 Puritan. Sure that was Judas then with the red beard.
2 Puritan. I would not feed my daughter with that spoon for all the world, for fear of coloring her hair; red hair the brethren like not, it consumes them much. 'Tis not the sisters' color.

Enter Nurse *with comfits and wine.*

Allwit. Well said, Nurse;
About, about with them among the gossips.

III.ii.5 Amsterdam a special place of refuge for Puritans
7 forsooth for truth
8 low stools (pun on false humility associated with the Puritans)
11 chopping vigorous, strapping
15 up and down upper and lower lips
17 spiny thin, spindly
18 mettled spirited
19 seed (the purpose of the wife is to have children)
22 speed good fortune
27 the Spirit (1) Holy Spirit; millennial sects claimed the guidance of the Holy Spirit as protection; such antinomianism could lead to debauchery; (2) alcohol
28 s.d. *plate* gold or silver ware
28 chief gossip the two chief gossips are Sir Walter (who is the one the women dote on) and Moll
29 fatness richest part
33 clown peasant
36 She's she has
38 zeal (1) religious enthusiasm; (2) sexual joy
47 charge expense (too generous)
49–50 standing cup a stemmed goblet, a traditional christening gift
50 'postle spoons common christening gift of spoons with figures of apostles as handles (hence idolatrous to the Puritans)
51 gilt gold-covered silver (hence also deceptive and hypocritical)
52 red beard traditional sign of Judas (also thought lascivious; cf. line 55)
55 consumes (1) with anger; (2) with lechery (both deadly sins)
56 sisters' women of the Puritan faith
57 said done

[*Aside.*] Now out comes all the tasselled
handkerchers,
They are spread abroad between their knees
already;
Now in goes the long fingers that are washed
Some thrice a day in urine (my wife uses it).
Now we shall have such pocketing;
See how they lurch at the lower end.
[*1*] *Puritan.* Come hither, Nurse.
Allwit. [*Aside.*] Again! She has taken twice already.
[*1*] *Puritan.* I had forgot a sister's child that's sick.
[*Taking comfits.*]
Allwit. [*Aside.*] A pox! It seems your purity loves sweet things well that puts in thrice together. Had this been all my cost now I had been beggared. These women have no consciences at sweetmeats, where e'er they come; see and they have not culled out all the long plums too. They have left nothing here but short wriggle-tail comfits, not worth mouthing. No mar'l I heard a citizen complain once that his wife's belly only broke his back. Mine had been all in fitters seven years since, but for this worthy knight that with a prop upholds my wife and me, and all my estate buried in Bucklersberry.
Wife. [*Pledging them.*] Here, Mistress
Yellowhammer, and neighbors,
To you all that have taken pains with me,
All the good wives at once.
[*Wine is taken round.*]
[*1*] *Puritan*]. I'll answer for them.
They wish all health and strength,
And that you may courageously go forward,
To perform the like and many such,
Like a true sister with motherly bearing.
[*She drinks.*]
Allwit. [*Aside.*] Now the cups troll about to wet
the gossips' whistles;
It pours down, i'faith; they never think of
payment.
[*1*] *Puritan.* Fill again, nurse.
[*She drinks again.*]
Allwit. [*Aside.*] Now bless thee, two at once! I'll
stay no longer;
It would kill me and if I paid for't.
[*To Sir Walter.*] Will it please you to walk down
and leave the women?
Sir Walter. With all my heart, Jack.
Allwit. Troth, I cannot blame you.
Sir Walter. Sit you all, merry ladies.
All Gossips. Thank your worship, sir.
[*1*] *Puritan.* Thank your worship, sir.
Allwit. [*Aside.*] A pox twice tipple ye, you are last
and lowest!
Exit [Allwit *with* Sir Walter].
[*1*] *Puritan.* Bring hither that same cup, Nurse, I would fain drive away this-hup!-antichristian grief.
[*Drinks.*]
3 Gossip. See, gossip, and she lies not in like a
countess;
Would I had such a husband for my daughter!
4 Gossip. Is not she toward marriage?
3 Gossip. Oh, no, sweet gossip!
4 Gossip. Why, she's nineteen?
3 Gossip. Aye, that she was last Lammas;
But she has a fault, gossip, a secret fault.
[Nurse *fills the glass, then exit.*]
4 Gossip. A fault, what is't?
3 Gossip. I'll tell you when I have drunk.
[*Drinks.*]
4 Gossip. [*Aside.*] Wine can do that, I see, that friendship cannot.
3 Gossip. And now I'll tell you, gossip: she's too free.
4 Gossip. Too free?
3 Gossip. Oh, aye, she cannot lie dry in her bed.
4 Gossip. What, and nineteen?
3 Gossip. 'Tis as I tell you, gossip.

[*Enter* Nurse *and speaks to* Maudline.]

Maudline. Speak with me, Nurse? Who is't?
Nurse. A gentleman from Cambridge;
I think it be your son, forsooth.

---

59 **handkerchers** handkerchiefs used as napkins
62 **urine** (used as a cleansing lotion and cosmetic)
63 **pocketing** (to take home)
64 **lurch** (1) steal; (2) stagger; **lower end** far end (with sexual pun)
69 **sweet things** (as sexual innuendo)
70 **all my** at my (rather than Sir Walter's)
73 **culled** picked; **plums** sugarplums
74–5 **short . . . comfits** small sweets resembling shriveled penises (hence rejected)
75 **mar'l** marvel
77 **only** alone; **broke . . . back** (because her eating and sexual activity made her heavy)
78 **fitters** fragments
79 **prop** (1) financial support; (2) sexual satisfaction from Allwit's wife
80 **Bucklersberry** London street running from the Poultry to Walbrook, known for its grocers and apothecaries
89 **troll** be passed; circulated
100 **tipple** topple
106 **toward** interested in
109 **Lammas** August 1; time of the harvest festival in the church year
113 **do that** reveal things
116 **free** (1) incontinent; (2) sexually active

Maudline. 'Tis my son Tim, i'faith.
Prithee, call him up among the women;
[*Exit* Nurse.]
'Twill embolden him well,
For he wants nothing but audacity.
Would the Welsh gentlewoman at home were here now.
Lady. Is your son come, forsooth?
Maudline. Yes, from the university, forsooth.
Lady. 'Tis great joy on ye.
Maudline. There's a great marriage towards for him.
Lady. A marriage?
Maudline. Yes, sure, a huge heir in Wales,
At least to nineteen mountains,
Besides her goods and cattle.

Enter [Nurse *with*] Tim.

Tim. Oh, I'm betrayed!
Exit.
Maudline. What, gone again? Run after him, good Nurse;
[*Exit* Nurse.]
He's so bashful, that's the spoil of youth.
In the university they're kept still to men,
And ne'er trained up to women's company.
Lady. 'Tis a great spoil of youth, indeed.

Enter Nurse *and* Tim.

Nurse. Your mother will have it so.
Maudline. Why, son, why, Tim!
What, must I rise and fetch you? For shame, son!
Tim. Mother you do intreat like a freshwoman;
'Tis against the laws of the university
For any that has answered under bachelor
To thrust 'mongst married wives.
Maudline. Come, we'll excuse you here.
Tim. Call up my tutor, mother, and I care not.
Maudline. What, is your tutor come? Have you brought him up?
Tim. I ha' not brought him up, he stands at door.
Negatur. There's logic to begin with you, mother.
Maudline. Run, call the gentleman, Nurse, he's my son's tutor.
[*Exit* Nurse.]
Here, eat some plums.
Tim. Come I from Cambridge, and offer me six plums?
Maudline. Why, how now, Tim.
Will not your old tricks yet be left?
Tim. Served like a child,
When I have answered under bachelor?
Maudline. You'll never lin till I make your tutor whip you; you know how I served you once at the free school in Paul's churchyard?
Tim. Oh, monstrous absurdity!
Ne'er was the like in Cambridge since my time.
'Life, whip a bachelor? You'd be laughed at soundly;
Let not my tutor hear you!
'Twould be a jest through the whole university;
No more words, mother.

Enter Tutor.

Maudline. Is this your tutor, Tim?
Tutor. Yes surely, lady, I am the man that brought him in league with logic, and read the Dunces to him.
Tim. That did he, mother, but now I have 'em all in my own pate, and can as well read 'em to others.
Tutor. That can he, mistress, for they flow naturally from him.
Maudline. I'm the more beholding to your pains, sir.
Tutor. *Non ideo sane.*
Maudline. True, he was an idiot indeed
When he went out of London, but now he's well mended.
Did you receive the two goose pies I sent you?
Tutor. And eat them heartily, thanks to your worship.
Maudline. 'Tis my son Tim. I pray bid him welcome, gentlewomen.

---

132 **towards** in prospect
136 **cattle** chattel; property
139 **spoil** (1) ruination; (2) uselessness
140 **still** always
146 **freshwoman** (1) in analogy to freshman, first-year student at university; (2) unspoiled, inexperienced
148 **answered under** proceeded to Bachelor of Arts
151 **up** up to London
152 **up** upstairs
154 ***Negatur*** "it is denied" (from the academic disputation)
162 **lin** cease; learn
164 **free school** St. Paul's School founded for 153 poor scholars
165 **Oh . . . absurdity** (she is ignorant, thinking they have schoolboy whippings at the university)
173 **Dunces** (1) scholastic scholars who are followers of Duns Scotus (Cambridge offered philosophy instead, as Middleton's Oxford did not); (2) fools
176 **pate** head
178–9 **flow naturally** pun; (1) he teaches others; (2) he forgets all he is taught intellectually
182 ***Non . . . sane*** "Not on that account indeed" (common rhetorical formula)
185 **goose pies** (made with joints of goose, spices, apples, fried onions, and wine, but playing on Tim as a goose or fool)

Tim. "Tim"? Hark you, "Timothius," mother,
"Timothius."
Maudline. How, shall I deny your name?
"Timothius," quoth he?
Faith, there's a name! 'Tis my son Tim,
forsooth.
Lady. You're welcome, Master Tim.
Kiss.
Tim. [*Aside to Tutor.*] Oh, this is horrible! She wets
as she kisses!
Your handkercher, sweet tutor, to wipe them
off as fast as they come on.
2 Gossip. Welcome from Cambridge.
Kiss.
Tim. [*Aside to Tutor.*] This is intolerable! This woman has a villainous sweet breath, did she not stink of comfits. Help me, sweet tutor, or I shall rub my lips off.
Tutor. I'll go kiss the lower end the whilst.
Tim. Perhaps that's the sweeter, and we shall dispatch the sooner.
[*1*] *Puritan.* Let me come next. Welcome from the wellspring of discipline, that waters all the brethren.
Reels and falls.
Tim. Hoist, I beseech thee.
3 Gossip. Oh, bless the woman! Mistress
Underman!
[*1*] *Puritan.* 'Tis but the common affliction of the
faithful;
We must embrace our falls.
Tim. [*Aside to Tutor.*] I'm glad I 'scap'd it; it was
some rotten kiss, sure.
It dropped down before it came at me.

Enter Allwit *and* Davy.

Allwit. [*Aside.*] Here's a noise! Not parted yet?
Hyda, a looking glass! They have drunk so
hard in plate
That some of them had need of other vessels.
[*Aloud.*] Yonder's the bravest show.
All Gossips. Where? Where, sir?
Allwit. Come along presently by the Pissing-
conduit,
With two brave drums and a standard bearer.
All Gossips. Oh, brave!
Tim. Come, tutor.
Exeunt.
All Gossips. Farewell, sweet gossip.
Exeunt
Wife. I thank you all for your pains.
[*1*] *Puritan.* Feed and grow strong.
Exit.
[*The curtains around Mistress Allwit's bed are drawn. Exeunt* Maudline, Lady Kix *and* Puritans.]
Allwit. You had more need to sleep than eat;
Go take a nap with some of the brethren, go,
And rise up a well edified, boldified sister!
Oh, here's a day of toil well passed o'er,
Able to make a citizen hare-mad!
How hot they have made the room with their
thick bums.
Dost not feel it, Davy?
Davy. Monstrous strong, sir.
Allwit. What's here under the stools?
Davy. Nothing but wet, sir; some wine spilt here,
belike.
Allwit. Is't no worse, think'st thou?
Fair needlework stools cost nothing with
them, Davy.
Davy. [*Aside.*] Nor you neither, i'faith.
Allwit. Look how they have laid them,
E'en as they lie themselves, with their heels up;
How they have shuffled up the rushes too,
Davy,
With their short, figging, little shittle-cork
heels!
These women can let nothing stand as they
find it.
But what's the secret thou'st about to tell me,

196–7 sweet . . . comfits (in fact, comfits were taken to sweeten the breath)

203 wellspring . . . discipline (Cambridge was a center of Puritan learning)

205 Hoist pick her up

206 Mistress Underman (with bawdy reference)

208 embrace . . . falls accept our moral shortcomings (Calvinist doctrine here mocked)

210 It she; **dropped down** i.e., she fell on the floor

211 parted departed

212 Hyda a nonsense exclamation; **looking glass** euphemism for chamberpot; **plate** vessels used in the christening

214 bravest finest; **show** civic procession or entertainment

216 Pissing-conduit a small conduit close to the Royal Exchange at the intersection of Threadneedle Street and Cornhill named for its slender stream of water (here a pun)

217 two . . . bearer (the phallic outline provokes the gossips' interest)

224–5 Go . . . sister (plays on Anabaptist belief that any man and woman could lie together if they were asleep)

227 hare-mad (1) mad as a hare in March (the breeding season); (2) pun on hair (pudendum)

228 bums (1) cushion-rolls under the skirt; (2) rumps

232 wet (presumably from the overturned chamberpot)

234 needlework stools fashionable stools with patterned embroidered cushions

238 rushes floor coverings in houses (and on public playhouse stages)

239 figging (1) fidgety; (2) copulating; **shittle-cork** (1) wedge-shaped heels and soles of cork; (2) play on "shuttle-cock" or whore

240 let . . . stand (with sexual reference)

My honest Davy?
Davy. If you should disclose it, sir –
Allwit. Life, rip my belly up to the throat then, Davy.
Davy. My master's upon marriage.
Allwit. Marriage, Davy? Send me to hanging rather.
Davy. [*Aside*.] I have stung him.
Allwit. When, where? What is she, Davy?
Davy. E'en the same was gossip, and gave the spoon.
Allwit. I have no time to stay, nor scarce can speak;
I'll stop those wheels, or all the work will break.
Exit.
Davy. I knew t'would prick. Thus do I fashion still
All mine own ends by him and his rank toil.
'Tis my desire to keep him still from marriage;
Being his poor nearest kinsman, I may fare
The better at his death; there my hopes build,
Since my Lady Kix is dry, and hath no child.
Exit.

[III.iii]

Enter both the Touchwoods.

Touchwood Junior. Y'are in the happiest way to enrich yourself
And pleasure me, brother, as man's feet can tread in;
For though she be locked up, her vow is fixed
Only to me. Then time shall never grieve me,
For by that vow e'en absent I enjoy her,
Assuredly confirmed that none else shall,
Which will make tedious years seem gameful to me.
In the mean space, lose you no time, sweet brother;
You have the means to strike at this knight's fortunes
And lay him level with his bankrout merit,
Get but his wife with child, perch at tree top,
And shake the golden fruit into her lap.
About it before she weep herself to a dry ground,
And whine out all her goodness.
Touchwood Senior. Prithee, cease;
I find a too much aptness in my blood
For such a business, without provocation;
You might'well spared this banket of eryngoes,
Hartichokes, potatoes, and your buttered crab:
They were fitter kept for your own wedding dinner.
Touchwood Junior. Nay, and you'll follow my suit, and save my purse too,
Fortune dotes on me: he's in happy case
Finds such an honest friend i'the common place.
Touchwood Senior. Life, what makes thee so merry? Thou hast no cause
That I could hear of lately since thy crosses,
Unless there be news come, with new additions.
Touchwood Junior. Why there thou hast it right.
I look for her this evening, brother.
Touchwood Senior. How's that, "look for her"?
Touchwood Junior. I will deliver you of the wonder straight, brother.
By the firm secrecy and kind assistance
Of a good wench i'the house (who, made of pity,
Weighing the case her own) she's led through gutters,
Strange hidden ways, which none but love could find.
Or ha'the heart to venture; I expect her
Where you would little think.
Touchwood Senior. I care not where,
So she be safe, and yours.
Touchwood Junior. Hope tells me so:
But from your love and time my peace must grow.
Exit.

---

244 Life "On the life of God" (mild oath)
245 upon planning
247 stung (if Sir Walter marries, Allwit is out of a job, as is his wife)
252 prick (with sexual reference)
253 rank (1) excessive; (2) sweaty; (3) corrupt
III.iii.7 gameful (1) joyful; (2) sexually active
8 space time
10 bankrout merit merit bankrupt
11 his Sir Oliver
12 golden fruit the apples of the Hesperides, a sign of sexual delight; the harvester shaking fruit may suggest the Garden of Eden and Danaë, who was impregnated by a shower of gold
13 she ... ground i.e., she becomes old and barren
17 might 'well might as well; **eryngoes** candied roots of sea holly, thought an aphrodisiac
18 Hartichokes ... crab artichokes, yams, and buttered crab were all considered aphrodisiacs
20 suit (1) courtship; (2) cause
22 common place Court of Common Pleas; i.e., you're lucky to have a friend when you need one
24 crosses setbacks
25 new additions further news
29 straight straight away
31 good wench i.e., Susan
32 gutters house gutters (Susan will lead Moll out over the rooftop)

Touchwood Senior. You know the worst then, brother. Now to my Kix,
The barren he and she; they're i'the next room;
But to say which of their two humors hold them
Now at this instant, I cannot say truly.
Sir Oliver. Thou liest, barrenness!
Kix to his Lady within.
Touchwood Senior. Oh, is't that time of day? Give you joy of your tongue,
There's nothing else good in you. This their life
The whole day, from eyes open to eyes shut,
Kissing or scolding, and then must be made friends,
Then rail the second part of the first fit out,
And then be pleased again, no man knows which way;
Fall out like giants, and fall in like children;
Their fruit can witness as much.

Enter Sir Oliver Kix *and his* Lady.

Sir Oliver. 'Tis thy fault.
Lady. Mine, drouth and coldness?
Sir Oliver. Thine, 'tis thou art barren.
Lady. I barren! Oh life, that I durst but speak now,
In mine own justice, in mine own right! I barren!
'Twas otherways with me when I was at court;
I was ne'er call'd so till I was married.
Sir Oliver. I'll be divorced.
Lady. Be hanged! I need not wish it,
That will come too soon to thee. I may say
"Marriage and hanging goes by destiny,"
For all the goodness I can find in't yet.
Sir Oliver. I'll give up house, and keep some fruitful whore,
Like an old bachelor, in a tradesman's chamber;
She and her children shall have all.
Lady. Where be they?
Touchwood Senior. [*Coming forward.*] Pray cease;
When there are friendlier courses took for you
To get and multiply within your house,
At your own proper costs in spite of censure,
Methinks an honest peace might be established.
Sir Oliver. What, with her? Never.
Touchwood Senior. Sweet sir –
Sir Oliver. You work all in vain.
Lady. Then he doth all like thee.
Touchwood Senior. Let me intreat, sir –
Sir Oliver. Singleness confound her!
I took her with one smock.
Lady. But indeed you came not so single,
When you came from shipboard.
Sir Oliver. [*Aside.*] Heart, she bit sore there!
[*To Touchwood Senior.*] Prithee, make's friends.
Touchwood Senior. [*Aside.*] Is't come to that? The peal begins to cease.
Sir Oliver. [*To Lady Kix.*] I'll sell all at an outcry.
Lady. Do thy worst, slave!
[*To Touchwood Senior.*] Good sweet sir, bring us into love again.
Touchwood Senior. [*Aside.*] Some would think this impossible to compass.
– Pray let this storm fly over.
Sir Oliver. Good sir, pardon me. I'm master of this house,
Which I'll sell presently. I'll clap up bills this evening.
Touchwood Senior. Lady, friends – come?
Lady. If e'er ye loved woman, talk not on't, sir.
What, friends with him? Good faith, do you think I'm mad?
With one that's scarce the hinder quarter of a man?
Sir Oliver. Thou art nothing of a woman.
Lady. Would I were less than nothing.
Weeps.
Sir Oliver. Nay, prithee, what dost mean?
Lady. I cannot please you.

38 **You . . . brother** things can now only get better for you
40 **humors** moods
44 **life** how they live
47 **fit** (1) part; (2) struggle
49 **fall in** (1) make up; (2) copulate
52 **drouth** drought
54 **durst** dared
58 **divorced** (an idle threat suggesting the fictional script of their eternal quarrel; while divorce was occasionally permitted to the rich by an Act of Parliament, barrenness was not acceptable grounds)
60 **"Marriage . . . destiny"** (proverbial)
65 **they** i.e., such imaginary children
69 **your . . . costs** at our expense (he is thinking of Touchwood Sr.); **censure** (1) criticism; (2) mutual recrimination
75 **intreat** plead for you
76 **Singleness** (as a divorced woman)
77 **with . . . smock** virtually penniless
78 **not so single** i.e., you came ashore accompanied by lice
81 **make's** make us
82 **peal** literally, cannonfire; figuratively, quarrel
83 **outcry** auction, proclaimed by the common crier
86 **compass** manage
89 **clap up** put up notices
94 **nothing** (pun on male genitalia)
97 **please** satisfy sexually

Sir Oliver. I'faith, thou art a good soul, he lies that says it;
Buss, buss, pretty rogue.
[*Kisses her.*]
Lady. You care not for me.
Touchwood Senior. [*Aside.*] Can any man tell now which way they came in?
By this light, I'll be hanged then!
Sir Oliver. Is the drink come?
Touchwood Senior. (*Aside.*) Here's a little vial of almond-milk
That stood me in some three pence.
Sir Oliver. I hope to see thee, wench, within these few years,
Circled with children, pranking up a girl,
And putting jewels in their little ears;
Fine sport, i'faith!
Lady. Aye, had you been aught, husband,
It had been done ere this time.
Sir Oliver. "Had I been aught"! Hang thee, hadst thou been aught!
But a cross thing I ever found thee.
Lady. Thou art a grub to say so.
Sir Oliver. A pox on thee!
Touchwood Senior. [*Aside.*] By this light they are out again at the same door.
And no man can tell which way.
[*To Sir Oliver.*] Come, here's your drink, sir.
Sir Oliver. I will not take it now, sir,
And I were sure to get three boys ere midnight.
Lady. Why there thou show'st now of what breed thou com'st,
To hinder generation! Oh, thou villain,
That knows how crookedly the world goes with us
For want of heirs, yet put by all good fortune.
Sir Oliver. Hang, strumpet, I will take it now in spite!
Touchwood Senior. Then you must ride upon't five hours.
Sir Oliver. I mean so. – Within there?

Enter a Servant.

Servant. Sir?
Sir Oliver. Saddle the white mare;
I'll take a whore along, and ride to Ware.
Lady. Ride to the devil!
Sir Oliver. I'll plague you every way.
Look ye, do you see, 'tis gone.
Drinks.
Lady. A pox go with it!
Sir Oliver. Aye, curse and spare not now.
Touchwood Senior. Stir up and down, sir, you must not stand.
Sir Oliver. Nay, I'm not given to standing.
Touchwood Senior. So much the better, sir, for the –
Sir Oliver. I never could stand long in one place yet;
I learnt it of my father, ever figient.
How if I crossed this, sir?
Capers.
Touchwood Senior. Oh, passing good, sir, and would show well a'horseback; when you come to your inn, if you leaped over a joint-stool or two 'twere not amiss; (*Aside.*) – although you broke your neck, sir.
Sir Oliver. [*Still capering.*] What say you to a table thus high, sir?
Touchwood Senior. Nothing better, sir [*Aside.*] – if it be furnished with good victuals. You remember how the bargain runs about this business?
Sir Oliver. Or else I had a bad head; you must receive, sir, four hundred pounds of me at four several payments: one hundred pounds now in hand.
Touchwood Senior. Right, that I have, sir.
Sir Oliver. Another hundred when my wife is quick; the third when she's brought a-bed; and the last hundred when the child cries, for if it should be stillborn, it doth no good, sir.

---

98 it i.e., that you cannot please me
101 which . . . in (because the quarrelers keep changing positions)
104 almond-milk sweet almonds pounded with barley water
105 stood me in cost me
107 pranking dressing
110 aught anything; i.e., potent
111 ere before
113 cross argumentative
114 grub (1) maggot, therefore not productive; (2) thick-set person (alluding to sexual inadequacy)
116 out . . . door off to the same old fight
124 put by dismiss
125 strumpet (indicating he knows the plan with Touchwood Sr.)
126 ride upon't let it work on you for
130 Ware a town in Hertfordshire 20 miles N of London known for romantic encounters; the Saracen's Head had a notorious great bed now in the British Museum
136 Stir move, to activate the almond-milk
137 standing (1) remaining still; (2) remaining sexually erect
141 figient fidgety
142 crossed this (1) crossed legs in dance step; (2) jumped over a joint-stool, a fashionable caper or dance; his continued action is to get the potion for fertility to work
145 joint-stool one made to fit tightly without pegs or nails
151 victuals provisions
152 business (with sexual references)
153 bad head i.e., suffering from cuckold's horns
159 quick pregnant

Touchwood Senior. All this is even still; a little faster, sir.

Sir Oliver. Not a whit, sir,
I'm in an excellent pace for any physic.

Enter a Servant.

Servant. Your white mare's ready.

Sir Oliver. I shall up presently. [*Exit* Servant.]
– One kiss, and farewell.

Lady. Thou shalt have two, love.

Sir Oliver. Expect me about three. *Exit.*

Lady. With all my heart, sweet.

Touchwood Senior. [*Aside.*] By this light they have forgot their anger since,
And are as far in again as e'er they were.
Which way the devil came they? Heart, I saw 'em not,
Their ways are beyond finding out. – Come, sweet lady.

Lady. How must I take mine, sir?

Touchwood Senior. Clean contrary, yours must be taken lying.

Lady. Abed, sir?

Touchwood Senior. Abed, or where you will for your own ease;
Your coach will serve.

Lady. The physic must needs please. *Exeunt.*

Act IV

[IV.i]

Enter Tim *and* Tutor.

Tim. *Negatur argumentum*, tutor.

Tutor. *Probo tibi*, pupil, *stultus non est animal rationale.*

Tim. *Falleris sane.*

Tutor. *Quaeso ut taceas: probo tibi –*

Tim. *Quomodo probas, domine?*

Tutor. *Stultus non habet rationem, ergo non est animal rationale.*

Tim. *Sic argumentaris, domine: stultus non habet rationem, ergo non est animal rationale. Negatur argumentum* again, tutor.

Tutor. *Argumentum iterum probo tibi, domine: qui non participat de ratione nullo modo potest vocari rationalibus;* but *stultus non participat de ratione, ergo stultus nullo modo potest dicere rationalis.*

Tim. *Participat.*

Tutor. *Sic disputas: qui participat, quomodo participat?*

Tim. *Ut homo: probabo tibi in silagismo.*

Tutor. *Hunc proba.*

Tim. *Sic probo, domine: stultus est homo sicut tu et ego sum, homo est animal rationale, sicut stultus est animal rationale.*

Enter Maudline.

Maudline. Here's nothing but disputing all the day long with 'em.

Tutor. *Sic disputas: stultus est homo sicut tu et ego sum, homo est animal rationale, sicut stultus est animal rationale.*

Maudline. Your reasons are both good, what e'er they be;
Pray, give them o'er; faith, you'll tire yourselves.
What's the matter between you?

Tim. Nothing but reasoning about a fool, mother.

Maudline. About a fool, son? Alas, what need you trouble your heads about that? None of us all but knows what a fool is.

Tim. Why, what's a fool, mother?
I come to you now.

Maudline. Why, one that's married before he has wit.

Tim. 'Tis pretty, i'faith, and well guessed of a woman never brought up at the university;

163 even precisely so; exact; **faster** he is still capering to activate the medicine

172 since previously

174 Which . . . they? i.e., How did they switch moods again?

176 mine i.e., remedy

181 coach enclosed coach seats were notorious places for sexual activity (Dekker called them "running bawdy-houses")

IV.i.1–26 *Negatur . . . rationale* (typical Latin disputation at the university, in which both parties accept the definition of man as a rational animal): *Tim.* "I deny your proof, tutor." *Tutor.* "I am proving to you, pupil, that a fool is not a rational animal." *Tim.* "You are certainly mistaken." *Tutor.* "Please be silent: I am demonstrating to you –." *Tim.* "How do you prove it, sir?" *Tutor.* "A fool does not have reason, therefore he is not a rational animal." *Tim.* "You argue thus, sir: a fool does not have reason, therefore he is not a rational animal. I deny your proof again, tutor." *Tutor.* "I will demonstrate the proof to you again, sir; he who has no share of reason cannot by any means be called rational; but a fool has no share of reason, therefore a fool cannot by any means be said to be rational." *Tim.* "He does share it." *Tutor.* "So you maintain: but in what way does he who shares have a share?" *Tim.* "As a man, I will prove it to you by a syllogism." *Tutor.* "Prove it." *Tim.* "I prove it thus, sir: a fool is a man just as you and I are, a man is a rational animal, just as a fool is a rational animal" . . . *Tutor.* "So you maintain: a fool is a man just as you and I are, a man is a rational animal, just as a fool is a rational animal"

29 matter issue at dispute

32–3 None . . . but all of us

35 I . . . you (1) formula in rhetoric: "I pose the question to you"; (2) you above all should know what a fool is

36–7 one . . . wit (she returns the jibe)

but bring forth what fool you will, mother, I'll prove him to be as reasonable a creature as myself or my tutor here.

Maudline. Fie, 'tis impossible.

Tutor. Nay, he shall do't, forsooth.

Tim. 'Tis the easiest thing to prove a fool by logic; By logic I'll prove anything.

Maudline. What, thou wilt not?

Tim. I'll prove a whore to be an honest woman.

Maudline. Nay, by my faith, she must prove that herself, or logic will never do't.

Tim. 'Twill do't, I tell you.

Maudline. Some in this street would give a thousand pounds that you could prove their wives so.

Tim. Faith, I can, and all their daughters too, though they had three bastards. When comes your tailor hither?

Maudline. Why what of him?

Tim. By logic I'll prove him to be a man,
Let him come when he will.

Maudline. How hard at first was learning to him? Truly, sir, I thought he would never a' took the Latin tongue. How many Accidences do you think he wore out ere he came to his Grammar?

Tutor. Some three or four?

Maudline. Believe me, sir, some four and thirty.

Tim. Pish, I made haberdines of 'em in church porches.

Maudline. He was eight years in his Grammar, and stuck horribly at a foolish place there called *as in presenti.*

Tim. Pox, I have it here now.

[*Taps his head.*]

Maudline. He so shamed me once before an honest gentleman that knew me when I was a maid.

Tim. These women must have all out.

Maudline. "*Quid est grammatica?*" says the gentleman to him (I shall remember by a sweet, sweet token), but nothing could he answer.

Tutor. How now, pupil, ha? *Quid est grammatica?*

Tim. *Grammatica?* Ha, ha, ha!

Maudline. Nay, do not laugh, son, but let me hear you say it now. There was one word went so prettily off the gentleman's tongue, I shall remember it the longest day of my life.

Tutor. Come, *quid est grammatica?*

Tim. Are you not ashamed, tutor? *Grammatica?* Why, *recte scribendi atque loquendi ars*, sir-reverence of my mother.

Maudline. That was it, i'faith! Why now, son, I see you are a deep scholar; and, master tutor, a word, I pray.
[*Aside to Tutor.*] Let us withdraw a little into my husband's chamber; I'll send in the North Wales gentlewoman to him. She looks for wooing. I'll put together both, and lock the door.

Tutor. I give great approbation to your conclusion.

Exit [*with* Maudline].

Tim. I mar'l what this gentlewoman should be
That I should have in marriage: she's a stranger to me;
I wonder what my parents mean, i'faith,
To match me with a stranger so.
A maid that's neither kiff nor kin to me.
'Life, do they think I have no more care of my body
Than to lie with one that I ne'er knew?
A mere stranger,
One that ne'er went to school with me neither,
Nor ever playfellows together?
They're mightily o'erseen in't, methinks.
They say she has mountains to her marriage;
She's full of cattle, some two thousand runts.
Now what the meaning of these runts should be,
My tutor cannot tell me;
I have looked in *Rider's Dictionary* for the letter R,

---

40 **bring forth** (pun in its self-reference)

48 **I'll . . . woman** (cf. Act V)

59 **a man** tailors were considered unmanly; "Nine tailors make but one man" was a common proverb

63 **Accidences** books of Latin inflection, possibly William Lily's prescribed *Short Introduction* (Maudline will now attempt to draw the Tutor into her chamber)

65 **Grammar** books on Latin syntax, most likely Lily's *Brevissima Instituto* (1540)

68 **haberdines** (1) literally, dried cod (cant for scrotum); (2) a children's game where paper fish were raced by the forces of wind (apparently Tim tore up his schoolbooks to make them)

71–2 ***as in presenti*** the opening of Lily's didactic poem on the endings of verbs of the first conjugation in the *Brevissima*, Part II, "De Verbo"; it plays on *ass*; "An ass/arse in the presence"

75 **knew . . . maid** i.e., knew sexually

76 **have all out** (with bawdy reference)

77 ***Quid . . . grammatica?*** "What is grammar?"

79 **token** *ars* (art) or *arse* (line 88)

88 ***recte . . . ars*** "the art of writing and speaking correctly"

88–9 **sir-reverence** (1) formulaic apology for indelicate talk, for he blames his tutor for making him say *arse*; (2) human excrement

103 **kiff** kith, neighbors and friends

109 **o'erseen** mistaken

110 **mountains . . . marriage** (as a dowry)

111 **runts** a breed of small Welsh and Highlands cattle

114 ***Rider's Dictionary*** a Latin/English, English/Latin dictionary compiled by John Rider (1589) (it has no entry for *runts*)

And there I can hear no tidings of these runts neither;
Unless they should be Rumford hogs,
I know them not.

Enter Welsh Gentlewoman.

And here she comes.
If I know what to say to her now
In the way of marriage, I'm no graduate!
Methinks, i'faith, 'tis boldly done of her
To come into my chamber, being but a stranger;
She shall not say I'm so proud yet, but I'll speak to her.
Marry, as I will order it,
She shall take no hold of my words, I'll warrant her.

[*She curtseys.*]

She looks and makes a cur'sey.
[*To her.*] *Salve tu quoque, puella pulcherima,*
Quid vis nescio nec sane curo.
– Tully's own phrase to a heart!

Welsh Gentlewoman. [*Aside.*] I know not what he means;
A suitor, quotha?
I hold my life he understands no English.

Tim. *Fertur me hercule tu virgo,*
Wallia ut opibus abundis maximis.

Welsh Gentlewoman. [*Aside.*] What's this *fertur* and *abundundis*?
He mocks me sure, and calls me a bundle of farts.

Tim. [*Aside.*] I have no Latin word now for their runts;
I'll make some shift or other: [*To her.*] *Iterum dico, opibus abundat maximis montibus et fontibus et, ut ita dicam, rontibus: attamen vero homunculus ego sum natura simule arte bachalarius lecto profecto non parata.*

Welsh Gentlewoman. [*Aside.*] This is most strange.
May be he can speak Welsh.
– *Avedera whee comrage, derdue cog foginis?*

Tim. [*Aside.*] *Cog foggin?* I scorn to cog with her. I'll tell her so too, in a word near her own language: – *Ego non cogo.*

Welsh Gentlewoman. *Rhegosin a whiggin harle ron corid ambre.*

Tim. By my faith, she's a good scholar, I see that already.
She has the tongues plain; I hold my life she has traveled.
What will folks say? "There goes the learned couple!"
Faith, if the truth were known, she hath proceeded.

Enter Maudline.

Maudline. How now, how speeds your business?

Tim. [*Aside.*] I'm glad my mother's come to part us.

Maudline. How do you agree, forsooth?

Welsh Gentlewoman. As well as e'er we did before we met.

Maudline. How's that?

Welsh Gentlewoman. You put me to a man I understand not;
Your son's no Englishman, methinks.

Maudline. No Englishman! Bless my boy.
And born i'the heart of London?

Welsh Gentlewoman. I ha'been long enough in the chamber with him,
And I find neither Welsh nor English in him.

Maudline. Why, Tim, how have you used the gentlewoman?

Tim. As well as a man might do, mother, in modest Latin.

Maudline. Latin, fool?

Tim. And she recoiled in Hebrew.

Maudline. In Hebrew, fool? 'Tis Welsh.

Tim. All comes to one, mother.

Maudline. She can speak English too.

Tim. Who told me so much?

---

116 Rumford hogs (refers to the famous hog market at Rumford, Essex, 12 miles NE of London)

124 Marry "By the Virgin Mary" (a common oath)

127–8 *Salve . . . curo* "Greetings to you also, most beautiful maiden; what you want I do not know, nor indeed do I care"

129 Tully Cicero, author of popular rhetorics; **to a heart** to perfection

131 quotha said he (sarcastically)

133–4 *Fertur . . . maximis* "By Hercules, it is said, young lady, that in Wales you abound in great riches"

138 shift contrivance

138–42 *Iterum . . . parata* "Again I say, it abounds in great riches, in mountains and fountains and (to coin a phrase) in runts; but truly, I am a little man by nature and a bachelor by art, not really ready for bed" (Dog Latin) (this has been taken to indicate the play was acted by a boys' company; cf. grub, III.iii.114)

145 *Avedera . . . foginis* "Can you speak Welsh? For God's sake, are you pretending with me?" (Dog Welsh)

146 *Cog* (1) cheat; (2) lie (with pun on *lie sexually* guessing at *foggin*)

148 *Ego . . . cogo* "I won't come together with you"

149–50 *Rhegosin . . . ambre* "Some cheese and whey after taking a walk" (Welsh; cheese and whey were believed the favorite Welsh diet)

152 traveled (with pun on *travailed*, worked hard)

154 proceeded (1) taken a university degree; (2) gone beyond a state of virginity

169 recoiled responded

Heart, and she can speak English, I'll clap to her;
I thought you'd marry me to a stranger.

Maudline. You must forgive him, he's so inured to Latin,
He and his tutor, that he hath quite forgot
To use the Protestant tongue.

Welsh Gentlewoman. 'Tis quickly pardoned, forsooth.

Maudline. Tim, make amends and kiss her.
[*To her.*] He makes towards you, forsooth.

[Tim *kisses Welsh Gentlewoman.*]

Tim. Oh, delicious! One may discover her country by her kissing. 'Tis a true saying, "There's nothing tastes so sweet as your Welsh mutton." [*To Gentlewoman.*] It was reported you could sing.

Maudline. Oh, rarely, Tim, the sweetest British songs.

Tim. And 'tis my mind, I swear, before I marry,
I would see all my wife's good parts at once,
To view how rich I were.

Maudline. Thou shalt hear sweet music, Tim.
[*To her.*] Pray, forsooth.

Music and Welsh Song.

The Song

[*Welsh Gentlewoman*]. Cupid is Venus' only joy,
But he is a wanton boy,
A very, very wanton boy;
He shoots at ladies' naked breasts,
He is the cause of most men's crests,
I mean upon the forehead,
Invisible but horrid;
'Twas he first taught upon the way
To keep a lady's lips in play.

Why should not Venus chide her son
For the pranks that he hath done,
The wanton pranks that he hath done?
He shoots his fiery darts so thick,
They hurt poor ladies to the quick,
Ah, me, with cruel wounding!
His darts are so confounding
That life and sense would soon decay,
But that he keeps their lips in play.
Can there be any part of bliss
In a quickly fleeting kiss,
A quickly, quickly fleeting kiss?
To one's pleasure, leisures are but waste,
The slowest kiss makes too much haste,
[We always are behind it,]
And lose it ere we find it;
The pleasing sport they only know
That close above and close below.

Tim. I would not change my wife for a kingdom;
I can do somewhat too in my own lodging.

Enter Yellowhammer *and* Allwit [*disguised*].

Yellowhammer. Why, well said, Tim! The bells go merrily;
I love such peals a 'life; wife, lead them in a while;
Here's a strange gentleman desires private conference.

[*Exeunt* Maudline, Tim, *and* Welsh Gentlewoman.]

You're welcome, sir, the more for your name's sake,
Good Master Yellowhammer, I love my name well;
And which a'the Yellowhammers take you descent from,
If I may be so bold with you? Which, I pray?

Allwit. The Yellowhammers in Oxfordshire,
Near Abbington.

Yellowhammer. And those are the best Yellowhammers, and truest bred: I came from thence myself, though now a citizen. I'll be bold with you; you are most welcome.

Allwit. I hope the zeal I bring with me shall deserve it.

---

174 **clap** (1) stick; (2) clap hand on her or her contract; (3) seize vigorously; (4) pun on clap as gonorrhoea
175 **stranger** foreigner
178 **the Protestant tongue** the vernacular which the Reformation made the only liturgical language in England
182 **country** (with pun on pudendum)
184–5 **mutton** (1) a favorite Welsh meat; (2) cant term for whore
186 **sing** (with pun on common euphuism for copulation)
187 **rarely** excellently; **British** Welsh (cf. line 184)
189 **good parts** (1) talents; (2) accomplishments; (3) physical attributes
197 **crests** (1) cuckold's horns (line 198); (2) erections
201 **lips** (1) lips; (2) pudendum
205 **shoots . . . thick** (with reference to male penetrations)
206 **quick** the most tender part (with bawdy reference)
208 **darts** (1) arrows; (2) penis; **confounding** destructive
209 **That . . . decay** (a popular belief held that each act of intercourse shortened life by one day)
214 **leisures** periods of inactivity; intermissions
219 **close** unite
221 **lodging** account (with bawdy allusion)
222 **The . . . merrily** (proverbial); **bells** i.e., wedding bells
223 **peals** (1) of bells; (2) peels; matches of equals; (3) peels as pillages; **a'life** as life itself
224 **strange** (1) odd; (2) from a different region
230 **Abbington** Abingdon, Oxfordshire, a village 5 miles s of Oxford
233 **citizen** a London freeman in the goldsmiths' guild, one of the Twelve Great Livery Companies

Yellowhammer. I hope no less; what is your will, sir?

Allwit. I understand by rumors, you have a daughter,
Which my bold love shall henceforth title "cousin."

Yellowhammer. I thank you for her, sir.

Allwit. I heard of her virtues, and other confirmed graces.

Yellowhammer. A plaguy girl, sir.

Allwit. Fame sets her out with richer ornaments
Than you are pleased to boast of; 'tis done modestly.
I hear she's towards marriage.

Yellowhammer. You hear truth, sir.

Allwit. And with a knight in town. Sir Walter Whorehound.

Yellowhammer. The very same, sir.

Allwit. I am the sorrier for't.

Yellowhammer. The sorrier? Why, cousin?

Allwit. 'Tis not too far past, is't? It may be yet recalled?

Yellowhammer. Recalled? Why, good sir?

Allwit. Resolve me in that point; ye shall hear from me.

Yellowhammer. There's no contract passed.

Allwit. I am very joyful, sir.

Yellowhammer. But he's the man must bed her.

Allwit. By no means, cuz; she's quite undone then,
And you'll curse the time that e'er you made the match;
He's an arrant whoremaster, consumes his time and state.
[*Whispers.*] – whom in my knowledge he hath kept this seven years;
Nay, cuz, another man's wife too.

Yellowhammer. Oh, abominable!

Allwit. Maintains the whole house, apparels the husband.
Pays servants' wages, not so much but – [*Whispers.*]

Yellowhammer. Worse and worse! And doth the husband know this?

Allwit. Knows? Aye, and glad he may too, 'tis his living.
As other trades thrive, butchers by selling flesh,
Poulters by venting conies, or the like, cuz.

Yellowhammer. What an incomparable wittol's this!

Allwit. Tush, what cares he for that?
Believe me, cuz, no more than I do.

Yellowhammer. What a base slave is that!

Allwit. All's one to him. He feeds and takes his ease,
Was ne'er the man that ever broke his sleep
To get a child yet, by his own confession,
And yet his wife has seven.

Yellowhammer. What, by Sir Walter?

Allwit. Sir Walter's like to keep 'em, and maintain 'em,
In excellent fashion; he dares do no less, sir.

Yellowhammer. Life, has he children too?

Allwit. Children? Boys thus high,
In their Cato and Cordelius.

Yellowhammer. What! You jest, sir!

Allwit. Why, one can make a verse,
And is now at Eton College.

Yellowhammer. Oh, this news has cut into my heart, cuz!

Allwit. It had eaten nearer if it had not been prevented.
One Allwit's wife.

Yellowhammer. Allwit? Foot, I have heard of him;
He had a girl kurs'ned lately?

Allwit. Aye, that work did cost the knight above a hundred mark.

Yellowhammer. I'll mark him for a knave and villain for't;
A thousand thanks and blessings! I have done with him.

Allwit. [*Aside.*] Ha, ha, ha! This knight will stick by my ribs still;

---

242 confirmed established
243 plaguy troublesome
252 recalled rescinded
254 Resolve . . . point satisfy me on one issue
255 contract marital pledge was binding when made before witnesses and before a marriage ceremony
258 cuz general term denoting a family relationship
261 whom i.e., Allwit's wife
265 s.d. *Whispers* (unfinished remarks in this scene may have been caused on stage by censorship but when printed also allow parody)
269 Poulters (1) poulterers, who sold game and poultry; (2) cant term for pimps; **venting conies** selling rabbits; conies meant cheaters colloquially and less often (as rabbits were sexually active) the word meant whores
270 wittol acquiescent cuckold
279 like likely; **keep** support
283 Cato and Cordelius Dionysius Cato's *Disticha de Moribus* (about 300 AD); Cordier's *Colloquia Scholastica* (1564), widely used moralizing grammarschool books
286 Eton College grammar school in Buckinghamshire 23 miles w of London
288 nearer deeper; **prevented** anticipated
290 Foot "By God's foot"
292–3 a hundred mark (equivalent to £66.13s.4d)
296 stick . . . ribs i.e., stick with me

I shall not lose him yet, no wife will come;
Where'er he woos, I find him still at home. Ha, ha!

Exit.

Yellowhammer. Well grant all this; say now his deeds are black;
Pray what serves marriage but to call him back
I have kept a whore myself, and had a bastard,
By Mistress Anne, in *Anno* –
I care not who knows it; he's now a jolly fellow,
H'as been twice warden; so many his fruit be.
They were but base begot, and so was he;
The knight is rich; he shall be my son-in-law.
No matter, so the whore he keeps be wholesome.
My daughter takes no hurt then, so let them wed;
I'll have him sweat well e'er they go to bed.

Enter Maudline.

Maudline. Oh, husband, husband!
Yellowhammer. How now, Maudline?
Maudline. We are all undone! She's gone, she's gone!
Yellowhammer. Again? Death! Which way?
Maudline. Over the houses.
Lay the waterside; she's gone forever, else.
Yellowhammer. Oh vent'rous baggage!

Exit [*with* Maudline.]

[IV.ii]

Enter Tim *and* Tutor.

Tim. Thieves, thieves! My sister's stol'n!
Some thief hath got her.
Oh, how miraculously did my father's plate 'scape!
'Twas all left out, tutor.
Tutor. Is't possible?
Tim. Besides three chains of pearl and a box of coral.
My sister's gone; let's look at Trig stairs for her;
My mother's gone to lay the Common stairs
At Puddle Wharf, and at the dock below
Stands my poor silly father, Run, sweet tutor, run.

Exit [*with* Tutor].

[IV.iii]

Enter both the Touchwoods.

Touchwood Senior. I had been taken, brother, by eight sergeants.
But for the honest watermen; I am bound to them.
They are the most requiteful'st people living.
For as they get their means by gentlemen,
They are still the forwardest to help gentlemen.
You heard how one 'scaped out of the Blackfriars,
But a while since, from two or three varlets
Came into the house with all their rapiers drawn,
As if they'd dance the sword-dance on the stage,
With candles in their hands, like chandlers' ghosts,
Whilst the poor gentleman so pursued and bandied
Was by an honest pair of oars safely landed.
Touchwood Junior. I love them with my heart for't.

Enter three or four Watermen.

1 [*Waterman*]. Your first man, sir.
2 [*Waterman*]. Shall I carry you gentlemen with a pair of oars?
Touchwood Senior. These be the honest fellows.

297 **no . . . come** i.e., he'll not marry
300 **call him back** reform him
304 **warden** (1) churchwarden; (2) member of the governing body of a London company; (3) a kind of pear; **fruit** bastards (playing on *pear*)
307 **wholesome** healthy, free of venereal disease
309 **sweat well** undergo mercurial fumigation in the sweating-tub as a treatment for syphilis
314 **houses** roofs
315 **Lay** search
316 **vent'rous** bold
IV.ii.3 **my . . . plate** i.e., Moll's dowry
7 **Trig stairs** landing place at the bottom of Trig Lane (for embarkation)
8 **Common stairs** public stairs for embarkation 300 yards upstream from Trig Lane
9 **Puddle Wharf** watergate into the Thames for horses to drink water (and leave puddles or excrement); **dock** below Burg Wharf where London refuse was loaded; **below** downstream
10 **silly** helpless, pitiful
IV.iii.1 **had been** would have been; **sergeants** sheriff's officers
2 **watermen** boatmen for hire to cross the Thames
3 **requiteful'st** (1) eager to return favors; (2) accommodating
4 **get their means** earn their living
6 **Blackfriars** private London theater lit by candles (probably an in-joke)
7 **varlets** knaves, rogues
8 **rapiers** small sword for thrusting
10 **chandlers** candlemakers
11 **bandied** buffeted
14 **Your . . . sir** common waterman's cry

Take one pair, and leave the rest for her.
Touchwood Junior. Barn Elms.
Touchwood Senior. No more, brother.
1 [*Waterman*]. Your first man.
2 [*Waterman*]. Shall I carry your worship?
[*Exit* Touchwood Senior *with* 1 Waterman.]
Touchwood Junior. Go.
And you honest watermen that stay,
Here's a French crown for you;
[*Gives money.*]
There comes a maid with all speed to take water;
Row her lustily to Barn Elms after me.
2 [*Waterman*]. To Barn Elms, good sir. Make ready the boat, Sam.
We'll wait below.
Exit [2 Waterman, *and* Others].

Enter Moll.

Touchwood Junior. What made you stay so long?
Moll. I found the way more dangerous than I looked for.
Touchwood Junior. Away, quick! There's a boat waits for you;
And I'll take water at Paul's Wharf, and overtake you.
Moll. Good sir, do; we cannot be too safe.
[*Exeunt.*]

[IV.iv]

Enter Sir Walter, Yellowhammer, Tim, *and* Tutor.

Sir Walter. Life, call you this close keeping?
Yellowhammer. She was kept under a double lock.
Sir Walter. A double devil!
Tim. That's a buff sergeant, tutor; he'll ne'er wear out.
Yellowhammer. How would you have women locked?
Tim. With padlocks, father, the Venetian uses it; my tutor reads it.
Sir Walter. Heart, if she were so locked up, how got she out?
Yellowhammer. There was a little hole, looked into the gutter;
But who would have dreamt of that?
Sir Walter. A wiser man would.
Tim. He says true, father, a wise man for love will seek every hole; my tutor knows it.
Tutor. *Verum poeta dicit.*
Tim. *Dicit Virgilius*, father.
Yellowhammer. Prithee, talk of thy gills somewhere else; she's played the gill with me. Where's your wise mother now?
Tim. Run mad, I think; I thought she would have drowned herself; she would not stay for oars, but took a smelt boat. Sure, I think she be gone a-fishing for her!
Yellowhammer. She'll catch a goodly dish of gudgeons now,
Will serve us all to supper.

Enter Maudline *drawing* Moll *by the hair*, *and* Watermen.

Maudline. I'll tug thee home by the hair.
Watermen. Good mistress, spare her.
Maudline. Tend your own business.
Watermen. You are a cruel mother.
Exeunt [Watermen].
Moll. Oh, my heart dies!
Maudline. I'll make thee an example for all the neighbors' daughters.
Moll. Farewell, life!
Maudline. You that have tricks can counterfeit.
Yellowhammer. Hold, hold, Maudline!
Maudline. I have brought your jewel by the hair.
Yellowhammer. She's here, knight.
Sir Walter. Forbear or I'll grow worse.
Tim. Look on her, tutor; she hath brought her from the water like a mermaid. She's but half my sister now, as far as the flesh goes; the rest may be sold to fishwives.
Maudline. Dissembling, cunning baggage!
Yellowhammer. Impudent strumpet!

---

18 **Barn Elms** a park and manor house on the s bank of the Thames opposite Hammersmith, famous for romantic rendezvous and dueling
24 **French crown** French silver coin worth five shillings
25 **take water** embark
32 **Paul's Wharf** s of St. Paul's between Puddle Wharf and Trig Stairs
IV.iv.4 **buff sergeant** officer responsible for making arrests (buff was the tough leather of their jerkins that came to designate their own toughness)
6 **padlocks** chastity belts
7 **reads** has read about
9 **looked** opened
13 **tutor knows it** (the tutor has presumably cuckolded Yellowhammer)
14–15 ***Verum... Virgilius*** "The poet says true... Virgil says it, father" (misattribution of vulgarity to a high moral poet; Tim is making this up)
16 **gills** wenches
21 **smelt** (1) small fish; (2) cant for fools
23 **gudgeons** small, easily caught freshwater fish used for bait (could also mean fool)
24 **to** for
37 **worse** angrier
39 **mermaid** (cant for whore)
41 **fishwives** (cant for bawds)

Sir Walter. Either give over both, or I'll give over!
[*To Moll.*] Why have you used me thus, unkind mistress?
Wherein have I deserved?

Yellowhammer. You talk too fondly, sir. We'll take another course and prevent all; we might have done't long since. We'll lose no time now, nor trust to't any longer. Tomorrow morn as early as sunrise, we'll have you joined.

Moll. Oh, bring me death tonight, love-pitying Fates;
Let me not see tomorrow up upon the world.

Yellowhammer. Are you content, sir, till then she shall be watched?

Maudline. Baggage, you shall!

Exit [*with* Moll *and* Yellowhammer].

Tim. Why, father, my tutor and I will both watch in armor.

Tutor. How shall we do for weapons?

Tim. Take you no care for that; if need be I can send for conquering metal, tutor. Ne'er lost day yet; 'tis but at Westminster. I am acquainted with him that keeps the monuments. I can borrow Harry the Fifth's sword; 'twill serve us both to watch with.

Exit [*with* Tutor].

Sir Walter. I never was so near my wish, as this chance
Makes me; ere tomorrow noon,
I shall receive two thousand pounds in gold,
And a sweet maidenhead
Worth forty.

Enter Touchwood Junior *with a* Waterman.

Touchwood Junior. Oh, thy news splits me!

Waterman. Half drowned, she cruelly tugged her by the hair,
Forced her disgracefully, not like a mother.

Touchwood Junior. Enough, leave me, like my joys.

Exit Waterman.

[*To Sir Walter.*] Sir, saw you not a wretched maid pass this way?
Heart, villain, is that thou?

Sir Walter. Yes, slave, 'tis I!

Both draw and fight.

Touchwood Junior. I must break through thee then. There is no stop
That checks my tongue and all my hopeful fortunes,
That breast excepted, and I must have way.

Sir Walter. Sir, I believe 'twill hold your life in play.

[*He wounds Touchwood Junior.*]

Touchwood Junior. Sir, you'll gain the heart in my breast at first?

Sir Walter. There is no dealing, then? Think on the dowry for two thousand pounds.

Touchwood Junior. [*Striking at Sir Walter.*] Oh, now 'tis quit, sir.

Sir Walter. And being of even hand, I'll play no longer.

Touchwood Junior. No longer, slave?

Sir Walter. I have certain things to think on
Before I dare go further.

Touchwood Junior. But one bout?
I'll follow thee to death, but ha't out.

Exeunt.

Act V

[V.i]

Enter Allwit, *his* Wife, *and* Davy Dahumma.

Wife. A misery of a house!

Allwit. What shall become of us?

Davy. I think his wound be mortal.

Allwit. Think'st thou so, Davy?
Then am I mortal too, but a dead man, Davy;
This is no world for me, when e'er he goes;
I must e'en truss up all, and after him, Davy;
A sheet with two knots, and away!

---

43 **Either . . . over!** Stop admonishing her or I'll refuse to marry her
44 **used** (with sexual implications)
47 **fondly** foolishly
56 **watch** (with reference to London citizen's night watch); **in armor** colloquialism for made bold by drinking
61–3 **Westminster . . . monuments** master of monuments and guide at Westminster Abbey
63 **Harry . . . sword** a joke; Henry V's armor had been stolen
67 **I . . . gold** although never made clear, this inheritance depends on marriage (cf. Lady Kix, II.i.167–8)
68 **maidenhead** (denoting virginity)
69 **forty** the price of virgins on the London market
70 **splits me** causes me to shipwreck
78–9 **There . . . fortunes** I will speak up for myself against Sir Walter's suit
81 **in play** at hazard
83 **at first** i.e., at first thrust (from fencing)
84 **dealing** compromising; Sir Walter would bribe Touchwood Junior with part of Moll's dowry since he is the leading suitor given her parents' support
87 **quit** requited, paid back
88 **of even hand** at a draw
90 **certain . . . on** religious considerations (see I.i)
V.i.3 **his** Sir Walter's
5 **Then . . . man** colloquial for suffering grave misfortune
7 **truss up** pack it all in
8 **sheet . . . knots** shroud tied at head and foot

Enter Sir Walter, *led in hurt* [*by two* Servants].

Davy. Oh see, sir,
How faint he goes! Two of my fellows lead him.
Wife. [*Fainting.*] Oh, me!
Allwit. Hyday, my wife's laid down, too! Here's like to be
A good house kept, when we are altogether down.
Take pains with her, good Davy, cheer her up there.
Let me come to his worship, let me come.
[*Exeunt* Servants.]
Sir Walter. Touch me not, villain! My wound aches at thee,
Thou poison to my heart!
Allwit. He raves already,
His senses are quite gone, he knows me not.
Look up, an't like your worship; heave those eyes;
Call me to mind; is your remembrance left?
Look in my face. Who am I, an't like your worship?
Sir Walter. If anything be worse than slave or villain,
Thou art the man.
Allwit. Alas, his poor worship's weakness!
He will begin to know me by little and little.
Sir Walter. No devil can be like thee!
Allwit. Ah, poor gentleman,
Methinks the pain that thou endurest –
Sir Walter. Thou know'st me to be wicked, for thy baseness
Kept the eyes open still on all my sins;
None knew the dear account my soul stood charged with
So well as thou, yet like Hell's flattering angel
Would'st never tell me on't, let'st me go on,
And join with death in sleep. That if I had not waked
Now by chance, even by a stranger's pity,
I had everlastingly slept out all hope
Of grace and mercy.
Allwit. Now he is worse and worse.
Wife, to him, wife; thou wast wont to do good on him.
Wife. How is't with you, sir?
Sir Walter. Not as with you,
Thou loathsome strumpet! Some good pitying man
Remove my sins out of my sight a little;
I tremble to behold her. She keeps back
All comfort while she stays. Is this a time,
Unconscionable woman, to see thee?
Art thou so cruel to the peace of man,
Not to give liberty now? The devil himself
Shows a far fairer reverence and respect
To goodness than thyself. He dares not do this,
But parts in time of penitence, hides his face;
When man withdraws from him, he leaves the place.
Hast thou less manners, and more impudence,
Than thy instructor? Prithee, show thy modesty,
If the least grain be left, and get thee from me.
Thou should'st be rather locked many rooms hence
From the poor miserable sight of me.
If either love or grace had part in thee.
Wife. He is lost forever.
Allwit. Run, sweet Davy, quickly,
And fetch the children hither; sight of them
Will make him cheerful straight.
[*Exit* Davy.]
Sir Walter. [*To Mistress Allwit.*] Oh, death! Is this
A place for you to weep? What tears are those?
Get you away with them; I shall fare the worse
As long as they are a-weeping; they work against me;
There's nothing but thy appetite in that sorrow,
Thou weep'st for lust; I feel it in the slackness
Of comforts coming towards me.
I was well till thou began'st to undo me.
This shows like the fruitless sorrow of a careless mother
That brings her son with dalliance to the gallows.
And then stands by, and weeps to see him suffer.

Enter Davy *with the* Children.

Davy. There are the children, sir, an't like your worship;
Your last fine girl. In troth she smiles!

11 Hyday "Hey-day!" (common exclamation); **down** low
18 an't if it
19 left departed, gone
22 his . . . weakness (he is raving)
25 Methinks I understand
27 still always
28 dear account costly accounting of all my sins
35 do good on (1) comfort; (2) copulate with
41 Unconscionable (1) insensitive; (2) unthinking
65 dalliance (1) indulgence; (2) sexual sport

Look, look, in faith, sir.
Sir Walter. Oh, my vengeance!
Let me for ever hide my cursèd face
From sight of those that darkens all my hopes,
And stands between me and the sight of Heaven.
Who sees me now, he too and those so near me,
May rightly say, I am o'er-grown with sin.
Oh, how my offenses wrestle with my repentance!
It hath scarce breath!
Still my adulterous guilt hovers aloft,
And with her black wings beats down all my prayers
Ere they be half way up. What's he knows now
How long I have to live? Oh, what comes then?
My taste grows bitter; the round world, all gall now;
Her pleasing pleasures now hath poisoned me,
Which I exchanged my soul for.
Make way a hundred sighs at once for me.
Allwit. Speak to him, Nick.
Nick. I dare not, I am afraid.
Allwit. Tell him he hurts his wounds, Wat, with making moan.
Sir Walter. Wretched, death of seven.
Allwit. Come, let's be talking somewhat to keep him alive.
Ah, sirrah Wat, and did my lord bestow that jewel on thee,
For an epistle thou mad'st in Latin?
Thou art a good forward boy, there's great joy on thee.
Sir Walter. Oh, sorrow!
Allwit. [*Aside.*] Heart, will nothing comfort him?
If he be so far gone, 'tis time to moan.
Here's pen, and ink, and paper, and all things ready;
Will't please your worship for to make your will?
Sir Walter. My will? Yes, yes, what else? Who writes apace now?
Allwit. That can your man Davy, an't like your worship,
A fair, fast, legible hand.
Sir Walter. Set it down then:
[*Davy writes.*]
Imprimis. I bequeath to yonder wittol
Three times his weight in curses –
Allwit. How?
Sir Walter. All plagues of body and of mind –
Allwit. Write them not down, Davy.
Davy. It is his will; I must.
Sir Walter. Together also
With such a sickness, ten days ere his death.
Allwit. [*Aside.*] There's a sweet legacy,
I am almost choked with't.
Sir Walter. Next I bequeath to that foul whore his wife
All barrenness of joy, a drouth of virtue,
And dearth of all repentance; for her end,
The common misery of an English strumpet,
In French and Dutch, beholding ere she dies
Confusion of her brats before her eyes.
And never shed a tear for it.

Enter a Servant.

Servant. Where's the knight?
Oh, sir, the gentleman you wounded is newly departed!
Sir Walter. Dead? Lift, lift! Who helps me?
Allwit. Let the law lift you now, that must have all;
I have done lifting on you, and my wife too.
Servant. You were best lock yourself close.
Allwit. Not in my house, sir,
I'll harbor no such persons as men-slayers;
Lock yourself where you will.
Sir Walter. What's this?
Wife. Why, husband!
Allwit. I know what I do, wife.
Wife. You cannot tell yet;
For having killed the man in his defense,
Neither his life nor estate will be touched, husband.

---

69 **vengeance** as his shame, guilt, sin
73 **he** presumably God
81 **gall** bitter-tasting substance; spiritual bitterness
84 **hundred sighs** in a ritual of repentance
87 **death of seven** i.e., spiritual destruction of his seven bastards by Mistress Allwit
89 **my lord** the person who bestowed an honor on Wat (line 90)
91 **forward** precocious
96 **apace** with speed
114 **French** (misery) syphilis; **Dutch** (misery) gonorrhoea; perhaps also drunkenness
115 **Confusion** death; destruction
119 **lift** (1) up on the gallows; (2) plunder (murderer's goods were forfeit)
120 **lifting** (1) helping; (2) robbing; (3) copulating; **on** of
121 **best** best off to
125 **in his defense** (self-defense was adequate grounds to keep property)

Allwit. Away, wife! Hear a fool! His lands will hang him.
Sir Walter. Am I denied a chamber?
What say you, forsooth?
Wife. Alas, sir, I am one that would have all well,
But must obey my husband. Prithee, love,
Let the poor gentleman stay, being so sore wounded;
There's a close chamber at one end of the garret
We never use, let him have that, I prithee.
Allwit. We never use? You forget sickness then,
And physic times. Is't not a place for easement?

Enter a[*nother*] Servant.

Sir Walter. Oh, death! Do I hear this with part
Of former life in me? What's the news now?
Servant. Troth, worse and worse; you're like to lose your land
If the law save your life, sir, or the surgeon.
Allwit. [*Aside.*] Hark you there, wife.
Sir Walter. Why how, sir?
Servant. Sir Oliver Kix's wife is new quick'ned;
That child undoes you, sir.
Sir Walter. All ill at once!
Allwit. I wonder what he makes here with his consorts?
Cannot our house be private to ourselves,
But we must have such guests? I pray depart, sirs,
And take your murtherer along with you;
Good he were apprehended ere he go,
H'as killed some honest gentleman. Send for officers.
Sir Walter. I'll soon save you that labor.
Allwit. I must tell you, sir,
You have been somewhat bolder in my house
Than I could well like of; I suffered you
Till it stuck here at my heart; I tell you truly
I thought you had been familiar with my wife once.
Wife. With me? I'll see him hanged first. I defy him,
And all such gentlemen in the like extremity.
Sir Walter. If ever eyes were open, these are they;
Gamesters, farewell, I have nothing left to play.

Exit.

Allwit. And therefore get you gone, sir.
Davy. [*To Allwit.*] Of all wittols
Be thou the head! [*To Mistress Allwit.*] Thou, the grand whore of spitals!

Exit [*with* Servants].

Allwit. So, since he's like now to be rid of all,
I am right glad I am so well rid of him.
Wife. I knew he durst not stay when you named officers.
Allwit. That stopped his spirits straight.
What shall we do now, wife?
Wife. As we were wont to do.
Allwit. We are richly furnished, wife, with household stuff.
Wife. Let's let out lodgings then,
And take a house in the Strand.
Allwit. In troth, a match, wench.
We are simply stocked with cloth-of-tissue cushions,
To furnish out bay windows; push, what not that's quaint
And costly, from the top to the bottom.
'Life, for furniture, we may lodge a countess!
There's a close-stool of tawny velvet, too,
Now I think on't, wife,
Wife. There's that should be, sir;
Your nose must be in everything!
Allwit. I have done, wench;
And let this stand in every gallant's chamber:
"There's no gamester like a politic sinner,
For whoe'er games, the box is sure a winner."

Exit [*with* Mistress Allwit].

[V.ii]

Enter Yellowhammer *and his* Wife.

Maudline. Oh, husband, husband, she will die, she will die!
There is no sign but death.
Yellowhammer. 'Twill be our shame then.
Maudline. Oh, how she's changed in compass of an hour!

127 **Hear . . . fool!** "You're talking nonsense"; **His . . . him** those wanting his lands will see to his conviction
133 **close** secluded
136 **place . . . easement** a privy (for easing urinal tract and bowels)
143 **quick'ned** made pregnant
145 **makes** does; **consorts** companions, servants
155 **been familiar** had sexual relations
159 **Gamesters** (1) gamblers; (2) lechers
161 **head** paragon
170 **Strand** the fashionable area from Temple Bar to Charing Cross (but also known for high-class prostitutes); **match** deal, agreement
171 **simply** absolutely; **cloth-of-tissue** cloth with interwoven threads of gold and silver
172 **bay windows** (used by courtesans to show off their wares); **what not** whatever
175 **close-stool** chamberpot in a box or on a stool
180 **box** (bets were placed in a box as house charges when gamblers drew their first hands)

Yellowhammer. Ah, my poor girl! Good faith, thou wert too cruel
To drag her by the hair.
Maudline. You would have done as much, sir,
To curb her of her humor.
Yellowhammer. 'Tis curbed sweetly, she catched her bane o'th' water!

Enter Tim.

Maudline. How now, Tim?
Tim. Faith, busy, mother, about an epitaph
Upon my sister's death.
Maudline. Death! She is not dead, I hope?
Tim. No, but she means to be, and that's as good,
And when a thing's done, 'tis done;
You taught me that, mother.
Yellowhammer. What is your tutor doing?
Tim. Making one too, in principal pure Latin,
Culled out of *Ovid de Tristibus.*
Yellowhammer. How does your sister look? Is she not changed?
Tim. Changed? Gold into white money was never so changed
As is my sister's color into paleness.

Enter Moll [*led in by* Servants].

Yellowhammer. Oh, here she's brought; see how she looks like death!
Tim. Looks she like death, and ne'er a word made yet?
I must go beat my brains against a bed post,
And get before my tutor.
[*Exit.*]
Yellowhammer. Speak, how dost thou?
Moll. I hope I shall be well, for I am as sick at heart
As I can be.
Yellowhammer. 'Las, my poor girl!
The doctor's making a most sovereign drink for thee,
The worst ingredience, dissolved pearl and amber;
We spare no cost, girl.
Moll. Your love comes too late;
Yet timely thanks reward it. What is comfort,
When the poor patient's heart is past relief?
It is no doctor's art can cure my grief.
Yellowhammer. All is cast away then?
Prithee, look upon me cheerfully.
Maudline. Sing but a strain or two, thou wilt not think
How 'twill revive thy spirits. Strive with thy fit,
Prithee, sweet Moll.
Moll. You shall have my good will, mother.
Maudline. Why, well said, wench.

The Song

[*Moll sings.*] Weep eyes, break heart,
My love and I must part;
Cruel fates true love do soonest sever;
Oh, I shall see thee never, never, never!
Oh, happy is the maid whose life takes end,
Ere it knows parent's frown, or loss of friend.
Weep eyes, break heart,
My love and I must part.

Enter Touchwood Senior *with a letter.*

Maudline. Oh, I could die with music! Well sung, girl.
Moll. If you call it so, it was.
Yellowhammer. She plays the swan, and sings herself to death.
Touchwood Senior. By your leave, sir.
Yellowhammer. What are you, sir? Or what's your business, pray?
Touchwood Senior. I may be now admitted, though the brother
Of him your hate pursued. It spreads no further,
Your malice sets in death, does it not, sir?
Yellowhammer. In death?
Touchwood Senior. He's dead: 'twas a dear love to him,
It cost him but his life, that was all, sir.
He paid enough, poor gentleman, for his love.
Yellowhammer. [*Aside.*] There's all our ill removed, if she were well now.
Impute not, sir, his end to any hate
That sprang from us; he had a fair wound brought that.

V.ii.7 **humor** disposition
9 **bane** death (literally, a poison); **water** (pun on *Walter*, pronounced *water*)
15 **when . . . done** (proverbial)
18 **principal** choice
19 ***de Tristibus*** "Of Dismal Surroundings"; Ovid's book of mourning poems used as a set grammarschool text
21 **white money** silver
24 **ne'er . . . yet** I have not yet begun my elegy
26 **get before** (1) precede; (2) write better poetry than
29–30 **sovereign . . . amber** dissolved pearl and amber were considered aphrodisiacs
30 **ingredience** ingredients
38 **revive** (music was thought to have therapeutic powers); **fit** (1) mortal crisis; (2) attack of melancholy; (3) strain of music
40 **You . . . will** i.e., I'll do the best I can
52 **plays the swan** (swans were thought to sing while dying)
57 **sets** ends, declines
58 **dear** (1) expensive; (2) sweet

Touchwood Senior. That helped him forward, I must needs confess;
But the restraint of love, and your unkindess,
Those were the wounds that from his heart drew blood;
But being past help, let words forget it too.
Scarcely three minutes ere his eyelids closed
And took eternal leave of this world's light,
He wrote this letter, which by oath he bound me
To give to her own hands. That's all my business.

Yellowhammer. You may perform it then; there she sits.

Touchwood Senior. Oh, with a following look.

Yellowhammer. Aye, trust me, sir, I think she'll follow him quickly.

Touchwood Senior. Here's some gold
He willed me to distribute faithfully among your servants.

[*He distributes the gold.*]

Yellowhammer. 'Las, what doth he mean, sir?

Touchwood Senior. [*To Moll.*] How cheer you, mistress?

Moll. I must learn of you, sir.

Touchwood Senior. [*Giving letter.*] Here's a letter from a friend of yours,
And where that fails in satisfaction,
I have a sad tongue ready to supply.

Moll. How does he, ere I look on't?

Touchwood Senior. Seldom better, h'as a contented health now.

Moll. I am most glad on't.

[*She reads.*]

Maudline. [*To Touchwood Senior.*] Dead, sir?

Yellowhammer. He is. [*Aside.*] Now, wife, let's but get the girl
Upon her legs again, and to church roundly with her.

Moll. Oh, sick to death, he tells me.
How does he after this?

Touchwood Senior. Faith, feels no pain at all; he's dead, sweet mistress.

Moll. Peace close mine eyes!

[*She faints.*]

Yellowhammer. The girl, look to the girl, wife!

Maudline. Moll, daughter, sweet girl, speak!
Look but once up, thou shalt have all the wishes of thy heart
That wealth can purchase.

Yellowhammer. Oh, she's gone for ever! That letter broke her heart.

Touchwood Senior. As good now, then, as let her lie in torment,
And then break it.

Enter Susan.

Maudline. Oh, Susan, she thou loved'st so dear is gone!

Susan. Oh, sweet maid!

Touchwood Senior. This is she that helped her still.
I've a reward here for thee.

[*He gives Susan a note.*]

Yellowhammer. Take her in,
Remove her from our sight, our shame, and sorrow.

Touchwood Senior. Stay, let me help thee; 'tis the last cold kindness
I can perform for my sweet brother's sake.

[*Exeunt* Touchwood Senior *and* Susan, *with* Servants *carrying* Moll.]

Yellowhammer. All the whole street will hate us, and the world
Point me out cruel. It is our best course, wife,
After we have given order for the funeral,
To absent ourselves, till she be laid in ground.

Maudline. Where shall we spend that time?

Yellowhammer. I'll tell thee where, wench. Go to some private church.
And marry Tim to the rich Brecknock gentlewoman.

Maudline. Mass, a match!
We'll not lose all at once, somewhat we'll catch.

Exit [*with* Yellowhammer].

[V.iii]

Enter Sir Oliver *and* Servants.

Sir Oliver. Ho, my wife's quickened. I am a man for ever!
I think I have bestirred my stumps, i'faith.
Run, get your fellows all together instantly.
Then to the parish church, and ring the bells.

[*1*] *Servant.* It shall be done, sir.

[*Exit.*]

Sir Oliver. Upon my love I charge you, villain, that you make a bonfire before the door at night.

---

64 forward i.e., toward death
73 following i.e., about to follow Touchwood Jr. to death
78 cheer you are you feeling
88 roundly promptly
114 private secluded (where a licensed marriage can be conducted away from the public)
116 a match (1) "agreed!"; (2) a wedding
117 somewhat some dowry
V.iii.2 bestirred my stumps been busy (but with bawdy reference)
7 bonfire (used as a sign of an important event)

[2] *Servant.* A bonfire, sir?
Sir Oliver. A thwacking one, I charge you.
[2] *Servant.* [*Aside.*] This is monstrous.
[*Exit.*]
Sir Oliver. Run, tell a hundred pounds out for the gentleman
That gave my wife the drink, the first thing you do.
[3] *Servant.* A hundred pounds, sir?
Sir Oliver. A bargain! As our joys grows,
We must remember still from whence it flows,
Or else we prove ungrateful multipliers;
The child is coming, and the land comes after;
The news of this will make a poor Sir Walter.
I have strook it home, i'faith.
[3] *Servant.* That you have, marry, sir.
But will not your worship go to the funeral
Of both these lovers?
Sir Oliver. Both? Go both together?
[3] *Servant.* Aye, sir, the gentleman's brother will have it so;
'Twill be the pitifullest sight! there's such running,
Such rumors, and such throngs, a pair of lovers
Had never more spectators, more men's pities,
Or women's wet eyes.
Sir Oliver. My wife helps the number, then?
[3] *Servant.* There's such a drawing out of handkerchers;
And those that have no handkerchers, lift up aprons.
Sir Oliver. Her parents may have joyful hearts at this!
I would not have my cruelty so talked on,
To any child of mine, for a monopoly.
[3] *Servant.* I believe you, sir.
'Tis cast so too, that both their coffins meet,
Which will be lamentable.
Sir Oliver. Come, we'll see't.
Ex[*eunt*].

[V.iv]

Recorders dolefully playing. Enter at one door the coffin of the gentleman [*Touchwood Junior*], *solemnly decked, his sword upon it, attended by many in black* [*including* Sir Oliver Kix, Allwit, *and a* Parson], *his brother* [*Touchwood Senior*] *being the chief mourner. At the other door, the coffin of the virgin* [Moll], *with a garland of flowers, with epitaphs pinn'd on it, attended by maids and women* [*among them are* Lady Kix, Mistress Allwit, *and* Susan]. *Then set them down one right over against the other, while all the company seem to weep and mourn; there is a sad song in the music room.*

Touchwood Senior. Never could death boast of a richer prize
From the first parent; let the world bring forth
A pair of truer hearts. To speak but truth
Of this departed gentleman, in a brother,
Might, by hard censure, be called flattery,
Which makes me rather silent in his right
Than so to be delivered to the thoughts
Of any envious hearer starved in virtue,
And therefore pining to hear others thrive.
But for this maid, whom envy cannot hurt
With all her poisons, having left to ages
The true, chaste monument of her living name,
Which no time can deface, I say of her
The full truth freely, without fear of censure.
What nature could there shine, that might redeem
Perfection home to woman, but in her
Was fully glorious; beauty set in goodness
Speaks what she was, that jewel so infixed;
There was no want of anything of life
To make these virtuous precedents man and wife.
Allwit. Great pity of their deaths!
All. Ne'er more pity!
Lady. It makes a hundred weeping eyes, sweet gossip.
Touchwood Senior. I cannot think there's any one among you
In this full fair assembly, maid, man, or wife,
Whose heart would not have sprung with joy and gladness
To have seen their marriage day?
All. It would have made a thousand joyful hearts.
Touchwood Senior. Up then apace, and take your fortunes!

9 **thwacking** stupendous
11 **tell** count; **gentleman** Touchwood Sr.
19 **strook . . . home** (1) made the winning move (from fencing); (2) copulate
29 **helps** increases
34 **monopoly** a royal grant given for exclusive rights in a commodity; hence, a good income
36 **cast** arranged

V.iv.1 **s.d.** ***over against*** alongside; ***music room*** musicians' gallery over the stage
2 **first parent** Adam
5 **censure** critical judgment
8 **starved** lacking
15–16 **redeem Perfection** (following the fall of Eve)
16 **but** only
18 **Speaks** expresses; **infixed** firmly set
20 **precedents** models of

Make these joyful hearts, here's none but friends.
[*Moll and* Touchwood Junior *rise from their coffins.*]
All. Alive, sir? Oh, sweet, dear couple!
Touchwood Senior. Nay, do not hinder 'em now, stand from about 'em;
If she be caught again, and have this time,
I'll ne'er plot further for 'em, nor this honest chambermaid
That helped all at a push.
Touchwood Junior. [*To Parson.*] Good sir, apace!
Parson. Hands join now, but hearts forever,
Which no parent's mood shall sever.
[*To Touchwood Junior.*] You shall forsake all widows, wives, and maids;
[*To Moll.*] You, lords, knights, gentlemen, and men of trades;
And if, in haste, any article misses
Go interline it with a brace of kisses.
Touchwood Senior. Here's a thing trolled nimbly. Give you joy, brother!
Were't not better thou should'st have her
Than the maid should die?
Wife. To you, sweet mistress bride.
All. Joy, joy to you both.
Touchwood Senior. Here be your wedding sheets you brought along with you; you may both go to bed when you please to.
Touchwood Junior. My joy wants utterance.
Touchwood Senior. Utter all at night then, brother.
Moll. I am silent with delight.
Touchwood Senior. Sister, delight will silence any woman;
But you'll find your tongue again, among maidservants,
Now you keep house, sister.
All. Never was hour so filled with joy and wonder.
Touchwood Senior. To tell you the full story of this chambermaid,
And of her kindness in this business to us,
'Twould ask an hour's discourse. In brief, 'twas she
That wrought it to this purpose cunningly.
All. We shall all love her for't.

Enter Yellowhammer *and his* Wife.

Allwit. See who comes here now.
Touchwood Senior. A storm, a storm, but we are sheltered for it.
Yellowhammer. I will prevent you all, and mock you thus,
You, and your expectations. I stand happy,
Both in your lives, and your hearts' combination.
Touchwood Senior. Here's a strange day again!
Yellowhammer. The knight's proved villain,
(All's come out now) his niece an arrant baggage;
My poor boy Tim is cast away this morning,
Even before breakfast, married a whore
Next to his heart.
All. A whore?
Yellowhammer. His "niece," forsooth!
Allwit. [*Aside.*] I think we rid our hands in good time of him.
Wife. [*Aside.*] I knew he was past the best when I gave him over.
What is become of him pray, sir?
Yellowhammer. Who, the knight? He lies i'th' knight's ward now.
[*To Lady Kix.*] Your belly, lady, begins to blossom.
There's no peace for him;
His creditors are so greedy.
Sir Oliver. [*To Touchwood Senior.*] Master Touchwood, hear'st thou this news?
I am so endeared to thee for my wife's fruitfulness
That I charge you both, your wife and thee,
To live no more asunder for the world's frowns:
I have purse, and bed, and board for you;
Be not afraid to go to your business roundly;
Get children, and I'll keep them.
Touchwood Senior. Say you so, sir?
Sir Oliver. Prove me, with three at a birth, and thou darest now.
Touchwood Senior. Take heed how you dare a man, while you live, sir,
That has good skill at his weapon.

Enter Tim *and* Welsh Gentlewoman [*and* Tutor].

Sir Oliver. 'Foot, I dare you, sir!
Yellowhammer. Look, gentlemen, if ever you saw the picture

33 have this time lose this opportunity
35 at a push in a crisis (*push* also means copulate)
36 Hands join (to complete the marriage ceremony; cf. III.i.19)
37 mood anger
40 article contractual clause
41 interline write in; **brace** pair
42 trolled easily said; uttered swiftly
51 Utter (1) say; (2) ejaculate
64 prevent anticipate
71 Next to his heart closest to his affection
75 knight's ward in debtors' prison, the next to cheapest accommodation (at twopence)
83 roundly thoroughly (playing on round-bellied, or pregnant)
85 Prove test
87 skill . . . weapon (deliberately bawdy)

Of the unfortunate marriage, yonder 'tis.
Welsh Gentlewoman. Nay, good sweet Tim –
Tim. Come from the university,
To marry a whore in London, with my tutor too?
O tempora! O mors!
Tutor. Prithee, Tim, be patient!
Tim. I bought a jade at Cambridge;
I'll let her out to execution, tutor,
For eighteen pence a day, or Brainford horse races;
She'll serve to carry seven miles out of town well.
Where be these mountains? I was promised mountains,
But there's such a mist, I can see none of 'em.
What are become of those two thousand runts?
Let's have a bout with them in the meantime.
A vengeance runt thee!
Maudline. Good sweet Tim, have patience.
Tim. *Flectere si nequeo superos Acheronta movebo,* mother.
Maudline. I think you have married her in logic, Tim.
You told me once, by logic you would prove
A whore an honest woman; prove her so, Tim,
And take her for thy labor.
Tim. Troth, I thank you.
I grant you I may prove another man's wife so,
But not mine own.
Maudline. There's no remedy now, Tim,
You must prove her so as well as you may.
Tim. Why then, my tutor and I will about her
As well as we can.
Uxor non est meretrix, ergo falacis.
Welsh Gentlewoman. Sir, if your logic cannot prove me honest,
There's thing called marriage, and that makes me honest.
Maudline. Oh, there's a trick beyond your logic, Tim.
Tim. I perceive then a woman may be honest according to the English print, when she is a whore in the Latin. So much for marriage and logic! I'll love her for her wit; I'll pick out my runts there; and for my mountains, I'll mount upon –
Yellowhammer. So fortune seldom deals two marriages
With one hand, and both lucky; the best is,
One feast will serve them both! Marry, for room
I'll have the dinner kept in Goldsmiths' Hall,
To which, kind gallants, I invite you all.
[*Exeunt.*]

FINIS

94 ***O...mors*** (a parody of "O tempora, O mores," "Oh, times; oh, manners!")
96 **jade** (1) poor horse; (2) whore
97 **execution** hire
98 **Brainford** Brentford, Middlesex, notorious for assignations and horse-racing
104 **runt** reprove
105 ***Flectere...movebo*** "Since I cannot move the powers above, I shall work on the lower regions" (Virgil, *Aeneid* VII.312)
110 **labor** (1) pains; (2) sexual effort
114 **about her** (with a bawdy pun)
116 ***Uxor...falacis*** "A wife is not a whore, therefore you are wrong"
121–2 **English...Latin** merry trick: meretrix (Latin for whore) (a common joke)
121 **print** spelling
124 **mount** (1) ride on; (2) sexually mount
129 **Goldsmiths' Hall** hall of the Goldsmiths' Company on the E side of Foster Lane N of Cheapside at the end of Maiden Lane; Stow calls it "a proper house, but not large"

Bartholomew Fair

Ben Jonson

BARTHOLMEW FAYRE:

A COMEDIE, ACTED IN THE YEARE, 1614.

By the Lady *ELIZABETHS* SERVANTS.

And then dedicated to King IAMES, of *most Blessed Memorie*;

By the Author, BENIAMIN IOHNSON.

Si foret in terris, rideret Democritus: *nam*
Spectaret populum ludis attentiùs ipsis,
Vt sibi praebentem, mimo spectacula plura.
Scriptores autem narrare putaret assello
Fabellam surdo. Hor. lib. 2. Epist. 1.

LONDON,
Printed by *I. B.* for ROBERT ALLOT, and are to be sold at the signe of the *Beare*, in *Pauls* Church-yard. 1631.

Title-page of the play in the 1640 Folio.

Ben Jonson's most complicated and comprehensive play – half as long again as his other comedies with twice the number of speaking parts – is nevertheless compressed into the Prologue he wrote for a royal performance on November 1, 1614:

> Your Majesty is welcome to a Fair;
> Such place, such men, such language and such ware
> You must expect: with these, the zealous noise
> Of your land's Faction, scandalized at toys,
> As babies, hobby-horses, puppet-plays,
> And such like rage, whereof the petulant ways
> Yourself have known, and have been vexed with long.
> These for your sport, without particular wrong
> Or just complaint of any private man
> (Who of himself or shall think well or can),
> The Maker doth present, and hopes tonight
> To give you, for a fairing, true delight.

The invitation replicates counsel King James had given to Prince Henry in his advice book to his son, the *Basilikon Doron*, widely available in both Scotland and England:

> In respect whereof, and therewith also to allure them to a common amity among themselves, certain days in the year would be appointed, for delighting the people with public spectacles of all honest games and exercise of arms, as also for convening of neighbors, for entertaining friendship and heartliness, by honest feasting and merriment. For I cannot see what greater superstition can be in making plays and lawful games in May, and good cheer at Christmas, than in eating fish in Lent and upon Fridays, the papists as well using the one as the other.

Jonson's fairing, or present, for his King is a play that concerns amity and friendship, an honest spectacle; superstition made entertainment. Jonson also knew that the audience for his play would have come after attending evensong for All Saints' Day where other directives and desires would also be set in motion. The prayer in that service was taken from Wisdom 5: "Then shall the righteous man stand in great boldness before the face of such as have afflicted him.... And they repenting and groaning for anguish of spirit shall say within themselves, This was he whom we had sometimes in derision, and a proverb of reproach: We fools account his life madness." In *Bartholomew Fair* such scripture might define either Justice Overdo or Trouble-All, but evening service's other lesson, taken from Apocalypse 19, envisions an avenging judge whose words are compared to swords which Overdo alone echoes: "Mine own words turned against me, like swords." Such a subtle yet surprising transformation of scripture is a preparation for the lesson's other anticipation of Jonson's play: the marriage supper of the Lamb which foreshadows the dominance of Jonson's third main character, Quarlous.

Yet there is nothing about the atmosphere of Jonson's play that seems to draw on the Bible; his play set on St. Bartholomew's Day in August is one which captures all the grittiness of Smithfield where it is set: the sights, the smells, the noises, the cheating and sweating and pissing that characterize congested Jacobean London. Jonson's play seems not so much a coming to terms as the loosening of carnival: a time for mock liturgies, travestied saints' lives and parodic reenactments of Holy Writ. Jonson's invitation displays the interconnectedness between human indulgence and human exploitation; this play, whose script begins and ends with reference to the King, is a play of craft and cunning. The people who come to the fair and those who work at the fair are alike in their infectious desire and avarice. Cozening seems synonymous with living. Joan Trash sells stale cakes; Ursula sells more froth than beer; and Lantern Leatherhead (like Trash) never gives Bartholomew Cokes what he paid for. Their unholy activity presages unholy alliances and practices: the balladsinger Nightingale is in cahoots with the cutpurse Ezekiel Edgworth as, later, they team up with a costermonger to rob Cokes not only of his money but his clothes. Some months before the royal performance, Jonson had sold his play to a marginal playing company, Lady Elizabeth's Men, which the entrepreneur Philip Henslowe had amalgamated with the Children of the Queen's Revels; and there is a way in which the crude and selfish behavior of many of Jonson's characters appears childish. Jonson sensed this too, echoing Wasp in a comment he made later in *Discoveries*:

> What pretty things they are we wonder at! Like children that esteem every trifle and prefer a fairing before their fathers. What difference is between us and them but that we are dearer fools, coxcombs at a higher rate? They are pleased with cockleshells, whistles, hobby-horses, and such like; we with statues, marble pillars, pictures, gilded roofs where underneath is lathe and lime, perhaps loam.

Inspiration for this apparently bizarre mixture of the sacred and the secular, the significant with the trivial, comes from the eponymous fair itself. Bartholomew Fair derived from a royal charter granted by Henry I in 1133 to his former jester Rahere, who needed the revenue for the management and upkeep of the priory and hospital, both dedicated to St. Bartholomew, which he had founded in Smithfield, just northwest of the city walls of London. The Feast of St. Bartholomew was August 24 – the day on which Jonson sets his play – and it commemorates the apostle who had been flayed alive; a symbolic knife generally depicted his martyrdom. In the church of St. Bartholomew the Great before the Reformation in the mid-sixteenth century, an altar was dedicated to him and there were also doubtless relics (which reappear in Jonson's play as the indigestible pieces of gingerbread sold by Joan Trash that Busy sees as icons of popery). But for centuries Smithfield was identified with harsh justice – of the kind Overdo longs to install – which condemned and punished religious nonconformists – as Busy would do – both Catholic and Protestant. In 1537, for instance, John Forest, a friar, was burned at Smithfield for heresy and treason, while at the same time the forthright Protestant Hugh Latimer preached at Smithfield and there was burned a wooden image (called by some an idol) of Darvel (or David) Gatheren of Llandervel, Wales. Forest was only one of the many martyrs to be executed at Smithfield under Henry VIII, but such punishment became proverbial under the Catholic Queen Mary, whose scores of executions of Protestants led to the common notion that "the fires of Smithfield" were always burning. When Elizabeth came to the throne, she made Smithfield the place where Catholic relics and icons were destroyed and burned, purifying the nation of the Roman religion. Following the bloody Catholic massacre of thousands of French Huguenots in Paris on St. Bartholomew's Day in 1572, said to be the bloodiest day since Herod slaughtered the Innocents, many London booksellers displayed only Bibles on their stalls. August 24 thus came to represent religious conflict and the exercise of justice alongside the need for tolerance and the desire for freedom of thought and action.

Rahere's fair, like many others, probably had its origin as a gathering for worship in a sacred place and, like other country fairs, became an occasion for the sale of staples and livestock, for the crops of farmers, and for the hiring of workers. Bartholomew Fair became famous as a cloth fair, which took place within the walls of the priory, and as a horse fair as well. Both special traditions lie behind Jonson's play. The ownership of clothing and cloth is important to many characters in *Bartholomew Fair*, from Win Littlewit who first appears in a remarkable velvet hat to Grace Wellborn with her cut-work. Ursula attracts customers by offering them silk gowns, velvet petticoats, and wrought smocks; in Act V both Win and Mistress Overdo emerge transformed by the green gowns of prostitutes that cause them to resemble Punk Alice. The horse fair, meantime, has degenerated into the cozening tricks of the horse-courser Jordan Knockem. Such remains of an earlier day, however, are overshadowed by the pleasure fair outside the old priory walls. This too had its origins with Rahere, who had performed as a juggler, and his successor Thomas, who had delivered doggerel poetry and song like Nightingale and occasionally delivered sermons parodied in the language of Zeal-of-the-Land Busy. This is the fair Cokes longs to visit, with its cheap trinkets and baubles, its stale baked goods, and its traditional puppet plays, the enormities that concern Justice Overdo but that provide much of the congested action and boisterous upheavals in Jonson's play. John Stow recalls still another tradition. On the Eve of St. Bartholomew, grammarschool students met in the churchyard at Smithfield for a public speaking contest held on a platform under a tree (perhaps suggesting Ursula's booth under a bower). There they debated. The best scholars came from St. Anthony's Hospital (called "Anthony's pigs" by their rivals, the boys from St. Paul's School known as the "pigeons of Paul's" from the birds that flocked around St. Paul's Cathedral): together they suggest the pigs and "birds o' the game" at Ursula's booth, just as their debates are satirized by Jonson in the game of vapors, a shouting match of no real substance where the only meaningful thing is victory. And Smithfield also had lingering associations with the theater. The royal office of the Master of the Revels, which prepared plays and masques for the court – such as the forty-shilling wedding masque Bartholomew Cokes plans for Grace Wellborn with Leatherhead's fiddles and toys, Nightingale's doggerel, and Trash's gingerbread – had been near Smithfield until 1607. Moreover, Inigo Jones, Jonson's former colleague in staging masques, and now his rival, had been born in St. Bartholomew parish; according to their contemporary John Selden, the puppeteer Lantern had originally been named Inigo.

Just which of these traditions is most important to Jonson's conception of *Bartholomew Fair* may be an open question, but they all turn, in their inherent unruliness, on the need for order and the problem of jurisdiction. King James claimed the power to license plays and players in and around London and to override any local actions or ordinances against them; the City of London fought to curb any royal monopolies within its city walls and its liberties with ordinances of its own. While the City Fathers denounced those plays that provided revenue for the King, they felt quite differently about revenues for the City's coffers and when the cloth fair and its revenues passed to Lord Rich, who owned the priory following the dissolution of the monasteries and church lands in the mid-sixteenth century, they became especially eager to receive the revenues from the pleasure fair. That land became a part of the city's jurisdiction in 1608, a part of the liberties of London when the King offered the city a new charter that specified that the "circuit, bounds, liberties, franchises, and jurisdiction" of London be extended to incorporate the area around the priory, known for the fair, as well as Blackfriars and Whitefriars, known for their connections as playing houses, in return for the funds to build himself a new banqueting house. At times this new situation became contentious because the King controlled the theater and the City controlled the fair. Jonson's prologue to the King to come to Bartholomew Fair, and to see his play, is therefore anything but innocent.

Justice is, consequently, central to *Bartholomew Fair*, both in the legal jurisdiction that provides law and order and in religious toleration which controls religious conflict and bullying short of the martyrdom which Busy envisions for himself when in the stocks. Justice Overdo is the main agent for law and order, yet again Jonson develops his character with such complexity that we are left to determine just what his role is meant to signify. For one thing, he seems to represent the city's authority. His means of searching for legal infractions by disguising himself as a madman may refer directly to Thomas Hayes, the Lord Mayor of London in 1614. A letter by Hayes to the King's Lord Chamberlain on July 8, 1614, is summarized in the city's archives: "He had informed himself by means of spies, of many lewd houses, and had gone himself disguised to divers of them, and, finding these nurseries of villainy, had punished them according to their deserts, some by carting and whipping, and many by banishment." He was especially concerned with the cunning practices of alehouses where drinks were scanted and tobacco was adulterated, as at Ursula's: "The Bakers and Brewers had been drawn within bounds, so that, if the case continued, men might have what they paid for, viz. weight and measure." Another letter from Hayes on October 15 requires "every Alderman in his Ward to call before him the innholders, victuallers, ale-house-keepers, cooks and all those who brewed and sold again in bye-places, to examine the quantity and prices of such ale and beer as they had received into their houses and cellars since Christmas, 1613." Such practices and remarks may have occurred during the writing of Jonson's play or suggested additions or alterations to a play written in 1614 but not printed until 1631, but they were shared by Hayes's predecessor as Lord Mayor, Thomas Middleton (unrelated to the playwright). Middleton wrote the Lords of the King's Council on December 13, 1613, "I have of late taken some courses with the victuallers and brewers of the City, and done my best endeavor to work a reformation of those enormities" (a word Justice Overdo uses twenty-three times in the play). A pamphlet which draws on an earlier work by George Whetstone was also published in 1613 entitled *Look on Me, London: I am an Honest Englishman, ripping up the Bowels of Mischief, lurking in thy Sub-urbs and Precincts, Take Heed.* A poem on the title-page reads, "The Hangman's Halter, and the Beadle's Whip, Will make the Fool dance and the Knave to skip," and the work is pointedly dedicated to Middleton: "for in the first year of the King's Majesty's reign, your Lordship being then Sheriff of this city), you made your Visitations in the Suburbs, and outplaces of the Precincts of London, to inquire after evil livers and by Justice strove to rule out iniquity." Other characteristics of Overdo, however, seem to point in other directions. Both Jonson and King James share Overdo's love of disguise and acting, and the Justice's references to Cicero and his respect for the ideas of Horace sound very much like Jonson himself, while his insistence on his own undeniable authority, his desire to be admired by his people, and even his attack on tobacco could all refer to the King.

So might the play's concern with Puritanism. "The name of Puritan," King James wrote to his son in *Basilikon Doron*,

> doth properly belong only to that vile sect among the Anabaptists called the Family of Love, because they think themselves only pure.... Of this special sect I principally mean when I speak of Puritans...and partly, indeed, I give this style to such brainsick and heady preachers their disciples and followers, as refusing to be called of that sect, yet participate too much with their humors.

He may have had in mind a famous Banbury Puritan William Whatley, the "roaring boy of Banbury," who notoriously preached at fairs for the same reason Busy scolds fairgoers, to gather for God a "fairing of souls." Jonson himself had little patience for men like Busy. "Some Controverters in Divinity are like Swaggerers in a tavern," he writes in *Discoveries*, "that catch that which stands next them, the candlestick or pots; turn everything into a weapon. Oft-time they fight blindfold; and both beat the air. The one milks a he-goat, the other holds under a sieve.... These Fencers in Religion, I like not." But *Bartholomew Fair* incorporates more than Puritans by associating Busy with Banbury; in associating Cokes with Harrow, Jonson also points to Catholicism. In 1614 the settlement of Harrow was notorious as a refuge for recusants, especially in the infamous Bellamy family's manor house of Uxendon at Harrow on the

Hill, which harbored seminarians. The Jesuit Edmund Campion stayed there shortly before his arrest in 1581; Richard Bristow, the author of *Motives Inducing to the Catholic Faith*, was a resident; and both Anthony Babington in 1586 and the Jesuit poet Robert Southwell in 1592 were captured there and executed for treason or, depending on our point of view, made martyrs for their cause. The arguments and brawls that erupt in *Bartholomew Fair*, then, resonate the deeper divisions in Jonson's time that the fair made manifest: the battle between the crown and the city for revenue and jurisdiction and the struggle of Puritans and Catholics for men's souls. The freedom Cokes relishes is given a darker turn in the liberty Grace wants from him, the insistence of Leatherhead and Trash for their own piece of ground to do business, and the absolutism of Ursula's rule over her den of iniquity: all potentially provoke trouble and even rebellion. Jonson was himself converted for a decade to Catholicism while a prisoner in 1598; the priest who converted him there, Fr. Thomas Wright, wrote *The Passions of the Mind in General* later that year in which, in his attempt to find order, he located disorder in "the inordinate motions of Passions [which] are thorny briars sprung from the infected root of original sin" common to all faiths that resulted in the "prevention of reason" and the "rebellion to virtue." (The book was reissued in 1604 with a commendatory poem by Jonson.)

To exercise some means of control over such contentiousness, and to enforce regulations and settle disputes, a special court was convened for Bartholomew Fair to dispense instant justice. It was called the Court of Piepowders, presumably a long-standing corruption of the French *pieds poudreux*, referring to the "dusty feet" of the itinerant tradesmen and merchants whose lives and livelihoods depended on such fairs. Justice Overdo presides over this court in *Bartholomew Fair*, but like so many of his fellows in the play, he trivializes his position by measuring puddings, cans, and custards "with a stick; and their circumference, with a thread." His actions mirror the bungling of his assistants Haggis, Bristle, and Poacher; like them, he seems hopelessly isolated from the fair. His first speech (II.i) is a soliloquy (although Mooncalf may spy on him from the inner stage as he means to spy on others); the disguise he takes in order to become a part of the fair is that of a madman. His ineptitude is measurable from the start; he finds enormities in the bantering of Ursula, Nightingale, and Knockem in II.ii. and II.iii only to miss the genuine enormities of theft and prostitution in II.iv. Jonson's own judgment may be signaled by the fact that the only person who fears him, Trouble-All, is also mad. Overdo's inability to put his convictions into responsible practice finds its analogue in Zeal-of-the-Land Busy, who concentrates on the heresy of toys and gingerbread while failing to notice the real sins of the world, the Devil, and the flesh that Ursula practices by sheltering thieves; by encouraging pride, lechery, anger, avarice, and gluttony; and by procuring prostitutes; and in Humphrey Wasp whose quick temper and general irascibility make him immune to the theft of the precious marriage license he carries and an easy dupe for the game of vapors – a tutor who himself needs tutoring.

Indeed, we may well find that the only order in *Bartholomew Fair* is the persistent interest in commodification and corruption of people which Jonson seems to impose. His fair is a "fair field of folk" that engages much of Jacobean England. There are gentry (Winwife, Cokes, Grace), merchants and tradesmen (Busy and Dame Purecraft), professionals (Littlewit, Overdo, and Wasp) attempting to mingle with the thieves, pimps, and whores (Edgworth, Whit, and Punk Alice as well as Leatherhead, Trash, and Ursula). The fair draws them in from all over – Bristle is from Wales, Northern from Scotland, Whit from Ireland, and Puppy the wrestler is a "western man." Cokes is from the country, only visiting the city, while Quarlous is at home as the typical London rake. What brings them all together is their shared interest in market principles and contractual obligations rather than, say, the shared beliefs of religion or the higher principles of morality or art. Grace Wellborn – on stage much of the time but silent for most of it – embodies these forces as they converge. She is a ward of Justice Overdo, who bought her wardship from the King in the hopes of rearing her in return for the profit her marriage might bring him. In pursuing Grace, Winwife and Quarlous also hope to cash in on her value. By Jonson's time, the outdated feudal practice of wardships had become notorious. When the Earl of Pembroke was thought to be dying in 1595, it was reported that "the tribe of Hunsdon do lay wait for the wardship of the brave young lord." The son of the Earl of Dorset was speedily married to Anne Clifford a few days before her father's death to "prevent the Duke of Lennox and others that made earnest means for his wardship." Where King James stood on this abusive practice of purchasing orphans with family inheritances in order to cash in on their fortunes is unclear, but the first Parliament under James was clear enough: it claimed wards were "bought and sold like horses." In the course of Jonson's play, Grace manages to escape Overdo's demand that she marry the foolish Cokes by trading in herself as the subject of money only to become the object of a lottery; the play seems to ask us whether a sense of the market and her own market worth has made Grace irrational and foolish or one resigned to a market economy, willing to cut her losses and accept what profitable outcome she can or retire until the trading improves. Financial survival and exigency are also seen in the case of Dame Purecraft, a wealthy widow who is likewise fair game for an impoverished gentry or aspiring workers. In *The Arraignment of Lewd, Idle, Froward and Unconstant Women* (1615), Joseph Swetnam (under the pseudonym of Thomas Tel-truth) argued that such a widow would be the cause of a thousand troubles. Such widows were ridiculed as "a sort of cattle so odd that the best of the kind with all the perfections of nature and advantage of fortune are seldom an equal exchange for any man's peace and liberty." Quarlous prefers her money to that of Grace; but it may be Jonson's telling verdict that in pursuing Purecraft, Quarlous aligns himself with a hypocrite, an embezzler, and a bawd who makes money out of marrying not only widows but "our poor handsome young virgins."

At the center of the fair and of the play – the setting for Acts II, III, and IV – Ursula's pig tent fosters both commodification and corruptibility as she sells animal and human flesh indiscriminately: "Here you may ha' your punk and your pig in state, sir, both piping hot." Ursula has been punished by carting as Punk Alice, one of her wares, has been imprisoned in Bridewell, but for Jonson there may be little difference (except for incarceration) between their practices and Dame Purecraft's shady business practices or Busy's callous ruination of a Newgate-market grocer from whom he took currants without paying for them in the days he worked as a baker. Such business does not breed lasting partnerships necessarily; although Leatherhead and Trash agree to cooperate when Cokes offers to buy all they have, they are quick to quarrel when their alliance is unprofitable and their business falters; the game of vapors may be Ursula's way of distracting what otherwise might be more ruthless competition, and although her companions are quick to help her when she scalds herself with pigfat, they are also protecting their own self- interests in helping their proprietress who serves as their infernal patron. In fact *Bartholomew Fair* is stuffed with images drawn from hunting and falconry that underlie its repeated dramatic cycles of predator and prey. People are commodified, but in the world of the fair, every material object has its price. Joan Trash sells gingerbread made from dead honey; a newt may lurk in each bottle of Bartholomew ale; and a spider may be found in each pipeful of tobacco. These darker images allow us to see the darker side of the coaches, wires, and tires which fascinate Win and Mistress Overdo and the pears for which Cokes scrambles. Such acquisitiveness makes Cokes easy prey for Nightingale and Edgworth who together steal his silver in Act II, his gold in Act III, and with the aid of the costermonger his cloak, hat, and sword in Act IV. Worst of all, perhaps, is Quarlous, Grace's suitor and Winwife's rival, who, as the play progresses, blackmails Edgworth into stealing the marriage license for Grace from Wasp, adopts the identity of Trouble-All to find out whom Grace has chosen to marry, uses the disguise to prey on Overdo's mercy to win for himself a blank warrant, and finally asserts the right to judge the others (and forgive them!) in the play's final scenes. Preaching a sermon against widow-hunting in I.iii, he finds no trouble in pursuing Purecraft for her money. He is, throughout, cold, unscrupulous, and untroubled. In stripping the mad and helpless Trouble-All of all his clothes, however, and leaving him with Ursula's pan, he may also render judgment on himself. This moment comes after Leatherhead's conventional cry, "What do you lack?" in Acts II and III, is displaced by Trouble-All's far more troubling question, "Have you a warrant?" in Acts IV and V. When the frustrated Cokes cries out for many of those at the fair to the departing Trouble-All (even as he becomes Overdo's conscience) "you are a very coxcomb, do you hear?," Trouble-All's reply sounds like the play's sudden universalizing indictment: "I think I am; if Justice Overdo sign to it, I am, and so we are all," and adds, "he'll quit us all, multiply us all." The mad vision may be a chilling truth.

Acquisitiveness also culminates in the commodification of the puppet show of Act V which combines the world of Littlewit in London and the world of Leatherhead in Smithfield – the proctor of the episcopal court turned salacious scriptwriter and the master of make-believe as ardent businessman. Around them nearly everyone in the cast gathers before what Francis Bacon had attacked as an Idol of the Theater. In 1613, Robert Milles, an outspoken opponent of the stage, attacked Jonson in a sermon at Paul's Cross in which he denounced those Londoners who preferred "the idle and scurrile invention of an illiterate bricklayer to the holy, pure, and powerful word of God." The puppet play may be Jonson's satiric but forthright reply, his defense of plays. Surely Littlewit's and Leatherhead's performance exposes the foolishness of Cokes, who associates each of the puppets with one of his earlier material purchases at the fair. The corruption of Marlowe's Ovidian poem on Hero and Leander as ideal lovers (and Richard Edwardes's *Damon and Pythias* as ideal friends) becomes pure farce and slapstick, the spirit of fair and carnival out of artistic control. But is it? The story, reduced to an appetite for lechery, drink, and aggressive behavior, seems in an eerie and canny way to judge all of its spectators. Hero, for instance, who is excited by the naked legs of Leander during their chance encounter, is observed by Grace Wellborn, who has given herself to Winwife after knowing him for less than two hours. The tyranny of King Dionysius is observed, but without a flicker of recognition, by Justice Overdo (and by Quarlous), while Cupid as a tapster supplies an ironic commentary on Ursula's tent and its dispensing of drink. (As a former scrivener, Cupid also looks back to Littlewit in Act I and the Scrivener in the Induction before that.) Busy's attacking the show and then debating a puppet argues the issue of idolatry with an idol; but he also disputes the possibility of the Catholic concern with the Real Presence and allies his casuistry with the books on conscience that the Protestant writer William Perkins was putting in every household at the time. Most of the spectators seem reduced to puppets themselves, then controlled by Leatherhead, the puppeteer. In fact, he defends his show against Busy's charge that it is "licentious" by arguing that it has been "licensed by authority" and in "the hand of the Master of the Revels" himself: James's own government, it is said, has certified the puppet play and, by implication and by royal performance, the play in which it takes place. Thus officially licensed, it makes its own social, political, and religious pronouncements and it does so in *Bartholomew Fair* by being a "get-penny." The puppet play thus commodifies authority – the King himself – even as it points to the corruptibility of those who enjoy it.

Following the precedent of Dekker's *Shoemakers' Holiday* and its final focus on Shrove Tuesday, Jonson's *Bartholomew Fair* centers on holiday in which social and political customs are suspended while new social and political alliances are formed. Both works attempt to appropriate acquisitiveness and human failings through laughter and joy, yet the two works may strike us as fundamentally dissimilar. To employ one of Jonson's own puns, *Bartholomew Fair* keeps asking us openly if it is a foul play or a fair one, if it is a sobering indictment of human aspiration and behavior or a festival celebrating the rejuvenating energies of folly and the disorder that releases us, if only for a three-day period in late August. The play itself was staged publicly in 1614 in the Hope Theater which, at least three days of the week with the staging removed, served as a major bearbaiting arena. The site, that is, used humans and animals alike as performers. It was as "dirty as Smithfield and as stinking every whit." (The Lady Elizabeth's Men disbanded in 1615; after 1617, the Hope had no standard acting company.) Is the game of vapors – referred to in the play sixty-nine times – a form of human liberty or the invitation to anarchism? The play itself asks the question. "Sir, you'll allow me my Christian liberty. I may laugh, I hope," Quarlous says about his right to engage in such a contest, but Mistress Overdo sees it far differently: "What mean you? Are you rebels, gentlemen? Shall I send out a sergeant-at-arms or a writ o' rebellion against you? I'll commit you, upon my womanhood, for a riot, upon my justice-hood, if you persist." For her, the apparent danger is acute. And what do we make of the puppet play? Fairs were still the site of didactic moralities with puppets in Jonson's day, but here *Sodom and Gomorrah* seems to be replaced by something more political, like *The Gunpowder Plot* which, we are assured, is the smart man's current get-penny. Other questions are even more difficult. How, for instance, are we to distinguish between the practices of Ursula and those of Dame Purecraft? How is Cokes, largely stripped of his clothes, any different from the naked Trouble-All, stripped of his? How do we sort out Punk Alice, Win Littlewit, and Mistress Overdo once they dress identically; or do we? Do we agree with the puppet Dionysius that there is no essential difference between a player and a Puritan, or with Edgworth and Quarlous that there is no way to tell the morality of a performer from that of a spectator? How does Overdo as Mad Arthur relate to the mad Trouble-All or the maddened Busy, the ever-angry Wasp? The play's key words, *warrant* and *license*, loosened from Overdo's pocket and Littlewit's black box, grow increasingly metaphorical and metonymic. At the very end of *Bartholomew Fair*, when all at last seems at least temporarily settled, Cokes is quick to open it all up again by inviting the puppets to come to Justice Overdo's house and continue the play; since this act goes beyond the boundaries of the play itself, the imaginative script moves past Littlewit, Leatherhead, and even Jonson to be our own creation. Jonson himself sees this possibility, as he makes clear in *Discoveries*: "I have considered our whole life is like a play wherein every man, forgetful of himself, is in travail with expression of another. Nay, we so insist in imitating others as we cannot, when it is necessary, return to ourselves." As the Articles of Agreement in the play's Induction made clear from the start, *Bartholomew Fair* cannot – as a play, as any play – work until we exercise our moral response to it. But while the Scrivener and Book-Holder allow us to make whatever judgment we wish, Jonson is not so forgiving. To those in his audiences at the Hope and at court – and to us as readers – he remarks in the Induction that, witnessing the play, "as you have preposterously put to your seals already (which is your money), you will now add the other part of suffrage, your hands." He has commodified his own authority as playwright – the King's authority, too, through the Master of the Revels – and in doing so, may have seduced and commodified us. Thus Jonson suggests rather openly that the world of Bartholomew Fair may be our world too.

Further Reading

Bledsoe, Mary W., "The Function of Linguistic Enormity in Ben Jonson's *Bartholomew Fair,*" *Language and Style* 17:2 (Spring 1984): 149–60.

Burt, Richard, *Licensed by Authority: Ben Jonson and the Discourse of Censorship*. Ithaca and London: Cornell University Press, 1993.

Cave, Richard Allen, *Ben Jonson*, ch. 7; London: Macmillan, 1991.

Cope, Jackson I., "*Bartholomew Fair* as Blasphemy," *Renaissance Drama* 8 (1965): 127–52.

Haynes, Jonathan, *The Social Relations of Jonson's Theater*, ch. 5. Cambridge: Cambridge University Press, 1992.

Juneja, Renu, "Eve's Flesh and Blood in Jonson's *Bartholomew Fair,*" *Comparative Drama* 12:4 (Winter 1978–9): 340–53.

Kaplan, Joel H., "Dramatic and Moral Energy in Ben Jonson's *Bartholomew Fair,*" *Renaissance Drama* n.s. 3 (1970): 137–56.

Levin, Richard, "The Structure of *Bartholomew Fair,*" *PMLA* 80:3 (June 1965): 172–9.

McDermott, Kristen, "Versions of Femininity in *Bartholomew Fair,*" *Renaissance Papers* (1993): 91–115.

McPherson, David, "The Origins of Overdo: A Study in Jonsonian Invention," *Modern Language Quarterly* 37:3 (September 1976): 221–33.

Miller, Shannon, "Consuming Mothers/Consuming Merchants: The Carnivalesque Economy of Jacobean City Comedy," *Modern Language Studies* 26:2–3 (Spring and Summer 1996): 73–95.

Parker, R. B., "The Themes and Staging of *Bartholomew Fair,*" *University of Toronto Quarterly* 39:4 (July 1970): 293–309.

Slights, William W. E., *Ben Jonson and the Art of Secrecy*, ch. 7. Toronto: University of Toronto Press, 1994.

Teague, Frances, *The Curious History of "Bartholomew Fair"*, esp. chs. 1–2. Lewisburg: Bucknell University Press, 1985.

Bartholomew Fair

THE PROLOGUE TO THE KING'S MAJESTY.

Your Majesty is welcome to a Fair;
Such place, such men, such language and such
ware
You must expect: with these, the zealous noise
Of your land's Faction, scandalized at toys,
As babies, hobby-horses, puppet-plays,
And such like rage, whereof the petulant ways
Yourself have known, and have been vexed
with long.
These for your sport, without particular wrong
Or just complaint of any private man
(Who of himself or shall think well or can),
The Maker doth present, and hopes tonight
To give you, for a fairing, true delight.

THE PERSONS OF THE PLAY.

John Littlewit.	*A Proctor.*
Solomon.	*His man.*
Win Littlewit.	*His wife.*
Dame Purecraft.	*Her mother, and a widow.*
Zeal-of-the-Land Busy.	*Her suitor, a Banbury man.*
Winwife.	*His rival, a gentleman.*

TEXTUAL VARIANTS

Persons of the Play 2 (line missing in F) **25** Watchmen] F Watchman **Induction 99** a] F an **110** pennyworth] F pen'orth **111** pennyworth] F pen(worth **160** loathe] F loth **165** among] F amongst **I.i**] (All stage directions in F list entire cast for each scene in order of appearance at the beginning of the scene; these have been replaced by the editor with more specific directions. Scenes do not indicate a break of action but a change in characters. Both Jonsonian practices follow classical precedents.) **3** Here's] F Her's **44** among] F amongst **45** against] F again **46** than] F then **I.ii.4** Dost] F Does't **50** good do] F do good **64** impostors!] F impostors? **88** has] F ha's **I.iii.5** hours!] F hours? **14** lime] F lyam **50** friend] F friends **100** had] F hadst **170** broked] F broke **I.iv.52** t'other] F to'ther **105** years] F year **I.v.25** **30** Bedlam] F Bet'lem **110** your] F you **126** lose] F loose **128** than] F then **I.vi.66** than] F then **II.ii.22** cattle] F cattel **48** *Who'd*] F Who'ld **II.iii.24** wilt] F will't **II.iv.2** Knockem] F Knockhum **26** What's] F what **II.v.156** Dost] F Does't **II.vi.33** alligator] F alligarta **96** pounds] F pound **III.i.81** o'clock] F a clocke **III.ii.101** wife's] F wives **133** among] F amongst **III.iv.81** burden] F burthen **III.v.14** of] F on **35** than] F then **83** *than*] F then **150** *a far better*] F a better **192** *Than*] F Then **198** than] F then **211** marvel] F mar'le **243** than] F then **259 s.d.**] F has s.d. at line 251 **271** than] then **III.vi.44** and the] F and and the **73** o'] F a **102** be called] F be a called **IV.i.68** of] F on **98** 'has] F his **105** than] F then **IV.ii.45 s.d.** *while*] F whilst **65** than] F then **IV.iii.11** than] F then **13** than] F then **92** is, is taken] F is taken **102** Justice] F Judice **116** aye] F I **IV.iv.276** take] F talk **IV.vi.1** does] F do's **79** o'clock] F a clocke **V.ii.48** than] F then **49** than] F then **59** pounds] F pound **77** into] F in to **77** than] F then **92 s.d.** *considers*] F consider **93** pounds] F pound **149** pounds] F pound **V.iii.66** glad to] F glad **V.iv.159** *at*] F a **163** *that he*] F thhe **164** *is lovely Hero*] F *is Hero* **233** wore] F were **285** *Hold*] F Hld **294** *me my*] F *mmy* *'hone*] F *ohone* **301** *does*] F *do's* **322** they'll] F the'll **V.v.58** than] F then **109** *You'd*] F you'ld **123** among] F amongst **V.vi.100** in pardoning him] F in him **115** Look] F Loke

Playsource

Bartholomew Fair relies largely on Jonson's own observations of the variety and eccentricity of human nature and (as parody) on such dramatic conventions as the disguised judge or ruler, the cuckold, and the zealous Puritan.

Title-page

Bartholmew Fair common form of spelling for Bartholomew (pronounced Bartlemy) for an annual fair in Smithfield, an open area of five or six acres W of London and N of Moorfields, from 1120 to 1855 beginning on St. Bartholomew's Day (August 24)

Lady Elizabeth's Servants company of players named for the Princess and founded by a patent on April 27, 1611; in the autumn of 1614 they moved into the newly built Hope Theater on Bankside in Southwark

Si foret . . . surdo "If Democritus were still in the land of the living, he would laugh himself silly, for he would pay far more attention to the audience than to the play, since the audience offers the more interesting spectacle. But as for the author of the plays – he would conclude they were telling their tales to a deaf donkey" (Horace, *Epistles* II.1.194–200, omitting lines 195–6; *nam* [rather] appears incorrectly for *seu* [for] and *asello* for *assello*)

I.B. John Bale the printer

Paul's Churchyard center of London book trade and an outdoor pulpit where Puritans condemned plays

Prologue

(substituted for the Induction at a court performance for King James on November 1, 1614)

4 **Faction** (Puritans were increasingly active after the Hampton Court conference of 1604); **toys** trifles
5 **babies** dolls
6 **rage** frenzy; folly
8 **particular wrong** individual reference
10 **or . . . or** either . . . or
11 **Maker** author
12 **fairing** present bought or given at a fair

Persons of the Play

(cast of 36 [requiring 26 actors] is the largest in the Jonsonian canon)

1 **Proctor** legal agent; attorney
4 **Purecraft** unmitigated cunning
5 **Busy** (1) industrious; (2) diligent; (3) officiously meddling; **Banbury man** (Banbury, Oxfordshire, was famous for cakes, ale, and cheese as well as a center of Puritanism; the gluttonous Busy was originally a baker)

Quarlous. *His companion, a gamester.*
Bartholomew Cokes. *An Esquire of Harrow.*
Humphrey Wasp. *His man.*
Adam Overdo. *A Justice of Peace.*
Dame Overdo. *His wife.*
Grace Wellborn. *His ward.*
Lantern Leatherhead. *A Hobby-horse-seller.*
Joan Trash. *A Ginger-bread-woman.*
Ezekiel Edgworth. *A Cutpurse.*
Nightingale. *A Ballad singer.*
Ursula. *A Pig woman.*
Mooncalf. *Her Tapster.*
Jordan Knockem. *A Horse-courser, and Ranger of Turnbull.*
Val. Cutting. *A Roarer.*
Captain Whit. *A Bawd.*
Punk Alice. *Mistress of the game.*
Trouble-All. *A madman.*
Watchmen, three. Haggis, Bristle, *and* Pocher, *a beadle*].
Costermonger.
Mousetrap Man. *Also called a* Tinder-box-man].
Clothier. [Northern].
Wrestler. [Puppy].
Porters.
Doorkeepers. [Filcher, Sharkwell].
Corn-cutter.
Passengers.
Puppets.

The Induction on the Stage

[*Enter*] Stage-Keeper.

[*Stage-Keeper.*] Gentlemen, have a little patience, they are e'en upon coming, instantly. He that should begin the play, Master Littlewit, the Proctor, has a stitch new fallen in his black silk stocking; 'twill be drawn up ere you can tell twenty. He plays one o' the Arches, that dwells about the Hospital, and he has a very pretty part. But for the whole play, will you ha' the truth on't? (I am looking, lest the poet hear me, or his man, Master Brome, behind the arras) it is like to be a very conceited scurvy one, in plain English. When 't comes to the Fair once, you were e'en as good go to Virginia for anything there is of Smithfield. He has not hit the humors, he does not know 'em; he has not conversed with the Bartholomew-birds, as they say; he has ne'er a sword-and-buckler man in his Fair, nor a little Davy, to take toll o' the bawds there, as in my time, nor a Kind-heart, if anybody's teeth should chance to ache in his play. Nor a juggler with a well-educated ape to come over the chain, for the King of England, and back again for the Prince, and sit still on his arse for the Pope, and the King of Spain! None o' these fine sights! Nor has he the canvas-cut i' the night, for a hobby-horse-man to creep in to his she-neighbor, and take his leap there! Nothing! No, an' some writer

---

7 **Quarlous** (play on quarrellous [argumentative] and parlous [dangerously clever]); ***gamester*** (1) gambler; (2) playboy

8 **Cokes** fool; one easily duped; ***Harrow*** a village in Middlesex 12 miles NW of London

13 **Lantern** (1) lanterns were used to light puppet plays; (2) lantern men were those who emptied privies during the night

17 **Ursula** "she-bear" (Latin); pronounced Urs'la

18 **Mooncalf** (1) deformed person; (2) imbecile

19 **Jordan** chamberpot; figuratively, a fool; ***Horse-courser*** a shrewd dealer in horses; ***Ranger of Turnbull*** gamekeeper of Turnbull (Turnmill) Street, Clerkenwell, called "the most disreputable street in London"

20 **Cutting** name for a cutthroat; ***Roarer*** bully

21 **Whit** "little something" (euphuism for genitals); ***Bawd*** pimp

22 ***Mistress . . . game*** madam of the prostitutes

24 **Pocher** poacher, one who intrudes on the business of another; ***beadle*** parish constable; messenger or executor of mandates in a law court

25 **Costermonger** one who sells apples and pears

27 **Clothier** producer or tradesman of woollen cloth, historically the central commodity at the Fair

30 **Filcher** thief; **Sharkwell** shark; swindler

Induction

1 s.d. **Stage-Keeper** one who sets and sweeps the stage; stage manager

2 **e'en upon** almost

6 **tell** count; **Arches** (Court of Arches where Littlewit practices; it was the court of appeal from the diocesan courts held in Bow Church, London)

7 **Hospital** (1) St. Bartholomew's Hospital, Smithfield, which served the poor; (2) Christ's Hospital, a school for foundlings closer to Bow Church

8 **pretty** attractive; significant

10 **Master Brome** Richard Brome, playwright, then an apprentice to Jonson

11 ***arras*** tapestry hanging; one may have hung at the rear of the stage; **conceited** fanciful; ingenious; **scurvy**worthless; contemptible

15 **hit** met; **humors** idiosyncrasies

16 **Bartholomew-birds** rogue inhabitants

17–18 **sword- . . . man** swashbuckler; bully; a ruffian expert at swordplay

18 **little Davy** (a notorious bully; Stow says he falsely accused his master of treason, then killed him in a duel)

19 **bawds** whores

19–20 **Kindheart** (name of an itinerant tooth-drawer)

21–2 **juggler . . . ape** (the ape performed routines according to persons named by the juggler)

26 **canvas-cut** (1) illicit entrance; (2) term for pudenda

26–7 **hobby-horse-man** (1) purveyor of hobby-horses; (2) frequenter of hobby-horses (i.e., prostitutes)

28 **leap** copulation (technically of a stallion and a mare; brothels were known as leaping-houses); **some writer** (unidentified)

(that I know) had had but the penning o' this matter, he would ha' made you such a jig-a-jog i' the booths, you should ha' thought an earthquake had been i' the Fair! But these master-poets, they will ha' their own absurd courses; they will be informed of nothing! He has, sir-reverence, kicked me three or four times about the Tiring-house, I thank him, for but offering to put in, with my experience. I'll be judged by you, gentlemen, now, but for one conceit of mine! Would not a fine pump upon the stage ha' done well, for a property now? And a punk set under upon her head, with her stern upward, and ha' been soused by my witty young masters o' the Inns o' Court? What think you o' this for a show, now? He will not hear o' this! I am an ass! I! And yet I kept the stage in Master Tarlton's time, I thank my stars. Ho! an' that man had lived to have played in *Bartholomew Fair*, you should ha' seen him ha' come in, and ha' been cozened i' the cloth-quarter, so finely! And Adams, the rogue, ha' leaped and capered upon him, and ha' dealt his vermin about, as though they had cost him nothing. And then a substantial watch to ha' stolen in upon 'em, and taken 'em away, with mistaking words, as the fashion is, in the stage practice.

[*Enter*] Book-Holder, Scrivener, *to him.*

Book-Holder. How now? what rare discourse are you fallen upon? ha! Ha' you found any familiars here that you are so free? What's the business?

Stage-Keeper. Nothing, but the understanding gentlemen o' the ground here asked my judgment.

Book-Holder. Your judgment, rascal? For what? Sweeping the stage? Or gathering up the broken apples for the bears within? Away rogue, it's come to a fine degree in these spectacles when such a youth as you pretend to a judgment. [*Exit* Stage-Keeper.] And yet he may, i' the most o' this matter i' faith; for the author hath writ it just to his meridian, and the scale of the grounded judgments here, his play-fellows in wit. Gentlemen, not for want of a prologue, but by way of a new one, I am sent out to you here, with a scrivener, and certain articles drawn out in haste between our author and you; which if you please to hear, and as they appear reasonable, to approve of, the play will follow presently. Read, scribe, gi' me the counterpane.

Scrivener. Articles of Agreement, indented, between the spectators or hearers at the Hope on the Bankside, in the County of Surrey, on the one party, and the author of *Bartholomew Fair*, in the said place and county, on the other party, the one and thirtieth day of October, 1614, and in the twelfth year of the reign of our Sovereign Lord, James, by the grace of God King of England, France, and Ireland, Defender of the Faith; and of Scotland the seven and fortieth.

INPRIMIS, It is covenanted and agreed, by and between the parties above-said, and the said spectators, and hearers, as well the curious and envious as the favoring and judicious, as also the grounded judgments and understand-

30 **jig-a-jog** jogging (with obscene pun)

34–5 **sir-reverence** with all respect ("save your reverence")

36 **Tiring-house** backstage dressing area (attiring house)

37 **put in** intervene, support

38 **conceit** creation

40 **punk** whore

42 **soused** drenched (with water)

43 **masters** students, known for pranks and jests; **Inns o' Court** (Lincoln's Inn, Inner Temple, Middle Temple, and Gray's Inn, in the aggregate London's law schools populated by gallants and aristocrats and known for performing revels and satires)

46 **Master Tarlton** Richard Tarlton, d. 1588, a legendary clown who acted with the Queen's Men

49 **cozened** cheated

50 **cloth-quarter** (along the N wall of St. Bartholomew's Church and originally the most important part of the Fair; *Tarlton's Jests* [1611] tells how the actor was cheated of his clothes there, perhaps a source for a similar scene here with Cokes); **finely** cleverly; **Adams** John Adams, also an actor with the Queen's Men

51 **capered** danced

52 **dealt** scattered; **vermin** fleas (often in a man's padded hose)

53 **substantial** burly, strong

54 **watch** constables; guardians of the law

55 **mistaking words** malapropisms

57 **s.d. Book-Holder** prompter; **Scrivener** professional writer or copier of documents

58–9 **familiars** acquaintances

59 **free** uncensored in speech

61–2 **understanding . . . ground** (audience members who, paying least, stood on the ground under [below] the stage throughout the performance)

65 **bears** (the Hope Theater was also used for bearbaiting; it was built on the site of the famous Bear Garden)

66 **degree** (with reference to social station)

67 **youth as you** (perhaps a reference to foolish old age, or second childhood, since the Stage-Manager knew Tarlton); **pretend** lay claim

70 **just . . . meridian** exactly to the extent of his comprehension

71 **grounded** (1) well-grounded; (2) judgments of audience standing on the ground

79 **counterpane** duplicate half of the indenture

91 **INPRIMIS** "In the first place" (Latin)

92 **above-said** (formulary should be followed by ***that . . .***; since it is not, the agreement is meant as a parody of the form as well as a satire of the audience)

93 **curious** overly critical

94 **envious** hostile

ings, do for themselves severally covenant and agree to remain in the places their money or friends have put them in, with patience, for the space of two hours and a half and somewhat more. In which time the author promiseth to present them, by us, with a new sufficient play called *Bartholomew Fair*, merry, and as full of noise as sport, made to delight all and to offend none, provided they have either the wit or the honesty to think well of themselves.

It is further agreed that every person here have his or their free-will of censure to like or dislike at their own charge, the author having now departed with his right. It shall be lawful for any man to judge his six pennyworth, his twelve pennyworth, so to his eighteen pence, two shillings, half a crown, to the value of his place provided always his place get not above his wit. And if he pay for half a dozen, he may censure for all them too, so that he will undertake that they shall be silent. He shall put in for censures here as they do for lots at the lottery; marry, if he drop but sixpence at the door, and will censure a crown's worth, it is thought there is no conscience, or justice in that.

It is also agreed that every man here exercise his own judgment, and not censure by contagion, or upon trust, from another's voice or face that sits by him, be he never so first in the Commission of Wit. As also that he be fixed and settled in his censure, that what he approves or not approves today, he will do the same tomorrow, and if tomorrow, the next day, and so the next week, if need be; and not to be brought about by any that sits on the bench with him, though they indict and arraign plays daily. He that will swear *Jeronimo* or *Andronicus* are the best plays yet, shall pass unexcepted at here as a man whose judgment shows it is constant, and hath stood still these five and twenty or thirty years. Though it be an ignorance, it is a virtuous and staid ignorance; and next to truth, a confirmed error does well. Such a one the author knows where to find him.

It is further covenanted, concluded and agreed, that how great soever the expectation be, no person here is to expect more than he knows, or better ware than a Fair will afford; neither to look back to the sword-and-buckler-age of Smithfield, but content himself with the present. Instead of a little Davy to take toll o' the bawds, the author doth promise a strutting Horse-courser, with a leer drunkard, two or three to attend him, in as good equipage as you would wish. And then for Kindheart, the tooth-drawer, a fine oily pig woman with her tapster to bid you welcome, and a consort of roarers for music. A wise Justice of Peace *meditant* instead of a juggler with an ape. A civil cutpurse *searchant*. A sweet singer of new ballads *allurant*; and as fresh an Hypocrite as ever was broached *rampant*. If there be never a servant-monster i' the Fair, who can help it? he says; nor a nest of antics? He is loathe to make Nature afraid in his plays, like those that beget Tales, Tempests, and such like drolleries, to mix his head with other men's heels; let the

---

97–8 **places . . . in** (refers to seating according to the cost of admission)
101 **sufficient** adequate
105 **think . . . themselves** i.e., do not see themselves as objects of the play's satire
107 **censure** criticism; judgment
108 **charge** (1) expectations; (2) cost, expense
109–10 **departed . . . right** surrendered his authority (having sold the play to the company)
110–12 **six . . . crown** (these prices are inflationary and perhaps denote [1] a continuing parody; [2] special prices reflecting a new play written for a new house on the first night; a half crown was worth two shillings sixpence)
115 **so** provided
117 **lottery** (King James patronized a lottery in 1612 to raise money for the colonization of Virginia)
118 **marry** simply
122–3 **contagion** influence
125 **Commission . . . Wit** (an imagined body of critics empowered to pass judgment on plays)
130 **brought about** converted
131 **bench** (1) bench of ruling magistrates; (2) stage seating for the fashionable gallant or distinguished members of the audience)
132–3 ***Jeronimo* or *Andronicus*** (Kyd's *The Spanish Tragedy* and Shakespeare's *Titus Andronicus* [ca. 1590], notably revenge plays; by 1614 both were considerably outdated and Kyd's play revised)
134 **unexcepted at** unobjected to (legal term for those jurors admitted to serve despite possible prejudices)
145–6 **the . . . Smithfield** (reference to West Smithfield, popularly known as Ruffians' Hall and used for duels and quarrels until ca. 1578)
149 **leer** sly
150 **equipage** (1) retinue; (2) dress
155–7 ***meditant . . . searchant . . . allurant*** (Jonson's terms parodying heraldic terminology such as *rampant* [standing] and *couchant* [lying])
156 **cutpurse** (a petty thief; he stole purses of money by cutting the strap or string that held the purse to the belt)
159 **servant-monster** (clear reference to Caliban in Shakespeare's *The Tempest* [1611])
160 **nest of antics** group of clowns
162 **Tales, Tempests** (references to Shakespeare's late romances, *The Winter's Tale* [ca. 1610] and *The Tempest*); **drolleries** fantastic entertaimments (Jonson is insisting on the realism or perhaps authenticity of his own play)
163 **mix . . . heels** mix intellectual matter with frivolous dancing

concupiscence of jigs and dances reign as strong as it will among you. Yet if the puppets will please anybody, they shall be entreated to come in.

In consideration of which, it is finally agreed by the foresaid hearers and spectators that they neither in themselves conceal, nor suffer by them to be concealed, any state-decipherer or politic picklock of the scene, so solemnly ridiculous as to search out who was meant by the ginger-bread-woman, who by the hobby-horseman, who by the costermonger, nay, who by their wares; or that will pretend to affirm, on his own inspired ignorance, what Mirror of Magistrates is meant by the Justice, what great lady by the pig woman, what concealed statesman by the seller of mousetraps, and so of the rest. But that such person or persons so found be left discovered to the mercy of the author, as a forfeiture to the stage and your laughter aforesaid; as also, such as shall so desperately or ambitiously play the fool by his place aforesaid, to challenge the author of scurrility because the language somewhere savors of Smithfield, the booth, and the pig-broth; or of profaneness because a madman cries, "God quit you," or "bless you." In witness whereof, as you have preposterously put to your seals already (which is your money), you will now add the other part of suffrage, your hands. The play shall presently begin. And though the Fair be not kept in the same region that some here, perhaps, would have it, yet think that therein the author hath observed a special decorum, the place being as dirty as Smithfield and as stinking every whit.

Howsoever, he prays you to believe his ware is still the same, else you will make him justly suspect that he that is so loathe to look on a baby or a hobby-horse here, would be glad to take up a commodity of them at any laughter or loss in another place.

[*Exeunt.*]

Act I

Scene i.

[*Enter* Littlewit.]

[*Littlewit*]. A pretty conceit, and worth the finding! I ha' such luck to spin out these fine things still and, like a silkworm, out of myself. Here's Master Bartholomew Cokes, of Harrow o' th' Hill, i' th' county of Middlesex, esquire, takes forth his license to marry Mistress Grace Wellborn of the said place and county; and when does he take it forth? Today! The four and twentieth of August! Bartholomew day! Bartholomew upon Bartholomew! There's the device! Who would have marked such a leap-frog chance now? A very less than ames-ace on two dice! Well, go thy ways, John Littlewit, Proctor John Littlewit, one o' the pretty

---

164 **concupiscence of** eager desire for

171 **state-decipherer** professional state informer

172 **politic . . . scene** informers on lewd, seditious, or slanderous matters in plays (for which Jonson had been arrested in 1597 and 1605)

177–8 **Mirror of Magistrates** (1) paragon of magistrates; (2) reference to George Whetstone's *Mirour for Magestrates of Cyties* (1584), which proposes that good magistrates witness plays in disguise before accepting charges against them (as Justice Overdo will do in Act V); (3) a warning not to confuse Justice Overdo with Thomas Hayes, then Lord Mayor of London who also undertook this practice

182 **discovered** revealed

186 **challenge** accuse

189–90 **"God . . . you"** (such oaths using God's name were not permitted on stage by the Act of Abuses [1616]; cf. Trouble-All's oaths in the play)

191 **preposterously** in reversed order, back to front; **put to** affixed

193 **suffrage** approvals; **hands** (1) signature (to this agreement); (2) applause (for the play)

197 **decorum** propriety

198 **dirty** (Smithfield was then a field of dirt; it was finally drained and paved in 1615)

199 **stinking** (because of bearbaiting when the stage, built on trestles, was removed, generally every other week)

204–5 **take . . . place** (reference to a practice to get around a law limiting interest to 10 percent by supplying relatively worthless goods for part of the loan; here, those not willing to pay in laughter [money] will get inferior comedies elsewhere at their own expense [derision])

I.i (Although the large number of players and scattered incidents appear confusing, Jonson imposes a classical and logical order in presenting them. Act I builds cumulatively, by slowly introducing all those in London who will join to see the Fair in Smithfield; Act II builds cumulatively by adding those who work at the Fair and merging them with the groupings from Act I. Act III continues the merging and then begins to disintegrate original groupings to form new ones, as does Act IV, until everyone comes together in Act V. There are two exceptions: Justice Overdo is delayed until II.i and Trouble-All until IV.i, although both belong to London and Act I; this may be to emphasize their importance and to imply their relationship both at the Fair and before the play begins.)

1 **conceit** invention

2 **luck** native ability; **spin out** create

4 **Bartholomew** (the only time the full name is used, here in a legal document; elsewhere in F, *Bartolmew*)

10 **Bartholomew upon Bartholomew** (parody of Batman upon Bartholomew, a popular translation of a compendium serving as a reference work)

11 **device** clever connection

12 **chance** coincidence; **very less** truly less frequent

12–13 **ames-ace** ambs ace; i.e., double aces, or the lowest possible throw

wits o' Paul's, the Littlewit of London (so thou art called) and something beside. When a quirk or a quiblin does 'scape thee, and thou dost not watch, and apprehend it, and bring it afore the constable of conceit (there now, I speak quib too), let 'em carry thee out o' the Archdeacon's Court into his kitchen, and make a Jack of thee instead of a John. (There I am again, la!)

[*Enter* Win.]

Win, good morrow, Win. Aye, marry, Win! Now you look finely indeed, Win! This cap does convince! You'd not ha' worn it, Win, nor ha' had it velvet, but a rough country beaver with a copper-band like the coney-skin woman of Budge-row? Sweet Win, let me kiss it! And her fine high shoes, like the Spanish lady! Good Win, go a little, I would fain see thee pace, pretty Win! By this fine cap, I could never leave kissing on't.

Win. Come, indeed la, you are such a fool still!

Littlewit. No, but half a one, Win, you are the tother half. Man and wife make one fool, Win. (Good!) Is there the proctor, or doctor indeed, i' the diocese, that ever had the fortune to win him such a Win! (There I am again!) I do feel conceits coming upon me, more than I am able to turn tongue to. A pox o' these pretenders to wit, your Three Cranes, Mitre and Mermaid men! Not a corn of true salt, nor a grain of right mustard among them all. They may stand for places or so against the next witfall, and pay twopence in a quart more for their canary than other men. But gi' me the man can start up a justice of wit out of six-shillings beer, and give the law to all the poets and poet-suckers i' town, because they are the players' gossips! 'Slid, other men have wives as fine as the players, and as well dressed. Come hither, Win.

[*Kisses her.*]

Act I. Scene ii.

[*Enter to them* Winwife.]

[*Winwife.*] Why, how now, Master Littlewit! Measuring of lips or molding of kisses? Which is it?

Littlewit. Troth, I am a little taken with my Win's dressing here! Dost not fine, Master Winwife? How do you apprehend, sir? She would not ha' worn this habit. I challenge all Cheapside to show such another – Moorfields, Pimlico path, or the Exchange, in a summer evening – with a lace to boot, as this has. Dear Win, let Master Winwife kiss you. He comes a-wooing to our mother, Win, and may be our father perhaps, Win. There's no harm in him, Win.

Winwife. None i' the earth, Master Littlewit.

Littlewit. I envy no man my delicates, sir.

Winwife. Alas, you ha' the garden where they grow still! A wife here with a strawberry-breath, cherry-lips, apricot-cheeks, and a soft velvet head like a melicotton.

---

15 Paul's the middle aisle of St. Paul's Cathedral, London, a gathering place for gallants and wits as well as a weekday market and exchange for news and gossip

16 quirk quip

17 quiblin quibble; pun

19 conceit wit

20 quib affectedly

20–1 Archdeacon's Court (Court of Arches for cases referred from the diocese)

22 Jack (1) a knave; (2) mechanical device to turn a spit for roasting meat

24 marry truly

26 does convince overcome; overwhelm

28 beaver made of beaver's fur; **copper-band** (metal hatbands were common; copper was less elegant than gold or silver)

28–9 coney-skin woman purveyor of rabbit-skins

29 Budge-row (a street of shops seiling budge [lambskin with the wool turned outwards])

30 it you

30–1 the Spanish lady an unnamed contemporary woman known for her high fashion

31 go walk

34 fool (a playful reference following his childish talk)

41 pox postules (a common expression of impatience)

42–3 Three . . . Mermaid (London taverns especially frequented by playwrights; one author of the time notes Jonson's favorite was the Mermaid where he verbally sparred with Shakespeare; the Three Cranes in New Thames Street was named for cranes lifting wine on nearby Vintry Wharf; the Mitre was then in Fleet Street; the Mermaid was located between Bread Street and Fleet Street in Cheapside)

43 corn grain

43–4 salt . . . mustard i.e., pungency of wit

45 stand strive; **against** anticipating

46 *witfall* harvest of wit

47 canary a common sweet wine imported from the Canary Islands

48–9 six-shillings beer small beer sold at six shillings a barrel

50 poet-suckers beginning poets; fledglings

51 gossips acquaintances; companions; **'Slid** "by God's eyelid" (a common oath)

I.ii.3 Troth truth

4 Dost looks it

6 habit dress; **Cheapside** (street where mercers and haberdashers had shops)

7–8 Moorfields . . . Exchange (places of resort for the fashionable; [1] Moorfield walks NE of London's city walls had been laid out in 1606; [2] Pimlico in the nearby village of Hoxton near the sites of the old Theatre, Curtain, and Fortune playhouses, was known for cakes and ale; [3] the New Exchange in the Strand [1608–9], succeeding Gresham's celebrated in *Shoemakers' Holiday*, had milliners' and seamstresses' shops)

9 to boot in addition

14 delicates delights

18 melicotton peach grafted to a quince

Littlewit. Good i' faith! Now dullness upon me, that I had not that before him, that I should not light on't as well as he! Velvet head!

Winwife. But my taste, Master Littlewit, tends to fruit of a later kind – the sober matron, your wife's mother.

Littlewit. Aye! We know you are a suitor, sir. Win and I both wish you well. By this license here, would you had her, that your two names were as fast in it, as here are a couple. Win would fain have a fine young father i' law with a feather, that her mother might hood it, and chain it, with Mistress Overdo. But you do not take the right course, Master Winwife.

Winwife. No? Master Littlewit, why?

Littlewit. You are not mad enough.

Winwife. How? Is madness a right course?

Littlewit. I say nothing, but I wink upon Win. You have a friend, one Master Quarlous, comes here sometimes?

Winwife. Why? he makes no love to her, does he?

Littlewit. Not a tokenworth that ever I saw, I assure you, but –

Winwife. What?

Littlewit. He is the more madcap o' the two. You do not apprehend me.

Winwife. You have a hot coal i' your mouth now you cannot hold.

Littlewit. Let me out with it, dear Win.

Win. I'll tell him myself.

Littlewit. Do, and take all the thanks, and much good do thy pretty heart, Win.

Win. Sir, my mother has had her nativity-water cast lately by the cunning men in Cow Lane, and they ha' told her her fortune, and do insure her she shall never have happy hour, unless she marry within this sen'night, and when it is it must be a madman, they say.

Littlewit. Aye, but it must be a gentleman madman.

Win. Yes, so the tother man of Moorfields says.

Winwife. But does she believe 'em?

Littlewit. Yes, and has been at Bedlam twice since, every day, to inquire if any gentleman be there, or to come there, mad!

Winwife. Why, this is a confederacy, a mere piece of practice upon her, by these impostors!

Littlewit. I tell her so; or else say I that they mean some young madcap-gentleman (for the devil can equivocate as well as a shopkeeper), and therefore would I advise you to be a little madder than Master Quarlous, hereafter.

Winwife. Where is she? Stirring yet?

Littlewit. Stirring! Yes, and studying an old elder, come from Banbury, a suitor that puts in here at meal-tide, to praise the painful brethren or pray that the sweet singers may be restored; says a grace as long as his breath lasts him! Sometime the spirit is so strong with him it gets quite out of him, and then my mother, or Win, are fain to fetch it again with malmsey, or *aqua cœlestis.*

Win. Yes indeed, we have such a tedious life with him for his diet. And his clothes too; he breaks his buttons, and cracks seams at every saying he sobs out.

Littlewit. He cannot abide my vocation, he says.

Win. No, he told my mother a proctor was a claw of the Beast, and that she had little less than committed abomination in marrying me so as she has done.

Littlewit. Every line, he says, that a proctor writes, when it comes to be read in the Bishop's Court, is a long black hair, kembed out of the tail of Antichrist.

Winwife. When came this proselyte?

Littlewit. Some three days since.

Act I. Scene iii.

[*Enter to them* Quarlous.]

[*Quarlous.*] Oh, sir, ha' you ta'en soil here? It's well a man may reach you after three hours

30 **feather** a sign of high social standing
30–1 **hood . . . chain** (referring to her ostentatious pride in her husband's badges of office)
40 **tokenworth** the least possible amount (from tokens given by tradesmen to remedy the shortage of small change)
51–2 **nativity-water cast** (Win confuses casting a horoscope with casting [inspecting] urine for diagnosing disease)
52 **cunning men** fortune tellers; **Cow Lane** (running from Holborn to Snow Hill; presently King Street)
54 **insure** assure
55 **sen'night** seven nights; a week
60 **Bedlam** (the hospital of St. Mary of Bethlehem in Bishopsgate; an asylum for lunatics publicly open to visitors who found it amusing to watch the inmates)
63 **confederacy** conspiracy; **mere** entire
64 **practice** trickery; deceit
73 **meal-tide** mealtime (Busy is a glutton, but Littlewit also plays on the Puritan habit of substituting *tide* meaning *time* for *mass*, considered papist, as in *Christmas*); **painful** diligent; **brethren** (Puritan word for fellow believers)
74 **sweet . . . restored** (referring to Puritan preachers deprived of their livings for refusing to conform to the 1604 Constitution of the Church of England)
78 **fetch it** i.e., revive him; **malmsey** a strong sweet wine
79 ***aqua cœlestis*** "wine of heaven," a kind of brandy distilled from wine
80 **tedious** annoying
86 **Beast** (a reference to the Apocalypse or Revelation of St. John 13; Puritans identified the Beast with the Antichrist or the Pope in Rome)
91 **kembed** combed
I.iii.l **ta'en soil** taken refuge

running yet! What an unmerciful companion art thou, to quit thy lodging at such ungentlemanly hours! None but a scattered covey of fiddlers or one of these rag-rakers in dunghills, or some marrow-bone man at most, would have been up when thou wert gone abroad, by all description. I pray thee what ailest thou, thou canst not sleep? Hast thou thorns i' thy eyelids, or thistles i' thy bed?

Winwife. I cannot tell. It seems you had neither i' your feet, that took this pain to find me.

Quarlous. No, an' I had, all the lime-hounds o' the city should have drawn after you by the scent rather, Master John Littlewit! God save you, sir! 'Twas a hot night with some of us, last night, John. Shall we pluck a hair o' the same wolf today, Proctor John?

Littlewit. Do you remember, Master Quarlous, what we discoursed on last night?

Quarlous. Not I, John. Nothing that I either discourse or do at those times, I forfeit all to forgetfulness.

Littlewit. No? not concerning Win? Look you: there she is, and dressed as I told you she should be. Hark you, sir, had you forgot?

Quarlous. By this head, I'll beware how I keep you company, John, when I am drunk, and you have this dangerous memory! That's certain.

Winwife. Why, sir?

Quarlous. Why? We were all a little stained last night, sprinkled with a cup or two, and I agreed with Proctor John here to come and do somewhat with Win (I know not what 'twas) today; and he puts me in mind on't, now. He says he was coming to fetch me. Before truth, if you have that fearful quality, John, to remember when you are sober, John, what you promise drunk, John, I shall take heed of you, John. For this once, I am content to wink at you. Where's your wife? Come hither, Win.

He kisseth her.

Win. Why, John! Do you see this, John? Look you! Help me, John.

Littlewit. O Win, fie, what do you mean, Win? Be womanly, Win; make an outcry to your mother, Win? Master Quarlous is an honest gentleman and our worshipful good friend, Win; and he is Master Winwife's friend, too. And Master Winwife comes a suitor to your mother, Win, as I told you before, Win, and may perhaps be our father, Win. They'll do you no harm, Win, they are both our worshipful good friends. Master Quarlous! You must know Master Quarlous, Win; you must not quarrel with Master Quarlous, Win.

Quarlous. No, we'll kiss again and fall in.

Littlewit. Yes, do, good Win.

Win. I' faith you are a fool, John.

Littlewit. A fool-John she calls me. Do you mark that, gentlemen? Pretty littlewit of velvet! A fool-John!

Quarlous. She may call you an apple-John, if you use this.

Winwife. Pray thee forbear, for my respect somewhat.

Quarlous. Hoy-day! How respective you are become o' the sudden! I fear this family will turn you reformed, too. Pray you come about again. Because she is in possibility to be your daughter-in-law, and may ask you blessing hereafter, when she courts it to Tottenham to eat cream. Well, I will forbear, sir; but, i' faith, would thou wouldst leave thy exercise of widow-hunting once, this drawing after an old reverend smock by the splay-foot! There cannot be an ancient tripe or trillibub i' the town but thou art straight nosing it; and 'tis a fine occupation thou'lt confine thyself to when thou hast got one – scrubbing a piece of buff, as if thou hadst the perpetuity of Pannier-alley to stink in, or perhaps, worse, currying a carcass that thou hast bound thyself to alive. I'll be sworn, some of them that thou art

---

6 **rag-rakers** scavengers collecting rags for resale
7 **marrow-bone man** scavenger collecting old bones
14 **lime-hounds** lyam-hounds; bloodhounds held on a leash (lyam)
15 **drawn after** tracked
17 **hot** hectic
18–19 **pluck . . . wolf** repeat the activity to cure the consequences (cf. "Hair of the dog that bit you"; proverbial)
32 **stained** drunk
42 **wink at you** overlook matters
58 **fall in** (1) agree; (2) be reconciled; (3) copulate
63 **fool-John** (applying *fool* as a term of endearment)
64 **apple-John** (1) an apple thought best when two years old and shriveled; (2) a cant term for impotence; (3) possibly a pun on "apple-squire," a pimp
65 **use this** behave in this way
68 **respective** concerned with good manners
70 **reformed** i.e., Puritan
73–4 **courts . . . cream** (Tottenham Court, an old manor house in Tottenham Court Road, was noted for cream, cakes, and ale)
75 **exercise** (1) practice; (2) occupation
76 **once** entirely; once and for all
77 **smock** (derogatory term for loose woman); **splay-foot** foot that turns outward
78 **tripe or trillibub** entrails
82 **buff** bare skin (literally, ox-hide leather); **perpetuity** perpetual tenure
82–3 **Pannier-alley** (a passage opening out of Paternoster Row in Newgate Street known for the sale of skins and tripe)
83–4 **currying** (1) rubbing down, as of a horse; (2) flattering

or hast been a suitor to are so old as no chaste or married pleasure can ever become 'em. The honest instrument of procreation has, forty years since, left to belong to 'em. Thou must visit 'em as thou wouldst do a tomb, with a torch, or three handfuls of link flaming hot, and so thou mayst hap to make 'em feel thee, and after, come to inherit according to thy inches. A sweet course for a man to waste the brand of life for, to be still raking himself a fortune in an old woman's embers; we shall ha' thee, after thou hast been but a month married to one of 'em, look like the quartan ague and the black jaundice met in a face, and walk as if thou had borrowed legs of a spinner, and voice of a cricket. I would endure to hear fifteen sermons a week 'fore her, and such coarse and loud ones as some of 'em must be; I would e'en desire of Fate I might dwell in a drum and take in my sustenance with an old broken tobacco-pipe and a straw. Dost thou ever think to bring thine ears or stomach to the patience of a dry grace as long as thy tablecloth, and droned out by thy son here, that might be thy father, till all the meat o' thy board has forgot it was that day i' the kitchen? Or to brook the noise made, in a question of predestination, by the good laborers and painful eaters assembled together, put to 'em by the matron, your spouse, who moderates with a cup of wine, ever and anon, and a sentence out of Knox between? Or the perpetual spitting, before and after a sober-drawn exhortation of six hours, whose better part was the hum-ha-hum? Or to hear prayers groaned out, over thy iron-chests, as if they were charms to break 'em? And all this for the hope of two apostle-spoons to suffer! And a cup to eat a caudle in! For that will be thy legacy. She'll ha' conveyed her state, safe enough from thee, an' she be a right widow.

Winwife. Alas, I am quite off that scent now.

Quarlous. How so?

Winwife. Put off by a brother of Banbury, one that, they say, is come here and governs all already.

Quarlous. What do you call him? I knew divers of those Banburians when I was in Oxford.

Winwife. Master Littlewit can tell us.

Littlewit. Sir! Good Win, go in, and if Master Bartholomew Cokes his man come for the license (the little old fellow), let him speak with me. What say you, gentlemen?

[*Exit* Win.]

Winwife. What call you the reverend elder you told me of? Your Banbury man.

Littlewit. Rabbi Busy, sir. He is more than an elder, he is a prophet, sir.

Quarlous. Oh, I know him! A baker, is he not?

Littlewit. He was a baker, sir, but he does dream now, and see visions; he has given over his trade.

Quarlous. I remember that, too. Out of a scruple he took that (in spiced conscience) those cakes he made were served to bridales, maypoles, morrises, and such profane feasts and meetings; his Christian name is Zeal-of-the-land.

Littlewit. Yes, sir, Zeal-of-the-land Busy.

Winwife. How, what a name's there!

Littlewit. Oh, they have all such names, sir. He was witness for Win here (they will not be called godfathers), and named her Win-the-fight; you thought her name had been Winifred, did you not?

---

89 **left to belong** ceased to be of interest
91 **link** pitch used for torches
94 **inches** size or length (of penis)
95 **brand** fire; vital spirits; **raking** (obscene term for sexual penetration)
98–9 **quartan ague** (fever in which the paroxysm occurs every fourth day)
99 **jaundice** (illness caused by obstruction of the bile and called by the color [black, yellow] of the skin that results)
100 **spinner** spider
108 **patience** endurance; suffering; **dry** (1) boring; (2) long (hence thirst-inducing)
113 **predestination** (a Calvinist belief, associated with Puritans, that persons were born saved [elect] or damned [reprobate] regardless of their intentions or deeds)
115 **moderates** (1) plays hostess; (2) arbitrates
116 **sentence** (1) maxim; (2) passage
117 **Knox** (John Knox, ca. 1505–72, a Scottish reformer and Presbyterian popular with Puritans)
120 **hum-ha-hum** (a representation of the whining pitch of Puritan preaching)
121 **iron-chests** locked containers for valuables
123 **apostle-spoons** silver spoons with a figure of an apostle on the handle, a common baptismal or christening gift
124 **caudle** warm drink given invalids
125 **conveyed** (1) willed; (2) transferred; **state** estate; property
127 **scent** i.e., your meaning
129 **Put off** (1) dismissed for; (2) replaced with
148 **spiced** scrupulous; tender
149–50 **bridales . . . morrises** (cultural practices attacked by Puritans as pagan and sacrilegious); **bridales** wedding feasts; **maypoles** (poles for dancing about on May Day, usually decorated with ribbons held by the dancers); **morrises** (morris dances done to tambourines with bells attached to the dancers)
150 **profane** pagan; ***feasts*** holidays; celebrations
151 **Christian** first (not a family name)

Winwife. I did indeed.

Littlewit. He would ha' thought himself a stark reprobate if it had.

Quarlous. Aye, for there was a blue-starch-woman o' the name at the same time. A notable hypocritical vermin it is; I know him. One that stands upon his face, more than his faith, at all times; ever in seditious motion, and reproving for vain-glory; of a most lunatic conscience, and spleen, and affects the violence of singularity in all he does. (He has undone a grocer here in Newgate-market that broked with him, trusted him with currants, as arrant a zeal as he, that's by the way). By his profession, he will ever be i' the state of innocence, though, and childhood; derides all antiquity; defies any other learning than inspiration; and what discretion soever years should afford him, it is all prevented in his original ignorance. Ha' not to do with him for he is a fellow of a most arrogant and invincible dullness, I assure you. Who is this?

Act I. Scene iv.

[*Enter to them* Wasp, Win.]

[*Wasp.*] By your leave, gentlemen, with all my heart to you, and God you good morrow. Master Littlewit, my business is to you. Is this license ready?

Littlewit. Here, I ha' it for you in my hand, Master Humphrey.

Wasp. That's well, nay, never open, or read it to me, it's labor in vain, you know. I am no clerk; I scorn to be saved by my book. I' faith I'll hang first. Fold it up o' your word and gi' it me; what must you ha' for't?

Littlewit. We'll talk of that anon, Master Humphrey.

Wasp. Now, or not at all, good Master Proctor. I am for no anon's, I assure you.

Littlewit. Sweet Win, bid Solomon send me the little black box within, in my study.

Wasp. Aye, quickly, good mistress, I pray you. For I have both eggs o' the spit, and iron i' the fire. Say what you must have, good Master Littlewit.

[*Exit* Win.]

Littlewit. Why, you know the price, Master Numps.

Wasp. I know? I know nothing. Aye, what tell you me of knowing, now I am in haste? Sir, I do not know, and I will not know, and I scorn to know, and yet (now I think on't) I will, and do know, as well as another. You must have a mark for your thing here and eightpence for the box. I could ha' saved twopence i' that, an' I had bought it myself, but here's fourteen shillings for you. Good Lord! How long your little wife stays! Pray God, Solomon, your clerk, be not looking i' the wrong box, Master Proctor.

Littlewit. Good i' faith! No, I warrant you, Solomon is wiser than so, sir.

Wasp. Fie, fie, fie, by your leave, Master Littlewit, this is scurvy, idle, foolish and abominable. With all my heart, I do not like it.

Winwife. Do you hear? Jack Littlewit, what business does thy pretty head think this fellow may have, that he keeps such a coil with?

Quarlous. More than buying of ginger-bread i' the Cloister here, for that we allow him, or a gilt pouch i' the Fair?

Littlewit. Master Quarlous, do not mistake him. He is his master's both-hands, I assure you.

Quarlous. What? to pull on his boots a-mornings, or his stockings, does he?

Littlewit. Sir, if you have a mind to mock him, mock him softly, and look t' other way. For if he apprehend you, flout him once, he will fly at you presently. A terrible testy old fellow, and his name is Wasp too.

---

162 **blue-starch-woman** (laundress whose practice of whitening clothes with blue starch was associated by Puritans with the sin of pride)
164 **vermin** (cant pejorative term)
165 **stands . . . face** relies on his effrontery
166 **in seditious motion** causing trouble; disobedient
166–7 **reproving for** attacking
169 **undone** ruined
170 **Newgate-market** (originally a market for corn and meal, it was a place for most foodstuffs by 1614)
170 **broked** did business
171 **currants** raisins (for which Busy declined to pay)
172 **zeal** zealot; **profession** declaration of religious principle and belief
174 **childhood** i.e., natural innocent state of a child of God
177 **prevented** precluded by; forestalled

I.iv.2 **God you** "God give you" (a common greeting)
9 **saved . . . book** (i.e., reading a Latin verse [usually the beginning of Psalm 51] to insure literacy and prevent death by hanging; this "neck-verse" saved Jonson's life in 1598 when he was accused of killing the actor Gabriel Spencer in a duel)
12 **anon** in due course
19 **eggs . . . fire** (two proverbs arguing the need for haste)
23 **Numps** (diminutive of Humphrey)
29 **mark** a weight worth thirteen shillings and fourpence ($\frac{2}{3}$ of a pound sterling), with a play on *signature*
34 **box** (with obscene pun on pudendum)
43 **keeps . . . with** makes such a fuss about
45 **Cloister** (the Cloisters of Christ Church which, near Smithfield, held additional markets during the Fair)
48 **both-hands** factotum
54 **presently** at once

Quarlous. Pretty insect! Make much on him.

Wasp. A plague o' this box, and the pox too, and on him that made it, and her that went for't, and all that should ha' sought it, sent it, or brought it! Do you see, sir?

Littlewit. Nay, good Master Wasp.

Wasp. Good Master Hornet, turd i' your teeth, hold you your tongue; do not I know you? Your father was a 'pothecary, and sold glisters, more than he gave, I wusse: and turd i' your little wife's teeth too. Here she comes; 'twill make her spit, as fine as she is, for all her velvet-custard on her head, sir.

[*Reenter* Win.]

Littlewit. Oh! be civil, Master Numps.

Wasp. Why, say I have a humor not to be civil; how then?
Who shall compel me? You?

Littlewit. Here is the box, now.

Wasp. Why, a pox o' your box, once again. Let your little wife stale in it, an' she will. Sir, I would have you to understand, and these gentlemen too, if they please –

Winwife. With all our hearts. Sir.

Wasp. That I have a charge. Gentlemen.

Littlewit. They do apprehend, sir.

Wasp. Pardon me, sir, neither they nor you can apprehend me, yet. (You are an ass.) I have a young master, he is now upon his making and marring; the whole care of his welldoing is now mine. His foolish schoolmasters have done nothing but run up and down the country with him, to beg puddings and cake-bread of his tenants, and almost spoiled him. He has learned nothing but to sing catches, and repeat *Rattle bladder rattle*, and *O, Madge*. I dare not let him walk alone, for fear of learning of vile tunes, which he will sing at supper and in the sermon-times! If he meet but a carman i' the street, and I find him not talk to keep him off on him, he will whistle him, and all his tunes over, at night in his sleep! He has a head full of bees! I am fain now, for this little time I am absent, to leave him in charge with a gentlewoman; 'tis true, she is a Justice of Peace his wife, and a gentlewoman o' the hood, and his natural sister. But what may happen, under a woman's government, there's the doubt. Gentlemen, you do not know him. He is another manner of piece than you think for! But nineteen years old, and yet he is taller than either of you, by the head, God bless him.

Quarlous. Well, methinks, this is a fine fellow!

Winwife. He has made his master a finer by this description, I should think.

Quarlous. 'Faith, much about one; it's cross and pile, whether for a new farthing.

Wasp. I'll tell you, gentlemen –

Littlewit. Will't please you drink, Master Wasp?

Wasp. Why, I ha' not talked so long to be dry, sir. You see no dust or cobwebs come out o' my mouth, do you? You'd ha' me gone, would you?

Littlewit. No, but you were in haste e'en now, Master Numps.

Wasp. What an' I were? So I am still, and yet I will stay too; meddle you with your match, your Win, there, she has as little wit as her husband, it seems. I have others to talk to.

Littlewit. She's my match indeed, and as little wit as I, good!

Wasp. We ha' been but a day and a half in town, gentlemen, 'tis true; and yesterday i' the afternoon, we walked London to show the city to the gentlewoman he shall marry, Mistress Grace. But, afore I will endure such another half day with him, I'll be drawn with a good gib-cat through the great pond at home, as his uncle Hodge was! Why, we could not meet that heathen thing, all day, but stayed him. He would name you all the signs over, as he went, aloud: and where he spied a parrot, or a monkey, there he was pitched with all the little-long-coats about him, male and female.

---

62 **Hornet** (implying Littlewit is a cuckold)
64 **glisters** enemas
65 **I wusse** surely; I know for certain
68 **velvet-custard** (velvet hat shaped like a custard pie, an open pie of meat or fruit covered with a thickened broth or milk)
70 **humor** inclination
75 **stale** piss
87 **puddings** sausages; **cake-bread** bread with the consistency of cake
89 **catches** common songs, usually rounds
90 ***Rattle . . . rattle*** (a nonsense verse, beginning, "Three blue beans in a blue bladder, rattle, bladder, rattle"; ***O, Madge*** (a ballad about a barn owl named Madge)
93 **carman** carter; carrier (who was noted for whistling)
95 **whistle** whistle for
97 **bees** (1) whims; fantasies (proverbial); (2) reference to the morality play *Respublica*, where Avarice's brain swarms with bees; **fain** obliged
100 **o' the hood** (as a sign of her husband's dignity as Justice)
103–4 **another . . . piece** a different kind of person
104 **think** bargain
110–11 **cross and pile** (two sides of a coin, from French *croix* and *pile*; cf. "heads and tails"; a toss-up)
111 **whether . . . farthing** i.e., "it makes little difference" (proverbial)
130–1 **drawn . . . home** (referring to a bet in which a fool agrees to have a tom-cat [gib-cat] haul him through or across a pond with a packthread)
133 **stayed** stopped; prevented
134 **signs** (of the zodiac)
136 **pitched** fixed
137 ***long-coats*** children in petticoats

No getting him away! I thought he would ha' run mad o' the black boy in Bucklersbury that takes the scurvy, roguy tobacco, there.

Littlewit. You say true, Master Numps; there's such a one indeed.

Wasp. It's no matter whether there be or no, what's that to you?

Quarlous. He will not allow of John's reading at any hand.

Act I. Scene v.

[*Enter to them* Cokes, Mistress Overdo, Grace.]

Cokes. Oh, Numps! Are you here, Numps? Look where I am, Numps! And Mistress Grace, too! Nay, do not look angerly, Numps; my sister is here, and all, I do not come without her.

Wasp. What the mischief! Do you come with her? Or she with you?

Cokes. We came all to seek you, Numps.

Wasp. To seek me? Why, did you all think I was lost? Or run away with your fourteen shillings worth of small ware here? Or that I had changed it i' the Fair for hobby-horses? 'Sprecious – to seek me!

Mrs. Overdo. Nay, good Master Numps, do you show discretion, though he be exorbitant, as Master Overdo says, an't be but for conservation of the peace.

Wasp. Marry gip, goody she-Justice, Mistress French-hood! Turd i' your teeth; and turd i' your French-hood's teeth, too, to do you service, do you see? Must you quote your Adam to me! You think you are Madam Regent still, Mistress Overdo, when I am in place? No such matter, I assure you; your reign is out, when I am in, dame.

Mrs. Overdo. I am content to be in abeyance, sir, and be governed by you. So should he, too, if he did well; but 'twill be expected you should also govern your passions.

Wasp. Will't so forsooth? Good Lord! How sharp you are! With being at Bedlam yesterday? Whetstone has set an edge upon you, has he?

Mrs. Overdo. Nay, if you know not what belongs to your dignity, I do, yet, to mine.

Wasp. Very well, then.

Cokes. Is this the license, Numps? For love's sake, let me see't. I never saw a license.

Wasp. Did you not so? Why, you shall not see't, then.

Cokes. An' you love me, good Numps.

Wasp. Sir, I love you, and yet I do not love you, i' these fooleries. Set your heart at rest; there's nothing in't but hard words. And what would you see't for?

Cokes. I would see the length and the breadth on't, that's all; and I will see't now, so I will.

Wasp. You sha' not see it, here.

Cokes. Then I'll see't at home, and I'll look upo' the case here.

Wasp. Why, do so; a man must give way to him a little in trifles, gentlemen. These are errors, diseases of youth which he will mend when he comes to judgment and knowledge of matters. I pray you conceive so, and I thank you. And I pray you pardon him, and I thank you again.

Quarlous. Well, this dry nurse, I say still, is a delicate man.

Winwife. And I am for the cosset, his charge! Did you ever see a fellow's face more accuse him for an ass?

Quarlous. Accuse him? It confesses him one without accusing. What pity 'tis yonder wench should marry such a cokes!

Winwife. 'Tis true.

Quarlous. She seems to be discreet, and as sober as she is handsome.

Winwife. Aye, and if you mark her, what a restrained scorn she casts upon all his behavior, and speeches!

---

139 Bucklersbury (London street known for shops selling tobacco; the *black boy* was pictured on the signs of such shops)
145 reading comment
145–6 at . . . hand on any account
I.v.11 changed exchanged
12 'Sprecious "By God's [Christ's] precious blood!" (a common oath)
14 exorbitant abnormal
17 Marry gip "By Mary Gipcy" (St. Mary of Egypt; an exclamatory expression that confused *gip* as *get along with you*); **goody** goodwife (a form of address for humble married women)
18 French-hood (a new fashion in which the front band depressed over the forehead and raised in folds or loops over the temples, popular with citizens' wives)
21–2 Madam Regent i.e., the woman ruler
25 in abeyance (a legal term for the position of waiting for or being without a claimant or owner)
31 Whetstone (unidentified, but conjectured to be a particular keeper or inmate; clearly Wasp is punning on the whetstone's function of sharpening cutting tools)
39 An' as
52 judgment majority; of age
57 delicate courteous; critical
58 cosset spoiled child
61 confesses acknowledges
63 cokes dunce
65 sober serious; solemn
67 mark observe

Cokes. Well, Numps, I am now for another piece of business more. The Fair, Numps, and then –

Wasp. Bless me! Deliver me. Help, hold me! The Fair!

Cokes. Nay, never fidge up and down, Numps, and vex itself. I am resolute Bartholomew, in this; I'll make no suit on't to you. 'Twas all the end of my journey, indeed, to show Mistress Grace my Fair. I call't my Fair, because of Bartholomew; you know my name is Bartholomew, and Bartholomew Fair.

Littlewit. That was mine afore, gentlemen. This morning. I had that i' faith, upon his license. Believe me, there he comes after me.

Quarlous. Come, John, this ambitious wit of yours, I am afraid, will do you no good i' the end.

Littlewit. No? Why, sir?

Quarlous. You grow so insolent with it, and overdoing, John, that if you look not to it, and tie it up, it will bring you to some obscure place in time, and there 'twill leave you.

Winwife. Do not trust it too much, John; be more sparing, and use it but now and then. A wit is a dangerous thing, in this age; do not overbuy it.

Littlewit. Think you so, gentlemen? I'll take heed on't, hereafter.

Win. Yes, do, John.

Cokes. A pretty little soul, this same Mistress Littlewit! Would I might marry her!

Grace. [*Aside.*] So would I, or anybody else, so I might 'scape you.

Cokes. Numps, I will see it, Numps, 'tis decreed; never be melancholy for the matter.

Wasp. Why, see it, sir, see it, do see it! Who hinders you? Why do you not go see it? 'Slid, see it.

Cokes. The Fair, Numps, the Fair.

Wasp. Would the Fair and all the drums and rattles in't were i' your belly for me; they are already i' your brain. He that had the means to travel your head now should meet finer sights than any are i' the Fair and make a finer voyage on't, to see it all hung with cockle-shells, pebbles, fine wheatstraws, and here and there a chicken's feather and a cobweb.

Quarlous. Good faith, he looks, methinks, an' you mark him, like one that were made to catch flies, with his Sir Cranion legs.

Winwife. And his Numps, to flap 'em away.

Wasp. God be wi' you, sir. There's your bee in a box, and much good do't you.

[*Gives him the box and offers to leave.*]

Cokes. Why, a "your friend, and Bartholomew"; an' you be so contumacious.

Quarlous. What mean you, Numps?

Wasp. I'll not be guilty, I, gentlemen.

Mrs. Overdo. You will not let him go, brother, and lose him?

Cokes. Who can hold that will away? I had rather lose him than the Fair, I wusse.

Wasp. You do not know the inconvenience, gentlemen, you persuade to, nor what trouble I have with him in these humors. If he go to the Fair, he will buy of everything to a baby there; and household-stuff for that too. If a leg or an arm on him did not grow on, he would lose it i' the press. Pray heaven I bring him off with one stone! And then he is such a ravener after fruit! You will not believe what a coil I had, t'other day, to compound a business between a Cather'ne-pear-woman and him, about snatching! 'Tis intolerable, gentlemen!

Winwife. Oh, but you must not leave him, now, to these hazards, Numps.

Wasp. Nay, he knows too well I will not leave him, and that makes him presume. Well, sir, will you go now? If you have such an itch i' your feet to foot it to the Fair, why do you stop; am I your tarriers? Go, will you go? Sir, why do you not go?

Cokes. Oh, Numps! have I brought you about? Come, Mistress Grace, and sister, I am resolute Bat, i' faith, still.

Grace. Truly, I have no such fancy to the Fair, nor ambition to see it. There's none goes thither of any quality or fashion.

---

74 **fidge . . . down** grow anxious; pace restlessly
75 **itself** yourself
87 **insolent** extravagant
88–9 **tie it up** restrain yourself
93 **overbuy** (1) overuse; (2) become too dependent on; (3) pay too much for
117 **Sir Cranion** crane-fly, known for its long legs ("daddy-long-legs"; Cokes may have been a tall and gangly actor, while Wasp was unusually short)
121 **"your . . . Bartholomew"** farewell (transferred from the farewell in a letter)
122 **contumacious** contemptuous; willfully disobedient; quarrelsome
127 **Who . . . away?** (proverbial)
132 **buy of** buy something of
135 **press** crowd
136 **stone** testicle; i.e., with some bodily parts remaining
137 **coil** trouble; fuss
139 **Cather'ne-pear** Catherine pear, a small and early variety
147 **tarriers** obstructors; delayers
149 **brought . . . about** brought you around; gotten your consent
151 **Bat** (1) short for Bartholomew; (2) lump of earth or stone
154 **quality** (1) social standing; (2) features of character

Cokes. Oh, Lord, sir! You shall pardon me, Mistress Grace, we are enow of ourselves to make it a fashion. And for qualities, let Numps alone; he'll find qualities.

[*Exeunt* Cokes, Wasp, Grace, Mistress Overdo.]

Quarlous. What a rogue in apprehension is this! To understand her language no better.

Winwife. Aye, and offer to marry to her? Well, I will leave the chase of my widow for today, and directly to the Fair. These flies cannot, this hot season, but engender us excellent creeping sport.

Quarlous. A man that has but a spoonful of brain would think so. Farewell, John.

[*Exeunt* Quarlous, Winwife.]

Littlewit. Win, you see, 'tis in fashion to go to the Fair, Win. We must to the Fair, too, you and I, Win. I have an affair i' the Fair, Win, a puppet-play of mine own making – say nothing – that I writ for the motion-man, which you must see, Win.

Win. I would I might, John, but my mother will never consent to such a "profane motion," she will call it.

Littlewit. Tut, we'll have a device, a dainty one. (Now, Wit, help at a pinch, good Wit come, come, good Wit, an't be thy will.) I have it, Win, I have it, i' faith, and 'tis a fine one. Win, long to eat of a pig, sweet Win, i' the Fair. Do you see? I' the heart o' the Fair; not at Pie-corner. Your mother will do anything, Win, to satisfy your longing, you know; pray thee long, presently, and be sick o' the sudden, good Win. I'll go in and tell her. Cut thy lace i' the meantime, and play the hypocrite, sweet Win.

Win. No, I'll not make me unready for it. I can be hypocrite enough, though I were never so strait-laced.

Littlewit. You say true. You have been bred i' the family and brought up to't. Our mother is a most elect hypocrite, and has maintained us all this seven year with it, like gentlefolks.

Win. Aye, let her alone, John, she is not a wise willful widow for nothing, nor a sanctified sister for a song. And let me alone, too. I ha' somewhat o' the mother in me, you shall see. Fetch her, fetch her. Ah, ah.

[*Exit* Littlewit.]

Act I. Scene vi.

[*Enter to her*] Purecraft, Littlewit.

[*Purecraft.*] Now, the blaze of the beauteous discipline fright away this evil from our house! How now, Win-the-fight, child; how do you? Sweet child, speak to me.

Win. Yes, forsooth.

Purecraft. Look up, sweet Win-the-fight, and suffer not the enemy to enter you at this door; remember that your education has been with the purest. What polluted one was it that named first the unclean beast, pig, to you, child?

Win. Uh, uh.

Littlewit. Not I, o' my sincerity, mother. She longed above three hours, ere she would let me know it. Who was it, Win?

Win. A profane black thing with a beard, John.

Purecraft. Oh, resist it, Win-the-fight, it is the Tempter, the wicked Tempter. You may know it by the fleshly motion of pig. Be strong against it, and its foul temptations, in these assaults whereby it broacheth flesh and blood, as it were, on the weaker side; and pray against its carnal provocations, good child, sweet child, pray.

Littlewit. Good mother, I pray you, that she may eat some pig, and her belly full, too; and do not you cast away your own child, and perhaps one of mine, with your tale of the Tempter. How do you, Win? Are you not sick?

---

156 **enow** enough
157–8 **let . . . alone** i.e., leave it to Numps
159 **apprehension** understanding
163–4 **flies . . . creeping** (refers to belief that insects propagated spontaneously in the heat of the sun; Cokes and Wasp are said to provide spontaneous comedy at the Fair)
172 **motion-man** puppet-master
175 **motion** act; practice
182–3 **Pie-corner** (the site of Magpie Tavern in West Smithfield, a place of cookshops outside the Fair)
188 **make me unready** undress
194 **seven year** (cf. v.ii.62–79)
196–7 **sanctified sister** an official in the sect's governance
198 **mother** (1) as a mother; (2) cravings of pregnancy; (3) hysteria (believed caused by a loosened womb); (4) like her mother Dame Purecraft in irrationality

I.vi.1 **blaze** fervent religious belief
1–2 **discipline** (i.e., the strict Puritan religious practice, pleasing in the sight of God)
2 **evil** (1) Win's longing for pig; (2) Win's fertility (which it represents)
5 **forsooth** in truth
6–7 **suffer not the enemy** (permit not the Devil; Puritans were known for employing the language of warfare)
7 **at this door** i.e., the stomach (with a sexual pun)
9 **polluted one** non-Puritan (with pun on menstruation; cf. lines 20–1 below)
10 **unclean** (by kosher law; Lev. 11.7)
18 **motion** prompting
20 **broacheth** breaks into
26–7 **perhaps . . . mine** (Littlewit suggests Win is actually pregnant)

Win. Yes, a great deal, John (uh, uh).

Purecraft. What shall we do? Call our zealous brother Busy hither, for his faithful fortification in this charge of the adversary; child, my dear child, you shall eat pig, be comforted, my sweet child.

[*Exit* Littlewit.]

Win. Aye, but i' the Fair, mother.

Purecraft. I mean i' the Fair, if it can be anyway made, or found lawful. Where is our brother Busy? Will he not come? Look up, child.

[*Reenter* Littlewit.]

Littlewit. Presently, mother, as soon as he has cleansed his beard. I found him, fast by the teeth i' the cold turkey-pie i' the cupboard, with a great white loaf on his left hand and a glass of malmsey on his right.

Purecraft. Slander not the brethren, wicked one.

Littlewit. Here he is now, purified, mother.

[*Enter* Busy.]

Purecraft. Oh, brother Busy! your help here to edify, and raise us up in a scruple. My daughter Win-the-fight is visited with a natural disease of women, called "A longing to eat pig."

Littlewit. Aye sir, a Bartholomew pig; and in the Fair.

Purecraft. And I would be satisfied from you, religiously-wise, whether a widow of the sanctified assembly, or a widow's daughter, may commit the act, without offense to the weaker sisters.

Busy. Verily, for the disease of longing, it is a disease, a carnal disease, or appetite, incident to women. And as it is carnal, and incident, it is natural, very natural. Now pig, it is a meat, and a meat that is nourishing, and may be longed for, and so consequently eaten; it may be eaten; very exceeding well eaten; but in the Fair, and as a Bartholomew-pig, it cannot be eaten, for the very calling it a Bartholomew-pig, and to eat it so, is a spice of idolatry, and you make the Fair no better than one of the high places. This, I take it, is the state of the question. A high place.

Littlewit. Aye, but in state of necessity. Place should give place, Master Busy. (I have a conceit left, yet.)

Purecraft. Good brother, Zeal-of-the-land, think to make it as lawful as you can.

Littlewit. Yes sir, and as soon as you can, for it must be, sir; you see the danger my little wife is in, sir.

Purecraft. Truly, I do love my child dearly, and I would not have her miscarry, or hazard her first fruits, if it might be otherwise.

Busy. Surely, it may be otherwise, but it is subject to construction, subject, and hath a face of offense with the weak, a great face, a foul face, but that face may have a veil put over it, and be shadowed, as it were – it may be eaten, and in the Fair, I take it, in a booth, the tents of the wicked. The place is not much, not very much, we may be religious in midst of the profane, so it be eaten with a reformed mouth, with sobriety, and humbleness, not gorged in with gluttony, or greediness. There's the fear. For, should she go there, as taking pride in the place, or delight in the unclean dressing, to feed the vanity of the eye or the lust of the palate, it were not well, it were not fit, it were abominable, and not good.

Littlewit. Nay, I knew that afore, and told her on't; but courage, Win, we'll be humble enough; we'll seek out the homeliest booth i' the Fair, that's certain; rather than fail, we'll eat it o' the ground.

Purecraft. Aye, and I'll go with you myself, Win-the-fight, and my brother, Zeal-of-the-land, shall go with us too, for our better consolation.

Win. Uh, uh.

Littlewit. Aye, and Solomon too, Win; the more the merrier, Win. [*Aside to Win.*] We'll leave Rabbi Busy in a booth. Solomon, my cloak.

[*Enter* Solomon.]

Solomon. Here, sir.

Busy. In the way of comfort to the weak, I will go, and eat. I will eat exceedingly, and prophesy; there may be a good use made of it, too, now I

40 **fast** fastened

42, 43 **on** in

45 **purified** (pun on Busy's washed face)

47 **edify** enlighten (a common Puritan term); **raise . . . scruple** assist us in a question of conscience

56–68 **Verily . . . place** (this and subsequent speeches by Busy parody Puritan sermons and biblical exegesis, and demonstrate pride in revealed truths of God and human logic)

65 **spice** kind; species; **idolatry** (because using a saint's name)

67 **high places** (where the Israelites worshipped idols; cf. Lev. 26:30)

69–70 **Place . . . place** (Littlewit puns on Busy's place [a location of idolatry according to scripture] as social rank or place yielding in precedence to another)

79 **first fruits** first child (by having evil thoughts)

81–2 **face of offense** apparent stumbling-block

90 **fear** danger

95 **abominable** (a term associated with Puritan description of evil); **abominable . . . good** cliché (cf. Prov. 20:23)

110 **exceedingly** (another favorite Puritan word); **prophesy** have religious visions

think on't. By the public eating of swine's flesh, to profess our hate and loathing of Judaism, whereof the brethren stand taxed. I will therefore eat, yea, I will eat exceedingly.

Littlewit. Good, i' faith, I will eat heartily, too, because I will be no Jew; I could never away with that stiffnecked generation. And truly, I hope my little one will be like me, that cries for pig so, i' the mother's belly.

Busy. Very likely, exceeding likely, very exceeding likely.

[*Exeunt.*]

Act II

Scene i.

[*Enter* Justice Overdo.]

Justice Overdo. Well, in Justice' name, and the King's, and for the Commonwealth! Defy all the world, Adam Overdo, for a disguise, and all story; for thou hast fitted thyself, I swear. Fain would I meet the Lynceus now, that eagle's eye, that piercing Epidaurian serpent (as my Quintus Horace calls him), that could discover a Justice of Peace (and lately of the Quorum) under this covering. They may have seen many a fool in the habit of a Justice, but never till now a Justice in the habit of a fool. Thus we must do, though, that wake for the public good; and thus hath the wise magistrate done in all ages. There is a doing of right out of wrong, if the way be found. Never shall I enough commend a worthy worshipful man, sometime a capital member of this city, for his high wisdom in this point, who would take you, now the habit of a porter; now of a carman; now of the dog-killer, in this month of August; and in the winter, of a seller of tinder-boxes; and what would he do in all these shapes? Marry, go you into every alehouse, and down into every cellar; measure the length of puddings, take the gauge of black pots and cans, aye, and custards, with a stick; and their circumference, with a thread; weigh the loaves of bread on his middle-finger. Then would he send for 'em, home; give the puddings to the poor, the bread to the hungry, the custards to his children; break the pots, and burn the cans, himself. He would not trust his corrupt officers; he would do't himself. Would all men in authority would follow this worthy precedent! For, alas, as we are public persons; what do we know? Nay, what can we know? We hear with other men's ears; we see with other men's eyes; a foolish constable or a sleepy watchman, is all our information. He slanders a gentleman by the virtue of his place (as he calls it), and we, by the vice of ours, must believe him. As, a while gone, they made me, yea me, to mistake an honest zealous pursuivant for a seminary, and a proper young Bachelor of Music for a bawd. This we are subject to, that live in high place. All our intelligence is idle, and most of our intelligencers knaves; and, by your leave, ourselves thought little better, if not arrant fools, for believing 'em. I, Adam Overdo, am resolved therefore to spare spy-money hereafter, and make mine own discoveries. Many are the yearly enormities of this Fair, in whose courts of Pie-powders I have had the honor during the three days sometimes to sit as judge. But this is the special day for detection of those

---

114 **Judaism . . . taxed** (Jews forebade the eating of pork but Busy rationalizes his greed and love of pork to show Puritans have no sympathy with Judaism; Puritans were often accused of Judaism because they relied so heavily on Old Testament scripture and thought, and because they were exceptionally tolerant of Jews)

117–18 **away with** tolerate; agree with

118 **stiffnecked generation** stubborn sect (cf. Deut. 9:13; Acts 7, 51)

II.i.2 **Commonwealth** (1) country; (2) common good

4 **fitted** furnished

5 **Lynceus** (an Argonaut known for exceptional vision)

6–7 **Epidaurian . . . him)** (serpent worshipped as sacred to Aesculapius, god of medicine, in Epidaurus; Horace, *Satires* I.3.26–7)

9 **Quorum** (justices who because of their learning were necessary to constitute a bench of magistrates); **covering** disguise

10 **habit** robes

11 **habit of a fool** motley

12 **wake** stay awake; watch out

16–23 **worthy . . . shapes** (despite Induction, this probably refers specifically to Thomas Hayes, Lord Mayor of London in 1614, who investigated the city in disguise, as well as his predecessor Thomas Middleton)

17 **capital** leading

20 **dog-killer** one hired by the city to kill dogs in times of plague under the mistaken assumption that they, not rats, spread the disease

24–8 **measure . . . middle-finger** (overseeing accuracy of weights and measures was a concern of the magistracy)

25–6 **black pots and cans** serving measures for ale

44 **pursuivant** state official with powers of arrest; **seminary** priest trained abroad by the Roman Catholic church to convert the English

47 **intelligence** information; **idle** baseless

47–8 **intelligencers** spies; informers

49 **arrant** wandering

53 **enormities** serious offenses and irregularities

53–4 **courts of Pie-powders** (summary courts held at fairs and markets to administer justice to itinerant tradesmen and their customers)

foresaid enormities. Here is my black book for the purpose, this the cloud that hides me: under this cover I shall see, and not be seen. On, Junius Brutus. And as I began, so I'll end: in Justice' name, and the King's; and for the Commonwealth!

Act II. Scene ii.

[*Enter* Leatherhead, Trash, Passengers.]

Leatherhead. The Fair's pestilence dead, methinks; people come not abroad, today, whatever the matter is. Do you hear, Sister Trash, Lady o' the Basket? Sit farther with your ginger-bread-progeny there, and hinder not the prospect of my shop, or I'll ha' it proclaimed i' the Fair what stuff they are made on.

Trash. Why, what stuff are they made on, Brother Leatherhead? Nothing but what's wholesome, I assure you.

Leatherhead. Yes, stale bread, rotten eggs, musty ginger, and dead honey, you know.

Justice Overdo. [*Aside.*] Aye! Have I met with enormity so soon?

Leatherhead. I shall mar your market, old Joan.

Trash. Mar my market, thou too-proud pedlar? Do thy worst; I defy thee, aye, and thy stable of hobby-horses. I pay for my ground as well as thou dost; an' thou wrong'st me, for all thou art parcel-poet, and an inginer, I'll find a friend shall right me, and make a ballad of thee and thy cattle all over. Are you puffed up with the pride of your wares? Your arsedine?

Leatherhead. Go to, old Joan, I'll talk with you anon; and take you down, too, afore Justice Overdo. He is the man must charm you; I'll ha' you i' the Pie-powders.

Trash. Charm me? I'll meet thee face to face afore his worship when thou dar'st; and though I be a little crooked o' my body, I'll be found as upright in my dealing as any woman in Smithfield. Aye, charm me!

Justice Overdo. [*Aside.*] I am glad to hear my name is their terror, yet; this is doing of Justice.

Leatherhead. What do you lack? What is't you buy? What do you lack? Rattles, drums, halberts, horses, babies o' the best?
Fiddles o'th' finest?

[*Enter* Costermonger, Nightingale.]

Costermonger. Buy any pears, pears, fine, very fine pears!

Trash. Buy any ginger-bread, gilt ginger-bread!

Nightingale. Hey, now the Fair's a filling!
Oh, for a tune to startle
The birds o' the booths here billing
Yearly with old Saint Bartle!
The drunkards they are wading,
The punks and chapmen trading;
Who'd see the Fair without his lading?
Buy any ballads; new ballads?

[*Enter* Ursula.]

Ursula. Fie upon't! Who would wear out their youth and prime thus, in roasting of pigs, that had any cooler vocation? Hell's a kind of cold cellar to't, a very fine vault, o' my conscience! What, Mooncalf!

Mooncalf. [*Within.*] Here, Mistress.

Nightingale. How now, Urs'la? In a heat, in a heat?

Ursula. My chair, you false faucet you; and my morning's draught, quickly. A bottle of ale to quench me, rascal. I am all fire and fat, Nightingale; I shall e'en melt away to the first woman, a rib again, I am afraid. I do water the ground in knots as I go, like a great garden-pot; you may follow me by the S's I make.

---

57 **black book** record book
58 **cloud** disguise
60 **Junius Brutus** Lucius Junius Brutus, who defeated the Tarquins and founded the Roman republic; he disguised himself as an idiot yet was known for inflexibility in later life regarding the law
II.ii.1 **pestilence dead** plague victims
3–4 **Lady . . . Basket** (Trash sells gingerbread men from a basket she carries)
7 **stuff** ingredients; **on** of
12 **dead** flavorless
16 **pedlar** traveling tradesmen who carried goods in a pack on their backs
20 **parcel-poet** part-time poet; **inginer** engineer; designer or contriver of shows (he is a puppeteer)
22 **cattle** wares; shows
23 **arsedine** gold-colored alloy of copper and zinc used to ornament toys
25 **take . . . down** humiliate
26 **charm** subdue; quiet (as if by magic)
35 **What . . . lack?** (the conventional phrase of shopkeepers and pedlars)
36 **halberts** weapons with spearheads and pointed blades
41 **gilt** gold leaf used to decorate gingerbread
46 ***wading*** staggering
47 ***chapmen*** itinerant merchants; traders
48 ***lading*** freight
56 **heat** (with obscene pun)
57 **faucet** tap for a barrel
58 **draught** drink
60–1 **first woman** i.e., Eve
62 **knots** intricate designs of crossing lines (used to plant knot gardens)
62–3 **garden-pot** sprinkling can

Nightingale. Alas, good Urs; was 'Zekiel here this morning?

Ursula. 'Zekiel? What 'Zekiel?

Nightingale. 'Zekiel Edgworth, the civil cutpurse, you know him well enough. He that talks bawdy to you still: I call him my secretary.

Ursula. He promised to be here this morning, I remember.

Nightingale. When he comes, bid him stay. I'll be back again presently.

Ursula. Best take your morning's dew in your belly, Nightingale.

Mooncalf *brings in the chair.*

Come, sir, set it here; did not I bid you should get this chair let out o' the sides for me, that my hips might play? You'll never think of anything, till your dame be rump-galled. 'Tis well, changeling; because it can take in your grasshopper's thighs, you care for no more. Now, you look as you had been i' the corner o' the booth, fleaying your breech with a candle's end, and set fire o' the Fair. Fill, stot: fill.

Justice Overdo. [*Aside.*] This pig woman do I know, and I will put her in for my second enormity. She hath been before me, punk, pinnace and bawd, anytime these two and twenty years, upon record i' the Pie-powders.

Ursula. Fill again, you unlucky vermin.

Mooncalf. 'Pray you be not angry, mistress; I'll ha' it widened anon.

Ursula. No, no, I shall e'en dwindle away to't ere the Fair be done, you think, now you ha' heated me? A poor vexed thing I am. I feel myself dropping already, as fast as I can: Two stone o' suet a day is my proportion; I can but hold life and soul together, with this (here's to you, Nightingale) and a whiff of tobacco, at most. Where's my pipe now? Not filled? Thou arrant incubee.

Nightingale. Nay, Urs'la, thou'lt gall between the tongue and the teeth with fretting, now.

Ursula. How can I hope that ever he'll discharge his place of trust – tapster, a man of reckoning under me – that remembers nothing I say to him?

[*Exit* Nightingale.]

But look to't, sirrah, you were best. Threepence a pipeful, I will ha' made of all my whole half-pound of tobacco, and a quarter of a pound of coltsfoot mixed with it too, to itch it out. I that have dealt so long in the fire, will not be to seek in smoke now. Then six and twenty shillings a barrel I will advance o' my beer, and fifty shillings a hundred o' my bottle-ale; I ha' told you the ways how to raise it. Froth your cans well i' the filling, at length, rogue, and jog your bottles o' the buttock, sirrah, then skink out the first glass ever and drink with all companies, though you be sure to be drunk; you'll misreckon the better, and be less ashamed on't. But your true trick, rascal, must be to be ever busy, and mis-take away the bottles and cans in haste before they be half drunk off, and never hear anybody call (if they should chance to mark you), till you ha' brought fresh, and be able to forswear 'em. Give me a drink of ale.

Justice Overdo. [*Aside.*] This is the very womb and bed of enormity! Gross as herself! This must all down for enormity, all, every whit on't.

One knocks.

Ursula. Look who's there, sirrah! Five shillings a pig is my price – at least. If it be a sow-pig, sixpence more. If she be a great-bellied wife and long for't, sixpence more for that.

Justice Overdo. [*Aside.*] *O tempora! O mores!* I would not ha' lost my discovery of this one grievance for my place, and worship o' the bench. How is the poor subject abused here! Well, I will fall in

69 **secretary** confidant; one entrusted with another's secrets
74 **morning's dew** habitual drink
78 **play** fit
79 **rump-galled** chafed buttocks
80 **changeling** ugly substitute child exchanged by fairies for a stolen one
83–4 **fleaying . . . end** (a process for removing fleas)
84 **stot** steer or heifer (contemptuous; with probable pun on stoat, weasel)
86 **put** call
87 **pinnace** go-between
97 **stone** measure of weight equaling fourteen pounds; **proportion** estimate
101 **incubee** child of a woman impregnated by an incubus
102 **gall** make sore by chafing
105 **reckoning** distinction
111 **coltsfoot** (plant traditionally used to adulterate tobacco)
114 **advance** raise the price
117 **at length** held as far as possible below the spigot (to produce the most froth and conserve ale)
118 **jog** (to increase foam still more)
119 **skink** pour
123 **mis-take** take away prematurely
126 **mark** note
127 **forswear** renounce; abandon
132 **sirrah** (a term of contempt or reprimand)
133 **sow-pig** female pig
134 **great-bellied** pregnant
136 ***O . . . mores*** "What an age! What behavior!" (Cicero, *In Catilinam* I.i.2)
137 **grievance** wrong; transgression
138 **worship** honor; respect; **bench** court of justice

with her, and with her Mooncalf, and win out wonders of enormity. [*To Ursula.*] By thy leave, goodly woman, and the fatness of the Fair, oily as the King's constable's lamp, and shining as his shoeing-horn! Hath thy ale virtue or thy beer strength? That the tongue of man may be tickled? And his palate pleased in the morning? Let thy pretty nephew here go search and see.

Ursula. What new roarer is this?

Mooncalf. Oh, Lord! Do you not know him, mistress? 'Tis mad Arthur of Bradley, that makes the orations. Brave master, old Arthur of Bradley, how do you? Welcome to the Fair; when shall we hear you again to handle your matters? With your back again' a booth, ha? I ha' been one o' your little disciples, i' my days!

Justice Overdo. Let me drink, boy, with my love, thy Aunt, here, that I may be eloquent. But of thy best, lest it be bitter in my mouth, and my words fall foul on the Fair.

Ursula. Why dost thou not fetch him drink? And offer him to sit?

Mooncalf. Is't ale, or beer, Master Arthur?

Justice Overdo. Thy best, pretty stripling, thy best; the same thy dove drinketh, and thou drawest on holy days.

Ursula. Bring him a sixpenny bottle of ale; they say, a fool's handsel is lucky.

Justice Overdo. Bring both, child. Ale for Arthur, and beer for Bradley.
Ale for thine Aunt, boy.

[*Exit* Mooncalf.]

[*Aside.*] My disguise takes to the very wish and reach of it. I shall, by the benefit of this, discover enough, and more – and yet get off with the reputation of what I would be: a certain middling thing, between a fool and a madman.

Act II. Scene iii.

[*Enter* Knockem *to them.*]

[*Knockem.*] What! my little lean Urs'la! My She-bear! Art thou alive yet? With thy litter of pigs to grunt out another Bartholomew Fair? Ha!

Ursula. Yes, and to amble afoot, when the Fair is done, to hear you groan out of a cart, up the heavy hill.

Knockem. Of Holborn, Urs'la, meanst thou so? For what? For what, pretty Urs?

Ursula. For cutting halfpenny purses, or stealing little penny dogs out o' the Fair.

Knockem. Oh, good words, good words, Urs.

Justice Overdo. [*Aside.*] Another special enormity. A cutpurse of the sword, the boot, and the feather! Those are his marks.

[*Reenter* Mooncalf.]

Ursula. You are one of those horse-leeches that gave out I was dead, in Turnbull-street, of a surfeit of bottle-ale and tripes?

Knockem. No, 'twas better meat, Urs; cow's udders, cow's udders!

Ursula. Well, I shall be meet with your mumbling mouth one day.

Knockem. What? Thou'lt poison me with neuft in a bottle of ale, wilt thou? Or a spider in a tobacco-pipe, Urs? Come, there's no malice in these fat folks, I never fear thee, an' I can 'scape thy lean Mooncalf here. Let's drink it out, good Urs, and no vapors!

[*Exit* Ursula.]

Justice Overdo. Dost thou hear, boy? (There's for thy ale, and the remnant for thee.) Speak in thy faith of a faucet, now; is this goodly person before us here, this vapors, a knight of the knife?

Mooncalf. What mean you by that, Master Arthur?

Justice Overdo. I mean a child of the horn-thumb, a babe of booty, boy; a cutpurse.

Mooncalf. Oh, Lord, sir! far from it! This is Master Dan Knockem Jordan, the ranger of Turnbull. He is a horse-courser, sir.

Justice Overdo. Thy dainty dame, though, called him cutpurse.

---

140 win out expose
147 nephew (general term for close relationship)
151–2 Arthur of Bradley (Overdo's disguise; Arthur was the hero of a mid-sixteenth-century ballad, "The Wedding of Arthur of Bradley")
153 again against
157 Aunt (general term for gossip)
163 stripling boy
164 dove darling
167 handsel first money taken for the day
171 takes succeeds
II.iii.6–7 groan . . . hill (convicted criminals were carted from Newgate Prison up Holborn Hill to the gallows at Tyburn)
16 horse-leeches (1) farriers; (2) large bloodsucking leeches; (3) predators
21 meet even
23 neuft newt
25–6 there's . . . folks (fat people were proverbially said to be good-natured)
28 vapors nonsense (cf. below IV.iv.38f.; also whims, vagaries [originally fumes from the stomach or other organs]; Knockem uses it to mean whatever he wishes, although for him it usually means fantastic ideas or a ridiculous urge to quarrel or brag)
32–3 knight . . . knife (reference to the main tool of the cutpurse)
35 horn-thumb horn thimble (used by cutpurses to protect themselves)

Mooncalf. Like enough, sir, she'll do forty such things in an hour (an' you listen to her) for her recreation if the toy take her i' the greasy kerchief. It makes her fat, you see. She battens with it.

Justice Overdo. [*Aside.*] Here might I ha' been deceived now, and ha' put a fool's blot upon myself, if I had not played an after-game o' discretion.

Ursula *comes in again dropping.*

Knockem. Alas, poor Urs, this's an ill season for thee.

Ursula. Hang yourself, hackney-man.

Knockem. How? How? Urs, vapors! Motion breed vapors?

Ursula. Vapors? Never tusk nor twirl your dibble, good Jordan, I know what you'll take to a very drop. Though you be captain o' the roarers, and fight well at the case of pisspots, you shall not fright me with your lion-chap, sir, nor your tusks; you angry? You are hungry. Come, a pig's head will stop your mouth and stay your stomach at all times.

Knockem. Thou art such another mad merry Urs still! Troth, I do make conscience of vexing thee now i' the dog-days, this hot weather, for fear of foundering thee i' the body; and melting down a pillar of the Fair. Pray thee take thy chair again and keep state; and let's have a fresh bottle of ale, and a pipe of tobacco; and no vapors. I'll ha' this belly o' thine taken up, and thy grass scoured, wench. Look! Here's Ezekiel Edgworth; a fine boy of his inches as any is i' the Fair! Has still money in his purse and will pay all with a kind heart; and good vapors.

Act II. Scene iv.

[*Enter to them* Edgworth, Nightingale, Corn-cutter, Tinderbox-man, Passengers.]

Edgworth. That I will, indeed, willingly, Master Knockem; fetch some ale, and tobacco.

[*Exit* Mooncalf.]

Leatherhead. What do you lack, gentlemen? Maid, see a fine hobby-horse for your young master. Cost you but a token a week his provender.

Corn-cutter. Ha'you any corns i' your feet and toes?

Tinderbox-man. Buy a mousetrap, a mousetrap, or a tormentor for a flea.

Trash. Buy some ginger-bread.

Nightingale. Ballads, ballads! Fine new ballads:
Hear for your love, and buy for your money!
A delicate ballad o' *The Ferret and the Coney!*
A Preservative again' the Punks' Evil!
Another of *Goose-green Starch, and the Devil!*
A Dozen of Divine Points, and *The Godly Garters!*
The Fairing of Good Counsel, of an ell and three quarters!
What is't you buy?
The Windmill blown down by the witch's fart!
Or *Saint George, that oh! did break the dragon's heart!*

[*Reenter* Mooncalf.]

Edgworth. Master Nightingale, come hither; leave your mart a little.

Nightingale. Oh, my secretary! What says my secretary?

Justice Overdo. Child o' the bottles, what's he? What's he?

Mooncalf. A civil young gentleman, Master Arthur, that keeps company with the roarers, and disburses all still. He has ever money in his purse; he pays for them, and they roar for him. One

---

44 **toy** whim

45 **kerchief** head (from the cloth used to cover it as a protection against heat); **battens** thrives

48 **blot** censure

49 **after-game** a second game played to reverse the outcome

50 s.d. ***dropping*** (1) dripping with grease; (2) bent from exhaustion

53 **hackney-man** one who keeps riding-horses for hire

54–5 **Motion . . . vapors?** does movement cause tantrums?

56 **tusk** to form into a tuft; **dibble** small spade-beard

59 **fight . . . pisspots** (proverbial; but Ursula substitutes *pisspots* for *pistols*)

60 **lion-chap** lion's jaw (with beard)

66 **dog-days** (unusually hot summer days in July and August associated with the rising of the dog-star)

67 **foundering** (causing a horse to collapse from being overworked)

69 **keep state** act like a queen under a canopy of state

72 **taken up** reduced (farrier's term); **scoured** purged

II.iv.1 s.d. **Passengers** passers-by

5 **provender** fodder for cattle

8 **tormentor** trap

11 **Hear . . . money** (cf. proverb "not to be had for love nor money")

12 ***The . . . Coney*** i.e., the Swindler and the Dupe

13 ***Punks' Evil*** venereal disease; syphilis

14 ***Goose-green . . . Devil*** (a ballad about a woman of Antwerp who wished the Devil would take her whenever her ruffs were starched again; he came as a handsome man, offered her ruffs, and broke her neck when she wore them); **Goose-green** yellowish-green (from gooseturd-green)

15 ***Dozen . . . Points*** (a ballad of twelve maxims sent by a gentlewoman to her lover as a New Year's gift); ***Godly Garters*** (a ballad about garters worn by men who serve God in fear of Him)

16 **ell** (a measure of 45 inches)

23 **mart** trade

24 **secretary** (as one who transacts business for another)

31 **roar** yell (to distract crowds from the cutpurse)

does good offices for another. They call him the secretary, but he serves nobody. A great friend of the ballad-man's – they are never asunder.

Justice Overdo. What pity 'tis so civil a young man should haunt this debauched company! Here's the bane of the youth of our time apparent. A proper penman, I see't in his countenance; he has a good clerk's look with him, and I warrant him a quick hand.

Mooncalf. A very quick hand, sir.

[*Exit.*]

Edgworth. All the purses and purchase I give you today by conveyance bring hither to Urs'la's presently. Here we will meet at night in her lodge, and share. Look you choose good places for your standing i' the Fair when you sing, Nightingale.

This they whisper, that Overdo *hears it not.*

Ursula. Aye, near the fullest passages; and shift 'em often.

Edgworth. And i' your singing, you must use your hawk's eye nimbly, and fly the purse to a mark still – where 'tis worn and o' which side – that you may gi' me the sign with your beak, or hang your head that way i' the tune.

Ursula. Enough, talk no more on't. Your friendship, masters, is not now to begin. Drink your draught of indenture, your sup of covenant, and away. The Fair fills apace, company begins to come in, and I ha' ne'er a pig ready, yet.

Knockem. Well said! Fill the cups, and light the tobacco. Let's give fire i' th' works, and noble vapors.

Edgworth. And shall we ha' smocks, Urs'la, and good whimsies, ha?

Ursula. Come, you are i' your bawdy vein! The best the Fair will afford, 'Zekiel, if bawd Whit keep his word.

[*Reenter* Mooncalf.]

How do the pigs, Mooncalf?

Mooncalf. Very passionate, mistress, one on 'em has wept out an eye. Master Arthur o' Bradley is melancholy here; nobody talks to him. Will you any tobacco, Master Arthur?

Justice Overdo. No, boy, let my meditations alone.

Mooncalf. He's studying for an oration now.

Justice Overdo. [*Aside.*] If I can, with this day's travel, and all my policy, but rescue this youth, here, out of the hands of the lewd man and the strange woman I will sit down at night, and say with my friend Ovid, *Jamque opus exegi, quod nec Jovis ira, nec ignis, &c.*

Knockem. Here, 'Zekiel; here's a health to Urs'la, and a kind vapor. Thou hast money i' thy purse still; and store! How dost thou come by it? Pray thee, vapor thy friends some in a courteous vapor.

Edgworth. Half I have, Master Dan Knockem, is always at your service.

Justice Overdo. [*Aside.*] Ha, sweet nature! What goshawk would prey upon such a lamb?

Knockem. Let's see what 'tis, 'Zekiel! Count it, come, fill him to pledge me.

Act II. Scene v.

[*Enter* Winwife, Quarlous, *to them.*]

[*Winwife.*] We are here before 'em, methinks.

Quarlous. All the better. We shall see 'em come in now.

Leatherhead. What do you lack, gentlemen, what is't you lack? A fine horse? A lion? A bull? A bear? A dog, or a cat? An excellent fine Bartholomew-bird? Or an instrument? What is't you lack?

Quarlous. 'Slid! here's Orpheus among the beasts, with his fiddle and all!

Trash. Will you buy any comfortable bread, gentlemen?

---

35 asunder apart
38 bane destroyer
41 quick hand (Overdo refers to writing, Mooncalf to thievery)
43 purchase booty
44 conveyance sleight-of-hand
49 fullest passages most crowded passageways
52 fly . . . mark spot the mark [target] precisely (metaphors are from hawking)
54 beak nose
56–7 Your . . . begin (allusion to the conspiracy between the doctor and the apothecaries in the General Prologue to Chaucer's *Canterbury Tales*, lines 427–8)
58 draught pun on (1) drink (often accompanying such a singing); (2) draft; (3) pledge
64 smocks prostitutes
65 whimsies whores (also cant for female genitalia)
70 passionate self-pitying
71 wept . . . eye (an indication that the roasted pig is nearly done)
77 travel journey, but with a pun on ***travail***, work; **policy** shrewd contrivance (the word was associated with Machiavelli)
79 strange woman harlot
80–1 *Jamque . . . &c.* "And now I have finished a work which neither the anger of Jove, nor fire, nor sword, nor devouring time will ever destroy" (Ovid, *Metamorphoses* X. 871–2)
84 store plenty
92 fill . . . pledge fill his glass for a toast
II.v.8 Orpheus . . . beasts (the mythic poet and singer Orpheus could charm even the beasts with his lyre; a commonplace reference)
10 comfortable digestible and nutritious; refreshing

Quarlous. And Ceres selling her daughter's picture in gingerwork!

Winwife. That these people should be so ignorant to think us chapmen for 'em! Do we look as if we would buy ginger-bread? Or hobby-horses?

Quarlous. Why, they know no better ware than they have, nor better customers than come. And our very being here makes us fit to be demanded, as well as others. Would Cokes would come! There were a true customer for 'em.

Knockem. How much is't? Thirty shillings? Who's yonder! Ned Winwife? And Tom Quarlous, I think! Yes. (Gi' me it all, gi' me it all.) Master Winwife! Master Quarlous! Will you take a pipe of tobacco with us? (Do not discredit me now, 'Zekiel.)

Winwife. Do not see him! He is the roaring horse-courser. Pray thee, let's avoid him; turn down this way.

Quarlous. 'Slud, I'll see him, and roar with him too an' he roared as loud as Neptune; pray thee go with me.

Winwife. You may draw me to as likely an inconvenience when you please, as this.

Quarlous. Go to, then, come along. We ha'nothing to do, man, but to see sights now.

Knockem. Welcome Master Quarlous and Master Winwife! Will you take any froth, and smoke with us?

Quarlous. Yes, sir, but you'll pardon us if we knew not of so much familiarity between us afore.

Knockem. As what, sir?

Quarlous. To be so lightly invited to smoke and froth.

Knockem. A good vapor! Will you sit down, sir? This is old Urs'la's mansion. How like you her bower? Here you may ha' your punk and your pig in state, sir, both piping hot.

Quarlous. I had rather ha' my punk cold, sir.

Justice Overdo. [*Aside.*] There's for me; punk! and pig!

Ursula. What, Mooncalf? You rogue.

She calls within.

Mooncalf. By and by; the bottle is almost off, mistress. Here, Master Arthur.

Ursula. I'll part you and your play-fellow there i' the guarded coat, an' you sunder not the sooner. [*Exit.*]

Knockem. Master Winwife, you are proud, methinks; you do not talk, nor drink. Are you proud?

Winwife. Not of the company I am in, sir, nor the place, I assure you.

Knockem. You do not except at the company, do you? Are you in vapors, sir?

Mooncalf. Nay, good Master Dan Knockem, respect my mistress' bower, as you call it. For the honor of our booth, none o' your vapors here.

She comes out with a firebrand.

Ursula. Why, you thin lean polecat you, an' they have a mind to be i' their vapors, must you hinder 'em? What did you know, vermin, if they would ha' lost a cloak or such a trifle? Must you be drawing the air of pacification here, while I am tormented within, i' the fire, you weasel?

Mooncalf. Good mistress, 'twas in the behalf of your booth's credit that I spoke.

Ursula. Why? Would my booth ha' broke if they had fallen out in't, sir? Or would their heat ha' fired it? In, you rogue, and wipe the pigs, and mend the fire that they fall not, or I'll both baste and roast you till your eyes drop out, like 'em. (Leave the bottle behind you, and be curst a while.)

[*Exit* Mooncalf.]

Quarlous. Body o' the Fair! What's this? Mother o' the bawds?

Knockem. No, she's mother o' the pigs, sir, mother o' the pigs!

Winwife. Mother o' the Furies, I think, by her firebrand.

Quarlous. Nay, she is too fat to be a Fury, sure; some walking sow of tallow!

---

11 **Ceres** goddess of grains and harvest; **selling . . . picture** (Ceres wandered for nine days seeking her lost daughter Proserpine who had been carried off to Hades by Pluto, god of the underworld)

14 **chapmen** customers

30 **'Slud** "By God's [i.e. Christ's] blood" (a common oath)

31 **Neptune** (god of the ocean, associated with horses and wild tempests)

33–4 **inconvenience** mischief; trick

41 **afore** previously

43 **lightly** casually

46 **mansion** (1) ironic, since her booth is not grand, though sprawling; (2) perhaps a reference to a stage "mansion" used as stage property or backdrop

47 **bower** (Ursula's stage booth may be shaded by boughs, but the word puns on bower as a place of secret rendezvous)

49 **cold** safe ("hot" punks suffered from syphilis)

52 **off** finished

55 **guarded** trimmed with braid or lace; **sunder** part

61 **except at** approve of

67 **polecat** (cant for prostitute)

75 **credit** reputation

76 **broke** (1) fallen apart; (2) gone bankrupt

77 **fallen out** quarreled

78 **wipe** baste

80 **baste . . . roast** (1) cook; (2) beat

81 **curst** damned (with play on *excommunicated*)

87 **Furies** (mythical goddesses of vengeance and retribution from the underworld)

90 **sow** a measure equal to 300 pounds in weight

Winwife. An inspired vessel of kitchen-stuff!

She drinks this while.

Quarlous. She'll make excellent gear for the coach-makers here in Smithfield to anoint wheels and axle-trees with.

Ursula. Aye, aye, gamesters, mock a plain plump soft wench o' the suburbs, do, because she's juicy and wholesome. You must ha' your thin pinched ware, pent up i' the compass of a dog-collar (or 'twill not do), that looks like a long laced conger set upright, and a green feather, like fennel i' the joll on't.

Knockem. Well said, Urs, my good Urs; to 'em, Urs!

Quarlous. Is she your quagmire, Dan Knockem? Is this your bog?

Nightingale. We shall have a quarrel presently.

Knockem. How? Bog? Quagmire? Foul vapors! Hum'h!

Quarlous. Yes, he that would venture for't, I assure him, might sink into her, and be drowned a week ere any friend he had could find where he were.

Winwife. And then he would be a fortnight weighing up again.

Quarlous. 'Twere like falling into a whole shire of butter. They had need be a team of Dutchmen, should draw him out.

Knockem. Answer 'em, Urs; where's thy Bartholomew-wit, now? Urs, thy Bartholomew-wit?

Ursula. Hang 'em, rotten, roguy cheaters! I hope to see 'em plagued one day (poxed they are already, I am sure) with lean playhouse poultry that has the bony rump sticking out like the ace of spades or the point of a partizan, that every rib of 'em is like the tooth of a saw; and will so grate 'em with their hips and shoulders as, take 'em altogether, they were as good lie with a hurdle.

Quarlous. Out upon her, how she drips! She's able to give a man the sweating sickness with looking on her.

Ursula. Marry, look off, with a patch o' your face; and a dozen i' your breech, though they be o' scarlet, sir. I ha' seen as fine outsides as either o' yours bring lousy linings to the broker's, ere now, twice a week!

Quarlous. Do you think there may be a fine new cucking-stool i' the Fair, to be purchased? One large enough, I mean. I know there is a pond of capacity for her.

Ursula. For your mother, you rascal. Out, you rogue, you hedge-bird, you pimp, you pannier-man's bastard, you!

Quarlous. Ha, ha, ha.

Ursula. Do you sneer, you dog's-head, you trendle-tail! You look as you were begotten a'top of a cart in harvest-time, when the whelp was hot and eager. Go snuff after your brother's bitch, Mistress Commodity. That's the livery you wear. 'Twill be out at the elbows shortly. It's time you went to't for the tother remnant.

Knockem. Peace, Urs, peace, Urs. They'll kill the poor whale, and make oil of her. Pray thee, go in.

Ursula. I'll see 'em poxed first, and piled, and double piled.

Winwife. Let's away; her language grows greasier than her pigs.

Ursula. Dost so, snotty nose? Good Lord! Are you sniveling? You were engendered on a she-beggar in a barn, when the bald thrasher, your sire, was scarce warm.

Winwife. Pray thee, let's go.

Quarlous. No, faith; I'll stay the end of her, now. I know she cannot last long; I find by her similes she wanes apace.

Ursula. Does she so? I'll set you gone. Gi' me my pig-pan hither a little. I'll scald you hence, an' you will not go.

[*Exit.*]

---

91 **inspired . . . kitchen- stuff** (container of dripping that has been given the breath of life; cf. Gen. 2:7)

92 **gear** material

96 **suburbs** (usually a reference to Southwark, across the Thames from London, a center for playhouses, entertainment, prostitution, and crime)

100 **laced** (1) streaked; (2) slashed (for cooking); **conger** large eel

101 **joll** head of a fish

103–4 **quagmire . . . bog** (horse-dealers kept part of their grounds under water to hide deficiencies of horses with poor legs who were kept standing there for show)

111–12 **weighing up** raising up (as with a ship's anchor)

113 **shire** county (i.e., a large area)

114 **Dutchmen** (proverbial eaters of butter)

120 **playhouse poultry** prostitutes who frequented playhouses

121–2 **ace of spades** (as to shape); **partizan** long-handled spear

125 **hurdle** portable frame with horizontal bars

127 **sweating sickness** epidemic fever, often fatal

129–30 **patch . . . breech** (symptoms of syphilis)

132 **bring . . . broker's** (1) bring lice-infected underwear to the pawnbroker's; (2) bring diseased breeches (i.e., genitals) to the bawd's; **broker's** dealer in second-hand clothing

135 **cucking-stool** dunking device used to shame and punish bawds

136 **pond** (the Horsepool at West Smithfield)

137 **of capacity** large enough

139 **hedge-bird** vagrant (one born under a hedge)

139–40 **pannier-man's** hawker's; pitchman's

142–3 **trendle-tail** cur; mongrel (with curled tail)

144 **whelp** puppy

146 **bitch** female dog

152 **piled** (1) bald (from the pox); (2) afflicted with piles; (3) threadbare

164 **set you gone** get you going

165 **an'** if

Knockem. Gentlemen, these are very strange vapors! And very idle vapors, I assure you.

Quarlous. You are a very serious ass, we assure you.

Knockem. Hum'h! Ass? And serious? Nay, then, pardon me my vapor. I have a foolish vapor, gentlemen. Any man that does vapor me the ass, Master Quarlous –

Quarlous. What then, Master Jordan?

Knockem. I do vapor him the lie.

Quarlous. Faith, and to any man that vapors me the lie, I do vapor that.

[*Strikes him.*]

Knockem. Nay, then, vapors upon vapors.

Edgworth, Nightingale. 'Ware the pan, the pan, the pan, she comes with the pan, gentlemen. God bless the woman.

Ursula *comes in, with the scalding-pan. They fight. She falls with it.*

Ursula. Oh!

[*Exeunt* Quarlous, Winwife.]

Trash. What's the matter?

Justice Overdo. Goodly woman!

Mooncalf. Mistress!

Ursula. Curse of hell, that ever I saw these fiends! Oh! I ha' scalded my leg, my leg, my leg, my leg. I ha' lost a limb in the service! Run for some cream and salad oil, quickly! Are you under-peering, you baboon? Rip off my hose, an' you be men, men, men!

Mooncalf. Run you for some cream, good mother Joan. I'll look to your basket.

[*Exit* Trash.]

Leatherhead. Best sit up i' your chair, Urs'la. Help, gentlemen.

Knockem. Be of good cheer, Urs; thou hast hindered me the currying of a couple of stallions here that abused the good race-bawd o' Smithfield; 'twas time for 'em to go.

Nightingale. I'faith, when the pan came, they had made you run else. (This had been a fine time for purchase, if you had ventured.)

Edgworth. Not a whit. These fellows were too fine to carry money.

Knockem. Nightingale, get some help to carry her leg out o' the air; take off her shoes; body o' me, she has the mallanders, the scratches, the crown scab, and the quitter bone i' the tother leg.

Ursula. Oh! the pox, why do you put me in mind o' my leg, thus, to make it prick and shoot? Would you ha' me i' the Hospital afore my time?

Knockem. Patience, Urs. Take a good heart, 'tis but a blister, as big as a windgall. I'll take it away with the white of an egg, a little honey, and hog's grease; ha' thy pasterns well rolled, and thou shalt pace again by tomorrow. I'll tend thy booth and look to thy affairs the while. Thou shalt sit i' thy chair, and give directions, and shine Ursa major.

[*Exeunt* Knockem, Mooncalf, Ursula.]

Act II. Scene vi.

[*Enter* Cokes, Wasp, Mistress Overdo, Grace.]

[*Justice Overdo.*] These are the fruits of bottle-ale, and tobacco! the foam of the one, and the fumes of the other! Stay, young man, and despise not the wisdom of these few hairs that are grown gray in care of thee.

Edgworth. Nightingale, stay a little. Indeed I'll hear some o' this!

Cokes. Come, Numps, come, where are you? Welcome into the Fair, Mistress Grace.

Edgworth. 'Slight, he will call company, you shall see, and put us into doings presently.

Justice Overdo. Thirst not after that frothy liquor, ale, for who knows, when he openeth the stopple, what may be in the bottle? Hath not a snail, a spider, yea, a newt been found there? Thirst not after it, youth; thirst not after it.

Cokes. This is a brave fellow, Numps, let's hear him.

Wasp. 'Sblood, how brave is he? In a guarded coat? You were best truck with him; e'en strip, and truck presently, it will become you. Why will you hear him? Because he is an ass, and may be akin to the Cokeses?

---

176 lie (with pun on *lye* or urine)
191 under-peering looking up under my skirts
198 currying beating
199 race-bawd mother bawd; breeder of bawds
203 purchase theft
204 fine clever
208–9 mallanders . . . bone hoof and leg diseases in horses
216 windgall soft tumor on a horse's leg
217–18 white . . . hog's grease farrier's remedies for diseases in horses
218 pasterns parts of the horse's foot between the fetlock and the hoof; **rolled** bandaged
219 pace walk
222 Ursa major (constellation known as the Great Bear)
II.vi.10 'Slight "By God's light" (a common oath)
14 stopple stem of a tobacco pipe
17 brave fine, exceptional
19 brave well-dressed
20 truck make an exchange (of clothing)
21 strip more quickly

Cokes. Oh, good Numps!

Justice Overdo. Neither do thou lust after that tawny weed, tobacco.

Cokes. Brave words!

Justice Overdo. Whose complection is like the Indian's that vents it!

Cokes. Are they not brave words, sister?

Justice Overdo. And who can tell if, before the gathering and making up thereof, the alligator hath not pissed thereon?

Wasp. 'Heart, let 'em be brave words, as brave as they will! An' they were all the brave words in a country, how then? Will you away yet? Ha' you enough on him? Mistress Grace, come you away, I pray you, be not you accessary. If you do lose your license, or somewhat else, sir, with listening to his fables, say Numps is a witch, with all my heart, do, say so.

Cokes. Avoid, i' your satin doublet, Numps.

Justice Overdo. The creeping venom of which subtle serpent, as some late writers affirm, neither the cutting of the perilous plant, nor the drying of it, nor the lighting, or burning, can any way persway or assuage.

Cokes. Good, i' faith! Is't not, sister?

Justice Overdo. Hence it is that the lungs of the tobacconist are rotted, the liver spotted, the brain smoked like the backside of the pig woman's booth, here, and the whole body within, black as her pan you saw e'en now, without.

Cokes. A fine similitude, that, sir! Did you see the pan?

Edgworth. Yes, sir.

Justice Overdo. Nay, the hole in the nose here of some tobacco-takers, or the third nostril (if I may so call it), which makes that they can vent the tobacco out like the ace of clubs, or rather the flower-de-lys, is caused from the tobacco, the mere tobacco! When the poor innocent pox, having nothing to do there, is miserably, and most unconscionably slandered.

Cokes. Who would ha' missed this, sister?

Mrs. Overdo. Not anybody but Numps.

Cokes. He does not understand.

Edgworth. Nor you feel.

He picketh his purse.

Cokes. What would you have, sister, of a fellow that knows nothing but a basket-hilt, and an old fox in't? The best music i' the Fair will not move a log.

Edgworth. In, to Urs'la, Nightingale, and carry her comfort. See it told. This fellow was sent to us by fortune for our first fairing.

[*Exit* Nightingale.]

Justice Overdo. But what speak I of the diseases of the body, children of the Fair?

Cokes. That's to us, sister. Brave, i' faith!

Justice Overdo. Hark, Oh, you sons and daughters of Smithfield! and hear what malady it doth the mind. It causeth swearing; it causeth swaggering, it causeth snuffling, and snarling, and now and then a hurt.

Mrs. Overdo. He hath something of Master Overdo, methinks, brother.

Cokes. So me thought, sister, very much of my brother Overdo – and 'tis when he speaks.

Justice Overdo. Look into any angle o' the town – the Straits, or the Bermudas – where the quarreling lesson is read, and how do they entertain the time, but with bottle-ale and tobacco? The lecturer is o' one side, and his pupils o' the other; but the seconds are still bottle-ale and tobacco, for which the lecturer reads and the novices pay. Thirty pounds a week in bottle-ale! Forty in tobacco! And ten more in ale again. Then for a suit to drink in, so much, and (that being slavered) so much for another suit, and then a third suit, and a fourth suit! And still the bottle-ale slavereth, and the tobacco stinketh!

Wasp. Heart of a madman! Are you rooted here? Will you never away? What can any man find out in this bawling fellow to grow here for? He is a full handful higher, sin' he heard him. Will you fix here? And set up a booth? Sir?

---

29 **vents** sells
41 **witch** wizard; magician (because he foresaw events)
42 **Avoid** go off (as in "Avoid, Satan" playing on *witch*)
44 **some . . . writers** (King James was one of those who attacked the use of tobacco in his *Counterblaste* [1604])
47 **persway** diminish
50 **tobacconist** smoker
55 **similitude** (comparison made for moral instruction)
58–9 **hole . . . nostril** (effects of syphilis [which Overdo ascribes to tobacco])
60 **vent** exhale
63 **mere** pure; only
71 **basket-hilt** hilt of a sword with a basket-like protection for the hand
72 **fox** sword
75 **told** counted
76 **fairing** present; gift
83 **snuffling** contemptuous sniffing
89 **angle** corner
90 **Straits . . . Bermudas** (disreputable district of narrow alleys near Charing Cross frequented by criminals)
90–1 **quarreling lesson** (instruction in dueling with sword and dagger by fencing academies developed in the 1590s)
91 **entertain** occupy
94 **seconds** standbys
99 **slavered** soiled with saliva and sweat

Justice Overdo. I will conclude briefly –

Wasp. Hold your peace, you roaring rascal; I'll run my head i' your chops else. You were best build a booth and entertain him, make your will, an' you say the word and him your heir! Heart, I never knew one taken with a mouth of a peck afore. By this light, I'll carry you away o' my back, an' you will not come.

He gets him up on pick-pack.

Cokes. Stay, Numps, stay, set me down. I ha' lost my purse, Numps; oh, my purse! One o' my fine purses is gone.

Mrs. Overdo. Is't indeed, brother?

Cokes. Aye, as I am an honest man, would I were an arrant rogue, else! A plague of all roguy, damned cutpurses for me.

Wasp. Bless 'em with all my heart, with all my heart, do you see! Now, as I am no infidel that I know of, I am glad on't. Aye I am; here's my witness! Do you see, sir? I did not tell you of his fables, I? No, no, I am a dull malthorse, I, I know nothing. Are you not justly served i' your conscience now? Speak i' your conscience. Much good do you with all my heart, and his good heart that has it, with all my heart again.

Edgworth. [*Aside.*] This fellow is very charitable; would he had a purse too! But I must not be too bold all at a time.

Cokes. Nay, Numps, it is not my best purse.

Wasp. Not your best! Death! Why should it be your worst? Why should it be any, indeed, at all? Answer me to that, gi' me a reason from you, why it should be any?

Cokes. Nor my gold, Numps; I ha' that yet. Look here else, sister.

Wasp. Why so, there's all the feeling he has!

Mrs. Overdo. I pray you, have a better care of that, brother.

Cokes. Nay, so I will, I warrant you; let him catch this that catch can. I would fain see him get this, look you here.

Wasp. So, so, so, so, so, so, so, so! Very good.

Cokes. I would ha' him come again, now, and but offer at it. Sister, will you take notice of a good jest? I will put it just where th' other was, and if we ha' good luck, you shall see a delicate fine trap to catch the cutpurse, nibbling.

Edgworth. [*Aside.*] Faith, and he'll try ere you be out o' the Fair.

Cokes. Come, Mistress Grace, prithee be not melancholy for my mischance; sorrow wi' not keep it, sweetheart.

Grace. I do not think on't, sir.

Cokes. 'Twas but a little scurvy white money, hang it. It may hang the cutpurse one day. I ha' gold left to gi' thee a fairing, yet, as hard as the world goes. Nothing angers me but that nobody here looked like a cutpurse, unless 'twere Numps.

Wasp. How? I? I look like a cutpurse? Death! Your sister's a cutpurse! And your mother and father and all your kin were cutpurses! And here is a rogue is the bawd o' the cutpurses, whom I will beat to begin with.

They speak all together; and Wasp *beats the* Justice.

Justice Overdo. Hold thy hand, child of wrath, and heir of anger, make it not Childermass day in thy fury, or the feast of the French Bartholomew, parent of the Massacre.

Cokes. Numps, Numps!

Mrs. Overdo. Good Master Humphrey!

Wasp. You are the Patrico, are you? The patriarch of the cutpurses? You share, sir, they say; let them share this with you. Are you i' your hot fit of preaching again? I'll cool you.

Justice Overdo. Murther, murther, murther!

[*Exeunt.*]

Act III

Scene i.

[*Enter* Whit, Haggis, Bristle, Leatherhead, Trash.]

[*Whit.*] Nay, 'tish all gone, now! Dish 'tish, phen tou vilt not be phitin call, Mashter Offisher! Phat ish a man te better to lishen out noishes for tee an' tou art in an oder 'orld – being very

110 chops mouth
111 entertain maintain
114 a peck (as a measure; the capacity of two gallons)
116 s.d. *pick-pack* (hoists him on his own back)
128 malthorse (heavy horse used for pulling brewers' wagons)
152 offer at make an attempt for
159–60 wi' . . . it will not bring it back
162 white money silver
175 Childermass day (feast day of the Holy Innocents, December 28)
176–7 French . . . Massacre (the Catholic massacre of Huguenots in Paris on August 24, 1572, the subject of a play by Marlowe)
180 Patrico hedge-priest of gypsies and vagabonds
III.i.1 'tish 'tis (Whit's lines are an inconsistent attempt to imitate Irish brogue); **phen** when
2 phitin within
3–4 Phat . . . 'orld (Whit has arranged to inform the watch where to make arrests in return for a share of the profits)

shuffishient noishes and gallantsh too, one o' their brabblesh would have fed ush all dish fortnight; but tou art so bushy about beggersh still, tou hast no leishure to intend shentlemen, an't be.

Haggis. Why, I told you, Davy Bristle.

Bristle. Come, come, you told me a pudding, Toby Haggis; a matter of nothing; I am sure it came to nothing! You said, "Let's go to Urs'la's," indeed; but then you met the man with the monsters, and I could not get you from him. An old fool, not leave seeing yet?

Haggis. Why? Who would ha' thought anybody would ha' quarreled so early? Or that the ale o' the Fair would ha' been up so soon?

Whit. Phy, phat a clock tost tou tink it ish, man?

Haggis. I cannot tell.

Whit. Tou art a vishe vatchman, i' te mean teeme.

Haggis. Why? Should the watch go by the clock, or the clock by the watch, I pray?

Bristle. One should go by another, if they did well.

Whit. Tou art right now! Phen didst tou ever know or hear of a shuffishient vatchman but he did tell the clock, phat business soever he had?

Bristle. Nay, that's most true, a sufficient watchman knows what o'clock it is.

Whit. Shleeping, or vaking! ash well as te clock himshelf, or te jack dat shtrikes him!

Bristle. Let's inquire of Master Leatherhead, or Joan Trash here. Master Leatherhead, do you hear, Master Leatherhead?

Whit. If it be a Ledderhead, 'tish a very tick Ledderhead, tat sho mush noish vill not piersh him.

Leatherhead. I have a little business now; good friends, do not trouble me.

Whit. Phat? Because o' ty wrought neet-cap, and ty phelvet sherkin, man? Phy? I have sheen tee in ty ledder sherkin ere now, mashter o' de hobby-horses, as bushy and as stately as tou sheem'st to be.

Trash. Why, what an' you have, Captain Whit? He has his choice of jerkins, you may see by that, and his caps too, I assure you, when he pleases to be either sick, or employed.

Leatherhead. God a mercy, Joan, answer for me.

Whit. Away, be not sheen i' my company; here be shentlemen, and men of vorship.

[*Exeunt* Haggis, Bristle.]

Act III. Scene ii.

[*Enter to them* Quarlous, Winwife.]

[*Quarlous.*] We had wonderful ill luck to miss this prologue o' the purse, but the best is, we shall have five Acts of him ere night; he'll be spectacle enough! I'll answer for't.

Whit. Oh, Creesh! Duke Quarlous, how dosht tou? Tou dosht not know me, I fear? I am te vishesht man, but Justish Overdo, in all Bartholomew Fair, now. Gi' me twelvepence from tee, I vill help tee to a vife vorth forty marks for't, an't be.

Quarlous. Away, rogue, pimp, away.

Whit. And she shall show tee as fine cut-'ork for't in her shmock too, as tou cansht vish, i' faith; vilt tou have her, vorshipful Vinvife? I vill help tee to her, here, be an't be, in te pig-quarter. Gi' me ty twel'pence from tee.

Winwife. Why, there's twel'pence; pray thee, wilt thou be gone?

Whit. Tou art a vorthy man, and a vorshipful man still.

Quarlous. Get you gone, rascal.

Whit. I do mean it, man. Prinsh Quarlous, if tou hasht need on me, tou shalt find me here, at Urs'la's; I vill see phat ale and punk ish i' te pigshty for tee, bless ty good vorship.

[*Exit.*]

Quarlous. Look! Who comes here! John Littlewit!

Winwife. And his wife, and my widow, her mother; the whole family.

Quarlous. 'Slight, you must gi' em all fairings now!

Winwife. Not I, I'll not see 'em.

Quarlous. They are going a-feasting. What schoolmaster's that is with 'em?

Winwife. That's my rival, I believe, the baker!

---

6 **brabblesh** brabbles, brawls
7 **bushy** Zeal-of-the-Land Busy
8 **intend** pay attention to
11 **a pudding** (1) a lot of tripe (colloquial); (2) colloquial for nothing; (3) pun on haggis, a kind of pudding
15 **monsters** freaks
22 **vishe** wise
33 **jack** the mechanical figure that strikes the bell on a public clock
38 **noish** noise; **piersh** pierce, awaken
42 **neet-cap** nightcap
44 **sherkin** jerkin, a man's close-fitting jacket or short-coat
47 **an'** if
52 **sheen** seen
III.ii.5 Creesh Christ
7 **vishesht** wisest
9 **vife** wife
12 **cut-'ork** lace ("cut-work")
20 **still** ever
22 **Prinsh** prince

[*Enter* Busy, Purecraft, Littlewit, Win.]

Busy. So, walk on in the middle way, fore-right, turn neither to the right hand, nor to the left. Let not your eyes be drawn aside with vanity nor your ear with noises.

Quarlous. Oh, I know him by that start!

Leatherhead. What do you lack? What do you buy, pretty Mistress! A fine hobby-horse to make your son a tilter? a drum to make him a soldier? A fiddle, to make him a reveler? What is't you lack? Little dogs for your daughters! Or babies, male or female?

Busy. Look not toward them, hearken not. The place is Smithfield, or the field of smiths, the grove of hobby-horses and trinkets; the wares are the wares of devils. And the whole Fair is the shop of Satan! They are hooks, and baits, very baits, that are hung out on every side, to catch you, and to hold you as it were, by the gills, and by the nostrils, as the fisher doth. Therefore, you must not look, nor turn towards them – the heathen man could stop his ears with wax, against the harlot o' the sea. Do you the like, with your fingers, against the bells of the Beast.

Winwife. What flashes comes from him!

Quarlous. Oh, he has those of his oven! A notable hot baker 'twas, when he plied the peel. He is leading his flock into the Fair now.

Winwife. Rather driving 'em to the pens; for he will let 'em look upon nothing.

[*Enter* Knockem, Whit.]

Knockem. Gentlewomen, the weather's hot! Whither walk you? Have a care o' your fine velvet caps; the Fair is dusty. Take a sweet delicate booth, with boughs, here, i' the way, and cool yourselves i' the shade, you and your friends. The best pig and bottle-ale i' the Fair, sir. Old Urs'la is cook. There you may read; the pig's head speaks it.

Littlewit is gazing at the sign; which is the Pig's Head with a large writing under it.

Poor soul, she has had a stringhalt, the maryhinchco. But she's prettily amended.

Whit. A delicate show-pig, little mistress, with shweet sauce, and crackling, like de bay-leaf i' de fire, la! Tou shalt ha' de clean side o' de table-clot and dy glass vash'd with phatersh of Dame Annessh Cleare.

[*Exit.*]

Littlewit. This's fine, verily: "Here be the best pigs: and she does roast 'em as well as ever she did," the pig's head says.

Knockem. Excellent, excellent, mistress, with fire o' juniper and rosemary branches! The oracle of the pig's head, that, sir.

Purecraft. Son, were you not warned of the vanity of the eye? Have you forgot the wholesome admonition so soon?

Littlewit. Good mother, how shall we find a pig if we do not look about for't? Will it run off o' the spit into our mouths, think you? As in Lubberland? And cry, "We, we"?

Busy. No, but your mother, religiously wise, conceiveth it may offer itself by other means to the sense, as by way of steam, which I think it doth here in this place. Huh, huh – yes, it doth.

Busy scents after it like a hound.

And it were a sin of obstinacy, great obstinacy, high and horrible obstinacy, to decline, or resist the good titillation of the famelic sense, which is the smell. Therefore be bold (huh, huh, huh), follow the scent. Enter the tents of the unclean, for once, and satisfy your wife's frailty. Let your frail wife be satisfied; your

---

34 fore-right forthright; straight forward
38 start language
41 tilter (1) jouster; a ride at the quintain; (2) lecher; (3) rake
42 reveler law student at the Inns of Court
46 place . . . smiths (the correct etymology is "Smetherfelda," smooth field)
52 fisher fisherman
54–5 heathen man . . . sea (Busy misquotes the *Odyssey* where Homer's Odysseus stopped the ears of his crew with wax but had himself tied to the mast of their ship so as to hear the alluring song of the Sirens)
57 bells (Puritans opposed church bells as papist)
58 flashes insights
60 peel baker's shovel for putting loaves in the oven and taking them out
67 delicate succulent
71 s.d. ***Pig's Head*** (Ursula's sign identifies her business for the illiterate)
72–3 stringhalt . . . maryhinchco (diseases affecting horses' hind legs)
74 show-pig sow-pig
77–8 phatersh . . . Cleare (waters from a spring at Hoxton named for a rich widow, Dame Annis (Agnes), who drowned herself there ca. 1300 following a disastrous second marriage to a courtier who spent her fortune and brought her to poverty)
79 verily truly
83 juniper . . . branches (branches burned to purify and give fragrance to the air)
91 Lubberland (Cockaign, an imaginary land of plenitude and idleness where roasted pigs run about asking to be eaten; proverbial)
98 famelic exciting hunger

zealous mother, and my suffering self, will also be satisfied.

Littlewit. Come, Win, as good winny here as go farther and see nothing.

Busy. We 'scape so much of the other vanities by our early ent'ring.

Purecraft. It is an edifying consideration.

Win. This is scurvy, that we must come into the Fair and not look on't.

Littlewit. Win, have patience, Win, I'll tell you more anon.

Knockem. Mooncalf, entertain within there; the best pig i' the booth, a pork-like pig. These are Banbury-bloods, o' the sincere stud, come a pig-hunting. Whit, wait, Whit, look to your charge.

Busy. A pig prepare, presently, let a pig be prepared to us.

[*He leads off Littlewit, Win, Purecraft.*]

[*Enter* Mooncalf, Ursula.]

Mooncalf. 'Slight, who be these?

Ursula. Is this the good service, Jordan, you'd do me?

Knockem. Why, Urs? Why, Urs? Thou'lt ha' vapors i' thy leg again presently; pray thee go in, 't may turn to the scratches else.

Ursula. Hang your vapors, they are stale, and stink like you. Are these the guests o' the game you promised to fill my pit withal today?

Knockem. Aye, what ail they, Urs?

Ursula. Ail they? They are all sippers, sippers o' the city; they look as they would not drink off two penn'orth of bottle-ale among 'em.

Mooncalf. A body may read that i' their small printed ruffs.

Knockem. Away, thou art a fool, Urs, and thy Mooncalf too, i' your ignorant vapors, now! Hence, good guests, I say right hypocrites, good gluttons. In, and set a couple o' pigs o' the board, and half a dozen of the biggest bottles afore 'em, and call Whit. I do not love to hear innocents abused. Fine ambling hypocrites! and a stone-puritan, with a sorrel head, and beard, good mouthed gluttons. Two to a pig; away.

[*Exit* Mooncalf.]

Ursula. Are you sure they are such?

Knockem. O' the right breed, thou shalt try 'em by the teeth, Urs. Where's this Whit?

[*Reenter* Whit.]

Whit. *Behold, man, and see, what a worthy man am ee!*
With the fury of my sword, and the shaking of my beard,
I will make ten thousand men afeard.

Knockem. Well said, brave Whit; in, and fear the ale out o' the bottles into the bellies of the brethren and the sisters. Drink to the cause, and pure vapors.

[*Exeunt* Knockem, Whit, Ursula.]

Quarlous. My roarer is turned tapster, methinks. Now were a fine time for thee, Winwife, to lay aboard thy widow. Thou'lt never be master of a better season or place; she that will venture herself into the Fair, and a pig-box, will admit any assault, be assured of that.

Winwife. I love not enterprises of that suddenness, though.

Quarlous. I'll warrant thee, then, no wife out o' the widow's hundred. If I had but as much title to her, as to have breathed once on that strait stomacher of hers, I would now assure myself to carry her, yet, ere she went out of Smithfield. Or she should carry me, which were the fitter sight, I confess. But you are a modest undertaker, by circumstances, and degrees; come, 'tis disease in thee, not judgment. I should offer at all together. Look, here's the poor fool again that was stung by the wasp, erewhile.

---

105 **winny** stay
116 **sincere stud** true breed (morally uncorrupted; i.e., Puritans)
117–18 **Whit... charge** (Whit is supposed to find women for Ursula's friends; Knockem is asking him to keep an eye on Win, whom he later persuades to go to the puppet show in disguise with Edgworth)
120 **to** for
130 **what ail they** what's wrong with them?
134–5 **small... ruffs** (a style particular to Puritans)
135 **printed** precisely fitted
143 **stone-puritan** lecherous male Puritan (cf. stone-horse, stallion); **sorrel** chestnut-colored (applied to horses)
149–51 ***Behold... afeard*** (unidentified; but may be from a common St. George play)
152 **fear** frighten
154 **cause** Puritanism
155 **pure** Puritan
157–8 **lay aboard** make advances to (in nautical terms, to bring one ship alongside another)
159 **season** time
165 **widow's hundred** (reference to property or inheritance; a hundred was a subdivision of an English county having its own court)
167 **stomacher** (ornamental covering of a woman's chest under a laced bodice)
168 **carry** win
171 **undertaker** executor; one who undertakes something
173 **offer... together** go all the way; risk everything

Act III. Scene iii.

[*Enter*] Justice.

[*Justice Overdo.*] I will make no more orations, shall draw on these tragical conclusions. And I begin now to think that, by a spice of collateral justice, Adam Overdo deserved this beating; for I, the said Adam, was one cause (a by-cause) why the purse was lost; and my wife's brother's purse too, which they know not of yet. But I shall make very good mirth with it at supper (that will be the sport), and put my little friend Master Humphrey Wasp's choler quite out of countenance. When, sitting at the upper end o' my table, as I use, and drinking to my brother Cokes and Mistress Alice Overdo, as I will, my wife, for their good affection to old Bradley, I deliver to 'em it was I that was cudgeled, and show 'em the marks. To see what bad events may peep out o' the tail of good purposes! The care I had of that civil young man I took fancy to this morning (and have not left it yet) drew me to that exhortation which drew the company, indeed, which drew the cutpurse; which drew the money; which drew my brother Cokes his loss; which drew on Wasp's anger; which drew on my beating: a pretty gradation! And they shall ha' it i' their dish, i' faith, at night for fruit. I love to be merry at my table. I had thought once, at one special blow he ga' me, to have revealed myself! But then (I thank thee, fortitude) I remembered that a wise man (and who is ever so great a part o' the Commonwealth in himself) for no particular disaster ought to abandon a public good design. The husbandman ought not, for one unthankful year, to forsake the plow; the shepherd ought not, for one scabbed sheep, to throw by his tar-box; the pilot ought not, for one leak i' the poop, to quit the helm; nor the alderman ought not, for one custard more at a meal, to give up his cloak; the constable ought not to break his staff, and forswear the watch, for one roaring night; nor the piper o' the parish (*ut parvis componere magna solebam*) to put up his pipes for one rainy Sunday. These are certain knocking conclusions, out of which I am resolved, come what come can – come beating, come imprisonment, come infamy, come banishment, nay, come the rack, come the hurdle, welcome all – I will not discover who I am till my due time; and yet still all shall be, as I said ever, in Justice' name, and the King's, and for the Commonwealth!

Winwife. What does he talk to himself, and act so seriously? Poor fool!

[*Exit* Justice.]

Quarlous. No matter what. Here's fresher argument, intend that.

Act III. Scene iv.

[*Enter to them* Cokes, Mistress Overdo, Grace, Wasp.]

[*Cokes.*] Come, Mistress Grace, come sister; here's more fine sights yet, i' faith. God's lid, where's Numps?

Leatherhead. What do you lack, gentlemen? What is't you buy? Fine rattles! Drums? Babies? Little dogs? And birds for ladies? What do you lack?

Cokes. Good honest Numps, keep afore. I am so afraid thou'lt lose somewhat, my heart was at my mouth when I missed thee.

Wasp. You were best buy a whip i' your hand to drive me.

Cokes. Nay, do not mistake, Numps, thou art so apt to mistake. I would but watch the goods. Look you now, the treble fiddle was e'en almost like to be lost.

Wasp. Pray you take heed you lose not yourself. Your best way were e'en get up and ride for more surety. Buy a token's worth of great pins to fasten yourself to my shoulder.

III.iii.1–2 shall draw on to lead to
3 collateral concomitant
4–5 by-cause secondary or incidental cause
8 sport entertainment
9 choler anger; irascibility
10–11 upper end (privileged place, for the host or most distinguished guests)
20–2 which ... loss (a parody of lawyer's reasoning; cf. lines 32–43 below)
25 fruit e.g., dessert; the final entertaining conversation
29–31 who ... himself (Cicero's ideal statesman; a commonplace)
32–3 husbandman farmer
35–6 tar-box (tar salve was used as a cure for skin diseases of sheep)
37 poop stern of a ship
38 custard guest (i.e., one extra serving)
39 cloak office; position (as host)
41 roaring noisy; unruly; **piper ... parish** (piper employed by a parish to play at church-ales and other functions)
41–2 *ut ... solebam* "thus it was my habit to compare great things to small ones" (Virgil, *Eclogues* I. 23, with *sic* for *ut*)
44 knocking decisive
47 rack instrument of torture in which limbs were pulled outwards
48 hurdle a sledge used to drag traitors publicly to their executions
52 What why
54 fresher more recent;
55 intend listen to
III.iv.14 treble fiddle violin with the highest pitch

Leatherhead. What do you lack, gentlemen? Fine purses, pouches, pincases, pipes? What is't you lack? A pair o' smiths to wake you i' the morning? Or a fine whistling bird?

Cokes. Numps, here be finer things than any we ha' bought, by odds! And more delicate horses, a great deal! Good Numps, stay, and come hither.

Wasp. Will you scourse with him? You are in Smithfield; you may fit yourself with a fine easy-going street-nag for your saddle again' Michaelmas term, do. Has he ne'er a little odd cart for you to make a caroche on i' the country, with four pied hobby-horses? Why the measles should you stand here, with your train, cheaping of dogs, birds, and babies? You ha' no children to bestow 'em on? Ha' you?

Cokes. No, but again' I ha' children, Numps, that's all one.

Wasp. Do, do, do, do; how many shall you have, think you? An' I were as you, I'd buy for all my tenants, too. They are a kind o' civil savages that will part with their children for rattles, pipes, and knives. You were best buy a hatchet or two, and truck with 'em.

Cokes. Good Numps, hold that little tongue o' thine, and save it a labor. I am resolute Bat, thou know'st.

Wasp. A resolute fool you are, I know, and a very sufficient coxcomb; with all my heart; nay, you have it, sir, an' you be angry, turd i' your teeth, twice (if I said it not once afore), and much good do you.

Winwife. Was there ever such a self-affliction? And so impertinent?

Quarlous. Alas! his care will go near to crack him. Let's in and comfort him.

Wasp. Would I had been set i' the ground, all but the head on me, and had my brains bowled at, or threshed out, when first I underwent this plague of a charge!

Quarlous. How now, Numps! Almost tired i' your protectorship? Overparted? Overparted?

Wasp. Why, I cannot tell, sir; it may be I am; does't grieve you?

Quarlous. No, I swear does't not, Numps, to satisfy you.

Wasp. Numps? 'Sblood, you are fine and familiar! How long ha' we been acquainted, I pray you?

Quarlous. I think it may be remembr'ed, Numps, that? 'Twas since morning sure.

Wasp. Why, I hope I know't well enough, sir; I did not ask to be told.

Quarlous. No? Why then?

Wasp. It's no matter why; you see with your eyes, now, what I said to you today? You'll believe me another time?

Quarlous. Are you removing the Fair, Numps?

Wasp. A pretty question! And a very civil one! Yes, faith, I ha' my lading you see, or shall have anon; you may know whose beast I am by my burden. If the pannier-man's jack were ever better known by his loins of mutton, I'll be flayed and feed dogs for him when his time comes.

Winwife. How melancholy Mistress Grace is yonder! Pray thee, let's go enter ourselves in grace with her.

Cokes. Those six horses, friend, I'll have –

Wasp. How!

Cokes. And the three Jew's trumps; and half a dozen o'birds, and that drum (I have one drum already) and your smiths (I like that device o' your smiths, very pretty well) and four halberts – and (le' me see) that fine painted great lady and her three women for state, I'll have.

Wasp. No, the shop. Buy the whole shop, it will be best; the shop, the shop!

Leatherhead. If his worship please.

Wasp. Yes, and keep it during the Fair, bobchin.

Cokes. Peace, Numps. Friend, do not meddle with him, an' you be wise, and would show your head above board. He will sting through your wrought nightcap, believe me. A set of these violins I would buy too, for a delicate young

22 **A . . . smiths** a clock with a pair of jacks to make the chime
28 **scourse** discourse, bargain
30 **again'** against; in preparation for
31 **Michaelmas term** law term following Michaelmas (September 29)
32 **caroche** fashionable carriage
33 **pied** spotted
35 **cheaping of** bargaining for
37 **again'** anticipating when
38 **that's all one** it's the same thing
41 **civil savages** civilized simpletons
44 **truck** deal
49 **coxcomb** fool (from the cock's comb on his costume)
55 **crack him** drive him insane
62 **Overparted** (given a larger part than you can handle)
81 **pannier-man** at the Inns of Court, one who brought provisions from the market; **jack** servant; knave
83 **flayed** skinned
86 **grace** (1) favor; (2) conversation
90 **trumps** harps
96 **state** ceremonial display
100 **bobchin** idle chatterer; imbecile; one socially inferior
103 **above board** in company (with pun on board as the tray for his wares)
105 **delicate** fine

noise I have i' the country, that are every one a size less than another, just like your fiddles. I would fain have a fine young masque at my marriage, now I think on't. But I do want such a number o' things! And Numps will not help me now, and I dare not speak to him.

Trash. Will your worship buy any ginger-bread, very good bread, comfortable bread?

Cokes. Ginger-bread! Yes, let's see.

He runs to her shop.

Wasp. There's the tother springe!

Leatherhead. Is this well, goody Joan? To interrupt my market? In the midst? And call away my customers? Can you answer this, at the Pie-powders?

Trash. Why? If his mastership have a mind to buy, I hope my ware lies as open as another's. I may show my ware as well as you yours.

Cokes. Hold your peace; I'll content you both. I'll buy up his shop, and thy basket.

Wasp. Will you, i'faith?

Leatherhead. Why should you put him from it, friend?

Wasp. Cry you mercy! You'd be sold too, would you? What's the price on you? Jerkin, and all as you stand? Ha' you any qualities?

Trash. Yes, good-man angry-man, you shall find he has qualities, if you cheapen him.

Wasp. God's so, you ha' the selling of him! What are they? Will they be bought for love or money?

Trash. No indeed, sir.

Wasp. For what then? Victuals?

Trash. He scorns victuals, sir; he has bread and butter at home, thanks be to God! And yet he will do more for a good meal if the toy take him i' the belly. Marry, then, they must not set him at lower end; if they do, he'll go away, though he fast. But put him atop o' the table, where his place is, and he'll do you forty fine things. He has not been sent for, and sought out, for nothing, at your great city-suppers, to put down Coriat, and Cokely, and been laughed at for his labor. He'll play you all the puppets i' the town over, and the players, every company, and his own company too. He spares nobody!

Cokes. I'faith?

Trash. He was the first, sir, that ever baited the fellow i' the bear's skin, an't like your worship. No dog ever came near him, since. And for fine motions!

Cokes. Is he good at those, too? Can he set out a masque, trow?

Trash. Oh, Lord, Master! sought to, far and near, for his inventions! And he engrosses all, he makes all the puppets i' the Fair.

Cokes. Dost thou (in troth), old velvet Jerkin? Give me thy hand.

Trash. Nay, sir, you shall see him in his velvet jerkin, and a scarf, too, at night, when you hear him interpret Master Littlewit's motion.

Cokes. Speak no more, but shut up shop presently, friend. I'll buy both it and thee too to carry down with me, and her hamper beside. Thy shop shall furnish out the masque, and hers the banquet. I cannot go less, to set out anything with credit. What's the price, at a word, o' thy whole shop, case and all as it stands?

Leatherhead. Sir, it stands me in six and twenty shillings sevenpence halfpenny, besides three shillings for my ground.

Cokes. Well, thirty shillings will do all, then! And what comes yours to?

Trash. Four shillings and elevenpence, sir, ground and all, an't like your worship.

Cokes. Yes, it does like my worship very well, poor woman, that's five shillings more. What a masque shall I furnish out for forty shillings (twenty pound Scotch)! And a banquet of ginger-bread! There's a stately thing! Numps! Sister! And my wedding gloves too! (That I never thought on afore.) All my wedding gloves, ginger-bread! Oh, me! What a device will there be, to make 'em eat their fingers'

---

106 noise3consort of musicians

108 masque group of masquers

115 springe snare (used to catch birds)

130 qualities accomplishments

132 cheapen (1) bargain for; (2) examine

133 God's so (from *cazzo*, Italian for penis)

136 Victuals (1) supplies; (2) food

139 toy attraction

141 lower end (of the table; for guests of lower station)

146 Coriat (Thomas Coryate [1557?–1617], known for his travels through Europe recorded in *Coryats Crudities* [1611] to which Jonson contributed mock-commendatory verses); **Cokely** (a jester well known for his improvisations)

152–3 baited . . . skin (in *The Knave of Hearts* [1612], Samuel Rowlands tells of an actor at the Fortune who played a bear)

156 set out stage

157 trow do you believe?

158 sought resorted, appealed

159 engrosses monopolizes

164 at night this evening

165 interpret ventriloquize

170 banquet dessert; **I . . . less** it's the least I can do (from gambling term in primero, meaning "match the highest bid")

172 stands costs

183 twenty pound Scotch (when Scotland and England were joined in 1603 the Scots pound was valued at one-twelfth the English pound)

185 wedding gloves (the groom's customary gift to guests at his wedding)

ends! And delicate brooches for the bridemen! And all! And then I'll ha' this posy put to 'em: "For the best grace," meaning Mistress Grace. My wedding posy!

Grace. I am beholden to you, sir, and to your Bartholomew-wit.

Wasp. You do not mean this, do you? Is this your first purchase?

Cokes. Yes, faith, and I do not think, Numps, but thou'lt say, it was the wisest act that ever I did in my wardship.

Wasp. Like enough! I shall say anything, I!

Act III. Scene v.

[*Enter to them* Justice, Edgworth, Nightingale.]

[*Justice Overdo.*] [*Aside.*] I cannot beget a project with all my political brain yet. My project is how to fetch off this proper young man from his debauched company. I have followed him all the Fair over, and still I find him with this songster; and I begin shrewdly to suspect their familiarity. And the young man of a terrible taint, poetry! with which idle disease if he be infected, there's no hope of him, in a state-course. *Actum est* of him for a commonwealths-man, if he go to't in rhyme once.

Edgworth. [*To Nightingale.*] Yonder he is buying o' ginger-bread. Set in quickly, before he part with too much of his money.

Nightingale. *My masters and friends, and good people, draw near, &c.*

Cokes. Ballads! Hark, hark! Pray thee, fellow, stay a little; good Numps, look to the goods. What ballads hast thou? Let me see, let me see myself!

He runs to the ballad-man.

Wasp. Why, so! He's flown to another lime-bush; there he will flutter as long more, till he ha' ne'er a feather left. Is there a vexation like this, gentlemen? Will you believe me now, hereafter? Shall I have credit with you?

Quarlous. Yes, faith, shalt thou, Numps, an' thou art worthy on't, for thou sweatest for't. I never saw a young pimp errant and his squire better matched.

Winwife. Faith, the sister comes after 'em well, too.

Grace. Nay, if you saw the Justice her husband, my guardian, you were fitted for the mess; he is such a wise one his way –

Winwife. I wonder we see him not here.

Grace. Oh, he is too serious for this place, and yet better sport than the other three, I assure you, gentlemen, where'er he is, though 't be o' the bench.

Cokes. How dost thou call it? *A caveat against cutpurses*! A good jest, i' faith; I would fain see that demon, your cutpurse you talk of, that delicate-handed devil. They say he walks hereabout. I would see him walk, now. Look you, sister, here, here, let him come, sister, and welcome.

He shows his purse boastingly.

Ballad-man, does any cutpurses haunt hereabout? Pray thee, raise me one or two. Begin and show me one.

Nightingale. Sir, this is a spell against 'em, spick and span new; and 'tis made as 'twere in mine own person, and I sing it in mine own defense. But 'twill cost a penny alone, if you buy it.

Cokes. No matter for the price. Thou dost not know me, I see; I am an odd Bartholomew.

Mrs. Overdo. Has't a fine picture, brother?

Cokes. Oh, sister, do you remember the ballads over the nursery-chimney at home o' my own pasting up? There be brave pictures. Other manner of pictures than these, friend.

Wasp. Yet these will serve to pick the pictures out o' your pockets, you shall see.

Cokes. So I heard 'em say. Pray thee mind him not, fellow; he'll have an oar in everything.

Nightingale. It was intended, sir. As if a purse should chance to be cut in my presence, now, I may be blameless, though, as by the sequel will more plainly appear.

Cokes. We shall find that i' the matter. Pray thee, begin.

---

189 bridemen (male attendants to the groom)
190 posy motto (inscribed in the ring)
194 Bartholomew-wit (derisory)
III.v.2 political shrewd, policy-directed
3 fetch off rescue; **proper** fine
9–10 state-course place in the commonwealth
10 ***Actum est*** of "it's all up with"
10–11 commonwealths-man good citizen
11 go to't indulge
13 Set in move in
20 lime-bush snare; attraction (a bush smeared with lime as a trap)
21 more again
24 have credit your agreement
27 pimp errant (Nightingale, as wandering purveyor); **squire** Cokes
29 sister Mistress Overdo
31 mess group of four persons (from common seating plans at banquets)
41 walks lurks (as a demonic spirit that haunts the Fair)
46 raise me bring before me
53 odd (1) particular; (2) unusual
59 pictures coins (showing the King's head)

Nightingale. To the tune of *Paggington's Pound*, sir.

Cokes. Fa, la la la, la la la, fa la la la. Nay, I'll put thee in tune, and all! Mine own country dance! Pray thee, begin.

Nightingale. It is a gentle admonition, you must know, sir, both to the purse-cutter and the purse-bearer.

Cokes. Not a word more, out o' the tune, an' thou lov'st me. Fa, la la la, la la la, fa la la la. Come, when?

Nightingale. *My masters and friends and good people draw near,*
And look to your purses, for that I do say;

Cokes. Ha, ha, this chimes! Good counsel at first dash.

Nightingale. *And though little money, in them you do bear,*
It cost more to get, than to lose in a day.

Cokes. – Good! –

Nightingale. *You oft have been told,*
Both the young and the old;
And bidden beware of the cutpurse so bold;

Cokes. – Well said! He were to blame that would not, i' faith. –

Nightingale. *Then if you take heed not, free me from the curse,*
Who both give you warning, for and the cutpurse.
Youth, youth, thou hadst better been starved by thy nurse,
Than live to be hanged for cutting a purse.

Cokes. – Good i' faith, how say you, Numps? Is there any harm i' this?—

Nightingale. *It hath been upbraided to men of my trade,*
That oftentimes we are the cause of this crime.

Cokes. – The more coxcombs they that did it, I wusse. –

Nightingale. *Alack and for pity, why should it be said?*
As if they regarded or places, or time.
Examples have been
Of some that were seen,
In Westminster Hall, yea, the pleaders between,
Then why should the judges be free from this curse,
More than my poor self, for cutting the purse?

Cokes. – God a mercy for that! Why should they be more free indeed? –

Nightingale. *Youth, youth, thou hadst better been starved by thy nurse,*
Than live to be hanged for cutting a purse.

Cokes. – That again, good ballad-man, that again.

He sings the burden with him.

Oh, rare! I would fain rub mine elbow now, but I dare not pull out my hand. On, I pray thee; he that made this ballad shall be poet to my masque. –

Nightingale. *At Worc'ster, 'tis known well, and even i' the jail,*
A knight of good worship did there show his face,
Against the foul sinners, in zeal for to rail,
And lost (ipso facto) *his purse in the place.*

Cokes. – Is it possible? –

Nightingale. *Nay, once from the seat*
Of judgment so great,
A judge there did lose a fair pouch of velvet.

Cokes. – I' faith? –

Nightingale. *O Lord for thy mercy, how wicked or worse*
Are those that so venture their necks for a purse!
Youth, youth, &c.

Cokes. *Youth, youth, &c.*
Pray thee, stay a little, friend; yet o' thy conscience,
Numps, speak; is there any harm i' this?

Wasp. To tell you true, 'tis too good for you, 'less you had grace to follow it.

Justice Overdo. [*Aside.*] It doth discover enormity. I'll mark it more. I ha' not liked a paltry piece of poetry so well, a good while.

Cokes. *Youth, youth, &c.*
Where's this youth, now? A man must call upon him for his own good, and yet he will not appear. Look here, here's for him; handy-dandy, which hand will he have?

He shows his purse.

On, I pray thee, with the rest; I do hear of him, but I cannot see him, this Master Youth, the cutpurse.

Nightingale. *At plays and at sermons, and at the sessions,*
'Tis daily their practice such booty to make.

---

69 ***Paggington's Pound*** ("Packington's Pound," an old country dance still extant)
76 **out o'** extraneous to; not a part of
81 **chimes** rings true; harmonizes
81–2 **at ... dash** from the street
97–8 ***It ... crime*** (ballad singers were commonly thought to be confederate with cutpurses)
97 ***upbraided*** alleged
105 ***Westminster Hall*** (as site of the Courts of Common Pleas, Chancery, and the King's Bench)
112 **s.d. *burden*** chorus
113 **rub mine elbow** (sign of pleasure)
115 **poet to** poet for
122–4 ***Nay, ... velvet*** (reference to the contemporary play on Sir Thomas More which recounts a similar incident in which More proved general vulnerability by asking an alleged cutpurse to take the purse of the judge, which he managed)
130 **stay** pause
132 **'less** unless
133 **grace** the good sense
140–1 **handy-dandy** (refers to a children's guessing game about which hand secretly held something)
145 ***sessions*** law sessions when the court sits

Yea, under the gallows, at executions,
They stick not the stare-abouts' purses to take.
Nay, one without grace,
At a far better place,
At court, and in Christmas, before the King's face.

Cokes. – That was a fine fellow! I would have him, now. –

Nightingale. *Alack then for pity, must I bear the curse,*
That only belongs to the cunning cutpurse?

Cokes. But where's their cunning, now, when they should use it? They are all chained now, I warrant you.

Youth, youth, thou hadst better, &c.

The rat-catcher's charm! Are all fools and asses to this? A pox on 'em, that they will not come! That a man should have such a desire to a thing, and want it.

Quarlous. 'Fore God, I'd give half the Fair, an' 'twere mine, for a cutpurse for him to save his longing.

Cokes. Look you, sister, here, here, where is't now? Which pocket is't in, for a wager?

He shows his purse again.

Wasp. I beseech you leave your wagers, and let him end his matter, an't may be.

Cokes. Oh, are you edified, Numps?

Justice Overdo. [*Aside.*] Indeed, he does interrupt him too much. There Numps spoke to purpose.

Cokes. Sister, I am an ass, I cannot keep my purse.

[*He shows it*] *again.*

– On, on; I pray thee, friend.

Winwife. Will you see sport? look, there's a fellow gathers up to him, mark.

Edgworth gets up to him and tickles him in the ear with a straw twice to draw his hand out of his pocket.

Quarlous. Good, i' faith! Oh, he has lighted on the wrong pocket.

Winwife. He has it, 'fore God, He is a brave fellow; pity he should be detected. –

Nightingale. *But Oh, you vile nation of cutpurses all,*
Relent and repent, and amend and be sound,
And know that you ought not, by honest men's fall,
Advance your own fortunes, to die above ground,
And though you go gay,
In silks as you may,
It is not the high way to heaven (as they say).
Repent then, repent you, for better, for worse;
And kiss not the gallows for cutting a purse.
Youth, youth, thou hadst better been starved by thy nurse,
Than live to be hanged for cutting a purse.

All. An excellent ballad! An excellent ballad!

Edgworth. Friend, let me ha' the first, let me ha' the first, I pray you.

Cokes. Pardon me, sir. First come, first served; and I'll buy the whole bundle too.

Winwife. That conveyance was better than all. Did you see't? He has given the purse to the ballad-singer.

Quarlous. Has he?

Edgworth. Sir, I cry you mercy; I'll not hinder the poor man's profit. Pray you, mistake me not.

Cokes. Sir, I take you for an honest gentleman, if that be mistaking; I met you today afore. Ha! Hum'h! Oh! God! My purse is gone, my purse, my purse, &c.

Wasp. Come, do not make a stir and cry yourself an ass through the Fair afore your time.

Cokes. Why, hast thou it, Numps? Good Numps, how came you by it? I marvel!

Wasp. I pray you seek some other gamester to play the fool with: you may lose it time enough, for all your Fair-wit.

Cokes. By this good hand, glove and all, I ha' lost it already, if thou hast it not. Feel else, and Mistress Grace's handkerchief, too, out o' the tother pocket.

Wasp. Why, 'tis well; very well, exceeding pretty, and well.

Edgworth. Are you sure you ha' lost it, sir?

Cokes. Oh, God! yes, as I am an honest man, I had it but e'en now, at "Youth, youth."

Nightingale. I hope you suspect not me, sir.

Edgworth. Thee? That were a jest indeed! Dost thou think the gentleman is foolish? Where hadst thou hands, I pray thee? Away, ass, away.

[*Exit* Nightingale.]

Justice Overdo. [*Aside.*] I shall be beaten again, if I be spied.

Edgworth. Sir, I suspect an odd fellow, yonder, is stealing away.

149–50 ***Nay . . . face*** (the cutpurse John Selden stole a purse during a celebration of the sacrament in the King's Chapel at Whitehall on Christmas Day 1611; he was hanged on January 7, 1612)

159 rat-catcher's charm (refers to belief that bards could kill rats or drive them away by musical verses; Cokes feels he can charm pickpockets as the Pied Piper of Hamelin charmed rats)

162 to for; **want** lack; be unable to get

169 matter (1) business; (2) performance

185 ***above ground*** on the scaffold

209 through throughout

228 shall ought to

230 suspect take note of

Mrs. Overdo. Brother, it is the preaching fellow! You shall suspect him. He was at your tother purse, you know! Nay, stay, sir, and view the work you ha' done; an' you be beneficed at the gallows, and preach there, thank your own handiwork.

Cokes. Sir, you shall take no pride in your preferment. You shall be silenced quickly.

Justice Overdo. What do you mean, sweet buds of gentility?

Cokes. To ha' my pennyworths out on you. Bud! No less than two purses a day, serve you? I thought you a simple fellow, when my man Numps beat you i' the morning, and pitied you –

Mrs. Overdo. So did I, I'll be sworn, brother; but now I see he is a lewd, and pernicious enormity (as Master Overdo calls him.)

Justice Overdo. [*Aside.*] Mine own words turned upon me, like swords.

Cokes. Cannot a man's purse be at quiet for you, i' the master's pocket, but you must entice it forth, and debauch it?

[*Justice is carried off.*]

Wasp. Sir, sir, keep your debauch and your fine Bartholomew-terms to yourself; and make as much on 'em as you please. But gi' me this from you, i' the meantime: I beseech you, see if I can look to this.

Wasp takes the license from him.

Cokes. Why, Numps?

Wasp. Why? Because you are an ass, sir, there's a reason the shortest way, an' you will needs ha' it. Now you ha' got the trick of losing, you'd lose your breech, an't 'twere loose. I know you, sir, come, deliver, you'll go and crack the vermin you breed now, will you? 'Tis very fine, will you ha' the truth on't? They are such retchless flies as you are, that blow cutpurses abroad in every corner; your foolish having of money makes 'em. An' there were no wiser than I, sir, the trade should lie open for you, sir, it should i' faith, sir. I would teach your wit to come to your head, sir, as well as your land to come into your hand, I assure you, sir.

Winwife. Alack, good Numps.

Wasp. Nay, gentlemen, never pity me, I am not worth it. Lord send me at home once, to Harrow o' the Hill again. If I travel any more, call me Coriat, with all my heart.

[*Exeunt* Wasp, Cokes *and* Mistress Overdo.]

Quarlous. Stay, sir, I must have a word with you in private. Do you hear?

Edgworth. With me, sir? What's your pleasure, good sir?

Quarlous. Do not deny it. You are a cutpurse, sir; this gentleman here, and I saw you, nor do we mean to detect you, though we can sufficiently inform ourselves toward the danger of concealing you. But you must do us a piece of service.

Edgworth. Good gentlemen, do not undo me; I am a civil young man, and but a beginner, indeed.

Quarlous. Sir, your beginning shall bring on your ending for us. We are no catchpoles nor constables. That you are to undertake, is this: you saw the old fellow with the black box here?

Edgworth. The little old governor, sir?

Quarlous. That same. I see you have flown him to a mark already. I would ha' you get away that box from him and bring it us.

Edgworth. Would you ha' the box and all, sir? Or only that, that is in't? I'll get you that and leave him the box to play with still (which will be the harder o' the two), because I would gain your worship's good opinion of me.

Winwife. He says well. 'Tis the greater mastery, and 'twill make the more sport when 'tis missed.

Edgworth. Aye, and 'twill be the longer a-missing, to draw on the sport.

Quarlous. But look you do it now, sirrah, and keep your word, or –

235–7 an' . . . handiwork (some preachers made a practice of hearing speeches of repentance at the gallows and some, like Henry Goodcole, preacher at Newgate, then published them for the edification of others)

235–6 beneficed . . . preach (condemned to be hanged and to sermonize on repentance before your death)

242 pennyworths revenge

254 debauch it induce it to depart

268 retchless heedless; **blow** beget

270–1 An' . . . I if I had my way

271–2 the . . . you you would be apprenticed to a trade

280 Coriat fool (Coryat was, according to Jonson, a well-known bore)

286–7 nor . . . you yet we do not mean to expose you

288 toward about

292 civil respectable; well-behaved

295 for us for all we care; **catchpoles** sheriff's officer or sergeant (a petty law officer empowered to make arrests)

295–6 constables officers of the peace

296 That that which

298 governor tutor

299–300 flown . . . mark identified him

307 mastery feat, exercise of skill

Edgworth. Sir, if ever I break my word with a gentleman, may I never read word at my need. Where shall I find you?

Quarlous. Somewhere i' the Fair hereabouts. Dispatch it quickly. I would fain see the careful fool deluded! Of all beasts, I love the serious ass; he that takes paints to be one, and plays the fool with the greatest diligence that can be.

Grace. Then you would not choose, sir, but love my guardian, Justice Overdo, who is answerable to that description in every hair of him.

Quarlous. So I have heard. But how came you, Mistress Wellborn, to be his ward, or have relation to him, at first?

Grace. Faith, through a common calamity, he bought me, sir; and now he will marry me to his wife's brother, this wise gentleman that you see, or else I must pay value o' my land.

Quarlous. 'Slid, is there no device of disparagement, or so? Talk with some crafty fellow, some picklock o' the Law! Would I had studied a year longer i' the Inns of Court, an't had been but i' your case.

Winwife. [*Aside.*] Aye, Master Quarlous, are you proffering?

Grace. You'd bring but little aid, sir.

Winwife. [*Aside.*] I'll look to you i' faith, gamester. [*To all.*] An unfortunate foolish tribe you are fall'n into, lady, I wonder you can endure 'em.

Grace. Sir, they that cannot work their fetters off must wear 'em.

Winwife. You see what care they have on you, to leave you thus.

Grace. Faith, the same they have of themselves, sir. I cannot greatly complain, if this were all the plea I had against 'em.

Winwife. 'Tis true! But will you please to withdraw with us a little, and make them think they have lost you. I hope our manners ha' been such hitherto, and our language, as will give you no cause to doubt yourself in our company.

Grace. Sir, I will give myself no cause; I am so secure of mine own manners, as I suspect not yours.

Quarlous. Look where John Littlewit comes.

Winwife. Away. I'll not be seen by him.

Quarlous. No, you were not best. He'd tell his mother, the widow.

Winwife. Heart, what do you mean?

Quarlous. Cry you mercy, is the wind there? Must not the widow be named?

[*Exeunt* Grace, Winwife, Quarlous.]

Act III. Scene vi.

[*Enter to them* Littlewit, Win.]

[*Littlewit.*] Do you hear, Win, Win?

Win. What say you, John?

Littlewit. While they are paying the reckoning, Win, I'll tell you a thing, Win. We shall never see any sights i' the Fair, Win, except you long still, Win; good Win, sweet Win, long to see some hobby-horses, and some drums, and rattles, and dogs, and fine devices, Win. The bull with the five legs, Win; and the great hog: now you ha' begun with pig, you may long for anything, Win, and so for my motion, Win.

Win. But we sha' not eat o' the bull and the hog, John, how shall I long then?

Littlewit. Oh, yes! Win, you may long to see, as well as to taste, Win. How did the 'pothecary's wife, Win, that longed to see the anatomy, Win? Or the lady, Win, that desired to spit i' the great lawyer's mouth, after an eloquent pleading? I assure you they longed, Win; good Win, go in, and long.

[*Exeunt* Littlewit, Win.]

Trash. I think we are rid of our new customer, brother Leatherhead, we shall hear no more of him.

They plot to be gone.

Leatherhead. All the better! Let's pack up all, and be gone before he find us.

---

315 read word (i.e., the "neck-verse" to avoid execution; cf. I.iv.9)

329 bought me (Grace's guardianship was sold to Justice Overdo by the Court of Wards, which administered the estates of all minors inheriting from tenants of the King; this abusive practice, established under Henry VIII, reached larger proportions during the reign of Elizabeth I)

331 or . . . land (if the ward refused the guardian's choice of spouse, the guardian was entitled to recover the settlement of the marriage from the ward)

332–3 disparagement (a situation where, if the guardian sought marriage of the ward with one of inferior rank, the match would not go forward; Grace could keep her property if she could show her marriage to Cokes was to someone of lower station)

334 picklock one who finds loopholes

338 proffering (1) making an offer of marriage; (2) making sexual advances

339 little aid insufficient means

340 look to you keep an eye on you

354 doubt have fears for

356 secure confident in; **manners** ethics

360 were . . . best had best not

363 is . . . there? "is that the case?" (proverbial)

III.vi.3 reckoning bill

16 anatomy skeleton

17–18 to . . . mouth (as a form of reward and encouragement; proverbial)

Trash. Stay a little; yonder comes a company. It may be we may take some more money.

[*Enter*] Knockem, Busy.

Knockem. Sir, I will take your counsel, and cut my hair and leave vapors. I see that tobacco, and bottle-ale, and pig, and Whit, and very Urs'la herself, is all vanity.

Busy. Only pig was not comprehended in my admonition, the rest were. For long hair, it is an ensign of pride, a banner, and the world is full of those banners, very full of banners. And bottle-ale is a drink of Satan's, a diet-drink of Satan's, devised to puff us up and make us swell in this latter age of vanity, as the smoke of tobacco to keep us in mist and error. But the fleshly woman (which you call Urs'la) is above all to be avoided, having the marks upon her of the three enemies of man: the world, as being in the Fair; the devil, as being in the fire; and the flesh, as being herself.

[*Enter* Purecraft.]

Purecraft. Brother Zeal-of-the-land, what shall we do? My daughter, Win-the-fight, is fall'n into her fit of longing again.

Busy. For more pig? There is no more, is there?

Purecraft. To see some sights i' the Fair.

Busy. Sister, let her fly the impurity of the place, swiftly, lest she partake of the pitch thereof. Thou art the seat of the Beast, oh, Smithfield, and I will leave thee. Idolatry peepeth out on every side of thee.

Knockem. An excellent right hypocrite! Now his belly is full, he falls a-railing and kicking, the jade. A very good vapor! I'll in, and joy Urs'la with telling how her pig works; two and a half he eat to his share. And he has drunk a pailfull. He eats with his eyes as well as his teeth.

[*Exit.*]

Leatherhead. What do you lack, gentlemen? What is't you buy? Rattles, drums, babies –

Busy. Peace, with thy apocryphal wares, thou profane publican: thy bells, thy dragons, and thy Toby's dogs. Thy hobby-horse is an idol, a very idol, a fierce and rank idol; and thou the Nebuchadnezzar, the proud Nebuchadnezzar of the Fair, that sett'st it up for children to fall down to and worship.

Leatherhead. Cry you mercy, sir, will you buy a fiddle to fill up your noise?

[*Reenter* Littlewit, Win.]

Littlewit. Look, Win. Do. Look o' God's name, and save your longing. Here be fine sights.

Purecraft. Aye, child, so you hate 'em, as our Brother Zeal does, you may look on 'em.

Leatherhead. Or what do you say to a drum, sir?

Busy. It is the broken belly of the Beast, and thy bellows there are his lungs, and these pipes are his throat, those feathers are of his tail, and thy rattles, the gnashing of his teeth.

Trash. And what's my ginger-bread? I pray you.

Busy. The provender that pricks him up. Hence with thy basket of popery, thy nest of images and whole legend of ginger-work.

Leatherhead. Sir, if you be not quiet the quicklier, I'll ha' you clapped fairly by the heels, for disturbing the Fair.

Busy. The sin of the Fair provokes me; I cannot be silent.

Purecraft. Good brother Zeal!

Leatherhead. Sir, I'll make you silent, believe it.

Littlewit. I'd give a shilling you could, i' faith, friend.

Leatherhead. Sir, give me your shilling; I'll give you my shop, if I do not, and I'll leave it in pawn with you, i' the meantime.

Littlewit. A match i' faith, but do it quickly, then.

[*Exit* Leatherhead.]

Busy. Hinder me not, woman.

He speaks to the widow.

I was moved in spirit to be here, this day, in this Fair, this wicked, and foul Fair – and fitter

28–9 cut my hair (supposedly a sign of reformation)
33 For as for
36 diet-drink prescribed drink; medicine
57 jade lively horse (a colloquial term of contempt); **vapor** (medically, fumes in a distempered stomach, thought to be caused by tobacco or drink)
58 works succeeds; **two . . . half** i.e., portions (he has eaten two and a half suckling pigs)
64 apocryphal spurious (Puritans rejected the Apocrypha as sacred scripture)
65 publican one who is excommunicated from the church
65–6 bells . . . dogs (from Tobit 5:16 in the Apocrypha)
68 Nebuchadnezzar (King of Babylon who restored the temple of Baal; Dan. 3)
72 noise consort
83 pricks him up stimulates him; makes him high-spirited (proverbial)
84 popery (Zeal attacks the gingerbread as pagan or papist images; they were evidently cut to look like St. Bartholomew)
85 legend (reference to *The Golden Legend*, a medieval collection of saints' lives)
87 clapped struck together (so as to make a clapping sound)
93 you could if you could

may it be called a foul, than a Fair – to protest against the abuses of it, the foul abuses of it, in regard of the afflicted saints that are troubled, very much troubled, exceedingly troubled, with the opening of the merchandise of Babylon again and the peeping of popery upon the stalls, here, here, in the high places. See you not Goldylocks, the purple strumpet, there, in her yellow gown and green sleeves? The profane pipes, the tinkling timbrels? A shop of relics!

Littlewit. Pray you forbear, I am put in trust with 'em.

Busy. And this idolatrous grove of images, this flasket of idols which I will pull down – *Overthrows the ginger-bread.*

Trash. Oh, my ware, my ware, God bless it!

Busy. In my zeal, and glory to be thus exercised!

Leatherhead *enters with officers.*

Leatherhead. Here he is. Pray you lay hold on his zeal, we cannot sell a whistle for him in tune. Stop his noise, first!

Busy. Thou canst not. 'Tis a sanctified noise. I will make a loud and most strong noise, till I have daunted the profane enemy. And for this cause –

Leatherhead. Sir, here's no man afraid of you or your cause. You shall swear it, i' the stocks, sir.

Busy. I will thrust myself into the stocks, upon the pikes of the land.

Leatherhead. Carry him away.

Purecraft. What do you mean, wicked men?

Busy. Let them alone; I fear them not.

[*Exeunt officers, with* Busy, *followed by* Purecraft.]

Littlewit. Was not this shilling well ventured, Win, for our liberty? Now we may go play, and see over the Fair, where we list, ourselves. My mother is gone after him, and let her e'en go, and loose us.

Win. Yes, John, but I know not what to do.

Littlewit. For what, Win?

Win. For a thing, I am ashamed to tell you, i' faith, and 'tis too far to go home.

Littlewit. I pray thee be not ashamed, Win. Come, i' faith, thou shall not be ashamed; is it anything about the hobby-horse-man? An't be, speak freely.

Win. Hang him, base bobchin, I scorn him. No, I have very great what sha' call 'um, John

Littlewit. Oh, is that all, Win? We'll go back to Captain Jordan; to the pig woman's, Win; he'll help us, or she with a dripping pan, or an old kettle, or something. The poor greasy soul loves you, Win, and after, we'll visit the Fair all over, Win, and see my puppet play, Win; you know it's a fine matter, Win.

[*Exeunt* Littlewit, Win.]

Leatherhead. Let's away I counseled you to pack up afore, Joan.

Trash. A pox of his Bedlam purity. He has spoiled half my ware. But the best is, we lose nothing, if we miss our first merchant.

Leatherhead. It shall be hard for him to find, or know us, when we are translated, Joan.

[*Exeunt.*]

Act IV

Scene i.

[*Enter* Trouble-All, Bristle, Haggis, Cokes, Justice.]

Trouble-All. My Masters, I do make no doubt but you are officers.

Bristle. What then, sir?

Trouble-All. And the King's loving and obedient subjects.

Bristle. Obedient, friend? Take heed what you speak, I advise you: Oliver Bristle advises you. His loving subjects, we grant you; but not his obedient at this time, by your leave. We know ourselves a little better than so; we are to command, sir, and such as you are to be obedient. Here's one of his obedient subjects going to the stocks, and we'll make you such another, if you talk.

Trouble-All. You are all wise enough i' your places, I know.

---

104 saints fellow Puritans
109–10 Goldylocks . . . green (Puritans wore black, considering bright colors to be profane)
110 green sleeves (the sign or costume of a prostitute)
112 relics idolatrous objects of worship
117 flasket long shallow basket
117–18 *Overthrows* (cf. Christ overturning the tables in the temple; John 2:15)
122 for because of
129 swear it do your swearing
130 thrust myself (i.e., accept punishment willingly, as a martyr)
131 pikes weapons with iron or steel heads on a pole (Busy envisions himself a martyr)
149 what . . . 'um (she needs to urinate)
151 Captain Jordan chamberpot; in fact, Ursula will offer her the bottom of an old bottle
161 miss avoid; **merchant** customer
163 are translated (1) have gone elsewhere; (2) have put on disguises; (3) are transformed
IV.i.7 Oliver Bristle (Jonson calls him "Davy" Bristle at III.i.10)
10 so that

Bristle. If you know it, sir, why do you bring it in question?

Trouble-All. I question nothing, pardon me. I do only hope you have warrant for what you do, and so quit you, and so multiply you.

He goes away again.

Haggis. What's he? Bring him up to the stocks there. Why bring you him not up?

[Trouble-All] *comes again.*

Trouble-All. If you have Justice Overdo's warrant, 'tis well; you are safe; that is the warrant of warrants. I'll not give this button for any man's warrant else.

Bristle. Like enough, sir; but let me tell you, an' you play away your buttons thus, you will want 'em ere night, for any store I see about you. You might keep 'em, and save pins, I wusse.

[Trouble-All] *goes away.*

Justice Overdo. [*Aside.*] What should he be, that doth so esteem and advance my warrant? He seems a sober and discreet person! It is a comfort to a good conscience to be followed with a good fame in his sufferings. The world will have a pretty taste by this, how I can bear adversity; and it will beget a kind of reverence toward me hereafter, even from mine enemies, when they shall see I carry my calamity nobly, and that it doth neither break me nor bend me.

Haggis. Come, sir, here's a place for you to preach in. Will you put in your leg?

They put him in the stocks.

Justice Overdo. That I will, cheerfully.

Bristle. O' my conscience, a seminary! He kisses the stocks.

Cokes. Well, my masters, I'll leave him with you; now I see him bestowed, I'll go look for my goods, and Numps.

Haggis. You may, sir, I warrant you; where's the tother bawler? Fetch him, too, you shall find 'em both fast enough.

[*Exit* Cokes.]

Justice Overdo. [*Aside.*] In the midst of this tumult, I will yet be the author of mine own rest, and not minding their fury, sit in the stocks in that calm as shall be able to trouble a triumph.

[Trouble-All] *comes again.*

Trouble-All. Do you assure me upon your words? May I undertake for you, if I be asked the question, that you have this warrant?

Haggis. What's this fellow, for God's sake?

Trouble-All. Do but show me Adam Overdo, and I am satisfied.

Goes out.

Bristle. He is a fellow that is distracted, they say; one Trouble-all. He was an officer in the court of Pie-powders, here last year, and put out of his place by Justice Overdo.

Justice Overdo. Ha!

Bristle. Upon which he took an idle conceit, and's run mad upon't. So that, ever since, he will do nothing but by Justice Overdo's warrant. He will not eat a crust, nor drink a little, nor make him in his apparel ready. His wife, sir-reverence, cannot get him make his water, or shift his shirt, without his warrant.

Justice Overdo. [*Aside.*] If this be true, this is my greatest disaster! How am I bound to satisfy this poor man, that is of so good a nature to me, out of his wits, where there is no room left for dissembling!

[Trouble-All] *comes in.*

Trouble-All. If you cannot show me Adam Overdo, I am in doubt of you. I am afraid you cannot answer it.

Goes again.

Haggis. Before me, neighbor Bristle, (and now I think on't better) Justice Overdo is a very parantory person.

Bristle. Oh, are you advised of that? And a severe Justicer, by your leave.

Justice Overdo. [*Aside.*] Do I hear ill o' that side, too?

---

21 **quit . . . you** "God reward you and increase your family" (formulaic)
30 **ere night** i.e., when it is colder; **store** supply
33 **should** might
34 **advance** extol
45 **leg** (the stocks secure prisoners here by one leg, not two, allowing Wasp to escape)
56 **rest** (1) peace of mind; (2) arrest
58 **trouble** mar; deny
71 **took . . . conceit** became victimized by a groundless delusion; **idle** foolish
74–5 **make . . . ready** get dressed
76 **make his water** urinate; **shift** change
85 **answer** justify
86 **Before me** "upon my word" (colloquial)
88 **parantory** peremptory (malapropism)
91 **hear ill** have an evil reputation

Bristle. He will sit as upright o' the bench, an' you mark him, as a candle i' the socket, and give light to the whole court in every business.

Haggis. But he will burn blue, and swell like a boil (God bless us) an' he be angry.

Bristle. Aye, and he will be angry, too, when 'has list, that's more. And when he is angry, be it right or wrong, he has the law on's side, ever. I mark that, too.

Justice Overdo. [*Aside.*] I will be more tender hereafter. I see compassion may become a Justice, though it be a weakness, I confess; and nearer a vice than a virtue.

Haggis. Well, take him out o' the stocks again. We'll go a sure way to work, we'll ha' the ace of hearts of our side, if we can.

They take the Justice out. [*Enter* Pocher, Busy, Purecraft.]

Pocher. Come, bring him away to his fellow there. Master Busy, we shall rule your legs, I hope, though we cannot rule your tongue.

Busy. No, minister of darkness, no, thou canst not rule my tongue; my tongue it is mine own, and with it I will both knock and mock down your Bartholomew-abhominations, till you be made a hissing to the neighbor parishes round about.

Haggis. Let him alone, we have devised better upon't.

Purecraft. And shall he not into the stocks then?

Bristle. No, mistress, we'll have 'em both to Justice Overdo, and let him do over 'em as is fitting. Then I, and my gossip Haggis, and my beadle Pocher are discharged.

Purecraft. Oh, I thank you, blessed, honest men!

Bristle. Nay, never thank us, but thank this madman that comes here; he put it in our heads.

[Trouble-All] *comes again.*

Purecraft. Is he mad? Now heaven increase his madness, and bless it, and thank it. Sir, your poor handmaid thanks you.

Trouble-All. Have you a warrant? An' you have a warrant, show it.

Purecraft. Yes, I have a warrant out of the word, to give thanks for removing any scorn intended to the brethren.

[*Exeunt all but* Trouble-All.]

Trouble-All. It is Justice Overdo's warrant that I look for. If you have not that, keep your word; I'll keep mine. Quit ye, and multiply ye.

Act IV. Scene ii.

[*Enter to him, severally* Edgworth, Nightingale, Cokes, Costermonger.]

[*Edgworth.*] Come away, Nightingale, I pray thee.

Trouble-All. Whither go you? Where's your warrant?

Edgworth. Warrant for what, sir?

Trouble-All. For what you go about; you know how fit it is; an' you have no warrant, bless you, I'll pray for you. That's all I can do.

Goes out.

Edgworth. What means he?

Nightingale. A madman that haunts the Fair, do you not know him? It's marvel he has not more followers after his ragged heels.

Edgworth. Beshrew him, he startled me. I thought he had known of our plot. Guilt's a terrible thing! Ha' you prepared the costermonger?

Nightingale. Yes, and agreed for his basket of pears. He is at the corner here, ready. And your prize, he comes down, sailing, that way, all alone, without his protector. He is rid of him, it seems.

Edgworth. Aye, I know; I should ha' followed his Protectorship for a feat I am to do upon him; but this offered itself so i' the way I could not let it 'scape. Here he comes. Whistle; be this sport called "Dorring the Dottrell."

Nightingale. Wh, wh, wh, wh, &c.

Nightingale whistles.

Cokes. By this light, I cannot find my gingerbread-wife, nor my hobby-horse-man, in all the Fair, now, to ha' my money again. And I do not know the way out on't, to go home for more. Do you hear, friend, you that whistle? What tune is that you whistle?

Nightingale. A new tune. I am practicing, sir.

Cokes. Dost thou know where I dwell, I pray thee? Nay, on with thy tune, I ha' no such haste for an answer. I'll practice with thee.

---

96 blue pale (thought to be an evil omen)
98–9 'has list he pleases
108 of our on our
115 abhominations (correctly abomination; a parody of Puritan misspelling which derived from the [false] etymology of *ad hominem, inhuman*)
116 hissing (as object of scorn and rebuke; cf. Jer. 19:8)
123 discharged freed from responsibility
132 the word the Bible

IV.ii.12 Beshrew curse; a plague on
15 agreed settled on a price
17 prize prey
22 i' the way opportunely
24 "Dorring . . . Dottrell" "hoaxing the simpleton" (to dor was "to make a fool of"; a dottrell is a species of plover known for its foolishness)
28 again returned

Costermonger. Buy any pears, very fine pears, pears fine.

Nightingale sets his foot afore him, and he falls with his basket.

Cokes. God's so! A muss, a muss, a muss, a muss.

Costermonger. Good gentleman, my ware, my ware. I am a poor man. Good sir, my ware.

Nightingale. Let me hold your sword, sir, it troubles you.

Cokes. Do, and my cloak, an' thou wilt; and my hat, too.

Cokes falls a-scrambling while they run away with his things.

Edgworth. A delicate great boy, methinks; he outscrambles 'em all. I cannot persuade myself but he goes to grammar-school yet; and plays the truant today.

Nightingale. Would he had another purse to cut, 'Zekiel.

Edgworth. Purse? A man might cut out his kidneys, I think, and he never feel 'em, he is so earnest at the sport.

Nightingale. His soul is half-way out on's body at the game.

Edgworth. Away, Nightingale, that way.

[Nightingale *runs off with his sword, cloak, and hat.*]

Cokes. I think I am furnished for Cather'ne pears for one undermeal. Gi' me my cloak.

Costermonger. Good gentleman, give me my ware.

Cokes. Where's the fellow I ga' my cloak to? My cloak? and my hat? ha! God's lid, is he gone? Thieves, thieves! Help me to cry, gentlemen.

He runs out.

Edgworth. Away, costermonger, come to us to Urs'la's. [*Exit* Costermonger] Talk of him to have a soul? 'Heart, if he have any more than a thing given him instead of salt, only to keep him from stinking, I'll be hanged afore my time, presently. Where should it be, trow? In his blood? He has not so much to'ard it in his whole body as will maintain a good flea; and if he take this course, he will not ha' so much land left as to rear a calf within this twelvemonth. Was there ever green plover so pulled! That his little overseer had been here now, and been but tall enough, to see him steal pears in exchange for his beaver-hat and his cloak thus! I must go find him out, next, for his black box, and his patent (it seems) he has of his place; which I think the gentleman would have a reversion of, that spoke to me for it so earnestly.

[*Exit.*]

He [Cokes] *comes again.*

Cokes. Would I might lose my doublet, and hose too, as I am an honest man, and never stir, if I think there be anything but thieving, and cozening, i' this whole Fair. Bartholomew-fair, quoth he; an' ever any Bartholomew had that luck in't that I have had, I'll be martyred for him, and in Smithfield, too.

Throws away his pears.

I ha' paid for my pears, a rot on 'em, I'll keep 'em no longer; you were choke-pears to me; I had been better ha' gone to mum-chance for you, I wusse. Methinks the Fair should not have used me thus; an' 'twere but for my name's sake, I would not ha' used a dog o' the name so. Oh, Numps will triumph, now!

Trouble-All *comes again.*

Friend, do you know who I am? Or where I lie? I do not myself, I'll be sworn. Do but carry me home, and I'll please thee; I ha' money enough there. I ha' lost myself, and my cloak and my hat, and my fine sword, and my sister, and Numps, and Mistress Grace (a gentlewoman that I should ha' married), and a cutwork handkerchief she ga' me, and two purses today. And my bargain o'hobby-horses and ginger-bread which grieves me worst of all.

Trouble-All. By whose warrant, sir, have you done all this?

Cokes. Warrant? Thou art a wise fellow, indeed, as if a man need a warrant to lose anything with.

Trouble-All. Yes, Justice Overdo's warrant, a man may get and lose with. I'll stand to't.

Cokes. Justice Overdo? Dost thou know him? I lie there, he is my brother-in-law, he married my sister. Pray thee, show me the way. Dost thou know the house?

38 **muss** scramble
58 **undermeal** afternoon snack
64–7 **Talk . . . stinking** (just as salt keeps meat from rotting, so does the soul prevent the body from stinking)
73 **plover** wading or shore bird; **pulled** plucked clean
78 **patent** a document conferring an office
79 **reversion** the right of succeeding to, or next occupying, an estate
85 **Bartholomew** (Bartholomew Leggatt, martyred at Smithfield in 1611)
86–7 **martyred . . . too** ("Bloody Mary" Tudor martyred Protestants at Smithfield during her brief Catholic rule [1553–8])
89 **choke-pears** (1) unpalatable pears; (2) a rebuke
90 **mum-chance** (dicing game popular with costermongers); **for** instead of
97 **lie** lodge; **carry** escort
98 **please** satisfy
102–3 **cut-work** embroidered

Trouble-All. Sir, show me your warrant; I know nothing without a warrant, pardon me.

Cokes. Why, I warrant thee, come along. Thou shalt see I have wrought pillows there, and cambric sheets, and sweet bags, too. Pray thee guide me to the house.

Trouble-All. Sir, I'll tell you; go you thither yourself, first, alone; tell your worshipful brother your mind; and but bring me three lines of his hand, or his clerk's, with "Adam Overdo" underneath. Here I'll stay you. I'll obey you, and I'll guide you presently.

Cokes. [*Aside.*] 'Slid, this is an ass, I ha' found him. Pox upon me, what do I talking to such a dull fool? [*To him.*] Farewell. You are a very coxcomb, do you hear?

Trouble-All. I think I am; if Justice Overdo sign to it, I am, and so we are all; he'll quit us all, multiply us all.

[*Exeunt.*]

Act IV. Scene iii.

[*Enter* Grace. Quarlous, Winwife *enter with their swords drawn.*]

[*Grace.*] Gentlemen, this is no way that you take. You do but breed one another trouble, and offense, and give me no contentment at all. I am no she that affects to be quarreled for, or have my name or fortune made the question of men's swords.

Quarlous. 'Slood, we love you.

Grace. If you both love me, as you pretend, your own reason will tell you but one can enjoy me; and to that point, there leads a directer line than by my infamy, which must follow if you fight. 'Tis true, I have professed it to you ingenuously that, rather than to be yoked with this bridegroom is appointed me, I would take up any husband, almost upon any trust. Though subtlety would say to me, I know, he is a fool, and has an estate, and I might govern him and enjoy a friend beside. But these are not my aims; I must have a husband I must love, or I cannot live with him. I shall ill make one of these politic wives!

Winwife. Why, if you can like either of us, lady, say which is he and the other shall swear instantly to desist.

Quarlous. Content, I accord to that willingly.

Grace. Sure you think me a woman of an extreme levity, gentlemen, or a strange fancy, that (meeting you by chance in such a place as this, both at one instant, and not yet of two hours' acquaintance, neither of you deserving, afore the other, of me) I should so forsake my modesty (though I might affect one more particularly) as to say, "This is he," and name him.

Quarlous. Why, wherefore should you not? What should hinder you?

Grace. If you would not give it to my modesty, allow it yet to my wit; give me so much of woman, and cunning, as not to betray myself impertinently. How can I judge of you, so far as to a choice, without knowing you more? You are both equal and alike to me, yet; and so indifferently affected by me, as each of you might be the man if the other were away. For you are reasonable creatures, you have understanding and discourse. And if fate send me an understanding husband, I have no fear at all but mine own manners shall make him a good one.

Quarlous. Would I were put forth to making for you, then.

Grace. It may be you are, you know not what's toward you. Will you consent to a motion of mine, gentlemen?

Winwife. Whatever it be, we'll presume reasonableness, coming from you.

Quarlous. And fitness, too.

Grace. I saw one of you buy a pair of tables e'en now.

Winwife. Yes, here they be, and maiden ones too, unwritten in.

Grace. The fitter for what they may be employed in. You shall write, either of you, here, a word,

---

118 **warrant** guarantee
119 **wrought** embroidered
120 **cambric** (fine white linen originally from Cambray, Flanders); **sweet bags** sachets; bags with fragrant herbs to perfume linen
126 **stay** await
128 **found** discovered (his true nature)
IV.iii.4 **affects** likes
8 **pretend** claim
14 **is** who is; **me** to me
15 **take up** accept
15–16 **upon . . . trust** without further question
17 **he** Cokes
18 **friend** lover
21 **politic** cunning; scheming; duplicitous
37 **wit** intelligence
38 **cunning** worldly knowledge
39 **impertinently** unbecomingly; immodestly
42 **indifferently** impartially; **affected** regarded
43 **For** because
45 **discourse** (ability to reason and speak reasonably)
48 **put . . . making** apprenticed to be trained
51 **toward** in store for; **motion** proposal
56 **tables** writing tablets
61 **either** each

or a name, what you like best; but of two, or three syllables at most: and the next person that comes this way (because destiny has a high hand in business of this nature) I'll demand, which of the two words he or she doth approve; and according to that sentence, fix my resolution, and affection, without change.

Quarlous. Agreed, my word is conceived already.

Winwife. And mine shall not be long creating after.

Grace. But you shall promise, gentlemen, not to be curious to know, which of you it is, is taken; but give me leave to conceal that till you have brought me, either home or where I may safely tender myself.

Winwife. Why, that's but equal.

Quarlous. We are pleased.

Grace. Because I will bind both your endeavors to work together, friendly, and jointly, each to the other's fortune, and have myself fitted with some means to make him that is forsaken a part of amends.

Quarlous. These conditions are very courteous. Well, my word is out of the *Arcadia*, then: "Argalus."

Winwife. And mine out of the play, "Palemon."

Trouble-All *comes again.*

Trouble-All. Have you any warrant for this, gentlemen?

Quartous, Winwife. Ha!

Trouble-All. There must be a warrant had, believe it.

Winwife. For what?

Trouble-All. For whatsoever it is, anything indeed, no matter what.

Quarlous. 'Slight, here's a fine ragged prophet, dropp'd down i' the nick!

Trouble-All. Heaven quit you, gentlemen.

Quarlous. Nay, stay a little. Good lady, put him to the question.

Grace. You are content, then?

Winwife, Quarlous. Yes yes.

Grace. Sir, here are two names written –

Trouble-All. Is Justice Overdo, one?

Grace. How, sir? I pray you read 'em to yourself. It is for a wager between these gentlemen, and with a stroke or any difference, mark which you approve best.

Trouble-All. They may be both worshipful names for ought I know, mistress, but Adam Overdo had been worth three of 'em, I assure you, in this place; that's in plain English.

Grace. This man amazes me! I pray you, like one of 'em, sir.

Trouble-All. I do like him there, that has the best warrant, Mistress, to save your longing, (and multiply him) it may be this. [*Marks the book.*] But I am aye still for Justice Overdo, that's my conscience. And quit you.

[*Exit.*]

Winwife. Is't done, lady?

Grace. Aye, and strangely, as ever I saw! What fellow is this, trow?

Quarlous. No matter what, a fortune-teller we ha' made him. Which is't, which is't?

Grace. Nay, did you not promise, not to inquire?

[*Enter* Edgworth.]

Quarlous. 'Slid, I forgot that. Pray you, pardon me. Look, here's our Mercury come. The license arrives i' the finest time, too! 'Tis but scraping out Cokes his name, and 'tis done.

Winwife. How now, lime-twig? Hast thou touched?

Edgworth. Not yet, sir; except you would go with me, and see't, it's not worth speaking on. The act is nothing without a witness. Yonder he is, your man with the box fallen into the finest company, and so transported with vapors; they ha' got in a northern clothier, and one Puppy, a western man, that's come to wrestle before my Lord Mayor anon, and Captain Whit, and one Val Cutting, that helps Captain Jordan to roar, a circling boy, with whom your Numps is so taken that you may strip him of his clothes, if you will. I'll undertake to geld him for you, if

75 **tender** take care of

76 **but equal** fair enough, equitable

81–2 **a part of** some

85 **"Argalus"** (Sidney's exemplar of a faithful husband in the prose romance *Arcadia* [1590])

86 **"Palemon"** (knightly lover in [1] Shakespeare's and Fletcher's *Two Noble Kinsmen* [1613]; [2] Samuel Daniel's *The Queen's Arcadia* [played at a royal visit to Oxford in 1605], ultimately derived from the "Knight's Tale" in Chaucer)

94 **prophet** (i.e., one who will discern [or choose] the winner)

95 **i' the nick** just in time

103 **to yourself** silently

105 **difference** distinguishing mark

111 **like** prefer

117 **conscience** conviction

125 **Mercury** (messenger of the gods, known as a thief)

126 **finest** fittest

128 **lime-twig** thief; **touched** (carried out the theft by erasing Cokes's name)

129 **except** unless

135 **western man** (Cornwall was famous for wrestlers)

135–6 **before . . . Mayor** (wrestling before the Lord Mayor of London was a tradition of Bartholomew Fair on the opening afternoon of the three-day fair [August 24–6])

138 **circling boy** (meaning unclear; perhaps a boy who joins the circle as a decoy or one who bullies opponents into a circle)

140 **geld** castrate

you had but a surgeon ready, to sear him. And Mistress Justice, there, is the goodest woman! She does so love 'em all over, in terms of Justice and the style of authority, with her hood upright – that I beseech you come away, gentlemen, and see't.

Quarlous. 'Slight, I would not lose it for the Fair. What'll you do, Ned?

Winwife. Why, stay here about for you. Mistress Wellborn must not be seen.

Quarlous. Do so, and find out a priest i' the mean-time. I'll bring the license. Lead, which way is't?

Edgworth. Here, sir, you are o' the backside o' the booth already. You may hear the noise.

[*Exeunt.*]

Act IV. Scene iv.

[*Enter* Knockem, Northern, Puppy, Cutting, Whit, Wasp, Mistress Overdo.]

[*Knockem.*] Whit, bid Val Cutting continue the vapors for a lift, Whit, for a lift.

Northern. I'll ne mare, I'll ne mare, the eale's too meeghty.

Knockem. How now! My Galloway Nag, the staggers? Ha! Whit, gi' him a slit i' the forehead. Cheer up, man; a needle and thread to stitch his ears. I'd cure him now an' I had it, with a little butter, and garlic, long-pepper, and grains. Where's my horn? I'll gi' him a mash, presently, shall take away this dizziness.

Puppy. Why, where are you, zurs? Do you vlinch, and leave us i' the zuds, now?

Northern. I'll ne mare, I is e'en as vull as a paiper's bag, by my troth, aye.

Puppy. Do my northern cloth zhrink i' the wetting, ha?

Knockem. Why, well said, old flea-bitten, thou'lt never tire, I see.

They fall to their vapors, again.

Cutting. No, sir, but he may tire, if it please him.

Whit. Who told dee sho? That he vuld never teer, man?

Cutting. No matter who told him so, so long as he knows.

Knockem. Nay, I know nothing, sir; pardon me there.

[*Enter* Edgworth, Quarlous.]

Edgworth. They are at it still, sir, this they call vapors.

Whit. He shall not pardon dee, captain, dou shalt not be pardoned. Pre'de shweetheart, do not pardon him.

Cutting. 'Slight, I'll pardon him, an' I list, whoso-ever says nay to't.

Quarlous. Where's Numps? I miss him.

Wasp. Why, I say nay to't.

Quarlous. Oh, there he is!

Knockem. To what do you say nay, sir?

Here they continue their game of vapors, which is nonsense. Every man to oppose the last man that spoke, whether it concerned him, or no.

Wasp. To anything, whatsoever it is, so long as I do not like it.

Whit. Pardon me, little man, dou musht like it a little.

Cutting. No, he must not like it at all, sir; there you are i' the wrong.

Whit. I tink I be, he must not like it, indeed.

Cutting. Nay, then he both must and will like it, sir, for all you.

Knockem. If he have reason, he may like it, sir.

Whit. By no meansh, captain, upon reason, he may like nothing upon reason.

Wasp. I have no reason, nor I will hear of no reason, nor I will look for no reason, and he is an ass that either knows any or looks for't from me.

Cutting. Yes, in some sense you may have reason, sir.

Wasp. Aye, in some sense, I care not if I grant you.

Cutting. Pardon me, thou ougsht to grant him nothing, in no shensh, if dou do love dyshelf, angry man.

Wasp. Why then, I do grant him nothing; and I have no sense.

---

141 sear cauterize
142 goodest most important
146 away along
IV.iv.2 for a lift in preparation for a theft (their plans will culminate when Knockem and Edgworth rob Wasp)
3–4 ne . . . meeghty "No more, the ale's too mighty" (attempt at northern dialect)
5 Galloway Nag (a breed of small horse from sw Scotland known for endurance)
5–6 staggers (disease of horses known by a staggering gait)
6–10 gi' . . . grains (recommended cure for staggers)
9 long-pepper (a strong pepper)
10 grains refuse of malt; **horn** (horn-shaped vessel used to administer medicine to horses)
12 vlinch flinch
13 i' the zuds in the suds (i.e., in trouble)
14–15 paiper's bag bagpipe
16–17 Do . . . wetting (northern cloth was notorious for shrinking)
18–19 flea-bitten . . . tire (proverbial)
21 teer tire
30 Pre'de pray thee
43 musht must
61 shensh sense

Cutting. 'Tis true, thou hast no sense indeed.

Wasp. 'Slid, but I have sense, now I think on't better, and I will grant him anything, do you see?

Knockem. He is i' the right, and does utter a sufficient vapor.

Cutting. Nay, it is no sufficient vapor, neither, I deny that.

Knockem. Then it is a sweet vapor.

Cutting. It may be a sweet vapor.

Wasp. Nay, it is no sweet vapor, neither, sir; it stinks, and I'll stand to't.

Whit. Yes, I think it doesh shtink, Captain. All vapor doesh shtink.

Wasp. Nay, then it does not stink, sir, and it shall not stink.

Cutting. By your leave, it may, sir.

Wasp. Aye, by my leave, it may stink; I know that.

Whit. Pardon me, thou knowesht nothing; it cannot by thy leave, angry man.

Wasp. How can it not?

Knockem. Nay, never question him, for he is i' the right.

Whit. Yesh, I am i' de right, I confesh it; so ish de little man too.

Wasp. I'll have nothing confessed that concerns me. I am not i' the right, nor never was i' the right, nor never will be i' the right, while I am in my right mind.

Cutting. Mind? Why, here's no man minds you, sir, nor anything else.

They drink again.

Puppy. Vriend, will you mind this that we do?

Quarlous. Call you this vapors? This is such belching of quarrel as I never heard. Will you mind your business, sir?

Edgworth. You shall see, sir.

Northern. I'll ne mair, my waimb warks too mickle with this auready.

Edgworth. Will you take that, Master Wasp, that nobody should mind you?

Wasp. Why? What ha' you to do? Is't any matter to you?

Edgworth. No, but methinks you should not be unminded, though.

Wasp. Nor I wu' not be, now I think on't. Do you hear, new acquaintance, does no man mind me, say you?

Cutting. Yes, sir, every man here minds you, but how?

Wasp. Nay, I care as little how, as you do; that was not my question.

Whit. No, noting was ty question; tou art a learned man, and I am a valiant man, i' faith la. Tou shalt speak for me, and I vill fight for tee.

Knockem. Fight for him, Whit? A gross vapor; he can fight for himself.

Wasp. It may be I can, but it may be, I wu' not, how then?

Cutting. Why, then you may choose.

Wasp. Why, and I'll choose whether I'll choose or no.

Knockem. I think you may, and 'tis true; and I allow it for a resolute vapor.

Wasp. Nay, then, I do think you do not think, and it is no resolute vapor.

Cutting. Yes, in some sort he may allow you.

Knockem. In no sort, sir. Pardon me, I can allow him nothing. You mistake the vapor.

Wasp. He mistakes nothing, sir, in no sort.

Whit. Yes, I pre dee now, let him mistake.

Wasp. A turd i' your teeth, never pre dee me, for I will have nothing mistaken.

Knockem. Turd, ha, turd? A noisome vapor. Strike, Whit.

They fall by the ears.

[Edgworth *steals the license out of the box, and exit.*]

Mrs. Overdo. Why, gentlemen, why gentlemen, I charge you upon my authority, conserve the peace. In the King's name, and my husband's, put up your weapons; I shall be driven to commit you myself, else.

Quarlous. Ha, ha, ha.

Wasp. Why do you laugh, sir?

Quarlous. Sir, you'll allow me my Christian liberty. I may laugh, I hope.

Cutting. In some sort you may, and in some sort you may not, sir.

Knockem. Nay, in some sort, sir, he may neither laugh nor hope, in this company.

Wasp. Yes, then he may both laugh and hope in any sort, an't please him.

Quarlous. Faith, and I will then, for it doth please me exceedingly.

Wasp. No exceeding neither, sir.

Knockem. No, that vapor is too lofty.

98–9 mind . . . business get on with the job (of stealing Cokes's license)
101 mair more; **waimb . . . mickle** stomach is too upset
105 What . . . do? what business is it of yours?
108 unminded left unnoticed
130 sort (1) sense; (2) company
139 s.d. *fall . . . ears* fight
143 commit imprison
148 In . . . sort to some extent
156 exceeding excess

Quarlous. Gentlemen, I do not play well at your game of vapors.
I am not very good at it, but –

Cutting. Do you hear, sir? I would speak with you in circle!

He draws a circle on the ground.

Quarlous. In circle, sir? What would you with me in circle?

Cutting. Can you lend me a piece, a jacobus, in circle?

Quarlous. 'Slid, your circle will prove more costly than your vapors, then. Sir, no, I lend you none.

Cutting. Your beard's not well turned up, sir.

Quarlous. How, rascal? Are you playing with my beard? I'll break circle with you.

They draw all, and fight.

Puppy, Northern. Gentlemen, gentlemen!

Knockem. Gather up, Whit, gather up, Whit, good vapors.

[*Exit.*]

Mrs. Overdo. What mean you? Are you rebels, gentlemen? Shall I send out a sergeant-at-arms or a writ o' rebellion against you? I'll commit you, upon my womanhood, for a riot, upon my justice-hood, if you persist.

[*Exeunt* Quarlous, Cutting.]

Wasp. Upon your justice-hood? Marry, shit o' your hood; you'll commit? Spoke like a true Justice of Peace's wife, indeed, and a fine female lawyer! Turd i' your teeth for a fee, now.

Mrs. Overdo. Why, Numps, in Master Overdo's name, I charge you.

Wasp. Good Mistress Underdo, hold your tongue.

Mrs. Overdo. Alas, poor Numps!

Wasp. "Alas!" And why "alas" from you, I beseech you? Or why "poor Numps," Goody Rich? Am I come to be pitied by your tuft taffeta now? Why, mistress, I knew Adam, the clerk, your husband, when he was Adam scrivener, and writ for twopence a sheet, as high as he bears his head now, or you your hood, dame. What are you, sir?

The watch comes in [*accompanied by Whit*].

Bristle. We be men, and no infidels; what is the matter here, and the noises? Can you tell?

Wasp. Heart, what ha' you to do? Cannot a man quarrel in quietness, but he must be put out on't by you? What are you?

Bristle. Why, we be His Majesty's Watch, sir.

Wasp. Watch? 'Sblood, you are a sweet watch, indeed. A body would think, an' you watched well o' nights, you should be contented to sleep at this time o' day. Get you to your fleas, and your flock-beds, your rogues, your kennels, and lie down close.

Bristle. Down? Yes, we will down, I warrant you; down with him in His Majesty's name, down, down with him, and carry him away to the pigeon-holes.

Mrs. Overdo. I thank you, honest friends, in the behalf o' the Crown, and the peace, and in Master Overdo's name, for suppressing enormities.

Whit. Stay, Bristle, here ish a noder brash o' drunkards, but very quiet, special drunkards, will pay dee five shillings very well. Take 'em to dee, in de graish o' God. One of 'em does change cloth for ale in the Fair here, te oder ish a strong man, a mighty man, my Lord Mayor's man, and a wrashler. He has wrashled so long with the bottle, here, that the man with the beard hash almost streek up hish heelsh.

Bristle. 'Slid, the Clerk o' the Market has been to cry him all the Fair over, here, for my Lord's service.

Whit. Tere he ish, pre de taik him hensh, and make ty best on him.

[*Exit watch with* Wasp, Northern, Puppy.]

How now, woman o' shilk, vat ailsh ty shweet faish? Art tou melancholy?

Mrs. Overdo. A little distempered with these enormities. Shall I entreat a courtesy of you, Captain?

---

163 s.d. *draws a circle* (an indirect challenge to fight which Quarlous does not understand)

165 jacobus (a sovereign gold coin issued by King James; Cutting knows Quarlous will refuse and provide a pretext for more insults)

171–2 playing . . . beard (final insult precipitating fight)

190 Goody Goodwife

191–2 tuft taffeta (taffeta woven with raised stripes or spots)

193–4 Adam scrivener (possible allusion to Chaucer's scrivener whom the poet accuses of carelessness)

200–1 put . . . on't debarred from it

207 flock-beds (beds made of coarse tufts of wool or cotton)

212 pigeon-holes stocks

217 brash brace (pair)

220 graish grace

224–5 the man . . . beard (a pot-bellied drinking jug with a narrow neck and decorated with a bearded face)

225 streek . . . heelsh overthrown him (struck up his heels)

226 Clerk . . . Market (official appointed to take tolls and manage the general business of the Fair for its proprietors)

227 cry summon

227–8 Lord's service (service of Lord Rich's family to whom the precincts of the Fair were assigned when St. Bartholomew's was dissolved)

229 hensh hence

231 o'shilk of silk (cf. line 236)

233 distempered upset

Whit. Entreat a hundred, velvet voman, I vill do it. Shpeak out.

Mrs. Overdo. I cannot with modesty speak of it out, but –

Whit. I vill do it, and more, and more, for dee. What, Urs'la, an't be bitch, an't be bawd, an't be!

[*Enter* Ursula.]

Ursula. How now, rascal? What roar you for, old pimp?

Whit. Here, put up de cloaks, Ursh; de purchase; pre dee now, shweet Ursh, help dis good brave voman to a jordan, an't be.

Ursula. 'Slid, call your Captain Jordan to her, can you not?

Whit. Nay, pre dee leave dy consheits, and bring the velvet woman to de –

Ursula. I bring her! Hang her! Heart, must I find a common pot for every punk i' your purlieus?

Whit. Oh, good voordsh, Ursh, it ish a guest o' velvet, i' fait la.

Ursula. Let her sell her hood and buy a sponge, with a pox to her, my vessel is employed, sir. I have but one, and 'tis the bottom of an old bottle. An honest proctor and his wife are at it within; if she'll stay her time, so.

Whit. As soon ash tou canshth, shweet Ursh. Of a valiant man I tink I am the patientsh man i' the world, or in all Smithfield.

[*Reenter* Knockem.]

Knockem. How now, Whit? Close vapors stealing your leaps? Covering in corners, ha?

Whit. No fait, captain, dough tou beesht a vishe man, dy vit is a mile hence, now. I vas procuring a shmall courtesy, for a woman of fashion here.

Mrs. Overdo. Yes, captain, though I am Justice of Peace's wife, I do love men of war, and the sons of the sword, when they come before my husband.

Knockem. Say'st thou so, filly? Thou shalt have a leap presently; I'll horse thee myself, else.

Ursula. Come, will you bring her in now? And let her take her turn?

Whit. Gramercy, good Ursh, I tank dee.

Mrs. Overdo. Master Overdo shall thank her.

[*Exit.*]

Act IV. Scene v.

[*Enter to them* Littlewit, Win.]

[*Littlewit.*] Good Gammer Urs, Win and I are exceedingly beholden to you, and to Captain Jordan, and Captain Whit. Win, I'll be bold to leave you i' this good company, Win, for half an hour, or so, Win, while I go and see how my matter goes forward, and if the puppets be perfect. And then I'll come and fetch you, Win.

Win. Will you leave me alone with two men, John?

Littlewit. Aye, they are honest gentlemen, Win, Captain Jordan, and Captain Whit, they'll use you very civilly, Win; God b' w' you, Win.

[*Exit.*]

Ursula. What's her husband gone?

Knockem. On his false gallop, Urs, away.

Ursula. An' you be right Bartholomew-birds, now show yourselves so. We are undone for want of fowl i' the Fair here. Here will be 'Zekiel Edgworth, and three or four gallants with him at night, and I ha' neither plover nor quail for 'em. Persuade this between you two, to become a bird o' the game, while I work the velvet woman within (as you call her).

[*Exit.*]

Knockem. I conceive thee, Urs! go thy ways. Dost thou hear, Whit? Is't not pity my delicate dark chestnut here – with the fine lean head, large forehead, round eyes, even mouth, sharp ears, long neck, thin crest, close withers, plain back, deep sides, short fillets, and full flanks; with a round belly, a plump buttock, large thighs, knit knees, straight legs, short pasterns, smooth hoofs, and short heels – should lead a dull honest woman's life that might live the life of a lady?

Whit. Yes, by my fait and trot it is, captain. De honesht woman's leef is a scurvy dull leef, indeed, la.

---

244 purchase booty
252 purlieus area of brothels
264 Covering copulating (a farrier's term)
265 fait faith
IV.v.1 Gammer grandmother (title of respect)
7 perfect prepared
15 false gallop (1) canter; (2) unwise journey
18 fowl (birds; cant for wenches)
20 neither . . . quail loose women
22 work entice
26–32 fine . . . heels (a deliberate echo of Shakespeare's *Venus and Adonis*, lines 295–300)
28 plain flat
33 honest (1) respectable; (2) chaste
34 lady (1) woman of high station; (2) as "lady of pleasure" used for women of low station
35 trot truth
36 leef life

Win. How, sir? Is an honest woman's life a scurvy life?

Whit. Yes, fait, shweetheart, believe him, de leef of a bondwoman! But if dou vilt harken to me, I vill make tee a free-woman, and a lady. Dou shalt live like a lady, as te captain saish.

Knockem. Aye, and be honest too, sometimes; have her wires, and her tires, her green gowns, and velvet petticoats.

Whit. Aye, and ride to Ware and Rumford i' dy coash, shee de players, be in love vit 'em; sup vit gallantsh; be drunk; and cost dee noting.

Knockem. Brave vapors!

Whit. And lie by twenty on 'em, if dou pleash, shweetheart.

Win. What, and be honest still? That were fine sport.

Whit. Tish common, shweetheart. Tou may'st do it, by my hand; it shall be justified to ty husband's faish, now. Tou shalt be as honest as the skin between his hornsh, la!

Knockem. Yes, and wear a dressing, top, and top-gallant, to compare with e'er a husband on 'em all, for a fore-top. It is the vapor of spirit in the wife to cuckold nowadays, as it is the vapor of fashion, in the husband, not to suspect. Your prying cat-eyed-citizen is an abominable vapor.

Win. Lord, what a fool have I been!

Whit. Mend then, and do everything like a lady, hereafter; never know ty husband from another man.

Knockem. Nor any one man from another, but i' the dark.

Whit. Aye, and then it ish no dishgrash to know any man.

[*Reenter* Ursula.]

Ursula. Help, help here.

Knockem. How now? What vapor's there?

Ursula. Oh, you are a sweet ranger! And look well to your walks! Yonder is your punk of Turnbull, Ramping Alice, has fall'n upon the poor gentlewoman within, and pulled her hood over her ears, and her hair through it.

Alice *enters, beating the Justice's wife.*

Mrs. Overdo. Help, help, i' the King's name.

Alice. A mischief on you! They are such as you are that undo us and take our trade from us, with your tuft taffeta haunches.

Knockem. How now, Alice!

Alice. The poor common whores can ha' no traffic, for the privy rich ones; your caps and hoods of velvet call away our customers, and lick the fat from us.

Ursula. Peace, you foul ramping jade, you –

Alice. Od's foot, you bawd in grease, are you talking?

Knockem. Why, Alice, I say.

Alice. Thou sow of Smithfield, thou.

Ursula. Thou tripe of Turnbull.

Knockem. Cat-a-mountain-vapors! Ha!

Ursula. You know where you were tawed lately, both lashed and slashed you were in Bridewell.

Alice. Aye, by the same token, you rid that week, and broke out the bottom o' the cart, night-tub.

Knockem. Why, lion face! Ha! Do you know who I am? Shall I tear ruff, slit waistcoat, make rags of petticoat? Ha! Go to, vanish, for fear of vapors. Whit, a kick, Whit, in the parting vapor. [*They kick out Alice.*] Come, brave woman, take a good heart, thou shalt be a lady, too.

Whit. Yes, fait, dey shall all both be ladies, and write Madam. I vill do't myself for dem. Do, is the vord, and D is the middle letter of Madam, DD, put 'em together and make deeds, without which all words are alike, la.

---

41 **bond-woman** bound woman, servant

43 **saish** says

45 **wires** frames used to stiffen ruffs and support the hair; **tires** (1) headdresses; (2) attire generally

45–6 **green gowns** (denoting a prostitute and taken from a gown colored by grass stain)

47 **Ware** (a place famous for its eleven-foot bed); **Rumford** (a village close to London notorious for assignations)

58 **between . . . hornsh** (horns signified a cuckold)

59–60 **top, and top-gallant** in full sail

61 **fore-top** (1) top of a foremast; (2) forepart of the head (or wig)

67 **Mend** reform yourself

68–9 **from another** from having known another

83 **undo** ruin

84 **tuft . . . haunches** (artificial silk haunches to improve the figure)

87 **for** because of; **privy** (1) private; (2) clandestine

89 **lick . . . us** deprive us of our best customers ("to lick the fat from one's lips" was proverbial)

90 **ramping** roaring back

91 **Od's foot** "by God's foot" (a common oath); **in grease** (in prime condition for killing)

96 **Cat-a-mountain** leopard or panther

97 **tawed** (softened by beating, a tanner's term; hence beaten)

98 **slashed** cut with the scourge; **Bridewell** (London prison for confining and punishing sexual offenders)

99 **rid** (rode in the public cart for shaming whores)

100–1 **night-tub** (tub for collecting the night's slops and excrement)

103–4 **tear . . . petticoat** (Knockem threatens to rip off Alice's clothes); **waistcoat** (the sign of a prostitute if no gown was worn over it)

110 **write** sign or style themselves as

Knockem. 'Tis true, Urs'la, take 'em in, open thy wardrobe, and fit 'em to their calling. Green gowns, crimson petticoats, green women! My Lord Mayor's green women! Guests o' the game, true bred. I'll provide you a coach, to take the air in.

Win. But do you think you can get one?

Knockem. Oh, they are as common as wheelbarrows where there are great dunghills. Every pettifogger's wife has 'em, for first he buys a coach, that he may marry, and then he marries that he may be made cuckold in't. For if their wives ride not to their cuckolding, they do 'em no credit. Hide, and be hidden; ride, and be ridden, says the vapor of experience.

[*Exeunt* Ursula, Win, Mistress Overdo.]

Act IV. Scene vi.

[*Enter* Trouble-All.]

[*Trouble-All.*] By what warrant does it say so?

Knockem. Ha! Mad child o' the Pie-powders, art thou there? Fill us a fresh can, Urs; we may drink together.

Trouble-All. I may not drink without a warrant, captain.

Knockem. 'Slood, thou'll not stale without a warrant, shortly. Whit, give me pen, ink and paper. I'll draw him a warrant presently.

Trouble-All. It must be Justice Overdo's!

Knockem. I know, man. Fetch the drink, Whit.

Whit. I pre dee now, be very brief, captain; for de new ladies stay for dee.

Knockem. Oh, as brief as can be, here 'tis already. Adam Overdo.

Trouble-All. Why, now, I'll pledge you, captain.

Knockem. Drink it off. I'll come to thee, anon, again.

[*Exeunt.*]

[*Enter* Quarlous, Edgworth.]

Quarlous. Well, sir. You are now discharged. Beware of being spied, hereafter.

Quarlous *to the cutpurse.*

Edgworth. Sir, will it please you, enter in here, at Urs'la's; and take part of a silken gown, a velvet petticoat, or a wrought smock. I am promised such; and I can spare any gentleman a moiety.

Quarlous. Keep it for your companions in beastliness; I am none of 'em, sir. If I had not already forgiven you a greater trespass, or thought you yet worth my beating, I would instruct your manners to whom you made your offers. But go your ways, talk not to me; the hangman is only fit to discourse with you. The hand of beadle is too merciful a punishment for your trade of life. [*Exit* Edgworth.] I am sorry I employed this fellow; for he thinks me such: *Facinus quos inquinat, æquat.* But it was for sport. And would I make it serious, the getting of this license is nothing to me without other circumstances concur. I do think how impertinently I labor, if the word be not mine that the ragged fellow marked; and what advantage I have given Ned Winwife in this time now, of working her, though it be mine. He'll go near to form to her what a debauched rascal I am, and fright her out of all good conceit of me: I should do so by him, I am sure, if I had the opportunity. But my hope is in her temper, yet; and it must needs be next to despair that is grounded on any part of a woman's discretion. I would give, by my troth, now, all I could spare (to my clothes, and my sword) to meet my tattered soothsayer again, who was my judge i' the question, to know certainly whose word he has damned or saved. For, till then, I live but under a reprieve. I must seek him. Who be these?

Enter Wasp *with the officers.*

Wasp. Sir, you are a Welsh cuckold, and a prating runt, and no constable.

Bristle. You say very well. Come put in his leg in the middle roundel, and let him hole there.

Wasp. You stink of leeks, metheglin, and cheese, you rogue.

Bristle. Why, what is that to you, if you sit sweetly in the stocks in the meantime? If you have a mind to stink too, your breeches sit close enough to your bum. Sit you merry, sir.

116 **green women** whores
123 **pettifogger** inferior lawyer
128 **ridden** mounted sexually by a man
IV.vi.7 **stale** urinate
21 **take part** partake in
23 **moiety** portion
34 **such** such a one as he is; ***Facinus ... æquat*** "Crime puts those it corrupts on the same footing" (Lucan, *Pharsalia* V. 290)
36 **without** if
38 **impertinently** pointlessly
41 **working** persuading
42 **form** formulate; state explicitly
44 **conceit** opinion
49 **to** all but
56 **runt** one who is ignorant or uncultivated
58 **roundel** hole in the stocks
59 **leeks** (symbol of St. David, patron saint of Wales); **metheglin** Welsh mead

Quarlous. How now, Numps?

Wasp. It is no matter, how; pray you look off.

Quarlous. Nay, I'll not offend you, Numps. I thought you had sat there to be seen.

Wasp. And to be sold, did you not? Pray you mind your business, an' you have any.

Quarlous. Cry you mercy, Numps. Does your leg lie high enough?

Bristle. How now, neighbor Haggis, what says Justice Overdo's worship to the other offenders?

Haggis. Why, he says just nothing, what should he say? Or where should he say? He is not to be found, man. He ha' not been seen i' the Fair, here, all this live-long day, never since seven o'clock i' the morning. His clerks know not what to think on't. There is no court of Piepowders yet. Here they be returned.

[*Enter others of the watch with* Justice *and* Busy.]

Bristle. What shall be done with 'em, then, in your discretion?

Haggis. I think we were best put 'em in the stocks, in discretion (there they will be safe in discretion) for the valor of an hour, or such a thing, till his worship come.

Bristle. It is but a hole matter if we do, neighbor Haggis; come, sir, here is company for you. Heave up the stocks.

Wasp. [*Aside.*] I shall put a trick upon your Welsh diligence, perhaps.

As they open the stocks, Wasp puts his shoe on his hand, and slips it in for his leg.

Bristle. Put in your leg, sir.

Quarlous. What, Rabbi Busy! Is he come?

They bring Busy, and put him in.

Busy. I do obey thee; the lion may roar, but he cannot bite. I am glad to be thus separated from the heathen of the land, and put apart in the stocks for the holy cause.

Wasp. What are you, sir?

Busy. One that rejoiceth in his affliction, and sitteth here to prophesy the destruction of Fairs and May-games, Wakes, and Whitsun-ales, and doth sigh and groan for the reformation of these abuses.

[*They put Justice in the stocks.*]

Wasp. And do you sigh, and groan too, or rejoice in your affliction?

Justice Overdo. I do not feel it; I do not think of it; it is a thing without me. Adam, thou art above these batteries, these contumelies. *In te manca ruit fortuna*, as thy friend Horace says; thou art one, *Quem neque pauperies, neque mors, neque vincula terrent.* And therefore, as another friend of thine says (I think it be thy friend Persius), *Non te quæsiveris extra.*

Quarlous. What's here! A stoic i' the stocks? The fool is turned philosopher.

Busy. Friend, I will leave to communicate my spirit with you if I hear any more of those superstitious relics, those lists of Latin, the very rags of Rome and patches of Popery.

Wasp. Nay, an' you begin to quarrel, gentlemen, I'll leave you. I ha' paid for quarreling too lately. Look you, a device, but shifting in a hand for a foot. God b' w' you.

He gets out.

Busy. Wilt thou then leave thy brethren in tribulation?

Wasp. For this once, sir.

[*Exit.*]

Busy. Thou art a halting neutral – stay him there, stop him – that will not endure the heat of persecution.

Bristle. How now, what's the matter?

Busy. He is fled; he is fled and dares not sit it out.

Bristle. What, has he made an escape? Which way? Follow, neighbor Haggis.

[*Exit* Haggis.]

[*Enter*] Purecraft.

Purecraft. Oh, me! In the stocks! Have the wicked prevailed?

Busy. Peace, religious sister, it is my calling, comfort yourself, an extraordinary calling, and done for my better standing, my surer standing, hereafter.

83 **discretion** judgment

85 **discretion** prudence

86 **discretion** separation; **valor** length; quantity

102 **Whitsun-ales** (parish Whitsuntide celebrations with feasting and sport; the Puritans opposed this as pagan)

107–8 **it...me** i.e., no man can miss what his sense of righteousness would not consider (cf. Epictetus, *Encheiridion* 1.1)

109 **batteries** series of blows; **contumelies** abuses

109–10 ***In...fortuna*** "Fortune maims herself when she attacks you" (Horace, *Satires* II.7.88)

111–12 ***Quem...terrent*** "whom neither poverty, nor death, nor shackles can affright" (Horace, *Satires* II.7.84)

113–14 ***Non...extra*** "Look to no one outside yourself" (Persius, *Satires* I.7)

115 **stoic...stocks** (pun on stoics who accept Roman philosophy of indifference to worldly suffering = senseless, stocklike)

117 **leave** cease

119 **lists** fag-ends or strips of cloth (Puritans condemned Latin as the Pope's language)

123 **device** trick; **shifting in** substituting

139 **standing** reputation for service in God

The madman enters.

Trouble-All. By whose warrant, by whose warrant, this?

Quarlous. Oh, here's my man dropped in, I looked for.

Justice Overdo. Ha!

Purecraft. Oh, good sir, they have set the faithful, here, to be wondered at; and provided holes for the holy of the land.

Trouble-All. Had they warrant for it? Showed they Justice Overdo's hand? If they had no warrant, they shall answer it.

[*Reenter* Haggis.]

Bristle. Sure, you did not lock the stocks sufficiently, neighbor Toby!

Haggis. No? See if you can lock 'em better.

Bristle. They are very sufficiently locked, and truly, yet something is in the matter.

Trouble-All. True, your warrant is the matter that is in question; by what warrant?

Bristle. Madman, hold your peace; I will put you in his room else, in the very same hole, do you see?

Quarlous. How! Is he a madman?

Trouble-All. Show me Justice Overdo's warrant, I obey you.

Haggis. You are a mad fool, hold your tongue.

[*Exeunt* Haggis, Bristle.]

Trouble-All. In Justice Overdo's name, I drink to you, and here's my warrant.

Shows his can.

Justice Overdo. [*Aside.*] Alas, poor wretch! How it earns my heart for him!

Quarlous. [*Aside.*] If he be mad, it is in vain to question him. I'll try, though. [*To him.*] Friend, there was a gentlewoman showed you two names, some hour since, Argalus and Palemon, to mark in a book; which of 'em was it you marked?

Trouble-All. I mark no name but Adam Overdo; that is the name of names; he only is the sufficient magistrate; and that name I reverence. Show it me.

Quarlous. [*Aside.*] This fellow's mad, indeed. I am further off, now, than afore.

Justice Overdo. [*Aside.*] I shall not breathe in peace till I have made him some amends.

Quarlous. [*Aside.*] Well, I will make another use of him, is come in my head: I have a nest of beards in my trunk, one something like his.

The watchmen come back again.

Bristle. This mad fool has made me that I know not whether I have locked the stocks or no; I think I locked 'em.

Trouble-All. Take Adam Overdo in your mind, and fear nothing.

Bristle. 'Slid, madness itself, hold thy peace, and take that.

Trouble-All. Strikest thou without a warrant? Take thou that.

The madman fights with 'em, and they leave open the stocks.

Busy. We are delivered by miracle; fellow in fetters, let us not refuse the means. This madness was of the spirit. The malice of the enemy hath mocked itself.

[*Exeunt* Busy *and* Justice.]

Purecraft. Mad, do they call him! The world is mad in error, but he is mad in truth. I love him o' the sudden (the cunning man said all true) and shall love him more and more. How well it becomes a man to be mad in truth! O, that I might be his yoke-fellow, and be mad with him, what a many should we draw to madness in truth with us.

[*Exit.*]

The watch, missing them, are affrighted.

Bristle. How now! All 'scaped? Where's the woman? It is witchcraft! Her velvet hat is a witch, o' my conscience, or my key t'one! The madman was a devil, and I am an ass; so bless me, my place, and mine office.

[*Exeunt.*]

Act V

Scene i.

[*Enter* Leatherhead, Filcher, Sharkwell.]

[*Leatherhead.*] Well, Luck and Saint Bartholomew! Out with the sign of our invention, in the

143 **I** whom I

147 **wondered** (1) marveled; (2) bewildered

169 **earns** grieves

176–9 **I . . . reverence** (cf. Eph. 1:21; Phil. 2:9)

183–5 **I . . . his** (the first indication that Quarlous will disguise himself [as Trouble-All] to see what is written on Grace Wellborn's tablet)

184 **nest** collection; **trunk** padded breeches (trunk-hose)

195 **We . . . miracle** (passage alludes to the stocking of Paul and Silas; cf. Acts 16:19–34)

199 **Mad . . . him!** (Purecraft is thinking of Quarlous in disguise)

204 **yoke-fellow** partner (in marriage)

210 **t'one** the one or the other

V.i.1 s.d. (as puppetmaster, the hobby-horse man, Leatherhead, takes on a new name [Lantern] and disguise – the very epitome of the Fair – so he will not be recognized by Cokes from whom he has stolen money; (cf. V.iii.61–2)

2 **sign . . . invention** (1) the painted cloth showing the subject of the puppet show; (2) the playbill describing the matter of the show

name of Wit, and do you beat the drum the while. All the foul i' the Fair, I mean all the dirt in Smithfield (that's one of Master Littlewit's carriwitchets now), will be thrown at our banner today if the matter does not please the people. Oh, the motions that I, Lantern Leatherhead, have given light to, i' my time, since my Master Pod died! *Jerusalem* was a stately thing; and so was *Nineveh*, and *The City of Norwich*, and *Sodom and Gomorrah*, with the rising o' the prentices and pulling down the bawdy houses there, upon Shrove Tuesday; but *The Gunpowder Plot*, there was a get-penny! I have presented that to an eighteen-, or twenty-pence audience, nine times in an afternoon. Your home-born projects prove ever the best, they are so easy, and familiar; they put too much learning i' their things now o' days. And that I fear will be the spoil o' this. Littlewit? I say, Micklewit, if not too mickle! Look to your gathering there, good man Filcher.

Filcher. I warrant you, sir.

Leatherhead. An' there come any gentlefolks, take twopence a piece, Sharkwell.

Sharkwell. I warrant you, sir, threepence an' we can.

[*Exeunt.*]

Act V. Scene ii.

The Justice *comes in like a porter.*

Justice Overdo. This later disguise, I have borrowed of a porter, shall carry me out to all my great and good ends; which, however interrupted, were never destroyed in me. Neither is the hour of my severity yet come, to reveal myself where in, cloud-like, I will break out in rain and hail, lightning and thunder, upon the head of enormity. Two main works I have to prosecute: first, one is to invent some satisfaction for the poor, kind wretch, who is out of his wits for my sake; and yonder I see him coming. I will walk aside, and project for it.

[*Enter* Winwife, Grace.]

Winwife. I wonder where Tom Quarlous is, that he returns not; it may be he is struck in here to seek us.

Grace. See, here's our madman again.

[*Enter*] Quarlous, [Purecraft. Quarlous] *in the habit of the madman is mistaken by* Mistress Purecraft.

Quarlous. [*Aside.*] I have made myself as like him as his gown and cap will give me leave.

Purecraft. Sir, I love you, and would be glad to be mad with you in truth.

Winwife. How! My widow in love with a madman?

Purecraft. Verily, I can be as mad in spirit as you.

Quarlous. By whose warrant? Leave your canting. Gentlewoman, have I found you? (Save ye, quit ye, and multiply ye.) Where's your book? 'Twas a sufficient name I marked, let me see't, be not afraid to shew't me.

He desires to see the book of Mistress Grace.

Grace. What would you with it, sir?

Quarlous. Mark it again, and again, at your service.

Grace. Here it is, sir, this was it you marked.

Quarlous. Palemon? Fare you well, fare you well.

Winwife. How, Palemon!

---

6 **carriwitchets** puns; jokes

6–8 **thrown . . . people** (in public playhouses, fruit was thrown onto the stage by disapproving members of the audience)

9 **light** birth

10 **Master Pod** (a marginal note by Jonson acknowledges Pod as Lantern's predecessor; Jonson refers to Master Pod in other works as well)

10–12 ***Jerusalem . . . Gomorrah*** (all popular themes for puppet shows: the destruction of Jerusalem by the Romans; the fate of Nineveh [Jonah 3]; the building of Norwich [the only non-biblical text here; Norwich was a center of the cloth trade]; and the destruction of Sodom and Gomorrah [Gen. 19:24–8])

13–14 **rising . . . Tuesday** (apprentices of London habitually rioted on Shrove Tuesday; shortage of food is now thought to be one possible cause apart from the tradition celebrated in Dekker's play here)

15 ***The . . . Plot*** (no play is extant, but this Catholic plot against the life and government of King James was exposed and defeated on November 5, 1605 and as Guy Fawkes Day – named for one of the conspirators – had become a national holiday); **get-penny** economic success

16–18 **eighteen- . . . afternoon** (the numbers are in the aggregate)

18 **projects** shows

19 **familiar** easily understood

21 **spoil** ruin; **this** puppet shows

22 **Micklewit** Great Wit

23 **gathering** entrance fees

23–7 **Filcher . . . Sharkwell** (their names suggest they overcharge)

V.ii.2 **carry . . . to** allow me to execute

5 **severity** (trial which must result in his unmasking himself)

6–8 **cloud-like . . . enormity** (his self-assigned role is described in a way that recalls Shakespeare's Prospero)

8 **prosecute** undertake

9 **invent** find

10 **wretch** (Trouble-All)

12 **project** devise a means

14 **struck** gone

23 **canting** (Puritan language)

25 **book** (the writing tablet with the names of "Argalus" and "Palemon")

Grace. Yes, faith, he has discovered it to you now, and therefore 'twere vain to disguise it longer; I am yours, sir, by the benefit of your fortune.

Winwife. And you have him, Mistress, believe it, that shall never give you cause to repent her benefit, but make you rather to think that in this choice she had both her eyes.

Grace. I desire to put it to no danger of protestation.

[*Exeunt* Grace *and* Winwife.]

Quarlous. Palemon the word and Winwife the man?

Purecraft. Good sir, vouchsafe a yoke-fellow in your madness; shun not one of the sanctified sisters that would draw with you in truth.

Quarlous. Away, you are a herd of hypocritical proud ignorants, rather wild, than mad. Fitter for woods, and the society of beasts, than houses, and the congregation of men. You are the second part of the society of canters, outlaws to order and discipline, and the only privileged church-robbers of Christendom. [*To himself.*] Let me alone. Palemon, the word, and Winwife the man?

Purecraft. [*Aside.*] I must uncover myself unto him, or I shall never enjoy him for all the cunning men's promises. [*To him.*] Good sir, hear me, I am worth six thousand pounds. My love to you is become my rack; I'll tell you all, and the truth, since you hate the hypocrisy of the party-colored brotherhood. These seven years I have been a willful holy widow only to draw feasts and gifts from my entangled suitors. I am also, by office, an assisting sister of the deacons, and a devourer instead of a distributor of the alms. I am a special maker of marraiges for our decayed brethren with our rich widows; for a third part of their wealth, when they are married, for the relief of the poor elect, as also our poor handsome young virgins with our wealthy bachelors, or widowers; to make them steal from their husbands, when I have confirmed them in the faith and got all put into their custodies. And if I ha' not my bargain, they may sooner turn a scolding drab into a silent minister than make me leave pronouncing reprobation and damnation unto them. Our elder, Zeal-of-the-land, would have had me, but I know him to be the capital knave of the land, making himself rich by being made feoffee in trust to deceased brethren, and cozening their heirs by swearing the absolute gift of their inheritance. And thus, having cased my conscience, and uttered my heart, with the tongue of my love – enjoy all my deceits together. I beseech you. I should not have revealed this to you, but that in time I think you are mad; and I hope you'll think me so too, sir?

Quarlous. Stand aside; I'll answer you presently.

He considers with himself of it.

Why should not I marry this six thousand pounds, now I think on't? And a good trade too, that she has beside, ha? The tother wench, Winwife, is sure of; there's no expectation for me there! Here I may make myself some saver; yet, if she continue mad, there's the question. It is money that I want; why should I not marry the money, when 'tis offered me? I have a license and all; it is but razing out one name and putting in another. There's no playing with a man's fortune! I am resolved! I were truly mad, an' I would not! [*To her.*] Well, come

35 **benefit** kindness

39 **she . . . eyes** (the goddess Fortune was usually represented as blindfolded)

40–1 **protestation** (a protest at an allegation the truth of which cannot be confirmed or denied, yet not ignored; Grace would seem immodest if she agreed with Winwife, but foolish if she did not; she would seem smug not to reply; she therefore declines the protest)

44 **vouchsafe** grant; bestow

51 **second . . . canters** (i.e., thieves who spoke a special jargon; cf. line 23 above)

56 **uncover** reveal

56–90 **I . . . sir?** (this speech is Jonson's most direct revelation and criticism of Puritan hypocrisy and behavior; it also suggests why Dame Purecraft is so drawn to Busy)

57 **enjoy** (with sexual overtones)

57–8 **cunning men's** (as part of the criminal underworld)

60 **rack** torment

62 **party-colored** hypocritical

68 **decayed** (impaired or fallen in fortune; here, because they lost their livings)

71 **elect** (those predestined for salvation according to Puritan doctrine)

76 **drab** whore

77 **silent minister** (one put out of a living as a result of the Hampton Court conference in 1604)

78 **reprobation** (those predestined for damnation according to Puritan doctrine)

80 **had** (1) married; (2) sexually possessed

82 **feoffee in trust** (trustee invested with a freehold estate)

83 **cozening** cheating

84 **absolute** (not open to challenge or lawsuit)

87 **deceits** practices; schemes

88 **in time** at present

93 **good trade** (as marriage-broker)

96 **saver** compensation (for loss; a gambling term)

100 **razing** erasing

your ways, follow me, an' you will be mad, I'll show you a warrant!

He takes her along with him.

Purecraft. Most zealously, it is that I zealously desire.

The Justice calls him.

Justice Overdo. Sir, let me speak with you.

Quarlous. By whose warrant?

Justice Overdo. The warrant that you tender, and respect so; Justice Overdo's! I am the man, friend Trouble-all, though thus disguised (as the careful magistrate ought) for the good of the republic, in the Fair, and the weeding out of enormity. Do you want a house or meat, or drink, or clothes? Speak whatsoever it is, it shall be supplied you; what want you?

Quarlous. Nothing but your warrant.

Justice Overdo. My warrant? For what?

Quarlous. To be gone, sir.

Justice Overdo. Nay, I pray thee, stay. I am serious, and have not many words, nor much time to exchange with thee; think what may do thee good.

Quarlous. Your hand and seal will do me a great deal of good; nothing else in the whole Fair, that I know.

Justice Overdo. If it were to any end, thou should'st have it willingly.

Quarlous. Why, it will satisfy me; that's end enough to look on. An' you will not gi' it me, let me go.

Justice Overdo. Alas! thou shalt ha' it presently. I'll but step into the scrivener's hereby, and bring it. Do not go away.

The Justice *goes out.*

Quarlous. [*Aside.*] Why, this madman's shape will prove a very fortunate one, I think! Can a ragged robe produce these effects? If this be the wise Justice, and he bring me his hand, I shall go near to make some use on't.

[Justice] *returns.*

He is come already!

Justice Overdo. Look thee! here is my hand and seal, "Adam Overdo"; if there be anything to be written, above in the paper, that thou want'st now, or at any time hereafter, think on't. It is my deed; I deliver it so. Can your friend write?

Quarlous. Her hand for a witness, and all is well.

Justice Overdo. With all my heart.

He urgeth Mistress Purecraft.

Quarlous. [*Aside.*] Why should not I ha' the conscience to make this a bond of a thousand pounds, now? or what I would else?

Justice Overdo. Look you, there it is; and I deliver it as my deed again.

Quarlous. Let us now proceed in madness.

He takes her in with him.

Justice Overdo. Well, my conscience is much eased; I ha' done my part, though it doth him no good, yet Adam hath offered satisfaction! The sting is removed from hence. Poor man, he is much altered with his affliction; it has brought him low! Now, for my other work, reducing the young man I have followed so long in love, from the brink of his bane to the center of safety. Here, or in some such like vain place, I shall be sure to find him. I will wait the good time.

Act V. Scene iii.

[*Enter* Cokes, Sharkwell, Filcher.]

[*Cokes.*] How now? What's here to do? Friend, art thou the Master of the Monuments?

Sharkwell. 'Tis a motion, an't please your worship.

Justice Overdo. [*Aside.*] My fantastical brother-in-law, Master Bartholomew Cokes!

Cokes. A motion, what's that?

He reads the bill.

"The ancient modern history of *Hero and Leander*, otherwise called *The Touch-stone of true Love*, with as true a trial of friendship between Damon and Pythias, two faithful friends o' the Bankside?" Pretty, i' faith, what's the meaning on't? Is't an interlude? Or what is't?

Filcher. Yes, sir; please you come near, we'll take your money within.

Cokes. Back with these children; they do so follow me up and down.

The boys o' the Fair follow him.

---

110 **tender** have regard for
112–13 **as . . . ought** as befits a responsible magistrate
113 **republic** state; commonwealth
119 **warrant** license
137 **hand** (document with his signature)
147–8 **conscience** good sense; sound judgment
158 **reducing** bringing back
160 **bane** destruction
161 **vain** indulgent
162–3 **good time** propitious moment

V.iii.1 **What's . . . do?** what's going on?
2 **Master . . . Monuments** (literally, the guide to tombs and effigies in Westminster Cathedral; but Cokes means a guide to the puppets as pagan effigies)
4 **fantastical** fanciful
7–11 **"The . . . Bankside"** (this bill of particulars parodies that of earlier Elizabethan court entertainments, as the puppet show travesties Marlowe's popular poem on Hero and Leander [published in 1598])
12 **interlude** (play usually staged in households of nobility or gentry)

[*Enter* Littlewit.]

Littlewit. By your leave, friend.

Filcher. You must pay, sir, an' you go in.

Littlewit. Who, I? I perceive thou know'st not me; call the master o' the motion.

Sharkwell. What, do you not know the author, fellow Filcher? You must take no money of him; he must come in *gratis*: Master Littlewit is a voluntary; he is the author.

Littlewit. Peace, speak not too loud, I would not have any notice taken that I am the author till we see how it passes.

Cokes. Master Littlewit, how dost thou?

Littlewit. Master Cokes! You are exceeding well met. What, in your doublet and hose, without a cloak or a hat?

Cokes. I would I might never stir, as I am an honest man, and by that fire, I have lost all i' the Fair, and all my acquaintance too. Didst thou meet anybody that I know, Master Littlewit? My man Numps, or my sister Overdo, or Mistress Grace? Pray thee, Master Littlewit, lend me some money to see the interlude, here. I'll pay thee again, as I am a gentleman. If thou'lt but carry me home, I have money enough there.

Littlewit. Oh, sir, you shall command it; what, will a crown serve you?

Cokes. I think it will. What do we pay for coming in, fellows?

Filcher. Twopence, sir.

Cokes. Twopence? there's twelvepence, friend; nay, I am a gallant, as simple as I look now, if you see me with my man about me, and my artillery, again.

Littlewit. Your man was i' the stocks, e'en now, sir.

Cokes. Who, Numps?

Littlewit. Yes, faith.

Cokes. For what, i' faith? I am glad o' that; remember to tell me on't anon; I have enough, now! What manner of matter is this, Master Littlewit? What kind of actors ha' you? Are they good actors?

Littlewit. Pretty youths, sir, all children both old and young. Here's the master of 'em –

[*Enter* Leatherhead.]

Leatherhead. (Call me not Leatherhead, but Lantern.)

Leatherhead whispers to Littlewit.

Littlewit. Master Lantern, that gives light to the business.

Cokes. In good time, sir, I would fain see 'em, I would be glad to drink with the young company; which is the tiring-house?

Leatherhead. Troth sir, our tiring-house is somewhat little; we are but beginners, yet, pray pardon us; you cannot go upright in't.

Cokes. No? Not now my hat is off? What would you have done with me, if you had had me, feather and all, as I was once today? Ha' you none of your pretty impudent boys, now, to bring stools, fill tobacco, fetch ale, and beg money, as they have at other houses? Let me see some o' your actors.

Littlewit. Show him 'em, show him 'em. Master Lantern, this is a gentleman that is a favorer of the quality.

Justice Overdo. [*Aside.*] Aye, the favoring of this licentious quality is the consumption of many a young gentleman, a pernicious enormity.

Cokes. What, do they live in baskets?

Leatherhead. They do lie in a basket, sir, they are o' the small players.

He brings them out in a basket.

Cokes. These be players minors, indeed. Do you call these players?

Leatherhead. They are actors sir, and as good as any, none dispraised, for dumb shows. Indeed, I am the mouth of 'em all!

---

20 **master** author (Littlewit)
22–3 **of him** from his associates
24 **voluntary** amateur; one who serves without pay
33 **fire** possibly (1) the fire of experience and tribulation; (2) the fire in Ursula's booth; (3) the fire of temptation and sin
43 **crown** (a five-shilling coin)
48 **simple** humble; poor
50 **artillery** equipage
55 **enough** (1) to think about; (2) money for the moment
59 **Pretty youths** (the puppet play may also parody the newly popular boys' companies; Richard Edwardes's *Damon and Pythias* was written for the Children of the Chapel in the 1560s; Jonson's company, Lady Elizabeth's Men, was half-constituted by the Children of the Revels)
61–2 **(Call . . . Lantern)** (Leatherhead cannot reveal his identity to Cokes)
63 **gives light** (pun on his name)
65 **In good time** well met; **fain** gladly
67 **tiring-house** (area behind the stage where actors dressed [attired themselves])
69 **little** (because puppets take no room; Cokes has not yet fathomed this; and cf. Busy in V.v)
70 **go** stand
74 **impudent** presumptuous; shameless
80 **quality** the actors
82 **consumption** (1) financial ruin; (2) moral corruption
86 **small players** (they are hand puppets, not marionettes)
90 **dumb shows** pantomimes (that were occasionally in plays in playhouses, as in *The Spanish Tragedy* and *The Duchess of Malfi*)
91 **mouth** voice

Cokes. Thy mouth will hold 'em all, I think. One Taylor would go near to beat all this company, with a hand bound behind him.

Littlewit. Aye, and eat 'em all, too, an' they were in cake-bread.

Cokes. I thank you for that, Master Littlewit, a good jest! Which is your Burbage now?

Leatherhead. What mean you by that, sir?

Cokes. Your best actor. Your Field?

Littlewit. Good, i'faith! You are even with me, sir.

Leatherhead. This is he that acts young Leander, sir. He is extremely beloved of the womenkind, they do so affect his action, the green gamesters that come here; and this is lovely Hero; this with the beard, Damon; and this, pretty Pythias: this is the ghost of King Dionysius in the habit of a scrivener, as you shall see anon, at large.

Cokes. Well, they are a civil company, I like 'em for that; they offer not to fleer, nor jeer, nor break jests, as the great players do. And then, there goes not so much charge to the feasting of 'em, or making 'em drunk, as to the other, by reason of their littleness. Do they use to play perfect? Are they never flustered?

Leatherhead. No, sir, I thank my industry and policy for it; they are as well-governed a company, though I say it – and here is young Leander, is as proper an actor of his inches; and shakes his head like an hostler.

Cokes. But do you play it according to the printed book? I have read that.

Leatherhead. By no means, sir.

Cokes. No? How then?

Leatherhead. A better way, sir; that is too learned and poetical for our audience; what do they know what Hellespont is? "Guilty of true love's blood?" Or what Abydos is? Or "the other Sestos hight"?

Cokes. Th' art i' the right, I do not know myself.

Leatherhead. No, I have entreated Master Littlewit to take a little pains to reduce it to a more familiar strain for our people.

Cokes. How, I pray thee, good Master Littlewit?

Littlewit. It pleases him to make a matter of it, sir. But there is no such matter, I assure you. I have only made it a little easy, and modern for the times, sir, that's all; as, for the Hellespont, I imagine our Thames here; and then Leander I make a dyer's son, about Puddle Wharf; and Hero a wench o' the Bank-side, who going over one morning, to old Fish Street, Leander spies her land at Trig Stairs, and falls in love with her. Now do I introduce Cupid, having metamorphosed himself into a drawer, and he strikes Hero in love with a pint of sherry; and other pretty passages there are, o' the friendship, that will delight you, sir, and please you of judgment.

Cokes. I'll be sworn they shall; I am in love with the actors already, and I'll be allied to them presently. (They respect gentlemen, these fellows.) Hero shall be my fairing: but, which of my fairings? Le' me see – i' faith, my fiddle! and Leander my fiddle-stick. Then Damon, my drum; and Pythias, my pipe, and the ghost of Dionysius, my hobby-horse. All fitted.

Act V. Scene iv.

[*Enter to them* Winwife, Grace.]

[*Winwife.*] Look, yonder's your Cokes gotten in among his playfellows; I thought we could not miss him at such a spectacle.

---

93 **Taylor** (possibly [1] the actor Joseph Taylor, a member of this play company; [2] the poet John Taylor, who challenged the pamphleteer William Fennor to a battle of wits in October 1614 but did not appear himself)

95 **in** made of

98 **Burbage** (Richard Burbage [died ca. 1619], in Shakespeare's company the King's Men as their leading actor)

100 **Field** (Nathan Field [1587–?1619], the chief actor of Lady Elizabeth's Servants when they staged *Bartholomew Fair*; Cokes is here showing off his knowledge of the theater; Jonson is playing with the thin line between art and reality, actor and audience)

101 **You . . . me** now I see what you mean (i.e., who is my leading actor?)

104 **affect** appreciate; approve; **action** (with sexual pun)

104–5 **green gamesters** young (perhaps inexperienced) wenches

109 **at large** in full

111 **fleer** mock

112 **great** adult

115–16 **Do . . . perfect?** are their memories perfect?

120 **of . . . inches** for his size

121 **hostler** innkeeper (with a pun on William Ostler, a member of the King's Men)

122–3 **printed book** (Marlowe's poem; it was reprinted with Chapman's addition in 1600, 1606, and 1613)

130 **hight** called (these phrases are all taken from Marlowe's poem)

133 **reduce** simplify

136 **make . . . it** suggest it was a difficult job

141 **Puddle Wharf** (one of London's watergates between Blackfriars and Paul's stairs, across the Thames from the Hope Theater)

142 **Bank-side** (where the major playhouses were – and where Jonson's audiences were attending the play)

143 **old Fish Street** (the major wet-fish market within the city walls of London)

144 **Trig Stairs** (stairs leading to the river next to Puddle Wharf)

146 **drawer** tapster

147 **strikes Hero** causes Hero to fall; **with** by means of

152 **be . . . them** make them members of my family (by associating each one of them with one of his purchases)

158 **fitted** accommodated; accounted for

Grace. Let him alone, he is so busy he will never spy us.

Leatherhead. Nay, good sir.

Cokes *is handling the puppets.*

Cokes. I warrant thee, I will not hurt her, fellow; what, dost think me uncivil? I pray thee be not jealous: I am toward a wife.

Littlewit. Well, good Master Lantern, make ready to begin, that I may fetch my wife, and look you be perfect; you undo me else, i' my reputation.

Leatherhead. I warrant you, sir, do not you breed too great an expectation of it among your friends; that's the only hurter of these things.

Littlewit. No, no, no.

[*Exit.*]

Cokes. I'll stay here, and see; pray thee, let me see.

Winwife. How diligent and troublesome he is!

Grace. The place becomes him, methinks.

Justice Overdo. [*Aside.*] My ward, Mistress Grace, in the company of a stranger? I doubt I shall be compelled to discover myself, before my time!

[*Enter* Knockem, Edgworth, Win, Whit, Mistress Overdo.]

The door-keepers speak.

Filcher. Twopence apiece, gentlemen, an excellent motion.

Knockem. Shall we have fine fireworks, and good vapors?

Sharkwell. Yes, captain, and waterworks, too.

Whit. I pree dee, take a care o' dy shmall lady, there, Edgworth; I will look to dish tall lady myself.

Leatherhead. Welcome, gentlemen, welcome, gentlemen.

Whit. Predee, mashter o' de monshtersh, help a very sick lady, here, to a chair, to shit in.

Leatherhead. Presently, sir.

They bring Mistress Overdo a chair.

Whit. Good fait now, Urs'la's ale and *aqua vitae* ish to blame for't; shit down, shweetheart, shit down, and shleep a little.

Edgworth. Madam, you are very welcome hither.

Knockem. Yes, and you shall see very good vapors.

Justice Overdo. [*Aside.*] Here is my care come! I like to see him in so good company; and yet I wonder that persons of such fashion should resort hither!

By Edgworth.

Edgworth. This is a very private house, madam.

Leatherhead. Will it please your ladyship sit, madam?

The cutpurse courts Mistress Littlewit.

Win. Yes, good-man. They do so all-to-be-madam me, I think they think me a very lady!

Edgworth. What else, madam?

Win. Must I put off my mask to him?

Edgworth. Oh, by no means.

Win. How should my husband know me, then?

Knockem. Husband? An idle vapor; he must not know you, nor you him; there's the true vapor.

Justice Overdo. [*Aside.*] Yea, I will observe more of this. [*To Whit.*] Is this a lady, friend?

Whit. Aye, and dat is anoder lady, shweetheart; if dou hasht a mind to 'em give me twelvepence from tee, and dou shalt have eider-oder on 'em!

Justice Overdo. [*Aside.*] Aye? This will prove my chiefest enormity; I will follow this.

Edgworth. Is not this a finer life, lady, than to be clogged with a husband?

Win. Yes, a great deal. When will they begin, trow, in the name o' the motion?

Edgworth. By and by, madam; they stay but for company.

Knockem. Do you hear, puppet-master, these are tedious vapors; when begin you?

Leatherhead. We stay but for Master Littlewit, the author, who is gone for his wife; and we begin presently.

Win. That's I, that's I.

Edgworth. That was you, lady; but now you are no such poor thing.

Knockem. Hang the author's wife, a running vapor! Here be ladies will stay for ne'er a Delia of 'em all.

Whit. But hear me now, here ish one o' de ladish, ashleep; stay till she but vake, man.

V.iv.10 toward about to marry
20 troublesome laborious
23 doubt fear
27 fireworks (fireworks on the Thames and elsewhere was common entertainment on special occasions)
29 waterworks (pageants on the Thames)
30 shmall lady (Win Littlewit)
31 tall lady (Mistress Overdo)
38 *aqua vitae* ardent spirits (such as whiskey or brandy)
46 s.d. *By* referring to
47 private house (1) house that provides us privacy; (2) private theater
50–1 all . . . me persist in calling me "Madam"
62 eider-oder on one or the other of
67 clogged obstructed
69 trow do you think
81 Delia (anagram of *ideal* and the subject of a well-known sonnet sequence by Samuel Daniel [1592])

[*Enter to them* Wasp.] *The door-keepers again.*

Wasp. How now, friends? What's here to do?

Filcher. Twopence apiece, sir, the best motion in the Fair.

Wasp. I believe you lie; if you do, I'll have my money again, and beat you.

Winwife. Numps is come!

Wasp. Did you see a master of mine come in here, a tall young squire of Harrow o' the Hill, Master Bartholomew Cokes?

Filcher. I think there be such a one within.

Wasp. Look he be, you were best; but it is very likely. I wonder I found him not at all the rest. I ha' been at the Eagle, and the Black Wolf, and the Bull with the Five Legs and Two Pizzles (he was a calf at Uxbridge Fair, two years agone), and at the Dogs that dance the Morris and the Hare o' the Tabor; and missed him at all these! Sure this must needs be some fine sight, that holds him so, if it have him.

Cokes. Come, come, are you ready now?

Leatherhead. Presently, sir.

Wasp. Hoyday, he's at work in his doublet and hose; do you hear, sir? Are you employed, that you are bare-headed, and so busy?

Cokes. Hold your peace, Numps; you ha' been i' the stocks, I hear.

Wasp. Does he know that? Nay, then the date of my authority is out; I must think no longer to reign, my government is at an end. He that will correct another must want fault in himself.

Winwife. Sententious Numps! I never heard so much from him before.

Leatherhead. Sure, Master Littlewit will not come; please you take your place, sir, we'll begin.

Cokes. I pray thee do, mine ears long to be at it, and my eyes too. Oh, Numps, i' the stocks, Numps? Where's your sword, Numps?

Wasp. I pray you intend your game; sir, let me alone.

Cokes. Well, then, we are quit for all. Come, sit down, Numps; I'll interpret to thee. Did you see Mistress Grace? It's no matter, neither, now I think on't, tell me anon.

Winwife. A great deal of love and care he expresses.

Grace. Alas! Would you have him to express more than he has? That were tyranny.

Cokes. Peace, ho; now, now.

Leatherhead. *Gentles, that no longer your expectations may wander,*
Behold our chief actor, amorous Leander.
With a great deal of cloth lapped about him like a scarf,
For he yet serves his father, a dyer at Puddle Wharf,
Which place we'll make bold with, to call it our Abydus,
As the Bankside is our Sestos, and let it not be denied us.
Now, as he is beating, to make the dye take the fuller,
Who chances to come by, but fair Hero, in a sculler;
And seeing Leander's naked leg, and goodly calf,
Cast at him, from the boat, a sheep's eye, and a half.
Now she is landed, and the sculler come back;
By and by, you shall see what Leander doth lack.

Puppet Leander. *Cole, Cole, old Cole.*

Leatherhead. *That is the sculler's name without control.*

Puppet Leander *Cole, Cole; I say, Cole.*

Leatherhead. *We do hear you.*

Puppet Leander *Old Cole.*

Leatherhead. *Old Cole? Is the dyer turned collier? How do you sell?*

Puppet Leander *A pox o' your manners; kiss my hole here, and smell.*

Leatherhead. *Kiss your hole, and smell? There's manners indeed.*

Puppet Leander *Why, Cole, I say, Cole.*

Leatherhead. *It's the sculler you need!*

Puppet Leander *Aye, and be hanged.*

Leatherhead. *Be hanged; look you yonder,*
Old Cole, you must go hang with Master Leander.

Puppet Cole. *Where is he?*

Puppet Leander *Here, Cole, what fairest of fairs*
Was that fare, that thou landedst but now at Trig-stairs?

Cokes. What was that, fellow? Pray thee tell me; I scarce understand 'em.

Leatherhead. *Leander does ask, sir, what fairest of fairs*
Was the fare that he landed, but now, at Trig-stairs?

Puppet Cole. *It is lovely Hero.*

Puppet Leander *Nero?*

Puppet Cole. *No, Hero.*

97–101 Eagle . . . Tabor (attractions at the Fair; cf. III.vi.8–9)
98 Pizzles penises
106 Hoyday (nonsense cry of excitement; properly "heyday")
106–7 doublet and hose (waistcoat and stockings without cloak; typical male attire but also a state of undress)
107 Are . . . employed (my authority with him has come to an end)
114 want be free of
122 intend pay attention to; **game** entertainment (i.e., the puppet play)
124 quit even (from acquitted)
134 *lapped* wrapped
138 *fuller* more completely
139 *sculler* (a boat propelled by oars; properly *scull*)
141 *sheep's . . . half* (proverbial for an amorous or lecherous look)
144 *Cole* (cant for *pander*)
145 *sculler's* oarsman's; ***control*** doubt
149 *collier* (1) coalseller; (2) term of abuse (colliers were black from coal and legendary cheaters)
150 *hole* (obscene reference)
165 *Nero* a corrupt Roman emperor

Leatherhead. *It is Hero*
Of the Bankside, he saith, to tell you truth without erring,
Is come over into Fish-street to eat some fresh herring,
Leander says no more, but as fast as he can,
Gets on all his best clothes; and will after to the Swan.

Cokes. Most admirable good, is't not?

Leatherhead. *Stay, sculler.*

Puppet Cole. *What say you?*

Leatherhead. *You must stay for Leander, and carry him to the wench.*

Puppet Cole. *You rogue, I am no pander.*

Cokes. He says he is no pander. 'Tis a fine language; I understand it, now.

Leatherhead. *Are you no pander, Goodman Cole?*
Here's no man says you are,
You'll grow a hot Cole, it seems; pray you, stay for your fare.

Puppet Cole. *Will he come away?*

Leatherhead. *What do you say?*

Puppet Cole. *I'd ha' him come away.*

Leatherhead. *Would you ha' Leander come away? Why 'pray, sir, stay.*
You are angry, Goodman Cole; I believe the fair maid
Came over wi' you o' trust. Tell us, sculler, are you paid?

Puppet Cole. *Yes, Goodman Hogrubber o' Pickt-hatch.*

Leatherhead. *How, Hogrubber, o' Pickt-hatch?*

Puppet Cole. *Aye, Hogrubber o' Pickt-hatch. Take you that.*

The Puppet strikes him over the pate.

Leatherhead. *O, my head!*

Puppet Cole. *Harm watch, harm catch.*

Cokes. Harm watch, harm catch, he says; very good i' faith, the Sculler had like to ha' knocked you, sirrah.

Leatherhead. Yes, but that his fare called him away.

Puppet Leander *Row apace, row apace, row, row, row, row, row.*

Leatherhead. *You are knavishly loaden, sculler; take heed where you go.*

Puppet Cole. *Knave i' your face, Goodman rogue.*

Puppet Leander *Row, row, row, row, row, row.*

Cokes. He said knave i' your face, friend.

Leatherhead. Aye, sir, I heard him. But there's no talking to these watermen; they will ha' the last word.

Cokes. God's my life! I am not allied to the sculler, yet; he shall be Dauphin, my boy. But my Fiddle-stick does fiddle in and out too much; I pray thee speak to him on't. Tell him,
I would have him tarry in my sight, more.

Leatherhead. I pray you, be content; you'll have enough on him, sir.
Now, gentles, I take it, here is none of you so stupid,
But that you have heard of a little god of love called Cupid.
Who out of kindness to Leander, hearing he but saw her,
This present day and hour, doth turn himself to a drawer.
And because he would have their first meeting to be merry,
He strikes Hero in love to him, with a pint of sherry.
Which he tells her, from amorous Leander is sent her,
Who after him, into the room of Hero, doth venter.

Puppet Jonas. *A pint of sack; score a pint of sack i' the Coney.*

Puppet Leander *goes into Mistress Hero's room.*

Cokes. Sack? You said but e'en now it should be sherry.

Puppet Jonas. *Why so it is; sherry, sherry, sherry.*

Cokes. "Sherry, sherry, sherry." By my troth he makes me merry. I must have a name for Cupid, too. Let me see, thou mightst help me now, an'thou wouldest, Numps, at a dead lift, but thou art dreaming o' the stocks still! Do not think on't. I have forgot it; 'tis but a nine days' wonder, man; let it not trouble thee.

Wasp. I would the stocks were about your neck, sir; condition I hung by the heels in them till the wonder wore off from you, with all my heart.

Cokes. Well said, resolute Numps. But hark you, friend, where is the friendship, all this while, between my drum, Damon, and my pipe, Pythias?

Leatherhead. You shall see by and by, sir!

---

171 ***Swan*** (a tavern or inn; not the theater)
187 ***o'trust*** (promising to pay later)
188 ***Hogrubber*** (abusive term; means *swineherd*); ***Pickt-hatch*** (an area of London known for thieves and prostitutes)
190 **s.d.** ***pate*** head
193 ***Harm . . . catch*** "if you do harm, you suffer harm" (proverbial)
194–5 **ha' . . . knocked** (seemed on the point of beating)
203 **watermen** (the monopoly of men who transported people across the Thames for a fee)
203–4 **watermen . . . word** (proverbial)
206 **he . . . boy** (apparently a line from an unidentified ballad)
206–7 **my Fiddle-stick** (i.e., Leander)
219 ***venter*** venture
220 ***score*** put on account; ***i' the Coney*** (rooms in the tavern were named, not numbered)
221–2 **Sack . . . sherry** (sack was the generic term for all white wines, including sherry)
227 **at . . . lift** in a pinch
229–30 **a . . . wonder** transient, trifling; a short-lived sensation
232 **condition** on the condition that

Cokes. You think my hobby-horse is forgotten, too? No, I'll see 'em all enact before I go; I shall not know which to love best, else.

Knockem. This gallant has interrupting vapors, troublesome vapors, Whit, puff with him.

Whit. No, I pre dee, captain, let him alone. He is a child i' faith, la.

Leatherhead. *Now, gentles, to the friends, who in number are two,*
And lodged in that ale-house, in which fair Hero does do.
Damon (for some kindness done him the last week)
Is come fair Hero, in Fish-street, this morning to seek.
Pythias does smell the knavery of the meeting,
And now you shall see their true friendly greeting.

Puppet Pythias. *You whore-masterly slave, you.*

Cokes. Whore-masterly slave, you? Very friendly, and familiar, that.

Puppet Damon. *Whore-master i' thy face,*
Thou hast lien with her thyself, I'll prove't i' this place.

Cokes. Damon says Pythias has lien with her, himself, he'll prove't in this place.

Leatherhead. *They are whore-masters both, sir, that's a plain case.*

Puppet Pythias. *You lie, like a rogue.*

Leatherhead. *Do I lie, like a rogue?*

Puppet Pythias. *A pimp, and a scab.*

Leatherhead. *A pimp, and a scab?*
I say between you, you have both but one drab.

Puppet Damon. *You lie again.*

Leatherhead. *Do I lie again?*

Puppet Damon. *Like a rogue again.*

Leatherhead. *Like a rogue again?*

Puppet Pythias. *And you are a pimp, again.*

Cokes. And you are a pimp again, he says.

Puppet Damon. *And a scab, again.*

Cokes. And a scab again, he says.

Leatherhead. *And I say again, you are both whore-masters again,*
And you have both but one drab again.

They fight.

Puppets Damon, Pythias. *Dost thou, dost thou, dost thou?*

Leatherhead. *What, both at once?*

Puppet Pythias. *Down with him, Damon.*

Puppet Damon. *Pink his guts, Pythias.*

Leatherhead. *What, so malicious?*
Will ye murder me, masters both, i' mine own house?

Cokes. Ho! well acted my drum, well acted my pipe, well acted still.

Wasp. Well acted, with all my heart.

Leatherhead. *Hold, hold your hands.*

Cokes. Aye, both your hands, for my sake! For you ha' both done well.

Puppet Damon. *Gramercy, pure Pythias.*

Puppet Pythias. *Gramercy, dear Damon.*

Cokes. Gramercy to you both, my pipe and my drum.

Puppets Damon, Pythias. *Come now, we'll together to breakfast to Hero.*

Leatherhead. *'Tis well, you can now go to breakfast to Hero,*
You have given me my breakfast, with 'hone and 'honero.

Cokes. How is't, friend; ha' they hurt thee?

Leatherhead. Oh, no!
Between you and I, sir, we do but make show.
Thus, gentles, you perceive, without any denial,
'Twixt Damon and Pythias here, friendship's true trial.
Though hourly they quarrel thus, and roar each with other,
They fight you no more, than does brother with brother.
But friendly together, at the next man they meet,
They let fly their anger, as here you might see't.

Cokes. Well, we have seen't, and thou hast felt it, whatsoever thou sayest. What's next? What's next?

Leatherhead. *This while young Leander, with fair Hero is drinking,*
And Hero grown drunk, to any man's thinking!
Yet was it not three pints of sherry could flaw her,
Till Cupid, distinguished like Jonas the drawer,
From under his apron, where his lechery lurks,
Put love in her sack. Now mark how it works.

Puppet Hero. *Oh, Leander, Leander, my dear, my dear Leander,*
I'll forever be thy goose, so thou'lt be my gander.

Cokes. Excellently well said, Fiddle, she'll ever be his goose, so he'll be her gander. Was't not so?

Leatherhead. Yes, sir, but mark his answer, now.

Puppet Leander. *And sweetest of geese, before I go to bed,*
I'll swim o'er the Thames, my goose, thee to tread.

Cokes. Brave! He will swim o'er the Thames, and tread his goose, tonight, he says.

---

240 **my . . . forgotten** (another phrase from a popular song)
244 **puff** quarrel
248 ***do*** work
257 ***lien*** lain
263 ***scab*** scoundrel (with reference to syphilis)
279 ***Pink*** stab; pierce
288 ***Gramercy*** Grant me mercy; ***pure*** good; fine
292 ***to*** with
294 ***'hone . . . 'honero*** alas (a Scottish and Irish expression of grief)
309 ***flaw her*** make her drunk
310 ***distinguished*** dressed
312 ***sack*** (1) sherry; (2) loose gown
319 ***tread*** press (with obscene reference)

Leatherhead. Aye, peace, sir; they'll be angry, if they hear you eavesdropping, now they are setting their match.

Puppet Leander. *But lest the Thames should be dark, my goose, my dear friend,*
Let thy window be provided of a candle's end.

Puppet Hero. *Fear not, my gander, I protest, I should handle*
My matters very ill, if I had not a whole candle.

Puppet Leander. *Well, then, look to't, and kiss me to boot.*

Leatherhead. *Now, here come the friends again, Pythias and Damon,*
And under their cloaks, they have of bacon, a gammon.

Damon *and* Pythias *enter.*

Puppet Pythias. *Drawer, fill some wine here.*

Leatherhead. *How, some wine there?*
There's company already, sir, pray forbear!

Puppet Damon. *'Tis Hero.*

Leatherhead. *Yes, but she will not be taken,*
After sack, and fresh herring, with your Dunmow-bacon.

Puppet Pythias. *You lie, it's Westfabian.*

Leatherhead. *Westphalian you should say.*

Puppet Damon. *If you hold not your peace, you are a coxcomb, I would say.*

Leander *and* Hero *are kissing.*

Puppet Pythias. *What's here? What's here? Kiss, kiss, upon kiss.*

Leatherhead. *Aye, wherefore should they not? What harm is in this?*
'Tis Mistress Hero.

Puppet Damon. *Mistress Hero's a whore.*

Leatherhead. *Is she a whore? Keep you quiet, or sir knave out of door.*

Puppet Damon. *Knave out of door?*

Puppet Hero. *Yes, knave, out of door.*

Puppet Damon. *Whore out of door.*

Here the Puppets quarrel and fall together by the ears.

Puppet Hero. *I say, knave, out of door.*

Puppet Damon. *I say, whore, out of door.*

Puppet Pythias. *Yea, so say I too.*

Puppet Hero. *Kiss the whore o' the arse.*

Leatherhead. *Now you ha' something to do: you must kiss her o' the arse, she says.*

Puppets Damon, Pythias. *So we will, so we will.*
[*They kick her.*]

Puppet Hero. *Oh, my haunches, Oh, my haunches, hold, hold.*

Leatherhead. *Stand'st thou still?*
Leander, where art thou? Stand'st thou still like a sot,
And not offer'st to break both their heads with a pot?
See who's at thine elbow there! Puppet Jonas and Cupid.

Puppet Jonas. *Upon 'em, Leander, be not so stupid.*

They fight.

Puppet Leander. *You goat-bearded slave!*

Puppet Damon. *You whore-master knave.*

Puppet Leander. *Thou art a whore-master.*

Puppet Jonas. *Whore-masters all.*

Leatherhead. *See, Cupid with a word has ta'en up the brawl.*

Knockem. These be fine vapors!

Cokes. By this good day they fight bravely! Do they not, Numps?

Wasp. Yes, they lacked but you to be their second, all this while.

Leatherhead. *This tragical encounter, falling out thus to busy us,*
It raises up the ghost of their friend Dionysius.
Not like a monarch, but the master of a school,
In a scrivener's furred gown, which shows he is no fool.
For therein he hath wit enough to keep himself warm.
"O Damon," he cries, "and Pythias; what harm
Hath poor Dionysius done you in his grave,
That after his death, you should fall out thus, and rave,
And call amorous Leander whore-master knave"?

Puppet Damon. *I cannot, I will not, I promise you, endure it.*

Act V. Scene v.

[*Enter*] *to them* Busy.

Busy. Down with Dagon, down with Dagon; 'tis I, will no longer endure your profanations.

Leatherhead. What mean you, sir?

Busy. I will remove Dagon there, I say, that idol, that heathenish idol, that remains (as I may say) a beam, a very beam, not a beam of the sun, nor a beam of the moon, nor a beam of a balance,

324 setting . . . match planning an intimate meeting

332 s.d. Damon *and* Pythias (a play on the love of two friends by Richard Edwardes in 1564 at odds with the heterosexual love of Marlowe's Hero and Leander)

337 *Dunmow-bacon* (associated with marital infidelity; Dunmow, Essex, was said to award bacon to those who could show they had not quarreled during the first year of marriage; the point here is that after her food and drink Hero will become lecherous)

338 *Westphalian* (a pun on Westphalia, Germany, known for ham and bacon)

357 *sot* drunkard

358 *pot* (1) alepot; (2) chamberpot

361 *goat-bearded* lecherous (colloquial)

372–3 *Dionysius . . . school* (Dionysius the Younger [367–343 BC], a tyrant of Syracuse who became a schoolmaster)

375 *wit . . . warm* (proverbial)

V.v.1 Dagon (the Philistines' national god, half-man and half-fish [1 Sam. 5], which Busy sees as analogous to the puppets as idols)

7 beam of a balance (beam from which scales are hung)

neither a house-beam, nor a weaver's beam, but a beam in the eye, in the eye of the brethren; a very great beam, an exceeding great beam; such as are your stage-players, rhymers, and morris dancers, who have walked hand in hand, in contempt of the brethren and the cause, and been borne out by instruments of no mean countenance.

Leatherhead. Sir, I present nothing but what is licensed by authority.

Busy. Thou art all license, even licentiousness itself, Shimei!

Leatherhead. I have the Master of the Revels' hand for't, sir.

Busy. The Master of Rebels' hand, thou hast; Satan's! Hold thy peace, thy scurrility, shut up thy mouth, thy profession is damnable, and in pleading for it, thou dost plead for Baal. I have long opened my mouth wide, and gaped, I have gaped as the oyster for the tide, after thy destruction but cannot compass it by suit, or dispute; so that I look for a bickering, ere long, and then a battle.

Knockem. Good Banbury-vapors.

Cokes. Friend, you'd have an ill match on't, if you bicker with him here; though he be no man o' the fist, he has friends that will go to cuffs for him. Numps, will not you take our side?

Edgworth. Sir, it shall not need; in my mind, he offers him a fairer course, to end it by disputation! Hast thou nothing to say for thyself, in defense of thy quality?

Leatherhead. Faith, sir, I am not well studied in these controversies, between the hypocrites and us. But here's one of my motion, Puppet Dionysius, shall undertake him, and I'll venture the cause on't.

Cokes. Who? My hobby-horse? Will he dispute with him?

Leatherhead. Yes, sir, and make a hobby-ass of him, I hope.

Cokes. That's excellent! Indeed, he looks like the best scholar of 'em all. Come, sir, you must be as good as your word, now.

Busy. I will not fear to make my spirit and gifts known! Assist me, zeal; fill me, fill me, that is, make me full.

Winwife. What a desperate, profane wretch is this! Is there any ignorance, or impudence like his? To call his zeal to fill him against a puppet?

Quarlous. I know no fitter match than a puppet to commit with an hypocrite!

Busy. First, I say unto thee, idol, thou hast no calling.

Puppet Dionysius. *You lie, I am called Dionysius.*

Leatherhead. The motion says you lie, he is called Dionysius i' the matter, and to that calling he answers.

Busy. I mean no vocation, idol, no present lawful calling.

Puppet Dionysius. *Is yours a lawful calling?*

Leatherhead. The motion asketh, if yours be a lawful calling?

Busy. Yes, mine is of the spirit.

Puppet Dionysius. *Then idol is a lawful calling.*

Leatherhead. He says, then idol is a lawful calling! For you called him idol, and your calling is of the spirit.

Cokes. Well disputed, hobby-horse!

Busy. Take not part with the wicked, young gallant. He neigheth and hinnyeth, all is but hinnying sophistry. I call him idol again. Yet, I say, his calling, his profession is profane, it is profane, idol.

Puppet Dionysius. *It is not profane!*

Leatherhead. It is not profane, he says.

Busy. It is profane.

Puppet Dionysius. *It is not profane.*

Busy. It is profane.

Puppet Dionysius. *It is not profane.*

---

8 **weaver's beam** (a cylinder in the loom)

9 **beam ... eye** mote in the eye (Matt. 7:3–5)

14 **borne out** supported; **instruments** agents (of the Devil)

15 **mean countenance** low rank

17 **licensed by authority** (approved for playing officially by the King's Master of the Revels)

19 **Shimei** (the son of Gera who stoned the Israelites; he cursed David who said he had God's authority for it, just as Busy curses [2 Sam. 16:5–13])

26 **Baal** (heathen god of the Midianites whose altar was cast down by Gideon [Judg. 6:25–32]; here Busy would be Gideon)

27–8 **gaped ... tide** (proverbial)

28 **compass** encompass

30 **bickering** i.e., skirmish

39 **quality** profession

40 **studied** taught; prepared

43 **undertake him** take him on

58 **s.p. *Quarlous*** (the F text gives this line to Quarlous; some editors argue that the compositor misread *Qua.* for *Gra.* and that the speech belongs to Grace)

59 **commit** do battle

61 **calling** Christian vocation (acting was not considered work, and players were associated with rogues and vagabonds by Puritans and, without a patron, by governmental statute)

62 ***called*** named; ***Dionysius*** Greek god of (1) wine; (2) fairs and celebrations; (3) theater

64 **matter** playtext

79 **sophistry** false logic; specious but fallacious reasoning

Leatherhead. Well said, confute him with "not," still. You cannot bear him down with your base noise, sir.

Busy. Nor he me, with his treble creaking, though he creak like the chariot wheels of Satan; I am zealous for the cause –

Leatherhead. As a dog for a bone.

Busy. And I say, it is profane, as being the page of Pride, and the waiting-woman of Vanity.

Puppet Dionysius. *Yea? What say you to your tire-women, then?*

Leatherhead. Good.

Puppet Dionysius. *Or feather-makers i' the Friars, that are o' your faction of faith? Are not they with their perukes, and their puffs, their fans, and their huffs, as much pages of Pride, and waiters upon Vanity? What say you? What say you? What say you?*

Busy. I will not answer for them.

Puppet Dionysius. *Because you cannot, because you cannot. Is a bugle-maker a lawful calling? Or the confect-maker's (such you have there)? Or your French fashioner? You'd have all the sin within yourselves, would you not? Would you not?*

Busy. No, Dagon.

Puppet Dionysius. *What then, Dagonet? Is a puppet worse than these?*

Busy. Yes, and my main argument against you, is, that you are an abomination: for the male, among you, putteth on the apparel of the female, and the female of the male.

Puppet Dionysius. *You lie, you lie, you lie abominably.*

Cokes. Good, by my troth, he has given him the lie thrice.

Puppet Dionysius. *It is your old stale argument against the players, but it will not hold against the puppets; for we have neither male nor female among us. And that thou may'st see, if thou wilt, like a malicious purblind zeal as thou art!*

The Puppet takes up his garment.

Edgworth. By my faith, there he has answered you, friend; by plain demonstration.

Puppet Dionysius. *Nay, I'll prove, against e'er a Rabbin of 'em all, that my standing is as lawful as his; that I speak by inspiration, as well as he; that I have as little to do with learning as he; and do scorn her helps as much as he.*

Busy. I am confuted, the cause hath failed me.

Puppet Dionysius. *Then be converted, be converted.*

Leatherhead. Be converted, I pray you, and let the play go on!

Busy. Let it go on. For I am changed, and will become a beholder with you!

Cokes. That's brave i' faith; thou hast carried it away, hobby-horse; on with the play!

The Justice discovers himself.

Justice Overdo. Stay, now do I forbid, I, Adam Overdo! Sit still, I charge you.

Cokes. What, my brother-i'-law!

Grace. My wise guardian!

Edgworth. Justice Overdo!

Justice Overdo. It is time, to take enormity by the forehead, and brand it; for I have discovered enough.

Act V. Scene vi.

[*Enter to them,* Quarlous (*like the madman*), Purecraft (*a while after*).]

Quarlous. Nay, come, mistress bride. You must do as I do, now. You must be mad with me, in truth. I have here Justice Overdo for it.

Justice Overdo. Peace, good Trouble-all; come hither, and you shall trouble none. I will take the charge of you and your friend too; you also, young man, shall be my care. Stand there.

To the cutpurse and Mistress Littlewit.

Edgworth. Now, mercy upon me.

The rest are stealing away.

Knockem. Would we were away, Whit; these are dangerous vapors. Best fall off with our birds, for fear o' the cage.

Justice Overdo. Stay, is not my name your terror?

88 **confute him** prove him to be wrong
91 **creaking** speaking in an irritating tone
97–8 ***tire-women*** dressmakers
100 ***feather-makers . . . Friars*** (traders in feathers who lived near Blackfriars were Puritans and opponents often noted they should not be dealing in such finery)
102 ***perukes*** wigs; ***puffs*** (bunches of ribbons, feathers, or hair)
103 **huffs** (shoulder padding in dresses)
107 ***bugle-maker*** (one who makes tube-shaped glass beads)
108 ***confect-maker*** (maker of sweetmeats)
109 ***fashioner*** tailor; dressmaker
112 ***Dagonet*** (King Arthur's fool)
115–17 **male . . . male** (the chief Puritan argument against plays, by then in countless pamphlets and sermons; ultimately from Deut. 22:5)
124–5 ***purblind zeal*** dim-sighted zealot
129 ***Rabbin*** (chief rabbi or teacher); ***standing*** profession
130 ***inspiration*** i.e., imagination
133 **I . . . me** (Busy may be defeated because Dionysius cites scripture: cf. Gal. 3:28)
139–40 **carried . . . away** brought it off
140 **s.d. *discovers* reveals; uncovers**
146–7 **take . . . forehead** (play on taking opportunity or occasion by the forelock; proverbial)
V.vi.10 **fall off** withdraw; **birds** companions
11 **cage** prison

Whit. Yesh, faith, man, and it ish for tat we would be gone, man.

[*Enter*] Littlewit.

Littlewit. Oh, gentlemen! Did you not see a wife of mine? I ha' lost my little wife, as I shall be trusted; my little pretty Win. I left her at the great woman's house in trust yonder, the pig woman's, with Captain Jordan, and Captain Whit, very good men, and I cannot hear of her. Poor fool, I fear she's stepped aside. Mother, did you not see Win?

Justice Overdo. If this grave matron be your mother, sir, stand by her, *et digito compesce labellum*, I may perhaps spring a wife for you, anon. Brother Bartholomew, I am sadly sorry to see you so lightly given, and such a disciple of enormity; with your grave governor Humphrey. But stand you both there, in the middle place; I will reprehend you in your course. Mistress Grace, let me rescue you out of the hands of the stranger.

Winwife. Pardon me, sir; I am a kinsman of hers.

Justice Overdo. Are you so? Of what name, sir?

Winwife. Winwife, sir.

Justice Overdo. Master Winwife? I hope you have won no wife of her, sir. If you have, I will examine the possibility of it, at fit leisure. Now, to my enormities: look upon me, Oh, London! And see me, Oh, Smithfield! The example of justice, and Mirror of Magistrates; the true top of formality, and scourage of enormity. Hearken unto my labors, and but observe my discoveries; and compare Hercules with me, if thou darest, of old; or Columbus; Magellan; or our country-man Drake of later times. Stand forth you weeds of enormity, and spread. (*To Busy.*) First, Rabbi Busy, thou super-lunatical hypocrite. (*To Lantern.*) Next, thou other extremity, thou profane professor of puppetry, little better than poetry. (*To the horse-courser, and cutpurse.*) Then thou strong debaucher, and seducer of youth; witness this easy and honest young man. (*Then Captain Whit and Mistress Littlewit.*) Now thou esquire of dames, madams, and twelvepenny ladies: now my green madam herself, of the price. Let me unmask your ladyship.

Littlewit. Oh, my wife, my wife, my wife!

Justice Overdo. Is she your wife? *Redde te Harpocratem!*

Enter Trouble-All, [Ursula, Nightingale].

Trouble-All. By your leave, stand by, my masters, be uncovered.

Ursula. Oh, stay him, stay him, help to cry, Nightingale; my pan, my pan.

Justice Overdo. What's the matter?

Nightingale. He has stolen Gammer Urs'la's pan.

Trouble-All. Yes, and I fear no man but Justice Overdo.

Justice Overdo. Urs'la? Where is she? Oh, the sow of enormity, this! (*To Ursula and Nightingale.*) Welcome, stand you there; you, songster, there.

Ursula. An' please your worship, I am in no fault. A gentleman stripped him in my booth, and borrowed his gown and his hat; and he ran away with my goods, here, for it.

Justice Overdo. (*To Quarlous.*) Then this is the true madman, and you are the enormity!

Quarlous. You are i' the right, I am mad, but from the gown outward.

Justice Overdo. Stand you there.

Quarlous. Where you please, sir.

Mistress Overdo is sick; and her husband is silenced.

Mrs. Overdo. Oh, lend me a basin, I am sick, I am sick; where's Master Overdo? Bridget, call hither my Adam.

Justice Overdo. How?

Whit. Dy very own wife, i' fait, worshipful Adam.

Mrs. Overdo. Will not my Adam come at me? Shall I see him no more then?

20–1 **hear of her** learn of her whereabouts

21 **fool** sweet (term of endearment); **stepped aside** wandered off

24–5 ***et . . . labellum*** "and check any movement of your lips with your finger" (Juvenal, *Satires* I.160); i.e., don't reveal yourself

25 **spring** (properly to cause [a partridge] to rise from cover)

27 **lightly given** casually supervised

30 **course** term

32 **stranger** (Edgworth)

42 **formality** legal procedure

44 **Hercules** (as reputed for strength and cleverness in accomplishing his twelve labors)

45–6 **Columbus . . . Drake** (the most famous explorers and voyagers in Jonson's time; Magellan and Drake had sailed around the world and Drake's ship, *The Golden Hind*, was a tourist attraction in the Thames near London)

47–8 **weeds . . . spread** (Justice Overdo's bestial metaphors turn to vegetative here)

54 **easy** (1) credulous; (2) easily duped

57 **price** cost of enormities

60 ***Redde . . . Harpocratem!*** "Transform yourself into Harpocrates" (god of silence)

62 **be uncovered** (1) remove your hats in respect to your superiors; (2) be revealed for what you are

73 **in no fault** not to blame

74 **gentleman** (Quarlous)

84 **Bridget** (not in list of players; apparently this servant is a delusion of Ursula's as she awakens in a drunken stupor)

88 **at** to

Quarlous. Sir, why do you not go on with the enormity? Are you oppressed with it? I'll help you. Hark you, sir, i' your ear – your "innocent young man," you have ta'en such care of, all this day, is a cutpurse, that hath got all your brother Cokes his things, and helped you to your beating, and the stocks; if you have a mind to hang him now, and show him your magistrate's wit, you may. But I should think it were better recovering the goods, and to save your estimation in pardoning him. I thank you, sir, for the gift of your ward, Mistress Grace; look you, here is your hand and seal, by the way. Master Winwife, give you joy, you are Palemon, you are possessed of the gentlewoman, but she must pay me value, here's warrant for it. And honest madman, there's thy gown and cap again; I thank thee for my wife. (*To the widow.*) Nay, I can be mad, sweetheart, when I please, still; never fear me. And careful Numps, where's he? I thank him for my license.

Wasp. How!

Wasp misseth the license.

Quarlous. 'Tis true, Numps.

Wasp. I'll be hanged then.

Quarlous. Look i' your box, Numps. [*To Justice.*] Nay, sir, stand not you fixed here, like a stake in Finsbury to be shot at, or the whipping post i' the Fair, but get your wife out o' the air, it will make her worse else; and remember you are but Adam, flesh and blood! You have your frailty. Forget your other name of Overdo, and invite us all to supper. There you and I will compare our discoveries; and drown the memory of all enormity in your biggest bowl at home.

Cokes. How now, Numps, ha' you lost it? I warrant, 'twas when thou wert i' the stocks. Why dost not speak?

Wasp. I will never speak while I live, again, for ought I know.

Justice Overdo. Nay, Humphrey, if I be patient, you must be so too; this pleasant conceited gentleman hath wrought upon my judgment, and prevailed. I pray you take care of your sick friend, Mistress Alice, and my good friends all –

Quarlous. And no enormities.

Justice Overdo. I invite you home with me to my house, to supper. I will have none fear to go along, for my intents are *ad correctionem, non ad destructionem; ad œdificandum, non ad diruendum.* So lead on.

Cokes. Yes, and bring the actors along, we'll ha' the rest o' the play at home!

[*Exeunt.*]

The end.

THE EPILOGUE.

Your Majesty hath seen the play, and you
Can best allow it from your ear, and view.
You know the scope of writers, and what store
Of leave is given them, if they take not more,
And turn it into license. You can tell
If we have used that leave you gave us, well.
Or whether we to rage, or license break,
Or be profane, or make profane men speak?
This is your power to judge, great sir, and not
The envy of a few. Which if we have got,
We value less what their dislike can bring,
If it so happy be, t' have pleased the King.

---

91 oppressed with overcome by
100 estimation reputation
105 pay me value (because Quarlous has become the guardian of Grace)
109 fear me doubt it
116–17 like . . . at (Finsbury Field, N of the city walls, was the site of public archery practice as well as military maneuvers)
117 whipping post (used to shame scolds)
124 bowl i.e., punchbowl
132 pleasant conceited; merrily disposed
140–1 *ad . . . diruendum* "to correct, not to destroy; to build up, not to tear down" (these words echo [1] King James's published speech to Parliament on March 21, 1610; [2] St. Paul in 2 Cor. 13:10)
143 actors (literally, puppets; but generally, self-reflexive on all of them)

Epilogue

(raises metatheatricality another level)
2 allow (1) sanction; (2) license
4 leave (1) permission; (2) freedom

The Duchess of Malfi

John Webster

THE TRAGEDY

OF THE DVTCHESSE Of Malfy.

As it was Presented priuatly, at the Black-Friers; and publiquely at the Globe, By the Kings Maiesties Seruants.

The perfect and exact Coppy, with diuerse *things Printed, that the length of the Play would* not beare in the Presentment.

VVritten by *John Webster.*

Hora. ——*Si quid*----
——*Candidus Imperti si non his vtere mecum.*

Jo: gatos

LONDON:

Printed by NICHOLAS OKES, [illegible] IOHN WATERSON, and are to be sold [illegible] the signe of the Crowne, in *Paules* Church-yard, 1623.

Frontispiece, 1623.

"I am Duchess of Malfi still": this courageous claim for the power of individual will, the most famous line in non-Shakespearean drama, rings through the centuries to Ibsen's *A Doll's House* and beyond. Yet just how we should interpret these words in Webster's play remains a matter of debate. The Duchess' forceful vow of autonomy may be a formidable denial of the powerful challenges of an evil Machiavellian – or worse, a meaningless – world. Or it may be the remark of a culturally sanctioned aristocratic arrogance to Bosola, a spy and intelligencer far beneath her in station. His reply ignores her claim. "That makes thy sleeps so broken. 'Glories, like glow-worms, afar off shine bright, But looked to near, have neither heat, nor light,'" a response she herself admits is "very plain." Even so, resistance has been, all along, her fundamental principle and course of action with a society and a family who continually attempt, with little success, to command and constrain her: "If all my royal kindred Lay in my way . . ., I'd make them my low footsteps." As the regent of a duchy she possesses an authority of her own. Her desires and decisions maintain an integrity that withstands assaults on her behavior and even her reason; she will not disclose her clandestine marriage and she will not be driven mad by terror and dread. Yet the full resonance of "I am Duchess of Malfi still" might be seen by Jacobean audiences as precarious rather than assertive: *still* then meant *always*, but it also could mean *yet*. For the Duchess is not only aware of the nature and utility of ambiguity; she is skilled at it: "as a tyrant doubles with his words, And fearfully equivocates, so we Are forced to express our violent passions In riddles, and in dreams, and leave the path Of simple virtue which was never made To seem the thing it is not." For *The Duchess of Malfi* is not only a play about assertion; it is also about precariousness. Scenes turn on surveillance, on a dropped horoscope, on the Duchess's misplaced trust in telling Bosola the identity of her husband. Self-conscious of "The misery of us that are born great" in her secret wedding scene with Antonio, she tells him "We are forced to woo." In Jacobean times, the pronunciation of *woo* was the pronunciation of *woe*. The ring that the Duchess takes from her finger at that moment, replacing the dead Duke with the steward Antonio, anticipates the noose Bosola will place about her neck: both encircle; both entrap. Such complications can make our initial reactions to the Duchess, and to the play, inadequate. Indeed, Webster may have chosen the highly charged life of the Duchess of Malfi to make clandestine observations of his own on the cultural practices and beliefs of Jacobean England.

Webster never names the Duchess of Malfi – as if her position more than her person were his main subject – but his play is based in historical events. Enrico d'Aragona, the half-brother of King Federico of Naples, had three children. When his oldest, Lodovico, became a cardinal, his younger son Carlo succeeded to the title of Marquis of Gerace. Their sister Giovanna was married in 1490, at about the age of twelve, to Alfonso Piccolomini, who became Duke of Amalfi in 1493 and died of the gout five years later. Giovanna was left with a daughter and a son born posthumously, for whom she ruled the duchy of Amalfi as regent. During the next few years, the Duchess paid off debts incurred by former rulers. Upon Federico's death in 1504, Antonio Bologna, his major-domo, was offered a similar position in the Duchess' household. She fell quickly and deeply in love with him and secretly married him, bearing him a son. For years the marriage and birth went undetected but the birth of a second child aroused the suspicions of her brothers. When they set spies on her, Antonio fled with the children to Ancona and the Duchess, unbearably lonely, announced a pilgrimage to Loretto. This, however, was a ruse to rejoin her family; at Ancona, she gave birth to a third child. There she announced her marriage to her household and one of the servants, astonished, reported the situation to the Cardinal. Antonio made plans to flee to a friend in Siena for safety, but when the Cardinal banished them in the summer of 1511, the family headed toward Venice. Overtaken, the Duchess persuaded Antonio to take their eldest child to Milan, where they arrived safely in the late summer of 1512; the Duchess and her two younger children were returned to Amalfi. Their fate after that is unknown, but they were not seen again. Presumably they were killed, along with the Duchess's waiting-woman, shortly before Antonio was killed in the streets of Milan in 1513.

Clandestine marriages were not unknown in England. Pledges of matrimony before a witness, known as a wedding ceremony *per verba de presenti*, were legal, although they were not sanctified by the church. Clandestine marriages between masters and servants were another matter, punishable not by death but by imprisonment. One prominent instance was that of the poet John Donne, secretary to Sir Thomas Egerton, Lord Keeper of the Great Seal, who secretly married the

Lord Keeper's niece Anne More in December 1601. The marriage was discovered two months later and Donne was committed to Fleet Prison for conspiracy to violate the civil and common law, and years of poverty followed. But sentiment was hardly unanimous. Egerton was genuinely sorry about the affair and spoke of "passionate petitioners" who interceded for Donne's reinstatement; Francis Walley, Egerton's stepson, offered the couple asylum in his own manor house after the poet's release. Webster may have this incident in mind, but at the time of his play a more telling parallel was that of King James's first cousin Arbella Stuart, at the time of Elizabeth's death a rival claimant to the throne of England. James attempted to arrange numerous marriages for Arbella, but in 1610 she secured his permission to choose her own husband so long as she did not marry a foreign prince. But when she announced her betrothal to William Seymour, a young Oxford scholar, James forbade the marriage. Although Seymour promised the King they would not complete their ceremony without royal approval, in fact he and Arbella Stuart were married clandestinely in the middle of the night in Stuart apartments at Greenwich before witnesses so that the legitimacy of the marriage could not be challenged. Both were imprisoned, Stuart in private custody in Lambeth Palace and Seymour in the Tower of London. But the two escaped and Stuart was captured off the French coast near Calais; she was then committed to the Tower of London where she died four years later, in 1615, of self-induced starvation. The sensationalism of this marriage was increased with rumors that Stuart was pregnant and that her imprisonment was driving her mad. In 1613 John Chamberlain reported her "distraction"; in July 1614 he noted "some business about the Lady Arbella, who they say is far out of frame this midsummer moon." The whole affair angered the King. He told his Privy Council that Stuart had violated the duties of her rank, that Stuart as a member of the royal family should not be governed by "caprice," and that as his ward she had no right to determine her own marriage in common law; to the Bishop of Durham he declared the marriage an indignity that damaged his honor. Privately, to a petition of mercy, he accused her of having "eaten of the forbidden tree."

Clandestine marriages were a growing social issue in Jacobean England, but of even more concern was the increasing number of widows: in the early seventeenth century, between one-third and one-half of the brides in some London parishes were widows. So widespread was the concern that Jeremy Taylor addresses it directly in his *Rule and Exercise of Holy Living*:

> For Widows, the fontinel of whose desires hath been opened by the former permissions of the marriage-bed, they must remember,
>
> 1. That God hath now restrained the former license, bound up their eyes, and shut up their heart into a narrower compass, and hath given them sorrow to be a bridle to their desires. A widow must be a mourner; and she that is not, cannot so well secure the chastity of her proper state.
>
> 2. It is against public honesty to marry another man, so long as she is with child by her former husband; and of the same fame it is in a lesser proportion to marry within the year of mourning. But anciently it was infamous for her to marry until by common account the body was dissolved into its first principle of earth.
>
> 3. A widow must restrain her memory and her fancy, not recalling or recounting her former permissions and freer licenses with any present delight, for then she opens that sluice which her husband's death and her own sorrow have shut up.
>
> 4. A widow that desires her widowhood should be a state pleasing to God, must spend her time as devoted virgins should – in fastings, and prayers, and charity.
>
> 5. A widow must forbid herself to use those temporal solaces which in her former estate were innocent but now are dangerous.

Webster himself, in fact, seems to be of mixed minds concerning the proper conduct of widows like the Duchess. In 1615, the year following his play, he wrote two sketches for Thomas Overbury's *Characters*. The first, "A Virtuous Widow," notes she

> is the palm tree that thrives not after the supplanting of her husband. For her children's sake she first marries, for she married that she might have children, and for their sakes she marries no more. She is like the purest gold, only employed for princes' medals; she never receives but one man's impression. The large jointure moves her not; titles of honor cannot sway her. To change her name were, she thinks, to commit a sin should make her ashamed of her husband's calling. She thinks she hath traveled all the world in one man; the rest of her time therefore she directs to heaven. Her main superstition is, she thinks her husband's ghost would walk should she not perform his will; she would do it were there no prerogative court. She gives much to pious uses without any hope to merit by them and, as one diamond fashions another, so is she wrought into works of charity with the dust or ashes of her husband.... To conclude, she is a relic that without any superstition in the world, though she might not be kissed, yet may be reverenced.

But the second portrait, of "An Ordinary Widow," sees the custom of his day as otherwise. This widow "is like the heralds' hearse-cloth. She serves to many funerals with a very little altering the color. The end of her husband begins in tears; and the end of her tears begins in a husband." While she many fancy "one of the biggest of the Guard," she will settle for "a Knight of the old rent"; she is "no morning woman; the evening a good fire and sack may make her listen to a husband, and if ever she be made sure, 'tis upon a full stomach to bedward." This was, indeed, "ordinary": about a third of the marriages at the time of *The Duchess of Malfi* were remarriages.

The Duchess' actions, then, could be seen as an insistence on private happiness, a lack of self-discipline, a violation of rank and decorum, willful irresponsibility concerning her children, and even as an act of impiety since she uses a pilgrimage to the Shrine of Our Lady of Loretto as, in part at least, a deception. This last act may signal what Webster's opposing character sketches of a widow also reveal: a deep cultural fissure in religious attitudes towards a widow's proper actions. Following the scriptural teachings of St. Paul and their interpretation by Church Fathers such as St. Jerome, the Catholic church argued that the widow should remain chaste; a "widowhood ought to be kept holily," protecting both property and lineage. In his *Instruction for a Christian Woman* reprinted in Elizabethan and Jacobean times, the popular Spanish humanist Juan Luis Vives conceded remarriage but clearly opposed it: "For to condemn and reprove utterly second marriages, it were a point of heresy. Howbeit, that better is to abstain than marry again is not only counseled by Christian pureness, that is to say, by divine wisdom, but also by pagan, that is to say, by worldly wisdom." According to Vives, a widow should take Christ as "her husband immortal" and spend her remaining life in devout seclusion. For him the alternative was the lusty widow, "wanton, hot, and full of play" who "taketh an husband but to the intent that she will lie with him, nor except his lust prick her." He means to keep in check such lack of self-governance:

> many be glad that their husbands be gone, as who were rid out of yoke and bondage, and they rejoice that they be out of dominion and bond and have recovered their liberty. But they be of a foolish opinion, for the ship is not at liberty that lacketh a governor but rather destitute; neither a child that lacketh his tutor, but rather wandering without order and reason.

Protestants, however, explicitly and forthrightly rejected such counsel. Thomas Becon, one of the best-known Reformist preachers in the later sixteenth century, remarks that second marriages were never disallowed "til the Devil and the Pope began to bear rule, which envy no state so much as the holy state of honorable matrimony." For Becon their insistence on a widow's life of chastity was the "dregs of Antichrist and a mere doctrine of devils." Since he subscribes to the homilies of the Established Church, he also supports the homily on matrimony which sees marriage as a lawful and spiritual means of propagation, the prevention of fornication, and mutual companionship and solace. For him, "God is no less the author of the second, third, fourth &c. marriages than of the first." Somewhat later William Gouge declares that widows (and widowers) are "as free as they who were never before married." In his *Christian Oeconomie* of 1613, the popular but conservative Puritan William Perkins argues that a widow can marry without consent although it is "fit and convenient" that she seek it out of "duty and honor" to her parents; another Puritan, Andrew Kingsmill, openly permits his sister to choose for herself "for you know best where your show wringeth you; neither need you any counselor to bid you cut where it wringeth you." The Duchess' brothers disagree. "You are a widow," Ferdinand begins, "You know already what man is; and therefore Let not youth, high promotion, eloquence" – and the Cardinal interrupts him to finish, "No, nor anything without the addition, honor, Sway your high blood." "Without the addition" sounds more permissive, seems to give the Duchess a loophole; and almost at once the brothers seem to disagree with each other. Her possible behavior raises anxiety in Ferdinand – "Marry! they are most luxurious Will wed twice"; "Their livers are more spotted Than Laban's sheep" – but the Cardinal would threaten her: "that motion lasts no longer Than the turning of an hour-glass. The funeral sermon And it both end together." Almost as if to prove his point, the Duchess' words of invitation to Antonio, kneeling at her petition to marry – "This is flesh, and blood, sir; 'Tis not the figure cut in alabaster Kneels at my husband's tomb" – eerily anticipates her only other moment of kneeling, as if in alabaster herself, a Catholic image of martyrdom: "Come, violent death, Serve for mandragora to make me sleep! Go tell my brothers, when I am laid out, They then may feed in quiet." This unexpected reaction, like the dead hand and waxen effigies and dancing of madmen preceding it, like so much in Webster's play, can be unnerving. So too her final command to her waiting-woman: "Farewell, Cariola;... I pray thee, look thou giv'st my little boy Some syrup for his cold, and let the girl Say her prayers, ere she sleep." The everydayness of the words, the sudden flash of maternal instinct, surprise us. They call into sharp relief the fundamental loneliness of the Duchess. In what has always seemed a claustrophobic play she is distant from the pilgrims of Loretto, divorced from her family, and separated from her sole remaining servant. Yet why, at this moment of submission, awareness, and resourcefulness, does she neglect to remember Antonio and her first son, who will take up her title?

For the Duchess of Malfi is never without a sense of station and rank, of order and degree and propriety, of a sense (even if she would redefine it) of family honor. This may be one thing that initially attracts her to Antonio. As he says at the outset in praising the French court,

> In seeking to reduce both state and people
> To a fixed order, their judicious King
> Begins at home: quits first his royal palace
> Of flatt'ring sycophants, of dissolute
> And infamous persons (which he sweetly terms
> His Master's masterpiece, the work of heaven)
> Consid'ring duly, that a prince's court
> Is like a common fountain, whence should flow
> Pure silver drops in general.

Such an appreciation of appropriate service in the smooth management of a kingdom suggests why he was chosen by the King to oversee his household and points to the wisdom of the Duchess in making him her steward. His sense of place is deeply ingrained, as is that of the Duchess, in their subtle and sensitive scene of courtship and proposal. The Duchess begins by seating him, placing him below her as his station warrants. But slowly she elevates him before kneeling before him. "You are an upright treasurer"; "I intend to make you overseer"; "I'd have you first provide for a good husband, Give him all"; "Yes, your excellent self." Finding his eye bloodshot, she attempts to cure it with "my wedding ring, And I did vow never to part with it, But to my second husband." Antonio grows increasingly uncomfortable, increasingly aware of his "unworthiness." "Conceive not I am so stupid but I aim Whereto your favors tend. But he's a fool That, being a-cold, would thrust his hands i'th'fire To warm them." Their clandestine betrothal and marriage, the legal contract *per verba de presenti*, is performed before Cariola as a hidden (but legal) witness. But the subsequent departure for the marriage bed where the Duchess will "shroud my blushes in your bosom, Since 'tis the treasury of all my secrets" frightens the waiting-woman; this treasurer will, knowing such secrets, prepare his own shroud. He may become, in his own words, "Some cursed example" which "near the head, 'Death, and diseases through the whole land spread.' " "Whether the spirit of greatness or of woman Reign most in her," Cariola observes as a kind of chorus to the scene, "I know not, but it shows A fearful madness. I owe her much of pity." What Cariola fails to recognize, however, is one of the basic questions which Webster's play deliberately raises: whether a political state like the duchy of Malfi should be governed by those of traditional rank and nobility or by those whose talents best equip them to manage state affairs – whether a country should reward degree over (or instead of) merit. Put this way, Webster's play addresses a flashpoint in the governance of England. Ever since Elizabeth I raised mere gentry like Sir William Cecil to the level of nobility and a ruling position on her Privy Council because of his astute statesmanship and sheer ability to oversee the entanglements of her inherited rule, the English court had attracted a number of eager aspirants whose abilities rather than station were the primary qualifications. What Elizabeth began, James exacerbated, creating and elevating a number of political allies to the ranks of nobility and knighting hundreds of others to establish a power base of his own, a Stuart succeeding a Tudor ruler, much as the Duchess means to establish her own governance, freed from the traditions and restrictions her brothers would impose upon her. To Webster's diverse audiences at the private Blackfriars Theater and at the public Globe playhouse, Antonio's sudden promotion interrogates pressing political issues, then, as well as social and religious ones. It may be for this reason that Webster is at pains to suggest Antonio's good character, his able horsemanship, his moral judgments, and his devotion to service. Merit has advantages. Yet in a crisis Antonio panics. Delio has to provide him with a cover story; the Duchess supplies another. He loses the horoscope. Ferdinand's eventual sneer asks us to reconsider him: "Antonio! A slave that only smelled of ink and counters, And ne'er in's life looked like a gentleman, But in the audit-time." Merit may not be a good premise for rule after all. The other profile in the play of a man who rises by merit alone is Antonio's adversary Bosola, who served "seven years in the galleys For a notorious murder."

Antonio's alternate means to influence may in itself be sufficient grounds for the Cardinal's enmity, quite apart from the Duchess' open resistance and remarriage. But the Cardinal is also vulnerable to Antonio's recognition of his true nature. The "brave fellow" that Delio praises as one who "Will play his five thousand crowns at tennis, dance, Court ladies, and [fight] single combats," Antonio knows as one whose "inward character" belies his "form." For Antonio, the Cardinal "is a melancholy churchman" who "strews in his way flatterers, panders, intelligencers, atheists, and a thousand such political monsters." To Orazio Businо, chaplain to the Venetian embassy, the Cardinal was a typical English attack on the Roman church.

> On another occasion they showed a cardinal in all his grandeur, in the formal robes appropriate to his station, splendid and rich, with his train in attendance, having an altar erected on the stage, where he pretended to make a prayer, organizing a procession; and then they produced him in public with a harlot on his knee. They showed

> him giving poison to one of his sisters, in a question of honor. Moreover, he goes to war, first laying down his cardinal's habit on the altar, with the help of his chaplains, with great ceremoniousness; finally he has his sword bound on and dons the soldier's sash with so much panache you could not imagine it better done. And all this was acted in condemnation of the grandeur of the Church, which they despise and which in this kingdom they hate to the death.

But in placing the Cardinal's transformation from priest to soldier in a spectacular dumb show at the center of his play, Webster makes it analogous with the Duchess' own politically strategic retreat to Loretto, the other part of the dumb show. Both the Cardinal and the Duchess suggest uneasy conjunctions of church and state. Unlike the passionate Duchess, however, the Cardinal shows a coldness of nature that will later permit him to conceive of ways to torture the Duchess when she is confined back in Malfi. He seems a total Machiavellian, a connoisseur of evil and villainy. Yet such secular punishments – which debase the Duchess' marriage and family – also have their religious dimension, for his acts, centering on her moment of death, also raise questions of moral judgment, of salvation and damnation. With such thoughts, the Cardinal can seem not so much a Catholic or a power politician as a Calvinist reprobate. According to Calvin's *Institutes*, the basis for the English Geneva Bible and its marginal exegeses, a reprobate is a man who is

> so entirely alienated from the righteousness of God that he cannot conceive, desire, or design anything but what is wicked, distorted, foul, impure, and iniquitous; that his heart is so thoroughly envenomed by sin, that it can breathe out nothing but corruption and rottenness; that if some men occasionally make a show of goodness, their mind is ever interwoven with hypocrisy and deceit, their soul inwardly bound with the fetters of wickedness.

Webster's possible colonization of a Roman prelate as a more familiar Calvinist sinner may be another way to signal the play's issues as fundamentally English.

The play's persistent concern with poisons and gilded pills, with syrups and purgation suggests a sick society and, indeed, a whole sense of illness haunts *The Duchess of Malfi*. Referring to the Galenic theory of humoral medicine, some critics have seen the Duchess as sanguine, Ferdinand as choleric, the Cardinal as phlegmatic, and Bosola as melancholic. But Ferdinand's obsession to cure his sister seems abnormal even so. "Apply desperate physic," he tells his brother,

> We must not now use balsamum, but fire,
> The smarting cupping-glass, for that's the mean
> To purge infected blood, such blood as hers.

Yet her corruption for him is more corrupted behavior than diseased body:

> Methinks I see her laughing –
> Excellent hyena! Talk to me somewhat, quickly,
> Or my imagination will carry me
> To see her in the shameful act of sin. . . .
> Happily with some strong thighed bargeman;
> Or one o'th' wood-yard, that can quoit the sledge,
> Or toss the bar, or else some lovely squire
> That carries coals up to her privy lodgings.

His concern seems more like repulsion at her conduct, not so much in what he sees her do as what he imagines her doing. Such thoughts lie behind the phallic poniard of their father that he offers her, "loth to see't look rusty, 'cause 'twas his":

> I would have you to give o'er these chargeable revels;
> A visor and a mask are whispering-rooms
> That were ne'er built for goodness. Fare ye well,
> And women like that part which, like the lamprey,
> Hath ne'er a bone in't.

His obscene reference to the penis, sudden and unaccounted for, he later justifies by accusing his sister of witchcraft. He wishes to enter her bedchamber and recoils at the thought of what he might find there. Antonio's residence there, rather than his political privilege, is what energizes and enervates him by turn, rent as he is by incestuous desire and the shame and guilt that accompany it. Incest within government can take many forms, but for Ferdinand it is direct and real. He identifies himself at one point with the Duchess' first husband – "thou hast ta'en that massy sheet of lead That hid thy husband's bones, and folded it About my heart" – but at her death (not his) he cannot look at her –

> Cover her face, mine eyes dazzle: she died young

– and yet he must:

> Let me see her face again.
> Why didst not thou pity her? What an excellent
> Honest man mightst thou have been
> If thou hadst borne her to some sanctuary!
> Or, bold in a good cause, opposed thyself
> With thy advanced sword above thy head,
> Between her innocence and my revenge!
> I bade thee, when I was distracted of my wits,
> Go kill my dearest friend, and thou hast done't.

His reason, he says, was "to have gained An infinite mass of treasure by her death," but the sheer inadequacy of such a motive is interrupted by a stranger, more accurate one, "her marriage!" His disintegrating mind seeks solace in the madness of lycanthropy, the new vision of his wolf-like state allowing him to range about graveyards, forever digging up corpses and covering them up again. Such a delusion is consonant with the chilliness that elsewhere in the play has rubbed our own nerves raw, but this self-punishment may also be something else for Webster than a frightening metaphor. Ferdinand is made one with his culture's myth of Lycaon who ruled over the Age of Iron, fallen from grace and the Age of Gold, punished by Jove for treachery, violence, and murder.

> Lycaon fled terrified until he reached the safety of the silent countryside. There he uttered howling noises, and his attempts to speak were all in vain. His clothes changed into bristling hairs, his arms to legs, and he became a wolf. His savage nature showed in his rabid jaws, and he now directed against the flocks his innate lust for killing. He had a mania, even yet, for shedding blood. But though he was a wolf, he retained some traces of his original shape. The grayness of his hair was the same, his face showed the same violence, his eyes gleamed as before, and he presented the same picture of ferocity.

His new form of violence extends his tyranny over others. Surely this is a comment on Ferdinand, but what does it say for the reverence paid to the bloodlines of nobility? Or of the establishment of new bloodlines through meritocracy?

The Duchess of Malfi has about 325 lines in her play; her murderer Bosola has at least 200 more than that. His role, not hers, is dominant, and his role as malcontent may show where Webster's chief focus lies. An intellectual who has studied at the famed University of Padua, a spy who observes the secrets of men, Bosola has a sense of superiority that supplies him with irreducible cynicism. It also allows him an indelible pride that motivates his rise in power as his just deserts, distinguishing him from the more modest Antonio. For Webster's audiences, he would represent the new men in James's government whose naked ambition made them dangerous. We can sense a playgoer's potential reaction to Bosola by a description of just such a new man in the anonymous pamphlet entitled *The Just Downfall of Ambition, Adultery, and Murder* published around 1616:

> if he rise from obscurity (as many have done), he laboreth to be skillful in those things which are most pleasing to the greater sort and tolerable among the Commons. His study is for praise, and not for virtue; his looks like Mausolus' Tomb, fair and comely without but within nothing but rotten bones and corrupt practices. His apparel increaseth with his fortune, and as worldly affairs direct him so suiteth he both fashions and affections; in his study he affecteth singularity and is proud in being author of a new stratagem. If he chance to come into the eye of the world, he then creeps into the favor of some great personage, in feeding whose humors (to relieve his wants) he makes intrusion into some heritage and matcheth not according to his birth but to the increase of his fortune and by that means, by hook or crook, he attaineth to some place in the court.

In 1613 James's court saw a great number of masques, and of three given on St. Valentine's Day to celebrate the marriage of his daughter Elizabeth to the Elector Palatine, two had antimasques danced by madmen similar to the antimasque Bosola oversees in IV.ii on Ferdinand's orders. As a malcontent, Bosola had initially enjoyed sharing his cynicism with Castruchio and the Old Lady.

> Man stands amazed to see his deformity
> In any other creature but himself.
> But in our own flesh, though we bear diseases
> Which have their true names only ta'en from beasts,
> As the most ulcerous wolf and swinish measle;
> Though we are eaten up of lice and worms,
> And though continually we bear about us
> A rotten and dead body, we delight
> To hide it in rich tissue.

In the mad scene, Bosola's "rich tissue" has become a series of disguises – first an old man himself, then a tomb-maker, and finally a bellman with the coffin, cords, and bells of "the common bellman That usually is sent to condemned persons The night before they suffer" at Newgate Prison in London. Such disguises shade Bosola from confronting the Duchess directly, yet they lead to a kind of litany with her that, solemn, exalted, Christian in its tonalities, comes as close as Webster's play does to incorporating orthodox religion. In this prolonged scene of the rite of mortification, Bosola seems initially unmoved himself but all that changes when Ferdinand refuses to reward him. "Let me quicken your memory," Bosola warns him. "You are falling into ingratitude. I challenge The reward due to my service." Ferdinand's abrupt dismissal of Bosola and his inability to bring the Duchess back to life – the "cords of life" of "sacred innocence" irretrievably "broke" – prompt Bosola, in his unerring honesty, to locate in his own "guilty conscience" a "black register wherein is writ All our good deeds and bad, a perspective That shows us hell!" Displacing Cariola as the eavesdropper in a scene between the Cardinal and Julia that eerily resembles that between the Duchess and Antonio at the play's beginning, Bosola rededicates himself, this time to "a most just revenge" on the Cardinal and Ferdinand. All along, Webster has been accumulating those conventions of the revenge play first launched by Thomas Kyd in *The Spanish Tragedy*, with the need for justice, a stockpiling of horrors, two dumb shows, and delusions of ghosts and echoes. Nor is it a departure to make a malcontent the agent of revenge. What is new is to assign heroism to a condemned murderer, an upstart courtier who is also a criminal. Hieronimo's bloody revenge cleansed a Spanish court analogous to the English, but Bosola's "perfect" revenge ends merely "in a little point, a kind of nothing."

The rich if confusing portraits of the aspiring courtier in Antonio and Bosola, like the range of responses to the Duchess herself, are Webster's way of calling the whole world he dramatizes into question. No one in the play is given greater agency than Bosola, yet he remarks at one point, "We are merely the stars' tennis-balls, struck and banded Which way please them." But earlier he had consoled the Duchess by telling her, "Look you, the stars shine still." Even the Duchess is at a loss before the political, social, and religious world of the play; for her the doors of life and death "go on such strange geometrical hinges, You may open them both ways." Deliberately, analogically, Webster sets his play in the court, the bedchamber, the shrine, the prison, and the grave, fusing them all in the gloom of night. Behind the play lies an observation of Montaigne:

> The souls of emperors and cobblers are all cast in one same mold. Considering the importance of princes' actions, and their weight, we persuade ourselves they are brought forth by some as weighty and important causes. We are deceived. They are moved, stirred, and removed in their motions by the same springs and wards that we are in ours. The same reason that makes us chide and brawl, and fall out with any of our neighbors, causeth a war to follow between princes. The same reason that makes us whip or beat a lackey maketh a prince, if he apprehend it, to spoil and waste a whole province.

In such a world as that of this play, what sense can finally be given to an assertion such as "I am Duchess of Malfi still"? Like her echo warning Antonio of danger some time after her death, she is invoked again by way of the crown, perhaps, in Delio's concluding lines: "Integrity of life is fame's best friend, Which nobly, beyond death, shall crown the end." But the lines from Horace he is paraphrasing argue that integrity protects us from physical harm; and the Duchess was scarcely invulnerable. Moreover, he promises the duchy to the wrong son, for as Jacobeans well knew, the children of a second marriage could not inherit the titles of a first. Indeed, if we are to imagine a triumphant Duchess, we must do so listening to Delio speak from the midst of a pile of corpses.

FURTHER READING

Bartels, Emily C., "Strategies of Submission: Desdemona, the Duchess, and the Assertion of Desire," *Studies in English Literature 1500–1600* 36:2 (Spring 1996): 417–33.

Boklund, Gunnar, *"The Duchess of Malfi": Sources, Themes, Characters*. Cambridge, Mass.: Harvard University Press, 1962.

Calderwood, James L., "*The Duchess of Malfi*: Styles of Ceremony," *Essays in Criticism* 12 (1962): 133–47.

DiMiceli, Caroline, "Sickness and Physic in Some Plays by Middleton and Webster," *Cahiers Elisabethains* 26 (October 1984): 41–78.

Ekeblad (Ewbank), Inga-Stina, "The 'Impure Art' of John Webster," *Review of English Studies* 9 (1958): 253–67.

Enterline, Lynn, "'Hairy on the In-side': *The Duchess of Malfi* and the Body of Lycanthropy," *The Yale Journal of Criticism* 7:2 (Fall 1994): 85–129.

Forker, Charles R., *Skull Beneath the Skin: The Achievement of John Webster*. Carbondale and Edwardsville: Southern Illinois University Press, 1986.

Jankowski, Theodora A., "Defining/Confining the Duchess: Negotiating the Female Body in John Webster's *The Duchess of Malfi*," *Studies in Philology* 87:2 (Spring 1990): 221–45.

Luckyj, Christina, *A Winter's Snake: Dramatic Form in the Tragedies of John Webster*. Athens and London: The University of Georgia Press, 1989.

Mikesell, Margaret Lael, "Catholic and Protestant Widows in *The Duchess of Malfi*," *Renaissance and Reformation* 7:4 (November 1983): 265–79.

Peterson, Joyce E., *Curs'd Example: "The Duchess of Malfi" and Commonweal Tragedy*. Columbia and London: University of Missouri Press, 1978.

Selzer, John L., "Merit and Degree in Webster's *The Duchess of Malfi*," *English Literary Renaissance* 11:1 (Winter 1981): 70–80.

Steen, Sara Jayne, "The Crime of Marriage: Arbella Stuart and *The Duchess of Malfi*," *Sixteenth Century Journal* 22:1 (Spring 1991): 61–76.

Whigham, Frank, "Sexual and Social Mobility in *The Duchess of Malfi*," *PMLA* 100:2 (March 1985): 167–86.

The Duchess of Malfi

[DEDICATION]

To the Right Honorable, George Harding, Baron Berkeley of Berkeley Castle, and Knight of the Order of the Bath to the Illustrious Prince Charles.

My Noble Lord,

That I may present my excuse why, being a stranger to your Lordship, I offer this poem to your patronage, I plead this warrant: men who never saw the sea, yet desire to behold that regiment of waters, choose some eminent river to guide them thither, and make that, as it were, their conduct or postilion; by the like ingenious means has your fame arrived at my knowledge, receiving it from some of worth who both in contemplation and practice owe to your Honor

TEXTUAL VARIANTS

S.d.] Q lists all the characters in each scene at the beginning of the scene; this text gives the names of the characters in separate entrances and exits **I.i.6** their] Q there **30** than] Q then **57** and] Q an **58** dependencies] Q dependences **60** than] Q then **62** than] Q then **63** dogs,] Q dogs, and whores **I.ii.32** Israel] Q Ismail **35** surgeons] Q chirurgeons **89** than] Q then **90** flatterers] Q flatters **113** ne'er] Q ne'ur shrewd] Q shewed **120** your] Q you **126** Than] Q Then **135** than] Q then **151** now are] Q now **153** leaguer] Q leagues **prefix** *Duch.*] Q Ferdinand **169** Than] Q Then **198** they'd] Q they'll'd to hell] Q hell **202** on't] Q out **208** o'er] Q are vile] vild **236** Than] Q Then **250** eaves] Q Eves **255** than] Q then **264** I'd] Q I'll'd **275** I'd] Q I'll'd **303** revenue] Q reuinew **312** Than] Q Then **314** distraction] Q destruction **316** you] Q yon **356** visitants] Q visitans **373** ne'er] Q ne'ur **375** woo . . . woo] Q woe . . . woe **385** than] Q then **389** off] Q of **420** ne'er] Q neu'r **424** bind] Q build **II.i.25–58**] Q sets as poetry **51** than] Q then **102** fashion] Q shashion **104–112**] Q sets as poetry **111** than] Q then **114–28**] Q sets as poetry **122** than] Q then **136** peels] pills **137** swoon] Q sound **140** courtiers] Q courties **148** than] Q then **150** Methought] Q My thought **II.ii.l** tetchiness] Q teatchives **15** bears] Q beare **22** Danäes] Q Danes **32** Shut] Q Shht **45** Ha, ha, ha] Q Hh, ha, ha **56** officers] Q offices **72** credibly] Q creadably **81** looks] Q looke **II.iii.9** screamed] Q schreamd **10** Who's] Q whose **50** quit] Q quite **65** *Caetera*] Q caeteta **69** cased] Q caside **77** ne'er] nea'r **II.iv.5** Here] Q Hebre **12** turnings] Q turning **30** pray thee] Q pray the **II.v.2** prodigy] Q progedy **3** damned] Q dampn'd **11** Than] Q Then **14** here 't] Q here' it **30** mother's] Q mother **III.i.16** insensibly] Q inseucibly **27** be] Q he **37** dream of] Q dream off **39** to bespeak] Q to be b-speake **51** of] Q off **54** were] Q where **70** horrid] Q horred **78** blood] Q bood **III.ii.25** flight] Q slight **26** Syrinx] Q Sirina **27** Anaxarete] Q Anaxorate **41** apprehension] Q approbation **73** eclipse] Q esclipze **78** mak'st us] Q mak'st **88** confederacy] Q consideracy **89** to thee] Q to the **91** hear'st] Q hearst **95** damn] dampue **99** vile] Q vilde **112** ta'en] Q ta'ne massy] Q massity **117** Too] Q to **123** it] It **134** shook] Q shooked **142 s.d.**] Q has s.d. at line 141 **170** lets] Q let's **176** jewels] Q Iewlls **177** enginous] Q engeneous **202** As loth] Q A-loth **203** confiscate] Q confifcate **238** intelligencers] Q and Intelligencers **240** livery] Q Liuery **243** doom] Q doome **252** On] Q one **260** than] Q then **274** Than] Q Then **310** Whither] Q Whether **III.iii.17** be gone] Q begon **20** keeps] Q keepe painters] Q pewterers **21** he'll] Q hel **40** wreck] Q wrack **76** ne'er] Q neu'r life] Q like **78** hundred] Q hundreth **III.iv**] This scene is omitted from Q4 and may have been omitted from the acting version as well since the play is so long **1** than] Q then **45** brother's] Q brothers **47** Off] Q of **III.v.63** Than] Q Then **89** Than] Q Then **94** what] Q What **97** move] Q more **99 prefix** *Bos*] Q [omits] **102** Whither] Q Whether **111** such a] Q such **IV.i.5** Than] Q shun **8** than] Q then **10** than] Q then **90** itself] Q it **91** vapors] Q vipers **123** Than] Q Then **IV.ii.66** *bell*] Q bill **83** tithe] Q tythe **147** than] Q then than] Q then **202** *bathe*] Q bath **283** agree] Q ageee **284** Than] Q Then **292** done 't] Q don't **345** than] Q then **351** were] Q wete **361** mercy] Q merry **V.i.70** fraught] Q fraight **V.ii.83** anatomies] Q anotomies **89** too] Q to **122** I'd] Q I'lld **180** compliment] Q complement **188** woo] Q woe **235** quit of] Q quit off **269** than] Q then **308** Fortune] Q fortune **317** bier] Q beare **329** rode] Q rod **335 s.d.**] Q has s.d. at line 334 **V.iii.31** Than] Q Then **33** passages] Q passes **V.iv.11** our] Q out **34** quiet] Q quiein **V.v.28** Let's] Lets's **43** than] Q then **54** been] Q bin **64 s.d.**] Q sets on line **84** this] Q his **115** than] Q then

Playsource

The Duchess of Malfi, which closely follows the historic life of Giovanna d'Aragona who was married in 1490 at the age of twelve to Alfonso Piccolomini, son and heir of the first Duke of Amalfi, was widely known. Webster probably turned to the version in William Painter's *Second Tome of the Palace of Pleasure* (1567) derived, with heavy moral comment against the Duchess as a lascivious widow, from the second tome of François de Belleforest's *Histoires Tragiques*, itself derived from the more balanced account in the twenty-sixth part of the first part of Matteo Bandellow's *Novella* (1554). Other accounts of the time condemn the Duchess: Thomas Beard in *The Theatre of God's Judgments* (1597), where she is treated under the heading "Of whoredomes committed under Colour of Marriage"; George Whetstone's *An Heptameron of Civil Discourses* (1582); and Simon Goulart's version translated by Edward Grimeston in his *Admirable and Memorable Histories* (1607). Brief references may also be found in H. C.'s *The Forest of Fancy* (1579) and Robert Greene's *Gwyndonius, the Card of Fancy* (1584), in which the Duchess' choice of husband is praised.

Dedication

1 George Harding (1601–58), 13th Baron Berkeley, student of Christ Church Oxford, was a friend of the King's Men; at the time of the first Q (1623), he was twenty-two years of age. Two years earlier, Robert Burton dedicated his *Anatomy of Melancholy* to Harding

6 poem imaginative work

7 warrant defense

11 conduct conductor; **postilion** escort

13–15 some . . . service perhaps the King's Men who earlier, as the Lord Chamberlain's Men, had served Harding's grandfather and father, the first and second Lord Hunsdons their clearest service. I do not altogether look up at your title, the ancientest nobility being but a relic of time past, and the truest honor indeed being for a man to confer honor on himself, which your learning strives to propagate and shall make you arrive at the dignity of a great example. I am confident this work is not unworthy your Honor's perusal; for by such poems as this, poets have kissed the hands of great princes and drawn their gentle eyes to look down upon their sheets of paper when the poets themselves were bound up in their winding sheets. The like courtesy from your Lordship shall make you live in your grave and laurel spring out of it, when the ignorant scorners of the Muses (that like worms in libraries seem to live only to destroy learning) shall wither, neglected and forgotten. This work and myself I humbly present to your approved censure, it being the utmost of my wishes to have your Honorable self my weighty and perspicuous comment, which grace so done me, shall ever be acknowledged

By your Lordship's
in all duty and observance,
John Webster.

[Commendatory Verses]

In the just worth of that well-deserver, Mr. John Webster, and upon this masterpiece of tragedy.

In this thou imitat'st one rich and wise,
That sees his good deeds done before he dies;
As he by works, thou by this work of fame,
Hast well provided for thy living name.
To trust to others' honorings is worth's crime –
Thy monument is rais'd in thy life-time;
And 'tis most just; for every worthy man
Is his own marble and his merit can
Cut him to any figure, and express
More art than Death's cathedral palaces
Where royal ashes keep their court. Thy note
Be ever plainness, 'tis the richest coat.
Thy epitaph only the title be –
Write "Duchess," that will fetch a tear for thee,
For whoe'er saw this Duchess live and die,
That could get off under a bleeding eye?

In Tragœdiam.
Ut lux ex tenebris ictu percussa Tonantis,
Illa, ruina malis, claris fit vita poetis.
Thomas Middletonus,
Poeta & Chron. Londinensis.

To his friend, Mr. John Webster, upon his *Duchess of Malfi.*

I never saw thy Duchess till the day
That she was lively bodied in thy play;
Howe'er she answered her low-rated love,
Her brothers' anger did so fatal prove,
Yet my opinion is she might speak more,
But never, in her life, so well before.
Wil. Rowley.

To the reader of the author, and his *Duchess of Malfi.*

Crown him a poet, whom nor Rome, nor Greece,
Transcend in all theirs, for a masterpiece:
In which, whiles words and matter change, and
 men
Act one another, he, from whose clear pen
They all took life, to memory hath lent
A lasting fame, to raise his monument.
John Ford.

The Actors' Names

Bosola, *J. Lowin.*
Ferdinand, 1. *R. Burbidge.* 2. *J. Taylor.*
Cardinal, 1. *H. Cundaile.* 2. *R. Robinson.*

---

15 **clearest** absolute; most complete
15–16 **look up at** have respect for
26–7 **winding sheets** shrouds
28 **laurel** a symbol of the poet
33 **approved censure** tested judgment
35 **perspicuous** discerning

Commendatory Verses

19–21 ***In . . . poetis*** "To Tragedy: As light from darkness springs at the Thunderer's stroke May she, bringing ruin to the wicked, bring life to famous poets" (a common sentiment)
23 ***Poeta . . . Londinensis*** Thomas Middleton was named City Chronicler for London on September 6, 1620; see also "Brief Lives"
27 **bodied** embodied
28 **answered** justified
32 ***Rowley*** (see "Brief Lives")
35 **nor Rome** neither Rome
37–8 **whiles . . . another** while style changes, theater continues
38 **clear** (1) pure; (2) illustrious
39 **all** i.e., words and matter
41 ***John Ford*** (see "Brief Lives")

The Actors' Names

0 This is the first published play to assign roles; some parts are missing (Castruchio, Roderigo, Grisolan, Old Lady) suggesting (1) doubling, in which only major parts are listed; (2) printed and acting scripts differ and shortened productions may have omitted some minor roles
1 **Bosola** (this character is exceptionally placed since characters are traditionally listed by gender and then by descending rank)
2–4 (multiple names suggest alternating casts)

Antonio, 1. *W. Ostler.* 2. *R. Benfield.*
Delio, *J. Underwood.*
Forobosco, *N. Towley.*
Malateste.
The Marquis of Pescara, *J. Rice.*
Silvio, *T. Pollard.*
The several madmen, *N. Towley, J. Underwood, etc.*
The Duchess, *R. Sharpe.*
The Cardinal's Mistress, *J. Tomson.*
The Doctor, }
Cariola, } *R. Pallant.*
Court Officers.
Three young children.
Two Pilgrims.

Act I

Actus Primus, Scena Prima.

[*Enter* Antonio *and* Delio.]

Delio. You are welcome to your country, dear Antonio.
You have been long in France, and you return
A very formal Frenchman in your habit.
How do you like the French court?
Ant. I admire it;
In seeking to reduce both state and people
To a fixed order, their judicious King
Begins at home: quits first his royal palace
Of flatt'ring sycophants, of dissolute
And infamous persons (which he sweetly terms
His Master's masterpiece, the work of heaven)
Consid'ring duly, that a prince's court
Is like a common fountain, whence should flow
Pure silver drops in general. But if't chance
Some cursed example poison 't near the head,
"*Death, and diseases through the whole land spread.*"
And what is't makes this blessed government
But a most provident Council, who dare freely
Inform him the corruption of the times?
Though some o'th' court hold it presumption
To instruct princes what they ought to do,
It is a noble duty to inform them
What they ought to foresee.

[*Enter* Bosola.]

Here comes Bosola,
The only court-gall. Yet I observe his railing
Is not for simple love of piety;
Indeed, he rails at those things which he wants,
Would be as lecherous, covetous, or proud,
Bloody, or envious, as any man,
If he had means to be so.

[*Enter* Cardinal.]

Here's the Cardinal.
Bos. I do haunt you still.
Card. So.
Bos. I have done you
Better service than to be slighted thus.
Miserable age, where only the reward
Of doing well is the doing of it.
Card. You enforce your merit too much.
Bos. I fell into the galleys in your service, where for two years together, I wore two towels instead of a shirt, with a knot on the shoulder after the fashion of a Roman mantle. Slighted thus? I will thrive some way. Blackbirds fatten best in hard weather; why not I, in these dog-days?
Card. Would you could become honest.
Bos. With all your divinity, do but direct me the way to it. [*Exit* Cardinal.] I have known many travel far for it, and yet return as arrant knaves as they went forth, because they carried themselves always along with them. Are you gone? Some fellows, they say, are possessed with the devil, but this great fellow were able to possess the greatest devil, and make him worse.

6 **Forobosco** a character who is mentioned in the play (II.ii.35) but who seems never to appear; a "ghost" character
I.i.1 **your country** i.e., Spain
3 **habit** clothing
5 **reduce** bring; **state and people** ruler and ruled
6 **fixed order** regular rule
7 **quits** rids
8 **sycophants** parasites
9 **infamous** noteworthy in evil or shame
12 **common** shared by all
13 **silver** precious; showy; **in general** everywhere
14 **head** source
17 **provident** foreseeing
19 **hold** consider
23 **court-gall** bitter satirist of the court; **railing** reviling; complaining; uttering abusive and contemptuous language
27 **envious** malicious
29 **haunt** follow after; **still** always
31 **only . . . reward** the only reward
33 **enforce** stress, emphasize
34 **I . . . service** "what I performed for you was punishable by imprisonment in slave-ships"
37 **after . . . mantle** (he attempts to dress with dignity despite the clothing)
39–40 **dog-days** the forty days following August 11, reckoned the hottest days of the year when the sun is near Sirius, the dog-star
44 **arrant** wandering, itinerant
45–6 **themselves** their possessions

Ant. He hath denied thee some suit?

Bos. He, and his brother, are like plum-trees that grow crooked over standing pools; they are rich, and o'erladen with fruit, but none but crows, pies, and caterpillars feed on them. Could I be one of their flattering panders, I would hang on their ears like a horse-leech till I were full, and then drop off. I pray, leave me. Who would rely upon these miserable dependencies in expectation to be advanced tomorrow? What creature ever fed worse than hoping Tantalus? Nor ever died any man more fearfully than he that hoped for a pardon? There are rewards for hawks, and dogs, when they have done us service; but for a soldier, that hazards his limbs in a battle, nothing but a kind of geometry is his last supportation.

Delio. Geometry?

Bos. Aye, to hang in a fair pair of slings, take his latter swing in the world upon an honorable pair of crutches from hospital to hospital; fare ye well, sir. And yet do not you scorn us, for places in the court are but like beds in the hospital, where this man's head lies at that man's foot, and so lower, and lower.

[*Exit.*]

Delio. I knew this fellow seven years in the galleys
For a notorious murder, and 'twas thought
The Cardinal suborned it: he was released
By the French general, Gaston de Foix,
When he recovered Naples.

Ant. 'Tis great pity
He should be thus neglected. I have heard
He's very valiant. This foul melancholy
Will poison all his goodness, for, I'll tell you
If too immoderate sleep be truly said
To be an inward rust unto the soul,
It then doth follow want of action
Breeds all black malcontents, and their close rearing,
Like moths in cloth, do hurt for want of wearing.

[I.ii]

[*Enter* Silvio, Castruchio, Julia, Roderigo, *and* Grisolan.]

Delio. The presence 'gins to fill. You promised me
To make me the partaker of the natures
Of some of your great courtiers.

Ant. The Lord Cardinal's
And other strangers', that are now in court?
I shall:

[*Enter* Ferdinand.]

Here comes the great Calabrian Duke.

Ferd. Who took the ring oftenest?

Sil. Antonio Bologna, my Lord.

Ferd. Our sister Duchess' great master of her household? Give him the jewel. When shall we leave this sportive action and fall to action indeed?

Cast. Methinks, my Lord,
You should not desire to go to war in person.

Ferd. Now for some gravity! Why, my Lord?

Cast. It is fitting a soldier arise to be a prince, but not necessary a prince descend to be a captain.

Ferd. No?

Cast. No, my Lord, he were far better do it by a deputy.

Ferd. Why should he not as well sleep, or eat, by a deputy? This might take idle, offensive, and base office from him, whereas the other deprives him of honor.

---

50 **suit** petition
52 **standing** still, stagnant
54 **crows . . . caterpillars** (as scavengers); **pies** magpies
55 **panders** bawds
56–7 **hang . . . full** (1) eavesdrop; (2) join them; **horse-leech** blood-sucker
58–9 **dependencies** (1) conditions; (2) positions of subjection or servitude; (3) appointment in reversion
61 **Tantalus** proverbial for a hoping and disappointed person; according to legend, Tantalus was punished in Hades by having to stand in a lake which receded when he attempted to get a drink; near a tree with fruit that eluded his reach; and under a huge rock that might fall on him
62–3 **hoped . . . pardon** i.e., was publicly executed when hoping for a last-minute release
66 **a . . . geometry** hanging awkwardly (the crutches are likened to compasses or dividers)
67 **supportation** (1) propping up; (2) bearing of expense
70 **swing** (1) forced movement; (2) fling, indulgence
78 **suborned** secretly arranged
79 **Gaston de Foix** (he was only twelve when Naples was recovered in 1501)
82 **melancholy** a mental disease fashionable among the disaffected gentry
86 **want** lack
87 **black** (1) color of his traditional clothes; (2) excess of black bile thought to cause a melancholy humor; **close rearing** secret breeding
I.ii.1 **presence** presence chamber used for official occasions at court
2 **partaker** sharer (in the understanding)
6 **ring** (1) prize in chivalric sport of riding the ring (carrying it away on a lance); (2) anticipatory pun on the wedding ring, the noose, and the Duchess' pudenda
8 **great** chief
9 **jewel** prize
10 **fall to action** enter into military engagement
22 **office** function

Cast. Believe my experience: that realm is never long in quiet where the ruler is a soldier.

Ferd. Thou told'st me thy wife could not endure fighting.

Cast. True, my Lord.

Ferd. And of a jest she broke, of a captain she met full of wounds – I have forgot it.

Cast. She told him, my Lord, he was a pitiful fellow, to lie, like the children of Israel, all in tents.

Ferd. Why, there's a wit were able to undo all the surgeons o' the city, for although gallants should quarrel, and had drawn their weapons, and were ready to go to it, yet her persuasions would make them put up.

Cast. That she would, my Lord –

Ferd. How do you like my Spanish jennet?

Rod. He is all fire.

Ferd. I am of Pliny's opinion, I think he was begot by the wind. He runs as if he were ballasted with quicksilver.

Sil. True, my Lord, he reels from the tilt often.

Rod., Gris. Ha, ha, ha!

Ferd. Why do you laugh? Methinks you that are courtiers should be my touch-wood, take fire, when I give fire; that is, laugh when I laugh, were the subject never so witty –

Cast. True, my Lord, I myself have heard a very good jest, and have scorned to seem to have so silly a wit as to understand it.

Ferd. But I can laugh at your fool, my Lord.

Cast. He cannot speak, you know, but he makes faces. My lady cannot abide him.

Ferd. No?

Cast. Nor endure to be in merry company, for she says too much laughing and too much company fills her too full of the wrinkle.

Ferd. I would then have a mathematical instrument made for her face, that she might not laugh out of compass. I shall shortly visit you at Milan, Lord Silvio.

Sil. Your Grace shall arrive most welcome.

Ferd. You are a good horseman, Antonio. You have excellent riders in France; what do you think of good horsemanship?

Ant. Nobly, my Lord, as out of the Grecian horse issued many famous princes, so, out of brave horsemanship, arise the first sparks of growing resolution that raise the mind to noble action.

Ferd. You have bespoke it worthily.

[*Enter* Cardinal, Duchess, Cariola, *with* Attendant.]

Sil. Your brother, the Lord Cardinal, and sister Duchess.

Card. Are the galleys come about?

Gris. They are, my Lord.

Ferd. Here's the Lord Silvio, is come to take his leave.

Delio. Now sir, your promise: what's that Cardinal?
I mean his temper? They say he's a brave fellow,
Will play his five thousand crowns at tennis, dance,
Court ladies, and one that hath fought single combats.

Ant. Some such flashes superficially hang on him for form; but observe his inward character: he is a melancholy churchman; the spring in his face is nothing but the engendering of toads. Where he is jealous of any man, he lays worse plots for them than ever was imposed on Hercules, for he strews in his way flatterers, panders, intelligencers, atheists, and a thousand such political monsters. He should have

26–7 **wife . . . fighting** (implies Castruchio's marriage is a battleground)
29 **broke, of** cracked about
32–3 **all in tents** (1) in canvas shelters; (2) in surgical dressings; (3) intentions
36–8 **drawn . . . up** (with sexual puns)
38 **put up** sheathe them
40 **jennet** light Spanish horse
42 **Pliny's opinion** that along the Tagus River and around Lisbon mares conceived from the west wind and gave birth to swift colts (Pliny's *Natural History* was translated in 1601)
43 **ballasted** weighted; **quicksilver** mercury
45 **reels . . . often** (1) the ballast rights the tilt; (2) tilt as copulation; **reels** staggers
48 **touch-wood** tinder (line is a class marker between princes who command and courtiers who seek favor by pleasing)
53 **silly** foolish
60 **wrinkle** (1) crease; (2) moral blemish
63 **out of compass** immoderately
69 **Grecian horse** Trojan horse which held Greek troops thus craftily allowed inside the gates of Troy
76 **Are . . . about?** "have the ships reversed their course?"
81 **brave** (1) bold; (2) extravagant
82 **Will** who will
83 **single combats** duels
84 **flashes** showy feats
85 **form** outer demeanor
86 **spring** i.e., of water
87 **the . . . toads** (bitter temperament was said to have poisoned the blood, resulting in toad-like complexions)
88 **jealous** suspicious
90 **Hercules** a mythological hero who, choosing a life of toil, underwent twelve great labors or challenges; he was said to suffer from bouts of insanity
91 **panders** bawds; **intelligencers** spies; **atheists** (here impious men generally)
92 **political** scheming, crafty

been Pope; but instead of coming to it by the primitive decency of the church, he did bestow bribes so largely, and so impudently, as if he would have carried it away without heaven's knowledge. Some good he hath done.

Delio. You have given too much of him. What's his brother?

Ant. The Duke there? A most perverse and turbulent nature.
What appears in him mirth, is merely outside;
If he laugh heartily, it is to laugh
All honesty out of fashion.

Delio. Twins?

Ant. In quality:
He speaks with others' tongues, and hears men's suits
With others' ears; will seem to sleep o'th' bench
Only to entrap offenders in their answers;
Dooms men to death by information,
Rewards by hearsay.

Delio. Then the law to him
Is like a foul black cobweb to a spider –
He makes it his dwelling, and a prison
To entangle those shall feed him.

Ant. Most true.
He ne'er pays debts, unless they be shrewd turns,
And those he will confess that he doth owe.
Last, for his brother, there, the Cardinal –
They that do flatter him most say oracles
Hang at his lips. And verily I believe them,
For the devil speaks in them.
But for their sister, the right noble Duchess –
You never fixed your eye on three fair medals,
Cast in one figure, of so different temper.
For her discourse, it is so full of rapture
You only will begin then to be sorry
When she doth end her speech; and wish, in wonder,
She held it less vain-glory to talk much,
Than you penance to hear her. Whilst she speaks,
She throws upon a man so sweet a look,
That it were able raise one to a galliard
That lay in a dead palsy, and to dote
On that sweet countenance; but in that look,
There speaketh so divine a continence
As cuts off all lascivious and vain hope.
Her days are practiced in such noble virtue
That sure her nights – nay more, her very sleeps –
Are more in heaven than other ladies' shrifts.
Let all sweet ladies break their flatt'ring glasses,
And dress themselves in her.

Delio. Fie, Antonio,
You play the wire-drawer with her commendations.

Ant. I'll case the picture up only thus much –
All her particular worth grows to this sum:
She stains the time past, lights the time to come.

Cari. You must attend my Lady, in the gallery,
Some half an hour hence.

Ant. I shall.

Ferd. Sister, I have a suit to you

Duch. To me, sir?

Ferd. A gentleman here, Daniel de Bosola;
One that was in the galleys.

Duch. Yes, I know him.

Ferd. A worthy fellow h' is: pray let me entreat for
The provisorship of your horse.

Duch. Your knowledge of him
Commends him, and prefers him.

Ferd. Call him hither.
[*Exit* Attendant.]
We now are upon parting. Good Lord Silvio,
Do us commend to all our noble friends
At the leaguer.

Sil. Sir, I shall.

Duch. You are for Milan?

Sil. I am

94 **decency...church** Popes were elected by strict rules that prevented bribery and lobbying
96 **carried it away** won the election
98 **give...much** said enough
104–5 **speaks...ears** neither tells what he thinks nor prejudicial when hearing cases
107 **information** private intelligence
109 **law...him** "the law, like a cobweb, traps the little and allows the greater to escape" (proverbial)
113 **shrewd** cunning, malicious
116 **oracles** wise sayings
117 **Hang** are ever ready
120 **medals** i.e., something stamped from a mold
121 **in one figure** after one original; **temper** (1) alloy of medals; (2) temperament – of people
125 **vain-glory** unnecessary pride
126 **penance** pay the price
128 **galliard** lively court dance
129 **palsy** paralysis
134 **her...sleeps** even in her sleep (or dreams)
135 **shrifts** confessions of sin
136 **glasses** mirrors
137 **dress...her** use her as the ideal model
138 **wire-drawer** one who makes much of little
139 **case** conclude; **picture** verbal description
141 **stains** eclipses, puts in shade
142 **gallery** long room used for exercise
145 **suit** petition, request
149 **provisorship** manager
150 **Commends...prefers** recommends him preferentially
153 **leaguer** military camp

Duch. Bring the caroches: we'll bring you down to the haven.
[*Exeunt all except* Cardinal *and* Ferdinand.]
Card. Be sure you entertain that Bosola
For your intelligence. I would not be seen in't;
And therefore many times I have slighted him
When he did court our furtherance, as this morning.
Ferd. Antonio, the great master of her household
Had been far fitter.
Card. You are deceived in him,

[*Enter* Bosola.]

His nature is too honest for such business.
He comes. I'll leave you.
[*Exit.*]
Bos. I was lured to you.
Ferd. My brother here, the Cardinal, could never
Abide you.
Bos. never since he was in my debt.
Ferd. May be some oblique character in your face
Made him suspect you!
Bos. Doth he study physiognomy?
There's no more credit to be given to th'face
Than to a sick man's urine, which some call
The physician's whore, because she cozens him.
He did suspect me wrongfully.
Ferd. For that
You must give great men leave to take their times.
Distrust doth cause us seldom be deceived.
You see, the oft shaking of the cedar-tree
Fastens it more at root.
Bos. Yet take heed,
For to suspect a friend unworthily
Instructs him the next way to suspect you,
And prompts him to deceive you.
Ferd. There's gold.
Bos. So:
What follows? Never rained such show'rs as these
Without thunderbolts in the tail of them.
Whose throat must I cut?
Ferd. Your inclination to shed blood rides post
Before my occasion to use you. I give you that
To live i'th' court, here; and observe the Duchess,
To note all the particulars of her 'havior;
What suitors do solicit her for marriage
And whom she best affects. She's a young widow;
I would not have her marry again.
Bos. No, sir?
Ferd. Do not you ask the reason, but be satisfied;
I say I would not.
Bos. It seems you would create me
One of your familiars.
Ferd. Familiar? What's that?
Bos. Why, a very quaint invisible devil, in flesh.
An intelligencer.
Ferd. Such a kind of thriving thing
I would wish thee; and ere long, thou mayst arrive
At a higher place by't.
Bos. Take your devils
Which hell calls angels. These cursed gifts would make
You a corrupter, me an impudent traitor,
And should I take these they'd take me to hell .
Ferd. Sir, I'll take nothing from you that I have given.
There is a place that I procured for you
This morning: the Provisorship o'th' horse.
Have you heard on't?
Bos. No.
Ferd. 'Tis yours; is't not worth thanks?

---

155 **caroches** stately coaches; **bring** accompany
156 **entertain** employ
157 **intelligence** spy
159 **court our furtherance** ask me for promotion
163 **lured** (1) summoned; (2) made obedient by training (from hawking)
166 **oblique** (1) perverse; (2) improper
167 **physiognomy** the judging of character by facial features
168 **credit** reliability, validity
169 **urine** (used to test for illness)
170 **cozens** deceives
172 **take . . . times** go at their own speed
173 **Distrust . . . deceived** "He who trusts not is not deceived" (proverbial)
174–5 **oft . . . root** "small strokes are safe when great trees are toppled by storm" (proverbial)
177 **next** nearest, most direct
178 **gold** a nugget of good advice
179–80 **Never . . . them** (refers to Jupiter appearing to the imprisoned Danaë in a shower of gold)
182 **post** hastily
187 **affects** likes; is drawn to
191 **familiars** (1) members of the household; (2) intimate friends; (3) spirits attendant on witches
192 **quaint** cunning
194 **ere** before
195 **higher place** (a play on devils and hell, but anticipatory of his concern regarding the Duchess' bewitching powers)
196 **angels** gold coins with St. Michael killing the dragon (the Devil) stamped on one side; cf. line 199
197 **impudent** shameless
200 **place** position at court
202 **thanks** (with a clear indication of obligation)

Bos. I would have you curse yourself now, that your bounty,
Which makes men truly noble, e'er should make
Me a villain. Oh, that to avoid ingratitude
For the good deed you have done me, I must do
All the ill man can invent! Thus the devil
Candies all sins o'er; and what heaven terms vile,
That names he complimental.
Ferd. Be yourself.
Keep your old garb of melancholy; 'twill express
You envy those that stand above your reach,
Yet strive not to come near 'em. This will gain
Access to private lodging where yourself
May, like a politic dormouse –
Bos. As I have seen some
Feed in a lord's dish, half asleep, not seeming
To listen to any talk; and yet these rogues
Have cut his throat in a dream. What's my place?
The provisorship o'th' horse? Say then, my corruption
Grew out of horse-dung. I am your creature.
Ferd. Away.
Bos. Let good men, for good deeds, covet good fame,
Since place and riches oft are bribes of shame.
Sometimes the devil doth preach.
Exit.

[*Enter* Duchess *and* Cardinal.]

Card. We are to part from you, and your own discretion
Must now be your director.
Ferd. You are a widow.
You know already what man is; and therefore
Let not youth, high promotion, eloquence –
Card. No, nor anything without the addition, honor,
Sway your high blood.
Ferd. Marry! they are most luxurious
Will wed twice.
Card. Oh, fie!
Ferd. Their livers are more spotted
Than Laban's sheep.
Duch. Diamonds are of most value,
They say, that have passed through most jewelers' hands.
Ferd. Whores, by that rule, are precious.
Duch. Will you hear me?
I'll never marry.
Card. So most widows say.
But commonly that motion lasts no longer
Than the turning of an hour-glass. The funeral sermon
And it end both together.
Ferd. Now hear me:
You live in a rank pasture here, i'th' court.
There is a kind of honey-dew that's deadly;
'Twill poison your fame. Look to't. Be not cunning,
For they whose faces do belie their hearts
Are witches ere they arrive at twenty years.
Aye and give the devil suck.
Duch. This is terrible good counsel.
Ferd. Hypocrisy is woven of a fine small thread,
Subtler than Vulcan's engine. Yet, believe't,
Your darkest actions – nay, your privat'st thought –
Will come to light.
Card. You may flatter yourself,
And take your own choice: privately be married;

203–9 I . . . complimental (the stock complaint of the malcontent or melancholic, both railing and self-pitying; Bosola uses it to gain extra consideration)
208 Candies sugars, sweetens
209 complimental refinement
210 garb appearance
214 politic shrewd, cunning; **dormouse** a rodent who hibernates for renewed life each spring (Pliny)
215 in . . . dish at the lord's table
217 in a dream when asleep
218 provisorship one who supplies provisions
219 creature (1) absolute servant; (2) solely the object of your creation
221–3 Let . . . preach (the insolence of this speech suggests it may be directed to the audience)
223 Sometimes . . . preach "the Devil can cite scripture for his purpose" (proverbial)
225–7 You . . . eloquence (Ferdinand as already part of a separate conversation may suggest he briefly left the stage to meet with his brother and sister)
228 addition title
229 high blood noble lineage; **Marry!** "By the Virgin Mary" (a common oath); **luxurious** lecherous
230 Will who will; **fie** (an expression of strong admonishment); **livers** (as the seat of violent passions)
231 Laban's sheep parti-colored sheep by which Laban managed to increase his reward from Jacob through a trick (Gen. 30:31–43)
235 motion resolution
238 rank lustful, licentious
239 honey-dew a sweet, sticky substance found on leaves
240 fame (1) reputation; (2) achievements
244 terrible good wise yet unnerving
246 Vulcan's engine a net in which he caught Mars and Venus, his wife, in adultery; **engine** contrivance, device

Under the eaves of night.
Ferd. Think't the best voyage
That e'er you made; like the irregular crab,
Which though't goes backward, thinks that it goes right
Because it goes its own way. But observe,
Such weddings may more properly be said
To be executed than celebrated.
Card. The marriage night
Is the entrance into some prison.
Ferd. And those joys,
Those lustful pleasures, are like heavy sleeps
Which do fore-run man's mischief –
Card. Fare you well.
Wisdom begins at the end; remember it.
[*Exit.*]
Duch. I think this speech between you both was studied,
It came so roundly off.
Ferd. You are my sister.
This was my father's poniard; do you see?
I'd be loth to see't look rusty, 'cause 'twas his.
I would have you to give o'er these chargeable revels;
A visor and a mask are whispering-rooms
That were ne'er built for goodness. Fare ye well,
And women like that part which, like the lamprey,
Hath ne'er a bone in't.
Duch. Fie, sir!
Ferd. Nay,
I mean the tongue. Variety of courtship.
What cannot a neat knave with a smooth tale
Make a woman believe? Farewell, lusty widow.
[*Exit.*]
Duch. Shall this move me? If all my royal kindred
Lay in my way unto this marriage,
I'd make them my low footsteps. And even now,
Even in this hate, as men in some great battles
By apprehending danger have achieved
Almost impossible actions – I have heard soldiers say so –
So I, through frights, and threat'nings, will assay
This dangerous venture. Let old wives report
I winked and chose a husband, Cariola,

[*Enter* Cariola.]

To thy known secrecy I have given up
More than my life, my fame.
Cari. Both shall be safe,
For I'll conceal this secret from the world
As warily as those that trade in poison
Keep poison from their children.
Duch. Thy protestation
Is ingenious and hearty; I believe it.
Is Antonio come?
Cari. He attends you.
Duch. Good dear soul,
Leave me. But place thyself behind the arras,
Where thou mayst overhear us. Wish me good speed,
For I am going into a wilderness
Where I shall find nor path nor friendly clew
To be my guide.
[*Cariola withdraws behind the arras.*]

[*Enter* Antonio.]

I sent for you, sit down.
Take pen and ink, and write. Are you ready?
Ant. Yes:
Duch. What did I say?
Ant. That I should write somewhat.
Duch. Oh, I remember –
After these triumphs, and this large expense,
It's fit, like thrifty husbands, we inquire
What's laid up for tomorrow.
Ant. So please your beauteous excellence.
Duch. Beauteous?

250 **eaves** shelter
255 **executed** (1) completed; (2) put participants to death
260 **Wisdom . . . end** (1) proverb concerning prudence; (2) a warning
261 **studied** prepared
262 **roundly** (1) smoothly; (2) forcefully
263 **poniard** dagger
264 **look rusty** remain unused
265 **chargeable** (1) expensive; (2) of which you have been charged (or assumed)
266 **whispering-rooms** private chambers
268 **that part** (perhaps a reference to the penis); **lamprey** fish similar to eels
271 **neat** clever, accomplished; **knave** (1) male servant; (2) person without principles; **tale** (1) story; (2) tail or penis
272 **lusty** (1) merry; (2) vigorous; (3) lecherous
275 **footsteps** stepping-stones
276 **in . . . hate** confronting such adversity (from her brothers)
279 **assay** attempt
281 **winked** (1) shut my eyes; (2) closed my eyes to something wrong
287 **ingenious** intelligent (and so reassuring); **hearty** heartfelt
288 **attends** awaits
289 **arras** tapestry hanging to cover a door but at some distance from the wall
290 **speed** luck, fortune
292 **nor** no; **clew** ball of thread, such as Theseus used to trace his way through a labyrinth to kill the Minotaur
297 **triumphs** festivities
298 **husbands** husbandmen, managers of households; stewards

Indeed I thank you. I look young for your sake.
You have ta'en my cares upon you.
Ant. I'll fetch your Grace
The particulars of your revenue, and expense.
Duch. Oh, you are an upright treasurer. But you mistook,
For when I said I meant to make inquiry
What's laid up for tomorrow, I did mean
What's laid up yonder for me.
Ant. Where?
Duch. In heaven.
I am making my will (as 'tis fit princes should,
In perfect memory) and I pray, sir, tell me
Were not one better make it smiling, thus,
Than in deep groans, and terrible ghastly looks,
As if the gifts we parted with procured
That violent distraction?
Ant. Oh, much better.
Duch. If I had a husband now, this care were quit.
But I intend to make you overseer;
What good deed shall we first remember? Say.
Ant. Begin with that first good deed began i'th' world
After man's creation, the sacrament of marriage.
I'd have you first provide for a good husband,
Give him all.
Duch. All?
Ant. Yes, your excellent self.
Duch. In a winding sheet?
Ant. In a couple.
Duch. Saint Winifred, that were a strange will!
Ant. 'Twere strange if there were no will in you
To marry again.
Duch. What do you think of marriage?
Ant. I take't, as those that deny purgatory –
It locally contains, or heaven, or hell;
There's no third place in't.
Duch. How do you affect it?
Ant. My banishment, feeding my melancholy,
Would often reason thus –
Duch. Pray let's hear it.
Ant. Say a man never marry, nor have children,
What takes that from him? Only the bare name
Of being a father, or the weak delight
To see the little wanton ride a-cock-horse
Upon a painted stick, or hear him chatter
Like a taught starling.
Duch. Fie, fie, what's all this?
One of your eyes is blood-shot. Use my ring to't,
They say 'tis very sovereign, 'twas my wedding ring,
And I did vow never to part with it,
But to my second husband.
Ant. You have parted with it now.
Duch. Yes, to help your eyesight.
Ant. You have made me stark blind.
Duch. How?
Ant. There is a saucy and ambitious devil
Is dancing in this circle.
Duch. Remove him.
Ant. How?
Duch. There needs small conjuration when your finger
May do it thus. Is it fit?
[*She puts her ring upon his finger:*] *he kneels.*
Ant. What said you?
Duch. Sir,
This goodly roof of yours is too low built.
I cannot stand upright in't, nor discourse,
Without I raise it higher. Raise yourself,
Or if you please, my hand to help you. So.
[*Raises him.*]
Ant. Ambition, Madam, is a great man's madness
That is not kept in chains and close-pent rooms,
But in fair lightsome lodgings, and is girt
With the wild noise of prattling visitants
Which makes it lunatic, beyond all cure.
Conceive not I am so stupid but I aim

---

313 **procured** produced
314 **violent distraction** madness
315 **were quit** would not exist
316 **But** thus; **overseer** (1) executor of her will; (2) husband of her household
322 **couple** (play on winding sheet [shroud] as wedding sheets; line 319)
323 **Saint Winifred** a seventh-century Welsh saint; when she denied her lover, he beheaded her but she was restored by St. Bruno, her mother's brother; **will** (1) act; (2) passion; (3) testament
326 **those . . . purgatory** i.e., Protestants
327 **or . . . or** either . . . or
328 **affect** feel about
329 **banishment** (solitude was thought to promote melancholy)
334 **wanton** rogue (a term of endearment)
336 **taught starling** (starlings were often caged as pets)
337 **use . . . ring** (as a charm)
338 **sovereign** powerful, efficacious
346 **circle** i.e., the ring (magicians raised spirits, or familiars, in charmed circles)
349 **roof** i.e., head
351 **Without** unless
354 **close-pent** (1) locked; (2) secret
355 **girt** surrounded
356 **prattling** talking; **visitants** (possibly referring to courtiers, as he might be made a duke)
357 **lunatic** a mad vision
358 **aim** (1) know; (2) conjecture; (3) desire

Whereto your favors tend. But he's a fool
That, being a-cold, would thrust his hands i'th' fire
To warm them.

Duch. So, now the ground's broke,
You may discover what a wealthy mine
I make you Lord of.

Ant. Oh, my unworthiness!

Duch. You were ill to sell yourself.
This dark'ning of your worth is not like that
Which tradesmen use i'th' city; their false lights
Are to rid bad wares off. And I must tell you
If you will know where breathes a complete man –
I speak it without flattery – turn your eyes
And progress through yourself.

Ant. Were there nor heaven nor hell,
I should be honest. I have long served virtue,
And ne'er ta'en wages of her.

Duch. Now she pays it!
The misery of us that are born great –
We are forced to woo, because none dare woo us.
And as a tyrant doubles with his words,
And fearfully equivocates, so we
Are forced to express our violent passions
In riddles, and in dreams, and leave the path
Of simple virtue which was never made
To seem the thing it is not. Go, go brag
You have left me heartless – mine is in your bosom,
I hope 'twill multiply love there. You do tremble.
Make not your heart so dead a piece of flesh
To fear, more than to love me. Sir, be confident –
What is't distracts you? This is flesh, and blood, sir;
'Tis not the figure cut in alabaster
Kneels at my husband's tomb. Awake, awake, man!
I do here put off all vain ceremony,
And only do appear to you a young widow
That claims you for her husband, and like a widow,
I use but half a blush in't.

Ant. Truth speak for me.
I will remain the constant sanctuary
Of your good name.

Duch. I thank you, gentle love,
And 'cause you shall not come to me in debt,
Being now my steward, here upon your lips
I sign your *Quietus est.*
[*Kisses him.*]
This you should have begged now;
I have seen children oft eat sweetmeats thus,
As fearful to devour them too soon.

Ant. But for your brothers?

Duch. Do not think of them.
All discord, without this circumference,
Is only to be pitied, and not feared.
Yet, should they know it, time will easily
Scatter the tempest.

Ant. These words should be mine,
And all the parts you have spoke, if some part of it
Would not have savored flattery.

Duch. Kneel. [Cariola *comes from behind the arras.*]

Ant. Hah?

Duch. Be not amazed, this woman's of my counsel.
I have heard lawyers say, a contract in a chamber
Per verba de presenti is absolute marriage.
Bless, heaven, this sacred Gordian, which let violence
Never untwine.

Ant. And may our sweet affections, like the spheres,
Be still in motion.

Duch. Quickening, and make

---

361 **ground's broke** intentions are clear
362 **mine** inheritance
365 **dark'ning** (1) belittling; (2) obscuring
366–7 **their . . . off** they deceptively promote wares to sell them
368 **complete** perfect
370 **progress through** renew (with play on royal progress)
371 **nor . . . nor** neither . . . nor
372 **should be honest** (1) am truthful; (2) am moral; (3) am chaste
373 **pays** rewards
376 **doubles** deceives
377 **fearfully** with apprehension
389 **vain** worthless; **ceremony** (1) politeness; (2) rituals
397 ***Quietus est*** "it is discharged"; the phrase was most common concerning the soul of someone dying
399 **sweetmeats** sugared cakes or candy
402 **circumference** (1) bounds; (2) embrace; (3) with allusion to wedding ring
406 **parts** (1) matters; (2) duties as the suitor
412 ***Per . . . presenti*** "by words about the present"; legal marriage by verbal contract with or without a witness; some considered this fornication, however, until it was further solemnized in religious ceremony, although intercourse was, strictly speaking, permissible; **absolute** (1) full; (2) true
413 **heaven** (here and elsewhere perhaps this means God but was changed because of censorship); **Gordian** a firm knot (from that of King Gordius of Phrygia who used it to tie his oxen, the oracle declaring that anyone who managed to untie the knot would rule all Asia. Alexander the Great did cut the knot with his sword)
415 **spheres** planets, which made music because of their perfect relationship
416 **still** always; **Quickening** coming alive

The like soft music.
Ant. That we may imitate the loving palms,
Best emblem of a peaceful marriage,
That ne'er bore fruit, divided.
Duch. What can the church force more?
Ant. That Fortune may not know an accident,
Either of joy or sorrow, to divide
Our fixed wishes.
Duch. How can the church bind faster?
We now are man and wife, and 'tis the church
That must but echo this. Maid, stand apart;
I now am blind.
Ant. What's your conceit in this?
Duch. I would have you lead your fortune by the hand,
Unto your marriage bed.
(You speak in me this, for we now are one)
We'll only lie, and talk together, and plot
T'appease my humorous kindred; and if you please,
Like the old tale, in "Alexander and Lodowick,"
Lay a naked sword between us, keep us chaste: –
Oh, let me shroud my blushes in your bosom,
Since 'tis the treasury of all my secrets.
[*Exeunt* Duchess *and* Antonio.]
Cari. Whether the spirit of greatness or of woman
Reign most in her, I know not, but it shows
A fearful madness. I owe her much of pity.
Exit.

Act II

Actus II, Scena i.

[*Enter* Bosola *and* Castruchio.]

Bos. You say you would fain be taken for an eminent courtier?

Cast. 'Tis the very main of my ambition.

Bos. Let me see, you have a reasonable good face for't already, and your night-cap expresses your ears sufficient largely. I would have you learn to twirl the strings of your band with a good grace; and in a set speech, at th' end of every sentence, to hum, three or four times, or blow your nose till it smart again, to recover your memory; when you come to be a president in criminal causes, if you smile upon a prisoner, hang him, but if you frown upon him and threaten him, let him be sure to 'scape the gallows.

Cast. I would be a very merry president!

Bos. Do not sup o'nights, 'twill beget you an admirable wit.

Cast. Rather it would make me have a good stomach to quarrel, for they say your roaring boys eat meat seldom, and that makes them so valiant. But how shall I know whether the people take me for an eminent fellow?

Bos. I will teach a trick to know it: give out you lie a-dying, and if you hear the common people curse you, be sure you are taken for one of the prime night-caps –

[*Enter an* Old Lady.]

You come from painting now?

Old Lady. From what?

Bos. Why, from your scurvy face-physic; to behold thee not painted inclines somewhat near a miracle. These, in thy face here, were deep ruts and foul sloughs the last progress. There was a lady in France, that having had the smallpox, flayed the skin off her face to make it more level; and whereas before she looked like a nutmeg-grater, after she resembled an abortive hedgehog.

Old Lady. Do you call this painting?

Bos. No, no, but careening of an old morphewed lady, to make her disembogue again – there's rough-cast phrase to your plastic.

Old Lady. It seems you are well acquainted with my closet.

418–20 That . . . divided (Pliny notes that single palm trees do not bear fruit)
418, 422 (Antonio's phrasing echoes the Book of Common Prayer)
421 force enforce, confirm
424 faster more tightly
427 blind (perhaps referring to the icon of Lady Fortune); **conceit** (1) idea; (2) meaning
431 humorous ill-humored
432 "Alexander and Lodowick" (two men who looked alike, one marrying a princess in the name of the other but keeping a sword between his wife and himself so as not to betray his friend sexually)
434 shroud hide, veil
438 fearful (1) frightened; (2) frightening
II.i.1 fain gladly
2 courtier lawyer
3 main purpose, end
5 night-cap white skull-cap worn by sergeants at law; **expresses** presses out
7 strings . . . band tabs of your neck-band
11–12 president presiding officer
20 stomach (1) appetite; (2) anger
20–1 roaring boys undisciplined bullies
28 night-caps i.e., lawyers
31 scurvy face-physic undesirable face-painting
34 sloughs literally, muddy ditches; here layers of dead skin; **progress** state journey, an occasion for ostentatious display
41 but only; **careening** scraping clean; **morphewed** scurfy
42 disembogue come out into the open sea
43 plastic fashioning
45 closet private room

Bos. One would suspect it for a shop of witchcraft, to find in it the fat of serpents, spawn of snakes, Jews' spittle, and their young children's ordure – and all these for the face. I would sooner eat a dead pigeon, taken from the soles of the feet of one sick of the plague, than kiss one of you fasting. Here are two of you, whose sin of your youth is the very patrimony of the physician, makes him renew his footcloth with the spring and change his high-prized courtesan with the fall of the leaf. I do wonder you do not loathe yourselves. Observe my meditation now:

What thing is in this outward form of man
To be beloved? We account it ominous
If nature do produce a colt, or lamb,
A fawn, or goat, in any limb resembling
A man; and fly from't as a prodigy.
Man stands amazed to see his deformity
In any other creature but himself.
But in our own flesh, though we bear diseases
Which have their true names only ta'en from beasts,
As the most ulcerous wolf and swinish measle;
Though we are eaten up of lice and worms,
And though continually we bear about us
A rotten and dead body, we delight
To hide it in rich tissue. All our fear–
Nay, all our terror – is lest our physician
Should put us in the ground to be made sweet.
Your wife's gone to Rome; you two couple, and get you
to the wells at Lucca, to recover your aches.

[*Exeunt* Castruchio *and* Old Lady.]

I have other work on foot. I observe our Duchess
Is sick o' days. She pukes, her stomach seethes,
The fins of her eyelids look most teeming blue,
She wanes i'th' cheek and waxes fat i'th' flank;
And, contrary to our Italian fashion,
Wears a loose-bodied gown. There's somewhat in't!
I have a trick may chance discover it,
A pretty one. I have bought some apricocks,
The first our spring yields.

[*Enter* Antonio *and* Delio, *talking apart.*]

Delio. And so long since married?
You amaze me.

Ant. Let me seal your lips forever,
For did I think that anything but th' air
Could carry these words from you, I should wish
You had no breath at all.
[*To Bosola.*] Now sir, in your contemplation?
You are studying to become a great wise fellow?

Bos. O sir, the opinion of wisdom is a foul tetter that runs all over a man's body. If simplicity direct us to have no evil, it directs us to a happy being, for the subtlest folly proceeds from the subtlest wisdom. Let me be simply honest.

Ant. I do understand your inside.

Bos. Do you so?

Ant. Because you would not seem to appear to th' world puffed up with your preferment. You continue this out-of-fashion melancholy. Leave it, leave it.

Bos. Give me leave to be honest in any phrase, in any compliment whatsoever. Shall I confess myself to you? I look no higher than I can reach. They are the gods that must ride on wingèd horses; a lawyer's mule of a slow pace will both suit my disposition and business, for mark me, when a man's mind rides faster than his horse can gallop, they quickly both tire.

Ant. You would look up to heaven, but I think
The devil, that rules i'th' air, stands in your light.

---

49 **ordure** excrement
50–1 **dead . . . plague** (holding a bird against a plague sore until it drew the poison to its heart and died was one recommended cure for the plague)
52 **fasting** in the morning when the breath is especially bad
53 **patrimony** estate, well-being
54 **footcloth** a rich cloth laid over the back of a horse to protect the rider from mud and dust; a new one annually would be a sign of wealth
59 **form** appearance
63 **prodigy** omen, portent
68 **ulcerous wolf** ulcers or cancerous growths (cf. Act V); **swinish measle** measles, often confused with a skin disease in swine resembling leprosy
71 **dead** i.e., dying
72 **tissue** fine cloth, often with gold or silver threads
76 **Lucca** a famous health spa 13 miles NE of Pisa
78 **seethes** is agitated
79 **fins** rims; **teeming** fruitful, perhaps denoting pregnancy
82 **somewhat** something hidden
84 **apricocks** apricots
92 **opinion of** reputation for; **tetter** sore
93 **simplicity** i.e., lack of learning
98 **inside** thoughts
102 **out-of-fashion** now unnecessary, as Provisor of the Horse
110–11 **when . . . gallop** (perhaps referring to Antonio's skill at horsemanship)
113 **devil . . . air** (cf. Ephesians 2:2)

Bos. Oh, sir, you are lord of the ascendant, chief man with the Duchess, a Duke was your cousin-german removed. Say you were lineally descended from King Pepin, or he himself, what of this? Search the heads of the greatest rivers in the world, you shall find them but bubbles of water. Some would think the souls of princes were brought forth by some more weighty cause than those of meaner persons. They are deceived; there's the same hand to them. The like passions sway them, the same reason that makes a vicar go to law for a tithe-pig and undo his neighbors makes them spoil a whole province, and batter down goodly cities with the cannon.

[*Enter* Duchess *with* Attendants *and* Ladies.]

Duch. Your arm, Antonio. Do I not grow fat?
I am exceeding short-winded. Bosola,
I would have you, sir, provide for me a litter,
Such a one as the Duchess of Florence rode in.
Bos. The Duchess used one when she was great with child.
Duch. I think she did. Come hither, mend my ruff.
Here, when? Thou art such a tedious lady; and
Thy breath smells of lemon peels. Would thou hadst done!
Shall I swoon under thy fingers? I am
So troubled with the mother.
Bos. [*Aside.*] I fear too much.
Duch. I have heard you say that the French courtiers
Wear their hats on 'fore the King.
Ant. I have seen it.
Duch. In the presence?
Ant. Yes
Duch. Why should not we bring up that fashion?
'Tis ceremony more than duty that consists
In the removing of a piece of felt.
Be you the example to the rest o' th' court,
Put on your hat first.
Ant. You must pardon me;
I have seen, in colder countries than in France,
Nobles stand bare to th' prince; and the distinction
Methought showed reverently.
Bos. I have a present for your Grace.
Duch. For me, sir?
Bos. Apricocks, Madam.
Duch. Oh, sir, where are they?
I have heard of none to-year.
Bos. [*Aside.*] Good, her color rises.
Duch. Indeed, I thank you; they are wondrous fair ones.
What an unskillful fellow is our gardener!
We shall have none this month.
Bos. Will not your grace pare them?
Duch. No, they taste of musk, methinks; indeed they do.
Bos. I know not; yet I wish your Grace had pared 'em.
Duch. Why?
Bos. I forgot to tell you the knave gard'ner
(Only to raise his profit by them the sooner)
Did ripen them in horse-dung.
Duch. Oh, you jest!
You shall judge; pray taste one.
Ant. Indeed, Madam,
I do not love the fruit.
Duch. Sir, you are loth
To rob us of our dainties. 'Tis a delicate fruit;
They say they are restorative.
Bos. 'Tis a pretty art,
This grafting.
Duch. 'Tis so: a bettering of nature.
Bos. To make a pippin grow upon a crab,
A damson on a blackthorn. [*Aside.*] How greedily she eats them!
A whirlwind strike off these bawd-farthingales,
For, but for that, and the loose-bodied gown,
I should have discovered apparently

114 **lord . . . ascendant** most important person, playing on the astrological term for the planetary ruler of the ascending sign of the zodiac (ironic since she would also then have special influence on any newly born child)
115–16 **cousin-german removed** first cousin once removed
117 **King Pepin** King of the Franks and founder of the papal states who died in 768
118 **heads** sources
122 **meaner** of lower class
123 **the . . . hand** i.e., God's (in creating them)
125–6 **tithe-pig** animals and goods were often used as parish tithes (one-tenth of the income)
126 **spoil** plunder
131 **litter** a small enclosed carriage borne by men or animals
134 **ruff** a collar usually of starched linen
135 **when?** (an exclamation of impatience); **tedious** troublesome, slow
136 **lemon peels** (taken to freshen the breath)
138 **the mother** hysteria (punning on her pregnancy) characterized by a sense of swelling and suffocation
143 **bring up** promote
149 **bare** bare-headed
153 **to-year** this year
159 **pared** prepared
165 **dainties** (1) choice foods; (2) luxuries; (3) social pleasures
167 **grafting** (as term for copulation)
168 **pippin** sweet dessert apple; **crab** sour crab apple tree
169 **damson** small black or purple plum; **blackthorn** a wild thorn tree that bears black fruit
170 **bawd** deceiving; **farthingales** hooped petticoats
172 **apparently** visibly, manifestly

The young springal cutting a caper in her belly.
Duch. I thank you, Bosola, they were right good ones,
If they do not make me sick.
Ant. How now, Madam?
Duch. This green fruit and my stomach are not friends.
How they swell me!
Bos. [*Aside.*] Nay, you are too much swelled already.
Duch. Oh, I am in an extreme cold sweat!
Bos. I am very sorry:
Duch. Lights to my chamber. Oh, good Antonio,
I fear I am undone.

Exit Duchess.

Delio. Lights there, lights!

[*Exeunt all except* Antonio *and* Delio.]

Ant. Oh, my most trusty Delio, we are lost!
I fear she's fall'n in labor; and there's left
No time for her remove.
Delio. Have you prepared
Those ladies to attend her? and procured
That politic safe conveyance for the midwife
Your Duchess plotted?
Ant. I have.
Delio. Make use then of this forced occasion.
Give out that Bosola hath poisoned her
With these apricocks. That will give some color
For her keeping close.
Ant. Fie, fie, the physicians
Will then flock to her.
Delio. For that you may pretend
She'll use some prepared antidote of her own,
Lest the physicians should re-poison her.
Ant. I am lost in amazement. I know not what to think on't.

Exeunt.

Scena ii.

[*Enter* Bosola.]

Bos. So, so: there's no question but her tetchiness and most vulturous eating of the apricocks are apparent signs of breeding –

[*Enter* Old Lady.]

Now?
Old Lady. I am in haste, sir.
Bos. There was a young waiting-woman had a monstrous desire to see the glass-house.
Old Lady. Nay, pray let me go.
Bos. And it was only to know what strange instrument it was should swell up a glass to the fashion of a woman's belly.
Old Lady. I will hear no more of the glass-house. You are still abusing women!
Bos. Who, I? No, only (by the way now and then) mention your frailties. The orange tree bears ripe and green fruit, and blossoms all together; and some of you give entertainment for pure love; but more, for more precious reward. The lusty spring smells well; but drooping autumn tastes well. If we have the same golden showers that rained in the time of Jupiter the Thunderer, you have the same Danäes still, to hold up their laps to receive them. Didst thou never study the mathematics?
Old Lady. What's that, sir?
Bos. Why, to know the trick how to make a many lines meet in one center. Go, go; give your foster-daughters good counsel. Tell them that the devil takes delight to hang at a woman's girdle, like a false rusty watch, that she cannot discern how the time passes.

[*Exit* Old Lady.]

[*Enter* Antonio, Delio, Roderigo, Grisolan.]

Ant. Shut up the court gates.
Rod. Why, sir? What's the danger?
Ant. Shut up the posterns presently; and call
All the officers o' th' court.
Gris. I shall instantly.

[*Exit.*]

Ant. Who keeps the key o' th' park gate?
Rod. Forobosco.
Ant. Let him bring 't presently.

[*Enter* Grisolan *with* Officers.]

1st. Off. Oh, gentlemen o'th' court, the foulest treason!

173 **springal** stripling (i.e., baby)
186 **politic** carefully arranged; **conveyance** escort
188 **forced** enforced, unwanted
190 **color** pretext
191 **close** secret, private
II.ii.1 **tetchiness** irritability
2 **most vulturous** greedily
3 **apparent** known, obvious
7 **glass-house** i.e., glass factory; one was near Blackfriars
15 **your** i.e., woman's
20 **tastes** (as the time of harvest)
20–2 **the . . . still** since Jupiter came to Danaë in a golden shower, she was considered a type for the mercenary woman
27 **lines . . . center** (sexual pun on the center of the woman's body, her genitalia)
28 **foster-daughters** charges (the Old Lady is a midwife)
30 **girdle** belt
33 **posterns** small back or side doors; **presently** immediately
35 **Forobosco** (apparently a guard; he never appears)

Bos. [*Aside*.] If that these apricocks should be poisoned now,
Without my knowledge!

1st. Off. There was taken even now a Switzer in the Duchess' bedchamber.

2nd. Off. A Switzer?

1st. Off. With a pistol in his great cod-piece.

Bos. Ha, ha, ha!

1st. Off. The cod-piece was the case for't.

2nd. Off. There was a cunning traitor. Who would have searched his cod-piece?

1st. Off. True, if he had kept out of the ladies' chambers. And all the molds of his buttons were leaden bullets.

2nd. Off. Oh, wicked cannibal! a fire-lock in's cod-piece!

1st. Off. 'Twas a French plot, upon my life.

2nd. Off. To see what the devil can do!

Ant. All the officers here?

Off. We are

Ant. Gentlemen,
We have lost much plate, you know, and but this evening
Jewels, to the value of four thousand ducats
Are missing in the Duchess' cabinet.
Are the gates shut?

Off. Yes.

Ant. 'Tis the Duchess' pleasure
Each officer be locked into his chamber
Till the sun-rising; and to send the keys
Of all their chests, and of their outward doors,
Into her bedchamber. She is very sick.

Rod. At her pleasure.

Ant. She entreats you take 't not ill: the innocent
Shall be the more approved by it.

Bos. Gentlemen o'th' wood-yard, where's your Switzer now?

1st. Off. By this hand, 'twas credibly reported by one o' the black guard.

[*Exeunt all except* Antonio *and* Delio.]

Delio. How fares it with the Duchess?

Ant. She's exposed
Unto the worst of torture, pain, and fear –

Delio. Speak to her all happy comfort.

Ant. How I do play the fool with mine own danger!
You are this night, dear friend, to post to Rome;
My life lies in your service.

Delio. Do not doubt me.

Ant. Oh, 'tis far from me: and yet fear presents me
Somewhat that looks like danger.

Delio. Believe it,
'Tis but the shadow of your fear, no more.
How superstitiously we mind our evils!
The throwing down salt, or crossing of a hare,
Bleeding at nose, the stumbling of a horse,
Or singing of a cricket, are of power
To daunt whole man in us. Sir, fare you well;
I wish you all the joys of a blessed father.
And, for my faith, lay this unto your breast –
Old friends, like old swords, still are trusted best.

[*Exit*.]

Enter Cariola.

Cari. Sir, you are the happy father of a son.
Your wife commends him to you.

Ant. Blessèd comfort.
For heaven-sake, tend her well; I'll presently
Go set a figure for's nativity.

Exeunt.

Scena iii.

[*Enter* Bosola, *with a dark lantern*.]

Bos. Sure I did hear a woman shriek; list, hah?
And the sound came, if I received it right,
From the Duchess' lodgings. There's some stratagem
In the confining all our courtiers
To their several wards. I must have part of it;
My intelligence will freeze else. List again!

---

41 **Switzer** Swiss mercenary
44 **pistol** (with play on *pizzle*, penis); **cod-piece** a pouch covering the male genitalia often enlarged and ornamented which could hold handkerchiefs, money, even fruit
50 **molds** shapes
51 **bullets** (with pun on male testicles)
52 **cannibal** bloodthirsty savage; **fire-lock** firing-chamber of pistol (with play on testicles driving forth semen)
54 **French** (known for courtesy, passion, and the pox)
59 **plate** money, tableware, and other valuables; **but** only
60 **ducats** gold or silver coins
61 **cabinet** private case for valuables
69 **approved** (1) vindicated; (2) commended
70 **Gentlemen . . . wood-yard** a mocking title (1) yard where wood is cut; (2) a disreputable part of Whitehall
73 **black guard** lowest rank of servants in a noble household
78 **to post** speed by horse
79 **lies in** depends upon
82 **shadow** imaginary image
84 **crossing . . . hare** omen of disordered senses or a witch's presence
85–6 **stumbling . . . cricket** (as traditional omens presaging death)
87 **whole** (1) fortified; (2) resolved
89 **faith** (1) loyalty; (2) trustworthiness
94 **set . . . nativity** cast a horoscope
II.iii.1 s.d. ***dark lantern*** lantern with a shield to hide its light
1 **list** listen
5 **several** (1) various; (2) separate; **wards** apartments; **part** knowledge
6 **freeze** be useless

It may be 'twas the melancholy bird,
Best friend of silence and of solitariness,
The owl, that screamed so.

[*Enter* Antonio.]

Hah? Antonio?
Ant. I heard some noise. Who's there? What art thou? Speak.
Bos. Antonio? Put not your face nor body
To such a forced expression of fear;
I am Bosola, your friend.
Ant. Bosola!
[*Aside.*] This mole does undermine me. [*To him.*] Heard you not
A noise even now?
Bos. From whence?
Ant. From the Duchess' lodging.
Bos. Not I; did you?
Ant. I did, or else I dreamed.
Bos. Let's walk towards it.
Ant. No; it may be 'twas
But the rising of the wind.
Bos. Very likely.
Methinks 'tis very cold, and yet you sweat;
You look wildly.
Ant. I have been setting a figure
For the Duchess' jewels.
Bos. Ah; and how falls your question?
Do you find it radical?
Ant. What's that to you?
'Tis rather to be questioned what design,
When all men were commanded to their lodgings,
Makes you a night-walker.
Bos. In sooth I'll tell you.
Now all the court's asleep, I thought the devil
Had least to do here. I came to say my prayers,
And if it do offend you I do so,
You are a fine courtier.
Ant. [*Aside.*] This fellow will undo me.
[*To him.*] You gave the Duchess apricocks today,
Pray heaven they were not poisoned!
Bos. Poisoned? A Spanish fig
For the imputation.
Ant. Traitors are ever confident,
Till they are discovered. There were jewels stol'n, too.
In my conceit, none are to be suspected
More than yourself.
Bos. You are a false steward.
Ant. Saucy slave! I'll pull thee up by the roots.
Bos. May be the ruin will crush you to pieces.
Ant. You are an impudent snake indeed, sir,
Are you scarce warm, and do you show your sting?

. . . .

Ant. You libel well, sir.
Bos. No sir, copy it out,
And I will set my hand to't.
Ant. [*Aside.*] My nose bleeds.
One that were superstitious would count
This ominous, when it merely comes by chance.
Two letters, that are wrought here for my name,
Are drowned in blood!
Mere accident. [*To him.*] For you, sir, I'll take order.
I'th' morn you shall be safe. [*Aside.*] 'Tis that must color
Her lying-in. [*To him.*] Sir, this door you pass not;
I do not hold it fit that you come near
The duchess' lodgings till you have quit yourself.
[*Aside.*] "The great are like the base – nay, they are the same – When they seek shameful ways, to avoid shame."

Exit.

Bos. Antonio hereabout did drop a paper –
Some of your help, false friend. Oh, here it is.
What's here? A child's nativity calculated!

9 **owl** (a bird associated with death)
14 **mole** (as someone who lives and functions in the dark; also meaning spy); **undermine** betray
20 **setting a figure** casting a horoscope, also a means to determine thieves, places stolen goods were hidden, and to predict loss or recovery
22 **radical** fit for a decision
25 **night-walker** a common name for rogue or thief
29 **fine** fastidious; **undo** outsmart, outmaneuver
31 **Spanish fig** (1) a poisoned fruit; (2) a phallic and obscene gesture thrusting a thumb between two fingers
34 **conceit** judgment, opinion
37 **ruin** falling down
39 **scarce warm** newly heated by promotion
39–40 Lines seem to be missing at this point since lines 40–1 are otherwise unprepared for; they suggest Antonio is willing to sign a copy of the child's horoscope as proof he wishes to catch the thief and establish his own innocence, yet he would be unlikely to show it to Bosola although ironically he drops it later when reaching for his handkerchief
40 **No . . . out** if this is a libel, write up the charge
41 **set my hand to** sign
44 **Two letters** i.e., monogram on the handkerchief
46 **accident** coincidence (that his name is covered in the blood from his nosebleed); **order** appropriate actions
47 **safe** safely confined; in custody; **color** (1) disguise; (2) with play on blood at childbirth
50 **quit** acquitted
55 **false friend** (the dark lantern)

[*Reads.*] *The duchess was delivered of a son, 'tween the hours twelve and one, in the night: Anno Dom. 1504* that's this year – *decimo nono Decembris* – that's this night – *taken according to the meridian of Malfi* – that's our Duchess! happy discovery! *The lord of the first house, being combust in the ascendant, signifies short life: and Mars being in a human sign, joined to the tail of the Dragon in the eighth house, doth threaten a violent death. Caetera non scrutantur.*
Why now 'tis most apparent! This precise fellow
Is the Duchess' bawd. I have it to my wish;
This is a parcel of intelligency
Our courtiers were cased up for! It needs must follow
That I must be committed on pretense
Of poisoning her, which I'll endure, and laugh at.
If one could find the father now! But that
Time will discover. Old Castruchio
I'th' morning posts to Rome; by him I'll send
A letter that shall make her brothers' galls
O'erflow their livers. This was a thrifty way.
"Though lust do masque in ne'er so strange disguisc,
She's oft found witty, but is never wise."
[*Exit.*]

Scena iv.

[*Enter* Cardinal *and* Julia.]

Card. Sit. Thou art my best of wishes. Prithee tell me
What trick didst thou invent to come to Rome
Without thy husband.
Julia. Why, my Lord, I told him
I came to visit an old anchorite
Here, for devotion.
Card. Thou art a witty false one –
I mean to him.
Julia. You have prevailed with me
Beyond my strongest thoughts I would not now
Find you inconstant.
Card. Do not put thyself
To such a voluntary torture, which proceeds
Out of your own guilt.
Julia. How, my Lord?
Card. You fear
My constancy because you have approved
Those giddy and wild turnings in yourself.
Julia. Did you e'er find them?
Card. Sooth, generally for women.
A man might strive to make glass malleable,
Ere he should make them fixed.
Julia. So, my Lord –
Card. We had need go borrow that fantastic glass
Invented by Galileo the Florentine,
To view another spacious world i'th' moon
And look to find a constant woman there.
Julia. This is very well, my Lord.
Card. Why do you weep?
Are tears your justification? The self-same tears
Will fall into your husband's bosom, Lady,
With a loud protestation that you love him
Above the world. Come, I'll love you wisely,
That's jealously, since I am very certain
You cannot me make cuckold.
Julia. I'll go home
To my husband.
Card. You may thank me, Lady,
I have taken you off your melancholy perch,
Bore you upon my fist, and showed you game,
And let you fly at it. I pray thee, kiss me.
When thou wast with thy husband, thou wast watched
Like a tame elephant – still you are to thank me –
Thou hadst only kisses from him, and high feeding,
But what delight was that? 'Twas just like one
That hath a little fing'ring on the lute,
Yet cannot tune it. Still, you are to thank me.

57–65 ***The . . . scrutantur*** the child's horoscope (ultimately nonsense, but combust means losing influence; Mars is the god of war but not one of the human signs [Gemini, Virgo, Sagittarius, Aquarius]; tail of the Dragon is the point where the moon crosses the sun's orbit in its descent)
65 ***caetera . . . scrutantur*** "the rest is not investigated"
66 **precise** scrupulous; **fellow** name for a social inferior
68 **parcel** item
70 **committed** imprisoned
74 **posts** rides
75 **galls** sense of bitterness
76 **thrifty** i.e., thriving
77 **masque** take part in a masque
II.iv.2 trick strategy
4 **anchorite** hermit
5 **devotion** (1) spiritual or (2) sexual exercise
11 **approved** experienced
13 **Sooth** in truth; **generally for** universally in
16–17 **that . . . Florentine** (Galileo's telescope proved the earth was not the center of the known universe)
19 **constant** (a joke; the moon was the sign of change and inconstancy)
25 **jealously** (1) ardently; (2) suspiciously
26 **You . . . cuckold** (because as a priest he is unmarried)
28–30 **I . . . it** (she is compared to a trained falcon who is rewarded for its behavior)
31 **watched** (1) kept in sight; (2) kept awake
32 **elephant** (as a figure for unmanageability)
33 **high feeding** luxuries (but not passion)

Julia. You told me of a piteous wound i'th' heart,
And a sick liver, when you wooed me first,
And spake like one in physic.
Card. Who's that?
Rest firm. For my affection to thee,
Lightning moves slow to't.

[*Enter* Servant.]

Serv. Madam, a gentleman,
That's come post from Malfi desires to see you.
Card. Let him enter; I'll withdraw.
Exit.
Serv. He says,
Your husband, old Castruchio, is come to
Rome,
Most pitifully tired with riding post.
[*Exit.*]

[*Enter* Delio.]

Julia. [*Aside.*] Signior Delio! 'Tis one of my old
suitors.
Delio. I was bold to come and see you.
Julia. Sir, you are welcome.
Delio. Do you lie here?
Julia. Sure, your own experience
Will satisfy you, no. Our Roman prelates
Do not keep lodging for ladies.
Delio. Very well.
I have brought you no commendations from
your husband,
For I know none by him.
Julia. I hear he's come to Rome!
Delio. I never knew man and beast, of a horse and
a knight,
So weary of each other. If he had had a good
back,
He would have undertook to have borne his
horse,
His breech was so pitifully sore.
Julia. Your laughter
Is my pity.
Delio. Lady, I know not whether
You want money, but I have brought you some.
Julia. From my husband?
Delio. No, from mine own allowance.
Julia. I must hear the condition, ere I be bound to
take it.
Delio. Look on't, 'tis gold. Hath it not a fine color?
Julia. I have a bird more beautiful.
Delio. Try the sound on't.
Julia. A lute-string far exceeds it;
It hath no smell, like cassia or civet,
Nor is it physical, though some fond doctors
Persuade us seethe 't in cullises. I'll tell you,
This is a creature bred by –

[*Enter* Servant.]

Serv. Your husband's come,
Hath delivered a letter to the Duke of Calabria,
That, to my thinking, hath put him out of his
wits.
[*Exit*].
Julia. Sir, you hear –
Pray let me know your business and your suit
As briefly as can be.
Delio. With good speed. I would wish you
(At such time as you are non-resident
With your husband) my mistress.
Julia. Sir, I'll go ask my husband if I shall,
And straight return your answer.
Exit.
Delio. Very fine!
Is this her wit or honesty that speaks thus?
I heard one say the Duke was highly moved
With a letter sent from Malfi. I do fear
Antonio is betrayed. How fearfully
Shows his ambition now! Unfortunate fortune!
"They pass through whirlpools and deep woes
do shun,
Who the event weigh, ere the action's done."
Exit.

Scena v.

[*Enter*] Cardinal, *and* Ferdinand *with a letter.*

Ferd. I have this night digged up a mandrake.
Card. Say you?

---

39 in physic under medical care; **Who's that?** (Cardinal hears the approaching servant)
41 to't in comparison (lightning, however, was usually considered destructive)
46 one . . . suitors (this reassignment of Delio's role, until now merely that of a loyal servant, will along with Julia make this a play of intrigue)
48 lie reside
54 if . . . back (may suggest impotency)
57 my pity to me pitiful
64 cassia a coarse kind of cinnamon; **civet** musky perfume of the civet cat
65 physical medicinal; **fond** foolish
66 seethe boil; **cullises** broths
71 suit request
77 honesty (1) truthfulness; (2) chastity
83 event outcome
II.v.1 digged uprooted by intense effort ("pulled" is the expectation); **mandrake** a poisonous root of the mandragora plant used as a narcotic or emetic; the forked shape was said to resemble a man. The power of this image unsettles the scene (and our sense of Ferdinand); the root was said to feed on blood (and commonly found near a gallows); to shriek when pulled from the ground; to madden those who sought it

Ferd. And I am grown mad with't.
Card. What's the prodigy?
Ferd. Read there – a sister damned; she's loose i'th' hilts.
Grown a notorious strumpet.
Card. Speak lower.
Ferd. Lower?
Rogues do not whisper 't now, but seek to publish 't
(As servants do the bounty of their lords)
Aloud; and with a covetous searching eye
To mark who note them. Oh, confusion seize her!
She hath had most cunning bawds to serve her turn,
And more secure conveyances for lust
Than towns of garrison for service.
Card. Is't possible?
Can this be certain?
Ferd. Rhubarb, oh, for rhubarb
To purge this choler! Here's the cursèd day
To prompt my memory, and here 't shall stick
Till of her bleeding heart I make a sponge
To wipe it out.
Card. Why do you make yourself
So wild a tempest?
Ferd. Would I could be one,
That I might toss her palace 'bout her ears,
Root up her goodly forests, blast her meads,
And lay her general territory as waste
As she hath done her honour.
Card. Shall our blood,
The royal blood of Arragon and Castile,
Be thus attainted?
Ferd. Apply desperate physic:
We must not now use balsamum, but fire,
The smarting cupping-glass, for that's the mean
To purge infected blood, such blood as hers.
There is a kind of pity in mine eye,
I'll give it to my handkercher; and now 'tis here,
I'll bequeath this to her bastard.
Card. What to do?
Ferd. Why, to make soft lint for his mother's wounds
When I have hewed her to pieces.
Card. Cursed creature!
Unequal nature, to place women's hearts
So far upon the left side!
Ferd. Foolish men,
That e'er will trust their honor in a bark
Made of so slight, weak bulrush as is woman,
Apt every minute to sink it!
Card. Thus ignorance, when it hath purchased honor,
It cannot wield it.
Ferd. Methinks I see her laughing –
Excellent hyena! Talk to me somewhat, quickly,
Or my imagination will carry me
To see her in the shameful act of sin.
Card. With whom?
Ferd. Happily with some strong thighed bargeman;
Or one o'th' wood-yard, that can quoit the sledge,
Or toss the bar, or else some lovely squire
That carries coals up to her privy lodgings.
Card. You fly beyond your reason.
Ferd. Go to, mistress!
'Tis not your whore's milk that shall quench my wildfire,
But your whore's blood.
Card. How idly shows this rage which carries you,
As men conveyed by witches through the air,

2 **prodigy** (1) ill omen; (2) monstrous occasion
3 **loose . . . hilts** (1) totally unreliable; (2) sexually open to anyone; **hilts** handles of swords (with obscene pun)
7 **covetous . . . eye** looking for pay for silence or intelligence
8 **confusion** ruin
9 **turn** purpose, plan
11 **service** (1) supplies; (2) military service; (3) copulation or sexual service
12 **Rhubarb** a customary prescription for choler or extreme anger
13 **the cursèd day** i.e., in the horoscope, sent by Bosola with his letter
19 **blast** wither; **meads** meadows
23 **attainted** (1) stained (as in a title); (2) inferior; (3) corrupted; **physic** medicine
24 **balsamum** balm (to soothe the pain)
25 **cupping-glass** a glass vessel which develops a vacuum through the application of heat to draw off bad blood
26 **blood** (here sexual appetite)
28 **handkercher** handkerchief
30 **lint** soft material for dressing wounds
32 **Unequal** unjust
33 **left side** (understood as a sign of a deceitful heart)
34 **bark** small boat or vessel
37 **purchased** gotten, obtained
39 **hyena** a nocturnal animal known for a cry which resembles a mad laugh; the female was believed capable of killing a sleeping man by stretching her body on him
42 **Happily** haply, perhaps
43 **quoit the sledge** throw the hammer (in sport, but with sexual implications)
44 **toss the bar** (with obscene pun); **squire** personal servant
45 **carries coals** proverbial for doing any dirty work; here Ferdinand imagines secret sexual encounters
46 **Go to** i.e., go to it
47 **wildfire** uncontrollable passion
49 **idly** (1) foolishly; (2) irrelevantly

On violent whirlwinds! This intemperate noise
Fitly resembles deaf men's shrill discourse,
Who talk aloud, thinking all other men
To have their imperfection.
Ferd. Have not you
My palsy?
Card. Yes. I can be angry
Without this rupture. There is not in nature
A thing that makes man so deformed, so beastly,
As doth intemperate anger. Chide yourself.
You have divers men who never yet expressed
Their strong desire of rest but by unrest,
By vexing of themselves. Come, put yourself
In tune.
Ferd. So; I will only study to seem
The thing I am not. I could kill her now,
In you, or in myself, for I do think
It is some sin in us heaven doth revenge
By her.
Card. Are you stark mad?
Ferd. I would have their bodies
Burned in a coal-pit, with the ventage stopped,
That their cursed smoke might not ascend to heaven.
Or dip the sheets they lie in, in pitch or sulfur,
Wrap them in't, and then light them like a match;
Or else to boil their bastard to a cullis,
And give 't his lecherous father, to renew
The sin of his back.
Card. I'll leave you.
Ferd. Nay, I have done –
I am confident, had I been damned in hell
And should have heard of this, it would have put me
Into a cold sweat. In, in; I'll go sleep.
Till I know who leaps my sister, I'll not stir.
That known, I'll find scorpions to string my whips,
And fix her in a general eclipse.

Exeunt.

Act III

Actus III, Scena I.

Enter Antonio *and* Delio.

Ant. Our noble friend, my most beloved Delio!
Oh, you have been a stranger long at court;
Came you along with the Lord Ferdinand?
Delio. I did, sir; and how fares your noble Duchess?
Ant. Right fortunately well. She's an excellent
Feeder of pedigres; since you last saw her,
She hath had two children more, a son and daughter.
Delio. Methinks 'twas yesterday. Let me but wink,
And not behold your face, which to mine eye
Is somewhat leaner. Verily, I should dream
It were within this half-hour
Ant. You have not been in law, friend Delio,
Nor in prison, nor a suitor at the court,
Nor begged the reversion of some great man's place,
Nor troubled with an old wife, which doth make
Your time so insensibly hasten.
Delio. Pray, sir, tell me,
Hath not this news arrived yet to the ear
Of the Lord Cardinal?
Ant. I fear it hath.
The Lord Ferdinand, that's newly come to court,
Doth bear himself right dangerously.
Delio. Pray why?
Ant. He is so quiet, that he seems to sleep
The tempest out, as dormice do in winter.
Those houses that are haunted are most still,
Till the devil be up.
Delio. What say the common people?
Ant. The common rabble do directly say
She is a strumpet.
Delio. And your graver heads,
Which would be politic, what censure they?
Ant. They do observe I grow to infinite purchase
The left-hand way, and all suppose the Duchess

55 **palsy** paralysis
58 **Chide** admonish
59 **have** have seen, have known of
66 **their bodies** i.e., of the Duchess and her lover
67 **coal-pit** used to make charcoal; **ventage** ventilation
71 **cullis** broth
76 **I'll . . . sleep** (his passion has exhausted him)
77 **leaps** sexually mounts
78 **scorpions . . . whips** (cf. 1 Kings 12:11); **scorpions** knotted or barbed scourges
79 **general** total
III.i.2 **long** (presumably two years have passed since the Duchess now has three children)
8 **wink** close my eyes
14 **reversion of** right to succeed to
16 **insensibly** (1) imperceptively; (2) foolishly
23 **still** quiet
27 **censure** judge
28 **purchase** wealth
29 **left-hand way** (1) indirectly; (2) by gift

Would amend it, if she could. For, say they,
Great princes, though they grudge their officers
Should have such large and unconfined means
To get wealth under them, will not complain
Lest thereby they should make them odious
Unto the people – for other obligation
Of love, or marriage, between her and me,
They never dream of.

[*Enter* Ferdinand *and* Duchess.]

Delio. The Lord Ferdinand
Is going to bed.
Ferd. I'll instantly to bed,
For I am weary. I am to bespeak
A husband for you.
Duch. For me, sir! Pray, who is't?
Ferd. The great Count Malateste.
Duch. Fie upon him;
A count! He's a mere stick of sugar-candy,
You may look quite thorough him. When I choose
A husband, I will marry for your honor.
Ferd. You shall do well in't. How is't, worthy Antonio?
Duch. But sir, I am to have private conference with you
About a scandalous report, is spread
Touching mine honor.
Ferd. Let me be ever deaf to't.
One of Pasquil's paper bullets, court-calumny,
A pestilent air which princes' palaces
Are seldom purged of. Yet, say that it were true,
I pour it in your bosom my fixed love
Would strongly excuse, extenuate, nay, deny
Faults, were they apparent in you. Go. Be safe
In your own innocency.
Duch. Oh blessed comfort!
This deadly air is purged.

Exeunt [*all except* Ferdinand].

Ferd. Her guilt treads on
Hot-burning coulters.

[*Enter* Bosola.]

Now Bosola,
How thrives our intelligence?
Bos. Sir, uncertainly.
'Tis rumored she hath had three bastards, but
By whom, we may go read i'th' stars.
Ferd. Why some
Hold opinion all things are written there.
Bos. Yes, if we could find spectacles to read them.
I do suspect there hath been some sorcery
Used on the Duchess.
Ferd. Sorcery! To what purpose?
Bos. To make her dote on some desertless fellow
She shames to acknowledge.
Ferd. Can your faith give way
To think there's power in potions, or in charms,
To make us love, whether we will or no?
Bos. Most certainly.
Ferd. Away. These are mere gulleries, horrid things
Invented by some cheating mountebanks
To abuse us. Do you think that herbs or charms
Can force the will? Some trials have been made
In this foolish practice; but the ingredients
Were lenitive poisons, such as are of force
To make the patient mad; and straight the witch
Swears, by equivocation, they are in love.
The witchcraft lies in her rank blood. This night
I will force confession from her. You told me
You had got, within these two days, a false key
Into her bed-chamber.
Bos. I have.
Ferd. As I would wish.
Bos. What do you intend to do?
Ferd. Can you guess?
Bos. No –
Ferd. Do not ask then.
He that can compass me, and know my drifts,
May say he hath put a girdle 'bout the world
And sounded all her quicksands.
Bos. I do not
Think so.
Ferd. What do you think then, pray?
Bos. That you

---

34 **odious** hateful
45 **worthy** (ironic, since Ferdinand thinks him his sister's pander)
49 **Pasquil's . . . bullets** lampoons, from a mutilated statue in Rome called Pasquil where topical and satirical verses were placed; **calumny** false charges or imputations
52 **I . . . bosom** I confide in you
56–7 **Her . . . coulters** walking barefoot on hot ploughshares was a practice in ancient English law to vindicate a woman's chastity
62 **spectacles** eye-glasses
70 **gulleries** tricks
71 **mountebanks** quack doctors who sold remedies at fairs and town marketplaces
73 **will** (1) sexual appetite; (2) intention
75 **lenitive** smoothly working and therefore unnoticed; sometimes aphrodisiac
84 **compass** comprehend
85 **put . . . world** (proverbial)

Are your own chronicle too much; and grossly
Flatter yourself.
Ferd. Give me thy hand. I thank thee.
I never gave pension but to flatterers
Till I entertained thee. Farewell.
"That friend a great man's ruin strongly checks
Who rails into his belief all his defects."
Exeunt.

Scena II.

[*Enter* Duchess, Antonio *and* Cariola.]

Duch. Bring me the casket hither, and the glass.
You get no lodging here tonight, my Lord.
Ant. Indeed, I must persuade one.
Duch. Very good.
I hope in time 'twill grow into a custom
That noblemen shall come with cap and knee,
To purchase a night's lodging of their wives.
Ant. I must lie here.
Duch. Must? you are a Lord of Misrule.
Ant. Indeed, my rule is only in the night.
Duch. To what use will you put me?
Ant. We'll sleep together.
Duch. Alas, what pleasure can two lovers find in sleep?
Cari. My lord, I lie with her often; and I know
She'll much disquiet you –
Ant. See, you are complained of.
Cari. – For she's the sprawling'st bedfellow.
Ant. I shall like her the better for that.
Cari. Sir, shall I ask you a question?
Ant. I pray thee, Cariola.
Cari. Wherefore still when you lie with my Lady
Do you rise so early?
Ant. Laboring men
Count the clock oft'nest, Cariola;
Are glad when their task's ended.
Duch. I'll stop your mouth.
[*Kisses him.*]
Ant. Nay, that's but one. Venus had two soft doves
To draw her chariot. I must have another.
[*Kisses her.*]
When wilt thou marry, Cariola?
Cari. Never, my Lord.
Ant. Oh, fie upon this single life! Forgo it!
We read how Daphne, for her peevish flight,
Became a fruitless bay-tree; Syrinx turned
To the pale empty reed; Anaxarete
Was frozen into marble: whereas those
Which married, or proved kind unto their friends,
Were, by a gracious influence, transshaped
Into the olive, pomegranate, mulberry;
Became flow'rs, precious stones, or eminent stars.
Cari. This is a vain poetry. But I pray you, tell me,
If there were proposed me wisdom, riches, and beauty,
In three several young men, which should I choose?
Ant. 'Tis a hard question. This was Paris' case
And he was blind in't, and there was great cause;
For how was't possible he could judge right,
Having three amorous goddesses in view,
And they stark naked? 'Twas a motion
Were able to benight the apprehension
Of the severest counselor of Europe.
Now I look on both your faces so well formed,
It puts me in mind of a question I would ask.
Cari. What is't?
Ant. I do wonder why hard-favored ladies,
For the most part, keep worse-favored waiting-women
To attend them, and cannot endure fair ones.
Duch. Oh, that's soon answered.
Did you ever in your life know an ill painter

---

88 chronicle record
92–3 "That . . . defects" one who openly criticizes a friend can prevent his misfortune
III.ii.1 casket (to put away jewels for the night); **glass** mirror (to prepare for bed)
5 cap and knee i.e., with cap in hand on bended knee
7 Lord of Misrule (1) one who presides over revels; (2) one who turns the world temporarily upside-down in mock celebrations; (3) lord of mistresses
25–6 Daphne . . . bay-tree Daphne asked the gods for help when she was pursued by Apollo and they turned her into a laurel tree (English bay-tree)
25 peevish willful
26–7 Syrinx . . . reed chased by Pan, Syrinx threw herself into a river where she was metamorphosed into a reed from which Pan made pipes to play
27–8 Anaxarete . . . marble Venus metamorphosed Anaxarete to stone for being unmoved when the forsaken Iphis hanged himself at her door
29 friends i.e., lovers
31 olive . . . mulberry fruitful (as opposed to fruitless and frozen metamorphoses of previous virginal lovers); **mulberry** the red of the mulberry fruit is said to be from the blood of Pyramus, who killed himself because he thought his love Thisbe was dead
33 vain worthless
34 proposed me put to me
35 several different
36 Paris' case Paris was asked to judge among Athene (wisdom), Hera (riches), and Aphrodite (beauty)
40 motion (1) proposal; (2) spectacle, show; (3) display
41 Were that would have been; **benight** put in darkness
45 hard-favored not well-favored

Desire to have his dwelling next door to the
shop
Of an excellent picture-maker? 'twould
disgrace
His face-making, and undo him. I prithee,
When were we so merry? My hair tangles.
Ant. Pray thee, Cariola, let's steal forth the room
And let her talk to herself; I have divers times
Served her the like, when she hath chafed
extremely
I love to see her angry. Softly, Cariola.
Exeunt.
Duch. Doth not the color of my hair 'gin to
change?
When I wax gray, I shall have all the court
Powder their hair with arras, to be like me.
You have cause to love me; I entered you into
my heart
Before you would vouchsafe to call for the
keys.

[*Enter* Ferdinand *behind.*]

We shall one day have my brothers take you
napping.
Methinks his presence, being now in court,
Should make you keep your own bed. But
you'll say
Love mixed with fear is sweetest. I'll assure
you
You shall get no more children till my brothers
Consent to be your gossips. Have you lost
your tongue?
[*Turns and sees Ferdinand.*]
'Tis welcome.
For know, whether I am doomed to live or die,
I can do both like a prince.
Ferdinand gives her a poniard.
Ferd. Die then, quickly!
Virtue, where art thou hid? What hideous
thing
Is it that doth eclipse thee?
Duch. Pray, sir, hear me –
Ferd. Or is it true, thou art but a bare name,
And no essential thing?
Duch. Sir –
Ferd. Do not speak.
Duch. No, sir.
I will plant my soul in mine ears to hear you.
Ferd. Oh, most imperfect light of human reason,
That mak'st us so unhappy to foresee
What we can least prevent! Pursue thy wishes,
And glory in them. There's in shame no
comfort
But to be past all bounds and sense of shame.
Duch. I pray, sir, hear me. I am married.
Ferd. So –
Duch. Happily, not to your liking. But for that,
Alas, your shears do come untimely now
To clip the bird's wings that's already flown!
Will you see my husband?
Ferd. Yes, if I could change
Eyes with a basilisk.
Duch. Sure, you came hither
By his confederacy.
Ferd. The howling of a wolf
Is music to thee, screech-owl. Prithee, peace!
Whate'er thou art, that hast enjoyed my sister
For I am sure thou hear'st me – for thine own
sake
Let me not know thee. I came hither prepared
To work thy discovery, yet am now persuaded
It would beget such violent effects
As would damn us both. I would not for ten
millions
I had beheld thee; therefore use all means
I never may have knowledge of thy name;
Enjoy thy lust still, and a wretched life,
On that condition. And for thee, vile woman,
If thou do wish thy lecher may grow old
In thy embracements, I would have thee build
Such a room for him as our anchorites
To holier use inhabit. Let not the sun
Shine on him, till he's dead. Let dogs and
monkeys
Only converse with him, and such dumb
things
To whom nature denies use to sound his
name;
Do not keep a paraquito, lest she learn it.
If thou do love him, cut out thine own tongue
Lest it bewray him.
Duch. Why might not I marry?
I have not gone about, in this, to create
Any new world or custom.
Ferd. Thou art undone.
And thou hast ta'en that massy sheet of lead

60 **arras** powder of the orris-root
62 **vouchsafe** prefer
68 **gossips** godparents
69 **'Tis welcome** (i.e., the poniard that Ferdinand holds)
73 **eclipse** embrace
75 **essential** real
83 **Happily** haply, perhaps
87 **basilisk** a fabulous beast able to strike people dead with a single look
89 **to thee** i.e., compared to thee
102 **anchorites** hermits
106 **use** the ability
107 **paraquito** small parrot
109 **bewray** reveal; expose

That hid thy husband's bones, and folded it
About my heart.
Duch. Mine bleeds for't.
Ferd. Thine? Thy heart?
What should I name 't, unless a hollow bullet
Filled with unquenchable wild-fire?
Duch. You arc, in this,
Too strict. And were you not my princely brother
I would say too willful. My reputation
Is safe.
Ferd. Dost thou know what reputation is?
I'll tell thee to small purpose, since th' instruction
Comes now too late.
Upon a time, Reputation, Love, and Death
Would travel o'er the world; and it was concluded
That they should part, and take three several ways.
Death told them, they should find him in great battles,
Or cities plagued with plagues; Love gives them counsel
To inquire for him 'mongst unambitious shepherds,
Where dowries were not talked of, and sometimes
'Mongst quiet kindred that had nothing left
By their dead parents: "Stay," quoth Reputation,
"Do not forsake me; for it is my nature
If once I part from any man I meet
I am never found again." And so, for you.
You have shook hands with Reputation,
And made him invisible. So fare you well.
I will never see you more
Duch. Why should only I,
Of all the other princes of the world,
Be cased up like a holy relic? I have youth,
And a little beauty.
Ferd. So you have some virgins
That are witches: I will never see thee more.
Exit.

Enter Antonio *with a pistol*[, *and* Cariola].

Duch. You saw this apparition?
Ant. Yes. We are
Betrayed. How came he hither? I should turn
This to thee, for that.
Cari. Pray sir, do. And when
That you have cleft my heart, you shall read there
Mine innocence.
Duch. That gallery gave him entrance.
Ant. I would this terrible thing would come again,
That, standing on my guard, I might relate
My warrantable love.
She shews the poniard.
Ha, what means this?
Duch. He left this with me.
Ant. And it seems did wish
You would use it on yourself?
Duch. His action seemed
To intend so much.
Ant. This hath a handle to't
As well as a point. Turn it towards him,
And so fasten the keen edge in his rank gall.
[*Knocking within.*]
How now! Who knocks? More earthquakes?
Duch. I stand
As if a mine beneath my feet, were ready
To be blown up.
Cari. 'Tis Bosola.
Duch. Away!
Oh, misery! Methinks unjust actions
Should wear these masks and curtains, and not we.
You must instantly part hence; I have fashioned it already.
Exit Antonio.

Enter Bosola.

Bos. The duke your brother is ta'en up in a whirlwind,
Hath took horse and's rid post to Rome.
Duch. So late?
Bos. He told me, as he mounted into th' saddle,
You were undone.
Duch. Indeed, I am very near it.
Bos. What's the matter?
Duch. Antonio, the master of our household,
Hath dealt so falsely with me, in's accounts:
My brother stood engaged with me for money
Ta'en up of certain Neapolitan Jews,
And Antonio lets the bonds be forfeit.

115 **hollow bullet** cannon ball (filled with explosives)
118 **willful** passionate
122 **Upon** once more
134 **shook hands with** bade farewell to
140 **you have** there are
142 **apparition** (1) specter; (2) illusion
144 **This** (i.e., the pistol); **to thee** (i.e., Cariola)
157–318 **'Tis . . . hand** (Cariola remains silently on stage emphasizing the Duchess' increased isolation)
158 **unjust** faithless, dishonest
167 **in's** in his
168 **stood . . . me** stood security for me

Bos. Strange! [*Aside.*]This is cunning
Duch. And hereupon
My brother's bills at Naples are protested
Against. Call up our officers.
Bos. I shall.
Exit.

[*Enter* Antonio.]

Duch. The place that you must fly to is Ancona,
Hire a house there. I'll send after you
My treasure and my jewels. Our weak safety
Runs upon enginous wheels; short syllables
Must stand for periods. I must now accuse you
Of such a feigned crime as Tasso calls
Magnanima menzogna: a noble lie
'Cause it must shield our honors. Hark! they are coming.

[*Enter* Bosola *and* Officers.]

Ant. Will your Grace hear me?
Duch. I have got well by you. You have yielded me
A million of loss; I am like to inherit
The people's curses for your stewardship.
You had the trick in audit-time to be sick,
Till I had signed your *quietus*; and that cured you
Without help of a doctor. Gentlemen,
I would have this man be an example to you all.
So shall you hold my favor; I pray let him,
For h'as done that, alas, you would not think of,
And, because I intend to be rid of him,
I mean not to publish. Use your fortune elsewhere.
Ant. I am strongly armed to brook my overthrow,
As commonly men bear with a hard year.
I will not blame the cause on't; but do think
The necessity of my malevolent star
Procures this, not her humor. Oh the inconstant
And rotten ground of service! [*To the witnesses present.*] You may see:
'Tis ev'n like him, that in a winter night
Takes a long slumber o'er a dying fire,
As loth to part from't; yet parts thence as cold
As when he first sat down.
Duch. We do confiscate,
Towards the satisfying of your accounts,
All that you have.
Ant. I am all yours. And 'tis very fit
All mine should be so.
Duch. So, sir; you have your pass.
Ant. You may see, gentlemen, what 'tis to serve
A prince with body, and soul.
Exit.

Bos. Here's an example for extortion. What moisture is drawn out of the sea, when foul weather comes, pours down and runs into the sea again.

Duch. I would know what are your opinions of this Antonio.

2nd. Off. He could not abide to see a pig's head gaping: I thought your Grace would find him a Jew.

3rd Off. I would you had been his officer, for your own sake.

4th Off. You would have had more money.

1st. Off. He stopped his ears with black wool; and to those came to him for money, said he was thick of hearing.

2nd. Off. Some said he was an hermaphrodite, for he could not abide a woman.

4th. Off. How scurvy proud he would look, when the treasury was full! Well, let him go

1st. Off. Yes, and the chippings of the buttery fly after him, to scour his gold chain.

Duch. Leave us.
Exeunt Officers.

What do you think of these?
Bos. That these are rogues, that in's prosperity,
But to have waited on his fortune, could have wished
His dirty stirrup riveted through their noses,

172 My brother's bills Ferdinand's promissory notes
172–3 protested Against not acceptable
177 Runs . . . wheels (as a sign of life's instability and uncertainty); **enginous wheels** crafty stratagems
179–80 feigned . . . *menzogna* (refers to a passage in Tasso's *Jerusalem Delivered* where Soprina accepts blame for rescuing a statue of the Virgin Mary to protect Christians against wholesale persecution)
184 like likely
190 let him i.e., leave him alone
191 h'as he has
194 brook endure
210–13 What . . . again (Antonio's wealth has been confiscated upon the accusation of his embezzlement and so returns again to the Duchess)
216–18 He . . . Jew (conflation of proverbs, "Some cannot abide to see a pig's head gaping" and "Invite not a Jew either to pig or pork")
222 black wool a recommended cure for deafness
224 thick hard
227 scurvy shabbily, discourteously
229 chippings crumbs, drippings; **buttery** a room for storing provisions; servery
230 gold chain (steward's badge of office)
233 in's in his (i.e., Antonio's)

And followed after's mule like a bear in a ring;
Would have prostituted their daughters to his lust;
Made their first-born intelligencers; thought none happy
But such as were born under his blessed planet,
And wore his livery. And do these lice drop off now?
Well, never look to have the like again.
He hath left a sort of flatt'ring rogues behind him –
Their doom must follow. Princes pay flatterers
In their own money; flatterers dissemble their vices
And they dissemble their lies. That's justice –
Alas, poor gentleman!

Duch. Poor? he hath amply filled his coffers.

Bos. Sure
He was too honest. Pluto, the god of riches,
When he's sent by Jupiter to any man
He goes limping, to signify that wealth
That comes on god's name comes slowly. But when he's sent
On the devil's errand, he rides post and comes in by scuttles.
Let me show you what a most unvalued jewel
You have, in a wanton humor, thrown away,
To bless the man shall find him. He was an excellent
Courtier, and most faithful, a soldier that thought it
As beastly to know his own value too little
As devilish to acknowledge it too much.
Both his virtue and form deserved a far better fortune.
His discourse rather delighted to judge itself, than show itself.
His breast was filled with all perfection,
And yet it seemed a private whisp'ring-room,
It made so little noise of't.

Duch. But he was basely descended.

Bos. Will you make yourself a mercenary herald,
Rather to examine men's pedigres than virtues?
You shall want him,
For know an honest statesman to a prince
Is like a cedar, planted by a spring:
The spring bathes the tree's root, the grateful tree
Rewards it with his shadow. You have not done so.
I would sooner swim to the Bermudas on
Two politicians' rotten bladders, tied
Together with an intelligencer's heart-string,
Than depend on so changeable a prince's favor.
Fare thee well, Antonio; since the malice of the world
Would needs down with thee, it cannot be said yet
That any ill happened unto thee,
Considering thy fall was accompanied with virtue.

Duch. Oh, you render me excellent music.

Bos. Say you?

Duch. This good one that you speak of is my husband.

Bos. Do I not dream? Can this ambitious age
Have so much goodness in't, as to prefer
A man merely for worth, without these shadows
Of wealth and painted honors? Possible?

Duch. I have had three children by him.

Bos. Fortunate lady!
For you have made your private nuptial bed
The humble and fair seminary of peace.
No question but many an unbeneficed scholar
Shall pray for you for this deed, and rejoice
That some preferment in the world can yet
Arise from merit. The virgins of your land,
That have no dowries, shall hope your example
Will raise them to rich husbands. Should you want

---

236 **in a ring** i.e., lead by a ring in the nose
240 **lice ... off** a commonplace image for sycophants (lice were commonly believed to leave a body as soon as the blood failed)
242 **sort** gang, company
248 **Pluto** i.e., Plutus (Pluto was god of the underworld)
252 **scuttles** trapdoors
253 **unvalued** (1) invaluable; (2) not regarded as of value
254 **wanton humor** undisciplined mood
255 **shall** who shall
260 **discourse** (1) talk; (2) wit; (3) reasoning
262 **whisp'ring-room** quarters
264 **herald** one who settles questions of precedence and pedigree
267 **know** take note that
271 **Bermudas** the site of a shipwreck in 1609 that led to a published report; the islands were known for strange inhabitants and music and the nearby sea for storms
272 **rotten** (and therefore leaky)
276 **down with** overthrow
282 **prefer** (1) advance; (2) choose; (3) support
283–4 **shadows Of** insubstantial
284 **painted** false, superficial
287 **seminary** nursery
288 **unbeneficed scholar** scholar without benefit of an ecclesiastical appointment
289 **pray for** say prayers for
292 **example** decision

Soldiers, 'twould make the very Turks and Moors
Turn Christians, and serve you for this act.
Last, the neglected poets of your time,
In honor of this trophy of a man,
Raised by that curious engine, your white hand,
Shall thank you, in your grave, for't; and make that
More reverend than all the cabinets
Of living princes. For Antonio,
His fame shall likewise flow from many a pen,
When heralds shall want coats to sell to men.

Duch. As I taste comfort in this friendly speech,
So would I find concealment.

Bos. Oh, the secret of my Prince,
Which I will wear on th' inside of my heart.

Duch. You shall take charge of all my coin and jewels,
And follow him; for he retires himself
To Ancona.

Bos. So.

Duch. Whither, within few days,
I mean to follow thee.

Bos. Let me think:
I would wish your Grace to feign a pilgrimage
To our Lady of Loretto, scarce seven leagues
From fair Ancona; so may you depart
Your country with more honor, and your flight
Will seem a princely progress, retaining
Your usual train about you.

Duch. Sir, your direction
Shall lead me by the hand.

Cari. In my opinion,
She were better progress to the baths
At Lucca, or go visit the Spa
In Germany, for, if you will believe me,
I do not like this jesting with religion,
This feigned pilgrimage.

Duch. Thou art a superstitious fool.
Prepare us instantly for our departure.
Past sorrows, let us moderately lament them,
For those to come, seek wisely to prevent them.

Exit [*with* Cariola].

Bos. A politician is the devil's quilted anvil.
He fashions all sins on him, and the blows
Are never heard; he may work in a lady's chamber,
As here for proof. What rests, but I reveal
All to my Lord? Oh, this base quality
Of intelligencer! why, every quality i'th' world
Prefers but gain or commendation.
Now, for this act I am certain to be raised,
"And men that paint weeds to the life are praised."

Exit.

Scena iii.

[*Enter* Cardinal *with* Malateste, Ferdinand *with* Delio *and* Silvio, *and* Pescara.]

Card. Must we turn soldier then?

Mal. The Emperor,
Hearing your worth that way, ere you attained
This reverend garment, joins you in commission
With the right fortunate soldier, the Marquis of Pescara,
And the famous Lannoy.

Card. He that had the honor
Of taking the French king prisoner?

Mal. The same.
Here's a plot drawn for a new fortification
At Naples.

Ferd. This great Count Malateste, I perceive,
Hath got employment?

Delio. No employment, my Lord;
A marginal note in the muster-book, that he is
A voluntary lord.

Ferd. He's no soldier?

---

297 trophy exemplar
298 curious skillful; **engine** device
299 Shall . . . for't write commemorative poems
300 reverend venerated; **cabinets** private rooms
303 want coats lack coats of arms (or crests); in 1609 the Heralds' College was investigated for selling spurious pedigrees
305 concealment secrecy
312 feign pretend; dissimulate
313 Lady of Loretto (where a house, supposedly that in which Jesus' mother lived, was located; it was threatened by the Turks in 1291)
316 princely progress state journey
317 train retinue
320 Lucca a town near Pisa famous for its curative waters; **Spa** a town 16 miles s of Liège, Belgium (often thought to be a part of Germany) known for its waters
326 Past . . . them i.e., "Let us moderately lament past sorrows"
331 rests remains
332 quality job, profession
334 Prefers promotes; **but** only
335 raised promoted, elevated in the opinions of others
336 weeds clothes
III.iii.1 Emperor Charles V, then Holy Roman Emperor
4 Marquis . . . Pescara Ferdinando Francisco d'Aroles (1489–1525)
5 Lannoy Charles de Lannoy, Viceroy of Naples (ca. 1487–1527); he received Francis I's sword in surrender in 1525 at Pavia
12 voluntary volunteer

Delio. He has worn gunpowder in's hollow tooth,
For the toothache.
Sil. He comes to the leaguer with a full intent
To eat fresh beef and garlic, means to stay
Till the scent be gone, and straight return to court.
Delio. He hath read all the late service
As the City Chronicle relates it,
And keeps two painters going, only to express
Battles in model.
Sil. Then he'll fight by the book.
Delio. By the almanac, I think –
To choose good days, and shun the critical.
That's his mistress' scarf.
Sil. Yes, he protests
He would do much for that taffeta.
Delio. I think he would run away from a battle
To save it from taking prisoner.
Sil. He is horribly afraid
Gunpowder will spoil the perfume on't.
Delio. I saw a Dutchman break his pate once
For calling him pot-gun; he made his head
Have a bore in't, like a musket.
Sil. I would he had made a touch-hole to't.
He is indeed a guarded sumpter-cloth,
Only for the remove of the court.

[*Enter* Bosola.]

Pes. Bosola arrived! what should be the business?
Some falling out among the cardinals?
These factions among great men, they are like
Foxes; when their heads are divided
They carry fire in their tails, and all the country
About them goes to wreck for't.
Sil. What's that Bosola?
Delio. I knew him in Padua, a fantastical scholar, like such who study to know how many knots was in Hercules' club, of what color Achilles' beard was, or whether Hector were not troubled with the toothache; he hath studied himself half blear-eyed to know the true symmetry of Caesar's nose by a shoeing-horn; and this he did to gain the name of a speculative man.
Pes. Mark Prince Ferdinand:
A very salamander lives in's eye,
To mock the eager violence of fire.
Sil. That Cardinal hath made more bad faces with his oppression than ever Michael Angelo made good ones; he lifts up's nose, like a foul porpoise before a storm –
Pes. The Lord Ferdinand laughs.
Delio. Like a deadly cannon
That lightens ere it smokes.
Pes. These are your true pangs of death,
The pangs of life that struggle with great statesmen.
Delio. In such a deformed silence, witches whisper
Their charms.
Card. Doth she make religion her riding-hood
To keep her from the sun and tempest?
Ferd. That!
That damns her. Methinks her fault and beauty
Blended together show, like leprosy,
The whiter, the fouler. I make it a question
Whether her beggarly brats were ever christened.
Card. I will instantly solicit the state of Ancona
To have them banished.
Ferd. You are for Loretto?

---

13 **worn gunpowder** i.e., saltpeter in gunpowder
15 **leaguer** military camp
16 **fresh beef and garlic** food presumed to increase martial drive
17 **scent** (of military adventure); **straight** directly
18 **late service** recent military efforts
20 **express** i.e., depict
21 **model** (1) drawings to scale; (2) ground-plan; **by the book** (1) according to rule; (2) theoretically
22 **almanac** reference work used to determine optimum conditions
24 **scarf** (Delio notes the token worn by Malateste)
25 **taffeta** glassy material of silk
27 **taking** i.e., being taken
28 **on't** of it
30 **pot-gun** a child's toy here used to describe (or label) a braggart
32 **touch-hole** (where the powder is ignited)
33 **guarded sumpter-cloth** decorated saddle-cloth used on special occasions
34 **Only . . . court** merely to adorn the court on its royal progress
37–40 **These . . . for't** reference to Samson, who tied the tails of 300 foxes and set them afire when let loose in Philistines' corn, destroying their grain, vines, and olives (Judges 15:4–5)
40 **wreck** ruin
41–9 **I . . . man** ambitious men, often highly intelligent, made desirable followers
41 **Padua** a city famous for its university; **fantastical** irrational, given to quibbling over worthless issues
43 **Hercules** mythic hero
43–4 **Achilles . . . Hector** epic heroes fighting for Greece and Troy in the Trojan War
46–7 **symmetry** proportions
48 **speculative** theorizing
51 **salamander** (standard symbol for fiery sexual or destructive passion)
53 **bad faces** (referring to Cardinal's victims)
54 **Michael Angelo** Florentine painter (the reference is to the 300 faces in his frescoes in the Pope's Sistine Chapel)
55–6 **he . . . storm** "The porpoise plays before a storm" (proverbial)
58 **lightens** lights up, flashes
61 **deformed** distorted
69 **solicit** request; **state** rulers

I shall not be at your ceremony. Fare you well.
Write to the Duke of Malfi, my young nephew
She had by her first husband, and acquaint him
With's mother's honesty.

Bos. I will.

Ferd. Antonio!
A slave that only smelled of ink and counters,
And ne'er in's life looked like a gentleman,
But in the audit-time. Go, go presently,
Draw me out an hundred and fifty of our horse,
And meet me at the fort-bridge.

Exeunt.

Scena iv.

[*Enter*] Two Pilgrims *to the Shrine of our Lady of Loretto.*

1st. Pil. I have not seen a goodlier shrine than this,
Yet I have visited many.

2nd. Pil. The Cardinal of Arragon
Is this day to resign his Cardinal's hat;
His sister Duchess likewise is arrived
To pay her vow of pilgrimage. I expect
A noble ceremony.

1st. Pil. No question. They come.

Here the ceremony of the Cardinal'*s installment in the habit of a soldier, performed in delivering up his cross, hat, robes and ring at the shrine, and investing him with sword, helmet, shield and spurs; then* Antonio, *the* Duchess *and their* Children, *having presented themselves at the shrine, are (by a form of banishment in dumb-show expressed towards them by the* Cardinal *and the state of Ancona) banished: during all which ceremony, this ditty is sung, to very solemn music, by divers* Churchmen; *and then exeunt* [*all, except the* Two Pilgrims].

The author disclaims this ditty to be his.

Arms and honors deck thy story
To thy fame's eternal glory!
Adverse fortune ever fly thee,
No disastrous fate come nigh thee!

I alone will sing thy praises,
Whom to honor virtue raises,
And thy study, that divine is,
Bent to martial discipline is.
Lay aside all those robes lie by thee;
Crown thy arts with arms, they'll beautify thee.

Oh, worthy of worthiest name, adorned in this manner,
Lead bravely thy forces on under war's warlike banner!
Oh, mayst thou prove fortunate in all martial courses!
Guide thou still, by skill, in arts and forces!
Victory attend thee nigh whilst Fame sings loud thy pow'rs;
Triumphant conquest crown thy head, and blessings pour down show'rs!

1st. Pil. Here's a strange turn of state! who would have thought
So great a lady would have matched herself
Unto so mean a person? Yet the Cardinal
Bears himself much too cruel.

2nd. Pil. They are banished.

1st. Pil. But I would ask what power hath this state
Of Ancona to determine of a free prince?

2nd. Pil. They are a free state sir, and her brother showed
How that the Pope, fore-hearing of her looseness,
Hath seized into th' protection of the church
The dukedom which she held as dowager.

1st. Pil. But by what justice?

2nd. Pil. Sure, I think by none,
Only her brother's instigation.

1st. Pil. What was it with such violence he took
Off from her finger?

2nd. Pil. 'Twas her wedding ring,
Which he vowed shortly he would sacrifice
To his revenge.

1st. Pil. Alas, Antonio!
If that a man be thrust into a well,
No matter who sets hand to't, his own weight
Will bring him sooner to th' bottom. Come, let's hence.
Fortune makes this conclusion general.
"All things do help th' unhappy man to fall."

Exeunt.

Scena v.

[*Enter* Antonio, Duchess, Children, Cariola, Servants.]

Duch. Banished Ancona?

Ant. Yes, you see what pow'r

74 **honesty** (1) chastity; (2) behavior (sarcastically)
75 **slave** i.e., one of no social status; **counters** discs used in counting
77 **presently** at once
III.iv.18–21 **The ... his** (Webster may disavow these songs as doggerel)
18 ***deck*** cover
22 ***I ... praises*** I will sing only in your praise
27 **arts** learning
30 ***courses*** encounters
36 **mean** low-born
39 **determine of** judge
40 **free state** Ancona was a semi-independent republic protected by the papacy
45 **her brother's** the Cardinal's
51 **No ... to't** (i.e., it does not matter who pushes)

Lightens in great men's breath.
Duch. Is all our train
Shrunk to this poor remainder?
Ant. These poor men,
Which have got little in your service, vow
To take your fortune. But your wiser buntings,
Now they are fledged, are gone.
Duch. They have done wisely.
This puts me in mind of death. Physicians thus,
With their hands full of money, use to give o'er
Their patients.
Ant. Right the fashion of the world,
From decayed fortunes every flatterer shrinks;
Men cease to build where the foundation sinks.
Duch. I had a very strange dream tonight.
Ant. What was't?
Duch. Methought I wore my coronet of state,
And on a sudden all the diamonds
Were changed to pearls.
Ant. My interpretation
Is, you'll weep shortly, for to me the pearls
Do signify your tears.
Duch. The birds that live i' th' field
On the wild benefit of nature, live
Happier than we; for they may choose their mates,
And carol their sweet pleasures to the spring.

[*Enter* Bosola *with a letter.*]

Bos. You are happily o'erta'en.
Duch. From my brother?
Bos. Yes, from the Lord Ferdinand, your brother,
All love and safety.
Duch. Thou dost blanch mischief,
Wouldst make it white. See, see, like to calm weather
At sea, before a tempest, false hearts speak fair
To those they intend most mischief.
A letter. [*Reads.*] "Send Antonio to me; I want his head in a business."
A politic equivocation!
He doth not want your counsel, but your head;
That is, he cannot sleep till you be dead.
And here's another pitfall, that's strewed o'er
With roses; mark it, 'tis a cunning one:
[*Reads*]
"I stand engaged for your husband, for several debts at Naples; let not that trouble him, I had rather have his heart than his money."
And I believe so too.
Bos. What do you believe?
Duch. That he so much distrusts my husband's love,
He will by no means believe his heart is with him
Until he see it. The devil is not cunning enough
To circumvent us in riddles.
Bos. Will you reject that noble and free league
Of amity and love which I present you?
Duch. Their league is like that of some politic kings,
Only to make themselves of strength and pow'r
To be our after-ruin. Tell them so.
Bos. And what from you?
Ant. Thus tell him: I will not come.
Bos. And what of this?
Ant. My brothers have dispersed
Bloodhounds abroad; which till I hear are muzzled,
No truce, though hatched with ne'er such politic skill
Is safe, that hangs upon our enemies' will.
I'll not come at them.
Bos. This proclaims your breeding.
Every small thing draws a base mind to fear,
As the adamant draws iron; fare you well, sir,
You shall shortly hear from's.
Exit.
Duch. I suspect some ambush.
Therefore, by all my love, I do conjure you
To take your eldest son and fly towards Milan.
Let us not venture all this poor remainder
In one unlucky bottom.
Ant. You counsel safely.
Best of my life, farewell. Since we must part

III.v.5 **buntings** common birds with cone-shaped bills related to larks
8 **give o'er** abandon
9 **Right** exactly
13 **coronet** small or inferior crown
19 **benefit** gift
21 **carol** sing happily
22 **happily** fortunately
24 **blanch** fear; **mischief** evil
25 **it** your face
29 **politic** cunning; **equivocation** double meaning
32 **pitfall** concealed or covered hole to capture animals
42 **league** covenant
44 **league** alliance
46 **after-ruin** future downfall
48 **this** (i.e., the letter); **brothers** (i.e., brothers-in-law)
52 **at them** within their reach
54 **adamant** magnetic lodestone
59 **remainder** (i.e., their possessions)
60 **bottom** ship's hold

Heaven hath a hand in't; but no otherwise
Than as some curious artist takes in sunder
A clock or watch when it is out of frame,
To bring 't in better order.

Duch. I know not which is best,
To see you dead, or part with you. Farewell, boy;
Thou art happy, that thou hast not understanding
To know thy misery, for all our wit
And reading brings us to a truer sense
Of sorrow. In the eternal church, sir,
I do hope we shall not part thus.

Ant. Oh, be of comfort!
Make patience a noble fortitude,
And think not how unkindly we are used.
"Man, like to cassia, is proved best, being bruised."

Duch. Must I, like to a slave-born Russian,
Account it praise to suffer tyranny?
And yet, Oh, Heaven, thy heavy hand is in't.
I have seen my little boy oft scourge his top
And compared myself to't. Naught made me e'er
Go right but heaven's scourge-stick.

Ant. Do not weep.
Heaven fashioned us of nothing; and we strive
To bring ourselves to nothing. Farewell, Cariola,
And thy sweet armful; if I do never see thee more,
Be a good mother to your little ones,
And save them from the tiger. Fare you well.

Duch. Let me look upon you once more; for that speech
Came from a dying father. Your kiss is colder
Than that I have seen an holy anchorite
Give to a dead man's skull.

Ant. My heart is turned to a heavy lump of lead,
With which I sound my danger. Fare you well.

Exit [, *with his elder* Son].

Duch. My laurel is all withered.

Cari. Look, Madam, what a troop of armed men
Make toward us.

Enter Bosola *with a* Guard [*with visards*].

Duch. Oh, they are very welcome:
When Fortune's wheel is overcharged with princes,
The weight makes it move swift. I would have my ruin
Be sudden. I am your adventure, am I not?

Bos. You are; you must see your husband no more.

Duch. What devil art thou, that counterfeits heaven's thunder?

Bos. Is that terrible? I would have you tell me
Whither is that note worse that frights the silly birds
Out of the corn, or that which doth allure them
To the nets? you have hearkened to the last too much.

Duch. Oh, misery! like to a rusty o'ercharged cannon,
Shall I never fly in pieces? Come; to what prison?

Bos. To none.

Duch. Whither then?

Bos. To your palace.

Duch. I have heard
That Charon's boat serves to convey all o'er
The dismal lake, but brings none back again.

Bos. Your brothers mean you safety, and pity.

Duch. Pity!
With such a pity men preserve alive
Pheasants and quails, when they are not fat enough
To be eaten.

Bos. These are your children?

Duch. Yes.

Bos. Can they prattle?

Duch. No.
But I intend, since they were born accursed,
Curses shall be their first language.

Bos. Fie, Madam,
Forget this base, low fellow.

Duch. Were I a man
I'd beat that counterfeit face into thy other.

---

63 **curious** skillful; **sunder** parts, pieces
71 **eternal church** the Church Triumphant
73 **Make** regard
74 **unkindly** unnaturally
79 **scourge** whip; **top** a spinning toy
90 **dead . . . skull** as an aid in meditating on death
92 **sound** (1) measure; (2) pronounce
93 **laurel . . . withered** proverbially, laurel withered at a king's death
94–5 **Look . . . us** (Cariola's silence makes her analogous to the Duchess' children)
95 **s.d. *visards*** masks
96 **overcharged** weighed down
97 **swift** (descent is swift compared to ascent)
98 **adventure** (1) business, purpose; (2) quarry
102 **note** sound; **silly** ignorant
104 **hearkened** heard (and been attracted); **too much** and are caught
108 **Charon** ferryman who took dead souls across the River Styx and River Acheron
114 **prattle** talk

Bos. One of no birth –
Duch. Say that he was born mean.
Man is most happy when's own actions
Be arguments and examples of his virtue.
Bos. A barren, beggarly virtue.
Duch. I prithee, who is greatest? Can you tell?
Sad tales befit my woe. I'll tell you one.
A salmon, as she swam unto the sea,
Met with a dog-fish, who encounters her
With this rough language. "Why art thou so bold
To mix thyself with our high state of floods,
Being no eminent courtier, but one
That for the calmest and fresh time o'th' year
Dost live in shallow rivers, rank'st thyself
With silly smelts and shrimps? and darest thou
Pass by our dog-ship, without reverence?"
"Oh," quoth the salmon, "sister, be at peace.
Thank Jupiter we both have passed the net!
Our value never can be truly known
Till in the fisher's basket we be shown;
I'th' market then my price may be the higher,
Even when I am nearest to the cook and fire."
So, to great men, the moral may be stretched:
"Men oft are valued high, when th'are most wretched."
But come, whither you please. I am armed 'gainst misery,
Bent to all sways of the oppressor's will.
"There's no deep valley, but near some great hill."

Exeunt.

Act IV

Actus IV, Scena i.

[*Enter* Ferdinand *and* Bosola.]

Ferd. How doth our sister Duchess bear herself
In her imprisonment?
Bos. Nobly; I'll describe her:
She's sad, as one long used to't; and she seems
Rather to welcome the end of misery
Than shun it: – a behavior so noble
As gives a majesty to adversity.
You may discern the shape of loveliness
More perfect in her tears than in her smiles;
She will muse four hours together, and her silence,
Methinks, expresseth more than if she spake.
Ferd. Her melancholy seems to be fortified
With a strange disdain.
Bos. 'Tis so: and this restraint
(Like English mastiffs, that grow fierce with tying)
Makes her too passionately apprehend
Those pleasures she's kept from.
Ferd. Curse upon her!
I will no longer study in the book
Of another's heart. Inform her what I told you.

Exit.

[*Enter* Duchess.]

Bos. All comfort to your Grace!
Duch. I will have none.
Pray thee, why dost thou wrap thy poisoned pills
In gold and sugar?
Bos. Your elder brother, the Lord Ferdinand,
Is come to visit you, and sends you word,
'Cause once he rashly made a solemn vow
Never to see you more, he comes i'th' night;
And prays you, gently, neither torch nor taper
Shine in your chamber. He will kiss your hand,
And reconcile himself. But, for his vow,
He dares not see you.
Duch. At his pleasure.
Take hence the lights;

[*Bosola removes lights.*]

[*Enter* Ferdinand.]

he's come.
Ferd. Where are you?
Duch. Here sir.
Ferd. This darkness suits you well.
Duch. I would ask you pardon.
Ferd. You have it;
For I account it the honorabl'st revenge,
Where I may kill, to pardon. Where are your cubs?
Duch. Whom?

---

121 arguments proofs
126 dog-fish small shark
128 floods (i.e., water)
132 smelts small fish
141 wretched depressed (cf. Ps. 121)
143 Bent (1) determined to withstand; (2) yielding to
144 some ... hill (possibly a reference to Ps. 121: 1–2)
IV.i.2 imprisonment house arrest
7 shape image
13 English mastiffs large, powerful watchdogs
14 apprehend imagine
15 Curse damnation (in response to "pleasures" as wholly sexual)
16 study ... book contemplate
21 elder (in Webster's source, Ferdinand is older than the Duchess; in the play, they are twins; the Cardinal is younger)
25 prays requests
32–3 I ... pardon "To pardon is divine revenge" (proverbial)

Ferd. Call them your children;
For though our national law distinguish bastards
From true legitimate issue, compassionate nature
Makes them all equal.
Duch. Do you visit me for this?
You violate a sacrament o'th' church
Shall make you howl in hell for't.
Ferd. It had been well
Could you have lived thus always; for indeed
You were too much i' th' light. But no more.
I come to seal my peace with you. Here's a hand
Gives her a dead man's hand.
To which you have vowed much love; the ring upon't
You gave.
Duch. I affectionately kiss it.
Ferd. Pray do and bury the print of it in your heart.
I will leave this ring with you for a love-token;
And the hand, as sure as the ring; and do not doubt
But you shall have the heart too; when you need a friend
Send it to him that owed it; you shall see
Whether he can aid you.
Duch. You are very cold.
I fear you are not well after your travel.
Hah! lights! Oh, horrible!
Ferd. Let her have lights enough.
Exit.
Duch. What witchcraft doth he practice that he hath left
A dead man's hand here?
Here is discovered, behind a traverse, the artificial figures of Antonio and his children, appearing as if they were dead.
Bos. Look you: here's the piece from which 'twas ta'en.
He doth present you this sad spectacle
That now you know directly they are dead.
Hereafter you may wisely cease to grieve
For that which cannot be recovered.
Duch. There is not between heaven and earth one wish
I stay for after this. It wastes me more
Than were't my picture, fashioned out of wax,
Stuck with a magical needle and then buried
In some foul dunghill; and yon's an excellent property
For a tyrant, which I would account mercy.
Bos. What's that?
Duch. If they would bind me to that lifeless trunk,
And let me freeze to death.
Bos. Come, you must live.
Duch. That's the greatest torture souls feel in hell –
In hell that they must live, and cannot die.
Portia, I'll new-kindle thy coals again,
And revive the rare and almost dead example
Of a loving wife.
Bos. Oh, fie! despair? Remember
You are a Christian.
Duch. The church enjoins fasting;
I'll starve myself to death.
Bos. Leave this vain sorrow.
Things being at the worst begin to mend;
The bee when he hath shot his sting into your hand
May then play with your eyelid.
Duch. Good comfortable fellow
Persuade a wretch that's broke upon the wheel
To have all his bones new set; entreat him live
To be executed again. Who must dispatch me?
I account this world a tedious theater,

39 **sacrament . . . church** i.e., marriage
40 **Shall** which shall
42 **i' th' light** publicly exposed, vulnerable (plays on "light" meaning "wanton")
44 **s.d.** ***dead . . . hand*** a powerful charm used to cure madness
50 **owed** owned
56 **s.d.** ***traverse*** (used to indicate drawing back a curtain on a "discovery space")
57 **sad** grave
58 **directly** plainly; without doubt
62–5 **It . . . dunghill** (refers to custom of burying wax dolls stuck with pins like daggers in the belief that as they were consumed or wasted in the soil's heat so would the person represented)
65 **yon's** yonder is; **property** device
66 **I . . . mercy** such a release from suffering would be considered kind (merciful)
68–9 **bind . . . death** a symbol for an ill-matched marriage (from emblem books)
68 **lifeless trunk** i.e., Antonio's body
72–4 **Portia . . . wife** Brutus' wife Portia committed suicide by putting hot coals in her mouth after his assassination of Caesar and his own death at the Battle of Philippi
74–5 **despair . . . Christian** despair as the human taking of God's gift of life was the greatest of sins (and insured damnation)
76 **starve . . . death** according to some churchmen, this method of suicide was permissible under certain circumstances; **vain** useless
77 **Things . . . mend** (proverbial)
78–9 **shot . . . eyelid** (stinging once, bees cannot sting again)
80 **comfortable fellow** jailer (the Duchess does not recognize Bosola)
81 **broke . . . wheel** a form of torture used often for confession more than punishment
84 **world . . . theater** "all the world's a stage" (for trying the soul)

For I do play a part in't 'gainst my will.
Bos. Come, be of comfort, I will save your life.
Duch. Indeed I have not leisure to tend so small a business.
Bos. Now, by my life, I pity you.
Duch. Thou art a fool then,
To waste thy pity on a thing so wretched
As cannot pity itself. I am full of daggers.
Puff! let me blow these vapors from me.

[*Enter* Servant.]

What are you?
Serv. One that wishes you long life.
Duch. I would thou wert hanged for the horrible curse
Thou hast given me.

[*Exit* Servant.]

I shall shortly grow one
Of the miracles of pity. I'll go pray. No,
I'll go curse.
Bos. Oh, fie!
Duch. I could curse the stars.
Bos. Oh, fearful!
Duch. And those three smiling seasons of the year
Into a Russian winter – nay the world
To its first chaos.
Bos. Look you, the stars shine still.
Duch. Oh, but you must
Remember, my curse hath a great way to go.
Plagues, that make lanes through largest families,
Consume them! –
Bos. Fie, lady!
Duch. Let them, like tyrants
Never be remembered but for the ill they have done;
Let all the zealous prayers of mortified
Churchmen forget them!
Bos. Oh, uncharitable!
Duch. Let heaven, a little while, cease crowning martyrs,
To punish them!
Go howl them this: and say I long to bleed;
"It is some mercy, when men kill with speed."

Exit.

[*Enter* Ferdinand.]

Ferd. Excellent! As I would wish; she's plagued in art.
These presentations are but framed in wax,
By the curious master in that quality,
Vincentio Lauriola, and she takes them
For true substantial bodies.
Bos. Why do you do this?
Ferd. To bring her to despair.
Bos. Faith, end here
And go no farther in your cruelty;
Send her a penitential garment to put on
Next to her delicate skin, and furnish her
With beads and prayer-books.
Ferd. Damn her! that body of hers,
While that my blood ran pure in't, was more worth
Than that which thou wouldst comfort, called a soul –
I will send her masques of common courtesans,
Have her meat served up by bawds and ruffians,
And, 'cause she'll needs be mad, I am resolved
To remove forth the common hospital
All the mad-folk, and place them near her lodging;
There let them practice together, sing, and dance,
And act their gambols to the full o'th' moon.
If she can sleep the better for it, let her –
Your work is almost ended.
Bos. Must I see her again?
Ferd. Yes.
Bos. Never.
Ferd. You must.
Bos. Never in mine own shape,
That's forfeited by my intelligence,

---

90 **daggers** (1) mental disturbances; (2) sharp pains
91 **vapors** mists (which for Webster often accompanied death)
95 **miracles** wonders
97 **three . . . seasons** spring, summer, fall as times of growth and harvest
102 **Plagues** (refers to guns in warfare; proverbial)
105 **mortified** those knowing extreme penance
111 **in art** by artifice
112 **presentations . . . wax** wax effigies of the dead were placed on the coffins of great persons in funeral processions; some were then on display in Westminster Abbey
113 **curious** expert; **quality** craft
114 **Vincentio Lauriola** (unknown; probably Webster's invention)
117 **Faith** in faith (a common expression)
119 **penitential garment** (in which she would be paraded through the streets as an adulteress)
121 **beads** a rosary
122 **more worth** sacrilegious; the body was thought a temporary covering for an eternal soul as God's spirit
124 **masques** courtly spectacles ending in dancing with members of the audience
127 **forth** forth from
129–30 **practice . . . gambols** (he is thinking of perverse and grotesque sexual acts)
130 **full . . . moon** (1) as a special time of madness; (2) as the time he will succeed in driving the Duchess mad
135 **forfeited . . . intelligence** betrayed my actions as intelligencer

And this last cruel lie. When you send me next,
The business shall be comfort.
Ferd. Very likely;
Thy pity is nothing of kin to thee. Antonio
Lurks about Milan; thou shalt shortly thither
To feed a fire, as great as my revenge,
Which ne'er will slack till it have spent his fuel.
"Intemperate agues make physicians cruel."
Exeunt.

Scena ii.

[*Enter* Duchess *and* Cariola.]

Duch. What hideous noise was that?
Cari. 'Tis the wild consort
Of madmen, Lady, which your tyrant brother
Hath placed about your lodging. This tyranny,
I think, was never practiced till this hour.
Duch. Indeed I thank him. Nothing but noise and folly
Can keep me in my right wits, whereas reason
And silence make me stark mad. Sit down;
Discourse to me some dismal tragedy.
Cari. Oh, 'twill increase your melancholy.
Duch. Thou art deceived,
To hear of greater grief would lessen mine.
This is a prison?
Cari. Yes, but you shall live
To shake this durance off.
Duch. Thou art a fool;
The robin-redbreast and the nightingale
Never live long in cages.
Cari. Pray dry your eyes.
What think you of, Madam?
Duch. Of nothing;
When I muse thus, I sleep.
Cari. Like a madman, with your eyes open?
Duch. Dost thou think we shall know one another
In th'other world?
Cari. Yes, out of question.
Duch. Oh, that it were possible we might
But hold some two days' conference with the dead,
From them I should learn somewhat I am sure
I never shall know here. I'll tell thee a miracle:
I am not mad yet, to my cause of sorrow.
Th'heaven o'er my head seems made of molten brass,
The earth of flaming sulfur, yet I am not mad.
I am acquainted with sad misery,
As the tanned galley-slave is with his oar;
Necessity makes me suffer constantly,
And custom makes it easy. Who do I look like now?
Cari. Like to your picture in the gallery,
A deal of life in show, but none in practice;
Or rather like some reverend monument
Whose ruins are even pitied.
Duch. Very proper.
And Fortune seems only to have her eyesight
To behold my tragedy. How now!
What noise is that?

[*Enter* Servant.]

Serv. I am come to tell you
Your brother hath intended you some sport.
A great physician, when the Pope was sick
Of a deep melancholy, presented him
With several sorts of madmen, which wild object,
Being full of change and sport forced him to laugh,
And so th' imposthume broke. The self-same cure
The Duke intends on you.
Duch. Let them come in.
Serv. There's a mad lawyer, and a secular priest,
A doctor that hath forfeited his wits
By jealousy; an astrologian
That in his works said such a day o'th' month
Should be the day of doom, and failing of't,
Ran mad; an English tailor, crazed i'th' brain
With the study of new fashion; a gentleman usher
Quite beside himself, with care to keep in mind
The number of his Lady's salutations,
Or "How do you," she employed him in each morning;
A farmer too, an excellent knave in grain,

137 business purpose
137–8 Very . . . thee i.e., "Hardly! pity is not your nature"
141 his its
142 agues fevers
IV.ii.1 consort (1) group of musicians; (2) harmonious music
3 tyranny i.e., torture
12 durance (1) duration; (2) enduring
19 out of question without doubt
25–6 Th'heaven . . . sulfur (cf. Deuteronomy 28: 15–34)
32 A . . . show lifelike in appearance
33 monument effigy
34 proper appropriate
35 only . . . eyesight (an extraordinary condition, since Fortune was thought to be blind)
42 change and sport variety and entertainment
43 imposthume abscess
45 secular i.e., not monastic
49 doom the Last Judgment
55 in grain (1) dealing in grain; (2) ingrained; (3) incorrigible

Mad 'cause he was hindered transportation
And let one broker that's mad loose to these,
You'd think the devil were among them.

Duch. Sit, Cariola. Let them loose when you please,
For I am chained to endure all your tyranny.

Enter Madmen.

Here, by a Madman, *this song is sung, to a dismal kind of music.*

Oh, let us howl some heavy note,
Some deadly dogged howl,
Sounding as from the threat'ning throat
Of beasts, and fatal fowl!
As ravens, screech-owls, bulls, and bears,
We'll bell and bawl our parts,
Till irksome noise have cloyed your ears
And corrosived your hearts.
At last when as our choir wants breath,
Our bodies being blest,
We'll sing like swans, to welcome death,
And die in love and rest.

1st. Madman. Doomsday not come yet? I'll draw it nearer by a perspective, or make a glass that shall set all the world on fire upon an instant. I cannot sleep; my pillow is stuffed with a litter of porcupines.

2nd. Madman. Hell is a mere glass-house where the devils are continually blowing up women's souls, on hollow irons, and the fire never goes out.

3rd. Madman. I will lie with every woman in my parish the tenth night. I will tithe them over, like hay-cocks.

4th. Madman. Shall my pothecary outgo me because I am a cuckold? I have found out his roguery. He makes alum of his wife's urine, and sells it to puritans that have sore throats with over-straining.

1st. Madman. I have skill in heraldry.

2nd. Madman. Hast?

1st. Madman. You do give for your crest a woodcock's head, with the brains picked out on't, you are a very ancient gentleman.

3rd. Madman. Greek is turned Turk; we are only to be saved by the Helvetian translation.

1st. Madman. Come on, sir, I will lay the law to you.

2nd. Madman. Oh, rather lay a corrosive; the law will eat to the bone.

3rd. Madman. He that drinks but to satisfy nature is damned.

4th. Madman. If I had my glass here, I would show a sight should make all the women here call me mad doctor.

1st. Madman. What's he, a rope-maker?

[*Points at 3rd. Madman.*]

2nd. Madman. No, no, no, a snuffling knave, that while he shows the tombs will have his hand in a wench's placket.

3rd. Madman. Woe to the caroche that brought home my wife from the masque at three o'clock in the morning! It had a large featherbed in it.

4th. Madman. I have pared the devil's nails forty times, roasted them in raven's eggs, and cured agues with them.

3rd. Madman. Get me three hundred milch-bats to make possets, to procure sleep.

---

56 **hindered transportation** (perhaps alluding to regulations against exporting grain when there were shortages, as in a proclamation of January 18, 1613)
57 **broker** (1) peddler; (2) pawnbroker; (3) procurer
60 **chained** forced (but only severe cases of madness were actually chained in London)
61 **s.d. *dismal*** (1) foreboding; (2) dissonant; (3) stylistically awkward
66 ***bell*** bellow
67 ***irksome*** physically painful
68 ***corrosived*** (1) corroded; (2) vexed
69 ***wants*** lacks
71–2 ***sing . . . rest*** (it was believed swans stopped their harsh cries and sang sweetly just before their deaths)
74 **perspective** perspective glass or telescope; **glass** magnifying glass
78 **glass-house** house where glassmaking furnaces were located; one was near Blackfriars
83 **tithe** decimate (alluding to tithe, or tenths, given to the church)
84 **hay-cocks** conical haystacks
85 **pothecary** apothecary, druggist
88–9 **that . . . over-straining** i.e., sung too many psalms too loudly
92 **give** display heraldically
92–3 **woodcock's** (1) a notoriously foolish bird; (2) a cuckold
94 **ancient gentleman** have the pedigreed lineage of the gentry
95 **Greek . . . Turk** holy language is turned heathen
96 **Helvetian** Genevan (Calvinist translation which gave Puritans the Geneva Bible in 1560, the most popular translation of Elizabeth I's reign)
97 **lay** expose; preach
99 **corrosive** (1) literally, caustic medicine; (2) figuratively, sharp grief or (3) sharp remedy
101–2 **He . . . damned** i.e., only drunkards are blessed
106 **rope-maker** (with possible allusion to the hangman)
109 **placket** (1) petticoat; (2) opening in a skirt
110 **caroche** a stately coach
112–13 **featherbed** alluding to (1) luxury of large coaches; (2) coaches as places known for sexual encounters
114–15 **pared . . . times** (proverbial)
117 **milch-bats** nocturnal creatures that supposedly yield milk
118 **possets** drinks of hot milk curdled with ale or wine and with added spices and sugar

4th. Madman. All the college may throw their caps at me, I have made a soap-boiler costive. It was my masterpiece.

Here the dance, consisting of 8 Madmen, *with music answerable thereunto; after which* Bosola, *like an old man, enters* [*and the* Madmen *leave*].

Duch. Is he mad too?
Serv. Pray question him. I'll leave you. [*Exit.*]
Bos. I am come to make thy tomb.
Duch. Hah, my tomb!
Thou speak'st as if I lay upon my death-bed,
Gasping for breath. Dost thou perceive me sick?
Bos. Yes, and the more dangerously, since thy sickness is insensible.
Duch. Thou art not mad, sure; dost know me?
Bos. Yes.
Duch. Who am I?
Bos. Thou art a box of worm-seed at best, but a salvatory of green mummy. – What's this flesh? A little crudded milk, fantastical puff-paste; our bodies are weaker than those paper prisons boys use to keep flies in; more contemptible, since ours is to preserve earth-worms. Didst thou ever see a lark in a cage? Such is the soul in the body. This world is like her little turf of grass, and the heaven o'er our heads, like her looking-glass, only gives us a miserable knowledge of the small compass of our prison.
Duch. Am not I thy Duchess?
Bos. Thou art some great woman, sure, for riot begins to sit on thy forehead, clad in gray hairs, twenty years sooner than on a merry milk-maid's. Thou sleepest worse than if a mouse should be forced to take up her lodging in a cat's ear. A little infant that breeds its teeth should it lie with thee, would cry out, as if thou wert the more unquiet bedfellow.
Duch. I am Duchess of Malfi still.
Bos. That makes thy sleeps so broken.
"Glories, like glow-worms, afar off shine bright,
But looked to near, have neither heat, nor light."
Duch. Thou art very plain.
Bos. My trade is to flatter the dead, not the living. I am a tomb-maker.
Duch. And thou com'st to make my tomb?
Bos. Yes.
Duch. Let me be a little merry; of what stuff wilt thou make it?
Bos. Nay, resolve me first of what fashion?
Duch. Why, do we grow fantastical in our death-bed? Do we affect fashion in the grave?
Bos. Most ambitiously! Princes' images on their tombs do not lie, as they were wont, seeming to pray up to heaven, but with their hands under their cheeks, as if they died of the tooth-ache; they are not carved with their eyes fixed upon the stars, but as their minds were wholly bent upon the world, the selfsame way they seem to turn their faces.
Duch. Let me know fully therefore the effect
Of this thy dismal preparation,
This talk fit for a charnel.
Bos. Now I shall.

[*Enter* Executioners, *with*] *a coffin, cords and a bell.*

Here is a present from your princely brothers,
And may it arrive welcome, for it brings
Last benefit, last sorrow.
Duch. Let me see it.
I have so much obedience in my blood,
I wish it in their veins, to do them good.
Bos. This is your last presence-chamber.

---

119 college community (such as of clergy or learned scholars)
119–20 throw . . . me pursue
120 soap-boiler soapmaker; **costive** constipated
121 masterpiece i.e., soapmakers would not normally be constipated since soap was an ingredient in suppositories designed to loosen the bowels
127 insensible imperceptible; unfelt
131 worm-seed a plant whose dried flowers were used in a medicine to treat intestinal worms (with possible play on "semen")
132 salvatory box for holding ointment; **green mummy** a medicine prepared from mummies
133 crudded curdled
133–4 puff-paste a fragile and airy confection
136 preserve keep alive
139 turf of grass grass placed in a bird's cage to simulate a natural habitat
144 riot dissipation
146–7 merry milkmaid's proverbial reference for simple, carefree living
149 breeds its has its first
163 resolve satisfy
165 affect (1) aspire to; (2) assume
166–73 Princes . . . faces (this Renaissance fashion in tomb sculpture began in England in the 1560s)
174 effect purpose
176 charnel charnel-house, burial place
179 benefit benefaction
182 presence-chamber (with reference to the earlier royal presence-chamber in I.ii and II.i)

Cari. Oh, my sweet lady!
Duch. Peace, it affrights not me.
Bos. I am the common bellman
That usually is sent to condemned persons
The night before they suffer.
Duch. Even now thou said'st
Thou wast a tomb-maker.
Bos. 'Twas to bring you
By degrees to mortification. Listen:
Hark, now everything is still,
The screech-owl, and the whistler shrill
Call upon our dame, aloud,
And bid her quickly don her shroud.
Much you had of land and rent,
Your length in clay's now competent.
A long war disturbed your mind,
Here your perfect peace is signed.
Of what is't fools make such vain keeping?
Sin their conception, their birth weeping;
Their life a general mist of error,
Their death a hideous storm of terror.
Strew your hair with powders sweet,
Don clean linen, bathe your feet,
And (the foul fiend more to check)
A crucifix let bless your neck.
'Tis now full tide, 'tween night and day;
End your groan, and come away.
Cari. Hence villains, tyrants, murderers! alas!
What will you do with my Lady? Call for help.
Duch. To whom? To our next neighbors? They are mad-folks.
Bos. Remove that noise.
Duch. Farewell, Cariola.
In my last will I have not much to give;
A many hungry guests have fed upon me,
Thine will be a poor reversion.
Cari. I will die with her.
Duch. I pray thee, look thou giv'st my little boy
Some syrup for his cold, and let the girl
Say her prayers, ere she sleep.
[*Executioners force Cariola off.*]
Now what you please –
What death?
Bos. Strangling. Here are your executioners.
Duch. I forgive them.
The apoplexy, catarrh, or cough o'th' lungs
Would do as much as they do.
Bos. Doth not death fright you?
Duch. Who would be afraid on't?
Knowing to meet such excellent company
In th' other world.
Bos. Yet, methinks,
The manner of your death should much afflict you,
This cord should terrify you?
Duch. Not a whit.
What would it pleasure me to have my throat cut
With diamonds? Or to be smothered
With cassia? Or to be shot to death with pearls?
I know death hath ten thousand several doors
For men to take their exits; and 'tis found
They go on such strange geometrical hinges,
You may open them both ways. Any way, for heaven-sake,
So I were out of your whispering. Tell my brothers
That I perceive death, now I am well awake,
Best gift is they can give, or I can take.
I would fain put off my last woman's fault,
I'd not be tedious to you.
Execut. We are ready.
Duch. Dispose my breath how please you, but my body
Bestow upon my women, will you?
Execut. Yes.
Duch. Pull, and pull strongly, for your able strength
Must pull down heaven upon me –
Yet stay; heaven-gates are not so highly arched
As princes' palaces, they that enter there
Must go upon their knees. [*Kneels.*] Come, violent death,

---

184 common bellman one who makes a speech outside the cell of condemned prisoners on the eve of their execution or the next day as they are carted to Tyburn, reminding the condemned of mortality and the importance of repentance
188 mortification (1) condition of austerity; (2) self-inflicted pain
190 ***whistler*** widgeon or lapwing whose shrill cry, as with the sound of the screech-owl, was an omen of death
191 ***our dame*** night
193 ***rent*** income, revenues
194 ***competent*** sufficient
196 ***perfect peace*** eternal rest
197 ***vain*** useless; ***keeping*** (1) holding; (2) defending
199 ***mist*** (1) confusion; (2) uncertainty
201–6 ***Strew... away*** (preparation for death suggested here parallels the more customary epithalamion about a bride preparing for marriage)
204 ***crucifix... neck*** (worn so as to ward off all evil)
206 ***come away*** (invitation to violent death echoes the ardent bridegroom's request to consummate marriage)
214 reversion bequest
218 What death? i.e., what means do you propose for my death?
220 apoplexy a sudden malady caused by the arrest of blood to the brain; loss of consciousness; **catarrh** inflammation of nose and throat
234 both ways i.e., (1) by pulling or pushing; (2) by suicide or murder
238 last... fault talking; that a woman's tongue is the last thing to die was proverbial

Serve for mandragora to make me sleep!
Go tell my brothers, when I am laid out,
They then may feed in quiet.

They strangle her.

Bos. Where's the waiting woman?
Fetch her; some other strangle the children.

[Executioners *fetch Cariola, and one goes to strangle the children.*]

Look you, there sleeps your mistress.
Cari. Oh, you are damned
Perpetually for this. My turn is next,
Is't not so ordered?
Bos. Yes, and I am glad
You are so well prepared for't.
Cari. You are deceived, sir,
I am not prepared for't, I will not die.
I will first come to my answer, and know
How I have offended.
Bos. Come, dispatch her.
You kept her counsel, now you shall keep ours.
Cari. I will not die, I must not, I am contracted
To a young gentleman.
Execut. Here's your wedding ring.
Cari. Let me but speak with the Duke. I'll discover
Treason to his person.
Bos. Delays; throttle her.
Execut. She bites, and scratches!
Cari. If you kill me now
I am damned; I have not been at confession
This two years: –
Bos. When?
Cari. I am quick with child.
Bos. Why, then,
Your credit's saved.

[*The Executioners strangle Cariola.*]

Bear her into th' next room;
Let this lie still.

[*Exeunt* Executioners *with the body of Cariola.*]

[*Enter* Ferdinand.]

Ferd. Is she dead?
Bos. She is what
You'd have her. But here begin your pity –

Shows the Children strangled.

Alas, how have these offended?
Ferd. The death
Of young wolves is never to be pitied.
Bos. Fix your eye here.
Ferd. Constantly.
Bos. Do you not weep?
Other sins only speak; murder shrieks out:
The element of water moistens the earth,
But blood flies upwards, and bedews the heavens.
Ferd. Cover her face, mine eyes dazzle: she died young.
Bos. I think not so: her infelicity
Seemed to have years too many.
Ferd. She and I were twins
And should I die this instant, I had lived
Her time to a minute.
Bos. It seems she was born first.
You have bloodily approved the ancient truth,
That kindred commonly do worse agree
Than remote strangers.
Ferd. Let me see her face again.
Why didst not thou pity her? What an excellent
Honest man mightst thou have been
If thou hadst borne her to some sanctuary!
Or, bold in a good cause, opposed thyself
With thy advanced sword above thy head,
Between her innocence and my revenge!
I bade thee, when I was distracted of my wits,
Go kill my dearest friend, and thou hast done 't.
For let me but examine well the cause:
What was the meanness of her match to me?
Only I must confess, I had a hope,
Had she continued widow, to have gained
An infinite mass of treasure by her death.
And that was the main cause: her marriage,
That drew a stream of gall, quite through my heart.
For thee, (as we observe in tragedies
That a good actor many times is cursed

---

247 **mandragora** mandrake (as narcotic)

248 **laid out** (1) for burial; (2) on a table; (3) as in the wedding night of the madmen's song, consummation

249 **feed in quiet** "Better enjoy a little with quietness than possess much with trouble" (proverbial)

257–8 **I...offended** for legal defense, I must first know the charges

260 **contracted** pledged

261 **wedding ring** i.e., in the noose

262 **discover** reveal

264–6 **If...years** dying without final absolution will forever condemn her soul to hell

266 **When?** (when will my orders be obeyed?); **quick** pregnant

267 **credit's saved** reputation is preserved for you will not give birth to an illegitimate child

270–1 **The...pitied** "The death of a young wolf does never come too soon" (proverbial)

277–8 **her...many** i.e., her misfortune lasted a very long time

282 **approved** confirmed

287 **sanctuary** place of security exempt from arrest

289 **advanced** held aloft

292 **friend** (1) companion; (2) lover; (3) paramour

294 **meanness** socially inferior class

299 **gall** bitterness

For playing a villain's part) I hate thee for't.
And for my sake say thou hast done much ill well.
Bos. Let me quicken your memory, for I perceive
You are falling into ingratitude. I challenge
The reward due to my service.
Ferd. I'll tell thee
What I'll give thee –
Bos. Do.
Ferd. I'll give thee a pardon
For this murder.
Bos. Hah?
Ferd. Yes. And 'tis
The largest bounty I can study to do thee.
By what authority didst thou execute
This bloody sentence?
Bos. By yours –
Ferd. Mine? was I her judge?
Did any ceremonial form of law
Doom her to not-being? Did a complete jury
Deliver her conviction up i'th' court?
Where shalt thou find this judgment registered
Unless in hell? See – like a bloody fool
Th' hast forfeited thy life, and thou shalt die for't.
Bos. The office of justice is perverted quite
When one thief hangs another. Who shall dare
To reveal this?
Ferd. Oh, I'll tell thee:
The wolf shall find her grave, and scrape it up
Not to devour the corpse, but to discover
The horrid murder.
Bos. You, not I, shall quake for't.
Ferd. Leave me –
Bos. I will first receive my pension.
Ferd. You are a villain.
Bos. When your ingratitude
Is judge, I am so.
Ferd. Oh, horror!
That not the fear of him which binds the devils
Can prescribe man obedience!
Never look upon me more.
Bos. Why fare thee well.
Your brother and yourself are worthy men;
You have a pair of hearts are hollow graves,
Rotten, and rotting others and your vengeance,
Like two chained bullets, still goes arm in arm.
You may be brothers; for treason, like the plague,
Doth take much in a blood. I stand like one
That long hath ta'en a sweet and golden dream:
I am angry with myself, now that I wake.
Ferd. Get thee into some unknown part o'th' world
That I may never see thee.
Bos. Let me know
Wherefore I should be thus neglected? Sir,
I served your tyranny; and rather strove
To satisfy yourself, than all the world;
And though I loathed the evil, yet I loved
You that did counsel it; and rather sought
To appear a true servant than an honest man.
Ferd. I'll go hunt the badger by owl-light;
'Tis a deed of darkness.

Exit.

Bos. He's much distracted. Off my painted honor!
While with vain hopes our faculties we tire,
We seem to sweat in ice, and freeze in fire.
What would I do, were this to do again?
I would not change my peace of conscience
For all the wealth of Europe. She stirs; here's life.
Return, fair soul, from darkness, and lead mine
Out of this sensible hell. She's warm, she breathes.
Upon thy pale lips I will melt my heart
To store them with fresh color. Who's there?
Some cordial drink! Alas, I dare not call.
So pity would destroy pity. Her eye opes,
And heaven in it seems to ope, that late was shut,

304 **quicken** refresh
305 **challenge** demand
309 **study** think; **do** give
321 **The . . . up** wolves were thought to uncover the bodies of those murdered and leave them exposed
324 **pension** payment
327 **him** God
328 **man** man's
331 **are** that are
333 **chained bullets** (cannon balls linked by a chain were used in naval warfare to destroy masts and rigging)
335 **Doth . . . blood** destroy many kindred
336 **ta'en** experienced
345 **honest** moral
346 **I'll . . . owl-light** (the badger is nocturnal)
348 **painted** (1) false; (2) specious; (3) superficial
349 **vain hopes** (i.e., for advancement)
351–3 **What . . . Europe** if I were asked to do this again, I would not exchange my peace of conscience to do it (registering a change of attitude)
355 **sensible hell** world of senses; palpable
357 **Who's there?** (Bosola's stricken mind, thinking the Duchess still lives, now imagines assistance has arrived)
358 **cordial** heart-restoring
359 **So . . . pity** i.e., piteous (calling out would recall pitiless Ferdinand)

To take me up to mercy.
Duch. Antonio!
Bos. Yes, Madam, he is living.
The dead bodies you saw were but feigned statues;
He's reconciled to your brothers; the Pope hath wrought
The atonement.
Duch. Mercy!
She dies.
Bos. Oh, she's gone again. There the cords of life broke.
Oh, sacred innocence, that sweetly sleeps
On turtles' feathers, whilst a guilty conscience
Is a black register wherein is writ
All our good deeds and bad, a perspective
That shows us hell! That we cannot be suffered
To do good when we have a mind to it!
This is manly sorrow;
These tears, I am very certain, never grew
In my mother's milk. My estate is sunk
Below the degree of fear. Where were
These penitent fountains while she was living?
Oh, they were frozen up! Here is a sight
As direful to my soul as is the sword
Unto a wretch hath slain his father. Come, I'll bear thee hence
And execute thy last will; that's deliver
Thy body to the reverent dispose
Of some good women. That the cruel tyrant
Shall not deny me. Then I'll post to Milan
Where somewhat I will speedily enact
Worth my dejection.
Exit [, *with the body of the Duchess*].

Act V

Actus v, Scena i.

[*Enter* Antonio *and* Delio.]

Ant. What think you of my hope of reconcilement
To the Arragonian brethren?
Delio. I misdoubt it,
For though they have sent their letters of safe conduct
For your repair to Milan, they appear
But nets to entrap you. The Marquis of Pescara,
Under whom you hold certain land in cheat,
Much 'gainst his noble nature, hath been moved
To seize those lands, and some of his dependants
Are at this instant making it their suit
To be invested in your revenues.
I cannot think they mean well to your life
That do deprive you of your means of life,
Your living.
Ant. You are still an heretic
To any safety I can shape myself.

[*Enter* Pescara.]

Delio. Here comes the Marquis. I will make myself
Petitioner for some part of your land,
To know whither it is flying.
Ant. I pray do.
[*He retires.*]
Delio. Sir, I have a suit to you.
Pes. To me?
Delio. An easy one:
There is the Citadel of Saint Bennet,
With some demesnes, of late in the possession
Of Antonio Bologna. Please you bestow them on me?
Pes. You are my friend; but this is such a suit
Nor fit for me to give, nor you to take.
Delio. No, sir?
Pes. I will give you ample reason for't
Soon in private.

[*Enter* Julia.]

Here's the Cardinal's mistress.
Julia. My Lord, I am grown your poor petitioner,
And should be an ill beggar had I not
A great man's letter here, the Cardinal's,

---

365 **atonement** reconciliation
366 **cords of life** heart strings; when the heart breaks, the person dies
368 **turtles'** turtle-doves' (as birds concerned about their mates)
369 **register** account book
371 **suffered** allowed
375 **estate** condition
376 **Below . . . degree** past
377 **These . . . fountains** (of weeping)
383 **reverent dispose** worshipful disposal
385 **post** hurry
387 **dejection** overthrow
V (all scenes in this act take place at night)

V.i.2 misdoubt distrust
4 **repair** return
6 **cheat** escheat (land possessed on the condition that if one dies without heirs or commits treason or a felony, it returns to the previous owner)
8 **seize** take possession of (a technical term)
13 **heretic** one opposed
17 **whither . . . flying** who is assuming possession
19 **Bennet** Benedict
20 **demesnes** land occupied by the owner
21 **Please you** would you
23 **Nor fit** unfit

To court you in my favor.

[*Gives letter.*]

Pes. He entreats for you
The Citadel of Saint Bennet, that belonged
To the banished Bologna.

Julia. Yes.

Pes. I could not have thought of a friend I could
Rather pleasure with it. 'Tis yours.

Julia. Sir, I thank you.
And he shall know how doubly I am engaged
Both in your gift, and speediness of giving,
Which makes your grant the greater.

Exit.

Ant. [*Aside.*] How they fortify
Themselves with my ruin!

Delio. Sir, I am
Little bound to you.

Pes. Why?

Delio. Because you denied this suit to me, and gave't
To such a creature.

Pes. Do you know what it was?
It was Antonio's land. Not forfeited
By course of law, but ravished from his throat
By the Cardinal's entreaty. It were not fit
I should bestow so main a piece of wrong
Upon my friend; 'tis a gratification
Only due to a strumpet, for it is injustice.
Shall I sprinkle the pure blood of innocents
To make those followers I call my friends
Look ruddier upon me? I am glad
This land, ta'en from the owner by such wrong,
Returns again unto so foul an use
As salary for his lust. Learn, good Delio,
To ask noble things of me, and you shall find
I'll be a noble giver.

Delio. You instruct me well.

Ant. [*Aside.*] Why, here's a man now would fright impudence
From sauciest beggars.

Pes. Prince Ferdinand's come to Milan
Sick, as they give out, of an apoplexy;
But some say 'tis a frenzy. I am going
To visit him.

Exit.

Ant. 'Tis a noble old fellow.

[*He advances.*]

Delio. What course do you mean to take, Antonio?

Ant. This night I mean to venture all my fortune
(Which is no more than a poor ling'ring life)
To the Cardinal's worst of malice. I have got
Private access to his chamber, and intend
To visit him, about the mid of night,
As once his brother did our noble Duchess.
It may be that the sudden apprehension
Of danger – for I'll go in mine own shape –
When he shall see it fraught with love and duty,
May draw the poison out of him, and work
A friendly reconcilement. If it fail,
Yet it shall rid me of this infamous calling;
For better fall once, than be ever falling.

Delio. I'll second you in all danger, and howe'er,
My life keeps rank with yours.

Ant. You are still my loved, and best friend.

Exeunt.

Scena ii.

[*Enter* Pescara *and a* Doctor.]

Pes. Now doctor, may I visit your patient?

Doc. If't please your Lordship. But he's instantly
To take the air here in the gallery
By my direction.

Pes. Pray thee, what's his disease?

Doc. A very pestilent disease, my Lord,
They call lycanthropia.

Pes. What's that?
I need a dictionary to't.

Doc. I'll tell you:
In those that are possessed with't there o'erflows
Such melancholy humor, they imagine
Themselves to be transformed into wolves,
Steal forth to churchyards in the dead of night,
And dig dead bodies up. As two nights since
One met the Duke, 'bout midnight in a lane
Behind Saint Mark's church, with the leg of a man
Upon his shoulder, and he howed fearfully;

44 **so . . . wrong** so great a portion of what has been wrongfully obtained
46 **strumpet** prostitute
49 **ruddier** more favorably
52 **salary** payment
55 **fright** refuse
56 **sauciest** most persistent
58 **give out** people say
59 **frenzy** a delirious madness induced by extreme anger or choler

60 **old fellow** (in fact, Pescara died in 1525 aged thirty-six)
64 **malice** power to harm
70 **fraught** filled
73 **calling** vocation, position
75 **howe'er** whatever happens
V.ii.3 **take . . . air** treatment of melancholics included exposure only to warm, moist air and moderate exercise; **gallery** long room in a house designed for walking
5 **pestilent** (1) deadly; (2) poisonous

Said he was a wolf, only the difference
Was, a wolf's skin was hairy on the outside,
His on the inside; bade them take their swords,
Rip up his flesh, and try. Straight I was sent
for,
And having ministered to him, found his
Grace
Very well recovered.
Pes. I am glad on't.
Doc. Yet not without some fear
Of a relapse. If he grow to his fit again
I'll go a nearer way to work with him
Than ever Paracelsus dreamed of. If
They'll give me leave I'll buffet his madness
out of him.

[*Enter* Ferdinand, Malateste, *and* Cardinal; Bosola *follows and watches, apart.*]

Stand aside; he comes.
Ferd. Leave me.
Mal. Why doth your Lordship love this
solitariness?
Ferd. Eagles commonly fly alone: they are crows, daws, and starlings that flock together. Look, what's that follows me?
Mal. Nothing, my Lord.
Ferd. Yes.
Mal. 'Tis your shadow.
Ferd. Stay it, let it not haunt me.
Mal. Impossible: if you move, and the sun shine –
Ferd. I will throttle it.
[*Throws himself down on his shadow.*]
Mal. Oh, my Lord: you are angry with nothing.
Ferd. You are a fool! How is't possible I should catch my shadow unless I fall upon't? When I go to hell, I mean to carry a bribe; for look you, good gifts evermore make way for the worst persons.
Pes. Rise, good my Lord.
Ferd. I am studying the art of patience.
Pes. 'Tis a noble virtue.
Ferd. To drive six snails before me, from this town to Moscow; neither use goad nor whip to them, but let them take their own time. The patientest man i'th' world match me for an experiment – and I'll crawl after like a sheep-biter.
Card. Force him up.
[*They raise him.*]
Ferd. Use me well, you were best. What I have done, I have done; I'll confess nothing.
Doc. Now let me come to him. Are you mad, my Lord? Are you out of your princely wits?
Ferd. What's he?
Pes. Your doctor.
Ferd. Let me have his beard sawed off and his eyebrows filed more civil.
Doc. I must do mad tricks with him, for that's the only way on't. I have brought your Grace a salamander's skin, to keep you from sun-burning.
Ferd. I have cruel sore eyes.
Doc. The white of a cockatrix's egg is present remedy.
Ferd. Let it be a new-laid one, you were best.
Hide me from him; physicians are like kings,
They brook no contradiction.
Doc. Now he begins to fear me; now let me alone with him.
Card. How now, put off your gown!
Doc. Let me have some forty urinals filled with rose-water. He and I'll go pelt one another with them now he begins to fear me. Can you fetch a frisk, sir? Let him go, let him go upon my peril. I find by his eye he stands in awe of me; I'll make him as tame as a dormouse.
Ferd. Can you fetch your frisks, sir? I will stamp him into a cullis, flay off his skin, to cover one of the anatomies this rogue hath set i'th' cold yonder, in Barber-Chirurgeons' Hall. Hence, hence, you are all of you like beasts for sacrifice; there's nothing left of you, but tongue, and belly, flattery, and lechery. [*Exit.*]

---

24 **nearer** quicker, more direct
25 **Paracelsus** a famous medical authority and magician (1493–1541)
26 **They'll** if they will; **buffet** whip
29 **Why . . . solitariness?** company was prescribed for melancholics; solitude was avoided
31 **daws** jackdaws
31–41 **Look . . . upon't?** (in Whitney's emblem book [1586], guilt is shown holding a sword and fearful of his shadow)
36 **Stay** stop
43–4 **good . . . persons** (with reference to the common practice of bribing jailers)
52 **sheep-biter** dog who worries or tends sheep
61 **civil** becoming, refined
62 **mad tricks** a common, but disputed, method of treating madness
64 **salamander's skin** (this was thought to resist fire, as salamanders were said to live in it)
67 **cockatrix's egg** (the imaginary cockatrice produced eggs that, if eaten, caused death; cf. Isaiah 59: 4–8); **present** immediate
71 **brook** tolerate
74 **put . . . gown** (to prepare for other, more violent treatments)
78 **fetch a frisk** cut a caper (a quick dance step)
80 **dormouse** (as a small, timid animal)
81 **stamp** trample
82 **cullis** broth; **flay** strip
83 **anatomies** (dead bodies, especially of executed criminals, were often taken to the Barber-Surgeons' Hall near Cripplegate in London to be dissected in lecture/demonstrations or displayed in the museum there)
86–7 **tongue, and belly** i.e., flattery and appetite (in ancient rituals, entrails were left as an offering to the gods)

Pes. Doctor, he did not fear you throughly.
Doc. True, I was somewhat too forward.
[*Exit.*]
Bos. Mercy upon me, what a fatal judgment
Hath fall'n upon this Ferdinand!
Pes. Knows your Grace
What accident hath brought unto the Prince
This strange distraction?
Card. [*Aside.*] I must feign somewhat. [*To them.*] Thus they say it grew:
You have heard it rumored for these many years,
None of our family dies, but there is seen
The shape of an old woman, which is given
By tradition to us to have been murdered
By her nephews for her riches; such a figure
One night, as the prince sat up late at's book,
Appeared to him. When crying out for help,
The gentlemen of's chamber found his Grace
All on a cold sweat, altered much in face
And language; since which apparition,
He hath grown worse and worse, and I much fear
He cannot live.
Bos. Sir, I would speak with you.
Pes. We'll leave your Grace,
Wishing to the sick Prince, our noble Lord,
All health of mind and body.
Card. You are most welcome.
[*Exeunt all except* Cardinal *and* Bosola.]
[*Aside.*] Are you come? So: this fellow must not know
By any means I had intelligence
In our Duchess' death; for, though I counseled it,
The full of all th' engagement seemed to grow
From Ferdinand. [*To him.*] Now, sir, how fares our sister?
I do not think but sorrow makes her look
Like to an oft-dyed garment. She shall now
Taste comfort from me. Why do you look so wildly?
Oh, the fortune of your master here, the Prince,
Dejects you. But be you of happy comfort;
If you'll do one thing for me I'll entreat,
Though he had a cold tomb-stone o'er his bones,
I'd make you what you would be.
Bos. Anything –
Give it me in a breath, and let me fly to 't:
They that think long, small expedition win,
For musing much o'th' end, cannot begin.

[*Enter* Julia.]

Julia. Sir, will you come in to supper?
Card. I am busy, leave me.
Julia. [*Aside.*] What an excellent shape hath that fellow!
Exit.
Card. 'Tis thus: Antonio lurks here in Milan;
Inquire him out, and kill him. While he lives
Our sister cannot marry, and I have thought
Of an excellent match for her. Do this, and style me
Thy advancement.
Bos. But by what means shall I find him out?
Card. There is a gentleman called Delio,
Here in the camp that hath been long approved
His loyal friend. Set eye upon that fellow,
Follow him to mass – may be Antonio,
Although he do account religion
But a school-name, for fashion of the world
May accompany him; or else go inquire out
Delio's confessor, and see if you can bribe
Him to reveal it; there are a thousand ways
A man might find to trace him. As to know
What fellows haunt the Jews for taking up
Great sums of money, for sure he's in want;
Or else to go to th' picture-makers and learn
Who bought her picture lately. Some of these
Happily may take –
Bos. Well, I'll not freeze i'th' business;

88 **throughly** thoroughly
92 **accident** circumstance
93 **distraction** madness
96 **but** except
105–6 **I . . . live** (the Cardinal may already have determined the need for Ferdinand to die and so invents this story; cf. lines 231–2 below)
113 **full . . . engagement** (1) responsibility; (2) blame as intelligencer; **seemed** must seem
116 **oft-dyed** decaying, ravaged
121 **Though . . . bones** even if consequently he were dead
123 **Give . . . to 't** (1) tell me and I will be quick to act; (2) restore your sister's life (breath) and I am content
124 **small expedition** little progress
127 **shape** figure, body
131–2 **style . . . advancement** name me (as the means for) your preferment
134 **camp** military encampment; **approved** confirmed
139 **school-name** a creation of the Church Fathers
144 **Jews** (as synonym for usurers); **taking up** borrowing
147 **bought . . . lately** (apparently he thinks Antonio will seek some remembrance of his wife)
148 **Happily** haply, perhaps

I would see that wretched thing, Antonio,
Above all sights i'th' world.
Card. Do, and be happy.
Exit.
Bos. This fellow doth breed basilisks in's eyes,
He's nothing else but murder. Yet he seems
Not to have notice of the Duchess' death.
'Tis his cunning: I must follow his example;
There cannot be a surer way to trace
Than that of an old fox.

[*Enter* Julia *pointing a pistol at him.*]

Julia. So, sir, you are well met.
Bos. How now?
Julia. Nay, the doors are fast enough.
Now, sir, I will make you confess your
treachery.
Bos. Treachery?
Julia. Yes, confess to me
Which of my women 'twas you hired to put
Love-powder into my drink?
Bos. Love-powder!
Julia. Yes,
When I was at Malfi –
Why should I fall in love with such a face else?
I have already suffered for thee so much pain,
The only remedy to do me good
Is to kill my longing.
Bos. Sure your pistol holds
Nothing but perfumes or kissing-comfits.
Excellent lady,
You have a pretty way on't to discover
Your longing. Come, come, I'll disarm you,
And arm you thus, yet this is wondrous
strange.
Julia. Compare thy form, and my eyes together,
You'll find my love no such great miracle.
Now you'll say
I am wanton. This nice modesty in ladies
Is but a troublesome familiar
That haunts them.
Bos. Know you me, I am a blunt soldier.
Julia. The better –
Sure, there wants fire where there are no lively
sparks
Of roughness.
Bos. And I want compliment.
Julia. Why ignorance
In courtship cannot make you do amiss
If you have a heart to do well.
Bos. You are very fair.
Julia. Nay, if you lay beauty to my charge,
I must plead unguilty.
Bos. Your bright eyes
Carry a quiver of darts in them, sharper
Than sunbeams.
Julia. You will mar me with commendation,
Put yourself to the charge of courting me
Whereas now I woo you.
Bos. [*Aside.*] I have it, I will work upon this
creature –
[*To her.*] Let us grow most amorously familiar.
If the great Cardinal now should see me thus,
Would he not count me a villain?
Julia. No; he might count me a wanton,
Not lay a scruple of offense on you;
For if I see and steal a diamond,
The fault is not i'th' stone, but in me the thief
That purloins it. I am sudden with you;
We that are great women of pleasure use to cut
off
These uncertain wishes, and unquiet longings,
And in an instant join the sweet delight
And the pretty excuse together. Had you been
i'th' street,
Under my chamber window, even there
I should have courted you.
Bos. Oh, you are an excellent lady.
Julia. Bid me do somewhat for you presently,
To express I love you.
Bos. I will, and if you love me,
Fail not to effect it.
The Cardinal is grown wondrous melancholy;
Demand the cause. Let him not put you off
With feigned excuse; discover the main
ground on't.
Julia. Why would you know this?
Bos. I have depended on him,
And I hear that he is fall'n in some disgrace
With the Emperor. If he be, like the mice

149–50 **I'll . . . world** (this reply can be seen as equivocal)
150 **happy** rewarded
153 **have notice** be aware
155 **way to trace** path to follow
167 **kissing-comfits** sweetmeats used to sweeten the breath
169 **pretty** (1) clever; (2) unusual; **discover** show
171 **arm** embrace
172 **form** shape
175 **nice** fastidious
176 **familiar** familiar spirit; familiar devil (usually companions associated with witches or the damned as in *Dr. Faustus*)
179 **wants fire** is little passion
179–80 **sparks . . . roughness** aggressive moves
180 **want compliment** lack manners
182 **If . . . well** (1) if your love is awakened; (2) if you are sexually aroused
194 **scruple** tiniest amount
198 **use** make our practice
204 **presently** at once
212–13 **mice . . . houses** (proverbial)

That forsake falling houses, I would shift
To other dependance.
Julia. You shall not need follow the wars;
I'll be your maintenance.
Bos. And I your loyal servant –
But I cannot leave my calling.
Julia. Not leave
An ungrateful general, for the love of a sweet lady?
You are like some, cannot sleep in feather-beds,
But must have blocks for their pillows.
Bos. Will you do this?
Julia. Cunningly.
Bos. Tomorrow I'll expect th' intelligence.
Julia. Tomorrow? Get you into my cabinet,
You shall have it with you. Do not delay me,
No more than I do you; I am like one
That is condemned. I have my pardon promised,
But I would see it sealed. Go, get you in,
You shall see me wind my tongue about his heart
Like a skein of silk.

[*Exit* Bosola.]

[*Enter* Cardinal, *followed by* Servants.]

Card. Where are you?
Serv. Here.
Card. Let none upon your lives
Have conference with the Prince Ferdinand,
Unless I know it.

[*Exeunt* Servants.]

– [*Aside.*] In this distraction
He may reveal the murder.
Yon's my ling'ring consumption.
I am weary of her; and by any means
Would be quit of.
Julia. How now, my Lord?
What ails you?
Card. Nothing.
Julia. Oh, you are much altered.
Come, I must be your secretary, and remove
This lead from off your bosom. What's the matter?
Card. I may not tell you.
Julia. Are you so far in love with sorrow,
You cannot part with part of it? Or think you
I cannot love your Grace when you are sad,
As well as merry? Or do you suspect
I, that have been a secret to your heart
These many winters, cannot be the same
Unto your tongue?
Card. Satisfy thy longing.
The only way to make thee keep my counsel
Is not to tell thee.
Julia. Tell your echo this,
Or flatterers that like echoes still report
What they hear though most imperfect, and not me.
For, if that you be true unto yourself,
I'll know.
Card. Will you rack me?
Julia. No, judgment shall
Draw it from you. It is an equal fault
To tell one's secrets unto all or none.
Card. The first argues folly.
Julia. But the last tyranny.
Card. Very well; why imagine I have committed
Some secret deed which I desire the world
May never hear of.
Julia. Therefore may not I know it?
You have concealed for me as great a sin
As adultery. Sir, never was occasion
For perfect trial of my constancy
Till now. Sir, I beseech you.
Card. You'll repent it.
Julia. Never.
Card. It hurries thee to ruin. I'll not tell thee –
Be well advised, and think what danger 'tis
To receive a prince's secrets. They that do,
Had need have their breasts hooped with adamant
To contain them. I pray thee yet be satisfied;
Examine thine own frailty; 'tis more easy
To tie knots than unloose them. 'Tis a secret
That, like a ling'ring poison, may chance lie
Spread in thy veins, and kill thee seven year hence.
Julia. Now you dally with me.
Card. No more; thou shalt know it.
By my appointment, the great Duchess of Malfi
And two of her young children, four nights since,
Were strangled.
Julia. Oh, heaven, sir, what have you done?

219 some some who
226 sealed i.e., signed and sealed; fully executed
235 quit rid
237 secretary confidant
238 lead weight
251 if...yourself if you keep faith with me, as your other self
252 rack torture
266 adamant diamond; the hardest metal
270–1 chance...veins perhaps lie dormant in your blood

Card. How now? How settles this? think you your bosom
Will be a grave, dark and obscure enough,
For such a secret?
Julia. You have undone yourself, Sir.
Card. Why?
Julia. It lies not in me to conceal it.
Card. No?
Come, I will swear you to't upon this book.
Julia. Most religiously.
Card. Kiss it.
[*She kisses the book.*]
Now you shall never utter it; thy curiosity
Hath undone thee. Thou'rt poison'd with that book;
Because I knew thou couldst not keep my counsel,
I have bound thee to't by death.

[*Enter* Bosola.]

Bos. For pity-sake, hold!
Card. Ha, Bosola!
Julia. I forgive you –
This equal piece of justice you have done,
For I betrayed your counsel to that fellow.
He overheard it; that was the cause I said
It lay not in me to conceal it.
Bos. Oh, foolish woman,
Couldst not thou have poisoned him?
Julia. 'Tis weakness,
Too much to think what should have been done. I go,
I know not whither.
[*Dies.*]
Card. Wherefore com'st thou hither?
Bos. That I might find a great man, like yourself,
Not out of his wits as the Lord Ferdinand,
To remember my service.
Card. I'll have thee hewed in pieces.
Bos. Make not yourself such a promise of that life
Which is not yours to dispose of.
Card. Who placed thee here?
Bos. Her lust, as she intended.
Card. Very well,
Now you know me for your fellow murderer.
Bos. And wherefore should you lay fair marble colors
Upon your rotten purposes to me?
Unless you imitate some that do plot great treasons,
And when they have done, go hide themselves i'th' graves
Of those were actors in't?
Card. No more, there is a fortune attends thee.
Bos. Shall I go sue to Fortune any longer?
'Tis the fool's pilgrimage.
Card. I have honors in store for thee.
Bos. There are a many ways that conduct to seeming
Honor, and some of them very dirty ones.
Card. Throw to the devil
Thy melancholy: the fire burns well,
What need we keep a stirring of't, and make
A greater smother? Thou wilt kill Antonio?
Bos. Yes.
Card. Take up that body.
Bos. I think I shall
Shortly grow the common bier for churchyards.
Card. I will allow thee some dozen of attendants
To aid thee in the murder.
Bos. Oh, by no means.
Physicians that apply horse-leeches to any rank swelling use to cut off their tails that the blood may run through them the faster. Let me have no train when I go to shed blood, lest it make me have a greater when I ride to the gallows.
Card. Come to me after midnight, to help to remove that body to her own lodging. I'll give out she died o'th' plague; 'twill breed the less inquiry after her death.
Bos. Where's Castruchio, her husband?
Card. He's rode to Naples to take possession
Of Antonio's citadel.
Bos. Believe me, you have done a very happy turn.
Card. Fail not to come. There is the master-key
Of our lodgings; and by that you may conceive
What trust I plant in you.
Bos. You shall find me ready.
Exit Cardinal.
Oh, poor Antonio, though nothing be so needful
To thy estate as pity, yet I find

276 How . . . this? what do you mean by this?
279 It . . . me I am unable
287 equal even-handed
294 I . . . whither (sermons often preached of life as a journey to an unknown destination, an undiscovered country)
297 remember reward
302 fair marble colors i.e., a good face (dry and rotten wood was often painted to resemble marble)
304 treasons i.e., betrayals
305–6 go . . . in't conceal their involvement by killing their accomplices
310 conduct lead
315 smother smoke
317 common . . . churchyards commonplace conveyers of the dead
320 horse-leeches insects used to suck out contaminated blood
323–4 lest . . . gallows lest I increase chances of being caught
331 turn (1) act of good will; (2) trick
336 estate condition, fortune

Nothing so dangerous. I must look to my footing.
In such slippery ice-pavements, men had need
To be frost-nailed well; they may break their necks else.
The precedent's here afore me. How this man
Bears up in blood! Seems fearless! Why, 'tis well:
Security some men call the suburbs of hell,
Only a dead wall between. Well, good Antonio,
I'll seek thee out, and all my care shall be
To put thee into safety from the reach
Of these most cruel biters, that have got
Some of thy blood already. It may be
I'll join with thee, in a most just revenge.
The weakest arm is strong enough that strikes
With the sword of justice. Still, methinks the Duchess
Haunts me: there, there! –
'Tis nothing but my melancholy.
Oh, Penitence, let me truly taste thy cup,
That throws men down, only to raise them up.
Exit.

Scena iii.

[*Enter* Antonio *and* Delio.] [*There is an*] Echo *from the* Duchess' *grave.*

Delio. Yon's the Cardinal's window. This fortification
Grew from the ruins of an ancient abbey;
And to yon side o'th' river lies a wall,
Piece of a cloister, which in my opinion
Gives the best echo that you ever heard,
So hollow, and so dismal, and withal
So plain in the distinction of our words,
That many have supposed it is a spirit
That answers.
Ant. I do love these ancient ruins.
We never tread upon them but we set
Our foot upon some reverend history.
And questionless, here in this open court,
Which now lies naked to the injuries
Of stormy weather, some men lie interred
Loved the church so well, and gave so largely to't,
They thought it should have canopied their bones
Till doomsday. But all things have their end:
Churches and cities, which have diseases like to men,
Must have like death that we have.
Echo. *Like death that we have.*
Delio. Now the echo hath caught you.
Ant. It groaned methought, and gave
A very deadly accent.
Echo. *Deadly accent.*
Delio. I told you 'twas a pretty one: you may make it
A huntsman, or a falconer, a musician,
Or a thing of sorrow.
Echo. *A thing of sorrow.*
Ant. Aye, sure; that suits it best.
Echo. *That suits it best.*
Ant. 'Tis very like my wife's voice.
Echo. *Aye, wife's voice.*
Delio. Come, let us walk farther from't.
I would not have you go to th' Cardinal's tonight;
Do not.
Echo. *Do not.*
Delio. Wisdom doth not more moderate wasting sorrow
Than time. Take time for't; be mindful of thy safety.
Echo. *Be mindful of thy safety.*
Ant. Necessity compels me.
Make scrutiny throughout the passages
Of your own life; you'll find it impossible
To fly your fate.
Echo. *– Oh, fly your fate!*
Delio. Hark – the dead stones seem to have pity on you
And give you good counsel.
Ant. Echo, I will not talk with thee,
For thou art a dead thing.
Echo. *Thou art a dead thing.*
Ant. My Duchess is asleep now,
And her little ones, I hope, sweetly. Oh, heaven,
Shall I never see her more?
Echo. *Never see her more.*

339 **frost-nailed** given hob-nailed boots
341 **Bears . . . blood** keeps up courage
342 **Security** over-confidence; **suburbs** beginning
343 **dead** (1) inert; (2) unbroken
346 **biters** (1) backbiters who betray you; (2) bloodsuckers who use you up
347 **Some . . . blood** i.e., his children
352 **melancholy** sadness of remorse which replaces the earlier bitterness of the malcontent
353–4 **Oh . . . up** i.e., repentance is bitter but it can lead to salvation
V.iii.6 **dismal** foreboding
11 **reverend** venerable
15 **Loved** who loved
18 **diseases** disturbances

Ant. I marked not one repetition of the echo
But that, and on the sudden, a clear light
Presented me a face folded in sorrow.
Delio. Your fancy, merely.
Ant. Come; I'll be out of this ague;
For to live thus is not indeed to live.
It is a mockery, and abuse of life –
I will not henceforth save myself by halves;
Lose all, or nothing.
Delio. Your own virtue save you!
I'll fetch your eldest son, and second you.
It may be that the sight of his own blood
Spread in so sweet a figure may beget
The more compassion.
Ant. However, fare you well.
Though in our miseries Fortune have a part,
Yet in our noble suff'rings she hath none –
Contempt of pain, that we may call our own.
Exeunt.

Scena iv.

[*Enter* Cardinal, Pescara, Malateste, Roderigo, *and* Grisolan.]

Card. You shall not watch tonight by the sick Prince,
His Grace is very well recovered.
Mal. Good my Lord, suffer us.
Card. Oh, by no means;
The noise, and change of object in his eye,
Doth more distract him. I pray, all to bed,
And though you hear him in his violent fit,
Do not rise, I entreat you.
Pes. So Sir, we shall not.
Card. Nay, I must have you promise
Upon your honors, for I was enjoined to't
By himself; and he seemed to urge it sensibly.
Pes. Let our honors bind this trifle.
Card. Nor any of your followers.
Mal. Neither.
Card. It may be to make trial of your promise
When he's asleep, myself will rise, and feign
Some of his mad tricks, and cry out for help,
And feign myself in danger.
Mal. If your throat were cutting,
I'd not come at you, now I have protested against it.
Card. Why, I thank you.
[*Withdraws.*]

Gris. 'Twas a foul storm tonight.
Rod. The Lord Ferdinand's chamber shook like an osier.
Mal. 'Twas nothing but pure kindness in the devil
To rock his own child.
Exeunt [*all except the* Cardinal].
Card. The reason why I would not suffer these
About my brother is because at midnight
I may with better privacy convey
Julia's body to her own lodging.
Oh, my conscience!
I would pray now, but the devil takes away my heart
For having any confidence in prayer.
About this hour I appointed Bosola
To fetch the body. When he hath served my turn,
He dies.
Exit.

[*Enter* Bosola.]

Bos. Hah? 'twas the Cardinal's voice. I heard him name
Bosola, and my death. Listen, I hear one's footing.

[*Enter* Ferdinand.]

Ferd. Strangling is a very quiet death.
Bos. [*Aside.*] Nay then, I see I must stand upon my guard.
Ferd. What say' to that? Whisper, softly. Do you agree to't?
So it must be done i'th' dark. The Cardinal
Would not for a thousand pounds the doctor should see it.
Exit.
Bos. My death is plotted; here's the consequence of murder:
"We value not desert, nor Christian breath,
When we know black deeds must be cured with death."

[*Enter* Antonio *and* Servant.]

Serv. Here stay, Sir, and be confident, I pray.
I'll fetch you a dark lantern.
Exit.
Ant. Could I take him at his prayers,
There were hope of pardon.
Bos. Fall right my sword! [*Stabs him.*]

44 clear light (perhaps a vision or apparition)
45 folded enveloped
47 ague fever
53 his i.e., the Cardinal's
54 Spread displayed
V.iv.3 suffer allow

11 bind . . . trifle confirm our obedience to such a trivial matter
17 protested pledged
19 osier wicker basket
28 For from
36 say' say you

I'll not give thee so much leisure as to pray.
Ant. Oh, I am gone! Thou hast ended a long suit
In a minute.
Bos. What art thou?
Ant. A most wretched thing,
That only have thy benefit in death,
To appear myself.

[*Enter* Servant *with a light.*]

Serv. Where are you, Sir?
Ant. Very near my home. Bosola!
Serv. Oh, misfortune!
Bos. Smother thy pity, thou art dead else. Antonio!
The man I would have saved 'bove mine own life!
We are merely the stars' tennis-balls, struck and banded
Which way please them. Oh, good Antonio,
I'll whisper one thing in thy dying ear
Shall make thy heart break quickly. Thy fair Duchess
And two sweet children –
Ant. Their very names
Kindle a little life in me.
Bos. Are murdered!
Ant. Some men have wished to die
At the hearing of sad tidings. I am glad
That I shall do't in sadness; I would not now
Wish my wounds balmed, nor healed, for I have no use
To put my life to. In all our quest of greatness,
Like wanton boys whose pastime is their care,
We follow after bubbles, blown in th'air.
Pleasure of life, what is't? Only the good hours
Of an ague; merely a preparative to rest,
To endure vexation. I do not ask
The process of my death; only commend me
To Delio.
Bos. Break heart!
Ant. And let my son fly the courts of princes.
[*Dies.*]
Bos. Thou seem'st to have loved Antonio?
Serv. I brought him hither,
To have reconciled him to the Cardinal.
Bos. I do not ask thee that.
Take him up, if thou tender thine own life,
And bear him where the Lady Julia
Was wont to lodge. Oh, my fate moves swift!
I have this Cardinal in the forge already.
Now I'll bring him to th' hammer. Oh, direful misprision!
I will not imitate things glorious,
No more than base. I'll be mine own example.
On, on, and look thou represent, for silence,
The thing thou bear'st.
Exeunt.

Scena v.

[*Enter* Cardinal, *with a book.*]

Card. I am puzzled in a question about hell:
He says, in hell there's one material fire,
And yet it shall not burn all men alike.
Lay him by; how tedious is a guilty conscience!
When I look into the fish-ponds in my garden,
Methinks I see a thing, armed with a rake,
That seems to strike at me:

[*Enter* Bosola, *and* Servant *with Antonio's body.*]

Now! art thou come?
Thou look'st ghastly:
There sits in thy face some great determination,
Mixed with some fear.
Bos. Thus it lightens into action:
I am come to kill thee.
Card. Hah? help! our guard!
Bos. Thou art deceived;
They are out of thy howling.
Card. Hold, and I will faithfully divide
Revenues with thee.
Bos. Thy prayers and proffers
Are both unseasonable.
Card. Raise the watch!
We are betrayed!
Bos. I have confined your flight:
I'll suffer your retreat to Julia's chamber,
But no further.
Card. Help! we are betrayed!

[*Enter, above* Pescara, Malateste, Roderigo, *and* Grisolan.]

47 **suit** (1) petition; (2) quest
49 **benefit** assistance
50 **appear** (1) be; (2) reveal
51 **home** eternal resting place (i.e., death)
54 **banded** bandied; randomly struck
62 **sadness** earnest
70 **process** story
76 **tender** care for, value
80 **misprision** (1) concealment (of treason); (2) mistake
83–4 **represent . . . bear'st** be as silent as the corpse you carry
V.v.l s.d. ***with a book*** (a common way of staging a melancholic)
4 **Lay . . . by** put this aside; **tedious** (1) troublesome; (2) painful; (3) wearisome
8 **ghastly** (1) ghostly; (2) fearful
9 **determination** resolution
10 **lightens** ignites, enlivens
16 **watch** night guard

Mal. Listen.
Card. My dukedom for rescue!
Rod. Fie upon his counterfeiting!
Mal. Why, 'tis not the Cardinal.
Rod. Yes, yes, 'tis he.
But I'll see him hanged ere I'll go down to him.
Card. Here's a plot upon me, I am assaulted! I am lost,
Unless some rescue!
Gris. He doth this pretty well!
But it will not serve to laugh me out of mine honor.
Card. The sword's at my throat.
Rod. You would not bawl so loud then.
Mal. Come, come.
Let's go to bed. He told us thus much aforehand.
Pes. He wished you should not come at him. But believe't,
The accent of the voice sounds not in jest.
I'll down to him, howsoever, and with engines
Force ope the doors.
[*Exit above.*]
Rod. Let's follow him aloof,
And note how the Cardinal will laugh at him.

[*Exeunt, above,* Malateste, Roderigo, *and* Grisolan.]

Bos. There's for you first –
He kills the Servant.
'Cause you shall not unbarricade the door
To let in rescue.
Card. What cause hast thou to pursue my life?
Bos. Look there.
Card. Antonio!
Bos. Slain by my hand unwittingly.
Pray, and be sudden; when thou killed'st thy sister,
Thou took'st from Justice her most equal balance,
And left her naught but her sword.
Card. Oh, mercy!
Bos. Now it seems thy greatness was only outward;
For thou fall'st faster of thyself than calamity
Can drive thee. I'll not waste longer time. There!
[*Stabs him.*]
Card. Thou hast hurt me!
Bos. Again!
[*Stabs him again.*]
Card. Shall I die like a leveret
Without any resistance? Help, help, help!
I am slain!

[*Enter* Ferdinand.]

Ferd. Th'alarum! Give me a fresh horse.
Rally the vaunt-guard, or the day is lost.
Yield, yield! I give you the honor of arms,
Shake my sword over you. Will you yield?
Card. Help me, I am your brother.
Ferd. The devil?
My brother fight upon the adverse party?
There flies your ransom.
He wounds the Cardinal, and in the scuffle gives Bosola his death-wound.
Card. Oh, Justice!
I suffer now for what hath former been:
"Sorrow is held the eldest child of sin."
Ferd. Now you're brave fellows. Caesar's fortune was harder than Pompey's; Caesar died in the arms of prosperity, Pompey at the feet of disgrace. You both died in the field. The pain's nothing. Pain many times is taken away with the apprehension of greater, as the toothache with the sight of a barber that comes to pull it out. There's philosophy for you.
Bos. Now my revenge is perfect.
He kills Ferdinand.
Sink, thou main cause
Of my undoing! The last part of my life
Hath done me best service.
Ferd. Give me some wet hay, I am broken-winded.
I do account this world but a dog-kennel.
I will vault credit, and affect high pleasures,
Beyond death.
Bos. He seems to come to himself,
Now he's so near the bottom.
Ferd. My sister! Oh, my sister! There's the cause on't:
"Whether we fall by ambition, blood, or lust,
Like diamonds, we are cut with our own dust."

---

31 **engines** implements
35 **'Cause** so that
43 **fall'st faster** i.e., the Cardinal proves more cowardly when confronted with death
45 **leveret** young hare (and so weak and no challenge in hunting)
47–53 (Ferdinand imagines he is fighting a battle)
48 **vaunt-guard** vanguard
49 **I . . . arms** I treat you as a soldier (allowing him the chance to surrender)
53 **flies . . . ransom** being dead, ransom is no longer possible
56 **brave** splendid
62 **barber** barber-surgeons also practiced dentistry
67 **wet hay** a customary cure for broken-winded horses
69 **vault credit** overleap (1) expectation; (2) reputation; **affect** aspire to
70 **come to himself** recover his wits
71 **the bottom** (1) of Fortune's wheel; (2) death
73 **blood** family
73–4 **"Whether . . . dust"** (having thought of his sister and lust, Ferdinand's reference here may be to the two of them rather than humanity generally; as diamonds cut diamonds)

[*Dies.*]

Card. Thou hast thy payment too.
Bos. Yes, I hold my weary soul in my teeth,
'Tis ready to part from me. I do glory
That thou, which stood'st like a huge pyramid
Begun upon a large and ample base,
Shalt end in a little point, a kind of nothing.

[*Enter* Pescara, Malateste, Roderigo, *and* Grisolan.]

Pes. How now, my Lord?
Mal. Oh, sad disaster!
Rod. How comes this?
Bos. Revenge for the Duchess of Malfi, murdered
By th' Arragonian brethren; for Antonio,
Slain by this hand; for lustful Julia,
Poisoned by this man; and lastly, for myself,
That was an actor in the main of all
Much 'gainst mine own good nature, yet i'th' end
Neglected.
Pes. How now, my Lord?
Card. Look to my brother:
He gave us these large wounds, as we were struggling
Here i'th' rushes. And now, I pray, let me
Be laid by, and never thought of.

[*Dies.*]

Pes. How fatally, it seems, he did withstand
His own rescue.
Mal. Thou wretched thing of blood,
How came Antonio by his death?
Bos. In a mist. I know not how –
Such a mistake as I have often seen
In a play. Oh, I am gone! –
We are only like dead walls, or vaulted graves,
That ruined, yields no echo. Fare you well.
It may be pain, but no harm to me to die
In so good a quarrel. Oh, this gloomy world!
In what a shadow, or deep pit of darkness,
Doth womanish and fearful mankind live!
Let worthy minds ne'er stagger in distrust
To suffer death, or shame for what is just.
Mine is another voyage.

[*Dies.*]

Pes. The noble Delio, as I came to th' palace,
Told me of Antonio's being here, and showed me
A pretty gentleman, his son and heir.

Enter Delio [*with* Antonio's Son].

Mal. Oh, sir, you come too late!
Delio. I heard so, and
Was armed for't ere I came. Let us make noble use
Of this great ruin; and join all our force
To establish this young, hopeful gentleman
In's mother's right. These wretched eminent things
Leave no more fame behind 'em than should one
Fall in a frost, and leave his print in snow;
As soon as the sun shines, it ever melts,
Both form, and matter. I have ever thought
Nature doth nothing so great, for great men,
As when she's pleased to make them lords of truth:
"Integrity of life is fame's best friend,
Which nobly, beyond death, shall crown the end."

Exeunt

[FINIS.]

76 in . . . teeth (common belief held that the soul left the body at death through the mouth)
86 main chief part
90 rushes (green rushes were used as floor coverings in houses and on theater stages)
98 dead continuous
101 quarrel claim
111 ere before
114 right (1) inheritance; (2) position
121 Integrity (1) wholeness; (2) honesty; (3) innocence

The Changeling

Thomas Middleton and William Rowley

Illustration from the 1657 edition of *The Triumphs of Gods Revenge* showing some major episodes and two views of the castle in Reynolds's "A Spanish History."

The raw power and intensity of *The Changeling* is unparalleled in Jacobean tragedy: nowhere else do we find such naked passion unleashed before the terrible physical and mental attraction of unalloyed evil. From the outset the gentleman servant De Flores is obsessed with his master's daughter, the beautiful Beatrice-Joanna: "I'll please myself with sight Of her at all opportunities"; "Her fingers touched me! She smells all amber." As he contemplates raping her, the thought of it "ravishes" him just as he thinks it will ravish her:

Oh, my blood!
Methinks I feel her in mine arms already,
Her wanton fingers combing out this beard,
And being pleased, praising this bad face.
Hunger and pleasure, they'll commend sometimes
Slovenly dishes, and feed heartily on 'em;
Nay, which is stranger, refuse daintier for 'em.
Some women are odd feeders.

Other unexpected images of desire can also convey his agony: "I live in pain now. That shooting eye Will burn my heart to cinders." Her response to him is equally forceful and equally complex. For Beatrice, De Flores is a "dog-face," a "serpent," a "villain," a "slave," a "standing toad-pool," even a "sepulcher," yet "This ominous ill-faced fellow more disturbs me Than all my other passions." Recognizing De Flores' reputation for loyal service to her father, Beatrice asks him to service her too and the very language of her request – "There's horror in my service, blood and danger" – suggests that, at least unconsciously, she knows all three words also signify copulation. Equally ardent, equally selfish, they transform each other into an unholy alliance. Now his language takes on an invitation that harbors consent to forthcoming sexual consummation:

Come, rise, and shroud your blushes in my bosom;
Silence is one of pleasure's best receipts.
Thy peace is wrought forever in this yielding.
'Las, how the turtle pants! Thou'lt love anon
What thou so fear'st and faint'st to venture on.

Subject to consuming passion, De Flores nevertheless sees things clearly; subject to a consuming selfishness, Beatrice does not. She is at first bewildered and frightened of the consequences of his service, of the "misery of sin." Yet in reminding her she is "A woman dipped in blood," De Flores may only be pronouncing what she herself seemed to confess earlier, separately unholy intentions wedding them in an unholy deed. De Flores requires that she

Look but into your conscience, read me there.
'Tis a true book, you'll find me there your equal,
Push, fly not to your birth, but settle you
In what the act has made you, y'are no more now;
Y'are the deed's creature; by that name
You lost your first condition, and I challenge you,
As peace and innocency has turned you out,
And made you one with me.

The wedding ring of Alonzo that Beatrice had hoped to escape with his death is returned to her in a ghastly and phallic form. These indelible scenes of temptation and reward – II.ii and III.iv – which rival Marlowe's *Dr. Faustus* in their extraordinary power and penetrating psychology remain even now compelling and intoxicating, threatening and yet irresistible in their emotional force and undertow. The language is at once lucidly explicit and overridden with implication and ambiguity, their heated negotiations unmatched elsewhere in Renaissance drama in energy and economy. Seduction and possession both exploit and degrade, release and imprison. Their fatal attraction to conspire in murder is only their first joint venture: fornication, spying, trespassing, bribery, and adultery will follow. "The east is not more beauteous than his service," Beatrice tells us; but even as she says this, De Flores' equally burning passion sets fire to Diaphanta's chambers and turns her, quite literally, to cinders. Creating such dreadful deeds, Beatrice and De Flores, as the play's central changelings, give the play's title its eternal shudder even as those same deeds recreate them. Yet who instigates this fatal attraction? Is it in the very nature of men and women? in the forceful regulations and restraints of a society that will not permit exceptions? in a protective society that finally cannot avoid the occasion for evil in a world of moral drift where moral corruption is always potentially present? Insofar as such questions are not limited to time and place, the play makes us complicit, too.

In their surprisingly seamless collaboration, Thomas Middleton and William Rowley thus transform the domestic murder and adultery central to *Arden of Faversham* and *A Woman Killed with Kindness* to a higher, if no less credible, pitch. The hackneyed scene of the dropped glove so common to tales of courtly love, for instance, used to initiate Horatio's courtship of Bel-imperia in *The Spanish Tragedy*, here becomes the first dark revelation of publicly undisclosed thoughts – Beatrice's fascination with her power over the repulsive De Flores and his own sexually graphic if frustrated yearnings: "She had rather wear my pelt tanned in a pair Of dancing pumps than I should thrust my fingers Into her sockets here." Like Kyd's earlier work, *The Changeling* is also a revenge play with its ghost and its dumb show, with its impatient Don Andrea revisited in the impatience of the frustrated revenger Tomazo. That said, however, the Spain of *The Changeling*, while confined to Alsemero's fortified castle and Alibius' guarded wards of madmen and fools as Kyd's play is confined to the Spanish court, is nevertheless a far more complicated place. In this, both are reliable cultural representations. At the time of *The Spanish Tragedy*, Catholic Spain was England's singularly dominant enemy, her threat for a time concentrated in the awful contemplations of the Armada of 1588. Under James, matters had gotten murkier when, on August 18, 1604, he signed a treaty with Spain permitting the English freedom of trade in European territories belonging to Spain and seemed to further their rapprochement by planning several royal marriages in the years following – between the infanta Ana and Prince Henry, then between the infanta Maria and Henry, and finally between Maria and Charles. Countering such attempts at reconciliation were continued fears of Spanish invasion, new English acts initiated by the Gunpowder Plot against Catholics, the execution of Ralegh after acts of piracy, and Spinola's invasion of western Germany that threatened James's daughter Elizabeth and her husband Frederick and Frederick's patrimony as the Elector Palatine. Such internal actions came to a head in 1621, just two years before *The Changeling*, when Parliament urged James to head a Protestant alliance against Spain and renounce any further marriage negotiations and James responded by suspending Parliament and imprisoning several members. Players patronized by Elizabeth of Bohemia, James's daughter, put on *The Changeling*, doubtless finding point in the hated Spaniard's comment to Alsemero in the opening scene about the Battle of Gibraltar "with those rebellious Hollanders," the leaders of the Protestant forces united with England and Germany against Spain at the same time nothing more is made of that conflict in the play. The whole sense of *changeling*, then, by which Beatrice challenges Spanish decrees of marriage in league with De Flores, captures the sense of potential subversion at the same time that it avoids any concrete instance that might bring on royal censorship. In the play's thus mirroring the unsettled attitudes toward Spain in 1623, can we argue that the nature of the changeling takes on a more useful function? Or does it merely deflect or postpone a necessity for commitment?

Indeed, the play insistently examines the function and nature of changelings in a procession of disguises, false reports, deceptions, spying, and distrust. Action proceeds by substitution – Alsemero replaces Alonzo in Beatrice's affections only to be displaced in turn by De Flores. Beatrice herself is displaced by Diaphanta on her wedding night. Perhaps even more unexpected, Isabella disguises herself as a madwoman in which she plays out what others would make of her in order to show Antonio the folly of his own madness. But naming Antonio in the cast of characters as "the changeling" may only be a decoy of the printed text, for in the play there is little difference between him and Franciscus: both men feign folly or madness to gain access to Isabella, yet both must finally rely on their constant wisdom or sanity to have any chance of winning her. In changing from devoted warrior to devoted lover, Alsemero claims to "keep the same church, same devotion," yet by Act IV we learn he has no faith at all, traveling with a medical kit that enables him to test women for virginity. Vermandero vows allegiance to Alonzo de Piracquo as the most eligible suitor for his daughter, yet he has no trouble replacing Alonzo with Alsemero when he thinks the former has taken flight: what remains constant for him is a match that is good for him as well as for his daughter while the particular person seems not to matter. Even Tomazo, with his reliable suspicions of Beatrice as a bride for his brother, once converted to a frenzied revenger changes only in degree, not in position. So too the shifting words on which key passages are ineluctably based – words such as *blood*, *will*, *deed*, *modesty*, *honor*, *honesty*, and *service* – rely on fixed social meanings from which they depart yet to which reference must always keep being made. In his *Art of English Poesie* (1589) with its listings of schemes and tropes the rhetorician George Puttenham uses *changeling* to describe what should be stable rituals that take place after a wedding:

> In the morning when it was fair broad day, and that by likelihood all turns were sufficiently served, the last acts of the interlude being ended, and that the bride must within few hours arise and apparell herself, no more as a virgin, but as a wife, and about dinner time must by order come forth *Sicut sponsa de thalamo*, very demurely and stately to be seen and acknowledged of her parents and kinsfolks whether she were the same woman or a changeling, or dead or alive, or maimed by any accident nocturnal.

But the matter of virginity is difficult to determine just as, after marriage, chastity is. "Chastity is the principal virtue of a woman and counterpoised with all the rest; if she have that, no man will look for any other," Juan Luis Vives writes; "She that is chaste is fair, well favored, rich, fruitful, noble, and all best things that can be named; and contrary, she that is unchaste, is a sea and treasure of all illness." But in the shifting world of *The Changeling* where women may be morally and intellectually superior to men, servants superior to their masters and gentry more reliable than aristocracy, such matters are all susceptible to doubt and transmutation. The striking castle of Santa Bárbara, high on a cliff above Alicante, where most of the play is set, was an actual fortress associated with the martyred virgin of Anatolia, patron saint of artillery. As Vermandero boasts, "our citadels Are placed conspicuous to outward view, On promonts' tops; but within are secrets." In courtly love terminology, such a fortress is the woman's chaste body, always vulnerable to attack in *The Changeling* even when there are cannon called "murderers at the gate." Such a courtly lexicon is invaded in the play by a vocabulary even more threatening in its physical and visual directness of capture and possession: even isolated courtly castles must keep their artillery at the ready.

This authentic Spanish setting which the playwrights take from the knowledgeable author of their source, John Reynolds, is itself permeable. De Flores in an aside likens himself to bulls in the bearbaiting arenas of Southwark – "I shall have a mad qualm within this hour again, I know't, and like a common Garden-bull, I do but take breath to be lugged again" – while off in his asylum Lollio reckons time as they do in London: "You may hear what time of day it is; the chimes of Bedlam goes." In *The Changeling* the world of Spain-watching can be the world of English-watching too. For playgoers at the Phoenix Theater in 1623 the hidden murder of Alonzo in the labyrinthine passages of the castle of Santa Bárbara, deeply hidden, might resemble the murder of Thomas Overbury at the instigation of Frances Howard, the Countess of Essex, who wished to free herself from an early marriage in order to wed the Earl of Somerset. The sensational trials of the Countess and Somerset were held in 1615, but their situation was not all that seems echoed in the story of Beatrice and De Flores. The Countess had also been forced to undergo a chastity test to obtain an annulment of her first marriage; and, according to widespread rumors, she had sent one of her cousins veiled, Diaphanta-like, to substitute for her. In a world where changeability supplants tradition and discipline as a means of survival, even the most vital matters are destabilized, evading meaning itself. When Alsemero attempts to assign significance to events at the close of *The Changeling* –

> Oh, the place itself e'er since
> Has crying been for vengeance, the temple
> Where blood and beauty first unlawfully
> Fired their devotion, and quenched the right one;
> 'Twas in my fears at first, 'twill have it now

– it is clear that he means to find a lesson even in condemning himself, but it is finally unclear what "place" he has in mind, since these lines can apply equally well to the church where he first saw Beatrice, the nuptial bed where he was betrayed, and even the city of Alicante which he had thought was made safe by the armed castle of Santa Bárbara. Observing the embodiment of all these in De Flores, Tomazo agrees:

> methinks honesty was hard bested
> To come there for a lodging – as if a queen
> Should make her palace of a pest-house.
> I find contrariety in nature
> Betwixt that face and me. The least occasion
> Would give me game upon him; yet he's so foul,
> One would scarce touch him with a sword he loved.

In such a precipitous and pestilent world, Jasperino speaks chorically when he observes that "truth is full of peril."

For many Jacobeans, it was Calvin who spoke of the theaters of the world where man was stunned, dazzled, even blinded by the allurements of the world only to discover the depths of his own reprobation. One solace which *The Changeling* addresses is predestination. It is neatly summarized by Beatrice as "my loathing Was prophet to the rest, but ne'er believed," yet she herself could not subscribe to it; for De Flores, it is not a matter of explanation so much as it is of total submission – for him rape can be ravishment, and lust made acceptable as love. Still another response was readily available in the popular book of the day, *Aristotle's Master-Piece*, where the matter of sexuality was a family and, by extension, a state matter.

> 'Tis a duty incumbent upon parents to be careful in bringing up their children in the ways of virtue and have ever a regard that they fully note their honor and reputation, especially the females, and most of all the virgins, when they grow up to be marriageable, for if through the unnatural severity of rigid parents they be crossed and frustrated in their love, many of them out of a mad humor, if temptation lies in their way throw themselves into the unchaste arms of a subtle charming tempter, being through the softness of good nature and strong desire to pursue their appetites, easily induced to believe men's flatteries and feigned vows of promised marriage to cover the shame, and then too late the parents find the effects of their rash severity, which brought a lasting stain upon their family.

In *The Arraignment of Lewd, Idle, Froward, and Unconstant Women* (1615), Joseph Swetnam makes such matters biblical and thereby universal: "Women are all necessary evils," he writes; thus Moses "also saith, that [women] were made of the rib of a man, and that their froward nature showeth, for a rib is a crooked thing, good for nothing else; and women are crooked by nature." Thus confronted, Vermandero grows insistent in his demands. Naked will cuts through changeability in fierce if contested dominance. (In fact his vow that "I'll have my will" has its unsettling resonance in the words of King James: "We needed not to be measured by any other rule, but our own princely will.") But a dominant will underlies most of the actions and all of the characters in *The Changeling* in their attempts to gain a foothold on life. Moreover, the exercise of will, like the practicing of sin, becomes dangerously habitual and in the changeable world of the play can become a dangerous liability as well. De Flores, for example, finds in Beatrice's willful transfer of affections to Alsemero an indication of his own future success: "For if a woman Fly from one point, from him she makes a husband," he argues to himself, "She spreads and mounts then like arithmetic, One, ten, a hundred, a thousand, ten thousand, Proves in time sutler to an army royal."

Still even De Flores fails to envision the depths of Beatrice's instincts for willful satisfaction and self-protection. Her first line in the play seems in retrospect calculated – "You are a scholar, sir?" – for later, desperate to find someone or something to trust, she turns to his "right physician's closet" at the start of Act IV. It is "Set round with vials, every one her mark too," she observes, adding perversely, revealingly, "Bless me!" The test for virginity which she locates almost at once may sound absurd to us, but it would seem otherwise to Jacobean playgoers. In 1618 the pharmacopoeia of the Royal College of Physicians for the Solomonic King James contained – and relied on – powdered human skulls, balsam of bats, and earthworms, while William Harvey still believed in telegony and Kenelm Digby promoted his Powder of Sympathy. In the *Eighteen Books of the Secrets of Art and Nature*, Dr. R. Read enters under the heading "How to know whether a woman be chaste, and whether she ever lay with a man or be with child,"

> Antiquity affords us some experiments of this thing, and so doth this later age, with things that are to be admired.... The jet stone (which is very frequent with us wherewith we make beads withal to pray and to number and sum up our prayers), some scrapings of it or the stone beaten in a mortar and sifted, so being brought into very fine powder, and then drank with wine or water; if the woman do make water presently and cannot hold it, that is a sign she hath lost her maidenhead. If she were never deflowered, she will hold her water and her retentive faculty is strengthened by it. White amber is as good as the former (or crystal), which they call electrum, if being powdered, it be drank with wine fasting, and so taken inwardly, for if she be polluted this will make her make water. We may try it sooner by the fume of purslane seed or leaves of the great burdock strewed upon burning coals and put under her for a fume, and if that fly upward, it will discover the truth of the matter.

Yet such learning – like the learning in *Dr. Faustus* – could be a matter of the delusion of providentiality, its knowledge forbidden, and enactment on it blasphemy. In *The Changeling* such matters of science are also matters of the soul and, as in *Faustus*, we find in such arcane matters clear signs of damnation. At this same time, seeing the ghost of Alonzo bleeding anew, De Flores experiences a "mist of conscience."

What appears confusing and subtle in the main plot of *The Changeling*, its critics have long argued, is made literal and clear in the subplot; the escapades of the madhouse usher out of the asylum to reverberate throughout the play. What does it mean, for example, to see Franciscus' autobiography as a knight errant available to perform any service for his fair lady alongside Beatrice and De Flores seeking a different kind of service at every turning? The shifting relationship of Lollio, Alibius, Antonio, and Franciscus to Isabella seems to echo that of De Flores, Alonzo, and Alsemero to Beatrice; Lollio's eavesdropping echoes that of De Flores, the attempted seduction of the one resembling the successful seduction of the other; the confinement of Isabella by her husband in a madhouse resonates in Vermandero's confinement of Beatrice in the physician's closet. Even Isabella's disguise as a madwoman has its uncanny similarity to the test with glass M (for maid). In each case, the subplot forces us to change perspective, to reposition ourselves in regard to the main plot. But the subplot itself divides in two – between the perspective of the fool and that of the madman. According to the English Court of Wards and Liveries the distinction between idiots and lunatics was that between nature and nurture: fools were those "mentally subnormal from birth"; lunatics were those "whose intellect and memory [failed] sometime after birth." The fool, like Antonio, has a weak grasp of the very real world around him; the lunatic, as in Franciscus' crazed chatter, fashions a world all his own and lives on the premise that it is the only real one. Against such clear definitions within the changeable world of the play, we can put the paranoid Alibius, fearful of the safety of his young wife while locking her in the asylum alongside the foolish lechery of Lollio that is more words than action. But where, the play keeps asking us, do we place Vermandero's obsession over his daughter's marriage in such a system? Or Alsemero's sudden passion for Beatrice? De Flores' genius at discerning the intentions of others alongside Alonzo's, or even Alonzo or Jasperino? The question is made difficult because in this play about the society at Alicante, the constant asides tell us that most of those who inhabit the play are isolated, condemned to the privacy of their own reveries and preoccupations, their own speculations and fantasies. Indeed, how advisable is it finally for a culture – whether that of Vermandero's Alicante or James's England – to become entangled in the lives of its citizenry?

Such a question becomes central to Act V. In the playwrights' source, Reynolds traverses the whole play in his comment that "It is both a grief and a scandal to any true Christian's heart that the church ordained for thanksgiving and prayer unto God should be made a stews, or at least a place for men to meet and court ladies." In *The Changeling* the sacred social space of the church is in the course of the play transformed into the secular social ritual of barley-brake. But the figural center of that ring game, recalling Alonzo's ringed finger, is called hell as De Flores comes to realize in his confession to Alsemero: "I coupled with your mate At barley-brake; now we are left in hell," and Vermandero makes the metaphor more unnerving yet: "We are all there; it circumscribes here"; "An host of enemies entered my citadel Could not amaze like this." To keep such sentiments from disappearing into platitudes, Beatrice at last steps forward to save her father by condemning herself forever.

Oh come not near me, sir, I shall defile you.
I am that of your blood was taken from you
For your better health; look no more upon't,
But cast it to the ground regardlessly.
Let the common sewer take it from distinction.

Her words are as courageous as they are futile; as no one paid her attention before, so no one effectually does now. Vermandero is wrapped in self-pity: "Oh, my name is entered now in that record Where till this fatal hour 'twas never read." Alsemero uses her words only to exonerate himself: "justice hath so right The guilty hit, that innocence is quit By proclamation, and may joy again." Even Tomazo is "satisfied," his thoughts centered on the recognition that "my injuries Lie dead before me; I can exact no more." One by one, Antonio, Franciscus, Isabella, and Alibius step forth as changelings who moralize all that has happened in their own self-interest. In the end *The Changeling*, inherently so politically radical, may seem to turn, changeling-like itself, socially conservative. Alsemero has no hesitation (and no compunction) in stepping forward to displace Vermandero's dead daughter as his living, loyal son, reconstituting the family as a confraternity of men no longer threatened by the presence of women. In rejoining and apparently forgiving her husband, Isabella too seems maddened again in erasing all that has happened. All of them have experienced the mutilation of Alonzo and Diaphanta, the bleeding corpses of Beatrice and De Flores, yet their responses, while restoring order, do not seem so much a matter of common sense as of willed blindness. Middleton and Rowley ask us, at the play's end, what we are to make of a society that, once again, seems intact. Is it the best, the only, solution for a world populated by changelings? Or is it, rather, a world of folly; indeed, of lunacy, which a stunningly inadequate epilogue only underscores?

Further Reading

Bromham, A. A. and Zara Bruzzi, *"The Changeling" and the Years of Crisis, 1619–1624: A Hieroglyph of Britain*. London: Pinter Publishers, 1990.

Bueler, Lois E., "The Rhetoric of Change in *The Changeling*," *English Literary Renaissance* 14:1 (Winter 1984): 95–113.

Burks, Deborah G., "'I'll Want My Will Else': *The Changeling* and Women's Complicity with Their Rapists," *ELH* 62:4 (Winter 1995): 759–90.

Daalder, Joost, "Folly and Madness in *The Changeling*," *Essays in Criticism* 38:1 (January 1988): 1–21.

Doob, Penelope B. R., "A Reading of *The Changeling*," *English Literary Renaissance* 3:1 (Winter 1973): 183–206.

Eaton, Sara, "Beatrice-Joanna and the Rhetoric of Love in *The Changeling*," *Theatre Journal* 36:3 (October 1984): 371–82.

Jordan, Robert, "Myth and Psychology in *The Changeling*," *Renaissance Drama* 3 (1970): 157–65.

Kowsar, Mohammad, "Middleton and Rowley's *The Changeling*: The Besieged Temple," *Criticism* 28:2 (Spring 1986): 145–64.

Little, Arthur, L., Jr., "'Transshaped Women': Virginity and Hysteria in *The Changeling*," in *Themes in Drama: Madness in Drama* (Cambridge: Cambridge University Press, 1993), pp. 19–42.

Malcolmson, Cristina, "'As Tame as the Ladies': Politics and Gender in *The Changeling*," *English Literary Renaissance* 20:2 (Spring 1990): 320–39.

Mooney, Michael E., "'Framing' as Collaborative Technique: Two Middleton–Rowley Plays," in *Drama in the Renaissance: Comparative and Critical Essays*, ed. Clifford Davidson, C. J. Giankaris, and John H. Stroupe (New York: AMS Press, 1986), pp. 300–14.

Randall, Dale B. J., "Some New Perspectives on the Spanish Setting of *The Changeling* and Its Source," *Medieval and Renaissance Drama in England* 3 (1986): 189–216.

——, "Some Observations on the Theme of Chastity in *The Changeling*," *English Literary Renaissance* 14:2 (Autumn 1984): 346–66.

Ricks, Christopher, "The Moral and Poetic Structure of *The Changeling*," *Essays in Criticism* 10 (1960): 290–306.

The Changeling

DRAMATIS PERSONÆ.

Vermandero, *father to Beatrice.*
Tomazo de Piracquo, *a noble lord.*
Alonzo de Piracquo, *his brother, suitor to Beatrice.*
Alsemero, *a nobleman, afterwards married to Beatrice.*
Jasperino, *his friend.*
Alibius, *a jealous doctor.*
Lollio, *his man.*
Pedro, *friend to Antonio.*
Antonio, *the changeling.*
Franciscus, *the counterfeit madman.*
De Flores, *servant to Vermandero.*
Madmen.
Servants.
Beatrice-Joanna, *daughter to Vermandero.*
Diaphanta, *her waiting-woman.*
Isabella, *wife to Alibius.*
The Scene: *Alicant.*

Textual Variants

Act I] Q Actus Primus **I.i.59 s.d.** Servants] Q Servants, Joanna **65** than] Q then **66** Turks] Q Turk **104** Will't] Q Wilt **110** than] Q then **115** Than] Then **119** The] Q Ahe of, the] Q of the **242** than] Q then **I.ii.69** Than] Q Then **94** the] Q his **144** than] Q then **159 s.d.**] Q has s.d. at line 153 **232–4**] Q sets as poetry **Act II**] Q Actus Secundus **II.i.9** Than] Q Then **54** Than] Q Then **138** him,] Q him, in his passions **142** and] Q an **II.ii.7** locked] Q lock **12** Than] Q Then **103** for't now,] Q for't, now **124** received] Q receive **Act III**] Q Actus Tertius **III.iii.28** last-come] Q last come **44 s.d.** *Enter* Franciscus] Q Enter Loll[io]. Franciscus **50** it is] Q 'tis **53–6**] Q sets as poetry **84** than] Q then **124–6**] Q sets as poetry **146** he] Q she **179–81**] Q sets as poetry **192–5**] Q sets as poetry **224** No,] Q Now **238** than] Q then **III.iv.30** Than] then **70** slept at ease] not in Q **91** 'twixt] Q betwixt **112** it not,] Q it, **129** than] Q then **163** may you] Q may **Act IV**] Q Actus Quartus **IV.i.100** Than] Q Then **IV.ii.15 s.d.** *Exit* Servant] Q has s.d. at line 16 **60** 'Twill] Q I will **112** I've made] Q I've **129 s.d.**] Q has s.d. at line 140 **131** 'Tis] Q T's **148** Keeps] Q Keep **IV.iii.2** at once] Q once **38** than] Q then **52** Why] Q We **74** pizzles] Q peestles **89** month's] Q moneths **100–1**] Q sets as poetry **111–14**] Q sets as poetry **111** rises] Q rise **116** he] Q she **118** than] Q then **130** straits] Q streets **178** t'other] Q to'ther **180** cast off] Q cast **Act V**] Q Actus Quintus **V.i.11 s.d.** *Strikes*] Q Strike **21** an] Q a **22** thanked] Q thank **25** Phosphorus] Q Bosphorus **72** than] Q then **77 s.d.** *Enter* Diaphanta] Q has s.d. at line 76 **113 s.d.**] Q has s.d. following "How now?" **V.ii.16** touch him] Q touch **18** near] Q ne'er **29** Than] Q Then **42** near] Q ne'er **81** Briamata] Q Bramanta **V.iii.61** Than] Q Then **71** than] Q then **89 s.d.** *Enter* De Flores] Q has s.d. at line 90 **108** It] Q I **155** hung] Q hang

following Epilogue

PLAYES *newly Printed.*

The *Wild-goose-Chase*, a Comedy; written by *Francis Beamont* and *John Fletcher*, Gent.

The *Widdow*, a Comedy; written by *Ben: Johnson, John Fletcher*, and *Thomas Midleton*, Gent.

PLAYES *in the Press.*

Five Playes written by M[r] *James Shirley*, being All of his that were Acted at the *Black-Fryers*: Together with the *Court-Secret*, written by the same Author, but never yet Acted.

Also, *The Spanish Gypsies.*

Playsource

The Changeling relies for its main plot on John Reynolds's *The Triumphs of God's Revenge against the Crying and Execrable Sin of Wilful and Premeditated Murder*, Book I, History IV. In the source, De Flores is a gallant young gentleman whose murder of Alonzo is rewarded by Beatrice's kisses. After three months of marriage, Alsemero becomes inexplicably jealous of Beatrice, alienating her. Alsemero kills Beatrice and De Flores when he discovers them committing adultery and then kills Alonzo's brother, Tomazo. At Alsemero's execution, he reveals that Beatrice and De Flores killed Alonzo, and their bodies are dug up from the grave and burned. The character of De Flores may also owe something to *Gerardo The Unfortunate Spaniard* by Leonard Digges.

Title

changeling (1) substitute child (usually ugly) for the desirable one stolen by the fairies; (2) a person covertly put in charge of another; (3) an inferior; (4) someone who wavers; (5) an inconstant woman. Critics have applied the term to Beatrice, De Flores, and/or Diaphanta, Antonio, and Franciscus; cf. the roll call in V.iii

Dramatis Personae

2 **Tomazo** his name may derive from the biblical doubting Thomas; cf. John 20:25

6 **Alibius** translates "He who is elsewhere"

11 **De Flores** translates "deflower"

14 **Beatrice** translates "she who makes happy"; **Joanna** translates "the Lord's grace"

15 **Diaphanta** translates (1) transparent; (2) fiery

16 **Isabella** translates "God has sworn"

17 **Alicant** (Alicante), a Valencian seaport on the E coast of Spain

Act I

[I.i]

Enter Alsemero.

Als. 'Twas in the temple where I first beheld her,
And now again the same. What omen yet
Follows of that? None but imaginary.
Why should my hopes or fate be timorous?
The place is holy, so is my intent.
I love her beauties to the holy purpose,
And that, methinks, admits comparison
With man's first creation, the place blest,
And is his right home back, if he achieve it.
The church hath first begun our interview,
And that's the place must join us into one,
So there's beginning and perfection too.

Enter Jasperino.

Jas. Oh sir, are you here? Come, the wind's fair with you,
Y'are like to have a swift and pleasant passage.
Als. Sure y'are deceived, friend, 'tis contrary
In my best judgment.
Jas. What, for Malta?
If you could buy a gale among the witches,
They could not serve you such a lucky pennyworth
As comes a' God's name.
Als. Even now I observed
The temple's vane to turn full in my face;
I know 'tis against me.
Jas. Against you?
Then you know not where you are.
Als. Not well indeed.
Jas. Are you not well, sir?
Als. Yes, Jasperino,
Unless there be some hidden malady
Within me that I understand not.
Jas. And that
I begin to doubt, sir; I never knew
Your inclinations to travels at a pause
With any cause to hinder it till now.
Ashore you were wont to call your servants up,
And help to trap your horses for the speed;
At sea I have seen you weigh the anchor with 'em,
Hoist sails for fear to lose the foremost breath,
Be in continual prayers for fair winds,
And have you changed your orisons?
Als. No, friend,
I keep the same church, same devotion.
Jas. Lover I'm sure y'are none, the stoic was
Found in you long ago. Your mother nor
Best friends, who have set snares of beauty (aye,
And choice ones, too), could never trap you that way.
What might be the cause?
Als. Lord, how violent
Thou art! I was but meditating of
Somewhat I heard within the temple.
Jas. Is this violence? 'Tis but idleness
Compared with your haste yesterday.
Als. I'm all this while a-going, man.

Enter Servants.

Jas. Backwards, I think, sir. Look, your servants.
1 Ser. The seamen call; shall we board your trunks?
Als. No, not today.
Jas. 'Tis the critical day, it seems, and the sign in Aquarius.
2 Ser. [*Aside.*] We must not to sea today; this smoke will bring forth fire.
Als. Keep all on shore; I do not know the end
(Which needs I must do) of an affair in hand
Ere I can go to sea.
1 Ser. Well, your pleasure.
2 Ser. [*Aside.*] Let him e'en take his leisure, too; we are safer on land.

Exeunt Servants.

I.i. 6 **the holy purpose** marriage
8 **the place blest** Eden (he compares marriage to the recovery of Eden before the fall)
10 **interview** meeting
12 **perfection** wedlock
14 **like** likely
17 **If . . . witches** common belief held that witches could sell winds
18 **pennyworth** bargain
19 **As . . . name** gratis: (1) God's gift; (2) naturally (because of God)
20–1 **The . . . me** the weather-vane of the church ironically turns against Alsemero although the wind is fair (a clear omen)
26 **doubt** fear, suspect
30 **trap** put on trappings or harness; **for . . . speed** to hasten them
31 **'em** the crew
34 **orisons** prayers
35 **church . . . devotion** manner, outlook
36 **stoic** one undisturbed by passion
40 **violent** suddenly concerned
42 **Somewhat** something
47 **board** load; put aboard
50 **critical** crucial, decisive; **Aquarius** the sign of the zodiac especially favorable to travel by water (the sun has entered the sign of the Water-Carrier)
52–3 **this . . . fire** will have serious consequences; **fire** sexual passion
54 **end** purpose
57 **your pleasure** as you desire

Enter Beatrice, Diaphanta, *and* Servants. [*Alsemero greets Beatrice and kisses her.*]

Jas. [*Aside.*] How now! The laws of the Medes are changed sure. Salute a woman? He kisses too. Wonderful! Where learnt he this? And does it perfectly, too; in my conscience he ne'er rehearsed it before. Nay, go on, this will be stranger and better news at Valencia than if he had ransomed half Greece from the Turks.

Bea. You are a scholar, sir?
Als. A weak one, lady.
Bea. Which of the sciences is this love you speak of?
Als. From your tongue I take it to be music.
Bea. You are skillful in't, can sing at first sight.
Als. And I have showed you all my skill at once.
I want more words to express me further,
And must be forced to repetition.
I love you dearly.
Bea. Be better advised, sir.
Our eyes are sentinels unto our judgments,
And should give certain judgment what they see;
But they are rash sometimes, and tell us wonders
Of common things, which when our judgments find,
They can then check the eyes, and call them blind.
Als. But I am further, lady; yesterday
Was mine eyes' employment, and hither now
They brought my judgment, where are both agreed.
Both houses then consenting, 'tis agreed;
Only there wants the confirmation
By the hand royal. That's your part, lady.
Bea. Oh, there's one above me, sir. [*Aside.*] For five days past
To be recalled! Sure, mine eyes were mistaken,
This was the man was meant me; that he should come
So near his time, and miss it!

Jas. [*Aside.*] We might have come by the carriers from Valencia, I see, and saved all our sea-provision. We are at farthest sure. Methinks I should do something too; I meant to be a venturer in this voyage. Yonder's another vessel. I'll board her; if she be lawful prize, down goes her top-sail.

[*Greets* Diaphanta.]

Enter De Flores.

De F. Lady, your father –
Bea. Is in health, I hope.
De F. Your eye shall instantly instruct you, Lady.
He's coming hitherward.
Bea. What needed then
Your duteous preface? I had rather
He had come unexpected; you must stall
A good presence with unnecessary blabbing.
And how welcome for your part you are,
I'm sure you know.
De F. [*Aside.*] Will't never mend this scorn
One side nor other? Must I be enjoined
To follow still whilst she flies from me? Well,
Fates, do your worst; I'll please myself with sight
Of her at all opportunities
If but to spite her anger. I know she had
Rather see me dead than living, and yet
She knows no cause for't but a peevish will.
Als. You seemed displeased, Lady, on the sudden.
Bea. Your pardon, sir, 'tis my infirmity,
Nor can I other reason render you,
Than his or hers, of some particular thing
They must abandon as a deadly poison,

60 **laws . . . Medes** laws that never change (cf. Dan. 6:8)
61 **Salute** greet by kissing
63 **in . . . conscience** truthfully; upon my word (colloquial)
65 **Valencia** (Alsemero's residence, a port on the E coast of Spain about 75 miles N of Alicante)
65–6 **if . . . Turks** (Greece was then part of the Turkish empire)
68 **sciences** fields of learning
72 **want** lack
75 **eyes** (metaphor for sexual arousal)
79 **check** restrain, rebuke
80 **further** more advanced (in love than love at first sight)
83 **Both houses** sight and judgment (compared to decisions by both Houses of Parliament)
85 **hand royal** (the bill needs only her signature to become law)
86 **one above** (1) Vermandero; (2) God
86–7 **For . . . recalled** to rescind her engagement five days previously to Alonzo
90 **carriers** land transporters
92 **farthest** (1) most distant from our goal; (2) wildly off course
94 **venturer** one who shares risks and profits; **voyage** business
94–5 **another vessel** Diaphanta
95 **board her** (with sexual pun); **lawful prize** single and eligible (a vessel no regulation prohibits from capturing)
96 **down . . . top-sail** a sign of surrender (with sexual pun)
101 **stall** (1) forestall; (2) spoil the discovery of
102 **good presence** i.e., Vermandero
105 **One . . . other** one way or another (i.e., whatever I do)
106 **still** always
109 **to . . . anger** in compensation for my frustrated desire
111 **peevish** perverse
115 **Than . . . hers** reasons anyone could provide; **of** concerning
116 **abandon** reject

Which to a thousand other tastes were wholesome;
Such to mine eyes is that same fellow there,
The same that report speaks of, the basilisk.
Als. This is a frequent frailty in our nature;
There's scarce a man among a thousand sound
But hath his imperfection. One distastes
The scent of roses, which to infinites
Most pleasing is, and odoriferous;
One oil, the enemy of poison;
Another wine, the cheerer of the heart,
And lively refresher of the countenance.
Indeed this fault (if so it be) is general,
There's scarce a thing but is both loved and loathed.
Myself (I must confess) have the same frailty.
Bea. And what may be your poison, sir? I am bold with you.
Als. What might be your desire. Perhaps a cherry.
Bea. I am no enemy to any creature
My memory has but yon gentleman.
Als. He does ill to tempt your sight, if he knew it.
Bea. He cannot be ignorant of that, sir,
I have not spared to tell him so; and I want
To help myself, since he's a gentleman
In good respect with my father, and follows him.
Als. He's out of his place then now.
[*They talk apart.*]

Jas. I am a mad wag, wench.

Dia. So methinks; but for your comfort I can tell you, we have a doctor in the city that undertakes the cure of such.

Jas. Tush, I know what physic is best for the state of mine own body.

Dia. 'Tis scarce a well-governed state, I believe.

Jas. I could show thee such a thing with an ingredient that we two would compound together, and if it did not tame the maddest blood i' th' town for two hours after, I'll ne'er profess physic again.

Dia. A little poppy, sir, were good to cause you sleep.

Jas. Poppy! I'll give thee a pop i' th' lips for that first, and begin there. [*Kisses her.*] Poppy is one simple indeed, and cuckoo (what you call't) another. I'll discover no more now, another time I'll show thee all.

Bea. My father, sir.

Enter Vermandero *and* Servants.

Ver. Oh, Joanna, I came to meet thee,
Your devotion's ended?
Bea. For this time, sir.
[*Aside.*] I shall change my saint, I fear me. I find
A giddy turning in me. [*To Ver.*] Sir, this while
I am beholding to this gentleman,
Who left his own way to keep me company,
And in discourse I find him much desirous
To see your castle. He hath deserved it, sir,
If ye please to grant it.
Ver. With all my heart, sir.
Yet there's an article between – I must know
Your country. We use not to give survey
Of our chief strengths to strangers; our citadels
Are placed conspicuous to outward view,
On promonts' tops; but within are secrets.
Als. A Valencian, sir.
Ver. A Valencian?
That's native, sir; of what name, I beseech you?
Als. Alsemero, sir.
Ver. Alsemero; not the son
Of John de Alsemero?
Als. The same, sir.

---

119 report common talk; **basilisk** a fabulous reptile that could kill by a glance
121 sound healthy
123 infinites infinite numbers of persons
124 odoriferous fragrant
125 oil (as laxative to remove poison)
132 cherry (as arbitrary illustration; trivial as in "not worth a cherry")
134 yon gentleman De Flores (cf. his name; Beatrice-Joanna is still a virgin)
135 tempt make trial of
137 want have need
139 respect repute
140 out . . . place (1) too forward; (2) not acting properly as a servant
141 mad wag high-spirited, playful person; **wench** woman
143 doctor Alibius
145 physic medicine (but with sexual pun)
147 well-governed (1) healthy; (2) disciplined
148 such a thing copulation
148–9 ingredient semen (with ovaries)
149 compound make with mortar and pestle (deliberate phallic imagery)
150 maddest blood great sexual passions
153 poppy opium
154 sleep (with pun on copulation)
157 simple unaltered herb as medicine
157–8 cuckoo . . . another cuckoo-flower (whose shape resembles a penis; with play on *cuckoo* as madness)
158 discover reveal
159 show thee all (1) tell thee everything; (2) (sexual pun)
163 change . . . saint i.e., find a new beloved
164 giddy (1) dizzying; (2) insane
165 beholding indebted
170 article between stipulation
171 use not are unaccustomed
172 strengths fortifications
174 promonts' promontories; **secrets** (ironic; he does not understand Alsemero's real interest in Beatrice-Joanna)

Ver. My best love bids you welcome.
Bea. [*Aside.*] He was wont
To call me so, and then he speaks a most
Unfeigned truth.
Ver. Oh, sir, I knew your father;
We two were in acquaintance long ago,
Before our chins were worth Iulan down,
And so continued till the stamp of time
Had coined us into silver. Well, he's gone;
A good soldier went with him.
Als. You went together in that, sir.
Ver. No, by Saint Jacques, I came behind him.
Yet I have done somewhat too; an unhappy day
Swallowed him at last at Gibraltar
In fight with those rebellious Hollanders,
Was it not so?
Als. Whose death I had revenged,
Or followed him in fate, had not the late league
Prevented me.
Ver. Aye, aye, 'twas time to breathe.
Oh, Joanna, I should ha' told thee news,
I saw Piracquo lately.
Bea. [*Aside.*] That's ill news.
Ver. He's hot preparing for this day of triumph;
Thou must be a bride within this sevennight.
Als. [*Aside.*] Ha!
Bea. Nay, good sir, be not so violent. With speed
I cannot render satisfaction
Unto the dear companion of my soul,
Virginity, whom I thus long have lived with,
And part with it so rude and suddenly;
Can such friends divide, never to meet again,
Without a solemn farewell?
Ver. Tush, tush, there's a toy.
Als. [*Aside.*] I must now part, and never meet again
With any joy on earth; [*To Ver.*] sir, your pardon,
My affairs call on me.
Ver. How, sir? By no means;
Not changed so soon, I hope? You must see my castle,
And her best entertainment, ere we part.
I shall think myself unkindly used else.
Come, come, let's on; I had good hope your stay
Had been a while with us in Alicant;
I might have bid you to my daughter's wedding.
Als. [*Aside.*] He means to feast me, and poisons me beforehand;
[*To Ver.*] I should be dearly glad to be there, sir,
Did my occasions suit as I could wish.
Bea. I shall be sorry if you be not there
When it is done, sir. But not so suddenly.
Ver. I tell you, sir, the gentleman's complete,
A courtier and a gallant, enriched
With many fair and noble ornaments;
I would not change him for a son-in-law
For any he in Spain, the proudest he,
And we have great ones, that you know.
Als. He's much
Bound to you, sir.
Ver. He shall be bound to me,
As fast as this tie can hold him; I'll want
My will else.
Bea. [*Aside.*] I shall want mine if you do it.
Ver. But come, by the way I'll tell you more of him.
Als. [*Aside.*] How shall I dare to venture in his castle,
When he discharges murderers at the gate?
But I must on, for back I cannot go.
Bea. [*Aside.*] Not this serpent gone yet?
[*Drops a glove.*]
Ver. Look, girl, thy glove's fallen;
Stay, stay. De Flores, help a little.
[*Exeunt* Vermandero, Alsemero, Jasperino, *and* Servants.]

---

179 **best love** (1) heartiest joy; (2) Beatrice-Joanna; **He** Vermandero
183 **Before . . . down** before we had beards (derived from Julian Ascanius, the son of Aeneas)
185 **Had . . . silver** had turned our beards gray
187 **went together** were equally good soldiers
188 **Saint Jacques** St. James of Compostela, patron saint of Spain
190 **Gibraltar** (the Dutch decisively defeated the Spanish fleet at the Battle of Gibraltar on April 25, 1607)
193 **the late league** (reference is to the truce signed at The Hague on April 9, 1609)
194 **Prevented** forestalled; **time . . . breathe** (the truce put a pause to hostilities; an English audience would have wished Spain defeated)
197 **day of triumph** i.e., the wedding day
198 **sevennight** week; **Ha!** "so that's it!"
205 **toy** trifle
210 **ere** before
215 **poisons me beforehand** (by announcing Beatrice-Joanna's marriage to Alonzo)
219 **suddenly** soon
220 **complete** perfect
221 **gallant** accomplished lover
223 **change** exchange
224 **he** man
226 **bound** (1) tied; (2) indebted
227 **want** not have
230 **by** along
232 **murderers** small cannon (with ironic anticipation)
234 **serpent** (1) sign of disgust; (2) as with Eve, unconscious attraction
234 **s.d.** ***Drops*** (1) accidentally; (2) deliberately as a token for Alsemero; (3) in confusion over De Flores' continued presence
235 **Stay** (to Beatrice-Joanna)

De F. Here, Lady.
[*Offers the glove.*]
Bea. Mischief on your officious forwardness!
Who bade you stoop? They touch my hand no more.
There, for t'other's sake I part with this,
[*Takes off the other glove and throws it down.*]
Take 'em and draw thine own skin off with 'em.
Exeunt [Beatrice *and* Diaphanta.]
De F. Here's a favor come, with a mischief! Now I know
She had rather wear my pelt tanned in a pair
Of dancing pumps than I should thrust my fingers
Into her sockets here, I know she hates me,
Yet cannot choose but love her.
No matter. If but to vex her, I'll haunt her still;
Though I get nothing else, I'll have my will.
Exit.

[I.ii]

Enter Alibius *and* Lollio.

Alib. Lollio, I must trust thee with a secret,
But thou must keep it.
Lol. I was ever close to a secret, sir.
Alib. The diligence that I have found in thee,
The care and industry already past,
Assures me of thy good continuance.
Lollio, I have a wife.
Lol. Fie, sir, 'tis too late to keep her secret. She's known to be married all the town and country over.
Alib. Thou goest too fast, my Lollio, that knowledge
I allow no man can be barred it;
But there is a knowledge which is nearer,
Deeper and sweeter, Lollio.
Lol. Well, sir, let us handle that between you and I.
Alib. 'Tis that I go about, man; Lollio,
My wife is young.
Lol. So much the worse to be kept secret, sir.
Alib. Why, now thou meet'st the substance of the point.
I am old, Lollio.
Lol. No, sir, 'tis I am old Lollio.
Alib. Yet why may not this concord and sympathize?
Old trees and young plants often grow together,
Well enough agreeing.
Lol. Aye, sir, but the old trees raise themselves higher and broader than the young plants.
Alib. Shrewd application! There's the fear, man;
I would wear my ring on my own finger;
Whilst it is borrowed it is none of mine,
But his that useth it.
Lol. You must keep it on still then; if it but lie by, one or other will be thrusting into't.
Alib. Thou conceiv'st me, Lollio.
Here thy watchful eye
Must have employment; I cannot always be
At home.
Lol. I dare swear you cannot.
Alib. I must look out.
Lol. I know't, you must look out, 'tis every man's case.
Alib. Here I do say must thy employment be,
To watch her treadings, and in my absence
Supply my place.
Lol. I'll do my best, sir, yet surely I cannot see who you should have cause to be jealous of.
Alib. Thy reason for that, Lollio? 'Tis a comfortable question.
Lol. We have but two sorts of people in the house, and both under the whip, that's fools and madmen; the one has not wit enough to be knaves, and the other not knavery enough to be fools.
Alib. Ay, those are all my patients, Lollio.
I do profess the cure of either sort.
My trade, my living 'tis, I thrive by it;

---

239 own skin (1) with reference to De Flores' unsightly appearance; (2) revitalize yourself (as a snake grows a second skin)
240 favor love token; **mischief** sign of disfavor
242 pumps slippers; **fingers** (with a pun on penis)
243 sockets fingers of gloves (with a pun on vagina)
245 If . . . still if sexually frustrated, I will harass her
I.ii.3 close to (1) neighbor to; (2) able to conceal; **secret** private parts (as in line 8)
13 knowledge carnal knowledge
15 handle discuss (with sexual pun)
16 that precisely my point
19 now . . . point it is difficult to keep a young wife
22 this (a marriage between an old man and a young woman)
25–6 raise . . . higher i.e., by a cuckold's horns
27 Shrewd i.e., painful but precise
28 ring (1) wedding ring; (2) wife's vagina; **finger** (with pun on *penis*)
33 conceiv'st understand
35 employment (with pun on *copulation*)
36 At home (with pun on sexual intimacy)
38 look out (1) be vigilant; (2) go (on business)
40 case (1) care; (2) problem; (3) vagina; (4) brothel
42 treadings (1) movements; (2) sexual acts
43 Supply take (in supervision; in sexual contacts)
45 jealous suspicious
46 comfortable (1) comforting; (2) reassuring

But here's the care that mixes with my thrift.
The daily visitants, that come to see
My brainsick patients, I would not have
To see my wife. Gallants I do observe
Of quick enticing eyes, rich in habits,
Of stature and proportion very comely:
These are most shrewd temptations, Lollio.

Lol. They may be easily answered, sir. If they come to see the fools and madmen, you and I may serve the turn, and let my mistress alone. She's of neither sort.

Alib. 'Tis a good ward; indeed, come they to see
Our madmen or our fools, let 'em see no more
Than what they come for. By that consequent
They must not see her. I'm sure she's no fool.

Lol. And I'm sure she's no madman.

Alib. Hold that buckler fast, Lollio. My trust
Is on thee, and I account it firm and strong.
What hour is't, Lollio?

Lol. Towards belly-hour, sir.

Alib. Dinner time? Thou mean'st twelve o'clock.

Lol. Yes, sir, for every part has his hour. We wake at six and look about us, that's eye-hour; at seven we should pray, that's knee-hour; at eight walk, that's leg-hour; at nine gather flowers and pluck a rose, that's nose-hour; at ten we drink, that's mouth-hour; at eleven lay about us for victuals, that's hand-hour; at twelve go to dinner, that's belly-hour.

Alib. Profoundly, Lollio! It will be long
Ere all thy scholars learn this lesson, and
I did look to have a new one entered. Stay,
I think my expectation is come home.

Enter Pedro, *and* Antonio *like an idiot.*

Ped. Save you, sir; my business speaks itself.
This sight takes off the labor of my tongue.

Alib. Aye, aye, sir;
'Tis plain enough. You mean him for my
patient.

Ped. And if your pains prove but commodious,
To give but some little strength to the sick
And weak part of nature in him, these are
[*Gives money.*]
But patterns to show you of the whole pieces
That will follow to you, beside the charge of
diet, washing, and other necessaries
Fully defrayed.

Alib. Believe it, sir, there shall no care be wanting.

Lol. Sir, an officer in this place may deserve something; the trouble will pass through my hands.

Ped. 'Tis fit something should come to your hands then, sir.

[*Gives him money.*]

Lol. Yes, sir, 'tis I must keep him sweet, and read to him; what is his name?

Ped. His name is Antonio; marry, we use but half to him, only Tony.

Lol. Tony, Tony, 'tis enough, and a very good name for a fool; what's your name, Tony?

Ant. He, he, he! Well, I thank you, cousin; he he, he!

Lol. Good boy! Hold up your head. He can laugh, I perceive by that he is no beast.

Ped. Well, sir,
If you can raise him but to any height,
Any degree of wit, might he attain
(As I might say) to creep but on all four
Towards the chair of wit, or walk on crutches,
'Twould add an honor to your worthy pains,
And a great family might pray for you,
To which he should be heir, had he discretion
To claim and guide his own. Assure you, sir,
He is a gentleman.

Lol. Nay, there's nobody doubted that; at first sight I knew him for a gentleman. He looks no other yet.

Ped. Let him have good attendance and sweet lodging.

Lol. As good as my mistress lies in, sir; and as you allow us time and means, we can raise him to the higher degree of discretion.

---

56 **care** responsibility; **thrift** profit
57 **daily visitants** (the madmen of Bethlehem Hospital were considered a popular entertainment)
60 **habits** clothes
61 **comely** attractive
62 **shrewd** (1) mischievous; (2) strong
65 **serve the turn** be adequate for such spectators (joking)
67 **ward** defense (a term from fencing)
69 **consequent** conclusion (as in a syllogism)
70 **They . . . fool** (Alibius is in charge of lunatics only; Lollio is only in charge of the fools)
72 **buckler** shield
81 **pluck a rose** (euphemism for) urinate
82–3 **lay about** search
83 **victuals** provisions
88 **expectation** suspicion
89 **s.d. *like an idiot*** (presumably wearing a long coat and conical cap)
89 **Save you** "God save you" (a common greeting)
90 **takes off** makes needless
93 **commodious** beneficial
96 **patterns** samples; **whole pieces** substantial coins
105 **sweet** clean
108 **Tony** cant term for fool
113–14 **He . . . beast** (common belief held that humans were distinguished from other animals by their ability to laugh)
126 **I . . . gentleman** (1) (said to please Alibius); (2) (sound because Lollio recognizes the disguise; cf. line 132)

Ped. Nay, there shall no cost want, sir.

Lol. He will hardly be stretched up to the wit of a magnifico.

Ped. Oh no, that's not to be expected, far shorter Will be enough.

Lol. I'll warrant you make him fit to bear office in five weeks. I'll undertake to wind him up to the wit of constable.

Ped. If it be lower than that it might serve turn.

Lol. No, fie, to level him with a headborough, beadle, or watchman were but little better than he is. Constable, I'll able him. If he do come to be a justice afterwards, let him thank the keeper. Or I'll go further with you; say I do bring him up to my own pitch, say I make him as wise as myself.

Ped. Why, there I would have it.

Lol. Well, go to, either I'll be as arrant a fool as he, or he shall be as wise as I, and then I think 'twill serve his turn.

Ped. Nay, I do like thy wit passing well.

Lol. Yes, you may, yet if I had not been a fool, I had had more wit than I have, too. Remember what state you find me in.

Ped. I will, and so leave you. Your best cares, I beseech you.

Alib. Take you none with you; leave 'em all with us.

Exit Pedro.

Ant. Oh, my cousin's gone, cousin, cousin, oh!

Lol. Peace, peace, Tony, you must not cry, child. You must be whipped if you do. Your cousin is here still, I am your cousin, Tony.

Ant. He, he, then I'll not cry, if thou be'st my cousin, he, he, he.

Lol. I were best try his wit a little that I may know what form to place him in.

Alib. Aye, do, Lollio, do.

Lol. I must ask him easy questions at first. Tony; how many true fingers has a tailor on his right hand?

Ant. As many as on his left, cousin.

Lol. Good; and how many on both?

Ant. Two less than a deuce, cousin.

Lol. Very well answered. I come to you again, cousin Tony; how many fools goes to a wise man?

Ant. Forty in a day sometimes, cousin.

Lol. Forty in a day? How prove you that?

Ant. All that fall out amongst themselves, and go to a lawyer to be made friends.

Lol. A parlous fool! He must sit in the fourth form at least, I perceive that. I come again, Tony: how many knaves make an honest man?

Ant. I know not that, cousin.

Lol. No, the question is too hard for you. I'll tell you, cousin, there's three knaves may make an honest man, a sergeant, a jailer, and a beadle. The sergeant catches him, the jailer holds him, and the beadle lashes him; and if he be not honest then, the hangman must cure him.

Ant. Ha, ha, ha, that's fine sport, cousin!

Alib. This was too deep a question for the fool, Lollio.

Lol. Yes, this might have served yourself, though I say't; once more, and you shall go play, Tony.

Ant. Aye, play at push-pin, cousin, ha, he!

Lol. So thou shalt; say how many fools are here.

Ant. Two, cousin, thou and I.

Lol. Nay, y'are too forward there, Tony; mark my question. How many fools and knaves are here? A fool before a knave, a fool behind a knave, between every two fools a knave; how many fools, how many knaves?

Ant. I never learned so far, cousin.

Alib. Thou putt'st too hard questions to him, Lollio.

Lol. I'll make him understand it easily; cousin, stand there.

Ant. Aye, cousin.

Lol. Master, stand you next the fool.

---

133 **Nay...sir** (1) we will pay whatever the cost; (2) don't economize on your care

134 **hardly** with difficulty; **stretched up** (1) advanced to; (2) treated as; **magnifico** magistrate

136 **shorter** lesser treatment

140 **wit...constable** (constables were often considered fools, intellectually inept)

142 **headborough** petty constable (lowest parochial authority)

143 **beadle** parish constable (lowest judicial authority); **watchman** (lowest civil authority)

144 **able** train

145 **justice** (stage justices were often portrayed as stupid)

147 **pitch** level of competence

150 **go to** (a common expression of admonishment); **arrant** wandering

151 **wise** clever

152 **serve...turn** be sufficient for him

153 **passing** extremely

156 **state** condition; position (as keeper of facts)

160 **cousin** (term for any close relation)

166 **try** test

167 **form** class in school

170 **true** honest; **tailor** (tailors were commonly believed to be dishonest)

174 **Two...deuce** i.e., none

176 **goes to** (1) makes up; (2) visits

182 **A...fool!** (only fools think lawyers would help when in fact they keep litigation going); **parlous** i.e., perilous, dangerously sly

187 **make** (1) create; (2) constitute

195 **served yourself** been appropriate for

197 **push-pin** (1) a children's game played with small pins; (2) a sexual pun

200 **forward** eager

202 **before** in front of

Alib. Well, Lollio?

Lol. Here's my place. Mark now, Tony, there a fool before a knave.

Ant. That's I, cousin.

Lol. Here's a fool behind a knave, that's I, and between us two fools there is a knave, that's my master; 'tis but we three, that's all.

Ant. We three, we three, cousin!

Madmen *within.*

1 Within. Put's head i' th' pillory, the bread's too little.

2 Within. Fly, fly, and he catches the swallow.

3 Within. Give her more onion, or the devil put the rope about her crag.

Lol. You may hear what time of day it is; the chimes of Bedlam goes.

Alib. Peace, peace, or the wire comes!

3 Within. Cat-whore, cat-whore, her permasant, her permasant!

Alib. Peace, I say; their hour's come, they must be fed, Lollio.

Lol. There's no hope of recovery of that Welsh madman, was undone by a mouse, that spoiled him a permasant; lost his wits for't.

Alib. Go to your charge, Lollio; I'll to mine.

Lol. Go you to your madmen's ward, let me alone with your fools.

Exit.

Alib. And remember my last charge, Lollio.

Lol. Of which your patients do you think I am? Come, Tony, you must among your school-fellows now; there's pretty scholars among 'em, I can tell you. There's some of 'em at *stultus, stulta, stultum.*

Ant. I would see the madmen, cousin, if they would not bite me.

Lol. No, they shall not bite thee, Tony.

Ant. They bite when they are at dinner, do they not, coz?

Lol. They bite at dinner indeed, Tony. Well, I hope to get credit by thee; I like thee the best of all the scholars that ever I brought up. And thou shalt prove a wise man, or I'll prove a fool myself.

Exeunt.

Act II

[II.i]

Enter Beatrice *and* Jasperino *severally.*

Bea. Oh sir, I'm ready now for that fair service,
Which makes the name of friend sit glorious on you.
Good angels and this conduct be your guide,
[*Gives a paper.*]
Fitness of time and place is there set down, sir.

Jas. The joy I shall return rewards my service.

Exit.

Bea. How wise is Alsemero in his friend!
It is a sign he makes his choice with judgment.
Then I appear in nothing more approved,
Than making choice of him;
For 'tis a principle, he that can choose
That bosom well, who of his thoughts partakes,
Proves most discreet in every choice he makes.
Methinks I love now with the eyes of judgment,
And see the way to merit, clearly see it.
A true deserver like a diamond sparkles,
In darkness you may see him, that's in absence,
Which is the greatest darkness falls on love;

216 knave (i.e., Alibius stands between Lollio and Antonio, who are both considered fools)
218 we three (a common joke on a picture of two fools called "we three" to include the spectator)
220 pillory (a wooden frame with holes for head and hands used in public punishments)
220–1 too little (rations are inadequate)
222 Fly . . . swallow (i.e., something seems possible that is not; proverbial)
223 Give . . . onion (a cry for food; "If thou hast not a capon, feed on onion" was proverbial)
224 rope (1) hangman's rope; (2) rope of onions; **crag** neck
226 chimes (patients' cries for food)
227 wire wire whips
228–9 Cat-whore . . . permasant! (complaint about a cat behaving like a whore in allowing a mouse to steal its cheese); **permasant** Parmesan cheese
232–3 Welsh madman (the Welsh were proverbial for their fondness for cheese)
233 was who was
235 charge duty, responsibility
238 charge instruction (to keep watch of Isabella, his wife)
239 which i.e., fool or madman
241 pretty clever
242–3 at . . . *stultum* (i.e., they have mastered the Latin for the three genders of fool)
245 bite steal from
248 coz (shortened form of *cousin*)
II.i.1 s.d. *severally* separately
3 conduct paper with directions
5 return take back to Alsemero
8 approved justified
11 bosom intimate friend
14 to to recognize
16 In . . . him diamonds were thought luminous
17 falls that falls

Yet is he best discerned then
With intellectual eyesight; what's Piracquo
My father spends his breath for? And his blessing
Is only mine, as I regard his name,
Else it goes from me, and turns head against me,
Transformed into a curse. Some speedy way
Must be remembered. He's so forward, too,
So urgent that way, scarce allows me breath
To speak to my new comforts.

Enter De Flores.

De F. [*Aside.*] Yonder's she.
Whatever ails me, now a-late especially,
I can as well be hanged as refrain seeing her;
Some twenty times a day, nay, not so little,
Do I force errands, frame ways and excuses
To come into her sight, and I have small reason for't,
And less encouragement; for she baits me still
Every time worse than other, does profess herself
The cruellest enemy to my face in town,
At no hand can abide the sight of me,
As if danger or ill luck hung in my looks.
I must confess my face is bad enough,
But I know far worse has better fortune,
And not endured alone, but doted on.
And yet such pick-haired faces, chins like witches',
Here and there five hairs, whispering in a corner,
As if they grew in fear one of another,
Wrinkles like troughs, where swine-deformity swills
The tears of perjury that lie there like wash
Fallen from the slimy and dishonest eye,
Yet such a one plucked sweets without restraint,
And has the grace of beauty to his sweet.
Though my hard fate has thrust me out to servitude,
I tumbled into th'world a gentleman.
She turns her blessèd eye upon me now,
And I'll endure all storms before I part with't.

Bea. [*Aside.*] Again!
This ominous ill-faced fellow more disturbs me
Than all my other passions.

De F. [*Aside.*] Now't begins again;
I'll stand this storm of hail though the stones pelt me.

Bea. Thy business? What's thy business?

De F. [*Aside.*] Soft and fair,
I cannot part so soon now.

Bea. [*Aside.*] The villain's fixed.
[*To De F.*] Thou standing toad-pool!

De F. [*Aside.*] The shower falls amain now.

Bea. Who sent thee? What's thy errand? Leave my sight.

De F. My Lord your father charged me to deliver
A message to you.

Bea. What, another since?
Do't and be hanged then, let me be rid of thee.

De F. True service merits mercy.

Bea. What's thy message?

De F. Let beauty settle but in patience,
You shall hear all.

Bea. A dallying, trifling torment!

De F. Signor Alonzo de Piracquo, Lady,
Sole brother to Tomazo de Piracquo –

Bea. Slave, when wilt make an end?

De F. [*Aside.*] Too soon I shall.

Bea. What all this while of him?

De F. The said Alonzo,
With the foresaid Tomazo –

Bea. Yet again?

De F. Is new alighted.

Bea. Vengeance strike the news!
Thou thing most loathed, what cause was there in this

20–1 **My . . . for** on whose behalf my father speaks; **And . . . name** my father will bless a wedding only if it maintains the family reputation
22 **head** direction
24 **remembered** brought to mind; **He's** Vermandero's; **forward** eager
26 **comforts** joys
27 **a-late** of late
30 **force** invent; **frame** devise
32 **baits** (1) attracts (from fishing); (2) taunts (from bullbaiting)
34 **in town** publicly
35 **At no hand** by no means
40 **pick-haired** bristled
43 **swine-deformity** pig-like resemblance; **swills** swallows down
44 **perjury** hypocrisy; **wash** watery discharge
46 **plucked sweets** enjoys a woman's (sexual) favor
47 **to his sweet** from the perspective of his beloved
49 **tumbled** was born
54 **passions** (1) sufferings; (2) strong emotions; (3) sexual desires
56 **Soft and fair** speak calmly and well
57 **fixed** obstinate
58 **standing toad-pool** stagnant water breeding ugly creatures (perhaps referring to De Flores' skin as well as his features); **shower** (of abuse); **amain** forcefully
61 **since** yet; still
64 **settle . . . patience** be but patient
65 **dallying** time-wasting
68 **Slave** wretch

To bring thee to my sight?
De F. My Lord your father
Charged me to seek you out.
Bea. Is there no other
To send his errand by?
De F. It seems 'tis my luck
To be i' th'way still.
Bea. Get thee from me.
De F. [*Aside.*] So;
Why, am not I an ass to devise ways
Thus to be railed at? I must see her still!
I shall have a mad qualm within this hour again,
I know't, and like a common Garden-bull,
I do but take breath to be lugged again.
What this may bode I know not; I'll despair the less,
Because there's daily precedents of bad faces
Beloved beyond all reason; these foul chops
May come into favor one day 'mong his fellows.
Wrangling has proved the mistress of good pastime;
As children cry themselves asleep, I ha' seen
Women have chid themselves abed to men.
Exit De Flores.
Bea. I never see this fellow, but I think
Of some harm towards me, danger's in my mind still;
I scarce leave trembling of an hour after.
The next good mood I find my father in,
I'll get him quite discarded. Oh, I was
Lost in this small disturbance, and forgot
Affliction's fiercer torrent that now comes
To bear down all my comforts.

Enter Vermandero, Alonzo, Tomazo.

Ver. Y'are both welcome,
But an especial one belongs to you, sir,
To whose most noble name our love presents
The addition of a son, our son Alonzo.
Alon. The treasury of honor cannot bring forth
A title I should more rejoice in, sir.
Ver. You have improved it well; daughter, prepare,
The day will steal upon thee suddenly.
Bea. [*Aside.*] Howe'er, I will be sure to keep the night,
If it should come so near me.
[*Beatrice and Vermandero talk apart.*]
Tom. Alonzo.
Alon. Brother?
Tom. In troth I see small welcome in her eye.
Alon. Fie, you are too severe a censurer
Of love in all points, there's no bringing on you;
If lovers should mark everything a fault,
Affection would be like an ill-set book,
Whose faults might prove as big as half the volume.
Bea. That's all I do entreat.
Ver. It is but reasonable;
I'll see what my son says to't. Son Alonzo,
Here's a motion made but to reprieve
A maidenhead three days longer; the request
Is not far out of reason, for indeed
The former time is pinching.
Alon. Though my joys
Be set back so much time as I could wish
They had been forward, yet since she desires it,
The time is set as pleasing as before.
I find no gladness wanting.
Ver. May I ever meet it in that point still.
Y'are nobly welcome, sirs.
Exeunt Vermandero *and* Beatrice.
Tom. So; did you mark the dullness of her parting now?
Alon. What dullness? Thou art so exceptious still!
Tom. Why, let it go then, I am but a fool
To mark your harms so heedfully.

---

76 **still** again; repeatedly
78 **railed at** insulted, maligned
79 **mad qualm** obsessive desire (*qualm* can also mean attack of illness)
80 **Garden-bull** bull baited at Paris Garden or Bear Garden, both in the theater district of Southwark
81 **lugged** literally, pulled by the ears; i.e., tormented
82 **bode** foretell
84 **chops** jaws (metonymy for the face)
85 **his** its
88 **chid** chided
91 **of** for
93 **discarded** dismissed
99 **addition** title
100 **treasury** keeping-place; dignity
102 **improved** added to
103 **The day** (of marriage)
104 **keep the night** (1) be on the alert during the wedding night; (2) retain control during the night
106 **troth** truth
107 **severe a censurer** strict a critic
108 **points** (1) respects; (2) punctuation marks; **bringing . . . you** bringing you around to a more agreeable position
110 **ill-set** put badly or erroneously into type
111 **faults** misprints; table of errata
114 **motion** proposal
117 **pinching** inadequate; **joys** (with sexual pun)
122 **meet it** agree
124 **dullness** indifference; mindlessness
125 **exceptious** objecting
127 **heedfully** warningly, sensitively

Alon. Where's the oversight?
Tom. Come, your faith's cozened in her, strongly cozened;
Unsettle your affection with all speed
Wisdom can bring it to, your peace is ruined else.
Think what a torment 'tis to marry one
Whose heart is leaped into another's bosom.
If ever pleasure she receive from thee,
It comes not in thy name, or of thy gift;
She lies but with another in thine arms,
He the half-father unto all thy children
In the conception; if he get 'em not,
She helps to get 'em for him, and how dangerous
And shameful her restraint may go in time to,
It is not to be thought on without sufferings.
Alon. You speak as if she loved some other, then.
Tom. Do you apprehend so slowly?
Alon. Nay, and that
Be your fear only, I am safe enough.
Preserve your friendship and your counsel, brother,
For times of more distress; I should depart
An enemy, a dangerous, deadly one
To any but thyself, that should but think
She knew the meaning of inconstancy,
Much less the use and practice; yet w'are friends.
Pray let no more be urged. I can endure
Much, till I meet an injury to her;
Then I am not myself. Farewell, sweet brother,
How much w'are bound to heaven to depart lovingly.
Exit.
Tom. Why, here is love's tame madness; thus a man
Quickly steals into his vexation.
Exit.

[II.ii]

Enter Diaphanta *and* Alsemero.

Dia. The place is my charge; you have kept your hour,
And the reward of a just meeting bless you.
I hear my lady coming; complete gentleman,
I dare not be too busy with my praises,
Th'are dangerous things to deal with.
Exit.
Als. This goes well;
These women are the ladies' cabinets,
Things of most precious trust are locked into 'em.

Enter Beatrice.

Bea. I have within mine eye all my desires;
Requests that holy prayers ascend heaven for,
And brings 'em down to furnish our defects,
Come not more sweet to our necessities
Than thou unto my wishes.
Als. W'are so like
In our expressions, lady, that unless I borrow
The same words, I shall never find their equals.
[*Kisses her.*]
Bea. How happy were this meeting, this embrace,
If it were free from envy! This poor kiss,
It has an enemy, a hateful one,
That wishes poison to't. How well were I now
If there were none such name known as Piracquo?
Nor no such tie as the command of parents,
I should be but too much blessed.
Als. One good service
Would strike off both your fears, and I'll go near it, too,
Since you are so distressed. Remove the cause,
The command ceases, so there's two fears blown out
With one and the same blast.
Bea. Pray let me find you, sir.
What might that service be so strangely happy?

---

127 Where's . . . oversight? what have I failed to see?
128 cozened deceived
129 Unsettle detach
133 pleasure sexual joy
135 She . . . arms she imagines sleeping with someone other than she actually is
137 get beget
139 her . . . to her behavior may be if she is restrained
142 and if
149 yet still
151 injury insult
153 bound grateful
155 steals proceeds with ignorance
II.ii.1 charge responsible care

2 just mutually arranged
3 complete perfect
4 busy open
6 cabinets confidants (from cabinets containing private matters or valuable possessions such as jewels)
10 our defects what we lack
16 envy enmity
17 enemy i.e., Alonzo
22 strike off as with (1) fetters; (2) items of indebtedness; **go near it** be more explicit
23 Remove the cause i.e., eliminate Alonzo
25 blast (as with gunpowder); **find** comprehend
26 happy fortunate

Als. The honorablest piece 'bout man, valor.
I'll send a challenge to Piracquo instantly.
Bea. How? Call you that extinguishing of fear,
When 'tis the only way to keep it flaming?
Are not you ventured in the action,
That's all my joys and comforts? Pray, no more, sir.
Say you prevailed. Y'are danger's and not mine then;
The law would claim you from me, or obscurity
Be made the grave to bury you alive.
I'm glad these thoughts come forth; oh, keep not one
Of this condition, sir; here was a course
Found to bring sorrow on her way to death.
The tears would ne'er ha' dried, till dust had choked 'em.
Blood-guiltiness becomes a fouler visage,
[*Aside.*] And now I think on one. I was to blame,
I ha' marred so good a market with my scorn;
'T had been done questionless; the ugliest creature
Creation framed for some use, yet to see
I could not mark so much where it should be!
Als. Lady –
Bea. [*Aside.*] Why, men of art make much of poison,
Keep one to expel another; where was my art?
Als. Lady, you hear not me.
Bea. I do especially, sir;
The present times are not so sure of our side
As those hereafter may be; we must use 'em then
As thrifty folks their wealth, sparingly now,
Till the time opens.
Als. You teach wisdom, lady.
Bea. Within there; Diaphanta!

Enter Diaphanta.

Dia. Do you call, Madam?
Bea. Perfect your service, and conduct this gentleman
The private way you brought him.
Dia. I shall, Madam.
Als. My love's as firm as love e'er built upon.
Exeunt Diaphanta *and* Alsemero.

Enter De Flores.

De F. [*Aside.*] I have watched this meeting, and do wonder much
What shall become of t'other; I'm sure both
Cannot be served unless she transgress; happily
Then I'll put in for one. For if a woman
Fly from one point, from him she makes a husband,
She spreads and mounts then like arithmetic,
One, ten, a hundred, a thousand, ten thousand,
Proves in time sutler to an army royal.
Now do I look to be most richly railed at,
Yet I must see her.
Bea. [*Aside.*] Why, put case I loathed him
As much as youth and beauty hates a sepulcher,
Must I needs show it? Cannot I keep that secret,
And serve my turn upon him? See, he's here.
[*To him.*] De Flores.
De F. [*Aside.*] Ha, I shall run mad with joy;
She called me fairly by my name De Flores,
And neither rogue nor rascal!
Bea. What ha' you done
To your face a-late? Y'have met with some good physician;

27 piece attribute
31 ventured risked
33 Y'are danger's you belong only to danger
34 The law (of dueling); **obscurity** the need to hide
36–7 keep . . . condition hide not a single thought
37 course course of action
38 on her way i.e., all the way to Beatrice-Joanna's
39 dust (dust of the grave)
40 becomes makes
41 one i.e., De Flores
42 marred . . . market had put off one who could help me (proverbial)
43 questionless (1) without question; (2) without hesitation
44 framed . . . use (refers to the general belief that all persons are created for some purpose)
45 mark perceive; **it** (the use of De Flores)
46 art knowledge
47 expel neutralize
48 especially in a special way
49 sure clearly supportive
52 opens becomes more favorable
54 Perfect complete
58 t'other Alonzo
59 happily (puns on *haply*, perhaps)
60 put in for one offer my services (with sexual implications)
61 point penis
62 spreads and mounts (alludes to birds but also with sexual implications)
64 sutler (1) camp follower who sells provisions to soldiers; (2) cant term for prostitute; **royal** i.e., large
66 put case suppose
69 serve . . . him make use of him for myself

Y'have pruned yourself, methinks, you were
not wont
To look so amorously.
De F. [*Aside.*]　　　Not I;
'Tis the same physnomy, to a hair and pimple,
Which she called scurvy scarce an hour ago.
How is this?
Bea.　　　Come hither; nearer, man!
De F. [*Aside.*] I'm up to the chin in heaven.
Bea.　　　Turn, let me see;
Faugh, 'tis but the heat of the liver, I perceiv't.
I thought it had been worse.
De F. [*Aside.*]　　　Her fingers touched me!
She smells all amber.
Bea. I'll make a water for you shall cleanse this
Within a fortnight.
De F.　　　With your own hands, Lady?
Bea. Yes, mine own, sir; in a work of cure
I'll trust no other.
De F. [*Aside.*]　　　'Tis half an act of pleasure
To hear her talk thus to me.
Bea.　　　When w'are used
To a hard face, 'tis not so unpleasing;
It mends still in opinion, hourly mends,
I see it by experience.
De F. [*Aside.*]　　　I was blest
To light upon this minute; I'll make use on't.
Bea. Hardness becomes the visage of a man well,
It argues service, resolution, manhood,
If cause were of employment.
De F.　　　'Twould be soon seen,
If e'er your Ladyship had cause to use it.
I would but wish the honor of a service
So happy as that mounts to.
Bea.　　　We shall try you.
Oh, my De Flores!
De F. [*Aside.*]　　　How's that?
She calls me hers already, *my* De Flores!
[*To Bea.*] You were about to sigh out
somewhat, Madam.
Bea. No, was I? I forgot. Oh!
De F.　　　There 'tis again,
The very fellow on't.
Bea.　　　You are too quick, sir.
De F. There's no excuse for't now, I heard it
twice, Madam;
That sigh would fain have utterance, take pity
on't,
And lend it a free word; 'las, how it labors
For liberty! I hear the murmur yet
Beat at your bosom.
Bea.　　　Would creation –
De F. Aye, well said, that's it.
Bea.　　　Had formed me man.
De F. Nay, that's not it.
Bea.　　　Oh, 'tis the soul of freedom!
I should not then be forced to marry one
I hate beyond all depths. I should have power
Then to oppose my loathings, nay, remove 'em
Forever from my sight.
De F.　　　Oh blest occasion!
Without change to your sex, you have your
wishes.
Claim so much man in me.
Bea.　　　In thee, De Flores?
There's small cause for that.
De F.　　　Put it not from me,
It's a service that I kneel for to you.
[*Kneels.*]
Bea. You are too violent to mean faithfully;
There's horror in my service, blood and
danger;
Can those be things to sue for?
De F.　　　If you knew
How sweet it were to me to be employed
In any act of yours, you would say then
I failed, and used not reverence enough
When I received the charge on't.
Bea. [*Aside.*]　　　This is much, methinks;
Belike his wants are greedy, and to such
Gold tastes like angels' food. [*To De F.*] Rise.
De F. I'll have the work first.
Bea. [*Aside.*]　　　Possible his need
Is strong upon him. [*Gives him money.*] There's
to encourage thee.
As thou art forward and thy service dangerous,

74 **pruned** preened; improved; adorned
75 **amorously** (1) lovely; (2) lusty
76 **physnomy** physiognomy, face
77 **scurvy** (1) scabby; (2) revolting
80 **heat . . . liver** inflammation of the organ that produces (1) passion; (2) violence
81 **worse** (infected by venereal disease)
82 **amber** ambergris, the basis of perfume
83 **water** medicinal lotion
86 **act of pleasure** (similar to) copulation
87 **used** accustomed
88 **hard** ugly
94 **cause** i.e., there were cause; **employment** (puns on copulation)
97 **mounts** amounts; **try** take the sexual measure of
102 **quick** ardent; sexually active
104 **fain** truly
107 **creation** (i.e., procreation as De Flores hears her)
113 **occasion** opportunity
118 **to mean faithfully** to intend to do what you claim
125 **Belike** probably
126 **angels' food** manna (cf. Ps. 78:25)
127 **Possible** possibly
129 **forward** bold

Thy reward shall be precious.
De F. That I have thought on;
I have assured myself of that beforehand,
And know it will be precious; the thought ravishes.
Bea. Then take him to thy fury.
De F. I thirst for him.
Bea. Alonzo de Piracquo.
De F. His end's upon him;
He shall be seen no more.
[*Rises.*]
Bea. How lovely now
Dost thou appear to me! Never was man
Dearlier rewarded.
De F. I do think of that.
Bea. Be wondrous careful in the execution.
De F. Why, are not both our lives upon the cast?
Bea. Then I throw all my fears upon thy service.
De F. They ne'er shall rise to hurt you.
Bea. When the deed's done,
I'll furnish thee with all things for thy flight;
Thou may'st live bravely in another country.
De F. Aye, aye, we'll talk of that hereafter.
Bea. [*Aside.*] I shall rid myself
Of two inveterate loathings at one time,
Piracquo, and his dog-face.
Exit.
De F. Oh, my blood!
Methinks I feel her in mine arms already,
Her wanton fingers combing out this beard,
And being pleased, praising this bad face.
Hunger and pleasure, they'll commend sometimes
Slovenly dishes, and feed heartily on 'em;
Nay, which is stranger, refuse daintier for 'em.
Some women are odd feeders. I'm too loud.
Here comes the man goes supperless to bed,
Yet shall not rise to-morrow to his dinner.

Enter Alonzo.

Alon. De Flores.
De F. My kind, honorable Lord?
Alon. I am glad I ha' met with thee.
De F. Sir.
Alon. Thou canst show me
The full strength of the castle?
De F. That I can, sir.
Alon. I much desire it.
De F. And if the ways and straits
Of some of the passages be not too tedious for you,
I will assure you, worth your time and sight, my Lord.
Alon. Pah, that shall be no hindrance.
De F. I'm your servant, then.
'Tis now near dinner-time; 'gainst your Lordship's rising
I'll have the keys about me.
Alon. Thanks, kind De Flores.
De F. [*Aside.*] He's safely thrust upon me beyond hopes.
Exeunt.

Act III

[III.i]

Enter Alonzo *and* De Flores. (*In the act-time* De Flores *hides a naked rapier.*)

De F. Yes, here are all the keys; I was afraid, my Lord,
I'd wanted for the postern; this is it.
I've all, I've all, my Lord. This for the sconce.
Alon. 'Tis a most spacious and impregnable fort.
De F. You'll tell me more, my Lord. This descent
Is somewhat narrow. We shall never pass
Well with our weapons; they'll but trouble us.
Alon. Thou say'st true.
De F. Pray, let me help your Lordship.
Alon. 'Tis done. Thanks, kind De Flores.
De F. Here are hooks, my lord,
To hang such things on purpose.
[*He hangs up the swords.*]
Alon. Lead, I'll follow thee.
Exeunt at one door and enter at the other.

---

131 that that reward (presumably sexual favors)
132 it . . . precious (he understands he will end her virginity)
137 Dearlier (1) at more cost; (2) at more pain and danger
139 cast outcome (from throw of dice)
141 deed's (1) the murder; (2) the sexual act
143 bravely splendidly
146 blood aroused sexual passion
149 pleased gratified
150 pleasure sexual desire; **commend** recommend
151 Slovenly base; **feed** (with sexual implications)
154–5 Here . . . dinner (i.e., Alonzo will be killed before sexual consummation)
159 straits narrow parts
160 tedious (1) troublesome; (2) difficult
162 Pah (later ***Push***) (nonsense exclamation of impatience)
163 'gainst before; **rising** (from dinner)
III.i.1 s.d. *act-time* between acts (De Flores hides a rapier to kill Alonzo while openly wearing a sword he will later openly remove)
2 I'd wanted I was without the key; **postern** small back door (of the fortification)
3 sconce small fort or earthwork
5 tell i.e., compliment, be pleased
8 let me help (presumably with the sword belt)

[III.ii]

De F. All this is nothing; you shall see anon
A place you little dream on.
Alon. I am glad
I have this leisure. All your master's house
Imagine I ha' taken a gondola.
De F. All but myself, sir, [*Aside.*] which makes up my safety.
[*To Alon.*] My Lord, I'll place you at a casement here
Will show you the full strength of all the castle.
Look, spend your eye awhile upon that object.
Alon. Here's rich variety, De Flores.
De F. Yes, sir.
Alon. Goodly munition.
De F. Aye, there's ordnance, sir,
No bastard metal, will ring you a peal like bells
At great men's funerals; keep your eye straight, my Lord,
Take special notice of that sconce before you,
There you may dwell awhile.
[*Takes up the rapier.*]
Alon. I am upon't.
De F. And so am I.
[*Stabs him.*]
Alon. De Flores! Oh, De Flores,
Whose malice hast thou put on?
De F. Do you question
A work of secrecy? I must silence you.
[*Stabs him.*]
Alon. Oh, oh, oh.
De F. I must silence you.
[*Stabs him.*]
So, here's an undertaking well accomplished.
This vault serves to good use now. Ha! what's that
Threw sparkles in my eye? Oh, 'tis a diamond
He wears upon his finger. It was well found,
This will approve the work. What, so fast on?
Not part in death? I'll take a speedy course then,
Finger and all shall off. [*Cuts off the finger.*] So, now I'll clear
The passages from all suspect or fear.
Exit with body.

[III.iii]

Enter Isabella *and* Lollio.

Isa. Why, sirrah? Whence have you commission
To fetter the doors against me?
If you keep me in a cage, pray whistle to me,
Let me be doing something.
Lol. You shall be doing, if it please you; I'll whistle to you if you'll pipe after.
Isa. Is it your Master's pleasure, or your own,
To keep me in this pinfold?
Lol. 'Tis for my Master's pleasure, lest being taken in another man's corn, you might be pounded in another place.
Isa. 'Tis very well, and he'll prove very wise.
Lol. He says you have company enough in the house, if you please to be sociable, of all sorts of people.
Isa. Of all sorts? Why, here's none but fools and madmen.
Lol. Very well; and where will you find any other, if you should go abroad? There's my Master and I to boot too.
Isa. Of either sort one, a madman and a fool.
Lol. I would ev'n participate of both then, if I were as you; I know y'are half mad already, be half foolish too.
Isa. Y'are a brave saucy rascal! Come on, sir,
Afford me then the pleasure of your bedlam;
You were commending once today to me
Your last-come lunatic, what a proper
Body there was without brains to guide it,
And what a pitiful delight appeared
In that defect, as if your wisdom had found
A mirth in madness. Pray, sir, let me partake,
If there be such a pleasure.
Lol. If I do not show you the handsomest, discreetest madman, one that I may call the understanding madman, then say I am a fool.

III.ii.1 anon soon
2 dream on conceive of
4 gondola small boat
6 casement recessed opening for viewing fortifications
7 full strength (deliberate irony; cf. lines 14–15)
10 munition weapons; **ordnance** large artillery
11 bastard adulterated; **peal** discharge
14 dwell (1) pause; (2) inhabit (De Flores will bury him there)
16 malice hatred
22 well found (the vault is fairly dark)
23 approve confirm; **fast** tightly
26 suspect suspicion
III.iii.1 sirrah a form of address to an inferior
3 whistle (as to a bird)
4 doing copulating (with sexual pun on *pipe* as penis)
6 pipe after follow my lead
8 pinfold place of confinement for stray livestock
11 pounded (1) impounded; (2) pounded as with a pestle or penis; **another place** vagina
14 house i.e., the madhouse
19 abroad out of the house
20 to ... too in addition
21 Of ... one i.e., one of each
22 participate i.e., sexually
25 brave fine; **saucy** impudent
26 bedlam madhouse
28 last-come most recent; **proper** well-endowed; handsome
34–5 discreetest i.e., showing qualities I describe

Isa. Well, a match, I will say so.

Lol. When you have a taste of the madman, you shall (if you please) see Fools' College, o'th' side; I seldom lock there, 'tis but shooting a bolt or two, and you are among 'em. *Exit. Enter presently.* Come on, sir, let me see how handsomely you'll behave yourself now.

Enter Franciscus.

Fran. How sweetly she looks! Oh, but there's a wrinkle in her brow as deep as philosophy; Anacreon, drink to my mistress' health, I'll pledge it. Stay, stay, there's a spider in the cup! No, 'tis but a grape-stone. Swallow it, fear nothing, poet; so, so, lift higher.

Isa. Alack, alack, it is too full of pity
To be laughed at; how fell he mad? Canst thou tell?

Lol. For love, mistress. He was a pretty poet too, and that set him forwards first; the muses then forsook him. He ran mad for a chambermaid, yet she was but a dwarf neither.

Fran. Hail, bright Titania!
Why stand'st thou idle on these flow'ry banks?
Oberon is dancing with his Dryades;
I'll gather daisies, primrose, violets,
And bind them in a verse of poesie.

Lol. Not too near; you see your danger. [*Shows the whip.*]

Fran. Oh, hold thy hand, great Diomed,
Thou feed'st thy horses well, they shall obey thee;
Get up, Bucephalus kneels. [*Kneels.*]

Lol. You see how I awe my flock; a shepherd has not his dog at more obedience.

Isa. His conscience is unquiet, sure that was
The cause of this. A proper gentleman.

Fran. Come hither, Esculapius; hide the poison. [*Rises.*]

Lol. Well, 'tis hid.

Fran. Didst thou never hear of one Tiresias,
A famous poet?

Lol. Yes, that kept tame wild-geese.

Fran. That's he; I am the man.

Lol. No!

Fran. Yes; but make no words on't. I was a man
Seven years ago.

Lol. A stripling I think you might.

Fran. Now I'm a woman, all feminine.

Lol. I would I might see that.

Fran. Juno struck me blind.

Lol. I'll ne'er believe that; for a woman, they say, has an eye more than a man.

Fran. I say she struck me blind.

Lol. And Luna made you mad; you have two trades to beg with.

Fran. Luna is now big-bellied, and there's room
For both of us to ride with Hecate;
I'll drag thee up into her silver sphere,
And there we'll kick the dog, and beat the bush,
That barks against the witches of the night.
The swift lycanthropi that walks the round,
We'll tear their wolvish skins, and save the sheep. [*Tries to seize Lollio.*]

Lol. Is't come to this? Nay, then my poison comes forth again. Mad slave, indeed; abuse your keeper!

Isa. I prithee hence with him, now he grows dangerous.

---

37 **a match** agreed; **say** (she only agrees to remark)
40 **shooting** pulling back
42 **s.d. *presently*** at once
46–9 **Anacreon . . . poet** (Anacreon, the Greek poet, was said to have choked to death on a grapestone while drinking a cup of wine)
47–8 **spider . . . cup** (proverbial for a poisoned cup)
50 **full of pity** pitiful
54 **first** (i.e., he was first made mad because he was a poet)
56 **but . . . neither** only a dwarf
57–61 **Hail . . . poesie** (Franciscus alludes to Titania, Queen of Fairies in Shakespeare's *Midsummer Night's Dream*, to insinuate Alibius [Oberon, King of the Fairies] is unfaithful [with Dryades])
59 **dancing** colloquialism for copulating; **Dryades** wood nymphs
61 **poesie** (1) poetry; (2) flowers
63 **Diomed** Diomedes, King of the Bistonians, who fed human flesh to his horses (references are to Lollio)
65 **Get up** mount (as on a horse); **Bucephalus** the gigantic horse of Alexander the Great which only he was able to mount
70 **Esculapius** (the Greek god of healing and medicine); **poison** (Lollio's whip)
72 **Tiresias** the Theban prophet blinded by Juno for revealing that love was more pleasurable to women than men; he changed into a woman for seven years, then back to a man
74 **wild-geese** prostitutes
77 **make . . . on't** don't get alarmed by this
79 **stripling** adolescent
81 **I . . . that** (Lollio prefers ocular proof)
84 **eye** perception (with pun on vagina)
86 **Luna** the moon, a proverbial source of madness; **two trades** (1) madness; (2) blindness
88 **big-bellied** (1) full; (2) pregnant
89 **ride** (1) move; (2) copulate; **Hecate** Greek goddess of witchcraft, often identified with the moon
91 **dog . . . bush** both dog and bush were said to belong to the Man in the Moon
93 **lycanthropi** those suffering from lycanthropia, a madness in which men thought themselves to be wolves
96 **abuse** attack (as a wolf)
98 **prithee** pray thee

Fran. Sings.

Sweet love, pity me,
Give me leave to lie with thee.

Lol. No, I'll see you wiser first: to your own kennel.

Fran. No noise, she sleeps, draw all the curtains round;
Let no soft sound molest the pretty soul
But love, and love creeps in at a mouse-hole.

Lol. I would you would get into your hole.

Exit Franciscus.

Now, Mistress, I will bring you another sort. You shall be fooled another while; Tony, come hither, Tony; look who's yonder, Tony.

Enter Antonio.

Ant. Cousin, is it not my aunt?

Lol. Yes, 'tis one of 'em, Tony.

Ant. He, he, how do you, uncle?

Lol. Fear him not, mistress, 'tis a gentle nigget; you may play with him, as safely with him as with his bauble.

Isa. How long hast thou been a fool?

Ant. Ever since I came hither, cousin.

Isa. Cousin? I'm none of thy cousins, fool.

Lol. Oh mistress, fools have always so much wit as to claim their kindred.

Madman within. Bounce, bounce, he falls, he falls!

Isa. Hark you, your scholars in the upper room
Are out of order.

Lol. Must I come among you there? Keep you the fool, mistress; I'll go up and play left-handed Orlando among the madmen.

Exit.

Isa. Well, sir.

Ant. 'Tis opportuneful now, sweet lady! Nay,
Cast no amazing eye upon this change.

Isa. Ha!

Ant. This shape of folly shrouds your dearest love,
The truest servant to your powerful beauties,
Whose magic had this force thus to transform me.

Isa. You are a fine fool indeed.

Ant. Oh, 'tis not strange.
Love has an intellect that runs through all
The scrutinous sciences, and like
A cunning poet, catches a quantity
Of every knowledge, yet brings all home
Into one mystery, into one secret
That he proceeds in.

Isa. Y'are a parlous fool.

Ant. No danger in me. I bring nought but love,
And his soft-wounding shafts to strike you with.
Try but one arrow; if it hurt you,
I'll stand you twenty back in recompense.

[*Kisses her.*]

Isa. A forward fool too!

Ant. This was love's teaching:
A thousand ways he fashioned out my way,
And this I found the safest and the nearest
To tread the Galaxia to my star.

Isa. Profound, withal! Certain, you dreamed of this;
Love never taught it waking.

Ant. Take no acquaintance
Of these outward follies; there is within
A gentleman that loves you.

Isa. When I see him,
I'll speak with him; so in the meantime keep
Your habit, it becomes you well enough.
As you are a gentleman, I'll not discover you;
That's all the favor that you must expect.

---

100 ***lie with*** copulate
102 **No . . . sleeps** (perhaps referring to Cordelia at the end of Shakespeare's *King Lear*)
105 **hole** (an obscene pun)
107 **fooled** (1) be entertained or (2) made to look foolish (by someone else)
110 **Cousin** (common term of address); **aunt** sometimes used to mean bawd or procurer
112 **uncle** colloquial for panderer
113 **nigget** idiot, fool
114 **play with** (1) fondle; (2) copulate
115 **bauble** a fool's stick, often with a clown's head (phallic in shape and here used obscenely)
117 **cousin** (used as a pretense to gain access)
119 **wit** understanding
121 **Bounce** i.e., Bang, like a discharged gun
125 **left-handed** (1) half-heartedly; (2) clumsily
126 **Orlando** the presumably love-mad protagonist of Ariosto's *Orlando Furioso*
128 **opportuneful** seasonable
129 **amazing** startled; amazed; **change** change of attitude
131 **shape** guise; **shrouds** (1) conceals; (2) disguises
136 **scrutinous** searching
137 **cunning** (1) skillful; (2) clever
139 **mystery** trained skill known to the apprenticed (guilds were called mysteries); **secret** secret part
140 **proceeds** (both mentally and sexually); **parlous** (1) dangerous; (2) mischief-making
141 **love** Cupid
144 **stand** give
145 **forward** (1) impudent; (2) aggressive
146 **fashioned out** contrived; **my way** my approach
148 **Galaxia** Milky Way
149 **Profound, withal!** "ingenious, as well!"
150 **Take . . . acquaintance** disregard
151 **follies** pretenses at madness
154 **habit** dress (of a fool)
155 **discover** reveal, report
156 **favor** reward

When you are weary, you may leave the school,
For all this while you have but played the fool.

Enter Lollio.

Ant. And must again. He, he, I thank you, cousin;
I'll be your valentine to-morrow morning.
Lol. How do you like the fool, mistress?
Isa. Passing well, sir.
Lol. Is he not witty, pretty well for a fool?
Isa. If he hold on as he begins, he is like
To come to something.
Lol. Aye, thank a good tutor. You may put him to't; he begins to answer pretty hard questions. Tony, how many is five times six?
Ant. Five times six is six times five.
Lol. What arithmetician could have answered better? How many is one hundred and seven?
Ant. One hundred and seven is seven hundred and one, cousin.
Lol. This is no wit to speak on; will you be rid of the fool now?
Isa. By no means; let him stay a little.
Madman within. Catch there, catch the last couple in hell!
Lol. Again? Must I come among you? Would my master were come home! I am not able to govern both these wards together.

Exit.

Ant. Why should a minute of love's hour be lost?
Isa. Fie, out again! I had rather you kept
Your other posture. You become not your tongue
When you speak from your clothes.
Ant. How can he freeze,
Lives near so sweet a warmth? Shall I alone
Walk through the orchard of the Hesperides,
And cowardly not dare to pull an apple?
This with the red cheeks I must venture for.

[*Tries to kiss her.*]

Enter Lollio *above.*

Isa. Take heed, there's giants keep 'em.
Lol. [*Aside.*] How now, fool, are you good at that? Have you read Lipsius? He's past *Ars Amandi*; I believe I must put harder questions to him, I perceive that –
Isa. You are bold without fear too.
Ant. What should I fear,
Having all joys about me? Do you smile,
And love shall play the wanton on your lip,
Meet and retire, retire and meet again.
Look you but cheerfully, and in your eyes
I shall behold mine own deformity,
And dress myself up fairer; I know this shape
Becomes me not, but in those bright mirrors
I shall array me handsomely.
Lol. Cuckoo, cuckoo!

Exit.

[*Enter*] Madmen *above, some as birds, others as beasts.*

Ant. What are these?
Isa. Of fear enough to part us;
Yet are they but our schools of lunatics,
That act their fantasies in any shapes
Suiting their present thoughts; if sad, they cry;
If mirth be their conceit, they laugh again;
Sometimes they imitate the beasts and birds,
Singing, or howling, braying, barking; all
As their wild fancies prompt 'em.

[*Exeunt* Madmen *above.*]

---

157 school (reference to acting as a grammarschool practice; role-playing)
160 I'll . . . morning (with reference to Ophelia in *Hamlet*)
162 Passing exceedingly
165 come to something (1) succeed with me (a message encoded to Antonio; cf. *tutor*, line 166, and *hard questions*, line 167 as unknowing puns); (2) (with sexual pun)
175 fool (Lollio has decided Antonio is a fool, not a madman)
177–8 Catch . . . hell (refers to barley-brake, a country circle game in which couples attempt to run through the center ["hell"] without being caught)
184 out dropping your disguise
185 posture pose; **become not** (1) are not like; (2) dishonor
186 from out of keeping with; **clothes** inmates' regulation dress
188–9 Walk . . . apple (one of Hercules' tasks was to kill the dragon guarding the orchard of golden apples known as Hesperides)
189 pull pick
191 giants guardians (refers to Lollio and Alibius)
193 Lipsius (pun on lips; Justus Lipsius, 1547–1606, was a famous scholar known for his inconstancy; born Catholic, he later converted to Lutheranism, then Calvinism, before renouncing both for Stoicism. This changeling nature may also explain the coin in Joseph Hall's *Mundus Alter et Idem*, translated into English as *The Discovery of a New World* about 1609, in which a scholar appears on the obverse and a chameleon with the motto *Const. Lips.* appears on the reverse; ***Ars Amandi*** Ovid's book on the art of love (and seduction)
197 Do . . . smile do but smile
198 the wanton lasciviously
202 shape guise
203 mirrors Isabella's eyes
205 Cuckoo (term for cuckold; he condemns himself)
206 s.d. *birds . . . beasts* (presumably refers to noises they make, not costumes)
206 Of fear fearful
208 fantasies (1) imaginations; (2) delusions
210 conceit fancy

Enter Lollio.

Ant. These are no fears.
Isa. But here's a large one, my man.
Ant. Ha, he, that's fine sport indeed, cousin.
Lol. I would my master were come home, 'tis too much for one shepherd to govern two of these flocks; nor can I believe that one churchman can instruct two benefices at once; there will be some incurable mad of the one side, and very fools on the other. Come, Tony.
Ant. Prithee, cousin, let me stay here still.
Lol. No, you must to your book now; you have played sufficiently.
Isa. Your fool is grown wondrous witty.
Lol. Well, I'll say nothing; but I do not think but he will put you down one of these days.

Exeunt Lollio *and* Antonio.

Isa. Here the restrained current might make breach,
Spite of the watchful bankers; would a woman stray,
She need not gad abroad to seek her sin,
It would be brought home one ways or other:
The needle's point will to the fixed north;
Such drawing arctics women's beauties are.

Enter Lollio.

Lol. How dost thou, sweet rogue?
Isa. How now?
Lol. Come, there are degrees, one fool may be better than another.
Isa. What's the matter?
Lol. Nay, if thou giv'st thy mind to fool's-flesh, have at thee!

[*Tries to kiss her.*]

Isa. You bold slave, you!
Lol. I could follow now as t'other fool did.
"What should I fear,
Having all joys about me? Do you but smile,
And love shall play the wanton on your lip,
Meet and retire, retire and meet again.
Look you but cheerfully, and in your eyes
I shall behold my own deformity,
And dress myself up fairer; I know this shape
Becomes me not –" And so as it follows; but is not this the more foolish way? Come, sweet rogue; kiss me, my little Lacedemonian. Let me feel how thy pulses beat; thou hast a thing about thee would do a man pleasure, I'll lay my hand on't.
Isa. Sirrah, no more! I see you have discovered
This love's knight-errant, who hath made adventure
For purchase of my love; be silent, mute,
Mute as a statue, or his injunction
For me enjoying shall be to cut thy throat.
I'll do it, though for no other purpose,
And be sure he'll not refuse it.
Lol. My share, that's all; I'll have my fool's part with you.
Isa. No more! Your master.

Enter Alibius.

Alib. Sweet, how dost thou?
Isa. Your bounden servant, sir.
Alib. Fie, fie, sweetheart,
No more of that.
Isa. You were best lock me up.
Alib. In my arms and bosom, my sweet Isabella,
I'll lock thee up most nearly. Lollio,
We have employment, we have task in hand;
At noble Vermandero's, our castle-captain,
There is a nuptial to be solemnized
(Beatrice-Joanna, his fair daughter, bride),
For which the gentleman hath bespoke our pains.
A mixture of our madmen and our fools,
To finish, as it were, and make the fag

214 **large one** real threat; **my man** Lollio (her servant)
215 **Ha . . . cousin** (Antonio plays a madman again)
218–19 **one . . . benefices** (refers to clerical pluralism used to increase income)
220 **of** on
228 **put . . . down** (1) defeat you in the argument; (2) to copulate
230 **bankers** workmen who build dykes or banks of dirt
232 **brought home** delivered
233 **needle's point** (on the compass, but also with phallic implications); **will** will move
234 **drawing arctics** magnetic poles
241 **have at thee** "here I come"
242 **slave** wretch
243 **I . . . did** having overheard you, I can play your part
252 **the . . . way** (1) a silly way to court you; (2) my straightforward, sexual way
253 **Lacedemonian** (1) someone given to understatement; (2) prostitute
253–4 **Let . . . beat** (with sexual pun)
255 **thing** female genitalia; **do** provide through copulation
256 **lay** (1) wager; (2) place
259 **purchase** (1) obtaining; (2) reward
262 **no other purpose** i.e., to have Alibius rid me of you
266 **bounden** (1) obedient; (2) confined
267 **were best** had better; **lock** (with a chastity belt)
270 **most nearly** (1) more closely; (2) intimately
274 **bride** being the bride
275 **bespoke . . . pains** commissioned our assistance
277 **fag** last part

Of all the revels, the third night from the first;
Only an unexpected passage over,
To make a frightful pleasure, that is all,
But not the all I aim at; could we so act it,
To teach it in a wild distracted measure,
Though out of form and figure, breaking
time's head,
It were no matter, 'twould be healed again
In one age or other, if not in this.
This, this, Lollio, there's a good reward begun,
And will beget a bounty, be it known.

Lol. This is easy, sir, I'll warrant you. You have about you fools and madmen that can dance very well; and 'tis no wonder, your best dancers are not the wisest men; the reason is, with often jumping they jolt their brains down into their feet, that their wits lie more in their heels than in their heads.

Alib. Honest Lollio, thou giv'st me a good
reason,
And a comfort in it.
Isa. Y'have a fine trade on't,
Madmen and fools are a staple commodity.
Alib. Oh wife, we must eat, wear clothes, and live;
Just at the lawyer's haven we arrive,
By madmen and by fools we both do thrive.

Exeunt.

[III.iv]

Enter Vermandero, Alsemero, Jasperino, *and* Beatrice.

Ver. Valencia speaks so nobly of you, sir,
I wish I had a daughter now for you.
Als. The fellow of this creature were a partner
For a king's love.
Ver. I had her fellow once, sir,
But heaven has married her to joys eternal;
'Twere sin to wish her in this vale again.
Come, sir, your friend and you shall see the
pleasures
Which my health chiefly joys in.
Als. I hear the beauty of this seat largely.
Ver. It falls much short of that.

Exeunt. Manet Beatrice.

Bea. So, here's one step
Into my father's favor; time will fix him.
I have got him now the liberty of the house.
So wisdom by degrees works out her freedom;
And if that eye be darkened that offends me
(I wait but that eclipse), this gentleman
Shall soon shine glorious in my father's liking,
Through the refulgent virtue of my love.

Enter De Flores.

De F. [*Aside.*] My thoughts are at a banquet for
the deed;
I feel no weight in't, 'tis but light and cheap
For the sweet recompense that I set down
for't.
Bea. De Flores.
De F. Lady?
Bea. Thy looks promise cheerfully.
De F. All things are answerable – time,
circumstance,
Your wishes, and my service.
Bea. Is it done then?
De F. Piracquo is no more.
Bea. My joys start at mine eyes; our sweet'st
delights
Are evermore born weeping.
De F. I've a token for you.
Bea. For me?
De F. But it was sent somewhat unwillingly,
I could not get the ring without the finger.

[*Shows her the finger.*]

Bea. Bless me! What hast thou done?
De F. Why, is that more
Than killing the whole man? I cut his heart-
strings.
A greedy hand thrust in a dish at court,
In a mistake hath had as much as this.
Bea. 'Tis the first token my father made me send
him.
De F. And I made him send it back again

---

278 Of...first (the wedding celebration will continue for three days)
279–80 Only...all (the fools and madmen will rush in for a harmless but grotesque [frightening and pleasurable] dance)
282 teach present
283 time's head measure of the set tempo
287 bounty generous payment
296 on't in it
299 lawyer's haven (i.e., lawyers are also fools and madmen)
300 thrive make our living
III.iv.3 fellow match
4 fellow i.e., Beatrice-Joanna's mother, now dead
6 vale vale of tears, earthly life
8 health well-being
9 seat estate, residence; **largely** by common report
11 fix (1) conquer; (2) make him a fixture
14 if...me (cf. Matt. 18:9)
17 refulgent radiant
18 banquet celebration; **the deed** Alonzo's death
20 For as for; **set down** specified, as in an account
22 answerable fitting
26 token (1) proof of my deed; (2) love token
30 heart-strings (strings were believed to hold the heart)
31 greedy hand (reference to cutting off Alonzo's finger which is unimportant compared to his loss of life); **dish** (woman as sexual food)
32 had...this would have the same result

For his last token; I was loath to leave it,
And I'm sure dead men have no use of jewels.
He was as loath to part with't, for it stuck
As if the flesh and it were both one substance.
Bea. At the stag's fall the keeper has his fees.
'Tis soon applied, all dead men's fees are yours, sir.
I pray, bury the finger, but the stone
You may make use on shortly; the true value,
Take't of my truth, is near three hundred ducats.
De F. 'Twill hardly buy a capcase for one's conscience, though,
To keep it from the worm, as fine as 'tis.
Well, being my fees I'll take it;
Great men have taught me that, or else my merit
Would scorn the way on't.
Bea. It might justly, sir.
Why, thou mistak'st, De Flores, 'tis not given
In state of recompense.
De F. No, I hope so, Lady,
You should soon witness my contempt to't then!
Bea. Prithee, thou look'st as if thou wert offended.
De F. That were strange, Lady; 'tis not possible
My service should draw such a cause from you.
Offended? could you think so? That were much
For one of my performance, and so warm
Yet in my service.
Bea. 'Twere misery in me to give you cause, sir.
De F. I know so much, it were so, misery
In her most sharp condition.
Bea. 'Tis resolved then;
Look you sir, here's three thousand golden florins.
I have not meanly thought upon thy merit.
De F. What, salary? Now you move me.
Bea. How, De Flores?
De F. Do you place me in the rank of verminous fellows,
To destroy things for wages? Offer gold?
The life blood of man! Is anything
Valued too precious for my recompense?
Bea. I understand thee not.
De F. I could ha' hired
A journeyman in murder at this rate,
And mine own conscience might [have slept at ease],
And have had the work brought home.
Bea. [*Aside.*] I'm in a labyrinth;
What will content him? I would fain be rid of him.
[*To De F.*] I'll double the sum, sir.
De F. You take a course
To double my vexation, that's the good you do.
Bea. [*Aside.*] Bless me! I am now in worse plight than I was;
I know not what will please him. [*To De F.*] For my fear's sake,
I prithee make away with all speed possible.
And if thou be'st so modest not to name
The sum that will content thee, paper blushes not;
Send thy demand in writing; it shall follow thee,
But prithee take thy flight.
De F. You must fly too then.
Bea. I?
De F. I'll not stir a foot else.
Bea. What's your meaning?
De F. Why, are not you as guilty, in (I'm sure)
As deep as I? And we should stick together.
Come, your fears counsel you but ill, my absence
Would draw suspect upon you instantly;
There were no rescue for you.
Bea. [*Aside.*] He speaks home.
De F. Nor is it fit we two, engaged so jointly,

---

36 **jewels** (1) signs of virginity; (2) maidenhead
38 **one substance** in marriage (Matt. 19:5)
39 **keeper** gamekeeper, who was entitled to certain parts of the animals he slaughtered
43 **of . . . truth** at my word; **ducats** valuable gold coins
44 **capcase** small traveling case; wallet
45 **worm** pangs of remorse
47 **my merit** (as opposed to trickery)
48 **way on't** reward given
50 **In state** by way
54 **cause** accusation, reproach
58 **misery** ingratitude
59 **misery** suffering
61 **golden florins** gold coins (or perhaps a note of payment in that amount)
62 **meanly** ungenerously
63 **salary** financial reward; **move** provoke, anger
66 **Is anything** can anything be
68–71 **I . . . home** (metaphor based on giving out piecework for later delivery to the contractor)
69 **journeyman** trained assassin
71 **brought home** waited at home for the hired killer to deliver the deed; **labyrinth** quandary
77 **make away** flee
84 **stick together** (1) as partners or accomplices; (2) as a finger and ring
86 **suspect** suspicion
87 **home** (1) truly; (2) forcefully
88 **engaged so** (1) jointly collaborating so closely; (2) betrothed

Should part and live asunder.
[*Tries to kiss her.*]
Bea. How now, sir?
This shows not well.
De F. What makes your lip so strange?
This must not be 'twixt us.
Bea. [*Aside.*] The man talks wildly.
De F. Come, kiss me with a zeal now.
Bea. [*Aside.*] Heaven, I doubt him!
De F. I will not stand so long to beg 'em shortly.
Bea. Take heed, De Flores, of forgetfulness,
'Twill soon betray us.
De F. Take you heed first;
Faith, y'are grown much forgetful, y'are to blame in't.
Bea. [*Aside.*] He's bold, and I am blamed for't!
De F. I have eased you
Of your trouble. Think on't, I'm in pain,
And must be eased of you; 'tis a charity,
Justice invites your blood to understand me.
Bea. I dare not.
De F. Quickly!
Bea. Oh, I never shall!
Speak it yet further off that I may lose
What has been spoken, and no sound remain on't.
I would not hear so much offense again
For such another deed.
De F. Soft, lady, soft;
The last is not yet paid for! Oh, this act
Has put me into spirit; I was as greedy on't
As the parched earth of moisture, when the clouds weep.
Did you not mark, I wrought myself into't,
Nay, sued and kneeled for't. Why was all that pains took?
You see I have thrown contempt upon your gold,
Not that I want it not, for I do piteously:
In order I will come unto't, and make use on't,
But 'twas not held so precious to begin with;
For I place wealth after the heels of pleasure,
And were I not resolved in my belief
That thy virginity were perfect in thee,
I should but take my recompense with grudging,
As if I had but half my hopes I agreed for.
Bea. Why, 'tis impossible thou canst be so wicked,
Or shelter such a cunning cruelty,
To make his death the murderer of my honor!
Thy language is so bold and vicious,
I cannot see which way I can forgive it
With any modesty.
De F. Push, you forget yourself!
A woman dipped in blood, and talk of modesty!
Bea. Oh, misery of sin! Would I had been bound
Perpetually unto my living hate
In that Piracquo, than to hear these words.
Think but upon the distance that creation
Set 'twixt thy blood and mine, and keep thee there.
De F. Look but into your conscience, read me there.
'Tis a true book, you'll find me there your equal.
Push, fly not to your birth, but settle you
In what the act has made you, y'are no more now;
You must forget your parentage to me.
Y'are the deed's creature; by that name
You lost your first condition, and I challenge you,
As peace and innocency has turned you out,
And made you one with me.
Bea. With thee, foul villain?
De F. Yes, my fair murd'ress; do you urge me?
Though thou writ'st maid, thou whore in thy affection!
'Twas changed from thy first love, and that's a kind
Of whoredom in thy heart; and he's changed now,
To bring thy second on, thy Alsemero,

90 **shows** lacks; **strange** cold, distant
92 **doubt** (1) suspect; (2) fear; (3) distrust
93 **beg . . . shortly** seek my earned favor much longer
94 **forgetfulness** (reminding him he is merely a servant)
96 **forgetful** (1) of your guilt; (2) of your obligation to me; **to blame** too blameworthy
98 **in pain** suffering in love
99 **eased** sexually relieved; **charity** a gift to one sexually deprived
100 **blood** sexual impulse; **understand** satisfy
102 **lose** forget
104 **offense** i.e., offensive suggestions
105 **such another** any such; **Soft** not so fast; wait a moment
106 **act** (of blood)
109 **wrought** forced
113 **In order** in due course
115 **pleasure** sexual consummation
122 **his** Alonzo's; **honor** chastity
126 **modesty** i.e., losing your virginity
129 **than** rather than
130 **creation** the social rank
133 **equal** (1) in violence; (2) in determination
136 **to** to replace it with
137 **the deed's creature** (1) recreated or reformed by this deed; (2) enslaved to the deed
138 **challenge** claim
139 **turned you out** dismissed you (from innocence; from Paradise)
141 **urge** incite
142 **writ'st maid** would call yourself virgin; **affection** passion
143 **first love** i.e., Alonzo
144 **changed** (from life to death)

Whom (by all sweets that ever darkness tasted)
If I enjoy thee not, thou ne'er enjoy'st;
I'll blast the hopes and joys of marriage,
I'll confess all; my life I rate at nothing.
Bea. De Flores!
De F. I shall rest from all lovers' plagues then;
I live in pain now. That shooting eye
Will burn my heart to cinders.
Bea. Oh sir, hear me.
De F. She that in life and love refuses me,
In death and shame my partner she shall be.
Bea. Stay, hear me once for all; [*Kneels.*] I make thee master
Of all the wealth I have in gold and jewels.
Let me go poor unto my bed with honor,
And I am rich in all things.
De F. Let this silence thee:
The wealth of all Valencia shall not buy
My pleasure from me;
Can you weep fate from its determined purpose?
So soon may you weep me.
Bea. Vengeance begins;
Murder I see is followed by more sins.
Was my creation in the womb so cursed,
It must engender with a viper first?
De F. Come, rise, and shroud your blushes in my bosom;
[*Raises her.*]
Silence is one of pleasure's best receipts.
Thy peace is wrought forever in this yielding.
'Las, how the turtle pants! Thou'lt love anon
What thou so fear'st and faint'st to venture on.
Exeunt.

Act IV

[IV.i]

[*Dumb Show.*]

Enter Gentlemen, Vermandero *meeting them with action of wonderment at the flight of* Piracquo. *Enter* Alsemero, *with* Jasperino, *and* Gallants; Vermandero *points to him, the* Gentlemen *seeming to applaud the choice*; [*Exeunt in procession*] Alsemero, Jasperino *and* Gentlemen; Beatrice *the bride following in great state, accompanied with* Diaphanta, Isabella *and other* Gentlewomen: De Flores *after all, smiling at the accident*; Alonzo's *ghost appears to* De Flores *in the midst of his smile, startles him, showing him the hand whose finger he had cut off. They pass over in great solemnity.*

Enter Beatrice.

Bea. This fellow has undone me endlessly,
Never was bride so fearfully distressed;
The more I think upon th'ensuing night,
And whom I am to cope with in embraces,
One that's ennobled both in blood and mind,
So clear in understanding (that's my plague now),
Before whose judgment will my fault appear
Like malefactors' crimes before tribunals –
There is no hiding on't, the more I dive
Into my own distress; how a wise man
Stands for a great calamity! There's no venturing
Into his bed, what course soe'er I light upon,
Without my shame, which may grow up to danger;
He cannot but in justice strangle me
As I lie by him, as a cheater use me;
'Tis a precious craft to play with a false die
Before a cunning gamester. Here's his closet,
The key left in't, and he abroad i' th' park.
Sure 'twas forgot; I'll be so bold as look in't.
[*Opens closet.*]
Bless me! A right physician's closet'tis,
Set round with vials, every one her mark too.

146 sweets sexual pleasures
151 plagues torments
152 shooting (1) communicating; (2) provocative
163 Vengeance (1) payment; (2) the consequences of sin
165–6 Was . . . first? was I cursed at birth to know a viper before knowing a man?
167 shroud hide (but with unconscious anticipation of the possible outcome)
168 receipts recipes
170 turtle turtle-dove, a bird of love known to protect its mate; **anon** at once
IV.i.1 s.d. 2 *wonderment* Vermandero assumes Alonzo has abandoned Beatrice-Joanna
s.d.9 *accident* turn of events
s.d. 11 pass over cross over the stage (or upper stage) and exit
1 fellow (colloquial for someone of lower rank and little worth); **undone** (1) ravished; (2) ruined; **endlessly** (1) infinitely; (2) eternally
2 distressed (1) anxious; (2) deprived
4 cope (1) contend; (2) pun on copulate
5 One i.e., Alsemero
9–10 dive Into (1) plunge; (2) contemplate; (3) comprehend
11 Stands for represents (because he will be harder to deceive)
13 grow . . . danger increase to a dangerous state
15 use copulate with
16 precious (1) delicate; (2) subtle; (3) risky; **die** (singular of dice)
17 closet private room, study
20 right true
21 vials small bottles; **her mark** its label

Sure he does practice physic for his own use,
Which may be safely called your great man's wisdom.
What manuscript lies here? "The Book of Experiment,
Called Secrets in Nature"; so 'tis, 'tis so;
"How to know whether a woman be with child or no."
I hope I am not yet; if he should try, though!
Let me see, folio forty-five. Here 'tis;
The leaf tucked down upon't, the place suspicious.
"If you would know whether a woman be with child or not, give her two spoonfuls of the white water in glass C –"
Where's that glass C? Oh yonder, I see't now –
"and if she be with child, she sleeps full twelve hours after, if not, not."
None of that water comes into my belly.
I'll know you from a hundred; I could break you now,
Or turn you into milk, and so beguile
The master of the mystery, but I'll look to you.
Ha! That which is next is ten times worse.
"How to know whether a woman be a maid or not";
If that should be applied, what would become of me?
Belike he has a strong faith of my purity,
That never yet made proof; but this he calls
"A merry sleight, but true experiment, the author Antonius Mizaldus. Give the party you suspect the quantity of a spoonful of the water in the glass M, which upon her that is a maid makes three several effects: 'twill make her incontinently gape, then fall into a sudden sneezing, last into a violent laughing; else dull, heavy, and lumpish." Where had I been?
I fear it, yet 'tis seven hours to bedtime. 54

Enter Diaphanta.

Dia. Cuds, Madam, are you here?
Bea. [*Aside.*] Seeing that wench now,
A trick comes in my mind; 'tis a nice piece
Gold cannot purchase. [*To Dia.*] I come hither, wench,
To look my Lord.
Dia. [*Aside.*] Would I had such a cause to look him too!
[*To Bea.*] Why, he's i' th' park, Madam.
Bea. There let him be.
Dia. Aye, Madam, let him compass
Whole parks and forests, as great rangers do;
At roosting time a little lodge can hold 'em.
Earth-conquering Alexander, that thought the world
Too narrow for him, in the end had but his pit-hole.
Bea. I fear thou art not modest, Diaphanta.
Dia. Your thoughts are so unwilling to be known, Madam;
'Tis ever the bride's fashion towards bed-time,
To set light by her joys, as if she owed 'em not.
Bea. Her joys? Her fears, thou would'st say.
Dia. Fear of what?
Bea. Art thou a maid, and talk'st so to a maid? 71
You leave a blushing business behind,
Beshrew your heart for't!
Dia. Do you mean good sooth, Madam?
Bea. Well, if I'd thought upon the fear at first,
Man should have been unknown.
Dia. Is't possible?
Bea. I will give a thousand ducats to that woman
Would try what my fear were, and tell me true

22 **physic** medicine; **for ... use** to protect against poison
24–5 **"The ... Nature"** *De Arcanis Naturae* by Antonius Mizaldus (1520–78), a book of science and pseudo-science that does not include the tests used here (although tests for virginity and pregnancy were in some of his works); the format suggests instead a commonplace book
26–52 **"How ... lumpish"** (Beatrice-Joanna is reading and reflecting on the book's contents)
32 **water** medicinal liquid; **glass** i.e., a glass bottle or container
37 **you** i.e., glass C
38 **Or ... milk** (by changing the contents or label)
39 **mystery** secret; **look to** keep watchful of
42 **applied** i.e., tested on me
43 **Belike** probably
44 **That** who
45 **sleight** method, trick
49 **several** separate, different
50 **incontinently gape** yawn uncontrollably
52 **else** otherwise
52–3 **Where ... been?** "what would have happened if I had not discovered this?"
55 **Cuds** "God's" (a mild oath)
56 **trick** strategy; **nice piece** (1) good plan; (2) scrupulous woman
57 **look** look for
61 **compass** ride around
62 **parks** colloquial for female bodies; **rangers** (1) park keepers; (2) rakes; (3) colloquial for penises
63 **lodge** colloquial for vagina
64 **Alexander** Alexander the Great (356–323 BC)
65 **end** colloquial for vagina; **pit-hole** (1) grave; (2) vagina
66 **modest** chaste
69 **owed** owned
71 **maid** virgin
73 **Beshrew** curse; **mean ... sooth** tell the truth
75 **Man ... unknown** (1) I would have wished men did not exist; (2) I would not ever know a man
77 **try** experience

To-morrow, when she gets from't. As she likes
I might perhaps be drawn to't.
Dia. Are you in earnest?
Bea. Do you get the woman, then challenge me,
And see if I'll fly from't; but I must tell you
This by the way, she must be a true maid,
Else there's no trial, my fears are not hers else.
Dia. Nay, she that I would put into your hands,
Madam, Shall be a maid.
Bea. You know I should be shamed else,
Because she lies for me.
Dia. 'Tis a strange humor.
But are you serious still? Would you resign
Your first night's pleasure, and give money too?
Bea. As willingly as live; [*Aside.*] alas, the gold
Is but a by-bet to wedge in the honor.
Dia. I do not know how the world goes abroad
For faith or honesty; there's both required in this.
Madam, what say you to me, and stray no further?
I've a good mind, in troth, to earn your money.
Bea. Y'are too quick, I fear, to be a maid.
Dia. How? Not a maid? Nay, then you urge me, Madam;
Your honorable self is not a truer
With all your fears upon you –
Bea. [*Aside.*] Bad enough then.
Dia. Than I with all my lightsome joys about me.
Bea. I'm glad to hear't then; you dare put your honesty
Upon an easy trial?
Dia. Easy? Anything.
Bea. I'll come to you straight. [*Goes to the closet.*]
Dia. [*Aside.*] She will not search me, will she,
Like the forewoman of a female jury?
Bea. Glass M: aye, this is it; look, Diaphanta,
You take no worse than I do.
[*Drinks.*]
Dia. And in so doing,
I will not question what 'tis, but take it.
[*Drinks.*]
Bea. [*Aside.*] Now if the experiment be true, 'twill praise itself,
And give me noble ease. Begins already;
[*Diaphanta gapes.*]
There's the first symptom; and what haste it makes
To fall into the second, there by this time!
[*Diaphanta sneezes.*]
Most admirable secret! On the contrary,
It stirs not me a whit, which most concerns it.
Dia. Ha, ha, ha!
Bea. [*Aside.*] Just in all things and in order
As if 'twere circumscribed; one accident
Gives way unto another.
Dia. Ha, ha, ha!
Bea. How now, wench?
Dia. Ha, ha, ha! I am so, so light at heart – ha, ha, ha! – so pleasurable!
But one swig more, sweet Madam!
Bea. Aye, to-morrow;
We shall have time to sit by't.
Dia. Now I'm sad again.
Bea. [*Aside.*] It lays itself so gently, too! [*To Dia.*] Come, wench,
Most honest Diaphanta I dare call thee now.
Dia. Pray tell me, Madam, what trick call you this?
Bea. I'll tell thee all hereafter; we must study
The carriage of this business.
Dia. I shall carry't well,
Because I love the burthen.
Bea. About midnight
You must not fail to steal forth gently,
That I may use the place.
Dia. Oh, fear not, Madam,
I shall be cool by that time. The bride's place,
And with a thousand ducats! I'm for a justice now,

78 gets from't removes herself from intercourse
80 challenge me demand the money from me
82 true maid virgin
83 fears anxieties
86 lies (1) substitutes; (2) lies down to make love; (3) tells lies; (4) cheats; (5) colloquial for copulates; **humor** disposition, whim
90 by-bet added incentive (literally, a side bet)
91 how . . . abroad how truthful the world is
94 troth truth
95 quick lively; sexually ardent
96 urge insult
98 Bad . . . then judged by Beatrice-Joanna, Diaphanta must be unchaste
99 lightsome lighthearted
102 straight directly
103 Like . . . jury (refers to the trial of the Countess of Essex in 1613 who sued before a group of women for divorce on grounds of non-consummation)
107 praise itself show its excellence
111 admirable wonderful
112 concerns needs to know
113 Just precise
114 circumscribed confined, specified; **accident** symptom
118 by't and leisurely enjoy it
119 lays itself subsides
120 honest chaste
123 carriage management (way it is carried out)
124 burthen burden, or the main theme (as in a song)

I bring a portion with me; I scorn small fools.
Exeunt.

[IV.ii]

Enter Vermandero *and* Servant.

Ver. I tell thee, knave, mine honor is in question,
A thing till now free from suspicion,
Nor ever was there cause; who of my gentlemen
Are absent? Tell me and truly how many and who.
Ser. Antonio, sir, and Franciscus.
Ver. When did they leave the castle?
Ser. Some ten days since, sir, the one intending to
Briamata, th'other for Valencia.
Ver. The time accuses 'em; a charge of murder
Is brought within my castle gate, Piracquo's murder;
I dare not answer faithfully their absence.
A strict command of apprehension
Shall pursue 'em suddenly, and either wipe
The stain off clear, or openly discover it.
Provide me wingèd warrants for the purpose.
Exit Servant.
See, I am set on again.

Enter Tomazo.

Tom. I claim a brother of you.
Ver. Y'are too hot,
Seek him not here.
Tom. Yes, 'mong your dearest bloods,
If my peace find no fairer satisfaction;
This is the place must yield account for him,
For here I left him, and the hasty tie
Of this snatched marriage gives strong testimony
Of his most certain ruin.
Ver. Certain falsehood!
This is the place indeed; his breach of faith
Has too much marred both my abused love,
The honorable love I reserved for him,
And mocked my daughter's joy; the prepared morning
Blushed at his infidelity. He left
Contempt and scorn to throw upon those friends
Whose belief hurt 'em. Oh, 'twas most ignoble
To take his flight so unexpectedly,
And throw such public wrongs on those that loved him.
Tom. Then this is all your answer?
Ver. 'Tis too fair
For one of his alliance; and I warn you
That this place no more see you.
Exit.

Enter De Flores.

Tom. The best is,
There is more ground to meet a man's revenge on.
Honest De Flores!
De F. That's my name indeed!
Saw you the bride? Good sweet sir, which way took she?
Tom. I have blest mine eyes from seeing such a false one.
De F. [*Aside.*] I'd fain get off, this man's not for my company.
I smell his brother's blood when I come near him.
Tom. Come hither, kind and true one; I remember
My brother loved thee well.
De F. Oh, purely, dear sir!
[*Aside.*] Methinks I am now again a-killing on him,
He brings it so fresh to me.
Tom. Thou canst guess, sirrah,
(One honest friend has an instinct of jealousy)
At some foul guilty person?
De F. 'Las, sir, I am so charitable, I think none
Worse than myself. You did not see the bride then?
Tom. I prithee name her not. Is she not wicked?
De F. No, no, a pretty, easy, round-packed sinner,
As your most ladies are, else you might think
I flattered her; but, sir, at no hand wicked,

129 portion large dowry (with pun on virginity); **scorn . . . fools** desire large fools (to guarantee the deception)
IV.ii.8 Briamata Vermandero's country estate
11 faithfully (1) confidently; (2) in good faith
12 apprehension arrest
14 discover uncover, reveal
16 set on harassed (he sees Tomazo)
18 bloods kin
22 snatched hastened, sudden
25 marred (1) tainted; (2) spoiled
30 belief mistaken confidence
33 fair kind
34 alliance (1) kindred; (2) lineage
36 There . . . on there are other ways to get revenge
40 fain happily
43 purely completely
46 instinct . . . jealousy instinctive suspicion
51 easy i.e., easy of virtue; **round-packed** (1) plump and firm; (2) full and shapely
52 your most most your
53 at . . . hand by no means

Till th'are so old their chins and noses meet,
And they salute witches. I am called, I think, sir.
[*Aside*.] His company ev'n o'erlays my conscience.

Exit.

Tom. That De Flores has a wondrous honest heart;
He'll bring it out in time, I'm assured on't.
Oh, here's the glorious master of the day's joy.
'Twill not be long till he and I do reckon.

Enter Alsemero.

Sir!
Als. You are most welcome.
Tom. You may call that word back;
I do not think I am, nor wish to be.
Als. 'Tis strange you found the way to this house then.
Tom. Would I'd ne'er known the cause! I'm none of those, sir,
That come to give you joy, and swill your wine;
'Tis a more precious liquor that must lay
The fiery thirst I bring.
Als. Your words and you
Appear to me great strangers.
Tom. Time and our swords
May make us more acquainted; this the business:
I should have a brother in your place;
How treachery and malice have disposed of him,
I'm bound to inquire of him which holds his right,
Which never could come fairly.
Als. You must look
To answer for that word, sir.
Tom. Fear you not,
I'll have it ready drawn at our next meeting.
Keep your day solemn. Farewell, I disturb it not;
I'll bear the smart with patience for a time.

Exit.

Als. 'Tis somewhat ominous this. A quarrel entered
Upon this day; my innocence relieves me,

Enter Jasperino.

I should be wondrous sad else. – Jasperino,
I have news to tell thee, strange news.
Jas. I ha' some too,
I think as strange as yours; would I might keep
Mine, so my faith and friendship might be kept in't!
Faith, sir, dispense a little with my zeal,
And let it cool in this.
Als. This puts me on,
And blames thee for thy slowness.
Jas. All may prove nothing;
Only a friendly fear that leapt from me, sir.
Als. No question it may prove nothing; let's partake it, though.
Jas. 'Twas Diaphanta's chance (for to that wench
I pretend honest love, and she deserves it)
To leave me in a back part of the house,
A place we chose for private conference;
She was no sooner gone, but instantly
I heard your bride's voice in the next room to me;
And lending more attention, found De Flores
Louder than she.
Als. De Flores? Thou art out now.
Jas. You'll tell me more anon.
Als. Still I'll prevent thee;
The very sight of him is poison to her.
Jas. That made me stagger too, but Diaphanta
At her return confirmed it.
Als. Diaphanta!
Jas. Then fell we both to listen, and words passed
Like those that challenge interest in a woman.
Als. Peace, quench thy zeal; 'tis dangerous to thy bosom.
Jas. Then truth is full of peril.
Als. Such truths are.

---

55 **salute** are called
56 **o'erlays** oppresses; **conscience** (also means *mind*)
58 **it** (i.e., the truth about Alonzo)
59 **glorious** proud, vainglorious
60 **reckon** settle our differences
66 **more... liquor** blood; **lay** satisfy, allay
68 **strangers** strange, unexpected reactions
72 **his right** (1) his wife, Beatrice; (2) his title of husband
74 **that word** (1) "fairly"; (2) your accusation generally
75 **it** (1) reply; (2) sword (to make good the challenge)
76 **day solemn** wedding day sacred (with appropriate ceremony)
77 **smart** pain, grief
80 **sad** (1) grieved; (2) concerned
83 **so** provided that
84 **zeal** i.e., zealous service, loyalty
85 **it... this** (i.e., not relay the sorry news); **puts me on** provokes me
88 **partake** share
89 **wench** woman
90 **pretend** offer, propose; **honest** (1) genuine; (2) chaste (Diaphanta is still a virgin)
92 **conference** (1) meeting; (2) sexual encounter (if so, it did not materialize)
96 **out** mistaken
97 **You'll... anon** you'll soon think otherwise; **prevent** forestall
99 **stagger** doubt
101 **fell... both** we both proceeded
102 **challenge** claim

Oh, were she the sole glory of the earth,
Had eyes that could shoot fire into kings' breasts,
And touched, she sleeps not here! Yet I have time,
Though night be near, to be resolved hereof;
And prithee do not weigh me by my passions.
Jas. I never weighed friend so.
Als. Done charitably.
That key will lead thee to a pretty secret, [*Gives key.*]
By a Chaldean taught me, and I've made
My study upon some; bring from my closet
A glass inscribed there with the letter M,
And question not my purpose.
Jas. It shall be done, sir. *Exit.*
Als. How can this hang together? Not an hour since,
Her woman came pleading her lady's fears,
Delivered her for the most timorous virgin
That ever shrunk at man's name, and so modest,
She charged her weep out her request to me,
That she might come obscurely to my bosom.

Enter Beatrice.

Bea. [*Aside.*] All things go well; my woman's preparing yonder
For her sweet voyage, which grieves me to lose;
Necessity compels it; I lose all else.
Als. [*Aside.*] Push, modesty's shrine is set in yonder forehead.
I cannot be too sure though. [*To her.*] My Joanna!
Bea. Sir, I was bold to weep a message to you,
Pardon my modest fears.
Als. [*Aside.*] The dove's not meeker,
She's abused, questionless.

Enter Jasperino [*with glass*].

Oh, are you come, sir?
Bea. [*Aside.*] The glass, upon my life! I see the letter.
Jas. Sir, this is M.
Als. 'Tis it.
Bea. [*Aside.*] I am suspected.
Als. How fitly our bride comes to partake with us!
Bea. What is't, my lord?
Als. No hurt.
Bea. Sir, pardon me,
I seldom taste of any composition.
Als. But this upon my warrant you shall venture on.
Bea. I fear 'twill make me ill.
Als. Heaven forbid that.
Bea. [*Aside.*] I'm put now to my cunning; th'effects I know,
If I can now but feign 'em handsomely. [*Drinks.*]
Als. [*To Jas.*] It has that secret virtue it ne'er missed, sir,
Upon a virgin.
Jas. Treble qualitied?
[*Beatrice gapes, then sneezes.*]
Als. By all that's virtuous it takes there, proceeds!
Jas. This is the strangest trick to know a maid by.
Bea. Ha, ha, ha!
You have given me joy of heart to drink, my Lord.
Als. No, thou hast given me such joy of heart,
That never can be blasted.
Bea. What's the matter, sir?
Als. [*To Jas.*] See, now 'tis settled in a melancholy,
Keeps both the time and method; [*To her.*] my Joanna!
Chaste as the breath of heaven, or morning's womb,
That brings the day forth; thus my love encloses thee.
[*Embraces her.*] *Exeunt.*

[IV.iii]

Enter Isabella *and* Lollio.

Isa. Oh heaven! Is this the waiting moon?
Does love turn fool, run mad, and all at once?
Sirrah, here's a madman, akin to the fool too,

107 touched unchaste; **here** in my bed
108 resolved settled; knowing
109 weigh judge; **passions** outbursts
111 pretty ingenious, shrewd
112 Chaldean soothsayer, astrologer (cf. Dan. 2)
113 some i.e., secrets
116 since ago
117 fears (for her first sexual encounter)
118 Delivered ... for described her as
121 obscurely (1) in the dark; (2) unseen
123 sweet voyage copulation
129 abused maligned; **questionless** without doubt
134 composition medicine of more than one ingredient
135 warrant guarantee
138 handsomely (1) convincingly; (2) easily
140 Treble qualified producing three effects
141 takes takes effect
146 blasted destroyed
148 time sequence; **method** effect
IV.iii.3 madman i.e., the disguised Franciscus; **fool** i.e., the disguised Antonio

A lunatic lover.

Lol. No, no, not he I brought the letter from?

Isa. Compare his inside with his out, and tell me. [*Gives him the letter.*]

Lol. The out's mad, I'm sure of that; I had a taste on't. [*Reads.*] "To the bright Andromeda, chief chambermaid to the Knight of the Sun, at the sign of Scorpio, in the middle region, sent by the bellows mender of Aeolus. Pay the post." This is stark madness.

Isa. Now mark the inside. [*Takes the letter and reads.*] "Sweet lady, having now cast off this counterfeit cover of a madman, I appear to your best judgment a true and faithful lover of your beauty."

Lol. He is mad still.

Isa. "If any fault you find, chide those perfections in you, which have made me imperfect; 'tis the same sun that causeth to grow, and enforceth to wither –"

Lol. Oh, rogue!

Isa. "– Shapes and transshapes, destroys and builds again; I come in winter to you dismantled of my proper ornaments. By the sweet splendor of your cheerful smiles, I spring and live a lover."

Lol. Mad rascal still!

Isa. "Tread him not under foot, that shall appear an honor to your bounties. I remain – mad till I speak with you, from whom I expect my cure. Yours all, or one beside himself, Franciscus."

Lol. You are like to have a fine time on't; my master and I may give over our professions. I do not think but you can cure fools and madmen faster than we, with little pains too.

Isa. Very likely.

Lol. One thing I must tell you, mistress. You perceive that I am privy to your skill; if I find you minister once and set up the trade, I put in for my thirds, I shall be mad or fool else.

Isa. The first place is thine, believe it, Lollio;
If I do fall –

Lol. I fall upon you.

Isa. So.

Lol. Well, I stand to my venture.

Isa. But thy counsel now; how shall I deal with 'em?

Lol. Why, do you mean to deal with 'em?

Isa. Nay, the fair understanding, how to use 'em.

Lol. Abuse 'em! That's the way to mad the fool, and make a fool of the madman, and then you use 'em kindly.

Isa. 'Tis easy, I'll practice; do thou observe it;
The key of thy wardrobe.

Lol. There; fit yourself for 'em, and I'll fit 'em both for you. [*Gives her the key.*]

Isa. Take thou no further notice than the outside.

Exit.

Lol. Not an inch; I'll put you to the inside.

Enter Alibius.

Alib. Lollio, art there? Will all be perfect, think'st thou?
To-morrow night, as if to close up the solemnity,
Vermandero expects us.

Lol. I mistrust the madmen most; the fools will do well enough; I have taken pains with them.

Alib. Tush, they cannot miss; the more absurdity,

---

6 **Compare . . . out** (1) compare Franciscus and his disguise; (2) compare the contents of the letter with what is written on the outside

7 **taste** (perhaps Franciscus' violence against Lollio at III.iii.94 s.d.)

8–11 **"To . . . post"** Andromeda was rescued from the dragon by Perseus (the name Franciscus gives himself)

9 **chambermaid** (chambermaids were often thought to be lascivious; chambering was a term for copulating)

9 **Knight . . . Sun** (1) Franciscus' self-appointed name; (2) the hero of a popular Spanish romance, *The Mirror of Knighthood* (nine parts, printed in England, 1578–1601)

10 **Scorpio** sign governing the body's sexual organs (the middle region)

11 **Aeolus** god of the winds; the bellows mender would enhance activity, bellow being a term for phallus; **post** messenger

25–6 **dismantled . . . ornaments** not in my proper clothes

30–1 **appear . . . honor** means to be honorable

33 **beside himself** distracted by love

37 **I . . . but** I am sure that

42 **privy to** made aware of

43 **minister** (1) provide medical treatment; (2) respond to this love letter

44 **my thirds** (obscene pun; Lollio would ask for one-third of the profit, shared equally with Alibius and her lover)

46–7 **fall . . . upon** (1) yield; (2) claim

48 **So** yes, but it will not happen

49 **stand to** (with sexual pun)

50 **deal** (1) treat; (2) copulate

53 **fair** decent, modest

54 **Abuse** deceive

56 **kindly** (1) appropriately; (2) affectionately; (3) generously

57 **practice** (1) scheme; (2) do it

59 **fit** (1) dress; (2) prepare; (3) sexually arouse

61–2 **Take . . . outside** treat me as a madwoman

63 **I'll . . . inside** (1) I'll give you access to your lover; (2) I'll make you have intercourse

65 **solemnity** celebration

67 **mistrust** am worried about

70 **miss** fail

The more commends it, so no rough behaviors
Affright the ladies; they are nice things, thou know'st.

Lol. You need not fear, sir; so long as we are there with our commanding pizzles, they'll be as tame as the ladies themselves.

Alib. I will see them once more rehearse before they go.

Lol. I was about it, sir; look you to the madmen's morris, and let me alone with the other. There is one or two that I mistrust their fooling; I'll instruct them, and then they shall rehearse the whole measure.

Alib. Do so; I'll see the music prepared. But Lollio,
By the way, how does my wife brook her restraint?
Does she not grudge at it?

Lol. So, so; she takes some pleasure in the house, she would abroad else. You must allow her a little more length, she's kept too short.

Alib. She shall along to Vermandero's with us;
That will serve her for a month's liberty.

Lol. What's that on your face, sir?

Alib. Where, Lollio? I see nothing.

Lol. Cry you mercy, sir, 'tis your nose; it showed like the trunk of a young elephant.

Alib. Away, rascal! I'll prepare the music, Lollio.

Exit Alibius.

Lol. Do, sir, and I'll dance the whilst; Tony, where art thou, Tony?

Enter Antonio.

Ant. Here, cousin; where art thou?

Lol. Come, Tony, the footmanship I taught you.

Ant. I had rather ride, cousin.

Lol. Aye, a whip take you; but I'll keep you out. Vault in; look you, Tony: fa, la la, la la.

[*Dances.*]

Ant. Fa, la la, la la.

[*Dances.*]

Lol. There, an honor.

Ant. Is this an honor, coz?

[*Bows.*]

Lol. Yes, and it please your worship.

Ant. Does honor bend in the hams, coz?

Lol. Marry, does it; as low as worship, squireship, nay, yeomanry itself sometimes, from whence it first stiffened. There rise, a caper.

Ant. Caper after an honor, coz?

Lol. Very proper; for honor is but a caper, rises as fast and high, has a knee or two, and falls to th'ground again. You can remember your figure, Tony?

Exit.

Ant. Yes, cousin; when I see thy figure, I can remember mine.

Enter Isabella [*like a madwoman*].

Isa. Hey, how he treads the air! Shough, shough, t'other way!
He burns his wings else; here's wax enough below, Icarus,
More than will be canceled these eighteen moons;
He's down, he's down, what a terrible fall he had!
Stand up, thou son of Cretan Dedalus,
And let us tread the lower labyrinth;
I'll bring thee to the clue.

Ant. Prithee, coz, let me alone.

Isa. Art thou not drowned?
About thy head I saw a heap of clouds,
Wrapped like a Turkish turban; on thy back
A crooked chamelion-colored rainbow hung
Like a tiara down unto thy hams.

---

71 **so** so long as
72 **nice** fastidious
74 **pizzles** bulls' penises (used as whips)
78 **morris** morris dance
79 **one or two** Franciscus (and Antonio)
81 **measure** dance
83 **brook** tolerate
84 **grudge** complain
85 **pleasure** (with pun on sexual activity)
87 **length . . . short** (with play on size of penis)
92 **Cry . . . mercy** "I beg your pardon" (colloquial); **nose** (1) perhaps analogous to the cuckold's horns; (2) being led by the nose (?)
99 **ride** make love
101 **Vault** jump (into the dance; with pun on vaulting a horse which he would ride sexually)
103 **honor** bow
105 **and** if
106 **hams** hips
107 **Marry** yes, indeed (from "by Mary," a common oath); **worship** those of a higher class; nobility
109 **stiffened** (1) ascended; (2) grew formal; (3) became an erection; **caper** wild leap in dancing
111–13 **rises . . . again** quick ascent presages quick descent
114 **figure** dance steps
116 **Shough** "shoo" (an exclamation to drive away poultry)
117 **Icarus** the son of Daedalus, whose waxen wings melted when he flew too near the sun
118 **canceled** (reference to wax seals on legal documents)
121–2 **tread . . . clue** (reference now is to the story of Theseus who unwound a thread given him by Ariadne in order to retrace his steps out of the labyrinth [here, the madhouse] after killing the Minotaur who ruled it [Alibius].
122 **clue** thread
127 **chamelion-colored** i.e., of no real color, but ever-changing (deliberate nonsense)
128 **tiara** peaked cap or turban

Let me suck out those billows in thy belly;
Hark, how they roar and rumble in the straits!
Bless thee from the pirates.

Ant. Pox upon you, let me alone!

Isa. Why shouldst thou mount so high as Mercury,
Unless thou hadst reversion of his place?
Stay in the moon with me, Endymion,
And we will rule these wild rebellious waves
That would have drowned my love.

Ant. I'll kick thee if again thou touch me,
Thou wild unshapen antic; I am no fool,
You bedlam!

Isa. But you are, as sure as I am, mad.
Have I put on this habit of a frantic,
With love as full of fury to beguile
The nimble eye of watchful jealousy,
And am I thus rewarded?

[*Reveals herself.*]

Ant. Ha! Dearest beauty!

Isa. No, I have no beauty now,
Nor never had, but what was in my garments.
You a quick-sighted lover? Come not near me!
Keep your caparisons, y'are aptly clad;
I came a feigner to return stark mad.

Exit.

Enter Lollio.

Ant. Stay, or I shall change condition,
And become as you are.

Lol. Why, Tony, whither now? Why, fool?

Ant. Whose fool, usher of idiots? You coxcomb!
I have fooled too much.

Lol. You were best be mad another while then.

Ant. So I am, stark mad. I have cause enough;
And I could throw the full effects on thee,
And beat thee like a fury!

Lol. Do not, do not; I shall not forbear the gentleman under the fool, if you do; alas, I saw through your fox-skin before now. Come, I can give you comfort. My mistress loves you, and there is as arrant a madman i'th' house as you are a fool, your rival, whom she loves not. If after the masque we can rid her of him, you earn her love, she says, and the fool shall ride her.

Ant. May I believe thee?

Lol. Yes, or you may choose whether you will or no.

Ant. She's eased of him; I have a good quarrel on't.

Lol. Well, keep your old station yet, and be quiet.

Ant. Tell her I will deserve her love.

[*Exit.*]

Lol. And you are like to have your desire.

Enter Franciscus.

Fran. [*Sings.*] "Down, down, down a-down a-down, and then with a horse-trick,
To kick Latona's forehead, and break her bowstring."

Lol. This is t'other counterfeit; I'll put him out of his humor. [*Takes out letter and reads.*] "Sweet lady, having now cast off this counterfeit cover of a madman, I appear to your best judgment a true and faithful lover of your beauty." This is pretty well for a madman.

Fran. Ha! What's that?

Lol. "Chide those perfections in you which made me imperfect."

Fran. I am discovered to the fool.

Lol. I hope to discover the fool in you, ere I have done with you. "Yours all, or one beside himself, Franciscus." This madman will mend sure.

Fran. What do you read, sirrah?

Lol. Your destiny, sir; you'll be hanged for this trick, and another that I know.

---

129 those billows sea water (into which Icarus fell)
130 straits the sea between Crete and Greece where Icarus was said to have drowned
131 Bless thee may God protect you
133 Mercury the gods' messenger who wore winged sandals
134 thou . . . reversion are named his successor
135 Endymion a beautiful boy whom Luna (the moon) loved
139 unshapen deformed; **antic** madwoman
140 bedlam lunatic
141 frantic mad person
148 caparisons garish clothes
149 feigner to pretender but now
150 I . . . condition I shall become authentically mad
153 usher (1) doorkeeper; (2) teacher (literally, assistant schoolmaster); **coxcomb** fool (the coxcomb was the fool's hat)
159–60 I . . . fool I will not tolerate bad behavior, even if you are a gentleman in disguise
161 fox-skin cunning disguise
163 arrant wandering
166 ride sexually mount
171 She's . . . him I'll get rid of him for her; **good . . . on't** valid reason for fighting him
172 station position (as a fool)
176 horse-trick (1) horse-play; (2) copulation
177 To . . . bowstring Latona was the mother of Diana, but here he means Diana who hunted with bow and arrow
187 discovered revealed; **fool** i.e., Lollio
188 discover expose
192–3 you'll . . . know (fraud and adultery)
193 trick i.e., disguise and letter (also *horse-trick*, line 176); **another** i.e., *horse-trick* (line 176)

Fran. Art thou of counsel with thy mistress?
Lol. Next her apron strings.
Fran. Give me thy hand.
Lol. Stay, let me put yours in my pocket first. [*Puts away the letter.*] Your hand is true, is it not? It will not pick? I partly fear it, because I think it does lie.
Fran. Not in a syllable.
Lol. So; if you love my mistress so well as you have handled the matter here, you are like to be cured of your madness.
Fran. And none but she can cure it.
Lol. Well, I'll give you over then, and she shall cast your water next.
Fran. Take for thy pains past.
[*Gives him money.*]
Lol. I shall deserve more, sir, I hope; my mistress loves you, but must have some proof of your love to her.
Fran. There I meet my wishes.
Lol. That will not serve; you must meet her enemy and yours.
Fran. He's dead already!
Lol. Will you tell me that, and I parted but now with him?
Fran. Show me the man.
Lol. Aye, that's a right course now, see him before you kill him in any case, and yet it needs not go so far neither; 'tis but a fool that haunts the house and my mistress in the shape of an idiot; bang but his fool's coat well-favoredly, and 'tis well.
Fran. Soundly, soundly!
Lol. Only reserve him till the masque be past, and if you find him not now in the dance yourself, I'll show you. In, in! My master!
Fran. He handles him like a feather. Hey!
[*Exit dancing.*]

Enter Alibius.

Alib. Well said; in a readiness, Lollio?
Lol. Yes, sir.
Alib. Away then, and guide them in, Lollio;
Entreat your mistress to see this sight.
[*Exit* Lollio.]
Hark, is there not one incurable fool
That might be begged? I have friends.
Lol. [*Within.*] I have him for you, one that shall deserve it too.
Alib. Good boy, Lollio.

[*Enter* Isabella, *then* Lollio *with* Madmen *and* Fools.] *The* Madmen *and* Fools *dance.*

'Tis perfect; well, fit but once these strains,
We shall have coin and credit for our pains.
Exeunt.

Act V

[V.i]

Enter Beatrice. *A clock strikes one.*

Bea. One struck, and yet she lies by't! – Oh, my fears!
This strumpet serves her own ends, 'tis apparent now,
Devours the pleasure with a greedy appetite,
And never minds my honor or my peace,
Makes havoc of my right. But she pays dearly for't.
No trusting of her life with such a secret
That cannot rule her blood to keep her promise.
Beside, I have some suspicion of her faith to me
Because I was suspected of my Lord,
And it must come from her. Hark, by my horrors,
Another clock strikes two.
Strikes two.

Enter De Flores.

De F. Pist, where are you?

194 of counsel in confidence
198 hand handwriting
199 pick (1) you are not a pickpocket; (2) your letter is true
204 madness (also infatuation)
206 give . . . over stop trying to treat (or cure) you
207 cast . . . water examine your urine specimen
212 There . . . wishes here is a more satisfying payment
215 He's dead then he's as good as dead
216 but just
219 see identify
292–3 bang . . . well-favoredly just hit him soundly
225 reserve spare
227 My master! (Alibius approaches)
228 him himself
229 said done
233–4 there . . . begged to beg a fool was to petition the Court of Wards and Liveries for the custody of an idiot and the profits of his property
235 him Antonio
238 fit . . . strains apply efforts appropriately to the music
V.i.1 and . . . by't and still she continues having intercourse
2 ends (with pun on pudendum)
4 peace peace of mind
5 right marital right
6 such . . . secret (of the bed-trick)
7 blood sexual impulses
9 of by

Bea. De Flores!
De F. Aye, is she not come from him yet?
Bea. As I am a living soul, not.
De F. Sure the devil
Hath sowed his itch within her; who'd trust
A waiting-woman?
Bea. I must trust somebody.
De F. Push, they are termagants,
Especially when they fall upon their masters
And have their ladies' first-fruits; th'are mad whelps,
You cannot stave 'em off from game royal; then
You are so harsh and hardy, ask no counsel,
And I could have helped you to an apothecary's daughter,
Would have fall'n off before eleven, and thanked you, too.
Bea. Oh me, not yet? This whore forgets herself.
De F. The rascal fares so well; look, y'are undone,
The day-star, by this hand! See Phosphorus plain yonder.
Bea. Advise me now to fall upon some ruin,
There is no counsel safe else.
De F. Peace, I ha't now;
For we must force a rising, there's no remedy.
Bea. How? Take heed of that.
De F. Tush, be you quiet,
Or else give over all.
Bea. Prithee, I ha' done then.
De F. This is my reach. I'll set some part a-fire
Of Diaphanta's chamber.
Bea. How? Fire, sir?
That may endanger the whole house.
De F. You talk of danger when your fame's on fire?
Bea. That's true; do what thou wilt now.
De F. Push, I aim
At a most rich success, strikes all dead sure;
The chimney being afire, and some light parcels
Of the least danger in her chamber only,
If Diaphanta should be met by chance then,
Far from her lodging (which is now suspicious),
It would be thought her fears and affrights then
Drove her to seek for succor. If not seen
Or met at all, as that's the likeliest,
For her own shame she'll hasten towards her lodging;
I will be ready with a piece high-charged,
As 'twere to cleanse the chimney. There 'tis proper now,
But she shall be the mark.
Bea. I'm forced to love thee now,
'Cause thou provid'st so carefully for my honor.
De F. 'Slid, it concerns the safety of us both,
Our pleasure and continuance.
Bea. One word now, prithee;
How for the servants?
De F. I'll dispatch them
Some one way, some another in the hurry,
For buckets, hooks, ladders; fear not you;
The deed shall find its time, and I've thought since
Upon a safe conveyance for the body, too.
How this fire purifies wit! Watch you your minute.
Bea. Fear keeps my soul upon't, I cannot stray from't.

Enter Alonzo's Ghost.

De F. Ha! What art thou that tak'st away the light
'Twixt that star and me? I dread thee not;
'Twas but a mist of conscience. All's clear again.
Exit.
Bea. Who's that, De Flores? Bless me! It slides by;
[*Exit* Ghost.]

14 **itch** sexual desire; inclination to evil
16 **termagants** fierce, violent women
17 **fall upon** sexually lie with
18 **first-fruits** the bride's maidenhead
18–19 **th'are . . . royal** they are like maddened young dogs who cannot be stopped from hunting on the king's game preserves
20 **harsh and hardy** rough and rash
22 **fall'n off** stopped
25 **Phosphorus** Venus, the morning-star indicating dawn
26 **fall upon** devise; **ruin** catastrophe
28 **For . . . rising** unless we create a disturbance
30 **give over all** surrender all hope
31 **reach** plan
34 **fame** reputation
36 **strikes . . . sure** makes all finally safe
37–8 **some . . . only** the small items in her room are incapable of igniting the whole house
45 **piece high-charged** heavily loaded gun
46 **proper** fitting; expected
47 **mark** target
49 **'Slid** "By God's eyelid" (a common oath)
50 **continuance** (their sexual liaison will continue)
54 **deed . . . time** "I'll kill her at the right moment"
55 **conveyance** removal
56 **fire** (1) flames; (2) passion; **purifies wit** stimulates craft; **your minute** i.e., to return to Alsemero's bed
57 **upon't** upon that moment

Some ill thing haunts the house; 't has left behind it
A shivering sweat upon me; I'm afraid now.
This night hath been so tedious; oh, this strumpet!
Had she a thousand lives, he should not leave her
Till he had destroyed the last. List, oh my terrors!
Three struck by Saint Sebastian's!

Struck three o'clock.

Within. Fire, fire, fire!
Bea. Already? How rare is that man's speed!
How heartily he serves me! His face loathes one,
But look upon his care, who would not love him?
The east is not more beauteous than his service.
Within. Fire, fire, fire!

Enter De Flores; Servants *pass over, ring a bell.*

De F. Away, dispatch! Hooks, buckets, ladders; that's well said;
The fire-bell rings, the chimney works; my charge;
The piece is ready.

Exit.

Bea. Here's a man worth loving –

Enter Diaphanta.

Oh, y'are a jewel!
Dia. Pardon frailty, Madam;
In troth I was so well, I ev'n forgot myself.
Bea. Y'have made trim work.
Dia. What?
Bea. Hie quickly to your chamber;
Your reward follows you.
Dia. I never made
So sweet a bargain.

Exit.

Enter Alsemero.

Als. Oh my dear Joanna,
Alas, art thou risen too? I was coming,
My absolute treasure.
Bea. When I missed you,
I could not choose but follow.
Als. Th'art all sweetness!
The fire is not so dangerous.
Bea. Think you so, sir?
Als. I prithee, tremble not. Believe me, 'tis not.

Enter Vermandero, Jasperino.

Ver. Oh bless my house and me!
Als. My Lord your father.

Enter De Flores *with a piece.*

Ver. Knave, whither goes that piece?
De F. To scour the chimney.

Exit.

Ver. Oh, well said, well said;
That fellow's good on all occasions.
Bea. A wondrous necessary man, my Lord.
Ver. He hath a ready wit; he's worth 'em all, sir.
Dog at a house of fire; I ha' seen him singed ere now:

The piece goes off.

Ha, there he goes.
Bea. [*Aside.*] 'Tis done.
Als. Come, sweet, to bed now;
Alas, thou wilt get cold.
Bea. Alas, the fear keeps that out;
My heart will find no quiet till I hear 96
How Diaphanta, my poor woman, fares;
It is her chamber, sir, her lodging chamber.
Ver. How should the fire come there?
Bea. As good a soul as ever lady countenanced,
But in her chamber negligent and heavy;
She 'scaped a mine twice.
Ver. Twice?
Bea. Strangely twice, sir.
Ver. Those sleepy sluts are dangerous in a house,
And they be ne'er so good.

Enter De Flores.

De F. Oh, poor virginity!
Thou hast paid dearly for't.
Ver. Bless us! What's that?
De F. A thing you all knew once – Diaphanta's burned. 106

64 **tedious** painful and unending
66 **destroyed . . . last** exhausted her sexual appetite; **terrors** (1) of being discovered; (2) of such sexual voraciousness
67 **Saint Sebastian's** clock in nearby church
69 **rare** (1) excelling; (2) exceptional
72 **The east** i.e., the sunrise
77 **jewel** (1) gem (sarcastically); (2) chastity itself (ironically)
78 **troth** truth; **was** performed
79 **trim work** a good job of it (sarcastically); **Hie** hurry
91 **wondrous necessary** (1) with deliberate irony; (2) to cover the scheme with De Flores
93 **Dog at** skilled with
100 **countenanced** (1) saw; (2) favored; (3) employed
101 **heavy** (1) sluggish; (2) a heavy sleeper
102 **mine** danger, blast (as in landmine); conflagration
104 **And . . . good** no matter how good as servants
104–5 **Oh . . . for't** (De Flores may enter carrying Diaphanta)

Bea. My woman, oh, my woman!
De F. Now the flames
Are greedy of her; burned, burned, burned to death, sir!
Bea. Oh my presaging soul!
Als. Not a tear more!
I charge you by the last embrace I gave you
In bed before this raised us.
Bea. Now you tie me;
Were it my sister, now she gets no more.

Enter Servant.

Ver. How now?
Ser. All danger's past, you may now take your rests, my Lords; the fire is throughly quenched. Ah, poor gentlewoman, how soon was she stifled!
Bea. De Flores, what is left of her inter,
And we as mourners all will follow her:
I will entreat that honor to my servant,
Ev'n of my Lord himself.
Als. Command it, sweetness.
Bea. Which of you spied the fire first?
De F. 'Twas I, Madam.
Bea. And took such pains in't, too? A double goodness!
'Twere well he were rewarded.
Ver. He shall be;
De Flores, call upon me.
Als. And upon me, sir.
Exeunt. [*Manet* De Flores.]
De F. Rewarded? Precious, here's a trick beyond me!
I see in all bouts, both of sport and wit,
Always a woman strives for the last hit.
Exit.

[V.ii]

Enter Tomazo.

Tom. I cannot taste the benefits of life
With the same relish I was wont to do.
Man I grow weary of, and hold his fellowship
A treacherous bloody friendship; and because
I am ignorant in whom my wrath should settle,
I must think all men villains, and the next
I meet (whoe'er he be) the murderer
Of my most worthy brother. – Ha! What's he?

Enter De Flores, *passes over the stage.*

Oh, the fellow that some call honest De Flores;
But methinks honesty was hard bested
To come there for a lodging as if a queen
Should make her palace of a pest-house.
I find a contrariety in nature
Betwixt that face and me. The least occasion
Would give me game upon him; yet he's so foul,
One would scarce touch him with a sword he loved
And made account of; so most deadly venomous,
He would go near to poison any weapon
That should draw blood on him; one must resolve
Never to use that sword again in fight,
In way of honest manhood, that strikes him;
Some river must devour't, 'twere not fit
That any man should find it. – What, again?

Enter De Flores.

He walks a' purpose by, sure, to choke me up,
To infect my blood.
De F. My worthy noble Lord!
Tom. Dost offer to come near and breathe upon me?
[*Strikes him.*]
De F. A blow!
[*Draws his sword.*]
Tom. Yea, are you so prepared?
I'll rather like a soldier die by th'sword,
Than like a politician by thy poison.
[*Draws.*]
De F. Hold, my Lord, as you are honorable.
Tom. All slaves that kill by poison are still cowards.
De F. [*Aside.*] I cannot strike; I see his brother's wounds
Fresh bleeding in his eye, as in a crystal.

111 **tie** constrain
112 **no more** no greater grief
115 **throughly** thoroughly
121 **my Lord** (Alsemero)
126 **Precious** "by God's precious body" (a common oath); **beyond me** "that is even better than I could have devised"
127 **sport** (1) games; (2) sexual play; **wit** i.e., combat of wits
V.ii.10 **hard bested** hard-pressed
12 **pest-house** hospital for victims of the plague
14 **occasion** opportunity, cause
15 **game upon** reason to attack
17 **so** De Flores is so
24 **choke . . . up** suffocate by his mere presence
29 **politician** schemer (the word is from Machiavelli)
31 **slaves** wretches; **still** always
33 **Fresh bleeding** (popular belief held that a corpse began bleeding again whenever the murderer approached); **as . . . crystal** as in a crystal ball

[*To Tom.*] I will not question this, I know y'are noble.
I take my injury with thanks given, Sir,
Like a wise lawyer; and as a favor,
Will wear it for the worthy hand that gave it.
[*Aside.*] Why this from him, that yesterday appeared
So strangely loving to me?
Oh, but instinct is of a subtler strain,
Guilt must not walk so near his lodge again;
He came near me now.

Exit.

Tom. All league with mankind I renounce forever,
Till I find this murderer; not so much
As common courtesy but I'll lock up.
For in the state of ignorance I live in,
A brother may salute his brother's murderer,
And wish good speed to th'villain in a greeting.

Enter Vermandero, Alibius *and* Isabella.

Ver. Noble Piracquo!
Tom. Pray keep on your way, sir,
I've nothing to say to you.
Ver. Comforts bless you, sir.
Tom. I have forsworn compliment; in troth I have, sir;
As you are merely man, I have not left
A good wish for you, nor any here.
Ver. Unless you be so far in love with grief
You will not part from't upon any terms,
We bring that news will make a welcome for us.
Tom. What news can that be?
Ver. Throw no scornful smile
Upon the zeal I bring you, 'tis worth more, sir.
Two of the chiefest men I kept about me
I hide not from the law, or your just vengeance.
Tom. Ha!
Ver. To give your peace more ample satisfaction,
Thank these discoverers.
Tom. If you bring that calm,
Name but the manner I shall ask forgiveness in
For that contemptuous smile upon you.
I'll perfect it with reverence that belongs
Unto a sacred altar.

[*Kneels.*]

Ver. Good sir, rise;

[*Raises him.*]

Why, now you overdo as much a'this hand,
As you fell short a' t'other. Speak, Alibius.
Alib. 'Twas my wife's fortune (as she is most lucky
At a discovery) to find out lately
Within our hospital of fools and madmen
Two counterfeits slipped into these disguises;
Their names, Franciscus and Antonio.
Ver. Both mine, sir, and I ask no favor for 'em.
Alib. Now that which draws suspicion to their habits,
The time of their disguisings agrees justly
With the day of the murder.
Tom. Oh blessed revelation!
Ver. Nay more, nay more, sir. I'll not spare mine own
In way of justice; they both feigned a journey
To Briamata, and so wrought out their leaves;
My love was so abused in't.
Tom. Time's too precious
To run in waste now; you have brought a peace
The riches of five kingdoms could not purchase.
Be my most happy conduct; I thirst for 'em.
Like subtle lightning will I wind about 'em,
And melt their marrow in 'em.

Exeunt.

[V.iii]

Enter Alsemero *and* Jasperino.

Jas. Your confidence, I'm sure, is now of proof.

---

34 **question this** call you to account
36–7 **Like . . . it** (as a lawyer sustains humiliation so as to file charges later)
41 **Guilt . . . again** the guilty party must avoid the scene of the crime
42 **came near me** nearly discovered me
43 **league** alliance; connection
45 **common** everyday; **lock up** refrain from
47 **salute** greet
48 **speed** success
51 **compliment** habitual courtesies
55 **You** that you
58 **zeal** good will
59 **Two . . . men** (Franciscus and Antonio)
60 **I . . . vengeance** i.e., you may have public or private justice
63 **these discoverers** Isabella and Alibius; **calm** means of atonement or satisfaction
66 **perfect** complete
75 **mine** my servants; **favor** lenience
76 **habits** disguises
77 **justly** exactly
81 **wrought . . . leaves** received permission to be absent
82 **love** trust
85 **conduct** guide
86–7 **Like . . . 'em** (lightning was thought to melt the bones' marrow without disfiguring the body)
V.iii.1 **confidence** distrust in Beatrice-Joanna; **of proof** (1) confirmed; (2) as defense

The prospect from the garden has showed
Enough for deep suspicion.
Als. The black mask
That so continually was worn upon't
Condemns the face for ugly ere't be seen
Her despite to him, and so seeming – bottomless.
Jas. Touch it home, then. 'Tis not a shallow probe
Can search this ulcer soundly. I fear you'll find it
Full of corruption; 'tis fit I leave you.
She meets you opportunely from that walk.
She took the back door at his parting with her.
Exit Jasperino.
Als. Did my fate wait for this unhappy stroke
At my first sight of woman? She's here.

Enter Beatrice.

Bea. Alsemero!
Als. How do you?
Bea. How do I?
Alas! How do you? You look not well.
Als. You read me well enough, I am not well.
Bea. Not well, sir? Is't in my power to better you?
Als. Yes.
Bea. Nay, then, y'are cured again.
Als. Pray resolve me one question, Lady.
Bea. If I can.
Als. None can so sure. Are you honest?
Bea. Ha, ha, ha! That's a broad question, my Lord.
Als. But that's not a modest answer, my Lady.
Do you laugh? My doubts are strong upon me.
Bea. 'Tis innocence that smiles, and no rough brow
Can take away the dimple in her cheek.
Say I should strain a tear to fill the vault,
Which would you give the better faith to?
Als. 'Twere but hypocrisy of a sadder color,
But the same stuff; neither your smiles nor tears
Shall move or flatter me from my belief.
You are a whore!
Bea. What a horrid sound it hath!
It blasts a beauty to deformity;
Upon what face soever that breath falls,
It strikes it ugly. Oh, you have ruined
What you can ne'er repair again.
Als. I'll all demolish, and seek out truth within you,
If there be any left. Let your sweet tongue
Prevent your heart's rifling; there I'll ransack
And tear out my suspicion.
Bea. You may, sir,
'Tis an easy passage; yet, if you please,
Show me the ground whereon you lost your love.
My spotless virtue may but tread on that,
Before I perish.
Als. Unanswerable!
A ground you cannot stand on. You fall down
Beneath all grace and goodness, when you set
Your ticklish heel on't; there was a visor
O'er that cunning face, and that became you.
Now impudence in triumph rides upon't;
How comes this tender reconcilement else
'Twixt you and your despite, your rancorous loathing,
De Flores? He that your eye was sore at sight of,
He's now become your arm's supporter, your
Lip's saint!
Bea. Is there the cause?
Als. Worse: your lust's devil,
Your adultery!
Bea. Would any but yourself say that,
'Twould turn him to a villain.
Als. 'Twas witnessed
By the counsel of your bosom, Diaphanta.
Bea. Is your witness dead then?
Als. 'Tis to be feared
It was the wages of her knowledge; poor soul,
She lived not long after the discovery.

3 **black mask** (women often wore masks to protect their skin)
7 **Touch . . . home** make a thorough investigation
10 **that walk** (they have apparently seen Beatrice-Joanna strolling with De Flores)
13 **At . . . woman** with my first love
18 **y'are** consider yourself
19 **resolve** answer
20 **sure** knowledgeably; **honest** chaste (i.e., faithful to only one man)
21 **broad** coarse; unfocused
23 **doubts** suspicions, fears
24 **rough brow** frown
25 **her** innocence (personified in previous line; Beatrice-Joanna deflects the charge and so remains truthful here)
26 **strain a tear** force myself to weep; **vault** arch of the sky
28 **sadder** graver
29 **the . . . stuff** cut from the same cloth
38 **your . . . rifling** my tearing open your heart to see into it
40 **passage** (to the truth of my heart)
41 **ground** (1) basis; (2) cause; (3) premise; **your love** your love for me
42 **tread on** deny, demolish
43 **Unanswerable** beyond any response you can make in denial
46 **ticklish** (1) fickle; (2) easily aroused; **visor** mask
47 **became** was flattering to
48 **impudence** shamelessness
50 **despite** object of derision
52–3 **your . . . saint** one you worship (with attention and kissing)
53 **there** that
54 **adultery** partner in adultery
56 **counsel . . . bosom** trusted confidant

Bea. Then hear a story of not much less horror
Than this your false suspicion is beguiled with;
To your bed's scandal, I stand up innocence,
Which even the guilt of one black other deed
Will stand for proof of. Your love has made me
A cruel murd'ress.
Als. Ha!
Bea. A bloody one;
I have kissed poison for't, stroked a serpent:
That thing of hate, worthy in my esteem
Of no better employment, and him most worthy
To be so employed, I caused to murder
That innocent Piracquo, having no
Better means than that worst, to assure
Yourself to me.
Als. Oh, the place itself e'er since
Has crying been for vengeance, the temple
Where blood and beauty first unlawfully
Fired their devotion, and quenched the right one;
'Twas in my fears at first, 'twill have it now.
Oh, thou art all deformed!
Bea. Forget not, sir,
It for your sake was done; shall greater dangers
Make the less welcome?
Als. Oh, thou shouldst have gone
A thousand leagues about to have avoided
This dangerous bridge of blood; here we are lost.
Bea. Remember I am true unto your bed.
Als. The bed itself's a charnel, the sheets shrouds
For murdered carcasses; it must ask pause
What I must do in this. Meantime, you shall
Be my prisoner only. Enter my closet;
Exit Beatrice.
I'll be your keeper yet. Oh, in what part
Of this sad story shall I first begin? – Ha!

Enter De Flores.

This same fellow has put me in. De Flores!
De F. Noble Alsemero?
Als. I can tell you
News, sir; my wife has her commended to you.
De F. That's news indeed, my Lord; I think she would
Commend me to the gallows if she could,
She ever loved me so well. I thank her.
Als. What's this blood upon your band, De Flores?
De F. Blood? No, sure, 'twas washed since.
Als. Since when, man?
De F. Since t'other day I got a knock
In a sword and dagger school; I think 'tis out.
Als. Yes, 'tis almost out, but 'tis perceived, though.
I had forgot my message. This it is:
What price goes murder?
De F. How, sir?
Als. I ask you, sir;
My wife's behindhand with you, she tells me,
For a brave bloody blow you gave for her sake
Upon Piracquo.
De F. Upon? 'Twas quite through him, sure;
Has she confessed it?
Als. As sure as death to both of you,
And much more than that.
De F. It could not be much more;
'Twas but one thing, and that – she's a whore.
Als. It could not choose but follow; oh cunning devils!
How should blind men know you from fair-faced saints?
Bea. within. He lies, the villain does belie me!
De F. Let me go to her, sir.
Als. Nay, you shall to her.
Peace, crying crocodile, your sounds are heard!
Take your prey to you; get you in to her, sir.
Exit De Flores.
I'll be your pander now; rehearse again
Your scene of lust, that you may be perfect
When you shall come to act it to the black audience
Where howls and gnashings shall be music to you.
Clip your adult'ress freely, 'tis the pilot

62 **To** in response to the accusation of
64 **Your love** my love for you
66 **stroked** copulated with
72 **the place** the temple
75 **quenched . . . one** demolished true love and devotion
76 **'twill . . . now** (1) my suspicions are confirmed; (2) I'll have satisfaction (in vengeance) now
79 **gone** detoured
80 **about** out of your way
83 **charnel** charnel-house where the bones of the dead were placed
87 **yet** for the time being
89 **put me in** show me where to begin
91 **her . . . you** (asked to be remembered)
95 **band** (1) collar; (2) cuff
98 **out** gone
102 **behindhand** indebted
103 **brave** (1) courageous; (2) splendid
109 **blind men** men were thought blinded by passion
110 **belie** trick
111 **Nay . . . her** you shall not go near her
112 **crocodile** (crocodiles were thought to shed false tears when seizing their victims)
114 **pander** go-between; pimp
116 **black audience** devils in hell
118 **Clip** embrace; **pilot** substitute for Charon, who ferried the dead to Hades

Will guide you to the Mare Mortuum,
Where you shall sink to fathoms bottomless.

Enter Vermandero, Alibius, Isabella, Tomazo, Franciscus, *and* Antonio.

Ver. Oh, Alsemero, I have a wonder for you.
Als. No, sir, 'tis I, I have a wonder for you.
Ver. I have suspicion near as proof itself
For Piracquo's murder.
Als. Sir, I have proof
Beyond suspicion for Piracquo's murder.
Ver. Beseech you hear me; these two have been disguised
E'er since the deed was done.
Als. I have two other
That were more close disguised than your two could be,
E'er since the deed was done.
Ver. You'll hear me! These, mine own servants
Als. Hear me; – those nearer than your servants,
That shall acquit them, and prove them guiltless.
Fran. That may be done with easy truth, sir.
Tom. How is my cause bandied through your delays!
'Tis urgent in blood, and calls for haste;
Give me a brother alive or dead.
Alive, a wife with him; if dead, for both
A recompense for murder and adultery.
Bea. within. Oh, oh, oh!
Als. Hark, 'tis coming to you.
De F. within. Nay, I'll along for company.
Bea. within. Oh, oh!
Ver. What horrid sounds are these?
Als. Come forth, you twins of mischief!

Enter De Flores *bringing in* Beatrice [*wounded*].

De F. Here we are. If you have any more
To say to us, speak quickly, I shall not
Give you the hearing else; I am so stout yet,
And so, I think, that broken rib of mankind.
Ver. An host of enemies entered my citadel
Could not amaze like this. Joanna! Beatrice! Joanna!
Bea. Oh come not near me, sir, I shall defile you.
I am that of your blood was taken from you
For your better health; look no more upon't,
But cast it to the ground regardlessly.
Let the common sewer take it from distinction.
Beneath the stars, upon yon meteor
Ever hung my fate, 'mong things corruptible;
I ne'er could pluck it from him. My loathing
Was prophet to the rest, but ne'er believed;
Mine honor fell with him, and now my life.
Alsemero, I am a stranger to your bed,
Your bed was cozened on the nuptial night,
For which your false bride died.
Als. Diaphanta!
De F. Yes; and the while I coupled with your mate
At barley-brake; now we are left in hell.
Ver. We are all there; it circumscribes here.
De F. I loved this woman in spite of her heart;
Her love I earned out of Piracquo's murder.
Tom. Ha! My brother's murderer!
De F. Yes, and her honor's prize
Was my reward; I thank life for nothing
But that pleasure. It was so sweet to me
That I have drunk up all, left none behind
For any man to pledge me.
Ver. Horrid villain!
Keep life in him for further tortures.
De F. No!
I can prevent you; here's my penknife still.
It is but one thread more. [*Stabs himself.*] And now 'tis cut.
Make haste, Joanna, by that token to thee
Canst not forget, so lately put in mind;
I would not go to leave thee far behind.
Dies.

---

119 **Mare Mortuum** Dead Sea (pictured here as hell)
126 **two** Franciscus and Antonio
127 **two other** Beatrice-Joanna and De Flores
128 **close** impenetrably
129 **deed** (1) murder; (2) adultery
130 **hear** listen to
134 **bandied** tossed about frivolously; neglected
135 **blood** blood vengeance
138 **adultery** (Tomazo means marriage to Alsemero rather than his brother to whom she was pledged)
139 **'tis** revenge
145 **stout** resolute
146 **broken...mankind** Beatrice (cf. Gen. 2:21–3)
148 **amaze** confound; make a maze of the nefarious activities in the citadel
149 **defile** infect
150–1 **I...health** (reference is to bloodletting as the cure for illness)
153 **from distinction** anything identifying it separately
154 **stars** pure, fixed lights in heaven; **meteor** burst of light, sublunary, and transient (here De Flores)
163 **barley-brake** i.e., they are the couple imprisoned in hell in the game
165 **heart** disposition (towards me)
167 **honor** (1) maidenhead; (2) reputation
171 **pledge** offer a toast to
175 **token** De Flores' self-inflicted wound showing his loyalty
177 **I...behind** (he knows she is mortally wounded)

Bea. Forgive me, Alsemero, all forgive;
'Tis time to die, when 'tis a shame to live.
Dies.
Ver. Oh, my name is entered now in that record
Where till this fatal hour 'twas never read.
Als. Let it be blotted out, let your heart lose it,
And it can never look you in the face,
Nor tell a tale behind the back of life
To your dishonor; justice hath so right
The guilty hit, that innocence is quit
By proclamation, and may joy again.
Sir, you are sensible of what truth hath done;
'Tis the best comfort that your grief can find.
Tom. Sir, I am satisfied. My injuries
Lie dead before me; I can exact no more,
Unless my soul were loose, and could o'ertake
Those black fugitives that are fled from thence,
To take a second vengeance; but there are wraths
Deeper than mine. 'Tis to be feared about 'em.
Als. What an opacous body had that moon
That last changed on us! Here's beauty changed
To ugly whoredom; here, servant obedience
To a master sin, imperious murder.
I, a supposed husband, changed embraces
With wantonness, but that was paid before;
Your change is come too, from an ignorant wrath
To knowing friendship. Are there any more on's?
Ant. Yes, Sir; I was changed, too, from a little ass as I was, to a great fool as I am, and had like to ha' been changed to the gallows but that you know my innocence always excuses me.
Fran. I was changed from a little wit to be stark mad,
Almost for the same purpose.
Isa. Your change is still behind,
But deserve best your transformation:
You are a jealous coxcomb, keep schools of folly,
And teach your scholars how to break your own head.
Alib. I see all apparent, wife, and will change now
Into a better husband, and never keep
Scholars that shall be wiser than myself.
Als. Sir, you have yet a son's duty living
Please you, accept it; let that your sorrow
As it goes from your eye, go from your heart;
Man and his sorrow at the grave must part.

EPILOGUE

Als. All we can do to comfort one another,
To stay a brother's sorrow for a brother,
To dry a child from the kind father's eyes,
Is to no purpose, it rather multiplies.
Your only smiles have power to cause re-live
The dead again, or in their rooms to give
Brother a new brother, father a child;
If these appear, all griefs are reconciled.
Exeunt omnes.

---

180 **record** heavenly accounting
182 **lose** forget
186 **quit** acquitted
188 **sensible** aware; **done** shown
193 **black fugitives** damned souls of Beatrice-Joanna and De Flores
194–5 **wraths . . . mine** the punishments of hell
196 **opacous** clouded, ominous
196–7 **that . . . us** the last month provided us
201 **wantonness** i.e., Diaphanta; **paid before** punished earlier by her earlier death
202 **Your** Tomazo's
203 **on's** of us
207 **innocence** (1) guiltlessness; (2) foolishness
209 **behind** to come
212 **break . . . head** make you a cuckold
215 **wiser** more clever
216 **son's duty** Alsemero will give Vermandero a son's loyalty
218 **from your eye** (by weeping)
220 **Epilogue** (spoken directly to the playhouse audience)
221 **stay** bring to a close
223 **multiplies** increases grief
226 **Brother . . . child** Alsemero will become their new brother and son

'Tis Pity She's a Whore

John Ford

John Ford's powerfully haunting masterpiece of the Caroline theater is about two young people who are deeply in love yet forbidden to marry: they are caught, remorselessly, between an older order of unbending orthodox belief and a newer world of emergent individualism and emancipated faith in human nature that persistently surrounds them. Written especially for the Phoneix (or Cockpit) Theater in Drury Lane, a small horseshoe-shaped theater that seated only 500, in a darkened room lit only by narrow windows and the flickering candles of wall sockets, chandeliers, and candelabra, Ford's play nevertheless reaches out to incorporate major works from the Elizabethan playhouses that were once performed in the open air to heterogeneous crowds four to six times greater. Like Faustus, Giovanni is a brilliant scholar from a great university – Bologna rather than Wittenberg – whose study of rhetoric, philosophy, and theology has led him to ask tough questions of traditional belief, to pick theological quibbles, and to assemble self-serving arguments that seriously challenge his mentor, Father Bonaventura. "I can tell you," Giovanni says to the compassionate Friar, "The Hell you often have prompted is nought else But slavish and fond superstitious fear; And I could prove it too." Like Faustus, Giovanni moves from euphoria to despair, from physical joy to self-induced terror from which his natural father and especially his sister – like Faustus' fellow scholars – are unable to save him. But at the same time Giovanni recalls *The Spanish Tragedy*: sensitive to insult, motivated by his own sense of family love and justice, Giovanni like Hieronimo is forced (justifiably, he would say) to murder those who refuse to listen to him. His cry, "Revenge is mine," is exacting in its echo of Hieronimo's earlier "*Vindicta mihi*." Sounds and scenes resonate unremittingly: when the idiot Bergetto is brutally slain, his servant runs through the street of Parma to the gates of the Cardinal's house, crying, like Hieronimo through the Spanish court, for help and for justice and finding none where it should always be at hand. Even Ford's *coup de théâtre* that ends the play, an emblem dripping blood, reminds us of young Edward III left on stage with the bloody head of Mortimer. Despite the fact that these had become staples of the public companies, their very success insured their dramatic as well as their commercial value. What is even more remarkable about *'Tis Pity She's a Whore* is Ford's special talent for combining spectacle with the most private, sensitive, and intimate matters. In this play, the terrible dislocations of a swiftly changing and fragmenting culture are captured in the intensely personal dislocations of incest.

'Tis Pity She's a Whore is extraordinary as the first play to deal openly and directly with incest and yet do so with an exquisite objectivity and tenderness. In the play's second scene, Giovanni reassures his sister Annabella that their socially illicit affair has God's sanction: "I have asked counsel of the holy Church, Who tells me I may love you, and 'tis just That since I may, I should." But we have been privy to that counsel in the opening scene, and that is not what the Friar said. Rather, he firmly opposed such a love: "nice philosophy May tolerate unlikely arguments, But Heaven admits no jests [exceptions]." Is Giovanni deliberately lying in order to make love to his sister? Or is he confusing that remark with another one made by the Friar; following Giovanni's initial objection – "Must I not do what all men else may – love?" his advisor has assented: "Yes, you may love, fair son" (or perhaps "Yes, you may love fair, son"). Or has Giovanni's pride in argumentation already led him into the moral drift of self-delusion? This is not an easy question to answer, yet it formulates a major premise of the play. Aquinas seems to side with Giovanni in *Summa Theologiae* I.viii.3.2:

> God is said to exist in things in two ways. Firstly, as an operative cause, and in this way he exists in everything he creates. Secondly, as an object attained by some activity exists within the acting subject, and this applies only to mental activities where the known exists in the knower, and the desired in the one who desires. In this latter way, therefore, God exists in a special fashion in those reasoning creatures that are actually knowing and loving him, or are disposed to do so.

In Ford's England, Richard Hooker cites Augustine:

> The works of Nature are all behoveful, beautiful, without superfluity or defect, even so theirs [that] be framed according to that which the Law of Reason teacheth .... Those Laws are investigable by Reason, without the help of Revelation supernatural and divine. Finally, in such sort they are investigable, that the knowledge of them is general, the world hath always been acquainted with them.

Such are exactly Giovanni's position and not especially (at least to him) radical at all: "Say that we had one father, say one womb (Curse to my joys!) gave both us life and birth; Are we not therefore each to other bound So much the more by nature? by the links Of blood, of reason? Nay, if you will have 't, Even of religion, to be ever one, One soul, one flesh, one love, one heart, one *all*?" Indeed, at their second meeting, the Friar seems to give way: "to be led alone By Nature's light – as were philosophers Of elder times – might give some defense" would seem to cut Giovanni some slack, especially in the Caroline years when various religious groups argued daily on the grounds of "moral probabilism." Yet the context tells us that for the Friar pagan philosophers spoke in this way because they had yet to learn of God's laws through Christian revelation. Their debate is already at stalemate, at a kind of intellectual exhaustion: "Dispute no more in this." Simply put – and beyond controversy – is the fact that (quite apart from Adam and Eve, which might undermine the Friar's argument), incest is evil because the scripture forbids it and what is forbidden by scripture is evil. Such tautological insistence from the church, however, denies Giovanni the powers of reason his education had trained in him. But the laws of nature to which Giovanni appeals, what Bacon calls the "idols of the marketplace," had their own tautologies; "It is credible," Bacon writes, "that there be natural laws as may be seen in other creatures, but in us they are lost: this goodly human reason engrafting itself among all men . . . confounding and topsy-turvying the visage of all things, according to her inconstant vanity and vain inconstancy," to which Agrippa adds, "The Law of Nature is that we should not die for thirst, for hunger, for cold . . . which, abandoning all the repentance of religion, and the works of repentance, doth appoint the pleasure of the epicure for the chiefest felicity." Following the skepticism of Sextus Empiricus reintroduced into the English university curriculum by the humanists in the sixteenth century and anticipating Descartes' premise of intensive subjectivity – "*cogito ergo sum*"; I think, therefore I am – Giordano Bruno had in his brief visit to England proposed the relativity of all sensory perceptions. In the charged intellectual and philosophical debates of the early Caroline years, then, there is some reason to see Giovanni as a spokesman of the times when he exclaims,

> why, I hold fate
> Clasped in my fist, and could command the course
> Of time's eternal motion; hadst thou been
> One thought more steady than an ebbing sea.

Only a change of heart in his natural sister might give Giovanni pause.

In fact, the ardent Protestant audiences of the time might have their own doubts about the wisdom of a Catholic priest. Moreover, his pragmatic advice to Giovanni – to fornicate freely in order to curb the drive towards incest – as well as his counsel to Annabella – to marry the adulterous Soranzo (as, we are told, all Parma knows) – are both morally suspect and theologically culpable. Even Giovanni takes strong exception: "Marriage? Why, that's to damn her; that's to prove Her greedy of variety of lust." We too need to judge the Friar, but Ford has given us other factors to consider: the Friar has given up his post in Bologna in his devotion to Giovanni; he is providing alternative outlets for the brother's and sister's passions in order to foreclose incest; and, in fact, it is not clear that he knows about Soranzo's previous affair with Hippolita. His combination of spiritual prayer and earthly distraction agrees with the prescription Robert Burton was contemporaneously prescribing in his *Anatomy of Melancholy* for the "love-melancholic." They do Giovanni little good. Caught between his religious training and his instinctive passions that alone provide all "harmony both in my rest and life," Giovanni redefines both by synthesizing them: "To make our love a god, and worship it!" Turning to Platonic love (as, at one point, Augustine had), he is also turning to the kind of love which Queen Henrietta Maria was promoting avidly at the English court as well as a philosophy he claimed to learn from the Friar:

> It is a principle, which you have taught
> When I was yet your scholar, that the frame
> And composition of the mind doth follow
> The frame and composition of body;
> So where the body's furniture is beauty,
> The mind's must needs be virtue; which allowed,
> Virtue itself is reason but refined,
> And love the quintessence of that; this proves
> My sister's beauty, being rarely fair,
> Is rarely virtuous; chiefly in her love,
> And chiefly in that love, her love to me.

Such thoughts provide a refrain in his remarks throughout the play: "She is like me and I like her"; "Oh, the glory Of two united hearts like hers and mine." For Giovanni, such Platonic spirituality renders carnality moral; in following natural philosophy, moreover, in which what is natural is also good, he is able to respond directly to the Friar's teaching that what is unnatural is evil. This remains problematic, however, for those coterie members who came to the Phoenix from court, for while Giovanni takes up a Platonic sense of love which the English Queen practices, he does so at the expense of that same Queen's Catholicism.

At least as serious, Giovanni's position breeds a sophistry that makes incest not only possible but acceptable. Yet by its very nature, incest is radically destructive of the early modern English state which, like the play, organizes its population by families. The government itself – in which Charles and Henrietta Maria extended the political role of Elizabeth and James as parents of the commonwealth – made this ideology fundamental. But the family remained the primary social, as well as the primary political, unit. Marriages occurred to unite families and legacies; diplomacy was executed through marriage; marriage established bloodlines and lineage. Not only was the family, often with servants an extended family, the primary living unit; it was also the primary reproductive unit. *'Tis Pity She's a Whore* is at great pains always to dramatize this: there is a way in which the public (if not the private) plot is one of marrying Annabella to one of three suitors – the Roman Grimaldi, the nobleman Soranzo, or the nobleman Bergetto – and there is a way in which they are in turn defined by familial ties: Annabella's father Florio shares his concerns with Bergetto's uncle Donado; Richardetto is not only concerned with vengeance on his wife Hippolita but with the marriage of his niece Philotis; even the loner Grimaldi seeks companionship with the Cardinal as Soranzo does with his loyal Spanish servant Vasques and Bergetto in turn with his beloved servant Poggio. Such relationships – all of them vulnerable to a threat from permissible incest – is what identifies and motivates them, just as family ties and associations identified and defined nearly every member of Ford's Phoenix Theater audiences.

Statistics for the actual incidence of incest in Caroline England are hard to come by; the jurisdiction of the ecclesiastical courts, such matters were then, as they are today, sensitive enough that they often went unreported. But in the cramped quarters of most homes, where siblings often shared beds and the sexual activities of parents might also be easily heard and perhaps sometimes actually witnessed, the danger must always have been real enough. Arthur Lake, the Bishop of Bath and Wells, notes just this need for strict prohibition of incest: "Had not God imprinted this reverence, the necessary cohabitation of parents and children, brethren and sisters, would yield too much opportunity and be too strong an incentive unto this unlawful conjunction, especially if you add thereunto the authority which parents have naturally over their children." As a matter of fact, like Friar Bonaventura, he found fornication itself less threatening. "Fornication," he claims in his *Sermons with Some Religious Meditations* (1629),

> violateth the good order that should be between single persons, through unruly lusts; adultery addeth thereunto a confusion of families, and taketh away the distinction of heirs and inheritance; but incest moreover abolisheth the reverence which is engraved by nature, to forbid that persons whom nature hath made so near should one uncover the others shame.

He echoes Thomas Beard's *Theatre of God's Judgments* (1597) which, if anything, had been even more severe: "Incest [is] a wicked and abhominable sin, and forbidden both by the law of God and man, insomuch that the very heathen held it in detestation," adding that it is "unlawful to marry those that are near unto us by any degree of kindred or affinity, as it is inhibited not only by the law of God, but also by civil and politic constitutions, whereunto all nations have ever by the sole instinct of nature agreed and accorded." The stiff fine accorded Sir Giles Allington who, in 1631, two years before the publication of *'Tis Pity She's a Whore*, was declared guilty of "intermarrying with Dorothy Dalton, daughter of Michael Dalton and his wife, which latter was half-sister to Sir Giles," brings the same forceful reaction from Joseph Mead: "It was the solemnest, the gravest and the severest censure that ever, they say, was made in that court." In Ford's play, the continued incest between Giovanni and Annabella will not only frustrate Florio's attempt to marry his daughter in order to provide for her before his death; it will bring an end to his family line. There is a way in which Bergetto's final poignant words – "Is this all mine own blood?" – resonates throughout the entire play, uniting his bloody death with those of the others – Hippolita, Annabella, Soranzo, Giovanni – in ways that eradicate all the class boundaries of rank and station, social institutions, and family identities by which Parman society – and Caroline society – managed to survive.

We must reevaluate all this, however, in light of the sympathy with which Ford treats Giovanni and Annabella at the same time he refuses to excuse the danger inherent in their attitudes and actions. Isolating Giovanni from the other suitors who parade, one by one, before Annabella's window in the play's second scene – selfish, quarreling, altogether undesirable – he unites Giovanni with Annabella in a ritual ceremony of love and marriage (they kneel to pledge vows to each other; she gives her brother her bridal ring) that fends off the implied possibilities and conditions of exogamous alliances. Ford suggests that, in some way, Annabella is better for doing so. In *The Second Part of the Christian Warfare* (1611), John Downame lists the causes of a fallen world in "the vanity of honors, riches, and pleasures" that denote these suitors: the sham because untested honor of Grimaldi who takes refuge in social rank; the material interests of Florio and Donado; the erotic pleasures sought by Soranzo, who has tired of Hippolita having, as she remarks, destroyed her chastity. Civility is the stated social ideal of Parma with its banquets, marriage plans, and masques, but such wedding arrangements and hospitality in fact mask adultery, violence, and betrayal that rent the city's very social fabric. The short scenes that might be thought to divide

Act III into discrete dramatic shards are in fact united in their impression and activity of secretive plots, rumors, hurried encounters that seem (despite Ford's ability to keep them straight for us) to be haphazard, undisciplined actions in a society that is in fact out of control. What does control it, and makes it more objectionable than the love of Giovanni and Annabella for each other, is the unifying force of private revenge – Hippolita's, Grimaldi's, Richardetto's, Soranzo's, Vasques' – that comes to a painful climax in the senseless death of Bergetto. What may seem to the characters in Ford's play a random misfortune, though, may to us seem a telling symbol of the death of innocence in a corrupt society. If so, then, what of the incest that frames and overrides such actions: is that too the death of innocence, or something so erotically charged, and so misbegotten, that it too measures the city's – and the culture's – corruption?

Both the innocence and the corruption come together in troubling ways in the bifocalism of III.ii, where Soranzo's active courtship of Annabella and her thoughtful and teasing responses on the main stage are witnessed by Giovanni as voyeur, eavesdropping on the balcony, and his own qualifications against Soranzo's, his own loyalty of his sister to him against his for her. This emblematic confrontation of rank, character, and motive must make us uneasy, too, but it is a flashpoint where we can begin to work out our own judgments. It forces us to assess, and perhaps reassess, the teasing, the tenderness, and the idealism of the incestuous relationship – its virtues, its validity, its stability, its very chances for survival. Until this scene, the privacy of brother and sister together, where all that matters is pure love, takes on a quiet dignity that may afford the relationship, and the lovers, a tragic status. After this scene, we are given a sharper, and alternative, perspective. We can, for instance, reassess Giovanni's ideas and motives for loving his sister. For one thing, her beauty has provided him an object worthy of worship. For another, he argues their blood relationship leads to an intimate, and deeper, more genuine, bond. For a third, his feelings are his destiny: he is fated to love Annabella, and this itself is a sufficient cause to do so. We may question, or disagree, with any or all of these positions; put together, however, they may be inconsistent, perhaps even incoherent. His behavior might suggest as much. When theology does not support his incestuous love, however sincere and well-intentioned, he turns to natural philosophy. When religion fails him, he becomes an atheist. When his sister admonishes him in a letter of blood and tears, he decries it to be forged. Faced with competing discourses he is no longer able to synthesize, Giovanni takes on the moral obdurance then characteristic of the Calvinist reprobate addicted, like Faustus, to sin and pleasure. As Ford writes of such a situation in his poem *Christ's Bloody Sweat*,

> 'tis almost impossible to change,
> From bad to good though God in mercy woe
> Mortality, to taste of mercy's treasure,
> Yet oh, 'tis hard to leave the baits of pleasure.

Ford's early audiences might have other reactions as well. Giovanni's love of books and solitude – since he has been away at school, Annabella has not seen him for years at the play's start – indicates he is a prime candidate for the illness of melancholy. He is especially prone to love-melancholy which, Burton writes in his *Anatomy* (1622, 1628, 1632), "commonly gallants, noblemen, and the most generous spirits are possessed with." He goes on to list symptoms: "burning lust, a disease, frenzy, madness, hell" which on occasion "begets rapes, incests, murders." By such terms, Giovanni is seriously ill and prone to madness; the very pressure he feels to redefine such terms as "love," "honor," "justice," and "revenge" illustrates the danger of an intellectual moving into a fatally solipsistic world of his own making.

Yet to what degree is Annabella complicit in all this? When we first see her, in the second scene, she is disdainful and dismissive of her various suitors, but on seeing Giovanni, whom she does not recognize, she is at once attracted to him, and descends from her balcony to meet him on his own level. Although Giovanni has already found the integrity and ability to confess his love of his sister before his confessor in the first scene, we sense the awkwardness and risk when he must repeat such a love to Annabella. Her teasing and doubting do not help, and he must hazard his life to the dagger in his hand to prove his sincerity. But what is, for us as for them, a tense scene, fraught with anxiety and yearning, gets its post-coital-like release in her own confession and assent.

> My captive heart had long ago resolved.
> I blush to tell thee – but I'll tell thee now –
> For every sigh that thou hast spent for me,
> I have sighed ten; for every tear shed twenty.

It is Annabella, not Giovanni, who initiates the prenuptial marriage contract:

> On my knees,
> Brother, even by our mother's dust, I charge you,
> Do not betray me to your mirth or hate.
> Love me, or kill me, brother,

and seals it with her vows and his and, in time, her mother's bridal ring. Yet in her only other appearance on the balcony, she again communicates with the man below – but this time it is the Friar and she gives him a letter for Giovanni that reveals her change of heart. Spurred by her apparent betrayal, Giovanni confronts her, once again pulling out his dagger even as once again he kisses her: "Thus die, and die by me, and by my hand." He follows her earlier directions, their shared vows, to the letter. "Revenge is mine; honor doth love command." His obsessive love has become painful in its possessiveness:

> to dispute,
> With – even in thy death – most lovely beauty,
> Would make me stagger to perform this act
> Which I most glory in.

How justified is he? And Annabella's disparate response –

> Forgive him, Heaven – and me my sins; farewell,
> Brother, unkind, unkind – mercy, great Heaven! – Oh
> – Oh!,

a plea for mercy for them both, how likely is that? The excruciating pain in such opposing acts of love renews in a major key Poggio's hopeless cries before the Cardinal's gate; but is this in any way a similar death of innocence? Indeed, Ford's play not only insists we address such a question; it hedges it in. As Annabella's tutoress, Putana has already excused and condoned the incestuous relationship, even encouraged it: "Nay, what a paradise of joy have you passed under! Why, now I commend thee, charge; fear nothing, sweetheart, what though he be your brother?... if a young wench feel the fit upon her, let her take anybody, father or brother, all is one." It is the way of Parma; it is the way of the world. Soranzo provides another perspective: when we meet him, he too is reading a book, by the love poet Sannazzaro, who writes the same Petrarchan lexicon he and Giovanni share; he too has some love for Annabella and, like Giovanni, talks of her possessively as his heroic will is also self-serving and concupiscent. Giovanni, it is true, kills Soranzo as an adulterer (all Parma knew of Hippolita; all Parma shall know of Annabella); yet after Giovanni's earlier marriage, known to canon law as the *sponsalia per verba de praesenti*, it is Soranzo and not Giovanni who has been cuckolded. Which of them is more culpable?

Still, *'Tis Pity She's a Whore* is best known for its final scene, with a startling and compelling image that once we see it, even in our mind's eye, can possess us forever. It may well be the most striking image in the whole of Renaissance English drama. Giovanni arrives at Soranzo's feast late – as, earlier, Hippolita had arrived at the banquet late, with murder on her mind – and he brandishes a heart dripping from his sword. For the audiences at the Phoenix, it would have been a real heart – that from a pig or sheep – yet it could evoke the same primal horror and revulsion. It is the word become flesh: incest and love and revenge made object and put on public display, what Henri Estienne called a device:

> A Device is nothing else but a rare and particular way of expressing oneself; the most compendious, most pleasing, most efficacious of all other that human wit can invent. It is indeed most compendious, since, by two or three words it surpasseth that which is contained in the greatest volumes. As a small beam of the sun is able to illuminate and replenish a cavern be it ever so vast, with the rays of its splendor, so a Device enlightens our whole understanding.

Giovanni himself may see it quite otherwise: "The glory of my deed Darkened the mid-day sun, made noon as night"; "The schoolmen teach that all this globe of earth Shall be consumed to ashes in a minute." But what does it *mean*; how does it press all meaning into a singular image that, unpacked, illumines not only Giovanni but the significance of Ford's play as well? Giovanni has, making metaphoric Petrarchan love poetry literal, possessed the heart of his beloved forever. He has, for Ford's audiences at the Phoenix, held up a heart still steaming just as executioners ritually did at the frequent public capital punishments of criminals and traitors. It could easily recall, too, the popular emblem books that rolled off the Jacobean and Caroline presses. In one such emblem of a heart impaled it signifies Love's Cruelty; it is this meaning for such an emblem which Clarke has in mind when he sends a similar painting to his beloved Susan in *Arden of Faversham*. It could also imagistically signify Love's Envy. In Catholic hagiography, it suggests the ecstatic suffering of St. Teresa, pictured with a fiery spear thrust into her heart as a reminder of Divine Love, here horribly parodic.

Such a shocking image, however, should not shock us, for it reorchestrates the play by pulling together warnings of such an act that recur throughout *'Tis Pity She's a Whore*. In the play's second scene, Giovanni has such thoughts to prove his love and fidelity:

> And here's my breast, strike home!
> Rip up my bosom, there thou shalt behold
> A heart in which is writ the truth I speak.

His double, Soranzo, has had similar thoughts when forcing Annabella to reveal the name of her lover:

> Not know it, strumpet! I'll rip up thy heart
> And find it there.

Even Friar Bonaventura echoes the lovers' pledges to "Love me, or kill me" when he admonishes Annabella; after "secret incests," and curses, he tells her,

you will wish each kiss your brother gave
Had been a dagger's point; then you shall hear
How he will cry, "Oh, would my wicked sister
Had first been damned, when she did yield to lust!"

At play's end, Giovanni assigns new yet similarly powerful meanings. The steaming heart presages revenge:

Soranzo, see this heart which was thy wife's.
Thus I exchange it royally for thine.

It is an "oracle." It is a matter of pride:

For nine months' space, in secret I enjoyed
Sweet Annabella's sheets; nine months I liv'd
A happy monarch of her heart and her.

It signifies the fall of this monarch's kingdom, the house of Florio presaged in his death:

How well this death becomes him in his griefs!
Why, this was done with courage. Now survives
None of our house but I, gilt [guilt?] in the blood
Of a fair sister and a hapless father.

It grotesquely images Soranzo's banquet and the host of the Catholic Mass:

I came to feast too, but I digged for food
In a much richer mine than gold or stone
Of any value balanced; 'tis a heart,
A heart, my lords, in which is mine entombed,

for when he struck Annabella, "this dagger's point ploughed up Her fruitful womb." He has committed not only incest and murder but infanticide; assuring the death of his family, he assures his own. The impaired heart suggests his own endangered. It is an emblem of suicide.

What meaning are we supposed to assign? How can we choose from such a dazzling and infernal set of propositions? Or should we, too, dispense with them, dispute them not? Does the illumination of the device transcend the poverty of language and inadequacy of explanation in its very theatricality? Does this take plays, and playgoing, to their farthest reaches?

The overriding religiosity of many of the possible significations of the pierced heart – like scriptural exegesis itself – takes us back to matters of faith as the play takes us, at the last, back to the Cardinal. He is faith's sole representative, having some time ago replaced the despairing Friar. The Pope's Nuncio has been decisive in his acts and words both. He has provided sanctuary for Grimaldi. He merely banishes the murderer Vasques: "to depart Within these three days; in this we do dispense With grounds of reason, not of thine offense." And he orders the bodies taken up for burial – although where is an open question – as he collects other remains for himself and the church:

Take up these slaughtered bodies, see them buried;
And all the gold and jewels, or whatsoever,
Confiscate by the canons of the Church,
We seize upon to the Pope's proper use.

He ends the play, too, with a question:

We still have time
To talk at large of all; but never yet
Incest and murder have so strangely met.
Of one so young, so rich in Nature's store,
Who could not say, *'Tis pity she's a whore*?

He names the play we have been examining; we have struggled under this Cardinal's aegis all along, just like the citizens of Parma. Yet the couplet seems woefully misspoken, the moral platitude grotesquely insufficient. Does this suggest that any attempt to summarize (or title) this play will fail to do it justice? Is *pity* or *whore* the wrong word; and who else would speak them? who else echo such judgments? Even "Nature's store" seems horribly ironic: that was Giovanni's reasoning in the first place – the temptation of Annabella that proved so fatal. Dealing with an impaled heart, we must also necessarily deal with the Cardinal.

Further Reading

Boehrer, Bruce, "'Nice Philosophy': *'Tis Pity She's a Whore* and the Two Books of God," *Studies in English Literature 1500–1900* 24:2 (Spring 1984): 355–71.

Clerico, Terri, "The Politics of Blood: John Ford's *'Tis Pity She's a Whore*," *English Literary Renaissance* 22:3 (Autumn 1992): 405–34.

Farr, Dorothy M., *John Ford and the Caroline Theatre*. London: Macmillan, 1979.

Hogan, A. P., "*'Tis Pity She's a Whore*: The Overall Design," *Studies in English Literature 1500–1600* 17:2 (Spring 1977): 303–16.

Ide, Richard S., "Ford's *'Tis Pity She's a Whore* and the Benefits of Belatedness," in *"Concord in Discord": The Plays of John Ford 1586–1986*, ed. Donald K. Anderson, Jr. (New York: AMS Press, 1986), pp. 61–81.

McCabe, Richard A., *Incest, Drama and Nature's Law 1550–1700*. Cambridge: Cambridge University Press, 1993.

Neill, Michael, ed., *John Ford: Critical Re-Visions*, esp. essays by Butler, Foster, Madelaine, and Neill. Cambridge: Cambridge University Press, 1988.

Smallwood, R. L., "*'Tis Pity She's a Whore* and *Romeo and Juliet*", *Cahiers Elisabethains* 20 (October 1981): 49–70.

Stavig, Mark, *John Ford and the Traditional Moral Order* (Madison: University of Wisconsin Press, 1968).

Wilks, John S., *The Idea of Conscience in Renaissance Tragedy*. London: Routledge, 1990.

Wymer, Rowland, *Webster and Ford*. London: Macmillan, 1995.

'Tis Pity She's a Whore

[The Epistle]

To the truly noble, John, Earl of Peterborough, Lord Mordaunt, Baron of Turvey.

My Lord,

Where a truth of merit hath a general warrant, there love is but a debt, acknowledgment a justice. Greatness cannot often claim virtue by inheritance; yet in this yours appears most eminent, for that you are not more rightly heir to your fortunes than glory shall be to your memory. Sweetness of disposition ennobles a freedom of birth; in both, your lawful interest adds honor to your own name, and mercy to my presumption. Your noble allowance of these first fruits of my leisure in the action emboldens my confidence of your as noble construction in this presentment; especially since my service must ever owe particular duty to your favors, by a particular engagement. The gravity of the subject may easily excuse the lightness of the title: otherwise I had been a severe judge against mine own guilt. Princes have vouchsafed grace to trifles, offered from a purity of devotion;

Textual Variants

Title-page adds "Acted by the Queen's Majesty's Servants at The Phoenix in Drury Lane" **Epistle 9** than] Q then **I.i.10** than] Q then **24** madman!] Q madman? **52** man!] Q man? **54** than] Q then **65** than] Q then **I.ii.18–20**] Q sets lines as poetry **36** mean] Q meaned **47** thy] Q this **49** had not] Q had **56** than] Q then **62–4**] Q sets lines as poetry **62** villainy] Q villain **88** Not one] Q one **124** than] Q then **163** **s.d.** *Exeunt*] Q Exit **211** The] Q they **229** strike] Q strick **I.iii.45** thither] Q hither **II.i.20** than] Q then **58–63**] Q sets lines as prose **II.ii.7** thee] Q the **59** thy] Q thee **89** than] Q then **100** accursed] Q curse **106** Than] Q Then **162–3**] Q sets lines as poetry **165–6** for witnesses] Q foe-witnesses **II.iii.54** kill] Q tell **63** ruined] Q mined **II.iv.31** than] Q then **37–9**] Q sets as poetry **II.v.8** my] Q thy **15** frame] Q fame **II.vi.50** have 't] Q have. **79** than] Q then **135–8**] Q sets as prose **135** alone, still?] Q alone, still, still? **III.i.8**] Q has *Poggio* for speech prefix **III.ii.31** I know] Q know **38–9**] Q sets as prose **66**] Q gives line to Giovanni **III.iii.14** qualms] Q quams **30** does] Q do **III.v.8–11**] Q sets as prose **12** Friar] Q Fryars **42** shall have] Q shall **IV.i.29** **s.d.** *Hautboys*] Q sets s.d. after line 35 **77** *inganna*] Q niganna **83** marriage] Q malice **IV.ii.28** lives] Q live **IV.iii.15** Why] Q Shey **59** *più*] Q pluis **90** author], Q authors **128** thou] thus **162** ferret] Q Secret **188** **s.d.**] Q has s.d. at line 192 **237** than] Q then **254–6**] Q sets as poetry **265** **s.d.** *Exeunt*] Q Exit **273–5**] Q sets as poetry **280–1**] Q sets as poetry **301** **s.d.** *Exeunt*] Q exit **V.i.45** than] Q then **53** than] then **V.iii.41** **s.d.**] Q has s.d. at line 42 **48** him] Q them **72**] Q omits speech prefix **76** rend] Q rent **V.iv.51** **s.d.** *Flourish*] Q has s.d. at line 54 **V.v.17** dining] Q dying **51** woo] Q woe **62** required] Q require **V.vi.6** than] Q then **85–7**] Q sets as poetry **94–5**] Q sets as poetry **99–101**] Q sets as prose **102** thee] the **170–5**] After "Finis" (169) Q adds: "The general commendation deserved by the actors in their presentment of this tragedy may easily excuse such few faults as are escaped in the printing; a common charity may allow him the ability of spelling, whom a secure confidence assures that he cannot ignorantly err in the application of sense" (i.e., no great charity is needed to assume that one who knows how to use words can also spell them)

Playsource

'Tis Pity She's a Whore has no known source, although critics have suggested many works dealing with incest: Sperone Speroni's play *Canace e Macareo* (1546), Rosset's *Histoires Tragiques* 5, Thomas Heywood's *Gunaikeion*, and Tirso de Molina's *La Venganza de Tamar*. But there are no certain resonances in any of these.

Dedicatory Epistle

1–2 ***John . . . Mordaunt*** Mordaunt (1599–1642) was drawn to King James's attention by his intelligence and beauty. Charles I made him first Earl of Peterborough on March 9, 1628. He sided with Parliament in the Civil War, however, and served the Earl of Essex as his general of ordnance, dying from consumption on June 18, 1642. Nothing is known of his relationship to Ford

13 **allowance** appraisal

14 **action** performance

15 **construction** interpretation, judgment; **presentment** (1) publication; (2) dedication

16–17 **particular . . . engagement** (reference is unknown)

18 **lightness** frivolity (perhaps the use of *pity*)

your lordship may likewise please to admit into your good opinion, with these weak endeavors, the constancy of affection from the sincere lover of your deserts in honor,

John Ford.

To my Friend, the Author.

With admiration I beheld this Whore
Adorned with beauty, such as might restore
(If ever being as thy Muse hath famed)
Her Giovanni, in his love unblamed.
The ready Graces lent their willing aid;
Pallas herself now played the chamber-maid
And helped to put her dressings on: secure
Rest thou, that thy name herein shall endure
To th' end of age; and Annabella be
Gloriously fair, even in her infamy.

Thomas Ellice.

The Scene

PARMA

The Actors' Names:

Bonaventura, *a friar.*
A Cardinal, *nuncio to the Pope.*
Soranzo, *a nobleman.*
Florio, *a citizen of Parma.*
Donado, *another citizen.*
Grimaldi, *a Roman gentleman.*
Giovanni, *son to Florio.*
Bergetto, *nephew to Donado.*
Richardetto, *a supposed physician.*
Vasques, *servant to Soranzo.*
Poggio, *servant to Bergetto.*
Banditti.
[Officers.
Attendants.]

Women:

Annabella, *daughter to Florio.*
Hippolita, *wife to Richardetto.*
Philotis, *his niece.*
Putana, *tutress to Annabella.*
[Ladies.]

Act I

[I.i]

Enter Friar *and* Giovanni.

Fri. Dispute no more in this, for know, young man,
These are no school-points; nice philosophy
May tolerate unlikely arguments,
But Heaven admits no jest; wits that presumed
On wit too much, by striving how to prove
There was no God, with foolish grounds of art,
Discovered first the nearest way to Hell;
And filled the world with devilish atheism.
Such questions, youth, are fond; for better 'tis
To bless the sun, than reason why it shines;
Yet He thou talk'st of is above the sun –
No more! I may not hear it.
Gio. Gentle father,
To you I have unclasped my burdened soul,
Emptied the storehouse of my thoughts and heart,
Made myself poor of secrets; have not left
Another word untold, which hath not spoke
All what I ever durst or think, or know;
And yet is here the comfort I shall have?
Must I not do what all men else may – love?
Fri. Yes, you may love, fair son.
Gio. Must I not praise
That beauty which, if framed anew, the gods
Would make a god of if they had it there,
And kneel to it, as I do kneel to them?
Fri. Why, foolish madman!
Gio. Shall a peevish sound,
A customary form, from man to man,
Of brother and of sister, be a bar
'Twixt my perpetual happiness and me?
Say that we had one father, say one womb
(Curse to my joys!) gave both us life and birth;
Are we not therefore each to other bound

Dedicatory Poem

6 **Graces** Zeus' three daughters, who awarded beauty, grace, and kindness

7 **Pallas** as patron of the arts

12 ***Thomas Ellice*** unknown; he may have been related to Robert Ellice of Gray's Inn to whom Ford's *The Lover's Melancholy* is dedicated

I.i.1 s.d. ***Friar*** (starting the play with a religious figure frames thought and action and anticipates the Cardinal's displacement of him at the play's end)

1 **Dispute** argue (a formal term in rhetoric and logic)

2 **nice** subtle

4 **admits** allows; **jest** (1) exception; (2) sophistry; **wits** men of learning

6 **art** argumentation

7–8 **first . . . atheism** i.e., putting the pride of their argumentative skills before God and His laws, they damned themselves from the start

7 **nearest** shortest

9 **fond** foolish

17 **what** that; **durst** dared to imagine

18 **here** (1) the friar's obdurance; (2) God's unbreakable laws

24 **peevish** (1) senseless; (2) spiteful

25 **customary form** cultural or conventional formality

So much the more by nature? by the links
Of blood, of reason? Nay, if you will have 't,
Even of religion, to be ever one,
One soul, one flesh, one love, one heart, one *all*?
Fri. Have done, unhappy youth, for thou art lost.
Gio. Shall then, for that I am her brother born,
My joys be ever banished from her bed?
No, father; in your eyes I see the change
Of pity and compassion; from your age,
As from a sacred oracle, distils
The life of counsel: tell me, holy man,
What cure shall give me ease in these extremes?
Fri. Repentance, son, and sorrow for this sin:
For thou hast moved a Majesty above
With thy unrangèd (almost) blasphemy.
Gio. Oh, do not speak of that, dear confessor.
Fri. Art thou, my son, that miracle of wit
Who once, within these three months, wert esteemed
A wonder of thine age, throughout Bononia?
How did the university applaud
Thy government, behavior, learning, speech,
Sweetness, and all that could make up a man!
I was proud of my tutelage, and chose
Rather to leave my books than part with thee;
I did so – but the fruits of all my hopes
Are lost in thee, as thou art in thyself.
Oh, Giovanni! hast thou left the schools
Of knowledge, to converse with lust and death?
For death waits on thy lust. Look through the world,
And thou shalt see a thousand faces shine
More glorious than this idol thou adorest.
Leave her, and take thy choice, 'tis much less sin,
Though in such games as those they lose that win.
Gio. It were more ease to stop the ocean
From floats and ebbs than to dissuade my vows.
Fri. Then I have done, and in thy willful flame
Already see thy ruin. Heaven is just;
Yet hear my counsel.
Gio. As a voice of life.
Fri. Hie to thy father's house, there lock thee fast
Alone within thy chamber, then fall down
On both thy knees, and grovel on the ground;
Cry to thy heart, wash every word thou utter'st
In tears, and, if 't be possible, of blood;
Beg Heaven to cleanse the leprosy of lust
That rots thy soul, acknowledge what thou art,
A wretch, a worm, a nothing; weep, sigh, pray
Three times a day, and three times every night;
For seven days' space do this, then if thou find'st
No change in thy desires, return to me.
I'll think on remedy. Pray for thyself
At home, whilst I pray for thee here – away!
My blessing with thee; we have need to pray.
Gio. All this I'll do, to free me from the rod
Of vengeance; else I'll swear my fate's my God.

Exeunt.

[I.ii]

Enter Grimaldi *and* Vasques *ready to fight.*

Vas. Come, sir, stand to your tackling, if you prove craven I'll make you run quickly.
Grim. Thou art no equal match for me.
Vas. Indeed, I never went to the wars to bring home news, nor cannot play the mountebank for a meal's meat, and swear I got my wounds in the field. See you these grey hairs? they'll not flinch for a bloody nose; wilt thou to this gear?

35 **Have done** be silent; **unhappy** unfortunate; **lost** without proper direction (but not yet damned; see line 43)
36 **for that** because
40 **oracle** (1) supernatural guide; (2) prophecy
41 **counsel** wise judgment
45 **unrangèd** uncontrolled
49 **Bononia** Bologna, famous for its university
51 **government** manner, behavior (self-government)
53–4 **I . . . thee** (before 1562 the faculty at the University of Bologna taught from their own houses or hired rooms since the university had no halls for classes)
53 **tutelage** (1) mentoring; (2) guardianship
62 **less sin** i.e., fornication is a lesser sin than incest; Montaigne, in "Of Moderation," trans. by John Florio in 1603, claims to have read in Aquinas that marriage between kin, which God forbids, leads to "immoderate" lust that carries the husband "beyond the bounds of reason"
65 **floats and ebbs** flowing and ebbing
68 **voice of life** (1) life-giving counsel; (2) as one who speaks for God
69 **Hie** go quickly
73 **tears . . . blood** i.e., grief straight from the heart
74–8 **Beg . . . this** (standard acts of contrition)
84 **I'll . . . God** (Giovanni will continue to displace God with Fate to explain his feelings and actions)
I.ii.1 **tackling** weapons
2 **craven** coward
3 **equal** social, not skilled in arms (honor dictated that gentlemen fought only gentlemen after a proper challenge)
5 **mountebank** impostor, charlatan (see next line)
6 **a meal's meat** food
9 **gear** business (of fighting)

Grim. Why, slave, think'st thou I'll balance my reputation with a cast-suit? Call thy master, he shall know that I dare –

Vas. Scold like a cot-quean, that's your profession. Thou poor shadow of a soldier, I will make thee know my master keeps servants thy betters in quality and performance; comest thou to fight, or prate?

Grim. Neither, with thee. I am a Roman and a gentleman; one that have got mine honor with expense of blood.

Vas. You are a lying coward and a fool; fight, or by these hilts I'll kill thee. [*Grimaldi draws.*] Brave, my lord! You'll fight.

Grim. Provoke me not, for if thou dost –

Vas. Have at you!

They fight; Grimaldi hath the worst.

Enter Florio, Donado, Soranzo.

Flo. What mean these sudden broils so near my doors?
Have you not other places but my house
To vent the spleen of your disordered bloods?
Must I be haunted still with such unrest
As not to eat or sleep in peace at home?
Is this your love, Grimaldi? Fie, 'tis naught.

Don. And Vasques, I may tell thee 'tis not well
To broach these quarrels; you are ever forward
In seconding contentions.

Enter above Annabella *and* Putana.

Flo. What's the ground?

Sor. That, with your patience, signiors, I'll resolve:
This gentleman, whom fame reports a soldier –
For else I know not – rivals me in love
To Signior Florio's daughter; to whose ears
He still prefers his suit, to my disgrace,
Thinking the way to recommend himself
Is to disparage me in his report.
But know, Grimaldi, though may be thou art
My equal in thy blood, yet this bewrays
A lowness in thy mind; which wert thou noble
Thou wouldst as much disdain as I do thee
For this unworthiness; and on this ground
I willed my servant to correct thy tongue,
Holding a man so base no match for me.

Vas. And had not your sudden coming prevented us, I had let my gentleman blood under the gills; I should have wormed you, sir, for running mad.

Grim. I'll be revenged, Soranzo.

Vas. On a dish of warm broth to stay your stomach – do, honest innocence, do! Spoon-meat is a wholesomer diet than a Spanish blade.

Grim. Remember this!

Sor. I fear thee not, Grimaldi.

Exit Grimaldi.

Flo. My lord Soranzo, this is strange to me,
Why you should storm, having my word engaged;
Owing her heart, what need you doubt her ear?
Losers may talk by law of any game.

Vas. Yet the villainy of words, Signior Florio, may be such as would make any unspleened dove choleric; blame not my lord in this.

Flo. Be you more silent;
I would not for my wealth my daughter's love
Should cause the spilling of one drop of blood.
Vasques, put up; let's end this fray in wine.

Exeunt [Florio, Donado, Soranzo, *and* Vasques].

Put. How like you this, child? Here's threat'ning, challenging, quarreling and fighting on every side, and all is for your sake; you had need look to yourself, charge, you'll be stol'n away sleeping else shortly.

---

11 **cast-suit** dependant (from a servant who wears his master's old clothes)
13 **cot-quean** shrew; harlot
16 **quality** (1) birth; (2) character
17 **prate** chatter
18 **Roman** of ancient Italian lineage
20 **blood** gentility
26 **broils** quarrels
28 **spleen** bodily organ producing secretions that cause anger
29 **still** always
31 **love** pleasure; habit; **naught** worthless
33 **broach** encourage; **forward** quick to be
34 **s.d.** ***above*** (on the upper balcony; the play is full of eavesdropping and of secret offstage conversations as well as the use of the discovery space)
34 **ground** issue disputed (cf. disputation at I.i)
35 **resolve** explain (Vasques is acting on his behalf)
37 **know not** have no other evidence
39 **prefers** (1) advances; (2) presses
43 **blood** social rank; **bewrays** reveals
44 **lowness** i.e., thoughts and behavior of the lower classes (*base*, line 48)
47 **correct . . . tongue** apologize for disparaging remarks of line 41
49 **prevented** interrupted
50 **let** opened up
51 **gills** loose flesh under jaws and ears where blood was believed to rise in moments of anger; **wormed** (the worm was the ligament in a puppy's tongue that was cut out to prevent rabies); **for** to prevent
54–5 **stay . . . stomach** (1) satisfy your need; (2) lower your pride
55 **honest innocence** false claimant; fool; **Spoon-meat** soft or liquid diet for the sick and toothless
59 **word** consent to marry his daughter
60 **Owing** owning; **doubt** think accusations might mislead
61 **talk . . . game** say anything to regain advantage (proverbial)
68 **put up** (i.e., put away your sword)
72 **charge** (i.e., person in my charge)

Ann. But tutress, such a life gives no content
To me, my thoughts are fixed on other ends;
Would you would leave me.

Put. Leave you? no marvel else; leave me no leaving, charge, this is love outright. Indeed I blame you not, you have choice fit for the best lady in Italy.

Ann. Pray do not talk so much.

Put. Take the worst with the best, there's Grimaldi the soldier, a very well-timbered fellow; they say he is a Roman, nephew to the Duke Mount Ferratto; they say he did good service in the wars against the Millanoys – but faith, charge, I do not like him, and be for nothing but for being a soldier. Not one among twenty of your skirmishing captains but have some privy maim or other that mars their standing upright. I like him the worse he crinkles so much in the hams. Though he might serve if there were no more men, yet he's not the man I would choose.

Ann. Fie, how thou pratest.

Put. As I am a very woman, I like Signior Soranzo well. He is wise, and what is more, rich; and what is more than that, kind; and what is more than all this, a nobleman; such a one, were I the fair Annabella myself, I would wish and pray for. Then he is bountiful; besides he is handsome, and, by my troth, I think wholesome – and that's news in a gallant of three and twenty. Liberal, that I know; loving, that you know; and a man sure, else he could never ha' purchased such a good name with Hippolita the lusty widow in her husband's lifetime – and 'twere but for that report, sweetheart, would a were thine! Commend a man for his qualities, but take a husband as he is a plain-sufficient, naked man. Such a one is for your bed, and such a one is Signior Soranzo, my life for 't.

Ann. Sure the woman took her morning's draught too soon.

Enter Bergetto *and* Poggio.

Put. But look, sweetheart, look what thing comes now. Here's another of your ciphers to fill up the number. Oh, brave old ape in a silken coat, observe.

Ber. Didst thou think, Poggio, that I would spoil my new clothes, and leave my dinner to fight?

Pog. No, sir, I did not take you for so arrant a baby.

Ber. I am wiser than so: for I hope, Poggio, thou never heard'st of an elder brother that was a coxcomb, didst, Poggio?

Pog. Never indeed, sir, as long as they had either land or money left them to inherit.

Ber. Is it possible, Poggio? Oh, monstrous! Why, I'll undertake, with a handful of silver, to buy a headful of wit at any time. But sirrah, I have another purchase in hand. I shall have the wench mine uncle says; I will but wash my face, and shift socks, and then have at her i'faith! – Mark my pace, Poggio. [*Walks affectedly.*]

Pog. Sir, I have seen an ass and a mule trot the Spanish pavin with a better grace, I know not how often.

Exeunt [Bergetto *and* Poggio].

Ann. This idiot haunts me too.

Put. Aye, aye, he needs no description. The rich magnifico that is below with your father, charge, Signior Donado his uncle, for that he means to make this his cousin a golden calf, thinks that you will be a right Israelite, and fall down to him presently; but I hope I have

---

74 **tutress** tutoress (cf. friar as Giovanni's equivalent)
77 **no ... else** of course you want me to; **leave ... no** do not talk to me of
79 **you ... for** you have first choice as
83 **well-timbered** well-proportioned; handsome
90 **privy maim** hidden injury
90–1 **standing upright** not impotent (obscene pun; cf. *skirmishing* and *privy maim*)
91–2 **crinkles ... hams** (1) bows; (2) withdraws
96 **very** (1) honest; (2) representative
102 **troth** truth (common vow)
102–3 **wholesome** healthy (i.e., without venereal disease)
104 **Liberal** generous (he has paid Putana – whose name means *whore* – to plead his suit)
106 **good name** high regard
108 **'twere ... for** if for nothing else but; **report** rumor
109 **a** he
110 **qualities** achievements
110–11 **is ... man** sufficient in manly functions
115 **draught** alcoholic drink (jestingly)
117 **ciphers** useless suitors
118 **brave** finely dressed; **old ... coat** "an ape is an ape though clad in scarlet" (proverbial)
122 **arrant** manifest
125 **elder brother** (as one who inherits)
126 **coxcomb** foolish person
131 **sirrah** form of address used for an inferior
133 **wench** woman, maid
134 **shift** change my; **have at her** bodily take her
135 **Mark ... pace** watch my walk
137 **pavin** pavan, a stately, graceful dance popular at the English court
139 **haunts** courts
141 **magnifico** grandee; magistrate
142 **for that** because
143 **cousin** kinsman; **golden calf** rich simpleton
144 **right Israelite** worshipping a golden calf (Exod. 32)
145 **presently** at once

tutored you better. They say a fool's bauble is a lady's playfellow; yet you having wealth enough, you need not cast upon the dearth of flesh at any rate. Hang him, innocent!

Enter Giovanni.

Ann. But see, Putana, see; what blessed shape
Of some celestial creature now appears?
What man is he, that with such sad aspect
Walks careless of himself?
Put. Where?
Ann. Look below.
Put. O, 'tis your brother, sweet –
Ann. Ha!
Put. 'Tis your brother.
Ann. Sure 'tis not he. This is some woeful thing
Wrapped up in grief, some shadow of a man.
Alas, he beats his breast, and wipes his eyes
Drowned all in tears; methinks I hear him sigh.
Let's down, Putana, and partake the cause;
I know my brother, in the love he bears me,
Will not deny me partage in his sadness.
My soul is full of heaviness and fear.
Exeunt [Annabella *and* Putana].
Gio. Lost, I am lost; my fates have doomed my death;
The more I strive, I love, the more I love,
The less I hope; I see my ruin, certain.
What judgment or endeavors could apply
To my incurable and restless wounds
I throughly have examined, but in vain.
Oh, that it were not in religion sin
To make our love a god, and worship it!
I have even wearied Heaven with prayers, dried up
The spring of my continual tears, even starved
My veins with daily fasts; what wit or art
Could counsel, I have practiced. But alas,
I find all these but dreams, and old men's tales
To fright unsteady youth; I'm still the same.
Or I must speak, or burst; 'tis not, I know,
My lust, but 'tis my fate that leads me on.
Keep fear and low faint-hearted shame with slaves!
I'll tell her that I love her, though my heart
Were rated at the price of that attempt.
Oh me! she comes.

Enter Annabella *and* Putana.

Ann. Brother!
Gio. [*Aside.*] If such a thing
As courage dwell in men, ye heavenly powers,
Now double all that virtue in my tongue.
Ann. Why brother, will you not speak to me?
Gio. Yes; how d'ee, sister?
Ann. Howsoever I am,
Methinks you are not well.
Put. Bless us, why are you so sad, sir?
Gio. Let me entreat you leave us awhile, Putana, –
Sister, I would be private with you.
Ann. Withdraw, Putana.
Put. I will. [*Aside.*] If this were any other company for her, I should think my absence an office of some credit; but I will leave them together.
Exit Putana.
Gio. Come sister, lend your hand, let's walk together.
I hope you need not blush to walk with me;
Here's none but you and I.
Ann. How's this?
Gio. Faith, I mean no harm.
Ann. Harm?
Gio. No, good faith; how is 't with 'ee?
Ann. [*Aside.*] I trust he be not frantic. [*To him.*] I am very well, brother.
Gio. Trust me, but I am sick; I fear so sick
'Twill cost my life.
Ann. Mercy forbid it! 'tis not so, I hope.
Gio. I think you love me, sister.
Ann. Yes, you know I do.
Gio. I know 't, indeed. – Y' are very fair.
Ann. Nay, then I see you have a merry sickness.
Gio. That's as it proves. The poets feign, I read,
That Juno for her forehead did exceed
All other goddesses; but I durst swear
Your forehead exceeds hers, as hers did theirs.

146–7 fool's bauble ... playfellow decorated stick (sometimes with ribbons or a carved head) carried by fools as a sign of their position (as a lady's playfellow it would be phallic; a dildo)
148–9 cast ... flesh take any (or the worst) of suitors
149 innocent idiot
159 partake learn
161 partage in a share of
168 throughly thoroughly
170 To ... god (the primal sin of Adam; cf. 1 Tim. 2:14)
173 art medical knowledge
176 fright admonish
177 Or either
179 slaves the lower classes
181 rated ... price berated as the cost
193–4 of ... credit deserving some reward
202 frantic mad
210 have ... sickness mean to jest with me
211 proves turns out (i.e., if you consent to my hopes and needs); **feign** pretend
212 Juno queen of the Roman gods (but Jupiter's sister as well as his wife)

Ann. Troth, this is pretty!
Gio. Such a pair of stars
As are thine eyes would, like Promethean fire,
If gently glanced, give life to senseless stones.
Ann. Fie upon 'ee!
Gio. The lily and the rose, most sweetly strange,
Upon your dimpled cheeks do strive for change.
Such lips would tempt a saint; such hands as those
Would make an anchorite lascivious.
Ann. D'ee mock me, or flatter me?
Gio. If you would see a beauty more exact
Than art can counterfeit or nature frame,
Look in your glass, and there behold your own.
Ann. Oh, you are a trim youth.
Gio. Here!
Offers his dagger to her.
Ann. What to do?
Gio. And here's my breast, strike home!
Rip up my bosom, there thou shalt behold
A heart in which is writ the truth I speak.
Why stand 'ee?
Ann. Are you earnest?
Gio. Yes, most earnest;
You cannot love –
Ann. Whom?
Gio. Me. My tortured soul
Hath felt affliction in the heat of death.
Oh, Annabella, I am quite undone:
The love of thee, my sister, and the view
Of thy immortal beauty hath untuned
All harmony both of my rest and life.
Why d'ee not strike?
Ann. Forbid it, my just fears;
If this be true, 'twere fitter I were dead.
Gio. True, Annabella? 'tis no time to jest.
I have too long suppressed the hidden flames
That almost have consumed me; I have spent
Many a silent night in sighs and groans,
Ran over all my thoughts, despised my fate,
Reasoned against the reasons of my love,
Done all that smoothed-cheek Virtue could advise,
But found all bootless. 'Tis my destiny
That you must either love, or I must die.
Ann. Comes this in sadness from you?
Gio. Let some mischief
Befall me soon, if I dissemble aught.
Ann. You are my brother, Giovanni.
Gio. You
My sister, Annabella; I know this;
And could afford you instance why to love
So much the more for this; to which intent
Wise Nature first in your creation meant
To make you mine, else 't had been sin and foul
To share one beauty to a double soul.
Nearness in birth or blood doth but persuade
A nearer nearness in affection.
I have asked counsel of the holy Church,
Who tells me I may love you, and 'tis just
That since I may, I should; and will, yes will:
Must I now live, or die?
Ann. Live; thou hast won
The field, and never fought; what thou hast urged,
My captive heart had long ago resolved.
I blush to tell thee – but I'll tell thee now –
For every sigh that thou hast spent for me,
I have sighed ten; for every tear shed twenty.
And not so much for that I loved, as that
I durst not say I loved; nor scarcely think it.
Gio. Let not this music be a dream, ye gods,
For pity's sake I beg 'ee!
Ann. On my knees,
She kneels.
Brother, even by our mother's dust, I charge you,
Do not betray me to your mirth or hate.
Love me, or kill me, brother.
Gio. On my knees,
He kneels.
Sister, even by my mother's dust I charge you,
Do not betray me to your mirth or hate.
Love me, or kill me, sister.
Ann. You mean good sooth then?
Gio. In good troth I do,

217 **Promethean fire** heavenly fire stolen by Prometheus to give life to men and women he fashioned from clay
220 **strange** intense
221 **change** (1) precedence; (2) interchange
223 **anchorite** (1) cloistered nun; (2) hermit
227 **glass** mirror
228 **trim** fine (and perhaps jolly; she still hopes he is teasing)
232 **stand 'ee** hesitate
233 **Me** (according to the friar's and God's commandments)
234 **in the heat** to the point
238 **rest** (1) final peace; (2) present peace of mind
247 **smoothed-cheek** (young like himself and therefore understanding)
248 **bootless** useless
250 **sadness** earnest; **mischief** evil
251 **dissemble aught** pretend anything else (other than the truth)
254 **afford . . . instance** show you example (or reason)
258 **double soul** (refers to neoplatonic theory which defined love as the union of two like souls)
259 **persuade** (1) argue for; (2) prove
261–2 **I . . . you** (Giovanni lies by not telling the whole truth from I.i)
265 **The field** my love (conventional)
270 **for that** because
280 **mean . . . sooth** tell the truth

And so do you I hope. Say, I'm in earnest.
Ann. I'll swear 't, and I.
Gio. And I, and by this kiss –
Kisses her.
Once more; yet once more. Now, let's rise. By this
I would not change this minute for Elysium.
What must we now do?
Ann. What you will.
Gio. Come then;
After so many tears as we have wept,
Let's learn to court in smiles, to kiss and sleep.
Exeunt.

[I.iii]

Enter Florio *and* Donado.

Flo. Signior Donado, you have said enough,
I understand you, but would have you know
I will not force my daughter 'gainst her will.
You see I have but two, a son and her;
And he is so devoted to his book,
As I must tell you true, I doubt his health.
Should he miscarry, all my hopes rely
Upon my girl. As for worldly fortune,
I am, I thank my stars, blessed with enough;
My care is how to match her to her liking.
I would not have her marry wealth, but love,
And if she like your nephew, let him have her:
Here's all that I can say.
Don. Sir, you say well,
Like a true father, and for my part, I,
If the young folks can like – 'twixt you and me –
Will promise to assure my nephew presently
Three thousand florins yearly during life,
And after I am dead, my whole estate.
Flo. 'Tis a fair proffer, sir; meantime your nephew
Shall have free passage to commence his suit.
If he can thrive, he shall have my consent.
So for this time I'll leave you, signior.
Exit.
Don. Well,
Here's hope yet, if my nephew would have wit;
But he is such another dunce, I fear
He'll never win the wench. When I was young
I could have done 't i'faith, and so shall he
If he will learn of me; and in good time
He comes himself.

Enter Bergetto *and* Poggio.

How now, Bergetto, whither away so fast?

Ber. Oh, uncle, I have heard the strangest news that ever came out of the mint – have I not, Poggio?

Pog. Yes indeed, sir.

Don. What news, Bergetto?

Ber. Why look ye uncle? My barber told me just now that there is a fellow come to town who undertakes to make a mill go without the mortal help of any water or wind, only with sandbags! And this fellow hath a strange horse, a most excellent beast, I'll assure you, uncle, my barber says, whose head, to the wonder of all Christian people, stands just behind where his tail is – is 't not true, Poggio?

Pog. So the barber swore forsooth.

Don. And you are running thither?

Ber. Aye, forsooth, uncle.

Don. Wilt thou be a fool still? Come sir, you shall not go; you have more mind of a puppet-play than on the business I told ye. Why, thou great baby, wou't never have wit? wou't make thyself a May-game to all the world?

Pog. Answer for yourself, master.

Ber. Why uncle, should I sit at home still and not go abroad to see fashions like other gallants?

Don. To see hobby-horses! What wise talk I pray had you with Annabella, when you were at Signior Florio's house?

Ber. Oh, the wench: Ud's sa'me, uncle, I tickled her with a rare speech, that I made her almost burst her belly with laughing.

Don. Nay, I think so, and what speech was 't?

Ber. What did I say, Poggio?

---

284 Elysium in mythology, the dwelling place of the blessed
I.iii.6 doubt fear for
7 miscarry come to harm
24 another a perfect
27 in good at a suitable
31 out of the mint i.e., most recent
35 barber (as a traditional source of gossip)
37–9 mill . . . sandbags (apparently a machine with perpetual motion)
39–43 strange . . . tail (a common trick; the horse's tail was tied to the manger)
44 forsooth truly
48 mind of care for
51 May-game i.e., joke, entertainment
54 fashions fashionable events and practices
55 hobby-horses men in horses' costumes (thought to be signs of fertility) in morris dances (performed on May Day and other festive occasions)
58 Ud's sa'me "God save me" (common expression)
59 rare excellent
62 What . . . Poggio? (i.e., he may have given no speech at all and expects Poggio to cover for him)

Pog. Forsooth, my master said that he loved her almost as well as he loved parmasent, and swore – I'll be sworn for him – that she wanted but such a nose as his was, to be as pretty a young woman as any was in Parma.

Don. Oh, gross!

Ber. Nay, uncle, then she asked me whether my father had any more children than myself; and I said, "No, 'twere better he should have had his brains knocked out first."

Don. This is intolerable.

Ber. Then said she, "Will Signior Donado your uncle leave you all his wealth?"

Don. Ha! that was good, did she harp upon that string?

Ber. Did she harp upon that string, aye, that she did. I answered, "Leave me all his wealth? Why, woman, he hath no other wit, if he had he should hear on 't to his everlasting glory and confusion; I know," quoth I, "I am his white boy, and will not be gulled"; and with that she fell into a great smile, and went away. Nay, I did fit her.

Don. Ah, sirrah, then I see there is no changing of nature. Well, Bergetto, I fear thou wilt be a very ass still.

Ber. I should be sorry for that, uncle.

Don. Come, come you home with me; since you are no better a speaker, I'll have you write to her after some courtly manner, and enclose some rich jewel in the letter.

Ber. Aye, marry, that will be excellent.

Don. Peace, innocent!
Once in my time I'll set my wits to school.
If all fail, 'tis but the fortune of a fool.

Ber. Poggio, 'twill do, Poggio!

Exeunt.

Act II

[II.i]

Enter Giovanni *and* Annabella, *as from their chamber.*

Gio. Come Annabella, no more sister now

But love, a name more gracious; do not blush,
Beauty's sweet wonder, but be proud, to know
That yielding thou hast conquered, and inflamed
A heart whose tribute is thy brother's life.

Ann. And mine is his. Oh, how these stol'n contents
Would print a modest crimson on my cheeks,
Had any but my heart's delight prevailed!

Gio. I marvel why the chaster of your sex
Should think this pretty toy called maidenhead
So strange a loss, when being lost, 'tis nothing,
And you are still the same.

Ann. 'Tis well for you;
Now you can talk.

Gio. Music as well consists
In th' ear, as in the playing.

Ann. O, y' are wanton!
Tell on 't, y' are best, do.

Gio. Thou wilt chide me, then?
Kiss me, so; thus hung Jove on Leda's neck,
And sucked divine ambrosia from her lips.
I envy not the mightiest man alive,
But hold myself in being king of thee
More great, than were I king of all the world.
But I shall lose you, sweetheart.

Ann. But you shall not.

Gio. You must be married, mistress.

Ann. Yes, to whom?

Gio. Someone must have you.

Ann. You must.

Gio. Nay, some other.

Ann. Now, prithee, do not speak so without jesting;
You'll make me weep in earnest.

Gio. What, you will not!
But tell me, sweet, canst thou be dared to swear
That thou wilt live to me, and to no other?

Ann. By both our loves I dare; for didst thou know,
My Giovanni, how all suitors seem

---

64 parmasent Parmesan cheese
66 wanted . . . nose (obscene pun; loss of a nose was a sign of advanced syphilis); **wanted** lacked
80 wit thought
81 glory i.e., shame; **confusion** damnation
82 white favorite
83 gulled cheated
84 fit handle; answer
II.i.1 s.d. *chamber* (apparently above on the balcony)
5 tribute . . . life has renewed his life (desire to live)
6 contents pleasures
10 maidenhead (he has taken her virginity)
11 strange valuable
12 well all right (for you to say)
13 you can talk you can brag about your manhood or conquest
14 in . . . playing enjoyment is as great in the doing as in the telling (i.e., I will not publicly talk about it); **wanton** naughty; sexually undisciplined (teasing)
16 Jove . . . Leda in seeking refuge in Leda's bosom (she had taken the form of a swan) Jove seduced her (perhaps meant to be a classical precedent for their act)
17 ambrosia sweet food of the gods providing immortality
23 have you (a pun: [1] marry you legally; [2] seduce you)
25 What . . . not! (he is astonished, especially now, that she would even conceive marrying someone else)
26 dared sufficiently bold
27 to for

To my eyes hateful, thou wouldst trust me then.
Gio. Enough, I take thy word; sweet, we must part.
Remember what thou vow'st; keep well my heart.
Ann. Will you begone?
Gio. I must.
Ann. When to return?
Gio. Soon.
Ann. Look you do.
Gio. Farewell.

Exit.

Ann. Go where thou wilt, in mind I'll keep thee here,
And where thou art, I know I shall be there.
Guardian!

Enter Putana.

Put. Child, how is 't child? Well, thank Heaven, ha?
Ann. Oh, guardian, what a paradise of joy
Have I passed over!
Put. Nay, what a paradise of joy have you passed under! Why, now I commend thee, charge; fear nothing, sweetheart, what though he be your brother? Your brother's a man I hope, and I say still, if a young wench feel the fit upon her, let her take anybody, father or brother, all is one.
Ann. I would not have it known for all the world.
Put. Nor I, indeed, for the speech of the people; else 'twere nothing.
Flo. (*Within.*) Daughter Annabella!
Ann. Oh, me, my father! – Here, sir! – Reach my work.
Flo. (*Within.*) What are you doing?
Ann. So, let him come now.

Enter Florio, Richardetto *like a Doctor of Physic, and* Philotis *with a lute in her hand.*

Flo. So hard at work, that's well! You lose no time.
Look, I have brought you company. Here's one,
A learned doctor, lately come from Padua,
Much skilled in physic; and for that I see
You have of late been sickly, I entreated
This reverend man to visit you some time.
Ann. Y' are very welcome, sir.
Rich. I thank you, mistress;
Loud fame in large report hath spoke your praise,
As well for virtue as perfection.
For which I have been bold to bring with me
A kinswoman of mine, a maid, for song
And music, one perhaps will give content.
Please you to know her?
Ann. They are parts I love,
And she for them most welcome.
Phil. Thank you, lady.
Flo. Sir, now you know my house, pray make not strange;
And if you find my daughter need your art,
I'll be your paymaster.
Rich. Sir, what I am
She shall command.
Flo. You shall bind me to you.
Daughter, I must have conference with you
About some matters that concerns us both.
Good master doctor, please you but walk in,
We'll crave a little of your cousin's cunning;
I think my girl hath not quite forgot
To touch an instrument, she could have done 't;
We'll hear them both.
Rich. I'll wait upon you, sir.

Exeunt.

[II.ii]

Enter Soranzo *in his study, reading a book.*

Sor. "Love's measure is extreme, the comfort pain,
The life unrest, and the reward disdain."
What's here? Look 't o'er again, 'tis so, so writes;
This smooth licentious poet in his rhymes.

---

37 **Look** be certain
44 **over** through (the joy of the first sexual consummation)
45–6 **passed under** (obscene pun)
49 **fit** urge; sexual drive
51 **all is one** it makes no difference
56 **Reach . . . work** hand me my needlework (an icon of obedient womanly duty)
58 **s.d. *Physic*** medicine
60 **Padua** (the medical school there was highly regarded)
63 **reverend** respectable
65 **large** widespread
66 **perfection** (1) beauty; (2) accomplishments
70 **parts** talents, abilities
72 **not strange** yourself at home
75 **bind . . . you** be beholden (grateful) to you
79 **cunning** skill
81 **touch** (1) play; (2) sexually arouse (with pun on *instrument*)
II.ii.1 measure moderation (he is reading Petrarchan poetry known for its paradoxes)
4 **licentious** (1) erotic; (2) taking artistic license by using paradox

But Sannazar, thou liest, for had thy bosom
Felt such oppression as is laid on mine,
Thou wouldst have kissed the rod that made thee smart.
To work then, happy Muse, and contradict
What Sannazar hath in his envy writ: [*Writes.*]
"Love's measure is the mean, sweet his annoys,
His pleasures life, and his reward all joys."
Had Annabella lived when Sannazar
Did in his brief encomium celebrate
Venice, that queen of cities, he had left
That verse which gained him such a sum of gold,
And for one only look from Annabell
Had writ of her, and her diviner cheeks.
Oh, how my thoughts are –

Vas. (*Within.*) Pray forbear, in rules of civility, let me give notice on 't; I shall be taxed of my neglect of duty and service.

Sor. What rude intrusion interrupts my peace?
Can I be nowhere private?

Vas. (*Within.*) Troth, you wrong your modesty.

Sor. What's the matter, Vasques, who is 't?

Enter Hippolita *and* Vasques.

Hip. 'Tis I:
Do you know me now? Look, perjured man, on her
Whom thou and thy distracted lust have wronged.
Thy sensual rage of blood hath made my youth
A scorn to men and angels; and shall I
Be now a foil to thy unsated change?
Thou know'st, false wanton, when my modest fame
Stood free from stain or scandal, all the charms
Of Hell or sorcery could not prevail
Against the honor of my chaster bosom.
Thine eyes did plead in tears, thy tongue in oaths
Such and so many, that a heart of steel
Would have been wrought to pity, as was mine.
And shall the conquest of my lawful bed,
My husband's death urged on by his disgrace,
My loss of womanhood, be ill-rewarded
With hatred and contempt? No, know Soranzo,
I have a spirit doth as much distaste
The slavery of fearing thee, as thou
Dost loathe the memory of what hath passed.

Sor. Nay, dear Hippolita –

Hip. Call me not dear,
Nor think with supple words to smooth the grossness
Of my abuses. 'Tis not your new mistress,
Your goodly Madam Merchant, shall triumph
On my dejection. Tell her thus from me,
My birth was nobler, and by much more free.

Sor. You are too violent.

Hip. You are too double
In your dissimulation. Seest thou this,
This habit, these black mourning weeds of care?
'Tis thou art cause of this, and hast divorced
My husband from his life and me from him,
And made me widow in my widowhood.

Sor. Will you yet hear?

Hip. More of thy perjuries?
Thy soul is drowned too deeply in those sins, 59
Thou need'st not add to th' number.

Sor. Then I'll leave you;
You are past all rules of sense.

Hip. And thou of grace.

---

5 **Sannazar** Jacopo Sannazzaro (1455–1530), Neapolitan pastoral poet
7 **kissed the rod** accepted the punishment (with pun on rod as whip or penis)
9 **envy** ill-will
10 **mean** true measure
11 **life** bliss
13–15 **encomium . . . gold** words of praise (his six-line verse on Venice paid him 600 crowns)
20 **taxed of** reprimanded for
27 **Do . . . Look** (she probably lifts a mourning veil)
28 **distracted** (1) maddened; (2) wrongly directed
29 **sensual . . . blood** violence of sexual passion
31 **foil** contrast
32 **wanton** libertine; **modest fame** reputation for modesty
40 **urged on** hastened
41 **womanhood** i.e., status
43 **distaste** dislike
47 **grossness** indecency
48 **my abuses** misuses of me
49 **Madam Merchant** Annabella (whose wealthy father is a merchant)
50 **dejection** (1) downfall; (2) rejection
51 **free** honorable
52 **violent** severe
54 **habit** her mourning clothes; **weeds** garments
57 **made . . . widowhood** (1) estranged me from my husband before his death; (2) deserted me after his death (there may be an indication that their relationship, which the husband knew, contributed to his death)
61 **sense** reason; **grace** mercy

Vas. Fie mistress, you are not near the limits of reason. If my lord had a resolution as noble as virtue itself, you take the course to unedge it all. Sir, I beseech you do not perplex her, griefs, alas, will have a vent; I dare undertake Madam Hippolita will now freely hear you.

Sor. Talk to a woman frantic! Are these the fruits of your love?

Hip. They are the fruits of thy untruth, false man!
Didst thou not swear, whilst yet my husband lived,
That thou wouldst wish no happiness on earth
More than to call me wife? Didst thou not vow
When he should die to marry me? For which
The devil in my blood, and thy protests,
Caused me to counsel him to undertake
A voyage to Ligorne – for that we heard
His brother there was dead, and left a daughter
Young and unfriended, who with much ado
I wished him to bring hither. He did so,
And went; and as thou know'st, died on the way.
Unhappy man to buy his death so dear
With my advice! yet thou for whom I did it
Forget'st thy vows, and leav'st me to my shame.

Sor. Who could help this?

Hip. Who? Perjured man, thou couldst,
If thou hadst faith or love.

Sor. You are deceived:
The vows I made, if you remember well,
Were wicked and unlawful, 'twere more sin
To keep them than to break them; as for me,
I cannot mask my penitence. Think thou
How much thou hast digressed from honest shame
In bringing of a gentleman to death
Who was thy husband; such a one as he,
So noble in his quality, condition,
Learning, behavior, entertainment, love,
As Parma could not show a braver man.

Vas. You do not well, this was not your promise.

Sor. I care not, let her know her monstrous life.
Ere I'll be servile to so black a sin
I'll be accursed. Woman, come here no more,
Learn to repent and die; for by my honor
I hate thee and thy lust; you have been too foul.

[*Exit.*]

Vas. This part has been scurvily played.

Hip. How foolishly this beast contemns his fate,
And shuns the use of that which I more scorn
Than I once loved, his love; but let him go,
My vengeance shall give comfort to his woe.

She offers to go away.

Vas. Mistress, mistress, Madam Hippolita; pray, a word or two.

Hip. With me, sir?

Vas. With you if you please.

Hip. What is 't?

Vas. I know you are infinitely moved now, and you think you have cause. Some I confess you have, but sure not so much as you imagine.

Hip. Indeed!

Vas. Oh, you were miserably bitter, which you followed even to the last syllable; faith, you were somewhat too shrewd. By my life, you could not have took my lord in a worse time since I first knew him; tomorrow you shall find him a new man.

Hip. Well, I shall wait his leisure.

Vas. Fie, this is not a hearty patience, it comes sourly from you; troth, let me persuade you for once.

Hip. [*Aside.*] I have it, and it shall be so; thanks, opportunity! [*To him.*] Persuade me to what?

Vas. Visit him in some milder temper; oh, if you could but master a little your female spleen, how might you win him!

Hip. He will never love me. Vasques, thou hast been a too trusty servant to such a master, and I believe thy reward in the end will fall out like mine.

Vas. So perhaps too.

Hip. Resolve thyself it will. Had I one so true, so truly honest, so secret to my counsels, as thou hast been to him and his, I should think it a slight acquittance, not only to make him master of all I have, but even of myself.

62–3 **not . . . reason** quite unreasonable
63 **resolution** sense of purpose
64 **unedge** undo
75 **protests** protestations; promises
77 **voyage** journey (in this instance by land); **Ligorne** Livorno, a seaport across a mountain range one hundred miles from Padua
90 **mask my penitence** hide my sense of remorse
91 **honest shame** honor; modesty
94 **quality** rank; **condition** estate, wealth
96 **braver** finer
97 **promise** agreement (she is falsifying [*do not well*] their confidentiality)
103 **scurvily played** badly acted
104 **contemns** disregards
107 **his woe** i.e., the woe he has caused
118 **followed** continued
119 **shrewd** shrewish; scolding
122 **new** different
134 **fall** turn
137 **Resolve thyself** be certain
140 **acquittance** discharge of debt; reward

Vas. Oh, you are a noble gentlewoman!

Hip. Wou't thou feed always upon hopes? Well, I know thou art wise, and seest the reward of an old servant daily what it is.

Vas. Beggary and neglect.

Hip. True; but Vasques, wert thou mine, and wouldst be private to me and my designs, I here protest myself, and all what I can else call mine, should be at thy dispose.

Vas. [*Aside.*] Work you that way, old mole? Then I have the wind of you. [*To her.*] I were not worthy of it, by any desert that could lie within my compass; if I could –

Hip. What then?

Vas. I should then hope to live in these my old years with rest and security.

Hip. Give me thy hand, now promise but thy silence,
And help to bring to pass a plot I have;
And here in sight of Heaven, that being done,
I make thee lord of me and mine estate.

Vas. Come, you are merry; this is such a happiness that I can neither think or believe.

Hip. Promise thy secrecy, and 'tis confirmed.

Vas. Then here I call our good genii for witnesses, whatsoever your designs are, or against whomsoever, I will not only be a special actor therein, but never disclose it till it be effected.

Hip. I take thy word, and with that, thee for mine;
Come then, let's more confer of this anon.
On this delicious bane my thoughts shall banquet:
Revenge shall sweeten what my griefs have tasted.

Exeunt.

[II.iii]

Enter Richardetto *and* Philotis.

Rich. Thou seest, my lovely niece, these strange mishaps,
How all my fortunes turn to my disgrace,
Wherein I am but as a looker-on,
Whiles others act my shame, and I am silent.

Phil. But uncle, wherein can this borrowed shape
Give you content?

Rich. I'll tell thee, gentle niece:
Thy wanton aunt in her lascivious riots
Lives now secure, thinks I am surely dead
In my late journey to Ligorne for you,
As I have caused it to be rumored out;
Now would I see with what an impudence
She gives scope to her loose adultery,
And how the common voice allows hereof;
Thus far I have prevailed.

Phil. Alas, I fear
You mean some strange revenge.

Rich. Oh, be not troubled;
Your ignorance shall plead for you in all.
But to our business: what you learned for certain
How Signior Florio means to give his daughter
In marriage to Soranzo?

Phil. Yes, for certain.

Rich. But how find you young Annabella's love
Inclined to him?

Phil. For aught I could perceive,
She neither fancies him or any else.

Rich. There's mystery in that which time must show.
She used you kindly?

Phil. Yes.

Rich. And craved your company?

Phil. Often.

Rich. 'Tis well, it goes as I could wish;
I am the doctor now, and as for you,
None knows you; if all fail not we shall thrive.
But who comes here?

Enter Grimaldi.

I know him, 'tis Grimaldi,
A Roman and a soldier, near allied
Unto the Duke of Montferrato; one
Attending on the Nuncio of the Pope
That now resides in Parma, by which means
He hopes to get the love of Annabella.

Grim. Save you, sir.

Rich. And you, sir.

Grim. I have heard
Of your approvèd skill, which through the city
Is freely talked of, and would crave your aid.

Rich. For what, sir?

Grim. Marry sir, for this –

---

149 protest declare
152 have . . . you understand your drift
162–3 happiness good fortune
165 good genii guardian spirits (classical mythology)
170 anon right away
171 bane poison; **banquet** (ironically looks forward to the masque in Act IV as a banquet of the senses)

II.iii.5 borrowed shape disguise (as a doctor)
7 lascivious riots sexual indulgences
8 secure unsuspecting
13 common voice popular opinion; **allows** judges
16 ignorance innocence; **plead** protect
31 Nuncio . . . Pope i.e., papal representative
34 Save you "God save you" (traditional greeting)

But I would speak in private.

Rich. Leave us, cousin.

Exit Philotis.

Grim. I love fair Annabella, and would know
Whether in arts there may not be receipts
To move affection.

Rich. Sir, perhaps there may,
But these will nothing profit you.

Grim. Not me?

Rich. Unless I be mistook, you are a man
Greatly in favor with the Cardinal.

Grim. What of that?

Rich. In duty to His Grace,
I will be bold to tell you, if you seek
To marry Florio's daughter, you must first
Remove a bar 'twixt you and her.

Grim. Who's that?

Rich. Soranzo is the man that hath her heart,
And while he lives, be sure you cannot
speed.

Grim. Soranzo – what, mine enemy, is 't he?

Rich. Is he your enemy?

Grim. The man I hate worse than confusion!
I'll kill him straight.

Rich. Nay, then take mine advice,
Even for His Grace's sake the Cardinal.
I'll find a time when he and she do meet,
Of which I'll give you notice, and to be sure
He shall not 'scape you, I'll provide a poison
To dip your rapier's point in. If he had
As many heads as Hydra had, he dies.

Grim. But shall I trust thee, doctor?

Rich. As yourself,
Doubt not in aught. [*Aside.*] Thus shall the
fates decree,
By me Soranzo falls, that ruined me.

Exeunt.

[II.iv]

Enter Donado, Bergetto *and* Poggio.

Don. Well, sir, I must be content to be both your secretary and your messenger myself. I cannot tell what this letter may work, but as sure as I am alive, if thou come once to talk with her, I fear thou wou't mar whatsoever I make.

Ber. You make, uncle? Why, am not I big enough to carry mine own letter, I pray?

Don. Aye, aye, carry a fool's head o' thy own; why, thou dunce, wouldst thou write a letter, and carry it thyself?

Ber. Yes, that I would, and read it to her with my own mouth; for you must think if she will not believe me myself when she hears me speak, she will not believe another's handwriting. Oh, you think I am a blockhead, uncle! No sir, Poggio knows I have indited a letter myself, so I have.

Pog. Yes truly, sir, I have it in my pocket.

Don. A sweet one, no doubt; pray let's see 't.

Ber. I cannot read my own hand very well, Poggio; read it, Poggio.

Don. Begin.

Poggio reads.

Pog. "Most dainty and honey-sweet mistress, I could call you fair, and lie as fast as any that loves you, but my uncle being the elder man I leave it to him, as more fit for his age, and the color of his beard; I am wise enough to tell you I can board where I see occasion, or if you like my uncle's wit better than mine, you shall marry me; if you like mine better than his, I will marry you in spite of your teeth; so commending my best parts to you, I rest
Yours upwards and downwards, or you may choose, Bergetto."

Ber. Ah, ha! here's stuff, uncle!

Don. Here's stuff indeed to shame us all; pray whose advice did you take in this learned letter?

Pog. None, upon my word, but mine own.

Ber. And mine, uncle, believe it, nobody's else; 'twas mine own brain, I thank a good wit for 't.

Don. Get you home, sir, and look you keep within doors till I return.

Ber. How? that were a jest indeed. I scorn it, i'faith.

Don. What, you do not?

Ber. Judge me, but I do now.

Pog. Indeed, sir, 'tis very unhealthy.

38 **cousin** i.e., niece (*cousin* meant any relative)
40 **arts** medicine; **receipts** recipes (love potions)
41 **move** arouse
42 **nothing** not at all
48 **bar** impediment
50 **speed** succeed
53 **confusion** damnation
54 **straight** directly
60 **Hydra** (in classical mythology, a monster who grew two heads replacing any one cut off)
II.iv.2 **secretary** letter-writer
9 **fool's head** jester's bauble
17 **indited** composed
29 **board** engage closely (in conversation or embraces); **occasion** an opportunity
32 **in...teeth** despite the opposition

Don. Well sir, if I hear any of your apish running to motions and fopperies till I come back, you were as good no; look to 't.

Exit Do[nado].

Ber. Poggio, shall 's steal to see this horse with the head in 's tail?

Pog. Aye, but you must take heed of whipping.

Ber. Dost take me for a child, Poggio? Come, honest Poggio.

Exeunt.

[II.v]

Enter Friar *and* Giovanni.

Fri. Peace! thou hast told a tale whose every word
Threatens eternal slaughter to the soul;
I'm sorry I have heard it. Would mine ears
Had been one minute deaf, before the hour
That thou camest to me! Oh, young man cast away,
By the religious number of mine order,
I day and night have waked my aged eyes
Above my strength, to weep on thy behalf;
But Heaven is angry, and be thou resolved,
Thou art a man remarked to taste a mischief.
Look for 't; though it come late, it will come sure.

Gio. Father, in this you are uncharitable;
What I have done, I'll prove both fit and good.
It is a principle, which you have taught
When I was yet your scholar, that the frame
And composition of the mind doth follow
The frame and composition of body;
So where the body's furniture is beauty,
The mind's must needs be virtue; which allowed,
Virtue itself is reason but refined,
And love the quintessence of that; this proves
My sister's beauty, being rarely fair,
Is rarely virtuous; chiefly in her love,
And chiefly in that love, her love to me.
If hers to me, then so is mine to her;
Since in like causes are effects alike.

Fri. Oh, ignorance in knowledge! Long ago,
How often have I warned thee this before!
Indeed, if we were sure there were no Deity,
Nor Heaven nor Hell, then to be led alone
By Nature's light – as were philosophers
Of elder times – might instance some defense.
But 'tis not so. Then, madman, thou wilt find
That Nature is in Heaven's positions blind.

Gio. Your age o'errules you. Had you youth like mine,
You'd make her love your Heaven, and her divine.

Fri. Nay, then I see th' art too far sold to Hell;
It lies not in the compass of my prayers
To call thee back; yet let me counsel thee:
Persuade thy sister to some marriage.

Gio. Marriage? Why, that's to damn her; that's to prove
Her greedy of variety of lust.

Fri. Oh, fearful! If thou wilt not, give me leave
To shrive her; lest she should die unabsolved.

Gio. At your best leisure, father; then she'll tell you
How dearly she doth prize my matchless love;
Then you will know what pity 'twere we two
Should have been sundered from each other's arms.
View well her face, and in that little round
You may observe a world of variety:
For color, lips; for sweet perfumes, her breath;
For jewels, eyes; for threads of purest gold,
Hair; for delicious choice of flowers, cheeks;
Wonder in every portion of that throne.
Hear her but speak, and you will swear the spheres
Make music to the citizens in Heaven;
But, father, what is else for pleasure framed
Lest I offend your ears shall go unnamed.

Fri. The more I hear, I pity thee the more,

52 **motions** puppet shows; **fopperies** follies
52–3 **you . . . no** you'll regret it
54 **shall 's** shall we
II.v.5 **cast away** i.e., lost, damned
6 **number** company
9 **resolved** assured
10 **remarked** marked out; **mischief** disaster
14–26 **It . . . alike** (what sounds like correct logic is actually sophistic, or false, reasoning here; the misuse of mind and knowledge suggests Giovanni's irrationality, self-defense, and even self-damnation)
18 **furniture** adornment
21 **quintessence** result (purest essence)
23 **rarely** excellently
28 **warned** forbidden
31 **philosophers** (i.e., pagan philosophers like Aristotle who did not take grace into account in their logic)
32 **instance** supply
34 **positions** doctrines; **blind** (classical logic is ignorant of God's mercy)
41 **damn her** (as an adulteress; cf. Ten Commandments, which have no prohibition concerning incest)
44 **shrive** confess her formally; **unabsolved** with the stain of sin; unrepentant and unforgiven
54 **throne** regal place
55–6 **spheres . . . music** (Ptolemaic cosmology held that the nine planets revolved around the earth in relationships that produced musical harmony)
57 **else for pleasure** the bodily parts that engage in lovemaking (which are in Annabella equally glorious and beautiful)

That one so excellent should give those parts
All to a second death. What I can do
Is but to pray; and yet I could advise thee,
Wouldst thou be ruled.

Gio. In what?

Fri. Why, leave her yet:
The throne of Mercy is above your trespass;
Yet time is left you both –

Gio. To embrace each other,
Else let all time be struck quite out of number;
She is like me, and I like her resolved.

Fri. No more, I'll visit her; this grieves me most,
Things being thus, a pair of souls are lost.

Exeunt.

[II.vi]

Enter Florio, Donado, Annabella, Putana.

Flo. Where's Giovanni?

Ann. Newly walked abroad,
And, as I heard him say, gone to the friar,
His reverend tutor.

Flo. That's a blessèd man,
A man made up of holiness; I hope
He'll teach him how to gain another world.

Don. Fair gentlewoman, here's a letter sent
To you from my young cousin; I dare swear
He loves you in his soul. Would you could hear,
Sometimes, what I see daily, sighs and tears,
As if his breast were prison to his heart!

Flo. Receive it, Annabella.

Ann. Alas, good man!

[*Takes the letter.*]

Don. What's that she said?

Put. And please you, sir, she said "Alas, good man!" [*Aside to Don.*] Truly, I do commend him to her every night before her first sleep, because I would have her dream of him; and she hearkens to that most religiously.

Don. [*Aside to Put.*] Say'st so? Godamercy, Putana, there's something for thee, and prithee do what thou canst on his behalf; sha'not be lost labor, take my word for 't.

Put. [*Aside to Don.*] Thank you most heartily, sir; now I have a feeling of your mind, let me alone to work.

Ann. Guardian!

Put. Did you call?

Ann. Keep this letter.

Don. Signior Florio, in any case bid her read it instantly.

Flo. Keep it, for what? Pray read it me here right.

Ann. I shall, sir.

She reads.

Don. How d'ee find her inclined, signior?

Flo. Troth sir, I know not how; not all so well
As I could wish.

Ann. Sir, I am bound to rest your cousin's debtor.
The jewel I'll return; for if he love,
I'll count that love a jewel.

Don. Mark you that?
Nay, keep them both, sweet maid.

Ann. You must excuse me,
Indeed I will not keep it.

Flo. Where's the ring,
That which your mother in her will bequeathed,
And charged you on her blessing not to give 't
To any but your husband? Send back that.

Ann. I have it not.

Flo. Ha! have it not, where is 't?

Ann. My brother in the morning took it from me,
Said he would wear 't today.

Flo. Well, what do you say
To young Bergetto's love? Are you content
To match with him? Speak.

Don. There's the point indeed.

Ann. [*Aside.*] What shall I do? I must say something now.

Flo. What say, why d'ee not speak?

Ann. Sir, with your leave,
Please you to give me freedom?

Flo. Yes, you have 't.

Ann. Signior Donado, if your nephew mean
To raise his better fortunes in his match,
The hope of me will hinder such a hope.
Sir, if you love him, as I know you do,
Find one more worthy of his choice than me.
In short, I'm sure I sha'not be his wife.

Don. Why, here's plain dealing; I commend thee for't,
And all the worst I wish thee, is Heaven bless thee!
Your father yet and I will still be friends,
Shall we not, Signior Florio?

---

61 second death damnation or spiritual death follows bodily death
64 throne . . . trespass (i.e., God's mercy is beyond your control [and sin])
65 Yet still
66 number sequence
II.vi.1 Newly . . . abroad i.e., he's just left
18 Godamercy "well done" (colloquial)
23 feeling sense (responding to his offer of payment, line 19)
30 right right away
50 freedom (1) permission to speak freely; (2) free choice of husband
52 raise . . . fortunes improve his social position

Flo. Yes, why not?
Look, here your cousin comes.

Enter Bergetto *and* Poggio.

Don. [*Aside.*] Oh, coxcomb, what doth he make here?

Ber. Where's my uncle, sirs?

Don. What's the news now?

Ber. Save you, uncle, save you; you must not think I come for nothing, masters; and how, and how is 't? What, you have read my letter? Ah, there I – tickled you i'faith!

Pog. [*Aside.*] But 'twere better you had tickled her in another place.

Ber. Sirrah sweetheart, I'll tell thee a good jest, and riddle what 'tis.

Ann. You say you'd tell me.

Ber. As I was walking just now in the street, I met a swaggering fellow would needs take the wall of me; and because he did thrust me, I very valiantly called him rogue. He hereupon bade me draw; I told him I had more wit than so; but when he saw that I would not, he did so maul me with the hilts of his rapier, that my head sung whilst my feet capered in the kennel.

Don. [*Aside.*] Was ever the like ass seen?

Ann. And what did you all this while?

Ber. Laugh at him for a gull, till I see the blood run about mine ears, and then I could not choose but find in my heart to cry; till a fellow with a broad beard – they say he is a new-come doctor – called me into this house, and gave me a plaster – look you, here 'tis; and sir, there was a young wench washed my face and hands most excellently, i'faith I shall love her as long as I live for 't – did she not, Poggio?

Pog. Yes, and kissed him too.

Ber. Why la now, you think I tell a lie, uncle, I warrant.

Don. Would he that beat thy blood out of thy head, had beaten some wit into it! for I fear thou never wilt have any.

Ber. Oh, uncle, but there was a wench would have done a man's heart good to have looked on her; by this light, she had a face methinks worth twenty of you, Mistress Annabella.

Don. [*Aside.*] Was ever such a fool born?

Ann. I am glad she liked you, sir.

Ber. Are you so? by my troth, I thank you forsooth.

Flo. Sure 'twas the doctor's niece, that was last day with us here.

Ber. 'Twas she, 'twas she!

Don. How do you know that, simplicity?

Ber. Why, does not he say so? If I should have said no, I should have given him the lie, uncle, and so have deserved a dry-beating again; I'll none of that.

Flo. A very modest, well-behaved young maid as I have seen.

Don. Is she indeed?

Flo. Indeed she is, if I have any judgment.

Don. Well, sir, now you are free; you need not care for sending letters now. You are dismissed; your mistress here will none of you.

Ber. No? why, what care I for that? I can have wenches enough in Parma for half-a-crown apiece, cannot I, Poggio?

Pog. I'll warrant you, sir.

Don. Signior Florio,
I thank you for your free recourse you gave
For my admittance; and to you, fair maid,
That jewel I will give you 'gainst your marriage.
Come, will you go sir?

Ber. Aye, marry will I. Mistress, farewell mistress;
I'll come again tomorrow. Farewell, mistress.

Exeunt Donado, Bergetto *and* Poggio.

Enter Giovanni.

Flo. Son, where have you been? What, alone, alone, still?
I would not have it so, you must forsake
This over-bookish humor. Well, your sister
Hath shook the fool off.

Gio. 'Twas no match for her.

Flo. 'Twas not indeed; I meant it nothing less.
Soranzo is the man I only like.
Look on him, Annabella! Come, 'tis supper-time,
And it grows late.

Exit.

Gio. Whose jewel's that?

62 **doth he make** is he doing
72 **Sirrah** (not customarily used to address women)
76 **take the wall** (to avoid gutter in center of street; to take the path being used by someone else was tantamount to a challenge)
82 **capered** danced (moved quickly to get away)
82–3 **kennel** gutter
86 **gull** dupe
91 **plaster** bandage
106 **liked** pleased
114 **given . . . lie** called him a liar (another challenge to a duel)
115 **dry** (1) bloodless; (2) severe
125 **half-a-crown** thought to be the standard price for a prostitute
131 **'gainst** in anticipation of
137 **humor** disposition
139 **meant . . . less** did not intend it
140 **only like** prefer

Ann. Some sweetheart's.
Gio. So I think.
Ann. A lusty youth,
Signior Donado, gave it me to wear
Against my marriage.
Gio. But you shall not wear it.
Send it him back again.
Ann. What, you are jealous?
Gio. That you shall know anon, at better leisure;
Welcome, sweet night! the evening crowns the day.

Exeunt.

Act III

[III.i]

Enter Bergetto *and* Poggio.

Ber. Does my uncle think to make me a baby still? No, Poggio, he shall know I have a sconce now.

Pog. Aye, let him not bob you off like an ape with an apple.

Ber. 'Sfoot, I will have the wench, if he were ten uncles, in despite of his nose, Poggio.

Pog. Hold him to the grindstone, and give not a jot of ground; she hath in a manner promised you already.

Ber. True, Poggio, and her uncle the doctor swore I should marry her.

Pog. He swore, I remember.

Ber. And I will have her, that's more; didst see the codpiece-point she gave me, and the box of marmalade?

Pog. Very well, and kissed you, that my chops watered at the sight on 't. There's no way but to clap up a marriage in hugger mugger.

Ber. I will do 't, for I tell thee, Poggio, I begin to grow valiant methinks, and my courage begins to rise.

Pog. Should you be afraid of your uncle?

Ber. Hang him, old doting rascal, no. I say I will have her.

Pog. Lose no time, then.

Ber. I will beget a race of wise men and constables that shall cart whores at their own charges, and break the Duke's peace ere I have done myself. Come away!

Exeunt.

[III.ii]

Enter Florio, Giovanni, Soranzo, Annabella, Putana *and* Vasques.

Flo. My lord Soranzo, though I must confess
The proffers that are made me have been great
In marriage of my daughter, yet the hope
Of your still rising honors havc prevailed
Above all other jointures. Here she is.
She knows my mind, speak for yourself to her;
And hear you, daughter, see you use him nobly.
For any private speech I'll give you time;
Come, son, and you the rest, let them alone,
Agree as they may.
Sor. I thank you, sir.
Gio. [*Aside.*] Sister, be not all woman: think on me.
Sor. Vasques!
Vas. My lord?
Sor. Attend me without.

Exeunt omnes, manent Soranzo *and* Annabella.

Ann. Sir, what's your will with me?
Sor. Do you not know what I should tell you?
Ann. Yes,
You'll say you love me.
Sor. And I'll swear it, too;
Will you believe it?
Ann. 'Tis not point of faith.

Enter Giovanni *above.*

Sor. Have you not will to love?
Ann. Not you.
Sor. Whom then?

---

144 **lusty** vigorous; manly
149 **crowns** completes
III.i.2 **sconce** head
4 **bob** put
4–5 **like . . . apple** by distracting you (obscene remark: apes were thought of as lecherous, apples as an aphrodisiac)
6 **'Sfoot** "by God's foot" (a common oath)
15 **codpiece-point** lace for tying the codpiece, material at the front of breeches to cover the genital area often enlarged and ornamental
15 **box** pot
16 **marmalade** any kind of preserve
17 **chops** chaps, jaws
19 **hugger mugger** secret
21 **courage** (with obscene pun on penis)
27 **constables** (usually thought of as dull-witted)
28 **cart whores** (public display of whores in carts or, whipped, walking behind them was a common form of humiliating punishment); **charges** expenses
29 **break . . . peace** create a disturbance; **ere** before; **done** done so
III.ii.5 **jointures** (1) marriages; (2) marriage settlements
11 **all** entirely; **woman** (1) faithless; (2) temperamental; (3) coy
14 **Attend** wait for
15 **should** plan to
17 **faith** religious doctrine

Ann. That's as the Fates infer.
Gio. [*Aside.*] Of those I'm regent now.
Sor. What mean you, sweet?
Ann. To live and die a maid.
Sor. Oh, that's unfit.
Gio. [*Aside.*] Here's one can say that's but a woman's note.
Sor. Did you but see my heart, then would you swear –
Ann. That you were dead.
Gio. [*Aside.*] That's true, or somewhat near it.
Sor. See you these true love's tears?
Ann. No.
Gio. [*Aside.*] Now she winks.
Sor. They plead to you for grace.
Ann. Yet nothing speak.
Sor. Oh, grant my suit!
Ann. What is 't?
Sor. To let me live –
Ann. Take it.
Sor. – still yours.
Ann. That is not mine to give.
Gio. [*Aside.*] One such another word would kill his hopes.
Sor. Mistress, to leave those fruitless strifes of wit,
I know I have loved you long, and loved you truly;
Not hope of what you have, but what you are
Have drawn me on. Then let me not in vain
Still feel the rigor of your chaste disdain.
I'm sick, and sick to th' heart.
Ann. Help, aqua-vitae!
Sor. What mean you?
Ann. Why, I thought you had been sick!
Sor. Do you mock my love?
Gio. [*Aside.*] There, sir, she was too nimble.
Sor. [*Aside.*] 'Tis plain, she laughs at me! – These scornful taunts
Neither become your modesty, or years.
Ann. You are no looking-glass, or if you were
I'd dress my language by you.
Gio. [*Aside.*] I'm confirmed.
Ann. To put you out of doubt, my lord, methinks
Your common sense should make you understand
That if I loved you, or desired your love,
Some way I should have given you better taste;
But since you are a nobleman, and one
I would not wish should spend his youth in hopes,
Let me advise you here to forbear your suit,
And think I wish you well, I tell you this.
Sor. Is 't you speak this?
Ann. Yes, I myself: yet know –
Thus far I give you comfort – if mine eyes
Could have picked out a man, among all those
That sued to me, to make a husband of,
You should have been that man; let this suffice.
Be noble in your secrecy, and wise.
Gio. [*Aside.*] Why, now I see she loves me.
Ann. One word more:
As ever virtue lived within your mind,
As ever noble courses were your guide,
As ever you would have me know you loved me,
Let not my father know hereof by you.
If I hereafter find that I must marry,
It shall be you or none.
Sor. I take that promise.
Ann. Oh, oh, my head!
Sor. What's the matter, not well?
Ann. Oh, I begin to sicken!
Gio. [*Aside.*] Heaven forbid!
Exit from above.
Sor. Help, help, within there, ho!
Look to your daughter, Signior Florio.

Enter Florio, Giovanni, Putana.

Flo. Hold her up, she swoons.
Gio. Sister, how d'ee?
Ann. Sick, brother, are you there?
Flo. Convey her to her bed instantly, whilst I send for a physician; quickly, I say.
Put. Alas, poor child!
Exeunt, manet Soranzo.

Enter Vasques.

Vas. My lord.
Sor. Oh Vasques, now I doubly am undone,
Both in my present and my future hopes.
She plainly told me that she could not love,
And thereupon soon sickened, and I fear
Her life's in danger.
Vas. [*Aside.*] By'r Lady sir, and so is yours, if you knew all. [*Aloud.*] 'Las, sir, I am sorry for that;

19 infer allow
22 note part
25 winks closes her eyes (so as not to see)
29 One . . . word another comment like that
35 aqua-vitae literally, water of life; brandy or other spirits to revive him (joking)
41 you yours
45 better taste a hint
53 husband (may ironically mean cuckold; he is hardly a man she could desire)
61 I . . . marry i.e., for convenience, while privately loving Giovanni

may be 'tis but the maid's sickness, an overflux of youth – and then, sir, there is no such present remedy as present marriage. But hath she given you an absolute denial?

Sor. She hath and she hath not; I'm full of grief,
But what she said I'll tell thee as we go.

Exeunt.

[III.iii]

Enter Giovanni *and* Putana.

Put. Oh, sir, we are all undone, quite undone, utterly undone, and shamed forever; your sister, oh, your sister!

Gio. What of her? For Heaven's sake speak, how does she?

Put. Oh, that ever I was born to see this day!

Gio. She is not dead, ha, is she?

Put. Dead! no, she is quick; 'tis worse, she is with child. You know what you have done, Heaven forgive 'ee! 'tis too late to repent, now Heaven help us!

Gio. With child? How dost thou know 't?

Put. How do I know 't? Am I at these years ignorant what the meanings of qualms and water-pangs be? of changing of colors, queasiness of stomachs, pukings, and another thing that I could name? Do not, for her and your credit's sake, spend the time in asking how and which way 'tis so. She is quick. Upon my word, if you let a physician see her water y' are undone.

Gio. But in what case is she?

Put. Prettily amended: 'twas but a fit, which I soon espied, and she must look for often henceforward.

Gio. Commend me to her, bid her take no care;
Let not the doctor visit her, I charge you,
Make some excuse till I return – oh, me,
I have a world of business in my head!
Do not discomfort her.
How does this news perplex me! If my father
Come to her, tell him she's recovered well,
Say 'twas but some ill diet. D'ee hear, woman?
Look you to 't.

Put. I will, sir.

Exeunt.

[III.iv]

Enter Florio *and* Richardetto.

Flo. And how d'ee find her, sir?

Rich. Indifferent well.
I see no danger, scarce perceive she's sick,
But that she told me she had lately eaten
Melons, and as she thought, those disagreed
With her young stomach.

Flo. Did you give her aught?

Rich. An easy surfeit-water, nothing else.
You need not doubt her health; I rather think
Her sickness is a fullness of her blood –
You understand me?

Flo. I do; you counsel well,
And once within these few days will so order 't
She shall be married, ere she know the time.

Rich. Yet let not haste, sir, make unworthy choice,
That were dishonor.

Flo. Master doctor, no,
I will not do so neither; in plain words,
My lord Soranzo is the man I mean.

Rich. A noble and a virtuous gentleman.

Flo. As any is in Parma. Not far hence
Dwells Father Bonaventure, a grave friar,
Once tutor to my son; now at his cell
I'll have 'em married.

Rich. You have plotted wisely.

Flo. I'll send one straight to speak with him tonight.

Rich. Soranzo's wise, he will delay no time.

Flo. It shall be so.

Enter Friar *and* Giovanni.

Fri. Good peace be here and love!

Flo. Welcome, religious friar, you are one
That still bring blessing to the place you come to.

---

80 **maid's sickness** (1) chlorosis (green sickness; anemia), thought to be caused by sexual need; (2) morning sickness (ironically but not knowingly)

80–1 **overflux of youth** excessive youthful behavior

82 **present** immediate

III.iii.8 **quick** alive

14–15 **water-pangs** impulses to urinate

16 **another thing** i.e., no menstruation has occurred

17 **credit's** reputation's

21 **case** state

22 **Prettily amended** somewhat better

25 **no care** not to worry

28 **business** matters needing attention

III.iv.1 **Indifferent** tolerably

5 **aught** anything (for it, as a doctor)

6 **surfeit-water** mild cure for indigestion

8 **fullness . . . blood** i.e., readiness for sexual intercourse; it was thought prolonged abstinence could lead to melancholy and the "falling sickness"

11 **know** be prepared for

16 **A . . . gentleman** (ironic)

17 **As . . . Parma** (unconsciously ironic)

20 **plotted** planned

25 **still** always

Gio. Sir, with what speed I could, I did my best
To draw this holy man from forth his cell
To visit my sick sister, that with words
Of ghostly comfort in this time of need
He might absolve her, whether she live or die.
Flo. 'Twas well done, Giovanni, thou herein
Hast showed a Christian's care, a brother's love.
Come, Father, I'll conduct you to her chamber,
And one thing would entreat you.
Fri. Say on, sir.
Flo. I have a father's dear impression,
And wish, before I fall into my grave,
That I might see her married, as 'tis fit;
A word from you, grave man, will win her more
Than all our best persuasions.
Fri. Gentle sir,
All this I'll say, that Heaven may prosper her.
Exeunt.

[III.v]

Enter Grimaldi.

Grim. Now if the doctor keep his word, Soranzo,
Twenty to one you miss your bride. I know
'Tis an unnoble act, and not becomes
A soldier's valor; but in terms of love,
Where merit cannot sway, policy must.
I am resolved, if this physician
Play not on both hands, then Soranzo falls.

Enter Richardetto.

Rich. You are come as I could wish: this very night
Soranzo, 'tis ordained, must be affied
To Annabella; and for aught I know,
Married.
Grim. How!
Rich. Yet your patience.
The place, 'tis Friar Bonaventure's cell.
Now I would wish you to bestow this night
In watching thereabouts; 'tis but a night;
If you miss now! Tomorrow I'll know all.
Grim. Have you the poison?
Rich. Here 'tis in this box,
Doubt nothing, this will do 't; in any case,
As you respect your life, be quick and sure.
Grim. I'll speed him.
Rich. Do; away, for 'tis not safe
You should be seen much here, ever, my love.
Grim. And mine to you.
Exit Gri[maldi].
Rich. So, if this hit, I'll laugh and hug revenge;
And they that now dream of a wedding-feast
May chance to mourn the lusty bridegroom's ruin.
But to my other business: niece Philotis!

Enter Philotis.

Phil. Uncle?
Rich. My lovely niece, you have bethought 'ee?
Phil. Yes, and as you counseled,
Fashioned my heart to love him, but he swears
He will tonight be married; for he fears
His uncle else, if he should know the drift,
Will hinder all, and call his coz to shrift.
Rich. Tonight? why, best of all; but let me see,
Aye – ha – yes, – so it shall be: in disguise
We'll early to the friar's, I have thought on 't.

Enter Bergetto *and* Poggio.

Phil. Uncle, he comes!
Rich. Welcome, my worthy coz.
Ber. Lass, pretty lass, come buss, lass. [*Kisses her.*]
Aha, Poggio!
Phil. There's hope of this yet.
Rich. You shall have time enough, withdraw a little,
We must confer at large.
Ber. Have you not sweetmeats, or dainty devices for me?
Phil. You shall have enough, sweetheart.
Ber. Sweetheart! mark that, Poggio; by my troth I cannot choose but kiss thee once more for that word "sweetheart." [*Kisses her.*] Poggio, I have a monstrous swelling about my stomach, whatsoever the matter be.
Pog. You shall have physic for 't, sir.

---

29 ghostly spiritual
35 impression (1) instinct; (2) person like myself
III.v.4 terms circumstances
5 policy cunning
7 Play . . . hands is not deceiving me
9 affied betrothed
12 place . . . cell (so Florio at III.iv.19–20; in fact, the betrothal will take place in Annabella's chamber when Florio suddenly thinks it best at III.iv.33)
14 but a only one
19 speed dispatch
22 hit succeeds; **hug** embrace
28 Fashioned disciplined; formed; **him** Bergetto
30 drift intention
31 call . . . shrift call his kinsman Bergetto to final accounting before God
32 best of all all the better
36 buss kiss
40 at large (1) fully; (2) together
46 swelling (1) of courage; (2) of sexual urging

Rich. Time runs apace.
Ber. Time's a blockhead! [*Kisses her.*]
Rich. Be ruled: when we have done what's fit to do,
Then you may kiss your fill, and bed her too.
Exeunt.

[III.vi]

Enter the Friar *in his study, sitting in a chair,* Annabella *kneeling and whispering to him, a table before them and wax lights; she weeps, and wrings her hands.*

Fri. I am glad to see this penance; for believe me,
You have unripped a soul so foul and guilty,
As I must tell you true, I marvel how
The earth hath borne you up; but weep, weep on,
These tears may do you good; weep faster yet,
Whiles I do read a lecture.
Ann. Wretched creature!
Fri. Aye, you are wretched, miserably wretched,
Almost condemned alive. There is a place
(List, daughter!) in a black and hollow vault,
Where day is never seen; there shines no sun,
But flaming horror of consuming fires;
A lightless sulfur, choked with smoky fogs
Of an infected darkness. In this place
Dwell many thousand, thousand sundry sorts
Of never-dying deaths. There damnèd souls
Roar without pity, there are gluttons fed
With toads and adders; there is burning oil
Poured down the drunkard's throat, the usurer
Is forced to sup whole draughts of molten gold;
There is the murderer forever stabbed,
Yet can he never die; there lies the wanton
On racks of burning steel, whiles in his soul
He feels the torment of his raging lust.
Ann. Mercy, oh, mercy!
Fri. There stands these wretched things
Who have dreamt out whole years in lawless sheets
And secret incests, cursing one another.
Then you will wish each kiss your brother gave
Had been a dagger's point; then you shall hear
How he will cry, "Oh, would my wicked sister
Had first been damned, when she did yield to lust!"
But soft, methinks I see repentance work
New motions in your heart; say, how is 't with you?
Ann. Is there no way left to redeem my miseries?
Fri. There is, despair not; Heaven is merciful,
And offers grace even now. 'Tis thus agreed,
First, for your honor's safety that you marry
The Lord Soranzo; next, to save your soul,
Leave off this life, and henceforth live to him.
Ann. Aye, me!
Fri. Sigh not, I know the baits of sin
Are hard to leave; oh, 'tis a death to do 't.
Remember what must come! are you content?
Ann. I am.
Fri. I like it well, we'll take the time.
Who's near us there?

Enter Florio, Giovanni.

Flo. Did you call, Father?
Fri. Is Lord Soranzo come?
Flo. He stays below.
Fri. Have you acquainted him at full?
Flo. I have,
And he is overjoyed.
Fri. And so are we;
Bid him come near.
Gio. [*Aside.*] My sister weeping, ha!
I fear this friar's falsehood. [*To them.*] I will call him.
Exit.
Flo. Daughter, are you resolved?
Ann. Father, I am.

Enter Giovanni, Soranzo *and* Vasques.

Flo. My lord Soranzo, here
Give me your hand; for that I give you this.
[*Joins their hands.*]
Sor. Lady, say you so too?
Ann. I do, and vow
To live with you and yours.

III.vi.1 s.d. ***his study*** (probably an error for her bedchamber)
2 unripped disclosed
4 borne (as opposed to *swallowed* you in sin to hell; *marvel* suggests the Friar sees this as a significant act of God's grace)
6 read...lecture (1) deliver a sermon on repentance; (2) reprimand you
9 List listen
9–23 in...lust (the Friar gives the traditional picture of the eternal torments characterizing the Christian Hell; he omits incest since there is no traditional iconography connected with it)
13 infected poisonous, corrupted
19 draughts drafts
30 first...damned (presumably he would have sinned less having only sinned once; a theological self-delusion)
32 motions stirrings
36–7 First...soul (the Friar here, like the Cardinal later, puts worldly resolutions before spiritual ones)
38 live to him live faithfully as a lawful wife with sanctioned sexual behavior
42 the time (1) wait patiently; (2) look for the redemptive moment (which her conscience will tell them); (3) take this moment when Annabella is contrite to perform the betrothal
51–3 Give...yours (a formal ceremony of betrothal, each partner making a legally binding promise to the other)

Fri. Timely resolved.
My blessing rest on both! More to be done,
You may perform it on the morning sun.
Exeunt.

[III.vii]

Enter Grimaldi *with his rapier drawn, and a dark lantern.*

Grim. 'Tis early night as yet, and yet too soon
To finish such a work; here I will lie
To listen who comes next.
He lies down.

Enter Bergetto *and* Philotis *disguised, and after* Richardetto *and* Poggio.

Ber. We are almost at the place I hope, sweetheart.
Grim. [*Aside.*] I hear them near, and heard one say "sweetheart";
'Tis he. Now guide my hand, some angry Justice,
Home to his bosom. [*Aloud.*] Now have at you, sir!
Strikes Bergetto and exit.

Ber. Oh, help, help, here's a stitch fallen in my guts; oh, for a flesh-tailor quickly! – Poggio!
Phil. What ails my love?
Ber. I am sure I cannot piss forward and backward, and yet
I am wet before and behind; lights, lights, ho, lights!
Phil. Alas, some villain here has slain my love!
Rich. Oh, Heaven forbid it! Raise up the next neighbors
Instantly, Poggio, and bring lights.
Exit Poggio.
How is 't, Bergetto? slain? It cannot be;
Are you sure y' are hurt?
Ber. Oh, my belly seethes like a porridge-pot; some cold water, I shall boil over else. My whole body is in a sweat, that you may wring my shirt; feel here – why, Poggio!

Enter Poggio *with* Officers, *and lights and halberts.*

Pog. Here; alas, how do you?
Rich. Give me a light – what's here? All blood! Oh, sirs,
Signior Donado's nephew now is slain!
Follow the murderer with all the haste
Up to the city, he cannot be far hence;
Follow, I beseech you.
Off. Follow, follow, follow!
Exeunt Officers.
Rich. Tear off thy linen, coz, to stop his wounds;
Be of good comfort, man.
Ber. Is all this mine own blood? Nay then, good-night with me; Poggio, commend me to my uncle, dost hear? Bid him for my sake make much of this wench – Oh, I am going the wrong way sure, my belly aches so – Oh, farewell, Poggio – Oh, ——Oh,——
Dies.

Phil. Oh, he is dead!
Pog. How! dead?
Rich. He's dead indeed.
'Tis now too late to weep; let's have him home,
And with what speed we may find out the murderer.
Pog. Oh, my master, my master, my master!
Exeunt.

[III.viii]

Enter Vasques *and* Hippolita.

Hip. Betrothed?
Vas. I saw it.
Hip. And when's the marriage-day?
Vas. Some two days hence.
Hip. Two days? Why man, I would but wish two hours
To send him to his last and lasting sleep;
And Vasques, thou shalt see, I'll do it bravely.
Vas. I do not doubt your wisdom, nor, I trust, you my secrecy: I am infinitely yours.
Hip. I will be thine in spite of my disgrace.
So soon? Oh, wicked man, I durst be sworn
He'd laugh to see me weep.
Vas. And that's a villainous fault in him.
Hip. No, let him laugh; I'm armed in my resolves,
Be thou still true.

---

54 More (the actual marriage ceremony)
III.vii.1 s.d. *dark lantern* one that burns although the light is concealed by a shutter
3 s.d. *lies down* (to hear approaching footsteps)
6 angry Justice (justice of vengeance)
8–9 stitch . . . guts (wounds causing bleeding)
9 flesh-tailor surgeon
14 next nearest
22 s.d. *halberts* poles with spears at one end, the weapons carried in England by the night watch
25 the i.e., possible
28 coz i.e., niece
32–3 make much take care
33–4 going . . . way i.e., dying, not responding or improving
III.viii.6 bravely with style

Vas. I should get little by treachery against so hopeful a preferment as I am like to climb to.

Hip. Even to my bosom, Vasques; let my youth
Revel in these new pleasures. If we thrive,
He now hath but a pair of days to live.

Exeunt.

[III.ix]

Enter Florio, Donado, Richardetto, Poggio *and* Officers.

Flo. 'Tis bootless now to show yourself a child,
Signior Donado; what is done, is done.
Spend not the time in tears, but seek for justice.

Rich. I must confess, somewhat I was in fault,
That had not first acquainted you what love
Passed 'twixt him and my niece; but as I live,
His fortune grieves me as it were mine own.

Don. Alas, poor creature, he meant no man harm,
That I am sure of.

Flo. I believe that too;
But stay, my masters, are you sure you saw
The murderer pass here?

Off. And it please you sir, we are sure we saw a ruffian, with a naked weapon in his hand all bloody, get into my Lord Cardinal's Grace's gate, that we are sure of; but for fear of his Grace, bless us! [*They cross themselves.*] we durst go no further.

Don. Know you what manner of man he was?

Off. Yes, sure I know the man, they say a is a soldier; he that loved your daughter, sir, an 't please ye, 'twas he for certain.

Flo. Grimaldi, on my life!

Off. Aye, aye, the same.

Rich. The Cardinal is noble, he no doubt
Will give true justice.

Don. Knock someone at the gate.

Pog. I'll knock, sir.

Poggio knocks.

Servant (*Within*). What would 'ee?

Flo. We require speech with the Lord Cardinal
About some present business. Pray inform
His Grace that we are here.

Enter Cardinal *and* Grimaldi.

Car. Why, how now, friends! what saucy mates are you
That know nor duty nor civility?
Are we a person fit to be your host?
Or is our house become your common inn,
To beat our doors at pleasure? What such haste
Is yours, as that it cannot wait fit times?
Are you the masters of this commonwealth,
And know no more discretion? Oh, your news
Is here before you. You have lost a nephew,
Donado, last night by Grimaldi slain.
Is that your business? Well sir, we have knowledge on 't;
Let that suffice.

Grim. In presence of Your Grace,
In thought I never meant Bergetto harm;
But Florio, you can tell, with how much scorn
Soranzo backed with his confederates
Hath often wronged me. I to be revenged
(For that I could not win him else to fight)
Had thought by way of ambush to have killed him,
But was unluckily therein mistook;
Else he had felt what late Bergetto did.
And though my fault to him were merely chance,
Yet humbly I submit me to Your Grace,
[*Kneeling.*]
To do with me as you please.

Car. Rise up, Grimaldi.
[*He rises.*]
You citizens of Parma, if you seek
For justice: know, as Nuncio from the Pope,
For this offense I here receive Grimaldi
Into His Holiness' protection.
He is no common man, but nobly born;
Of princes' blood, though you, Sir Florio,
Thought him too mean a husband for your daughter.
If more you seek for, you must go to Rome,
For he shall thither. Learn more wit, for shame.
Bury your dead. Away, Grimaldi; leave 'em.

Exeunt Cardinal *and* Grimaldi.

Don. Is this a churchman's voice? Dwells Justice here?

15–16 against ... hopeful in comparison to so promising
16 preferment promotion; **like** likely
17 my youth (Soranzo [in contempt] or herself)
III.ix.1 bootless useless; **show ... child** act childishly
12 And if
29 present urgent
31 saucy mates impudent vulgar men
32 nor duty neither duty
35 such kind of
37 masters magistrates; **commonwealth** community
50 late just now
51 merely wholly
60 mean of too low rank (his rank is higher than Florio's)

Flo. Justice is fled to Heaven and comes no nearer.
Soranzo, was 't for him? Oh, impudence!
Had he the face to speak it, and not blush?
Come, come Donado, there's no help in this,
When cardinals think murder's not amiss;
Great men may do their wills, we must obey,
But Heaven will judge them for 't another day.
Exeunt.

Act IV

[IV.i]

A banquet. Hautboys. Enter the Friar, Giovanni, Annabella, Philotis, Soranzo, Donado, Florio, Richardetto, Putana *and* Vasques.

Fri. These holy rites performed, now take your times,
To spend the remnant of the day in feast;
Such fit repasts are pleasing to the saints
Who are your guests, though not with mortal eyes
To be beheld. Long prosper in this day,
You happy couple, to each other's joy!
Sor. Father, your prayer is heard. The hand of goodness
Hath been a shield for me against my death;
And, more to bless me, hath enriched my life
With this most precious jewel – such a prize,
As earth hath not another like to this.
Cheer up, my love; and gentlemen, my friends,
Rejoice with me in mirth: this day we'll crown
With lusty cups to Annabella's health.
Gio. Aside. Oh, torture! were the marriage yet undone,
Ere I'd endure this sight, to see my love
Clipped by another, I would dare confusion,
And stand the horror of ten thousand deaths.
Vas. Are you not well, sir?
Gio. Prithee fellow, wait,
I need not thy officious diligence.
Flo. Signior Donado, come, you must forget
Your late mishaps, and drown your cares in wine.
Sor. Vasques!
Vas. My lord?
Sor. Reach me that weighty bowl.
Here, brother Giovanni, here's to you;
Your turn comes next, though now a bachelor:
Here's to your sister's happiness and mine!
[*Drinks, and offers him the bowl.*]
Gio. I cannot drink.
Sor. What?
Gio. 'Twill indeed offend me.
Ann. Pray, do not urge him if he be not willing.
Hautboys.
Flo. How now, what noise is this?
Vas. Oh, sir, I had forgot to tell you: certain young maidens of Parma, in honor to Madam Annabella's marriage, have sent their loves to her in a masque, for which they humbly crave your patience and silence.
Sor. We are much bound to them, so much the more
As it comes unexpected. Guide them in.

Enter Hippolita *and* Ladies *in white robes [all masked], with garlands of willows. Music, and a dance.*

Sor. Thanks, lovely virgins; now might we but know
To whom we have been beholding for this love,
We shall acknowledge it.
Hip. Yes, you shall know.
[*Unmasks.*]
What think you now?
Omnes. Hippolita!
Hip. 'Tis she.
Be not amazed; nor blush, young lovely bride,
I come not to defraud you of your man.
[*To Sor.*] 'Tis now no time to reckon up the talk
What Parma long hath rumored of us both.
Let rash report run on; the breath that vents it
Will, like a bubble, break itself at last.
[*To Ann.*] But now to you, sweet creature; lend 's your hand.
Perhaps it hath been said that I would claim
Some interest in Soranzo, now your lord;
What I have right to do, his soul knows best.
But in my duty to your noble worth,

---

65 **Justice . . . Heaven** Astraea, goddess of justice, returned to heaven when the actions of men on earth changed the golden age to the age of iron
66 **for him** i.e., was he the intended victim?
IV.i.1 s.d. *Hautboys* oboes
1 **holy rites** the sacrament of matrimony
3 **saints** souls of the faithful
14 **lusty cups** cups of strong wine
17 **Clipped** embraced; **confusion** damnation
19 **Prithee** pray thee; **wait** (said to the server to continue serving)
20 **officious diligence** special attention
27 **offend** (1) cause physical sickness; (2) displease
29 **noise** music
33 **masque** (wedding masques were a common convention)
35 **bound** obliged
37 **s.d. *willows*** (signs of a forsaken lover)
38 **beholding** indebted; **love** act of kindness

Sweet Annabella, and my care of you,
Here take, Soranzo, take this hand from me.
I'll once more join what by the holy Church
Is finished and allowed. Have I done well?

Sor. You have too much engaged us.

Hip. One thing more:
That you may know my single charity,
Freely I here remit all interest
I e'er could claim, and give you back your vows;
And to confirm 't – reach me a cup of wine –
My lord Soranzo, in this draught I drink
Long rest t'ee! [*Aside to Vas.*] Look to it, Vasques.

Vas. [*Aside to Hip.*] Fear nothing.

He gives her a poisoned cup; she drinks.

Sor. Hippolita, I thank you, and will pledge
This happy union as another life.
Wine there!

Vas. You shall have none, neither shall you pledge her.

Hip. How!

Vas. Know now, mistress she-devil, your own mischievous treachery hath killed you; I must not marry you.

Hip. Villain!

Omnes. What's the matter?

Vas. Foolish woman, thou art now like a firebrand, that hath kindled others and burned thyself. *Troppo sperar, inganna*, thy vain hope hath deceived thee. Thou art but dead. If thou hast any grace, pray.

Hip. Monster!

Vas. Die in charity, for shame! – This thing of malice, this woman, had privately corrupted me with promise of marriage, under this politic reconciliation to poison my lord, whiles she might laugh at his confusion on his marriage-day. I promised her fair, but I knew what my reward should have been; and would willingly have spared her life, but that I was acquainted with the danger of her disposition, and now have fitted her a just payment in her own coin. There she is, she hath yet——and end thy days in peace, vile woman; as for life there's no hope, think not on 't.

Omnes. Wonderful justice!

Rich. Heaven, thou art righteous.

Hip. Oh, 'tis true,
I feel my minute coming; had that slave
Kept promise – (Oh, my torment!) thou this hour
Hadst died, Soranzo. – Heat above hell-fire! –
Yet ere I pass away – cruel, cruel flames! –
Take here my curse among you: may thy bed
Of marriage be a rack unto thy heart;
Burn, blood, and boil in vengeance. Oh, my heart,
My flame's intolerable! – May'st thou live
To father bastards, may her womb bring forth
Monsters, and die together in your sins
Hated, scorned and unpitied! – Oh, – Oh –

Dies.

Flo. Was e'er so vile a creature?

Rich. Here's the end
Of lust and pride.

Ann. It is a fearful sight.

Sor. Vasques, I know thee now a trusty servant,
And never will forget thee. Come, my love,
We'll home, and thank the Heavens for this escape.
Father and friends, we must break up this mirth;
It is too sad a feast.

Don. Bear hence the body.

Fri. [*Aside to Gio.*] Here's an ominous change;
Mark this, my Giovanni, and take heed!
I fear the event: that marriage seldom's good,
Where the bride-banquet so begins in blood.

Exeunt.

[IV.ii]

Enter Richardetto *and* Philotis.

Rich. My wretched wife, more wretched in her shame
Than in her wrongs to me, hath paid too soon
The forfeit of her modesty and life.

---

55 **allowed** confirmed
56 **engaged** (1) obliged; (2) taken our time
57 **single charity** sincere love
58 **remit** renounce; **interest** (1) claim (his pledge to marry her would in England be a pre-nuptial contract, making his marriage to Annabella illegal); (2) concern
62 **Look** see
65 **union** accord
71–2 **must not** am not destined to
77 ***Troppo . . . inganna*** "too much hoping deceived"
78 **but** as good as
83–4 **politic** hypocritical
85 **confusion** destruction; death
87 **should** would
96 **minute** appointed moment of death
101 **rack** instrument of torture
116 **event** outcome
IV.ii.1 **wife** Hippolita
3 **forfeit** penalty

And I am sure, my niece, though vengeance hover,
Keeping aloof yet from Soranzo's fall,
Yet he will fall, and sink with his own weight.
I need not (now my heart persuades me so)
To further his confusion. There is One
Above begins to work, for, as I hear,
Debates already 'twixt his wife and him
Thicken and run to head; she, as 'tis said,
Slightens his love, and he abandons hers.
Much talk I hear. Since things go thus, my niece,
In tender love and pity of your youth,
My counsel is that you should free your years
From hazard of these woes, by flying hence
To fair Cremona, there to vow your soul
In holiness a holy votaress;
Leave me to see the end of these extremes.
All human worldly courses are uneven;
No life is blessed but the way to Heaven.

Phil. Uncle, shall I resolve to be a nun?

Rich. Aye, gentle niece, and in your hourly prayers
Remember me, your poor unhappy uncle.
Hie to Cremona now, as fortune leads,
Your home your cloister, your best friends your beads;
Your chaste and single life shall crown your birth:
Who dies a virgin lives a saint on earth.

Phil. Then farewell, world, and worldly thoughts, adieu!
Welcome, chaste vows, myself I yield to you.

Exeunt.

[IV.iii]

Enter Soranzo *unbraced, and* Annabella *dragged in.*

Sor. Come, strumpet, famous whore, were every drop
Of blood that runs in thy adulterous veins
A life, this sword – dost see 't? – should in one blow
Confound them all. Harlot, rare, notable harlot,
That with thy brazen face maintain'st thy sin,
Was there no man in Parma to be bawd
To your loose cunning whoredom else but I?
Must your hot itch and plurisy of lust,
The heyday of your luxury, be fed
Up to a surfeit, and could none but I
Be picked out to be cloak to your close tricks,
Your belly-sports? Now I must be the dad
To all that gallimaufry that's stuffed
In thy corrupted bastard-bearing womb?
Why must I?

Ann. Beastly man, why 'tis thy fate.
I sued not to thee, for, but that I thought
Your over-loving lordship would have run
Mad on denial. Had ye lent me time,
I would have told 'ee in what case I was;
But you would needs be doing.

Sor. Whore of whores!
Darest thou tell me this?

Ann. Oh, yes, why not?
You were deceived in me: 'twas not for love
I chose you, but for honor. Yet know this,
Would you be patient yet, and hide your shame,
I'd see whether I could love you.

Sor. Excellent quean!
Why, art thou not with child?

Ann. What needs all this,
When 'tis superfluous? I confess I am.

Sor. Tell me by whom.

Ann. Soft, sir, 'twas not in my bargain.
Yet somewhat, sir, to stay your longing stomach
I'm content t' acquaint you with. The man,
The more than man that got this sprightly boy –
For 'tis a boy, that for your glory, sir,
Your heir shall be a son –

Sor. Damnable monster!

8 confusion destruction
10 Debates quarrels, disagreements
11 Thicken multiply; **run . . . head** build to a crisis
12 Slightens disdains
18 votaress nun
19 extremes dire actions
20 uneven (1) difficult; (2) unjust
25 Hie hasten
26 beads rosary
27 crown fulfill
IV.iii.1 s.d. ***unbraced*** clothes unfastened (presumably his coat)
4 Confound destroy; **rare** (1) exceptional; (2) excellent
5 maintain'st (1) defends; (2) continues
6 bawd pander
8 plurisy excess
9 heyday excitement; **luxury** lechery
11 close (1) secret; (2) intimate; **tricks** (1) acts; (2) techniques
13 gallimaufry confused jumble
16 sued not to did not woo
19 case condition
20 needs be doing (1) couldn't wait; (2) pun on intercourse
23 honor reputation
25 quean whore
29 stay . . . stomach appease your appetite

Ann. Nay, and you will not hear, I'll speak no more.
Sor. Yes, speak, and speak thy last.
Ann. A match, a match;
This noble creature was in every part
So angel-like, so glorious, that a woman,
Who had not been but human as was I,
Would have kneeled to him, and have begged for love.
You, why you are not worthy once to name
His name without true worship, or indeed,
Unless you kneeled, to hear another name him.
Sor. What was he called?
Ann. We are not come to that.
Let it suffice that you shall have the glory
To father what so brave a father got.
In brief, had not this chance fall'n out as 't doth,
I never had been troubled with a thought
That you had been a creature; but for marriage,
I scarce dream yet of that.
Sor. Tell me his name!
Ann. Alas, alas, there's all;
Will you believe?
Sor. What?
Ann. You shall never know.
Sor. How!
Ann. Never. If you do, let me be cursed.
Sor. Not know it, strumpet! I'll rip up thy heart
And find it there.
Ann. Do, do.
Sor. And with my teeth
Tear the prodigious lecher joint by joint.
Ann. Ha, ha, ha, the man's merry.
Sor. Dost thou laugh?
Come whore, tell me your lover, or by truth
I'll hew thy flesh to shreds. Who is 't?
Ann. "*Che morte più dolce che morire per amore?*" *Sings.*
Sor. Thus will I pull thy hair, and thus I'll drag
Thy lust-belepered body through the dust.
Yet tell his name.
Ann. "*Morendo in gratia a lui, morirei senza dolore.*" *Sings.*
Sor. Dost thou triumph? The treasure of the earth
Shall not redeem thee, were there kneeling kings
Did beg thy life, or angels did come down
To plead in tears, yet should not all prevail
Against my rage. Dost thou not tremble yet?
Ann. At what? to die? No, be a gallant hangman,
I dare thee to the worst, strike, and strike home;
I leave revenge behind, and thou shalt feel 't.
Sor. Yet tell me ere thou diest, and tell me truly,
Knows thy old father this?
Ann. No, by my life.
Sor. Wilt thou confess, and I will spare thy life?
Ann. My life! I will not buy my life so dear.
Sor. I will not slack my vengeance.

Enter Vasques.

Vas. What d'ee mean, sir?
Sor. Forbear, Vasques, such a damnèd whore
Deserves no pity.
Vas. Now the gods forfend!

And would you be her executioner, and kill her in your rage too? Oh, 'twere most unmanlike! She is your wife; what faults hath been done by her before she married you were not against you. Alas, poor lady, what hath she committed, which any lady in Italy in the like case would not? Sir, you must be ruled by your reason, and not by your fury, that were unhuman and beastly.

Sor. She shall not live.

Vas. Come, she must. You would have her confess the author of her present misfortunes, I warrant 'ee; 'tis an unconscionable demand, and she should lose the estimation that I, for my part, hold of her worth, if she had done it. Why, sir, you ought not of all men living to know it. Good sir, be reconciled; alas, good gentlewoman!

Ann. Pish, do not beg for me, I prize my life
As nothing; if the man will needs be mad,
Why let him take it.
Sor. Vasques, hear'st thou this?

Vas. Yes, and commend her for it: in this she shows the nobleness of a gallant spirit, and beshrew my heart but it becomes her rarely. [*Aside to Sor.*] Sir, in any case smother your

34 and if
35 match bargain
37 a any
45 brave splendid
48 had . . . creature existed; **but** as
55 prodigious monstrous
59 *"Che . . . amore?"* "what death is sweeter than to die for love?"
61 lust-belepered leper-like with lust
63 *"Morendo . . . dolore"* "dying in the grace of God, I would die without pain"
69 hangman executioner
76 slack (1) forgo; (2) delay
78 forfend forbid
84 in the like case i.e., pregnant and unmarried
102 beshrew curse
103 in any case by any means

revenge; leave the scenting-out your wrongs to me; be ruled, as you respect your honor, or you mar all. [*Aloud.*] Sir, if ever my service were of any credit with you, be not so violent in your distractions. You are married now; what a triumph might the report of this give to other neglected suitors! 'Tis as manlike to bear extremities, as godlike to forgive.

Sor. Oh, Vasques, Vasques, in this piece of flesh,
This faithless face of hers, had I laid up
The treasure of my heart! Hadst thou been virtuous,
Fair, wicked woman, not the matchless joys
Of life itself had made me wish to live
With any saint but thee. Deceitful creature,
How hast thou mocked my hopes, and in the shame
Of thy lewd womb even buried me alive!
I did too dearly love thee.

Vas. This is well;
Aside [*to him*].
Follow this temper with some passion, be brief and moving: 'tis for the purpose.

Sor. Be witness to my words, thy soul and thoughts,
And tell me, didst not think that in my heart
I did too superstitiously adore thee?

Ann. I must confess, I know you loved me well.

Sor. And wouldst thou use me thus? Oh, Annabella,
Be thou assured, whatsoe'er the villain was
That thus hath tempted thee to this disgrace,
Well he might lust, but never loved like me:
He doted on the picture that hung out
Upon thy cheeks, to please his humorous eye;
Not on the part I loved, which was thy heart,
And as I thought, thy virtues.

Ann. Oh, my lord!
These words wound deeper than your sword could do.

Vas. Let me not ever take comfort, but I begin to weep myself, so much I pity him; why, madam, I knew when his rage was overpassed what it would come to.

Sor. Forgive me, Annabella: though thy youth
Hath tempted thee above thy strength to folly,
Yet will not I forget what I should be,
And what I am, a husband; in that name
Is hid divinity. If I do find
That thou wilt yet be true, here I remit
All former faults, and take thee to my bosom.

Vas. By my troth, and that's a point of noble charity.

Ann. Sir, on my knees –

Sor. Rise up, you shall not kneel;
Get you to your chamber, see you make no show
Of alteration; I'll be with you straight.
My reason tells me now, that 'tis as common
To err in frailty as to be a woman.
Go to your chamber.

Exit Annabella.

Vas. So, this was somewhat to the matter; what do you think of your heaven of happiness now, sir?

Sor. I carry Hell about me, all my blood
Is fired in swift revenge.

Vas. That may be, but know you how, or on whom? Alas, to marry a great woman, being made great in the stock to your hand, is a usual sport in these days; but to know what ferret it was that haunted your cony-berry – there's the cunning.

Sor. I'll make her tell herself, or –

Vas. Or what? You must not do so, let me yet persuade your sufferance a little while. Go to her, use her mildly, win her if it be possible to a voluntary, to a weeping tune; for the rest, if all hit, I will not miss my mark. Pray sir, go in; the next news I tell you shall be wonders.

Sor. Delay in vengeance gives a heavier blow.

Exit.

---

107 **of . . . credit** deserved any reward
116 **life itself** heaven
121 **temper** state of mind (of regret); **passion** outburst
125 **too . . . adore** i.e., idolize
131–2 **picture . . . cheeks** outward beauty
132 **humorous** capricious
138 **overpassed** expended
145 **remit** forgive
147 **a point** an instance
150 **alteration** distress
154 **matter** purpose
161 **made great** (1) made higher in rank; (2) made large with child; **stock** (1) body; (2) rabbit-burrow (rabbit, or cony, was a term of endearment)
161 **to . . . hand** ready for
162 **ferret** predator
163 **cony-berry** rabbit burrow; **cony** (colloquialism for female sexual organ)
164 **cunning** skill
167 **sufferance** forbearance
169 **voluntary** (1) an improvisational piece of music; (2) a spontaneous confession
170 **if all hit** if everything goes right

Vas. Ah, sirrah, here's work for the nonce! I had a suspicion of a bad matter in my head a pretty whiles ago; but after my madam's scurvy looks here at home, her waspish perverseness and loud fault-finding, then I remembered the proverb, that "where hens crow and cocks hold their peace there are sorry houses." 'Sfoot, if the lower parts of a she-tailor's cunning can cover such a swelling in the stomach, I'll never blame a false stitch in a shoe whiles I live again. Up, and up so quick? and so quickly too? 'Twere a fine policy to learn by whom; this must be known: and I have thought on't – here's the way, or none.

Enter Putana.

– What, crying, old mistress? alas, alas, I cannot blame 'ee. We have a lord, Heaven help us, is so mad as the devil himself, the more shame for him.

Put. Oh, Vasques, that ever I was born to see this day! Doth he use thee so too sometimes, Vasques?

Vas. Me! why, he makes a dog of me; but if some were of my mind, I know what we would do. As sure as I am an honest man, he will go near to kill my lady with unkindness; say she be with child, is that such a matter for a young woman of her years to be blamed for?

Put. Alas, good heart, it is against her will full sore.

Vas. I durst be sworn, all his madness is for that she will not confess whose 'tis; which he will know, and when he doth know it, I am so well acquainted with his humor that he will forget all straight. Well I could wish she would in plain terms tell all, for that's the way indeed.

Put. Do you think so?

Vas. Foh, I know 't; provided that he did not win her to 't by force. He was once in a mind that you could tell, and meant to have wrung it out of you, but I somewhat pacified him for that; yet sure you know a great deal.

Put. Heaven forgive us all, I know a little, Vasques.

Vas. Why should you not? who else should? Upon my conscience, she loves you dearly, and you would not betray her to any affliction for the world.

Put. Not for all the world, by my faith and troth, Vasques.

Vas. 'Twere pity of your life if you should; but in this you should both relieve her present discomforts, pacify my lord, and gain yourself everlasting love and preferment.

Put. Dost think so, Vasques?

Vas. Nay, I know't; sure 'twas some near and entire friend.

Put. 'Twas a dear friend indeed; but –

Vas. But what? Fear not to name him; my life between you and danger; faith, I think 'twas no base fellow.

Put. Thou wilt stand between me and harm?

Vas. Ud's pity, what else? You shall be rewarded too; trust me.

Put. 'Twas even no worse than her own brother.

Vas. Her brother Giovanni, I warrant 'ee!

Put. Even he, Vasques; as brave a gentleman as ever kissed fair lady. Oh, they love most perpetually.

Vas. A brave gentleman indeed; why, therein I commend her choice. [*Aside.*] Better and better. [*To her.*] You are sure 'twas he?

Put. Sure; and you shall see he will not be long from her too.

Vas. He were to blame if he would: but may I believe thee?

Put. Believe me! why, dost think I am a Turk or a Jew? No, Vasques, I have known their dealings too long to belie them now.

Vas. Where are you? there within, sirs!

Enter Banditti.

Put. How now, what are these?

Vas. You shall know presently. Come sirs, take me this old damnable hag, gag her instantly, and put out her eyes. Quickly, quickly!

Put. Vasques, Vasques!

Vas. Gag her I say, 'sfoot d'ee suffer her to prate? what d'ee fumble about? Let me come to her,

---

174 nonce present
181 lower . . . cunning elements of a dressmaker's skill (with obscene pun)
184 Up swollen (in the belly); **quick** alive
185 policy strategy
190 mad i.e., angry
193 he i.e., the Devil
200 of . . . years of youthful exuberance and normal sexuality
206 humor disposition
208 way solution (to calm him and provide reconciliation)
229 entire (1) devoted; (2) trusted
230 dear (1) beloved; (2) costly
231 my life i.e., I would put my life on the line
235 Ud's God's
239 brave fine
240–1 perpetually (1) continually; (2) eternally
249–50 a Turk or a Jew i.e., an infidel, someone unfaithful or treacherous
254 presently soon enough
258 prate chatter

I'll help your old gums, you toad-bellied bitch! [*He gags Putana.*] Sirs, carry her closely into the coal-house and put out her eyes instantly. If she roars slit her nose. D'ee hear, be speedy and sure.

Exeunt [Banditti] *with* Putana.

Why, this is excellent and above expectation. Her own brother? Oh, horrible! To what a height of liberty in damnation hath the devil trained our age; her brother, well! There's yet but a beginning. I must to my lord, and tutor him better in his points of vengeance; now I see how a smooth tale goes beyond a smooth tail – but, soft: what thing comes next?

Enter Giovanni.

Giovanni! as I would wish; my belief is strengthened, 'tis as firm as winter and summer.

Gio. Where's my sister?

Vas. Troubled with a new sickness, my lord; she's somewhat ill.

Gio. Took too much of the flesh, I believe.

Vas. Troth, sir, and you I think have e'en hit it; but my virtuous lady –

Gio. Where's she?

[*Gives him money.*]

Vas. In her chamber; please you visit her? She is alone, your liberality hath doubly made me your servant, and ever shall, ever –

Exit Giovanni.

Enter Soranzo.

Sir, I am made a man, I have plied my cue with cunning and success; I beseech you, let's be private.

Sor. My lady's brother's come, now he'll know all.

Vas. Let him know 't: I have made some of them fast enough.
How have you dealt with my lady?

Sor. Gently, as thou hast counseled. Oh, my soul
Runs circular in sorrow for revenge!
But Vasques, thou shalt know –

Vas. Nay, I will know no more: for now comes your turn to know; I would not talk so openly with you. Let my young master take time enough, and go at pleasure; he is sold to death, and the devil shall not ransom him. Sir, I beseech you, your privacy.

Sor. No conquest can gain glory of my fear.

Exeunt.

Act V

[V.i]

Enter Annabella *above.*

Ann. Pleasures farewell, and all ye thriftless minutes
Wherein false joys have spun a weary life;
To these my fortunes now I take my leave.
Thou precious Time, that swiftly ridest in post
Over the world, to finish up the race
Of my last fate; here stay thy restless course,
And bear to ages that are yet unborn
A wretched woeful woman's tragedy.
My conscience now stands up against my lust
With depositions charactered in guilt,

Enter Friar.

And tells me I am lost. Now I confess,
Beauty that clothes the outside of the face
Is cursèd if it be not clothed with grace.
Here like a turtle, mewed up in a cage
Unmated, I converse with air and walls,
And descant on my vile unhappiness.
Oh, Giovanni, that hast had the spoil
Of thine own virtues and my modest fame,
Would thou hadst been less subject to those stars
That luckless reigned at my nativity!
Oh, would the scourge due to my black offense
Might pass from thee, that I alone might feel
The torment of an uncontrollèd flame!

261 **closely** secretly
267 **liberty** license
268 **trained** (1) instructed; (2) seduced
272 **tail** (1) woman; (2) woman's genitalia; **soft** listen
274 **firm** (1) certain; (2) predictable
279 **Took... flesh** (1) ate too much meat; (2) had too much sex
280 **hit it** had the reason
282 **s.d. *Gives... money*** (treating Vasques as a pander, Giovanni makes Annabella a prostitute)
284 **liberality** (1) generosity; (2) licentiousness
286 **I... man** I have won; **plied** played; **cue** part
298 **he** i.e., his soul
301 **No... fear** (a puzzling remark; perhaps "whatever defeats I suffer, I will not show fear")
V.i.4 **in post** at full speed
9 **against** to bear witness against
10 **depositions** written testimony; **charactered** lettered; **guilt** (with pun on *gilt*, decorative letters on documents of importance)
14 **turtle** turtle-dove, a bird symbolizing love for its mate; **mewed** shut
16 **descant** (1) sing; (2) complain
17 **had** (1) plundered; (2) destroyed
21 **would** that
23 **flame** (1) of passion; (2) of Hell

Fri. [*Aside.*] What's this I hear?
Ann. That man, that blessed friar,
Who joined in ceremonial knot my hand
To him whose wife I now am, told me oft
I trod the path to death, and showed me how.
But they who sleep in lethargies of lust
Hug their confusion, making Heaven unjust,
And so did I.
Fri. [*Aside.*] Here's music to the soul!
Ann. Forgive me, my good genius, and this once
Be helpful to my ends. Let some good man
Pass this way, to whose trust I may commit
This paper double-lined with tears and blood;
Which being granted, here I sadly vow
Repentance, and a leaving of that life
I long have died in.
Fri. Lady, Heaven hath heard you,
And hath by providence ordained that I
Should be his minister for your behoof.
Ann. Ha, what are you?
Fri. Your brother's friend the friar;
Glad in my soul that I have lived to hear
This free confession 'twixt your peace and you.
What would you, or to whom? Fear not to speak.
Ann. Is Heaven so bountiful? then I have found
More favor than I hoped. Here, holy man:
Throws a letter.
Commend me to my brother, give him that,
That letter; bid him read it and repent.
Tell him that I – imprisoned in my chamber,
Barred of all company, even of my guardian,
Who gives me cause of much suspect – have time
To blush at what hath passed; bid him be wise,
And not believe the friendship of my lord.
I fear much more than I can speak. Good Father,
The place is dangerous, and spies are busy,
I must break off – you'll do 't?
Fri. Be sure I will,
And fly with speed; my blessing ever rest
With thee, my daughter; live to die more blessed!
Exit.

Ann. Thanks to the heavens, who have prolonged my breath
To this good use; now I can welcome death.
Exit.

[V.ii]

Enter Soranzo *and* Vasques.

Vas. Am I to be believed now? First, marry a strumpet that cast herself away upon you but to laugh at your horns? To feast on your disgrace, riot in your vexations, cuckold you in your bride-bed, waste your estate upon panders and bawds?

Sor. No more, I say no more!
Vas. A cuckold is a goodly tame beast, my lord.
Sor. I am resolved; urge not another word,
My thoughts are great, and all as resolute
As thunder; in mean time I'll cause our lady
To deck herself in all her bridal robes,
Kiss her, and fold her gently in my arms.
Begone – yet hear you, are the banditti ready
To wait in ambush?

Vas. Good sir, trouble not yourself about other business than your own resolution. Remember that time lost cannot be recalled.

Sor. With all the cunning words thou canst, invite
The states of Parma to my birthday's feast;
Haste to my brother rival and his father,
Entreat them gently, bid them not to fail;
Be speedy and return.

Vas. Let not your pity betray you till my coming back; think upon incest and cuckoldry.

Sor. Revenge is all the ambition I aspire,
To that I'll climb or fall; my blood's on fire.
Exeunt.

[V.iii]

Enter Giovanni.

Gio. Busy opinion is an idle fool,
That, as a school-rod keeps a child in awe,
Frights the unexperienced temper of the mind.
So did it me; who ere my precious sister
Was married, thought all taste of love would die
In such a contract. But I find no change

28 **lethargies** moral laxness
29 **confusion** damnation; **unjust** unable to reward by justice
31 **good genius** guardian angel
34 **double-lined with** lined with both
35 **sadly** solemnly
37 **died** i.e., died spiritually by acts of copulation (dying)
39 **behoof** advantage
50 **Who** which; **suspect** suspicion
V.ii.3 **horns** (sign of being cuckolded)
4 **riot** delight
20 **states** dignitaries
25 **aspire** intend
V.iii.1 **opinion** (1) talk; (2) rumor
4 **ere** before

Of pleasure in this formal law of sports.
She is still one to me, and every kiss
As sweet and as delicious as the first
I reaped, when yet the privilege of youth
Entitled her a virgin. Oh, the glory
Of two united hearts like hers and mine!
Let poring book-men dream of other worlds,
My world, and all of happiness, is here,
And I'd not change it for the best to come:
A life of pleasure is Elysium.

Enter Friar.

Father, you enter on the jubilee
Of my retired delights. Now I can tell you,
The Hell you oft have prompted is nought else
But slavish and fond superstitious fear;
And I could prove it, too –

Fri. Thy blindness slays thee;
Look there, 'tis writ to thee.

Gives the letter.

Gio. From whom?

Fri. Unrip the seals and see;
The blood's yet seething hot, that will anon
Be frozen harder than congealed coral.
Why d'ee change color, son?

Gio. 'Fore Heaven, you make
Some petty devil factor 'twixt my love
And your religion-maskèd sorceries.
Where had you this?

Fri. Thy conscience, youth, is seared,
Else thou wouldst stoop to warning.

Gio. 'Tis her hand,
I know 't; and 'tis all written in her blood.
She writes I know not what – death? I'll not fear
An armèd thunderbolt aimed at my heart.
She writes we are discovered – pox on dreams
Of low faint-hearted cowardice! Discovered?
The devil we are! which way is 't possible?
Are we grown traitors to our own delights?
Confusion take such dotage, 'tis but forged!
This is your peevish chattering, weak old man.

Enter Vasques.

Now, sir, what news bring you?

Vas. My lord, according to his yearly custom keeping this day a feast in honor of his birthday, by me invites you thither; your worthy father, with the Pope's reverend Nuncio and other magnificoes of Parma, have promised their presence. Will't please you to be of the number?

Gio. Yes, tell him I dare come.

Vas. Dare come?

Gio. So I said; and tell him more, I will come.

Vas. These words are strange to me.

Gio. Say I will come.

Vas. You will not miss?

Gio. Yet more? I'll come! Sir, are you answered?

Vas. So I'll say; my service to you.

Exit.

Fri. You will not go, I trust.

Gio. Not go! for what?

Fri. Oh, do not go! This feast, I'll gage my life,
Is but a plot to train you to your ruin;
Be ruled, you sha'not go.

Gio. Not go? Stood Death
Threat'ning his armies of confounding plagues,
With hosts of dangers hot as blazing stars,
I would be there. Not go! Yes, and resolve
To strike as deep in slaughter as they all,
For I will go.

Fri. Go where thou wilt. I see
The wildness of thy fate draws to an end,
To a bad, fearful end. I must not stay
To know thy fall; back to Bononia I
With speed will haste, and shun this coming blow.
Parma, farewell; would I had never known thee,
Or aught of thine! Well, youngman, since no prayer
Can make thee safe, I leave thee to despair.

Exit.

Gio. Despair, or tortures of a thousand hells,
All's one to me. I have set up my rest.
Now, now, work serious thoughts on baneful plots.

7 **this . . . sports** our relationship
8 **one** perfectly united
17 **on the jubilee** at the height; at the celebration
18 **retired** secluded
19 **prompted** urged me to think of
26 **congealed coral** (the seaplant coral was thought to harden when exposed to air)
28 **factor** intermediary
30 **seared** incapable of feeling because hardened by sinful habit
31 **stoop** submit
39 **dotage** nonsense
40 **peevish** (1) senseless; (2) spiteful
53 **miss** fail
57 **gage** wager
58 **train** lure
61 **blazing stars** comets, thought to be ominous portents
73 **set . . . rest** take final stand (from primero, a card game)
74 **baneful** poisonous

Be all a man, my soul; let not the curse
Of old prescription rend from me the gall
Of courage, which enrolls a glorious death.
If I must totter like a well-grown oak,
Some under-shrubs shall in my weighty fall
Be crushed to splits. With me they all shall perish.

Exit.

[V.iv]

Enter Soranzo, Vasques *and* Banditti.

Sor. You will not fail, or shrink in the attempt?

Vas. I will undertake for their parts. Be sure, my masters, to be bloody enough, and as unmerciful as if you were preying upon a rich booty on the very mountains of Liguria. For your pardons, trust to my lord; but for reward you shall trust none but your own pockets.

Ban. omnes. We'll make a murder.

Sor. Here's gold, here's more. Want nothing. What you do
Is noble, and an act of brave revenge.
I'll make ye rich, banditti, and all free.

Ban. omnes. Liberty! Liberty!

Vas. Hold, take every man a vizard. When ye are withdrawn, keep as much silence as you can possibly. You know the watchword, till which be spoken, move not; but when you hear that, rush in like a stormy flood; I need not instruct ye in your own profession.

Ban. omnes. No, no, no.

Vas. In, then; your ends are profit and preferment – away!

Exeunt Banditti.

Sor. The guests will all come, Vasques?

Vas. Yes sir, and now let me a little edge your resolution: You see nothing is unready to this great work, but a great mind in you. Call to your remembrance your disgraces, your loss of honor, Hippolita's blood, and arm your courage in your own wrongs; so shall you best right those wrongs in vengeance which you may truly call your own.

Sor. 'Tis well; the less I speak, the more I burn,
And blood shall quench that flame.

Vas. Now you begin to turn Italian! This beside, when my young incest-monger comes, he will be sharp set on his old bit. Give him time enough, let him have your chamber and bed at liberty; let my hot hare have law ere he be hunted to his death, that if it be possible he may post to Hell in the very act of his damnation.

Enter Giovanni.

Sor. It shall be so; and see, as we would wish,
He comes himself first. Welcome, my much-loved brother,
Now I perceive you honour me; y' are welcome.
But where's my father?

Gio. With the other states,
Attending on the Nuncio of the Pope
To wait upon him hither; how's my sister?

Sor. Like a good housewife, scarcely ready yet;
Y' are best walk to her chamber.

Gio. If you will.

Sor. I must expect my honorable friends;
Good brother, get her forth.

Gio. You are busy, sir.

Exit.

Vas. Even as the great devil himself would have it! Let him go and glut himself in his own destruction.

Flourish

Hark, the Nuncio is at hand. Good sir, be ready to receive him.

Enter Cardinal, Florio, Donado, Richardetto *and* Attendants.

Sor. Most reverend lord, this grace hath made me proud
That you vouchsafe my house; I ever rest
Your humble servant for this noble favor.

75–6 **curse...prescription** (concerning incest; see Deut. 27:22; Lev. 20:17; *old* = Old Testament)

76 **gall** bitterness (but gall was used as the basis for making ink; hence *enrolls* at line 77)

80 **splits** splinters

V.iv.2 **undertake** vouch

5 **Liguria** i.e., travelers crossing the Liguria mountains between Parma and Genoa

11 **free** (the banditti are outlaws; Soranzo promises to pardon them of their crimes)

13 **vizard** mask

22 **edge** sharpen

32 **turn Italian** (Italians were known for the capacity and intensity for revenge)

34 **sharp set** keen; eager; **old bit** i.e., making love to Annabella

36 **hot hare** ([1] rabbits known for sexual activity; [2] as their quarry); **law** "the start" given the quarry before the chase begins

38 **post** speed; **damnation** (to kill someone in an act of sin insures damnation)

40 **brother** i.e., brother-in-law

42 **father** father-in-law

44 **wait upon** attend

47 **expect** wait (here) for

48 **get** bring

54 **grace** honor

55 **vouchsafe** confer upon

Car. You are our friend, my lord; His Holiness
Shall understand how zealously you honor
Saint Peter's Vicar in his substitute.
Our special love to you.
Sor. Signiors, to you
My welcome, and my ever best of thanks
For this so memorable courtesy.
Pleaseth Your Grace to walk near?
Car. My lord, we come
To celebrate your feast with civil mirth,
As ancient custom teacheth; we will go.
Sor. Attend His Grace, there! signiors, keep your way.
Exeunt.

[V.v]

Enter Giovanni *and* Annabella *lying on a bed.*

Gio. What, changed so soon? Hath your new sprightly lord
Found out a trick in night-games more than we
Could know in our simplicity? Ha, is 't so?
Or does the fit come on you, to prove treacherous
To your past vows and oaths?
Ann. Why should you jest
At my calamity, without all sense
Of the approaching dangers you are in?
Gio. What danger's half so great as thy revolt?
Thou art a faithless sister, else thou know'st
Malice, or any treachery beside,
Would stoop to my bent brows; why, I hold fate
Clasped in my fist, and could command the course
Of time's eternal motion; hadst thou been
One thought more steady than an ebbing sea.
And what? You'll now be honest, that's resolved?
Ann. Brother, dear brother, know what I have been,
And know that now there's but a dining-time
'Twixt us and our confusion. Let's not waste
These precious hours in vain and useless speech.

Alas, these gay attires were not put on
But to some end; this sudden solemn feast
Was not ordained to riot in expense;
I that have now been chambered here alone,
Barred of my guardian, or of any else,
Am not for nothing at an instant freed
To fresh access. Be not deceived, my brother,
This banquet is an harbinger of death
To you and me, resolve yourself it is,
And be prepared to welcome it.
Gio. Well then,
The schoolmen teach that all this globe of earth
Shall be consumed to ashes in a minute.
Ann. So I have read too.
Gio. But 'twere somewhat strange
To see the waters burn. Could I believe
This might be true, I could believe as well
There might be Hell or Heaven.
Ann. That's most certain.
Gio. A dream, a dream: else in this other world
We should know one another.
Ann. So we shall.
Gio. Have you heard so?
Ann. For certain.
Gio. But d'ee think
That I shall see you there, you look on me;
May we kiss one another, prate or laugh,
Or do as we do here?
Ann. I know not that,
But good, for the present, what d'ee mean
To free yourself from danger? Some way, think
How to escape; I'm sure the guests are come.
Gio. Look up, look here; what see you in my face?
Ann. Distraction and a troubled countenance.
Gio. Death, and a swift repining wrath – yet look,
What see you in mine eyes?
Ann. Methinks you weep.
Gio. I do indeed. These are the funeral tears
Shed on your grave; these furrowed up my cheeks
When first I loved and knew not how to woo.
Fair Annabella, should I here repeat
The story of my life, we might lose time.

59 Saint . . . substitute the Pope, represented by the Nuncio
66 keep . . . way walk on
V.v.4 fit (of remorse)
11 stoop . . . brows yield to my frown
15 honest chaste
17 dining-time the period for a normal meal
21 solemn ceremonial
22 riot . . . expense to waste money
25–6 freed . . . access allowed to receive visitors again
30 schoolmen medieval theologians
30–1 globe . . . minute (cf. Rev. 20–1)
39 you . . . me that you will find me there
40 prate talk idly
41 do i.e., make love
42 good dear (as a form of address)
46 Distraction (1) disturbance; (2) temporary madness
47 repining angry

Be record all the spirits of the air,
And all things else that are; that day and night,
Early and late, the tribute which my heart
Hath paid to Annabella's sacred love
Hath been these tears, which are her mourners now.
Never till now did Nature do her best
To show a matchless beauty to the world,
Which in an instant, ere it scarce was seen,
The jealous Destinies required again.
Pray, Annabella, pray; since we must part,
Go thou white in thy soul, to fill a throne
Of innocence and sanctity in Heaven.
Pray, pray my sister.

Ann. Then I see your drift;
Ye blessed angels, guard me!

Gio. So say I.
Kiss me. If ever after-times should hear
Of our fast-knit affections, though perhaps
The laws of conscience and of civil use
May justly blame us, yet when they but know
Our loves, that love will wipe away that rigor
Which would in other incests be abhorred.
Give me your hand; how sweetly life doth run
In these well-colored veins! how constantly
These palms do promise health! But I could chide
With Nature for this cunning flattery.
Kiss me again – forgive me.

Ann. With my heart.

Gio. Farewell.

Ann. Will you be gone?

Gio. Be dark, bright sun,
And make this midday night, that thy gilt rays
May not behold a deed will turn their splendor
More sooty than the poets feign their Styx!
One other kiss, my sister.

Ann. What means this?

Gio. To save thy fame, and kill thee in a kiss.

Stabs her.

Thus die, and die by me, and by my hand.
Revenge is mine; honor doth love command.

Ann. Oh, brother, by your hand?

Gio. When thou art dead
I'll give my reasons for 't; for to dispute
With thy – even in thy death – most lovely beauty,
Would make me stagger to perform this act
Which I most glory in.

Ann. Forgive him, Heaven – and me my sins; farewell,
Brother, unkind, unkind – mercy, great Heaven! – Oh – Oh!

Dies.

Gio. She's dead; alas, good soul; the hapless fruit
That in her womb received its life from me,
Hath had from me a cradle and a grave.
I must not dally. This sad marriage-bed,
In all her best, bore her alive and dead.
Soranzo, thou hast missed thy aim in this,
I have prevented now thy reaching plots,
And killed a love, for whose each drop of blood
I would have pawned my heart. Fair Annabella,
How over-glorious art thou in thy wounds,
Triumphing over infamy and hate!
Shrink not, courageous hand; stand up, my heart,
And boldly act my last and greater part!

Exit with the body.

[V.vi]

A Banquet. Enter Cardinal, Florio, Donado, Soranzo, Richardetto, Vasques *and* Attendants; *they take their places.*

Vas. [*Aside to Sor.*] Remember, sir, what you have to do; be wise and resolute.

Sor. [*Aside to Vas.*] Enough, my heart is fixed. [*To Car.*] Pleaseth Your Grace
To taste these coarse confections? Though the use
Of such set entertainments more consists
In custom than in cause, yet, reverend sir,
I am still made your servant by Your presence.

Car. And we your friend.

Sor. But where's my brother Giovanni?

---

54 **spirits . . . air** evil spirits thought to be in attendance on evil thoughts
64 **white . . . soul** according to neoplatonic (but not Christian) belief, the soul was not defiled by bodily sin
66 **drift** intention
70 **civil use** civilized customs
72 **wipe . . . rigor** cleanse away the shame of violence
75 **constantly** confidently
82 **Styx** river on entering the underworld whose waters were thought to be poisonous
86 **honor . . . command** their honor requires self-judgment and payment for their behavior
93 **unkind** unnatural; cruel
94 **hapless** luckless
98 **best** (1) behavior; (2) finery (her wedding dress); (3) sacrifice
99 **missed . . . in** not had your chance at
100 **prevented** forestalled; **reaching** far-reaching; all-consuming
102 **pawned** ransomed
103 **over-glorious** beautiful beyond measure
V.vi.4 **coarse confections** plain dishes
6 **cause** substantial benefit
7 **made . . . by** obliged to you for
9 **Giovanni** (rather, he should inquire about Annabella as hostess; clearly his mind is on the banditti)

Enter Giovanni *with a heart upon his dagger.*

Gio. Here, here Soranzo! trimmed in reeking
  blood
That triumphs over death; proud in the spoil
Of love and vengeance! Fate, or all the powers
That guide the motions of immortal souls
Could not prevent me.
Car. What means this?
Flo. Son Giovanni!
Sor. [*Aside.*] Shall I be forestalled?
Gio. Be not amazed. If your misgiving hearts
Shrink at an idle sight, what bloodless fear
Of coward passion would have seized your
  senses,
Had you beheld the rape of life and beauty
Which I have acted? My sister, oh, my sister!
Flo. Ha! what of her?
Gio. The glory of my deed
Darkened the mid-day sun, made noon as
  night.
You came to feast, my lords, with dainty fare;
I came to feast too, but I digged for food
In a much richer mine than gold or stone
Of any value balanced: 'tis a heart,
A heart, my lords, in which is mine entombed.
Look well upon 't; d'ee know 't?
Vas. What strange riddle's this?
Gio. 'Tis Annabella's heart, 'tis; why d'ee startle?
I vow 'tis hers: this dagger's point ploughed up
Her fruitful womb, and left to me the fame
Of a most glorious executioner.
Flo. Why, madman, art thyself?
Gio. Yes, father, and that times to come may
  know
How as my fate I honored my revenge,
List, Father, to your ears I will yield up
How much I have deserved to be your son.
Flo. What is 't thou say'st?
Gio. Nine moons have had their changes,
Since I first throughly viewed and truly loved
Your daughter and my sister.
Flo. How! alas,
My lords, he's a frantic madman!
Gio. Father, no.
For nine months' space, in secret I enjoyed
Sweet Annabella's sheets; nine months I liv'd
A happy monarch of her heart and her.
Soranzo, thou know'st this. Thy paler cheek
Bears the confounding print of thy disgrace;
For her too fruitful womb too soon bewrayed
The happy passage of our stol'n delights,
And made her mother to a child unborn.
Car. Incestuous villain!
Flo. Oh, his rage belies him!
Gio. It does not, 'tis the oracle of truth;
I vow it is so.
Sor. I shall burst with fury;
Bring the strumpet forth!
Vas. I shall, sir.
Exit.
Gio. Do, sir; have you all no faith
To credit yet my triumphs? Here I swear
By all that you call sacred, by the love
I bore my Annabella whilst she lived,
These hands have from her bosom ripped this
  heart.

Enter Vasques.

Is 't true or no, sir?
Vas. 'Tis most strangely true.
Flo. Cursèd man! – have I lived to –
Dies.
Car. Hold up Florio;
Monster of children, see what thou hast done,
Broke thy old father's heart! Is none of you
Dares venture on him?
Gio. Let 'em. Oh, my father,
How well his death becomes him in his griefs!
Why, this was done with courage. Now
  survives
None of our house but I, gilt in the blood
Of a fair sister and a hapless father.
Sor. Inhuman scorn of men, hast thou a thought
T' outlive thy murders?
Gio. Yes, I tell thee yes;
For in my fists I bear the twists of life.
Soranzo, see this heart which was thy wife's.
Thus I exchange it royally for thine,
[*Stabs him.*]
And thus, and thus; now brave revenge is mine.
[*Soranzo falls.*]

---

10 **trimmed** decorated; **reeking** steaming hot
11 **spoil** (1) destruction; (2) plunder
16 **misgiving** apprehensive
17 **idle sight** mere spectacle
25 **stone** precious stone; jewel
26 **balanced** i.e., weighed for determining value
30 **startle** take fright
34 **art thyself?** are you in your right mind?
38 **son** (plays on son-in-law)
40 **throughly** thoroughly
47 **confounding** shaming
48 **bewrayed** revealed
51 **rage** madness; **belies him** makes him lie
64 **venture on** (1) challenge; (2) restrain; (3) defeat
67 **gilt** covered (gilded)
71 **twists of life** i.e., the threads of life controlled by the Three Fates in classical mythology

Vas. I cannot hold any longer: you sir, are you grown insolent in your butcheries? Have at you!

Fight.

Gio. Come, I am armed to meet thee.

Vas. No, will it not be yet? if this will not, another shall. –
Not yet? I shall fit you anon. – Vengeance!

Enter Banditti.

Gio. Welcome! come more of you, whate'er you be,
I dare your worst.

[*They surround and wound him.*]

Oh, I can stand no longer. Feeble arms,
Have you so soon lost strength?

[*Falls.*]

Vas. Now you are welcome, sir! Away, my masters; all is done. Shift for yourselves; your reward is your own. Shift for yourselves.

Ban. Away, away!

Exeunt Banditti.

Vas. How d'ee, my lord? See you this? How is 't?

Sor. Dead; but in death well pleased, that I have lived
To see my wrongs revenged on that black devil.
Oh, Vasques, to thy bosom let me give
My last of breath; let not that lecher live –
Oh!

Dies.

Vas. The reward of peace and rest be with him, my ever dearest lord and master.

Gio. Whose hand gave me this wound?

Vas. Mine, sir, I was your first man; have you enough?

Gio. I thank thee; thou hast done for me
But what I would have else done on myself.
Art sure thy lord is dead?

Vas. Oh, impudent slave,
As sure as I am sure to see thee die.

Car. Think on thy life and end, and call for mercy.

Gio. Mercy? Why, I have found it in this justice.

Car. Strive yet to cry to Heaven.

Gio. Oh, I bleed fast;
Death, thou art a guest long looked-for, I embrace
Thee and thy wounds. Oh, my last minute comes.
Where'er I go, let me enjoy this grace,
Freely to view my Annabella's face.

Dies.

Don. Strange miracle of justice!

Car. Raise up the city, we shall be murdered all!

Vas. You need not fear, you shall not. This strange task being ended, I have paid the duty to the son which I have vowed to the father.

Car. Speak, wretched villain, what incarnate fiend
Hath led thee on to this?

Vas. Honesty, and pity of my master's wrongs. For know, my Lord, I am by birth a Spaniard, brought forth my country in my youth by Lord Soranzo's father, whom whilst he lived I served faithfully; since whose death I have been to this man, as I was to him. What I have done was duty, and I repent nothing but that the loss of my life had not ransomed his.

Car. Say fellow, know'st thou any yet unnamed
Of counsel in this incest?

Vas. Yes, an old woman, sometimes guardian to this murdered lady.

Car. And what's become of her?

Vas. Within this room she is; whose eyes after her confession I caused to be put out, but kept alive, to confirm what from Giovanni's own mouth you have heard. Now, my Lord, what I have done you may judge of, and let your own wisdom be a judge in your own reason.

Car. Peace! First, this woman, chief in these effects,
My sentence is that forthwith she be ta'en
Out of the city, for example's sake,
There to be burned to ashes.

Don. 'Tis most just.

Car. Be it your charge, Donado, see it done.

Don. I shall.

Vas. What for me? If death, 'tis welcome. I have been honest to the son, as I was to the father.

Car. Fellow, for thee: since what thou didst was done
Not for thyself, being no Italian,
We banish thee for ever, to depart

---

76 **insolent** excessive;

76–7 **Have at you!** (cf. I.ii where Soranzo refuses to fight Grimaldi)

79 **No, . . . yet?** I have not yet killed you?

80 **fit** fix (with the banditti); **anon** soon; **Vengeance!** (watchword for the banditti; see V.iv.15)

119 **Spaniard** (the Spanish were reputed for cloaking malice with friendship)

128 **Of counsel** involved

129 **sometimes** formerly

137–8 **in . . . reason** of your own sentence

Within three days; in this we do dispense
With grounds of reason, not of thine offense.

Vas. 'Tis well. This conquest is mine, and I rejoice that a Spaniard outwent an Italian in revenge.

Exit.

Car. Take up these slaughtered bodies, see them buried;
And all the gold and jewels, or whatsoever,
Confiscate by the canons of the Church,
We seize upon to the Pope's proper use.

Rich. [*Discovers himself.*] Your Grace's pardon.
Thus long I lived disguised
To see the effect of pride and lust at once
Brought both to shameful ends.

Car. What, Richardetto, whom we thought for dead?

Don. Sir, was it you –

Rich. Your friend.

Car. We shall have time
To talk at large of all; but never yet
Incest and murder have so strangely met.
Of one so young, so rich in Nature's store,
Who could not say, *'Tis pity she's a whore?*

Exeunt.

[FINIS.]

151–2 dispense . . . offense grant a pardon because of the motives
159 proper personal

165 at large at greater length
167 Nature's store natural endowments

Further Background Reading

Substantial work in political, social, religious, economic, and theatrical history of Renaissance England has in recent years turned to fresh documentary evidence and changed our perspectives on the culture in which the plays in this collection were written and first performed. Readers may find the following books especially helpful in understanding Tudor and Stuart plays and entertainments.

Abbott, Mary, *Life Cycles in England 1560–1720: Cradle to Grave*. London and New York: Routledge, 1996.

Archer, Ian, *The Pursuit of Stability: Social Relations in Elizabethan London*. Cambridge: Cambridge University Press, 1990.

Beier, A. L., *Masterless Men: The Vagrancy Problem in England 1560–1640*. London: Methuen, 1985.

Brigden, Susan, *London and the Reformation*. Oxford: Clarendon Press, 1989.

Clare, Janet, *"Art Made Tongue-Tied by Authority": Elizabethan and Jacobean Censorship*. Manchester: Manchester University Press, 1990.

Collinson, Patrick, *The Birthpangs of Protestant England: Religious and Cultural Change in the Sixteenth and Seventeenth Centuries*. New York: St. Martin's Press, 1988.

——, *Elizabethan Essays*. London: Hambledon Press, 1994.

——, *The Religion of Protestants: The Church in English Society 1559–1625*. Oxford: Clarendon Press, 1982.

Coward, Barry, *The Stuart Age: England 1603–1714*, 2nd edn. London: Longman, 1994.

Cox, John D. and David Scott Kastan, eds., *A New History of Early English Drama*. New York: Columbia University Press, 1997.

Cressy, David, *Birth, Marriage and Death: Ritual, Religion and the Life-Cycle in Tudor and Stuart England*. Oxford: Oxford University Press, 1997.

Erickson, Amy Louise, *Women and Property in Early Modern England*. London and New York: Routledge, 1993.

Fletcher, Anthony, *Gender, Sex and Subordination in England 1500–1800*. London and New Haven: Yale University Press, 1995.

—— and John Stevenson, eds., *Order and Disorder in Early Modern England*. Cambridge: Cambridge University Press, 1985.

Gowing, Laura, *Domestic Dangers: Women, Words, and Sex in Early Modern England*. Oxford: Clarendon Press, 1996.

Gurr, Andrew, *Playgoing in Shakespeare's London*. Cambridge: Cambridge University Press, 1987.

Guy, John, ed., *The Reign of Elizabeth I: Court and Culture in the Last Decade*. Cambridge: Cambridge University Press, 1995.

Hanson, Elizabeth, *Discovering the Subject in Renaissance England*. Cambridge: Cambridge University Press, 1998.

Harris, Jonathan Gil, *Foreign Bodies and the Body Politic: Discourses of Social Pathology in Early Modern England*. Cambridge: Cambridge University Press, 1998.

Haynes, Alan, *Invisible Power: The Elizabethan Secret Services 1570–1603*. Stroud: Alan Sutton Publishing, 1992.

Heal, Felicity and Clive Holmes, *The Gentry in England and Wales 1500–1700*. London: Macmillan, 1994.

Hirst, Derek, *England in Conflict: 1603–1660*. Cambridge, Mass.: Harvard University Press, 1999.

Houlbrooke, Ralph A, *The English Family 1450–1700*. London and New York: Longman, 1984, 1993.

Ingram, Martin, *Church Courts, Sex and Marriage in England 1570–1640*. Cambridge: Cambridge University Press, 1986.

James, Mervyn, *Society, Politics and Culture: Studies in Early Modern England*. Cambridge: Cambridge University Press, 1986.

Kishlansky, Mark, *A Monarchy Transformed: Britain 1603–1714*. London: Penguin, 1996.

Laurence, Anne, *Women in History 1500–1760: A Social History*. New York: St. Martin's Press, 1994.

Maltby, Judith, *Prayer Book and People in Elizabethan and Early Stuart England*. Cambridge: Cambridge University Press, 1998.

Orlin, Lena Cowen, *Private Matters and Public Culture in Post-Reformation England*. Ithaca: Cornell University Press, 1994.

Palmer, Daryl W., *Hospitable Performances: Dramatic Genre and Cultural Practice in Early Modern England*. West Lafayette, Ind.: Purdue University Press, 1992.

Peck, Linda Levy, *Court Patronage and Corruption in Early Stuart England*. Boston: Unwin Hyman, 1990.

——, ed., *The Intellectual Milieu of the Jacobean Court*. Cambridge: Cambridge University Press, 1992.

Perry, Curtis, *The Making of Jacobean Culture*. Cambridge: Cambridge University Press, 1997.

Rappaport, Steve, *Worlds within Worlds: Structures of Life in Sixteenth-Century London*. Cambridge: Cambridge University Press, 1989.

Sharpe, J. A., *Crime in Early Modern England 1550–1750*. London and New York: Longman, 1984.

Smith, Bruce R., *Homosexual Desire in Shakespeare's England: A Cultural Poetics*. Chicago: University of Chicago Press, 1991.

Underdown, David, *Fire from Heaven: Life in an English Town in the Seventeenth Century*. New Haven: Yale University Press, 1992.

——, *Revel, Riot and Rebellion: Popular Politics and Culture in England 1603–1660*. Oxford: Clarendon Press, 1985.

Wrightson, Keith, *English Society 1580–1680*. New Brunswick, NJ: Rutgers University Press, 1982.

Appendix: Cultural Documents

I: The History of a Most Horrible Murder Commited at Faversham in Kent

II: The Life and Raigne of King Edward of Carnarvan

III: The infortunate mariage of a Gentleman, called Antonio Bologna, wyth the Duchesse of Malfi, and the pitifull death of them both

IV: Music from the Plays

I

The History of a Most Horrible Murder Commited at Faversham in Kent*

There dwelt at Fevershame in the county of Kent a gentleman callyd Mastar Arden, a tall gentleman, and of a comly personage. This Ardene had a mothar dwellynge in Norwiche who went abeggynge, but he assayde all meanes posseble to kepe hir from it, whiche wowld not be. Notwithestondynge, he gave a stipend delyvered to Mastar to hir use and, when Mastar Aldriche was maior of Norwiche, she was robbyd, and a princypall chest browght out into hir backe syde [rear premises or outbuilding] and certeyne lynnyn that was in it lefte scateryd abrode to the vallew of forty or fyfty shillyngs. This robery beinge commyttyd in the nyght, she, beynge deaf, hard it not. Next day, whan it was knowne that she was robbed, the maior with others came to hir howse, and serchinge they found Lx£ lyeinge in sondry places tyed up in severall litle clowtes [pieces of cloth] not above ten grotes [fourpence] in one clowte. Than she was restreyned from hir beggynge, and willed to chuse who shuld with hir porcion kepe hir durynge hir lyfe, and to have for his labowr that whiche remayned of the Lx£ unspent at hir deathe and so it was done. Notwithstandynge, she nevar inioyed after she was restreynyd from hir beggynge, and dyed within half a yere aftar, but many yeres aftar the deathe of hir sonne, whereof we have here to speake.

This Master Arden married a well-favoryd yonge gentlewoman and a tal[e] who was the Lord Northes wyves dowghter. And hir husband and she havynge therefore often recowrse to my Lord Northes, ther was one Mosby, who was a taylor by his occupation, a blacke swart man, who in procese of tyme was made one of the chefeste gentlemen about the Lord Northe. And ther he grew to be familiar withe Mystris Arden. Notwithstondynge for some dyslykynge he had of hir, he fell out with hir. Howbeit she beygne very desyrows to be in favowr agayne with Mosby, sent hym a payre of sylvar dice, by one Adam Fowle dwellyng at the Flowre de Luce in Fevershame. Aftar this he resorted to hir agayne and would very often tymes lye at Arden's howse, insomoche that within the space of ij yeres aftar they wer made frinds, he had to do with Mistris Arden. Mastar Arden, perceyvynge ryght well theyr mutuall familiaritie to be muche greatar then theyr honestie, was yet so greatly gyven to seke his advauntage, and caryd so lytle how he came by it, that in hope of atteynynge some benefite of the Lord Northe by meanes of this Mosby who could do muche with hym, he winked at that shamefull dysorder and bothe parmyttyd and also invited hym very often to be in his howse. And thus it contynuyd a good space before any practyse agaynst Arden. At length she was so enflamyd with the love of Mosby that she lothyd [loathed] hir husbond and therefore wyshed, and aftar practysed, how to brynge hym to his end. Now she was acqwayntyd with a certayne payntor dwellynge in the towne of Faversham, who had skyll of poysens, whiche she demaundyd, and he denyed not. "Ye[a]," sayd she, "but I would have suche a one, made as shuld moste spedyly dyspatche the eatar therof." Then he made hir suche one and wylled hir to put it in the botom of a poringer and then to powr mylke upon it, whiche she forgettynge powryd the mylke first and aftarward the poyson. Now Mastar Arden purposed that day to ryd [ride] to Canterbury and thowght first to breake his fast and she browght hym this mylke and butar, and he havynge eatyd [eaten] a sponefull or two therof, he muche myslykynge the collar [color] and taste, sayd to his wyfe, "Mystris Ales, what mylke have yow gyven me here?" Wherewith she tyltyd it ovar with hir hand saynge, "I wene [think] nothinge can please yow." Then as he rode to Cantorbery, he fell in a great vomittynge and a laske [diarrhoea], and so porgyd upwards and downewards that he was preservyd for that tyme. Then fell she to be acqwayntyd with one Grene of Feversham, who was one of Ser Anthony Agers servauntes, and Mastar Arden had got extorciously [by extortion] a peace of ground from hym on the backesyde of the abbey, and ther had blowes passed betwene them and great threttyngs. Therefore she, knowynge that Greene for this cawse hated Mastar Arden, began to practyse with hym how to make hir husbond owt of the way, and concludyd that yf he could get any that would kyll hym, the party shuld have x£ for a reward. This Grene havynge doyngs for Ser Antony Ager, who was vitellor [victualer] to Bulleyn [Boulogne] had occasyon to go up to London to his mastar, and bycawse he had some charge with hym, he desyred one Bradshow a goldsmythe of Fevarsham to accompany hym to Gravesend and he would content hym for his paynes. This Bradshawe beinge a very honest man was content and rode with hym, and when they came to Raynam Doune they chansed to see iij or iiij servyngemen comynge from Leedes, and than Bradshew espyed commynge up the hyll from Rochestar-wards one Blacke Will a tirible [terrible] ruffian with a sword and a buckler, and another with a great stafe over his necke. "Than," sayde Bradshew to Grene, "we are happye that here comythe some company from Ledes, for here commethe as murtheringe a knave as any is in England, and it had not bene for

* An account by John Stow transcribed with minimal modernization from British Library Harleian MS 452. Plut XLVIII B, fols. 34ff.

them we myght have chansed to have escaped hardly of owr money and lyves. "Yea, thought Grene, as he aftarward confessyd, such a one is for my purpose." Wherefore he asked, "Whiche, is he?" "Yondar is he," quoth Bradshaw, "the same that hathe the swerde and bucklar. His name is Blacke Will." "How know yow that?" sayd Grene. Bradshow answeryd, "I knowe hym at Bulleyn, when we bothe servyd. He was a souldyar and I was Ser Richard Candishes man. And ther he commytted many haynous murthurs on such as travayled betwene Bulleyne and Fraunce." By this tyme the othar companye of servyngemen came to them, and they goynge alltogethar met with Blacke Will and his fellowe. The servyngmen knewe Black Will and salutyd hym, demaundyd whethar he went. He aunsweryd, "by Gods blod I know not, nor I care not but even as my staffe fallethe I goo". They sayd, "Yf thow wilt turne backe agayne to Gravesend we will gyve the thy suppar." "By God blowd," sayd he, "I care not, I am content," so he turnynge with them, took acqwantance of Bradshowe, sayeng, "Fellow Bradshewe, how dost thow?" He unwillinge to renew acqwantance with suche a shamles ruffian, sayd, "Why do you knowe me?" "Ye[a] that I do," quothe he, "dyd not we serve in Bulleyn togethar?" "Ye must perdon me" quoth Bradshowe, "for I have forgoten yow." Than Grene talked with Blacke [Will] and sayd "Whan yow have suppyd, come to my hosteis howse at suche a signe and I will gyve you secke [sack] and sugar." "By Gods blode," sayd he, "I thanke yow. I will come and take it." Accordynge to promyse, he came to Grene and there they made good chere. Then Blacke Will and Grene went and talked togethar aparte from Bradshaw and ther concludyd that yf Blacke Will would kyll Mastar Arden he shuld have x£ for his labowre. Than he answeryd, by Gods wounds that yf he knew hym, he would dispache hym. "Mary [to be sure], to morow," quoth Grene, "I will shew hym [to] the in Powles [St. Paul's Cathedral, London]. Then they lefte theyr talke, and Grene bad hym go to his hostes howse, and so he dyd [did]. Then Grene wrote a lettar to Mistris Arden and amongst other things put in these words, we have got a man for owr purpose, we may thanke my brother Bradshewe. Now Bradshew not knowyng anythinge of this toke the lettar of hym, and in the mornynge departyd home agayne and delyveryd the lettar to Mystris Arden, and Grene and Blacke Will went up to London at the tyde. At the tyme apoyntyd, Grene shewed Blacke Will Master Arden walkyng in Powles. Then sayd Blacke Will, "What is he that goethe after hym?" "Mary," sayd Grene, "one of his men." "Gods blowde," sayd Blacke Will, "I will kyll them bothe." "Nay," sayde Grene, "do not so for he is of counsell with us in this matar." "By Gods blowd," sayd he, "I care not for that. I will kyll them bothe." "Nay," sayd Grene, "in any wyse do not do so." Than Blacke Will thowght to have kyllyd Mastar Arden in Powls churcheyard, but ther wer so many gentlemen that accompanyed hym to dynner that he missed of his purpose. Grene shewed all this talke to Master Ardens man, whos name was Michaell, which evar after stode in dowbt of Blacke Will lest he shuld kyll hym. The cawse that this Michaell conspired with the rest agaynst his mastar was for that it was determyned he shuld mary a kynsewoman of Mosbyes. Now Mastar Arden lay at a certayn parsonage of his in London, and so Mychell his man and Grene agreyd that Blacke Will shuld come at nyght to the parsonage where he shuld find the dores open and so he myght morthar Mastar Arden. Now Mychell havynge his mastar to bed lefte open the dores accordynge to the apoyntment made before. His mastar, beinge in bed, asked yf he had shut the dores, and he sayd yea. Now he, fearynge lest Blacke Will would kyll hym as well as his mastar aftar he was a bedde, rose up agayne and shut the dores so that Blacke Will comynge thethar and fyndynge the dores shut departyd, beynge disapoyntyd that tyme allso. The next day, Blacke Will cam to Grene marvelowsly chafed and vexyd bycaws he was so decyvyd, and swore wounds and blowd that where he met Arden's man he will kyll hym first, for that he had so deceyvyd hym. "No," sayd Grene, "do not so for I will first know the cawse of shuttynge the dores," and so pacified Blacke Will. Than Grene went and talked with Ardens man and asked why he dyd not leave open the dores accordynge to his promyse. "Mary," sayde he, "I will show yow the cawse. My master dyd yesternyght that he nevar dyd before, for aftar I was a bed he rose up and shut the dores and in the morninge rated me mervellously for not shuttynge the dores," whereat they war content. Arden beynge ready to goo homewards his man sayde to Grene, "This nyght will my mastar goo downe," whereupon it was agreed that Blacke Will shuld kyll hym on Raynam downe. When Mastar Arden cam to Rochestar, his man fearinge still that Blacke Will would kyll hym with his mastar, pricked his horse of purpos, and made hym halt, to the end he myght protracte tyme, and tary behynd his mastar. So ridynge before his mastar thrwghe Rochestar, his mastar asked hym why his horse haltyd. He sayde he knew not. "Well" quoth Arden, "when ye come at the smythes dwellyng before (between Rochestar and the hill fote ovar agaynst Chetham), remove his shoe and serche hym, and come aftar me." So Mastar Arden rode on and or evar he came at the place where Blacke Will layd wayte for hym there ovartoke Mastar Arden dyvars gentlemen of his acqwayntance who accompanied hym so that Blacke Will miste of his purpose. After that Mastar Arden was come home he sent (as he usually dyd) his man to Shepey to Ser Thomas Chenyes, than Lord Warden of the Cinque Portes, about certayn busynes. And at his commynge away he had a letar delyvered, sent by Sir Thomas Cheney to his mastar. When he came home his mystris toke the letter and perused it and cept it and willed hir man in any wyse that he shuld tell his mastar that he had a letter delyveryd hym by Ser Thomas Cheney and had lost it, addynge that he thowght it best that his mastar went next mornynge to Ser Thomas, becawse he knewe not the mattar. He sayd he wolde and therefore he willyd his man to be stiringe betymes. Than Blacke Will lying in Preston (where he and one George Shakebage, his companion), was kept all that while in a storehouse of Ser Anthony Ager, and that by Grene and thethar came Mystris Arden to se hym and browght and sent hym meate many tymes (wayting oportunytie for his purpos) was willed in any wise to be early in the mornynge in wayte for Mastar Arden, in a certayne brome close betwene Feversham and the fery whiche Arden must nedes passe thrwghe, and ther to do his feate. Now Blacke Will stirred in the mornynge betymes, but he myst the way and tarried in a wrong place. Than Mastar Arden and his man commynge on theyr way early in the mornynge toward Shornelaw [Shurland], as they wer almoste come to the brome close his man, allwayes fearinge that Blacke Will would kyll hym with his mastar, feynyd that he has lost his purce: Than sayd Arden, "Why, thow nowghty knave, couldst thow not kepe thy purse? What was there in it?" He sayd, "iij£." "Why, go thy wayes back agayne," sayd Arden, "and seke it for, beinge so early as it is, ther is no man stirringe, and therefore thou are sure to finde it agayne. Than come and overtake me at the ferie [ferry]". So by the meanes that Blacke Will has lost his way, Arden ther esckapyd [escaped] also. But Blacke Will thowght he would not myse hym homewards, but there accompanied hym so many gentlemen of my Lorde Wardens to Feversham that Blacke Will was disapoyntyd, Gods wonderful provydence hetharto.

Now Seint Valentyns fayre beinge at hand, the conspirators thowght surely to worke theyr feat at that tyme. Mosby thowght to picke some quarell with Arden at the fayre to fight with hym, for he sayd he could not fynd in his harte to kyll a gentleman, wheras Mystris Arden egged hym to kyll hir husband by some meanes, for he was so evell belovyd that no man would make inquire aftar his death. But Mosbye, perceyvynge that he could not by any meanes cawse Arden to fight with hym (for he had piked a qwarell with hym rydynge to or from London and callynge hym knave, vyllane and cokoolde, but Arden would not fight, this much Mosby confessyd in prison), went away in a great furye towards the Flowre de Luce to Adam Fowls wher he went to hoste. But er[e] he came thethar, a messengar cam to hym from Mistris Arden shewynge hym that she desyred hym of all loves to come agayne to hir and to go about the purpose that was in hand. So he came backe. Than they convayed Blacke Will into Arden's howse into a closet at the end of his parlowr, (before this, they had sent owt of the howse all the sarvauntes about dyvars errands, except those that were confederat to the morther). Then went Moseby and stode at the dore in a nyght gowne of sylke gyrdyd [girded, wrapped] about hym and this was about 6 and 7 of the cloke at nyght. Now Master Arden havynge bene at a neighbowrs of his called Dimpkin, dwellyng ovar agaynst his howse, and thir havinge made an end of certayne reconings betwen them, cam home to go to supper, and findynge Mosbye standynge at the dore asked hym yf it were suppertyme. He sayde "I thinke not, it is not redy yet." "Than let us goe and playe a game at tables in the meane ceason," sayd Mastar Arden. Now they went streyght into the parlor and as they cam by throwghe ye hall she was walkynge ther and Master Arden sayde, "How now, Mystrys Ales," but she made small answer to hym. In the meanetyme one cheyned the wicket dore of the entrye. Whan they came into the parlor Mosbye sat downe on the benche havynge his face toward the place where Blacke Will stoode and Mastar Arden stood with his face toward the same. Than Mychaell his man stode at his mastars backe holdynge a candell in his hand to shadow Blacke Will that Arden myght by no means perceyve hym commynge forthe. In theyr playe Mosbye sayde thus (whiche semyd to be a wacheworde for Black Wills comynge forthe), "Now may I take yow; see yf I will." "Take me," sayde Arden, "whiche way." With that, the terrible ruffian Blacke Will cam forthe, and cast a towell about his necke so to stope his breathe and strangle hym. Than Mosby, havynge at his gerdle a pressynge yron of 14 pound weight, stroke hym on the heade with the same so that he fell downe and gave a great grone insomuch that they thowght that they had kyllyd hym. Than they toke hym and caried hym away to lay hym in the countynge howse and in the berynge of hym downe, the pangs of deathe commynge on hym, he strugled and gronyd. Blacke Will stroke [struck] hym twharte [across] the browe a great gashe with his daggar and so kyllyd hym, and layd hym downe, tooke the money out of his purse and rynges from his fingars, cam out, and sayd as folowythe: "Now this feate is done, come, gyve me my monye." So Mistris Arden gave him x pound, and he voydyd the towne streyghtways, aftar he had gotten to Grene and had a horse there. Than came this good wyfe, and with a knyfe gave hir husbond 7 or 8 pricks in the brest becawse she would make him sure.

Aftar this, they toke hym as he was in his nyght-gowne, with his slyppers on his fete, to cary hym into a field without the garden ioynyd to the abbey grownde. Now they brought his body to the garden dore, but they could not find the kaye in half an houre. At lengthe findynge it, they openyd the dore and layde the cowrce [corpse] along in the filde (whiche filede he in his lyfetyme had got by like title as Ahab got Naboths vyneyard, for he had taken it from one Reade and his wyfe by vyolence, which oftentymes had sayd both to his face and in many othar places with teares that she besowght God the plage and vengeaunce myght lyght upon hym that all men myght wondar on hym). In the meane tyme there fell a great snowe insomuch that they commynge in agayne into the house thowght that the snow woulde have coveryd theyr fotynge but sodeynly by the good provydence of God, who would not suffar so detestable a murther longe hydden, it stint [ceased] snowynge [but] they, not consyderynge the same, but thinkynge all had been sure. Than they toke a clout and wyped where it was blowdy and strewyd agayne the russhes that was shuffled with struglynge and cast the clout with whiche they wyped the blowde and the knyfe that was blowdye wherewith she wounded hir husband into a tubbe by the wells syde, where aftarward they were found. Thus thys wickyd woman with hir complices most shamefully murderyd hir owne husbonde, who moste entirely loved hir all his lyfetyme. Then she sent streghtway for Pryme and Cole the grocers, with othar Londonars whiche were before the dede doynge bydde to come to suppar. Whan they cam she sayd, "I mervayle where Mastar Arden is. Well, we will not tary for hym. Come ye and sit downe. We will go to supar"; havynge supte, she sayde, "I merveyll where Mastar Arden is so longe I pray yow let us goe and play a game at the tables till he come. I am sure it will not be longe." So they went to the tables and hir dowghter playd on the vyrginalls and she herselfe danced till it waxed somewhat late and the Londonars lefte playnge, and went theyr wayes to theyr lodgynges. Than sent she abroad to make enquirie for Mastar Arden in dyvers places – namely, amonge the best in the towne where he was wont to be. But they aunsweryd they could tell nothinge of hym. Than she began to make an owtcrye and sayde, nevar woman had suche neighbowrs as I have, and wept, insomuche that hir neighbowrs cam in and found hir makynge great lamentacion, pretendynge to marvayle greatly where hir husband was, insomuche that the maior and othars came and made a searche. The fayre was wont to be kepte partely in the towne, and partely in the abbey, but Arden for his owne lucre had this present yere browght it to be wholye kepte within the abbey ground which he had purchased so that all the gaynes came to hym and none to the townesmen. For the which dede he had many a curse. Than the maior went about the fayre in his serche, and at lengthe came into the same grounde whereas Arden lay. Within a while, Prime the grocer sayd, "Staye, for methinke I se one lye here". So they lokte and perusynge the body found it was Mastar Arden lay deade. Than they lokynge about hym found some rusches of the parlowr stickynge in his slyppars, and by dyligent searche they espied certayne fotynge by meanes of the snowe betwene them and the garden dore. Then the maior sayde, "Let every man staye," and by his commaundement went about and commynge in the insyde from the howse thrwghe the garden to the place wher Arden lay deade, they perceyved evarmore footynge before them in the snowe. And so it apperyd playnly that he was browght alonge that waye from the howse throughe the garden and so forthe into the fielde where he laye. Than they went in and knowynge hir evell behavyowr in tymes past, they examonyd hir, but she defied them, and sayd, "I would you shuld know I am no suche woman." Then they examonyd hir sarvaunts and in examination by reason of a peace of his heare [hair] and blowde found about the howse in the way by whiche they caried hym, and the knyfe wherewithe she thrust hym in, and the clowte wherewith they wipt the blowde awaye, they all confessyd the matter. And Mistris Arden seynge [seeing] hir husbonds blowde, sayde, "O, the blowde of God helpe me, for this blowde have I shede." Than wer they all comyttyd to prison. Aftar this the maior with othars went presently to the Flower de Luce wher they found Mosby in bed, and as they came towards hym they espyed the blowde on his hose and on his purse. Than he asked the cawse of theyr comynge. They sayde, "Se here, yow may undarstond it by thes tokens," shewynge hym the blod on his hose and purse. Then he confessed the dede. So he and all the othar that had conspired agaynst Master Arden were layde in prison, savynge Grene and Blacke Will, who fled, and the payntar and George Shackebacke, who was gone before and nevar hard of aftar. Shortly after were sessyons kepte at Fevarshame, where all these prisonars wer arreygned and condempned. Then beynge demaundyd whethar they had any othar complices, Mystris Arden accusyd Bradshew upon occasyon of a lettar whiche he brought hir sent by Grene from Gravesend in whiche it was written, "We have gotten a man for owre purpose. We may thanke my brother Bradshew, as is afore declaryd," which words had none other meanynge, but only that by Bradshews describyng of Blacke Wills qwallities. Grene iudged hym to be a mete ~~mant~~ [suitable] instrument for the execution of the murther of Mastar Arden. Wherunto notwithstondyng (as Grene confessyd at his deathe certayne yeres aftar), this Bradshew was nevar made pryve. Howbeit, he was upon this accusation of Mistris Ardyn imediatly sent for to the sessyons and indited and the same fact layd to his charge and declaration made agaynst hym, as procuror of Blacke Will to kyll Mastar Arden, whiche came wholy of the ~~unadvised~~ mysundarstondyng of the words of the lettar as is aforesayde. Then he desyred to talke with the persons condempned, whiche was grauntyd. So he demaundyd whithar they did evar know hym or had any convarsatyon with hym. Thay all said no. Then the lettar beinge redd, he shewyd the trewthe, and upon what cawse he tolde Grene of Black Will. Notwithstondynge, he was condempned and suffred. So all thes condemporyd persons were dyversly executyd in severall places, for Mychell Mastar Ardens man was hanged in chaynes at Feversham; and one of the mayedens was brent there, who pitifully bewayled hir case and cryed out on hir Mystris who brought hir to this end and would not forgyve hir; Mosby and his systar wer hanged on a gallows in Smithefilde at London; Ardens wyfe was burned at Canterbury the 14 day of Marche 1550.

Vide exactores et certiorum personarum et locorum in quibus perierunt descriptiones quod a magistro Roberto Coleo de Bow petere licet. [See the charges and descriptions of the various persons and the places where they were put to death, which may be had of Master Robert Cole of Bow.]

Grene came agayne certyene yeres aftar and was hanged in chaynes in the higheway agaynst Feversham betwen Osprynge and Bowghten, and Blacke Will the ruffian was brent on a scaffold at Flysshynge in Zeland. Adam Foule of the Flowre de Luce in Feversham was about this mater caried up to London to prison with his legges bound undar an horse bealy [belly], for that Moseby was hard to say these words: "Had it not bene for Adam Fowle, I had not come to this trowble," meanynge that the bringynge of the sylvar dyse for a token to hym from Mistris Arden (whereof mencion is made before) occasyonyd hym to renew his famyliaritie with hir, but when the mattar was well skannyd, this mans innocentye preservyd hym. This one thinge semythe very notable towchinge Mastar Arden, in the place wher Mastar Arden was layde beynge deade, even all the whole proporcion of hym was sene two yeres aftar in suche sorte as his body lay in the filde, neythar dyd any grasse growe in all the space, where any parte of hym towchyd. so that a man myght saye, here lay his head, here lay an arme, her lay a legge and etc.

Nostri alius magnus contemplator post brennum
[Our other esteemed witness after the burning]

1
Mosby had a systar dwellynge hard by Master Ardens howse in a tenament of his. On the fayre even there was sent thethar Blacke Will, and Grene who came and met there with Mistris Arden hir man and hir mayde with Mosby and George Shackebagge, and ther they devysed to have hym kylled as he was aftarwarde; and, to this cowardly murtherynge of hym, Mosbye would not consent and so in a furye went away up Abbey Strete toward the Flower de Luce where he did often hoste.

2
Whan he came back agayne to hir, she knelyd downe to hym sayenge, "Yf thow lovest me thow wouldest be content seinge (as before) thow nedist not to dowbt, no man will care for his deathe" etc.,

3
Than they made clene the parlor, openyd the dores, servaunts cam hom, she sent for Londonars to com to suppar, they cam, they asked for Mastar Arden, she sayd he was in the towne at suppar, and Mosbys sister was sent for thethar at suppar tyme and ther they were merye. Aftar supar they play on the vyrgynals and dancyd and detractyd the tyme. She would have had the Londonars to play at tables, but they sayd they must go to theyr hostes, they shuld els be shut owt adores. When they were gon, they sent forthe hir servaunts on errants into the towne, all save hir man and mayde, that was of counsell, hir selfe, Mosbys sistar, and hir dowghtar. Then they went to cary hym owt to lay hym in a filde next to the churcheyard ioynynge to hys garden wall thrwghe the whiche he went to the churche. And whils they were thus provydynge, it began to snowe apace and when thay came to the garden gate they had forgotten the kaye, and one went in for the key, and being longe at last found it, and openyd the gate, and caried into the same filde as it were x paces from the garden gate toward the sextrye, and layd hym downe upon his backe streyght in his nyghtgowne with his slyppers, and betwene one of his slyppars and his fote a longe rushe which they left there, and went backe the way they went into the garden and into the howse.

Aftar they came before the commyssyonars beyng demaundyd whether there were any othar of theyr counseyll, Mosby of envy toward Adam Fowle, sayd, "I wowld I had nevar knowne hym. Yf he had not bene I nevar come to this." At this saynge Ser Thomas Moyle, Mastar Petit, and Hawkens of the garde beynge papistis and hatynge Adam Fowle for the gospell, sent Hawkens to aprehend hym and caried hym up to London with his legs bownd undar his horse bely, and left hym at the Marshalsey [prison]. And yf Mosby at his arraignement had not dischargyd hym, nevar to know any thinge of his doynge, he had surely suffred. The fielde in the whiche Arden was layd was one Cookes wydow, who maried one Reade a marinar who kept a taverne in the marketplace, and lay hard by the churche walle; and the West end butted upon Ardens garden wall in whiche end he was layd when he was slayne. He lay there on his backe with nothinge upon hym but his shirt, doblet and hose, and slyppars, and his nyghtgowne. He lay from mydnight till the mornynge and all the next day beinge the fayre day till nyght, all whiche day there were many hundreds of people came to wondar on hym. And this is marvelylows: that his picture was to be sene in the place above ij yeres aftar so playne as coulde be, for the grasse dyd not grow where his bodye, his heade and armes and lengs, dyd lye, but between his legges, betwene his armes and his body and the holoues [hollows] of his necke and rownd about his body it dyd grow, so many strangars came with in ij or iij years besyds the townes man to see the proportion of his bodye on the grownd and are witnesses at this day alyve. This filde he had taken by extortion from Cooks wydow, then Reads wyfe, and gyven them nothing for it, for the whiche the sayd Reads wyfe dyd not only shed many a teare, but also cursyd the same Arden, to his face continually, and in every place where she was prayenge, that a vengeaunce and plage myght lyght upon hym and that all the world myght wondar over hym, and cowld nevar be otharwyse perswadyd tyll God had sufferyd hym to come to this end.

II
The Life and Raigne of King Edward of Carnarvan.*

Edward the second, son to the first Edward, borne at Caernarvan, began his raigne the seuneth day of July, in the yeere of Christ 1307. He was faire of body, but vnstedfast of manners, and disposed to lightnesse, haunting the company of vile persons, and giuen onely to the pleasure of the body, not regarding to gouerne his common weale by discretion and justice, which caused great variance betweene him and his Lords. He tooke to be of his Councell Patricke Earle of Lincolne, and Otho de Gransone with other. He ordained Walter Reignald to be his Chancellour, and caused Walter Langton, Byshop of Chester, Treasurer of England, to bring the king his Fathers body from Carlisle to Waltham Crosse, and then to be arrested by Sir John Felton Constable of the tower, and sent to Wallingford, there to be shut up in prison, and his goods confiscate, because in his fathers lifetime he had reproued him of his insolent life, &c. Hee also called out of exile Pierce of Gaueston a stranger borne, which lately in his fathers dayes, had for certaine causes beene banished this land. He gaue to the said Pierce the Earledome of Cornwall, the Isle of Man, and the Lordship of Wallingford, otherwise assigned to Queen Isabell....

The king gaue vnto Pierce of Gaueston all such gifts and jewels as had bin giuen to him, with the crownes of his Father, his ancestors treasure and many other things, affirming that if he could, he should succeed him in the kingdome, calling him brother, not granting any thing without his consent. The Lords therefore enuying him, told the king that the father of this Pierce was a Traytor to the king of France, and was for the same executed, & that his mother was burned for a witch, and that the said Pierce was banished for consenting to his mothers witchcraft, and that he had now bewitched the king himselfe....

Then the king taking counsell of Pierce, Hugh Spencer the Treasurer, the Chancellor and others, he appointed to answere the Barons at the Parliament on Hocday [Hock Day, second Tuesday after Easter]. The Barons being departed out of London, the City gates were shut vp and chained, great watch kept, and Hugh Spencer made Constable of London. The king with Pierce of Gaueston went toward Wallingford castle with a great company of Soldiers, as well strangers [foreigners] as English, and Hugh Spencer [the elder] tarried still at London....

The king intended to giue Gascoigne to the French king, Scotland to Robert Bruse, Ireland and Wales to others, hoping thereby to haue ayd against his Barons....

The king sent for Pierce of Gaueston out of Ireland. He landed at Caernaan, on the Euen of Saint John Baptist, the king met him at the Castle of Flint with great joy: and gaue to him the Earle of Glocesters sister in mariage....

The Abbot of Saint Denis in France, being sent Legate from the Pope to demand the Legacy that king Edwards father gaue to the holy land, did earnestly request king Edward to remoue from him Pierce Gaueston, with whose conversation all the world was as it were infected....

Pierce of Gaueston conceiuing an affiance [confidence] in the fauour of king Edwards, & of the young earle of Glocester, whose sister he had maried, taking with him many strangers, returned into England, & a little before Christmas came to the kings presence, whom the king, forgetting all oathes and promised pacts, receiued as a heauenly guift.

K. Edward kept his Christmas at Yorke, where Pierce of Gaueston was present with his Outlandish [foreign] men, the king rejoycing, and being in a great jolity because he had receiued him in safety, all the Court and Queene being sorrowfull, because they saw the king not very sound. The mighty men of the land therefore sought how they might set an end to the trouble at hand, for they feared to raise warre, and durst not disquiet the king, yet the peril being weyed, they found that so long as Pierce liued, there could be no peace in the kingdom nor the king to abound in treasure, nor the Queene to enjoy the kings true loue. Thus after they had long considered the perils past, present, & to come, they determined rather to try all extremities, then to be despised and set at naught by a stranger. They chose a Captaine then for their busines to come, Thomas of Lancaster, noble in lineage, valiant in armes, excellent in fame for his manners and justice....

This yeere [1313] therefore by consent of the Prelates, and certaine Nobles, Hugh Spencer the sonne was appointed the kings Chamberlain in place of Pierce of Gaueston, whom they the rather preferred, because they knew the king hated him. Neverthelesse, not long after, by his great diligence, he brought himselfe into the kings fauour. The father of this Hugh being olde, was yet liuing, a knight of great vertue, in counsell wise, in armes valiant, whose confusion and shamefull end he won vnto himselfe by naturall loue though disordinate towards his son, who was in body very comely, in spirit proud, and in action most wicked, whose

* John Stow, *Annales, or A Generall Chronicle of England* (1592); the text is taken from the augmented edition with entries of later years by Edmund Howes (1631).

couetousnes and ambition, by the disheriting of Widowes and strangers, wrought the death of the Nobles, the fall of the king, with the vtter destruction of himselfe and his father....

King Edward held his Christmas [1321] at Circester, and after Christmas leauing Glocester and Worcester, he with his Army went to Shrewsbury and Bridgenorth. Both the Mortimers meeting the king, reuerently and peaceably submitted themselues vnto him. But the king sent them both to the Tower of London....

The 2. day of August [1322], the two Mortimers were adjudged to bee drawne and hanged at Westminster, for diuers robberies and murthers which the king layd against them, but no execution of that judgement was done, by reason of a writ that the king sent to Sir Richard de Swardstone, then Constable of the Tower, to stay the judgement, and the k. granted them their liues, to be in perpetuall prison....

These tormenters of Edward [Thomas Gurney and John Maltravers] exercised towards him many cruelties, vnto whome it was not permitted to ride, vnlesse it were by night, neither to see any man or to be seene of any. When hee rode, they forced him to bee bare-headed. When he would sleepe, they would not suffer him, neither when hee was hungry would they giue him such meate as he desired, but such as hee loathed. Euery word that hee spake, was contraried by them, who gaue it out most slanderously, that he was madde. And shortly to speake, in all matters they were quite contrary to his will, that either by cold, watching or vnwholesome meates, for melancholy [or] by some infirmity he might languish and die. But this man being by nature strong to suffer paines, and patient thorow Gods grace to abide all griefes, he endured all the deuises of his enemies, for as touching poysons, which they gaue him often to drinke, by the benefit of nature he dispatched away.

These Champions bring Edward towards Barkeley, being guarded with a rabble of helhounds, along by the Grange belonging to the Castle of Bristowe, where that wicked man Gurney making a crowne of hay, put it on his head, and the Souldiers that were present, scoffed, and mocked him beyond all measure, saying, "Tprut, auaunt sir king," making a kinde of noise with their mouthes, as though they had farted. They feared to be met of any that should know Edward, they bent their journey therefore towardes the left hand, riding along ouer the Marish [marshy] grounds lying by the riuer of Seuerne. Moreouer, deuising to disfigure him that hee might not bee knowne, they determined for to shaue as well the haire of his head, as also of his bearde. Wherefore, as in their journey they trauailed by a little water which ran in a ditch, they commanded him to light from his horse to bee shauen, to whom, being set on a moale-hill, a Barber came vnto him with a bason of colde water taken out of a ditch, to shaue him withall, saying vnto the king, that that water should serue for that time. To whom Edward answered, that would they, noulde [nor would] they, hee would haue warme water for his beard; and, to the end that hee might keepe his promise, hee beganne to weepe, and shed teares plentifully. At length they came to Barkley castle, where Edward was shut vp close like an anchorite. Isabell his wife taking it grieuously that her husbands life (which shee deadly hated) was prolonged, made her complaint to her Schoolemaster Adam de Orleton, faining that she had certaine dreames, the interpretation whereof she misliked, which if they were true, she feared least, that if her husband be at any time restored to his old dignity, that hee would burne her for a Traytor, or condemne her to perpetuall bondage. In like sort the Bishop being guilty in his owne conscience stood in the like feare. The like feare also stroke the hearts of other for the same offence; wherfore it seemed good to many of great dignity and bloud, aswell spirituall, as temporall, both men and women, that all such feare should bee taken away, desiring his death. Whereupon there were letters colourably [deceitfully] written to the keepers of Edward, greatly blaming them, for looking so slenderly to the king, suffering him to haue such liberty, and nourishing him too delicately.

Moreouer, there is a priuy motion made vnto them, but yet in such sort, as it might seeme halfe done, that the death of Edward would not be misliking vnto them, whether it were naturall or violent. And in this point, the great deceit of Sophisters stoode in force, set downe by the Bishop who wrote thus.

Edwardum accidere nolite timere bonum est,
Kill Edward doe not feare is a good thing:
Or thus:
To seeke to shead King Edwards bloud
Refuse to feare I count it good.

Which sophisticall saying is to be resolued into two propositions, whereof the first consisting of three words, to wit, *Edwardum accidere nolite*, doe not kill Edward, and the second of other three, that is *timere bonum est*, feare is a good thing, doe seeme to perswade subtilly from murthering of the king. But the receiuers of these letters, not ignorant of the writing, changed the meaning thereof to this sence, *Edwardum accidere nolite timere* to kill Edward doe not fear. And afterwards these words, *bonus est*, it is good, so that they being guilty, turned a good saying into euill.

The Bishop being thus determinately purposed touching the death of Edward, and warily prouiding for himselfe, if by any chance hee should bee accused thereof, craftily worketh that the authoritie which hee gaue by writing, might seeme to bee taken expressely contrary to his meaning, by reason of accenting and poynting [punctuating] of the same....

[*From The Life and Raigne of King Edward the III.*] There was a Parliament holden at Nottingham, where Roger Mortimer was in such glory and honour, that it was without all comparison. No man durst name him any other than Earle of March. A greater route of men waited on his heeles, than on the kings person. He would suffer the king to rise to him and would walke with the king equally, step by step, and cheeke by cheeke, neuer preferring the king, but would goe foremost himselfe with his officers.... By which means, a contention rose among the Noblemen, and great murmuring among the common people, who said, that Roger Mortimer, the Queens Paragon [companion], & the kings Master, sought all the means he could to destroy the kings bloud, and to vsurpe the Regall Maiestie. Which report troubled much the kings friends, to wit, William Mountacute [Montagu], and other, who for the safegard of the king, sware themselues to be true to his person, and drew vnto them Robert de Holland, who had of long time beene keeper of the Castle, vnto whom all secret corners of the same were knowne. Then vpon a certaine night, the king lying without the castle, both he and his friends were brought by torchlight through a secret way vnderground, beginning farre off from the sayd Castle, till they came euen to the Queenes chamber, which they by chance found open. They therefore being armed with naked swords in their hands, went forwards, leauing the king also armed without the doore of the Chamber, least that his Mother should espy him.... From thence, they went towarde the Queene mother, whom they found with the Earle of March ready to haue gone to bed. And hauing taken the sayd Earle, they ledde him out into the Hall, after whom the Queene followed, crying, "*Bel filz, bel filz, ayez pitie de gentil Mortimer*" Good sonne, good sonne, take pitty vpon gentle Mortimer. For she suspected that her sonne was there, though shee saw him not.... The next day in the morning verie early, they bring Roger Mortimer, and other his friends taken with him, with an horrible shout and crying... towards London, where hee was committed to the Tower, and afterward condemned at Westminster, in presence of the whole Parliament on Saint Andrewes euen next following, and then drawne to the Elmes [Tyburn] and there hanged on the common Gallowes....

III
The infortunate mariage of a Gentleman, called Antonio Bologna, wyth the Duchesse of Malfi, and the pitifull death of them both.*

The great Honor and authority men haue in thys World, and the greater their estimation is, the more sensible and notorious are the faultes by theim committed, and the greater is their slaunder. In lyke manner more difficult it is for that man to tolerate and sustayne Fortune, which al the dayes of his life hath lyued at his ease, if by chaunce he fall into any great necessity than for hym whych neuer felt but woe, mishap, and aduersity.... Thus I say, because a woman being as it were the Image of sweetnesse, curtesie and shamefastnesse, so soone as she steppeth out of the right tract, and abandoneth the sweete smel of hir duety and modesty, besides the denigration of hir honour, thrusteth her selfe into infinite Troubles, causeth ruine of sutch whych should bee honoured and praysed, if Womens Allurementes solicited theym not to Folly.... In the very tyme [of Henry VII] then lyued a Gentleman of Naples called Antonio Bologna, who hauing bin master of Household to Fredericke of Aragon, sometime king of Naples, after the French had expelled those of Aragon out of that Citty, the sayde Bologna retyred into Fraunce, and thereby recouered the goods, which hee possessed in his countrey. The Gentleman besides that he was valiant of his persone, a good man of Warre, and wel esteemed amongs the best, had a passing numbre of good graces, which made him to be loued and cherished of euery wight; and for riding and managing of greate horse, he had not his fellow in Italy: he could also play exceedynge well and trim vpon the Lute, whose fayning voyce so wel agreed therevnto, that the moste melancholike persons would forget their heauinesse, vpon hearing of his heauenly noyse: and besides these qualyties, he was of personage comely, and of good proportion.... This Gentleman was Mayster of the kinge of Naples household, and beyng a gentle person, a good Courtier, wel trained vp, and wyse for gouernment of himself in the Courte and in the seruice of Princes, the Duchesse of Malfi thought to intreate him that he would serue hir, in that office which he serued the King. This Duchesse was of the house of Aragon, and sister to the Cardinall of Aragon, which then was a rych and puissant personage. Being resolued, and persuaded, that Bologna was deuoutly affected to the house of Aragon, as one brought vp there from a Chylde: shee sent for him home to his House, and vpon hys repaire vsed vnto him these, or like Woordes: "Mayster Bologna, sith your ill fortune, nay rather the vnhap of our whole House is sutch, as your good Lord and Mayster hath forgon his state and dignity, and that you therwithall haue lost a good Maister, without other recompence but the prayse which euery man giueth you for your good seruice, I haue thought good to intreat you to doe me the honor, as to take charge of the gouernment of my House, and to vse the same, as you did that of the King you maister. I know well that the office is to vnworthy for your calling; notwithstanding you be not ignorant what I am, and how neare to him in bloud, to whom you haue bene a Seruaunte so faythfull and Louing; and albeit that I am no Queene, endued with greatest reuenue, yet with that little portyon I haue, I beare a Pryncely heart: and sutch as you by experience do knowe what I haue done, and dayly do to those which depart my seruice, recompensing them according to theyr paine and trauaile: magnificence is obserued as well in the Courts of poore Princes, as in the stately Palaces of great Kings and monarches."... The gentleman hearynge that curteous demaund of the Dutchesse, knowing himselfe how deepely bound he was to the name of Aragon, and led by some vnknowen prouocation to his great il luck, answered hir in this wise: "I would to God, Madame, that with so good reason and equity I were able to make denyall of your commaundment, as iustly you maye require the same: wherfore for the bounden duety which I owe to the name and memorie of the house of Aragon, I make promise that I shall not only sustaine the trauell, but also the daunger of my Lyfe, dayly to be offred for your seruice: but I feele in mynde I know not what, which commaundeth me to withdraw my selfe to lyue alone at home within my lyttle house, and to be content with that I haue, forgoing the sumptuous charge of Prynces houses, which Lyfe would be wel liked of my self, were it not for the feare that you Madame should be discontented with my refusall, and that you should conceiue, that I disdained your offred charge, or contempne your Court for respect of the great Office I bare in the Courte of the Kyng, my Lord and Mayster: for I cannot receiue more honour, than to serue hir, which is the paragon of that flock and royal race. Therefore at all aduentures I am resolued to obey your will."... Thys Lady waxed very weary of lying alone, and gryeued hir Hearte to by wythoute a match, specially in the Nyght, when the secrete silence and darkenesse of the same presented beefore the eyes of hir mind, the Image of the pleasure which she felt in the lyfe tyme of hir deceased Lord and Husband,

* William Painter, *The second Tome of the Palace of Pleasure, contayning store of goodlye Histories, Tragical matters, and other Morall argumentes, very requisite for delight and profyte* (second augmented edition, ?1575). This story is called "The Twenty-Third Nouell."

whereof now feelying hir selfe despoyled, she felt a contynuall Combat, and durst not attempte that which she desyred most, but eschued the thyng wherof hir Mind lyked best.... Who then could blame thys fayre Princesse, if (pressed wyth desire of match, to remoue the ticklish instigations of her wanton flesh, and hauing in hir presence a man so wise) shee did set hir minde on hym, or fantasy to mary him? Would not that party for calming of his thirst and hunger, being set at a table before sundry sorts of delicate viands, ease his hunger?.... Thus Bologna framed the plot for intertaynment of the Duchesse (albeit hir loue already was fully bent vpon him) and fortified hym selfe agaynst all perillous myshap and chaunce that might succeede, as ordinarily you see that Louers conceyue all things for their aduauntage, and fantasie dreames agreeable to their most desire, resemblinge the Mad and Bedlem persons which haue before their eyes, the figured Fansies whych cause the conceipt of their fury, and stay themselues vpon the vision of that which most troubleth their offended Brayne.... "Bologna shall be my Husband, for of a freend I purpose to make my loyall and lawful Husband, meaning thereby not to offend God and men together, and pretend to liue without offence of conscience, wherby my soule shall not be hindred for any thyng I do, by marying him whom I do straungely loue. I am sure not to be deceyued in loue. He loueth me so mutch or more as I do him, but he dareth not disclose the same, fearing to be refused and cast of with shame. Thus 2 vnited wils, and 2 hearts tied togethers with equal knot cannot chose but bryng forth fruites worthy of sutch society. Let men say what they list, I will doe none otherwyse than my heade and mynd haue already framed. Semblably I neede not make accompt to any persone for my fact, my body, and reputation beynge in full liberty and freedome. The bond of mariage made, shall couer the faulte whych men would fynde, and leauyng myne estate, I shall do no wrong but to the greatnesse of my house, which maketh me amongs men right honorable. But these honors he nothyng worth, where the Mynd is voyd of contentation, and wher the hearte pryckte forwarde by desire leaueth the Bodye and Mynde restlesse wythout quiet." ... Beholde the first Acte of this Tragedy ... for albeit theyr mariage was secrete, and therby politikely gouerned themselues in their stelthes and robberyes of Loue, and that Bologna more ofte helde the state of the Stewarde of the House by Daye, than of Lorde of the same, and by Nyghte supplyed that Place, yet in the ende, the thynge was perceyued whych they desyred to bee closely kepte ... the Duchess after many pleasures (being ripe and plentifull) became with childe, which at the firste astonned the maried couple: neuerthelesse the same so well was prouided for, as the first Childbed was kept secret, and none did know thereof ... the Duchesse beinge great with Childe agayne, and deliuered of a Girle, the businesse of the same was not so secretly done, but that it was discouered.... And this was the second Acte of this Tragicall Historie, to see a fugitife husband secretly to mary, especially hir, vpon whome hee ought not so mutch as to loke but with feare and reuerence.... True it is, that mariages be don in heauen and performed in earth, but that saying may not be applied to fooles, which gouerne them selues by carnall desires, whose scope is but pleasure, and the reward many times equall to their follie.... The Cardinall night nor day did sleepe, and his brother still did wayt to performe hys othe of reuenge.... These two infortunate, Husband and Wyfe, were chasid from all places.... He might well haue saued himself and his eldest sonne by flight, being both wel mounted vpon two good Turkey horsses, which ran so fast, as the quarrel out of a Crosbow. But he loued to mutch his wife and children, and woulde kepe them company both in lyfe and death ... she was greatly deceyued, and knew within shorte space after, the good will that hir Brethren bare hir: for so soone as these Gallants had conducted hir into the kyngdome of Naples, to one of the Castels of hir sonne, she was committed to pryson wyth hir chyldren, and she also that was the secretary of hir infortunate mariage.... And now hearken the most sorowfull scene of all the Tragedy. The little Chyldren which had seene all this furious game executed vpon their mother and hir mayde, as nature prouoked them, or as some presage of their myshap might leade them thereunto, kneeled vpon their knees before those Tyrants, and embracinge their Legges, wayled in sutch wyse, as I thinke that any other, except a pitilesse heart spoyled of all humanity, would haue had compassion. And impossible it was for them, to vnfolde the embrancementes of those innocent creature, whych seemed to foreiudge their death by Sauage lookes and Countenaunce of those Roysters.... But who can appease a heart determined to worke mischief, and hath sworne the death of another forced thereunto by some special commaundment? The Aragon brethren ment hereby nothing else, but to roote out the whole name and race of Bologna.... Sutch ende had the infortunate mariage of him, whych ought to haue contented himselfe wyth that degree and honor that he had acquired by the deedes and glory of his vertues, so mutch by ech wight recommended: we ought neuer to climb higher than our force permitteth, ne yet surmount the bounds of duty, and lesse suffer our selues to be haled fondly forth with desire of brutal sensuality.

IV Music from the Plays

The Knight of the Burning Pestle

Francis Beaumont

I. 382–3, 388–9

II. 485–8; III. 618–19

As— it fell out on a long sum - mer's day, Two

lo - vers, they sat on— a— hill; They sat— to - ge - ther that

long sum - mer's day,— And could— not talk— their— fill.

II. 493

Three merry men and three mer- ry men, And three mer - ry men be we. Oh,—

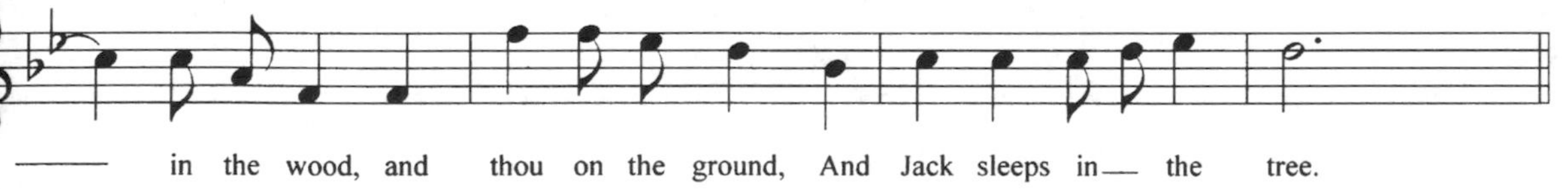
— in the wood, and thou on the ground, And Jack sleeps in— the tree.

II. 497

Troll, troll, troll the bowl to me.

II. 534–7

II. 540–1

II. 545–8

II. 556–7

But down, down, down, down I fall; but down, down, down, down I fall;
down, and a - rise, down and a - rise. I nev - er shall.
II. 577–85
Was e - ver knight for la - dy's sake So toss'd in love as I? Sir
Grey, For Phyl - lis fair, that la - dy bright, As e - ver man be - held with eye.
III. 29–42
Tell me, Dear - est what is love? 'Tis a light - ning from a -
bove, 'Tis an ar - row, 'Tis a fire, 'Tis a boy they call De - sire,
'Tis a grave Gapes to have Those poor fools that long to prove.

III. 540–4, 562–6

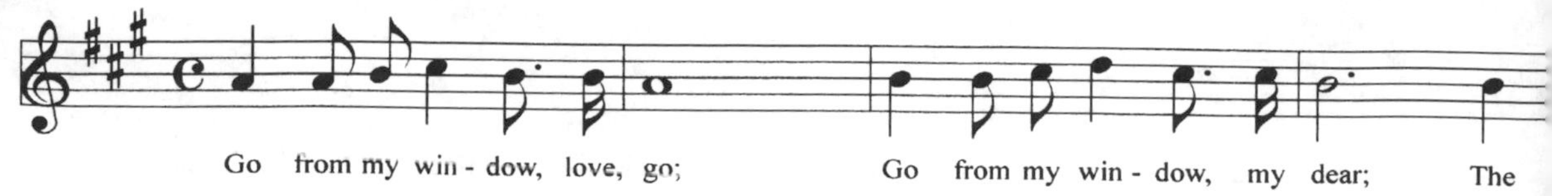

IV. 343–4

IV. 387–90

V. 204–5

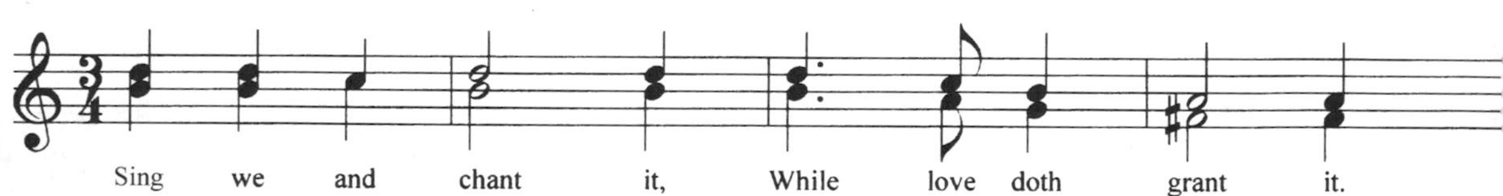

V. 241–5

V. 263
V. 265–7
If such dan - ger— be in play - ing, And sport must to—
earn - est turn, I will go no more a - may - ing
V. 281
For - tune my foe, why dost thou frown on me? And will thy
fa - vors ne - ver great - er be? Wilt thou, I say, for ev - er breed me
pain, And wilt thou not re - store my joys a - gain?

A Chaste Maid in Cheapside

Thomas Middleton

IV.i. 193–219

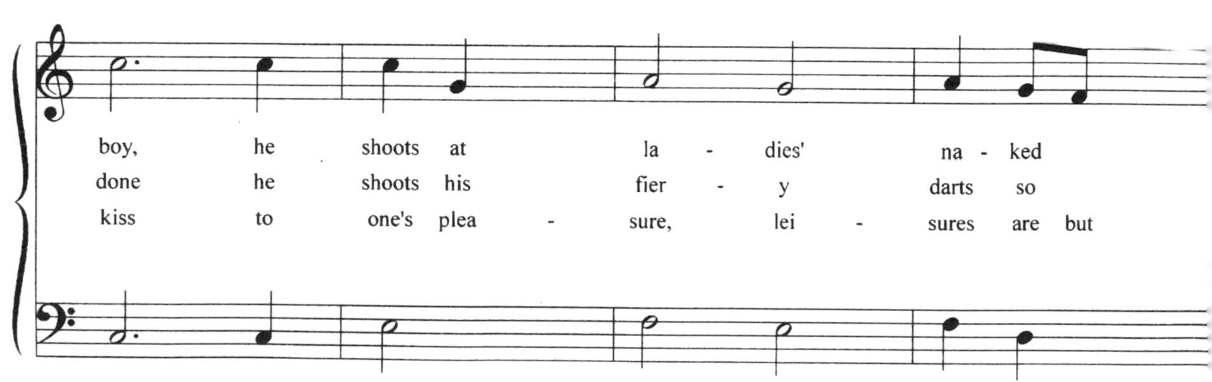

breasts, he is the cause of most men's crests
thick, they wound poor la - dies to the quick
waste, the slow - est kiss makes too much haste,

I mean u - pon the fore - head,
aye - me with cru - el wound - ing,
and lose it ere we find

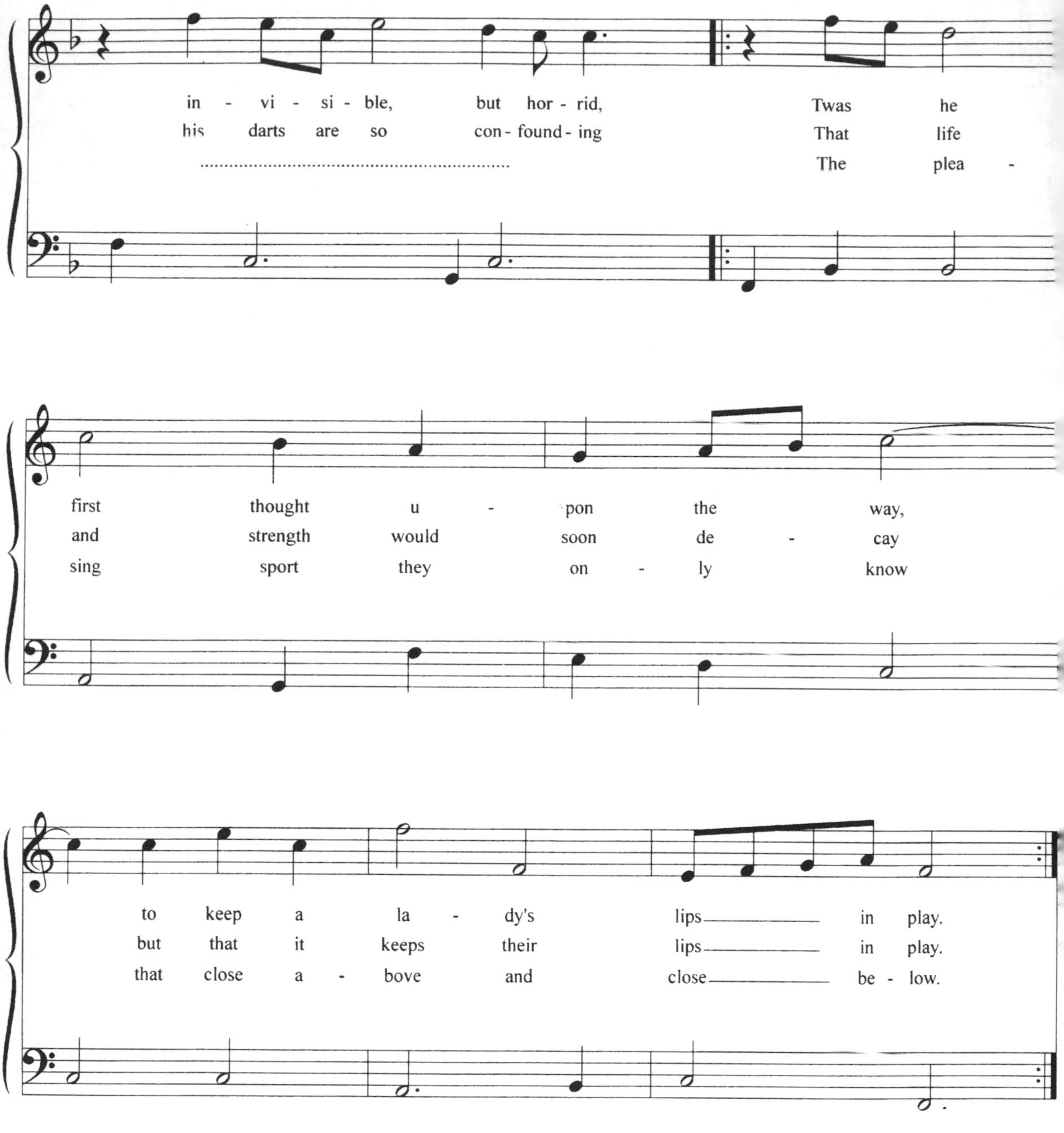

in - vi - si - ble, but hor - rid, Twas he
his darts are so con - found - ing That life
.... The plea -

first thought u - pon the way,
and strength would soon de - cay
sing sport they on - ly know

V.ii. 42–9

Weep eyes, weep eyes, break heart, break,

break, break heart, My Love, and I must part and

Fine
I must part, Cru - el Fates, true love do
soon - est sever. Oh, I shall see thee, ne - ver, ne - ver, never.

Oh hap - py is the Maid, whose life takes
end. Ere it knows Par - ents frown, or loss of friend.

The Duchess of Malfi

John Webster

IV.ii. 61–72

our parts, Till irk - some noise have cloy'd your
ears, And cor - ro - siv'd your hearts. At last when- as our
choir wants breath. Our bo - dies be- ing blessed, We'll sing like swans, we'll

sing like swans, to wel - come death, And die in love and rest.